THE
ENGLISH
LITERATURES
OF AMERICA,
1500–1800

THE
ENGLISH
LITERATURES
OF AMERICA,
1500–1800

EDITED BY
MYRA JEHLEN AND MICHAEL WARNER

Routledge
New York and London

Published in 1997 by
Routledge
29 West 35th Street
New York, NY 10001

Published in Great Britain by
Routledge
11 New Fetter Lane
London EC4P 4EE

Contents

The English Literatures of America, 1500–1800

In 1500, English was written by a small class of people in an island kingdom on the margin of Europe. By 1800, it was the language of a colonial system that stretched around the earth, from India and Australia to the Caribbean and Newfoundland. The Atlantic rim, in particular, had become the scene of a complex Anglophone world. *The English Literatures of America* is a guide to the written culture of that world; it includes texts by explorers, creole settlers, the peoples they subjugated, and Englishmen who viewed the Americas only from the banks of the Thames. The differences are significant enough to speak of many literatures rather than one. Yet all of texts in this book were caught up, to different degrees, in a new world of empire and commerce.

In the three centuries covered by this anthology, the oceans had become routinely navigable. The earth was remapped. Armies, commodities, missionaries, and deadly bacteria swept across seas in European ships. Voluntary and involuntary migrations created new peoples. The European powers developed new forms of government and commerce to organize their empires, and found themselves transformed in the process. New religions and new nationalisms appeared, both at home and in the colonies. The modern world had been invented—including the very idea of a modern world.

When the Scotsman William Robertson wrote his *History of America* (1777) toward the end of this period, it seemed natural to begin with an overview of "the progress of men, in discovering and peopling the various parts of the earth." Of course, the Americas had been peopled since antiquity, as Robertson knew. But to him the history of the New World was different from the endless succession of kingdoms, each erasing its predecessor, that had dominated classical or Renaissance historical writing. The Americas were a break between ancient and modern. Knowledge of them gave Europeans for the first time a knowledge of the whole world. And the history of that world could be told as a story of progress.

Robertson thought that this progress should be credited less to empire than to trade. With the spread of navigation and commerce, he wrote, "The ambition of conquest, or the necessity of procuring new settlements, were no longer the sole motives of visiting distant lands. The desire of gain became a new incentive to activity, roused adventurers, and sent them forth upon long voyages in search of countries whose products or wants might increase that circulation which nourishes and gives vigour to commerce. Trade proved a great source of discovery: it opened unknown seas, it penetrated into new regions, and contributed more than any other cause to bring men acquainted with the situation, the nature, and commodities of the different parts of the globe."

In a way, Robertson was right. The commercial empire of Europe had exceeded the political empires of the European nations. Spain, which had pioneered the art of conquering and administering other lands across the ocean, had been surpassed by England, which in the words of Fernand Braudel was "the first territorial state to complete its tranformation into a national economy or national market." Merchants —as well as soldiers, settlers, and subjects—made the Atlantic world. The early modern economy had become, for the first time, a global economy. India and the Americas contributed equally the staples of the remarkably intoxicating British empire: tea, coffee, sugar, tobacco, opium, rum. Pepper and calico made their way to the Appalachian frontiers. Cultural relations among different parts of the modern world increasingly took place through markets and commerce rather than through the administrators and courts of the state. Empire and commerce linked the world in different ways.

What Robertson did not say was that the contacts brought about by trade were themselves unequal. Unlike the contacts of political empire, the inequality brought about by commerce was an indirect result rather than direct subordination. But it remained a source of dominion. Europe as a whole became the center of a world economy. Tea, on its way from India to Long Island, went through London. Regions that had before been independent found themselves drawn into European circuits. Because of such indirect effects, an imperial culture does not depend on a political doctrine of empire. As late as 1782, on the verge of ceding an empire in America and consolidating one in India, the British House of Commons resolved that "to pursue schemes of conquest and extent of dominion, are measures repugnant to the wish, the honour, and the policy of this nation." Yet colonialism was well under way. For most of the texts in this anthology, the contexts of empire and trade are interwoven. Thomas Hariot, promoting the settlement of Virginia in 1588, spends most of his time describing its "commodities." When creole settlers two centuries later wanted to protest London taxes, they threw Indian tea into the Boston harbor.

The imperial culture of English America went far beyond even the administrative and commercial domains. It could be experienced as a geographical imagination, or as a moral language, or as style. William Robertson's history might serve as an example. Robertson, though a Scot by birth, writes from the seat of empire. His prose rings with the confidence that he and his readers are its most informed and freely enquiring members. Only a commercial civilization such as the one Robertson describes could result in the erudition and polish of *History of America*, let alone provide it with a receptive audience. His is the voice of cosmopolitanism.

A different style is to be found in the journal of Sarah Knight, a Boston school-teacher and shopkeeper of the early eighteenth century who had never been to Europe, but who was no less a subject of the British empire. As she traveled the countryside she could not help dreaming: "The way being smooth and even, the night warm and serene, and the Tall and thick Trees at a distance, especially when the moon glar'd light through the branches, fill'd my Imagination with the pleasent delusion of a Sumpteous citty, fill'd with famous Buildings and churches, with their spiring steeples, Balconies, Galleries and I know not what: Granduers which I had heard of, and which the stories of foreign countries had given me the Idea of."

Knight here longs for more than exotic sights. She longs for a better context for her own consciousness. Her journal is filled with anecdotes of the boorish behavior of the colonials around her. Writing is her resource for survival. When the drunken provincials in the room next door will not shut up, she writes satiric verse about them. She does so to remind herself that there is a larger world than the one these locals know. The closest she can come to living there is to fill her journal with wit and poetry, manufacturing an urbane consciousness with the borrowed resources of a style she imported through reading. But she cannot escape the double bind of the colonial: because the style that makes her journal urbane is a borrowed one, it also makes her provincial. The metropolis of her imagination is a jumbled picture, full of indistinct balconies, galleries, "and I know not what."

Twenty-five years before Knight wrote her journal, another Massachusetts Puritan named Mary Rowlandson wrote a famous narrative of her captivity among Indians. Rowlandson had not returned to England since her infancy. Yet she interrupts her wild tale with a note of familiarity: "I saw a place where English Cattle had been: that was a comfort to me, such as it was: quickly after that we came to an English Path, which so took with me, that I thought I could have freely lyen down and dyed. That day, a little after noon, we came to Squaukheag, where the Indians quickly spread themselves over the deserted English Fields."

This, too, is colonial language, and not just because of the value scale—English good, Indian bad. At a time when English and Indians were at war over the right to the land, Rowlandson defines Englishness through evidence of settlement, glimpsed only in transit as the wild Indians ceaselessly move through unfelled forests. Cattle, path, and fields make Englishness local, even while they struggle to make local places English. These imprints on the countryside are the markers of Rowlandson's identity, and she unhesitatingly calls them English even though she had not been within three thousand miles of England in the time of her memory, and wouldn't talk this way about Englishness if she had. Her captors tease her for the strength of her feeling: "What, will you love Englishmen still?"

Virtually every colonial writer in this anthology looks both homeward to the seat of imperial culture and outward to the localities that would remain for them subordinate. They were also gradually developing their own patterns of culture. Already in the seventeenth century, English writers made sport of colonials in different regions. In Ned Ward's satirical sketches of Jamaica (1698) and New England (1699), in Aphra Behn's play about Virginia (1689), or in Ebenezer Cooke's satirical poem of Maryland (1708), colonials had come to be recognizable as comic types. By 1705 Robert Beverley of Virginia could even embrace the stereotype with partial seriousness. "I am an *Indian*," he declared, though it may be doubted whether he ever meant to cast doubt on his own credentials as an Englishman. Toward the middle of the eighteenth century, the word "American" began to appear more frequently in reference to white creole settlers rather than to Indians. Ironically, just as the English finally emerged the victors in the long struggle over North America—the French ceded Canada in 1763— the sense of colonial identity had become strong enough to force a crisis in the imperial system, in a series of largely symbolic tax revolts. Colonial culture had begun to produce one of its least anticipated but most momentous effects: creole nationalism.

For the past two centuries, those colonists who happened to live in the future United States have been scrutinized for promising germs of Americanness; their provinciality has often been tactfully overlooked. Even Benjamin Franklin, regarded by many as the original American, spent twenty years of his life in London and as late as the 1760s fully intended to live there permanently as a happy Englishman. Portraits of him throughout most of his life show him in the powdered wig of a London gentleman. On his second trip to France, during the Revolutionary War, when he was seventy years old, Franklin changed his look. He shed the wig, wore his thinning hair long, sported a fur cap, glasses, a plain coat, and a walking stick. (Many French observers believed this to be a Quaker costume.) He was playing the American, a role he was inventing for the occasion.

Olaudah Equiano, by contrast, was dragged toward Englishness: he was taken from Africa to Montserrat and other West Indian islands; from thence to Georgia, South Carolina, Pennsylvania, Virginia, and finally to London. There, renamed Gustavus Vassa, he began to write English prose. Equiano himself was now not only an author but an English subject, no longer fully African or American. His life history outstripped the labels of identity in a way that paradoxically makes him more typical of his world than those who had a more comfortable home in it. In his long involuntary progress Equiano lived the full circuit of the commerce and colonies of the Atlantic rim. He saw and endured the force of its imperial order, perhaps more thoroughly than any other author in this volume.

By the same token it would be a stretch to call Samson Occom a Native American. That term was coined much later, a conscious gesture designed to exploit the symbolic resonance of American nationalism. Occom was a Mohegan; in English terms, he was an Indian, an American, a native. Only in the middle of his life did some Englishmen begin calling themselves American; and toward such disputes among the English as the Revolution he preferred to remain neutral. Toward English culture, however, he was far from neutral. He had made a significant break with most of his fellow Mohegans when he converted to Christianity; even more so when he pursued an English education and then traveled to England for two years. When he wrote a sketch of his own life, he began, "I was born a heathen and raised up in heathenism."

Robertson, Knight, Rowlandson, Franklin, Equiano, and Occom—all wrote from different positions in the same imperial culture. They might have had little else in common, but each writes in the language of England's dominion, and each invokes the reference points of empire, of the transatlantic economy, of Christendom, of modern history. By bringing these texts together in *The English Literatures of America*, we want to render as fully as possible the complex imperial culture of the early modern Atlantic world. To many readers, the emergence of American nationalism will be the central story here. We have tried to make both this and other stories available, even for the period after the revolution. Some of the places represented here remain British colonies to this day. Not everyone in the period was swept up in the unfolding time of world history, like the ever-modern Franklin; many lived in local worlds of less moment, relatively indifferent to markets, wars, printing, and other venues of the English Atlantic.

In the first chapter we depart from the rule that governs the rest of our selections; in that chapter we include modern translations of texts from other languages. By the time the English got involved in the New World, it was old news. They entered the project of empire after others had defined it. So it is with this anthology; the English enter in chapter 2. In subsequent chapters, the reader should remember that the other European empires of the Americas did not end when English one began.

It should also be remembered that the English movement into America was accompanied by a counterpoint of empire in India. In many ways, of course, America and India are contrasting images, as are British America and French or Spanish America. There is more than one kind of colonialism. Yet English involvement in "the two Indies" began at the same time, led by the same people, with the same infrastructures. The East India Company, chartered in 1600, was headed by Thomas Smith, who also governed the company chartered for Virginia in 1606. At the end of the period, too, British writers often made the comparison. Those who looked to colonial matters, such as Edumund Burke, spoke equally on America and India. Clive, before his death in 1774, was slated to quell American unrest following the Boston Tea Party; Cornwallis compensated for losing America by consolidating Bengal. Historian Peter Marshall notes that Cornwallis's triumphs in India after Yorktown were the turning-point in British public opinion on empire. After the early 1790s, he writes, "British activities in India were never again, at least before the twentieth century, to be subjected to prolonged hostile scrutiny from within the mainstreams of British opinion."

If the moment for challenging the empire had passed for the British, others took from the Revolutionary era a legacy of anticolonial thought. The name of Thomas Paine became almost sacred throughout Latin America. Yet the context of the empire as a whole—surely one of the most significant contexts for the material of this anthology—seldom appears in the work of North American writers. It is a notable silence. The Americans who rebelled against the colonial system quickly lost interest in it once free of its burdens. The century that followed the Revolution would ironically turn out to be the heyday of the imperial system. And the Americans themselves would eventually turn to thoughts of an empire of their own; the period of this anthology had scarcely closed when Lewis and Clark launched into the United States' vast new territorial possessions.

There are many such notable silences in the literatures of English America. This anthology, after all, is not a documentary history. Many aspects of Anglo-American history have been omitted here in a way that would be inexcusable in a historical record. We include, for example, very little from almanacs, one of the most popular kinds of colonial writing. And although we have taken pains to show that the imperial culture was never monolithic, it is not in the power of this anthology to bring about the utopia in which everyone gets to speak. Some, like the sexual dissidents mentioned by Francis Higginson and William Bradford, appear in the archives only when they are destroyed. Others—such as most servants, slaves, Indians, and English women—seldom appear in the archive except by borrowing from others an ill-fitting style, or an inadequate language of self-understanding, or tendentious forms of narrative. To read this anthology for historical awareness, one will need to read between the lines, remembering larger contexts and teasing out inarticulate voices.

There are many ways of using this book. We have arranged the material for the most part with an eye to chronology, so that a reader who moves from the beginning to the end will be able to appreciate the historical context. We have also done some other kinds of organizing. Some chapters focus on regions (4, 5); others on genre (8, 10, 14); others on contexts of discourse (2, 7, 9, 12, 13) or topic (6). To make these connections stronger, we have not hesitated to scatter an author's work across different chapters. The nearly omnipresent Benjamin Franklin appears in each of the final six chapters. We hope that the structure of the book helps to make sense of the texts in as many ways as possible. We invite readers to consider other ways of making intertextual connections; for example, grouping women writers for comparison, or tracing the changes in autobiographical narrative, or weighing rival standards of the beautiful. And we invite readers to experiment with anachronism.

In style and idiom, these writings belong to another linguistic as well as historic epoch. They can be strange and unfamiliar, in a way that can be both a difficulty and a source of pleasure. They should be read with care. Some texts articulate ideologies or relations of power that strike modern readers as repugnant. When the texts themselves are frankly patriarchal, or frankly imperial, or frankly ethnocentric, we have not shrunk from presenting them to modern readers. In many cases we have included exactly those texts that openly or inadvertently reveal relations of power. We do so in part to encourage a historical awareness. It would be naive to think that skilled writers always transcend, or resist, or subvert the inequalities of their world. It would also be naive to think that a dominant culture only dominates, that it has achieved supremacy without contradictions of its own, or without a moral or aesthetic vision that would carry broad force. And these can be a source of more than historical interest. The pleasures of language, rhetoric, narrative, and form do not evaporate wherever power appears.

The selections here are for the most part "thick" texts, not simple facts. Intermittently they illuminate many kinds of history, addressing multiple audiences and referring to multiple contexts. They have rhetorical ambitions. They have style. They are riven by contradictions, inaccuracies, or unintended revelations. They are interesting to read. They should be approached with the questions that go into close and critical reading: What does it feel like to read this? Whom does the text address, and to what end? Is there a pattern to its figures of speech, or to its narrative movement? What does it leave out, or forget, or revise? What are its driving tensions or contradictions? Does the tone shift? What is the speaker like? How does the text achieve a sense of ending?

Questions of this sort are difficult to apply to snippets. They work best when the reader can see a whole stretch of language that is bounded as a text. We have included as many complete texts as possible while still presenting a rich cultural context. Each chapter has at least one work in its entirety.

M.W.

"Preparation for War to Defend Commerce," Philadelphia, 1800.

Suggested readings: At the end of each chapter's introduction, we have added more specific suggestions for background reading. For the period as a whole, the best starting point may be Fernand Braudel's *Civilization and Capitalism, 15th to 18th Century*; readers may want to begin with the third volume, *The Perspective of the World*. A comprehensive narrative can be found in Angus Calder, *The Revolutionary Empires*. D. W. Meinig offers a geographical background in *Atlantic America, 1492–1800*. A model study of colonial culture is Serge Gruzinski's *La colonization imaginaire*, translated into English as *The Conquest of Mexico*. Benedict Anderson's *Imagined Communities* usefully introduces the problem of nationalism in a comparative context.

Acknowledgments: Our last task in this project is particularly pleasant: thanking those who have so generously helped us along the way. Early in the process, Routledge sent a questionnaire to colleagues in the field of colonial American studies. Many scholars, too many to list here, took the time to respond with invaluable advice and suggestions, and we are very grateful to them. Our students Max Cavitch and Elise Lemire were ideal assistants throughout the project, and Max Cavitch's final work on the manuscript was absolutely essential to its completion. Finally, we wish to thank our Rutgers colleagues—Emily Bartels, William Dowling, Richard Poirier, and Barry Qualls—for the contribution of their intelligence, knowledge, and friendship.

M.J. and M.W.

ONE

THE GLOBE AT 1500

Chapter 1

The Expansion of Europe

Introduction

The story of America has many beginnings, some of them centuries apart. October 12, 1492, the day a Genoese ship-captain named Christopher Columbus discovered a land Europeans didn't know existed, is one beginning, but neither the first nor the last. Columbus himself would have claimed it all began in the thirteenth century when a Venetian merchant, Marco Polo, travelled to the Chinese court of Kublai Khan. 1415 is another date with which the story could begin: the fall that year of the Muslim stronghold of Ceuta in North-West Africa to the Portuguese, followed by the decision to hold the captured territory as a colony, was the first instance of a European state's territorial expansion; and it launched the western empire of which the Americas became the major outpost. The taking of Ceuta set off a series of competitive ventures among which Columbus's attempt to find a sea-route to Asia was only one. In Ceuta, the king of Portugal was seeking the key to the Mediterranean; the Spanish sponsored Columbus hoping to best the Portuguese with a key to the Atlantic.

Looking over this history, Fernand Braudel concluded that Europe's most important discovery was not this or that new land, but how to navigate the Atlantic Ocean. The Chinese, Arabs, and Turks (whose capture of Constantinople in 1453, ending the era of religious crusades, could constitute still another beginning of Euro-American history) were as skilled voyagers as the Portuguese, Spanish, and English; but the latter mastered the Atlantic first, and in Braudel's view it was this that enabled them to overrun the globe. Thus the American landfall was less beginning than culmination, the final conquest of the ocean. Or rather it was the penultimate conquest, for, six years after Columbus, the successful passage of Vasco da Gama around the tip of Africa sealed Europe's control of the sea. For a while, it seemed that the discovery of America had been superseded, 1498 eclipsing 1492.

Even after the Spanish, worried by this Portuguese victory, had set about establishing themselves in Central and South America, the beginning of North American history as a predominantly English world awaited the seventeenth century. English empire-builders considered the East more promising and had to be prodded to look west. A century after Columbus planted the flag on the beach at San Salvador, the publication in 1589–90 of Richard Hakluyt's first compilation of diverse documents of discovery and exploration, *The Principal Navigations*, launched a program of English colonization. Actual settlement in the region that would be the United States waited another seventeen years, if we start with Virginia, and thirty more if we take the landing at Plymouth Rock as the beginning, which, in that case, takes place 128 years after Columbus discovered America.

There is nothing surprising in this delay; discoveries typically have to make their way. To its citizens, the fifteenth-century world seemed complete with Europe, Asia, and Africa. Prince Henry the Navigator's maritime ambitions hugged the coast of Africa. Moreover, for a long time the new territories in themselves held little interest for their discoverers, except as caches of potential treasure. That is, at first, the voyages out served mostly to confirm, or even generate, a sense of identity within Europe. Although, in the sixteenth century, Portugal took possession of foreign territory many times its size, it would be anachronistic to say that this represented the expansion of Portugal as such, of the Portuguese nation. The concept of national identity did not pre-exist colonial conquest; they developed concurrently. Columbus claimed Española in the name not of Spain but of the King and Queen of Castile, that way materially aiding them in their effort to establish a Spanish nation under their rule. In the same way, the capture of Ceuta represented consolidation as much as expansion, and the king's decision to annex foreign territory reciprocally implied Portugal's own territorial integrity at home. Portugal's integrity in turn projected Europe's, as the Christian continent, home-base for a group of Christian feodalities only emerging as states from a pan-European feudalism centered on Rome. The Spanish crown sponsored Columbus in part to celebrate the recapture of Granada, the last Muslim outpost on European soil. As Columbus concluded his agreement with the Spanish monarchs, they expelled all non-converted Jews, and with that double purging asserted a distinct and homogeneous national identity.

Since the eighteenth century, the conventional depiction of the discovery has featured two distinct and opposing worlds, the old and the new, both fully constituted and only awaiting the lifting of the curtain that obscured them from one another to begin unfolding a mutual destiny. But for much of the sixteenth century, the fact that new lands had been found in the western ocean had to beg for meaning and was sometimes ignored outright. The discoverer himself died still refusing to believe he had found anything that so radically altered the prevailing geography as two new continents. There was no America in America when Columbus arrived; neither was there a Spain in Spain, nor a Europe, as we understand any of these today.

Their modern identities grew out of interactions that changed all the participants, transforming them into entities defined by their relations to one another. Spain became Spain by vying for empire with Portugal, Europe grew into Europe when it began to conquer the other continents. Hakluyt, urging English colonization of America, warned that England would otherwise not acquire its rightful identity among the nations of Europe.

On the other side of the Atlantic, it took time for America to acquire even a geographical identity. This had to be put together piece by piece from reports of exploratory voyages, such as those gathered by a printer, Martin Waldseemüller, who in 1507, in the *Cosmographiae Introductio*, reprinted the letters of a Florentine traveller named Amerigo Vespucci. Waldseemüller was so impressed by Vespucci's account of his explorations that he proposed naming the continent after him. North America

Vespucci meeting America, late sixteenth century. Note the cannibal scene in the background.

received its name from Mercator a few years later when his map made clear the twinship of the two land-masses.

Named, claimed, proclaimed, reported, and mapped, America emerged in crucial relation to writing, books, and publishing. The significance of the invention of movable type in the middle of the fifteenth century cannot be told apart from the history of colonization, and *vice versa*. Printed accounts of explorations and conquests did not merely report the building of Europe's empire, they participated actively in it. The compilers of documents used texts as their colleagues did ships and guns. One way to recuperate a sense of this period of exceptional expansion and movement is to look at the body of these texts and at their relations, as they pass from Latin into and among various vernaculars, through an increasing traffic in translation which generated, simultaneously, a community of European knowledge and fierce competition among its members.

In 1500, then, Europe was coming into being as it went out to conquer other lands. The inhabitants of these other lands had their own identities and histories, though until recently these and what happened to them in the conflict have received less attention in Western historiography. Of course, though there was no America in the European sense when Columbus arrived, there *were* two continents in the Western hemisphere home to possibly as many as 80 to 100 million people. (By comparison, the population of Europe was no more than 60 million, and of the world probably 275 million.) There may have been fewer native Americans, one historian having estimated only 10 to 15 million. The reason for this drastic uncertainty is a second figure which must enter into any attempt to reconstruct what America was like in 1500. In the period immediately following the arrival of Europeans, as many as 90 percent of the native peoples died from violence, intolerable labor conditions, and diseases common in the rest of the world but hitherto unknown in the Americas. As a measure of this catastrophe, it is useful to recall that the Black Death that disoriented all fourteenth-century Europe—and continues to haunt the Western imagination—reduced Europe's population by 25 percent.

Very little is known of America before Columbus, and very little of the life and thinking of the Americans during the period of invasion. With the important exception of the civilizations of Central America, they left no written records. Still, without being able to reconstruct the societies and cultures of the native Americans, it is nonetheless imperative to place them on the scene, not as Columbus and his followers did, as negligible opponents or variably valuable resources, but as interlocutors. For the process of self-creation upon which Europeans embarked in the fifteenth and sixteenth centuries was at every stage an aggressive engagement. It was a violent global argument, and it is unintelligible heard as a monologue. The problem in reading the literature of colonization, which is overwhelmingly the literature of the colonizers, is to discern, within the tone of victorious authority, the accent lent by contingency and conflict.

M.J.

Suggested readings: J. H. Parry's brief overview, *The Establishment of the European Hegemony, 1415–1715: Trade and Exploration in the Age of the Renaissance*, is an excellent introduction to this period. J. H. Elliott, *The Old World and the New: 1492–1650* is similarly wide-ranging but more focused and analytical in its discussions. Edmundo O'Gorman's influential *The Invention of America* suggests its main thesis in the title, that America was not discovered as what it was, but invented as Europe would have it become. Inga Clendinnen's *Aztecs: An Interpretation* and Frank Lestringant's *Mapping the Renaissance World: The Geographical Imagination in the Age of Discovery* are important and accessible examples of the recent scholarship.

1. Marco Polo

from *The Travels of Marco Polo*
c. 1298

*Marco Polo (1254?–1324?), a Venetian merchant, travelled to Asia in 1271–95
(spending seventeen years in China) and described his experiences in a hugely
successful book. Its original title,* Divisamentu dou Monde *(Description of the
World), predicted the global ambitions that set off the age of colonization. When
European horizons began to widen in the fifteenth and sixteenth centuries,* The
Travels of Marco Polo *found an ever-enlarging audience; Columbus took a copy
along on his first voyage. This opening paragraph, promising both truth and
marvels, is particularly interesting for the way, from the start, such reports posit
the prime importance and value of knowledge.*

Ye emperors, kings, dukes, marquises, earls, and knights, and all other people
desirous of knowing the diversities of the races of mankind, as well as the
diversities of kingdoms, provinces and regions of all parts of the East, read
through this book, and ye will find in it the greatest and most marvellous characteristics of the peoples especially of Armenia, Persia, India, and Tartary, as they are severally related in the present work by Marco Polo, a wise and learned citizen of Venice,
who states distinctly what things he saw and what things he heard from others. For
this book will be a truthful one. It must be known, then, that from the creation of
Adam to the present day, no man, whether Pagan, or Saracen, or Christian, or other,
of whatever progeny or generation he may have been, ever saw or inquired into so
many and such great things as Marco Polo above mentioned. Who, wishing in his
secret thoughts that the things he had seen and heard should be made public by the
present work, for the benefit of those who could not see them with their own eyes, he
himself being in the years of our Lord 1295 in the prison at Genoa, caused the things
which are contained in the present work to be written by master Rustigielo, a citizen
of Pisa, who was with him in the same prison at Genoa.

2. Sir John Mandeville

from *The Travels of Sir John Mandeville* 1356

> *Nothing certain is known about Sir John Mandeville, who may have been invented along with the story of his travels. The Travels first appeared in Europe in the mid-fourteenth century and by 1500 hundreds of manuscript versions were circulating throughout Europe. That they were taken as truthful accounts of actual observations—along with Marco Polo, Columbus also studied Mandeville—suggests how mysterious the world was in the late middle ages, how little reliable knowledge existed. Reading that the inhabitants of the fictional Lamary go naked, practice free love, lack a concept of private property and are cannibals, all signature traits of New World savages, may raise questions about Columbus's descriptions ostensibly reporting his direct observation of the Arawaks and Caribs.*

OF THE EVIL CUSTOMS USED IN THE ISLE OF LAMARY. AND HOW THE EARTH AND THE SEA BE OF ROUND FORM AND SHAPE, BY PROOF OF THE STAR THAT IS CLEPT[1] ANTARCTIC, THAT IS FIXED IN THE SOUTH.

From that country go men by the sea ocean, and by many divers isles and by many countries that were too long for to tell of. And a fifty-two days journeys from this land that I have spoken of, there is another land, that is full great, that men clepe Lamary. In that land is full great heat. And the custom there is such, that men and women go all naked. And they scorn when they see any strange folk going clothed. And they say, that God made Adam and Eve all naked, and that no man should shame him to shew him such as God made him, for nothing is foul that is of kindly nature. And they say, that they that be clothed be folk of another world, or they be folk that trow not in God. And they say, that they believe in God that formed the world, and that made Adam and Eve and all other things. And they wed there no wives, for all the women there be common and they forsake no man. And they say they sin if they refuse any man; and so God commanded to Adam and Eve and to all that come of him, when he said, *Crescite et multiplicamini et replete terram.*[2] And therefore may no man say, This is my wife; nor any woman may say This is my husband. And when they have children, they may give them to what man they will that hath accompanied with them. And also all the land is common; for all that a man holdeth one year, another man hath it another year; and every man taketh what part

---

1. clept: called.
2. Increase and multiply and fill the earth. Gen. 1:22.

Illustration for Mandeville's Travels, 1508.
Mandeville's race of headless men is discussed
by Sir Walter Ralegh in chapter 2.

Illustration of cannibals, from a 1483 edition of
Mandeville.

that him liketh. And also all the goods of the land be common, corns and all other things: for everything there is kept in close, nothing there is under lock, and every man there taketh what he will without any contradiction, and as rich is one man there as is another.

But in that country there is a cursed custom, for they eat more gladly man's flesh than any other flesh; and yet is that country abundant of flesh, of fish, of corns, or gold and silver, and of all other goods. Thither go merchants and bring with them children to sell to them of the country, and they buy them. And if they be fat they eat them anon. And if they be lean they feed them till they be fat, and then they eat them. And they say, that it is the best flesh and the sweetest of all the world.

In that land, and in many other beyond that, no man may see the Star Transmontane, that is clept the Star of the Sea, that is unmovable and that is toward the north, that we clepe the Lode-star. But men see another star, the contrary to him, that is toward the south, that is clept Antarctic. And right as the ship-men take their advice here and govern them by the Lode-star, right so do ship-men beyond those parts by the star of the south, the which star appeareth not to us. And this star that is toward the north, that we clepe the Lode-star, appeareth not to them. For which cause men may well perceive, that the land and the sea be of round shape and form; for the part of the firmament sheweth in one country that sheweth not in another country. And men may well prove by experience and subtle compassment of wit, that if a man found passages by ships that would go to search the world, men might go by ship all about the world and above and beneath.

3. Niccolo Machiavelli

from *History of Florence*
1525

*Niccolo Machiavelli (1469–1527), a Florentine writer and statesman, is best
known as the author of* The Prince, *a treatise on the nature of the state and the
laws of politics. The uncompromisingly pragmatic stance of this treatise and
Machiavelli's often pessimistic view of psychology in the political realm earned him
an unjustified reputation for amorality. But in fact, while projecting an ideal Prince
who would rule autocratically and be unafraid to use violence if necessary to
remain in power, Machiavelli was a committed republican and a civic humanist
seeking to mitigate the corruption of Florentine politics. Here he advocates colonization by the establishment of local settlements rather than by long-distance
administrators, so that conquered territories may be cultivated to their full potential and their security ensured by the strongest of motives, self-protection. His
model colonies are thus small republics under the aegis of an empire, and they bear
a prophetic resemblance to the English colonies of North America. Yet, oddly,
Machiavelli does not mention the New World. The translation is from a 1732
English collection of writings on colonies.*

BOOK II

Nothing is more worthy and becoming an excellent Prince, a well dispos'd
Common-wealth, nor more for the Interest and Advantage of a Province,
than to erect new Towns, where Men may cohabit with more Convenience
both for Agriculture and Defence. For besides the Beauty and Ornament which
followed upon that Custom, it render'd such Provinces as were conquer'd more
dutiful and secure to the Conqueror, planted the void Places, and made a commodious
Distribution of the People; upon which living regularly and in Order, they did not
only multiply faster, but were more ready to invade, and more able for Defence. But
by the Negligence and Omission of Common-wealths and Principalities this Method
of establishing Colonies being at present disused, the Provinces are become weaker
and some of them ruined. For (as I said before) it is this Order alone that secures a
Countrey and supply's it with People. The Security consists in this, that in a new
Countrey a Colony placed by Authority, is a Fortress and Guard to keep the Natives
in Obedience; neither without this can a Province continue inhabited, or preserve a
just Distribution of the People, because all Places being not equally fertile or healthful,
where it is barren they desert; where unwholesome they die; and unless there be some
Way to invite or dispose new Men to the one as well as the other, that Province must
fail; the abandoning some Places leaving them desolate and weak, and the thronging

to others, making them indigent and poor. And forasmuch as these inconveniencies are not to be remedied by Nature, Art and Industry is to be applied; and we see many Countries which are naturally unhealthful, much better'd by the Multitude of Inhabitants; the Earth being purifi'd by their Tillage, and the Air by their Fires, which Nature alone could never have effected. Of this *Venice* is an Instance sufficient; for tho' seated in a sickly and watrish Place, the Concourse of so many People at one Time made it healthful enough. *Pisa* by reason of the Malignity of the Air was very ill inhabited till the Inhabitants of *Genoa* and its Territories, being defeated and dispossessed by the *Saracens*, it followed that being supplanted all of them at once, and repairing thither in such Numbers, that Town in a short Time became populous and potent. But the Custom of sending Colonies being laid aside, new Conquests are not so easily kept, void Places not so easily supplied; nor full and exurberant Places so easily evacuated. Whereupon many Places in the World, and particularly in *Italy*, are become desolate and deserted in respect of what in former Ages they have been, which is imputable to nothing but that Princes do not retain their ancient Appetite of true Glory, nor Common-wealths the laudable Customs of the Ancients.

4. Christopher Columbus

letter to the King and Queen of Castile (first voyage) 1493

> *Christopher Columbus (1451?–1506) made four voyages to America steadfastly denying that he was landing anywhere but off the coast of China. To his death the discoverer refused to believe he had discovered a new continent. There was method to this obstinacy: by clinging to the notion that the West Indies were just the western tip of the East Indies, Columbus could retain his original concept of the globe and not be forced to the radical redrawing of the map of the world required to make it accommodate two more continents.*
>
> *Others at the time were quicker to recognize the new lands as new, notably Amerigo Vespucci (see selection 5 below). But everyone began by trying to fit them into the known world, making modifications only when forced to. The letter reprinted here exemplifies the process by which new knowledge enters the scene set by old knowledge. Columbus arrives in an unknown world and at once begins to assimilate it to Europe; naming the islands gives him symbolic possession, and it also translates them into his language. He makes the alien familiar by describing it in terms of its uses: the land is wonderfully fertile, its fruits richer than any he has seen; there is a wild abundance of game in its woods, fish in its streams, birds in its trees; and its people seem made to be subjugated.*
>
> *The islands' inhabitants offer some resistance to being absorbed into the familiar cosmos. They are too clearly different from what Columbus knows of human ways*

to be renamed into familiarity. Indeed he grants them their own names: Arawaks
and later Caribs. The solution to the problem of nonetheless maintaining his world
view lies in reversing the terms: the Indians are defined by how they are not like
Europeans and the European remains intact as the definition of the human norm.

ALetter addressed to the noble Lord Raphael Sanchez, Treasurer to their most invincible Majesties, Ferdinand and Isabella, King and Queen of Spain, by Christopher Columbus, to whom our age is greatly indebted, treating of the islands of India recently discovered beyond the Ganges, to explore which he had been sent eight months before under the auspices and at the expense of their said Majesties.

Knowing that it will afford you pleasure to learn that I have brought my undertaking to a successful termination, I have decided upon writing you this letter to acquaint you with all the events which have occurred in my voyage, and the discoveries which have resulted from it. Thirty-three days after my departure from Cadiz I reached the Indian sea, where I discovered many islands, thickly peopled, of which I took possession without resistance in the name of our most illustrious Monarch, by public proclamation and with unfurled banners. To the first of these islands, which is called by the Indians Guanahani, I gave the name of the blessed Saviour (San Salvador), relying upon whose protection I had reached this as well as the other islands; to each of these I also gave a name, ordering that one should be called Santa Maria de la Concepcion, another Fernandina, the third Isabella, the fourth Juana, and so with all the rest respectively. As soon as we arrived at that, which as I have said was named Juana, I proceeded along its coast a short distance westward, and found it to be so large and apparently without termination, that I could not suppose it to be an island, but the continental province of Cathay.[3] Seeing, however, no towns or populous places on the sea coast, but only a few detached houses and cottages, with whose inhabitants I was unable to communicate, because they fled as soon as they saw us, I went further on, thinking that in my progress I should certainly find some city or village.

At length, after proceeding a great way and finding that nothing new presented itself, and that the line of coast was leading us northwards (which I wished to avoid, because it was winter, and it was my intention to move southwards; and because moreover the winds were contrary), I resolved not to attempt any further progress, but rather to turn back and retrace my course to a certain bay that I had observed, and from which I afterwards dispatched two of our men to ascertain whether there were a king or any cities in that province. These men reconnoitred the country for three days, and found a most numerous population, and great numbers of houses, though small, and built without any regard to order: with which information they returned to us. In the mean time I had learned from some Indians whom I had seized, that that country was certainly an island: and therefore I sailed towards the east, coasting to the distance of three hundred and twenty-two miles, which brought us to the extremity of it; from this point I saw lying eastwards another island, fifty-four miles distant from Juana, to which I gave the name of Española. I went thither, and

3. Cathay: China.

steered my course eastward as I had done at Juana, even to the distance of five hundred and sixty-four miles along the north coast. This said island of Juana is exceedingly fertile, as indeed are all the others; it is surrounded with many bays, spacious, very secure, and surpassing any that I have ever seen; numerous large and healthful rivers intersect it, and it also contains many very lofty mountains.

All these islands are very beautiful, and distinguished by a diversity of scenery; they are filled with a great variety of trees of immense height, and which I believe to retain their foliage in all seasons; for when I saw them they were as verdant and luxuriant as they usually are in Spain in the month of May,—some of them were blossoming, some bearing fruit, and all flourishing in the greatest perfection, according to their respective stages of growth, and the nature and quality of each: yet the islands are not so thickly wooded as to be impassable. The nightingale and various birds were singing in countless numbers, and that in November, the month in which I arrived there. There are besides in the same island of Juana seven or eight kinds of palm trees, which, like all the other trees, herbs, and fruits, considerably surpass ours in height and beauty. The pines also are very handsome, and there are very extensive fields and meadows, a variety of birds, different kinds of honey, and many sorts of metals, but no iron. In that island also which I have before said we named Española, there are mountains of very great size and beauty, vast plains, groves, and very fruitful fields, admirably adapted for tillage, pasture, and habitation. The convenience and excellence of the harbours in this island, and the abundance of the rivers, so indispensable to the health of man, surpass anything that would be believed by one who had not seen it. The trees, herbage, and fruits of Española are very different from those of Juana, and moreover it abounds in various kinds of spices, gold, and other metals.

The inhabitants of both sexes in this island, and in all the others which I have seen, or of which I have received information, go always naked as they were born, with the exception of some of the women, who use the covering of a leaf, or small bough, or an apron of cotton which they prepare for that purpose. None of them, as I have already said, are possessed of any iron, neither have they weapons, being unacquainted with, and indeed incompetent to use them, not from any deformity of body (for they are well-formed), but because they are timid and full of fear. They carry however in lieu of arms, canes dried in the sun, on the ends of which they fix heads of dried wood sharpened to a point, and even these they dare not use habitually; for it has often occurred when I have sent two or three of my men to any of the villages to speak with the natives, that they have come out in a disorderly troop, and have fled in such haste at the approach of our men, that the fathers forsook their children and the children their fathers. This timidity did not arise from any loss or injury that they had received from us; for, on the contrary, I gave to all I approached whatever articles I had about me, such as cloth and many other things, taking nothing of theirs in return: but they are naturally timid and fearful. As soon however as they see that they are safe, and have laid aside all fear, they are very simple and honest, and exceedingly liberal with all they have; none of them refusing any thing he may possess when he is asked for it, but on the contrary inviting us to ask them.

They exhibit great love towards all others in preference to themselves: they also give objects of great value for trifles, and content themselves with very little or nothing in return. I however forbad that these trifles and articles of no value (such as pieces of dishes, plates, and glass, keys, and leather straps) should be given to them, although if they could obtain them, they imagined themselves to be possessed of the most beautiful trinkets in the world. It even happened that a sailor received for a leather strap as much gold as was worth three golden nobles, and for things of more trifling value offered by our men, especially newly coined blancas, or any gold coins, the Indians would give whatever the seller required; as, for instance, an ounce and a half or two ounces of gold, or thirty or forty pounds of cotton, with which commodity they were already acquainted. Thus they bartered, like idiots, cotton and gold for fragments of bows, glasses, bottles, and jars; which I forbad as being unjust, and myself gave them many beautiful and acceptable articles which I had brought with me, taking nothing from them in return; I did this in order that I might the more easily conciliate them, that they might be led to become Christians, and be inclined to entertain a regard for the King and Queen, our Princes and all Spaniards, and that I might induce them to take an interest in seeking out, and collecting, and delivering to us such things as they possessed in abundance, but which we greatly needed.

They practice no kind of idolatry, but have a firm belief that all strength and power, and indeed all good things, are in heaven, and that I had descended from thence with these ships and sailors, and under this impression was I received after they had thrown aside their fears. Nor are they slow or stupid, but of very clear understanding; and those men who have crossed to the neighbouring islands give an admirable description of everything they observed; but they never saw any people clothed, nor any ships like ours. On my arrival at that sea, I had taken some Indians by force from the first island that I came to, in order that they might learn our language,[4] and communicate to us what they knew respecting the country; which plan succeeded excellently, and was a great advantage to us, for in a short time, either by gestures and signs, or by words, we were enabled to understand each other. These men are still travelling with me, and although they have been with us now a long time, they continue to entertain the idea that I have descended from heaven; and on our arrival at any new place they published this, crying out immediately with a loud voice to the other Indians, "Come, come and look upon beings of a celestial race": upon which both women and men, children and adults, young men and old, when they got rid of the fear they at first entertained, would come out in throngs, crowding the roads to see us, some bringing food, others drink, with astonishing affection and kindness. Each of these islands has a great number of canoes, built of solid wood, narrow and not unlike our double-banked boats in length and shape, but swifter in their motion: they steer them only by the oar. These canoes are of various sizes, but the greater number are constructed with eighteen banks of oars, and with these they cross to the other islands, which are of countless number, to carry on traffic with the people. I saw some of these canoes that held as many as seventy-eight rowers.

In all these islands there is no difference of physiognomy, of manners, or of language, but they all clearly understand each other, a circumstance very propitious for the real-

4. The literary historian Stephen Greenblatt has pointed out that Columbus's phrase is more accurately translated as "that they may learn to speak," implying that the Indians, in not speaking a European tongue, appear to the Spanish as if lacking language altogether.

ization of what I conceive to be the principal wish of our most serene King, namely, the conversion of these people to the holy faith of Christ, to which indeed, as far as I can judge, they are very favourable and well-disposed. I said before, that I went three hundred and twenty-two miles in a direct line from west to east, along the coast of the island of Juana; judging by which voyage, and the length of the passage, I can assert that it is larger than England and Scotland united; for independent of the said three hundred and twenty-two miles, there are in the western part of the island two provinces which I did not visit; one of these is called by the Indians Anam, and its inhabitants are born with tails. These provinces extend to a hundred and fifty-three miles in length, as I have learnt from the Indians whom I have brought with me, and who are well acquainted with the country. But the extent of Española is greater than all Spain from Catalonia to Fontarabia, which is easily proved, because one of its four sides which I myself coasted in a direct line, from west to east, measures five hundred and forty miles. This island is to be regarded with especial interest, and not to be slighted; for although as I have said I took possession of all these islands in the name of our invincible King, and the government of them is unreservedly committed to his said Majesty, yet there was one large town in Española of which especially I took possession, situated in a remarkably favourable spot, and in every way convenient for the purposes of gain and commerce. To this town I gave the name of Navidad del Señor, and ordered a fortress to be built there, which must by this time be completed, in which I left as many men as I thought necessary, with all sorts of arms, and enough provisions for more than a year. I also left them one caravel, and skillful workmen both in ship-building and other arts, and engaged the favor and friendship of the King of the island in their behalf, to a degree that would not be believed, for these people are so amiable and friendly that even the King took a pride in calling me his brother. But supposing their feelings should become changed, and they should wish to injure those who have remained in the fortress, they could not do so, for they have no arms, they go naked, and are moreover too cowardly; so that those who hold the said fortress, can easily keep the whole island in check, without any pressing danger to themselves, provided they do not transgress the directions and regulations which I have given them.

As far as I have learned, every man throughout these islands is united to but one wife, with the exception of the kings and princes, who are allowed to have twenty: the women seem to work more than the men. I could not clearly understand whether the people possess any private property, for I observed that one man had the charge of distributing various things to the rest, but especially meat and provisions and the like. I did not find, as some of us had expected, any cannibals amongst them, but on the contrary men of great deference and kindness. Neither are they black, like the Ethiopians: their hair is smooth and straight: for they do not dwell where the rays of the sun strike most vividly, -and the sun has intense power there, the distance from the equinoctial line being, it appears, but six-and-twenty degrees. On the tops of the mountains the cold is very great, but the effect of this upon the Indians is lessened by their being accustomed to the climate, and by their frequently indulging in the use of

---

5. Charis: Columbus refers here for the first time to the isle of the Caribs as he later calls them, that name in turn yielding "cannibals" when, beginning with Columbus, the Carib Indians were taken to be eaters of human flesh.

very hot meats and drinks. Thus, as I have already said, I saw no cannibals, nor did I hear of any, except in a certain island called Charis,[5] which is the second from Española on the side towards India, where dwell a people who are considered by the neighbouring islanders as most ferocious: and these feed upon human flesh. The same people have many kinds of canoes, in which they cross to all the surrounding islands and rob and plunder wherever they can; they are not different from the other islanders, except that they wear their hair long, like women, and make use of the bows and javelins of cane, with sharpened spear-points fixed on the thickest end, which I have before described, and therefore they are looked upon as ferocious, and regarded by the other Indians with unbounded fear; but I think no more of them than of the rest. These are the men who form unions with certain women, who dwell alone in the island Matenin, which lies next to Española on the side towards India; these latter employ themselves in no labour suitable to their own sex, for they use bows and javelins as I have already described their paramours as doing, and for defensive armour have plates of brass, of which metal they possess great abundance.

They assure me that there is another island larger than Española, whose inhabitants have no hair, and which abounds in gold more than any of the rest. I bring with me individuals of this island and of the others that I have seen, who are proofs of the facts which I state. Finally, to compress into few words the entire summary of my voyage and speedy return, and of the advantages derivable therefrom, I promise, that with a little assistance afforded me by our most invincible sovereigns, I will procure them as much gold as they need, as great a quantity of spices, of cotton, and of mastic[6] (which is only found in Chios), and as many men for the service of the navy as their Majesties may require. I promise also rhubarb and other sorts of drugs, which I am persuaded the men whom I have left in the aforesaid fortress have found already and will continue to find; for I myself have tarried no where longer than I was compelled to do by the winds, except in the city of Navidad, while I provided for the building of the fortress, and took the necessary precautions for the perfect security of the men I left there. Although all I have related may appear to be wonderful and unheard of, yet the results of my voyage would have been more astonishing if I had had at my disposal such ships as I required. But these great and marvelous results are not to be attributed to any merit of mine, but to the holy Christian faith, and to the piety and religion of our Sovereigns; for that which the unaided intellect of man could not compass, the spirit of God has granted to human exertions, for God is wont to hear the prayers of his servants who love his precepts even to the performance of apparent impossibilities.

Thus it has happened to me in the present instance, who have accomplished a task to which the powers of mortal men had never hitherto attained; for if there have been those who have anywhere written or spoken of these islands, they have done so with doubts and conjectures, and no one has ever asserted that he has seen them, on which account their writings have been looked upon as little else than fables. Therefore let the king and queen, our princes and their most happy kingdoms, and all the other

---

6. mastic: a tree resin and ingredient of a strong adhesive.

provinces of Christendom, render thanks to our Lord and Saviour Jesus Christ, who has granted us so great a victory and such prosperity. Let processions be made, and sacred feasts be held, and the temples be adorned with festive boughs. Let Christ rejoice on earth, as he rejoices in heaven in the prospect of the salvation of the souls of so many nations hitherto lost. Let us also rejoice, as well on account of the exaltation of our faith, as on account of the increase of our temporal prosperity, of which not only Spain, but all Christendom will be partakers.

Such are the events which I have briefly described. Farewell.

Lisbon, the 14th of March.

> Christopher Columbus,
> *Admiral of the Fleet of the Ocean.*

5. Amerigo Vespucci

letter to Pier Soderini, Confalonier of the Republic of Florence 1504

When this letter was translated into Latin to give it more weight, it was titled "Mondus Novus" to focus on Vespucci's claim that, in the Western ocean, he had discovered "new lands," "much continental land and innumerable islands": in short, a mondus novus, a new world. The "Mondus Novus" letter so impressed the Dutch scholar and printer Martin Waldseemüller that he reprinted it for sale, and later, upon publishing a map of the New World in 1507, he inscribed on it the name "Ameraca" for the first time, in recognition of Amerigo's perspicacity.

Vespucci's letter offers a remarkably evolved vision of the New World, repeating many of the features already depicted in Columbus's first letter, but complicating that account of blankly innocent savages with a discussion of their customs and beliefs. Rather than a state of absence of civilization, Vespucci projects an alternative one with its own characteristics. This recognition that the Indians possessed a culture did not prevent him from bringing home over two hundred slaves. On the contrary it helped justify doing so. With Vespucci, we have entered fully into the history of the New World.

Magnificent Lord. After humble reverence and due commendations, etc. It may be that your Magnificence will be surprised by my rashness and the affront to your wisdom, in that I should so absurdly bestir myself to write to your Magnificence the present so-prolix letter, knowing that your Magnificence is continually employed in high councils and affairs concerning the good government of this sublime Republic. And will hold me not only presumptuous, but also idly meddlesome in setting myself to write things, neither suitable to your station, nor entertaining, and written in barbarous style, and outside of every canon of literature.

1509 illustration for Vespucci's letter to Soderini.

But the confidence which I have in your virtues and in the truth of my writing, which are things are not found written neither by the ancients nor by modern writers, as your Magnificence will in the sequel perceive, makes me bold. The chief cause which moved me to write to you, was by the request of the present bearer, who is named Benvenuto Benvenuti our Florentine fellow citizen, very much, as it is proven, your Magnificence's servant, and my very good friend: who happening to be here in this city of Lisbon, begged that I should make communication to your Magnificence of the things seen by me in divers regions of the world, by virtue of four voyages which I have made in discovery of new lands: two by order of the King of Castile, King Don Ferrando VI, across the great gulph of the Ocean-sea towards the west; and the other two by command of the puissant King Don Manuel King of Portugal, towards the south. Telling me that your Magnificence would take pleasure thereof, and that herein he hoped to do you service. Wherefore I set me to do it: because I am assured that your Magnificence holds me in the number of your servants, remembering that in the time of our youth I was your friend, and now am your servant: and remembering our going to hear the rudiments of grammar under the fair example and instruction of the venerable monk friar of Saint Mark Fra Giorgio Antonio Vespucci, whose counsels and teaching would to God that I had followed, for as saith Petrarch, I should be another man than what I am. Howbeit soever, I grieve not, because I have ever taken delight in worthy matters. And although these trifles of mine may not be suitable to your virtues, I will say to you as said Pliny to Maecenas, you were sometime wont to take pleasure in my prattlings. Even though your Magnificence be continually busied in public affairs, you will take some hour of relaxation to consume a little time in laughable or amusing things: and as fennel is customarily given atop of delicious viands to fit them for better digestion, so may you, for a relief from your so heavy occupations, order this letter of mine to be read: so that they may withdraw you somewhat from the continual anxiety and assiduous reflection upon public affairs, and if I shall be prolix, I crave pardon, my Magnificent Lord.

Your Magnificence shall know that the motive of my coming into this realm of Spain was to traffic in merchandise: and that I pursued this intent about four years, during which I saw and knew the inconstant shiftings of Fortune, and how she kept changing those frail and transitory benefits, and how at one time she holds man on the summit of the wheel, and at another time drives him back from her, and despoils him of what may be called his borrowed riches. So that, knowing the continuous toil which man undergoes to win them, submitting himself to so many discomforts and risks, I resolved to abandon trade, and to fix my aim upon something more praiseworthy and stable. Whence it was that I made preparation for going to see part of the world and its wonders, and herefor the time and place presented themselves most opportunely to me, which was that the King Don Ferrando of Castile being about to despatch four ships to discover new lands towards the west, I was chosen by his Highness to go in that fleet to aid in making discovery: and we set out from the port of Cadiz on the 10 day of May 1497, and took our route through the great gulph of the Ocean-sea, in which voyage we were 18 months, and discovered much continental land and innumerable islands, and great part of them inhabited, of which there is no mention made by the ancient writers: I believe, because they had no knowledge thereof, for, if I remember well, I have read in some one of those writers that he considered that this Ocean-sea was an unpeopled sea: and of this opinion was Dante our poet in the xxvi. chapter of the Inferno, where he feigns the death of Ulysses, in which voyage I beheld things of great wondrousness, as your Magnificence shall understand. As I said above, we left the port of Cadiz four consort ships, and began our voyage in a direct course to the Fortunate Isles, which are called to-day *la gran Canaria*, which are situated in the Ocean-sea at the extremity of the inhabited west, set in the third climate, over which the North Pole has an elevation of 27 and a half degrees beyond their horizon, and they are 280 leagues distant from this city of Lisbon, by the wind between *mezzo di* and *libeccio*:[7] where we remained eight days, taking in provision of water, and wood, and other necessary things. And from here, having said our prayers, we weighed anchor, and gave the sails to the wind, beginning our course to westward, taking one quarter by southwest, and so we sailed on till at the end of 37 days we reached a land which we deemed to be a continent, which is distant westwardly from the isles of Canary about a thousand leagues beyond the inhabited region within the torrid zone. For we found the North Pole at an elevation of 16 degrees above its horizon, and it was according to the shewing of our instruments, 75 degrees to the west of the isles of Canary, whereat we anchored with our ships a league and a half from land: and we put out our boats freighted with men and arms.

We made towards the land, and before we reached it, had sight of a great number of people who were going along the shore, by which we were much rejoiced. And we observed that they were a naked race. They shewed themselves to stand in fear of us, I believe it was because they saw us clothed and of other appearance than their own. They all withdrew to a hill, and for whatsoever signals we made to them of peace and of friendliness, they would not come to parley with us, so that, as the night was now coming on, and as the ships were anchored in a dangerous place, being on a rough and shelterless coast, we decided to remove from there the next day, and to go in search of some harbour or bay, where we might place our ships in safety. And we sailed with the maestrale wind, thus running along the coast with the land ever in sight, continually in our course observing people along the shore. Till after having navigated for two days, we found a place sufficiently secure for the ships, and

---

7. between *mezzo di* and *libeccio*: between north and southwest.

anchored half a league from land, on which we saw a very great number of people. And this same day we put to land with the boats, and sprang on shore full 40 men in good trim, and still the land's people appeared shy of converse with us, and we were unable to encourage them so much as to make them come to speak with us. And this day we laboured so greatly in giving them of our wares, such as rattles and mirrors, beads, balls, and other trifles, that some of them took confidence and came to discourse with us. And after having made good friends with them, the night coming on, we took our leave of them and returned to the ships. And the next day when the dawn appeared we saw that there were infinite numbers of people upon the beach, and they had their women and children with them. We went ashore, and found that they were all laden with their worldly goods which are suchlike as, in its proper place, shall be related. And before we reached the land, many of them jumped into the sea and came swimming to receive us at a bowshot's length from the shore, for they are very great swimmers, with as much confidence as if they had for a long time been acquainted with us, and we were pleased with this their confidence.

For so much as we learned of their manner of life and customs, it was that they go entirely naked, as well the men as the women, without covering any shameful part, not otherwise than as they issued from their mother's womb. They are of medium stature, very well proportioned: their flesh is of a colour that verges into red like a lion's mane, and I believe that if they went clothed, they would be as white as we. They have not any hair upon the body, except the hair of the head which is long and black, and especially in the women, whom it renders handsome. In aspect they are not very good-looking, because they have broad faces, so that they would seem Tartar-like. They let no hair grow on their eyebrows, nor on their eyelids nor elsewhere, except the hair of the head, for they hold hairiness to be a filthy thing. They are very light-footed in walking and in running, as well the men as the women, so that a woman recks nothing of running a league or two, as many times we saw them do, and herein they have a very great advantage over us Christians. They swim beyond all belief, and the women better than the men, for we have many times found and seen them swimming two leagues out at sea without any thing to rest upon. Their arms are bows and arrows very well made, save that they have no iron nor any other kind of hard metal, and instead of iron they put animals' or fishes' teeth, or a spike of tough wood, with the point hardened by fire: they are sure marksmen, for they hit whatever they aim at: and in some places the women use these bows. They have other weapons, such as fire-hardened spears, and also clubs with knobs, beautifully carved. Warfare is used amongst them, against people not of their own language, very cruelly, without granting life to any one, except for greater suffering.

When they go to war, they take their women with them not that these may fight, but because they carry behind them their worldly goods, for a woman carries on her back for thirty or forty leagues a load which no man could bear, as we have many times seen them do. They are not accustomed to have any Captain, nor do they go in any ordered array, for every one is lord of himself. And the cause of their wars is not for lust of dominion, nor of extending their frontiers, nor for inordinate covetousness, but for some ancient enmity which in by-gone times arose amongst them. And when asked why they made war, they knew not any other reason to give us than that they did so to avenge the death of their ancestors, or of their parents.

These people have neither King, nor Lord, nor do they yield obedience to any one, for they live in their own liberty: and how they be stirred up to go to war is that when the enemies have slain or captured any of them, his oldest kinsman rises up and goes about the highways haranguing them to go with him and avenge the death of such his kinsman, and so are they stirred up by fellow-feeling. They have no judicial system, nor do they punish the ill-doer, nor does the father, nor the mother chastise the children, and marvellously seldom or never did we see any dispute among them. In their conversation they appear simple, and are very cunning and acute in that which concerns them. They speak little and in a low tone, they use the same articulations as we, since they form their utterances either with the palate, or with the teeth, or on the lips, except that they give different names to things. Many are the varieties of tongues, for in every 100 leagues we found a change of language, so that they are not understandable each to the other. The manner of their living is very barbarous, for they eat at no certain hours, and as oftentimes as they will. And it does not matter much to them that the will may come rather at midnight than by day, for they eat at all hours. And their repast is made upon the ground without a table-cloth or any other cover, for they have their meats either in earthen basins which they make therefor, or in the halves of pumpkins. They sleep in certain very large nettings made of cotton, suspended in the air. And although this their fashion of sleeping may seem uncomfortable, I say that it is sweet to sleep in those, and we slept better in them than in quilts.[8] They are a people of neat exterior, and clean of body, because of so continually washing themselves as they do. When, saving your reverence, they evacuate the stomach they do their utmost not to be observed, and as much as in this they are cleanly and bashful, so much the more are they filthy and shameless in making water, since, while standing speaking to us, without turning round or shewing any shame, they let go their nastiness, for in this they have no shame.

There is no custom of marriages amongst them. Each man takes as many women as he lists, and when he desires to repudiate them, he repudiates them without any imputation of wrong-doing to him, or of disgrace to the woman, for in this the woman has as much liberty as the man. They are not very jealous and are immoderately libidinous, and the women much more so than the men, so that for decency I omit to tell you the artifice they practice to gratify their inordinate lust. They are very fertile women, and do not shirk any work during their pregnancies, and their travails in childbed are so light that, a single day after parturition, they go abroad everywhere, and especially to wash themselves in the rivers, and are then as sound as fishes. They are so void of affection and cruel, that if they be angry with their husbands they immediately adopt an artificial method by which the embryo is destroyed in the womb, and procure abortion, and they slay an infinite number of creatures by that means. They are women of elegant persons very well proportioned, so that in their bodies there appears no ill-shapen part or limb. And although they go entirely naked, they are fleshy women, and, of their sexual organ, that portion which he who has never seen it may imagine, is not visible, for they conceal with their thighs everything

8. Vespucci is describing the hammock, which was unknown in Europe.

except that part for which nature did not provide, which is, speaking modestly, the pectignone. In fine, they have no shame of their shameful parts, any more than we have in displaying the nose and the mouth: it is marvellously rare that you shall see a woman's paps hang low, or her belly fallen in by too much childbearing, or other wrinkles, for they all appear as though they had never brought forth children.

They shewed themselves very desirous of having connexion with us Christians. Amongst those people we did not learn that they had any law, nor can they be called Moors nor Jews, and they are worse than pagans, because we never saw them offer any sacrifice, nor even had they a house of prayer. Their manner of living I judge to be Epicurean: their dwellings are in common, and their houses made in the style of huts, but strongly made, and constructed with very large trees, and covered over with palm-leaves, secure against storms and winds, and in some places of so great breadth and length, that in one single house we found there were 600 souls, and we saw a village of only thirteen houses where there were four thousand souls, every eight or ten years they change their place of habitation, and when asked why they did so, they said it was because of the soil which, from its filthiness, was already unhealthy and corrupted, and that it bred aches in their bodies, which seemed to us a good reason. Their riches consist of birds' plumes of many colours, or of rosaries which they make from fishbones, or of white or green stones which they put in their cheeks and in their lips and ears, and of many other things which we in no wise value: they use no trade, they neither buy nor sell. In fine, they live and are contented with that which nature gives them. The wealth that we enjoy in this our Europe and elsewhere, such as gold, jewels, pearls, and other riches, they hold as nothing, and although they have them in their own lands, they do not labour to obtain them, nor do they value them. They are liberal in giving, for it is rarely they deny you anything, and on the other hand, free in asking, when they shew themselves your friends. The greatest sign of friendship which they shew you is that they give you their wives and their daughters, and a father or a mother deems himself or herself highly honored, when they bring you a daughter, even though she be a young virgin, if you sleep with her, and hereunto they use every expression of friendship.

When they die, they use divers manners of obsequies, and some they bury with water and victuals at their heads, thinking that they shall have to eat. They have not nor do they use ceremonies of torches nor of lamentation. In some other places they use the most barbarous and inhuman burial, which is that when a suffering or infirm person is as it were at the last pass of death, his kinsmen carry him into a large forest, and attach one of those nets of theirs, in which they sleep, to two trees, and then put him in it, and dance around him for a whole day. And when the night comes on they place at his bolster, water with other victuals, so that he may be able to subsist for four or six days, and then they leave him alone and return to the village. And if the sick man helps himself, and eats, and drinks, and survives, he returns to the village, and his friends receive him with ceremony. But few are they who escape. Without receiving any further visit they die, and that is their sepulture. And they have many other customs which for prolixity are not related. They use in their sicknesses various forms of medicines, so different from ours that we marvelled how any one escaped. For many times I saw that with a man sick of fever, when it heightened upon him, they bathed him from head to foot with a large quantity of cold water; then they lit a great fire around him, making him turn and turn again every two hours, until they tired him and left him to sleep, and many were cured. With this they make much use of dieting, for they remain three days without eating, and also of blood-letting, but not from the arm, only from the thighs and the loins and the calf of the leg. Also they provoke vomiting with their herbs which are put into the mouth, and they use many other remedies which it would be long to relate. They are much vitiated in the phlegm and in the blood because of their food which consists chiefly of roots of herbs, and fruits and fish.

They have no seed of wheat nor other grain, and for their ordinary use and feeding, they have a root of a tree, from which they make flour, tolerably good, and they call it Iuca, and others call it Cazabi, and others Ignami. They eat little flesh except human flesh: for your Magnificence must know that herein they are so inhuman that they outdo every custom even of beasts, for they eat all their enemies whom they kill or capture, as well females as males, with so much savagery, that to relate it appears a horrible thing, how much more so to see it, as, infinite times and in many places, it was my hap to see it. And they wondered to hear us say that we did not eat our enemies, and this your Magnificence may take for certain, that their other barbarous customs are such that expression is too weak for the reality. And as in these four voyages I have seen so many things diverse from our customs, I prepared to write a common-place-book which I name Le Quattro Giornate, in which I have set down the greater part of the things which I saw, sufficiently in detail, so far as my feeble wit has allowed me, which I have not yet published, because I have so ill a taste for my own things that I do not relish those which I have written, notwithstanding that many encourage me to publish it, therein everything will be seen in detail, so that I shall not enlarge further in this chapter. As in the course of the letter we shall come to many other things which are particular, let this suffice for the general. At this beginning, we saw nothing in the land of much profit, except some show of gold. I believe the cause of it was that we did not know the language, but in so far as concerns the situation and condition of the land, it could not be better. We decided to leave that place, and to go further on, continuously coasting the shore, upon which we made frequent descents, and held converse with a great number of people. And after some days we went into a harbour where we underwent very great danger: and it pleased the Holy Ghost to save us, and it was in this wise.

We landed in a harbour, where we found a village built like Venice upon the water. There were about 44 large dwellings in the form of huts erected upon very thick piles, and they had their doors or entrances in the style of drawbridges, and from each house one could pass through all, by means of the drawbridges which stretched from house to house. And when the people thereof had seen us, they appeared to be afraid of us, and immediately drew up all the bridges, and while we were looking at this strange action, we saw coming across the sea about 22 canoes, which are a kind of boats of theirs, constructed from a single tree, which came towards our boats, as if they had been surprised by our appearance and clothes, and kept wide of us. And thus remaining, we made signals to them that they should approach us, encouraging them with every token of friendliness, and seeing that they did not come, we went to them, and they did not stay for us, but made to the land, and, by signs, told us to wait, and that they would soon return. And they went to a hill in the background, and did not delay long. When they returned, they led with them 16 of their girls, and entered with these into their canoes, and came to the boats, and in each boat they put 4 of the girls. How greatly we marvelled at this behaviour your Magnificence can imagine, and they placed themselves with their canoes among our boats, coming to speak with us, insomuch that we deemed it a mark of friendliness.

And while thus engaged, we beheld a great number of people advance swimming towards us across the sea, who came from the houses, and as if they were approaching us without any apprehension. Just then there appeared at the doors of the houses certain old women, uttering very loud cries and tearing their hair to exhibit grief, whereby they made us suspicious, and we each betook ourselves to arms. And instantly the girls whom we had in the boats, threw themselves into the sea, and the men of the canoes drew away from us, and began with their bows to shoot arrows at us. And those who were swimming each carried a lance held, as covertly as they could, beneath the water. So that, recognizing the treachery, we engaged with them, not merely to defend ourselves, but to attack them vigorously, and we overturned with our boats many of their skiffs or canoes, for so they call them, we made a slaughter, and they all flung themselves into the water to swim, leaving their canoes abandoned, with considerable loss on their side, they went swimming away to the shore. There were killed of them about 15 or 20, and many were left wounded. Of ours 5 were wounded, and all, by the grace of God, escaped. We captured two of the girls and two men, and we proceeded to their houses, and entered therein, and in them all we found nothing but two old women and a sick man, we took away from them many things, but of small value, and we would not burn their houses, because it seemed to us a burden upon our conscience. And we returned to our boats with five prisoners, and betook ourselves to the ships, and put a pair of irons on the feet of each of the captives, except the girls, and when the night came on, the two girls and one of the men escaped in the most subtle manner possible.

And next day we decided to quit that harbour and go further onwards. We proceeded continuously skirting the coast, until we had sight of another tribe distant perhaps some 80 leagues from the former tribe, and we found them very different in speech and customs. We resolved to cast anchor, and went ashore with the boats, and we saw on the beach a great number of people amounting probably to 4000 souls: and when we had reached the shore, they did not stay for us, and betook themselves to flight through the forests, abandoning their things.[9] We jumped on land, and took a pathway that led to the forest, and at the distance of a bow-shot we found their tents, where they had made very large fires, and two were cooking their victuals, and roasting several animals, and fish of many kinds, where we saw that they were roasting a certain animal which seemed to be a serpent, save that it had no wings, and was in its appearance so foul that we marvelled much at its loathsomeness.[10] Thus went we on through their houses, or rather tents, and found many of those serpents

9. This landing appears to be in the general area of French Guiana.   10. serpent: probably an iguana.

alive, and they were tied by the feet and had a cord around their snouts, so that they could not open their mouths, as is done in Europe with mastiff-dogs so that they may not bite. They were of such savage aspect that none of us dared to take one away, thinking that they were poisonous. They are of the bigness of a kid, and in length an ell and a half. Their feet are long and thick, and armed with big claws, they have a hard skin, and are of various colours. They have the muzzle and aspect of a serpent: and from their snouts there rises a crest like a saw which extends along the middle of the back as far as the tip of the tail. In fine we deemed them to be serpents and venomous, and they were used as food. We found that those people made bread out of little fishes which they took from the sea, first boiling them, pounding them, and making thereof a paste, or bread, and they baked them on the glowing embers, thus did they eat them. We tried it, and found that it was good. They had so many other kinds of eatables, and especially of fruits and roots, that it would be a large matter to describe them in detail, and seeing that the people did not return, we decided not to touch nor take away anything of theirs, so as better to reassure them. And we left in the tents for them many of our things, placed where they should see them, and returned by night to our ships.

And the next day, when it was light, we saw on the beach an infinite number of people, and we landed. And although they appeared timorous towards us, they took courage nevertheless to hold converse with us, giving us whatever we asked of them, and shewing themselves very friendly towards us, they told us that those were their dwellings, and that they had come hither for the purpose of fishing, and they begged that we would visit their dwellings and villages, because they desired to receive us as friends. And they engaged in such friendship because of the two captured men whom we had with us, as these were their enemies, insomuch that, in view of such importunity on their part, holding a council, we determined that 28 of us Christians in good array should go with them, and in the firm resolve to die if it should be necessary, and after we had been here some three days, we went with them inland. And at three leagues from the coast we came to a village of many people and few houses, for there were no more than nine, where we were received with such and so many barbarous ceremonies that the pen suffices not to write them down, for there were dances, and songs, and lamentations mingled with rejoicing, and great quantities of food. And here we remained the night, where they offered us their women, so that we were unable to withstand them, and after having been here that night and half the next day, so great was the number of people who came wondering to behold us that they were beyond counting, and the most aged begged us to go with them to other villages which were further inland, making display of doing us the greatest honour, wherefore we decided to go. And it would be impossible to tell you how much honour they did us, and we went to several villages, so that we were nine days journeying, so that our Christians who had remained with the ships were already apprehensive concerning us.

And when we were about 18 leagues in the interior of the land, we resolved to return to the ships, and on our way back, such was the number of people, as well men as women, that came with us as far as the sea, that it was a wondrous thing, and if any of us became weary of the march, they carried us in their nets very refreshingly, and in crossing the rivers, which are many and very large, they passed us over by skilful means so securely that we ran no danger whatever, and many of them came laden with the things which they had given us, which consisted of their sleeping-nets, and very rich feathers, many bows and arrows, innumerable popinjays of divers colours, and others brought with them loads of their household goods, and of animals. But a greater marvel will I tell you, that, when we had to cross a river, he deemed himself lucky who was able to carry us on his back, and when we reached the sea, our boats having arrived, we entered into them: and so great was the struggle which they made to get into our boats, and to come to see our ships, that we marvelled, and in our boats we took as many of them as we could, and made our way to the ships, and so many came swimming that we found ourselves embarrassed in seeing so many people in the ships, for there were over a thousand persons all naked and unarmed. They were amazed by our gear and contrivances, and the size of the ships, and with them there occurred to us a very laughable affair, which was that we decided to fire off some of our great guns, and when the explosion took place, most of them through fear cast themselves to swim, not otherwise than frogs on the margins of a pond, when they see something that frightens them, will jump into the water, just so did those people, and those who remained in the ships were so terrified that we regretted our action. However we reassured them by telling them that with those arms we slew our enemies. And when they had amused themselves in the ships the whole day, we told them to go away because we desired to depart that night, and so separating from us with much friendship and love, they went away to land.

Amongst that people and in their land, I knew and beheld so many of their customs and ways of living, that I do not care to enlarge upon them. For Your Magnificence must know that in each of my voyages I have noted the most wonderful things, and I have indited it all in a volume after the manner of a geography, and I intitle it Le Quattro Giornate, in which work the things are comprised in detail, and as yet there is no copy of it given out, as it is necessary for me to revise it. This land is very populous, and full of inhabitants, and of numberless rivers, animals, few resemble ours, excepting lions, panthers, stages, pigs, goats, and deer, and even these have some dissimilarities of form. They have no horses nor mules, nor, saving your reverence, asses nor dogs, nor any kind of sheep or oxen, but so numerous are the other animals which they have—and all are savage, and of none do they make use for their service—that they could not be counted. What shall we say of their different birds? which are so numerous, and of so many kinds, and of such various-coloured plumages, that it is a marvel to behold them. The land is very pleasant and fruitful, full of immense woods and forests: and it is always green, for the foliage never drops off. The fruits are so many that they are numberless and entirely different from ours. This land is within the torrid zone, close to or just under the parallel which marks the Tropic of Cancer, where the pole of the horizon has an elevation of 23 degrees, at the extremity of the second climate.

Many tribes came to see us, and wondered at our faces and our whiteness, and they asked us whence we came, and we gave them to understand that we had come from heaven, and that we were going to see the world, and they believed it. In this land we placed baptismal fonts, and an infinite number of people were baptized, and they called us in their language Carabi, which means men of great wisdom. We took our departure from that port, and the province is called Lariab, and we navigated along the coast, always in sight of land, until we had run 870 leagues of it, still going in the direction of the maestrale, north-west, making in our course many halts, and holding intercourse with many peoples. And in several places we obtained gold by barter but not much in quantity, for we had done enough in discovering the land and learning that they had gold.

We had now been thirteen months on the voyage, and the vessels and the tackling were already much damaged, and the men worn out by fatigue. We decided by general council to haul our ships on land and examine them for the purpose of stanching leaks, as they made much water, and of caulking and tarring them afresh, and returning towards Spain, and when we came to this determination, we were close to a harbour the best in the world, into which we entered with our vessels, where we found an immense number of people, who received us with much friendliness. And on the shore we made a bastion with our boats and with barrels and casks, and our artillery, which commanded every point, and our ships having been unloaded and lightened, we drew them upon land, and repaired them in everything that was needful. And the land's people gave us very great assistance, and continually furnished us with their victuals, so that in this port we tasted little of our own, which suited our game well, for the stock of provisions which we had for our return-passage was little and of sorry kind, where we remained 37 days, and went many times to their villages, where they paid us the greatest honour, and desiring to depart upon our voyage, they made complaint to us how at certain times of the year there came from over the sea to this their land, a race of people very cruel, and enemies of theirs, and by means of treachery or of violence slew many of them, and ate them: and some they made captives, and carried them away to their houses, or country, and how they could scarcely contrive to defend themselves from them, making signs to us that were an island-people and lived out in the sea about a hundred leagues away, and so piteously did they tell us this that we believed them, and we promised to avenge them of so much wrong, and they remained overjoyed herewith. And many of them offered to come along with us, but we did not wish to take them for many reasons, save that we took seven of them, on condition that they should come afterwards in canoes because we did not desire to be obliged to take them back to their country, and they were contented.

And so we departed from those people, leaving them very friendly towards us, and having repaired our ships, and sailing for seven days out to sea between north-east and east. And at the end of the seven days we came upon the islands, which were many, some inhabited, and others deserted. And we anchored at one of them, where we saw a numerous people who called it Iti. And having manned our boats with strong crews, and taken three guns in each, we made for land, where we found about 400 men, and many women, and all naked like the former. They were of good bodily presence, and seemed right warlike men, for they were armed with their weapons, which are bows, arrows, and lances, and most of them had square wooden targets, and bore them in such wise that they did not impede the drawing of the bow. And when we had come with our boats to about a bowshot of the land, they all sprang into the water to shoot their arrows at us and to prevent us from leaping upon shore, and they all had their bodies painted of various colours, and plumed with feathers. And the interpreters who were with us told us that when they displayed themselves so painted and plumed, it was to betoken that they wanted to fight, and so much did they persist in preventing us from landing, that we were compelled to play with our artillery. And when they heard the explosion, and saw some of their number fall dead, they all drew back to the land, wherefore, forming our Council, we resolved that 42 of our men should spring on shore, and, if they waited for us, fight them. Thus having leaped to land with our weapons, they advanced towards us, and we fought for about an hour, but we had little advantage of them, except that our arbalasters and gunners killed some of them, and they wounded certain of our men, and this was because they did not stand to receive us within reach of lance-thrust or sword-blow. And so much vigour did we put forth at last, that we came to sword-play, and when they tasted our weapons, they betook themselves to flight through the mountains and the forests, and left us conquerors of the field with many of them dead and a good number wounded. And for that day we took no other pains to pursue them, because we were very weary, and we returned to our ships, with so much gladness on the part of the seven men who had come with us that they could not contain themselves.

And when the next day arrived, we beheld coming across the land a great number of people, with signals of battle, continually sounding horns, and various other instruments which they use in their wars, and all painted and feathered, so that it was a very strange sight to behold them. Wherefore all the ships held council, and it was resolved that since this people desired hostility with us, we should proceed to encounter them and try by every means to make them friends. In case they would not have our friendship, that we should treat them as foes, and so many of them as we might be able to capture should all be our slaves. And having armed ourselves as best we could, we advanced towards the shore, and they sought not to hinder us from landing, I believe from fear of the cannons, and we jumped on land, 57 men in four squadrons, each one consisting of a captain and his company, and we came to blows with them. And after a long battle in which many of them were slain, we put them to flight, and pursued them to a village, having made about 250 of them captives, and we burnt the village, and returned to our ships with victory and 250 prisoners leaving many of them dead and wounded, and of ours there were no more than one killed, and 22 wounded, who all escaped, God be thanked. We arranged our departure, and the seven men, of whom five were wounded, took an island-canoe, and, with seven prisoners that we gave them, four women and three men, returned to their country full of gladness, wondering at our strength. And we thereupon made sail for Spain with 222 captive slaves, and reached the port of Cadiz on the 15 day of October 1498, where we were well received and sold our slaves. Such is what befell me, most noteworthy, in this my first voyage.

6. King Manuel I of Portugal

Letter to the King and Queen of Castile 1499

King Manuel I (1469–1521) reigned over a consolidating nation and an expanding empire, including important holdings in Brazil and India. Portuguese explorers were the first and most important at the start of the period of exploration. Here King Manuel has the pleasure of announcing the major victory of Vasco da Gama who in 1498 temporarily outdid the discovery of the New World by succeeding where Columbus had failed, reaching the East by an ocean route.

Most high and excellent Prince and Princess, most potent Lord and Lady! Your Highnesses already know that we had ordered Vasco da Gama, a nobleman of our household, and his brother Paulo da Gama, with four vessels to make discoveries by sea, and that two years have now elapsed since their departure. And as the principal motive of this enterprise has been, with our predecessors, the service of God our Lord, and our own advantage, it pleased Him in His mercy to speed them on their route. From a message which has now been brought to this city by one of the captains, we learn that they did reach and discover India and other kingdoms and lordships bordering upon it; that they entered and navigated its sea, finding large cities, large edifices and rivers, and great populations, among whom is carried on all the trade in spices and precious stones, which are forwarded in ships (which these same explorers saw and met with in good numbers and of great size) to Mecca, and thence to Cairo, whence they are dispersed throughout the world. Of these they have brought a quantity, including cinnamon, cloves, ginger, nutmeg, and pepper, as well as other kinds, together with the boughs and leaves of the same; also many fine stones of all sorts, such as rubies and others. And they also came to a country in which there are mines of gold, of which as of the spices and precious stones, they did not bring as much as they could have done, for they took no merchandise with them.

As we are aware that your Highnesses will hear of these things with much pleasure and satisfaction, we thought well to give this information. And your Highnesses may believe, in accordance with what we have learnt concerning the Christian people whom these explorers reached, that it will be possible, notwithstanding that they are not as yet strong in the faith or possessed of a thorough knowledge of it, to do much in the service of God and the exaltation of the Holy Faith, once they shall have been converted and fully fortified in it. And when they shall have thus been fortified in the faith there will be an opportunity for destroying the Moors of those parts. Moreover, we hope, with the help of God, that the great trade which now enriches the Moors of those parts, through whose hands it passes without the intervention of other persons or peoples, shall, in consequence of our regulations be diverted to the natives and ships of our own kingdom, so that henceforth all Christendom, in this part of Europe, shall be able, in a large measure, to provide itself with these spices and precious stones. This, with the help of God, who in His mercy thus ordained it, will cause our designs and intentions to be pushed with more ardour especially as respects the war upon the Moors of the territories conquered by us in these parts, which your Highnesses are so firmly resolved upon, and in which we are equally zealous.

And we pray your Highnesses, in consideration of this great favour, which, with much gratitude, we received from Our Lord, to cause to be addressed to Him those praises which are His due.

Most high and excellent Prince and Princess, most potent Lord and Lady, may the Lord our God ever hold your persons and kingdoms in His holy keeping.

Written at Lisbon, July 1499.

7.

Nahuatl accounts of the Spanish conquest of Mexico
assembled beginning in 1528

About 2,000 years ago, at the same time as the Romans were establishing their empire and Christianity was beginning its expansion in the Mediterranean world, the empire of the Maya was emerging in Mexico. This empire remained powerful into the eighth and ninth centuries to be followed by others, notably that of the Toltecs. The last Indian rulers of the area were the Aztecs who, from the fourteenth to the fifteenth century, built an empire embracing several million people, whose wealth and culture, embodied in its capital Tenochtitlan (today Mexico City), astounded the arriving conquistadors.

From their Toltec predecessors, the Aztecs had adopted the Nahuatl language, and a method of writing combining pictographs, ideographs, and quasi-phonetic symbols. After the conquest, Spanish friars developed a way to write Nahuatl in the Latin alphabet. Using this, scribes began recording, in 1528, only seven years after the fall of Tenochtitlan, a virtually unique Indian version of the conquest of America. The selections below include: a list of omens purported to have predicted the catastrophic arrival of the Spanish; a description of the Spanish seen as barbarians; accounts of fierce battles, in one of which the invaders are driven back (this defeat led to a two-year stalemate that ended only when an epidemic decimated the besieged Indians); and the final episode of the war, the capture of the Aztec king.

[THE OMENS]

The first bad omen: Ten years before the Spaniards first came here, a bad omen appeared in the sky. It was like a flaming ear of corn, or a fiery signal, or the blaze of daybreak; it seemed to bleed fire, drop by drop, like a wound in the sky. It was wide at the base and narrow at the peak, and it shone in the very heart of the heavens.

This is how it appeared: it shone in the eastern sky in the middle of the night. It appeared at midnight and burned till the break of day, but it vanished at the rising of the sun. The time during which it appeared to us was a full year, beginning in the year 12-House.

When it first appeared, there was great outcry and confusion. The people clapped their hands against their mouths; they were amazed and frightened, and asked themselves what it could mean.

1615 Italian engraving of the Aztec deity Tonacatecuhtli, based on a codex from Mexico.

The second bad omen: The temple of Huitzilopochtli burst into flames. It is thought that no one set it afire, that it burned down of its own accord. The name of its divine site was Tlacateccan (House of Authority).

And now it is burning, the wooden columns are burning! The flames, the tongues of fire shoot out, the bursts of fire shoot up into the sky!

The flames swiftly destroyed all the woodwork of the temple. When the fire was first seen, the people shouted: "Mexicanos, come running! We can put it out! Bring your water jars . . . !" But when they threw water on the blaze it only flamed higher. They could not put it out, and the temple burned to the ground.

The third bad omen: A temple was damaged by a lightning-bolt. This was the temple of Xiuhtecuhtli, which was built of straw, in the place known as Tzonmolco. It was raining that day, but it was only a light rain or a drizzle, and no thunder was heard. Therefore the lightning-bolt was taken as an omen. The people said: "The temple was struck by a blow from the sun."

The fourth bad omen: Fire streamed through the sky while the sun was still shining. It was divided into three parts. It flashed out from where the sun sets and raced straight to where the sun rises, giving off a shower of sparks like a red-hot coal. When the people saw its long train streaming through the heavens, there was a great outcry and confusion, as if they were shaking a thousand little bells.

The fifth bad omen: The wind lashed the water until it boiled. It was as if it were boiling with rage, as if it were shattering itself in its frenzy. It began from far off, rose high in the air and dashed against the walls of the houses. The flooded houses collapsed into the water. This was in the lake that is next to us.

The sixth bad omen: The people heard a weeping woman night after night. She passed by in the middle of the night, wailing and crying out in a loud voice: "My children, we must flee far away from this city!" At other times she cried: "My children, where shall I take you?"

The seventh bad omen: A strange creature was captured in the nets. The men who fish the lakes caught a bird the color of ashes, a bird resembling a crane. They brought it to Motecuhzoma in the Black House.

This bird wore a strange mirror in the crown of its head. The mirror was pierced in the center like a spindle whorl, and the night sky could be seen in its face. The hour was noon, but the stars and the *mamalhuaztli*[11] could be seen in the face of that mirror. Motecuhzoma took it as a great and bad omen when he saw the stars and the *mamalhuaztli*.

But when he looked at the mirror a second time, he saw a distant plain. People were moving across it, spread out in ranks and coming forward in great haste. They made war against each other and rode on the backs of animals resembling deer.

Motecuhzoma called for his magicians and wise men and asked them: "Can you explain what I have seen? Creatures like human beings, running and fighting . . . !" But when they looked into the mirror to answer him, all had vanished away, and they saw nothing.

The eighth bad omen: Monstrous beings appeared in the streets of the city: deformed men with two heads but only one body. They were taken to the Black House and shown to Motecuhzoma; but the moment he saw them, they all vanished away.

[The Spaniards See the Objects of Gold]

Then Motecuhzoma dispatched various chiefs. Tzihuacpopocatzin was at their head, and he took with him a great many of his representatives. They went out to meet the Spaniards in the vicinity of Popocatepetl and Iztactepetl, there in the Eagle Pass.

They gave the "gods" ensigns of gold, and ensigns of quetzal feathers, and golden necklaces. And when they were given these presents, the Spaniards burst into smiles; their eyes shone with pleasure; they were delighted by them. They picked up the gold and fingered it like monkeys; they seemed to be transported by joy, as if their hearts were illumined and made new.

The truth is that they longed and lusted for gold. Their bodies swelled with greed, and their hunger was ravenous; they hungered like pigs for that gold. They snatched at the golden ensigns, waved them from side to side and examined every inch of them. They were like one who speaks a barbarous tongue: everything they said was in a barbarous tongue.

[The Spaniards Attack the Celebrants]

At this moment in the fiesta, when the dance was loveliest and when song was linked to song, the Spaniards were seized with an urge to kill the celebrants. They all

11. *mamalhuaztli*: three stars in the constellation Taurus of great importance in Nahuatl religion.

ran forward, armed as if for battle. They closed the entrances and passageways, all the gates of the patio: the Eagle Gate in the lesser palace, the Gate of the Canestalk and the Gate of the Serpent of Mirrors. They posted guards so that no one could escape, and then rushed into the Sacred Patio to slaughter the celebrants. They came on foot, carrying their swords and their wooden or metal shields.

They ran in among the dancers, forcing their way to the place where the drums were played. They attacked the man who was drumming and cut off his arms. Then they cut off his head, and it rolled across the floor.

They attacked all the celebrants, stabbing them, spearing them, striking them with their swords. They attacked some of them from behind, and these fell instantly to the ground with their entrails hanging out. Others they beheaded: they cut off their heads, or split their heads to pieces.

They struck others in the shoulders, and their arms were torn from their bodies. They wounded some in the thigh and some in the calf. They slashed others in the abdomen, and their entrails all spilled to the ground. Some attempted to run away, but their intestines dragged as they ran; they seemed to tangle their feet in their own entrails. No matter how they tried to save themselves, they could find no escape.

Some attempted to force their way out, but the Spaniards murdered them at the gates. Others climbed the walls, but they could not save themselves. Those who ran into the communal houses were safe there for a while; so were those who lay down among the victims and pretended to be dead. But if they stood up again, the Spaniards saw them and killed them.

The blood of the warriors flowed like water and gathered into pools. The pools widened, and the stench of blood and entrails filled the air. The Spaniards ran into the communal houses to kill those who were hiding. They ran everywhere and searched everywhere; they invaded every room, hunting and killing.

[THE AZTECS RETALIATE]

When the news of this massacre was heard outside the Sacred Patio, a great cry went up: "Mexicanos, come running! Bring your spears and shields! The strangers have murdered our warriors!"

This cry was answered with a roar of grief and anger: the people shouted and wailed and beat their palms against their mouths. The captains assembled at once, as if the hour had been determined in advance. They all carried their spears and shields.

Then the battle began. The Aztecs attacked with javelins and arrows, even with the light spears that are used for hunting birds. They hurled their javelins with all their strength, and the cloud of missiles spread out over the Spaniards like a yellow cloak.

The Spaniards immediately took refuge in the palace. They began to shoot at the Mexicans with their iron arrows and to fire their cannons and arquebuses. And they shackled Motecuhzoma in chains.

[THE MASSACRE AT THE CANAL OF THE TOLTECS]

When the Spaniards reached the Canal of the Toltecs, in Tlaltecayohuacan, they hurled themselves headlong into the water, as if they were leaping from a cliff. The

Tlaxcaltecas, the allies from Tliliuhquitepec, the Spanish foot soldiers and horsemen, the few women who accompanied the army—all came to the brink and plunged over it.

The canal was soon choked with the bodies of men and horses; they filled the gap in the causeway with their own drowned bodies. Those who followed crossed to the other side by walking on the corpses.

When they reached Petlalco, where there was another canal, they crossed over on their portable bridge without being attacked by the Aztecs. They stopped and rested there for a short while, and began to feel more like men again. Then they marched on to Popotla.

Dawn was breaking as they entered the village. Their hearts were cheered by the brightening light of this new day: they thought the horrors of the retreat by night were all behind them. But suddenly they heard war cries and the Aztecs swarmed through the streets and surrounded them. They had come to capture Tlaxcaltecas for their sacrifices. They also wanted to complete their revenge against the Spaniards.

The Aztecs harried the army all the way to Tlacopan. Chimalpopoca, the son of Motecuhzoma, was killed in the action at Tlilyuhcan by an arrow from the crossbows. Tlaltecatzin, the Tepanec prince, was wounded in the same action and died shortly after. He had served the Spaniards as a guide and advisor, pointing out the best roads and short cuts.

[The Capture of Cuauhtemoc]

At a given signal, our forces attacked the enemy all at once. We pressed forward so swiftly that within a few hours we had totally defeated them. Our brigantines and canoes attacked their flotilla; they could not withstand us but scattered in every direction, with our forces pursuing them. Garcia de Olguin, who commanded one of the brigantines, was told by an Aztec prisoner that the canoe he was following was that of the king. He bore down on it and gradually caught up with it.

Cuauhtemoc, seeing that the enemy was overtaking him, ordered the boatman to turn the canoe toward our barkentine and prepare to attack it. He grasped his shield and *macana* and was determined to give battle. But when he realized that the enemy could overwhelm him with crossbows and muskets, he put down his arms and surrendered.

[The Imprisonment of Cuauhtemoc]

The Aztecs are besieged in the city;
the Tlatelolcas are besieged in the city!

The walls are black,
the air is black with smoke,
the guns flash in the darkness.
They have captured Cuauhtemoc;
they have captured the princes of Mexico.

The Aztecs are besieged in the city;
the Tlatelolcas are besieged in the city!

After nine days, they were taken to Coyoacan:
Cuauhtemoc, Coanacoch, Tetlepanquetzaltzin.
The kings are prisoners now.

Tlacotzin consoled them:
"Oh my nephews, take heart!
The kings are prisoners now;
they are bound with chains."

The king Cuauhtemoc replied:
"Oh my nephew, you are a prisoner;
they have bound you in irons.

"But who is that at the side of the Captain-General?
Ah, it is Dona Isabel, my little niece!
Ah, it is true: the kings are prisoners now!

"You will be a slave and belong to another:
the collar will be fashioned in Coyoacan,
where the quetzal feathers will be woven.

"Who is that at the side of the Captain-General?
Ah, it is Dona Isabel, my little niece!
Ah, it is true: the kings are prisoners now!"

TWO

The Sixteenth and Seventeenth Centuries

Chapter 2

Learning to Say "America" in English

INTRODUCTION

Like the Ming Chinese, the Ottoman Turks, the Spanish, and the Portuguese, the English at the close of the fifteenth century were showing interest in other lands. Cosmography became an arousing business. The transnational elite of cosmographers visited and corresponded with the Tudor court. Columbus, seeking backing for his route to India in the late 1480s, approached Henry VII as a likely source—though without success. The Cabota family left Venice for London, where the father and son would come to be known as John and Sebastian Cabot. Gradually the English began developing their own speculations about the navigable world. Expeditions went east, to Russia, looking for a northerly route to India. (Later, expeditions in the other direction would be financed by the same Muscovy Company.) They went overland to Persia, down the Atlantic coast to Africa, and, in the wake of the Spanish, to the tropics of the Western hemisphere. The English paid more attention than before to neighboring Atlantic islands, dramatically renewing efforts to dominate the Irish. They also began speculating about the more distant northwest lands where English boats had already been visiting on fishing expeditions. Could they find a route to India that way?

Still, throughout the sixteenth century, and well into the seventeenth, English efforts in the Western reaches of the Atlantic were tentative and feeble by comparison with the Spanish and Portuguese empires. With the wealthiest of the Amerindian cultures already enslaved, the English found little prospect in imitating the Iberian model of conquest. Even later, when they applied the classic model of colonialism on a grand scale in India, they did not do so in the Americas. As the texts collected here show, however, the English slowly developed in the Western hemisphere a different kind of colonial venture. Instead of sending an armed administration to control the wealth of a native population, the English began to consider sending their own population— something the Spanish and Portuguese never willingly did. The settlement method of colonialism, called "planting," was a new game entirely. It allowed the English finally to get out from under the Iberian shadow in the competition of empires.

This chapter covers the first phase of English expansion, when the new model of settlement colonies was still only a theory. The texts are not limited, therefore, to what would later become English colonies, for English interests before settlement were geographically rather vague. To the end of the century, English speculation continued to center on India and China. Because the English had not yet set up a territorial administration, they tended to use geographical names loosely: India, Cathay, Newfoundland, Virginia, America, New Albion, New Spain, and Terra Florida are overlapping if not interchangeable terms in many of these texts.

The writings collected here, unlike their French or Spanish counterparts, show only sporadic interest in Amerindians. English writing contains no equivalent of Sahagun, Las Casas, or the *Jesuit Relations*. These texts should not therefore be regarded as an encompassing record of the period. They are what the English themselves produced *as* their record. Written texts themselves, during the period covered here, were central to the growing self-understanding of the English as a nation and as an empire. The English were not yet developing colonies, but they *were* developing a record—written reports that they could circulate as part of a developing culture of cosmo-

"*America,*" Amsterdam, *1671.*

graphical alertness. London printers gradually became involved in marketing the new expertise. They published narratives, polemics, tributes, and—not least—translations of the most informative French and Spanish works. The summa of this great enterprise was Richard Hakluyt's great compilation, *The Principal Navigations, Voyages, Traffiques, and Discoveries of the English Nation.* Many of the texts in this chapter appeared in Hakluyt, though only about half of his collection was devoted to the Americas. Hakluyt does not seem to have intended a thorough documentation of the New World; his focus was on English forays outward, and his industrious editing indeed demonstrated the long reach of English envoys, in *all* parts of the known world. He himself also advanced some of the earliest theories for the English-American colonial mode.

Selections appear in a rough chronology; we seek to introduce readers to a public discussion as it developed. Some Englishmen would have known of nonEnglish writings, such as those of Columbus, which for a very long time went untranslated. An

English reader might have known such works either because he (or, occasionally, she) knew the languages of the Continent; or because many such texts circulated in Latin, the transnational language of learning. A striking example of the latter is *Utopia,* written by the Englishman Thomas More, but not published in English in his lifetime. In it, a character refers to books about the New World as being "in print and abroad in every man's hands"—even though More was writing in 1515, when no books about the New World yet existed in English. This chapter traces the growth of a *vernacular* literature, but it should be remembered that there were other kinds as well.

The English vernacular itself underwent enormous changes in the period covered by this chapter. Richard Hakluyt (and his compositors) routinely modernized the texts he collected at the end of the sixteenth century; in many cases his patterns of English usage remain current (-ly endings replace -lie, for instance). Early sixteenth-century texts looked archaic to him; they look even more so now. Those that pose the greatest challenge to modern readers we have given in both the original form and a modernized version. For other difficult texts we have modernized some spelling and punctuation. In the later and more substantial texts, especially Hariot, we have preserved the historical form of the texts as much as possible.

M.W.

Suggested readings: Samuel Eliot Morison, *The European Discovery of America*; Howard Mumford Jones, *O Strange New World*; Wayne Franklin, *Discoverers, Explorers, Settlers.*

1.

from *The Great Chronicle of London* 1502

Native Americans lived in England before the English lived in America. Like Columbus before him, John Cabot kidnapped natives and brought them back to court. Little else is known about these three Micmac Indians who thus found themselves in London, far from the place that was not yet known as America.

Thys yere alsoo were browgth unto the kyng iii men takyn In the Newe Found Ile land, that beffore I spak of In Wylliam Purchas tyme beyng mayer, These were clothid In beastis skynnys and ete Rawe Flesh and spak such spech that noo man cowde undyrstand theym, and In theyr demeanure lyke to bruyt bestis whom the kyng kept a tyme afftyr. Of whych upon ii yeris passid afftyr I sawe ii of theym apparaylyd afftyr Inglysh men In Westmynstyr paleys, which at that tyme I cowde not dyscern From Inglysh men tyll I was lernyd what men they were, But as For spech I hard noon of theym uttyr oon word.

[A MODERN PARAPHRASE]

This year also were brought unto the King three men, taken in the New-Found Island that before I spoke of, in William Purchas's time as mayor. They were clothed in beasts' skins, and ate raw flesh, and spoke such speech that no man could understand them. In their demeanor, they were like brute beasts. The King kept them a time after. After two years passed I saw two of them apparelled in the manner of Englishmen in Westminster Palace; at that time I could not tell them from Englishmen until I was told who they were. But as for speech I heard none of them utter one word.

2.

the first printed account of America in English 1511

The word "America" makes its first English appearance in 1509, as a passing refer-
ence in the translation of Sebastian Brandt's The Ship of Fools *(orig. 1494). The*
following account is based on a German broadside (a single printed sheet, like a
poster) of 1505. It reveals as much about European fantasy as it does about the
peoples of the Western hemisphere.

That lande is not nowe known for there have no masters wryten thereof nor it knowethe and it is named Armenica. there we sawe meny wonders of beestes and fowles yat we have never seen before. the people of this lande have no kynge nor lorde nor theyr god. But all thinges is comune . . . the men and women have on theyr heed necke Armes Knees and fete all with feders bounden for their bewtynes and fayrenes. These folke lyven lyke bestes without any resenablenes. . . . And they ete also on a nother. the man etethe hys wyfe his chylderne as we also have seen and they hange also the bodyes or persons fleeshe in the smoke as men do with us swynes fleshe. And that lande is ryght full of folke for they lyve commonly. iii.C. yere and more as with sykenesse they dye nat. they take much fysshe for they can goen under the water and feche so the fysshes out of the water. and theywerre also on upon a nother. for the olde men brynge the yonge men thereto that they gather a great company thereto of towe partyes and come the on ayene the other to the felde or bateyll and slee on the other with great hepes. And nowe holdeth the fylde they take the other prysoners. And they brynge them to deth and ete them and as the deed is eten then fley they the rest. And they been than eten also or otherwyse lyve they longer tymes and many yeres more than other people for they have costely spyces and rotes where they them selfe recover with and hele them as they be seke.

[A MODERN PARAPHRASE]

That land is not yet known, for no authorities have written about it nor known
about it; and it is named America. There we saw many wonders, of beasts and fowles
that we have never seen before. The people of this land have no king, nor lord, nor
their god. All things are shared in common. The men and women have bound feathers
on their head, neck, arms, knees, and feet, all for their beauty and fairness. These folk
live like beasts without any reason. And they also eat one another. The man eateth his
wife, and his children as we also have seen. They also hang the bodies or persons'

This German woodcut, 1505, was the source of the first printed account of America in English.

flesh in the smoke as men with us do swine's flesh. And that land is very full of people, for they live commonly 300 years and more, as with sickness they die not. They take much fish, for they can go under the water and fetch the fishes out of the water. And they war also one upon another. For the old men bring the young men, gather a great company in two parties, and come the one against the other on the field or battle, and slay one another with great heaps. And now they who hold the field take the others prisoner. And they put them to death and eat them, and when the dead are eaten then they flay the rest. And they are then eaten also, or otherwise they live longer times and many years more than other people, for they have costly spices and roots with which they recover themselves and heal them that are sick.

3. Sir Thomas More

from *Utopia*
1516

More (1478–1535), friend of Erasmus and other men of letters on the Continent, entered Parliament in 1504, later serving as Lord Chancellor. He began Utopia *while an envoy to Flanders in 1515. It was published the following year in Latin, but was not translated into English until long after his death. In 1534, he refused to swear loyalty to Henry VIII in a dispute with the Pope, and the following year he was beheaded for treason. Although the name* Utopia *means "no place," More presents the tale itself as another tale of marvels from the New World. But where others recount savagery, More imagines a perfect civilization. The text here is based on the first English translation, of 1551, somewhat modernized and with a few errors corrected.*

One day I chanced to see Peter talking with a certain stranger, a man well stricken in age, with a black sunburned face, a long beard, and a cloak cast casually about his shoulders. By his look and apparel I judged him to be a mariner.

But when Peter saw me, he came to me and saluted me. And as I was about to answer him, he said, "See you this man?" And therewith he pointed to the man that I saw him talking with before. "I was minded," quoth he, "to bring him straight home to you."

"He should have been very welcome to me," I said, "for your sake."

"Nay," quoth he, "for his own sake, if you knew him. For there is no man living today who can tell you of so many strange and unknown peoples and countries as this man can. And I know well that you love to hear of such news.

"He left his patrimony to his brethren (he is a Portuguese by birth). And for the desire he had to see and know the far countries of the world, he joined himself in company with Amerigo Vespucci, and in the last three of those four voyages, that are now in print and abroad in every man's hands,[1] he continued still in his company; except that in the last voyage he came not home again with him. For by importunate entreaty, that he got permission of master Amerigo (though it was sore against his will) to be one of the twenty-four who at the farthest point of the last voyage were left in the fort. He was therefore left behind at his request, as one that took more thought and care for traveling than dying; having habitually in his mouth these two sayings: 'He that hath no grave is covered with the sky' and, 'The way to heaven is the same distance out of all places.' Which fancy of his (if God had not bene his better friend) would surely have cost him dear. But after Vespucci's departure, when he had traveled through many countries with five companions from the fort, by strange chance he was carried to Ceylon, where he reached Calcutta. There he conveniently found some Portuguese ships, and at length arrived home again, beyond all expectation."

And at this I turned toward Raphael; and when we had greeted one another, and had spoken those common words that are customarily spoken at the first meeting and acquaintance of strangers, we went thence to my house, and there in my garden, upon a bench covered with green turfs, we sat down talking together.

There he told us that, after the departure of Vespucci, he and his fellows that tarried behind in the fort began, little by little, through fair and gentle speech, to win the love and favor of the people of that country; so much that within a short time, they not only dwelt amongst them without harm, but actually became very friendly with them.

"Under the equinox and on both sides of it, as far as the sun extends his course," quoth he, "lie great and wide deserts and wildernesses—parched, burned and dried up with continual and intolerable heat. All things are hideous terrible, loathsome, and

---

1. More refers to *Quatuor Americi Vesputii Navigationes*, not then available in English, from which he derives his information about the New World.

Utopia. Woodcut from the 1518 edition.

unpleasant to behold; all things uncultivated and uncomely, inhabited with wild beasts and serpents, or at the leastwise with people that are no less savage, wild, and noisome than the very beasts themselves. But a little farther beyond that all things begin little by little to wax pleasant; the air soft, temperate, and gentle; the ground covered with green grass; less wildness in the beasts. At the last ye come again to people, cities, and towns, wherein is continual trade and traffic, not only among themselves and with their neighbors, but also with merchants of far countries both by land and water."

Of such things did we busily inquire of him, and he likewise very willingly told us of the same. But as for monsters, because they are not news, of them we were not at all inquisitive. For nothing is easier to find, than barking Scyllaes, ravening Celaenos, and Laestrygones devourers of people, and such like great and incredible monsters.[2] But to find citizens ruled by good and wholesome laws, that is an exceeding rare and hard thing.

---

2. Scylla and Celaeno are in Virgil's *Aeneid*; Laestrygones in Homer's *Odyssey*.

4. John Rastell

from *A New Interlude and a Merry of the Nature of the Four Elements* 1519

> *Rastell, a printer and scholar, was also Thomas More's brother-in-law. In 1517, after reading* Utopia, *he obtained a patent from the king and sailed two ships for "distant parts of the world, remote from our Kingdom of England." With no seafaring experience, he made it no farther than Ireland. But on his return to London he wrote a dramatic dialogue in which one of the characters gives the following lesson on mapping the world.*

Loo estwarde beyonde ye great occyan
Here entereth the see callyd Mediterran
Of .ij. M. myle of lengthe
The Soudans contrey lyeth here by
The great Turke on ye north syde doth ly
A man of merveylous strengthe
This sayde north parte is callyd Europa
And this south parte callyd Affrica
This eest parte is callyd Ynde
But this newe landes founde lately
Ben callyd America by cause only
Americus dyd furst them fynde
Loo Ihrsin lyeth in this contrey
And this beyonde is the Red See
That moyses maketh of mencyon
This quarter is India minor
And this quarter India major
The lande of Prester Johnn
But northwarde this way as ye se
Many other straunge regions ther be
And people that we not knowe
But estwarde on the see syde
A prynce there is that rulyth wyde
Callyd the Cane of Catowe
And this is called the great eest see
whiche goth all a longe this wey

Towardes the newe landis agayne
But whether that see go thyther dyrectly
Or if any wyldernes bytwene them do ly
No man knoweth for certeyne
But these newe landes by all cosmografye
From the Cane of Catous lande cannot lye
Lytell paste a thousand myle
But from those new landes men may sayle playne
Estward & cum to Englande agaie
where we began ere whyle
Lo all this parte of the yerth whiche I
Have here discryvyd openly
The north parte we do it call
But the south parte on the other syde
ys as large as this full and as wyde
whiche we knowe nothynge at all
Nor whether ye moste parte be lande or see
Nor whether the people that there be
Be bestyall or connynge
Nor whether they knowe god or no
Nor howe they beleve nor what they do
Of this we knowe nothynge
Lo is not this a thynge wooderfull

[A MODERN PARAPHRASE]

Lo! Eastward beyond the great ocean,
Here begins the sea called the Mediterranean,
Of two thousand miles' length.
The Sultan's country lies here;
On the north side lies the Great Turk—
A man of marvellous strength.
This north part is called Europe,
And the south part is called Africa.
The east part is called India.
But these new lands, lately found,
Have been called America, merely because
Amerigo Vespucci found them first.
Lo! [obscure] lies in this country,
And this beyond it is the Red Sea,
Of which Moses makes mention.
This quarter is India Minor,
And this quarter is India Major,
The land of Prester John.
But northward, as you see,
There are many other strange regions,

And people that we do not know.
But eastward on the sea side,
There is a prince who rules wide,
Called the Khan of Cathay.
And this is called the Great East Sea,
Which goes along this way
Towards the new lands again.
But whether that sea goes there directly,
Or if any wilderness lies between them,
No man knows for certain.
But these new lands, according to cosmography,
Cannot lie much more than a thousand miles
From the Khan of Cathay's land.
From those new lands men can sail
Due east and come to England again,
Where we began a while ago.
Lo, all this part of the earth which I
Have here described clearly
We call the north part.
But the south part on the other side
Is fully as large as this, and as wide,
Of which we know nothing at all—
Neither whether it is mostly land or sea,
Nor whether the people that are there
Are bestial or civilized,
Nor whether they know God or not,
Nor how they believe, nor what they do,
Of this we know nothing.
Lo, is this not an astounding thing?

5. Richard Eden

from translation of Peter Martyr
1555

The following comment appears as a digression in the English translation of Peter Martyr's Decades of the New World, *the most famous compilation of New World writing. Eden's praise for the Spanish was politic; after Queen Mary's accession to the throne in 1553, England had again become officially Catholic, with such a vengeance that the queen would become known as "Bloody Mary." And in 1554, the year before Eden's translation, she had married King Philip of Spain, uniting England briefly to its greater rival for empire. The text is slightly modernized.*

Bbut whereas now, by the power of Neptune (I know not with what wind), I have been driven thus far from my navigations, I have thought good to turn my sails and to follow the ordinary course which I began, and by the example of this worthy captain King Ferdinando, encourage all others (to their power) to attempt the like voyages.

As for which, in few words to declare my opinion, if any man should ask me what I think these things will grow to in time, I will answer as doth the author of this book, [i.e., Martyr]: that when I consider how far our posterity shall see the Christian religion enlarged, I am not able with tongue or pen to express what I conceive hereof in my mind.

Yet one thing I see which enforceth me to speak and lament: that the harvest is so great and the workmen so few. The Spaniards have shewed a good example to all Christian nations to follow. But as god is great and wonderful in all his works, so besides the portion of land pertaining to the Spaniards, being eight times bigger than Italy (as we may read in the last book of the second Decade), and besides that which pertaineth to the Portuguese, there yet remaineth another portion of that mainland reaching toward the northeast, thought to be as large as the other, and yet known only by the sea coasts, neither inhabited by any Christian men.

Whereas nevertheless (as Gemma Phrisius writes) in this land there are many fair and fruitful regions, high mountains, and fair rivers, with abundance of gold and diverse kinds of beasts. Also cities and towers so well built, and people of such civility, that this part of the world seemeth little inferior to our Europe, if the inhabitants had only received our religion. They are witty people and refuse not bartering with strangers. These regions are called Terra Florida and Regio Baccalearum or Bacchallaos, of the which you may read somewhat in this book, in the voyage of the worthy old man yet living Sebastian Cabot, in the 6th book of the third Decade. But Cabot touched only in the north corner and most barbarous part hereof, from whence he was repulsed with Ice in the month of July. Nevertheless, the west and south parts of these regions have since been better searched by others, and found to be as we have said before.

The chief city in the southwest parts of these regions, is called Temixtecan, or Mexico, under the circle called the Tropic of Cancer, and strongly defended by the nature of the place. For it standeth in a very great lake, having about it innumerable bridges, and buildings to be compared to the works of Dedalus. The inhabitants also can write and read. Some writers connect this land to the firm land of Asia. But the truth is not yet known. And although the Spaniards have certain colonies in that part of this land that is now called Nova Hispania, yet the people for the most part are Idolaters.

How much therefore is it to be lamented, and how greatly doth it sound to the reproach of all Christendom, and especially to such as dwell nearest to these lands (as we do), being much nearer unto the same then are the Spaniards (as within 25 days sailing and less)—how much, I say, shall this sound unto our reproach and inexcusable slothfulness and negligence both before god and the world, that so large dominions of such tractable people and pure gentiles, not being hitherto corrupted with any other false religion (and therefore the easier to be allured to embrace ours) are now known unto us, and that we have respect neither for god's cause nor for our own commodity to attempt some voyages into these coasts, to do for our parts as the

Spaniards have done for theirs, and not ever like sheep to haunt one trade, and to do nothing worth memory among men or thanks before god, who may herein worthily accuse us for the slackness of our duty toward him?

6. John Sparke

from *The Voyage Made by Master John Hawkins* c. 1566

> *John Hawkins had persuaded London investors in 1562 to supply a voyage for taking slaves from Africa to the West Indies. After his return in 1563, the queen's objections to English involvement in the slave trade are said to have melted at the sight of his profits. The following is an account of Hawkins's next voyage, printed in Hakluyt's* Principal Navigations, *by "me John Sparke the younger, who went upon the same voyage, and wrote the same." Hawkins sailed in four ships, including the Jesus of Lubeck, which would later carry Ralegh's party to Roanoke.*

The 27th [of December] the Captaine was advertised[3] by the Portugals of a towne of the Negros called Bymba, being in the way as they returned, where was not only a great quantitie of gold, but also that there were not above forty men, and an hundred women and children of the Towne, so that if he would give the adventure upon the same, he might get a hundred slaves. With the which tidings he being glad, because the Portugals should not think him to be of so base a courage, but that he durst give them that, and greater attempts. And being thereunto also the more provoked with the prosperous success he had in other Islands adjacent, where he had put them all to flight, and taken in one boate twenty together, [he] determined to stay before the Town three or four hours, to see what he could do: and thereupon prepared his men in armor and weapons together, to the number of forty men well appointed, having to their guides certain Portugals, in a boat, who brought some of them to their death. We landing boat after boat, and divers of our men scattering themselves, contrary to the Captaine's will, by one or two in a company, for the hope that they had to find gold in their houses, ransacking the same, in the meantime the Negroes came upon them, and hurt many being thus scattered. Whereas if five or six had been together, they had been able, as their companions did, to give the overthrow to 40 of them. And being driven down to take their boats, they were followed so hardly[4] by a rout of Negroes, who by that took courage to pursue them to their boats, that not only some of them, but others standing on shore—not looking for any such matter by means that the Negroes did flee at first, and our company remained in the town—were suddenly so set upon that some with great hurt recovered their boats. Others, not able

---

3. advertised: notified.　　　　　　　　4. hardly: closely.

to recover the same, took the water, and perished by means of the ooze. While this was doing, the Captaine, who with a dozen men went through the town, returned, finding 200 Negroes at the water's side, shooting at them in the boats, and cutting them in pieces which were drowned in the water; at whose coming, they ran all away. So he entered his boats, and before he could put off from the shore, they returned again, and shot very fiercely and hurt divers of them. Thus we returned back somewhat discomforted, although the Captaine in a singular wise manner carried himself, with countenance very cheerful outwardly, as though he did little weigh the death of his men, nor yet the great hurt of the rest, although his heart inwardly was broken in pieces for it.

7. Lopez Vaz

the English in New Spain, from Hakluyt's *Principal Navigations* before 1586

Francis Drake's raid on Spanish trade in 1572 set the English on a collision course with the Spanish empire. The following account, according to Hakluyt, was written by the Portuguese Lopez Vaz, who had the manuscript with him when he was captured by the Earl of Cumberland in 1586. It shows, among other things, the importance of the runaway African slaves called címarróns, or, in later English parlance, maroons. In Palmares, in Brazil, these ex-slaves formed an independent kingdom that held off attacks by slaving nations until the end of the seventeenth century.

[FRANCIS DRAKE MEETS THE CIMARRÓNS, 1572]

There was a certain English man named Francis Drake ... who came to the sound of Darien, and having conference with certain Negroes which were fled from their masters of Panama, and Nombre de Dios, the Negroes did tell him that certain Mules came laden with gold and silver from Panama to Nombre de Dios. In company of these Negroes he went thereupon on land, and stayed in the way where the treasure should come, with an hundred shot.[5] And so he took two companies of mules, which came only with their drivers distrusting nothing. And he carried away the gold only, for they were not able to carry the silver through the mountains. Two days after, he came to the house of Crosses, where he killed six or seven merchants, but found no gold nor silver but much merchandize. So he set fire to the house, where was burnt above 200,000 Ducats in merchandize, and so went to his ship again. Within half an hour after he was shipboard. There came down to the sands three

5. an hundred shot: a hundred men armed with guns.

hundred shot of the Spaniards in the sight of his ships, purposing to seek him, but he cared little for them, being out of their reach, and so departed with his treasure.

[JOHN OXNAM FOLLOWS IN DRAKE'S STEPS, 1575]

There was another Englishman who, hearing of the spoil that Francis Drake had done upon the coast of Nueva España, and of his good adventure and safe return home, was thereby provoked to undertake the like enterprise, with a ship of 140 tons, and 70 men. He came thither, and had also conference with the foresaid Negroes. And hearing that the gold and silver which came upon the Mules from Panama to Nombre de Dios, was now conducted with soldiers, he determined to do that which never any man before enterprised. He landed in that place where Francis Drake before had had his conference with the Negroes. This man covered his ship after he had brought her aground with boughs of trees, and hid his great Ordinance[6] in the ground, and so not leaving any man in his ship, he took two small pieces of ordinance, and his calivers, and good store of victuals, and so went with the Negroes about twelve leagues into the mainland, to a river that goes to the South sea. And there he cut wood and made a Pinnace, which was five and forty foot by the keel. And having made this Pinnace, he went into the South sea, carrying six Negroes with him to be his guides, and so went to the Island of Pearls.

At last there came a small Bark by, which came from Peru from a place called Quito, which he took and found in her sixty thousand pesos of gold, and much victuals. But not contenting himself with this prize, he stayed long without sending away his prize or any of the men, and in the end of six days after, he took another Bark which came from Lima.

The Negroes that dwelt in the Island of Pearls, the same night that he went from them, went in Canoes to Panama. And the Governor within two days sent four barks with 100 men, 25 in every one, and Negroes to row with the captain John de Ortega, which went to the Island of Pearls, and there had intelligence which way the English men were gone. And following them, he [i.e., Ortega] met by the way the ships which the English men had taken, of whom he learned that the English men were gone up the river. Going thither, when he came to the mouth of the river, the captaine of Panama knew not which way to take, because there were three partitions in the river to go up in. And being determined to go up the greatest of the three rivers, he saw, coming down a lesser river, many feathers of hens, which the Englishmen had pulled to eat. And being glad thereof, he went up that river where he saw the feathers. After he had been in that river four days, he descried the Englishmen's pinnace upon the sands. . . .

And the Justice of Panama asked the English captain whether he had the Queen's license, or the license of any other Prince or Lord for his attempt. And he answered he had none. Whereupon he and all his company were condemned to die, and so were all executed, saving the Captain, the Master, the Pilot, and five boys which were carried to Lima. There the Captain was executed with the other two, but the boys are yet living.

---

6. Ordinance: artillery.

The King of Spain having intelligence of these matters, sent 300 men of war against those Negroes who had assisted those English men, who before were slaves unto the Spaniards, and as before is said, fled from their masters unto those mountains, and so joined themselves to the Englishmen, to the end that they might better revenge themselves on the Spaniards.

At their first coming, these 300 soldiers, took many of the Negroes, and executed great justice upon them. But after a season, the Negroes grew wise and wary, and prevented the Spaniards, so that none of them could be taken.

8. George Best

from *A True Discourse* 1578

George Best, a companion of Martin Frobisher, wrote the following account after the second of Frobisher's three attempts to find the Northwest Passage to China. The text, A True Discourse of the Late Voyages of Discoverie, for the Finding of a Passage to Cathaya, *was published in 1578. It is significant not only for its intriguing narrative, but for an early speculative theory of race, designed to prove to skeptics that Englishmen could live in America.*

[CLIMATE AND RACE]

Wee have among us in England black Moors, Æthiopians, out of all parts of Torrida Zona,[7] which after a small continuance, can well endure the cold of our Country. And why should not we as well abide the heat of their Country?

Some there are who think the middle Zone extremly hot, because the people of the country can, and do live without clothing, wherein they childishly are deceived. For our Clime rather tends to extremity of cold, because we cannot live without clothing. For our double lining, furring, and wearing so many clothes, is a remedy against extremity; and argues not the goodness of the habitation, but inconvenience and injury of cold. And that is rather the moderate, temperate, and delectable habitation, where none of these troublesome things are required, but that we may live naked and bare, as nature bringeth us forth.

Others again imagine the middle Zone to be extreme hot, because the people of Africa, especially the Ethiopians, are so coal black, and their hair like wool curled short, which blackness and curled hair they suppose to come only by the parching heat of the Sun. How this should be possible I cannot see. For even under the Equinox in America, and in the East Indies, and in the Molucca Islands, the people are not

---

7. Torrida Zona: Aristotle's name for the tropics.

Illustration of a narwhal, from Best's True Discourse.

black, but tawny and white, with long hair uncurled as we have. So that if the Ethiopians' blackness came by the heat of the Sun, why should not those Americans and Indians also be as black as they, seeing the Sun is equally distant from them both, they abiding in one Parallel?

I myself have seen an Ethiopian as black as a coal brought into England, who taking a fair English woman to wife, begat a son in all respects as black as the father was, although England was his native country, and an English woman his mother. Whereby it seems this blackness proceeds rather of some natural infection of that man, which was so strong, that neither the nature of the Clime, neither the good complexion of the mother concurring, could anything alter. And therefore we cannot impute it to the nature of the Clime.

And for a more fresh example, our people of Meta Incognita[8] (of whom and for whom this discourse is taken in hand) that were brought this last year into England, were all generally of the same color that many nations be, lying in the midst of the middle Zone. And this their color was not only in the face which was subject to Sun and air, but also in their bodies, which were still covered with garments as our are. Yea the very sucking child of twelve months' age had his skin of the very same color that most have under the Equinox, which cannot proceed by reason of the Clime, for they are at least ten degrees more towards the North than we in England are.
⁎ Whereby it follows, that there is some other cause than the Climate or the Sun's perpendicular reflection, that should cause the Ethiopians' great blackness. And the most probable cause to my judgement is, that this blackness proceeds of some natural infection of the first inhabitants of that Country, and so all the whole progeny of them descended, are still polluted with the same blot of infection. ⁎

Therefore it shall not be far from our purpose, to examine the first origin of these black men, and how by a lineal descent they have hitherto continued thus black.

It manifestly and plainly appears by holy Scripture, that after the general inundation and overflowing of the earth, there remained no more men alive but Noah and his three sons, Shem, Cham, and Japhet, who only were left to possess and inhabit the whole face of the earth. Therefore all the sundry descendants that until this present day have inhabited the whole earth, must needs come of the offspring either of Shem, Cham, or Japhet. The only sons of Noah, all three being white and their wives also, by course of nature should have begotten and brought forth white children. But the envy of our great and continual enemy the wicked Spirit is such, that as he could not

8. Meta Incognita: the New World.

suffer our old father Adam to live in the felicity and Angelic state wherein he was first created, but tempting him, sought and procured his ruin and fall; so again, finding at this flood none but a father and three sons living, he so caused one of them to transgress and disobey his father's commandment, that after him all his posterity should be accursed.

Thus you see, that the cause of the Ethiopians' blackness is the curse and natural infection of blood, and not the distemperature of the Climate. We may therefore very well be assured, that under the Equinox is the most pleasant and delectable place of the world to dwell in.

[THE CAPTIVE]

When the Savages heard the shot of one of our calivers (and yet having first bestowed their arrows) they ran away, our men speedily following them. But a servant of my Lord of Warwick, called Nicholas Conger—a good footman, and unencumbered with any furniture,[9] having only a dagger at his back—overtook one of them, and being a good Cornishman and a good wrestler, showed his companion such a Cornish trick, that he made his sides ache against the ground for a month after. And so being stayed, he [i.e., the Indian] was taken alive and brought away, but the others escaped. Thus with their strange and new prey our men repaired to their boates....

In one of the small Islands here we found a Tomb, wherein the bones of a dead man lay together, and our savage Captive being with us, & being demanded[10] by signs whether his countrymen had not slain this man and eaten his flesh so from the bones, he made signs to the contrary, and that he was slain with Wolves and wild beasts. Here also was found hid under stones a good store of fish, and sundry other things of the inhabitants; as sleds, bridles, kettles of fish-skins, knives of bone, and such other like. And our Savage declared unto us the use of all those things. And taking in his hand one of those country bridles, he caught one of our dogs and hampered him handsomely therein, as we do our horses. And with a whip in his hand, he taught the dog to draw in a sled as we do horses in a coach.

Here our captive being ashore with us, to declare the use of such things as we saw, we shewed him the picture of his countryman, which the last year was brought into England (whose counterfeit we had drawn, with boat and other furniture, both as he was in his own, & also in English apparel). He was upon the sudden much amazed thereat, and beholding advisedly[11] the same with silence a good while, as though he would strain courtesy whether should begin the speech (for he thought him no doubt a lively[12] creature) at length began to question with him, as with his companion. And finding him dumb and mute, he seemed to suspect him, as one disdainful, and would with a little help have grown into choler[13] at the matter, until at last by feeling and handling, he found him but a deceiving picture. And then with great noise and cries, he ceased not wondering, thinking that we could make men live or die at our pleasure.

9. furniture: equipment.
10. demanded: asked.
11. advisedly: carefully.

12. lively: living.
13. choler: anger.

[The English try matchmaking]

Our men marched up into the country, passing over two or three mountains, and by chance espied certain tents, and besetting them about, determined to take them if they could. . . .

But desperately returning upon our men, [the natives] resisted manfully, so long as their arrows and darts lasted. And after gathering up those arrows which our men shot at them, yea, and plucking our arrows out of their bodies encountered [us] afresh again, and maintained their cause until both weapons and life failed them. And when they found they were mortally wounded, being ignorant what mercy means, with deadly fury they cast themselves headlong from off the rocks into the sea, lest perhaps their enemies should receive glory or prey of their dead carcasses, for they supposed us likely to be Cannibals or eaters of men's flesh.

In this conflict one of our men was dangerously hurt in the belly with one of their arrows, and of them were slain five or six, the rest by flight escaping among the rocks, saving two women, whereof the one being old and ugly, our men thought she had been a devil or some witch, and therefore let her go. The other being young, and cumbered with a suckling child at her back, hiding herself behind the rocks, was espied by one of our men, who supposing she had been a man, shot through the hair of her head, and pierced through the child's arm. Whereupon she cried out, and our Surgeon meaning to heal her child's arm, applied salves thereunto. But she not acquainted with such kind of surgery, plucked those salves away, and by continual licking with her own tongue, not much unlike our dogs, healed up the child's arm.

Having now got a woman captive for the comfort of our man, we brought them both together, and every man with silence desired to behold the manner of their meeting and entertainment, which was more worth the beholding than can be well expressed by writing. At their first encountering they beheld each the other very wistfully a good space, without speech or word uttered, with great change of color and countenance, as though it seemed the grief and disdain of their captivity had taken away the use of their tongues and utterance. The woman at the first very suddenly, as though she disdained or regarded not the man, turned away, and began to sing as though she minded another matter: but being again brought together, the man broke up the silence first, and with stern and staid countenance, began to tell a long solemn tale to the woman, whereunto she gave good hearing, and interrupted him nothing, till he had finished. And afterwards, being grown into more familiar acquaintance by speech, they were turned together, so that (I think) the one would hardly have lived without the comfort of the other. And for so much as we could perceive, albeit they lived continually together, yet they did never use as man & wife, though the woman spared not to do all necessary things that appertained to a good housewife indifferently[14] for them both, as in making clean their Cabin, and every other thing that appertained to his ease. For when he was seasick, she would make him clean. She would kill and flea the dogs for their eating, and dress his meat. Only I think it worth

14. indifferently: equally.

the noting, the continence of them both. For the man would never shift himself, except he had first caused the woman to depart out of his cabin, and they both were most shamefaced, lest any of their privy parts should be discovered, either of themselves, or any other body.

9.

four views on plantation

By the 1570s, growing numbers of the English were determined to compete with the new world empires. Over the next several decades, a number of writers stepped forward to develop a theory for colonies. Most, including each of the following four authors, were directly involved in sending voyages to America. Since the arguments against colonization were seldom committed to writing, these texts are also our best guide to the other side of the debate, as for example when Richard Hakluyt—older cousin of the compiler—acknowledges an objection in his first sentence here.

Richard Hakluyt the elder
1578

Now admit that we might not be suffered by the Savages to enjoy any whole country or any more than the scope of a city. Yet if we might enjoy traffic,[15] and be assured of the same, we might be much enriched, our Navy might be increased, and a place of safety might there be found, if change of religion or civil wars should happen in this realm, which are things of great benefit.

But if we may enjoy any large territory of apt soil, we might so use the matter, as we should not depend upon Spain for oils, sacks, resins, oranges, lemons, Spanish skins, &c. Nor upon France for woad, basalt, and Gascoyne wines, nor on Eastland for flax, pitch, tar, masts, &c. So we should not so exhaust our treasure, and so exceedingly enrich our doubtful friends, as we do, but should purchase the commodities that we want for half the treasure that now we do. And we should, by our own industries and the benefits of the soil there, cheaply purchase oils, wines, salt, fruits, pitch, tar, flax, hemp, masts, boards, fish, gold, silver, copper, tallow, hides and many commodities.

15. traffic: trade.

Christopher Carleill

1583

The bad dealings of the Easterlings are sufficiently known to be such towards our Merchants of that trade, as they do not only offer them many injuries overlong to be written, but do seek all the means they can, to deprive them wholly of their occupying[16] that way. And to the same purpose they have, of late, clean debarred them their accustomed and ancient privileges in all their great Towns.

The traffics into Turkey—besides that by some it is thought a hard point[17] to have so much familiarity with the professed and obstinate Enemy of Christ—is likewise a voyage which can not be made but at the devotion, and as it were in the danger of many States, who for sundry respects are apt to quarrel with us upon sudden occasions. And the presents to be given away in Turkey this year cost little less then two thousand pounds. . . .

The trade into Barbary grows likewise to worse terms than before times. And when it was at the best our Merchants have been in danger of all their goods they had there, whenever the King happened to die. For until a new one were chosen, the liberty of all disordered persons is such, as they spoil & wrong whom they list[18] without any redress at all.

Touching Spain and Portugal, with whom we have very great trade, and much the greater, by means of their vending a good part of our wares into their Indies, . . . whensoever the King of Spain lists to take the opportunity, he may at these seasons deprive us not only of a great number of our very good Ships, but also of our most honest and able Mariners. . . .

But whoever shall look into the quality of this voyage, being directed to the latitude of 40 degrees, or thereabouts of that hithermost part of America, shall find it hath as many points of good moment belonging unto it, as may almost be wished for. . . .

As for the Merchandizing, which is the matter especially looked for, albeit that for the present, we are not certainly able to promise any such like quantity, as is now at the best time of the Moscovian trade brought from thence; so likewise there is not demanded any such proportion of daily expenses, as was at the first, and as yet is consumed in that of Moscovia and others. But when this of America shall have been haunted[19] and practiced, thirty years to an end, as the other hath been, I doubt not by God's grace, that for the ten Ships, that are now commonly employed once the year into Moscovia, there shall in this voyage twice ten be employed well, twice the year at the least. . . .

---

16. occupying: trading.
17. it is thought a hard point: it is considered a matter of conscience.
18. list: wish.
19. haunted: visited familiarly.

The Country people[20] being made to know, that for Wax and Honey, we will give them such trifling things, as they desire of us, and showing them once the means, how to provide the same, the labor thereof being so light, no doubt but in short time they will earnestly care to have the same in good quantity for us. . . . It is to bee assuredly hoped, that they will daily little by little forsake their barbarous and savage living, and grow to such order and civility with us, as there may be well expected from thence no less quantity, and diversity of Merchandize, than is now had out of Dutchlande, Italy, France, or Spain. . . .

To those who have any forward minds in well doing,[21] to the generality of mankind, I say thus much more, that Christian charity doth as greatly persuade the furtherance of this action, as any other that may be laid before us, inasmuch as thereby, we shall not only do a most excellent work, in respect of reducing[22] the savage people to Christianity and civility, but also in respect of our poor sort of people, which are very many amongst us, living altogether unprofitably, and often-times to the great disquiet of the better sort. For who knoweth not, how by the long peace, happy health, and blessed plentifulness, wherewith God hath endowed this Realm, that the people is so mightily increased, as a great number being brought up, during their youth in their parents' houses, without any instruction how to get their livings, after their parents' decease, are driven to some necessity, whereby very often, for want of better education they fall into sundry disorders, and so the good sort of people, as I said before, are by them ordinarily troubled, and themselves led on, to one shameful end or other? Whereas if there might be found some such kind of employ-ment as this, there would be no doubt but a greater part of them would be withheld from falling into such vile deeds; and instead prove greatly serviceable in those affairs, where they might be so employed.

Edward Hayes

1583

It behooveth every man of great calling, in whom is any instinct of inclination unto this attempt, to examine his own motives. If it proceeds from ambition or avarice, he may assure himself it cometh not of God, and therefore cannot have confidence of God's protection and assistance against the violence (else irresistible) both of sea, and infinite perils upon the land.

And the same, who feeleth this inclination in himself, by all likelihood may hope, or rather confidently repose in the preordinance of God, that in this last age of the world (or likely never) the time is complete of receiving also these Gentiles into his mercy; and that God will raise him an instrument to effect the same—it seeming probable by

---

20. the Country people: the Indians.   22. reducing: leading.
21. forward minds in well doing: dispositions to do good.

preceeding attempts made by the Spaniards and French sundry times, that the countries lying North of Florida, God hath reserved to be reduced unto Christian civility by the English nation. For not long after Christopher Columbus had discovered the Islands and continent of the West Indies for Spain, John and Sebastian Cabot made discovery also of the rest from Florida Northwards to the behoof of England.

And whensoever afterwards the Spaniards (very prosperous in all their Southern discoveries) did attempt anything into Florida and those regions inclining towards the North, they proved most unhappy, and were at length discouraged utterly by the hard and lamentable success of many both religious and valiant in arms, endeavoring to bring those Northerly regions also under the Spanish jurisdiction; as if God had prescribed limits unto the Spanish nation which they might not exceed—as by their own gestes[23] recorded may be aptly gathered.

The French can pretend less title unto these than the Spaniard. The English nation only hath right unto these countries of America from the cape of Florida Northward, by the privilege of first discovery, unto which Cabot was authorized by regal authority, and set forth by the expense of our late famous king Henry the seventh: which right also seemeth strongly defended on our behalf by the powerful hand of almighty God, withstanding the enterprises of other nations. It may greatly encourage us upon so just a ground, as is our right, and upon so sacred an intent, as to plant religion (our right and intent being meet foundations for the same) to prosecute effectually the full possession of those so ample and pleasant countries appertaining unto the crown of England. As is to be conjectured by infallible arguments of the world's end approaching, [those countries] are now arrived unto the time by God prescribed of their vocation, if ever their calling unto the knowledge of God may be expected. Which also is very probable by the revolution and course of God's word and religion, which from the beginning hath moved from the East, towards, & at last unto the West, where it is likely to end, unless it begin again where it did in the East, which were to expect a like world again. But we are assured of the contrary by the prophecy of Christ, whereby we gather, that after his word is preached throughout the world shall be the end. And as the Gospel when it descended Westward began in the South, and afterward spread into the North of Europe: even so, as the same hath begun in the South countries of America, no less hope may be gathered that it will also spread into the North.

---

23. gestes: deeds.

Sir George Peckham

1583

It will prove a general benefit unto our Country, that through this occasion, not only a great number of men which do now live idly at home, and are burdenous, chargeable and unprofitable to this Realm, shall hereby be set to work. But also children of 12 or 14 years of age or under, may be kept from idleness, in making a thousand kinds of trifling things, which will be good Merchandize for that Country. And moreover, our idle women, (which the Realm may well spare) shall also be employed in plucking, drying, and sorting Feathers, in pulling, beating, and working Hemp, and in gathering Cotton, and diverse things necessary for dyeing. All which things are to be found in those Countries most plentifully. And the men may employ themselves in dragging for Pearl, working for Mines, and in matters of husbandry, and likewise in hunting the Whale for traine,[24] and making Casks to put the same in; besides fishing for Cod, Salmon and Herring, drying, salting, and barrelling the same, and felling Trees, hewing and sawing them, and such like work, meet for those persons as are no men of art or science.

And it is very evident that planting there shall in time right amply enlarge her Majesty's Territories and Dominions; or, I might rather say, restore her to her Highness's ancient right and interest those Countries, into which a noble and worthy personage, lineally descended from the blood royal, born in Wales, named Madoc ap Owen Gwyneth, departing from the coast of England, about the year of our Lord 1170, arrived and there planted himself, and his Colonies, and afterward returned himself into England, leaving certain of his people there, as appeareth in an ancient Welch Chronicle, where he then gave to certain Islands, Beasts, and Fowls, sundry Welch names, as the Island of Pengwyn, which yet to this day beareth the same.

And the same in effect is confirmed by Montezuma, that mighty Emperor of Mexico, who in an Oration unto his subjects, for the better pacifying of them, made in the presence of Hernando Cortes, used these speeches following.

> My kinsmen, friends, and servants, you do well know that eighteen years I have been your King, as my Fathers and Grandfathers were, and always I have been unto you a loving Prince, and you unto me good and obedient subjects, and so I hope you will remain unto me all the days of my life. You ought to have in remembrance, that either you have heard of your fathers, or else our divines have instructed you that we are not naturally of this Country, nor yet is our Kingdom durable, because our Forefathers came

---

24. traine: oil.

from a far country, and their King and Captain who brought them hither, returned again to his natural country, saying, that he would send such as should rule and govern us, if by chance he himself returned not, etc.

These be the very words of Montezuma, set down in the Spanish Chronicles, which being thoroughly considered, because they have relation to some strange noble person, who long before had possessed those Countries, do all sufficiently argue, the undoubted title of her Majesty. For no other Nation can truly by any Chronicles they can find, make prescription of time for themselves, before the time of this Prince Madoc.

10. William Lightfoot

from *The Complaint of England* 1587

Just as the English began to be active in the New World, they began paying closer attention to criticism of the Spanish arising from within the Spanish empire itself. Instead of taking those criticisms as arguments against empire, the English took them as arguments about the Spanish national character. Thus arose "the black legend"— the image of Spanish inhumanity that would allow the English to understand themselves as a more civilized, and more deserving empire. This pamphlet is closely based on the work of the friar Bartolomé de Las Casas, whose denunciation of Spanish colonists had been translated as The Spanish Cruelties *only a few years before.*

The execrable tyrannies which the Spaniards have shewed on the Indians, as they do almost surmount credit,[26] so can they hardly be furnished with terms effectual to decipher them. They have dispeopled in [West] *India* more than ten realms, greater than all *Spain, Aragon, & Portugal*; which now remain as a wilderness abandoned & desolate, being before as populous as was possible. Within the space of forty years, they as in a common butchery slaughtered of innocent lambs, above twelve millions, men, women, & children.

At their first arrival they were entertained with performance of all serviceable courtesies, the Indians most humbly submitting themselves unto them, & after a sort adoring them as divine creatures descended from heaven. But after they were too well acquainted with their savage cruelties, they fled from them as from hateful furies broke loose out of hell.

The Spaniards customarily disported themselves in laying wagers which of them should with one thrust of a sword panch or bowel an *Indian* bravest[27] in the midst; or which one blow most deliverly strike off his head; or best dismember him with one stroke. They used to murder the lords & nobility, by broiling them on gridirons with a

---

26. surmount credit: surpass belief.   27. bravest: most directly.

soft fire underneath, that yelling and despairing in those lingering torments they might so give up the ghost.

Four or five of the Lords one time being roasted in this manner, their pitiful roaring and lamentation disquieted the Captain (the caitiff I should say) and broke his sleep. Whereupon for his better quiet he commanded them to be strangled. The Sergeant would not suffer them to die so easy a death. But himself putting bullets in

Atrocities of the Spaniards, from a 1614 edition of Bartolomé de Las Casas.

their mouth so they should not cry, roasted them softly after his desire.[28]

Such are the Spaniards, such are their fruits: fruits far worse than the fruits of *Sodom.*

11. Thomas Hariot

A Briefe and True Report of the New Found Land of Virginia 1588

> *Born at Oxford in 1560, Thomas Hariot (also Heriot or Harriot) became a distinguished mathematician, and was hired by Sir Walter Ralegh as a private tutor in that subject. He also wrote a treatise on navigation before being sent by Ralegh to the Roanoke colony in 1585, where he learned the Algonquian language and studied the Carolina resources before returning in 1586. (He returned to his scholarly work, mostly in mathematics, until his death in 1621.) The* Brief and True Report *was probably written in 1587, and may have been designed to promote a new voyage to Roanoke in that year. It was published as a small volume in 1588; a larger edition, illustrated with engravings by Theodor de Bry based on watercolors*

28. after his desire: as he desired.

*and drawings of John White, appeared in 1590. The text here is from Hakluyt's
Principal Navigations, which corrected some errors and made minor improvements
on the earlier versions. Hariot begins on a defensive note, trying to counter bad
word of mouth on the colony. And his promotional intent guides the text
throughout. Except for an oblique remark at the end, for example, he says nothing
of the brutal policies of Ralph Lane toward the Indians. And information about
both "merchantable commodities" and natives is presented with one clear goal: to
promote plantation.*

To the Adventurers, Favourers, and Welwillers of the enterprise
for the inhabiting and planting in Virginia.

Since the first undertaking by Sir Walter Ralegh to deale in the action of discovering of that countrey which is now called and knowen by the name of Virginia, many voyages having beene thither made at sundry times to his great charge; as first in the yere 1584, and afterwards in the yeres 1585, 1586, and now of late this last yeere 1587: there have bene divers and variable reports, with some slanderous and shamefull speeches bruted[29] abroad by many that returned from thence: especially of that discovery which was made by the colony transported by Sir Richard Grinvile in the yere 1585, being of all others the most principall, and as yet of most effect, the time of their abode in the countrey being a whole yere, when as in the other voyage before they stayed but six weeks, and the others after were onely for supply and transportation, nothing more being discovered than had bene before. Which reports have not done a little wrong to many that otherwise would have also favoured and adventured in the action, to the honour and benefit of our nation, besides the particular profit and credit which would redound to themselves the dealers therein, as I hope by the sequel of events, to the shame of those that have avouched the contrary, shall be manifest, if you the adventurers, favourers and welwillers doe but either increase in number, or in opinion continue, or having beene doubtfull, renew your good liking and furtherance to deale therein according to the woorthinesse thereof already found, and as you shall understand hereafter to be requisit. Touching which woorthinesse through cause of the diversity of relations and reports, many of your opinions could not be firme, nor the minds of some that are well disposed be setled in any certaintie.

I have therefore thought it good, being one that have beene in the discoverie, and in dealing with the naturall inhabitants specially imployed: and having therefore seene and knowen more then[30] the ordinary, to impart so much unto you of the fruits of our labours, as that you may know how injuriously the enterprise is slandered, and that in publique manner at this present, chiefly for two respects.

First, that some of you which are yet ignorant or doubtfull of the state thereof, may see that there is sufficient cause why the chiefe enterpriser[31] with the favour of her Majesty, notwithstanding such reports, hath not onely since continued the action by sending into the countrey againe, and replanting this last yeere a new Colony, but is

---

29. bruted: noised.
30. then: than.

31. chiefe enterpriser: Ralegh.

Title page of the 1590 folio edition of Hariot, illustrated by Theodor de Bry.

also ready, according as the times and meanes will affoord, to follow and prosecute the same.

Secondly, that you seeing and knowing the continuance of the action, by the view hereof you may generally know and learne what the countrey is, and thereupon consider how your dealing therein, if it proceed, may returne you profit and gaine, be it either by inhabiting and planting, or otherwise in furthering thereof.

And least[32] that the substance of my relation should be doubtfull unto you, as of others by reason of their diversitie, I will first open the cause[33] in a few words, wherefore they are so different, referring my selfe to your favourable constructions, and to be adjudged of, as by good consideration you shall finde cause.

Of our company that returned, some for their misdemeanour and ill dealing in the countrey have bene there worthily punished, who by reason of their bad natures, have maliciously not onely spoken ill of their Governours, but for their sakes slandered the countrey it selfe. The like also have those done which were of their consort.

Some being ignorant of the state thereof, notwithstanding since their returne amongst their friends & acquaintance, and also others, especially if they were in company where they might not be gainsayd, would seeme to know so much as no men more, and make no men so great travellers as themselves. They stood so much, as it may seeme, upon their credit and reputation, that having bene a twelvemoneth in the countrey, it would have bene a great disgrace unto them, as they thought, if they could not have sayd much, whether it were true or false. Of which some have spoken of more then ever they saw, or otherwise knew to be there. Other some[34] have not bene ashamed to make absolute deniall of that, which although not by them, yet by others is most certainly and there plentifully knowen, & other some make difficulties of those things they have no skill of.

The cause of their ignorance was, in that they were of that many that were never out of the Island where we were seated, or not farre, or at the least wise in few places els, during the time of our abode in the country: or of that many, that after gold & silver was not so soone found, as it was by them looked for, had litle or no care of any other thing but to pamper their bellies: or of that many which had litle understanding, lesse discretion, and more tongue then was needfull or requisite.

Some also were of a nice bringing up, only in cities or townes, or such as never (as I may say) had seene the world before. Because there were not to be found any English cities, nor such faire houses, nor at their owne wish any of their old accustomed dainty food, nor any soft beds of downe or feathers, the countrey was to them miserable, and their reports thereof according.

Because my purpose was but in briefe to open the cause of the variety of such speeches, the particularities of them, and of many envious, malicious, and slanderous reports and devices els;[35] by our owne countreymen besides, as trifles that are not worthy of wise men to be thought upon, I meane not to trouble you withall, but will passe to the commodities, the substance of that which I have to make relation of unto you.

---

32. least: lest.
33. open the cause: explain.

34. Other some: some others.
35. devices els: other devices.

The Treatise whereof, for your more ready view and easier understanding, I will divide into three speciall parts. In the first I will make declaration of such commodities there already found or to be raised, which will not onely serve the ordinary turnes of you which are and shall be the planters and inhabitants, but such an overplus sufficiently to be yeelded, or by men of skill to be provided, as by way of traffique and exchange with our owne nation of England, will inrich your selves the providers: those that shall deale with you, the enterprisers in generall, and greatly profit our owne countreymen, to supply them with most things which heretofore they have bene faine to provide either of strangers or of our enemies, which commodities, for distinction sake, I call Merchantable.

In the second I will set downe all the commodities which we know the countrey by our experience doth yeeld of it selfe for victuall and sustenance of mans life, such as are usually fed upon by the inhabitants of the countrey, as also by us during the time we were there.

In the last part I will make mention generally of such other commodities besides, as I am able to remember, and as I shall thinke behoovefull for those that shall inhabit, and plant there, to know of, which specially concerne building, as also some other necessary uses: with a briefe description of the nature and maners of the people of the countrey.

THE FIRST PART OF MERCHANTABLE COMMODITIES.

Silke of grasse, or Grasse silke.[36] There is a kind of grasse in the country, upon the blades whereof there groweth very good silke in forme of a thin glittering skin to be stript off. It groweth two foot & an halfe high or better: the blades are about two foot in length, and halfe an inch broad. The like groweth in Persia, which is in the selfe same climate as Virginia, of which very many of the Silke works that come from thence into Europe are made. Hereof if it be planted and ordered as in Persia, it cannot in reason be otherwise, but that there will rise in short time great profit to the dealers therein, seeing there is so great use and vent[37] thereof as well in our countrey as elsewhere. And by the meanes of sowing and planting it in good ground, it will be farre greater, better, and more plentifull then it is. Although notwithstanding there is great store thereof in many places of the countrey growing naturally and wild, which also by proofe here in England, in making a piece of Silke grogran,[38] we found to be excellent good.

Worme silke. In many of our journeys we found Silke-wormes faire and great, as bigge as our ordinary Walnuts. Although it hath not bene our hap[39] to have found such plenty, as elswhere to be in the countrey we have heard of, yet seeing that the countrey doth naturally breed and nourish them, there is no doubt but if arte be added in planting of Mulberie trees, and others, fit for them in commodious places, for their feeding & nourishing, and some of them carefully gathered & husbanded in

---

36. Here, as with many of the commodities he describes, Hariot seems to have confused a New World item—probably yucca, in this case—with a more familiar one.

37. vent: sale.
38. grogran: a coarse silk.
39. hap: fortune.

that sort, as by men of skil is knowen to be necessary: there wil rise as great profit in time to the Virginians, as thereof doth now to the Persians, Turks, Italians and Spanyards.

Flaxe and Hempe. The trueth is, that of Hempe and Flaxe there is no great store in any one place together, by reason it is not planted but as the soile doth yeeld of it selfe: and howsoever the leafe and stemme or stalke do differ from ours, the stuffe by judgement of men of skill is altogether as good as ours: and if not, as further proofe should finde otherwise, we have that experience of the soile, as that there cannot be shewed any reason to the contrary, but that it will grow there excellent well, and by planting will be yeelded plentifully, seeing there is so much ground whereof some may well be applied to such purposes. What benefit heereof may grow in cordage and linnens who cannot easily understand?

Allum. There is a veine of earth along the sea coast for the space of forty or fifty miles, whereof by the judgement of some that have made triall here in England, is made good Allum, of that kind which is called Roch allum. The richnesse of such a commodity is so well knowen, that I need not to say any thing thereof. The same earth doth also yeeld White coprasse, Nitrum, and Alumen plumeum,[40] but nothing so plentifully as the common Allum, which be also of price, and profitable.

Wapeih. A kind of earth so called by the naturall inhabitants, very like to Terra sigillata, and having bene refined, it hath bene found by some of our Physicians and Chyrurgians,[41] to be of the same kind of vertue, and more effectuall. The inhabitants use it very much for the cure of sores and wounds: there is in divers places great plenty, and in some places of a blew sort.

Pitch, Tarre, Rozen and Turpentine. There are those kinds of trees which yeeld them abundantly and great store. In the very same Island where we were seated, being fifteen miles of length, and five or sixe miles in breadth, there are few trees els but of the same kinde, the whole Island being full.

Sassafras, called by the inhabitants Winauk, a kind of wood of most pleasant and sweet smell, and of most rare vertues in physicke for the cure of many disease. It is found by experience to be far better and of more uses then the wood which is called Guaiacum,[42] or Lignum vitae. For the description, the maner of using, and the manifold vertues thereof, I refer you to the booke of Monardes, translated and entituled in English, The joyfull newes from the West Indies.

Cedar. A very sweet wood, and fine timber, whereof if nests of chests be there made, or timber thereof fitted for sweet and fine bedsteds, tables, desks, lutes, virginals, and many things els, (of which there hath bene proofe made already) to make up fraight with other principall commodities, will yeeld profit.

Wine. There are two kindes of grapes that the soile doth yeeld naturally, the one is small and sowre, of the ordinary bignesse as ours in England, the other farre greater and of himselfe lushious sweet. When they are planted and husbanded as they ought, a principall commodity of wines by them may be raised.

---

40. Minerals used for dyeing and for making gunpowder.
41. Chyrurgians: surgeons.

42. Guaiacum: a wood used to treat syphilis.

Oile. There are two sorts of Walnuts, both holding oile; but the one farre more plentifull then the other. When there are mils and other devices for the purpose, a commodity of them may be raised, because there are infinite store. There are also three severall kindes of berries in the forme of Oke-akornes, which also by the experience and use of the inhabitants, we find to yeeld very good and sweet oile. Furthermore, the beares of the countrey are commonly very fat, and in some places there are many. Their fatnesse, because it is so liquid, may well be termed oile, and hath many speciall uses.

Furres. All along the Sea coast there are great store of Otters, which being taken by weares[43] and other engines made for the purpose, wil yeeld good profit. We hope also of Marterne[44] furres, and make no doubt by the relation of the people, but that in some places of the countrey there are store, although there were but two skinnes that came to our hands. Luzernes[45] also we have understanding of, although for the time we saw none.

Deers skinnes dressed after the maner of Chamoes,[46] or undressed, are to be had of the naturall inhabitants thousands yerely by way of traffike for trifles, and no more waste or spoile of Deere then is and hath bene ordinarily in time before.

Civet-cats.[47] In our travels there was found one to have bin killed by a Savage or inhabitant, & in another place the smel where one or more had lately bene before,

---

43. weares: weirs, traps.
44. Marterne: marten, but more likely mink.
45. Luzernes: lynx.

46. Chamoes: chamois.
47. Civet-cats: unlike its relative, the skunk, the civet was valuable for making perfume.

whereby we gather, besides then by the relation of the people, that there are some in the country: good profit will rise by them.

Iron. In two places of the countrey specially, one about fourescore, & the other six score miles from the fort or place where we dwelt, we found nere the water side the ground to be rocky, which by the triall of a Minerall man was found to holde iron richly. It is found in many places of the country els: I know nothing to the contrary, but that it may be allowed for a good merchantable commodity, considering there the small charge for the labour & feeding of men, the infinite store of wood, the want of wood & deerenesse thereof in England, and the necessity of ballasting of ships.

Copper. An hundred and fifty miles into the maine in two townes we found with the inhabitants divers small plates of Copper, that had bene made as we understood by the inhabitants that dwell further into the country, where as they say are mountaines and rivers that yeeld also white graines of mettall, which is to be deemed Silver. For confirmation whereof, at the time of our first arrivall in the countrey, I saw, with some others with me, two small pieces of Silver grosly beaten, about the weight of a testron, hanging in the eares of a Wiroans[48] or chiefe lord that dwelt about fourescore miles from us: of whom through inquiry, by the number of dayes and the way, I learned that it had come to his hands from the same place or neere, where I after understood the Copper was made, and the white graines of metall found. The aforesayd Copper we also found by triall to holde Silver.

Pearle. Sometimes in feeding on Muscles we found some Pearle: but it was our happe to meet with ragges, or of a pide[49] colour: not having yet discovered those places where we heard of better and more plenty. One of our company, a man of skill in such matters, had gathered together from among the Savage people about five thousand: of which number he chose so many as made a faire chaine, which for their likenesse and uniformity in roundnesse, orientnesse, and pidenesse of many excellent colours, with equality in greatnesse, were very faire and rare: and had therefore beene presented to her Majesty, had we not by casualty, and through extremity of a storme lost them, with many things els in comming away from the countrey.

Sweet gummes of divers kinds, and many other Apothecary drugges, of which we will make speciall mention, when we shall receive it from such men of skill in that kinde, that in taking reasonable paines shal discover them more particularly then we have done, and then now I can make relation of, for want of the examples I had provided and gathered, and are now lost, with other things by casualty before mentioned.

Dies of divers kinds: There is Shoemake[50] well knowen, and used in England for blacke: the seed of an herbe called Wasebur, little small roots called Chappacor, and the barke of the tree called by the inhabitants Tangomockonomindge: which dies are for divers sorts of red: their goodnesse for our English clothes remaine yet to be prooved. The inhabitants use them only for the dying of haire, and colouring of their faces, and mantles made of Deere skinnes: and also for the dying of rushes to make artificiall works withall in their mats and baskets: having no other thing besides that

---

48. Wiroans: also werowance; a tribal elder.
49. pide: pied.

50. Shoemake: sumac.

they account of, apt to use them for. If they will not proove merchantable, there is no doubt but the planters there shall finde apt uses for them, as also for other colours which we know to be there.

Woad: a thing of so great vent[51] and uses amongst English Diers, which can not be yeelded sufficiently in our owne countrey for spare of ground, may be planted in Virginia, there being ground enough. The growth thereof need not to be doubted, when as in the Islands of the Acores[52] it groweth plentifully, which are in the same climate. So likewise of Madder.

We caried thither Suger-canes to plant, which being not so well preserved as was requisite, and besides the time of the yeere being past for their setting when we arrived, we could not make that proofe of them as we desired. Notwithstanding, seeing that they grow in the same climate, in the South part of Spaine, and in Barbary, our hope in reason may yet continue. So likewise for Orenges and Limmons. There may be planted also Quinses. Whereby may grow in reasonable time, if the action be diligently prosecuted, no small commodities in Sugars, Suckets, and Marmelades.

Many other commodities by planting may there also be raised, which I leave to your discreet and gentle considerations: and many also may be there, which yet we have not discovered. Two more commodities of great value, one of certeinty, and the other in hope, not to be planted, but there to be raised and in short time to be provided, and prepared, I might have specified. So likewise of those commodities already set downe I might have sayd more: as of the particular places where they are found, and best to be planted and prepared: by what meanes, and in what reasonable space of time they might be raised to profit, and in what proportion: but because others then welwillers might be there withall acquainted, not to the good of the action, I have wittingly omitted them: knowing that to those that are well disposed, I have uttered, according to my promise and purpose, for this part sufficient.

THE SECOND PART OF SUCH COMMODITIES AS VIRGINIA IS KNOWEN TO YEELD FOR VICTUALL AND SUSTENANCE OF MANS LIFE, USUALLY FED UPON BY THE NATURALL INHABTANTS; AS ALSO BY US, DURING THE TIME OF OUR ABODE: AND FIRST OF SUCH AS ARE SOWED AND HUSBANDED.

Pagatowr,[53] a kinde of graine so called by the inhabitants: the same in the West Indies is called Mayz: English men call it Guiny-wheat or Turkey-wheat, according to the names of the countreys from whence the like hath beene brought. The graine is about the bignesse of our ordinary English peaze,[54] and not much different in forme

---

51. vent: sale.
52. Acores: Azores.

53. Pagatowr: an Indian word for "things put in a pot to boil." Here, corn.
54. peaze: peas.

and shape: but of divers colours: some white, some red, some yellow, and some blew. All of them yeeld a very white and sweet flowre: being used according to his kinde, it maketh a very good bread. We made of the same in the countrey some Mault, whereof was brewed as good Ale as was to be desired. So likewise by the helpe of Hops, therof may be made as good Beere. It is a graine of marvellous great increase: of a thousand, fifteene hundred, and some two thousand folde. There are three sorts, of which two are ripe in eleven & twelve weeks at the most, sometimes in tenne, after the time they are set, and are then of height in stalke about six or seven foot. The other sort is ripe in foureteene, and is about tenne foot high, of the stalks some beare foure heads, some three, some one, and some two: every head conteining five, sixe, or seven hundred graines, within a few more or lesse. Of these graines, besides bread, the inhabitants make victuall, either by parching them, or seething them whole untill they be broken: or boiling the flowre with water into a pap.

Okindgier, called by us Beanes, because in greatnesse and partly in shape they are like to the beanes in England, saving that they are flatter, of more divers colours, and some pide. The leafe also of the stemme is much different. In taste they are altogether as good as our English peaze.

Wickonzowr, called by us Peaze, in respect of the Beanes, for distinction sake, because they are much lesse, although in forme they litle differ: but in goodnesse of taste much like, and are far better then our English Peaze. Both the beanes and peaze are ripe in ten weeks after they are set. They make them victuall either by boiling them all to pieces into a broth, or boiling them whole untill they be soft, and beginne to breake, as is used in England, either by themselves, or mixtly together: sometime they mingle of the Wheat with them: sometime also, being whole sodden, they bruse or pound them in a morter, and therof make loaves or lumps of doughish bread, which they use to eat for variety.

Macocquer, according to their several formes, called by us Pompions,[55] Melons, and Gourds, because they are of the like formes as those kinds in England. In Virginia such of severall formes are of one taste, and very good, and do also spring from one seed. There are of two sorts: one is ripe in the space of a moneth, and the other in two moneths.

There is an herbe which in Dutch is called Melden.[56] Some of those that I describe it unto take it to be a kinde of Orage: it groweth about foure or five foot high: of the seed thereof they make a thicke broth, and pottage of a very good taste: of the stalke by burning into ashes they make a kinde of salt earth, wherewithall many use sometimes to season their broths: other salt they know not. We our selves used the leaves also for pot-herbs.

There is also another great herbe, in forme of a Marigolde, about six foot in height, the head with the floure is a spanne in breadth. Some take it to be Planta Solis:[57] of the seeds hereof they make both a kinde of bread and broth.

All the aforesayd commodities for victual are set or sowed, sometimes in grounds apart and severally by themselves, but for the most part together in one ground

---

55. Pompions: pumpkins.
56. Melde in Dutch refers to the spinach and beet family.

57. Planta Solis: sunflower.

mixtly: the maner thereof, with the dressing and preparing of the ground, because I will note unto you the fertility of the soile, I thinke good briefly to describe.

The ground they never fatten with mucke, dung, or any other thing, neither plow nor digge it as we in England, but onely prepare it in sort as followeth. A few dayes before they sowe or set, the men with wooddEN instruments made almost in forme of mattocks or hoes with long handles: the women with short peckers or parers, because they use them sitting, of a foot long, and about five inches in breadth, doe onely breake the upper part of the ground to raise up the weeds, grasse, and olde stubbes of corne stalks with their roots. The which after a day or two dayes drying in the Sunne, being scrapt up into many small heaps, to save them labour for carying them away, they burne into ashes. And whereas some may thinke that they use the ashes for to better the ground, I say that then they would either disperse the ashes abroad, which wee observed they do not, except the heaps be too great, or els would take speciall care to set their corne where the ashes lie, which also wee finde they are carelesse of. And this is all the husbanding of their ground that they use.

Then their setting or sowing is after this maner. First for their corne, beginning in one corner of the plot, with a pecker they make a hole, wherein they put foure graines, with care that they touch not one another (about an inch asunder) & cover them with the molde[58] againe: and so thorowout the whole plot making such holes, and using them after such maner, but with this regard, that they be made in ranks, every ranke differing from other halfe a fadome or a yard, and the holes also in every ranke as much. By this meanes there is a yard spare ground betweene every hole: where according to discretion here and there, they set as many Beanes and Peaze; in divers places also among the seeds of Macocquer, Melden, and Planta solis.

The ground being thus set according to the rate by us experimented, an English acre conteining forty pearches in length, and foure in breadth, doth there yeeld in croppe or ofcome of corne, Beanes and Peaze, at the least two hundred London bushels, besides the Macocquer, Melden, and Planta solis; when as in England forty bushels of our Wheat yeelded out of such an acre is thought to be much.

I thought also good to note this unto you, that you which shall inhabit, and plant there, may know how specially that countrey corne is there to be preferred before ours: besides, the manifold wayes in applying it to victual, the increase is so much, that small labor & paines is needful in respect of that which must be used for ours. For this I can assure you that according to the rate we have made proofe of, one man may prepare and husband so much ground (having once borne corne before) with lesse then foure and twenty houres labour, as shall yeeld him victual in a large proportion for a twelvemoneth, if he have nothing els but that which the same ground will yeeld, and of that kinde onely which I have before spoken of: the sayd ground being also but of five and twenty yards square. And if need require, but that there is ground enough, there might be raised out of one and the selfesame ground two harvests or ofcomes: for they sow or set, and may at any time when they thinke good, from the midst of March untill the end of June: so that they also set when they have eaten of

---

58. molde: earth.

their first croppe. In some places of the
countrey notwithstanding they have two
harvests, as we have heard, out of one
and the same ground.

For English corne neverthelesse,
whether to use or not to use it, you that
inhabit may doe as you shall have
further cause to thinke best. Of the
growth you need not to doubt: for
Barley, Oats, and Peaze, we have seene
proofe of, not being purposely sowen,
but fallen casually in the woorst sort of ground, and yet to be as faire as any we have
ever seene heere in England. But of Wheat, because it was musty, and had taken salt
water, we could make no triall: and of Rie we had none. Thus much have I digressed,
and I hope not unnecessarily: now will I returne againe to my course, and intreat of
that which yet remaineth, apperteining to this chapter.

There is an herbe which is sowed apart by it selfe, and is called by the inhabitants
Uppowoc: in the West Indies it hath divers names, according to the severall places and
countreys where it groweth and is used: the Spanyards generally call it Tabacco. The
leaves thereof being dried and brought into pouder, they use to take the fume or
smoake thereof, by sucking it thorow pipes made of clay, into their stomacke and
head; from whence it purgeth superfluous fleame[59] and other grosse humours, and
openeth all the pores and passages of the body: by which meanes the use thereof not
onely preserveth the body from obstructions, but also (if any be, so that they have not
bene of too long continuance) in short time breaketh them: whereby their bodies are
notably preserved in health, and know not many grievous diseases, wherewithall we in
England are often times afflicted.

This Uppowoc is of so precious estimation amongst them, that they thinke their gods
are marvellously delighted therewith: whereupon sometime they make hallowed fires,
and cast some of the pouder therin for a sacrifice: being in a storme upon the waters, to
pacifie their gods, they cast some up into the aire and into the water: so a weare for fish
being newly set up, they cast some therein and into the aire: also after an escape of
danger, they cast some into the aire likewise: but all done with strange gestures,
stamping, sometime dancing, clapping of hands, holding up of hands, and staring up
into the heavens, uttering therewithall, and chattering strange words and noises.

We our selves, during the time we were there, used to sucke it after their maner, as
also since our returne, and have found many rare and woonderfull experiments of the
vertues thereof: of which the relation would require a volume by it selfe: the use of it
by so many of late men and women of great calling, as els, and some learned
Physicians also, is sufficient witnesse.

And these are all the commodities for sustenance of life, that I know and can
remember, they use to husband: all els that follow, are found growing naturally or
wilde.

59. fleame: phlegm.

OF ROOTS.

Openauk[60] are a kinde of roots of round forme, some of the bignesse of Walnuts, some farre greater, which are found in moist and marish grounds growing many together one by another in ropes, as though they were fastened with a string. Being boiled or sodden, they are very good meat. Monardes calleth these roots, Beads or Pater nostri of Santa Helena.

Okeepenauk are also of round shape, found in dry grounds: some are of the bignesse of a mans head. They are to be eaten as they are taken out of the ground: for by reason of their drinesse they will neither rost nor seethe.[61] Their taste is not so good as of the former roots: notwithstanding for want of bread, and sometimes for variety the inhabitants use to eat them with fish or flesh, and in my judgement they do as well as the housholde bread made of Rie here in England.

Kaishucpenauk, a white kinde of roots about the bignesse of hennes egges, and neere of that forme: their taste was not so good to our seeming as of the other, and therefore their place and maner of growing not so much cared for by us: the inhabitants notwithstanding used to boile and eat many.

Tsinaw,[62] a kind of root much like unto that which in England is called the China root brought from the East Indies. And we know not any thing to the contrary but that it may be of the same kinde. These roots grow many together in great clusters, and do bring foorth a brier stalke, but the leafe in shape farre unlike: which being supported by the trees it groweth neerest unto, will reach or climbe to the top of the highest. From these roots while they be new or fresh, being chopt into small pieces, and stampt, is strained with water a juice that maketh bread, and also being boiled, a very good spoonmeat in maner of a gelly, and is much better in taste, if it be tempered with oile. This Tsinaw is not of that sort, which by some was caused to be brought into England for the China root; for it was discovered since, and is in use as is aforesayd: but that which was brought hither is not yet knowen, neither by us nor by the inhabitants to serve for any use or purpose, although the roots in shape are very like.

Coscushaw some of our company tooke to be that kinde of root which the Spanyards in the West Indies call Cassavy, whereupon also many called it by that name: it groweth in very muddy pooles, and moist grounds. Being dressed according to the countrey maner, it maketh a good bread, and also a good spoonmeat, and is used very much by the inhabitants. The juice of this root is poison, & therefore heed must be taken before any thing be made therewithall: either the roots must be first sliced and dried in the Sunne, or by the fire, and then being punned into floure, will make good bread: or els while they are greene they are to be pared, cut in pieces, and stampt: loaves of the same to be layd here or over the fire untill it be sowre; and then being well punned againe, bread or spoonmeat very good in taste and holesome may be made thereof.

Habascon is a root of hote taste, almost of the forme and bignesse of a Parsnip: of it selfe it is no victuall, but onely a helpe, being boiled together with other meats.

---

60. Openauk: probably a kind of potato.
61. rost nor seethe: roast nor boil.

62. Tsinaw: an Indian pronunciation of China, a word they had probably learned from earlier English voyagers.

There are also Leeks, differing little from ours in England, that grow in many places of the countrey; of which, when we came in places where they were, we gathered and eat many, but the naturall inhabitants never.

Of Fruits.

Chestnuts there are in divers places great store: some they use to eat raw, some they stampe and boile to make spoonmeat, and with some being sodden, they make such a maner of dough bread as they use of their beanes before mentioned.

Walnuts. There are two kinds of Walnuts, and of them infinite store: in many places, where are very great woods for many miles together, the third part of trees are Walnut trees. The one kinde is of the same taste and forme, or little differing from ours of England, but that they are harder and thicker shelled: the other is greater, and hath a very ragged and hard shell: but the kernel great, very oily and sweet. Besides their eating of them after our ordinary maner, they breake them with stones, and punne them in morters with water, to make a milke which they use to put into some sorts of their spoonemeat: also among their sodde wheat, peaze, beanes and pompions, which maketh them have a farre more pleasant taste.

Medlars,[63] a kinde of very good fruit: so called by us chiefly for these respects: first in that they are not good untill they be rotten, then in that they open at the head as our Medlars, and are about the same bignesse: otherwise in taste and colour they are farre different; for they are as red as cheries, and very sweet: but whereas the chery is sharpe sweet, they are lushious sweet.

Mutaquesunnauk,[64] a kinde of pleasant fruit almost of the shape and bignesse of English peares, but that they are of a perfect red colour as well within as without. They grow on a plant whose leaves are very thicke, and full of prickles as sharpe as needles. Some that have beene in the Indies, where they have seene that kind of red die of great price, which is called Cochinile, to grow, doe describe his plant right like unto this of Metaquesunnauk; but whether it be the true Cochinile, or a bastard or wilde kinde, it cannot yet be certified, seeing that also, as I heard, Cochinile is not of the fruit, but found on the leaves of the plant: which leaves for such matter we have not so specially observed.

Grapes there are of two sorts, which I mentioned in the merchantable commodities.

Strawberies there are as good and as great as those which we have in our English gardens.

Mulberies, Applecrabs, Hurts or Hurtleberies, such as we have in England.

Sacquenummener, a kinde of berries almost like unto Capers, but somewhat greater, which grow together in clusters upon a plant or hearbe that is found in shallow waters: being boiled eight or nine houres according to their kinde, are very good meat and holesome; otherwise if they be eaten they will make a man for the time frantike or extremely sicke.

There is a kinde of Reed[65] which beareth a seed almost like unto our Rie or Wheat; and being boiled is good meat.

63. Medlars: persimmons.
64. Mutaquesunnauk: prickly pears.
65. Reed: possibly wild rice.

In our travels in some places we found Wilde peaze like unto ours in England, but that they were lesse, which are also good meat.

Of a kinde of fruit or berry in forme of Acornes.

There is a kinde of berry or acorne, of which there are five sorts that grow on severall kindes of trees: the one is called Sagatemener, the second Osamener, the third Pummuckoner. These kinde of acornes they use to drie upon hurdles made of reeds, with fire underneath, almost after the maner as we dry Malt in England. When they are to be used, they first water them untill they be soft, and then being sod, they make a good victuall, either to eat so simply, or els being also punned to makes loaves or lumps of bread. These be also the three kinds, of which I sayd before the inhabitants used to make sweet bile.

Another sort is called Sapummener, which being boiled or parched, doth eat and taste like unto Chesnuts. They sometime also make bread of this sort.

The fift sort is called Mangummenauk, and is the acorne of their kinde of Oake, the which being dried after the maner of the first sorts, and afterward watered, they boile them, and their servants, or sometime the chiefe themselves, either for variety or for want of bread, do eat them with their fish or flesh.

Of Beasts.

Deere, in some places there are great store: neere unto the Sea coast they are of the ordinary bignesse of ours in England, and some lesse: but further up into the countrey, where there is better food, they are greater: they differ from ours onely in this, their tailes are longer, and the snags of their hornes looke backward.

Conies. Those that we have seene, and all that we can heare of are of a gray colour like unto Hares: in some places there are such plenty that all the people of some townes make them mantles of the furre or flue of the skinnes of those which they usually take.

Saquenuckot and Maquowoc, two kinds of small beasts greater then Conies, which are very good meat. We never tooke any of them our selves but sometime eat of such as the inhabitants had taken and brought unto us.

Squirels, which are of a grey colour, we have taken and eaten.

Beares, which are of blacke colour. The beares of this countrey are good meat. The inhabitants in time of Winter do use to take & eat many: so also sometime did we. They are taken commonly in this sort: In some Islands or places where they are, being hunted for, as soone as they have spiall[66] of a man, they presently run away, and then being chased, they clime and get up the next tree they can: from whence with arrowes they are shot downe starke dead, or with those wounds that they may after easily be killed. We sometime shot them downe with our calievers.

I have the names of eight and twenty severall sorts of beasts, which I have heard of to be here and there dispersed in the countrey, especially in the maine:[67] of which

---

66. spiall: sight.   67. maine: mainland.

there are only twelve kinds that we have yet discovered; and of those that be good meat we know only them before mentioned. The inhabitants sometime kill the Lion, and eat him: and we sometime as they came to our hands of their Woolves or Woolvish dogs, which I have not set downe for good meat, least that some would understand my judgement therein to be more simple then needeth, although I could alleage the difference in taste of those kinds from ours, which by some of our company have bene experimented in both.

Of Fowle.

Turkie cocks and Turkie hennes, Stockdoves, Partridges, Cranes, Hernes, and in Winter great store of Swannes and Geese. Of all sorts of fowle I have the names in the countrey language of fourescore and sixe, of which number, besides those that be named, we have taken, eaten, & have the pictures as they were there drawn, with the names of the inhabitants, of severall strange sorts of water fowle eight, and seventeene kinds more of land fowle, although we have seene and eaten of many more, which for want of leasure there for the purpose, could not be pictured: and after we are better furnished and stored upon further discovery with their strange beasts, fish, trees, plants, and herbs, they shall be also published.

There are also Parrots, Faulcons, and Marlin hauks, which although with us they be not used for meat, yet for other causes I thought good to mention.

Of Fish.

For foure moneths of the yeere, February, March, Aprill and May, there are plenty of Sturgeons. And also in the same moneths of Herrings, some of the ordinary bignesse of ours in England, but the most part farre greater, of eighteene, twenty inches, and some two foot in length and better: both these kinds of fish in those moneths are most plentifull, and in best season, which we found to be most delicate and pleasant meat.

There are also Trouts, Porpoises, Rayes, Oldwives,[68] Mullets, Plaice,[69] and very many other sorts of excellent good fish, which we have taken and eaten, whose names I know not but in the countrey language: we have the pictures of twelve sorts more, as they were drawn in the countrey, with their names.

68. Oldwives: bream.   69. Plaice: flounder.

The inhabitants use to take them two maner of wayes; the one is by a kinde of weare made of reeds, which in that country are very strong: the other way, which is more strange, is with poles made sharpe at one end, by shooting them into the fish after the maner as Irish men cast darts, either as they are rowing in their boats, or els as they are wading in the shallowes for the purpose.

There are also in many places plenty of these kinds which follow:

Sea-crabs, such as we have in England.

Oisters, some very great, and some small, some round, and some of a long shape: they are found both in salt water and brackish, and those that we had out of salt water are farre better than the other, as in our countrey.

Also Muscles, Scalops, Periwinkles, and Crevises.

Seekanauk, a kinde of crusty shel-fish, which is good meat, about a foot in bredth, having a crusty taile, many legges like a crab, and her eyes in her backe. They are found in shallowes of waters, and sometime on the shore.

There are many Tortoises both of land and sea kinde, their backs and bellies are shelled very thicke; their head, feet, and taile, which are in appearance, seeme ougly, as though they were members of a serpent or venimous beasts; but notwithstanding they are very good meat, as also their eggs. Some have bene found of a yard in bredth and better.

And thus have I made relation of all sorts of victuall that we fed upon for the time we were in Virginia, as also the inhabitants themselves, as farre forth as I know and can remember, or that are specially woorthy to be remembered.

THE THIRD AND LAST PART OF SUCH OTHER THINGS AS ARE BEHOVEFULL FOR THOSE WHICH SHALL PLANT AND INHABITE TO KNOW OF, WITH A DESCRIPTION OF THE NATURE AND MANERS OF THE PEOPLE OF THE COUNTREY.

OF COMMODITIES FOR BUILDING AND OTHER NECESSARY USES.

Those other things which I am more to make rehearsal of, are such as concerne building, & other mechanicall necessary uses, as divers sorts of trees for house and ship-timber, and other uses else: Also lime, stone, and bricke, least that being not mentioned some might have bene doubted of, or by some that are malitious the contrary reported.

Okes there are as faire, straight, tall, and as good timber as any can be, and also great store, and in some places very great.

Walnut trees, as I have said before very many, some have bene seene excellent faire timber of foure and five fadome, and above fourescore foote streight without bough.

Firre trees fit for masts of ships, some very tall and great.

Rakiock, a kinde of trees so called that are sweete wood, of which the inhabitants that were neere unto us doe commonly make their boates or Canoas of the forme of trowes, onely with the helpe of fire, hatchets of stones, and shels: we have knowen some so great being made in that sort of one tree, that they have caried well 20. men at once, besides much baggage: the timber being great, tall, streight, soft, light, and yet tough ynough I thinke (besides other uses) to be fit also for masts of ships.

Cedar, a sweete wood good for seelings, chests, boxes, bedsteads, lutes, virginals, and many things els, as I have also said before. Some of our company which have wandered in some places where I have not bene, have made certaine affirmation of Cyprus, which for such and other excellent uses is also a wood of price and no small estimation.

Maple, and also Wich-hazle, whereof the inhabitants use to make their bowes.

Holly, a necessary thing for the making of birdlime.

Willowes good for the making of weares and weeles to take fish after the English maner, although the inhabitants use onely reedes, which because they are so strong as also flexible, doe serve for that turne very well and sufficiently.

Beech and Ashe, good for caske-hoopes, and if neede require, plowe, worke, as also for many things els.

Elme.

Sassafras trees.

Ascopo a kinde of tree very like unto Lawrell, the barke is hot in taste and spicie, it is very like to that tree which Monardes describeth to be Cassia Lignea of the West Indies.

There are many other strange trees whose names I know not but in the Virginian language, of which I am not now able, neither is it so convenient for the present to trouble you with particular relation: seeing that for timber and other necessary uses, I have named sufficient. And of many of the rest, but that they may be applied to good use, I know no cause to doubt.

Now for stone, bricke, and lime, thus it is. Neere unto the Sea coast where wee dwelt, there are no kinde of stones to be found (except a few small pebbles about foure miles off) but such as have bene brought from further out of the maine. In some of our voyages we have seene divers hard raggie stones, great pebbles, and a kinde of gray stone like unto marble of which the inhabitants make their hatchets to cleave wood. Upon inquirie wee heard that a little further up into the Countrey were of all sorts very many, although of quarries they are ignorant, neither have they use of any store whereupon they should have occasion to seeke any. For if every housholde have one or two to cracke nuts, grinde shels, whet copper, and sometimes other stones for hatchets, they have ynough: neither use they any digging, but onely for graves about three foote deepe: and therefore no marveile that they know neither quarries, nor lime-stones, which both may be in places neerer then they wot of.

In the meane time until there be discovery of sufficient store in some place or other convenient, the want of you which are & shalbe the planters therein may be as well supplied by bricke: for the making whereof in divers places of the Countrey there is clay both excellent good, and plentie, and also by lime made of oyster shels, and of others burnt, after the maner as they use in the Isles of Tenet and Shepy, and also in divers other places of England: Which kinde of lime is well known to be as good as any other. And of oyster shels there is plentie ynough: for besides divers other particular places where are abundance, there is one shallow Sound along the coast, where for the space of many miles together in length, and two or three miles in breadth, the ground is nothing els, being but halfe a foote or a foote under water for the most part.

A pair of Picts, primitive inhabitants of England, illustrated by de Bry for comparison with the Indians.

Thus much can I say furthermore of stones, that about 120. miles from our fort neere the water in the side of a hill, was found by a Gentleman of our company, a great veine of hard ragge stones, which I thought good to remember unto you.

OF THE NATURE AND MANERS OF THE PEOPLE.

It resteth[70] I speake a word or two of the naturall inhabitants, their natures and maners, leaving large discourse thereof until time more convenient hereafter: nowe only so farre foorth, as that you may know, how that they in respect of troubling our inhabiting and planting, are not to be feared, but that they shall have cause both to feare and love us, that shall inhabite with them.

They are a people clothed with loose mantles made of deere skinnes, and aprons of the same round about their middles, all els naked, of such a difference of statures only as wee in England, having no edge tooles or weapons of yron or steele to offend us withall, neither knowe they how to make any: those weapons that they have, are onely bowes made of Witch-hazle, and arrowes of reedes, flat edged truncheons also of wood about a yard long, neither have they any thing to defend themselves but targets made of barkes, and some armours made of sticks wickered together with thread.

Their townes are but small, and neere the Sea coast but fewe, some contayning but tenne or twelve houses; some 20 the greatest that we have seene hath bene but of 30

70. resteth: remains that.

houses: if they bee walled, it is onely done with barkes of trees made fast to stakes, or els with poles onely fixed upright, and close one by another.

Their houses are made of small poles, made fast at the tops in round forme after the maner as is used in many arbories in our gardens of England, in most townes covered with barkes, and in some with artificiall mats made of long rushes, from the tops of the houses downe to the ground. The length of them is commonly double to the breadth, in some places they are but 12 and 16 yards long, and in other some we have seene of foure and twentie.

In some places of the Countrey, one onely towne belongeth to the government of a Wiroans or chiefe Lord, in other some two or three, in some sixe, eight, and more: the greatest Wiroans that yet wee had dealing with, had but eighteene townes in his government, and able to make not above seven or eight hundred fighting men at the most. The language of every government is different from any other, and the further they are distant, the greater is the difference.

The town of Pomeiooc. De Bry's illustrations for the 1590 edition were based on drawings by John White, who had been in Virginia in 1585.

Their maner of warres amongst themselves is either by sudden surprising one an other most commonly about the dawning of the day, or moone-light, or els by ambushes, or some subtile devises. Set battels are very rare, except it fall out where there are many trees, where either part may have some hope of defense, after the delivery of every arrow, in leaping behind some or other.

If there fall out any warres betweene us and them, what their fight is likely to bee, wee having advantages against them so many maner of wayes, as by our discipline, cur strange weapons and devises else, especially Ordinance[71] great and small, it may easily bee imagined: by the experience wee have had in some places, the turning up of their heeles against us in running away was their best defence.

In respect of us they are a people poore, and for want of skill and judgement in the knowledge and use of our things, doe esteeme our trifles before things of greater value: Notwithstanding, in their proper maner (considering the want of such meanes as we have), they seeme very ingenious. For although they have no such tooles, nor any such crafts, Sciences and Artes as wee, yet in those things they doe, they shew excellencie of wit. And by how much they upon due consideration shall finde our maner of knowledges and crafts to exceed theirs in perfection, and speede for doing or execution, by so much the more is it probable that they should desire our friend-

71. Ordinance: artillery.

ship and love, and have the greater respect for pleasing and obeying us. Whereby may bee hoped, if meanes of good government be used, that they may in short time bee brought to civilitie, and the imbracing of true Religion.

Some religion they have already, which although it be farre from the trueth, yet being as it is, there is hope it may be the easier and sooner reformed.

They beleeve that there are many gods, which they call Mantoac, but of different sorts & degrees, one onely chiefe and great God, which hath bene from all eternitie. Who, as they affirme, when hee purposed to make the world, made first other gods of a principall order, to be as meanes and instruments to be used in the creation and government to follow, and after the Sunne, moone, and starres as pettie gods, and the instruments of the other order more principal. First (they say) were made waters, out of which by the gods was made all diversitie of creatures that are visible or invisible.

For mankinde they say a woman was made first, which by the working of one of the gods, conceived and brought foorth children: And in such sort they say they had their beginning. But how many yeeres or ages have passed since, they say they can make no relation, having no letters nor other such meanes as we to keepe Records of the particularities of times past, but onely tradition from father to sonne.

They thinke that all the gods are of humane shape, and therefore they represent them by images in the formes of men, which they call Kewasowok, one alone is called Kewas: them they place in houses appropriate or temples, which they call Machicomuck, where they worship, pray, sing, and make many times offring unto them. In some Machicomuck we have seene but one Kewas, in some two, and in other some three. The common sort thinke them to be also gods.

They beleeve also the immortalitie of the soule, that after this life as soone as the soule is departed from the body, according to the workes it hath done, it is either caried to heaven the habitacle of gods, there to enjoy perpetuall blisse and happinesse, or els to a great pitte or hole, which they thinke to be in the furthest parts of their part of the world toward the Sunne set, there to burne continually: the place they call Popogusso.

For the confirmation of this opinion, they tolde me two stories of two men that had bene lately dead and revived againe, the one happened but few yeeres before our comming into the Countrey of a wicked man, which having bene dead and buried, the next day the earth of the grave being seene to move, was taken up againe, who made declaration where his soule had bene, that is to say, very neere entring into Popogusso, had not one of the gods saved him, and gave him leave to returne againe, and teach his friends what they should do to avoyd that terrible place of torment. The other happened in the same yeere we were there, but in a towne that was 60 miles from us, and it was told me for strange newes, that one being dead, buried, and taken up againe as the first, shewed that although his body had lien dead in the grave, yet his soule was alive, & had travailed farre in a long broad way, on both sides whereof grew most delicate and pleasant trees, bearing more rare and excellent fruits, then ever hee had seene before, or was able to expresse, and at length came to most brave and faire houses, neere which he met his father that had bene dead before, who gave him great charge to goe backe againe, and shew his friendes what good they were to doe to enjoy the pleasures of that place, which when he had done he should after come againe.

What subtiltie soever be in the Wiro-
ances and priestes, this opinion worketh
so much in many of the common and
simple sort of people, that it maketh them
have great respect to their Governours,
and also great care what they doe, to
avoyd torment after death, and to enjoy
blisse, although notwithstanding there is
punishment ordeined for malefactours, as
stealers, whoremongers, and other sorts
of wicked doers, some punished with
death, some with forfeitures, some with
beating, according to the greatnesse of the
facts.

The town of Secota.

And this is the summe of their Religion,
which I learned by having speciall familiaritie with some of their priests. Wherein
they were not so sure grounded, nor gave
such credite to their traditions and stories,
but through conversing with us they were
brought into great doubts of their owne,
and no small admiration of ours, with
earnest desire in many, to learne more than wee had meanes for want of perfect utterance in their language to expresse.

Most things they sawe with us, as Mathematicall instruments, sea Compasses, the
vertue of the load-stone[72] in drawing yron, a perspective glasse[73] whereby was shewed
many strange sights, burning glasses, wilde firewoorkes, gunnes, hookes, writing and
reading, spring-clockes that seeme to goe of themselves and many other things that
wee had were so strange unto them, and so farre exceeded their capacities to comprehend the reason and meanes how they should be made and done, that they thought
they were rather the workes of gods then of men, or at the leastwise they had bene
given and taught us of the gods. Which made many of them to have such opinion of
us, as that if they knew not the trueth of God and Religion already, it was rather to
bee had from us whom God so specially loved, than from a people that were so
simple, as they found themselves to be in comparison of us. Whereupon greater
credite was given unto that wee spake of, concerning such matters.

Many times and in every towne where I came, according as I was able, I made declaration of the contents of the Bible, that therein was set foorth the true and onely God,
and his mightie workes, that therein was conteined the true doctrine of salvation
through Christ, with many particularities of Miracles and chiefe points of Religion, as I
was able then to utter, and thought fit for the time. And although I told them the booke
materially and of it selfe was not of any such vertue, as I thought they did conceive, but
onely the doctrine therein conteined: yet would many be glad to touch it, to embrace it,

---

72. load-stone: lodestone, magnet.

73. perspective glasse: telescope or magnifying glass.

to kisse it, to holde it to their breastes and heads, and stroke over all their body with it, to shew their hungry desire of that knowledge which was spoken of.

The Wiroans with whom we dwelt called Wingina, and many of his people would bee glad many times to be with us at our Prayers, and many times call upon us both in his owne towne, as also in others whither hee sometimes accompanied us, to pray and sing Psalmes, hoping thereby to be partaker of the same effects which we by that meanes also expected.

Twise this Wiroans was so grievously sicke that he was like to die, and as he lay languishing, doubting of any helpe by his owne priestes, and thinking hee was in such danger for offending us and thereby our God, sent for some of us to pray and bee a meanes to our God that it would please him either that he might live, or after death dwell with him in blisse, so likewise were the requests of many others in the like case.

On a time also when their corne began to wither by reason of a drought which happened extraordinarily, fearing that it had come to passe by reason that in some thing they had displeased us, many would come to us and desire us to pray to our God of England, that he would preserve their Corne, promising that when it was ripe we also should be partakers of the fruit.

There could at no time happen any strange sicknesse, losses, hurts, or any other crosse unto them, but that they would impute to us the cause or meanes thereof, for offending or not pleasing us. One other rare and strange accident, leaving others, wil I mention before I end, which moved the whole Countrey that either knew or heard of us, to have us in wonderfull admiration.

There was no towne where wee had any subtile devise practised against us, wee leaving it unpunished or not revenged (because we sought by all meanes possible to win them by gentlenesse) but that within a few dayes after our departure from every such Towne, the people began to die very fast, and many in short space, in some Townes about twentie, in some fourtie, and in one six score, which in trueth was very many in respect of their numbers.[74] This happened in no place that we could learne, but where we had bin, where they used some practise against us, & after such time. The disease also was so strange, that they neither knewe what it was, nor how to cure it, the like by report of the oldest men in the Countrey never happened before, time out of minde. A thing specially observed by us, as also by the naturall inhabitants themselves. Insomuch that when some of the inhabitants which were our friends, and especially the Wiroans Wingina, had observed such effects in foure or five Townes to followe their wicked practises, they were perswaded that it was the worke of our God through our meanes, and that we by him might kill and slay whom we would without weapons, and not come neere them. And thereupon when it had happened that they had understanding that any of their enemies had abused us in our journeys, hearing that we had wrought no revenge with our weapons, and fearing upon some cause the matter should so rest: did come and intreate us that we would be a meanes to our God that they as others that had dealt ill with us might in like sort die, alleadging how much it would bee for our credite and profite, as also theirs, and hoping furthermore that we would doe so much at their requests in respect of the friendship we professed them.

---

74. In almost every part of the New World, epidemics decimated native populations after encounters with Europeans.

Here, because Hariot mentions no symptoms of smallpox, the disease may have been the common cold.

Whose entreaties although wee shewed that they were ungodly, affirming that our God would not subject himselfe to any such prayers and requests of men: that indeede all things have bene and were to be done according to his good pleasure as he had ordeined: and that we to shewe our selves his true servants ought rather to make petition for the contrary, that they with them might live together with us, be made partakers of his trueth, and serve him in righteousnesse, but notwithstanding in such sort, that wee referre that, as all other things, to bee done according to his divine will and pleasure, and as by his wisedome he had ordeined to be best.

Yet because the effect fell out so suddenly and shortly after according to their desires, they thought neverthelesse it came to passe by our meanes, & that we in using such speeches unto them, did but dissemble the matter, and therefore came unto us to give us thankes in their maner, that although we satisfied them not in promise, yet in deedes and effect we had fulfilled their desires.

This marveilous accident in all the Countrey wrought so strange opinions of us, that some people could not tell whether to thinke us gods or men, and the rather because that all the space of their sicknes, there was no man of ours knowen to die, or that was specially sicke: they noted also that we had no women amongst us, neither that we did care for any of theirs.

Some therefore were of opinion that we were not borne of women, and therefore not mortal, but that we were men of an old generation many yeeres past, then risen againe to immortalitie.

Some would likewise seeme to prophecie that there were more of our generation yet to come to kill theirs and take their places, as some thought the purpose was, by that which was already done. Those that were immediately to come after us they imagined to be in the aire, yet invisible and without bodies, and that they by our intreatie and for the love of us, did make the people to die in that sort as they did, by shooting invisible bullets into them.

To confirme this opinion, their Phisitions (to excuse their ignorance in curing the disease) would not be ashamed to say, but earnestly make the simple people beleeve, that the strings of blood that they sucked out of the sicke bodies, were the strings wherewithall the invisible bullets were tied and cast. Some also thought that wee shot them our selves out of our pieces, from the place where wee dwelt, and killed the people in any Towne that had offended us, as wee listed, howe farre distant from us soever it were. And other some said, that it was the speciall worke of God for our sakes, as we our selves have cause in some sort to thinke no lesse, whatsoever some doe, or may imagine to the contrary, specially some Astrologers, knowing of the Eclipse of the Sunne which we saw the same yeere before in our voyage thitherward, which unto them appeared very terrible. And also of a Comet which began to appeare but a fewe dayes before the beginning of the saide sicknesse. But to exclude them from being the speciall causes of so speciall an accident, there are further reasons then I thinke fit at this present to be alleadged. These their opinions I have set downe the more at large, that it may appeare unto you that there is good hope they may be brought through discreete dealing and government to the imbracing of the trueth, and consequently to honour, obey, feare and love us.

And although some of our company towards the end of the yeere, shewed themselves too fierce in slaying some of the people in some Townes, upon causes that on our part might easily ynough have bene borne withall: yet notwithstanding, because it was on their part justly deserved, the alteration of their opinions generally and for the most part concerning us is the lesse to be doubted. And whatsoever els they may be, by carefulnesse of our selves neede nothing at all to be feared.

THE CONCLUSION.

Now I have (as I hope) made relation not of so few and small things, but that the Countrey (of men that are indifferent and well disposed) may bee sufficiently liked: If there were no more knowen then I have mentioned, which doubtlesse and in great reason is nothing to that which remaineth to be discovered, neither the soyle, nor commodities. As we have reason so to gather by the difference we found in our travailes, for although al which I have before spoken of, have bene discovered and experimented not farre from the Sea coast, where was our abode and most of our travailing: yet sometimes as we made our journeys further into the maine and Countrey; we found the soile to be fatter, the trees greater and to grow thinner, the ground more firme and deeper mould, more and larger champions,[75] finer grasse, and as good as ever we saw any in England; in some places rockie and farre more high and hilly ground, more plentie of their fruites, more abundance of beastes, the more inhabited with people, and of greater pollicie and larger dominions; with greater townes and houses.

Why may wee not then looke for in good hope from the inner parts of more and greater plentie, as well of other things, as of those which wee have already discovered? Unto the Spaniards happened the like in discovering the maine of the West Indies. The maine also of this Countrey of Virginia, extending some wayes so many hundreds of leagues, as otherwise then by the relation of the inhabitants wee have most certaine knowledge of, where yet no Christian prince hath any possession or dealing, cannot but yeelde many kinds of excellent commodities, which we in our discovery have not yet seene.

What hope there is els to bee gathered of the nature of the Climate, being answerable to the Iland of Japan, the land of China, Persia, Jury, the Ilands of Cyprus and Candy, the South parts of Greece, Italy and Spaine, and of many other notable and famous Countreys, because I meane not to be tedious, I leave to your owne consideration.

Whereby also the excellent temperature of the aire there at all seasons, much warmer then in England, and never so vehemently hot, as sometimes is under and betweene the Tropikes, or neere them, cannot be knowen unto you without further relation.

For the holsomnesse thereof I neede to say but thus much: that for all the want of provision, as first of English victuall, excepting for twentie dayes, we lived onely by drinking water, and by the victuall of the Countrey, of which some sorts were very strange unto us, and might have bene thought to have altered our temperatures in such sort, as to have brought us into some grievous and dangerous diseases: secondly the want of English meanes, for the taking of beastes, fish and foule, which by the

---

75. champions: meadows.

helpe onely of the inhabitants and their meanes could not bee so suddenly and easily provided for us, nor in so great number and quantities, nor of that choise as otherwise might have bene to our better satisfaction and contentment. Some want also we had of clothes. Furthermore in al our travailes, which were most specially and often in the time of Winter, our lodging was in the open aire upon the ground. And yet I say for all this, there were but foure of our whole company (being one hundreth and eight) that died all the yeere, and that but at the latter ende thereof, and upon none of the aforesaide causes. For all foure, especially three, were feeble, weake, and sickly persons before ever they came thither, and those that knew them, much marveled that they lived so long being in that case, or had adventured to travaile.

Seeing therefore the aire there is so temperate and holsome, the soyle so fertile, and yeelding such commodities, as I have before mentioned, the voyage also thither to and fro being sufficiently experimented to be perfourmed twise a yeere with ease, and at any season thereof: And the dealing of Sir Walter Ralegh so liberall in large giving and granting lande there, as is already knowen, with many helpes and furtherances else: (The least that he hath granted hath bene five hundreth acres to a man onely for the adventure of his person) I hope there remaines no cause whereby the action should be misliked.

If that those which shall thither travaile to inhabite and plant bee but reasonably provided for the first yeere, as those are which were transported the last, and being there, doe use but that diligence and care, that is requisit, and as they may with ease: There is no doubt, but for the time following, they may have victuals that are excellent good and plentie ynough, some more English sorts of cattel also hereafter, as some have bene before, and are there yet remayning, may, and shall be (God willing) thither transported. So likewise, our kinde of fruites, rootes, and hearbes, may be there planted and sowed, as some have bene already, and prove well: And in short time also they may raise so much of those sorts of commodities which I have spoken of, as shall both enrich themselves, as also others that shall deale with them.

And this is all the fruit of our labours, that I have thought necessary to advertise you of at this present: What else concerneth the nature and maners of the inhabitants of Virginia, the number with the particularities of the voyages thither made, and of the actions of such as have bene by Sir Walter Ralegh therein, and there imployed, many worthy to be remembered, as of the first discoverers of the Countrey, of our Generall for the time Sir Richard Grinvil, and after his departure of our Governour there Master Ralph Lane, with divers other directed and imployed under their government: Of the Captaines and Masters of the voyages made since for transportation, of the Governor and assistants of those already transported, as of many persons, accidents, and things els, I have ready in a discourse by it selfe in maner of a Chronicle, according to the course of times: which when time shall be thought convenient, shall be also published.

Thus referring my relation to your favorable constructions, expecting good successe of the action, from him which is to be acknowledged the authour and governour, not onely of this, but of all things els, I take my leave of you, this moneth of February 1588.

12. Richard Hakluyt the younger

a case of cannibalism among the English in 1536
1590

The Mr. Hore described here had persuaded a remarkable number of English
gentlemen in 1536 that Newfoundland would be a good place to visit. Samuel
Eliot Morison called the voyage, with only a slight exaggeration, the first tourist
trip to the New World. It remains something of a mystery why they became so
desperate, given the plentiful fishing of the area. The story appears in Hakluyt's
Principal Navigations.

One master Hore of London, a man of goodly stature and of great courage, and given to the study of Cosmography, in the 28th year of king Henry VIII and in the year of our Lord 1536, encouraged diverse Gentlemen and others, being assisted by the king's favor and good countenance, to accompany him in a voyage of discovery upon the Northwest parts of America.

There they grew into great want of victuals, and they found small relief more than what they had from the nest of an Osprey, that brought hourly to her young great plenty of diverse sorts of fishes. But such was the famine that increased amongst them from day to day, that they were forced to seek to relieve themselves with raw herbs and roots that they sought on the mainland. But the famine increasing, and the relief of herbs being to little purpose to satisfy their insatiable hunger, in the fields and deserts here and there, the fellow killed his mate while he stooped to take up a root for his relief, and cutting out pieces of his body whom he had murdered, broiled the same on the coals and greedily devoured them.

By this means the company decreased, and the officers knew not what was become of them. And it fortuned that one of the company, driven with hunger to seek abroad for relief, found out in the fields the savour of broiled flesh, and fell out with one, that he would suffer him and his fellows to starve, enjoying plenty (as he thought). And this matter growing to cruel speeches, he that had the broiled meat, burst out into these words: "If thou wouldst needs know, the broiled meat that I had was a piece of such a man's buttock."

The report of this brought to the ship, the Captain found what became of those that were missing, & was persuaded that some of them were neither devoured by wild beasts, nor yet destroyed by Savages. And hereupon he stood up and made a notable Oration, containing how much these dealings offended the Almighty; and vouched the Scriptures from first to last, what God had in cases of distress done for them that called upon him; and told them that the power of the Almighty was then no less, then in all former times it had been. And added, that if it had not pleased God to have helped them in that distress, that it had been better to have perished in body, and to have lived everlastingly, then to have relieved for a poor time their mortal bodies, and to be condemned everlastingly both body and soul to the unquenchable fire of hell. And thus having ended to that effect, he began to exhort to repentance, and besought all the company to pray, that it might please God to look upon their miserable present state, and for his own mercy to relieve the same.

The famine increasing, and the inconvenience of the men that were missing being found, they agreed amongst themselves—rather than all should perish—to cast lots who should be killed. And such was the mercy of God, that the same night there arrived a French ship in that port, well furnished with victual. And such was the policy[76] of the English, that they became masters of the same, and changing ships and victualing them, they set sail to come into England.

Master Thomas Butts was so changed in the voyage with hunger and misery, that Sir William his father and my Lady his mother knew him not to be their son, until they found a secret mark which was a wart upon one of his knees—as he told me, Richard Hakluyt of Oxford, himself, to whom I rode 200 miles only to learn the whole truth of this voyage from his own mouth, as being the only man now alive that was in this discovery.

13. Sir Walter Ralegh

from *The Discovery of the Large, Rich and Bewtiful Empire of Guiana 1596*

Sir Walter Ralegh, or Raleigh (1554?–1618), first achieved distinction in the campaign to subdue the Irish. After the death of his half-brother Sir Humphrey Gilbert, Ralegh received from the Queen a transfer of Gilbert's patent for colonization, and sent several expeditions to his colony in Roanoke from 1584 to 1590, when it was found to have disappeared. He then turned his attention to Guiana, with little success (though an English colony was later to survive on the Amazon for several years in the 1620s). Long a favorite of Queen Elizabeth, Ralegh fell briefly out of favor for marrying one of her maids. When James became king in 1603, Ralegh was imprisoned for treason. Until his execution in 1618, he remained in the Tower, where he wrote The History of the World.

B y my Indian interpreter, which I carried out of England, I made them understand that I was the servant of a Queen, who was the great *Cassique*[77] of the north, and a virgin, and had more *Cassiqui* under her than there were trees in their Island: that she was an enemy to the *Castellani*[78] in respect of their tyranny and oppression, and that she delivered all such nations about her, as were by them

76. policy: skill.
77. *Cassique*: chief.

78. *Castellani*: Castilians, Spaniards.

oppressed, and having freed all the coast of the northern world from their servitude had sent me to free them also, and withal to defend the country of *Guiana* from their invasion and conquest. I showed them her majesty's picture which they so admired and honored, as it had been easy to have brought them Idolatrous thereof.

The like and a more large discourse I made to the rest of the nations both in my passing to *Guiana*, and to those of the borders, so as in that part of the world her majesty is very famous and admirable, whom they now call *Ezrabeta Cassipuna Aquerewana*, which is as much as *Elizabeth*, the great princess or greatest commander.

[AMAZONS]

I made enquiry amongst the most ancient and best travelled of the *Orenoqueponi*, and I had knowledge of all the rivers between *Orinoco* and *Amazones*, and was very desirous to understand the truth of those warlike women, because of some it is believed, of others not.... In many histories they are verified to have been, and in divers ages and Provinces: But they which are not far from *Guiana* do accompany with men but once in a year, and for the time of one month, which I gather by their relation to be in April. At that time all the Kings of the borders assemble, and the *Queens* of the *Amazons*, and after the Queens have chosen, the rest cast lots for their *Valentines*. This one month, they feast, dance, and drink of their wines in abundance, and the Moon being done, they all depart to their own Provinces. If they conceive, and be delivered of a son, they return him to the father, if of a daughter they nourish it, and retain it, and as many as have daughters send unto the begetters a Present, all being desirous to increase their own sex and kind, but that they cut off the right dug of the breast I do not find to be true....

[THE MOST BEAUTIFUL COUNTRY]

On both sides of this river, we passed the most beautiful country that ever mine eyes had beheld: and whereas all that we had seen before was nothing but woods, prickles, bushes, and thorns, here we beheld plains of twenty miles in length, the grasses short and green, and in divers parts groves of trees by themselves, as if they had been by all the art and labor in the world so made of purpose: and still as we rowed, the Deer came down feeding by the water's side, as if they had been used to a keeper's call. Upon this river there were great store of fowl, and of many sorts: we saw in it divers sorts of strange fishes, and of marvellous bigness, but for *Lagartos* it exceeded, for there were thousands of those ugly serpents, and the people call it for the abundance of them the river of *Lagartos*, in their language. I had a *Negro* a very proper young fellow, that leaping out of the *Galley* to swim in the mouth of this river, was in all our sights taken and devoured with one of those *Lagartos*.[79]

[THE SPANISH]

The Spaniards to the end that none of the people in the passage towards *Guiana* or in *Guiana* itself might come to speech with us, persuaded all the nations, that we were

---

79. *Lagartos*: alligators.

Ralegh confers with the Arromaians. Engraved by Theodor de Bry.

man eaters, and *Cannibals*: but when the poor men and women had seen us, and that
we gave them meat, and to every one something or other, which was rare and strange
to them, they began to conceive the deceit and purpose of the *Spaniards*, who indeed
(as they confessed) took from them both their wives, and daughters daily, and used
them for satisfying of their own lusts, especially such as they took in this manner by
strength. But I protest before the majesty of the living God, that I neither know nor
believe, that any of our company one or other, ever knew any of their women, and yet
we saw many hundreds, and had many in our power, and of those very young, and
excellently favoured which came among us without deceit, stark naked.

[MANDEVILLE AND REALITY]

Next unto *Arui* there are two rivers *Arromaia* and *Caora*, and on that branch which
is called *Caora* are a nation of people, whose heads appear not above their shoulders,
which though it may be thought a mere fable, yet for mine own part I am resolved it is
true, because every child in the provinces of *Arromaia* and *Canuri* affirm the same:
they are called *Ewaipanoma*: they are reported to have their eyes in their shoulders,
and their mouths in the middle of their breasts, and that a long train of hair groweth
backward between their shoulders. The son of *Topiawari*, which I brought with me
into England, told me that they are the most mighty men of all the land, and use

bows, arrows, and clubs thrice as big as any of *Guiana*, or of the *Orenoqueponi*, and that one of the *Iwarawakeri* took a prisoner of them the year before our arrival there, and brought him into the borders of *Arromaia* his father's Country: And farther when I seemed to doubt of it, he told me that it was no wonder among them, but that they were as great a nation, and as common, as any other in all the provinces, and had of late years slain many hundreds of his father's people, and of other nations their neighbours, but it was not my chance to hear of them till I was come away, and if I had but spoken one word of it while I was there, I might have brought one of them with me to put the matter out of doubt. Such a nation was written of by *Mandeville*, whose reports were held for fables many years, and yet since the East *Indies* were discovered, we find his relations true of such things as heretofore were held incredible: whether it be true or no the matter is not great, neither can there be any profit in the imagination, for mine own part I saw them not, but I am resolved that so many people did not all combine, or forethink to make the report.

[EMPIRE IN THE WEST INDIES]

To conclude, *Guiana* is a Country that hath yet her Maidenhead, never sacked, turned, nor wrought, the face of the earth hath not been torn, nor the virtue and salt of the soil spent by manurance, the graves have not opened for gold, the mines not broken with sledges, nor their Images pulled down out of their temples. It hath never been entered by any army of strength, and never conquered or possessed by any Christian Prince. It is besides so defensible, that if two forts be builded in one of the Provinces which I have seen, the flood setteth so near the bank, where the channel also lieth, that no ship can pass up, but within a Pike's length of the Artillery, first of the one, and afterwards of the other: Which two Forts will be a sufficient Guard both to the Empire of *Inca*, and to an hundred other several kingdoms, lying within the said River, even to the city of *Quito* in *Peru*. . . .

The west Indies were first offered her Majesty's Grandfather by *Columbus* a stranger, in whom there might be doubt of deceit, and besides it was then thought incredible that there were such and so many lands and regions never written of before. This Empire is made known to her Majesty by her own vassal, and by him that oweth to her more duty than an ordinary subject, so that it shall ill sort with the many graces and benefits which I have received to abuse her highness, either with fables or imaginations. The country is already discovered, many nations won to her Majesty's love and obedience, and those Spaniards which have latest and longest laboured about the conquest, beaten out, discouraged and disgraced, which among these nations were thought invincible. Her majesty may in this enterprise employ all those soldiers and gentlemen that are younger brethren, and all captains and Chieftains that want employment, and the charge will be only the first setting out in victualling and arming them: for after the first or second year I doubt not but to see in London a Contractation house of more receipt for *Guiana*, than there is now in Seville for the West indies.

14. Michel de Montaigne

from "Of the Caniballes"
1580

Montaigne (1533–92) first published his Essays, *generally understood as creating the modern essay form, in 1580. The extracts printed here, though brief, show his characteristic irony. The text is from the 1603 English translation by John Florio.*

Three of that nation,[80] ignorant how dear the knowledge of our corruptions will one day cost their repose, security, and happiness, and how their ruin shall proceed from this commerce, which I imagine is already well advanced, (miserable as they are to have suffered themselves to be so cozened by a desire of new-fangled novelties, and to have quit the calmness of their climate, to come and see ours) were at *Rouen* in the time of our late King *Charles* the ninth,[81] who talked with them a great while. They were shewed our fashions, our pomp, and the forme of a faire City; afterward some demanded their advise, and would needs know of them what things of note and admirable they had observed amongst us: they answered three things, the last of which I have forgotten, and am very sorry for it, the other two I yet remember. They said, *First, they found it very strange, that so many tall men with long beards, strong and well armed, as were about the Kings person (it is very likely they meant the Switzers of his guard) would submit themselves to obey a beardless child, and that we did not rather choose one amongst them to command the rest.* Secondly (they have a manner of phrase whereby they call men but a moiety[82] one of another.) *They had perceived, there were men amongst us full gorged with all sorts of commodities, and others which hunger-starved, and bare with need and poverty, begged at their gates: and found it strange, these moieties so needy could endure such an injustice, and that they took not the others by the throat, or set fire on their houses.* I talked a good while with one of them, but I had so bad an interpreter, and who did so ill apprehend my meaning, and who through his foolishness was so troubled to conceive my imaginations, that I could draw no great matter from him.

---

80. three of that nation: the Americans who met Montaigne came from what is now Brazil.
81. the time of our late king: Montaigne visited the royal court at Rouen—where Charles IX had gone to suppress the Huguenots—in October of 1562.

82. moiety: half.

15. Michel de Montaigne

from "Of Coaches"
1580

Certain Spaniards coasting along the Sea in search of mines, fortuned to land in a very fertile, pleasant and well peopled country: unto the inhabitants whereof they declared their intent, and shewed their accustomed persuasions; saying: That they were quiet and well-meaning-men, coming from far-countries, being sent from the King of *Castile*, the greatest King of the habitable earth, unto whom the Pope, representing God on earth, had given the principality of all the *Indies*. That if they would become tributaries to him, they should bee most kindly used and courteously entreated: They required of them victuals for their nourishment; and some gold for the behoof of certain Physical experiments. Moreover, they declared unto them, the believing in one only God, and the truth of our religion, which they persuaded them to embrace, adding thereto some minatory threats. Whose answer was this: That *happily*[83] *they might be quiet and well meaning, but their countenance shewed them to be otherwise: As concerning their King, since he seemed to beg, he shewed* [himself] *to be poor and needy: And for the Pope, who had made that distribution, he expressed himself a man loving dissention, in going about to give unto a third man, a thing which was not his own: so to make it questionable and litigious amongst the ancient possessors of it. As for victuals, they should have part of their store: And for gold, they had but little, and that it was a thing they made very small account of, as merely unprofitable for the service of their life, whereas all their care was but how to passe it happily and pleasantly: and therefore, what quantity soever they should find, that only excepted which was employed about the service of their Gods, they might boldly take it. As touching one only God, the discourse of him had very well pleased them: but they would by no means change their religion, under which they had for so long time lived so happily: and that they were not accustomed to take any counsel, but of their friends and acquaintance. As concerning their menaces it was a sign of want of judgement, to threaten those, whose nature, condition, power and means was to them unknown. And therefore they should with all speed hasten to avoid their dominions (forsomuch as they were not wont to admit or take in good part the kindnesses and remonstrances of armed people, namely of strangers) otherwise they would deal with them as they had done with such others, showing them the heads of certain men sticking upon stakes about their City, which had lately been executed.* Lo here an example of the stammering of this infancy.

---

83. happily: by chance, fortunately.

16. Francis Bacon

"Of Plantations"
1625

Remembered as an essayist and philosopher, Francis Bacon (later Baron Verulam and Viscount St. Albans) also led a turbulent political career. Born in London in 1561, he entered Parliament in 1584 and became Lord Chancellor in 1618. Like most of the English who were concerned with America, Bacon had earlier been interested in the "plantation" of Ireland with English settlers, and in 1606 had drawn up a plan to this effect for King James I. The following essay, published in 1625, was probably composed while Bacon was Lord Chancellor or shortly there-after. It shows familiarity with the debates of the Virginia Company from 1619 to 1621, but seems to have been written before the Indian raid of 1622 (see chapter 3, selection 5). In 1621, Bacon was accused of taking bribes, and was imprisoned in the Tower. Upon his release he retired to his writing. He died in 1626. The text, originally a single long paragraph, has been reparagraphed for ease of reading.

*P*lantations are amongst Ancient, Primitive, and Heroicall Workes. When the World was young, it begate more Children; but now it is old, it begets fewer. For I may justly account new *Plantations*, to be the Children of former King-domes. I like a *Plantation* in a Pure Soile; that is, where People are not *Displanted*, to the end, to *Plant* in Others. For else, it is rather an Extirpation, than a *Plantation*.

Planting of Countries, is like *Planting* of Woods; For you must make account, to leese[84] almost Twenty yeeres Profit, and expect your Recompence, in the end. For the Principall Thing, that hath beene the Destruction of most *Plantations*, hath beene the Base, and Hastie drawing of Profit, in the first Yeeres. It is true, Speedie Profit is not to be neglected, as farre as may stand, with the Good of the *Plantation*, but no further.

It is a Shamefull and Unblessed Thing, to take the Scumme of People, and Wicked Condemned Men, to be the People with whom you *Plant*: And not only so, but it spoileth the *Plantation*; For they will ever live like Rogues, and not fall to worke, but be Lazie, and doe Mischiefe, and spend Victuals, and be quickly weary, and then Certifie over to their Country, to the Discredit of the *Plantation*. The People wherewith you *Plant*, ought to be Gardners, Plough-men, Labourers, Smiths, Carpenters, Joyners, Fisher-men, Fowlers, with some few Apothecaries, Surgeons, Cookes, and Bakers.

In a Country of *Plantation*, first looke about, what kinde of Victuall, the Countrie yeelds of it selfe, to Hand: As Chest-nuts, Wall-nuts, Pine-Apples, Olives, Dates, Plummes, Cherries, Wilde-Hony, and the like: and make use of them. Then consider,

---

84. leese: lose.

what Victuall or Esculent Things there are, which grow speedily, and within the yeere; As Parsnips, Carrets, Turnips, Onions, Radish, Artichokes of Jerusalem, Maiz, and the like. For Wheat, Barly, and Oats, they aske too much Labour: But with Pease, and Beanes, you may begin; Both because they aske lesse Labour, and because they serve for Meat, as well as for Bread. And of Rice likewise commeth a great Encrease, and it is a kinde of Meat. Above all, there ought to be brought Store of Bisket, Oat-meale, Flower, Meale, and the like, in the beginning, till Bread may be had. For Beasts, or Birds, take chiefly such, as are least Subject to Diseases, and Multiply fastest: As Swine, Goats, Cockes, Hennes, Turkies, Geese, House-doves, and the like. The Victuall in *Plantations*, ought to be expended, almost as in a Besieged Towne; That is, with certaine Allowance. And let the Maine Part of the Ground employed to Gardens or Corne, bee to a Common Stocke;[85] And to be Laid in, and Stored up, and then Delivered out in Proportion; Besides some Spots of Ground, that any Particular Person, will Manure, for his owne Private.

Consider likewise, what Commodities the Soile, where the *Plantation* is, doth naturally yeeld, that they may some way helpe to defray the Charge of the *Plantation*; So it be not, as was said, to the untimely Prejudice, of the maine Businesse; As it hath fared with *Tabacco* in *Virginia*. Wood commonly aboundeth but too much; And therefore, Timber is fit to be one. If there be Iron Ore, and Streames whereupon to set the Milles; Iron is a brave[86] Commoditie, where Wood aboundeth. Making of Bay Salt, if the Climate be proper for it, would be put in Experience. Growing Silke likewise, if any be, is a likely Commoditie. Pitch and Tarre, where store of Firres and Pines are, will not faile. So Drugs, and Sweet Woods, where they are, cannot but yeeld great Profit. Soape Ashes likewise, and other Things, that may be thought of. But moile not too much under Ground: For the Hope of Mines is very Uncertaine, and useth to make the *Planters* Lazie, in other Things.

For Government, let it be in the Hands of one, assisted with some Counsell: And let them have Commission, to exercise Martiall Lawes, with some limitation. And above all, let Men make that Profit of being in the Wildernesse, as they have God alwaies, and his Service, before their Eyes. Let not the Government of the *Plantation*, depend upon too many Counsellours, and Undertakers,[87] in the Countrie that *Planteth*, but upon a temperate Number: And let those be, rather Noblemen, and Gentlemen, than Merchants: For they looke ever to the present Gaine. Let there be Freedomes from Custome,[88] till the *Plantation* be of Strength: And not only Freedome from Custome, but Freedome to carrie their Commodities, where they may make their Best of them, except there be some speciall Cause of Caution. Cramme not in People, by sending too fast, Company, after Company; But rather hearken how they waste, and send Supplies proportionably; But so, as the Number may live well, in the *Plantation*, and not by Surcharge be in Penury.

It hath beene a great Endangering, to the Health of some *Plantations*, that they have built along the Sea, and Rivers, in Marish and unwholesome Grounds. Therefore, though you begin there, to avoid Carriage,[89] and other like Discommodities, yet build

---

85. Common Stocke: common rather than private property.
86. brave: worthy, excellent.
87. Undertakers: contractors.

88. Custome: import and export taxes.
89. Carriage: transportation.

Frontispiece to Bacon's The Great Instauration, *1620.*

still, rather upwards, from the Streames, than along. It concerneth likewise, the Health of the *Plantation*, that they have good Store of Salt with them, that they may use it, in their Victualls, when it shall be necessary.

If you *Plant*, where Savages are, doe not onely entertaine them with Trifles, and Gingles;[90] But use them justly, and gratiously, with sufficient Guard neverthelesse. And doe not winne their favour, by helping them to invade their Enemies, but for their Defence it is not amisse. And send oft of them, over to the Country, that *Plants*, that they may see a better Condition then their owne, and commend it when they returne. When the *Plantation* grows to Strength, then it is time, to *Plant* with Women, as well as with Men; That the *Plantation* may spread into Generations, and not be ever peeced[91] from without. It is the sinfullest Thing in the world, to forsake or destitute a *Plantation*, once in Forwardnesse. For besides the Dishonour, it is the Guiltinesse of Bloud, of many Commiserable Persons.

90. Gingles: jingles, rattles.

91. peeced: patched.

17. Anonymous

from *The Planter's Plea*
1630

[Definition of "colony"]

*B*y *a Colony we meane a societie of men drawne out of one state or people, and transplanted into another country.*

Colonies (as other conditions and states in humane society) have their warrant from Gods direction and command; who as soone as men were, set them their task, to replenish the earth, and to subdue it, *Gen.* 1:28. . . .

Neither is this sufficient to conceive that Gods intention is satisfied if some part of the earth be replenished, and used, though the rest be waste; because the same difficulty urgeth us still, that the rest of which we receive no fruit, was never intended to us, because it was never Gods minde wee should possesse it. If it were then the minde of God, that man should possesse all parts of the earth, it must be enforced[92] that we neglect our duty, and crosse his will, if we do it not, when wee have occasion and opportunitie: and withall do little lesse than despise his blessing.

92. it must be enforced: it must follow.

Chapter 3

The English Diaspora

Modern readers tend to suppose that crossing the Atlantic was a sharp break with the past, a new beginning. But the settlers themselves rarely saw their transit as final. In the texts of this chapter, English emigrants to new colonies work out the meaning of migration. *Diaspora* literally means dispersion, or scattering; its association with the dispersion of the Jews gives it the connotation of being away from a homeland. Not all the authors in this chapter would have compared themselves to the Jews as readily as the New England Puritans did, but all saw themselves as Englishmen away from England. None imagined that migration had made him American. Many, including John Smith and Edward Winslow, returned to England before they died, like Hariot before them.

In some colonies, particularly in the Caribbean, returning was the whole reason for going. Englishmen went in order to amass enough wealth to return to London in high style. This was the practice of Englishmen in India during the same period; through them the term *nabob* entered the language. The writers in this chapter had many different intentions when they went across the Atlantic to build colonies. But all of them continued to look homeward for inspiration and recognition.

Indeed, of the works in this chapter that were published during their authors' lifetimes, all were published in London (or, in one special case, Oxford). London remained, in a sense, the most important place in colonial America. Colonists who had never been to London while they lived in England were suddenly directly dependent on its administrative and military powers, its shipping routes, its markets, its credit networks, and the growing strength of its culture of public opinion. Many of the works in this chapter—notably those of John Smith, Edward Waterhouse, the Virginia Assembly, William Wood, Thomas Morton, and Edward Winslow

From the title page of Captain Smith's True Relation *(London, 1608).*

—were written and published in order to sway the opinion of officials and investors in the commercial capital. Like the promotional screeds of Hakluyt's generation, they describe the colonies to people who had not yet seen them. They are London texts as much as American ones.

The exceptions, significantly, are the two major works of the chapter that remained unpublished in the authors' lifetimes: Winthrop's "Modell of Christian Charity" and Bradford's *Of Plymouth Plantation*. These texts, which share important connections to chapters 5 and 6, are given here because they enunciate the meaning of migration for the first-generation participants. Winthrop's sermon does so dramatically; he preached it en route, hoping by its means to clarify the intentions of the act that his followers had already collectively undertaken. Bradford's history, apparently written for the rising generation, was more an exercise of memory—though it too attempts to clarify the intention of a settlement still in progress, and consequently does some revising as it remembers. Both Winthrop's sermon and Bradford's history, though unprinted, were in an important sense published, in that they circulated in manuscript and had a far-reaching influence.

The texts of this chapter range widely, in geography, in the class background of the authors (though not in their sex), and in the self-understanding that motivates them. Yet they all have in common the effort to determine the meaning of settlement. The chapter begins with William Strachey, for whom settlement is literally an accident, the result of a shipwreck that left him and his companions stranded on Bermuda, just as Ferdinand is stranded on the haunted island in *The Tempest*—the play that was based partly on Strachey's account. At the opposite extreme, Bradford and Winthrop describe migrations that were years in planning and deliberation, that took heavy capital investment and involved resettling whole communities.

Bradford's history is somewhat responsible for one of the most enduring myths of colonial American history: that the Pilgrims came to America in search of religious liberty. His own text, when read closely, makes it clear that they indeed wanted liberty for their own religion. But not for any other kind. As Bradford explicitly recounts, it was to escape the liberal tolerance of the Netherlands that they went someplace where they could keep a closer eye on their children.

Just up the coast, however, Thomas Morton had a rival vision of the meaning of emigration; for him, the remote trading posts of New England could offer a kind of secular liberty that was scandalous indeed to the Pilgrim Fathers. Morton's English companions were all male; they did not intend to sustain a separate people unto future generations. Partly for this reason, his account is remarkably untroubled about male homoerotics and miscegenation—two topics that induced deep panic among his Puritan neighbors. Less concerned to preserve an essentially racial identity than his neighbors, Morton also pursued a very different policy in his relations with the natives; certainly nothing agitated Plymouth so much as Morton's sale of firearms to Indians. Plymouth and Mount Wollaston were competing over the Indian fur trade, and the easier cultural assimilation of Mount Wollaston may have struck the Plymouth dealers as sharp business.

What the Indians themselves thought of the wave of settlement must remain mostly the subject of guesswork. Most were dying of diseases borne by the Europeans. (See chapter 2, selection 11.) "For the natives," John Winthrop wrote in 1634, "they are near all dead of the smallpox, so as the Lord hath cleared our title to what we possess." There is some evidence that Indians shared this view of how Massachusetts was won. Though they were recorded late in the seventeenth century, and may therefore be emerging traditions rather than mere records, the anecdotes at the end of this chapter about Indian prophecies show a grim and tragic view of history that sharply differs from white narratives of promise.

M.W.

Suggested readings: David Cressy, *Coming Over*; Bernard Bailyn, *Voyagers to the New World*; David Hackett Fischer, *Albion's Seed*; Neal Salisbury, *Manitou and Providence*.

1. William Strachey

from *A True Reportory of the Wrack and Redemption of Sir Thomas Gates, Knight* 1610

A member of the minor gentry, William Strachey (1572–1621) dabbled in London literary life, made voyages to Turkey and Constantinople, and finally turned to the Virginia Company in 1609. His ship, bound for Virginia, wrecked in the storm he so vividly describes here. By chance, the ship was blown to Bermuda, hitherto thought to be uninhabitable and haunted; it was known as Devil's Island. The crew settled the island under Sir Thomas Gates and Sir George Somers, or Summers, by whose name the islands would come to be known for the rest of the century; eventually they went on to rejoin the Virginia Company, where they took control away from Captain John Smith. Strachey's account, written in the form of a letter to a lady, is one of the best American narratives. It had one note-worthy reader in London: William Shakespeare, who used it as the basis for The Tempest *in 1611. Strachey's other main work,* The Historie of Travell into Virginia Britannia *(1612), was largely cribbed by Captain John Smith for Smith's* Generall History.

For four and twenty hours the storm, in a restless tumult, had blown so exceed-ingly, as we could not apprehend in our imaginations any possibility of greater violence. Yet did wee still find it not only more terrible, but more constant, fury added to fury, and one storm urging a second more outrageous than the former; whether it so wrought upon our fears, or indeed met with new forces. Sometimes strikes in our Ship amongst women, and passengers, not used to such hurly[1] and discomforts, made us look one upon the other with troubled hearts, and panting bosoms. Our clamors drowned in the winds, and the winds in thunder. Prayers might well be in the heart and lips, but drowned in the outcries of the Officers; nothing heard that could give comfort, nothing seen that might encourage hope. It is impos-sible for me, had I the voice of *Stentor*, and expression of as many tongues as his throat of voices, to express the outcries and miseries, not languishing, but wasting his spirits, and art constant to his own principles, but not prevailing.

Our sails wound up lay without their use, and if at any time we bore but a Hollocke, or half forecourse, to guide her before the Sea, six and sometimes eight men were not enough to hold the whipstaffe in the steerage, and the tiller below in the Gunner room, by which may be imagined the strength of the storm, in which

---

1. hurly: commotion.

the Sea swelled above the Clouds, and gave battle unto heaven. It could not be said to rain; the waters like whole Rivers did flood in the air. And this I did still observe: that whereas upon the Land, when a storm hath poured itself forth once in drifts of rain, the wind as beaten down, and vanquished therewith, not long after endures; here the glut of water (as if throttling the wind ere while) was no sooner a little emptied and qualified, but instantly the winds (as having gotten their mouths now free, and at liberty) spoke more loud, and grew more tumultuous, and malignant.

What shall I say? Winds and Seas were as mad, as fury and rage could make them. For mine own part, I had been in some storms before, as well upon the coast of *Barbary* and *Algeere*, in the *Levant*, and once more distressful in the *Adriatique* gulf, in a bottom of Candy. So as I may well say, *Ego quid sit ater Adriæ noui sinus, & quid albus Peccet Iapex.*[2] Yet all that I had ever suffered gathered together, might not hold comparison with this. There was not a moment in which the sudden splitting, or instant over-setting of the Ship was not expected.

Howbeit this was not all. It pleased God to bring a greater affliction yet upon us; for in the beginning of the storm we had received likewise a mighty leak. And the Ship in every joint almost, having spewed out her Oakum,[3] before we were aware (a casualty more desperate than any other that a Voyage by Sea draws with it) was grown five foot suddenly deep with water above her ballast, and we almost drowned within, whilst we sat looking when to perish from above. This imparting no less terror than danger, ran through the whole Ship with much fright and amazement, startled and turned the blood, and took down the braves of the most hardy Mariner of them all, insomuch as he that before happily felt not the sorrow of others, now began to sorrow for himself, when he saw such a pond of water so suddenly broken in, and which he knew could not (without present avoiding) but instantly sink him. So as joining (only for his own sake, not yet worth the saving) in the public safety, there might be seen Master, Master's Mate, Boatswain, Quarter Master, Coopers, Carpenters, and who not, with candles in their hands, creeping along the ribs viewing the sides, searching every corner, and listening in every place, if they could hear the water run. Many a weeping leak was this way found, and hastily stopped, and at length one in the Gunner room made up with I know not how many pieces of Beef; but all was to no purpose, the Leak (if it were but one) which drunk in our greatest Seas, and took in our destruction fastest, could not then be found, nor ever was, by any labor, counsel, or search. The waters still increasing, and the Pumps going, which at length choked with bringing up whole and continual Biscuit (and indeed all we had, ten thousand weight) it was conceived, as most likely, that the Leak might be sprung in the Bread-room, whereupon the Carpenter went down, and ripped up all the room, but could not find it so.

I am not able to give unto your Ladyship every man's thought in this perplexity, to which we were now brought. But to me, this Leakage appeared as a wound given to men that were before dead. The Lord knows, I had as little hope, as desire of life in

---

2. "Full well I know what Hadria's black gulf can be and what the sins of clear Iapyx." Horace, *Odes*.   3. Oakum: rope fibers used for caulking.

the storm; and in this it went beyond my will, because beyond my reason. Why should we labor to preserve life? Yet we did, either because so dear are a few lingering hours of life in all mankind, or that our *Christian* knowledges taught us how much we owed to the rites of Nature, as bound, not to be false to ourselves, nor to neglect the means of our own preservation; the most despairefull things amongst men, being matters of no wonder nor moment with him who is the rich Fountain and admirable Essence of all mercy.

Our Governor, upon the tuesday morning (at what time, by such who had been below in the hold, the Leak was first discovered) had caused the whole Company, about one hundred and forty, besides women, to be equally divided into three parts, and opening the Ship in three places (under the forecastle, in the waste, and hard by the Bitacke) appointed each man where to attend. And thereunto every man came duly upon his watch, took the Bucket, or Pump for one hour, and rested another. Then men might be seen to labor, I may well say, for life, and the better sort, even our Governor, and Admiral themselves, not refusing their turn, and to spell each the other, to give example to others. The common sort stripped naked, as men in Galleys, the easier both to hold out, and to shrink from under the salt water, which continually leapt in among them, kept their eyes waking, and their thoughts and hands working, with tired bodies, and wasted spirits, three days and four nights destitute of outward comfort, and desperate of any deliverance, testifying how mutually willing they were, yet by labor to keep each other from drowning albeit each one drowned whilst he labored.

[THE ENGLISH FIND BERMUDA]

Sir *George Summers*, when no man dreamed of such happiness, had discovered, and cried Land. . . . But having no hope to save [the ship] by coming to an anchor in the same, we were enforced to run her ashore, as near the land as we could, which brought us within three quarters of a mile of shore, and by the mercy of God unto us, making out our Boats, we had ere night brought all our men, women, and children, about the number of one hundred and fifty, safe into the Island.

We found it to be the dangerous and dreaded Island, or rather Islands of the *Bermuda*: whereof let me give your Ladyship a brief description, before I proceed to my narration. And that the rather, because they be so terrible to all that ever touched on them, and such tempests, thunders, and other fearful objects are seen and heard about them, that they be called commonly, *The Devils Lands*, and are feared and avoided of all sea travellers alive, above any other place in the world. Yet it pleased our merciful God, to make even this hideous and hated place, both the place of our safety, and means of our deliverance.

And hereby also, I hope to deliver the world from a foul and generall error: it being counted of most, that they can be no habitation for Men, but rather given over to Devils and wicked Spirits; whereas indeed we find them now by experience, to be as habitable and commodious as most Countries of the same climate and situation. Insomuch as if the entrance into them were as easy as the place itself is contenting, it had long ere this been inhabited, as well as other Lands. Thus shall we make it appear,

That Truth is the daughter of Time, and that men ought not to deny every thing which is not subject to their own sense.

[TROUBLE IN PARADISE]

And sure it was happy for us, who had now run this fortune, and were fallen into the bottom of this misery, that we both had our Governor with us, and one so solicitous and careful, whose both example (as I said) and authority, could lay shame, and command upon our people. Else I am persuaded we had most of us finished our days there, so willing were the major part of the common sort (especially when they found such a plenty of victuals) to settle a foundation of ever inhabiting there; as well appeared by many practices of theirs (and perhaps of some of the better sort). Lo, what are our affections and passions, if not rightly squared? How irreligious, and irregular they express us! Not perhaps so ill as we would be, but yet as we are. Some dangerous and secret discontents nourished amongst us, had like to have been the parents of bloody issues and mischiefs. They began first in the Seamen, who in time had fastened unto them (by false baits) many of our land-men likewise, and some of whom (for opinion of their Religion) was carried an extraordinary and good respect. The Angles wherewith chiefly they thus hooked in these disquieted Pools,[4] were: how that *in Virginia, nothing but wretchedness and labor must be expected, with many wants, and a churlish entreaty, there being neither that Fish, Flesh, nor Fowl, which here (without wasting on the one part, or watching on theirs, or any threatening, and air of authority) at ease, and pleasure might be enjoyed: and since both in the one, and the other place, they were (for the time) to lose the fruition both of their friends and Country, as good, and better were it for them, to repose and seat them where they should have the least outward wants the while.* This, thus preached, and published each to other, though by such who never had bin more onward towards *Virginia*, than (before this Voyage) a Sculler could happily row him (and what hath a more adamantine power to draw unto it the consent and attraction of the idle, untoward, and wretched number of the many, then liberty, and fullness of sensuality?) begat such a murmur, and such a discontent, and disunion of hearts and hands from this labor, and forwarding the means of redeeming us from hence, as each one wrought with his Mate how to divorce him from the same.

---

4. i.e., the hooks with which they fished in these troubled waters.

2. John Smith et al.

from *A Map of Virginia . . . and the Proceedings of the English Colonie* 1612

It is not easy to separate Captain John Smith (1580–1631) from his legend. The main source of information is his own rather incredible account, The True Travels, Adventures, and Observations of Captaine John Smith *(1630), some parts of which have been verified to everyone's surprise. In it he describes going off to war after his father's death in 1596; making a piratical voyage in the Mediterranean and getting rich following the capture of a Venetian trader; joining the Austrian army against the Turks, and eventually being stationed in Transylvania (it is from the Austrians that he acquired his title); challenging three Turkish officers to single combat, beheading all three; being captured in battle and carried off as a Turkish slave; being saved from slavery by a beautiful woman (the Lady Tragabigzanda) who fell in love with him and sent him to her brother in Russia; escaping from the brother and making his way back to Western Europe. Only after these adventures did Smith fall in with the Virginia Company, in 1606.*

In Virginia, Smith became the center of disputes among the English over self-government and Indian policy. Both sides in the dispute tried to win support from the Virginia Company in London. Smith presented his side in his first published work, A True Relation of Such Occurrences and Accidents of Noate as Hath Hapned in Virginia *(1608), arguing for the use of force to impress the Indians. Smith also describes his release from captivity among the Powhatans in the* True Relation, *but makes no mention of Pocahontas there. (See selection 6 below.)*

Injured by a gunpowder blast in 1609, Smith returned to London. He continued to be a party of contention, to such a degree that in 1612 his next work had to be printed in Oxford to avoid censorship. It is actually two books printed together: A Map of Virginia, With a Description of the Countrey, the Commodities, People, Government and Religion; *and* The Proceedings of the English Colonie in Virginia. *The selection given here comes from* The Proceedings. *According to the title page, the* Proceedings *was written not by Smith, but by eight other members of the company, whose names are sometimes signed at the end of chapters. Yet it seems clear that Smith had the strongest hand in the book's compilation, and he clearly emerges as the book's hero. Chapters 8 and 9, given below, are particularly interesting for their attempt to render dialogues between Smith and Powhatan, and between Smith and Opechancanough, on self-consciously classical models of eloquence.*

CAPTAIN SMITH'S JOURNEY TO PAMAUNKE.

Quartering in the next houses we found, we sent to Powhatan for provision, who sent us plentie of bread, Turkies, and Venison. The next day having feasted us after his ordinarie manner, he began to ask, when we would be gone, faining he sent not for us, neither had he any corn, and his people much less. Yet for 40 swords he would procure us 40 bushels. The President shewing him the men there present, that brought him the message and conditions, asked him how it chanced he became so forgetful. Thereat the king concluded the matter with a merry laughter, asking for our commodities, but none he liked without[5] guns and swords, valuing a basket of corne more pretious than a basket of copper, saying he could eat his corne, but not his copper.

Captaine Smith seeing the intent of this subtil Salvage began to deale with him after this manner,

Powhatan, though I had many courses to have made my provision, yet beleeving your promises to supply my wants, I neglected all, to satisfie your desire, and to testifie my love, I sent you my men for your building, neglecting my owne. What your people had you have engrossed, forbidding them our trade. And nowe you think by consuming the time, we shall consume for want, not having to fulfill your strange demands. As for swords, and guns, I told you long ago, I had none to spare. And you shall knowe, those I have, can keep me from want. Yet steale, or wrong you I will not, nor dissolve that friendship, we have mutually promised, except you constrain me by your bad usage.

The king having attentively listned to this discourse; promised, that both he and his Country would spare him what they could, the which within 2 days, they should receive.

Yet Captaine Smith, (saith the king) some doubt I have of your coming hither, that makes me not so kindly seek to relieve you as I would. For many do inform me, your coming is not for trade, but to invade my people and possess my Country, who dare not come to bring you corn, seeing you thus armed with your men. To clear us of this fear, leave aboard your weapons, for here they are needless, we being all friends and for ever Powhatans.

With many such discourses they spent the day, quartring that night in the kings houses. . . .

Whilst we expected the coming in of the country, we wrangled out of the king 10 quarters of corn for a copper kettle, the which the President perceived him much to affect, valued it at a much greater rate, but (in regard of his scarcety) hee would accept of as much more the next yeare, or else the country of Monacan, the king exceeding liberall of that he had not yielded him Monacan. Wherewith each seeming well contented; Powhatan began to expostulate the difference betwixt peace and war, after this manner.

Captaine Smith you may understand, that I, having seene the death of all my people thrice, and not one living of those 3 generations, but myself, I know the difference of

5. without: except.

peace and war, better than any in my Countrie. But now I am old, and ere long must die. My brethren, namely Opichapam, Opechankanough, and Kekataugh, my two sisters, and their two daughters, are distinctly each others successours. I wish their experiences no lesse than mine, and your love to them, no lesse then mine to you, but this brute[6] from Nansamund that you are come to destroy my Countrie, so much affrighteth all my people, as they dare not visit you. What will it avail you, to take that perforce, [which] you may quietly have with love, or to destroy them that provide you food? What can you get by war, when we can hide our provision and fly to the woodes, whereby you must famish by wronging us your friends; And why are you thus jealous of our loves, seeing us unarmed, and both do, and are willing still to feed you with that you cannot get but by our labours? Think you I am so simple not to knowe, it is better to eate good meate, lie well, and sleepe quietly with my women and children, laugh and be merrie with you, have copper, hatchets, or what I want, being your friend; than be forced to fly from all, to lie cold in the woods, feed upon acorns, roots, and such trash, and be so hunted by you, that I can neither rest, eat, nor sleepe; but my tired men must watch, and if a twig but breake, everyone cry there comes Captaine Smith, then must I fly I knowe not whither, and thus with miserable fear end my miserable life; leaving my pleasures to such youths as you, which through your rash unadvisedness, may quickly as miserably end, for want of that you never know how to find? Let this therefore assure you of our loves and every year our friendly trade shall furnish you with corn. And now also, if you would, come in friendly manner to see us, and not thus with your gunnes and swords, as to invade your foes.

To this subtil discourse the President thus replied.

Seeing you will not rightly conceive of our words, we strive to make you know our thoughts by our deeds. The vow I made you of my love, both my self and my men have kept. As for your promise I finde it every day violated, by some of your subjects. Yet we finding your love and kindness (our custom is so far from being ungratefull) that for your sake only, we have curbed our thirsting desire of revenge, else had they knowne as well the cruelty we use to our enemies as our true love and courtesy to our friends. And I think your judgement sufficient to conceive as well by the adventures we have undertaken, as by the advantage we have by our armes of yours, that had we intended you any hurt, long ere this we could have effected it. Your people coming to me at James towne, are entertained with their bowes and arrowes without exception, we esteeming it with you, as it is with us, to wear our armes as our apparell. As for the dangers of our enemies, in such wars consist our chiefest pleasure. For your riches we have no use; as for the hiding your provision, or by your flying to the woods, we shall not so unadvisedly starve as you conclude. Your friendly care in that behalfe is needlesse; for we have a rule to find beyond your knowledge.

Manie other discourses they had, til at last they began to trade, but the king seeing his will would not be admitted as a lawe, our guard dispersed, nor our men disarmed, he (sighing) breathed his mind, once more in this manner.

Captaine Smith, I never used any Werowances so kindlie as your self. Yet from you I receave the least kindnesse of any. Captaine Newport gave me swords, copper, cloths, a

6. brute: rumor.

bed, tooles, or what I desired, ever taking what I offered him, and would send away his guns when I intreated him. None doth deny to lay at my feet (or do) what I desire, but onelie you, of whom I can have nothing, but what you regard not. And yet you will have whatsoever you demand. Captain Newport you call father, and so you call me, but I see for all us both, you will do what you list, and we must both seek to content you. But if you intend so friendly as you say, send hence your arms that I may believe you, for you see the love I bear you, doth cause me thus nakedly to forget my self.

Smith seeing this Salvage but trifled the time to cut his throat, procured the Salvages to breake the ice, (that his boat might come to fetch both him and his corne) and gave order for his men to come ashore, to have surprised the king, with whom also he but trifled the time till his men landed, and to keepe him from suspition, entertained the time with this reply.

Powhatan, you must know as I have but one God, I honour but one king; and I live not here as your subject, but as your friend, to pleasure you with what I can. By the gifts you bestowe on me, you gaine more than by trade. Yet would you visit me as I do you, you should know it is not our customs to sell our curtesy as a vendible commodity. Bring all your Country with you for your guard. I will not dislike of it as being over jealous. But to content you, to morrow I will leave my arms, and trust to your promise. I call you father indeed, and as a father you shall see I will love you, but the small care you had of such a child, caused my men to perswade me to shift for my selfe.

By this time Powhatan having knowledge, his men were readie; whilst the ice was breaking, his luggage women, and children fled, and to avoid suspicion, left 2 or 3 of his women talking with the Captaine, whilst he secretly fled, and his men as secretlie beset the house, which being at the instant discovered to Captaine Smith, with his Pistol, Sword and Target, he made such a passage amongst those naked devils, that they fled before him some one way some another, so that without hurt he obtained the Corps du-guard. When they perceived him so well escaped, and with his 8 men (for he had no more with him), to the uttermost of their skill, they sought, by excuses to dissemble the matter. And Powhatan, to excuse his flight, and the suddaine coming of this multitude, sent our Captaine a greate bracelet, and a chaine of pearle, by an ancient Orator that bespoke us to this purpose, (perceiving them from our Pinnace, a barge and men departing and comming unto us.)

Captaine Smith, our Werowans is fled, fearing your guns, and knowing when the ice was broken there would come more men, sent those of his to guard his corne from the pilfering that might happen without your knowledge. Now though some be hurt by your misprison, yet he is your friend, and so wil continue. And since the ice is open he would have you send away your corn; and if you would have his company send also your armes, which so affrighteth his people, that they dare not come to you, as he hath promised they should.

Now having provided baskets for our men to carry the corn, they kindly offered their service to guard our arms, that none should steale them. A great many they were, of goodly well appointed fellows as grim as devils; yet the very sight of cocking our matches against them, and a few words, caused them to leave their bows and arrows to our guard, and bear down our corn on their own backs; we needed not importune them to make quick dispatch. But our own barge being left by the ebb, caused us to stay, till the midnight tide carried us safe aboard, having spent that half night with such mirth, as though we never had suspected or intended any thing, we left the Dutchmen to build, Brinton to kil fowle for Powhatan (as by his messengers he importunately desired) and left directions with our men to give Powhatan all the content they could, that we might enjoy his company at our return from Pamaunke.

How we escaped surprising at Pamaunke.

We had no sooner set sail, but Powhatan returned, and sent Adam and Francis (2 stout Dutch men) to the fort, who faining to Captaine Winne that all things were well, and that Captaine Smith had use for their armes, wherefore they requested newe (the which were given them) they told him their coming was for some extraordinary tooles and shift of apparell. By this colourable excuse, they obtained 6 or 7 more to their confederacie, such expert theefes, that presently furnished them with a great many swords, pike-heads, pieces, shot, powder and such like. They had Salvages at hand ready to carry it away, the next day they returned unsuspected, leaving their confederates to follow, and in the interim, to convey them a competency of all things they could, for which service they should live with Powhatan as his chiefe affected, free from those miseries that would happen the Colony. Samuell, their other consort, Powhatan kept for their pledge, whose diligence had provided them 300 of their kind of hatchets, the rest 50 swords, 8 pieces, and 8 pikes. Brinton, and Richard Salvage seeing the Dutch-men so strangly diligent to accommodate the Salvages with weapons attempted to have got to James Towne, but they were apprehended. Within 2 or 3 days we arrived at Pamaunke. The king[7] as many days entertained us with feasting and much mirth. And the day he appointed to begin our trade, the President, with Master Persie, Master West, Master Russell, Master Beheathland, Master Powell, Master Crashaw, Master Ford, and some others to the number of 15 went up to Opechancanoug's house (near a quarter of a mile from the river) where we found nothing but a lame fellow and a boy, and all the houses about, of all things abandoned. Not long we stayed ere the king arrived. And after him came divers of his people loaded with bowes and arrowes, but such pinching commodities, and those esteemed at such a value, as our Captaine began with him in this manner.

Opechancanough the great love you professe with your tongue, seemes mere deceit by your actions. Last year you kindly freighted our ship, but now you have invited me to starve with hunger. You know my want, and I your plenty, of which by some means I must have part. Remember it is fit for kings to keep their promise. Here are my commodities, wherof take your choice. The rest I will proportion, fit bargains for your people.

The king seemed kindly to accept his offer; and the better to colour his project, sold us what they had to our content, promising the next day more company, better provided. The barges, and Pinnas being committed to the charge of Master Phetiplace, the President with his old 15 marched up to the kings house, where we found 4 or 5

---

7. the king: Opechancanough.

Captain Smith's combat with Opechancanough. Detail from the illustrated map in Smith's General History, *1624.*

men newly come with great baskets. Not long after came the king, who with a strained cheerfulness held us with discourse, what paines he had taken to keepe his promise; til Master Russell brought us in news that we were all betrayed. For at least 6 or 700 of well appointed Indians had environed the house and beset the fields. The king conjecturing what Russell related, we could well perceive how the extremity of his feare betrayed his intent. Whereat some of our company seeming dismayed with the thought of such a multitude, the Captaine encouraged us after this manner.

Worthy countrymen, were the mischiefs of my seeming friends no more than the danger of these enemies, I little cared, were they as many more, if you dare do but as I. But this is my torment, that if I escape them, our malicious councill with their open mouthed minions, will make me such a peace-breaker (in their opinions) in England, as will break my neck. I could wish those here, that make these seem Saints, and me an oppressor. But this is the worst of all, wherein I pray aid me with your opinions. Should we begin with them and surprise this king, we cannot keep him and defend well our selves. If we should each kill our man and so proceed with all in this house, the rest will all fly. Then shall we get no more than the bodies that are slaine, and then starve for victuall. As for their fury it is the least danger; for well you know, (being alone assaulted with 2 or 300 of them) I made them compound to save my life, and we are now 16 and they but 700 at the most, and assure your selves God will so assist us, that if you dare but to stand to discharge your pieces, the very smoke will be sufficient to affright them. Yet however (if there be occasion) let us fight like men, and not die like sheep. But first I will deale with them, to bring it to passe, we may fight for some thing and draw them to it by conditions. If you like this motion, promise me you'll be valiant.

The time not permitting any argument, all vowed to execute whatsoever he attempted, or die; whereupon the captaine, approaching the king bespoke him in this manner.

I see Opechancanough your plot to murder me, but I feare it not, as yet your men and mine, have done no harme, but by our directions. Take therefore your arms; you see mine. My body shall be as naked as yours. The Isle in your river is a fit place, if you be contented. And the conqueror (of us two) shall be Lord and Master over all our men; otherwise draw all your men into the field; if you have not enough take time to fetch more, and bring what number you will, so every one bring a basket of corn, against all which I will stake the value in copper. You see I have but 15 men, and our game shall be the conquerer take all.

The king, being guarded with 50 or 60 of his chief men, seemed kindly to appease Smith's suspition of unkindnesse, by a great present at the door, they entreated him to receive. This was to draw him without[8] the door where the present was garded with at the least 200 men and 30 lying under a great tree (that lay thwart as a barricado) each his arrow nocked ready to shoot; some the President commanded to go and see what kind of deceit this was, and to receive the present, but they refused to do it. Yet divers offered whom he would not permit; but commanding Master Persie and Master West to make good the house, took Master Powell and Master Beheathland to guard the door, and in such a rage snatched the king by his vambrace[9] in the midst of his men, with his pistol ready bent against his breast. Thus he led the trembling king, (neare dead with feare) amongst all his people, who delivering the Captaine his bow and arrows, all his men were easily entreated to cast down their armes, little dreaming any durst in that manner have used their king; who then to escape himselfe, bestowed his presents in good sadnesse. And having caused all his multitude to approach disarmed, the President argued with them to this effect.

I see, you Pamaunkies, the great desire you have to cut my throat. And my long suffering your injuries, have enboldened you to this presumption. The cause I have forborne your insolencies, is the promise I made you (before the God I serve) to be your friend, till you give me just cause to be your enemie. If I keep this vow, my God will keep me; you cannot hurt me. If I breake it, he will destroy me. But if you shoot but one arrow, to shed one drop of blood of any of my men, or steal the least of these beads, or copper, (I spurn before me with my foot) you shall see, I will not cease revenge, (if once I begin) so long as I can hear where to find one of your nation that will not deny the name of Pamaunke. I am not now at Rasseweac (halfe drowned with mire) where you tooke me prisoner. Yet then for keeping your promise, and your good usage, and saving my life, I so affect you, that your denials of your treachery, doth half perswade me to mistake my self. But if I be the mark you aim at, here I stand, shoot he that dare. You promised to freight my ship ere I departed, and so you shall, or I mean to load her with your dead carcases. Yet if as friends you will come and trade, I once more promise not to trouble you, except you give me the first occasion.

Upon this away went their bows and arrows, and men, women, and children brought in their commodities. But 2 or three hours they so thronged about the President, and so overwearied him, as he retired himself to rest. . . .

Those temporall proceedings to some may seem too charitable; to such a daily daring treacherous people; to others, unpleasant that we washed not the ground with their bloods, nor showed such strange inventions in mangling, murdering, ransacking, and destroying, (as did the Spaniards) the simple bodies of those ignorant souls; nor delightful because not stuffed with relations of heaps, and mines of gold and silver, nor such rare commodities as the Portugals and Spaniards found in the East and West Indies. The want wherof hath begot us (that were the first undertakers) no less scorn and contempt, than their noble conquests and valiant adventures (beautified with it) praise and honor. Too much I confess the world cannot attribute to their ever memo-

---

8. without: outside.   9. vambrace: forearm armor.

rable merit. And to clear us from the worlds blind ignorant censure, these few words may suffice to any reasonable understanding.

It was the Spaniards good hap to happen in those parts, where were infinite numbers of people, who had manured the ground with that providence, that it afforded victual at all times. And time had brought them to that perfection, they had the use of gold and silver, and the most of such commodities, as their countries afforded. So that what the Spaniard got, was only the spoil and pillage of those country people, and not the labours of their own hands. But had those fruitfull Countries been as Salvage, as barbarous, as ill peopled, as little planted, laboured and manured as Virginia, their proper labours (it is likely) would have produced as small profit as ours. But had Virginia been peopled, planted, manured, and adorned, with such store of precious Jewels, and rich commodities, as was the Indies, then, had we not gotten and done as much as by their examples might be expected from us, the world might then have traduced us and our merits, and have made shame and infamy our recompense and reward.

But we chanced in a land, even as God made it. Where we found only an idle, improvident, scattered people; ignorant of the knowledge of gold, or silver, or any commodities; and careless of any thing but from hand to mouth, but for baubles of no worth; nothing to encourage us, but what accidentally we found nature afforded. Which ere we could bring to recompense our paines, defray our charges, and satisfy our adventurers, we were to discover the country, subdue the people, bring them to be tractable, civil, and industrious, and teach them trades, that the fruits of their labours might make us recompense, or plant such colonies of our own that must first make provision how to live of themselves, ere they can bring to perfection the commodities of the countrie, which doubtless will be as commodious for England, as the west Indies for Spain, if it be rightly managed; notwithstanding all our home-bred opinions, that will argue the contrarie, as formerly such like have done against the Spaniards and Portugals. But to conclude, against all rumor of opinion, I only say this, for those that the three first years began this plantation, notwithstanding all their factions, mutinies, and miseries, so gently corrected, and well prevented: peruse the Spanish Decades,[10] the relations of Master Hackluyt, and tell me how many ever with such small means, as a barge of 2 Tunnes; sometimes with 7, 8, 9, or but at most 15 men did ever discover so many fair and navigable rivers; subject so many several kings, people, and nations, to obedience, and contribution with so little blood shed.

And if in the search of those Countries, we had happened where wealth had been, we had as surely had it, as obedience and contribution, but if we have overskipped it, we will not envy them that shall chance to find it. Yet can we not but lament, it was our ill fortunes to end, when we had but only learned how to begin, and found the right course how to proceed.

10. Spanish Decades: see chapter 2, selection 5.

3. John Smith

from *A Description of New England* 1616

After his return from Virginia in 1609, Smith made two other brief voyages, both to the North Atlantic coast. He coined the name "New England" for the lands whose settlement he vigorously promoted in A Description of New England and in New Englands Trials (1622). In the selection below Smith shows that, although he clearly wished as much as any Englishman to emulate Cortes, he also had an advanced theory of English colonialism that differed sharply from the Spanish practice. Smith rejects the hope of quick mineral riches and genteel adventure that had guided the founding of Virginia, arguing instead for colonies based in transatlantic commerce and the labors of settlement. By the end of this selection, Smith's speculations lead to far-reaching questions about social order and about what makes life interesting. Historian Karen Kupperman has noted that in this work Smith becomes "the first to argue that the promise of America was a bourgeois society."

Worthy is that person to starve that here cannot live; if he have sense, strength and health. For there is no such penury of these blessings in any place, but that a hundred men may, in one hour or two, make their provisions for a day. And he that hath experience to manage well these affaires, with forty or thirty honest industrious men, might well undertake (if they dwell in these parts) to subject the Salvages, and feed daily two or three hundred men, with as good corn, fish, and flesh, as the earth hath of those kinds, and yet make that labor but their pleasure: provided that they have engins,[11] that be proper for their purposes.

Who can desire more content, that hath small meanes; or but only his merit to advance his fortune, than to tread, and plant that ground he hath purchased by the hazard of his life? If he have but the taste of virtue, and magnanimitie,[12] what to such a mind can be more pleasant, than planting and building a foundation for his Posterity, got from the rude earth, by God's blessing and his own industry, without prejudice to any? If he have any grain of faith or zeal in Religion, what can he do less hurtfull to any; or more agreeable to God, than to seek to convert those poor Salvages to know Christ, and humanity, whose labors with discretion will triple requite thy charge and paines? What so truely suits with honour and honestie, as the discovering things unknowne? erecting Townes, peopling Countries, informing the ignorant, reforming things unjust, teaching virtue; and gain to our Native mother-country a kingdom to attend her; find employment for those that are idle, because they know

---

11. engins: tools.   12. magnanimitie: greatness.

not what to do; so far from wronging any, as to cause Posterity to remember thee; and remembring thee, ever honour that remembrance with praise? Consider: What were the beginnings and endings of the Monarchies of the Chaldeans, the Syrians, the Grecians, and Romanes, but this one rule; What was it they would not do, for the good of the commonwealth, or their Mother-citie? For example, Rome: What made her such a Monarchesse, but only the adventures of her youth; not in riots at home, but in dangers abroad? and the justice and judgement out of their experience, when they grew aged. What was their ruin and hurt, but this: The excess of idleness, the fondness of Parents, the want of experience in Magistrates, the admiration of their undeserved honours, the contempt of true merit, their unjust jealousies, their politicke incredulities, their hypocriticall seeming goodness, and their deeds of secret lewdness? Finally, in fine, growing only formal temporists, all that their predecessors got in many years, they lost in few days. Those by their pains and virtues became Lords of the world; they by their ease and vices became slaves to their servants. This is the difference betwixt the use of Arms in the field, and on the monuments of stones; the golden age and the leaden age, prosperity and miserie, justice and corruption, substance and shadows, words and deeds, experience and imagination, making Commonwealths and marring Commonwealths, the fruits of virtue and the conclusions of vice.

Then, who would live at home idly (or think in himself any worth to live) only to eat, drink, and sleep, and so die? Or by consuming that carelessly, [which] his friends got worthily? Or by using that miserably, that maintained virtue honestly? Or, for being descended nobly, pine with the vain vaunt of great kindred, in penury? Or (to maintaine a silly show of bravery) toil out thy heart, soul, and time, basely, by shifts,[13] tricks, cards, and dice? Or by relating newes of others' actions, shark here or there for a dinner, or supper; deceive thy friends, by fair promises, and dissimulation, in borrowing where thou never intendest to pay; offend the lawes, surfeit with excess, burden thy Country, abuse thy self, despair in want, and then couzen thy kindred, yea even thine own brother, and wish thy parents' death (I will not say damnation) to have their estates? though thou seest what honours, and rewards, the world yet hath for them [who] will seek them and worthily deserve them.

I would be sorry to offend, or that any should mistake my honest meaning. For I wish good to all, hurt to none. But rich men for the most part are grown to that dotage, through their pride in their wealth, as though there were no accident could end it, or their life. And what hellish care do such take to make it their own miserie, and their Country's spoil, especially when there is most need of their employment? drawing by all manner of inventions, from the Prince and his honest subjects, even the vital spirits of their powers and estates: as if their Bagges,[14] or Bragges, were so powerfull a defence, the malicious could not assault them; when they are the only bait, to cause us not to be only assaulted; but betrayed and murdered in our own security, ere we well perceive it.

May not the miserable ruin of Constantinople, their impregnable walls, riches, and pleasures last taken by the Turk (which are but a bit, in comparison of their now mightiness) remember[15] us of the effects of private covetousness? at which time the

---

13. shifts: expediences.
14. Bagges: money.

15. remember: remind.

good Emperour held himself rich enough, to have such rich subjects, so formal in all excesse of vanity, all kind of delicacy, and prodigality. His poverty when the Turk besieged, the citizens (whose marchandizing thoughts were only to get wealth, little conceiving the desperate resolution of a valiant expert enemy) left the Emperour so long to his conclusions, having spent all he had to pay his young, raw, discontented Souldiers; that suddenly he, they, and their city were all a prey to the devouring Turke. And what they would not spare for the maintenance of them who adventured their lives to defend them, did serve onely their enemies to torment them, their friends, and country, and all Christendom to this present day. Let this lamentable example remember you that are rich (seeing there are such great thieves in the world to rob you) not grudge to lend some proportion, to breed them that have little, yet willing to learn how to defend you: for it is too late when the deed is a-doing. The Romans estate hath been worse than this: for the mere covetousness and extortion of a few of them, so moved the rest, that not having any employment but contemplation, their great judgements grew to so great malice, as themselves were sufficient to destroy themselves by faction: Let this move you to embrace imployment, for those whose educations, spirits, and judgements, want but your purses; not onely to prevent such accustomed dangers, but also to gain more thereby than you have. And you fathers that are either so foolishly fond, or so miserably covetous, or so willfully ignorant, or so negligently careless, as that you will rather maintain your children in idle wantonness, till they grow your masters; or become so basely unkind, as they wish nothing but your deaths; so that both sorts grow dissolute: and although you would wish them any where to escape the gallows, and ease your cares; though they spend you here one, two or three hundred pound a year; you would grudge to give half so much in adventure with them, to obtain an estate, which in a small time but with a little assistance of your providence, might be better than your own. But if an Angell should tell you that any place yet unknown can afford such fortunes, you would not believe him, no more than Columbus was believed there was any such Land as is now the well known abounding America; much lesse such large Regions as are yet unknown, as well in America, as in Affrica, and Asia, and Terra incognita; where were courses for gentlemen (and them that would be so reputed) more suiting their qualities, than begging from their Prince's generous disposition, the labours of his subjects, and the very marrow of his maintenance.

I have not been so ill bred, but I have tasted of Plenty and Pleasure, as well as Want and Miserie. Nor doth necessity yet, or occasion of discontent, force me to these endeavors. Nor am I ignorant what small thank I shall have for my paines; or that many would have the Worlde imagine them to be of great judgement, that can but blemish these my designes, by their witty objections and detractions. Yet (I hope) my reasons with my deeds, will so prevail with some, that I shall not want imployment in these affairs, to make the most blind see his own senselessnesse, and incredulity; Hoping that gain will make them affect that, which Religion, Charity, and the Common good cannot. It were but a poor device in me, To deceive my selfe; much more the King, and State, my Friends, and Countrey, with these inducements: which, seeing his Majestie hath given permission, I wish all sorts of worthy, honest, industrious spirits, would understand. And if they desire any further satisfaction, I will do my best to give it. Not to perswade them to goe onely; but goe with them. Not leave them there; but live with them there. I will not say, but by ill providing and undue managing, such courses may be taken, [as] may make us miserable enough. But if I may have the execution of what I have projected; if they want to eat, let them eat or never digest[16] Me. If I perform what I say, I desire but that reward out of the gains that may suit my pains, quality, and condition. And if I abuse you with my tongue, take my head for satisfaction. If any dislike at the years end, defraying their charge, by my consent they should freely return. I fear not want of company sufficient, were it but known what I know of those Countries; and by the proof of that wealth I hope yearly to returne, if God please to bless me from such accidents, as are beyond my power in reason to prevent. For I am not so simple, to think, that ever any other motive than wealth, will ever erect there a Commonweale; or draw companie from their ease and humours at home, to stay in New England to effect my purposes. And lest any should think the toil might be insupportable, though these things may be had by labour, and diligence: I assure my self there are those who delight extremely in vain pleasure, that take much more pains in England, to enjoy it, than I should do here to gain wealth sufficient. And yet I think they should not have half such sweet content. For our pleasure here is still gaines; in England charges and loss. Here nature and liberty affords us that freely, which in England we want, or it costeth us dearely. What pleasure can be more, than (being tired with any occasion a-shore) in planting Vines, Fruits, or Herbs, in contriving their own Grounds, to the pleasure of their own minds, their Fields, Gardens, Orchards, Buildings, Ships, and other works, etc. to recreate themselves before their own doors, in their own boats upon the Sea, where man woman and child, with a small hook and line, by angling, may take diverse sorts of excellent fish, at their pleasures? And is it not pretty sport, to pull up two pence, six pence, and twelve pence, as fast as you can haul and veer a line? He is a very bad fisher, who cannot kill in one day with his hook and line, one, two, or three hundred Cods: which dressed and dryed, if they be sold there for ten shillings the hundred, though in England they will give more then twenty; may not both the servant, the master, and marchant, be well content with this gain? If a man work but three days in seven, he may get more than he can spend, unless he will be excessive. Now that Carpenter, Mason, Gardiner, Taylor, Smith, Sailer, Forgers, or what other, may they not make this a pretty recreation though they fish but an houre in a day, to take more then they eate in a weeke: or if they will not eate it, because there is so much better choice; yet sell it, or change it, with the fisher men, or marchants, for any thing they want? And what sport doth yield a more pleasing content, and less hurt or charge than angling with a hook, and crossing the sweet air from Isle to Isle, over the silent streams of a calm Sea? wherein the most curious may finde pleasure, profit, and content. Thus, though all men be not fishers, yet all men, whatsoever, may in other matters do as well. For necessity doth in these cases so rule a Commonwealth, and each in their severall functions, as their labours in their qualities may be as profitable, because there is a necessary mutual use of all.

16. digest: understand.

For Gentlemen, what exercise should more delight them, than ranging daily those unknown parts, using fowling and fishing, for hunting and hawking? and yet you shall see the wild hawkes give you some pleasure, in seeing them swoope (six or seven after one another) an hour or two together, at the schools of fish in the fair harbours, as those a-shore at a fowl; and never trouble nor torment your selves, with watching, mewing, feeding, and attending them:

Gentlemen's sports. Engraving by de Bry.

nor kill horse and man with running and crying, See you not a hawk?

For hunting also: the woods, lakes, and rivers, afford not only chase sufficient, for any that delights in that kind of toil, or pleasure; but such beasts to hunt, that besides the delicacy of their bodies for food, their skins are so rich, as may well recompense thy daily labour, with a Captain's pay.

For labourers, if those that sowe hemp, rape, turnips, parsnips, carrots, cabbage, and such like; give 20, 30, 40, 50 shillings yearly for an acre of ground, and meat drink and wages to use it, and yet grow rich: when better, or at least as good ground, may be had and cost nothing but labour; it seems strange to me, any such should there grow poor.

My purpose is not to perswade children from their parents; men from their wives; nor servants from their masters: only, such as with free consent may be spared. But that each parish, or village, in Citie, or Countrey, that will but apparell their fatherless children, of thirteen or fourteen years of age, or young maried people, that have small wealth to live on; here by their labour may live exceeding well: provided alwaies that first there be a sufficient power to command them, houses to receive them, means to defend them, and meet provisions for them. For any place may be overlain[17] and it is most necessary to have a fortress (ere this grow to practice) and sufficient masters (as, Carpenters, Masons, Fishers, Fowlers, Gardiners, Husbandmen, Sawyers, Smiths, Spinsters, Taylors, Weavers, and such like) to take ten, twelve, or twenty, or as there is occasion, for Apprentises. The Masters by this may quickly grow rich; these may learne their trades themselves, to do the like; to a generall and an incredible benefit, for King, and Countrey, Master, and Servant.

It would be an historie of a large volume, to recite the adventures of the Spanyards, and Portugals, their affronts, and defeats, their dangers and miseries; which with such incomparable honour and constant resolution, so far beyond beliefe, they have attempted and endured in their discoveries and plantations, as may well condemn us, of too much imbecillitie, sloth, and negligence. Yet the Authors of those new inventions, were held as ridiculous, for a long time, as now are others, that do but seek to imitate their unparalleled virtues. And though we see daily their mountains of wealth (sprung from the plants of their generous indeavours) yet is our sensuality and untowardness such, and so great, that we either ignorantly believe nothing; or so curiously

17. overlain: overthrown.

contest, to prevent we knowe not what future events; that we either so neglect, or oppress and discourage the present, as we spoil all in the making, crop all in the blooming; and building upon fair sand, rather than rough rocks, judge that we know not, govern that we have not, fear that which is not; and for fear some should do too well, force such against their wills to be idle or as ill. And who is he who hath judgement, courage, and any industrie or qualitie with understanding, who will leave his Country, his hopes at home, his certain estate, his friends, pleasures, liberty, and the preferment sweet England doth afford to all degrees, were it not to advance his fortunes by enjoying his deserts? whose prosperity once appearing, will encourage others. But it must be cherished as a child, till it be able to go, and understand it self; and not corrected, nor oppressed above its strength, ere it know wherefore. A child can neither perform the office, nor deeds of a man of strength, nor indure that affliction He is able. Nor can an Apprentice at the first performe the part of a Master. And if twenty years be required to make a child a man, seven years limited an apprentice for his trade: if scarce an age be sufficient to make a wise man a States man; and commonly, a man dies ere he hath learned to be discreet: If perfection be so hard to be obtained, as of necessity there must be practice, as well as theorick: Let no man much condemn this paradox opinion, to say, that half seven years is scarce sufficient, for a good capacity, to learn in these affairs, how to carry himself: and who ever shall try in these remote places the erecting of a Colony, shall find at the end of seven years occasion enough to use all his discretion: and, in the Interim all the content, rewards, gaines, and hopes will be necessarily required, to be given to the beginning, till it be able to creep, to stand, and go, yet time enough to keep it from running, for there is no fear it will grow too fast, or ever to any thing; except liberty, profit, honor, and prosperity there found, more bind the planters of those affairs, in devotion to effect it; than bondage, violence, tyranny, ingratitude, and such double dealing, as binds free men to become slaves, and honest men turn knaves: which hath ever been the ruin of the most popular commonweales; and is very unlikely ever well to begin in a new.

Who seeth not what is the greatest good of the Spanyard, but these new conclusions, in searching those unknown parts of this unknown world? By which means he dives even into the very secrets of all his Neighbours, and the most part of the world: and when the Portugale and Spanyard had found the East and West Indies; how many did condemn themselves, that did not accept of that honest offer of Noble Columbus? who, upon our neglect, brought them to it, perswading our selves the world had no such places as they had found: and yet ever since we find, they still (from time to time) have found new Lands, new Nations, and trades, and still daily do find both in Asia, Africa, Terra incognita, and America; so that there is neither Soldier nor Mechanick, from the Lord to the begger, but those parts afford them all employment; and discharge their Native soil, of so many thousands of all sorts, that else, by their sloth, pride, and imperfections, would long ere this have troubled their neighbours, or have eaten the pride of Spaine it self.

Now he knows little, that knows not England may well spare many more people than Spaine, and is as well able to furnish them with all manner of necessaries. And seeing, for all they have, they cease not still to search for that they have not, and know not; It is strange we should be so dull, as not maintain that which we have, and pursue that we knowe. Surely I am sure many would take it ill, to be abridged of the titles and honours of their predecessors: when if but truly they would judge themselves; look how inferior they are to their noble virtues, so much they are unworthy of their honours and livings: which never were ordained for shows and shadows, to maintain idleness and vice; but to make them more able to abound in honor, by heroicall deeds of action, judgement, piety, and virtue. What was it, They would not do both in purse and person, for the good of the Commonwealth? which might move them presently to set out their spare kindred in these generous designes. Religion, above all things, should move us (especially the Clergy) if we were religious, to show our faith by our works; in converting those poor salvages, to the knowledge of God, seeing what pains the Spanyards take to bring them to their adulterated faith. Honor might move the Gentry, the valiant, and industrious; and the hope and assurance of wealth, all; if we were that we would seem, and be accounted. Or be we so far inferior to other nations, or our spirits so far dejected, from our ancient predecessors, or our minds so upon spoil, piracy, and such villany, as to serve the Portugall, Spanyard, Dutch, French, or Turk (as to the cost of Europe, too many do) rather than our God, our King, our Country, and our selves? excusing our idleness, and our base complaints, by want of employment; when here is such choice of all sorts, and for all degrees, in the planting and discovering these North parts of America.

4.

five letters from America

> The writers of the following five letters come from widely differing social classes. John Baldwin is barely literate. On the other hand, George Calvert was a distinguished courtier, given the title Lord Baltimore for his services in colonizing Ireland; after the unsuccessful attempt to settle Newfoundland that he describes here in a letter to King Charles, he would later receive Maryland as a royal grant. John Pory falls in between, struggling to maintain contact with London life through print, style, and wit. All five writers, in sharp contrast to the printed promotional literature, describe early colonization as a dolorous business. All long to be back in England, which they continue to regard as their home.

John Pory

a letter from Virginia
1619

owe that your lordship may knowe, that we are not the veriest beggers in the worlde, our cowekeeper here of James citty on Sundays goes accowtered all in freshe flaming silke; and a wife of one that in England had professed the black arte, not of a scholler, but of a collier of Croydon, weares her rough bever hatt with a faire perle hatband, and a silken suite thereto correspondent. But to leave the Populace, and to come higher; the Governour here, who at his first coming, besides a great deale of worth in his person, brought onely his sword with him, was at his late being in London, together with his lady, out of his meer gettings here, able to disburse very near three thousand pounde to furnishe himselfe for his voiage. And once within seven yeares, I am persuaded that the Governors place here may be as profitable as the lord Deputies of Irland. . .

At my first coming hither the solitary uncouthnes of this place, compared with those partes of Christendome or turky where I had bene; and likewise my being sequestred from all occurrents and passages which are so rife there, did not a little vexe me. And yet in these five moneths of my continuance here, there have come at one time or another eleven saile of ships into this river; but fraighted more with ignorance, then with any other marchandize. At length being hardned to this custome of abstinence from curiosity, I am resolved wholly to minde my busines here, and nexte after my penne, to have some good book alwayes in store, being in solitude the best and choicest company. Besides among these Christall rivers, and oderiferous woods I doe escape muche expense, envye, contempte, vanity, and vexation of minde. Yet good my lorde, have a little compassion upon me, and be pleased to sende mee what pampletts and relations of the Interim since I was with you, as your lordship shall thinke good, directing the same (if you please) in a boxe to Mr. Ralfe Yeardley, Apothecary (brother to Sir George Yeardley our governour), dwelling at the signe of the Hartychoke in great Woodstreet, to be sente to me by the first, together with his brothers thinges.

Richard Frethorne

a letter from Virginia
1623

Loving and kind father and mother:

My most humble duty remembered to you, hoping in God of your good health, as I myself am at the making hereof. This is to let you understand that I your Child am in a most heavy Case by reason of the nature of the

Country, [which] is such that it Causeth much sickness, as the scurvy and the bloody flux and diverse other diseases, which maketh the body very poor and Weak. And when we are sick, there is nothing to Comfort us; for since I came out of the ship I never ate anything but peas and loblollie (that is, water gruel). As for deer or venison, I never saw any since I came into this land. There is indeed some fowl, but We are not allowed to go and get it, but must Work hard both early and late for a mess of water gruel and a mouthful of bread and beef. A mouthful of bread for a penny loaf must serve for 4 men—which is most pitiful, if you did know as much as I, when people cry out day and night, Oh! that they were in England without their limbs; and would not care to lose any limb to be in England again, yea, though they beg from door to door.

For we live in fear of the Enemy every hour, yet we have had a Combat with them on the Sunday before Shrovetide, and we took two alive and made slaves of them. But it was by policy, for we are in great danger. For our Plantation is very weak, by reason of the death, and sickness, of our Company. For we came but Twenty for the merchants, and they half dead Just; as we look every hour when two more should go. Yet there came some four other men yet to live with us, of which there is but one alive, and our Lieutenant is dead, and his father, and his brother, and there was some 5 or 6 of the last year's 20 of us, of which there is but 3 left. So that we are fain to get other men to plant with us. And yet we are but 32 to fight against 3000 if they should Come. And the nighest help that We have is ten miles of us, and when the rogues overcame this place last, they slew 80 persons. How then shall we do? For we lie even in their teeth. They may easily take us but that God is merciful, and can save with few as well as with many; as he showed to Gilead. And like Gilead's soldiers, if they lapped water, we drink water which is but Weak.

And I have nothing to Comfort me, nor there is nothing to be gotten here but sickness and death, except that one had money to lay out in some things for profit. But I have nothing at all—no, not a shirt to my back, but two Rags; nor no clothes but one poor suit; nor but one pair of shoes; but one pair of stockings; but one Cap; but two bands. My Cloak is stolen by one of my own fellows, and to his dying hour would not tell me what he did with it. But some of my fellows saw him have butter and beef out of a ship, which my Cloak I doubt paid for. So that I have not a penny, nor a half-penny Worth to help me to either spice, or sugar, or strong Waters, without the which one cannot live here. For as strong beer in England doth fatten and strengthen them, so water here doth wash and weaken these here, only keeps life and soul together. But I am not half a quarter so strong as I was in England, and all is for want of victuals. For I do protest unto you, that I have eaten more in a day at home than I have allowed me here for a Week. You have given more than my day's allowance to a beggar at the door. And if Mr. Jackson had not relieved me, I should be in a poor Case. But he like a father and she like a loving mother doth still help me.

For when we go up to James Town (that is 10 miles of us), there lie all the ships that Come to land, and there they must deliver their goods. And when we went up to Town, as it may be, on Monday at noon, and come there by night, then load the next day by noon, and go home in the afternoon, and unload, and then away again in the night, and be up about midnight, then if it rained or blowed never so hard, we must lie in the boat on the water and have nothing but a little bread, for when we go into the boat we have a loaf allowed to two men, and it is all if we stayed there 2 days, which is hard, and must lie all that while in the boat.

But that Goodman Jackson pitied me and made me a Cabin to lie in always when I come up, and he would give me some poor jacks[18] home with me, which Comforted me more than peas or water gruel. Oh, they be very godly folks, and love me very well, and will do anything for me. And he much marvelled that you would send me a servant to the Company. He saith I had been better knocked on the head (and indeed so I find it now, to my great grief and misery) and saith that if you love me you will redeem me suddenly, for which I do entreat and beg.

And if you cannot get the merchants to redeem me for some little money, then for God's sake get a gathering or entreat some good folks to lay out some little sum of money in meal and cheese and butter and beef. Any eating meat will yield great profit. Oil and vinegar is very good; but, father, there is great loss in leaking. But for God's sake send beef and Cheese and butter, or the more of one sort and none of another. But if you send Cheese, it must be very old Cheese; and at the Cheesemonger's you may buy very good Cheese for twopence farthing or halfpenny, that will be liked very well. But if you send Cheese, you must have a care how you pack it in barrels. And you must put cooper's chips between every Cheese, or else the heat of the hold will rot them.

And look whatsoever you send me—be it never so much—look what I make of it. I will deal truly with you. I will send it over and beg the profit to redeem me. And if I die before it Come, I have entreated Goodman Jackson to send you the worth of it, who hath promised he will. If you send, you must direct your letters to Goodman Jackson, at James Town, a gunsmith. (You must set down his freight, because there be more of his name there.) Good Father, do not forget me, but have mercy and pity my miserable Case. I know if you did but see me you would weep to see me. For I have but one suit. Though it is a strange one, it is very well guarded. Wherefore, for God's sake, pity me. I pray you to remember my love to all my friends, and kindred. I hope all my Brothers and sisters are in good health, and as for my part I have set down my resolution that certainly Will be; that is, that the Answer of this letter will be life or death to me. There, good Father, send as soon as you can; and if you send me any thing let this be the mark.

ROT

Richard Frethorne
Martin's Hundred

18. poor jacks: fish.

John Baldwin

a letter from Virginia
1623

My love remembered unto you and to your wife I hope you are in good health as I am at this tyme. Mr. Sandys hath dealt unkindlie with us he maketh us serve him whether wee will or noe and how to helpe yt we doe not knowe for hee beareth all the sway, but I hope to doe well enough yf God blesse me this yeare. I thank god I have had my health very well here, all our company is livinge but three William Lanes Willm Smith which weare killed with the Indians goeinge to worke in the wood. They lay in a tree that was newlie felled where they killed them. Thomas Knowles is dead; but I thinke he had bene livinge now but we had a base fellow to our overseer, which was the occasion of his death: ffor he was sicke awhile and could not worke, and then he went to him and beate him that he fell downe presentlie and could not stand, and then they carryed him to bed, and there he lay sixe dayes and neither eate nor dranke Ffor the land it is a plentifull countrye. I like yt well yf the people were good that are in yt: but they are base all over for yf a man be sicke, putt them into a new house and there lett lie downe & starve, for noebody will come at him. I hard the Seafflower was come to the Bermudas. I pray you send me word yf I have ever a kinsman in her. William Allen is here, come servant for five yeare Thomas Cole is here, but he liveth very poorlie. I pray you remember my love to John harris and Thomas Wilkinson, and Hugh Wall, and Henry & Rowland Sheene and his mate Daniell, to Robert ffludd at Somersett, to Mr. Bagley and his wife and to Mr. Crosse thus I rest your everlovinge

John Baldwin.

POSTSCRIPT

It hath been a verye hard tyme with all men they had like to all starve this yeare: there was them that paid fortye shillings a bushell for sheld Corne. But howsoever, they dye like rotten sheepe noe man dies, but he is as full of maggotts as he can hould. They rott above ground.

George Calvert

a letter from Newfoundland 1629

Most Gracious and dread Soveraigne,

I have mett with greater difficultyes and encumbrances here which in this place are no longer to be resisted, but enforce me presently to quitt my residence, and to shift to some other warmer climate of this new world, where the wynters be shorter and lesse rigorous. For here, your Majesty may please to understand that I have fownd by too deare bought experience which other men for their private interests always concealed from me, that from the middst of October to the middst of May there is a sadd face of wynter upon all this land, both sea and land so frozen for the greatest part of the tyme as they are not penetrable no plant or vegetable thing appearing out of the earth untill it bee about the beginning of May, nor fish in the sea—besides the air, so intolerable cold as it is hardly to be endured. By meanes whereof, and of much salt water, my house hath beene an hospitall all this wynter, of 100 persons 50 sick at a tyme, my self being one and nyne or ten of them dyed. Hereupon I have had strong temptations to leave all proceedings in plantations, and being much decayed in my strength to retire my self to my former quiett; but my inclination carrying me naturally to these kynde of workes, and not knowing how better to employ the poore remaynder of my days than with other good subjects to further the best I may the enlarging your Majesty's empire in this part of the world, I am determined to committ this place to fishermen that are able to encounter storms and hard weather, and to remove my self with some 40 persons to your Majesty's dominion of Virginia, where if your Majesty will please to grant me a precinct of land with such privileges as the King your father my gracious master was pleased to grant me here, I shall endevor to the utmost of my power to deserve it and pray for your Majesty's long and happy raigne as

> your Majesty's most humble
> and faithfull subject and servant.
> George Baltimore.

Writer unknown

a letter from Massachusetts
1631

I know, loving Father, and do confess that I was an undutiful child unto you when I lived with you and by you, for the which I am much sorrowful and grieved for it, trusting in God that He will so guide me that I will never offend you so any more, and I trust in God that you will forgive me for it, and my writing unto you is to let you understand what a country this new Eingland is where we live.

Here are but few eingeines,[19] and a great sort of them died this winter. It was thought it was of the plague. They are a crafty people and they will cozen and cheat, and they are a subtle people, and whereas we did expect great store of beaver, here is little or none to be had, and their Sackemor John[20] weigheth it, and many of us truck with them and it layeth us many times in eight shillings a pound. They are proper men and clean-jointed men, and many of them go naked with a skin about their loins, but some of them get eingellische menes parell.[21]

And the country is very rocky and hilly and some champion ground,[22] and the soil is very fleet,[23] and here is some good ground and marsh ground, but here is no Michaelmas spring.[24] Cattle thrive well here, but they give small store of milk. The best cattle for profit is swines, and a good swine is here at five pounds price and a goat is worth three pounds, a gardene goat. Here is timber good store and acorns good store, and here is good store of fish, if we had boats to go eight or ten leagues to sea to fish in. Here are good store of wild fowl, but they are hard to come by. it is harder to get a shot than it is in ould eingland. And people here are subject to disease, for here have died of the scurvy and of the burning fever two hundred and odd, besides many layeth lame, and all Sudberey men are dead but three and the women and some children. And provisions here are at a wonderful rate. . . .

Therefore, loving Father, I would entreat you that you would send me a firkin of butter and a hogshead of malt unground, for we drink nothing but water, and a coarse cloth of four-pound price, so it be thick. And for the freight, if you of your love will send them, I will pay the freight, for here is nothing to be got without we had commodities to go into the east parts amongst the eingeines to truck,[25] for here where we live is no beaver, and here is no cloth to be had to make no apparel, and shoes are

---

19. eingeines: Indians.
20. Sackemor John: Sagamore John, an Indian chief.
21. eingellische menes parell: Englishmen's apparel.
22. champion ground: meadow.

23. fleet: shallow.
24. Michaelmas spring: fall growing season.
25. truck: trade.

at five shillings a pair for me, and that cloth that is worth two shillings eight pence a yard is worth here five shillings. So I pray, father, send me four or five yards of cloth to make us some apparel, and, loving Father, though I be far distant from you, yet I pray you remember me as your child, and we do not know how long we may subsist, for we cannot live here without provisions from ould eingland. Therefore, I pray, do not put away your shopstuff, for I think that in the end if I live it must be my living, for we do not know how long this plantation will stand, for some of the merchants that did uphold it have turned off their men and have given it over. Besides, God hath taken away the chiefest stud in the land, Mr. Johnson and the lady Arabella his wife, which was the chiefest man of estate in the land and one that would have done most good.

5. Edward Waterhouse

A Declaration of the State of the Colony in Virginia
1622

Very little is known about Edward Waterhouse. He was probably born in Berkshire, the nephew of Sir Edward Waterhouse, who held several prominent posts in Ireland and assisted Sir Henry Sidney and the Earl of Essex in their efforts to establish English settlements there. The younger Waterhouse was serving as the secretary to the Virginia colony in 1622 when it suffered its greatest public relations nightmare: an Indian massacre. (Its mastermind appears to have been Opechancanough, whose dialogue with Captain Smith appears in selection 2 above.) To Waterhouse fell the task of getting out an official version of the event, one that would not cast the entire settlement enterprise in doubt. He begins with a recap of promotional arguments. Then, echoing accounts of Cortes and Pizarro, he manages to tell the story of the massacre as an argument for more forceful colonization. The title page of the 1622 pamphlet is A Declaration of the State of the Colony and Affaires in Virginia. With a Relation of the

Depiction of the 1622 massacre by Theodor de Bry.

Barbarous Massacre in the time of peace and League, treacherously executed by
the Native Infidels upon the English, the 22 of *March* last. Together with the names
of those that were then massacred; that their lawfull heyres, by this notice given,
may take order for the inheriting of their lands and estates in Virginia.

To the Honorable Companie of Virginia.

The fame of our late unhappy accident in *Virginia*, hath spread it selfe, I doubt
not, into all parts abroad, and as it is talked of of all men, so no question of
many, and of most, it cannot but be misreported, some carryed away with
over-weak lightnesse to beleeve all they heare, how untrue soever; others out of their
dissaffection possibly to the *Plantation*, are desirous to make that, which is ill, worse;
and so the truth of the Action, which is only one, is varied and misreported. I have
thought it therefore a part of some acceptable service in me towards you, whose
favors have preferred me to be a member of your *Company*, to present you with these
my poore labours, the Collection of the truth hereof, drawne from the relation of
some of those that were beholders of that *Tragedie*, and who hardly escaped from
tasting of the same cup, as also from the Letters sent you by the *Governour* and other
Gentlemen of quality, and of the *Councell* in that Colonie, read openly here in your
Courts: That so the world may see that it was not the strength of a professed enemy
that brought this slaughter them, but contrived by the perfidious treachery of a false-
hearted people, that know not God nor faith. No generous Spirit will forbeare to goe
on for this accident that hath hapned to the Plantation, but proceed rather chearfully
in this honorable Enterprize, since the discovery of their bruitish falshood will prove
(as shall appeare by this Treatise following) many waies advantageable to us, and
make this forewarning a forearming forever to prevent a greater mischiefe.

Accept it from me, I most humbly beseech you, as the first fruits of my poore
service.

Time may happily make me able to yeeld you some other worke whose subject may
bee Joy, as this is a Theame of Sadnesse: Meanetime, I commit You and the *Noble
Colony* to Gods good blessing, as he that shall alwaies be

A true Votarie for your happinesse,
and servant to your commands,

Edward Waterhouse.

A Declaration of the state of the Colonie and Affaires in *Virginia*.

Although there have been many and sundry Treaties writ of *Virginia*, and the
Commodities thereof; whereat malitious men may take occasion to cavill, but
godly men will finde good cause to praise the Almighty, whose wonders are
seene in the deepe, through the which we have sailed to the discovery of this good
Land: Yet I have not thought it amisse (since I am to expresse some late Accidents)[26]

26. Accidents: events.

before-hand to summe up the benefits of that Countrey; partly because they daily encrease by new Discoveries made, to the glory of our most gratious King, and ever renowned to all posteritie, for the founding and supporting of this most Royall and blessed work of Plantation, to the great honor, wealth and happinesse of his most famous Kingdomes; and partly, because such is the customary daintinesse of Readers, that they seldome take the paines to gather together all that hath beene written of any subject, that so they might take the whole businesse into their consideration, (which is the onely way to make a true judgement,) but usually content themselves with one or two Bookes set out occasionally, and with reference to some former Treatises, whereby they gaine but a lame and parcell-knowledge, and so oftentimes both prejudice themselves and the truth.

The Countrey called Virginia (so named by the late Virgin-Queene *Elizabeth* of blessed memory) being the rightfull inheritance of his Majesty, as being first discovered at the costs and charges of that most prudent Prince of famous memory, *King Henry the Seaventh*, his Majesties great Grand-father; The Patent whereof still extant to be seene, was granted to *John Cabot* and divers other of his subjects, who went thither with sixe Saile of Ships, and discovered as farre as from *Cape Florida* to *New-found-land*, all along the Coast, and tooke possession thereof to the Kings use, about that time when *Ferdinando* and *Isabella* discovered the *Westerne Indies:* (by which title of first dicovery the King of *Portugal* and *Spaine* hold and enjoy their ample and rich Kingdomes in their *Indies East & West:*) A coast where *King Edward the Sixth* after planted his fishing to the *New-found-land* by publike Act in Parliament, and of which *Philip Amadas* and *Arthur Barlow* tooke againe possession to the use of the late *Queen Elizabeth:* and after them, *Sir Richard Greenfield, Sir Ralph Lane*, and *Sir Walter Rawleigh*; at what time severall Colonies were there placed. And since his Majesties most happy comming to the Crowne, being an absolute King of three of the most populous Kingdomes (which *Charles the Fifth* was wont to tearme *Officina gentium*, the shop or forge of men,) finding his Subjects to multiply by the blessed peace they enjoy under his happy government, did out of his high wisedome and Princely care of the good of his Subjects, grant a most gratious Patent to divers Honourable persons, and others of his loving Subjects, authorizing them thereby to goe on in the Plantation of this his lawfull and rightfull Kingdome of Virginia, which by the blessing of Almighty God is growne to good perfection.

This spatious and fruitful Country of Virginia, is (as is generally knowne to all) naturally rich, and exceedingly well watered, very temperate, and healthfull to the Inhabitants, abounding with as many naturall blessings, and replenished with as goodly Woods, and those full of Deere and sundry other beasts for mans sustenance; and the Seas and Rivers thereof (many therein being exceeding fayre and navigable) as full of excellent fish of divers sorts, and both water & land yeelding as great variety of fowle, as any Country in the world is knowne to afford. The situation whereof being neere the middest of the world, betweene the extremities of heate and colde, seemes to partake of the benefits of both, and therby becometh capable of the richest commodities of most parts of the Earth. From whence ariseth an assurance that (by the assistance and skill of industry) those rich Furres, Cordage, and other Commodities, which with difficulty and danger are now drawn from *Russia*, will be had in Virginia and the parts adjoyning, with ease and safety. And the Masts, Plancks, and Boards, the Pitch and Tarre, the Pot-ashes and Sope-ashes, the Hempe and Flaxe, which now are fetched from *Norway, Denmark, Poland* and *Germany,* will there be had in abundance. The Iron, which hath so wasted our English Woods, (that it selfe in short time must decay together with them) is to be had in Virginia (where wasting of Woods is an ease and benefit to the Planter) for all good conditions answerable to the best Iron of the world, whereof proofe hath beene made. The Wines, Fruits, and Salt of *France* and *Spaine*: the Silkes of *Persia* and *Italy*, will be had also in Virginia, in no kinde of worth inferiour, where are whole Woods of many miles together of Mulberry trees of the best kindes, the proper food of the Silke-worme, and a multitude of other naturall commodities. Of Woods, Roots and Berries, for excellent Dyes; of Plants and other Drugs for Physicall service; of sweet Woods, Oyles and Gummes, for pleasure and other use; of Cotton-wooll, Silke-grasse and Sugar-Canes, will there be had in abundance, with many other kindes. And for Corne, Cattell, and Fish, (which are the substance of the food of man) in no place better: the Graine also of our owne Country prospering there very well; but their Maize (being the naturall Graine of Virginia) doth farre exceed in pleasantnesse, strength, fertilitie, and generalitie of use, the Wheat of *England.*

The Cattell which were transported thither (being now growne neere to fifteene hundred) doe become much bigger of body then the breed from whence they came. The Horses also (through the benefit of the Climate, and nature of their feeding) more beautifull and fuller of courage. And such is the extraordinary fertilitie of that soyle, that the Does of their Deere (a kinde differing from ours in *England*, yet no way inferiour) yeeld two Fawnes at a fall or birth, and sometimes three. And the Fishings along our Coasts are in plenty of Fish equall to those of *New-foundland*, and in greatnesse and goodnesse much superiour, and twice in the yeare to be taken, in their going and returne, which is not else-where found in such plenty and varietie; So as there went this yeare from divers parts of this Kingdome, neere thirty Saile thither, who are well returned and richly fished.

To conclude (but out of certaine advertisements so often reiterated from thence, as well as by the constant relations of many hundreds now yearely comming & going) they avow, that it is a Country which nothing but ignorance can thinke ill of, and which no man but of a corrupt minde & ill purpose can defame, which as it paralelleth the most opulent and rich Kingdomes of the world, by lying in the same Latitude with them, so doth it promise richer Mynes of the best and most desired mettals with them, when the Colonie shall be of sufficient strength to open and defend them. And for the Passage thither, and Trade there, it is free from all restraint by forren Princes, whereunto most of our other accustomed trades are subject: there is neyther danger in the way, through the encountering of the Enemy or Pyrate, nor meeting with Rockes or Sholes (by reason of the fayre and safe passage thorow the maine Ocean) nor tediousnes of journey, which by reason of better knowledge then in former yeares (the fruit of time and observation) is oftner made and in fewer weekes, then formerly it was wont to be in monethes; which (with the blessing of God) produced in the last Summer this effect, that in the Fleet of nine Saile of ships, transporting above seaven hundred Passengers out of *England* and *Ireland*, for the Plantation, but one person (in whose roome[27] another at Sea was borne) miscarryed by the way. And for them after arivall, there are convenient lodgings now in building, and carefull attendance in Guests-houses providing, till those that arrive can provide for themselves.

In the three last yeares of 1619, 1620, and 1621, there hath beene provided and sent for Virginia forty two Saile of ships, three thousand five hundred and seaventy men and women for Plantation, with requisite provisions, besides store of Cattell, and in those ships have beene above twelve hundred Mariners imployed: There hath also beene sent in those yeares nine ships to the *Sommer Ilands* with about nine hundred people to inhabite there, in which ships two hundred and forty Mariners were imployed. In which space have beene granted fifty Patents to particular persons, for Plantation in Virginia, who with their Associates have undertaken therein to transport great multitudes of people and cattell thither, which for the most part is since performed, and the residue now in preparing, as by the severall Declarations of each yeare in their particulars, (manifested and approved in our generall and publike Quarter-Courts) and for the fuller satisfaction of all desirous to understand the particularities of such proceedings, hath beene by printing commended to the understanding of all.

The Letters written from the *Governor* and *Treasurer* in Virginia in the beginning of *March* last, (which came hither in *April*,) gave assurance of overcomming and bringing to perfection in this yeare, the Iron-works, Glasse-works, Salt-works, the plentifull sowing of all sorts of English graine with the Plough, having now cleared good quantitie of ground; setting of store of *Indian* Corne or Maize, sufficient for our selves, and for trucke with the Natives; restraint of the quantity of *Tobacco*, and amendment of it in the quality, learned by time and experience; The planting of Vines and Mulberry-trees neere to their houses, Figg-trees, Pomgranats, Potatoes, and Cottonwooll seedes, Pocoon, Indico, Sugar-Canes, Madder, Woade, Hempe, Flaxe, and Silke-grasse; and for the erecting of a fayre Inne in *James-Citie* for the better entertainment of new commers, whereto and to other publike workes, every old planter there offered freely and liberally to contribute. I write the words of their Letters. And how in a late Discovery made, a few moneths before by some of them to the Southward, they had past thorow great Forrests of Pines, fifteene or sixteene miles broad, and above threescore miles long, very fit for Mastes for shipping, and for Pitch and Tarre, and of other sorts of woods fit for Pot-ashes and Sope-ashes, and came unto a most fruitfull Country, blessed with abundance of Corne, reaped twice a yere (within the limits of Virginia) where also they understand of a Copper-myne, an essay whereof was sent, and upon tryall here found to be very rich; and met with a great deale of Silk-grasse there growing, which monethly may be cut, of which kindes, and Cotton-wooll, all the *Cambaya* and *Bengala* stuffes are made in the *East-Indies*: and of which kindes of Silke-grasse was heretofore made a peece of Grogeram[28] given to *Queene Elizabeth*. And how that in *December* last they had planted and cultivated in Virginia Vines of all sorts, (as well those naturally growing, as those other Plants sent them from these parts of Europe) Orenge and Lemon-trees, Figge-trees, Sugar-Canes, Cotton-wooll, Cassavi Rootes, (that make very good bread) Plantanes, Potatoes, and sundry other *Indian* fruits and plants not formerly seene in Virginia, which at the time

27. in whose roome: in whose place.　　　　28. Grogeram: coarse silk.

of their said Letters beganne to prosper very well: as also their Indico-seedes, for the true cure whereof there is lately caused a Treatise to be written.

Furthermore, they write that in a Voyage made by Lieutenant *Marmaduke Parkinson*, and other English Gentlemen, up the River of *Patomack* they saw a *China Boxe* at one of the Kings houses where they were: Being demanded where he had it, made answer, That it was sent him from a King that dwelt in the *West*, over the great Hils, some tenne dayes journey, whose Countrey is neare a great Sea, hee having that Boxe, from a people as he said, that came thither in ships, that weare cloaths, crooked swords, & somwhat like our men, dwelt in houses, and were called *Acanack-China*; and he offered our people, that he would send his Brother along with them to that King, which offer the Governor purposed not to refuse; and the rather, by reason of the continual constant relations of all those *Savages* in Virginia, of a Sea, and the way to it West, they affirming that the heads of all those seaven goodly Rivers, (the least whereof is greater then the River of *Thames*, and navigable above an hundred and fifty miles, and not above sixe or eight miles one from another) which fall all into one great Bay, have their rising out of a ridge of hils, that runnes all along South and North: whereby they doubt not but to finde a safe, easie, and good passage to the South Sea, part by water, and part by land, esteeming it not above an hundred and fifty miles from the head of the Falls, where wee are now planted; the Discovery whereof will bring forth a most rich trade to *Cathay, China, Japan*, and those other of the *East Indies*, to the inestimable benefit of this Kingdome.

But for the further proofe hereof, and of the North-west passage thither by Sea, I referre the Reader to the Treatie annexed at the end of this Booke,[29] written by that learned and famous *Mathematician, Mr. Henry Briggs*, which I having happily attained unto, have published for the common good.

Moreover, the Letters of Mr. *John Berkley*, sometimes of *Beverstone Castle* in the County of *Glocester*, (a Gentleman of an honorable Familie) likewise certifie, that a more fit place for Iron-workes (whereof he was made Master & over-seer) than in Virginia, both for wood, water, mynes, and stone, was not to be found: And that by *Whitsontide* then next (now past) the Company might relye upon good quantities of Iron made by him: which also by Letters from Mr. *George Sandis* the third of *March* last, was confirmed, with this farther description of the place (called *The falling Creeke*) to be so fitting for that purpose, as if Nature had applyed her selfe to the wish and direction of the Workeman; where also were great stones hardly seene else-where in Virginia, lying on the place, as though they had beene brought thither to advance the erection of those Workes.

The Letters of the *French Vignerons* or *Vine-men*, procured out of *France* & sent over into Virginia, did likewise assertaine, that no Countrey in the world was more proper for Vines, Silke, Rice, Olives, and other Fruits, then Virginia is: and that it fare excelled their owne Countrey of *Languedocke*; the Vines of divers sorts being in abundance naturally over all the Countrey: and they having planted some cuttings of Vines at *Michaelmas* last, in their Letters affirme that these bare Grapes already this Spring, to their great wonder, as being a thing they suppose not heard of in any other

29. [This and other appendices are omitted here.]

Countrey. A taste of Wine made of the wilde grape, they last yeare sent, with hope to send a good quantitie this next Vintage; and that the Mulberry-trees where they abode were in wonderfull abundance, and much excelling both in goodnesse and greatnesse those of their owne Country of *Languedocke*: and that those Silke-wormes they have, prosper exceeding well, and some Silke they hope to send this yeare, there wanting nothing to set up that rich Commodity but store of hands wherewith *England* doth abound. Of the fruit of which Mulberry-trees (as of a Plum there plentifully growing) they would make wholsome drinkes for the Colony and people there.

The Letters of Mr. *Porey*[30] (verified also from the *Governor* and *Councell*) advertisied of a late Discovery by him and others made into the great Bay Northward, (reserving the sounding of the bottome thereof for a second Voyage,) where hee left setled very happily neare an hundred English, with hope of a good trade for Furres there to be had. From thence was brought by Lieutenant *Perkinson*, in his voyage, some of that kind of Earth which is called *Terra Lemnia* (there to be had in great abundance) as good as that of *Turkey*.

By this (though it be but in part) the Reader may understand the great riches and blessings of this excellent Countrey, which even ordinary diligence and care must needes strangely improve. But that all men may see the unpartiall ingenuity of this Discourse, we freely confesse, that the Countrey is not so good, as the *Natives* are bad, whose barbarous Savagenesse needs more cultivation than the ground it selfe, being more overspread with incivilitie and treachery, than that with Bryers. For the land being tilled and used well by us, deceived not our expectation, but rather exceeded it farre, being so thankfull as to returne an hundred for one. But the *Savages* though never Nation used so kindly upon so small desert, have in stead of that *Harvest* which our paines merited, returned nothing but Bryers and thornes, pricking even to death many of their Benefactors: yet doubt wee not, but that as all wickednes is crafty to undoe it self, so these also, thorow our sides, have more wounded themselves than us, God Almighty making way for severitie there, where a fayre gentlenesse would not take place. The occasion whereof thus I relate from thence.

The last *May* there came Letters from *Sir Francis Wiat Governor* in Virginia, which did advertise that when in *November* last he arived in Virginia, and entred upon his Government, he found the Country setled in a peace (as all men there thought) sure and unviolable, not onely because it was solemnly ratified and sworne, and at the request of the Native King stamped in Brasse, and fixed to one of his Oakes of note, but as being advantagious to both parts; to the Savages as the weaker, under which they were safely sheltred and defended; to us, as being the easiest way then thought to pursue and advance our projects of buildings, plantings, and effecting their conversion by peaceable and fayre meanes. And such was the conceit of firme peace and amitie, as that there was seldome or never a sword worne, and a Peece[31] seldomer, except for a Deere or Fowle. By which assurance of securitie, the Plantations of particular Adventurers and Planters were placed scatteringly and straglingly as a choyce veyne of

---

30. Mr. *Porey*: see selection 4 above. 31. Peece: gun.

rich ground invited them, and the further from neighbors held the better. The houses generally set open to the Savages, who were alwaies friendly entertained at the tables of the English, and commonly lodged in their bed-chambers. The old planters (as they thought now come to reape the benefit of their long travels)[32] placed with wonderfull content upon their private dividents, and the planting of particular Hundreds and Colonies pursued with an hopefull alacrity, all our projects (saith he) in a faire way, and their familarity with the Natives, seeming to open a faire gate for their conversion to Christianitie.

The Country being in this estate, an occasion was ministred of sending to *Opachankano* the King of these Savages, about the middle of *March* last, what time the Messenger returned backe with these words from him, That he held the peace concluded so firme, as the Skie should sooner fall than it dissolve: yea, such was the treacherous dissimulation of that people who then had contrived our destruction, that even two dayes before the Massacre, some of our men were guided thorow the woods by them in safety: and one *Browne*, who then to learne the language lived among the *Warrascoyacks* (a Province of that King) was in friendly manner sent backe by them to Captaine *Hamor* his Master, and many the like passages, rather increasing our former confidence, than any wise in the world ministring the least suspition of the breach of the peace, or of what instantly ensued; yea, they borrowed our owne Boates to convey themselves crosse the River (on the bankes of both sides whereof all our Plantations were) to consult of the divellish murder that ensued, and of our utter extirpation, which God of his mercy (by the meanes of some of themselves converted to Christianitie) prevented: and as well on the Friday morning (the fatal day) the 22 of *March*, as also in the evening, as in other dayes before, they came unarmed into our houses, without Bowes or arrowes, or other weapons, with Deere, Turkies, Fish, Furres, and other provisions, to sell, and trucke with us, for glasse, beades, and other trifles: yea in some places, sate downe at Breakfast with our people at their tables, whom immediately with their owne tooles and weapons, eyther laid downe, or standing in their houses, they basely and barbarously murthered, not sparing eyther age or sexe, man, woman or childe; so sodaine in their cruell execution, that few or none discerned the weapon or blow that brought them to destruction. In which manner they also slew many of our people then at their severall workes and husbandries in the fields, and without their houses, some in planting Corne and Tobacco, some in gardening, some in making Bricke, building, sawing, and other kindes of husbandry, they well knowing in what places and quarters each of our men were, in regard of their daily familiarity, and resort to us for trading and other negotiations, which the more willingly was by us continued and cherished for the desire we had of effecting that great master-peece of workes, their conversion. And by this meanes that fatall Friday morning, there fell under the bloudy and barbarous hands of that perfidious and inhumane people, contrary to all lawes of God and men, of Nature & Nations, three hundred forty seven men, women, and children, most by their owne weapons; and not being content with taking away life alone, they fell after againe upon the dead, making as well as they could, a fresh murder, defacing, dragging, and

---

32. travels: travails.

mangling the dead carkasses into many pieces, and carrying some parts away in derision, with base and bruitish triumph.

Neither yet did these beasts spare those amongst the rest well knowne unto them, from whom they had daily received many benefits and favours, but spitefully also massacred them, without remorse or pitty, being in this more fell than Lyons and Dragons, which (as Histories record) have beene so farre from hurting, as they have both acknowledged, and gratefully requited their Benefactors; such is the force of good deeds, though done to cruell beasts, as to make them put off the very nature of beasts, and to put on humanity upon them. But these miscreants, contrariwise in this kinde, put not off onely all humanity, but put on a worse and more then unnaturall bruitishnesse. One instance of it, amongst too many, shall serve for all.

That worthy religious Gentleman, Master *George Thorpe* Esquire, Deputie of the Colledge lands, sometimes one of his Majesties Pentioners, and in one of the principall places of command in Virginia, did so truly and earnestly affect their conversion, and was so tender over them, that whosoever under his authority had given them but the least displeasure or discontent, he punished them severely. He thought nothing too deare for them, and as being desirous to binde them unto him by his many courtesies, hee never denyed them any thing that they asked him, insomuch that when these *Savages* complained unto him of the fiercenesse of our Mastives,[33] most implacable and terrible unto them, (knowing them by instinct it seemes, to be but treacherous and false-hearted friends to us, better then our selves) he to gratifie them in all things, for the winning of them by degrees, caused some of them to be killed in their presence, to the great displeasure of the owners, and would have had all the rest guelt[34] (had he not beene hindered) to make them the gentler and the milder to them. Hee was not onely too kinde and beneficiall to the common sort, but also to their King, to whom hee oft resorted, and gave many presents which hee knew to be highly pleasing to him. And whereas this king before dwelt onely in a cottage, or rather a denne or hog-stye, made with a few poles and stickes, and covered with mats after their wyld manner, to civilize him, he first built him a fayre house according to the English fashion, in which hee tooke such joy, especially in his locke and key, which hee so admired, as locking and unlocking his doore an hundred times a day, hee thought no device in all the world was comparable to it.

Thus insinuating himselfe to this King for his religious purposes, he conferred after with him oft, and intimated to him matters of our Religion; and thus far the *Pagan* confessed, moved by naturall Principles, that our God was a good God, and better much then theirs, in that he had with so many good things above them endowed us. Hee told him, if hee would serve our God, hee should bee partaker of all those good things wee had, and of farre greater then sense or reason ever could imagine. Hee wonne upon him, as hee thought in many things, so as hee gave him fayre hearing and good answer, and seemed to be much pleased with his discourse and in his company. And both hee and his people for the daily courtesies this good Gentleman did to one or other of them, did professe such outward love and respect unto him, as nothing could seeme more: but all was little regarded after by this Viperous brood, as the

---

33. Mastives: mastiffs, dogs.   34. guelt: neutered.

sequell shewed: for they not only wilfully murdered him, but cruelly and felly, out of devillish malice, did so many barbarous despights and foule scornes after to his dead corpse, as are unbefitting to be heard by any civil eare. One thing I cannot omit, that when this good Gentleman upon his fatall hower, was warned by his man (who perceived some treachery intended to them by these hell-hounds) to looke to himselfe, and withall ranne away for feare of the mischiefe he strongly apprehended, and so saved his owne life; yet his Master, out of the conscience of his owne good meaning, and faire deserts ever towards them, was so void of all suspition, and so full of confidence, that they had sooner killed him, then hee could or would beleeve they meant any ill against him. Thus the sinnes of these wicked Infidels, have made them unworthy of enjoying him, and the eternall good that he most zealously alwayes intended to them.

And thus these miserable wretches, not hee, hath lost by it, who to the comfort of us all, hath gayned a Crowne of endlesse blisse, and is assuredly become a glorious Martyr, in which thrice-happy and blessed state we leave him. But these miscreants, who have thus despised Gods great mercies so freely offered to them, must needs in time therefore be corrected by his justice: So as those who by the way of mercies would not be drawne unto him, shall some of them at length (no doubt) be brought unto him by his way of judgments: to which leaving them, I will knit againe together now the thred of my Discourse, and proceed to tell you. That at the time of this Massacre there were three or foure of our ships in *James-River*, and one in the next River, and daily more to come in, as three did within fourteene dayes after; one of which they endevored to have surprised, but in vaine, as had also beene their whole attempt, had any the least fore-knowledge beene in those places where the Massacre was committed: yet were the hearts of the English ever stupid, and averted from beleeving any thing that might weaken their hopes of speedy winning the Savages to Civilitie and Religion, by kinde usage and fayre conversing amongst them. Hee, and the whole Councell write further, That Almighty God (they doubt not) hath his great worke to doe in this Tragedy, and will thereout draw honor and glory to his great Name; safety, and a more flourishing estate to themselves, and the whole Plantation there; and the more speedy convertion of the Children of those Savages to himselfe, since hee so miraculously preserved so many of the English (there being, God be praysed, about eleven parts of twelve still remayning) whose desire to draw those people to Religion by the carelesse neglect of their owne safeties, seemes to have beene the greatest cause of their own ensuing destruction. Yet it pleased God to use some of them as instruments to save many of their lives, whose soules they had formerly saved, as at *James-Citie*, and other places, and the Pinnace trading in *Pamounkey* River, all whose lives were saved by a converted *Indian*, disclosing the plot in the instant (whereof though our sinnes (say they) made us unworthy to be instruments of so glorious a conversion in generall, yet his infinite wisedome can neverthelesse bring it to passe with some more of them, and with other Provinces there in his good time, and by such meanes as wee thinke most unlikely. For even in the delivery of us that now survive, no mans particular carefulnesse saved any one person, but the meere goodnesse of himselfe, freely and miraculously preserved whom it pleased him.

The letters of Mr. *George Sandis* a worthy Gentleman and Treasurer there, likewise have advertised (as many others from many particular persons of note and worth) besides the Relations of many returned in the Sea-flower (the ship that brought us this unwelcome newes) have beene heard at large in the publike Courts, that whilst all their affayres were full of successe, and such intercourse of familiaritie, as if the *Indians* and themselves had beene of one Nation, those treacherous Natives, after five yeares peace, by a generall combination in one day plotted to subvert their whole Colony, and at one instant of time, though our severall Plantations were an hundred and forty miles up one River on both sides.

But before I goe any further, for the better understanding of all things, you shall know that these wyld naked Natives live not in great numbers together, but dispersed, and in small companies; and where most together, not above two hundred, and that very rare, in other places fifty or forty, or thereabouts, and many miles distant from one another, in such places among the Woods where they either found, or might easiliest make some cleared plots of ground, which they imploy wholly in setting of Corne, whereby to sustaine their lives. These small and scattered Companies (as I have said) had warning given from one another in all their habitations to meete at the day and houre appointed for our destruction, at all our severall Townes and places seated upon the River; some were directed to goe to one place, some to another, all to be done at the same day and time, which they did accordingly: some entring their Houses under colour of trucking,[35] and so taking advantage, others drawing our men abroad upon faire pretences, and the rest suddenly falling upon those that were at their labours.

They certifie further, that besides Master *George Thorpe*, before mentioned, Master *John Berkeley*, Captaine *Nathanael Powel*, and his wife, (daughter of Master *William Tracy*, and great with childe) and Captaine *Maycock*, all Gentlemen of birth, vertue, and industry, and of the Councell there, suffered under this their cruelty and treason.

That the slaughter had beene universall, if God had not put it into the heart of an Indian belonging to one *Perry*, to disclose it, who living in the house of one *Pace*, was urged by another Indian his Brother (who came the night before and lay with him) to kill *Pace*, (so commanded by their King as he declared) as hee would kill *Perry*: telling further that by such an houre in the morning a number would come from divers places to finish the Execution, who failed not at the time: *Perries* Indian rose out of his bed and reveales it to *Pace*, that used him as a Sonne: And thus the rest of the Colony that had warning given them, by this meanes was saved. Such was (God bee thanked for it) the good fruit of an Infidell converted to Christianity; for though three hundred and more of ours died by many of these Pagan Infidels, yet thousands of ours were saved by the means of one of them alone which was made a Christian; Blessed be God for ever, whose mercy endureth for ever; Blessed bee God whose mercy is above his justice, and farre above all his workes: who wrought this deliverance whereby their soules escaped even as a Bird out of the snare of the Fowler.

---

35. trucking: trading.

Pace upon this discovery, securing his house, before day rowed over the River to *James*-City (in that place neere three miles in bredth) and gave notice thereof to the Governor, by which meanes they were prevented there, and at such other Plantations as was possible for a timely intelligence to be given; for where they saw us standing upon our Guard, at the sight of a Peece they all ranne away. In other places that could have no notice, some Peeces with munition (the use whereof they know not) were there carried away, and some few Cattell also were destroyed by them. And as Fame divulgeth (not without probable grounds) their King hath since caused the most part of the Gunpowder by him surprized; to bee sowne, to draw therefrom the like increase, as of his Maize or Corne, in Harvest next. And that it is since discovered,

that the last Summer *Opachankano* practised with a King of the Eastern shore (no well-willer of his) to furnish him with store of poison (naturally growing in his country) for our destruction, which he absolutely refused, though he sent him great store of Beades, and other presents to winne him thereunto: which he, with five or six of his great men, offered to be ready to justifie against him. That the true cause of this surprize was most by the instigation of the Devill, (enemy to their salvation) and the dayly feare that possest them, that in time we by our growing continually upon them, would dispossesse them of this Country, as they had beene formerly of the West Indies by the Spaniard; produced this bloody act. That never griefe and shame possessed any people more than themselves, to be thus butchered by so naked and cowardly a people, who dare not stand the presentment of a staffe in manner of a Peece, nor an uncharged Peece in the hands of a woman, from which they flye as so many Hares; much faster than from their tormenting Devill, whom they worship for feare, though they acknowledge they love him not.

Thus have you seene the particulars of this massacre, out of Letters from thence written, wherein treachery and cruelty have done their worst to us, or rather to themselves; for whose understanding is so shallow, as not to perceive that this must needs bee for the good of the Plantation after, and the losse of this blood to make the body more healthfull, as by these reasons may be manifest.

First, Because betraying of innocency never rests unpunished: And therefore *Agesilaus*,[36] when his enemies (upon whose oath of being faithful hee rested) had deceived him, he sent them thankes, for that by their perjury, they had made God his friend, and their enemy.

Secondly, Because our hands which before were tied with gentlenesse and faire usage, are now set at liberty by the treacherous violence of the Savages, not untying the Knot, but cutting it: So that we, who hitherto have had possession of no more ground than their waste, and our purchase at a valuable consideration to their owne contentment, gained; may now by right of Warre, and law of Nations, invade the Country, and destroy them who sought to destroy us: whereby wee shall enjoy their cultivated places, turning the laborious Mattocke[37] into the victorious Sword (wherein there is more both ease, benefit, and glory) and possessing the fruits of others labours.

---

36. *Agesilaus*: king of Sparta.   37. Mattocke: tool similar to an adze or a pick.

Now their cleared grounds in all their villages (which are situate in the fruitfullest places of the land) shall be inhabited by us, whereas heretofore the grubbing of woods was the greatest labour.

Thirdly, Because those commodities which the Indians enjoyed as much or rather more then we, shall now also be entirely possessed by us. The Deere and other beasts will be in safety, and infinitly increase, which heretofore not onely in the generall huntings of the King (whereat foure or five hundred Deere were usually slaine) but by each particular Indian were destroied at all times of the yeare, without any difference of Male, Damme, or Young. The like may be said of our owne Swine and Goats, whereof they have used to kill eight in tenne more then the English have done. There will be also a great increase of wild Turkies, and other waighty Fowle, for the Indians never put difference of destroying the Hen, but kill them whether in season or not, whether in breeding time, or sitting on their egges, or having new hatched, it is all one to them: whereby, as also by the orderly using of their fishing Weares,[38] no knowne Country in the world will so plentifully abound in victuall.

Fourthly, Because the way of conquering them is much more easie then of civilizing them by faire meanes, for they are a rude, barbarous, and naked people, scattered in small companies, which are helps to Victorie, but hinderances to Civilitie: Besides, that a conquest may be of many, and at once; but civility is in particular, and slow, the effect of long time, and great industry. Moreover, victorie of them may bee gained many waies; by force, by surprize, by famine in burning their Corne, by destroying and burning their Boats, Canoes, and Houses, by breaking their fishing Weares, by assailing them in their huntings, whereby they get the greatest part of their sustenance in Winter, by pursuing and chasing them with our horses, and blood-Hounds to draw after them, and Mastives to teare them, which take these naked, tanned, deformed Savages, for no other then wild beasts, and are so fierce and fell upon them, that they feare them worse then their old Devill which they worship, supposing them to be a new and worse kinde of Devils then their owne. By these and sundry other wayes, as by driving them (when they flye) upon their enemies, who are round about them, and by animating and abetting their enemies against them, may their ruine or subjection be soone effected.

So the Spaniard made great use for his owne turne of the quarrels and enmities that were amongst the Indians, as throughly understanding and following that Maxime of the Politician, *Divide & impera*, Make divisions and take Kingdomes: For thus he got two of the greatest Kingdomes of the West Indies, *Peru* and *Mexico*, by the Princes divisions, and the peoples differences. After the death of *Guainacapa* king of *Peru*, his sonnes *Attabalippa* and *Gascar* falling to war about the kingdom, & each of them striving to make the *Spaniard* to his friend, *Francis Pizzarro* managing those their divisions onely to his owne ends, easily stripped them both of that rich Kingdome, and became Master of *Peru*. And so likwise *Ferdinando Cortez* vanquished King *Motezuma*, and gained the Kingdome of *Mexico* from him, by the aid and furtherance of the neighboring people of the Province of *Tascala*, being deadly enemies to the *Mexicans*; for which service they of *Tascala* are freed by the *Spaniards* from all

38. Weares: traps, weirs.

Tributes to this time. In Virginia the many divers Princes and people there are at this day opposite in infinite factions one unto another, and many of them beare a mortall hatred to these our barbarous Savages, that have beene likely as false and perfidious heretofore to them, as unto us of late. So as the quarrels, and the causes of them, and the different humours of these people being well understood, it will be an easie matter to overthrow those that now are, or may bee our enemies hereafter, by ayding and setting on their enemies against them. And by these factions and differences of petty Princes, the *Romans* tooke their greatest advantage to overcome this Iland of *Great Britayne*, of which *Tacitus* sayes, *Ita dam singuli pugnant universi vincuntur*. And *Justin* hath the like saying of the cause of vanquishing the *Grecian* Cities.

Fiftly, Because the *Indians*, who before were used as friends, may now most justly be compelled to servitude and drudgery, and supply the roome[39] of men that labour, whereby even the meanest of the Plantation may imploy themselves more entirely in their Arts and Occupations, which are more generous, whilest Savages performe their inferiour workes of digging in mynes, and the like, of whom also some may be sent for the service of the *Sommer Ilands*.

Sixtly, This will for ever hereafter make us more cautelous and circumspect, as never to bee deceived more by any other treacheries, but will serve for a great instruction to all posteritie there, to teach them that *Trust is the mother of Deceipt*, and to learne them that of the *Italian, Chi non fida, non s'inganna*, Hee that trusts not is not deceived: and make them know that kindnesses are misspent upon rude natures, so long as they continue rude; as also, that Savages and Pagans are above all other for matter of Justice ever to be suspected. Thus upon this Anvile shall wee now beate out to our selves an armour of proofe, which shall for ever after defend us from barbarous Incursions, and from greater dangers that otherwise might happen. And so we may truly say according to the *French* Proverb, *A quelque chose malheur est bon*, Ill lucke is good for something.

Lastly, We have this benefit more to our comfort, because all good men doe now take much more care of us then before, since the fault is on their sides, not on ours, who have used so fayre a cariage, even to our owne destruction. Especially his *Majesties* most gratious, tender and paternall care is manifest herein, who by his Royall bounty and goodnesse, hath continued his many favors unto us, with a new, large, & Princely supply of Munition and Armes, out of his Majesties owne store in the Tower, being gratiously bestowed for the safety and advancement of the Plantation. As also his Royall favor is amply extended in a large supply of men and other necessaries throughout the whole Kingdome, which are very shortly to bee sent to Virginia.

Neyther must wee omit the Honourable City of *London*, who to shew their zeale at this time (as they have alwayes done upon all Honourable occasions to their endlesse praise) are now setting forth one hundred persons, at their owne charges, for the advancement of the Plantations. In the furtherance of which action, as the whole grave Senate of Aldermen have shewed much piety and wisedome, so in particular, the Right Honourable *Sir Edward Barkham* Knight, the now Lord Mayor, hath demon-

---

39. roome: place.

strated a most worthy mind. Besides many worthy Persons of birth and quality, and divers others at their owne costs are now preparing for Virginia. Neyther is any man to be dejected because of some such disasters as these that may seeme to thwart the businesse.

What growing State was there ever in the world which had not the like? *Rome* grew by opposition, and rose upon the backe of her enemies. Marke but the *Spaniard* who is in the same Continent with Virginia, and hath now perfected his worke; Marke and tell mee, if hee hath not had more counterbusses farre then wee, as out of their owne histories at large may be proved.

Columbus upon his returne from the *West Indies* into *Spaine*, having left his people with the *Indian* in peace, and promise of fayre usage towards them, yet at his comming backe againe, hee found no one man alive of them, but all by the Natives treacherously slaine.

After this againe, when the *Spanish Colony* was increased in great numbers, the *Indians* (from whom the *Spaniards* for trucking stuffe used to have all their corn) generally conspired together to plant no corne at all, intending therby to famish them, themselves living in the meane time upon *Cassavi* (a root to make bread) onely then knowne to themselves: This plot of theirs by the *Spaniards* over-sight (that foolishly depended upon Strangers for their bread) tooke such effect, and brought them to such misery by the rage of famine, that they spared no uncleane, no loathsome beast, no not the poysonous and hideous Serpents, but eate them up also, devouring one death to save them from another: And by this meanes the whole Colony well-neare surfetted, sickned, and dyed miserably.

After againe, upon fresh and great supplyes new made, an infinite company of them by their incontinency dyed of the *Indian* disease,[40] that hath now got a *French* name, which at first (as being a strange and unknowne malady) was deadly upon whomsoever it lighted. Besides (before they knew the cause and remedy) very many lost divers parts of their body, feet and hands principally, by a little vermine lesse then a Flea, and skipping like it, called *Nigua*, which got between the skinne and the flesh before they were aware, and there bred and multiplyed, making swellings and putrefactions, to the decay and losse of their bodily members.

What should I tell you that the Plantations divers times were neare undone, by the ambition, factions, and malice of the Commanders one unto another. *Columbus*, to whom they were beholding for all, with his brother, were sent home from the *West Indies* into *Spaine* bound with chaines: and some other great Commanders killed and murthered one another. *Pizzarro* was killed by *Almagros* sonne, and him *Vasco* beheaded, which *Vasco* was taken by *Blasco*, and this *Blasco* was likewise taken by *Pizzarroes* brother. Thus by their owne spightfull and ambitious quarrels did they well-neare shake the mayne pillars of that Plantation.

These and many other calamities and mischiefes, too long to relate now, hapned unto them more then ever did to us. And at one time their plantation was even at the last gaspe, all their Colony being resolved desperately to leave it, had not two ships unexpected come in with new supplyes: yet wee see for all these miseries, that they

---

40. *Indian* disease: syphilis.

have attained to their ends at last, Honor, power, and wealth; In so much as that Countrey, which (when they were dishartned with disasters) they beganne to be so weary of, that they were about to forsake it all, in short time after (seeing all stormes blowne over, and fayre weather shining upon them) they were so in love with their great fortunes, that they grew so jealous of them, as made them shut them up from the sight of any but themselves. And then they petitioned their King, by an inviolable Decree to annexe and unite the *West Indies* inseparably for ever to the Crowne of *Spaine*; which (for their better securitie and satisfaction) was accordingly performed and ratified, as it is to be seene in *Hereras* History of the *West Indies*. And whereas before, few could be hired to go to inhabite there, now with great suite they must obtaine it.

Thus have they in time by industry, patience, and constancy effected this great worke of theirs, notwithstanding to encrease their difficulties also, they were to deale with a most populous & numerous nation, which they overcame at last: So as *Oviedo* in his third Booke of the first Part of his *West Indie* History saith, that of a million of *Indians* at least, that were in *Hispaniola*, there were not (in little more then forty yeares space after the first beginning of the Plantation) five hundred of them & all their children living: for the *Indians* that lived there, after were brought out of the Continent into that Iland, or out of one Iland to be planted in another. On the other side, the Natives in Virginia are nothing populous, but thin and scattered Nations, as is knowne to all.

Here by the way to make a little Digression, since I have mentioned *Oviedo* who lived above twenty two yeares in the *West Indies*, I will acquaint you with his observation and judgement of the nature and disposition of the *Indians* there, that you may compare and see in what, and how farre, it agrees with that of the Natives of Virginia.

They are (saith hee) by nature sloathfull and idle, vitious, melancholy, slovenly, of bad conditions, lyers, of small memory, of no constancy or trust. In another place he saith, The *Indian* is by nature of all people the most lying and most inconstant in the world, sottish and sodaine:[41] never looking what dangers may happen afterwards, lesse capable then children of sixe or seaven yeares old, and lesse apt and ingenious. This is the generall disposition of most of them, though there be some (sayes he) that be wise and subtill. And indeede it should seeme so, when they could over-reach and goe beyond the *Spaniard* so much, to put that tricke of starving them (as aforesaid) upon them, to their so great and almost totall destruction.

But to come againe to that which I first intended: Since the *Spaniard* (as we see) in his Plantations hath gone thorow farre more hazards, and greater difficulties then ever wee have had, we therefore in looking to what is past, upon great reason ought like-wise not to be deterred, but so much the rather invited to proceede with constancy and courage. And if besides wee looke (as most men doe) after the riches of a Countrey to invite us on, aske those that have beene there, and have travelled farre and neare, and they will tell you, that no Countrey in the world doth naturally abound with more Commodities then Virginia doth. The Clymate is knowne to be more temperate, and the soyle more rich then that of the *West Indies* is: neyther doth

41. sodaine: sudden, unpredictable.

it want mynes of all sorts, no not of the richest, as is knowne to some now living, and shall be manifested when fit time shall serve. And yet to thinke that Gold and Silver mynes are in a Countrey (otherwise most rich and fruitfull) the greatest wealth of a Plantation, is but a popular error, as is that opinion likewise, That the Gold and Silver is the greatest wealth of the *West Indies* now at this present time. True it is indeed, that in the first Conquest the *Spaniards* got great and mighty treasure from the *Indians*, which they in long space had heaped up together, and in those times the *Indians* shewed them entyre and plentifull rich mynes, which by length of time (as is well known and published to the world by those that have beene there) are wasted and exhausted since, so as now the charge of getting those mettals is growne most excessive, besides the consuming and spoyling many men of their lives, which are deprived of them by the vapors that come out of the Gold and Silver mynes, which are most pestilent and deadly, as divers authors averre. Amongst others, a late Geographer speaking of the *West Indies*, and of those mynes there, saith, *Odor ex auri & argenti fodinis noxius admodum; neg tamen prohibuit aeris corruptissimi violentia Hispanos, ne in alio orbe novum moriendi locum quaererent.* So as all things considered by these mynes, what by the lives of many men lost in them, and what with the great charge otherwise in getting them, the cleare gaine to the Adventurers from these mettals (the Kings part defrayed) is but small to them, nothing neere so much I am sure, as is imagined. And were it not for other rich Commodities there that enable and enrich the Adventurers, those of the Contractation house were never able to subsist by this. For the greatest part of their gaine and profit I say consists not in these mynes, but in their other Commodities, partly native, and partly translated from other parts of the world, and planted in the *West Indies*: As in their mighty wealth of Sugars (the Sugar-Canes being transported first from the *Canaries*,) and in Ginger, and some other commodities derived from the *East Indies* thither: in their Cochanile, their Indico, their Cotton, their infinite store of Hydes and Skins, their Quick-silver, and Allom, Woad, and Brasillwood, &c. And their many other Dyes, Paints, *Petacaraua*, Tobacco, Gummes, Balmes, Oyles medecinall, and Perfumes, their *Sarsaparillia*, and many other physicall drugs, (for which, learned Physitians and skilfull Simplers were sent to take a survey, and make an exquisite draught of all the Plants in colours.) These I say and other the like commodities are the West Indies indeed unto the Adventurers, by which they are inabled to inrich themselves, and to sustaine the mighty charge of drawing out the Gold and Silver, to the great and cleare revenew of their King.

I had many things of importance to say more, but I will detain the Reader no longer now. To conclude then, seeing that *Virginia* is most abundantly fruitfull, and that this Massacre must rather be beneficiall to the Plantation then impaire it, let all men take courage, and put to their helping hands, since now the time is most seasonable and advantagious for the reaping of those benefits which the Plantation hath long promised: and for their owne good let them doe it speedily, that so by taking the prioritie of time, they may have also the prioritie of place, in choosing the best Seats of the Country, which now by vanquishing of the Indians, is like to offer a more ample and faire choice of fruitfull habitations, then hitherto our gentlenesse and faire comportment to the Savages could attaine unto. Wherein no doubt but all the favour that may be, shall be shewed to Adventurers and Planters. And for old Adventurers, there is due unto them and their heyres (according to the Orders of the Company) for each twelve pounds ten shillings formerly paid into the treasury, one hundred Acres of Land, upon a first division, and as much upon a second, the first being planted. And whosoever transports himselfe or any other, at his charge into Virginia, shall for himselfe and each person so transported, before Midsummer, 1625 have to him and his heyres for ever, fifty Acres of land upon a first Division, and as much more upon a second: the first fifty being cultivated or manured, if such person continue there three yeares, eyther at once or severall times, or dye after hee bee shipped for that Voyage.

Lastly, it is to be wished, that every good Patriot will take these things seriously into his thoughts, and consider how deeply the prosecution of this noble Enterprise concerneth the honor of his *Majestie* and the whole Nation, the propagation of Christian Religion, the enlargement, strength, and safety of his Majesties Dominions, the rich augmenting of his Revennues, the imploiment of his Subjects idle at home, the increase of men, Mariners and shipping, and the raising of such necessary commoditie, for the importation of which from forren Countries so great and incredible summes are continually issued and expended. Some may helpe with their purses, some with their persons, some with their favour, some with their counsell: especially amongst others, let Ministers in their publike and private prayers commend these

Plantations to the blessing of Almighty God:

To whom be all honor and glory,

for ever and ever,

Amen.

6. John Smith

from *The Generall Historie of Virginia* 1624

Contrary to legend and Walt Disney, there was no romantic affair between Smith and Pocahontas (1595?–1617). He does not even mention her in his early accounts of his captivity with Powhatan. His first version of the story comes seventeen years later, as part of a comprehensive tome on English America. At this point the Jamestown massacre had already occurred, led by Pocahontas's uncle. Pocahontas had married the colonist John Rolfe and returned with him to England, where as an Indian princess she had had an audience with King James I. She had also been dead for seven years. Some scholars have speculated that her intervention for Smith—if it happened at all—was part of a ritual allowing Smith to be adopted into the Powhatan tribe, and that Smith simply misinterpreted it as a real execution. Others have noted a pattern in Smith's autobiographical narratives; Pocahontas is actually the third beautiful native female to save him from death in his own accounts. No matter what did or did not happen, the Smith/Pocahontas legend, as Robert Tilton has argued, did not fully blossom until after the Revolution. In Smith's account, the more revealing moment may be the reproachful encounter he reports from her last year.

[THE STORY OF POCAHONTAS IN VIRGINIA]

A t last they brought [Captain Smith] to Meronocomoco, where was Powhatan their Emperor. Here more then two hundred of those grim Courtiers stood wondering at him, as he had beene a monster; till Powhatan and his trayne had put themselves in their greatest braveries.[42] Before a fire upon a seat like a bedsted, he sat covered with a great robe, made of Rarowcun[43] skinnes, and all the tayles hanging by. On either hand did sit a young wench of 16 or 18 yeares, and along on each side the house, two rowes of men, and behind them as many women, with all their heads and shoulders painted red; many of their heads bedecked with the white downe of Birds; but every one with something: and a great chayne of white beads about their necks. At his entrance before the King, all the people gave a great shout. The Queene of Appamatuck was appointed to bring him water to wash his hands, and another brought him a bunch of feathers, in stead of a Towell to dry them: having feasted him after their best barbarous manner they could, a long consultation was held, but the conclusion was, two great stones were brought before Powhatan: then as many as could layd hands on him, dragged him to them, and thereon laid his head, and being ready with their clubs, to beate out his braines, Pocahontas the Kings dearest daughter, when no intreaty could prevaile, got his head in her armes, and laid her owne upon his to save him from death: whereat the Emperour was contented he should live to make him hatchets, and her bells, beads, and copper; for they thought him as well of all occupations as themselves.[44]

[POCAHONTAS IN ENGLAND]

Being about this time preparing to set saile for New-England, I could not stay to doe her that service I desired, and she well deserved; but hearing shee was at Branford with divers of my friends, I went to see her: After a modest salutation, without any word, she turned about, obscured her face, as not seeming well contented; and in that humour her husband, with divers others, we all left her two or three houres, repenting my selfe to have writ she could speake English. But not long after, she began to talke, and remembred mee well what courtesies shee had done: saying, You did promise Powhatan what was yours should bee his, and he the like to you; you called him father being in his land a stranger, and by the same reason so must I doe you: which though I would have excused, I durst not allow of that title, because she was a Kings daughter; with a well set countenance she said, Were you not afraid to come into my fathers Countrie, and caused feare in him and all his people (but mee) and feare you here I should call you father; I tell you then I will, and you shall call me childe, and so I will bee for ever and ever your Countrieman. They did tell us alwaies you were dead, and I knew no other till I came to Plimoth; yet Powhatan did command Uttamato-makkin to seeke you, and know the truth, because your Countriemen will lie much. This Salvage, one of Powhatans Councell, being amongst them held an under-

---

42. braveries: fineries.
43. Rarowcun: racoon.

44. as well of all occupations: as good for all tasks.

Rescue of Smith by Pocahontas. Detail from Smith's Generall Historie.

standing fellow; the King purposely sent him, as they say, to number the people here, and informe him well what wee were and our state. Arriving at Plimoth, according to his directions, he got a long sticke, whereon by notches hee did thinke to have kept the number of all the men hee could see, but he was quickly wearie of that taske: Comming to London, where by chance I met him, having renewed our acquaintance, where many were desirous to heare and see his behavior, hee told me Powhatan did bid him to finde me out, to shew him our God, the King, Queene, and Prince, I so much had told them of: Concerning God, I told him the best I could, the King I heard he had seene, and the rest hee should see when he would; he denied ever to have seene the King, till by circumstances he was satisfied he had: Then he replyed very sadly, You gave Powhatan a white Dog, which Powhatan fed as himselfe, but your King gave me nothing, and I am better than your white Dog.

7.

The Tragicall Relation of the Virginia Assembly 1624

This document was produced as part of the ongoing struggle for official influence and public opinion among the different factions of the Virginia colony. It is notable not only for its contrast to promotional accounts, but also for its open admission of cannibalism among the English. Sir Thomas Smith, the main object of the Assembly's protest, was the dominant figure in London's colonial ventures; he also headed the East India Company.

In those 12 yeers of Sir Thomas Smith's goverment, we averr that the Colony for the most parte remayned in great want and misery under most severe and Crewell lawes sent over in printe,[45] and contrary to the expresse Letter of the Kinge in his most gracious Charter, and as mercylessly executed, often times without tryall or Judgment. The allowance in those tymes for a man was only eight ounces of meale and half a pinte of pease for a daye, the one and the other mouldy, rotten, full of Cobwebs and Maggotts loathsome to man and not fit for beasts, which forced many to flee for reliefe to the Savage Enemy, who being taken againe were putt to sundry deaths as by hanginge, shooting and breakinge uppon the wheele. And others were forced by famine to filch for their bellies, of whom one for steelinge of 2 or 3 pints of oatemeale had a bodkinge[46] thrust through his tounge and was tyed with a chaine to a tree untill he starved. If a man through his sicknes had not been able to worke, he had noe allowance at all, and soe consequently perished. Many through these extremities, being weery of life, digged holes in the earth and there hidd themselves till they famished.

Wee cannott for this our scarcity blame our Comanders heere, in respect that our sustenance was to come from England. For had they at that time given us better allowance we had perished in generall, so lamentable was our scarcity that we were constrayned to eate Doggs, Catts, ratts, Snakes, Toadstooles, horse hides and what nott. One man out of the mysery that he endured, killinge his wife powdered her up[47] to eate her, for which he was burned. Many besides fedd on the Corpses of dead men, and one who had gotten unsatiable, out of custome to that foode, could not be restrayned, untill such tyme as he was executed for it. And indeed soe miserable was our estate, that the happyest day that ever some of them hoped to see, was when the Indyans had killed a mare, they wishinge whilst she was a boiling that Sir Thomas Smith were uppon her backe in the kettle.

---

45. in printe: the *Laws Divine, Morall and Martiall* of 1612.
46. bodkinge: bodkin, dagger.
47. powdered her up: salted her body.

8. Francis Higginson

from his journal
1629

In 1629, Francis Higginson (1587–1630) was hired by the Massachusetts Bay
Company as its minister. He went over to Salem, a year in advance of the Great
Migration led by John Winthrop. His journal of the voyage circulated in manuscript
among the Massachusetts company, and his promotional treatise New Englands
Plantation *(1630) went through three editions in one year. Higginson died of a fever*
that same year, like so many of the early colonists. Almost nothing is known about
the "beastly sodomitical boys" outside of Higginson's remarks, which were deleted
when Thomas Hutchinson later printed the journal.

[TUESDAY, MAY 19]

This day towards night my daughter grew sicker, and many blue spots were seen upon her breast, which affrighted us. At the first we thought they had been the plague tokens, but we found afterwards that it was only an high measure of the infection of the pox, which were struck again into the child, and so it was god's will the child died about six of the clock at night, being the first in our ship that was buried in the bowels of the great Atlanticke Sea, which as it was a grief to us her parents and a terror to all the rest as being the beginning of a contagious disease and mortality. So in the same judgment it pleased God to remember mercy in that child, in freeing it from a world of misery wherein otherwise she had lived all her days. For being about four years old a year since, we know not by what means swayed in the back, so that it was broken and grew crooked, and the joints of her hips were loosed and her knees went crooked, pitiful to see, since which time she hath had a most lamentable pain in her belly and would ofttimes cry out in the day and in her sleep also, "My belly!" which declared some extraordinary distemper, so that in respect of her we had cause to take her death as a blessing from the Lord to shorten her misery.

[TUESDAY, JUNE 23]

This day we examined five beastly sodomitical boys, which confessed their wickedness not to be named. The fact was so foul we reserved them to be punished by the governor when we came to new England, who afterward sent them back to the company to be punished in old England, as the crime deserved.

9. John Winthrop

from "A Modell of Christian Charity" 1630

The legendary first governor of the Massachusetts Bay Colony, John Winthrop (1588–1649) was a member of the landed gentry before he emigrated, with a large entourage, in 1630. He was a lawyer as well as a devout Puritan, and is credited with noticing the legal loophole that allowed him to take the Massachusetts Bay Company's charter with him across the Atlantic, holding company meetings in the colony in order to gain greater freedom from watchful eyes in London. As governor, Winthrop played a key role in conflicts over political representation, economics, and theology, perhaps doing more than any other figure to shape colonial society. His positions in these controversies are detailed in his famous Journal, *and can be followed in chapters 5 and 6.*

"A Modell of Christian Charity," which follows the classic form of the Puritan sermon, was delivered by Winthrop en route to Massachusetts, aboard the Arbella, *flagship of the Great Migration. Though it circulated only in manuscript until the eighteenth century, it has become one of the*  *most famous texts in American history. Its final paragraph in particular continues to serve as a vision of national culture, as for example in a 1980 campaign speech by Ronald Reagan. But in 1630 it was not about a new nation; Winthrop and his followers continued to see themselves as English, and the last paragraph refers to the importance of their venture as an example to conflicting factions in England. More broadly, the sermon is about a new model of society, and Winthrop asks fundamental questions about what binds people together. Even in asking the question, he is making a very modern assumption about the kinds of self-interest and economic motives that pull people apart in commercial society. The sermon goes far in advancing contract relations as a fundamental model. But it is also about the limits of self-interest. Paradoxically, Winthrop elaborates a theory of society on the basis of the individual's natural love of self, which leads the individual to love anything that resembles him- or herself; i.e., another. This egalitarian impulse in the sermon is in some tension with its other main theme, stated at the outset: the justification of hierarchy and authority. In the end, Winthrop counts on a common sense of mission in an unfolding story. The city on the hill will not be just like any other city. Because it is an example, anchoring a divine perspective in human history, it is a world-historical experiment.*

Written
On Boarde the Arrabella,
On the Attlantick Ocean.
By the Honorable John Winthrop Esquire.

In His passage, (with the great Company of Religious people, of which Christian Tribes he was the Brave Leader and famous Governor;) from the Island of Great Brittaine, to New-England in the North America.

Anno 1630.

CHRISTIAN CHARITIE

A Modell Hereof

God Almightie in his most holy and wise providence hath soe disposed of the Condicion of mankinde, as in all times some must be rich some poore, some highe and eminent in power and dignitie; others meane[48] and in subjection.

The Reason Hereof

1. *First*, to hold conformity with the rest of his workes, being delighted to shewe forthe the glory of his wisdome in the variety and differance of the Creatures and the glory of his power, in ordering all these differences for the preservacion and good of the whole, and the glory of his greatnes; that as it is the glory of princes to have many officers, soe this great King will have many Stewards counting himselfe more honoured in dispenceing his gifts to man by man, then if hee did it by his owne immediate hand.

2. *Secondly*, That he might have the more occasion to manifest the worke of his Spirit: first, upon the wicked in moderateing and restraineing them: soe that the riche and mighty should not eate upp the poor, nor the poore, and dispised rise upp against theire superiours, and shake off theire yoake; 2ly in the regenerate in exerciseing his graces in them, as in the greate ones, theire love, mercy, gentlenes, temperance etc.; and the poore and inferiour sorte, theire faithe, patience, obedience etc.

3. Thirdly, That every man might have need of others, and from hence they might be all knitt more nearly together in the Bond of brotherly affeccion. From hence it appeares plainely that noe man is made more honourable than another or more wealthy etc., out of any perticuler and singuler respect to himselfe but for the glory of his Creator and the Common good of the Creature, Man. Therefore God still reserves the property of these gifts to himselfe as Ezek: 16. 17. he there calls wealthe his gold and his silver etc. Prov: 3. 9. he claims theire service as his due; honour the Lord with thy riches etc. All men being thus (by divine providence) rancked into two sortes, riche, and poore; under the first, are comprehended all such as are able to live comfortably by theire owne meanes duely improved; and all others are poore according to the former distribution. . . .

This Lawe of the Gospell propoundes likewise a difference of seasons and occasions. There is a time when a christian must sell all and give to the poore as they did in the Apostles times. There is a tyme allsoe when a christian (though they give not all yet) must give beyond theire abillity, as they of Macedonia. Cor: 2. 6. Likewise, community of perills calls for extraordinary liberallity and soe doth Community in some speciall service for the Churche. Lastly, when there is noe other meanes whereby

---

48. meane: lowly.

our Christian brother may be releived in this distresse, wee must help him beyond our ability, rather then tempt God, in putting him upon help by miraculous or extraordinary meanes.

This duty of mercy is exercised in the kindes, Giveing, lending, and forgiveing.

QUEST. What rule shall a man observe in giveing in respect of the measure?[49]

ANS. If the time and occasion be ordinary he is to give out of his aboundance—let him lay aside, as god hath blessed him. If the time and occasion be extraordinary he must be ruled by them; taeking this withall, that then a man cannot likely doe too much especially, if he may leave himselfe and his family under probable meanes of comfortable subsistance.

OBJECTION. A man must lay upp for posterity, the fathers lay upp for posterity and children; and he is worse then an Infidell that provideth not for his owne.[50]

ANS. For the first, it is plaine, that it being spoken by way of Comparison it must be meant of the ordinary and usuall course of fathers and cannot extend to times and occasions extraordinary. For the other place the Apostle speakes against such as walked inordinately, and it is without question, that he is worse then an Infidell whoe throughe his owne Sloathe and voluptuousnes shall neglect to provide for his family.

OBJECTION. The wise man's Eyes are in his head (saith Salomon)[51] and foreseeth the plague; therefore wee must forecast and lay upp against evill times when hee or his may stand in need of all he can gather.

ANS. This very Argument Salomon useth to perswade to liberallity. Eccle: [11.1] cast thy bread upon the waters etc.: for thou knowest not what evill may come upon the land Luke 16. make you freinds of the riches of Iniquity; you will aske how this shall be? Very well. For first he that gives to the poore lends to the lord, and he will repay him even in this life an hundred fold to him or his. The righteous is ever mercifull and lendeth and his seed enjoyeth the blessing. And besides, wee know what advantage it will be to us in the day of account, when many such Witnesses shall stand forthe for us to witnesse the improvement of our Tallent. And I would knowe of those whoe pleade soe much for layeing up for time to come, whether they hold that to be Gospell Math: 16. 19. Lay not upp for yourselves Treasures upon Earth etc. . . .

The lord lookes that when hee is pleased to call for his right in any thing wee have, our owne Interest wee have must stand aside, till his turne be served. For the other, wee need looke noe further then to that of John I: he whoe hath this worlds goodes and seeth his brother to neede, and shutts upp his Compassion from him, how dwelleth the love of god in him? Which comes punctually to this Conclusion: if thy brother be in want and thou canst help him, thou needst not make doubt what thou shouldst doe: if thou lovest god thou must help him.

QUEST. What rule must wee observe in lending?

ANS. Thou must observe whether thy brother hath present or probable, or possible meanes of repayeing thee, if ther be none of these, thou must give him according to his necessity, rather then lend him as hee requires. If he hath present meanes of repayeing thee, thou art to looke at him, not as an Act of mercy, but by way of Commerce,

---

49. i.e., how much shall a man give?
50. I Tim. 5:8.

51. Eccles. 2:14.

wherein thou arte to walke by the rule of Justice. But, if his meanes of repayeing thee be onely probable or possible, then is hee an object of thy mercy; thou must lend him, though there be danger of looseing it Deut: 15. 7. If any of thy brethren be poore etc. thou shalt lend him sufficient. That men might not shift off this duty by the apparant hazzard, he tells them that though the Yeare of Jubile were at hand (when he must remitt it, if hee were not able to repay it before) yet he must lend him and that chearefully.[52] It may not greive thee to give him (saith hee) and because some might object, "Why soe I should soone impoverishe my selfe and my family," he adds: with all thy Worke etc. for our Saviour Math: 5. 42. From him that would borrow of thee turne not away.

QUEST. What rule must wee observe in forgiving?

ANS. Whether thou didst lend by way of Commerce or in mercy, if he have noething to pay thee [thou] must forgive him (except in cause where thou hast a surety or a lawfull pleadge) Deut. 15. 2. Every seaventh yeare the Creditor was to quitt that which hee lent to his brother if hee were poore, as appeares verse 4: save when there shall be noe poore with thee.

In all these and like Cases Christ was a generall rule Math: 7.22. Whatsoever ye would that men should doe to you doe yee the same to them allsoe.

QUEST. What rule must wee observe and walke by in cause of Community of perill?

ANS. The same as before, but with more enlargement towards others and lesse respect towards our selves, and our owne right. Hence it was that in the primitive Churche they sold all, [and] had all things in Common. Neither did any man say that that which he possessed was his owne. Likewise in theire returne out of the Captivity, because the worke was greate for the restoreing of the church and the danger of enemies was Common to all, Nehemiah exhortes the Jewes to liberallity and readines in remitting theire debtes to theire brethren, and disposeth liberally of his owne to such as wanted, and stands not upon his owne due, which hee might have demaunded of them. Thus did some of our forefathers in times of persecucion here in England. And soe did many of the faithfull in other Churches, whereof wee keepe an honourable remembrance of them. And it is to be observed that both in Scriptures and latter stories of the Churches, that such as have beene most bountifull to the poore Saintes, especially in these extraordinary times and occasions, god hath left them highly Commended to posterity: as Zacheus, Cornelius, Dorcas, Bishop Hooper, the Cuttler of Brussells and divers others. Observe againe that the scripture gives noe caution to restraine any from being over liberall this way; but all men to the liberall and cherefull practise hereof by the sweetest promises as to instance one for many, Isaiah 58. 6. . . .

Haveing allready sett forth the practise of mercy according to the rule of gods lawe, it will be usefull to lay open the groundes of it allsoe being the other parte of the Commaundement; and that is, the affeccion from which this exercise of mercy must arise. The Apostle tells us that this love is the fullfilling of the law; not that it is enough to love our brother and soe noe further, but in regard of the excellency of his

---

52. Deut. 15:7–11; Lev. 25:35–42.

partes gieveing any motion to the other, as the Soule to the body, and the power it hath
to sett all the faculties on worke in the outward exercise of this duty. As when wee bid
one make the clocke strike, he doth not lay hand on the hammer, which is the immediate instrument of the sound, but setts on worke the first mover or maine wheele,
knoweing that will certainely produce the sound which hee intends; soe the way to
drawe men to the workes of mercy is not by force of Argument from the goodnes or
necessity of the worke. For though this course may enforce a rationall minde to some
present Act of mercy, as is frequent in experience, yet it cannot worke such a habit in
a Soule as shall make it prompt upon all occasions to produce the same effect, but by
frameing these affeccions of love in the hearte, which will as natively bring forthe the
other, as any cause doth produce the effect.

The diffinition which the Scripture gives us of love is this: Love is the bond of
perfection.[53] First, it is a bond, or ligament. 2ly, it makes the worke perfect. There is
noe body but consistes of partes and that which knitts these partes together gives the
body its perfeccion, because it makes eache parte soe contiguous to others as thereby
they doe mutually participate with eache other, both in strengthe and infirmity, in
pleasure and pain. To instance in the most perfect of all bodies, Christ and his church
make one body. The severall partes of this body, considered aparte before they were
united, were as disproportionate and as much disordering as soe many contrary qual-
lities or elements. But when christ comes and by his spirit and love knitts all these
partes to himselfe and each to others, it is become the most perfect and best proportioned body in the world Eph: 4. 16. . . .

The next consideracion is how this love comes to be wrought. Adam in his first
estate was a perfect modell of mankinde in all theire generacions, and in him his love
was perfected in regard of the habit. But Adam Rent in himselfe from his Creator, and
rent all his posterity allsoe one from another. Whence it comes that every man is borne
with this principle in him, to love and seeke himselfe only. And thus a man continueth
till Christ comes and takes possession of the soule, and infuseth another principle: love
to God and our brother. And this latter haveing continuall supply from Christ, as the
head and roote by which hee is united get the predominency in the soule, soe by little
and little expells the former I John 4. 7. Love cometh of god and every one that loveth
is borne of god, soe that this love is the fruite of the new birthe, and none can have it
but the new Creature. Now when this quallity is thus formed in the soules of men, it
workes like the Spirit upon the drie bones Ezek. 37. bone came to bone. It gathers
together the scattered bones or perfect old man Adam, and knitts them into one body
againe in Christ, whereby a man is become againe a liveing soule.

The third Consideracion is concerning the exercise of this love, which is twofold,
inward or outward. The outward hath beene handled in the former preface of this
discourse. For unfolding the other, wee must take in our way that maxime of philosophy: Simile simili gaudet or like will to like. For as it is things which are carved[54] with
disafeccion to eache other, the ground of it is from a dissimilitude or [*blank*] arising
from the contrary or different nature of the things themselves. Soe the ground of love is

53. Col. 3:14.

54. carved: evidently a copyist's mistake. Some editors suggest "turned."

an apprehension of some resemblance in the things loved to that which affects it. This is the cause why the Lord loves the Creature, soe farre as it hath any of his Image in it. He loves his elect because they are like himselfe. He beholds them in his beloved sonne. Soe a mother loves her childe, because shee thoroughly conceives a resemblance of herselfe in it. Thus it is betweene the members of Christ; each discerns by the worke of the spirit his owne Image and resemblance in another, and therefore cannot but love him as he loves himselfe. Now when the soule, which is of a sociable nature, findes any thing like to it selfe, it is like Adam when Eve was brought to him; shee[55] must have it one with herselfe. This is fleshe of my fleshe (saith shee), and bone of my bone. Shee conceives a greate delighte in it, therefore shee desires nearenes and familiarity with it. She hath a greate propensity to doe it good and receives such content in it, as feareing the miscarriage of her beloved shee bestowes it in the inmost closett of her heart. Shee will not endure that it shall want any good which shee can give it. If by occasion shee be withdrawne from the Company of it, shee is still lookeing towardes the place where shee left her beloved. If shee heare it groane shee is with it presently. If shee finde it sadd and disconsolate shee sighes and mournes with it. Shee hath noe such joy, as to see her beloved merry and thriveing. If shee see it wronged, shee cannot beare it without passion. Shee setts noe boundes of her affeccions, nor hath any thought of reward. Shee findes recompence enoughe in the exercise of her love towardes it.

Wee may see this Acted to life in Jonathan and David. Jonathan, a valiant man endued with the spirit of Christ, soe soone as hee Discovers the same spirit in David had presently his hearte knitt to him by this linement of love, soe that it is said he loved him as his owne soule. He takes soe great pleasure in him that hee stripps himselfe to adorne his beloved. His father's kingdome was not soe precious to him as his beloved David. David shall have it with all his hearte. Himselfe desires noe more but that hee may be neare to him to rejoyce in his good. Hee chooseth to converse with him in the wildernesse, even to the hazzard of his owne life, rather then with the greate Courtiers in his fathers Pallace. When hee sees danger towards him, hee spares neither care, paines, nor perill to divert it. When Injury was offered his beloved David, hee could not beare it, though from his owne father. And when they must parte for a Season onely, they thought theire heartes would have broake for sorrowe, had not theire affections found vent by aboundance of Teares.

Other instances might be brought to shewe the nature of this affeccion, as of Ruthe and Naomi and many others, but this truthe is cleared enough. If any shall object that it is not possible that love should be bred or upheld without hope of requitall, it is graunted. But that is not our cause. For this love is allwayes under reward. It never gives, but it allwayes receives with advantage. First, in regard that among the members of the same body, love and affection are reciprocall in a most equall and sweete kinde of Commerce. 2ly, in regard of the pleasure and content that the exercise of love carries with it as wee may see in the naturall body. The mouth is at all the paines to receive, and mince the foode which serves for the nourishment of all the other partes of the body. Yet it hath noe cause to complaine. For first, the other partes

---

55. shee: i.e., the soul.

send backe by secret passages a due proporcion of the same nourishment in a better forme for the strengthening and comforteing the mouthe. 2ly the labour of the mouthe is accompanied with such pleasure and content as farre exceedes the paines it takes. Soe is it in all the labour of love. Among christians, the partie loveing, reapes love againe as was shewed before, which the soule covetts more then all the wealthe in the world. Noething yeildes more pleasure and content to the soule then when it findes that which it may love fervently. For to love and live beloved is the soule's paradice, both heare and in heaven. In the State of Wedlock there be many comfortes to beare out the troubles of that Condicion. But let such as have tryed the most, say if there be any sweetnes in that Condicion comparable to the exercise of mutuall love.

From the former Considerations ariseth these Conclusions.

First, This love among Christians is a reall thing, not Imaginarie.

2ly. This love is as absolutely necessary to the being of the body of Christ, as the sinewes and other ligaments of a naturall body are to the being of that body.

3ly. This love is a divine spirituall nature—free, active, strong, Couragious, permanent, under valueing all things beneathe its propper object. And of all the graces this makes us nearer to resemble the virtues of our heavenly father.

4ly, It restes in the love and wellfare of its beloved, for the full and certaine knowledge of these truthes concerning the nature, use, [and] excellency of this grace. That which the holy ghost hath left recorded I. Cor. 13. may give full satisfaccion which is needfull for every true member of this lovely body of the Lord Jesus to worke upon theire heartes, by prayer, meditacion, continuall exercise at least of the speciall [power] of this grace till Christ be formed in them and they in him, all in eache other knitt together by this bond of love.

It rests now to make some application of this discourse by the present designe which gave the occasion of writeing of it. Herein are 4 things to be propounded: first the persons, 2ly, the worke, 3ly, the end, 4ly the meanes.

1. For the persons, wee are a Company professing our selves fellow members of Christ. In which respect onely, though wee were absent from eache other many miles, and had our imploymentes as farre distant, yet wee ought to account our selves knitt together by this bond of love, and live in the excercise of it, if wee would have comforte of our being in Christ. This was notorious in the practise of the Christians in former times, as is testified of the Waldenses from the mouth of one of the adversaries, Aeneas Sylvius: mutuo [solent amare] pene antequam norint; they use to love any of theire owne religion even before they were acquainted with them.

2ly. for the worke wee have in hand, it is by a mutuall consent through a speciall overruleing providence, and a more then an ordinary approbation of the Churches of Christ, to seeke out a place of Cohabitation and Consorteshipp under a due forme of Government both civill and ecclesiasticall. In such cases as this the care of the publique must oversway all private respects, by which not onely conscience, but meare Civill pollicy doth binde us. For it is a true rule that perticuler estates cannott subsist in the ruine of the publique.

3ly. The end is to improve our lives to doe more service to the Lord, to the comforte and encrease of the body of christe, whereof wee are members, that our selves and posterity may be the better preserved from the Common corrupcions of this evill world; to serve the Lord and worke out our Salvacion under the power and purity of his holy Ordinances.

4ly for the meanes whereby this must bee effected, they are 2fold, a Conformity with the worke and end wee aime at. These wee see are extraordinary. Therefore wee must not content our selves with usuall ordinary meanes. Whatsoever wee did or ought to have done when wee lived in England, the same must wee doe and more allsoe where wee goe. That which the most in theire Churches maineteine as a truthe in profession onely, wee must bring into familiar and constant practise, as in this duty of love wee must love brotherly without dissimulation. Wee must love one another with a pure hearte fervently. Wee must beare one anothers burthens. Wee must not looke onely on our owne things, but allsoe on the things of our brethren. Neither must wee think that the lord will beare with such faileings at our hands as hee dothe from those among whome wee have lived, and that for 3 Reasons.

1. In regard of the more neare bond of mariage, betweene him and us, wherein he hath taken us to be his after a most strickt and peculiar manner, which will make him the more Jealous of our love and obedience, soe he tells the people of Israell: you onely have I knowne of all the families of the Earthe, therefore will I punishe you for your Transgressions.

2ly, because the lord will be sanctified in them that come neare him. Wee know that there were many that corrupted the service of the Lord, some setting upp Alters before his owne, others offering both strange fire and strange Sacrifices allsoe. Yet there came noe fire from heaven, or other sudden Judgement upon them as did upon Nadab and Abihu, whoe yet wee may thinke did not sinne presumptously.

3ly When God gives a speciall Commission he lookes to have it stricktly observed in every Article. When hee gave Saule a Commission to destroy Amaleck, hee indented with him upon certaine Articles; and because hee failed in one of the least, and that upon a faire pretence, it lost him the kingdome, which should have been his reward, if hee had observed his Commission. Thus stands the cause between God and us: wee are entered into Covenant with him for this worke. Wee have taken out a Commission. The Lord hath given us leave to drawe our owne Articles. We have professed to enterprise these Accions upon these and these ends. Wee have hereupon besought him of favour and blessing. Now if the Lord shall please to heare us, and bring us in peace to the place wee desire, then hath hee ratified this Covenant and sealed our Commission, [and] will expect a strickt performance of the Articles contained in it. But if wee shall neglect the observacion of these Articles, which are the ends wee have propounded; and, dissembling with our God, shall fall to embrace this present world and prosecute our carnall intencions, seekeing great things for our selves and our posterity, the Lord will surely breake out in wrathe against us, be revenged of such a perjured people and make us knowe the price of the breache of such a Covenant.

Now the onely way to avoyde this shipwracke and to provide for our posterity is to followe the Counsell of Micah, to doe Justly, to love mercy, to walke humbly with our God. For this end, wee must be knitt together in this worke as one man. Wee must entertaine each other in brotherly Affeccion. Wee must be willing to abridge our selves of our superfluities, for the supply of others necessities. Wee must uphold a familiar Commerce together in all meekenes, gentlenes, patience and liberallity. Wee must delight in eache other, make others' Condicions our owne, rejoyce together, mourne together, labour, and suffer together, allwayes haveing before our eyes our Commission and Community in the worke, our Community as members of the same body. Soe shall wee keepe the unitie of the spirit in the bond of peace. The Lord will be our God and delight to dwell among us, as his owne people, and will commaund a blessing upon us in all our wayes, soe that wee shall see much more of his wisdome, power, goodnes, and truthe then formerly wee have beene acquainted with. Wee shall finde that the God of Israell is among us, when tenn of us shall be able to resist a thousand of our enemies, when hee shall make us a prayse and glory, that men shall say of succeeding plantacions: the lord make it like that of New England. For wee must Consider that wee shall be as a Citty upon a Hill. The eyes of all people are uppon vs; soe that if wee shall deale falsely with our god in this worke wee have undertaken, and soe cause him to withdrawe his present help from us, wee shall be made a story and a by-word through the world. Wee shall open the mouthes of enemies to speake evill of the wayes of god and all professours for Gods sake. Wee shall shame the faces of many of gods worthy servants, and cause theire prayers to be turned into Cursses upon us till wee be consumed out of the good land whether wee are goeing. And to shutt upp this discourse with that exhortacion of Moses, that faith-full servant of the Lord, in his last farewell to Israell, Deut. 30. Beloved, there is now sett before us life, and good, deathe and evill in that wee are Commaunded this day to love the Lord our God, and to love one another to walke in his wayes and to keepe his Commaundements and his Ordinance, and his lawes, and the Articles of our Covenant with him, that wee may live and be multiplyed, and that the Lord our God may blesse us in the land whither wee goe to possesse it. But if our heartes shall turne away soe that we will not obey, but shall be seduced and worshipp other Gods, our pleasures, and proffitts, and serve them; it is propounded unto us this day, wee shall surely perishe out of the good Land whither wee passe over this vast Sea to possesse it.

Therefore lett us choose life,
that wee, and our Seede,
may live; by obeyeing his
voyce, and cleaveing to him,
for hee is our life, and
our prosperity.

10. John Cotton

from *Gods Promise to His Plantations* 1630

Among the English Puritan clergy behind the migration to Massachusetts, none had more influence than John Cotton (1584-1652). Cotton himself did not leave England until 1633, but his farewell sermon to Winthrop's group offers a concise summary of the Massachusetts Puritans' sense of mission. Cotton's defensiveness about Indian rights shows that a criticism of colonial ventures was already implicitly felt, and was probably made vocally in a way that required explicit response.

Once established across the Atlantic, Cotton would become a central figure in the antinomian controversy (see chapter 6). He later became embroiled in a pamphlet war with Roger Williams over religious toleration, an idea he opposed as heretical. He wrote important defenses of the New England experiment during the English civil wars: The Way of the Churches of Christ in New England *(1645) and* The Way of the Congregational Churches Cleared *(1648).*

2 SAM. 7:10: *Moreover I will appoint a place for my people Israell, and I will plant them, that they may dwell in a place of their owne, and move no more.*

Now God makes room for a people 3 wayes:

First, when he casts out the enemies of a people before them by lawfull warre with the inhabitants, which God cals them unto: as in *Ps.* 44:2, *Thou didst drive out the heathen before them.* But this course of warring against others, & driving them out without provocation, depends upon speciall Commission from God, or else it is not imitable.

Secondly, when he gives a forreigne people favour in the eyes of any native people to come and sit downe with them either by way of purchase, as *Abraham* did obtaine the field of *Machpelah*; or else when they give it in courtesie, as *Pharaoh* did the land of *Goshen* unto the sons of *Jacob.*

Thirdly, when hee makes a Countrey though not altogether void of inhabitants, yet voyd in that place where they reside. Where there is a vacant place, there is liberty for the sonne of *Adam* or *Noah* to come and inhabite, though they neither buy it, nor aske their leaves. *Abraham* and *Isaac*, when they sojourned amongst the Philistines, they did not buy that land to feede their cattle, because they said There is roome enough. And so did *Jacob* pitch his Tent by *Sechem*, *Gen.* 34:21. There was *roome enough* as *Hamor* said, *Let them sit down amongst us.* And in this case if the people who were former inhabitants did disturbe them in their possessions, they complained to the King, as of wrong done unto them: As *Abraham* did because they took away his well, in *Gen.* 21:25. For his right whereto he pleaded not his immediate calling from God, (for that would have seemed frivolous amongst the Heathen) but his owne industry and culture in digging the well, verse 30. Nor doth the King reject his plea, with what had he to doe to digge wells in their soyle? but admitteth it as a Principle in Nature, That in a vacant soyle, hee that taketh possession of it, and bestoweth culture and husbandry upon it, his Right it is. And the ground of this is from the grand Charter given to *Adam* and his posterity in Paradise, *Gen* 1:28. *Multiply, and replenish the earth, and subdue it.* If therefore any sonne of Adam come and finde a place empty, he hath liberty to come, and fill, and subdue the earth there. This Charter was renewed to *Noah, Gen.* 9:1. *Fulfill the earth and multiply*: So that it is free from that comon Grant for any to take possession of vacant Countries. Indeed no Nation is to drive out another without speciall Commission from heaven, such as the Israelites had, unless the Natives do unjustly wrong them, and will not recompense the wrongs done in peacable sort, & then they may right themselves by lawfull war, and subdue the Countrey unto themselves.

11. Sir Henry Colt

journal of a voyage to the West Indies 1631

Although the West Indies, like New England, was the site of Puritan settlements, it had also been the favorite destination of more adventurous Englishmen since the Elizabethan period. In the seventeenth century the West Indian colonies saw the most spectacular growth and economic success in all of English America, despite frequent raids and wars with the French, Spanish, Portuguese, Dutch, and Indians. Sir Henry Colt, a member of the Essex gentry, led a well-funded expedition in 1631 to set up a plantation on St. Christopher's, commonly known as St. Kitts. He kept a journal for the benefit of his son, describing the voyage and the islands along the way. Little else is known of his fate; by 1635 he was reported dead.

[FINDING BARBADOS]

Tuesday the 28th of June brings us into the height of all our Journey; that is, into the latitude of 13 degrees and a half, 12 minutes. And now we equall the Barbados bearing just west upon us. But the longitude is now harder to find. It is easy to know when our body is even agaynst a house or a tree, but how many paces exactly we have thither is hard to tell. But sure we are it should be the first land we shall discover since our setting forth out of England if we finde it at all. This land is low, hard to find, and stands alone. The last year's example of the many ships that missed it do well declare the difficulty thereof. The Barbados may well admit of this simile: to be like sixpence throwne downe upon Newmarkett Heath. And you should command such a one to go and finde it out; for it lies due west from such a place 13 miles. Happy would your messenger be thought, if upon the full career of a horse he comes just to the place assigned him, and there to find it out.

[BARBADOS]

First you have such abundance of small gnats by the seashore, towards the sunn going downe, that bite so as no rest can be had without fires under your Hamaccas. You have also multitude of little black Aunts that hang in clusters about trees. You have seldome any rain, but 6 months in the year. We arrived in your winter months, the sun being far removed from you into the Tropick of Cancer North. Your daily showres of raine, windes, and cloudy, sultry heat, declares it was the worst time of all the year. But St. Christopher's little differs from you, but only the daily and violent storms is there more frequent.

You are all young men, and of good desert, if you would but bridle the excess of drinkinge, together with the quarrelsome conditions of your fiery spirits. You are devourers up of hot waters, and such good distillers thereof, that I am persuaded a ship of good burthen, laden therewith, could not returne from you but in stead of hot water you would freight it with cold. I, in the Imitation of this bad example of yours, and for your societye, was brought from 2 drams of hot water a meal, to 30. And in few days if I had continued this acquaintance, I do believe I should have been brought to the increase of 60.

But the worst of all was your manifold quarrells. Your young and hot bloods, should not have oil added to increase the flame, but rather cold water to quench it. As your quarrells have slight beginnings, so are they without much difficulty soon ended, but only to the trouble of your governour,[56] who, being but a young man, I have often wondered by myself alone, that he is not corrupted by you; but certainly he is naturally inclined to modesty and temperance. For in a few dayes you corrupted me, that have seen more, and lived many more years to be more wise and temperate.

Your servants also you keep too Idly; they continually pestered our ship without any occasion or acquaintance, lingering sometimes 24 hours with us, although no man spoke to them, to avoid labour, which I am persuaded few of you look after. For let us come to your plantations. Behold the order of them; first, in 10 days travail about them, I never saw any man at work. Your ground and plantations shows what you are; they lie like the ruins of some village lately burned—here a great timber tree half burned, in another place a rafter singed all black. There stands a stub of a tree above two yards high, all the earth covered black with cinders; nothing is clear. What [has been] digged or weeded for beautye? All are bushes, and long grasse, all thinges carrying the face of a desolate and disorderly show to the beholder.

56. governor: Henry Hawley.

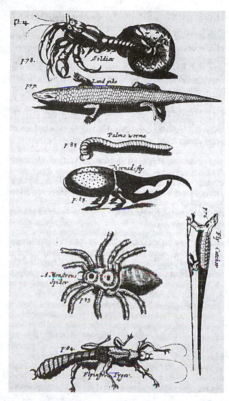

Creatures of the West Indies, 1666.

But you are all beholding to your climate, more than to your soile or Industry. For your soile, that is naught; nothing else but loose sand. Your ground which you esteem the best is but the leaves and ashes of your trees. Dig but half a foot deep and there will be found nothing else but Clay. Your water is thick and not of the best. Your under woods are not hard to be cleared, your great trees not many; but your rivers few or none, except such as you account out of vaine glory rivers, being no other than little pits; or if it holds water but for a small time it is named a river.

Yet for all this let no man Condemn you and yours. You might be all so happy, for you are able if you will to aide and help all others. Now, do but consider what you are owners of. Your aire and soile produceth with a mavelous swiftnesse. What can either the earth or sea afford that the meanest[57] man of you all might not have in abundance?

[SETTLING ST. CHRISTOPHER'S]

Tuesday 26 July towards night brings me ashore with all my Companye. We supped by moonlight upon a chest and lodged in our tent, placing out 2 Centinells for our guard to watch one hour and then to be relieved by two more. I was not used to lodge on land. The squeaking of lisards, and other thinges whose names I know not, made me take small rest, and also the rats come at first to visit us.

Wednesday 27 July. The next court of guard from the old fort early in the morninge comes to salute me with a volley of shot for my welcome, and now I must give over writing and drinke with them.

But now comes one of the greatest labours and cares; that is, for the sudden building of a house. Although I have chosen a situation between two rivers, for water is to be prized above anything else, yet was the place wonderfully discommodious. For timber we find not any; palmeto leaves for covering harder to be found; so that all things must be transported upon the shoulders of men, the way from the sea half a mile all uphill, the ground hard to clear. The first thing we Employ is the Axe, an Instrument that must set all others to work. It is worthy of Consideration what a

57. meanest: lowliest.

small, unthought of want [can] drive us to, where we cannot borrow. We had forgot to bring a helve out of England, the want of which kept us all Idle half a day. We must saw a helve, rive it, cut it, plane it. The wood we must cut down is the prickly tree, hard and tough. This being done, we come to the wood that we must deal with. The trees are but small, some hard some soft, but the withes of a nut that is green and round, as big as a warden, carrying a soft shell like a Chestnutt and 3 kernells in every nutt, reasonably good in taste; [they] give us the greatest Impediments; for the withes of these run up to the tops of trees and then down to the bottom, running about like ropes, so entangling the trees the one with the other, as we could not divide them without cutting down 4 or 5 together. We were also seated amongst plantaines and sugar canes that grow like reeds or canes in the ponds of England, very sweet in taste, but unwholesome. Also there was planted Anotto, a low tree with a cod which opens, and little small red berries appear wherewith the Indians colour themselves. This was anciently a plantation of the Indians, but now all overgrowne.

But I will leave my building until it comes to greater perfection, for stay I must at St. Christopher's all this winter until our ship return, and a pinnace is bought, that we might proceed to greater exploits. For rest we will not, until we have done some things worthy of ourselves, or die in the attempt thereof.

12.   William Wood

from *New England's Prospect* 1634

> *William Wood left England for Massachusetts, probably in 1629, when Salem was being settled. He was back in England by 1633, publishing* New England's Prospect *the following year. Almost nothing else is known about him. His book is one of the best early eyewitness accounts of the English American colonies—readable and informative. The first half describes the land and the settlements. The second half is devoted to ethnography, and although it contains some inaccuracies its descriptions of Indian life are more detailed than those of most of Wood's English contemporaries.*

OF THEIR WOMEN, THEIR DISPOSITIONS, EMPLOYMENTS, USAGE BY THEIR HUSBANDS, THEIR APPAREL, AND MODESTY.

To satisfy the curious eye of women readers, who otherwise might think their sex forgotten or not worthy a record, let them peruse these few lines wherein they may see their own happiness, if weighed in the woman's balance of these ruder Indians who scorn the tutorings of their wives or to admit them as their equals—though their qualities and industrious deservings may justly claim the preeminence and command better usage and more conjugal esteem, their persons and features being every way correspondent, their qualifications more excellent, being more loving, pitiful, and modest, mild, provident, and laborious than their lazy husbands.

Their employments be many: first their building of houses, whose frames are formed like our garden arbors, something more round, very strong and handsome, covered with close-wrought mats of their own weaving which deny entrance to any drop of rain, though it come both fierce and long, neither can the piercing north wind find a cranny through which he can convey his cooling breath. They be warmer than our English houses. At the top is a square hole for the smoke's evacuation, which in rainy weather is covered with a pluver.[58] These be such smoky dwellings that when there is good fires they are not able to stand upright, but lie all along under the smoke, never using any stools or chairs, it being as rare to see an Indian sit on a stool at home as it is strange to see an Englishman sit on his heels abroad. Their houses are smaller in the summer when their families be dispersed by reason of heat and occasions. In winter they make some fifty or threescore foot long, forty or fifty men being inmates under one roof. And as is their husbands' occasion, these poor tectonists[59] are often troubled like snails to carry their houses on their backs, sometime to fishing places, other times to hunting places, after that to a planting place where it abides the longest.

Another work is their planting of corn, wherein they exceed our English husbandmen, keeping it so clear with their clamshell hoes as if it were a garden rather than a corn field, not suffering a choking weed to advance his audacious head above their infant corn or an undermining worm to spoil his spurns. Their corn being ripe they gather it, and drying it hard in the sun convey it to their barns, which be great holes digged in the ground in form of a brass pot, sealed with rinds of trees, wherein they put their corn, covering it from the inquisitive search of their gourmandizing husbands who would eat up both their allowed portion and reserved seed if they knew where to find it. But our hogs having found a way to unhinge their barn doors and rob their garners, they are glad to implore their husbands' help to roll the bodies of trees over their holes to prevent those pioneers whose thievery they as much hate as their flesh.

Another of their employments is their summer processions to get lobsters for their husbands, wherewith they bait their hooks when they go afishing for bass or codfish. This is an everyday's walk, be the weather cold or hot, the waters rough or calm. They must dive sometimes over head and ears for a lobster, which often shakes them by their hands with a churlish nip and bids them adieu. The tide being spent, they trudge home two or three miles with a hundredweight of lobsters at their backs, and if none, a hundred scowls meet them at home and a hungry belly for two days after. Their husbands having caught any fish, they bring it in their boats as far as they can by water and there leave it; as it was their care to catch it, so it must be their wives' pains to fetch it home, or fast. Which done, they must dress it and cook it, dish it, and present it, see it eaten over their shoulders; and their loggerships[60] having filled their paunches, their sweet lullabies scramble for their scraps. In the summer these Indian women, when lobsters be in their plenty and prime, they dry them to keep for winter, erecting

---

58. pluver: rain cover.
59. tectonists: builders; here, the women.

60. loggerships: a play on lordships and loggerheads.

scaffolds in the hot sun-shine, making fires likewise underneath them (by whose smoke the flies are expelled) till the substance remain hard and dry. In this manner they dry bass and other fishes without salt, cutting them very thin to dry suddenly before the flies spoil them or the rain moist them, having a special care to hang them in their smoky houses in the night and dankish weather.

In summer they gather flags,[61] of which they make mats for houses, and hemp and rushes, with dyeing stuff of which they make curious baskets with inter-mixed colors and protrac-tures[62] of antic imagery. These baskets be of all sizes from a quart to a quarter,[63] in which they carry their luggage. In winter they are their husband's caterers, trudging to the clam banks for their belly timber, and their porters to lug home

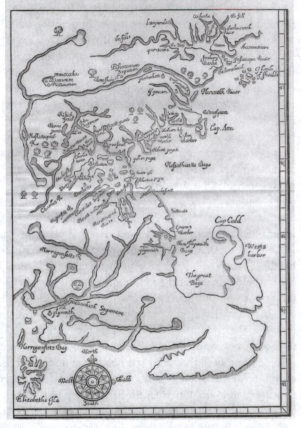

The South part of New-England, as it is Planted this yeare, 1634.

From William Wood, New England's Prospect, 1634.

their venison which their laziness exposes to the wolves till they impose it upon their wives' shoulders. They likewise sew their husbands' shoes and weave coats of turkey feathers, besides all their ordinary household drudgery which daily lies upon them, so that a big belly hinders no business, nor a childbirth takes much time, but the young infant being greased and sooted, wrapped in a beaver skin, bound to his good behavior with his feet up to his bum upon a board two foot long and one foot broad, his face exposed to all nipping weather, this little papoose travels about with his bare-footed mother to paddle in the icy clam banks after three or four days of age have sealed his passboard[64] and his mother's recovery.

For their carriage it is very civil, smiles being the greatest grace of their mirth; their music is lullabies to quiet their children, who generally are as quiet as if they had

61. flags: reeds.
62. protractures: designs.

63. quarter: eight bushels.
64. passboard: a play on board and passport.

neither spleen or lungs. To hear one of these Indians unseen, a good ear might easily mistake their untaught voice for the warbling of a well-tuned instrument, such command have they of their voices.

These women's modesty drives them to wear more clothes than their men, having always a coat of cloth or skins wrapped like a blanket about their loins, reaching down to their hams, which they never put off in company. If a husband have a mind to sell his wife's beaver petticoat, as sometimes he doth, she will not put it off until she have another to put on. Commendable is their mild carriage and obedience to their husbands, notwithstanding all this—their [husbands'] customary churlishness and savage inhumanity—not seeming to delight in frowns or offering to word it with their lords, not presuming to proclaim their female superiority to the usurping of the least title of their husbands' charter, but rest themselves content under their helpless condition, counting it the woman's portion.

Since the English arrival, comparison hath made them miserable, for seeing the kind usage of the English to their wives, they do as much condemn their husbands for unkindness and commend the English for their love, as their husbands—commending themselves for their wit in keeping their wives industrious—do condemn the English for their folly in spoiling good working creatures. These women resort often to the English houses, where *pares cum paribus congregatae*,[65] in sex I mean, they do somewhat ease their misery by complaining and seldom part without a relief. If her husband come to seek for his squaw and begin to bluster, the English woman betakes her to her arms, which are the warlike ladle and the scalding liquors, threatening blistering to the naked runaway, who is soon expelled by such liquid comminations.[66]

In a word, to conclude this woman's history, their love to the English hath deserved no small esteem, ever presenting them something that is either rare or desired, as strawberries, hurtleberries, raspberries, gooseberries, cherries, plums, fish, and other such gifts as their poor treasury yields them. But now it may be that this relation of the churlish and inhumane behavior of these ruder Indians towards their patient wives may confirm some in the belief of an aspersion which I have often heard men cast upon the English there, as if they should learn of the Indians to use their wives in the like manner and to bring them to the same subjection—as to sit on the lower hand and to carry water and the like drudgery. But if my own experience may out-balance an ill-grounded scandalous rumor, I do assure you, upon my credit and reputation, that there is no such matter, but the women find there as much love, respect, and ease as here in old England. I will not deny but that some poor people may carry their own water. And do not the poorer sort in England do the same, witness your London tankard bearers and your country cottagers? But this may well be known to be nothing but the rancorous venom of some that bear no good will to the plantation. For what need they carry water, seeing everyone hath a spring at his door or the sea by his house?

Thus much for the satisfaction of women, touching this entrenchment upon their prerogative, as also concerning the relation of these Indian squaws.

---

65. Equals gathered with equals.   66. comminations: threats.

13. Thomas Morton

from *New English Canaan*
1634

Thomas Morton (1579–1647) was a gentleman lawyer before joining Captain Wollaston at the trading settlement named Ma-Re-Mount (present-day Quincy) in 1624. Arrested by Myles Standish of nearby Plymouth in 1628 for selling guns to Indians, Morton was tried by the Plymouth authorities and deported to England. He returned the following year to Ma-Re-Mount, and the maypole episode dates from this second sojourn to New England. The Plymouth Puritans this time burned his house to the ground. On a third trip to New England, Morton fell afoul of Massachusetts before moving on to Maine, where he died in 1647. New English Canaan is, in its very title, a parody of the Puritans, though not of the American colonies. A quirky book, it is especially notable for Morton's restless but sometimes obscure wit, and for his deep identification with London literary culture even on the far outposts of the empire.

OF A GREAT MORTALITY THAT HAPPENED AMONGST THE NATIVES OF NEW ENGLAND, NEERE ABOUT THE TIME THAT THE ENGLISH CAME THERE TO PLANT.

The hand of God fell heavily upon them, with such a mortall stroake that they died on heapes as they lay in their houses. And the living, that were able to shift for themselves, would runne away and let them die, and let there Carkases ly above the ground without buriall. For in a place where many inhabited, there hath been but one left alive to tell what became of the rest. The livinge being (as it seemes) not able to bury the dead, they were left for Crowes, Kites and vermin to prey upon. And the bones and skulls upon the severall places of their habitations made such a spectacle after my comming into those partes, that, as I travailed in that Forrest nere the Massachussets, it seemed to mee a new found Golgatha.

But otherwise, it is the custome of those Indian people to bury their dead ceremoniously and carefully, and then to abandon that place, because they have no desire the place should put them in minde of mortality. And this mortality was not ended when the Brownists[67] of new Plimmouth were setled at Patuxet in New England: and by all likelyhood the sicknesse that these Indians died of was the Plague, as by conference with them since my arrivall and habitation in those partes, I have learned. And by this

---

67. Brownists: a derisory name for the Puritan sect that settled Plymouth.

meanes there is as yet but a small number of Salvages in New England, to that which hath beene in former time, and the place is made so much the more fitt for the English Nation to inhabit in, and erect in it Temples to the glory of God.

OF THEIR CUSTOME IN BURNING THE COUNTRY, AND THE REASON THEREOF.

The Salvages are accustomed to set fire of the Country in all places where they come, and to burne it twize a yeare, viz: at the Spring, and the fall of the leafe. The reason that mooves them to doe so, is because it would other wise be so overgrowne with underweedes that it would be all a coppice wood, and the people would not be able in any wise to passe through the Country out of a beaten path.

The meanes that they do it with, is with certaine minerall stones, that they carry about them in baggs made for that purpose of the skinnes of little beastes, which they convert into good lether, carrying in the same a peece of touch wood, very excellent for that purpose, of their owne making. These minerall stones they have from the Piquenteenes, (which is to the Southward of all the plantations in New England,) by trade and trafficke with those people.

The burning of the grasse destroyes the underwoods, and so scorcheth the elder trees that it shrinkes them, and hinders their grouth very much. So that hee that will looke to finde large trees and good tymber, must not depend upon the help of a wooden prospect to finde them on the upland ground; but must seeke for them, (as I and others have done,) in the lower grounds, where the grounds are wett, when the Country is fired, by reason of the snow water that remaines there for a time, untill the Sunne by continuance of that hath exhaled the vapoures of the earth, and dried up those places where the fire, (by reason of the moisture,) can have no power to doe them any hurt. And if he would endevoure to finde out any goodly Cedars, hee must not seeke for them on the higher grounds, but make his inquest for them in the vallies, for the Salvages, by this custome of theirs, have spoiled all the rest. For this custome hath bin continued from the beginninge.

And least[68] their firing of the Country in this manner should be an occasion of damnifying us, and indaingering our habitations, wee our selves have used carefully about the same times to observe the winds, and fire the grounds about our owne habitations; to prevent the Dammage that might happen by any neglect thereof, if the fire should come neere those howses in our absence.

For, when the fire is once kindled, it dilates and spreads it selfe as well against, as with the winde; burning continually night and day, untill a shower of raine falls to quench it.

And this custome of firing the Country is the meanes to make it passable; and by that meanes the trees growe here and there as in our parks: and makes the Country very beautifull and commodious.

---

68. least: lest.

That the Salvages live a contended life.

A Gentleman and a traveller, that had bin in the parts of New England for a time, when hee retorned againe, in his discourse of the Country, wondered, (as hee said,) that the natives of the land lived so poorely in so rich a Country, like to our Beggers in England. Surely that Gentleman had not time or leasure whiles hee was there truely to informe himselfe of the state of that Country, and the happy life the Salvages would leade weare they once brought to Christianity.

I must confesse they want the use and benefit of Navigation, (which is the very sinnus of a flourishing Commonwealth,) yet are they supplied with all manner of needefull things for the maintenance of life and lifelyhood. Foode and rayment are the cheife of all that we make true use of; and of these they finde no want, but have, and may have, them in a most plentifull manner.

If our beggers of England should, with so much ease as they, furnish themselves with foode at all seasons, there would not be so many starved in the streets, neither would so many gaoles be stuffed, or gallouses[69] furnished with poore wretches, as I have seene them.

But they of this sort of our owne nation, that are fitt to goe to this Canaan, are not able to transport themselves; and most of them [are] unwilling to goe from the good ale tap, which is the very loadstone of the lande by which our English beggers steere theire Course; it is the Northpole to which the flowre-de-luce[70] of their compasse points. The more is the pitty that the Commonalty of oure Land are of such leaden capacities as to neglect so brave a Country, that doth so plentifully feede manie lusty and brave, able men, women and children, that have not the meanes that a Civilized Nation hath to purchase foode and rayment; which that Country with a little industry will yeeld a man in a very comfortable measure, without overmuch carking.[71]

I cannot deny but a civilized Nation hath the preheminence of an uncivilized, by meanes of those instruments that are found to be common amongst civile people, and the uncivile want the use of, to make themselves masters of those ornaments that make such a glorious shew, that will give a man occasion to cry, *sic transit gloria Mundi*.[72]

Now since it is but foode and rayment that men that live needeth, (though not all alike,) why should not the Natives of New England be sayd to live richly, having no want of either? Cloaths are the badge of sinne; and the more variety of fashions is but the greater abuse of the Creature. The beasts of the forrest there doe serve to furnish them at any time when they please. Fish and flesh they have in greate abundance, which they both roast and boyle.

They are indeed not served in dishes of plate with variety of Sauces to procure appetite; that needs not there. The rarity of the aire, begot by the medicinable quality of the sweete herbes of the Country, always procures good stomakes to the inhabitants.

I must needs commend them in this particular, that, though they buy many commodities of our Nation, yet they keepe but fewe, and those of speciall use.

69. gallouses: gallows.
70. flowre-de-luce: fleur-de-lis, commonly used to mark North on compasses.
71. carking: burden.
72. Thus passes wordly glory.

They love not to bee cumbered with many utensilles, and although every proprietor knowes his owne, yet all things, (so long as they will last), are used in common amongst them: A bisket cake given to one, that one breakes it equally into so many parts as there be persons in his company, and distributes it. Platoes Commonwealth is so much practised by these people.

According to humane reason, guided onely by the light of nature, these people lead the more happy and freer life, being voyde of care, which torments the mindes of so many Christians. They are not delighted in baubles, but in useful things.

Their naturall drinke is of the Cristall fountaine, and this they take up in their hands, by joyning them close together. They take up a great quantity at a time, and drinke at the wrists. It was the sight of such a feate which made Diogenes hurle away his dishe, and, like one that would have this principall confirmed, *Natura paucis contentat,* used a dish no more.

I have observed that they will not be troubled with superfluous commodities. Such things as they finde they are taught by necessity to make use of, they will make choise of, and seeke to purchase with industry. So that, in respect that their life is so voyd of care, and they are so loving also that they make use of those things they enjoy, (the wife onely excepted,) as common goods, and are therein so compassionate that, rather than one should starve through want, they would starve all. Thus doe they passe awaye the time merrily, not regarding our pompe, (which they see dayly before their faces,) but are better content with their owne, which some men esteeme so meanely of.

They may be rather accompted to live richly, wanting nothing that is needefull; and to be commended for leading a contented life, the younger being ruled by the Elder, and the Elder ruled by the Powahs, and the Powahs are ruled by the Devill; and then you may imagin what good rule is like to be amongst them.

OF THE REVELLS OF NEW CANAAN.

The Inhabitants of Pasonagessit, (having translated the name of their habitation from that ancient Salvage name to Ma-re Mount, and being resolved to have the new name confirmed for a memorial to after ages,) did devise amongst themselves to have it performed in a solemne manner, with Revels and merriment after the old English custome; [they] prepared to sett up a Maypole upon the festivall day of Philip and Jacob, and therefore brewed a barrell of excellent beare and provided a case of bottles, to be spent, with other good cheare, for all commers of that day. And because they would have it in a compleat forme, they had prepared a song fitting to the time and present occasion. And upon Mayday they brought the Maypole to the place appointed, with drumes, gunnes, pistols and other fitting instruments, for that purpose; and there erected it with the help of Salvages, that came thether of purpose to see the manner of our Revels. A goodly pine tree of 80 foote longe was reared up, with a peare of buckshorns nayled on somewhat neare unto the top of it: where it stood, as a faire sea marke for directions how to finde out the way to mine Hoste of Ma-re Mount.

And because it should more fully appeare to what end it was placed there, they had a poem in readines made, which was fixed to the Maypole, to shew the new name confirmed upon that plantation; which, although it were made according to the occurrents[73] of the time, it, being Enigmatically composed, pussled the Seperatists[74] most pittifully to expound it, which, (for the better information of the reader,) I have here inserted.

THE POEM.[75]

> Rise Oedipeus, and, if thou canst, unfould
> What meanes Caribdis underneath the mould,
> When Scilla sollitary on the ground
> (Sitting in forme of Niobe,) was found,
> Till Amphitrites Darling did acquaint
> Grim Neptune with the Tenor of her plaint,
> And causd him send forth Triton with the sound
> Of Trumpet lowd, at which the Seas were found
> So full of Protean formes that the bold shore
> Presented Scilla a new parramore
> So stronge as Sampson and so patient
> As Job himselfe, directed thus, by fate,
> To comfort Scilla so unfortunate.
> I doe professe, by Cupids beautious mother,
> Heres Scogans choise[76] for Scilla, and none other;
> Though Scilla's sick with greife, because no signe
> Can there be found of vertue masculine.
> Esculapius come; I know right well
> His laboure's lost when you may ring her Knell.
> The fatall sisters doome none can withstand,
> Nor Cithareas powre, who poynts to land
> With proclamation that the first of May
> At Ma-re Mount shall be kept hollyday.

The setting up of this Maypole was a lamentable spectacle to the precise seperatists, that lived at new Plimmouth. They termed it an Idoll; yea, they called it the Calfe of Horeb, and stood at defiance with the place, naming it Mount Dagon; threatning to make it a woefull mount and not a merry mount.

The Riddle, for want[77] of Oedipus, they could not expound; onely they made some explication of part of it, and sayd it was meant by Sampson Job, the carpenter of the shipp that brought over a woman to her husband, that had bin there longe before and thrived so well that hee sent for her and her children to come to him; where shortly after hee died: having no reason, but because of the sound of those two words; when as, (the truth is,) the man they applyed it to was altogether unknowne to the Author.

---

73. occurrents: events.
74. Seperatists: Puritans who disowned the Church of England.
75. For Morton's explanation of this poem, see below.

76. *Scogans choise*: John Scogan, court buffoon under Edward IV, when ordered to be hung was allowed to choose the tree.
77. want: ignorance.

 There was likewise a merry song made, which, (to make their Revells more fashionable,) was sung with a Corus, every man bearing his part; which they performed in a dance, hand in hand about the Maypole, whiles one of the Company sung and filled out the good liquor, like gammedes[78] and Jupiter.

THE SONGE.

Cor.
Drinke and be merry, merry, merry boyes;
Let all your delight be in the Hymens joyes;
So to Hymen, now the day is come,
About the merry Maypole take a Roome.
        Make greene garlons, bring bottles out
        And fill sweet Nectar freely about.
        Uncover thy head and feare no harme,
        For here's good liquor to keepe it warme.
Then drinke and be merry, etc.
So to Hymen, etc.
        Nectar is a thing assign'd
        By the Deities owne minde
        To cure the hart opprest with greife,
        And of good liquors is the cheife.
Then drinke, etc.
So to Hymen, etc.
        Give to the Mellancolly man
        A cup or two of 't now and than;
        This physick will soone revive his bloud,
        And make him be of a merrier moode.
Then drinke, etc.
So to Hymen, etc.
        Give to the Nymphe thats free from scorne
        No Irish stuff nor Scotch over worne.
        Lasses in beaver coats come away,
        Yee shall be welcome to us night and day.
To drinke and be merry etc.
So to Hymen, etc.

This harmeles mirth made by younge men, (that lived in hope to have wifes brought over to them, that would save them a laboure to make a voyage to fetch any over,) was much distasted of[79] the precise Seperatists, that keepe much ado about the tyth of

---

78. gammedes: Ganymede, a beautiful Trojan boy taken by Jupiter as cupbearer; hence also catamite.

79. distasted of: disliked by.

Mint and Cummin,[80] troubling their braines more then reason would require about things that are indifferent: and from that time sought occasion against my honest Host of Ma-re Mount, to overthrow his undertakings and to destroy his plantation quite and cleane. But because they presumed with their imaginary gifts, (which they have out of Phaos box,) they could expound hidden misteries, to convince them of blindnes, as well in this as in other matters of more consequence, I will illustrate the poem, according to the true intent of the authors of these Revells, so much distasted by those Moles.

Oedipus is generally receaved for the absolute reader of riddles, who is invoaked. Silla and Caribdis are two dangerous places for seamen to incounter, neere unto Vennice; and have bin by poets formerly resembled to man and wife. The like licence the author challenged for a paire of his nomination, the one lamenting for the losse of the other as Niobe for her children. Amphitrite is an arme of the Sea, by which the newes was carried up and downe of a rich widow, now to be taken up or laid downe. By Triton is the same spread that caused the Suters to muster, (as it had bin to Penellope of Greece;) and, the Coast lying circular, all our passage to and froe is made more convenient by Sea then Land. Many aimed at this marke; but hee that played Proteus best and could comply with her humor must be the man that would carry her; and hee had need have Sampsons strength to deale with a Dallila, and as much patience as Job that should come there, for a thing that I did observe in the life-time of the former.

But marriage and hanging, (they say,) comes by desteny and Scogans choise tis better [than] none at all. Hee that playd Proteus, (with the helpe of Priapus,) put their noses out of joynt,[81] as the Proverbe is.

And this the whole company of the Revellers at Ma-re Mount knew to be the true sence and exposition of the riddle that was fixed to the Maypole, which the Seperatists were at defiance with. Some of them affirmed that the first institution thereof was in memory of a whore; not knowing that it was a Trophe erected at first in honor of Maja,[82] the Lady of learning which they despise, vilifying the two universities with uncivile termes, accounting what is there obtained by studdy is but unnecessary learning; not considering that learninge does inable mens mindes to converse with eliments of a higher nature then is to be found within the habitation of the Mole.

80. tyth of Mint and Cummin: proverbial for legalistic requirements.
81. A play on "joynt"; the actor playing Proteus evidently wore a phallus.

82. Maja: in Greek mythology, daughter of Atlas and mother of Hermes; in Italy, an earth goddess to whom sacrifices were made in May, which is named for her.

14.   William Bradford

another version of the maypole episode

On Bradford, see selection 15 below. Note that Bradford, not to be outdone by
Morton's literary wit, makes a few puns of his own.

About some three or four years before this time, there came over one Captain Wollaston (a man of pretty parts) and with him three or four more of some eminency, who brought with them a great many servants, with provisions and other implements for to begin a plantation . . .

After this they fell to great licentiousness and led a dissolute life, pouring out themselves into all profaneness. And Morton became Lord of Misrule, and maintained (as it were) a School of Atheism. And after they had got some goods into their hands, and got much by trading with the Indians, they spent it as vainly in quaffing and drinking, both wine and strong waters in great excess (and, as some reported) £10 worth in a morning. They also set up a maypole, drinking and dancing about it many days together, inviting the Indian women for their consorts, dancing and frisking together like so many fairies, or furies, rather; and worse practices. As if they had anew revived and celebrated the feasts of the Roman goddess Flora, or the beastly practices of the mad Bacchanalians. Morton likewise, to show his poetry composed sundry rhymes and verses, some tending to lasciviousness, and others to the detraction and scandal of some persons, which he affixed to this idle or idol maypole. They changed also the name of their place, and instead of calling it Mount Wollaston they call it Merrymount, as if this jollity would have lasted ever. But this continued not long, for after Morton was sent for England (as follows to be declared) shortly after came over that worthy gentleman Mr. John Endecott, who brought over a patent under the broad seal for the government of the Massachusetts. Who, visiting those parts, caused that maypole to be cut down and rebuked them for their profaneness and admonished them to look there should be better walking. So they or others now changed the name of their place again and called it Mount Dagon.

15. William Bradford

from *Of Plymouth Plantation* 1630–1650

William Bradford (1590–1657) was born in Yorkshire, and fell in with separatists at the age of twelve. He later joined the separatist church at Scrooby, emigrating with them to Holland in 1608. In 1620 he sailed on the Mayflower with the group that became known as the Pilgrims, following a phrase in the selection below. These English expatriates were bound for the Hudson River, but landed at Cape Cod and decided to stay at Plymouth, even though it left them with dubious land claims and legal rights for years to come. Bradford's wife Dorothy went overboard and drowned at the first landfall, in Provincetown harbor, in what may have been a suicide. Bradford served many terms as governor of Plymouth, for a total of thirty-three years, and has entered folklore as the patriarch of the first Thanksgiving—though the ritual holiday of that name is a nineteenth-century invention.

Of Plymouth Plantation was not published in Bradford's lifetime, though the manuscript was used by colonial historians. The manuscript disappeared following the Revolution, until an attentive scholar saw a reference to it and traced it to the library of the Bishop of London. It was first published in 1856. The manuscript appears to have been composed in two bursts of writing: the first, around 1630, was a continuous narrative; the second, from about 1644 to 1650, took the form of annals. Both parts were composed during periods of crisis in the Plymouth colony's sense of mission; in 1630 it was being upstaged by the more legitimate and better funded Massachusetts Bay Colony, while in the late 1640s the Revolution in Old England was making Puritan New England seem redundant. In both parts, Bradford addresses an audience of young men in the colony, who he thinks need to be reminded of the vision and trials of their fathers. (Women seldom appear in his story.) Bradford repeatedly stresses his sense of decline from the pure faith. Like Winthrop, he understood his life in world-historical terms; the characters of the opening drama in his narrative are Satan, God, and the church. This drama explains every episode that follows, including the genocidal war against the Pequots in 1637, and executions for sexual practices in 1642.

OF PLIMMOTH PLANTATION.

nd first of the occasion and inducements thereunto; the which, that I may truly unfould, I must begine at the very roote and rise of the same. The which I shall endevor to manefest in a plaine stile, with singuler regard unto the simple trueth in all things, at least as near as my slender judgmente can attaine the same.

CHAPTER I

It is well knowne unto the godly and judicious, how ever since the first breaking out
of the lighte of the gospell in our Honourable Nation of England, (which was the first
of nations whom the Lord adorned therewith, after that grosse darkness of popery
which had covered and overspred the Christian world) what warrs and oppositions
ever since, Satan hath raised, maintained, and continued against the Saints, from time
to time, in one sorte or other. Some times by bloody death and cruell torments; other
whiles imprisonments, banishments, and other hard usages; as being loath his
kingdom should goe downe, the trueth prevaile, and the churches of God reverte to
their anciente puritie, and recover their primitive order, libertie, and beauty.

But when he could not prevaile by these means, against the maine trueths of the
gospell, but that they began to take rooting in many places, being watered with the
blood of the martyrs, and blessed from heaven with a gracious encrease; He then
began to take him to his anciente strategemes, used of old against the first Christians.
That when by the bloody and barbarous persecutions of the Heathen Emperours, he
could not stoppe and subverte the course of the gospell, but that it speedily overspread, with a wonderful celerity, the then best known parts of the world, He then
began to sow errours, heresies and wonderful dissensions amongst the professours[83]
themselves (working upon their pride and ambition, with other corrupte passions inci-
dente to all mortall men, yea to the saints themselves in some measure), by which
wofull effects followed; as not only bitter contentions, and hartburnings, schismes,
with other horrible confusions, but Satan tooke occasion and advantage thereby to
foyst in a number of vile ceremonies, with many unproffitable canons and decrees,
which have since been as snares to many poore and peaceable souls even to this day.

So as in the anciente times, the persecutions by the heathen and their Emperours,
was not greater than of the Christians one against [the] other; the Arians and other
their complices against the orthodoxe and true Christians. As witnesseth Socrates[84] in
his second book. His words are these: *The violence truly* (saith he) *was no less than
that of ould practised towards the Christians when they were compelled and drawne
to sacrifice to idols; for many endured sundrie kinds of tormente, often rackings, and
dismemberings of their joynts; confiscating of their goods; some bereaved of their
native soyle; others departed this life under the hands of the tormentor; and some died
in banishmente, and never saw their countrie againe, etc.*

The like methode Satan hath seemed to hold in these later times, since the trueth
began to springe and spread after the great defection made by Antichrist, that man of
sinne.

For to let pass the infinite examples in sundrie nations and severall places of the
world, and instance in our owne, when as that old serpente could not prevaile by
those fiery flames and other his cruell tragedies, which he by his instruments put in use
every where in the days of queene Mary and before, he then began an other kind of
warre, and went more closely to worke; not only to oppugn, but even to ruinate and

---

83. professours: believers.

84. Socrates: not the philosopher, but Socrates Scholasticus, a
fifth-century Greek historian.

destroy the kingdom of Christ, by more secrete and subtile means, by kindling the flames of contention and sowing the seeds of discorde and bitter enmitie amongst the proffessors and seeming reformed themselves. For when he could not prevaile by the former means against the principal doctrines of faith, he bente his force against the holy discipline and outward regimente of the kingdom of Christ, by which those holy doctrines should be conserved, and true pietie maintained amongst the saints and people of God.

But that I may come more near my intendmente; when as by the travail and diligence of some godly and zealous preachers, and God's blessing on their labours, as in other places of the land, so in the North parts, many became inlightened by the word of God, and had their ignorance and sins discovered unto them, and begane by his grace to reforme their lives, and make conscience of their wayes, the worke of God was no sooner manifest in them, but presently they were both scoffed and scorned by the prophane multitude, and the ministers urged with the yoak of subscription, or else must be silenced. And the poore people were so vexed with apparators, and pursuants,[85] and the comissarie courts, as truly their affliction was not small; which, notwithstanding, they bore sundrie years with much patience, till they were occasioned (by the continuance and encrease of these troubles, and other means which the Lord raised up in those days) to see further into things by the light of the word of God. How not only these base and beggerly ceremonies were unlawfull, but also that the lordly and tyranous power of the prelates ought not to be submitted unto; which thus, contrary to the freedome of the gospell, would load and burden men's consciences, and by their compulsive power make a prophane mixture of persons and things in the worship of God. And that their offices and callings, courts and canons, etc. were unlawfull and antichristian; being such as have no warrante in the word of God; but the same that were used in poperie, and still retained. . . .

So many therefore of these proffessors as saw the evill of these things, in these parts, and whose hearts the Lord had touched with heavenly zeale for his trueth, they shooke off this yoake of antichristian bondage, and as the Lords free people, joyned them selves (by a covenant of the Lord) into a church estate, in the felowship of the gospell, to walke in all his wayes, made known, or to be made known unto them, according to their best endeavours, whatsoever it should cost them, the Lord assisting them. And that it cost them something this ensewing historie will declare.

These people became 2 distincte bodys or churches, and in regarde of distance of place did congregate severally.[86] For they were of sundrie townes and villages, some in Notingamshire, some of Lincolnshire, and some of Yorkshire, where they border nearest togeather. In one of these churches (besides others of note) was Mr John Smith, a man of able gifts, and a good preacher, who afterwards was chosen their pastor. But these afterwards falling into some errours in the Low Countries, there (for the most part) buried themselves, and their names.

But in this other church (which must be the subject of our discourse) besides other worthy men, was Mr. Richard Clifton, a grave and reverend preacher, who by his

---

85. apparators, and pursuants: officers of the ecclesiastical courts.   86. severally: separately.

paines and dilligens had done much good, and under God had ben a means of the conversion of many. And also that famous and worthy man Mr. John Robinson, who afterwards was their pastor for many years, till the Lord tooke him away by death. Also Mr. William Brewster a reverent man, who afterwards was chosen an elder of the church and lived with them till old age.

But after these things they could not long continue in any peaceable condition, but were hunted and persecuted on every side, so as their former afflictions were but as flea-bitings in comparison of these which now came upon them. For some were taken and clapt up in prison, others had their houses besett and watcht night and day, and hardly escaped their hands; and the most were faine to flie and leave their howses and habitations, and the means of their livelehood. Yet these and many other sharper things which afterward befell them, were no other then they looked for, and therfore were the better prepared to bear them by the assistance of God's grace and spirite.

Yet seeing themselves thus molested, and that there was no hope of their continuance there, by a joynte consente they resolved to goe into the Low-Countries, where they heard was freedome of Religion for all men; as also how sundrie from London, and other parts of the land, had been exiled and presecuted for the same cause, and were gone thither, and lived at Amsterdam, and in other places of the land. So affter they had continued togeither aboute a year, and kept their meetings every Sabbath in one place or other, exercising the worship of God amongst themselves, notwithstanding all the dilligence and malice of their adversaries, they seeing they could no longer continue in that condition, they resolved to get over into Holland as they could; which was in the year 1607 and 1608.

CHAPTER 4

SHOWING THE REASONS AND CAUSES OF THEIR REMOOVALL.

After they had lived in this citie[87] about some 11 or 12 years, (which is the more observable being the whole time of that famous truce between that state and the Spaniards,) and sundrie of them were taken away by death, and many others begane to be well striken in years, the grave mistress Experience haveing taught them many things, those prudent governours with sundrie of the sagest members begane both deeply to apprehend their present dangers, and wisely to foresee the future, and thinke of timely remedy. In the agitation of their thoughts, and much discourse of things here aboute, at length they began to incline to this conclusion, of remoovall to some other place. Not out of any newfangledness, or other such like giddie humor, by which men are oftentimes transported to their great hurt and danger, but for sundrie weightie and solid reasons; some of the cheefe of which I will hear breefly touch.

And first, they saw and found by experience the hardnes of the place and countrie to be such, as few in comparison would come to them, and fewer that would bide it out, and continew with them. For many that came to them, and many more that desired to be with them, could not endure that great labor and hard fare, with other

---

87. this citie: Leyden, in the Netherlands.

inconveniences which they underwent and were contented with. But though they loved their persons, approved their cause, and honoured their sufferings, yet they left them as it were weeping, as Orpah did her mother in law Naomi, or as those Romans did Cato in Utica, who desired to be excused and borne with, though they could not all be Catoes. For many, though they desired to injoye the ordinances of God in their puritie, and the libertie of the gospell with them, yet, alas, they admitted of bondage, with danger of conscience, rather than to indure these hardships. Yea, some preferred and chose the prisons in England, rather than this libertie in Holland, with these afflictions. But it was thought that if a better and easier place of living could be had, it would draw many, and take away these discouragments. Yea, their pastor would often say, that many of those who both wrote and preached now against them, if they were in a place where they might have libertie and live comfortably, they would then practise as they did.

2ly. They saw that though the people generally bore all these difficulties very cheerfully, and with a resolute courage, being in the best and strength of their years, yet old age began to steale on many of them, (and their great and continuall labours, with other crosses and sorrows, hastened it before the time,) so as it was not only probably thought, but apparently seen, that within a few years more they would be in danger to scatter, by necessities pressing them, or sinke under their burdens, or both. And therefore according to the divine proverb, that a wise man seeth the plague when it cometh, and hideth himselfe, Pro. 22. 3., so they like skillfull and beaten[88] souldiers were fearfull either to be intrapped or surrounded by their enimies, so as they should neither be able to fight nor flie; and therefore thought it better to dislodge betimes to some place of better advantage and less danger, if any such could be found.

Thirdly; as necessitie was a taskmaster over them, so they were forced to be such, not only to their servants, but in a sorte, to their dearest children; the which as it did not a little wound the tender hearts of many a loving father and mother, so it produced likewise sundrie sad and sorrowful effects. For many of their children, that were of best dispositions and gracious inclinations, having learned to bear the yoke in their youth, and willing to bear parte of their parents' burden, were, often times, so oppressed with their heavie labours, that though their minds were free and willing, yet their bodies bowed under the weight of the same, and became decrepit in their early youth; the vigor of nature being consumed in the very bud, as it were. But that which was more lamentable, and of all sorowes most heavie to be borne, was that many of their children, by these occasions, and the great licentiousness of youth in that countrie, and the manifold temptations of the place, were drawne away by evill examples into extravagante and dangerous courses, getting the reins off their necks, and departing from their parents. Some became souldiers, others took upon them far voiages by sea, and others some worse courses, tending to dissolutenes and the danger of their soules, to the great greefe of their parents and dishonour of God. So that they saw their posteritie would be in danger to degenerate and be corrupted.

Lastly, (and which was not least), a great hope and inward zeall they had of laying some good foundation, or at least to make some way therunto, for the propagating

---

88. beaten: toughened.

and advancing the gospell of the kingdom of Christ in those remote parts of the world; yea, though they should be but even as stepping-stones unto others for the performing of so great a work.

These, and some other like reasons, moved them to undertake this resolution of their removall; the which they afterward prosecuted with so great difficulties, as by the sequell will appear.

The place they had thoughts on was some of those vast and unpeopled countries of America, which are fruitfull and fit for habitation, being devoyd of all civill inhabitants, where there are only salvage and brutish men, which range up and downe, litle otherwise than the wild beasts of the same. This proposition being made publike and coming to the scanning of all, it raised many variable opinions amongst men, and caused many fears and doubts amongst themselves. Some, from their reasons and hopes conceived, laboured to stirr up and incourage the rest to undertake and prosecute the same. Others, againe, out of their fears, objected against it, and sought to divert from it, alleging many things, and those neither unreasonable nor unprobable; as that it was a great designe, and subject to many unconceivable perills and dangers; as, besides the casualties of the seas (which none can be freed from) the length of the voiage was such, as the weake bodys of women and other persons worne out with age and travaille (as many of them were) could never be able to endure. And yet if they should, the miseries of the land which they should be exposed unto, would be to hard to be borne; and likely, some or all of them together, to consume and utterly to ruinate them. For there they should be liable to famine, and nakednes, and the wante, in a manner, of all things. The change of air, diet, and drinking of water, would infecte their bodies with sore sickneses, and greevous diseases. And also those which should escape or overcome these difficulties, should yet be in continuall danger of the salvage people, who are cruell, barbarous, and most trecherous, being most furious in their rage, and merciless where they overcome; not being contente only to kill, and take away life, but delight to tormente men in the most bloodie manner that may be; flaying some alive with the shells of fishes, cutting of the members and joynts of others by piecemeal, and broiling on the coals, eate the collops of their flesh in their sight whilst they live; with other cruelties horrible to be related. And surely it could not be thought but the very hearing of these things could not but move the very bowels of men to grate within them, and make the weake to quake and tremble.

It was further objected, that it would require greater summes of money to furnish such a voiage, and to fitt them with necessaries, than their consumed estates would amounte too; and yett they must as well looke to be seconded with supplies, as presently to be transported. Also many precedents of ill success, and lamentable miseries befallen others in the like designes, were easie to be found, and not forgotten to be alleged; besides their owne experience, in their former troubles and hardships in their removall into Holland, and how hard a thing it was for them to live in that strange place, though it was a neighbour countrie, and a civill and rich commonwealth.

It was answered, that all great and honourable actions are accompanied with great difficulties, and must be both enterprised and overcome with answerable courages. It was granted the dangers were great, but not desperate; the difficulties were many, but not invincible. For though there were many of them likely, yet they were not certaine. It might be sundrie of the things feared might never befale. Others by provident care and the use of good means, might in a great measure be prevented. And all of them, through the help of God, by fortitude and patience, might either be borne, or overcome.

True it was, that such attempts were not to be made and undertaken without good ground and reason; not rashly or lightly as many have done for curiositie or hope of gaine, etc. But their condition was not ordinarie; their ends were good and honourable; their calling lawfull, and urgente. And therefore they might expecte the blessing of God in their proceding. Yea, though they should lose their lives in this action, yet might they have comforte in the same, and their endeavors would be honourable. They lived here but as men in exile, and in a poore condition; and as great miseries might possibly befall them in this place, for the 12 years of truce were now out, and there was nothing but beating of drums, and preparing for warr, the events wherof are allway uncertaine.[89] The Spaniard might prove as cruell as the salvages of America, and the famine and pestelence as sore here as there, and their libertie less to looke out for remedie. After many other perticuler things answered and alleged on both sides, it was fully concluded by the major parte, to put this designe in execution, and to prosecute it by the best means they could.

CHAPTER 5

SHEWING WHAT MEANS THEY USED FOR PREPARATION TO THIS WAIGHTIE VOYAGE.

And first after thir humble prayers unto God for his direction and assistance, and a generall conferrence held here aboute, they consulted what perticuler place to pitch upon, and prepare for. Some (and none of the meanest) had thoughts and were ernest for Guiana, or some of those fertill places in those hot climates. Others were for some parts of Virginia, where the English had all ready made entrance, and beginning. Those for Guiana alleged that the countrie was rich, fruitfull, and blessed with a perpetuall spring, and a florishing greenness; where vigorous nature brought forth all things in abundance and plentie without any great labour or art of man. So as it must needs make the inhabitants rich, seeing less provisions of clothing and other things would serve, than in more colder and less fruitfull countries must be had. As also that the Spaniards (having much more than they could possess) had not yet planted there, nor any where very near the same. But to this it was answered, that out of question the countrie was both fruitfull and pleasante, and might yeeld riches and maintenance to the possessors, more easily than the other; yet, other things considered, it would not be so fit for them. And first, that such hott countries are subject to greevous diseases, and many noysome impediments, which other more temperate places are freer from, and would not so well agree with our English bodys. Againe, if they should there live, and do well, the jealous Spaniard would never suffer them long, but would displant or overthrow them, as he did the French in Florida, who were seated

---

89. The truce between Holland and Spain, signed in 1609, was to expire in 1621.

further from his richest countries; and the sooner because they should have none to protect them, and their owne strength would be too small to resiste so potent an enemie, and so neare a neighbor.

On the other hand, for Virginia it was objected, that if they lived among the English which were there planted, or so near them as to be under their government, they should be in as great danger to be troubled and persecuted for the cause of religion, as if they lived in England, and it might be worse. And if they lived too far off, they should neither have succour, nor defence from them.

But at length the conclusion was, to live as a distinct body by themselves, under the generall Government of Virginia; and by their friends to sue to his majestie that he would be pleased to grant them freedome of Religion. And that this might be obtained, they were put in good hope by some great persons, of good rank and qualitie, that were made their friends. Whereupon 2 were chosen and sent in to England (at the charge of the rest) to sollicit this matter, who found the Virginia Company very desirous to have them go thither, and willing to grant them a patent, with as ample privileges as they had, or could grant to any, and to give them the best furtherance they could.

CHAPTER 7

OF THEIR DEPARTURE FROM LEYDEN, AND OTHER THINGS THERE ABOUTE, WITH THEIR ARIVALL AT SOUTH HAMTON, WHERE THEY ALL MET TOGETHER, AND TOOK IN THEIR PROVISIONS.

At length, after much travell and these debates, all things were got ready and provided. A small ship[90] was bought, and fitted in Holland, which was intended as to serve to help to transport them, so to stay in the countrie and attend upon fishing and such other affairs as might be for the good and benefit of the colonie when they came there. Another[91] was hired at London, of burden about 9 score; and all other things got in readiness.

So being ready to departe, they had a day of sollemn humiliation, their pastor taking his texte from Ezra 8. 21. *And there at the river, by Ahava, I proclaimed a fast, that we might humble ourselves before our God, and seeke of him a right way for us, and for our children, and for all our substance.* Upon which he spente a good parte of the day very profitably, and suitable to their presente occasion. The rest of the time was spente in powering out prayers to the Lord with great fervencie, mixed with abundance of tears.

And the time being come that they must departe, they were accompanied with most of their brethren out of the citie, unto a towne sundrie miles off called Delfts-Haven, where the ship lay ready to receive them. So they left that goodly and pleasante citie, which had been their resting place near 12 years; but they knew they were pilgrimes, and looked not much on those things, but lifted up their eyes to the heavens, their dearest countrie, and quieted their spirits.

90. The Speedwell.   91. The Mayflower.

When they came to the place they found the ship and all things ready; and such of their friends as could not come with them followed after them, and sundrie also came from Amsterdam to see them shipped and to take their leave of them. That night was spent with litle sleepe by the most, but with freindly entertainmente and christian discourse and other reall expressions of true christian love.

The next day, the wind being faire, they went aboard, and their friends with them, where truly dolefull was the sight of that sad and mournfull parting; to see what sighs and sobs and prayers did sound amongst them, what tears did gush from every eye, and pithy speeches pierced each heart; that sundry of the Dutch strangers that stood on the key as spectators, could not refraine from tears. Yet comfortable and sweete it was to see such lively and true expressions of dear and unfained love. But the tide (which stays for no man) calling them away that were thus loath to departe, their Reverend pastor falling downe on his knees, (and they all with him,) with waterie cheeks commended them with most fervent prayers to the Lord and his blessing. And then with mutuall embraces and many tears, they took their leaves one of an other; which proved to be the last leave to many of them.

CHAPTER 9

OF THEIR VOIAGE, AND HOW THEY PASSED THE SEA, AND OF THEIR SAFE ARRIVAL AT CAPE CODD.

Sept. 6. These troubles being blowne over, and now all being compact together in one shipe, they put to sea againe with a prosperous wind, which continued diverse days together, which was some incouragemente unto them. Yet according to the usuall manner many were afflicted with seasickness. And I may not omit hear a speciall worke of God's providence. There was a proud and very profane young man, one of the sea-men, of a lustie,[92] able body, which made him the more hauty. He would always be condemning the poor people in their sickness, and cursing them dayly with greevous execrations, and did not let to tell them, that he hoped to help to cast half of them over board before they came to their journey's end, and to make merry with what they had. And if he were by any gently reproved, he would curse and swear most bitterly. But it pleased God before they came half seas over, to smite this young man with a greevous disease, of which he dyed in a desperate manner, and so was himselfe the first that was thrown overboard. Thus his curses light on his owne head; and it was an astonishment to all his fellows, for they noted it to be the just hand of God upon him. . . .

But to omit other things, (that I may be brief) after long beating at sea they fell with that land which is called Cape Cod; the which being made and certainly known to be it, they were not a little joyfull. After some deliberation had amongst themselves and with the master of the ship, they tacked about and resolved to stand for the south-ward (the wind and weather being fair) to find some place about Hudson's river for their habitation. But after they had sailed that course about half the day, they fell

92. lustie: robust.

amongst dangerous shoals and roaring breakers, and they were so far intangled there with as they conceived themselves in great danger. And the wind shrinking upon them withall, they resolved to bear up againe for the Cape, and thought themselves hapy to get out of those dangers before night overtook them, as by Gods providence they did. And the next day they got into the Cape-harbor where they rode in safetie.

A word or two by the way of this cape; it was thus first named by Capten Gosnold and his company, 1602, and after by Captain Smith was called Cape James. But it retains the former name amongst seamen. Also that pointe which first shewed those dangerous shoals unto them, they called Pointe Care, and Tuckers Terrour. But the French and Dutch to this day call it Malabarr, by reason of those perilous shoals, and the losses they have suffered there.

Being thus arrived in a good harbor and brought safe to land, they fell upon their knees and blessed the God of heaven, who had brought them over the vast and furious ocean, and delivered them from all the perils and miseries therof, again to set their feet on the firm and stable earth, their proper element. And no marvell if they were thus joyfull, seeing wise Seneca was so affected with sailing a few miles on the coast of his owne Italy; as he affirmed, that he had rather remain twentie years on his way by land, than pass by sea to any place in a short time; so tedious and dreadfull was the same unto him.

But here I cannot but stay and make a pause, and stand half amazed at this poor people's present condition. And so I think will the reader too, when he well considers the same. Being thus passed the vast ocean, and a sea of troubles before in their prepa-ration (as may be remembered by that which went before), they had now no friends to welcome them, nor inns to entertain or refresh their weatherbeaten bodys, no houses or much less townes to repair too, to seeke for succour. It is recorded in scripture as a mercie to the apostle and his shipwrecked company, that the barbarians showed them no small kindness in refreshing them. But these savage barbarians, when they met with them (as after will appeare) were readier to fill their sides full of arrows than otherwise. And for the season it was winter, and they that know the winters of that countrie know them to be sharp and violent, and subject to cruell and fierce stormes, dangerous to travill to known places, much more to search an unknown coast. Besides, what could they see but a hidious and desolate wilderness, full of wild beasts and wild men? And what multitudes there might be of them they knew not. Neither could they, as it were, go up to the top of Pisgah, to view from this wilderness a more goodly countrie to feed their hopes, for which way soever they turned their eyes (save upward to the heavens) they could have little solace or content in respecte of any outward objects. For summer being done, all things stand upon them with a wetherbeaten face; and the whole coun-trie, full of woods and thickets, represented a wild and savage hue.

If they looked behind them, there was the mighty ocean which they had passed, and was now as a main bar and gulfe to separate them from all the civill parts of the world. If it be said they had a ship to succour them, it is true; but what heard they daily from the master and company? but that with speede they should looke out a place with their shallop, where they would be at some near distance; for the season was such as he would not stir from thence till a safe harbor was discovered by them where they would be, and he might go without danger; and that victualls consumed apace, but he must and would keep sufficient for themselves and their return. Yea, it was muttered by some, that if they got not a place in time, they would turn them and their goods ashore and leave them.

Let it also be considered what weak hopes of supply and succour they left behind them, that might bear up their minds in this sad condition and trialls they were under; and they could not but be very small. It is true, indeed, the affections and love of their brethren at Leyden was cordiall and entire towards them, but they had little power to help them, or themselves. And how the case stood between them and the marchants at their coming away, hath allready been declared. What could now sustain them but the spirit of God and his grace? May not and ought not the children of these fathers rightly say: *Our fathers were Englishmen which came over this great ocean, and were ready to perish in this wilderness; but they cried unto the Lord, and he heard their voyce, and looked on their adversitie, etc. Let them therefore praise the Lord, because he is good, and his mercies endure for ever. Yea, let them which have been redeemed of the Lord, shew how he hath delivered them from the hand of the oppressor. When they wandered in the desert wilderness out of the way, and found no citie to dwell in, both hungrie, and thirstie, their soul was overwhelmed in them. Let them confess before the Lord his loving kindness, and his wonderfull works before the sons of men.*

The 2. Booke.

The rest of this History (if God give me life, and opportunitie) I shall, for brevity's sake, handle by way of annalls, noting only the heads of principall things, and passages as they fell in order of time, and may seeme to be profitable to know, or to make use of. And this may be as the 2. Booke.

[1623: ECONOMIC EXPERIMENTS]

All this while no supply was heard of, neither knew they when they might expect any. So they began to think how they might raise as much corn as they could, and obtain a better crop than they had done, that they might not still thus languish in miserie. At length, after much debate of things, the Governor (with the advice of the cheefest amongst them) gave way that they should set corn every man for his own perticuler, and in that regard trust to themselves; in all other things to goe on in the generall way as before. And so assigned to every family a parcell of land, according to the proportion of their number for that end, only for present use (but made no division for inheritance), and ranged all boys and youth under some familie. This had very good success; for it made all hands very industrious, so as much more corn was planted than other wise would have been by any means the Governor or any other could use, and saved him a great deal of trouble, and gave far better content. The women now went willingly into the field, and took their little-ones with them to set corn, which before would allege weakness, and inabilitie; whom to have compelled would have been thought great tyranie and oppression.

The experience that was had in this common course and condition, tried sundrie years, and that amongst godly and sober men, may well evince the vanitie of that conceite of Plato's and other ancients, applauded by some of later times—that the taking away of propertie, and bringing in communitie into a common wealth, would make them happy and flourishing; as if they were wiser then God. For this communitie (so farr as it was) was found to breed much confusion and discontent, and retard much imployment that would have been to their benefite and comforte. For the young-men that were most able and fit for labour and service did repine that they should spend their time and strength to work for other men's wives and children, without any recompence. The strong, or man of parts, had no more in division of victuals and clothes, than he that was weak and not able to do a quarter the other could; this was thought injustice. The aged and graver men to be ranked and equalised in labours, and victuals, clothes, etc., with the meaner and younger sort, thought it some indignity and disrespect unto them. And for men's wives to be commanded to do service for other men, as dressing their meat, washing their clothes, etc., they deemed it a kind of slaverie, neither could many husbands well brook it. Upon the poynte all being to have alike, and all to do alike, they thought themselves in the like condition, and one as good as another; and so, if it did not cut off those relations that God hath set amongst men, yet it did at least much diminish and take off the mutuall respects that should be preserved amongst them. And would have been worse if they had been men of another condition. Let none object this is men's corruption, and nothing to the course iteselfe. I answer, seeing all men have this corruption in them, God in his wisdome saw another course fitter for them.

[1637: THE PEQUOT WAR]

In the fore parte of this year, the Pequots fell openly upon the English at Conightecute, in the lower parts of the river, and slew sundry of them, (as they were at work in the fields,) both men and women, to the great terrour of the rest; and wente away in great pride and triumph, with many high threats. They also assaulted a fort at the river's mouth, though strong and well defended. And though they did not there prevaile, yet it struck them with much fear and astonishmente to see their bould attempts in the face of danger; which made them in all places to stand upon their guard, and to prepare for resistance, and ernestly to solissit their friends and confederates in the Bay of Massachusets to send them speedy aide, for they looked for more forcible assaults. Mr. Vane, being then Governor, wrote from their Generall Courte to them here, to joyne with them in this warr; to which they were cordially willing. . . .

In the mean time, the Pequots, especially in the winter before, sought to make peace with the Narigansets, and used very pernicious arguments to move them thereunto: as that the English were strangers and began to overspread their countrie, and would deprive them therof in time, if they were suffered to grow and increase; and if the Narigansets did assist the English to subdue them, they did but make way for their own overthrow, for if they were rooted out, the English would soone take occasion to subjugate them; and if they would harken to them, they should not need to fear the strength of the English; for they would not come to open battle with them, but fire their houses, kill their cattle, and lie in ambush for them as they went abroad upon their occasions; and all this they might easily do without any or little danger to themselves. The which course being held, they well saw the English could not long subsiste, but they would either be starved with hunger, or be forced to forsake the countrie; with many the like things; insomuch that the Narigansets were once wavering, and were halfe minded to have made peace with them, and joyned against the English.

But againe when they considered, how much wrong they had received from the Pequots, and what an opportunitie they now had by the help of the English to right themselves, revenge was so sweete unto them, as it prevailed above all the rest; so as they resolved to joyne with the English against them, and did.

The Court here agreed forthwith to send 50 men at their own charge; and with as much speed as possiblie they could, got them armed, and had made them ready under sufficiente leaders, and provided a barke to carrie them provisions and tend upon them for all occasions; but when they were ready to march (with a supply from the Bay) they had word to stay, for the enemy was as good as vanquished, and there would be no need.

I shall not take upon me exactly to describe their proceedings in these things, because I expecte it will be fully done by themselves, who best know the carrage and circumstances of things; I shall therefore but touch them in generall. From Connightecute (who were most sencible of the hurt sustained, and the present danger), they sett out a partie of men, and an other partie met them from the Bay, at the Narigansets, who were to joyne with them. The Narigansets were ernest to be gone before the English were well rested and refreshte, especially some of them which came last. It should seeme their desire was to come upon the enemie suddenly, and undiscovered. There was a barke of this place, newly put in there, which was come from Conightecutte, who did incourage them to lay hold of the Indians' forwardness, and to shew as great forwardness as they, for it would incourage them, and expedition might prove to their great advantage.

So they went on, and so ordered their march, as the Indians brought them to a fort of the enemies (in which most of their cheefe men were) before day. They approached the same with great silence, and surrounded it both with English and Indians, that they might not break out; and so assaulted them with great courage, shooting amongst them, and entered the fort with all speed. And those that first entered found sharp resistance from the enemie, who both shot at and grappled with them. Others ran into their houses, and brought out fire, and sett them on fire, which soone tooke in their matts, and, standing close together, with the wind, all was quickly on a flame, and thereby more were burnt to death than was otherwise slain. It burnt their bowstrings, and made them unservicable. Those that escaped the fire were slain with the sword; some hewed to peeces, others run throw with their rapiers, so as they were quickly dispatcht, and very few escaped.

It was conceived they thus destroyed about 400 at this time. It was a fearfull sight to see them thus frying in the fire, and the streams of blood quenching the same, and horrible was the stinck and scent thereof; but the victory seemed a sweete sacrifice, and they gave the praise thereof to God, who had wrought so wonderfully for them, thus to inclose their enemies in their hands, and give them so speedy a victory over so proud and insulting an enemie.

The Narigansett Indians, all this while, stood round about, but aloof from all danger, and left the whole execution to the English, exept it were the stopping of any that broke away, insulting over their enemies in this their ruin and miserie, when they saw them dancing in the flames, calling them by a word in their owne language, signifing, O brave Pequots! which they used familierly among themselves in their own praise, in songs of triumph after their victories. After this service was thus happily accomplished, they marcht to the water side, where they met with some of their vessels, by which they had refreshing with victualls and other necessaries.

But in their march the rest of the Pequots drew into a body, and accosted them, thinking to have some advantage against them by reason of a neck of land. But when they saw the English prepare for them, they kept aloof, so as they neither did hurt, nor could receive any. After their refreshing and repair together for further counsell and directions, they resolved to pursue their victory, and follow the war against the rest, but the Narigansett Indians most of them forsooke them, and such of them as they had with them for guides, or otherwise, they found them very cold and backward in the business, either out of envie, or that they saw the English would make more profit of the victorie than they were willing they should, or else deprive them of such advantage as themselves desired by having them become tributaries unto them, or the like.

[1642: SODOMY]

Marvilous it may be to see and consider how some kind of wickednes did grow and breake forth here, in a land wher the same was so much witnesed against, and so narrowly looked unto, and severly punished when it was knowne; as in no place more, or so much, that I have known or heard of; insomuch as they have been somewhat censured, even by moderate and good men, for their severitie in punishments. And yet all this could not suppress the breaking out of sundrie notorious sins, (as this year, besides other, gives us too many said precedents and instances,) especially drunkennes and uncleanness; not only incontinencie betweene persons unmarried, for which many both men and women have been punished sharply enough, but some married persons also. But that which is worse, even sodomie and bugerie, (things fearfull to name,) have broke forth in this land, oftener then once. I say it may justly be marveled at, and cause us to fear and tremble at the consideration of our corrupte natures, which are so hardly[93] bridled, subdued, and mortified; nay, cannot by any other

93. hardly: difficultly.

means but the powerfull work and grace of God's spirite. But (besides this) one reason may be, that the Devil may carrie a greater spite against the churches of Christ and the gospell here, by how much the more they indeavour to preserve holyness and puritie amongst them, and strictly punisheth the contrary when it ariseth either in church or commonwealth; that he might cast a blemishe and staine upon them in the eyes of [the] world, who use to be rash in judgmente. I would rather think thus, than that Satane hath more power in these heathen lands, as some have thought, than in more Christian nations, especially over God's servants in them.

2. Another reason may be, that it may be in this case as it is with waters when their streames are stopped or dammed up, when they gett passage they flow with more violence, and make more noise and disturbance, than when they are suffered to run quietly in their owne chanels. So wikednes being here more stopped by strict laws, and the same more nearly looked unto, so as it cannot run in a common road of liberty as it would, and is inclined, it searches every where, and at last breaks out where it gets vent.

3. A third reason may be, here (as I am verily perswaded) is not more evills in this kind, nor nothing near so many by proportion; as in other places; but they are here more discovered and seen, and made publick by due search, inquisition, and due punishment; for the churches looke narrowly to their members, and the magistrates over all, more strictly than in other places. Besides, here the people are but few in comparison of other places, which are full and populous, and lye hid, as it were, in a wood or thickett, and many horrible evils by that means are never seen nor knowne; wheras here, they are, as it were, brought into the light, and set in the plaine field, or rather on a hill, made conspicuous to the view of all.

But to proceed; . . . There was a youth whose name was Thomas Granger. He was servant to an honest man of Duxbury, being about 16 or 17 years of age. (His father and mother lived at the same time at Scituate.) He was this year detected of buggery, and indicted for the same, with a mare, a cow, two goats, five sheep, two calves and a turkey. Horrible it is to mention, but the truth of the history requires it. He was first discovered by one that accidentally saw his lewd practice towards the mare. (I forbear particulars.) Being upon it examined and committed, in the end he not only confessed the fact with that beast at that time, but sundry times before and at several times with all the rest of the forenamed in his indictment. And this his free confession was not only in private to the magistrates (though at first he strived to deny it) but to sundry, both ministers and others; and afterwards, upon his indictment, to the whole Court and jury; and confirmed it at his execution. And whereas some of the sheep could not so well be known by his description of them, others with them were brought before him and he declared which were they and which were not. And accordingly he was cast by the jury and condemned, and after executed about the 8th of September, 1642.

A very sad spectacle it was. For first the mare and then the cow and the rest of the lesser cattle were killed before his face, according to the law, Leviticus xx.15; and then he himself was executed. The cattle were all cast into a great and large pit that was digged of purpose for them, and no use made of any part of them.

Upon the examination of this person and also of a former that had made some sodomitical attempts upon another, it being demanded of them how they came first to the knowledge and practice of such wickedness, the one confessed he had long used it in old England; and this youth last spoken of said he was taught it by another that had heard of such things from some in England when he was there, and they kept cattle together. By which it appears how one wicked person may infect many, and what care all ought to have what servants they bring into their families.

But it may be demanded how came it to pass that so many wicked persons and profane people should so quickly come over into this land, and mix themselves amongst them? seeing it was religious men that begane the work, and they came for religions sake. I confess this may be marveilled at, at least in time to come, when the reasons therof should not be known; and the more because here was so many hardships and wants met withall. I shall therefore indeavor to give some answer hereunto.

And first, according to that in the gospell, it is ever to be remembered that where the Lord begins to sow good seed, there the envious man will endeavor to sow tares.

2. Men being to come over into a wilderness, in which much labour and service was to be done about building and planting, etc., such as wanted help in that respect, when they could not have such as they would, were glad to take such as they could; and so, many untoward servants, sundry of them proved, that were thus brought over, both men and women kind; who, when their times were expired, became families of themselves, which gave increase hereunto.

3. Another and a main reason hearof was, that men, finding so many godly disposed persons willing to come into these parts, some began to make a trade of it, to transport passengers and their goods, and hired ships for that end; and then, to make up their freight and advance their profit, cared not who the persons were so they had money to pay them. And by this means the countrie became pestered with many unworthy persons, who, being come over, crept into one place or other.

4. Againe, the Lord's blessing usually following his people, as well in outward as spirituall things, (though afflictions be mixed withall,) do make many to adhere to the people of God, as many followed Christ, for the loaves sake, John 6. 26. and a mixed multitude came into the wilderness with the people of God out of Egypte of old, Exod. 12. 38; so also there were sent by their friends some under hope that they would be made better; others that they might be eased of such burthens, and they kept from shame at home that would necessarily follow their dissolute courses. And thus, by one means or other, in 20 years time, it is a question whether the greater part be not growne the worser.

16.

from *Mourt's Relation*
1622

The first published account of the Plymouth settlement was an anonymous narrative called A Relation or Journall of the beginning and proceedings of the English Plantation setled at *Plimoth* in New England, by certaine English Adventurers both Merchants and others *(London, 1622). It appears to be the work primarily of Edward Winslow and William Bradford, though it has long been known as* Mourt's Relation *because a preface is signed "G. Mourt," possibly George Morton. The following versions of the first encounter should be compared with Bradford's later version in* Of Plymouth Plantation.

Wednesday the 15 of *November*, they were set ashore, and when they had ordered themselves in the order of a single File, and marched about the space of a mile, by the Sea they espyed five or six people, with a Dogge, coming towards them, who were Savages, who when they saw them ran into the Wood and whistled the Dogge after them, &c. First, [the English] supposed them to be master *Jones*, the Master and some of his men, for they were ashore, and knew of their coming, but after they knew them to be *Indians* they marched after them into the Woods, lest other of the *Indians* should lie in Ambush; but when the *Indians* saw our men following them, they ran away with might and mayne, and our men turned out of the Wood after them, for it was the way they intended to go, but they could not come near them. . . .

From thence we went on & found much plaine ground, about fiftie Acres, fit for the Plow, and some signes where the *Indians* had formerly planted their corn. . . . Also we found a great Kettle, which had beene some Ship's kettle and brought out of *Europe*. There was also an heape of sand, made like the former, but it was newly done (we might see how they had paddled it with their hands); which we digged up, and in it we found a little old Basket full of fair *Indian* Corn, and digged further & found a fine great new Basket full of very fair corn of this year, with some 36 goodly ears of corn, some yellow, and some red, and others mixt with blue, which was a very goodly sight. The Basket was round, and narrow at the top. It held about three or four Bushels, which was as much as two of us could lift up from the ground, and was very handsomely and cunningly made. But whilst we were busy about these things, we set our men Sentinell in a round ring, all but two or three which digged up the corn. We were in suspence, what to do with it, and the Kettle, and at length after much consultation, we concluded to take the Kettle, and as much of the Corne as we could carry away with us; and when our Shallop came, if we could find any of the people, and come to parley with them, we would give them the Kettle againe, and satisfie them for their Corn. So we took all the ears and put a good deal of the loose Corn in the Kettle for two men to bring away on a staff. Besides, they that could put any into their Pockets filled the same. The rest we buried again, for we were so laden with Armour that we could carry no more.

17. Thomas Shepard

a Nauset prophecy, circa 1618
1648

Because North American Indians left no written accounts from the early colonial period, and because the English, unlike the French and Spanish, made little attempt to record what the Indians said, written sources for an Indian perspective on early settlement date from much later. Thomas Shepard (1605–49) was one of the principal clergy of Massachusetts following his emigration in 1635. In The Clear Sunshine of the Gospel Breaking Forth upon the Indians *(1648), he relates the following anecdote.*

A fourth and last observation wee took, was the story of an *Indian* in those parts, telling us of his dreame many yeers since, which he told us of openly before many witnesses when we sate at meat: the dreame is this, hee said "That about two yeers before the *English* came over into those parts there was a great mortality among the *Indians*, and one night he could not sleep above half the night, after which hee fell into a dream, in which he did think he saw a great many men come to those parts in cloths, just as the *English* now are apparelled, and among them there arose up a man all in black, with a thing in his hand which hee now sees was all one *English* mans book; this black man he said stood upon a higher place then all the rest, and on the one side of him were the *English*, on the other a great number of *Indians*: this man told all the *Indians* that God was *moosquantum* or angry with them, and that he would kill them for their sinnes, whereupon he said himself stood up, and desired to know of the black man what God would do with him and his *Squaw* and *Papooses*, but the black man would not answer him a first time, nor yet a second time, untill he desired the third time, and then he smil'd upon him, and told him that he and his *Papooses* should be safe, and that God would give unto them *Mitcheu*, (i.e.) victualls and other good things, and so hee awakened."

18. George Fox

an Indian prophecy
1672

A similar anecdote appears in the journal of George Fox (1624-91), the founder of the Quakers, who was travelling in the colonies at the time.

An Indian said, before the English came, that a white people should come in a great thing of the sea, and their people should be loving to them and receive them; but if they did hurt or wrong the white people, they would be destroyed. And this hath been seen and fulfilled, that when they did wrong the English they never prospered and have been destroyed. So that Indian was a prophet and prophesied truly.

Chapter 4

Seventeenth-Century Anglo-America: Virginia and the Indies

INTRODUCTION

The term "Anglo-America" in the title of this chapter identifies its major theme, the growth of a culture—of social and personal values, of habits of mind and writing—that is no longer simply English, nor even just English inflected by foreign experiences. The preceding two chapters showed explorers and conquerors traveling into situations that sometimes transformed them personally. However, their views of the world, their ways of thinking about it, remained essentially English, focussed on England, articulated in English terms with English references. In the mid-seventeenth century, though many and perhaps most colonists still crossed the Atlantic to make their fortune, rather than to settle permanently, their engagement with the colonies nonetheless began to change.

In addition to English attitudes, values, references, knowledge, and ambitions, the writers featured in this chapter gained others inspired by their experience in Virginia and the West Indies; for it is not colonization alone but also its particular location that gives these new attitudes a new coherence. English America, in the texts gathered here, begins to have a distinct character. A creole culture appears as the system of English ways adapts in the New World to an alternative way of life.

Richard Ligon, whose American exposure lasted only two years and who wrote his *True and Exact History* back in London, nonetheless sensed the emergence of this hybrid. Who can be successful in America, he asks at one point? His answer draws one of the earliest portraits of the typical American: one who is willing to abandon the pleasures of England and its inherited privileges, a man "made of middle earth," ready to work hard in his eagerness to climb the "Ladder . . . to a high degree." Neither honest rustic nor elegant gentleman, the successful American, according to Ligon, will climb to "Wealth and opulencie" but remain a man of the middling way.

If a creole culture was sufficiently evolved to suggest this typing to Ligon who was outside it, for insiders like Robert Beverley and the elder William Byrd it was fast becoming a way of life. These men who owned and ran Anglo-America, as the century progressed, stressed the distinctiveness of their situation more and more, not by abandoning their English identities but by claiming another as well, one Englishmen in England needed to have explained by Virginians who identified themselves as such, albeit in the educated prose of English gentlemen. Byrd's letter to his English friend illustrates this dual stance: the way the Virginia colonists are beginning to see them-

Seal of the Virginia Company.

selves not only living outside England but also *in* the colonies. Beverley signed his *History and Present State of Virginia,* "A Native and Inhabitant of the Place."

At the same time, the colonies were also developing regional identities. The divisions were permeable. It was John Smith, the colonizer of Virginia, who named New England and drew its first map. And just as the mock-epic conflict of William Bradford and Thomas Morton has immortalized the cavalier presence in New England, a text like "A Loving Invitation to Repentance, and Amendment of Life . . . etc." demonstrates the presence of Puritans in the south. Until the second half of the seventeenth century, Bermuda was predominantly Puritan, and there were always Puritans among the largest planters and merchants of the Indies generally; the settlement of Carolina was undertaken first by a group from Massachusetts Bay.

Still, dominant regional characters did emerge, reflecting local conditions more than the identity of the settlers. The first major sites of English colonization were in the subtropical areas of Virginia and the West Indies, which grew concurrently and developed similar cultures. Bermuda and Virginia were developed by the same company, and tobacco plantations formed the basic economy in both. Sugar plantations in Barbados engendered a similar culture. Society in both the West Indian islands and the mainland South was structured like a pyramid, with a small group of wealthy planters at the top and a growing group of African slaves at the bottom. The first generation of plantation workers had been indentured servants, often Irish; but, at mid-century, these were being rapidly replaced by slaves and the displaced whites seldom rose to the top of the pyramid.

The main West Indian colonies eventually included Bermuda, Bahamas, St. Christopher, Jamaica, and Barbados. The last was the focus of contemporary colonial ambition and considered among empire builders much more important than Virginia or Massachusetts, although in American histories from the nineteenth century on, Barbados has generally been relegated to the margins of the colonial story. In the seventeenth century, it was the most populated and also the most productive of the colonies, with a population of 50,000 (40,000 of whom were slaves), and more exports than all of the other North American colonies combined. The excerpt from Richard Ligon's work thus describes, in the plantation society and economy, the most prevalent form of English colonization in the first century of the empire.

The Virginia colony, with close ties to Barbados and living from the production of tobacco, as Barbados did from the production of sugar, is more properly placed in this context of Atlantic imperial commerce than in any primary relation to the continent, still less to Massachusetts and New England. The early Virginia settlers (to John Smith's great disapproval) were mainly intent on precious metals, tobacco, and overseas commerce. "Virginia" was an expanding territory fanning out from the mouth of the James River and around the Chesapeake Bay. Its outline and features growing ever vaguer, it extended toward and through the Piedmont to the Blue Ridge Mountains. On some contemporary maps, the word "Sea," written hopefully just above the sketch of the mountains, suggests the limits both of geographical knowledge and of interest in the continent as such. In this period, it was the French who had a continental vision. LaSalle, traveling down the whole length of the Mississippi in 1682, imagined a French America extending from the Gulf of Mexico to Canada. For their part, the English would not become predominant in North America until the Treaty of Paris in 1763. With 1,200 inhabitants in 1624 and still only 20,000 in 1654, the great majority engaged in the production of a cash crop, Virginia located its horizon of ambition overseas. Had it been found that North America was a narrow strip of land after all and traversed by a northwest passage to the East, most people in Virginia would have rejoiced.

M.J.

Suggested readings: R. C. Simmons's *The American Colonies: From Settlement to Independence* provides an overview of the period. Two histories of the colonization of the West Indies make up for relative neglect: Richard S. Dunn's *Sugar and Slaves: The Rise of the Planter Class in the English West Indies, 1624–1713* and Peter Hulme's *Colonial Encounters: Europe and the Native Caribbean*. For the continental colonies, Edmund S. Morgan's *American Slavery, American Freedom: The Ordeal of Colonial Virginia,* while dealing closely with the local situation, applies to the development of colonial society generally. In *The Invasion Within: The Contest of Cultures in Colonial North America,* James Axtell describes the three-sided battle for North America, among the English, the French, and the Indians.

1. James I

from *A Counter-Blaste to Tobacco* 1604

The first Stuart king of England, James I (1566–1625) was already king of Scotland when he succeeded Elizabeth I in 1603. Committed to royal power, peace in Europe, and colonial expansion in America, James I represents the temper of an era when the map of Europe would be stable for the foreseeable future while the map of the world was rapidly being covered by European names.

When tobacco first appeared from America it was widely touted as a miracle drug, a cure for digestive and respiratory diseases, an enhancer of moods and sexual energies, and withal a sign of sophistication. It should be noted that his scorn for tobacco and its users did not prevent the king from doing all he could to enrich the crown through its trade.

That the manifolde abuses of this vile custome of *Tobacco* taking, may the better be espied, it is fit, that first you enter into consideration both of the first orginiall thereof, and likewise of the reasons of the first entry thereof into this Countrey. For certainely as such customes, that have their first institution either from a godly, necessary, or honorable ground, and are first brought in, by the meanes of some worthy, vertuous, and great Personage, are ever, and most justly, holden in great and reverent estimation and account, by all wise, vertuous, and temperate spirits: So should it by the contrary, justly bring a great disgrace into that sort of customes, which having their originall from base corruption and barbarity, doe in like sort, make their first entry into a Countrey, by an inconsiderate and childish affectation of Noveltie, as is the true case of the first invention of *Tobacco* taking, and of the first entry thereof among us. For *Tobacco* being a common herbe, which (though under divers names) growes almost everywhere, was first found out by some of the barbarous *Indians*, to be a Preservative, or Antidot against the Pockes[1] a filthy disease, whereunto these barbarous people are (as all men know) very much subject, what through the uncleanly and adust[2] constitution of their bodies, and what through the intemperate heate of their Climate: so that as from them was first brought into Christendome, that most detestable disease, so from them likewise was brought this use of *Tobacco*, as a stinking and unsavorie Antidot, for so corrupted and execrable a Maladie, the stinking Suffumigation whereof they yet use against that disease, making so one canker or venime to eate out another.

---

1. Pockes: syphilis, which some believed to have originated in the New World.

2. adust: in seventeenth-century medicine, a state of the body characterized by dryness, heat, and thirst.

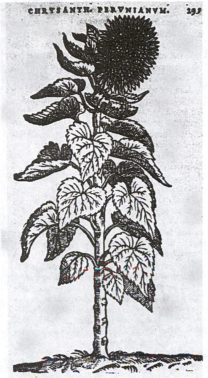

Sixteenth-century illustration of tobacco.

Tobacco smoking, from a broadside called "The Sucklington Faction" (London, 1641).

[THE ADVOCATES OF TOBACCO WILL CLAIM ANYTHING]

Such is the miraculous omnipotence of our strong tasted *Tobacco*, as it cures all sorts of diseases (which never any drugge could do before) in all persons, and at all times. It cures all maner of distellations, either in the head or stomacke (if you beleeve their Axiomes) although in very deede it doe both corrupt the braine, and by causing over quicke digestion, fill the stomacke full of crudities. It cures the Gowt in the feet, and (which is miraculous) in that very instant when the smoke thereof, as light, flies up into the head, the vertue thereof, as heavie, runs downe to the little toe. It helpes all sorts of Agues. It makes a man sober that was drunke. It refreshes a weary man, and yet makes a man hungry. Being taken when they goe to bed, it makes one sleepe soundly, and yet being taken when a man is sleepie and drowsie, it will, as they say, awake his braine, and quicken his understanding. As for curing of the Pockes, it serves for that use but among the pockie Indian slaves. Here in *England* it is refined, and will not deigne to cure heere any other then cleanly and gentlemanly diseases. Omnipotent power of *Tobacco*! And if it could by the smoke thereof chace our devils, as the smoke of *Tobias* fish did (which I am sure could smel no stronglier) it would serve for a precious Relicke, both for the superstitious Priests, and the insolent Puritanes, to cast out devils withall. . . .

Have you not reason then to bee ashamed, and to forbeare this filthie noveltie, so basely grounded, so foolishly received and so grossely mistaken in the right use thereof? In your abuse thereof sinning against God, harming yourselves both in persons and goods, and taking also thereby the markes and notes of vanitie upon you: by the custome thereof making your selves to be wondered at by all forraine civil Nations, and by all strangers that come among you, to be scorned and contemned. A custome lothsome to the eye, hatefull to the Nose, harmefull to the braine, dangerous to the Lungs, and in the blacke stinking fume thereof, neerest

resembling the horrible Stigian

smoke of the pit that is

bottomelesse.

2. John Smith

on tobacco, from the *Generall Historie* 1624

Although tobacco had virtually saved the Virginia colony, John Smith was not an enthusiast. The colonies should produce a variety of crops so as to be self-supporting. Instead, the Jamestown colony was abandoning all other enterprises for a single cash crop. Here he describes the colony itself apparently dissolving into tobacco culture.

In James towne he found but five or six houses, the Church downe, the Palizado's[3] broken, the Bridge in pieces, the Well of fresh water spoiled; the Store-house they used for the Church, the market-place, and streets, and all other spare places planted with Tobacco, the Salvages as frequent in their houses as themselves, whereby they were become expert in our armes, and had a great many in their custodie and possession, the Colonie dispersed all about, planting Tobacco.

---

3. Palizado's: a fence made of stakes driven into the ground.

3. Richard Ligon

from *A True and Exact History of the Island of Barbados*
1657

Very little is known of Richard Ligon (?–1662) other than that through some misalliances he found himself after 1647 with no prospects in England and decided, like many in his situation, to seek his fortune in Barbados. There things did not go much better and after three years, ill and as poor as ever, he returned to England and to debtors' prison. At Newgate, he wrote his True and Exact History, *a vivid description of island life and customs and an account of its sugar-based economy, including maps and illustrations, plans, diagrams, and budgets. Ligon's account of the Barbados colony has been called by Peter Hulme, a historian of the region, "probably the single most valuable source for the history of the English Caribbean islands in the seventeenth century."*

The descriptions of colonial society below are at once remarkably acute and entirely conventional, notably in their attitude toward Africans and women of all races. Witty and entrepreneurial, the text embodies its imperial context and its author's situation as an impoverished gentleman. Richard Ligon was not one of the empire's successes, which may have had something to do with his being one of its best historians.

Having been Censur'd by some (whose Judgements I cannot controll, and therefore am glad to allow) for my weakenesse and Indiscretion, that having never made proofe of the Sea's operation, and the severall faces that watry Element puts on, and the changes and chances that happen there, from Smooth to Rough, from Rough to Raging Seas, and High going Billowes, (which are killing to some Constitutions,) should in the last Scene of my life, undertake to run so long a Risco from *England* to the *Barbadoes*; And truly I should without their help conclude my selfe guilty of that Censure, had I not the refuge of an old proverb to fly to, which is, Need makes the old wife trot: for having lost (by a Barbarous Riot) all that I had gotten by the painfull travells and cares of my youth; by which meanes I was stript and rifled of all I had, left destitute of a subsistance, and brought to such an Exigent, as I must famish or fly; and looking about for friends, who are the best supporters in so staggering a condition, found none, or very few, whom griefs and afflictions had not deprest, or worne out, Banishment absented, or Death devour'd; so that in stead of these neere and Native comforters, I found my selfe a stranger in my owne Country, and therefore resolv'd to lay hold on the first opportunity that might convoy me to any other part of the World, how far distant soever, rather then abide here. I continued not many weekes in this expectation, when a friend, as willing to shift his ground as I, gave me an Overture which I accepted, and so upon the sixteenth day of *June 1647*, we embark'd in the Downes, on the good Ship called the *Achilles*; a vessell of 350 tunnes the Master *Thomas Crowder* of *London*; and no sooner were we all aboard, but we presently weighed Anchor, and put to Sea.

[THEY ARRIVE AT THE CAPE VERDE ISLANDS AND ARE ENTERTAINED]

Dinner being ended, and the Padre well neere wearie of his wayting, we rose, and made roome for better Companie; for now the Padre, and his blacke mistresse were to take their turnes; A Negro of the greatest beautie and majestie together that ever I saw in one woman. Her stature large, and excellently shap't, well favour'd, full eye'd, & admirably grac't; she wore on her head a roll of green taffatie, strip't with white and Philiamort,[4] made up in manner of a Turban; and over that a sleight vayle, which she tooke off at pleasure. On her bodie next her linen, a Peticoate of Orange Tawny and Skye Colour; not done with Straite stripes, but wav'd; and upon that a mantle of purple silke, ingrayld with straw Colour. This Mantle was large, and tyed with a knot of verie broad black Ribbon, with a rich Jewell on her right shoulder, which came under her left arme, and so hung loose and carelesly, almost to the ground. On her Legs, she wore buskins of wetched Silke, deckt with Silver lace, and Fringe; Her shooes, of white Leather, lac't with skie colour; and pinkt between those laces. In her eares, she wore Large Pendants, about her neck; and on her armes, fayre Pearles. But her eyes were her richest Jewells: for they were the largest, and most orientall, that I have ever seene.

Seing all these perfections in her onely at passage, but not yet heard her Speake; I was resolv'd after dinner, to make an Essay what a present of rich silver silke and gold Ribbon would doe, to perswade her to open her lips: Partly out of a Curiositie, to see whether her teeth were exactly white, and cleane, as I hop'd they were; for 'tis a generall opinion, that all *Negroes* have white teeth; but that is a Common error, for the black and white, being so neere together, they set off one another with the greater advantage. But looke neerer to them, and you shall find those teeth, which at a distance appear'd rarely white, are yellow and foul. This knowledge wrought this Curiositie in me, but it was not the mayne end of my enquirie; for there was now, but one thing more, to set her off in my opinion, the rarest black swanne that I had ever seen, and that was her language, & gracefull delivery of that, which was to unite and confirme a perfection in all the rest. And to that end I took a Gentleman that spoke good Spanish with me, and awaited her comming out, which was with far greater majesty, and gracefulness, then I have seen Queen *Anne*, descend from the Chaire of State, to dance the Measures with a Baron of England, at a Maske in the Banquetting house. And truly, had her followers and friends, with other perquisits (that ought to be the attendants on such a state and beautie) wayted on her, I had made a stop, and gone no farther. But finding her but slightly attended and considering she was but the Padres Mistres, & therefore the more accessible, I made my addresses to her, by my interpreter; & told her, I had some Trifles made by the people of *England*, which for

4. Philiamort: corruption of feuille morte, therefore the color of a dead or faded leaf.

their value were not worthy her acceptance, yet for their Novelty, they might be of some esteem, such having bin worn by the great Queens of *Europe*, & intreated her to vouchsafe to receive them. She with much gravity, and reserv'dness, opened the paper; but when she lookt on them, the Colours pleased her so, as she put her gravity into the loveliest smile that I have ever seen. And then shewed her rowes of pearls, so clean, white, Orient, and well shaped, as *Neptunes* Court was never pav'd with such as these; & to shew whether was whiter, or more Orient, those or the whites of her eyes, she turn'd them up, & gave me such a look, as was a sufficient return for a far greater present, and withall wisht, I would think of somewhat wherein she might pleasure me, and I should finde her both ready and willing. And so with a gracefull bow of her neck, she took her way towards her own house; which was not above a stones cast from the *Padres*. Other addresses were not to be made, without the dislike of the *Padre*, for they are there as jealous of their Mistrisses, as the *Italians* of their wives.

In the afternoon we took leave, and went aboard, where we remained three or four days; about which time, some passengers of the ship, who had no great store of linnen for shift, desired leave to go ashoare and took divers women along with them, to wash their linnen. But (it seem'd) the *Portugalls*, and *Negroes* too, found them handsome and fit for their turnes, and were a little Rude, I cannot say Ravisht them; for the Major part of them, being taken from Bridewell, Turnboule street, and such like places of education,[5] were better natur'd then to suffer such violence; yet complaints were made, when they came aboard, both of such abuses, and stealing their linnen.

But such a praise they gave of the place, as we all were desirous to see it: for, after the Raine, every day gave an increase to the beauty of the place, by the budding out of new fruits and flowers.

This was the valley on the left side of the Hill, more spacious and beautifull by much than that on the right hand, where the *Padre* dwelt. The next day, a dozen Gentlemen of our company, resolv'd to go and see this so much admired valley, and when our Saylers with their long boat went to fetch water, (as dayly they did,) we went along with them and landed there, in as high going Billows, as I have ever seen, so near the land. Much adoe we had, to be carried to land though on mens backs, and yet the grapple came as near the shoare as they durst bring it, for bulging against the bottome.

No sooner were we landed, but the Captaine of the Castle, with one souldier with him; came towards us, with a slow formall pace; who desired to speake with one of us alone. Colonel *Modiford*, being the chiefe man in the Company, went with an Interpreter to meet him; and being at the distance of speech, desired to know his pleasure; which he told him was this. That he understood divers of our women had bin ashoare, the day before; and received some injury, from the people of the Iland, and that it was conceiv'd, we were come Arm'd to take revenge on those that did the affront. He therefore advised us, either to make speedy returne to the boate that brought us: or to send back our swords and pistols, and commit our selves to his protection; and if one of those were not presently put in act, we should in a very short time have all our throats Cut.

We told him we had no intention of revenge for any wrong done, and that the only

5. Bridewell, Turnboule street: London places of prostitution.

cause of our landing, was to see the beauty of the place we had heard so much Commended, by our people that were ashore, of which they had given a very large testimony, both of the pleasantness and fruitfulness of it, and that our visit was out of love, both to the place and people. But for sending our weapons back to the boate, we desired his pardon; for this reason, that the Billows going so very high at that time, we could not send them to the boat without being dipt in the Sea water, which would spoyle them; and the most of them, being rich swords, and pistols, we were loath to have their beauty covered with rust, which the salt water would be the occasion of. We desired rather, that he would Command a souldier of his, to stay with a man of ours, and keep them safe, till our returne; which he being content to doe, we committed our selves to his protection, who put a guard upon us of 10 Souldiers, part *Portugalls* part *Negroes*; the most part of either kind, as proper men as I have seen, and as handsomely cloathed.

Their garments made with much Art, and all seem'd to be done by the Tayler; the Coverings for their heads, were not unlike Helmits; of blew and white strip't silke, some tawny, and yellow, others of other sorts of Colours; but all of one fashion, their doublets close to their bodies, with Cassocks, made of the fashion of the Kings guard: loose sleeves, which came to their elbowes, but large and gathered so as to fit loose from their armes; with foure large skirts, reaching down to the middle of their thighs; but these of a different colour from their suits, their breeches indifferently large, comming down below the knee; and the upper part, so wrought with Whalebones within, as to keep them hollow, from touching their backs; to avoid heat, which they were much troubled with; upon their leggs, buskins of the colour of their suits, yet some made a difference: their shoes Colour'd for the most part; some white, but very few blacke. Their weapons, as Swords, Pistols, Muskets, Pikes, and Partisans, kept very bright, and worne comelily and gracefully, which argued a decencie in the Commander, as their awfull respect did of his autheritie.

Being now under a Guard, we marcht into this valley, one of the delightfullest places that I have ever seen, for besides the high and loftie trees, as the *Palmeto, Royall, Coco, Cedar, Locust, Masticke, Mangrave, Bully, Redwood, Pickled yellow wood, Cassia, Fistula, Calabash, Cherry, Figg tree*, whose body is large inough for timber, *Cittrons, Custard apple, Gnavers, Macow, Cipres, Oranges, Limons, Lymes, Pomegrannat, Abotto, Prickled apple, Prickled peare, Papa*, these and more may be accounted wood: and yet a good part of them bearing excellent fruit; But then there are of a lesser sort, that beare the rarest fruit; whose bodyes cannot be accompted wood, as the Plantine, Pine, Bonano, Milon, water Milon, etc. and some few grapes, but those inconsiderabie, by reason they can never make wine: because they have no winter, and so by that meanes, they can never ripe together, but one is green, another ripe, another rotten, which reason will ever hold, that no wine can be made on Ilands, where there is no winter: or within twenty degrees of the line on either side. I have heard that wine is made in the *East Indies*, within lesse then fifteen Degrees; but tis of the Palme tree; out of whose body, they draw both wine and oyle; which wine will not keep above a day, but no wine of grapes, for the reasons afore said. Other kinds of trees, we found good to smell to, as Mirtle, Jesaman, Tamarisk, with a tree somewhat of that bignesse, bearing a very beautifull flower. The first halfe next the stalke, of a

Ligon's map of Barbados.

deep yellow or gold colour; the other halfe being the larger, of a rich Scarlet: shap'd like a Carnation, & when the flowers fall off, there grows a pod, with 7 or 8 seeds in it, divers of which, we carried to the *Barbados*, and planted there: and they grew and multiplied abundantly, and they call them there, the *St. Iago* flower, which is a beautifull, but not sweet flower.

From these woods of pleasant trees, we saw flying divers birds, some one way, some another, of the fairest, and most beautifull colours, that can be imagined in Nature: others whose Colours and shapes come short of these, did so except in sweetnesse, and loudness of voyce, as our Nightingals in England, are short of them, in either of those two properties; but in variety of tunes, our birds are beyond them, for in that they are defective.

In this valley of pleasure, adorn'd as you have heard, we march't with our Guard, faire and softly, near a quarter of a mile; before we came to the much praised fountaine; from whence we fetcht our water. The circle whereof, was about 60 foot, the Diameter about 20 from the ground to the top of the Well, (which was of freestone,) 3 foot and a halfe, from thence within, downe to the surface of the water, about 15 foot. The spring itselfe, not so much to be praised for the excellency of the taste, though cleare inough, as for the Nymphs that repaire thither. For whilst we stayed there seeing the Sayles fill their Casks; and withall Contemplating the glory of the place: there appeared to our view, many pretie young Negro Virgins, playing about the Well. But amongst those; two, that came downe with either of them a naturall Pitcher, a Calibash upon their arme, to fetch water from this fountaine. Creatures, of such shapes, as would have puzzel'd *Albert Durer*, the great Master of Proportion, but to have imitated; and *Tition*, or *Andrea de Sarta*, for softness of muscles, and Curiositie of Colouring, though with a studied diligence; and a love both to the partie and the worke. To expresse all the perfections of Nature, and Parts, these Virgins were owners of, would aske a more skillfull pen, or pencill then mine; Sure I am, though all were excellent, their motions were the highest, and that is a beautie no painter can expresse, and therefore my pen may well be silent; yet a word or two, would not be amisse, to expresse the difference between these and those of high. *Africa* as of Morcoco, Guinny, Binny, Cutchow, Angola, Æthiopia, and *Mauritania*, or those that dwell nere the *River* of *Gambia*, who are thick lipt, short nosd, and commonly low foreheads. But these, are compos'd of such features, as would marre the judgment of the best Paynters, to undertake to mend. Wanton, as the soyle that bred them, sweet as the fruites they fed on; for being come so neere, as their motions, and graces might perfectly be discern'd, I guest that Nature could not, without help of Art, frame such accomplisht beauties not onely of colours, and favour, but of motion too, which is the highest part of beautie. If dancing had bin in fashion in this *Iland*, I might have been perswaded, that they had bin taught those motions, by some who had studied that Art. But considering the *Padre's Musique* to be the best the *Iland* afforded, I could not but cast away that thought, and attribute all to pure nature; Innocent, as youthfull, their ages about 15.

Seing their beauties so fresh and youthfull, withall the perfections I have named, I thought good to trie, whether the uttering of their language, would be as sweet and harmonious, as their other partes were comely. And by the helpe of a Gentleman that spoke *Portugall*, I accosted them; and began to praise their beauties, shapes, and manner of dressings; which was extreamly prettie. Their haire not shorne as the *Negroes* in the places I have named, close to their heads; nor in quarters, and mases, as they use to weare it, which is ridiculous to all that see them, but themselves: But in a due proportion of length so as having their shortenings by the naturall Curles, they appeared as weirs, and artificiall, dressings to their faces. On the sides of their Cheeks, they plat little of it, of purpose to tie small Ribbon; or some small beads, of white Amber, or blew bugle, sometimes of the rare flowers that grow there; Their eares hung with Pendants, their necks and armes adorn'd with bracelets of Counterfeit pearles, and blew bugle; such as the *Portugalls* bestow on them, for these are free *Negroes*, and weare upon the small of one of their legs, the badge of their freedome; which is a small peece of silver, or tinne, as big as the stale of a spoone; which comes round about the leg: and by reason of the smoothnes, and lightnes, is no impediment to their going. Their cloathes, were petticoates of Strip't silk, next to their linen, which reach to their midle leg: and upon that a mantle, of blew taffitie, tied with a Ribbon on the right shoulder: which coming under the left arme, hung downe carelesly somewhat lower then the petticoate, so as a great part of the naturall beautie, of their backes and necks before, lay open to the view, their breast round, firme, and beautifully shaped.

Upon my addresses to them, they appeared a little disturb'd; and whispered to one another, but had not the Confidence to speake aloud. I had in my hat, a piece of silver and silke Ribbon, which I perceiv'd their well shap't eyes, often to dart at; but their modesties would not give them Confidence to aske. I tooke it out, and divided it between them, which they accepted with much alacritie; and in returne, dranke to one another my health in the liquor of the pure fountaine, which I perceiv'd by their wanton smiles, and jesticulations, and casting their eyes towards me: when they thought they had exprest enough they would take in their Countenances, and put themselves in the modestest postures that could be, but we having brought a Case of bottles, of English spirits, with us; I cald for some, and drunke a health to them, in a small dramme cup; and gave it to one of them; which they smelt to, and finding it too strong for their temper, pour'd some of it into one of their Calibashes: and put to it as much water, as would temper it to their palats; they dranke againe, but all this would not give them the Confidence to speake, but, in mute language, and extream prety motions, shewed, they wanted neither wit nor discretion, to make an answer. But it seem'd, it was not the fashion there, for young Maides to speak to strangers, in so publick a place.

I thought I had been sufficiently arm'd with the perfections I found in the *Padre*'s Mistresse, as to be free from the darts of any other Beauty of that place, and in so short a time: But I found the difference between young fresh Beauties, and those that are made up with the addition of State and Majesty: For though they counsell and perswade our Loves; yet, young Beauties force, and so commit rapes upon our affections. In summe, had not my heart been fixed fast in my breast, and dwelt there above sixty years, and therefore loath to leave his long kept habitation, I had undoubtedly left it between them for a Legacy. For, so equall were there Beauties, and my Love, as it was not, nor could be, particular to either.

I have heard it a question disputed, whether if a Horse, being plac'd at an equall distance, between two bottles of hey, equally good; and his appetite being equally fix'd upon either: Whether that Horse must not necessarily starve. For, if he feed on either, it must argue, that his appetite was more fixt on that; or else, that bottle was better than the other. Otherwise, what should move him to chose one before the other?

In this posture was I, with my two Mistresses; or rather, my two halves of one Mistresse: for, had they been conjoyned, and so made one, the poynt of my Love had met there; but, being divided, and my affection not forked, it was impossible to fix, but in one Centre.

In this doubtfull condition, I took my leave, with an assurance, that I should never finde two such parallel Paragons, in my whole search through the World.

[ACQUIRING A PLANTATION IN BARBADOS]

And so upon discourse with some of the most knowing men of the Iland, we found that it was farre better, for a man that had money, goods, or Credit, to purchase a plantation there ready furnisht, and stockt with Servants, Slaves, Horses, Cattle, Assinigoes,[6] Camels, etc. with a sugar worke, and an Ingenio[7] than to begin upon a place, where land is to be had for nothing, but a triviall Rent, and to indure all hardships, and a tedious expectation, of what profit or pleasure may arise, in many yeers patience: and that, not to be expected without large and frequent supplies from *England*; and yet fare, and labour hard. This knowledge, was a spurre to set on Colonel *Modiford*, who had both goods and credit, to make enquiry for such a purchase, which in very few dayes he

---

6. Assinigoes: small asses.   7. Ingenio: sugar mill.

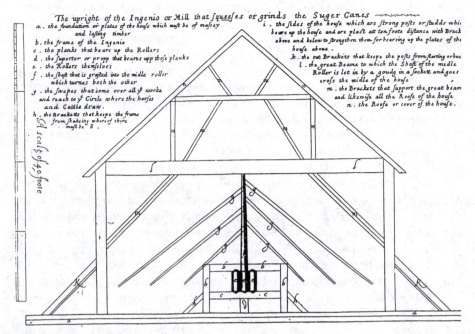

Ligon's drawing of the Ingenio or sugar mill.

lighted on; making a visit to the Governour Mr. *Phillip Bell*, met there with Major *William Hilliard*, an eminent planter of the Iland, and a Councellor, who had been long there, and was now desirous to sucke in some of the sweet ayre of *England*: And glad to find a man likely to performe with him, took him home to his house, and began to treat with him, for halfe the plantation upon which he lived; which had in it 500 Acres of Land, with a faire dwelling house, an Ingenio plac't in a roome of 400 foot square; a boyling house, filling roome, Cisterns, and Still-house; with a Carding house, of 100 foot long, and 40 foot broad; with stables, Smiths forge, and rooms to lay provisions, of Corne, and Bonavist;[8] Houses for *Negroes* and *Indian* slaves, with 96 *Negroes*, and three *Indian* women, with their Children; 28 Christians, 45 Cattle for worke, 8 Milch Cowes, a dosen Horses and Mares, 16 Assinigoes.

After a Months treaty, the bargaine was concluded, and Colonel *Modiford* was to pay for the Moity[9] of this plantation, £7000; to be payed, £1000, in hand, the rest £2000 a time, at sixe and sixe months, and Colonel *Modiford* to receive the profit of halfe the plantation as it rose, keeping the account together, both of the expence and profit.

In this plantation of 500 acres of land, there was imployed for sugar somewhat more then 200 acres; above 80 acres for pasture, 120 for wood, 20 for Tobacco, 5 for Ginger, as many for Cotton wool, and 70 acres for provisions; *viz.* Corne, Potatoes,

8. Bonavist: kidney beans.   9. Moity: half share.

Plantines, Cassavie[10] and Bonavist; some few acres of which for fruite; *viz*. Pines, Plantines, Milions, Bonanoes, Gnavers Water Milions, Oranges; Limons, Limes, etc. most of these onely for the table.

[BARBADOS SOCIETY]

The Iland is divided into three sorts of men, *viz*. Masters, Servants, and slaves. The slaves and their posterity, being subject to their Masters for ever; are kept and preferv'd with greater care then the servants, who are theirs but for five yeers, according to the law of the Iland. So that for the time, the servants have the worser lives, for they are put to very hard labour, ill lodging, and their dyet very sleight. When we came first on the Iland, some Planters themselves did not eate bone meat, above twice a weeke: the rest of the seven dayes, Potatoes, Loblolly[11] and Bonavist. But the servants no bone meat at all, unlesse an Oxe dyed: and then they were feasted, as long as that lasted, And till they had planted good store of Plantines, the *Negroes* were fed with this kind of food; but most of it Bonavist, and Loblolly, with some eares of Mayes toasted, which food (especially Loblolly,) gave them much discontent: But when they had Plantines enough to serve them, they were heard no more to complaine; for 'tis a food they take great delight in, and their manner of dressing and eating it, is this: 'tis gathered for them (somewhat before it be ripe, for so they desire to have it,) upon Saturday, by the keeper of the Plantine grove; who is an able *Negro*, and knowes well the number of those that are to be fed with this fruite; and as he gathers, layes them all together, till they fetch them away, which is about five a clock in the afternoon, for that day they breake off worke sooner by an houre: partly for this purpose, and partly for that the fire in the furnaces is to be put out, and the Ingenio and the roomes made cleane; besides they are to wash, shave and trim themselves again on Sunday. But 'tis a lovely sight to see a hundred handsome *Negroes*, men and women, with every one a grasse-green bunch of these fruits on their heads, every bunch twice as big as their heads, all comming in a train one after another, the black and green so well becomming one another. Having brought this fruit home to their own houses, and pilling off the skin of so much as they will use, they boyl it in water, making it into balls, and so they eat it. One bunch a week is a *Negres* allowance. To this, no bread nor drink, but water. Their lodging at night a board, with nothing under, nor any thing a top of them. They are happy people, whom so little contents. Very good servants, if they be not spoyled by the English. But more of them hereafter.

As for the usage of the Servants, it is much as the Master is, mercifull or cruell; Those that are mercifull, treat their Servants well, both in their meat, drink, and lodging, and give them such work, as is not unfit for Christians to do. But if the Masters be cruell, the Servants have very wearisome and miserable lives. Upon the arrivall of any ship, that brings servants to the Iland, the Planters go aboard; and having bought such of them as they like, send them with a guide to his Plantation; and

---

10. Cassavie: a plant grown for its nutritious roots which provided an important part of the slave diet.

11. Loblolly: thick gruel or spoon-meat.

being come, commands them instantly to make their Cabins, which they not knowing how to do, are to be advised by other of their servants, that are their seniors; but, if they be churlish, and will not shew them, or if materialls be wanting, to make them Cabins, then they are to lie on the ground that night. These Cabins are to be made of sticks, withes, and Plantine leaves, under some little shade that may keep the rain off; Their suppers being a few Potatoes for meat, and water or Mobbie[12] for drink. The next day they ar rung out with a Bell to work, at six a clock in the morning, with a severe Overseer to command them, till the Bell ring again, which is at eleven a clock; and then they return, and are set to dinner, either with a messe of Lob-lollie, Bonavist, or Potatoes. At one a clock, they are rung out again to the field, there to work till six, and then home again, to a supper of the same. And if it chance to rain, and wet them through, they have no shift, but must lie so all night. If they put off their cloths, the cold of the night will strike into them; and if they be not strong men, this ill lodging will put them into a sicknesse: if they complain, they are beaten by the Overseer; if they resist, their time is doubled. I have seen an Overseer beat a Servant with a cane about the head, till the blood has followed, for a fault that is not worth the speaking of; and yet he must have patience, or worse will follow. Truly, I have seen such cruelty there done to Servants, as I did not think one Christian could have done to another. But, as discreeter and better natur'd men have come to rule there, the servants lives have been much bettered; for now, most of the servants lie in Hamocks, and in warm rooms, and when they come in wet, have shift of shirts and drawers, which is all the cloths they were, and are fed with *bone meat* twice or thrice a week. Collonell *Walrond* seeing his servants when they came home, toyled with their labour, and wet through with their sweating, thought that shifting of their linnen not sufficient refreshing, nor warmth for their bodies, their pores being much opened by their sweating; and therefore resolved to send into *England* for rug Gownes, such as poor people wear in Hospitalls, that so when they had shifted themselves, they might put on those Gowns, and lie down and rest them in their Hamocks: For the Hamocks being but thin, and they having nothing on but shirts and drawers, when they awak'd out of their sleeps, they found themselves very cold; and a cold taken there, is harder to be recovered, than in *England*, by how much the body is infeebled by the great toyle, and the Sun's heat, which cannot but very much exhaust the spirits of bodies unaccustomed to it. But this care and charity of Collonell *Walrond's*, lost him nothing in the conclusion; for, he got such love of his servants, as they thought all too little they could do for him; and the love of the servants there, is of much concernment to the Masters, not only in their diligent and painfull labour, but in fore seeing and preventing mischiefes that often happen, by the carelessnesse and slothfulnesse of recklesse servants; sometimes by laying fire so negligently, as whole lands of Canes and Houses too, are burnt down and consumed, to the utter ruine and undoing of their Masters: For, the materialls there being all combustible, and apt to take fire, a little oversight, as the fire of a Tobacco-pipe, being knockt out against a drie stump of a tree, has set it on fire, and the wind fanning that fire, if a land of Canes be but neer, and they once take fire, all that are down the winde will be burnt up. Water there is

---

12. Mobbie: a spiritous liquor made from sweet potatoes.

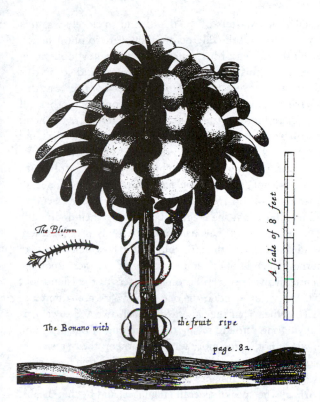

The Blossom

A scale of 8 feet

The Bonano with   the fruit ripe

page .82.

Ligon's drawing of the banana tree.

none to quench it, or if it were, a hundred *Negres* with buckets were not able to do it; so violent and spreading a fire this is, and such a noise it makes, as if two Armies, with a thousand shot of either side, were continually giving fire, every knot of every Cane, giving as great a report as a Pistoll. So that there is no way to stop the going on of this flame, but by cutting down and removing all the Canes that grow before it, for the breadth of twenty or thirty foot down the winde, and there the *Negres* to stand and beat out the fire, as it creeps upon the ground, where the Canes are cut down. And I have seen some *Negres* so earnest to stop this fire, as with their naked feet to tread, and with their naked bodies to tumble, and roll upon it; so little they regard their own smart or safety, in respect of their Masters benefit. The year before I came away, there were two eminent Planters in the Iland, that with such an accident as this, lost at least £10000 sterling, in the value of the Canes that were burnt; the one, Mr. *James Holduppe*, the other, Mr. *Constantine Silvester*: And the latter had not only his Canes, but his house burnt down to the ground. This, and much more mischiefe has been done, by the negligence and wilfulnesse of servants. And yet some cruell Masters will provoke their Servants so, by extream ill usage, and often and cruell beating them, as they grow desperate, and so joyne together to revenge themselves upon them.

A little before I came from thence, there was such a combination amongst them, as the like was never seen there before. Their sufferings being grown to a great height, & their daily complainings to one another (of the intolerable burdens they labour'd under) being spread throughout the Iland; at the last, some amongst them, whose spirits were not able to endure such slavery, resolved to break through it, or die in the act; and so conspired with some others of their acquaintance, whose sufferings were equall, if not above theirs; and their spirits no way inferiour, resolved to draw as many of the discontented party into this plot, as possibly they could; and those of this perswasion, were the greatest numbers of servants in the Iland. So that a day was appointed to fall upon their Masters, and cut all their throats, and by that means, to make themselves not only freemen, but Masters of the Iland. And so closely was this plot carried, as no discovery was made, till the day before they were to put it in act: And then one of them, either by the failing of his courage, or some new obligation from the love of his Master, revealed this long plotted conspiracy; and so by this timely advertisment, the Masters were saved: Justice *Hethersall* (whose servant this was) sending Letters to all his friends, and they to theirs, and so one to another, till they were all secured; and, by examination, found out the greatest part of them; whereof eighteen of the principall men in the conspiracy, and they the first leaders and contrivers of the plot, were put to death, for example to the rest. And the reason why they made examples of so many, was, they found these so haughty in their resolutions, and so incorrigible, as they were like enough to become actors in a second plot; and so they thought good to secure them; and for the rest, to have a speciall eye over them.

It has been accounted a strange thing, that the Negres, being more then double the numbers of the Christians that are there, and they accounted a bloody people, where they think they have power or advantages; and the more bloody, by how much they are more fearfull than others: that these should not commit some horrid massacre upon the Christians, thereby to enfranchise themselves, and become Masters of the Island. But there are three reasons that take away this wonder; the one is, They are not suffered to touch or handle any weapons: The other, That they are held in such awe and slavery, as they are fearfull to appear in any daring act; and seeing the mustering of our men, and hearing their Gun-shot, (than which nothing is more terrible to them) their spirits are subjugated to so low a condition, as they dare not look up to any bold attempt. Besides these, there is a third reason, which stops all designes of that kind, and that is, They are fetch'd from severall parts of *Africa*, who speake severall languages, and by that means, one of them understands not another: For, some of them are fetch'd from *Guinny* and *Binny*, some from *Cutchew*, some from *Angola*, and some from the River of *Gambra*. And in some of these places where petty Kingdomes are, they sell their Subjects, and such as they take in Battle, whom they make slaves; and some mean men sell their Servants, their Children, and sometimes their Wives; and think all good traffick, for such commodities as our Merchants sends them.

When they are brought to us, the Planters buy them out of the Ship, where they find them stark naked, and therefore cannot be deceived in any outward infirmity. They choose them as they do Horses in a Market; the strongest, youthfullest, and most beautiful, yield the greatest prices. Thirty pound sterling is a price for the best man Negre; and twenty five, twenty six, or twenty seven pound for a Woman; the Children are at easier rates. And we buy them so, as the sexes may be equall; for, if they have more men then women, the men who are unmarried will come to their Masters, and complain, that they cannot live without Wives, and desire him, they may have Wives. And he tells them, that the next ship that comes, he will buy them Wives, which satisfies them for the present; and so they expect the good time: which the Master performing with them, the bravest fellow is to choose first, and so in order, as they are in place; and every one of them knowes his better, and gives him the precedence, as Cowes do one another, in passing through a narrow gate; for the most of them are as neer beasts as may be, setting their souls aside. Religion they know none; yet most of them acknowledge a God, as appears by their motions and gestures: For, if one of them do another wrong, and he cannot revenge himselfe, he looks up to Heaven for vengeance, and holds up both his hands, as if the power must come from thence, that must do him right. Chast they are as any people under the Sun; for, when the men and women are together naked, they never cast their eyes towards the parts that ought to be covered; and those amongst us, that have Breeches and Petticoats, I never saw so much as a kisse, or embrace, or a wanton glance with their eyes between them. Jealous they are of their Wives, and hold it for a great injury and scorn, if another man make the least courtship to his Wife. And if any of

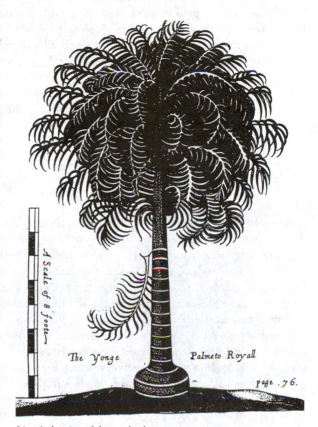

Ligon's drawing of the royal palm.

their Wives have two Children at a birth, they conclude her false to his Bed, and so no more adoe but hang her. We had an excellent Negre in the Plantation, whose name was *Macow*, and was our chiefe Musitian; a very valiant man, and was keeper of our Plantine-groave. This Negres Wife was brought to bed of two Children, and her Husband, as their manner is, had provided a cord to hang her. But the Overseer finding what he was about to do, enformed the Master of it, who sent for *Macow*, to disswade him from this cruell act, of murdering his Wife, and used all perswasions that possibly he could, to let him see, that such double births are in Nature, and that divers presidents were to found amongst us of the like; so that we rather praised our Wives, for their fertility, than blamed them for their falsenesse. But this prevailed little with him, upon whom custome had taken so deep an impression; but resolved, the next thing he did, should be to hang her. Which when the Master perceived, and that the ignorance of the man, should take away the life of the woman, who was innocent of the crime her Husband condemned her for, told him plainly, that if he hang'd her, he himselfe should be hang'd by her, upon the same bough; and therefore wish'd him to consider what he did. This threatning wrought more with him, then all the reasons of Philosophy that could be given him; and so let her alone; but he never car'd much for her afterward, but chose another which he lik'd better. For the Planters there deny not a slave, that is a brave fellow, and one that has extraordinary qualities, two or three Wives, and above that number they seldome go: But no woman is allowed above one Husband.

At the time the wife is to be brought abed, her husband removes his board (which is his bed) to another room (for many severall divisions they have, in their little houses, and none above sixe foot square). And leaves his wife to God, and her good fortune, in the room, and upon the board alone, and calls a neighbour to come to her, who gives little help to her deliverie, but when the child is borne, (which she calls her Pickaninnie) she helps to make a little fire nere her feet and that serves instead of Possets[13] Broaths, and Caudles.[14] In a fortnight, this woman is at worke with her Pickaninny at her back, as merry a soule as any there: If the overseer be discreet, shee is suffer'd to rest her selfe a little more than ordinary; but if not, shee is compelled to doe as others doe. Times they have of suckling their Children in the fields, and refreshing themselves; and good reason, for they carry burdens on their backs; and yet work too. Some women, whose Pickaninnies are three yeers old, will, as they worke at weeding, which is a stooping worke, suffer the hee Pickaninnie, to sit astride upon their backs, like St. *George* a horseback; and there spurre his mother with his heeles, and sings and crowes on her backe, clapping his hands, as if he meant to flye; which the mother is so pleas'd with, as shee continues her painfull stooping posture, longer than she would doe, rather than discompose her Joviall Pickaninnie of his pleasure, so glad she is to see him merry. The worke which the women doe, is most of it weeding, a stooping and painfull worke; at noon and night they are call'd home by the ring of a Bell, where they have two hours time for their repast at noone; and at night, they rest from sixe, till sixe a Clock next morning.

On Sunday they rest, and have the whole day at their pleasure; and the most of them use it as a day of rest and pleasure; but some of them who will make benefit of that dayes liberty, goe where the Mangrave trees grow, and gather the barke of which they make ropes, which they trucke away for other Commoditie, as shirts and drawers.

In the afternoons on Sundayes, they have their musicke, which is of kettle drums, and those of severall sises; upon the smallest the best musitian playes, and the other come in as Chorasses: the drum all men know, has but one tone; and therefore varietie of tunes have little to doe in this musick; and yet so strangely they varie their time, as 'tis a pleasure to the most curious eares, and it was to me one of the strangest noyses that ever I heard made of one tone; and if they had the varietie of tune, which gives the greater scope in musick, as they have of time, they would doe wonders in that Art. And if I had not faln sicke before my comming away, at least seven months in one sickness, I had given them some hints of tunes, which being understood, would have serv'd as a great addition to their harmonie; for time without tune, is not an eighth part of the science of Musick.

---

13. Posset: a drink of hot milk mixed with some kind of liquor.   14. Caudles: a warm drink of thin gruel with liquor.

[THE SUGAR CULTURE]

At the time we landed on this Iland, which was in the beginning of *September*, 1647, we were informed, partly by those Planters we found there, and partly by our own observations, that the great work of Sugar-making, was but newly practiced by the inhabitants there. Some of the most industrious men, having gotten Plants from *Fernamlock*, a place in *Brasill*, and made tryall of them at the *Barbadoes*; and finding them to grow, they planted more and more, as they grew and multiplyed on the place, till they had such a considerable number, as they were worth the while to set up a very small Ingenio and so make tryall what Sugar could be made upon that soyl. But, the secrets of the work being not well understood, the Sugars they made were very inconsiderable, and little worth, for two or three years. But they finding their errours by their daily practice, began a little to mend; and, by new directions from *Brasil*, sometimes by strangers, and now and then by their own people, (who being covetous of the knowledge of a thing, which so much concerned them in their particulars, and for the generall good of the whole Iland) were content sometimes to make a voyage thither, to improve their knowledge in a thing they so much desired. Being now made much abler to make their queries, of the secrets of that mystery, by how much their often failings, had put them to often stops and nonplusses in the work. And so returning with more Plants, and better Knowledge, they went on upon fresh hopes, but still short, of what they should be more skilfull in: for, at our arrivall there, we found them ignorant in three main points, that much conduced to the work; *viz*. The manner of Planting, the time of Gathering, and the right placing of their Coppers in their Furnaces; as also, the true way of covering their Rollers, with plates or Bars of Iron: All which being rightly done, advance much in the performance of the main work.

At the time of our arrivall there, we found many Sugar-works set up, and at work; but yet the Sugars they made, were but bare Muscavadoes[15] and few of them Merchantable commodities; so moist, and full of molosses, and so ill cur'd, as they were hardly worth the bringing home for *England*. But about the time I left the Iland, which was in 1650, they were much better'd; for then they had the skill to know when the Canes were ripe, which was not, till they were fifteen months old; and before, they gathered them at twelve, which was a main disadvantage to the making good Sugar; for, the liquor wanting of the sweetnesse it ought to have, caused the Sugars to be lean, and unfit to keep. Besides, they were grown greater proficients, both in boyling and curing them, and had learnt the knowledge of making them white, such as you call Lump Sugars here in *England*; but not so excellent as those they make in *Brasill*, nor is there any likelyhood they can ever make such: the land there being better, and lying in a Continent, must needs have constanter and steadier weather, and the Aire much drier and purer, than it can be in so small an Iland, as that of *Barbadoes*. And now, seeing this commodity, Sugar, hath gotten so much the start of all the rest of those, that were held the staple Commodities of the Iland, and so much over-top't them, as they are for the most part sleighted and neglected. And, for that few in *England* know the trouble and care of making it, I think it convenient, in the first place, to acquaint you, as far as

---

15. Muscavadoes: raw or unrefined sugar.

my memory will serve, with the whole processe of the work of Sugar-making, which is now grown the soul of Trade in this Iland. And leaving to trouble you and my self, with relating the errours our Predecessors so long wandred in, I will in briefe set down the right and best way they practised, when I left the Iland, which, I think, will admit of no greater or farther improvement.

But, before I will begin with that, I will let you see, how much the land there hath been advanc'd in the profit, since the work of Sugar began, to the time of our landing there, which was not above five or six years: For, before the work began, this Plantation of Major *Hilliards*, of five hundred acres, could have been purchased for four hundred pound sterling; and now the halfe of this Plantation, with the halfe of the Stock upon it, was sold for seven thousand pound sterling: and it is evident, that all the land there, which has been imployed to that work, hath found the like improvement. And, I believe, when the small Plantations in poor mens hands, often, twenty, or thirty acres, which are too small to lay to that work, be bought up by great men, and put together, into Plantations of five, six, or seven hundred acres, that two thirds of the Iland will be fit for Plantations of Sugar, which will make it one of the richest Spots of earth under the Sun.

[REFINING THE SUGARCANE]

The manner of grinding them, is this, the Horses and Cattle being put to their tackle: they go about, and by their force turne (by the sweeps) the middle roller; which being Cog'd to the other two, at both ends, turne them about; and they all three, turning upon their Centres, which are of Brass and Steele go very easily of themselves, and so easie, as a mans taking hold, of one of the sweeps, with his hand will turne all the rollers about with much ease. But when the Canes are put in between the rollers, it is a good draught for five Oxen or Horses; a *Negre* puts in the Canes of one side, and the rollers draw them through to the other side, where another *Negre* stands, and receives them; and returnes them back on the other side of the middle roller, which drawes the other way. So that having past twice through, that is forth and back, it is conceived all the juyce is prest out; yet the Spaniards have a press, after both the former grindings, to press out the remainder of the liquor, but they having but small works in Spaine, make the most of it, whilst we having far greater quantities are loath to be at that trouble. The Canes having past to and againe, there are young Negre girles that carry them away, and lay them on a heap, at the distance of six score paces or there abouts; where they make a large hill, if the worke have continued long; under the rollers, there is a receiver, as big as a large Tray; into which the liquor falls, and stayes not there, but runs under ground in a pipe or gutter of lead cover'd over close, which pipe or gutter, carries it into the Cistern, which is fixt neer the staires, as you go down from the Mill-house to the boyling house. But it must not remaine in that Cisterne above one day, lest it grow sower; from thence it is to passe through a gutter, (fixt to the wall) to the Clarifying Copper, as there is occasion to use it, and as the work goes on, and as it Clarifies in the first Copper, and the skumme rises, it is conveyed away by a passage, or gutter for that purpose; as also of the second Copper, both which skimmings, are not esteem'd worth the labour of stilling; because the skum is dirtie and grosse: But the skimmings of the other three Coppers, are conveyed down to the Still-house, there to remaine in the Cisterns, till it be a little sower, for till then it will not come over the helme. This liquor is remov'd, as it is refin'd, from one Copper to another, and the more Coppers it passeth through, the finer and purer it is, being continually drawn up, and keel'd by ladles, and skim'd by skimmers, in the Negres hands, till at last it comes to the tach; where it must have much labour, in keeling and stirring, and as it boyles, there is thrown into the four last Coppers, a liquor made of water and Withs which they call Temper, without which, the Sugar would continue a Clammy substance and never kerne. The quantities they put in are small, but being of a tart quality it turnes the ripeness and clamminesse of the Sugar to curddle and separate: which you will find, by taking out some drops of it, to Candy, and suddenly to grow hard; and then it has inough of the fire.

[Who should go to Barbados]

There are some that have heard of the pleasures of *Barbadoes*, but are loath to leave the pleasures of England behind them. These are of a sluggish humour, and are altogether unfit for so noble an undertaking; but if any such shall happen to come there, he shall be transmitted to the innumerable Armie of Pismires; and Ants, to sting him with such a reproof, as he shall wish himselfe any where rather than amongst them. So much is a sluggard detested in a Countrey, where Industry and Activity is to be exercised. The Dwarfe may come there, and twice a year vie in competition with the Giant: for set them both together upon a levell superficies,[16] and at noone, you shall not know by their shadowes who is the tallest man.

The Voluptuous man, who thinks the day not long enough for him to take his pleasure, Nor the sleepie man who thinks the longest night too short for him to dreame out his delights, are not fit to repose and solace themselves upon this Iland; for in the whole compasse of the Zodiacke, they shall neither find St. Barnabies day, or St. Lucies night. The Sun, running an eeven course, is there an indifferent Arbiter of the differences which are between those two Saints, and like a just and cleere sighted Judge, reconciles those extreams to a Medium, of 12 and 12 houres, which equality of time is utterly inconsistent to the humours and dispositions of these men.

But I speak this, to such as have their fancies so Aereall, and refin'd as not to be pleased with ordinary delight; but think to build and settle a felicity here: above the ordinary levell of mankind. Such spirits, are too volatile to fixe on businesse; and therefore I will leave them out, as useless in this Common-wealth. But such as are made of middle earth: and can be content to wave those pleasures, which stand as Blocks, and Percullisses,[17] in their way; and are indeed, the main Remoras[18] in their passage to their profits. Such may here find moderate delights, with moderate labour, and those taken moderately will conduce much to their healths, and they that have industry, to imploy that well, may make it the Ladder to clyme to a high degree, of Wealth and opulencie, in this sweet Negotiation of Sugar, provided they have a competent stock to

16. superficies: surfaces.
17. Percullisses: gates, portcullises.

18. Remoras: obstacles or impediments, from the sucking fish ancients believed able to stop ships.

begin with; such I mean as may settle them in a Sugar-work, and lesse then £14000 sterling, will not do that: in a Plantation of 500 acres of land, with a proportionable stock of Servants, Slaves, Horses, Camels, Cattle, Assinigoes, with an Ingenio, and all other houseing, thereunto belonging; such as I have formerly nam'd.

But one wil say, why should any man that has 14000 l. in his purse, need to runne so long a Risco, as from hence to the Barbadoes: when he may live with ease and plenty at home; to such a one I answer, that every drone can sit and eate the Honey of his own Hive: But he that can by his own Industry, and activity, (having youth and strength to friends,) raise his fortune, from a small beginning to a very great one, and in his passage to that, doe good to the publique, and be charitable to the poor, and this to be accomplished in a few years, deserves much more commendation and applause. And shall find his bread, gotten by his painfull and honest labour and industry, eate sweeter by much, than his that onely minds his ease, and his belly.

[A NEARLY FATAL VOYAGE BACK WHEN THE SHIP IS BECALMED]

At last, a little Virgin, who was a passenger in the Ship, stood up upon the quarter deck, like a she-Worthy, and said, that if they would be rul'd by her, she would not only be the contriver, but the acter of our deliverance. At whose speech, we all gave a strict attention, as ready to contribute our help to all she commanded; which was, that the Ship-Carpenter should make her a Distaffe and Spindle, and the Saylers combe out some of the Occome:[19] with which instruments and materialls, she doubted not, but to make such a quantity of thread, as to repair our then uselesse Sailes; which accordingly she did, and by her vertue (under God) we held our lives.

Though such an accident as this, and such a deliverance, deserve a gratefull commemoration; yet, this is not all the use we are to make of it, somewhat more may be considered, that may prevent dangers for the future; and that is, the great abuse of Captaines and Masters of Ships, who promise to their Passengers, such plenty of victualls, as may serve them the whole voyage: But, before they be halfe way, either pinch them of a great part, or give them that which is nastie and unwholsome. And therefore I could wish every man, that is to go a long voyage, to carry a reserve of his owne, of such viands, as will last, and to put that up safe; for, if it be not under lock and key, they are never the neer; for, the Saylers will as certainly take it, as you trust it to their honesties: Complaine to the Master, and you finde no remedy. One thing I have observed, let a Sayler steal any part of the Ships provision, he shall be sure to have severe punishment; but, if from a Passenger, though it concern him never so neerly, his remedy is to be laughed at. These enormities are fit to be complained on at the Trinity-house, that some redresse may be had; for, the abuses are grievous.

Out of this danger at Sea, it has pleased the God of all mercy to deliver me, as also from a grievous and tedious sicknesse on land, in a strange Country; For which, may his holy Name be eternally blessed and praised, for ever and ever.

I am now cast in Prison, by the subtle practices of some, whom I have formerly called Friends: But the eternall and mercifull God has been pleased to visit and

19. Occome: oakum.

comfort me, and to raise me up such friends, as have kept me from cold and hunger, whose charities in an Age, where cruelties and tyrannies are exercised in so high a measure, may be accounted a prodigie. But, I doubt not of my release out of this restraint, by the power of him, who is able to do all in all. For, as *David* said to *Saul*, that God, who had delivered him out of the paw of the Lion, and out of the paw of the Bear, would deliver him from that uncircumcised Philistine, *Goliah* of *Gath*: So may I now say; that God, which has delivered me from a sicknesse to death, on land, and from shipwrack and hazards at Sea, will also deliver me from this uncircumcised Philistine, the *Upper Bench*, than which, the

> burning fire of a Feavour, nor the raging waves of the Sea,
> are more formidable: But, we have seen and suffered
> greater things. And when the great Leveller of
> the world, Death, shall run his progresse, all
> Estates will be laid eeven.

4. Richard Pinder

from *A Loving Invitation to Repentance and Amendment of Life*
1660

All that is known of Richard Pinder is that he was the author of this jeremiad addressed to the slave-owning aristocracy of Barbados. Though we tend to associate Puritan thought and rhetoric with life in the New England colonies, they were in fact not foreign to the West Indies. Puritans were dominant in the Bermudas and aggressive colonizers of the surrounding territories. In 1631, for instance, they established a colony on Providence Island deep in Spanish territory. The Caribbean was Oliver Cromwell's major interest in the New World and Richard Pinder's prediction of doom for sinning planters does not condemn the slave-plantation enterprise, but only its abuses.

Oh *Barbados*! Listen oh Island! for the Lord hath a sore and great Controversie with thee, because of the Lewdness, and Abominations that are found in thee, which the Righteous soul hateth, and which the Lord is burdened with; that though he be mercifull, and full of pity, and bear long; yet nevertheless, the wicked cannot go unpunished, nor escape his sore and great Judgement: For so he hath determined, that the wicked shall bear the weight of their own wickedness. And oh Island, consider the wickedness that is committed in thee is great; that it is become even as a Mountain before the Lord of Hosts; that Vile, and Contemptible, thou art in his sight, because he hath replenished thee, and filled thee with earthly Fruit, and Substance; and yet though rebellest against him, as though thou couldest bring forth Fruit of thy self. O consider, and call to mind thy former dayes, wherein thou wast little in thine own eyes, and in the eyes of all that knew thee.

O all ye Inhabitants of this Island! many of you are Full, and Rich, and the sins of *Sodom* are found among you; fulness of Bread, and abundance of Idleness. Oh how is the Creatures of God abused, and destroyed among you, in satisfying your ungodly lusts? Do you think the Lord takes no notice of all your wickedness, and unchristian-like Practices? Are you not bad Examples unto all about you; both to the Heathen, and them that have the Name of Christians? Do you think you can escape the Lords Hand? Will all your Riches, and Greatness in the Earth, defend you from it? Oh no: his hand is Mighty, and his stroke will be Grievous; and assuredly it will fall heavy upon the Heads of the Wicked; and especially upon them whom he hath suffered long, as he hath done thee, oh Island: yet provoketh him to displeasure, thou dayly doth, by the Sins which dayly abound in thee, and are brought forth by the Tillers, and Manurers of thee: That though, oh Island, thou yieldst unto them Fruit, and Substance in abundance, yet against him (who causeth the pleasant showers to come upon thee) they rebell.

Oh bring thou forth Thorns and Thistles for their sake, that they may read their Figure, and see how unfruitfull they are unto him, who replenisheth thee, who is the God of the whole Earth, whom all ought to serve, and obey, and not their ungodly lusts, which oh Island, destroyes thy encrease; that I say bring thou forth, and be thou overspread with unfruitfull Weeds, that thy Inhabiters may read their Figure, and see how they cumber the ground, and how they are become as an unfruitfull Wilderness unto him, who hath been gracious unto them, in causing thee to yield encrease in abundance; but with it their hearts are made fat, and corrupted before the Lord, whom they ought to serve, and obey, with their whole heart, who is displeased with their ungodly lusts.

[SLAVERY ESPECIALLY LEADS TO SIN]

Unto you all, who are the Masters, and Owners of the severall Plantations, am I moved to write, and to lay some things before you to be considered of in the fear of the Lord. You, many of you, hath many under you as Slaves, and Bond-Men: Therefore consider your Places, and be not high minded, but fear; provoke not your Servants through cruell usage, for that the Lord hates; they are of the same Blood, and Mould, you are of; and you must give an account of your actions unto the Lord, as well as they, & with him there is no respect of persons. . . .

And truly it will be your burden one day, that you have spent so much precious time, in rioting, feasting, and drunkenness; through which you destroy Gods Creatures; when, as alas, many of your Servants, both white People, and Negroes, are like to perish, and be destroyed for want of the Creatures: and thus you burden the Creation, by being Subject unto your own Lusts: For consider; if the Wisdom of God did lead you, it would bring you to use his Creatures to his Glory; and then it would be your care, Oh ye Heads, and Owners of the severall Plantations, that none of your Servants, or Slaves did perish, or suffer, for want of the Creatures; and also it would be your care, if the Wisdom of God you lived in, which is the Wisdom of the Creation, that none of your Servants, nor any under you should abuse themselves, and the Creatures of God through drunkenness. And then if these things be your care, God would blesse you; but so long as you are bad examples your selves unto your Servants, you strengthen them in their wicked debauched wayes; and thus you become guilty before the Lord, both of their, and your own wickedness; then let amendment of life be brought forth, that you may become good examples to all under you, in patience, in moderation, and sobriety, in your Words and Actions; and that will be the way, whereby you may escape Gods sore Judgments, and be freed from his wrath to come.

[REPENT NOW]

Therefore take yet a word of advice, oh ye great, and rich ones in the earth. If you intend that God shall bless you, then put away far from you all high-mindedness, cruelty, and hard-heartedness, which at this day abounds among you in your severall Plantations. And you the Heads and Owners of them are deeply guilty of these things. Now to remove these, and such like things from your severall Plantations, this would be your way, Put such men in place, to be Overseers of your Servants, as fear God, and hate drunkenness, and swearing, and all such things, that they may rule over them in moderation, and not in Tyranny, and hard-heartedness; and this will be the way to beget love in your Servants unto you, and one to another; and so love being begotten in your Servants unto you, and one unto another, this will stop abundance of cruelty, and wickedness, which doth abound among you; and let not your Overseers (I warn you all) rule in such Tyranny over your Negroes; for if you do, you will bring blood upon you, and the cry of their blood shall enter into the eares of the Lord of Sabbath, (for he made them, & giveth them life) and it shall cause his wrath to break forth upon you; and if you thus provoke the Lord, by letting them, who are your Slaves, be wrongfully entreated, and unmercifully used, it is much, if the Lord bring them not, as a Rod upon you: however let the Lord be clear, and me clear in his sight, in that I warn you of it now, while you have time to mend it; and take heed you abuse not the long-suffering of God, but let it lead you to Repentance, & amendment of life; for if the long-suffering of God comes once to an end, that his Spirit leave striving with you, know then, That your State is miserable; for no other way can, either high or low, rich or poor, bond or free, come to be reconciled in peace with God, and escape his judgements, but by giving regard to be led by his Spirit, which striveth with them, in reproving of them for their sin, which separateth them from God.

5. Anonymous

Great News from the Barbadoes
1676

> *The slave rebellion of 1675 described in this pamphlet was the one that most alarmed Barbados whites. But between 1640 and 1713, there were six others in the West Indies large enough to be recorded. One rebellion in 1685–86 in Jamaica lasted a year. The Jamaica landscape offered better hopes of success and it was there that the majority of the uprisings occurred. Planters felt and indeed were threatened everywhere, and the title page of "Great Newes" which gloats over the thirty-five blacks "burned alive, Beheaded, and otherwise executed," participates in a deliberate savagery intended to intimidate the whole of the slave community. During the year-long insurrection on Jamaica, the historian Richard Dunn found, every rebel caught was killed, "burned alive, torn by dogs, or drawn and quartered."*

THE RELATION OF A CONSPIRACY IN THE *BARBADOES*.

This *Conspiracy* first broke out and was hatched by the *Cormantee* or *Gold-Cost Negro's* about Three years since, and afterwards Cunningly and Clandestinely carried, and kept secret, even from the knowledge of their own Wifes.

Their grand design was to choose them a King, one *Coffee* an Ancient Gold-Cost *Negro*, who should have been Crowned the 12th of *June* last past in a Chair of State exquisitely wrought and Carved after their Mode; with Bowes and Arrowes to be likewise carried in State before his Majesty their intended King: Trumpets to be made of Elephants Teeth and Gourdes to be sounded on several Hills, to give Notice of their general Rising, with a full intention to fire the Sugar-Canes, and so run in and Cut their Masters the Planters Throats in their respective Plantations whereunto they did belong.

Some affirm, they intended to spare the lives of the Fairest and Handsomest Women (their Mistresses and their Daughters) to be Converted to their own use. But some others affirm the contrary; and I am induced to believe they intended to Murther all the White People there, as well Men as Women: for *Anna* a house Negro Woman belonging to Justice *Hall*, over-hearing a Young *Cormantee Negro* about 18 years of age, and also belonging to Justice *Hall*, as he was working near the Garden, and discoursing with another *Cormantee Negro* working with him, told him boldly and plainly, *He would have no hand in killing the* Baccararoes[20] *or White Folks; And that he would tell his Master.* All which the aforesaid *Negro* Woman (being then acciden-

---

20. Baccararoes: original form of buckra, meaning white folks.

tally in the Garden) over-heard, and called to him the aforesaid Young *Negro* Man over the Pales,[21] and enquired and asked of him *What it was they so earnestly were talking about?* He answered and told her freely, *That it was a general Design amongst them the* Cormantee Negro's, *to kill all the* Baccararoes *or White People in the Island within a fortnight.* Which she no sooner understood, but went immediately to her Master and Mistris, and discovered the whole truth of what she heard, saying withal, *That it was great Pity so good people as her Master and Mistriss were, should be destroyed.* Which was the first discovery that I can learn came to the knowledge of the worthy Inhabitants of that Noble and most flourishing Island.

Afterwards the Discreet and Prudent Justice sent presently for the young *Negro* Man, who discovered and impeached several, as well his own Master's *Negro's* as others belonging to the adjacent Plantations who had a hand in this Plot.

Of all which the said Justice sending the true Information to that Noble Person (now Governour there) Sir *Jonathan Atkins,* he with his Life-Guard presently came to the house of the aforesaid Justice *Hall,* and granted him and others Commissions to apprehend the guilty and impeached *Negroes,* with the Ring-leaders of this fatal Conspiracy; which in pursuance was put in Execution with much Celerity and Secrecy, that the Heads and Chief of these ungrateful wretches (who I have often heard confess to live better in Servitude there, then at Liberty in their own Native Country) were apprehended and brought to Tryal at a Court of *Oyer* and *Terminer* granted by the aforesaid Governour to a Dozen or more of the Colonels and Field-Officers as Judges of that Island; Who after strict and due Examination of the matter of Fact of their Conspiracy, at first Seventeen were found guilty and Executed, (*viz.*) Six burnt alive, and Eleven beheaded, their dead bodies being dragged through the Streets at *Spikes* a pleasant Port-Town in that Island, and were afterwards burnt with those that were burned alive.

One of those that were burned alive being chained at the stake, was perswaded by that honest Gentleman Mr. *George,* the Deputy Provost-Marshall, *That since he was going to suffer death, Ingeniously to Confess the depth of their design.* The *Negro* calling for water to drink (which is a Custome they use before they tell or discover any thing) he just then going to speak and confess the truth of what he knew in this Matter; The next *Negro* Man chained to him (one *Tony,* a sturdy Rogue, a *Jew's Negro*) jogged him, and was heard to Chide him in these words, *Thou Fool, are there not enough of our Country-men killed already? Art thou minded to kill them all?* Then the aforesaid *Negro* that was going to make Confession, would not speak one word more.

Which the spectators observing cryed out to *Tony, Sirrah, we shall see you fry bravely by and by.* Who answered undauntedly, *If you Roast me today you cannot Roast me tomorrow*: (all those *Negro's* having an opinion that after their death they go into their own Countrey). Five and Twenty more have been since Executed. The particulars of whose due Punishment are not yet come to my hands.

Five impeached Hanged themselves, because they would not stand Tryal.

Threescore and odd more are in Custody at the *Hole,* a fine Haven and small Town in the said Island, and are not as yet brought to Tryal.

21. Pales: fence.

Thus escaped from Eminent dangers, this flourishing and Fertile Island, or to say more properly Spatious and profitable Garden, one of the chiefest of his Majesties Nurseries for Seamen.

This little Spot imploying every year above 100 good Merchant Ships, to carry off its product, *viz.* Sugar, Ginger, Cotton, and Indigo; of which I have heard it affirmed, That that Earth and Rich soyl being so thinly placed on most part of the said Island, as not exceeding above half a foot in depth, the said product since its first manuring carried off in several years, much exceeds in bulk and weight the surface of the Island, it being only a Rock. So leaving to others the giving an account of the great plenty of fresh Fish there, though of different shapes and names from ours, which it exceeds in pleasantness and nourishment, especially the Turtles there caught; their admirable Pork, Poultry etc. Their Wood Pidgeons, Turtle-Doves of several kinds, wild Fowls, Plovers, Thrushes, Crabs, Lobsters, Prawns, and all other necessary and pleasant Provisions in abundance, both Fish and Flesh. But above all, admirable (considering it is so small an Island) is the Populousness thereof, for I have seen at a General Rendezvous in *Hethersals*[22] Pasture 12000 well Armed fighting men, Horse and Foot, of the Train-Bands,[23] besides *Negro's* that waited on their Masters: And I have lately seen a list taken by Authority that amounts to above 80000 Souls. 'Tis fortified (besides the stone Wall all along the places of most danger for Landing, near the Seaside) with several strong uniform Forts Alla-Modern, well mounted with store of great Guns; so as considering the strength, Riches, Pleasant situation, Populousness and good Hospitality of those Noble Gentlemen there now inhabiting, I conclude it to be the finest and worthiest Island in the World.

6.

two accounts of Bacon's Rebellion

> At the height of the rebellion led by Nathaniel Bacon (1647–76) in 1676 against the colonial government of Virginia, hundreds of rebels burned down Jamestown and captured a twenty-gun ship on the James River. Had Bacon not then died of malaria, it is unclear how or at any rate how quickly this revolt of mostly poorer farmers and the landless would have ended. Because of its large plantations which produced great wealth for a few who owned the best lands, Virginia early developed a particularly unequal society. Newer settlers (like the well-born but late-arriving Bacon) or those who came as indentured servants, found themselves at a growing disadvantage. A decision in 1670 that only the landed could vote excluded a large number of laborers and frontiersmen. The best hope of this class of marginal settlers lay inland on the frontier, but there they confronted a hardening Indian resistance.

22. Hethersals: Thomas and John Hethersal were among the largest planters of Barbados.   23. Train-bands: militias.

The rebellion erupted after an Indian attack. The rebels accused Governor William Berkeley and his aristocratic peers of excessive friendliness to the Indians for the sake of the fur trade; and they began their insurrection with an attack on a native stronghold. Bacon's rebellion has generally been represented as an early battle for greater democracy. But while Bacon and his followers agitated for more political representation and fairer economic treatment, their rallying cry was a halt to treating with the Indians and a demand for their violent removal from the land. The historian Edmund Morgan wrote that Bacon gave the Virginia colony "the first lessons in the social usefulness of racism," when he united a wide range of disaffected whites by invoking a common hatred for the Indians.

Robert Beverley (1673?–1722) gives the governor's side of the story. Beverley, a leading member of the Virginia aristocracy and one of the wealthiest men in the colonies, was the son of one of Governor William Berkeley's most important supporters.

Nathaniel Bacon

Manifesto Concerning the Present Troubles in Virginia 1676

If vertue be a sin, if Piety be guilt, all the Principles of morality goodness and Justice be perverted, Wee must confesse That those who are now called Rebells may be in danger of those high imputations, Those loud and severall Bulls would affright Innocents and render the defense of our Brethren and the enquiry into our sad and heavy oppressions, Treason. But if there bee as sure there is, a just God to appeal to, if Religion and Justice be a sanctuary here, if to plead ye cause of the oppressed, if sincerely to aime at his Majesties Honour and the Publick good without any reservation or by Interest, if to stand in the Gap after soe much blood of our dear Brethren bought and sold, if after the losse of a great part of his Majesties Colony deserted and dispeopled, freely with our lives and estates to indeavor to save the remaynders bee Treason, God Almighty Judge and let the guilty dye. But since wee cannot in our hearts find one single spott of Rebellion or Treason, or that wee have in any manner aimed at the subverting the setled Government, or attempting of the Person of any either magistrate or private man, notwithstanding the severall Reproaches and Threats of some who, for sinister ends, were disaffected to us and censured our inocent and honest designes; and since all people in all places where wee have yet bin can attest our civill quiet, peaseable behaviour—farre different from that of Rebellion and tumultuous persons—let Trueth be bold and all the world know the real Foundations of pretended giult. Wee appeale to the Country itselfe, what and of what nature their Oppressions have bin, or by what Caball and mistery the designs of many of those whom wee call great men have bin transacted and caryed on. But let us trace these men in Authority and Favour to whose hands the dispensation of the Countries wealth has been commited; let us observe the sudden Rise of their Estates compared with the Quality in which they first entered this Country, or the Reputation they have held here amongst wise and discerning men. And lett us see wither their extractions and Education have not bin vile, and by what pretence of learning and vertue they could soe soon into Imployments of so great Trust and consequence.

Let us consider their sudden advancement and let us also consider wither any Publick work for our safety and defence or for the Advancement and propogation of Trade, liberall Arts or sciences is here Extant in any way adequate to our vast chardg. Now let us compare these things together and see what spounges have suckt up the Publique Treasure, and wither it hath not bin privately contrived away by unworthy Favourites and juggling Parasites whose tottering Fortunes have bin repaired and supported at the Publique chardg. Now if it be so Judg, what greater guilt can bee then to offer to pry into these and to unriddle the misterious wiles of a powerful Cabal. Let all people Judge what can be of more dangerous Import then to suspect the soe long Safe proceedings of Some of our Grandees and wither People may with safety open their Eyes in soe nice a Concerne.

Another main article of our Guilt is our open and manifest aversion of all, not onely the Foreign but the protected and Darling Indians. This wee are informed is Rebellion of a deep dye For that both the Governour and Councell are by Colonell Coales Assertion bound to defend the Queen and the Appamatocks with their blood. Now whereas we doe declare and can prove that they have bin for these Many years enemies to the King and Country, Robbers and Theeves and Invaders of his Majesties Right and our Interest and Estates, but yet have by persons in Authority bin defended and protected even against His Majesties loyall Subjects; and that in soe high a Nature that even the Complaints and oaths of his Majesties Most loyall Subjects, in a lawfull Manner proffered by them against those barborous Outlawes, have bin by the right Honourable Governour rejected and the Delinquents from his presence dismissed, not only with pardon and indemnitye, but with all incouragement and favour, Their Fire Arms soe destructfull to us and by our lawes prohibited, Commanded to be restored them, and open Declaration before Witness made That they must have Ammunition, although directly contrary to our law. Now what greater guilt can be then to oppose and indeavour the destruction of these Honest quiet neighbours of ours?

Another main article of our Guilt is our Design not only to ruine and extirpate all Indians in Generall but all Manner of Trade and Commerce with them. Judge who can be innocent that strike at this tender Eye of Interest. Since the Right honourable the Governour hath bin pleased by his Commission to warrant this Trade, who dare oppose it, or opposing it can be innocent? Although Plantations be deserted, the blood of our dear Brethren Spilt, on all Sides or complaints, continually Murder upon Murder renewed upon us, who may or dare think of the generall Subversion of all Mannor of Trade and Commerce with our enemies who can or dare impeach any of the Traders at the Heades of the Rivers if, contrary to the wholesome provision made by lawes for the countries safety, they dare continue their illegall practises and dare asperse ye right honourable Governours wisdome and Justice soe highly to pretend to have his warrant to break that law which himself made? Who dare say That these Men at the Heads of the Rivers buy and sell our blood, and doe still notwithstanding the late Act made to the contrary, admit Indians painted and continue to Commerce? Although these things can be proved yet who dare bee soe giulty as to doe it.

Another Article of our Guilt is To Assert all those neighbour Indians as well as others to be outlawed, wholly unqualifyed for the benefitt and Protection of the law; For that the law does reciprocally protect and punish, and that all people offending must either in person or Estate make equivalent satisfaction or Restitution, according to the manner and merit of ye Offences Debts or Trespasses. Now since the Indians cannot, according to the tenure and forme of any law to us known, be prosecuted, Seised or Complained against, Their Persons being difficulty distinguished or known, Their many nations languages, and their subterfuges such as makes them incapeable to make us Restitution or satisfaction, would it not be very guilty to say They have bin unjustly defended and protected these many years?

If it should be said that the very foundation of all these disasters, the Grant of the Beaver trade to the Right Honourable Governour, was illegall and not granteable by any power here present as being a monopoly, were not this to deserve the name of Rebell and Traytor?

Judge therefore all wise and unprejudiced men, who may or can faithfully or truely with an honest heart attempt ye country's good, their vindication and libertie without the aspersion of Traitor and Rebell, since as soe doing they must of necessity gall such tender and dear concernes. But to manifest Sincerity and loyalty to the World, and how much wee abhorre those bitter names, may all the world know that we doe unanimously desire to represent our sad and heavy grievances to his most sacred Majestie as our Refuge and Sanctuary, where wee doe well know that all our Causes will be impartially heard and Equall Justice administered to all men.

Robert Beverley

from *History and Present State of Virginia*
1705

The Occasion of Bacon's Rebellion is not easie to be discover'd: But 'tis certain there were many Things that concurr'd towards it. For it cannot be imagined, that upon the Instigation of Two or Three Traders only, who aim'd at a Monopoly of the *Indian* Trade, as some pretend to say, the whole Country would have fallen into so much Distraction; in which People did not only hazard their Necks by Rebellion: But endeavor'd to ruine a Governour, whom they all entirely loved, and had unanimously chosen; a Gentleman who had devoted his whole Life and Estate to the Service of the Country; and against whom in Thirty Five Years Experience, there had never been one single Complaint. Neither can it be supposed, that upon so slight Grounds, they would make Choice of a Leader they hardly knew, to oppose a Gentleman, that had been so long, and so deservedly the Darling of the People. So that in all Probability there was something else in the Wind, without which the Body of the Country had never been engaged in that Insurrection.

Four Things may be reckon'd to have been the main Ingredients towards this intestine Commotion, *viz.* First, The extream low Price of Tobacco, and the ill Usage of the Planters in the Exchange of Goods for it, which the Country, with all their earnest Endeavours, could not remedy. Secondly, The Splitting the Colony into Proprieties, contrary to the original Charters; and the extravagant Taxes they were forced to undergo, to relieve themselves from those Grants. Thirdly, The heavy Restraints and Burdens laid upon their Trade by Act of Parliament in *England*. Fourthly, The Disturbance given by the *Indians*. Of all which I beg Leave to speak in their Order.

First, Of the low Price of Tobacco, and the Disappointment of all sort of Remedy, I have spoken sufficiently before. Secondly, Of splitting the Country into Proprieties.

King *Charles* the Second, to gratifie some Nobles about him, made Two great Grants out of that Country. These Grants were not of the uncultivated Wood-Land only, but also of Plantations, which for many Years had been seated and improv'd, under the Encouragement of several Charters granted by his Royal Ancestors to that Colony. Those Grants were distinguished by the Names of the Northern and Southern Grants of *Virginia*, and the same Men were concern'd in both. They were kept dormant some Years after they were made, and in the Year 1674 begun to be put in Execution. As soon as ever the Country came to know this, they remonstrated against them; and the Assembly drew up an humble Address to his Majesty, complaining of the said Grants, as derogatory to the previous Charters and Privileges granted to that Colony, by his Majesty and his Royal Progenitors. They sent to *England* Mr. Secretary *Ludwell* and Colonel *Park*, as their Agents to address the King to vacate those Grants. And the better to defray that Charge, they laid a Tax of Fifty Pounds of Tobacco *per* Poll, for Two Years together, over and above all other Taxes, which was an excessive Burden. They likewise laid Amercements[24] of Seventy, Fifty, and Thirty Pounds of Tobacco on every Cause tried throughout the Country. Besides all this, they applied the Ballance, remaining due upon Account of the Two Shilling *per* Hogshead, and Fort Duties, to this Use. Which Taxes and Amercements fell heaviest on the poor People, the Effect of whose Labour wou'd not cloath their Wives and Children. This made them desperately uneasie, especially when, after a whole Year's Patience under all these Pressures, they had no Encouragement from their Agents in *England*, to hope for Remedy; nor any Certainty when they should be eased of those heavy Impositions.

Thirdly, Upon the Back of all these Misfortunes came out the Act of 25 *Car.* II. for better securing the Plantation Trade. By this Act several Duties were laid on the Trade from one Plantation to another. This was a new Hardship, and the rather, because the Revenue arising by this Act, was not applied to the Use of the Plantation wherein it was raised: But given clear away; nay, in that Country it seem'd to be of no other Use, but to create a good Income to the Officers; for the Collector had Half, the Comptroller a Quarter, and the remaining Quarter was subdivided into Salaries, till it was lost.

By the same Act also very great Duties were laid on the Fisheries of the Plantations, if manufactured by the *English* Inhabitants there; while the People of *England* were absolutely free from all Customs. Nay, tho' the Oil, Blubber, and Whale-Bone, which

24. Amercements: penalties left to the "mercy" of the inflicter.

were made by the Inhabitants of the Plantations, were carried to *England* by *English* Men, and in *English* built Ships, yet it was held to a considerable Duty.

These were the Afflictions that Country labour'd under, when the Fourth Accident happen'd, *viz.* The Disturbance offer'd by the *Indians* to the Frontiers.

This was occasion'd, First, By the *Indians* on the Head of the Bay. Secondly, By the *Indians* on their own Frontiers.

First, The *Indians* at the Head of the Bay drove a constant Trade with the *Dutch* in *Monadas*, now call'd *New-York*; and, to carry on this, they used to come and return every Year by their Frontiers of *Virginia*, to purchase Skins and Furs of the *Indians* to the Southward. This Trade was carried on peaceably while the *Dutch* held *Monadas*; and the *Indians* used to call on the *English*, to whom they would sell part of their Furs, and with the rest go on to *Monadas*. But after the *English* came to possess that Place, and understood the Advantages the *Virginians* made by the Trade of their *Indians*, they inspired them with such a Hatred to the Inhabitants of *Virginia*, that, instead of coming peaceably to trade with them, as they had done for several Years before, they afterwards never came, but only to commit Robberies and Murders upon the People.

Secondly, The *Indians* upon their own Frontiers were likewise inspir'd with ill Thoughts of 'em. For their *Indian* Merchants had lost a considerable Branch of their Trade they knew not how; and apprehended the Consequences of Sir *William Berkeley's* intended Discoveries, which were espoused by the Assembly, might take away the remaining Part of their Profit. This made them very troublesome to the Neighbour *Indians*; who on their part, observing an unusual Uneasiness in the *English*, and being terrified by their rough Usage, immediately suspected some wicked Design against their Lives, and so fled to their remoter Habitations. This confirm'd the *English* in the Belief, that they had been the Murderers, till at last they provoked them to be so in Earnest.

This Addition of Mischief to Minds already full of Discontent, made People ready to vent all their Resentment against the poor *Indians*. There was nothing to be got by Tobacco; neither could they turn any other Manufacture to Advantage; so that most of the poorer Sort were willing to quit their unprofitable Employments, and go Voluntiers against the *Indians*.

At first they flock'd together tumultuously, running in Troops from one Plantation to another without a Head; till at last the seditious Humour of Colonel *Nath. Bacon*, led him to be of the Party. This Gentleman had been brought up at one of the Inns of Court in *England*, and had a moderate Fortune. He was young, bold, active, of an inviting Aspect, and powerful Elocution. In a Word, he was every way qualified to head a giddy and unthinking Multitude. Before he had been Three Years in the Country, he was, for his extraordinary Qualifications, made one of the Council, and in great Honour and Esteem among the People. For this Reason he no sooner gave Countenance to this riotous Mob, but they all presently fix'd their Eyes upon him for their General, and accordingly made their Addresses to him. As soon as he found this, he harangued them publickly. He aggravated the *Indian* Mischiefs, complaining, that they were occasion'd for want of a due Regulation of their Trade. He recounted particularly the other Grievances and Pressures they lay under; and pretended, that he accepted of their Command with no other Intention, but to do them and the Country

Service, in which he was willing to encounter the greatest Difficulties and Dangers. He farther assured them, he would never lay down his Arms, till he had revenged their Sufferings upon the *Indians*, and redress'd all their other Grievances.

By these Insinuations he wrought his Men into so perfect a Unanimity, that they were one and all at his Devotion. He took care to exasperate them to the utmost, by representing all their Misfortunes. After he had begun to muster them, he dispatch'd a Messenger to the Governour, by whom he aggravated the Mischiefs done by the *Indians*, and desired a Commission of General to go out against them. This Gentleman was in so great Esteem at that Time with the Council, that the Governour did not think fit to give him a flat Refusal: But sent him Word, he would consult the Council, and return him a further Answer.

In the mean time, *Bacon* was expeditious in his Preparations, and having all Things in Readiness, began his March, depending on the Authority the People had given him. He would not lose so much Time, as to stay for his Commission; but dispatched several Messengers to the Governour to hasten it. On the other Hand, the Governour, instead of a Commission, sent positive Orders to him to disperse his Men, and come down in Person to him, upon Pain of being declared a Rebel.

This unexpected Order, was a great Surprize to *Bacon*, and not a little Trouble to his Men. However, he was resolved to prosecute his first Intentions, depending upon his Strength, and Interest with the People. Nevertheless, he intended to wait upon the Governour, but not altogether defenceless. Pursuant to this Resolution, he took about Forty of his Men down with him in a Sloop to *James-Town*, where the Governour was with his Council.

Matters did not succeed there to Mr. *Bacon's* Satisfaction; wherefore he express'd himself a little too freely. For which being suspended from the Council, he went away again in a Huff with his Sloop and Followers. The Governour fill'd a Long-Boat with Men, and pursued the Sloop so close, that Colonel *Bacon* removed into his Boat to make more Haste. But the Governour had sent up by Land to the Ships at *Sandy-Point*, where he was stopp'd, and sent down again. Upon his Return he was kindly received by the Governour, who, knowing he had gone a Step beyond his Instructions in having suspended him, was glad to admit him again of the Council; after which he hoped all Things might be pacified.

Notwithstanding this, Col. *Bacon* still insisted upon a Commission to be General of the Volunteers, and to go out against the *Indians*; from which the Governour endeavour'd to disswade him, but to no Purpose, because he had some secret Project in View. He had the Luck to be countenanced in his Importunities, by the News of fresh Murder and Robberies committed by the *Indians*. However, not being able to accomplish his Ends by fair Means, he stole privately out of Town; and having put himself at the Head of Six Hundred Volunteers, marched directly to *James-Town*, where the Assembly was then sitting. He presented himself before the Assembly, and drew up his Men in Battalia before the House wherein they sat. He urged to them his Preparations; and alledged, that if the Commission had not been delay'd so long, the War against the *Indians* might have been finish'd.

The Governour resented this insolent Usage worst of all, and now obstinately refused to grant him any thing, offering his naked Breast against the presented Arms of his Followers. But the Assembly, fearing the fatal Consequence of provoking a discontented Multitude ready arm'd, who had the Governour, Council and Assembly entirely in their Power, address'd the Governour to grant *Bacon* his Request. They prepar'd themselves the Commission, constituting him General of the Forces of *Virginia*, and brought it to the Governour to be sign'd.

With much Reluctancy his Excellency sign'd it, and thereby put the Power of War and Peace into *Bacon's* Hands. Upon this he march'd away immediately, having gain'd his End, which was in effect a Power to secure a Monopoly of the *Indian* Trade to himself and his Friends.

As soon as General *Bacon* had march'd to such a convenient Distance from *James-Town*, that the Assembly thought they might deliberate with Safety, the Governour, by their Advice, issued a Proclamation of Rebellion against him, commanding his Followers to surrender him, and forthwith disperse themselves. Not contented with this, he likewise gave Orders at the same time, for raising the Militia of the Country against him.

The People being much exasperated, and General *Bacon* by his Address and Eloquence having gain'd an absolute Dominion over their Hearts, they unanimously resolved, that not a Hair of his Head shou'd fall to the Ground, much less that they shou'd surrender him as a Rebel. Therefore, they kept to their Arms, and instead of proceeding against the *Indians*, they march'd back to *James-Town*; directing their Fury against such of their Friends and Country-men, as should dare to oppose them.

The Governour seeing this, fled over the Bay to *Accomack*, whither he hoped the Infection of *Bacon's* Conspiracy had not reach'd. But there, instead of People's receiving him with open Arms, in Remembrance of the former Services he had done them; they began to make Terms with him for Redress of their Grievances, and for the Ease and Liberty of Trade. Thus Sir *William*, who had been almost the Idol of the People, was, by reason of the loyal Part he acted, abandon'd by all; except some few, who went over to him from the Western Shore in Sloops and Boats. So that it was some time before he could make head against *Bacon*: But he left him to range through the Country at Discretion.

General *Bacon* at first held a Convention of such of the chief Gentlemen of the Country, as would come to him, especially of those about *Middle-Plantation*, who were near at Hand. At this Convention they made a Declaration to justifie his unlawful Proceedings; and obliged People to take an Oath of Obedience to him as their General. Then, by their Advice, on Pretence of the Governour's Abdication, he call'd an Assembly, by Writs sign'd by himself, and Four others of the Council.

The Oath was Word for Word as follows.

Whereas the Country hath raised an Army against our common Enemy the *Indians*, and the same under the Command of General *Bacon*, being upon the Point to march forth against the said common Enemy, hath been diverted, and necessitated to move to the Suppressing of Forces, by evil disposed Persons raised against the said General *Bacon*, purposely to foment and stir up Civil War among us, to the Ruine of this his Majesty's Country. And, *Whereas* it is notoriously manifest, that Sir *William Berkeley*, Knight, Governour of the Country, assisted, counselled and abetted by those evil disposed Persons aforesaid, hath not only commanded, fomented and stirr'd up the

People to the said Civil War; but failing therein, hath withdrawn himself, to the great Astonishment of the People, and the Unsettlement of the Country. And, *Whereas* the said Army, raised by the Country for the Causes aforesaid, remain full of Dissatisfaction in the Middle of the Country, expecting Attempts from the said Governour and the evil Counsellors aforesaid. And since no proper Means have been found out for the Settlement of the Distractions, and preventing the horrid Outrages and Murders daily committed in many Places of the Country by the barbarous Enemy; It hath been thought fit by the said General, to call unto him all such sober and discreet Gentlemen, as the present Circumstances of the Country will admit, to the *Middle-Plantation*, to consult and advise of re-establishing the Peace of the Country. So we the said Gentlemen, being this 3d of *August, 1676*, accordingly met, do advise, resolve, declare and conclude, and for our selves do swear in manner following.

First, That we will at all Times join with the said General *Bacon*, and his Army, against the common Enemy in all Points whatsoever.

Secondly, That whereas certain Persons have lately contrived and design'd the Raising Forces against the said General, and the Army under his Command, thereby to beget a Civil War; We will endeavour the Discovery and Apprehending of all and every of those evil disposed Persons, and them secure, untill further Order from the General.

Thirdly, And whereas it is credibly reported, that the Governour hath inform'd the King's Majesty, that the said General, and the People of the Country in Arms under his Command, their Aiders and Abettors, are Rebellious, and removed from their Allegiance; and that upon such like Information, he the said Governour hath advised and petition'd the King to send Forces to reduce them; We do further declare and believe in our Consciences, That it consists with the Welfare of this Country, and with our Allegiance to his most Sacred Majesty, that we the Inhabitants of *Virginia*, to the utmost of our Power, do oppose and suppress all Forces whatsoever of that Nature, until such time as the King be fully inform'd of the State of the Case, by such Person or Persons, as shall be sent from the said *Nathaniel Bacon*, in the Behalf of the People; and the Determination thereof be remitted hither. And we do swear, That we will him the said General, and the Army under his Command, aid and assist accordingly.

By this Time the Governor had got together a small Party to side with him. These he furnished with Sloops, Arms and Ammunition, in order to cross the Bay, and oppose the Malecontents. By this Means there happen'd some Skirmishes, in which several were kill'd, and others taken Prisoners. Thus they were going on by a Civil War to destroy one another, and lay waste their Infant Country; when it pleased God, after some Months Confusion, to put an End to their Misfortunes, as well as to *Bacon*'s Designs, by his natural Death.

He died at Dr. *Green*'s, in *Gloucester* County: But where he was bury'd was never yet discover'd; tho' afterward there was great Enquiry made, with Design to expose his Bones to publick Infamy.

7. Aphra Behn

The Widow Ranter; or the History of Bacon in Virginia
1689

*Aphra Behn (1640–89) is best known today for being the first woman to earn her
living by writing and for her novel* Oroonoko *(1688), the romantic story of an
African prince sold into slavery. In the seventeenth century, however, her reputation rested rather on her plays. The sorry plight of women both in and out of
marriage is a frequent theme in both her fiction and her drama; her first play is
entitled* The Forced Marriage, *and determined women like the Widow Ranter are
some of her best-realized characters. A committed Tory, Behn belongs to the group
of Restoration playwrights of whom Dryden is the pinnacle. Like them, she writes
sympathetically about the rebellious passions of the nobility and comically about
the bawdy doings of ordinary folk; herself deeply implicated in contemporary politics, she is a Restoration writer also in the political and generally polemical stance
of all her work.*

*The Widow Ranter, published posthumously, deploys the full range of her inter-
ests vividly, inventively, if also at times somewhat confusingly. With four plots
featuring virtually separate casts of characters, it is both tragic and comic,
romantic and ribald, and resoundingly political, indeed bringing out an aspect of
the rebellion that subsequent accounts have tended to obscure. Aphra Behn's
Bacon is, like the real one, an English gentleman and the social superior of the
Council. Unlike the Bacon conventionally cast in United States histories as the first
democratic rebel, this Bacon is a thorough Tory. At the same time, his and the
play's contempt for the colonial administration expresses Behn's memories of her
own sojourn in the colony of Surinam. This experience, which feeds Oroonoko as
well, seems to have disillusioned her about the empire, which she associates here
with corruption.*

*The Widow Ranter takes some liberties with the events of 1676. It alludes to
many of the events of Bacon's Rebellion, including the burning of Jamestown,
Bacon's disputed commission, Council corruption, and the Indian war. But
Governor Berkeley is absent from the play, and Bacon's fondness for Indians is
pure fiction. (It was Berkeley, in fact, who was accused of Indian-loving.) The play
establishes colonial atmosphere through references to the savannah and in an early
English usage of the word "barbicu." And it follows news reports of the troubles
overseas in its lampoon of colonial society, including the high premium on widows
and their estates in land-crazed Virginia. For the play's London audience, such
details coalesce into a new stereotype of Virginia's colonists as provincials—half
savage, violent, and clamorous with class aspirations.*

DRAMATIS PERSONAE

MEN

Cavarnio, *the Indian King*
Bacon, *General of the English*
Colonel Wellman, *deputy Governor*
Colonel Downright, *a Loyall Honest Counselor*
Hazard ⎤
Friendly ⎦ *Two friends known to one another many years in England*
Dareing ⎤
Fearless ⎦ *Lieutenant Generals to* Bacon
Dullman, *A Captain*
Timerous *Cornet*
Whimsey ⎤
Whiff ⎦ *Justices of the Peace, and very great Cowards*
Boozer, *a Lieutenant*
Bragg, *A Captain*
Grub, *One Complain'd on by* Capt. Whiff *for calling his Wife Whore*
Parson Dunce, *formerly a Farrier fled from England, And Chaplain to the Governour*
Cavaro, *an Indian warrior*
Clark
Boy
Jeffrey, *Coachman to the* Widow Ranter
Officer
Seaman
Indian
Souldier

WOMEN

Semernia, *Indian Queen, Belov'd by* Bacon
Madam Surelove, *Belov'd by* Hazard
Mrs. Crisante, *Daughter to Col.* Downright
Widow Ranter, *in Love with* Dareing
Mrs. Flirt
Mrs. Whimsey
Jenny, the Widow Ranter's *Maid*
Madam Surelove's *Maid*
Girl, *a singer*

Priests, Indians, Soldiers, with other Attendants.

SCENE: VIRGINIA IN BACON'S CAMP.

PROLOGUE

WRITTEN BY MR. JOHN DRYDEN

Spoken by a Woman

Plays you will have; and to supply your store,
Our poets trade to every foreign shore:
This is the product of Virginian ground,
And to the port of Covent-Garden bound.
Our cargo is, or should at least, be wit:
Bless us from you damned pirates of the pit:
And vizard-masks, those dreadful apparitions;
She-privateers, of venomous conditions,
That clap us oft aboard with French commissions.[25]
You sparks,[26] we hope, will wish us happy trading;
For you have ventures in our vessel's lading;
And though you touch at this or t'other nation;
Yet sure Virginia is your dear plantation.
Expect no polished scenes of love should rise
From the rude growth of Indian colonies.
Instead of courtship, and a tedious pother,
They only tip the wink at one another;
Nay often the whole nation, pig together.
You civil beaux, when you pursue the game,
With manners mince the meaning of—that same:
But every part has there its proper name.
Good heavens defend me, who am yet unbroken
From living there, where such bug[27] words are spoken:
Yet surely, Sirs, it does good stomachs show,
To talk so savourly of what they do.
But were I bound to that broad speaking land,
What e'er they said, I would not understand,
But innocently, with a lady's grace,
Would learn to whisk my fan about my face.
However, to secure you, let me swear,
That no such base mundungus[28] stuff is here.
We bring you of the best the soil affords:
Buy it for once, and take it on our words.
You would not think a country-girl the worse,
If clean and wholesome, though her linen's coarse.

---

25. These lines allude to pirates (privateers, with French commissions) and also, punningly, to prostitutes and venereal disease (clap, the French disease).
26. sparks: fashionable young men.
27. bug: frightening.
28. mundungus: "stinking tobacco," according to Johnson's dictionary.

Such are our scenes; and I dare boldly say,
You may laugh less at a far better play.
The story's true; the fact not long ago;
The hero of our stage was English too:
And bate him one small frailty of rebelling,
As brave as e'er was born at Iniskelling.[29]

ACT I

SCENE I

A Room with severall Tables. Enter Hazard *in a travelling Habit, and a Sea-Boy, carrying his Port-mantel.*[30]

HAZARD: What Town's this Boy?

JACK: James-Town, Master.

HAZARD: Take care my Trunk be brought ashore to Night, and there's for your Pains.

JACK: God bless you Master.

HAZARD: What do you call this House?

JACK: Mrs Flirts, Master, the best House for the Commendation in all Virginia.

HAZARD: That's well, has she any handsome Lady's Sirrah?

JACK: Oh! she's woundly handsome her self Master, and the Kindest Gentlewoman—look here she comes Master—

Enter Flirt *and* Nell.

God bless you Mistress, I have brought you a young Gentleman here.

FLIRT: That's well, honest Jack—Sir, you are most heartily Welcome.

HAZARD: [*Salutes her.*] Madam, your Servant.

FLIRT: Please you to walk into a Chamber Sir?

HAZARD: By and by, Madam, but I'le repose here awhile for the coolness of the Air.

FLIRT: This is a Publick Room, Sir, but 'tis at your Service.

HAZARD: Madam, you oblige me.

FLIRT: A Fine-spoken Person—A Gentleman I'le warrant him, come Jack, I'le give thee a Cogue[31] of Brandy for old acquaintance.

Exeunt Landlady and Boy. Hazard *Pulls out Pen, Ink and Paper, and goes to Write. Enter* Friendly.

FRIENDLY: Here Nell, a Tankard of Cool drink quickly.

NELL: You shall have it, Sir.

Exit Nell.

---

29. Iniskelling: also Enniskillen; site of a dramatic victory over Jacobite forces in 1689, the year this prologue was first published. Dryden here compares Bacon's Rebellion to the Glorious Revolution.

30. *Port-mantel*: traveler's case.
31. Cogue: dram.

FRIENDLY: Hah! who's that Stranger? he seems to be a Gentleman.

HAZARD: If I should give Credit to mine Eyes, that should be Friendly.

FRIENDLY: Sir, you seem a stranger, may I take the Liberty to present my Service to you?

HAZARD: If I am not mistaken Sir, you are the only Man in the world whom I would soonest Pledge, you'l Credit me if three year's Absence has not made you forget Hazard.

FRIENDLY: Hazard, my Friend! come to my Arms and Heart.

HAZARD: This Unexpected Happiness O're-Joys me. Who could have Imagin'd to have found thee in Virginia? I thought thou hadst been in Spain with thy Brother.

FRIENDLY: I was so till Ten Months since, when my Uncle Colonell Friendly dying here, left me a Considerable Plantation; And faith I find Diversions not altogether to be despis'd; the God of Love Reigns here, with as much Power, as in Courts or Popular Cities: but prithee what Chance, (Fortunate for me) drove thee to this part of the New World?

HAZARD: Why (faith) Ill Company, and that Common Vice of the Town, Gaming, soon ran out my Younger Brother's Fortune, for Imagining like some of the Luckier Gamesters to Improve my Stock at the Groom-Porter's;[32] Ventur'd on and lost all— My Elder Brother, an Errant Jew, had neither Friendship, nor Honour enough to Support me, but at last was mollified by perswasions and the hopes of being for ever rid of me, [and] sent me hither with a small Cargo to seek my fortune—

FRIENDLY: And begin the world withall.

HAZARD: I thought this a better Venture than to turn Sharping Bully, Cully in Prentices and Country-Squires, with my Pocket full of false dice, your high and low Flats and Bars, or turn broker to young Heirs; take up goods, to pay ten-fold at the Death of their Fathers, and take Fees on both sides; or sit up all night at the Groom-Porters begging his Honour to go a Guinney the better of the lay. No Friendly, I had rather starve abroad than live Pitty'd and despis'd at home.

FRIENDLY: Thou art in the Right, and art come just in the Nick of time to make thy Fortune—Wilt thou follow my advice?

HAZARD: Thou art too honest to Command any thing that I shall Refuse.

FRIENDLY: You must know then, there is about a Mile from James-Town a Young Gentlewoman—No matter for her Birth, her Breeding's the best this world affords. She is Marryed to one of the Richest Merchants here, he is Old and Sick, and now gone into England for the Recovery of his Health, where he'l e'en give up the Ghost; he has writ her word he finds no Amendment, and Resolves to stay another Year. The Letter I accidently took up and have about me; 'tis easily Counterfeited and will be of great use to us.

HAZARD: Now do I fancy I conceive thee.

FRIENDLY: Well, hear me first, you shall get another Letter writ like this Character,[33] which shall say, you are his Kinsman, that is come to Trafick in this Country, and 'tis his will you should be received into his House as such.

---

32. Groom-Porter: officer in charge of gaming. 33. Character: handwriting.

HAZARD: Well, and what will come of this?

FRIENDLY: Why thou art Young and Handsome; She Young and Desiring; 'twere easy to make her Love thee, and if the Old Gentleman chance to dye, you Guess the rest, you are no Fool.

HAZARD: Ay, but if he shou'd return—

FRIENDLY: If—Why if she Love you, that Other will be but a slender Bar to thy happiness; For if thou canst not Marry her, thou mayst lye with her, (and Gad) a Younger Brother may pick out a Pritty Livelyhood here that way, as well as in England—Or if this fail, there thou wilt find a perpetual Visiter the Widdow Ranter, a Woman brought from the Ship by Old Coll. Ranter. She served him half a year, and then he Marry'd her, and dying in a year more, left her worth Fifty thousand Pounds Sterling, besides Plate and Jewells: She's a great Gallant, But assuming the Humour of the Country Gentry, her Extravagancy is very Pleasant, she retains something of her Primitive Quallity still, but is good-natur'd and Generous.

HAZARD: I like all this well.

FRIENDLY: But I have a further End in this matter; you must know there is in the same House a Young Heiress, one Coll. Downright's Daughter, whom I Love, I think not in Vain. Her Father indeed has an Implacable hatred to me, for which Reason I can but seldom Visit her, and in this Affair I have need of a Friend in that House.

HAZARD: Me you're sure of.

FRIENDLY: And thus you'l have an Opportunity to Mannage both our Amours: here you will find Occasion to shew your Courage as well as Express your Love; For at this time the Indians by our ill Management of Trade, whom we have Armed against Our selves, Very frequently make War upon us with our own Weapons, Tho' often coming by the Worst are forced to make Peace with us again, but so, as upon every turn they fall to Massacring us wherever we ly exposed to them.

HAZARD: I have heard the news of this in England, which hastens the new Governour's arrivall here, who brings you fresh Supplys.[34]

FRIENDLY: Would he were landed, we hear he is a Noble Gentleman.

HAZARD: He has all the Qualities of a Gallant Man, besides he is Nobly Born.

FRIENDLY: This Country wants nothing but to be Peopl'd with a well-born Race to make it one of the best Collonies in the World. But for want of a Governour we are Ruled by a Council, some of which have been perhaps transported Criminals, who having Acquired great Estates are now become your Honour, and Right Worshipfull, and Possess all Places of Authority; there are amongst 'em some honest Gentlemen who now begin to take upon 'em, and Manage Affairs as they ought to be.

HAZARD: Bacon I think was one of the Councill.

FRIENDLY: Now you have named a Man indeed above the Common Rank, by Nature Generous; Brave Resolv'd, and Daring; who studying the Lives of the Romans and great Men, that have raised themselves to the most Elevated fortunes, fancies it easy for Ambitious men, to aim at any Pitch of Glory. I've heard him often say, Why cannot I Conquer the Universe as well as Alexander? or like another Romulus form a

34. Behn departs here from chronology. When Lord Culpeper was named as the new governor in 1677, Bacon was already dead.

new Rome, and make my self Ador'd?

HAZARD: Why might he not? great Souls are born in common men, sometimes as well as Princes.

FRIENDLY: This Thirst of Glory cherisht by Sullen Melancholly, I believe was the first Motive that made him in Love with the young Indian Queen, fancying no Hero ought to be without his Princess. And this was the Reason why he so earnestly prest for a Commission, to be made General against the Indians, which long was promis'd him, but they fearing his Ambition, still put him off, till the Grievances grew so high, that the whole Country flockt to him, and beg'd he would redress them. He took the opportunity, and Led them forth to fight, and vanquishing brought the Enemy to fair terms. But now instead of receiving him as a Conquerour, we treat him as a Traytor.

HAZARD: Then it seems all the Crime this brave Fellow has committed, is serving his Country without Authority.

FRIENDLY: 'Tis so, and however I admire the Man, I am resolv'd to be of the Contrary Party, that I may make an Interest in our new Governor. Thus stand affairs, so that after you have seen Madam Surelove, I'le present you to the Councill for a Commission.

HAZARD: But my Kinsman's Character—

FRIENDLY: He was a Lester-shire younger Brother, came over hither with a small fortune, which his Industry has increas'd to a thousand pounds a year, and he is now Coll. John Surelove, and one of the Councill.

HAZARD: Enough.

FRIENDLY: About it then, Madam Flirt to direct you.

HAZARD: You are full of your Madams here.[35]

FRIENDLY: Oh! 'tis the greatest affront imaginable, to call a woman Mistris, tho' but a retale Brandy-munger.—Adieu!—one thing more, tomorrow is our Country-Court. Pray do not fail to be there, for the rarity of the Entertainment. But I shall see you anon at Sureloves, where I'le Salute thee as my first meeting, and as an old acquaintance in England—here's company, farewell.

Exit Friendly. *Enter* Dullman, Timorous *and* Boozer. Hazard *sits at a Table and writes.*

DULLMAN: Here Nell—Well Lieutenant Boozer, what are you for?[36]

Enter Nell.

BOOZER: I am for Cooling Nants,[37] Major.

DULLMAN: Here Nell, a quart of Nants, and some Pipes and smoak.

TIMOROUS: And do ye hear Nell, bid your Mistress come in to Joke a little with us, for adzoors I was damnable drunk last night, and am better at the petticoat than the bottle to day.

DULLMAN: Drunk last night, and sick today, how comes that about Mr. Justice? you use to bear your Brandy well enough.

TIMOROUS: Ay your shier-Brandy[38] I'le grant you, but I was Drunk at Coll. Downrights with your high Burgundy Claret.

---

35. "Madam" connotes higher rank than "Mistress."
36. what are you for: what will you drink?
37. Nants: brandy, from Nantes.
38. shier-Brandy: local brandy.

DULLMAN: A Pox of that Paulter Liquor, your English French Wine, I wonder how the Gentlemen do to drink it.

TIMOROUS: Aye, so do I, 'tis for want of a little Virginia Breeding. How much more like a Gentleman 'tis, to drink as we do, brave Edifying Punch and Brandy,—but they say, the young Noble-men now and Sparks in England begin to reform, and take it for their mornings Draught, get Drunk by noon, and despise the Lowsey Juce of the Grape.

Enter Mrs. Flirt *and* Nell, *with drink, pipes, etc.*

DULLMAN: Come Landlady, come, you are so taken up with Parson Dunce, that your old friends can't Drink a Dram with you,—what no smutty Catch now, no Gibe or Joke to make the Punch go down Merrily, and advance Trading? Nay, they say, Gad forgive ye, you never miss going to Church when Mr. Dunce Preaches—but here's to you.

Drinks.

FLIRT: Lords, your Honours are pleas'd to be merry—but my service to your Honour.

Drinks.

HAZARD: [*Aside.*] Honours, who the Devill have we here? some of the wise Councill at least, I'd sooner took 'em for Hoggerds.

FLIRT: Say what you please of the Doctor, but I'le swear he's a fine Gentleman. He makes the Prettiest Sonnets, nay, and Sings'em himself to the rarest Tunes.

TIMOROUS: Nay the man will serve for both Soul and Body, for they say he was a Farrier[39] in England, but breaking[40] turn'd Life-guard man,[41] and his Horse dying— he Counterfeited a Deputation from the Bishop, and came over here a Substantiall Orthodox: but come, where stands the Cup?—here, my Service to you Major.

FLIRT: Your Honours are pleas'd—but me-thinks Doctor Dunce is a very Edifying Person, and a Gentleman, and I pretend to know a Gentleman,—For I my self am a Gentlewoman; my Father was a Barronet, but undone in the late Rebellion[42]—and I am fain to keep an Ordinary[43] now, Heaven help me.

TIMOROUS: Good lack, why see how Virtue may be bely'd—we heard your Father was a Taylor, but trusting for old Oliver's[44] Funerall, Broke, and so came hither to hide his head,—but my Service to you; what, you are never the worse?

FLIRT: Your Honours knows this is a Scandalous place, for they say your Honour was but a broken Excise-man, who spent the King's money to buy your Wife fine Petticoats, and at last not worth a Groat, you came over a poor Servant, though now a Justice of the Peace, and of the Honourable Council.

TIMOROUS: Adz zoors if I knew who 'twas said so, I'd sue him for *Scandalum Magnatum.*

DULLMAN: Hang 'em Scoundrells, hang 'em, they live upon Scandal, and we are Scandall-Proof,—They say too, that I was a Tinker, and running the Country, robb'd a Gentlemans House there, was put into Newgate, got a reprieve after Condemnation, and was Transported hither—And that you Boozer was a Common Pick-pocket, and

---

39. Farrier: one who doctors and shoes horses.
40. breaking: going bankrupt.
41. Life-guard man: bodyguard.
42. the late Rebellion: the English Civil Wars (1640–49).

43. Ordinary: tavern.
44. old Oliver: Cromwell, whose funeral in 1658 was never fully paid for.

being often flogg'd at the Carts-tale, afterwards turn'd Evidence, and when the times grew Honest was fain to fly.

BOOZER: Ay, Ay Major, if Scandal would have broke our hearts, we had not arriv'd to the Honour of being Privy-Counsellors— but come Mrs. Flirt, what never a Song to Entertain us?

FLIRT: Yes, and a Singer too newly come Ashore.

TIMOROUS: Adz zoors, let's have it then.

Enter a Girl, who sings, they bear the Bob.[45]

HAZARD: Here Maid, a Tankard of your Drink.

FLIRT: Quickly Nell, wait upon the Gentleman.

DULLMAN: Please you Sir to taste our Liquor—My service to you; I see you are a Stranger and alone, please you to come to our Table?

He rises and comes.

FLIRT: Come Sir, pray sit down here, these are very Honourable Persons I assure you,—This is Major Dullman, Major of his Excellencies own Regiment, when he Arrives, this is Mr. Timorous, Justice a Peace in *Corum*,[46] this Capt. Boozer, all of the Honourable Councill.

HAZARD: With your leave, Gentlemen. [*Sits.*]

TIMOROUS: My service to you, Sir. [*Drinks.*] What have you brought over any Cargo Sir, I'le be your Customer.

BOOZER: [*Aside.*] Ay, and cheat him too, I'le warrant him.

HAZARD: I was not bred to Merchandizing Sir, nor do intend to follow the Drudgery of Trading.

DULLMAN: Men of Fortune seldom travell hither Sir to see fashions.

TIMOROUS: Why Brother, it may be the Gentleman has a mind to be a Planter. Will you hire your self to make a Crop of Tobacco this year?

HAZARD: I was not born to work Sir.

TIMOROUS: Not work Sir, zoors your betters have workt Sir, I have workt my self Sir, both set and stript Tobacco, for all I am of the Honourable Councill. Not work quoth a—I suppose Sir you wear your fortune upon your Back Sir?

HAZARD: [*Rises*] Is it your Custom here Sir to affront Strangers? I shall expect satisfaction.

TIMOROUS: Why does any body here owe you any thing?

DULLMAN: No, unless he means to be paid for drinking with us—ha, ha, ha.

HAZARD: [*Flings down a Guinia.*] No Sir, I have money to pay for what I drink: here's my Club—my Guinia. I scorn to be oblig'd to such Scoundrells.

BOOZER: [*Rises in huff.*] Hum—Call Men of Honour Scoundrells.

TIMOROUS: Let him alone, let him alone Brother, how should he learn manners, he never was in Virginia before.

DULLMAN: He's some Covent-Garden Bully.

TIMOROUS: Or some broken Citizen turn'd Factor.[47]

HAZARD: [*Flings the Brandy in his Face.*] Sir you lye, and you're a Rascall.

---

45. *bear the Bob*: sing the chorus.
46. in *Corum*: for the Crown.
47. Factor: commercial agent.

TIMOROUS: Adz zoors he has spill'd all the Brandy.

Timorous *runs behind the door*, Dullman *and* Boozer *strike* Hazard.

HAZARD: I understand no Cudgel-Play, but wear a sword to right my self. [*Draws, they run off.*]

FLIRT: Good heavens, what quarelling in my House?

HAZARD: Do the Persons of Quallity in this Country treat strangers thus?

FLIRT: Alas Sir, 'tis a familiar way they have, Sir.

HAZARD: I'm glad to know it,—Pray Madam can you inform one how I may be furnisht with a Horse and a guide to Madam Sureloves?

FLIRT: A most Accomplisht Lady, and my very good friend you shall be Immediately—

SCENE II
The Council Chamber.

Enter Wellman, Downright, Dunce, Whimsey, Whiff, *and others.*

WELLMAN: Come Mr. Dunce, tho' you are no Councellour, yet your Council may be good in time of necessity, as now.

DUNCE: If I may give worthy advice, I do not look upon our danger to be so great from the Indians, as from young Bacon, whom the People have nick-nam'd Fright-all.

WHIMSEY: Ay, Ay, that same Bacon, I would he were well hang'd, I am afraid that under pretence of killing all the Indians he means to Murder us, Ly with our Wives, and hang up our little Children, and make himself Lord and King.

WHIFF: Brother Whimsey, not so hot, with leave of the Honourable Board, My Wife is of Opinion, that Bacon came seasonably to our Aid, and what he has done was for our defence; the Indians came down upon us, and Ravisht us all, Men, Women, and Children.

WELLMAN: If these Grievances were not redrest we had our reasons for it; it was not that we were insensible Capt. Whiff of what we suffer'd from the Insolence of the Indians: But all knew what we must expect from Bacon if that by Lawfull Authority he had Arriv'd to so great a Command as Generall, nor would we be huft out of our Commissions.

DOWNRIGHT: 'Tis most certain that Bacon did not demand a Commission out of a design of serving us, but to satisfy his Ambition and his Love, it being no secret that he passionately Admires the Indian Queen, and under the pretext of a War, intends to kill the King her Husband, Establish himself in her heart, and on all occasions make himself a more formidable Enemy, than the Indians are.

WHIMSEY: Nay, nay, I ever foresaw he would prove a Villain.

WHIFF: Nay, and he be thereabout, my Nancy shall have no more to do with him.

WELLMAN: But Gentlemen the People dayly flock to him, so that his Army is too Considerable for us to oppose by any thing but Policy.

DOWNRIGHT: We are sensible, Gentlemen, that our Fortunes, our Honours, and our Lives are at Stake, and therefore you are call'd together to consult what's to be done in this Grand Affair, till our Governour and Forces arrive from England. The Truce he made with the Indians will be out to Morrow.

WHIFF: Ay, and then he intends to have another bout with the Indians. Let's have Patience I say till he has thrumb'd[48] their Jackets, and then to work with your Politicks as soon as you please.

DOWNRIGHT: Colonel Wellman has answer'd that point, good Captain Whiff; 'tis the Event of this Battle we ought to dread, and if won or lost will be equally fatall for us, either from the Indians or from Bacon.

DUNCE: With the Permission of the Honourable Board I think I have hit upon an Expedient that may prevent this Battle: your Honours shall write a Letter to Bacon, where you shall acknowledge his Services, invite him kindly home, and offer him a Commission for General—

WHIFF: Just my Nancys Counsell—Doctor Dunce has spoken like a Cherubin, he shall have my voice for General, what say you Brother Whimsey?

DOWNRIGHT: I say, he is a Noble fellow, and fit for a General.

DUNCE: But conceive me right Gentlemen, as soon as he shall have render'd himself, seize him and strike off his Head at the Fort.

WHIFF: Hum! his head—Brother.

WHIMSEY: Ay, ay, Doctor Dunce speaks like a Cherubin.

WELLMAN: Mr. Dunce, your Counsell in extremity I confess is not amiss, but I should be loth to deal dishonourably with any man.

DOWNRIGHT: His Crimes deserve death, his life is forfeited by Law, but shall never be taken by my consent by Treachery: If by any Stratagem we could take him alive, and either send him for England to receive there his Punishment, or keep him Prisoner here till the Governour arrive, I should agree to't, but I question his coming in upon our Invitation.

DUNCE: Leave that to me—

WHIMSEY: Come, I'le warrant him, the Rogue's as stout as Hector, he fears neither Heaven nor Hell.

DOWNRIGHT: He's too Brave and Bold to refuse our summons, and I am for sending him for England and leaving him to the Kings Mercy.

DUNCE: In that you'l find more difficulty Sir. To take him off here will be more quick and sudden: for the people worship him.

WELLMAN: I'le never yield to so ungenerous an expedient. The seizing him I am content in the Extremity wherein we are, to follow. What say you Collonell Downright? Shall we send him a Letter now while this two days truce lasts, between him and the Indians?

DOWNRIGHT: I approve it.

ALL: And I, and I, and I.

DUNCE: If your Honours please to make me the Messenger, I'le use some arguments of my own to prevail with him.

WELLMAN: You say well Mr. Dunce, and we'l dispatch you presently.

Exit Wellman, Downright, *and all*
but Whimsey, Whiff, *and* Dunce.

48. thrumb'ed: beaten.

WHIFF: Ah Doctor, if you could but have persuaded Collonell Wellman and Collonel Downright to have hang'd him—

WHIMSEY: Why Brother Whiff you were for making him a Generall but now.

WHIFF: The Councills of wise Statesmen, Brother Whimsey, must change as causes do, d'ye see.

DUNCE: Your Honours are in the right, and whatever those two leading Councellors say, they would be glad if Bacon were dispatcht, but the punctillio of Honour is such a thing.

WHIMSEY: Honour, a Pox on't, what is that Honour that keeps such a Bustle in the world, yet never did good as I heard of?

DUNCE: Why 'tis a Foolish word only, taken up by great men, but rarely practis'd,—but if you would be great men indeed—

WHIFF: If we wou'd Doctor, name, name the way.

DUNCE: Why, you command each of you a company—when Bacon comes from the Camp, as I am sure he will, (and full of this silly thing call'd Honour will come unguarded too,) lay some of your men in Ambush along those Ditches by the Sevana about a Mile from the Town, and as he comes by, seize him, and hang him upon the next Tree.

WHIFF: Hum—hang him! a rare Plot.

WHIMSEY: Hang him—we'l do't, we'l do't, Sir, [*Aside*] and I doubt not but to be made Generrall for the Action—I'le take it all upon my self.

DUNCE: If you resolve upon this, you must about instantly—Thus I shall at once serve my Country, and revenge my self on the Rascall for affronting my Dignity once at the Councell-Table, by calling me Farrier.

Exit Doctor.

WHIFF: Do you know Brother what we are to do?

WHIMSEY: To do, yes, to hang a Generall, Brother, that's all.

WHIFF: All, but is it Lawfull to hang any Generall?

WHIMSEY: Lawfull, yes, that 'tis Lawfull to hang any Generall that fights against Law.

WHIFF: But in what he has done, he has serv'd the King and our Country, and preserv'd all our Lives and Fortunes.

WHIMSEY: That's all one, Brother, if there be but a Quirk in the Law offended in this Case, tho' he fought like Alexander and preserv'd the whole world from perdition, yet if he did it against Law, 'tis Lawful to hang him; why what Brother, is it fit that every impudent fellow that pretends to a little Honour, Loyalty, and Courage, should serve his King and Country against the Law? no, no, Brother, these things are not to be suffer'd in a Civil Government by Law Establish'd,—wherefore let's about it—

Exeunt.

Scene iii

Surelove's House.

Enter Ranter *and* Jeffery *her Coachman.*

RANTER

Here Jeffery, ye Drunken Dog, set your Coach and Horses up, I'le not go till the Cool of the Evening, I love to ride in Fresco.[49]

Enter a Boy.

JEFFERY: [*Aside.*] Yes, after hard drinking— It shall be done, Madam.

Exit.

RANTER: How now Boy, is Madam Surelove at home?

BOY: Yes Madam.

RANTER: Go and tell her I am here, Sirrah.

BOY: Who are you pray, forsooth?

RANTER: Why you Son of a Baboone don't you know me?

BOY: No Madam, I came over but in the last Ship.

RANTER: What from Newgate or Bridewell?[50] from shoving the Tumbler, Sirrah, Lifting or filing the Cly?[51]

BOY: I don't understand this Country-Language forsooth, yet.

RANTER: You Rogue, 'tis what we transport from England first—go ye Dog, go tell your Lady, the Widow Ranter is come to dine with her—

Exit Boy.

I hope I shall not find that Rogue Dareing here, Sniveling after Mrs. Crisante: if I do, by the Lord, I'le lay him thick. Pox on him why should I love the Dog, unless it be a Judgment upon me.

Enter Surelove and Crisante.

—My dear Jewel, how do'st do?—as for you Gentlewoman you are my Rivall, and I am in rancour against you till you have renounc'd my Dareing.

CRISANTE: All the Interest I have in him Madam, I resign to you.

RANTER: Ay—but your house lying so near the Camp, gives me Mortal fears—but prithee how thrives thy Amour with honest Friendly?

CRISANTE: As well as an Amour can, that is absolutely forbid by a Father on one side, and pursu'd by a good resolution on the other.

RANTER: Ha, Gad, I'le warrant for Friendlys resolution, what tho' his Fortune be not answerable to yours, we are bound to help one another—here, Boy—some Pipes and a Bowle of Punch, you know my humour Madam, I must Smoke and Drink in a Morning, or I am Mawkish all day.

SURELOVE: But will you drink Punch in a Morning?

RANTER: Punch, 'tis my Mornings draught, my Table-drink, my Treat, my Regalio, my every thing, ah my dear Surelove, if thou woud'st but refresh and Chear thy heart with Punch in a morning, thou wou'dst not look thus Clowdy all the Day.

Enter Pipes and a great Bowl, she falls to smoking.

---

49. in Fresco: on horseback, rather than in a carriage.
50. Newgate or Bridewell: London prisons.
51. shoving the Tumbler, etc.: mugging and pickpocketing.

SURELOVE: I have reason Madam to be Melancholy. I have receiv'd a Letter from my Husband, who gives me an account that he is worse in England than when he was here, so that I fear I shall see him no more, the Doctors can do no good on him.

RANTER: [*Drinks.*] A very good hearing. I wonder what the Devill thou hast done with him so long? an old fusty weather-beaten Skelleton, as dri'd as Stock-fish, and much of the Hue.—come, come, here's to the next, may he be young, Heaven, I beseech thee.

SURELOVE: You have reason to praise an old man, who dy'd and left you worth fifty thousand Pound.

RANTER: Ay Gad—and what's better Sweet-heart, dy'd in good time too, and left me young enough to spend this fifty thousand pound in better Company—rest his Soul for that too.

CRISANTE: I doubt 'twill be all laid out in Bacon's Mad Lieutenant Generall Dareing.

RANTER: Faith I think I could lend it the Rogue on good Security.

CRISANTE: What's that, to be bound Body for Body?

RANTER: Rather that he should love no bodies Body besides my own, but my Fortune is too good to trust the Rogue, my money makes me an Infidel.

CRISANTE: You think they all love you for that.

RANTER: For that, Ay what else? if it were not for that, I might sit still and sigh, and cry out, a Miracle! a Miracle! at sight of a Man within my doors.

Enter Maid.

MAID: Madam, here's a young Gentleman without would speak with you.

SURELOVE: With me, sure thou'rt mistaken, is it not Friendly?

MAID: No Madam 'tis a Stranger.

RANTER: 'Tis not Dareing that Rogue, is it?

MAID: No Madam.

RANTER: Is he handsome? does he look like a Gentleman?

MAID: He's handsome and seems a Gentleman.

RANTER: Bring him in then, I hate a conversation without a Fellow,—

Enter Hazard *with a Letter.*

[*Aside*] hah—a good handsome Lad indeed.

SURELOVE: With me Sir would you speak?

HAZARD: If you are Madam Surelove.

SURELOVE: So I am call'd.

HAZARD: Madam I am newly arriv'd from England, and from your Husband my kinsman bring you this—[*Gives a letter.*]

RANTER: Please you to sit Sir.

HAZARD: [*Aside.*] She's extreamly handsome—[*Sits down.*]

RANTER: Come Sir will you Smoke a Pipe?

HAZARD: I never do Madam—

RANTER: Oh fy upon't you must learn then, we all smoke here, 'tis a part of good breeding,—well, well, what Cargo, what goods have ye? any Poynts, Lace, rich Stuffs,

Jewells; if you have, I'le be your Chafferer.[52] I live hard by; any body will direct you to the widow Ranters.

HAZARD: I have already heard of you, Madam.

RANTER: What you are like all the young Fellows, the first thing they do when they come to a strange place, is to enquire what Fortunes there are.

HAZARD: Madam I had no such Ambition.

RANTER: Gad, then you're a fool, Sir, but come, my service to you; we rich Widdows are the best Commodity this Country affords, I'le tell you that.

[*This while* Surelove *reads the Letter*.]

SURELOVE: Sir, my Husband has recommended you here in a most particular manner, by which I do not only find the esteem he has for you, but the desire he has of gaining you mine, which on a double score I render you, first for his sake, next for those Merits that appear in your self.

HAZARD: Madam, the endeavours of my life shall be to express my Gratitude for this great Bounty.

Enter Maid.

MAID: Madam, Mr. Friendly's here.

SURELOVE: Bring him in.

HAZARD: Friendly,—I had a dear Friend of that name, who I hear is in these Parts— Pray Heaven it may be he.

Enter Friendly.

RANTER: How now Charles?

FRIENDLY: Madam your Servant—Hah! should not I know you for my dear friend Hazard. [*Embracing him.*]

HAZARD: Or you're to blame my Friendly.

FRIENDLY: Prethee what calm brought thee ashore?

HAZARD: Fortune *de la guarr*, but prethee ask me no questions in so good Company; where a minute lost from this Conversation is a misfortune not to be retriev'd.

FRIENDLY: [*Softly aside.*] Do'st like her Rogue—

HAZARD: Like her—I have sight, or sense—Why I adore her.

FRIENDLY: Mrs. Crisante, I heard your Father would not be here to day, which made me snatch this opportunity of seeing you.

RANTER: Come, Come, a Pox of this whining Love, it spoyls good company.

FRIENDLY: You know my dear friend, these opportunities come but seldom, and therefore I must make use of 'em.

RANTER: Come, come, I'le give you a better opportunity at my House to morrow, we are to eat a Buffalo there, and I'le secure the old Gentleman from coming.

FRIENDLY: Then I shall see Crisante once more before I go.

CRISANTE: Go—Heavens—whither my Friendly?

FRIENDLY: I have received a Commission to go against the Indians, Bacon being sent for home.

RANTER: But will he come when sent for?

---

52. Chafferer: agent.

FRIENDLY: If he refuse we are to Endeavour to force him.

CRISANTE: I do not think he will be forc'd, not even by Friendly.

FRIENDLY: And faith it goes against my Conscience to lift my Sword against him, for he is truly brave, and what he has done, a Service to the Country, had it but been by Authority.

CRISANTE: What pity 'tis there should be such false Maxims in the World, that Noble Actions however great, must be Criminall for want of a Law to Authorise 'em.

FRIENDLY: Indeed 'tis pity when Laws are faulty they should not be mended or abolisht.

RANTER: Hark'ye Charles, by Heaven if you kill my Dareing I'le Pistol you.

FRIENDLY: No, widdow I'le spare him for your sake.

They joyn with Surelove.

HAZARD: Oh she's all Divine, and all the Breath she utters serves but to blow my Flame. [*Enter Maid.*]

MAID: Madam dinner's on the Table—

SURELOVE: Please you, Sir, to walk in—come, Mr. Friendly.

She takes Hazard.

RANTER: Prithee good wench bring in the Punch-Bowle.

Exeunt.

ACT II

Scene i

A Pavillion.

Discovers the Indian King *and* Queen *sitting in State, with Guards of Indians, Men and Women attending:* to them Bacon *richly dress'd, attended by* Dareing, Fearless, *and other Officers. He bows to the* King *and* Queen, *who rise to receive him.*

KING: I am sorry Sir, we meet upon these terms, we who so often have embrac'd as friends.

BACON: [*Aside.*] How charming is the Queen! War, Sir, is not my business nor my pleasure: Nor was I bred in Arms; my Country's good has forc'd me to assume a Soldier's life: And 'tis with much regret that I Employ the first effects of it against my Friends; Yet whilst I may—Whilst this Cessation lasts, I beg we may exchange those Friendships, Sir, we have so often paid in happier Peace.

KING: For your part, Sir, you've been so Noble, that I repent the fatall difference that makes us meet in Arms. Yet tho' I'm young I'm sensible of Injuries; And oft have heard my Grandsire say—That we were Monarchs once of all this spacious World; Till you an unknown People landing here, Distress'd and ruin'd by destructive storms, Abusing all our Charitable Hospitality, Usurp'd our Right, and made your friends your slaves.

BACON: I will not justify the Ingratitude of my fore-fathers, but finding here my Inheritance, I am resolv'd still to maintain it so, And by my sword which first cut out my Portion, Defend each inch of Land with my last drop of Bloud.

QUEEN: [*Aside.*] Ev'n his threats have charms that please the heart.

KING: Come Sir, let this ungratefull Theme alone, which is better disputed in the Field.

QUEEN: Is it impossible there might be wrought an understanding betwixt my Lord and you? 'Twas to that end I first desired this truce, My self proposing to be Mediator, To which my Lord Cavarnio shall agree, Could you but Condescend—I know you're Noble: And I have heard you say our tender Sex could never plead in vain.

BACON: Alas! I dare not trust your pleading Madam! A few soft words from such a Charming mouth would make me lay the Conqueror at your feet as a Sacrifice for all the ills he has done you.

QUEEN: [*Aside.*] How strangely I am pleas'd to hear him talk.

KING: Semernia, see—the Dancers do appear. [*To Bacon.*] Sir will you take your seat?

He *leads the* Queen *to a seat, they sit and talk.*

BACON: Curse on his sports that interrupted me, My very soul was hovering at my Lip, ready to have discover'd all its secrets. But oh! I dread to tell her of my pain, And when I wou'd an Awfull trembling seizes me, And she can only from my dying eyes, read all the Sentiments of my Captive heart.

Sits down, the rest wait.

Enter Indians that dance Anticks;
After the Dance the King *seems in discourse with* Bacon,
the Queen *rises, and comes forth.*

QUEEN: The more I gaze upon this English Stranger, the more Confusion struggles in my Soul. Oft I have heard of Love, and oft this Gallant Man (When Peace had made him pay his idle Visits) Has told a thousand Tales of dying Maids. And ever when he spoke, my panting heart, with a Prophetick fear in sighs reply'd, I shall fall such a Victim to his Eyes.

Enter an Indian.

INDIAN: [*To the* King.] Sir here's a Messenger from the English Council Desires admittance to the General.

BACON: [*To the* King.] With your Permission Sir, he may advance.

Re-enter Indian with Dunce. *A Letter.*

DUNCE: [*Gives him a Letter.*] All health and Happyness attend your honour, This from the Honourable Council.

KING: I'le leave you till you have dispatch'd the Messenger, and then expect your presence in the Royal Tent.

Exeunt King, Queen, and Indians.

BACON: [*To Dareing.*] Lieutenant, read the Letter.

DAREING: [*Reads.*] *Sir, the necessity of what you have Acted makes it pardonable, and we could wish we had done the Country, and our selves so much Justice as to have given you that Commission you desired—We now finde it reasonable to raise more forces, to oppose these Insolences, which possibly yours may be too weak to accomplish, to which end the Council is ordered to meet this Evening, and desiring you will come and take your place there, and be pleas'd to accept from us a Commission to Command in Chief in this War—Therefore send those Soldiers under your Command to their respective houses, and hast, Sir, to your affectionate Friends—*

FEARLESS: Sir, I fear the hearts and Pen do not agree when this was writ.

DAREING: A plague upon their shallow Politicks! Do they think to play the old Game twice with us?

BACON: Away, you wrong the Council, who of themselves are Honourable Gentlemen, but the base Coward fear of some of them, puts the rest on tricks that suit not with their nature.

DUNCE: Sir, 'tis for noble ends you're sent for, and for your safety I'le engage my life.

DAREING: By Heaven and so you shall—and pay it too with all the rest of your wise-headed Council.

BACON: Your zeal is too Officious now: I see no Treachery, and can fear no danger.

DUNCE: Treachery! now Heavens forbid, are we not Christians Sir, All Friends and Countrymen! believe me Sir, 'tis Honour calls you to increase your fame, and he who would dissuade you is your Enemy.

DAREING: Go Cant, Sir to the Rabble—for us—we know you.

BACON: You wrong me when you but suspect for me; let him that acts dishonourably fear. My innocence, and my good sword's my guard.

DAREING: If you resolve to go, we will attend you.

BACON: What go like an Invader? No Dareing, the Invitation's friendly, and as a friend, attended only by my menial Servants, I'le wait upon the Council, that they may see that when I could Command it I came an humble Suppliant for their favour— You may return, and tell 'em I'le attend.

DUNCE: I kiss your Honour's hands— [*Goes out.*]

DAREING: 'Sdeath will you trust the faithless Council Sir, who have so long held you in hand with promises, That curse of Statesmen, that unlucky Vice that renders even Nobility despis'd?

BACON: Perhaps the Council thought me too aspiring, and would not add Wings to my Ambitious flight.

DAREING: A pox of their considering caps, and now they find that you can soar alone, they send for you to knip your spreading wings. Now by my soul, you shall not go alone.

BACON: Forbear, lest I suspect you for a mutineer; I am resolv'd to go.

FEARLESS: What, and send your Army home? a pretty fetch.

DAREING: By Heaven, we'le not disband—not till we see how fairly you are dealt with: if you have a Commission to be General, here we are ready to receive new orders: If not—we'll ring 'em such a Thundring Peal shall beat the Town about their treacherous Ears.

BACON: I do Command you not to stir a Man; Till you're inform'd how I am treated by 'em.—leave me all—

Exeunt Officers.

While Bacon *reads the letter again,*
To him the Indian Queen, *with* Women waiting.

QUEEN: Now while my Lord's asleep in his Pavilion I'le try my power with the General, for an Accommodation of a Peace: the very dreams of war fright my soft slumbers that us'd to be employ'd in kinder Business.

BACON: Ha!—The Queen—What happiness is this presents it self which all my Industry could never gain?

QUEEN: [*Approaching him.*] Sir—

BACON: Prest with the great Extreams of Joy and Fear I trembling stand, unable to approach her.

QUEEN: I hope you will not think it fear in me, tho' tim'rous as a Dove by nature fram'd: Nor that my Lord, whose youth's unskill'd in War, can either doubt his Courage, or his forces, that makes me seek a Reconciliation on any honourable terms of Peace.

BACON: Ah Madam! if you knew how absolutely you command my Fate, I fear but little honour would be left me, since what so e'er you ask me I should grant.

QUEEN: Indeed I would not ask your Honour, Sir, That renders you too Brave in my esteem. Nor can I think that you would part with that. No, not to save your Life.

BACON: I would do more to serve your least Commands than part with triviall Life.

QUEEN: Bless me! Sir, how came I by such a Power?

BACON: The Gods, and Nature gave it you in your Creation, form'd with all the Charms that ever grac'd your Sex.

QUEEN: Is't possible? am I so Beautifull?

BACON: As Heaven, or Angels there.

QUEEN: Supposing this, how can my Beauty make you so obliging?

BACON: Beauty has still a power over great Souls, And from the moment I beheld your eyes, my stubborn heart melted to compliance, and from a nature rough and turbulent, grew Soft and Gentle as the God of Love.

QUEEN: The God of Love! what is the God of Love?

BACON: [*Takes her by the Hand and gazes on her.*] 'Tis a resistless Fire, that's kindd'd thus—at every gaze we take from such fine Eyes, from such Bashful Looks, and such soft touches—it makes us sigh—and pant as I do now, and stops the Breath when e're we speak of Pain.

QUEEN: [*Aside*] Alas, for me if this should be Love!

BACON: It makes us tremble when we touch the fair one, And all the blood runs shiv'ring thro' the veins. The heart's surrounded with a feeble Languishment. The eyes are dying, and the Cheeks are pale. The tongue is faltring, and the body fainting.

QUEEN: [*Aside*] Then I'm undone, and all I feel is Love. If Love be Catching Sir, by looks and touches, Let us at distance parley— [*Aside*] or rather let me fly, For within view is too near—

BACON: Ah! she retires—displeas'd I fear with my presumptuous Love,—[*Kneels.*] Oh, pardon, fairest creature.

QUEEN: I'le talk no more, our words exchange our Souls, and every look fades all my blooming honour, like Sun beams, on unguarded Roses.—take all our Kingdoms— make our People Slaves, and let me fall beneath your Conquering Sword. But never let me hear you talk again or gaze upon your Eyes—

Goes out.

BACON: She Loves! by Heaven she Loves! And has not art enough to hide her Flame tho' she have Cruel honour to suppress it. However, I'le pursue her to the Banquet.

Exit.

SCENE II

The Widdow Ranters-Hall.

SURELOVE: This Madam Ranter is so prodigious a Treater,—oh! I hate a room that smells of a great Dinner, and what's worse a desert of Punch and Tobacco—what! are you taking leave so soon Cousin?

HAZARD: Yes Madam, but 'tis not fit I should let you know with what regret I go,—but business will be obey'd.

SURELOVE: Some Letters to dispatch to English Ladies you have left behind—come Cousin Confess.

HAZARD: I own I much admire the English Beauties but never yet have put their Fetters on—

SURELOVE: Never in Love—oh then you have pleasure to Come.

HAZARD: Rather a Pain when there's no hope attends it.

SURELOVE: Oh such diseases quickly cure themselves.

HAZARD: I do not wish to find it so; For even in Pain I find a pleasure too.

SURELOVE: You are infected then, and came abroad for cure.

HAZARD: Rather to receive my wounds Madam.

SURELOVE: Already Sir.—who e'er she be, she made good hast to Conquer, we have few here, boast that Dexterity.

HAZARD: What think you of Crisante, Madam?

SURELOVE: [*Coldly.*] I must confess your Love and your Dispair are there plac'd right, of which I am not fond of being made a Confident, since I am assur'd she can Love none but Friendly.

HAZARD: Let her Love on, as long as life shall last, let Friendly take her, and the Universe, so I had my next wish—[*Sighs*] Madam it is your self that I adore,—I should not be so vain to tell you this, but that I know you've found the secret out already from my sighs.

SURELOVE: Forbear Sir, and know me for your kinsman's wife, and no more.

HAZARD: Be Scornfull as you please, rail at my passion, and refuse to hear it; yet I'le Love on, and hope in spite of you, my Flame shall be so constant and Submissive, it shall compell your heart to some return.

SURELOVE: You're very Confident of your power I perceive, but if you chance to finde your self mistaken, say your opinion and your affectation were misapply'd, and not that I was Cruell.

Exit.

HAZARD: Whate're denyalls dwell upon your Tongue, your eyes assure me that your heart is tender. [*Goes out.*]

Enter the Bag-Piper, Playing before a great Boule of
Punch, carried between two Negro's, a Highlander
Dancing after it, The Widdow Ranter *led by* Timorous,
Crisante *by* Dullman; Mrs. Flirt *and* Friendly *all*
dancing after it; they place it on the Table.

DULLMAN: This is like the Noble Widdow all over I'faith.

TIMOROUS: [*Drinks*.] Ay, Ay, the widdows Health is a full Ladle, Major. [*While they drink about*.] —but a Pox on't what made that young Fellow here, that affronted us yesterday Major?

DULLMAN: Some damn'd Sharper that wou'd lay his Knife aboard your Widdow Cornet.[53]

TIMOROUS: Zoors if I thought so, I'd Arrest him for Salt and Battery, Lay him in Prison for a Swinging fine, and take no Baile.

DULLMAN: Nay, had it not been before my Mrs here, Mrs Crisante, I had swing'd him for his yesterday's affront,—ah my sweet Mistris Crisante—if you did but know what a power you have over me—

CRISANTE: Oh, you're a great Courtier Major.

DULLMAN: Would I were any thing for your sake Madam.

RANTER: Thou art any thing, but what thou shouldst be, prethee Major leave off being an old Buffoon, that is a Lover turn'd to ridicule by Age. Consider thy self a Meer rouling Tun of Nants,—a walking Chimney, ever Smoaking with Nasty Mundungus,—and then thou hast a Countenance like an old worm-eaten Cheese.

DULLMAN: Well widdow, you will Joake, ha, ha, ha—

TIMOROUS: Gad Zoors She's pure Company, ha, ha—

DULLMAN: No matter for my Countenance—Coll. Downright likes my Estate and is resolv'd to have it a Match.

FRIENDLY: Dear Widdow, take off your Damn'd Major, for if he speak another word to Crisante, I shall be put past all my patience, and fall foul upon him.

RANTER: S'life not for the world—Major I bar Love-making within my Territories, 'tis inconsistent with the Punch-Bowle. If you'l drink, do, if not, be gone.

TIMOROUS: Nay, Gad's Zooks if you enter me at the Punch-Boule, you enter me in Politicks—well 'tis the best Drink in Christendom for a Statesman.

> They drink about, the Bag-Pipe playing.

RANTER: Come, now you shall see what my high Land-Vallet can do—

> A *Scots Dance*.

DULLMAN: So—I see let the world go which way it will, widdow, you are resolv'd for Mirth,—but come—to the conversation of the times.

RANTER: The times, why what a Devill ailes the times, I see nothing in the times but a company of Coxcombs that fear without a Cause.

TIMOROUS: But if these fears were laid and Bacon were hang'd, I look upon Virginia to be the happiest part of the world, gads Zoors,—why, there's England—'tis nothing to't—I was in England about six years ago, and was shew'd the Court of Aldermen, some were nodding, some saying nothing, and others very little to purpose, but how could it be otherwise, for they had neither Bowle of Punch, Bottles of wine or Tobacco before 'em to put Life and Soul into 'em as we have here: then for the young Gentlemen—Their farthest Travels is to France or Italy, they never come hither.

DULLMAN: The more's the Pitty by my troth. [*Drinks*.]

---

53. i.e., some cheat who would live off the widow.

TIMOROUS: Where they learn to swear Mor-blew, Mor-dee.[54]

FRIENDLY: And tell you how much bigger the Louvre is than White-Hall, buy a suit A-la-mode, get a swinging Clap of some French Marquis, spend all their money and return just as they went.

DULLMAN: For the old fellows, their bus'ness is Usury, Extortion, and undermining young Heirs.

TIMOROUS: Then for young Merchants, their Exchange is the Tavern, their Ware-house the Play-house, and their Bills of Exchange Billet-Deaxs,[55] where to sup with their wenches at the other end of the Town,—now Judge you what a Condition poor England is in: for my part I look upon't as a lost Nation gads zoors.

DULLMAN: I have considered it, and have found a way to save all yet.

TIMOROUS: As how, I pray?

DULLMAN: As thus, we have men here of great Experience and Ability— now I would have as many sent into England as would supply all places, and Offices, both Civill and Military, de see,[56] their young Gentry should all Travell hither for breeding, and learn the misteries of State.

FRIENDLY: As for the old Covetous Fellows, I would have the Tradesmen get in their debts, break and turn Troupers.

TIMOROUS: And they'd soon be weary of Extortion gadz zoors.

DULLMAN: Then for the young Merchants, there should be a Law made, none should go beyond Ludgate.

FRIENDLY: [*Drinking all this while sometimes.*] You have found out the only way to preserve that great Kingdom.

TIMOROUS: Well, Gad zoors 'tis a fine thing to be a good Statesman.

FRIENDLY: Ay Cornet, which you had never been had you staid in old England.

DULLMAN: Why Sir we were somebody in England.

FRIENDLY: So I heard Major.

DULLMAN: You heard Sir, what have you heard, he's a kid-Napper that says he heard any thing of me—and so my service to you— I'le sue yon Sir for spoiling my Marriage, here by your Scandalls with Mrs. Crisante, but that shan't do Sir, I'le marry her for all that, and he's a Rascal that denies it.

FRIENDLY: S'death, you Lye Sir—I do.

TIMOROUS: Gad zoors Sir Lye to a Privy-Councellour, a Major of Horse, Brother, this is an affront to our Dignities, draw and I'le side with you.

They both draw on Friendly, the Ladies run off.

FRIENDLY: If I disdain to draw, 'tis not that I fear your base and Cowardly force, but for the respect I bear you as Magistrates, and so I leave you—[*Goes out.*]

TIMOROUS: An Arrant Coward Gad zoors.

DULLMAN: A mere paultroon, and I scorn to drink in's Company.

Exeunt, putting up their Swords.

---

54. Mor-dee: imitation of Mort-dieu, a French oath.
55. Billet-Deaxs: love notes (billets doux).
56. de see: do you see.

SCENE III

A Sevana, or Large Heath.
Enter Whimsey, Whiff, *and* Boozer,
With some Souldiers Arm'd.

WHIMSEY: Stand—stand—and hear the word of Command—do ye see yon Copse, and that Ditch that runs along Major Dullmans Plantation?

BOOZER: We do.

WHIMSEY: Place your Men there, and lye Flat on your Bellies, and when Bacon comes (if alone) seize him, dy'see.

WHIFF: Observe the Command now: *if alone* for we are not for bloud-shed.

BOOZER: I'le warrant you for our Parts.

Exeunt all but Whimsey *and* Whiff.

WHIMSEY: Now we have Ambusht our men, let's light our Pipes and sit down and take an Encouraging dram of the Bottle.

Pulls out a bottle of brandy out of his Pocket—they sit.

WHIFF: Thou art a Knave and hast Emptyed half the Bottle in thy Leathern Pockets, but come here's young Fright-all's health.

WHIMSEY: What, wilt drink a mans health thou'rt going to hang?

WHIFF: 'Tis all one for that, we'le drink his health first, and hang him afterwards, and thou shalt pledge me de see, and tho' 'twere under the Gallows.

WHIMSEY: Thou'rt a Traytor for saying so, and I defy thee.

WHIFF: Nay, since we are come out, like Loving Brothers to hang the Generall, let's not fall out among our selves, and so here's to you [*drinks*] though I have no great Maw to this business.

WHIMSEY: Prethee Brother Whiff, do not be so Villainous a Coward, for I hate a Coward.

WHIFF: Nay 'tis not that—But my Whiff, my Nancy dreamt to night she saw me hang'd.

WHIMSEY: 'Twas a Cowardly Dream, think no more on't, but as dreams are Expounded by Contraries, thou shalt hang the Generall.

WHIFF: Ay—but he was my friend, and I owe him at this time a hundred Pounds of Tobacco.

WHIMSEY: Nay, then I am sure thoud'st hang him if he were thy brother.

WHIFF: But hark—I think I hear the Neighing of horses, where shall we hide our selves, for if we stay here, we shall be Mawl'd damnably.

Exeunt both behind a Bush, peeping.
Enter Bacon, Fearless, *and three or four Footmen.*

BACON: Let the Groom lead the Horses o're the Sevana; we'le walk it on Foot, 'tis not a quarter of a Mile to the Town; and here the Air is cool.

FEARLESS: The Breazes about this time of the day begin to take Wing and fan refreshment to the Trees and Flowers.

BACON: And at these hours how fragrant are the Groves.

FEARLESS: The Country's well, were but the People so.

BACON: But come let's on—[*They pass to the Entrance.*]

WHIMSEY: There Boys—

The Soldiers come forth and fall on Bacon.

BACON: Ha! Ambush—[*Draws.*]

Fearless and Footmen draw, the Soldiers
after a while fighting take Bacon *and* Fearless
they having laid three or four Dead.

WHIFF: So, so, he's taken Now we may venture out.

WHIMSEY: But are you sure he's taken?

WHIFF: Sure can't you believe your Eyes, come forth, I hate a Coward—Oh Sir, have we caught your Mightiness?

BACON: Are you the Authors of this Valliant Act? None but such Villainous Cowards dar'st have attempted it.

WHIMSEY: Stop his railing Tongue.

WHIFF: No, no, let him rail, let him rail now his hands are tyed, ha, ha, Why, good Generall Fright-all, what was no body able d'ye think to tame the Roaring Lyon?

BACON: You'le be hanged for this!

WHIMSEY: Come, come, away with him to the next Tree.

BACON: What mean you, Villains?

WHIFF: Only to hang your Honour a little, that's all. We'le teach you Sir, to serve your Country against Law.

DAREING: Hah—my General betray'd—this I suspected.

As they go off, enter Dareing *with Soldiers.*
His Men come in, they fall on, release Bacon
and Fearless, *and his Man, who get Swords.*
Whimsey's *Party put* Whimsey *and* Whiff *before 'em*
striking 'em as they Endeavour to run on this side
or that, and forcing 'em to bear up, they are taken
after some Fighting.

FEARLESS: Did not the General tell you Rogues, you'd be all hang'd?

WHIFF: Oh, Nancy, Nancy, how prophetick are thy Dreams!

BACON: Come, lets on—

DAREING: S'death, what mean you Sir?

BACON: As I design'd—to present my self to the Council.

DAREING: By Heavens we'le follow then to save you from their Treachery. 'Twas this that has befallen you that I fear'd, which made me at a distance follow you.

BACON: Follow me still, but still at such a distance as your Aids may be assisting on all occasions—Fearless go back and bring your Regiment down, and Dareing let your Sergeant with his Party Guard these Villains to the Council.

Exeunt Bacon, Dareing, *and* Fearless.

WHIFF: A Pox on your Worship's Plot.

WHIMSEY: A Pox of your forwardness to come out of the hedge.

Exeunt Officers, with Whimsey *and* Whiff.

SCENE IV

The Council Table

Enter Coll. Wellman, Coll. Downright, Dullman

Timorous, *and about seven or eight more seat themselves.*

WELLMAN: You hear Mr. Dunce's opinion Gentlemen, concerning Bacon's coming upon our Invitation. He believes he will come, but I rather think, tho' he be himself undaunted, yet the persuasions of his two Lieutenant-Generalls, Dareing and Fearless may prevent him—Colonel, have you order'd our Men to be in Arms?

Enter a Souldier.

DOWNRIGHT: I have, and they'l attend further order on the Sevana.

SOULDIER: May it please your Honours, Bacon is on his way, he comes unattended by any but his Footmen, and Coll. Fearless.

DOWNRIGHT: Who is this Fellow?

WELLMAN: A Spy I sent to watch Bacon's Motions.

SOULDIER: But there is a Company of Soldiers in Ambush on this side of the Sevana to seize him as he passes by.

WELLMAN: That's by no order of the Council.

OMNES: No, no, no order.

WELLMAN: Nay, 'twere a good design if true.

TIMOROUS: Gad zoors wou'd I had thought on't for my Troup.

DOWNRIGHT: I am for no unfair dealing in any Extremity.

Enter Brag *in haste.*

BRAG: An't please your Honours, the saddest News—An Ambush being laid for Bacon, they rusht out upon him on the Sevana, and after some fighting took him and Fearless—

TIMOROUS: Is this your sad News—zoors wou'd I had had a hand in't.

BRAG: When on a sudden, Dareing and his Party fell in upon us, turn'd the tide—kill'd our men and took Captain Whimsey, and Captain Whiff Pris'ners; the rest ran away, but Bacon fought like fury.

TIMOROUS: A bloudy Fellow!

DOWNRIGHT: Whimsey and Whiff? they deserve death for Acting without order.

TIMOROUS: I'm of the Colonels Opinion, they deserve to hang for't.

DULLMAN: Why Brother, I thought you had wisht the Plot had been yours but now!

TIMOROUS: Ay, but the Case is alter'd since that, good Brother.

WELLMAN: Now he's Exasperated past all hopes of a Reconciliation.

DULLMAN: You must make use of the Statesman's refuge, wise dissimulation.

BRAG: For all this, Sir, he will not believe but that you mean Honourably, and no persuasions could hinder him from Coming, so he has dismisst all his Soldiers, and is entering the Town on foot.

WELLMAN: What pitty 'tis a brave Man should be Guilty of an ill Action.

BRAG: But the noise of his danger has so won the hearts of the Mobile,[57] that they encrease his Train as he goes, and follow him in the Town like a Victor.

57. Mobile: mob.

WELLMAN: Go wait his coming.[*Exit* Brag.] He grows too popular, and must be humbled.

TIMOROUS: I was ever of your mind, Colonel.

WELLMAN: Ay right or Wrong—but what's your Counsell now?

TIMOROUS: E'en as it us'd to be, I leave it to wiser heads.

Enter Brag.

BRAG: Bacon Sir is Entering.

TIMOROUS: Gad zoors wou'd I were safe in Bed.

DULLMAN: Colonel keep in your heat and treat Calmly with him.

WELLMAN: I rather wish you wou'd all follow me, I'd meet him at the head of all his noisy Rabble, and seize him from the rout.

DOWNRIGHT: What Men of Authority dispute with Rake-Hells? 'tis below us Sir.

TIMOROUS: To Stake our Lives and Fortunes against their nothing.

Enter Bacon, *after him the Rabble with Staves and Clubs bringing in* Whimsey *and* Whiff *bound.*

WELLMAN: What means this Insolence—What Mr. Bacon do you come in Arms?

BACON: I'de need Sir come in Arms, when men that should be Honourable can have so poor designs to take my life.

WELLMAN: Thrust out his following Rabble.

FIRST RABBLE: We'le not Stirr till we have the General safe back again.

BACON: Let not your Loves be too Officious—but retire—

FIRST RABBLE: At your Command we vanish—[*The Rabble retire.*]

BACON: I hope you'l pardon me, if in my own defence I seiz'd on these two Murderers.

DOWNRIGHT: You did well, Sir, 'twas by no Order they Acted,—stand forth and hear your Sentence—in time of war we need no Formall Tryalls to hang Knaves that Act without order.

WHIFF: Oh, Mercy Mercy Collonell—'twas Parson Dunce's Plot.

DOWNRIGHT: Issue out a warrant to seize Dunce Immediately—you shall be carry'd—to the Fort to Pray—

WHIMSEY: Oh Good your Honour I never Pray'd in all my Life.

DOWNRIGHT: From thence Drawn on a Sledg to the Place of Execution,—where you shall hang till you are dead—and then be cut down and—

WHIMSEY: [*Kneeling.*] Oh hold—hold—we shall never be able to endure half this.

WELLMAN: I think th'offence needs not so great Punishment, their Crime Sir is but equall to your own, acting without Commission.

BACON: 'Tis very well Explain'd Sir,—had I been Murder'd by Commission then, the Deed had been approv'd, and now perhaps, I am beholding to the Rabble for my Life—

WELLMAN: A fine pretence to hide a Popular fault, but for this once we Pardon them and you.

BACON: Pardon, for what? by Heaven I Scorn your Pardon, I've not offended Honour nor Religion.

WELLMAN: You have offended both in taking Arms.

BACON: Shou'd I stand by and see my Country ruin'd, my King dishonour'd, and his Subjects Murder'd hear the sad Crys of widdows and of Orphans? You heard it Lowd, but gave no pitying care to't. And till the war and Massacre was brought to my own door, my Flocks, and Heards surpriz'd, I bore it all with Patience. Is it unlawfull to defend my self against a Thief that breaks into my doors?

WELLMAN: And call you this defending of your self?

BACON: I call it doing of my self that right, which upon Just demand the Councill did refuse me. If my Ambition as you're pleas'd to call it, made me demand too Much, I left my self to you.

WELLMAN: Perhaps we thought it did.

BACON: Sir you affront my Birth,—I am a Gentleman, And yet my thoughts were humble—I wou'd have fought under the meanest of your Parasites—

TIMOROUS: [*To Dullman.*] There's a Bob for us Brother.

BACON: But still you put me off with promises—And when compell'd to stir my defence I call'd none to my aid, and those that came, 'twas their own wrongs that urg'd 'em.

DOWNRIGHT: 'Tis fear'd Sir, under this pretence you aim at Government.

BACON: I scorn to answer to so base an accusation. The height of my Ambition is to be an honest Subject.

WELLMAN: An honest Rebell, Sir—

BACON: You know you wrong me, and 'tis basely urg'd—but this is trifling—here are my Commissions.

Throws down Papers, Downright *reads.*

DOWNRIGHT: —To be General of the Forces against the Indians, and Blank Commissions for his Friends.

WELLMAN: Tear them in peices—are we to be imposed upon? Do ye come in Hostile manner to compel us?

DOWNRIGHT: Be not too rough Sir, let us argue with him—

WELLMAN: I am resolved I will not.

TIMOROUS: Then we are all Dead Men, Gudzoors! he will not give us time to say our Prayers.

WELLMAN: We every day expect fresh Force from England. Till then, we of our selves shall be sufficient to make Defence, against a sturdy Traytor.

BACON: [*Rises.*] Traytor! S'death Traytor—I defy ye, but that my Honour's yet above my Anger; I'd make you answer me that Traytor dearly.

WELLMAN: Hah—am I threatened—Guards secure the Rebel.

Guards seize him.

BACON: Is this your Honourable Invitation? Go—Triumph in your short Liv'd Victory, the next turn shall be mine.

Exeunt Guards with Bacon.

A noise of Fighting—Enter Bacon, Wellman,
his Guards Beat back by the Rabble,
Bacon *snatches a Sword from one,*
and keeps back the Rabble,
Timorous *gets under the Table.*

DOWNRIGHT: What means this Insolence!

RABBLE: We'l have our General, and knock that fellow's brains out, and hang up Collonel Wellman.

ALL: Ay ay, Hang up Wellman.

The Rabble seize Wellman, *and* Dullman *and the rest.*

DULLMAN: Hold, hold Gentlemen, I was always for the General.

RABBLE: Let's Barbicu this fat Rogue.

BACON: Begon, and know your distance to the Councel.

The Rabble let 'em go.

WELLMAN: [*In rage.*] I'd rather perish by the meanest hand, than owe my safety poorly thus to Bacon.

BACON: If you persist still in that mind I'le leave you, and Conquering, make you happy 'gainst your will.

Exeunt Bacon *and* Rabble, *hallowing*[58] *a Bacon, a Bacon.*

WELLMAN: Oh Villainous Cowards, who will trust his Honour with Sycophants so base? Let us to Arms—by Heaven I will not give my Body rest, till I've chastiz'd the boldness of this Rebel.

Exeunt Wellman, Downright, *and the rest, all but* Dullman.

Timorous *Peeps from under the Table.*

TIMOROUS: What is the Roystering Hector gone Brother?

DULLMAN: Ay, ay, and the Devil go with him.

Looking sadly, Timorous *comes out.*

TIMOROUS: Was there ever such a Bull of Bashan![59] Why, what if he should come down upon us and kill us all for Traytors?

DULLMAN: I rather think the Councel will Hang us all for Cowards—ah—oh—a Drum—a Drum—oh—[*He goes out.*]

TIMOROUS:

> This is the Misery of being Great,
>   We're Sacrific'd to every turn of State.

Exit.

---

58. hallowing: hollering.   59. Bull of Bashan: see Ps. 22:12–15.

ACT III

SCENE I

The Country Court, a great Table, with Papers, a Clerk writing.
Enter a great many people of all sorts,
then Friendly, *after him* Dullman.

FRIENDLY: How now Major; what, they say Bacon scar'd you all out of the Council yesterday: What say the People?

DULLMAN: Say? they Curse us all, and Drink young Frightall's Health, and swear they'll fight thro Fire and Brimstone for him.

FRIENDLY: And to morrow will hollow him to the Gallows, if it were his chance to come there.

DULLMAN: 'Tis very likely: Why, I am forc'd to be guarded to the Court now, the Rabble swore they would De-Wit[60] me, but I shall hamper some of 'em. Wou'd the Governour were here to bear the brunt on't, for they call us the Evil Counsellors.

Enter Hazard, *goes to* Friendly.

DULLMAN: Here's the young Rogue that drew upon us too, we have Rods in piss[61] for him i'faith.

Enter Timorous *with Bayliffs, whispers to* Dullman,
after which to the Bailiffs.

TIMOROUS: Gadzoors that's he, do your Office.

BAILIFF: We arrest you Sir, in the Kings name, at the suit of the Honourable Justice Timorous.

HAZARD: Justice Timorous, who the Devil's he?

TIMOROUS: I am the man Sir, de see, for want of a better; you shall repent Guds zoors your putting of tricks upon persons of my Rank and Quality.

After he has spoke, he runs back as afraid of him.

HAZARD: Your Rank and Quality!

TIMOROUS: Ay Sir, my Rank and Quality; first I am one of the Honourable Council, next a Justice of Peace in *Quorum*, Cornet of a Troop of Horse de see, and Church-warden.

FRIENDLY: From whence proceeds this Mr. Justice? You said nothing of this at Madam Ranters Yesterday; you saw him there, then you were good Friends!

TIMOROUS: Ay, however I have carried my Body swimmingly before my Mistress, de see, I had rancour in my Heart, Gads zoors.

FRIENDLY: Why, this Gentleman's a stranger, and but lately come a shore.

HAZARD: At my first Landing I was in company with this Fellow and two or three of his cruel Brethren, where I was affronted by them, some words past and I drew—

TIMOROUS: Ay ay Sir, you shall pay for't,—why—what Sir, cannot a Civil Magistrate affront a Man, but he must be drawn upon presently?

---

60. De-Wit: Johan DeWitt, a Dutch statesman, was killed by a mob in 1672.

61. Rods in piss: switches soaked in urine, for whipping.

FRIENDLY: Well Sir, the Gentleman shall answer your Sute, and I hope you'l take my Bail for him.

TIMOROUS: 'Tis enough—I know you to be a Civil Person.

Timorous and Dullman *take their Places,*
on a long Bench placed behind the Table,
to them Whimsey *and* Whiff, *they seat themselves,*
then Boozer *and two or three more;*
who seat them-selves: Then enter two, bearing
a Bowl of Punch and a great Ladle or two in it;
the rest of the Stage being fill'd with People.

WHIFF: Brothers it has been often been mov'd at the Bench, that a new Punch Bowl shou'd be provided, and one of a larger Circumference, when the Bench sits late about weighty affairs, oftentimes the Bowl is emptied before we end.

WHIMSEY: A good Motion, Clark set it down.

CLARK: Mr. Justice Boozer the Council has ordered you a writ of Ease and dismiss your Worship from the Bench.

BOOZER: Me from the Bench, for what?

WHIMSEY: The Complaint is Brother Boozer, for Drinking too much Punch in the time of hearing Tryals.

WHIFF: And that you can neither write nor read, nor say the Lords Prayer.

TIMOROUS: That your Warrants are like a Brewers Tally, a Notch on a Stick; if a special Warrant, then a Couple. Gods Zoors, when his Excellency comes he will have no such Justice.

BOOZER: Why Brother, tho' I can't read my self, I have had Dolton's Country-Justice read over to me two or three times, and understand the Law; this is your Malice Brother Whiff, because my Wife does not come to your Ware-House to buy her Commodities,—but no matter, to show I have no Malice in my heart, I drink your Health—I care not this, I can turn Lawyer and plead at the Board.

Drinks, all pledge him, and hum.

DULLMAN: Mr. Clark, come, to the Tryals on the Docket.

CLARK: [*Reads.*] The first is between his Worship Justice Whiff and one Grubb.

DULLMAN: Ay, that Grubb's a Common Disturber. Brother your Cause is a good Cause if well manag'd, here's to't. [*Drinks.*]

WHIFF: I thank you Brother Dullman,—read my Petition. [*Drinks.*]

CLARK: The Petition of Captain Thomas Whiff Sheweth, whereas Gilbert Grubb, calls his Worships Wife Ann Whiff Whore, and said he would prove it; your Petitioner desires the Worshipful Bench to take it into Consideration, and your Petitioner shall pray, etc.—Here's two witnesses have made Affidavit *Viva voce*, an't like your Worships.

DULLMAN: Call Grubb.

CLARK: Gilbert Grubb, come into the Court.

GRUBB: Here.

WHIMSEY: Well, what can you say for your self Mr. Grubb.

GRUBB: [*To* Whimsey] Why an't like your Worship, my wife invited some Neighbours wives to drink a Cagg of Syder, now your worships wife Madam Whiff being there fuddl'd, would have thrust me out of doors, and bid me go to my old Whore Madam Whimsey, meaning your Worship's Wife.

WHIMSEY: Hah! My wife called Whore, she's a Jade, and I'le arrest her husband here—in an Action of debts.

TIMOROUS: Gad zours she's no better than she should be I'le warrant her.

WHIFF: Look ye Brother Whimsey, be patient, you know the Humour of my Nancy when she's drunk, but when she's sober, she's a civil Person, and shall ask your pardon.

WHIMSEY: Let this be done and I am satisfied. And so here's to you. [*Drinks.*]

DULLMAN: Go on to the Tryal.

GRUBB: I being very angry said indeed, I would prove her a greater Whore than Madam Whimsey.

CLARK: An't like your Worships, he confesses the words in open Court.

GRUBB: Why, an't like your Worships, she has had two Bastards I'le prove it.

WHIFF: Sirrah, Sirrah, that was when she was a Maid, not since I married her, my marrying her made her Honest.

DULLMAN: Let there be an order of Court to Sue him, for *Scandalum Magnatum*.

TIMOROUS: Mr. Clark, let my Cause come next.

CLARK: The Defendant's ready Sir.

Hazard comes to the Board.

TIMOROUS: Brothers of the Bench take notice, that this Hector here coming into Mrs. Flirts Ordinary where I was, with my Brother Dullman and Lieutenant Boozer; we gave him good Councel to fall to Work, now my Gentleman here was affronted at this Forsooth, and makes no more to do but calls us Scoundrels, and drew his Sword on us, and had I not defended my self by running away, he had Murdered me, and Assassinated my two Brothers.

WHIMSEY: What witness have you Brother?

TIMOROUS: Here's Mrs. Flirt and her Maid Nell,—besides we may be witness for one another I hope, our words may be taken.

CLARK: Mrs. Flirt and Nell are Sworn.

They stand forth.

WHIMSEY: By the Oaths that you have taken, speak nothing but the Truth.

FLIRT: An't please your Worships, your Honours came to my House, where you found this Young Gentlemen; and your Honours invited him to Drink with your Honours: Where after some opprobrious words given him, Justice Dullman, and Justice Boozer struck him over the head; and after that indeed the Gentleman drew.

TIMOROUS: Mark that Brother he drew.

HAZARD: If I did, it was *se defendendo*.

TIMOROUS: Do you hear that Brothers, he did it in defiance.

HAZARD: Sir, you ought not to sit Judge and Accuser too.

WHIFF: The Gentlemans i'th'right Brother, you cannot do it according to the Law.

TIMOROUS: Gad zoors, what new tricks, new querks?

HAZARD: Gentlemen, take notice, he swears in Court.

TIMOROUS: Gad Zoors what's that to you Sir?

HAZARD: This is the second time of his swearing.

WHIMSEY: What, do you think we are Deaf Sir? Come, come proceed.

TIMOROUS: I desire he may be bound to his Good behaviour, Fin'd and deliver up his Sword, what say you Brother?

Jogs Dullman *who nods.*

WHIMSEY: He's asleep, drink to him and waken him,—you have miss'd the Cause by sleeping Brother. [*Drinks.*]

DULLMAN: [*Drinks.*] Justice may nod, but never sleeps Brother—you were at—Deliver his Sword—a good Motion, let it be done.

HAZARD: No Gentlemen, I wear a Sword to right my self.

TIMOROUS: That's fine i'faith, Gads Zoors, I've worn a Sword this Duzen year and never cou'd right my self.

WHIFF: Ay, 'twou'd be a fine World if Men shou'd wear Swords to right themselves, he that's bound to the Peace shall wear no Sword.

WHIMSEY: I say he that's bound to the Peace ought to wear no Peruke, they may change 'em for black or white, and then who can know them.

HAZARD: I hope Gentlemen I may be allowed to speak for my self.

WHIFF: Ay, what can you say for your self, did you not draw your Sword Sirrah?

HAZARD: I did.

TIMOROUS: 'Tis sufficient he confesses the Fact, and we'l hear no more.

HAZARD: You will not hear the Provocation given?

DULLMAN: 'Tis enough Sir, you drew—

WHIMSEY: Ay, ay, 'tis enough, he drew—let him be Fin'd.

FRIENDLY: The Gentleman shou'd be heard, he's a Kinsman too, to Collonel John Surelove.

TIMOROUS: Hum—Collonel Sureloves Kinsman.

WHIFF: Is he so, nay, then all the reason in the World he should be heard, Brothers.

WHIMSEY: Come, come Cornet, you shall be Friends with the Gentleman, this was some Drunken bout I'le warrant you.

TIMOROUS: Ha, ha, ha—so it was Gads Zoors.

WHIFF: Come drink to the Gentleman, and put it up.

TIMOROUS: Sir, my Service to you, I am heartily sorry for what's past, but it was in my Drink. [*Drinks.*]

WHIMSEY: You hear his acknowledgements Sir, and when he's sober he never quarrels, come Sir sit down, my Service to you.

HAZARD: I beg your Excuse Gentlemen—I have earnest business.

DULLMAN: Let us adjourn the Court, and prepare to meet the Regiments on the Sevana.

All go but Friendly *and* Hazard.

HAZARD: Is this the best Court of Judicature your Country affords?

FRIENDLY: To give it its due it is not. But how does thy Amour thrive?

HAZARD: As well as I can wish, in so short a time.

FRIENDLY: I see she regards thee with kind Eyes, Sighs and Blushes.

HAZARD: Yes, and tells me I am so like a Brother she had—to Excuse her kind concern,—then blush so prettily, that Gad I cou'd not forbear making a discovery of my Heart.

FRIENDLY: Have a care of that, come upon her by slow degrees, for I know she's Vertuous;—but come, let's to the Sevana; where I'le present you to the two Collonels, Wellman and Downright, the Men that manage all till the arrival of the Governour.

Exeunt.

SCENE II

The Sevana or Heath.

Enter Wellman, Downright, Boozer, *and* Officers.

WELLMAN: Have you dispatch'd the Scouts, to watch the Motions of the Enemies? I know that Bacon's Violent and Haughty, and will resent our vain attempts upon him; therefore we must be speedy in prevention.

DOWNRIGHT: What forces have you raised since our last order?

BOOZER: Here's a list of 'em, they came but slowly in, till we promised every one a Bottle of Brandy.

Enter Officer *and* Dunce.

OFFICER: We have brought Mr. Dunce here, as your Honour commanded us. After strict search we found him this Morning in Bed with Madam Flirt.

DOWNRIGHT: No matter; he'll exclaim no less against the vices of the Flesh, the next Sunday.

DUNCE: I hope Sir you will not credit the Malice of my Enemies.

WELLMAN: No more, you are free, and what you counsell'd about the Ambush was both prudent and seasonable, and perhaps I now wish it had taken effect.

Enter Friendly *and* Hazard.

FRIENDLY: I have brought an English Gentleman to kiss your hands, Sir, and offer you his service; he is young and brave, and Kinsman to Colonel Surelove.

WELLMAN: Sir, you are welcome and to let you see you are so, we will give you your Kinsmans command, Captain of a Troop of Horse-Guards, and which I'm sure will be continued to you when the Governour arrives.

HAZARD: I shall endeavour to deserve the Honour, Sir.

Enter Dullman, Timorous, Whimsey, *and* Whiff,
all in Buff, Scarf, and Feather.[62]

DOWNRIGHT: So Gentlemen, I see you're in a readiness.

TIMOROUS: Readiness! What means he, I hope we are not to be drawn out to go against the Enemy, Major.

DULLMAN: If we are, they shall look a new Major for me.

WELLMAN: We were debating, Gentlemen, what course were best to pursue against this Powerful Rebel.

FRIENDLY: Why, Sir, we have Forces enough, let's charge him instantly, delays are dangerous.

TIMOROUS: Why, what a damn'd fiery Fellow's this?

DOWNRIGHT: But if we drive him to Extremities, we fear his siding with the Indians.

DULLMAN: Colonel Downright has hit it; why should we endanger our Men against

62. *Buff, Scarf, and Feather*: Indian dress.

a desperate Termagant? If he love Wounds and Scars so well, let him exercise on our Enemies—but if he will needs fall upon us, 'tis then time enough for us to venture our lives and fortunes.

TIMOROUS: How, we go to Bacon! under favour I think 'tis his Duty to come to us, an you go to that, Gads Zoores.

FRIENDLY: If he do, 'twill cost you dear, I doubt Cornet.—I find by our List, Sir, we are four thousand men.

TIMOROUS: Gads Zoores, not enough for a Breakfast for that insatiate Bacon, and his two Lieutenant Generals Fearless and Dareing.

Whiff sits on the Ground with a Bottle of Brandy.

WHIMSEY: A Morsel, a Morsel.

WELLMAN: I am for an attack, what say you Gentlemen to an attack?— What, silent all? What say you, Major?

DULLMAN: [*Speaks big.*] I say, Sir, I hope my courage was never in dispute. But, Sir, I am going to Marry Collonel Downright's Daughter here—and should I be slain in this Battle 'twould break her heart;—besides, Sir, I should lose her Fortune.

WELLMAN: [*To Whimsey.*] I'm sure here's a Captain will never Flinch.

WHIMSEY: Who, I, an't like your Honour?

WELLMAN: Ay, you.

WHIMSEY: Who, I? ha, ha, ha; Why did your Honour think that I would fight?

WELLMAN: Fight, yes? Why else do you take Commissions?

WHIMSEY: Commissions! Oh Lord, Oh Lord, take Commissions to fight! ha, ha, ha; that's a jest, if all that take Commissions should fight—

WELLMAN: Why do you bear Arms then?

WHIMSEY: Why for the Pay; to be called Captain, noble Captain, to show, to cock and look big and bluff as I do; to be bow'd to thus as we pass, to domineer and beat our Souldiers: Fight, quoth a, ha, ha, ha.

FRIENDLY: But what makes you look so simply Cornet?

TIMOROUS: Why, a thing that I have quite forgot, all my accounts for England are to be made up, and I'm undone if they be neglected—else I wou'd not flinch for the stoutest he that wears a Sword—[*Looking big.*]

DOWNRIGHT: What say you, Captain Whiff?

WHIFF: [*Almost drunk.*] I am trying Colonel what Mettle I'm made on; I think I am Valiant, I suppose I have Courage, but I confess 'tis a little of the D— breed, but a little inspiration from the bottle, and the leave of my Nancy, may do wonders.

Enter a Seaman in haste.

SEAMAN: An't please your Honours, Frightall's Officers have seiz'd all the Ships in the River, and rid now round the Shore, and had by this time secur'd the Sandy Beach, and Landed men to Fire the Town, but that they are high in Drink aboard the Ship call'd the Good Subject; the Master of her sent me to let your Honours know, that a few men sent to his assistance will surprize them, and retake the Ships.

WELLMAN: Now, Gentlemen, here's a brave occasion for Emulation—why writ not the Master?

DULLMAN: Ay, had he writ, I had soon been amongst them i'faith; but this is some Plot to betray us.

SEAMAN: Keep me here, and kill me if it not be true.

DOWNRIGHT: He says well—there's a Brigantine and a Shallop ready, I'le Embark immediately.

FRIENDLY: No Sir, your Presence is here more necessary, let me have the Honour of this Expedition.

HAZARD: I'll go your Voluntier Charles.

WELLMAN: Who else offers to go?

WHIMSEY: A mere trick to Kidnap us, by Bacon,—if the Captain had writ—

TIMOROUS: Ay, ay, if he had writ—

WELLMAN: I see you're all base Cowards, and here Cashier ye from all Commands and Offices.

WHIMSEY: Look ye Collonel, you may do what you please, but you lose one of the best dress'd Officers in your whole Camp, Sir—

TIMOROUS: And in me, such a Head Piece.

WHIFF: I'le say nothing, but let the State want me.

DULLMAN: For my part I am weary of weighty Affairs.

> *In this while* Wellman, Downright,
> Friendly *and* Hazard *talk.*

WELLMAN: Command what Men you please, but Expedition makes you half a Conquerour.

> *Exit* Friendly *and* Hazard.

> *Enter another* Seaman *with a Letter, gives it to*
> Downright, *he and* Wellman *read it.*

DOWNRIGHT: Look ye now Gentlemen, the Master has writ.

DULLMAN: Has he—he might have writ sooner, while I was in Command,—if he had—

WHIMSEY: Ay, Major—if he had—but let them miss us—

WELLMAN: Collonel, haste with your Men, and Reinforce the Beach, while I follow with the Horse;—Mr. Dunce pray let that Proclamation be Read concerning Bacon, to the Souldiers.

DUNCE: It shall be done, Sir.

> *Exit* Downright *and* Wellman.

Gentlemen, how simply you look now.

> *The Scene opens and discovers a Body of Souldiers.*

TIMOROUS: —Why Mr. Parson I have a scruple of Conscience upon me, I am considering whether it be Lawful to Kill, tho it be in War; I have a great aversion to't, and hope it proceeds from Religion.

WHIFF: I remember the Fit took you just so, when the Dutch Besieged us, for you cou'd not then be perswaded to strike a stroke.

TIMOROUS: Ay, that was because they were Protestants as we are, but Gads Zoors had they been Dutch Papists I had maul'd them! But Conscience—

WHIMSEY: I have been a Justice of Peace this six years and never had a conscience in my Life.

TIMOROUS: Nor I neither, but in this damn'd thing of Fighting.

DUNCE: [*To the Souldiers.*] Gentlemen I am Commanded to read the Declaration of the Honourable Council to you.

ALL: Hum, hum, hum—

BOOZER: Silence—silence—

DUNCE: [*Reads.*] *By an order of Council Dated May the 10th 1670: To all Gentle-men Soulders, Merchants, Planters, and whom else it may concern. Whereas Bacon, contrary to Law and Equity, has to satisfy his own Ambition taken up Arms, with a pretence to fight the Indians, but indeed to molest and enslave the whole Colony, and to take away their Liberties and Properties; this is to declare, that whoever shall bring this Traytor Dead or alive to the Council shall have three hundred Pounds reward: And so God save the King.*

ALL: [*Hollow.*]

A Councel, a Councel! Hah—

Enter a Souldier *hastily.*

SOULDIER: Stand to your Arms Gentlemen, stand to your Arms, Bacon is Marching this way.

DUNCE: Hah—what numbers has he?

SOULDIER: About a hundred Horse, in his March he has surpriz'd Collonel Down-right, and taken him Prisoner.

ALL: [*Hollow.*] Let's fall on Bacon—let's fall on Bacon hay—

BOOZER: We'll hear him speak first—and see what he can say for himself.

ALL: Ay, ay, we'll hear Bacon speak—

Dunce pleads with them.

TIMOROUS: Well Major I have found a Stratagem shall make us four the Greatest Men in the Colony, we'll surrender our selves to Bacon, and say we Disbanded on purpose.

DULLMAN: Good—

WHIFF: Why, I had no other design in the World in refusing to Fight.

WHIMSEY: Nor I, d'ye think I wou'd have excus'd it with the fear of disordering my Cravat-String else—

DUNCE: Why Gentlemen, he designs to Fire James Town; Murder you all, and then lye with your Wives, and will you slip this opportunity of seizing him?

BOOZER: Here's a Termagant Rogue, Neighbours—we'll Hang the Dog.

ALL: Ay, Ay, hang Bacon, hang Bacon.

Enter Bacon, *and* Fearless, *some Souldiers leading in*
Downright *bound;* Bacon *stands and stares a while*
on the Regiments, who are silent all.

BACON: Well Gentlemen—in order to your fine Declaration you see I come to render my self—

DUNCE: How came he to know of our Declaration?

WHIFF: Rogues, Rogues among our selves—that inform.

BACON: What are ye silent all,—not a Man to lift his Hand in Obedience to the Council to murder this Traytor, that has exposed his Life so often for you? Hah what not for three hundred Pound,—you see I've left my Troops behind and come all wearied with the Toyles of War, worn out by Summers heats and Winters colds, March'd tedious Days and Nights thro Bogs and Fens as dangerous as your Clamors, and as Faithless,—what tho 'twas to preserve you all in safety, no matter, you shou'd obey the Grateful Council, and Kill this honest Man that has defended you?

ALL: Hum, hum hum.

WHIFF: The General speaks like a Gorgon.

TIMOROUS: Like a Cherubim, Man.

BACON: All silent yet—where's that might Courage that cryed so loud but now? A Council a Council, where is your Resolution, cannot three hundred Pound Excite your Valour, to seize that Traytor Bacon who has bled for you?—

ALL: [*Hollow.*] A Bacon, a Bacon, a Bacon—

DOWNRIGHT: Oh Villainous Cowards—Oh the Faithless Multitude!

BACON: What say you Parson—you have a forward Zeal!

DUNCE: I wish my Coat Sir did not hinder me, from acting as becomes my Zeal and Duty.

WHIMSEY: A plaguy Rugid[63] Dog—that Parson—

BACON: Fearless seize me that canting Knave from out the Herd, and next those Honourable Officers.

> *Points to* Dullman, Whimsey, Whiff, *and* Timorous.
> Fearless *seizes them, and gives them to the* Souldiers, *and takes*
> *the Proclamation from* Dunce *and shews* Bacon, *they read it.*

DULLMAN: Seize us, Sir, you shall not need, we laid down our Commissions on purpose to come over to your Honour.

WHIFF: We ever lov'd and honour'd your Honour.

TIMOROUS: So intirely, Sir—[*Aside*] that I wish I were safe in James Town for your sake, and your Honour were hang'd.

BACON: This fine Piece is of your Penning Parson—though it be countenanc'd by the Councils Names—Oh in gratitude— Burn—burn the Treacherous Town—Fire it immediately—

WHIMSEY: We'll obey you, Sir—

WHIFF: Ay, ay, we'll make a Bonfire on't, and Drink your Honours Health round about it.

> *They offer to go.*

BACON: Yet hold, my Revenge shall be more Merciful, I ordered that all the Women of Rank shall be seiz'd and brought to my Camp. I'll make their Husbands pay their Ransoms dearly; they'd rather have their Hearts bleed than their Purses.

FEARLESS: Dear General, let me have the seizing of Collonel Downright's Daughter; I would fain be Plundering for a Trifle call'd a Maiden-head.

BACON: On pain of Death treat them with all respect; assure them of the safety of their Honour. Now, all that will follow me, shall find a welcom, and those that will not, may depart in Peace.

ALL: Hay, a General, a General, a General.

> *Some Souldiers go off, some go to the side of* Bacon.
> *Enter* Dareing *and Souldiers, with* Crisante, Surelove,
> Mrs. Whimsey *and* Mrs. Whiff, *and several other* Women.

BACON: Successful Dareing, welcome, what Prizes have ye?

---

63. Rugid: rugged.

DAREING: The Fairest in the World Sir, I'm not for common Plunder.

DOWNRIGHT: Hah, my Daughter and my Kinswoman!—

BACON: 'Tis not with Women Sir, nor honest Men like you that I intend to Combat; their own Parents shall not be more indulgent, nor better safeguard to their Honours Sir: But 'tis to save the Expence of Blood, I seize on their most valu'd Prizes.

DOWNRIGHT: But Sir, I know your wild Lieutenant General has long lov'd my Crisante, and perhaps, will take this time to force her to consent.

DAREING: I own I have a Passion for Crisante, yet by my Generals Life—or her fair self—what now I Act is on the score of War. I scorn to force the Maid I do adore.

BACON: Believe me Ladies, you shall have Honourable Treatment here.

CRISANTE: We do not doubt it Sir, either from you or Dareing. If he love me—that will secure my Honour, or if he do not, he's too brave to injure me.

DAREING: I thank you for your just opinion of me, Madam.

CRISANTE: But Sir, 'tis for my Father I must plead; to see his Reverend Hands in Servile Chains—and then perhaps if stubborn to your will, his Head must fall a Victim to your Anger.

DOWNRIGHT: No my good Pious Girl, I cannot fear Ignoble usage from the General—And if thy Beauty can preserve thy Fame, I shall not mourn in my Captivity.

BACON: I'le ne'er deceive your kind opinion of me—Ladies I hope you're all of that opinion too.

SURELOVE: If seizing us Sir can advance your Honour, or be of any use considerable to you, I shall be proud of such a slavery.

MRS. WHIMSEY: I hope Sir we shan't be Ravish'd in your Camp.

DAREING: Fie Mrs. Whimsey, do Souldiers use to Ravish?

MRS. WHIFF: Ravish—marry I fear 'em not, I'de have 'em know I scorn to be Ravish'd by any Man!

FEARLESS: Ay a my Conscience Mrs. Whiff, you are too good natur'd.

DAREING: Madam, I hope you'l give me leave to name Love to you, and try by all submissive ways to win your heart!

CRISANTE: Do your worst Sir, I give you leave, if you assail me only with your Tongue.

DAREING: That's generous and brave, and I'le requite it.

Enter Souldier *in haste.*

SOULDIER: The Truce being ended, Sir, the Indians grow so insolent as to attack us even in our Camp, and have kill'd several of our Men.

BACON: 'Tis time to check their boldness. Dareing haste draw up our Men in order, to give 'em Battel. I rather had expected their submission.

The Country now may see what they're to fear,
Since we that are in Arms are not secure.

Exeunt, leading the Ladies.

ACT IV

S<small>CENE</small> 1

A Temple, with an Indian God placed upon it, Priests and Priestesses attending;
Enter Indian King *on one side attended by Indian Men, the* Queen *Enters on the other*
side with Women, all bow to the Idol, and divide on each side of the Stage, then the
Musick Playing lowder, the Priests and Priestesses Dance about the Idol, with ridicu-
lous Postures, and crying (as for Incantations.) Thrice repeated,

Agah Yerkin, Agah Boah,

Sulen Tawarapah, Sulen Tawarapah.

After this soft Musick plays again, then they Sing something fine, after which the
Priests lead the King *to the Altar, and the Priestesses, the* Queen; *they take off little*
Crowns from their Heads, and offer them at the Alter.

KING: Invoke the God, of our Quiocto to declare, what the Event shall be of this our
last War against the English General.

Soft music ceases.

The Musick changes to confused Tunes, to which the Priests and Priestesses Dance
Antickly Singing between; the same Incantation as before; and then Dance again, and
so invoke again alternately. Which Dance ended a Voice behind the Alter cries, while
soft Musick Plays—

The English General shall be,

A Captive to his Enemy;

And you from all your Toyles be freed,

When by your hand the Foe shall bleed:

And ere the Sun's swift course be run,

This mighty Conquest, shall be won.

KING: I thank the Gods for taking care of us: Prepare new Sacrifice against the
Evening; when I return a Conqueror, I will my self perform the Office of a Priest.

QUEEN: Oh Sir, I fear you'l fall a Victim first.

KING: What means Semernia, why are thy looks so Pale?

QUEEN: Alas the Oracles have double meanings, their sense is doubtful, and their
words Inigmas. I fear Sir I cou'd make a truer interpritation—

KING: How, Semernia! by all thy Love I charge thee as you respect my Life, to let me
know your thoughts.

QUEEN: Last Night I Dream'd a Lyon, fell with Hunger, spite of your Guards slew
you, and bore you hence.

KING: This is thy Sexes fear, and no interpretation of the Oracle.

QUEEN: I cou'd convince you farther.

KING: Hast thou a secret thou canst keep from me? Thy Soul a thought that I must
be stranger to? This is not like the Justice of Semernia, come unriddle me the Oracle.

QUEEN: The English General shall be, a captive to his Enemy; he is so Sir already to
my Beauty, he says he languishes for Love of me.

KING: Hah—the General my Rival—but go on—

QUEEN: And you from all your War be freed: Oh let me not explain that fatal line, for fear it mean, you shall be freed by Death.

KING: What, when by my hand the Foe shall bleed?—away—it cannot be—

QUEEN: No doubt my Lord, you'l bravely sell your Life, and deal some wounds where you'l receive so many.

KING: 'Tis Love Semernia makes thee Dream, while waking I'le trust the Gods, and am resolved for Battel.

Enter an Indian.

INDIAN: Haste, haste, Great Sir to Arms, Bacon with all his Forces is prepar'd, and both the Armies ready to engage.

KING: Haste to my General bid him charge em instantly. I'le bring up the supplies of stout Teroomians, those so well skill'd in the Envenom'd Arrow.

Exit Indian.

—Semernia—words but poorly do express the griefs of parting Lovers—'tis with dying Eyes, and a Heart trembling—thus—

Puts her Hand on his Heart.

They take a heavy leave,—one parting Kiss, and one Love pressing sigh, and then farewel—but not a long farewel; I shall return Victorious to thy Arms,—commend me to the Gods and still remember me.

Exit.

QUEEN: Alas! What pitty 'tis I saw the General, before my Fate had given me to the King—but now—like those that change their Gods, my faithless mind 'twixt my two opinions wavers; while to the Gods my Monarch I commend; my wandring thoughts in pitty of the General makes that zeal cold, declin'd— ineffectual;—If for the General, I implore the Deities, methinks my Prayers shou'd not ascend the Skies since Honour tells me 'tis an impious zeal.

> Which way so ever my Devotions move,
> I am too wretched to be heard above.

Goes in. All exeunt.

SCENE II

Shows a Field of Tents, seen at some distance thro' the Trees of a Wood, Drums, Trumpets and the noise of Battel, with hollowing. The Indians are seen with Battel-Axes to Retreat Fighting from the English and all go off, when they Re-enter immediately beating back the English, the Indian King *at the head of his Men, with Bows and Arrows;* Dareing *being at the head of the English: They Fight off; the noise continues less loud as more at distance.*

Enter Bacon *with his Sword drawn, meets*
Fearless *with his Sword drawn.*

FEARLESS: Haste, haste Sir to the Entrance of the Wood, Dareings Engaged past hope of a retreat, ventring too far, persuing of the Foe; the King in Ambush with his Poyson'd Archers, fell on and now we're dangerously distrest.

BACON: Dareing is Brave, but he's withal too rash, come on and follow me to his Assistance—[*Goes out.*]

A hollowing within, the Fight renews,
enter the Indians Beaten back by
Bacon, Dareing and Fearless; they Fight off,
the noise of Fighting continues a while,
this still behind the Wood.
Enter Indians Flying over the Stage, pursu'd by the King.

KING: Turn, turn ye fugitive Slaves, and face the Enemy; Oh Villains, Cowards, Deaf to all Command, by Heaven I had my Rival in my view and Aim'd at nothing but my Conquering him—now like a Coward I must fly with Cowards, or like a desperate Mad-Man fall, thus singly midst the numbers.

Follows the Indians.

Enter Bacon *inrag'd with his Sword drawn,*
Fearless, *and* Dareing *following him.*

BACON: —Where is the King, Oh ye perfidious Slaves, how have you hid him from my just Revenge—search all the Brakes, the Furzes and the Trees, and let him not escape on Pain of Death.

DAREING: We cannot do wonders Sir.

BACON: But you can run away.—

DAREING: Yes, when we see occasion—yet—shou'd any but my General tell me so—by Heaven he shou'd find I were no starter.

BACON: Forgive me, I'm Mad—the Kings escap'd, hid like a trembling slave in some close Ditch, where he will sooner starve than Fight it out.

Re-enter Indians running over the Stage, pursued by the King
who shoots them as they Fly, some few follow him.

KING: [*In rage.*] All's lost—the day is lost—and I'm betray'd—Oh Slaves, that even Wounds can't Animate.

BACON: The King!

KING: The General here, by all the Powers betray'd by my own Men.

BACON: Abandon'd as thou art I scorn to take thee basely, you shall have Souldier's chance Sir for your Life, since chance so luckily has brought us hither; without more aids we will dispute the day: this spot of Earth bears both our Armies Fates, I'le give you back the Victory I have won, and thus begin a new, on equal terms.

KING: That's Nobly said—the Powers have heard my wish! You Sir first taught me how to use a Sword, which heretofore has served me with success, but now—'tis for Semernia that it draws, a prize more valu'd than my Kingdom, Sir—

BACON: Hah Semernia!

KING: Your Blushes do betray your Passion for her.

DAREING: 'Sdeath we have Fought for this, to expose the Victor to the Conquer'd Foe?

FEARLESS: What, Fight a single Man—our Prize already?

KING: Not so young Man while I command a Dart.

BACON: Fight him, by Heaven, no reason shall disswade me, and he that interrupts me is a Coward, whatever be my Fate, I do command ye to let the King pass freely to his Tents.

DAREING: The Devil's in the General.

FEARLESS: 'Sdeath, his Romantick humour will undo us.

They Fight and pause.

KING: You Fight as if you meant to outdo me this way, as you have done in Generosity.

BACON: You're not behind hand with me Sir in courtesy, come here's to set us even—

Fight again.

KING: You bleed apace.

BACON: You've only Breath'd a Vein, and given me new Health and Vigour by it.

They Fight again, Wounds on both sides, the King staggers,
Bacon takes him in his Arms; the King drops his Sword.

BACON: How do you do, Sir?

KING: Like one—that's hovering between Heaven and Earth, I'm—mounting—some-where—upwards—but giddy with my flight,—I know not where.

BACON: Command my Surgions,—instantly—make haste! Honour returns and Love all Bleeding's fled.

Exit Fearless.

KING: Oh Semernia, how much more truth had thy Divinity than the Predictions of the flattering Oracles. Commend me to her—I know you'l—visit—your Fair Captive Sir, and tell her—oh—but Death prevents the rest. [*Dies.*]

Enter Fearless.

BACON: He's gone—and now like Caesar I cou'd weep over the Hero I my self destroy'd.

FEARLESS: I'm glad for your repose I see him there—'twas a Mad hot Brain'd Youth and so he dy'd.

BACON: Come bear him on your Shoulders to my Tent, from whence with all the solemn state we can, we will convey him to his own Pavillion.

Enter a Souldier.

SOULDIER: Some of our Troops pursuing of the Enemy even to their Temples, which they made their Sanctuary, finding the Queen at her Devotion there with all her Indian Ladies, I'd much ado to stop their violent rage from setting fire to the Holy Pile.

BACON: Hang em immediately that durst attempt it, while I my self will flye to rescue her.

Goes out. They bear off the Kings Body. Exeunt all.

Enter Whimsey, pulling in Whiff,
with a Halter about his Neck.

WHIMSEY: Nay I'm resolved to keep thee here till his Honour the General comes,— what to call him Traytor, and run away after he had so generously given us our freedom, and listed us Cadees for the next command that fell in his Army;—I'm resolv'd to Hang thee—

WHIFF: Wilt thou betray and Peach thy Friend? Thy Friend that kept thee Company all the while thou wert a Prisoner—Drinking at my own charge.—

WHIMSEY: No matter for that, I scorn Ingratitude and therefore will Hang thee—but as for thy drinking with me—I scorn to be behind hand with thee in Civility and therefore here's to thee.

Takes a Bottle of Brandy out of his Pocket, Drinks.

WHIFF: I can't drink.

WHIMSEY: A certain sign thou would be Hang'd.

WHIFF: [*Weeps.*] You us'd to be a my side when a Justice, let the cause be how it wou'd.

WHIMSEY: Ay—when I was a Justice I never minded Honesty, but now I'le be true to my General, and Hang thee to be a great man.—

WHIFF: If I might but have a fair Tryal for my Life—

WHIMSEY: [*Sits on a Drum Head.*] A fair Tryal!—come I'le be thy Judge—and if thou can'st clear thy self by Law I'le acquit thee, Sirrah, Sirrah, what can'st thou say for thy self for calling his Honour Rebel?

WHIFF: 'Twas when I was Drunk an't like your Honour.

WHIMSEY: That's no Plea, for if you kill a Man when you are Drunk you must be Hang'd when you are Sober, hast thou any thing else to say for thy self, why Sentence may not pass upon thee?

WHIFF: I desire the Benefit of the Clergy.

WHIMSEY: The Clergy, I never knew any body that ever did benefit by em, why thou canst not read a word!

WHIFF: Transportation then—

WHIMSEY: It shall be to England then—but hold—who's this?

DULLMAN: [*Creeping from a Bush.*] So the danger's over, I may venture out—Pox on't I would not be in this fear again, to be Lord Chief Justice of our Court.

Enter Timorous *with Battle-Ax, Bow and Arrows, and Feathers on his Head.*

Why how now Cornet—what in dreadful Equipage? Your Battle Ax bloody, with Bow and Arrows?

TIMOROUS: I'm in the posture of the times, Major—I cou'd not be Idle where so much Action was, I'm going to present my self to the General with these Trophies of my Victory here—

DULLMAN: Victory—what Victory—did I not see thee creeping out of yonder Bush, where thou wert hid all the Fight—stumble on a Dead Indian, and take away his Arms?

TIMOROUS: Why, didst thou see me?

DULLMAN: See thee Ay—and what a fright thou wert in, till thou were sure he was Dead.

TIMOROUS: Well, well, that's all one—Gads zoors if every Man that pass for Valiant in a Battel, were to give an account how he gained his Reputation, the World wou'd be but thinly stock'd with Heroes, I'le say he was a great War Captain, and that I kill'd him hand to hand, and who can disprove me?

DULLMAN: Disprove thee—why that Pale face of thine, that has so much of the Coward in't.

TIMOROUS: Shaw that's with loss of Blood—Hah I am overheard I doubt—who's yonder—[*Sees* Whimsey *and* Whiff] how, Brother Whiff in a Hempen Cravat-String?

WHIMSEY: He call'd the General Traytor and was running away, and I'm resolv'd to Peach.

DULLMAN: Hum—and one witness will stand good in Law, in case of Treason—

TIMOROUS: Gads zoors in case of Treason he'l be hang'd if it be proved against him, were there ne'er a witness at all, but he must be try'd by a Councel of War Man—come, come let's disarm him—

> *They take away his Arms, and pull a*
> *Bottle of Brandy out of his pocket.*

WHIFF: What, I hope you will not take away my Brandy Gentlemen, my last comfort.

TIMOROUS: Gads zoors it's come in good time—we'l Drink it off, here Major—

> *Drinks,* Whiff *takes him aside.*

WHIFF: Hark ye Cornet—you are my good Friend, get this matter made up before it comes to the General.

TIMOROUS: But this is Treason Neighbour.

WHIFF: If I Hang—I'le declare upon the Ladder, how you kill'd your War Captain.

TIMOROUS: Come Brother Whimsey—we have been all Friends and loving Magistrates together, let's Drink about, and think no more of this business.

DULLMAN: Ay, ay, if every sober man in the Nation, should be call'd to account of the Treason he speaks in's Drink the Lord have mercy upon us all—put it up—and let us like loving Brothers take an honest resolution to run away together; for this same Frightal minds nothing but Fighting.

WHIMSEY: I'm content, provided we go all to the Council and tell them (to make our Peace) we went in obedience to the Proclamation to kill Bacon, but the Traytor was so strongly guarded we could not effect it, but Mum—who's here?—

> *To them, Enter* Ranter *and* Jenny, *as Man and Footman.*

RANTER: Hah, our four Reverend Justices—I hope the Blockheads will not know me—Gentlemen, can you direct me to Lieutenant General Dareings Tents?

WHIFF: Hum, who the Devil's this—that's he you see coming this way, 'Sdeath yonder's Dareing—Let's slip away before he advances.

> *Exeunt all but* Ranter *and* Jenny.

JENNY: I am scar'd with those dead Bodies we have past over, for God's sake Madam, let me know your design in coming.

RANTER: Why? now I'le tell thee—my damn'd mad Fellow Dareing, who has my heart and soul—Loves Crisante, has stolen her, and carried her away to his Tents, she hates him, while I am dying for him.

JENNY: Dying Madam! I never saw you melancholy.

RANTER: Pox on't no, why should I sigh and whine, and make my self an Ass, and him conceited, no, instead of snivelling I'm resolved—

JENNY: What Madam?

RANTER: Gad, to beat the Rascal, and bring off Crisante.

JENNY: Beat him Madam? What, a woman beat a Lieutenant General?

RANTER: Hang 'em, they get a name in War, from command, not courage; but how know I but I may fight, Gad I have known a Fellow kickt from one end of the Town to t'other, believing himself a Coward, at last forc'd to fight, found he could, got a Reputation and bullyed all he met with, and got a name, and a great Commission.

JENNY: But if he should kill you Madam?

RANTER: I'le take care to make it as Comical a Duel as the best of 'em. As much in Love as I am, I do not intend to dy its Martyr.

Enter Dareing *and* Fearless.

FEARLESS: Have you seen Crisante since the fight?

DAREING: Yes, but she is still the same, as nice and coy as Fortune, when she's courted by the wretched, yet she denys me, so obligingly she keeps my Love still in its humble Calm.

RANTER: [*Sullenly.*] Can you direct me Sir, to one Dareings Tent?

DAREING: One Dareing—he has another Epithet to his Name!

RANTER: What's that, Rascal, or Coward?

DAREING: Hah, which of thy Stars young man has sent thee hither, to find that certain Fate they have decreed.

RANTER: I know not what my Stars have decreed, but I shall be glad if they have ordain'd me to Fight with Dareing,—by thy concern thou shou'dst be he?

DAREING: I am, prithee who are thou?

RANTER: Thy Rival, tho newly arriv'd from England, and came to Marry fair Crisante, whom thou hast Ravish'd, for whom I hear another Lady Dies.

DAREING: Dies for me?

RANTER: Therefore resign her fairly—or fight me fairly—

DAREING: Come on Sir—but hold—before I kill thee, prithee inform me who this Dying Lady is?

RANTER: Sir I owe ye no Courtesy, and therefore will do you none by telling you— come Sir for Crisante—draw.

They offer to fight, Fearless *steps in.*

FEARLESS: Hold—what mad Frolick's this?— [*to Ranter*] Sir you fight for one you never saw [*to Dareing*] and you for one that Loves you not.

DAREING: Perhaps she'l Love him as little.

RANTER: Gad put it to the Tryal, if you dare—if thou be'st Generous bring me to her, and whom she does neglect shall give the other Place.

DAREING: That's fair, put up thy Sword—I'll bring thee to her Instantly.

Exeunt.

SCENE III

A Tent.

Enter Crisante *and* Surelove.

CRISANTE: I'm not so much afflicted for my confinement as I am, that I cannot hear of Friendly.

SURELOVE: Art not persecuted with Dareing?

CRISANTE: Not at all, tho he tells me daily of his Passion I rally him, and give him neither hope nor despair,—he's here.

Enter Dareing, Fearless, Ranter *and* Jenny.

DAREING: Madam, the Complaisance I show in bringing you my Rival, will let you see how glad I am to oblige you in every way.

RANTER: I hope the danger I have expos'd my self to for the Honour of kissing your Hand, Madam, will render me something acceptable—here are my Credentials—

Gives her a Letter.

CRISANTE: [*Reads.*] *Dear Creature, I have taken this habit to free you from an impertinent Lover, and to secure the Damn'd Rogue Dareing to my self. Receive me as sent by Collonel Surelove from England to Marry you—favour me—no more—your Ranter.*

[*Aside*]—Hah, Ranter?

[*to* Ranter]—Sir, you have too good a Character from my Cousin Collonel Surelove, not to receive my welcome.

Gives Surelove *the letter.*

RANTER: Stand by General—

Pushes away Dareing *and looks big, and takes* Crisante *by the Hand, and kisses it.*

DAREING: 'Sdeath, Sir, there's room—enough—at first sight so kind? Oh Youth—Youth and Impudence, what Temptations are you—to Villanous Woman.

CRISANTE: I confess Sir we Women do not Love these rough Fighting Fellows, they're always scaring us with one Broil or other.

DAREING: Much good may it do you with your tame Coxcomb.

RANTER: Well Sir, then you yield the Prize?

DAREING: Ay, Gad, were she an Angel, that can prefer such a callow Fop as thou before a man—take her and domineer.

They all laugh.

—'Sdeath am I grown Ridiculous?

FEARLESS: [*Aside to* Dareing] Why hast thou not found the Jest? by Heaven 'tis Ranter, 'tis she that loves you, carry on the humour. Faith Sir, if I were you, I wou'd devote my self to Madam Ranter.

CRISANTE: Ay, she's the fittest Wife for you, she'll fit your Humour.

DAREING: Ranter—Gad I'd sooner marry a She Bear, unless for a Pennance for some horrid Sin, we should be eternally challenging one another to the Field, and ten to one she beats me there; or if I should escape there, she would kill me with Drinking.

RANTER: Here's a Rogue—does your Country abound with such Ladies?

DAREING: The Lord forbid, half a dozen wou'd ruine the Land, debauch all the men, and scandalize all the Women.

FEARLESS: No matter, she's rich.

DAREING: Ay that will make her Insolent.

FEARLESS: Nay she's generous too.

DAREING: Yes when she's Drunk, and then she'l lavish all.

RANTER: A Pox on him—how he vexes me.

DAREING: Then such a Tongue—she'l rail and smoak till she choke again, then six Gallons of Punch hardly recovers her, and never but then is she good Natur'd.

RANTER: I must lay him on—

DAREING: There's not a Blockhead in the Country that has not—

RANTER: —What—

DAREING: —Been Drunk with her.

RANTER: [*In huff*] I thought you had meant something else Sir.

DAREING: Nay—as for that—I suppose there's no great difficulty.

RANTER: 'Sdeath Sir you lye—and you are a Son of a Whore.

> *Draws and fences with him, and he runs back round the Stage.*

DAREING: Hold—hold Virago—dear Widow hold, and give me thy hand.

RANTER: Widow!

DAREING: 'Sdeath I knew thee by instinct Widow, tho I seemed not to do so, in revenge for the trick you put on me in telling me a Lady dy'd for me.

RANTER: Why, such an one there is, perhaps she may dwindle forty or fifty years— or so—but will never be her own Woman again that's certain.

SURELOVE: This we are all ready to testifie, we know her.

CRISANTE: Upon my Life 'tis true.

DAREING: Widow I have a shrewd suspicion, that you your self may be this dying Lady.

RANTER: Why so Coxcomb?

DAREING: Because you took such pains to put your self into my hands.

RANTER: Gad if your heart were but half so true as your guess, we should conclude a Peace before Bacon and the Council will—besides [To Crisante] this thing whines for Friendly and there's no hopes.

DAREING: Give me thy hand Widow, I am thine—and so intirely, I will never—be drunk out of thy Company—Dunce is in my Tent—prithee let's in and bind the bargain.

RANTER: Nay, faith, let's see the Wars at an end first.

DAREING: Nay, prithee, take me in the humour, while thy Breeches are on—for I never lik'd thee half so well in Petticoats.

RANTER: Lead on General, you give me good incouragement to wear them.

> *Exeunt.*

ACT V

SCENE I

The Sevana in sight of the Camp; the Moon rises.
   Enter Friendly, Hazard *and* Boozer, *and a Party of Men.*
FRIENDLY: We are now in the sight of the Tents.
BOOZER: Is not this a rash attempt, Gentlemen, with so small Force to set upon Bacon's whole Army?
HAZARD: Oh, they are drunk with Victory and Wine; there will be naught but Revelling to Night.
FRIENDLY: Would we cou'd learn in what Quarter the Ladies are lodg'd, for we have no other business but to release them—but hark—who comes here?
BOOZER: Some Scouts, I fear, from the Enemy.
   Enter Dullman, Timorous, Whimsey, *and* Whiff,
    creeping as in the dark.
FRIENDLY: Let's shelter our selves behind yonder Trees—lest we be surpriz'd.
TIMOROUS: Wou'd I were well at home—Gad zoors—if e'er you catch me a Cadeting again, I'll be content to be set in the fore-front of the Battel for Hawks Meat.
WHIMSEY: Thou'rt affraid of every Bush.
TIMOROUS: Ay, and good Reason too: Gad Zoors, there may be Rogues hid—prithee, Major, do thou advance.
DULLMAN: No, no, go on—no matter of ceremony in these cases of running away.
      They advance.
FRIENDLY: They approach directly to us, we cannot escape them—their numbers are not great—let us advance.
      They come up to them.
TIMOROUS: Oh I am annihilated.
WHIFF: Some of Frightall's Scouts, we are lost men.
      They push each other foremost.
FRIENDLY: Who goes there?
WHIMSEY: Oh, they'll give us no Quarter; 'twas long of you Cornet, that we ran away from our Colours.
TIMOROUS: Me—'twas the Majors Ambition here—to make himself a great Man with the Council again.
DULLMAN: Pox o' this Ambition, it has been the ruin of many a Gallant Fellow.
WHIFF: If I get home again, the height of mine shall be to top Tobacco; would I'd some Brandy.
TIMOROUS: Gads Zoors, would we had, 'tis the best Armour against fear—hum—I hear no body now—prithee advance a little.
WHIMSEY: What, before a Horse-Officer?
FRIENDLY: Stand, on your Lives—
TIMOROUS: Oh, 'tis impossible—I am dead already.
FRIENDLY: What are ye—speak—or I'll shoot!

WHIMSEY: Friends to thee—who the Devil are we friends to?

TIMOROUS: E'en who please you, Gad Zoors.

FRIENDLY: Hah—Gad Zoors—who's there, Timorous?

TIMOROUS: [*Gets behind.*] Hum—I know no such Scoundrel—

DULLMAN: Hah—that's Friendly's Voice.

FRIENDLY: Right—thine's that of Dullman—who's with you?

DULLMAN: Only Timorous, Whimsey and Whiff, all Valiantly running away from the Arch Rebel that took us Prisoners.

HAZARD: Can you inform us where the Ladies are lodg'd?

DULLMAN: In the hither Quarter in Dareings Tents; you'll know them by Lanthorns on every corner—there was never better time to surprize them—for this day Dareing's Marry'd, and there's nothing but Dancing and Drinking.

HAZARD: Married! To whom?

DULLMAN: That I ne'r inquir'd.

FRIENDLY: 'Tis to Crisante, Friend—and the reward of my attempt is lost. Oh, I am mad, I'll fight away my life, and my despair shall yet do greater wonders, than even my Love could animate me to. Let's part our Men, and beset his Tents on both sides.

> Friendly *goes out with a Party.*

HAZARD: Come, Gentlemen, let's on—

WHIFF: On Sir—we on Sir?—

HAZARD: Ay, you on, Sir—to redeem the Ladies.

WHIFF: Oh, Sir, I am going home for money to redeem my Nancy.

WHIMSEY: So am I, Sir.

TIMOROUS: I thank my Stars I am a Batchellor.—Why, what a plague is a Wife!

HAZARD: Will you March forward?

DULLMAN: [*Looking big.*] We have atchiev'd Honour enough already, in having made our Campaign here—

HAZARD: 'Sdeath, but you shall go—put them in the front, and prick them on—if they offer to turn back run them through.

> *The Souldiers prick them on with their Swords.*

TIMOROUS: Oh, horrid—

WHIFF: Oh, Nancy, thy Dream will yet come to pass.

HAZARD: Will you advance, Sir? [*Pricks Whiff.*]

WHIFF: Why, so we do, Sir; [*Aside.*] the Devil's in these fighting Fellows.

> *Exeunt.*
>
> *An Alarm at a distance.*

Within: To Arms, to Arms, the Enemy's upon us.

> *A Noise of fighting, after which enters* Friendly
> *with his Party, retreating and fighting from*
> Dareing *and some Souldiers,*
> Ranter *fighting like a Fury by his side,*
> *he putting her back in vain; they fight out.*
> *Re-enter* Dareing *and* Friendly *all bloody.*
> *Several Souldiers enter with Flambeaux.*

DAREING: Now, Sir—what injury have I ever done you, that you should use this Treachery against me?

FRIENDLY: To take advantage any way in War, was never counted Treachery—and had I Murder'd thee, I had not paid thee half the Debt I owe thee.

DAREING: You bleed too much to hold too long a Parley—come to my Tent, I'll take a charitable care of thee.

FRIENDLY: I scorn thy Courtesie, who against all the Laws of Honour and of Justice, hast ravish'd innocent Ladies.

DAREING: Sir, your upbraiding of my Honour shall never make me forfeit it, or esteem you less—Is there a Lady here you have a Passion for?

FRIENDLY: Yes, on a Nobler score than thou darest own.

DAREING: To let you see how you're mistaken, Sir, who e'er that Lady be whom you affect, I will resign, and give you both your Freedoms.

FRIENDLY: Why, for this Courtesie, which shows thee brave, in the next Fight I'le save thy Life, to quit the obligation.

DAREING: I thank you, Sir—come to my Tent—and when we've drest your Wounds, and yielded up the Ladies, I'll give you my Pass-port for your safe conduct back, and tell your Friends i'th' Town we'll Visit them i'th' Morning.

FRIENDLY: They'll meet you on your way, Sir—

DAREING: Come, my young Souldier, now thou'st won my Soul.

Exeunt.

*An Alarm beats: Enter at another Passage Boozer
with all the Ladies; they pass over the Stage,
while Hazard and Downright beating back a
Party of Souldiers. Dullman, Timorous, and Whiff,
prick'd on by their Party to fight, so that
they lay about them like Madmen.
Bacon, fearless and Dareing come in,
rescue their men, and fight out the other Party,
some falling dead.
Bacon, Fearless and Dareing return tired,
with their Swords drawn.
Enter Souldier running.*

SOULDIER: Return, Sir, where your Sword will be more useful—a Party of Indians, taking advantage of the Night, have set Fire on your Tents, and born away the Queen.

BACON: Hah, the Queen! By Heaven this Victory shall cost them dear; come, let us fly to rescue her.

Goes out.

SCENE II

Scene changes to Wellman's Tent.

WELLMAN: I cannot sleep my Impatience is so great, to ingage this haughty Enemy, before they have reposed their weary Limbs—Is not yon Ruddy Light the Mornings Dawn?

BRAG: 'Tis, and please your Honour.

WELLMAN: Is there no News of Friendly yet, and Hazard?

BRAG: Not yet—'tis thought they left the Camp to Night, with some design against the Enemy.

WELLMAN: What Men have they?

BRAG: Only Boozers Party, Sir.

WELLMAN: I know they are brave, and mean to surprize me with some handsom Action.

Enter Friendly.

FRIENDLY: I ask a thousand Pardons, Sir for quitting the Camp without your leave.

WELLMAN: Your Conduct and your Courage cannot Err; I see thou'st been in action by thy Blood.

FRIENDLY: Sir I'm ashamed to own these slender wounds, since without more my luck was to be taken, while Hazard did alone effect the business; the rescuing of the Ladies.

WELLMAN: How got ye Liberty?

FRIENDLY: By Dareing's generosity, who sends ye word he'l visit you this Morning.

WELLMAN: We are prepared to meet him.

Enter Downright, Hazard, *Ladies*, Whimsey,
Whiff, Dullman, Timorous *looking big*;
Wellman *Embraces* Downright.

WELLMAN: My worthy Friend how am I joyed to see you?

DOWNRIGHT: We owe our Liberties to these brave Youths, who can do wonders when they Fight for Ladies.

TIMOROUS: With our assistance Ladies.

WHIMSEY: For my part I'le not take it as I have done, Gad I find when I am Damnable Angry I can beat both Friend and Foe.

WHIFF: When I fight for my Nancy here—adsfish, I'm a Dragon.

MRS. WHIFF: Lord, you need not have been so hasty.

FRIENDLY: Do not upbraid me with your Eyes Crisante, but let these wounds assure you I endeavour'd to serve you, tho Hazard had the Honour on't.

WELLMAN: But Ladies we'l not expose you in the Camp,—a Party of our Men shall see you safely conducted to Madam Sureloves; 'tis but a little Mile from our Camp.

FRIENDLY: Let me have that Honour Sir.

CRISANTE: No, I conjure you let your Wounds be drest, obey me if you Love me, and Hazard shall conduct us home.

WELLMAN: He had the Toyl, 'tis fit he have the recompence.

WHIFF: He the Toil! Sir, what did we stand for Cyphers?

WHIMSEY: The very appearance I made in the front of the Battle, aw'd the Enemy.

TIMOROUS: Ay, ay, Let the Enemy say how I maul'd 'em—but Gads zoors I scorn to brag.

WELLMAN: Since you've regain'd your Honour so Gloriously—I restore you to your Commands, you lost by your seeming Cowardice.

DULLMAN: Valour is not always in Humour Sir.

WELLMAN: Come Gentlemen since they've resolv'd to engage us, let's set our Men in order to receive 'em.

Exeunt all but the four Justices.

TIMOROUS: Our Commissions again—you must be bragging, and see what comes on't; I was modest ye see and said nothing of my Prowess.

WHIFF: What a Devil, does the Collonel think we are made of Iron, continually to be beat on the Anvil?

WHIMSEY: Look Gentlemen here's two Evils—if we go we are dead Men if we stay we are hang'd—and that will disorder my Cravat string:—therefore the least Evil is to go—and set a good Face on the Matter as I do—

Goes out singing.

SCENE III

A thick Wood.

Enter Queen *dress'd like an Indian Man, with a Bow in her Hand and Quiver at her Back;* Anaria *her Confident disguis'd so too, and about a Dozen Indians led by* Cavaro.

QUEEN: I tremble yet, dost think we're safe Cavaro?

CAVARO: Madam these Woods are intricate and vast, and 'twill be difficult to find us out—or if they do, this habit will secure you from the fear of being taken.

QUEEN: Dost think if Bacon find us he will not know me? Alas, my fears and blushes will betray me.

ANARIA: 'Tis certain Madam if we stay we Perish; for all the Wood's surrounded by the Conqueror.

QUEEN: Alas 'tis better we should Perish here, than stay to expect the violence of his Passion: To which my heart's too sensibly inclin'd.

ANARIA: Why do you not obey its dictates then, why do you fly the Conqueror?

QUEEN: Not fly—not fly the Murderer of my Lord?

ANARIA: What world, what resolution can preserve you, and what he cannot gain by soft submission, force will at last o'ercome.

QUEEN: I wish there were in Nature one excuse, either by force or Reason to compel me:—For oh, Anaria—I adore this General,—take from my Soul a Truth—till now conceal'd—at twelve years Old—at the Pauwomungian[64] Court I saw this Conqueror. I saw him young and Gay as new born Spring, Glorious and Charming as the Mid-days Sun, I watch't his looks, and listned when he spoke, and thought him more than Mortal.

64. Pauwomungian: Pamunkey; a reference to the Indian tribe of the Jamestown area.

ANARIA: He has a graceful Form.

QUEEN: At last a Fatal Match concluded was, between my Lord and me. I gave my Hand, but oh how far my heart was from consenting, the angry Gods are witness.

ANARIA: 'Twas pity.

QUEEN: Twelve teadious Moons I pass'd in silent languishment; Honour endeavouring to destroy my Love, but all in vain, for still my pain return'd when ever I beheld my Conqueror, but now when I consider him as Murderer of my Lord— [*Fiercely*] I sigh and wish—some other fatal hand had given him his Death—but now there's a necessity, I must be brave and overcome my Heart: What if I do? ah whither shall I fly, I have no Amazonian fire about me, all my Artillery is sighs and Tears, the Earth my Bed, and Heaven my Canopy. [*Weeps.*]

After a noise of Fighting.

Hah, we are surpriz'd, oh whither shall I fly? And yet methinks a certain trembling joy, spite of my Soul, spite of my boasted Honour, runs shivering round my heart.

Enter an Indian.

INDIAN: Madam, your out guards are surpriz'd by Bacon, who hews down all before him, and demands the Queen with such a voice and Eyes so Fierce and Angry, he kills us with his looks.

CAVARO: Draw up your Poyson'd Arrows to the head, and aim them at his Heart, sure some will hit.

QUEEN: [*Aside.*] Cruel Cavaro,—wou'd 'twere fit for me to contradict thy Justice.

BACON: [*Within.*] The Queen, ye slaves, give me the Queen, and live!

He Enters furiously, beating back some Indians;
Cavaro's *Party going to shoot,*
the Queen *runs in.*

QUEEN: Hold, hold, I do Command ye.

Bacon *Flyes on em as they shoot and miss him,*
and fights like a fury, and
wounds the Queen *in the disorder;*
beats them all out.

—hold thy commanding Hand, and do not kill me, who wou'd not hurt thee to regain my Kingdom—

He snatchs her in his Arms she reels.

BACON: Hah—a Womans Voice,—what art thou? Oh my Fears!

QUEEN: Thy Hand has been too cruel to a Heart—whose Crime was only tender thoughts for thee.

BACON: The Queen! What is't my Sacrilegious hand has done?

QUEEN: The noblest office of a Gallant Friend, thou'st sav'd my Honour and hast given me Death.

BACON: Is't possible! ye unregarding Gods is't possible?

QUEEN: Now I may Love you without Infamy, and please my Dying Heart by gazing on you.

BACON: Oh, I am lost—for ever lost—I find my Brain turn with the wild confusion.

QUEEN: I faint—oh, lay me gently on the Earth.

BACON: [*Lays her down.*] Who waits—[*Turns in a rage to his Men.*] make of the

Trophies of the War a Pile, and set it all on Fire, that I may leap into consuming Flames—while all my Tents are burning round about me. [*Wildly.*] Oh thou dear Prize, for which alone I toyl'd! [*Weeps, and lyes down by her.*]

Enter Fearless *with his Sword drawn.*

FEARLESS: Hah, on the Earth—how do you, Sir?

BACON: What wou'dst thou?

FEARLESS: Wellman, with all the Forces he can gather, attacks us even in our very Camp. Assist us Sir or all is lost.

BACON: Why prithee let him make the World his Prize. I have no business with the Trifle now; it contains nothing that's worth my care, since my fair Queen—is Dead—and by my Hand.

QUEEN: So charming and obliging is thy moan, that I cou'd wish for Life to recompense it; but oh, Death falls—all cold—upon my Heart like Mildews on the Blossoms.

FEARLESS: By Heaven Sir, this Love will ruin all—rise, rise and save us yet.

BACON: Leave me, what e'er becomes of me—lose not thy share of Glory—prithee leave me.

QUEEN: Alas, I fear thy Fate is drawing on, and I shall shortly meet thee in the Clouds; till then—farewel—even Death is pleasing to me, while thus—I find it in thy Arms—

Dies.

BACON: There ends my Race of Glory and of Life.

An Alarm at distance—continues a while.

Hah—Why should I idly whine away my life, since there are Nobler ways to meet with Death?—Up, up, and face him then—Hark—there's the Souldiers knell—and all the Joys of Life—with thee I bid farewell—[*Goes out.*]

The Indians bear off the Body of the Queen.

The Alarm continues:

Enter Downright, Wellman,

and others, Swords drawn.

WELLMAN: They fight like men possest—I did not think to have found them so prepar'd.

DOWNRIGHT: They've good intelligence—but where's the Rebel?

WELLMAN: Sure he's not in the fight, oh that it were my happy chance to meet him, that while our men look on, we might dispatch the business of the War.—Come, let's fall in again now we have taken breath. [*They go out.*]

Enter Dareing *and* Fearless *hastily,*

with their Swords drawn,

meet Whimsey, Whiff, *with*

their Swords drawn, running away.

DAREING: [*In anger.*] How now, whether away?

WHIMSEY: Hah, Dareing here—we are pursuing of the Enemy, Sir, Stop us not in the pursuit of Glory [*Offers to go.*]

DAREING: Stay—I have not seen you in my ranks to day.

WHIFF: Lord, does your Honour take us for Starters?

FEARLESS: Yes, Sirrah, and believe you are now rubbing off—confess, or I'll run you through.

WHIFF: Oh Mercy Sir, Mercy, we'll confess.

WHIMSEY: What will you confess—we were only going behind yon Hedge to untruss a point;[65] that's all.

WHIFF: Ay, your Honours will smell out the truth if you keep us here long.

DAREING: Here, carry them Prisoners to my Tent.

Exeunt Souldiers with Whimsey *and* Whiff.
Enter Ranter *without a Hat, and Sword drawn,*
Dareing *angrily goes the other way.*

RANTER: A Pox of all ill luck, how came I to lose Dareing in the fight?—Ha—who's here?—Dullman and Timorous Dead—the Rogues are Counterfeits—I'll see what Moveables they Have about them, all's Lawful Prize in War.

Takes their Money, Watches and Rings; goes out.

TIMOROUS: What, Rob the Dead?—Why, what will this Villainous World come to!

Clashing of Swords, just as they were going to rise.
Enter Hazard *bringing in* Ranter.

HAZARD: Thou cou'dst expect no other Fate Young man, thy hands are yet too tender for a Sword.

RANTER: Thou look'st like a good natur'd Fellow, use me civilly, and Dareing shall Ransom me.

HAZARD: Doubt not a Generous Treatment. [*Goes out.*]

DULLMAN: So, the Coast is clear, I desire to remove my Quarters to some place of more safety—[*They rise and go off.*]

Enter Wellman *and Souldiers hastily.*

WELLMAN: 'Twas this way Bacon fled. Five hundred Pound for him who finds the Rebel. [*Goes out.*]

SCENE IV

Changes to a Wood.
Enter Bacon *and* Fearless, *with their Swords drawn, all bloody.*

BACON: 'Tis Just, ye Gods! That when ye took the Prize for which I fought, Fortune and you should all abandon me.

FEARLESS: Oh fly Sir to some place of safe retreat, for there's no mercy to be hop't if taken. What will you do, I know we are pursu'd, by Heaven I will not dye a shameful Death.

BACON: Oh they'll have pitty on thy Youth and Bravery, but I'm above their Pardon. [*A noise is heard.*]

VOICES WITHIN: This way—this way—hay—hallow.

FEARLESS: Alas Sir we're undone—I'll see which way they take.

Exit.

---

65. untruss a point: unfasten a garment (to urinate).

BACON: So near! Nay, then to my last shift.

Undoes the Pomel of his Sword.

Come, my good Poyson, like that of Hannibal; long I have born a noble Remedy for all the ills of Life. [*Takes Poyson.*] I have too long surviv'd my Queen and Glory, those two bright Stars that influenc'd my Life are set to all Eternity.

Lies down.

Enter Fearless, *runs to* Bacon *and looks on his Sword.*

FEARLESS: —Hah—what have ye done?

BACON: Secur'd my self from being a publick Spectacle upon the common Theatre of Death.

Enter Dareing *and Souldiers.*

DAREING: Victory, Victory, they fly, they fly, where's the Victorious General?

FEARLESS: Here—taking his last Adieu.

DAREING: Dying? Then wither all the Laurels on my Brows, for I shall never Triumph more in War, where is the Wounds?

FEARLESS: From his own hand by what he carried here, believing we had lost the Victory.

BACON: And is the Enemy put to flight my Hero?

Grasps his Neck.

DAREING: All routed Horse and Foot; I plac'd an Ambush, and while they were pursuing you, my Men fell on behind and won the day.

BACON: Thou almost makes me wish to Live again, If I cou'd live now Fair Semerina's Dead,—But oh—the baneful Drug is just and kind and hastens me away— Now while you are Victors make a Peace—with the English Councel—and never let Ambition—Love—or Interest, make you forget as I have done—your Duty—and Allegiance—farewel—a long farewel—

Dies embracing their Necks.

DAREING: So fell the Roman Cassius, by mistake—

Enter Souldiers with Dunce, Timorous *and* Dullman.

SOULDIER: An't please your Honour we took these Men running away.

DAREING: Let 'em loose—the Wars are at an end, see where the General lyes—that great Soul'd Man, no private Body e're contain'd a Nobler, and he that cou'd have conquer'd all America, finds only here his scanty length of Earth,—go bear the Body to his own Pavilion—

Souldiers go out with the Body.

Tho we are Conquerors we submit to treat, and yield upon condition, you Mr. Dunce shall bear our Articles to the Councel—

DUNCE: With joy I will obey you.

TIMOROUS: Good General let us be put in the agreement.

DAREING: You come too late Gentlemen to put into the Articles, nor am I satisfy'd you're worthy of it.

DULLMAN: Why did not you Sir see us ly dead in the Field?

DAREING: Yes, but I see no wound about you.

TIMOROUS: We were stun'd with being knock'd down, Gads zoors a Man may be kill'd with the Butt end of a Musquet, as soon as with the point of a Sword.

Enter Dunce.

DUNCE: The Council Sir wishes you Health and Happiness, and sends you these Sign'd by their Hands—[*Gives Papers.*]

DAREING: [*Reads*] *That you shall have a general Pardon for your self and Friends, that you shall have all new Commissions, and Dareing to command as General; that you shall have free leave to Interr your Dead General, in James Town, and to ratify this—we will meet you at Madam Surelove's House which stands between the Armies, attended only by our Officers.* The Councel's noble, and I'll wait upon them.

Exeunt.

SCENE V

A Grove near Madam Surelove's.

Enter Surelove *weeping*, Wellman, Crisante,
Mrs. Flirt, Ranter *as before*, Downright,
Hazard, Friendly, Boozer, Brag.

WELLMAN: How long Madam have you heard the News of Colonel Surelove's Death?

SURELOVE: By a Vessel last Night arriv'd.

WELLMAN: You shou'd not grieve when Men so old pay their debt to Nature; you are too Fair not to have been reserved for some young Loves Arms.

HAZARD: I dare not speak—but give me leave to hope.

SURELOVE: The way to oblige me to't, is never more to speak to me of Love till I shall think it fit—

WELLMAN: [to Downright.] Come, you shan't grant it—'tis a hopeful Youth.

DOWNRIGHT: [to Friendly.] You are too much my Friend to be denied— [to Crisante.] Crisante, do you love Friendly? nay do not blush—till you have done a fault, your Loving him is none— [to Friendly.] here take her young Man and with her all my Fortune—when I am Dead Sirrah—not a Groat before—unless to buy ye Baby-Clouts.

FEARLESS: He merits not this Treasure Sir, can wish for more.

Enter Dareing, Fearless, Dunce, *and* Officers, *and the rest;*
they meet Wellman *and* Downright *who Embrace em.*
Dullman *and* Timorous *stand.*

DAREING: Can you forgive us Sir our Disobedience?

WELLMAN: Your offering peace while yet you might command it, has made such kind impressions on us, that now you may command your Propositions; your Pardons are all Seal'd and new Commissions.

DAREING: I'm not Ambitious of that Honour Sir, but in obedience will accept your goodness, but Sir I hear I have a young Friend taken Prisoner by Captain Hazard whom I intreat you'l render me.

HAZARD: Sir—here I resign him to you. [*Gives him* Ranter.]

RANTER: Faith General you left me but scurvily in Battel.

DAREING: That was to see how well you cou'd shift for your self, now I find you can bear the brunt of a Campaign you are a fit Wife for a Souldier.

ALL: A Woman—Ranter—

HAZARD: Faith Madam I shou'd have given you kinder quarter if I had known my Happiness.

FLIRT: I have a humble Petition to you Sir.

SURELOVE: In which we are joyn.

FLIRT: [*Simpers.*] An't please you Sir, Mr. Dunce has long made Love to me and on promise of Marriage has—

DOWNRIGHT: What has he Mrs. Flirt?

FLIRT: Only been a little familiar with my Person Sir—

WELLMAN: Do you hear Parson—you must Marry Mrs. Flirt.

DUNCE: How Sir, a Man of my Coat Sir, Marry a brandy-Munger?

WELLMAN: [*Aside to him.*] Of your calling, you mean, a Farrier and no Parson— she'l leave her Trade—and spark it above all the Ladies at Church,—no more—take her and make her honest.

Enter Whimsey *and* Whiff *stript.*

CRISANTE: Bless me, what have we here?

WHIMSEY: Why, an't like your Honours, we were taken by the Enemy— hah Dareing here and Fearless?

FEARLESS: How now—Gentlemen were not you two Condemn'd to be Shot for running from your Colours.

DOWNRIGHT: From your Colours?

FEARLESS: Yes Sir, they were both listed in my Regiment.

DOWNRIGHT: Then we must hang them for deserting us.

WHIMSEY: So out of the Frying Pan—you know where Brother—

WHIFF: Ay he that's Born to be Hang'd—you know the rest, a Pox of these Proverbs.

WELLMAN: I know ye well—ye're all rank Cowards, but once more we forgive ye, your Places in the Councel shall be supply'd by these Gentlemen of Sense and Honour. The Governour when he comes shall find the Country in better hands than he expects to find it.

WHIMSEY: A very fair discharge.

WHIFF: I'm glad 'tis no worse, I'le home to my Nancy.

DULLMAN: Have we expos'd our Lives and Fortunes for this?

TIMOROUS: Gad zoors I never thriv'd since I was a States-man, left Planting, and fell to promising and Lying. I'le to my old Trade again, bask under the shade of my own Tobacco, and Drink my Punch in Peace.

WELLMAN:

> Come, my brave Youths, let all our Forces meet,
> To make this Country Happy, Rich and great;
> Let scanted Europe see that we enjoy
> Safer Repose, and larger Worlds than they.

EPILOGUE

[BY JOHN DRYDEN]

Spoken by a Woman

By this time you have liked, or damned our plot;
Which though I know, my Epilogue knows not:
For if it could foretell, I should not fail,
In decent wise, to thank you, or to rail.
But he who sent me here, is positive,
This farce of government is sure to thrive;
Farce is a food as proper for your lips,
As for green-sickness, crumped tobacco pipes.[66]
Besides, the author's dead, and here you sit,
Like the infernal judges of the pit:
Be mercifull; for 'tis in you this day,
To save or damn her soul; and that's her play.
She who so well could love's kind passion paint,
We piously believe, must be a saint:
Men are but bunglers, when they would express
The sweets of love, the dying tenderness;
But women, by their own abundance, measure,
And when they write, have deeper sense of pleasure.
Yet though her pen did to the mark arrive,
'Twas common praise, to please you, when alive;
But of no other woman you have read,
Except this one, to please you, now she's dead.
'Tis like the fate of bees, whose golden pains,
Themselves extinguished, in their hive remains.
Or in plain terms to speak, before we go,
What you young gallants, by experience, know,
This is an orphan child; a bouncing boy,
'Tis late to lay him out, or to destroy.
Leave your dog-tricks, to lie and to foreswear,
Pay you for nursing, and we'll keep him here.

66. crumped: curved. Tobacco was thought to cure chlorosis,
or green-sickness.

8. John Esquemeling

from *The Buccaneers of America* 1684

The title page of the 1684 English translation of The Buccaneers of America *added a clause to make this history of slaughter and looting more appealing to the English reader: "Wherein are contained more especially the Unparalleled Exploits of Sir Henry Morgan, our English Jamaican Hero, who sacked Porto Bello, burnt Panama, etc." By the time the book was published, indeed, the pirate Henry Morgan (1635–88) had become Sir Henry Morgan, Deputy Governor of Jamaica and respected tobacco planter. That before his ascension, he had "sacked Porto Bello, burnt Panama, etc." need not have unduly disturbed a right-thinking gentleman because the sacking and burning had also constituted service to the nation and the empire. The buccaneers (from "boucan," an Indian word meaning a grid for roasting pigs) were gangs of men privately organized (hence also "privateers") to capture Spanish ships on the high sea and steal their cargo. They were in the unofficial employ of their governments and played a major role in redressing the balance between Spain—which had been in the New World first and most energetically—and late-arriving England.*

Here Henry Morgan performs the first of the two exploits cited above by his English publisher and sacks Porto Bello.

Some nations may think that, the French having deserted Captain Morgan, the English alone could not have sufficient courage to attempt such great actions as before. But Captain Morgan, who always communicated vigour with his words, infused such spirits into his men as were able to put every one of them instantly upon new designs, they being all persuaded by his reasons that the sole execution of his orders would be a certain means of obtaining great riches. This persuasion had such influence upon their minds that with inimitable courage they all resolved to follow him. The same likewise did a certain Pirate of Campeche, who in this occasion joined with Captain Morgan to seek new fortunes under his conduct, and greater advantages than he had found before. Thus Captain Morgan in a few days gathered a fleet of nine sail, between ships and great boats, wherein he had four-hundred-and-threescore military men.

After that all things were in good posture of readiness, they put forth to sea, Captain Morgan imparting the design he had in his mind unto nobody for that present. He only told them on several occasions that he held as indubitable he should make a good fortune by that voyage, if strange occurrences altered not the course of his designs. They directed their course towards the continent, where they arrived in few days upon the coast of Costa Rica, with all their fleet entire. No sooner had they discovered land than Captain Morgan declared his intentions to the Captains, and presently after unto all the rest of the company. He told them he intended in that expedition to plunder Porto Bello, and that he would perform it by night, being resolved to put the whole city to the sack, not the least corner escaping his diligence. Moreover, to encourage them, he added: *This enterprize could not fail to succeed well, seeing he had kept it secret in his mind without revealing it to anybody; whereby they could not have notice of his coming.* Unto this proposition some made answer: *They had not a sufficient number of men wherewith to assault so strong and great a city.* But Captain Morgan replied: *If our number is small, our hearts are great. And the fewer persons we are, the more union and better shares we shall have in the spoil.* Hereupon, being stimulated with the ambition of those vast riches they promised themselves from their good success, they unanimously concluded to venture upon that design. But now, to the intent my reader may better comprehend the incomparable boldness of this exploit, it may be necessary to say something beforehand of the city of Porto Bello.

The city which bears this name in America is seated in the Province of Costa Rica, under the latitude of 10 degrees North, at the distance of 14 leagues from the Gulf of Darien, and 8 Westwards from the port called Nombre de Dios. It is judged to be the strongest place that the King of Spain possesses in all the West Indies, excepting two, that is to say Havana and Cartagena. Here are two castles, almost inexpungable, that defend the city, being situated at the entry of the port, so that no ship or boat can pass without permission. The garrison consists of three hundred soldiers, and the town constantly inhabited by four hundred families, more or less. The merchants dwell not here, but only reside for awhile, when the galleons come or go from Spain, by reason of the unhealthiness of the air, occasioned by certain vapours that exhale from the mountains. Notwithstanding, their chief warehouses are at Porto Bello, howbeit their habitations are all the year long at Panama, whence they bring the plate upon mules at such times as the fair begins, and when the ships belonging to the Company of Negroes arrive here to sell slaves.

Captain Morgan, who knew very well all the avenues of this city, as also all the neighbouring coasts, arrived in the dusk of the evening at the place called Puerto de Naos, distant ten leagues towards the West of Porto Bello. Being come unto this place, they mounted the river in their ships, as far as another harbour called Puerto Pontin, where they came to an anchor. Here they put themselves immediately into boats and canoes, leaving in the ships only a few men to keep them and conduct them the next day unto the port. About midnight they came to a certain place called Estera Longa Lemos, where they all went on shore, and marched by land to the first posts of the city. They had in their company a certain Englishman who had been formerly a prisoner in those parts and who now served them for a guide. Unto him, and three or four more, they gave commission to take the sentry, if possible, or kill him upon the place. But they laid hands on him and apprehended him with such cunning that he had no time to give warning with his musket or make any other noise. Thus they brought him, with his hands bound, unto Captain Morgan, who asked him: *How things went in the city, and what forces they had*; with many other circumstances, which he was desirous to know. After every question, they made him a thousand menaces to kill him, in case he declared not the truth. Thus they began to advance towards the city, carrying always the said sentry bound before them. Having marched about one quarter of a league, they came unto the castle that is nigh unto the city, which presently they closely surrounded, so that no person could get either in or out of the said fortress.

Being thus posted under the walls of the castle, Captain Morgan commanded the sentry whom they had taken prisoner to speak unto those that were within, charging them to surrender and deliver themselves up to his discretion—otherwise they should be all cut to pieces, without giving quarter to any one. But they would hearken to none of these threats, beginning instantly to fire; which gave notice unto the city, and this was suddenly alarmed. Yet, notwithstanding, although the Governor and soldiers of the said castle made as great resistance as could be performed, they were constrained to surrender unto the Pirates. These no sooner had taken the castle but they resolved to be as good as their words, in putting the Spaniards to the sword, thereby to strike a terror into the rest of the city. Hereupon, having shut up all the soldiers and officers as prisoners into one room, they instantly set fire to the powder (whereof they found great quantity), and blew up the whole castle into the air, with all the Spaniards that were within. This being done, they pursued the course of their victory, falling upon the city, which as yet was not in order to receive them. Many of the inhabitants cast their precious jewels and moneys into wells and cisterns, or hid them in other places underground, to excuse, as much as were possible, their being totally robbed. One party of the Pirates, being assigned to this purpose, ran immediately to the cloisters, and took as many religious men and women as they could find. The Governor of the city not being able to rally the citizens through the huge confusion of the town, retired unto one of the castles remaining, and thence began to fire incessantly at the Pirates. But these were not in the least negligent either to assault him or defend themselves with all the courage imaginable. Thus it was observable that, amidst the horror of the assault, they made very few shot in vain. For, aiming with great dexterity at the mouths of the guns, the Spaniards were certain to lose one or two men every time they charged each gun anew.

The assault of this castle where the Governor was continued very furious on both sides, from break of day until noon. Yea, about this time of the day the case was very dubious which party should conquer or be conquered. At last the Pirates, perceiving they had lost many men and as yet advanced but little towards the gaining either this or the other castles remaining, thought to make use of fireballs, which they threw with their hands, designing if possible to burn the doors of the castle. But, going about to put this into execution, the Spaniards from the wall let fall great quantities of stones and earthen pots full of powder and other combustible matter, which forced them to desist from that attempt. Captain Morgan, seeing this generous defence made by the Spaniards, began to despair of the whole success of the enterprize. Hereupon many faint and calm meditations came into his mind; neither could he determine which way to turn himself in that straitness of affairs. Being involved in these thoughts, he was suddenly animated to continue the assault by seeing the English colours put forth at one of the lesser castles, then entered by his men, of whom he presently after spied a troop that came to meet him, proclaiming victory with loud shouts of joy. This instantly put him upon new resolutions of making new efforts to take the rest of the castles that stood out against him, especially seeing the chiefest citizens were fled unto them and had conveyed thither great part of their riches, with all the plate belonging to the churches and other things dedicated to divine service.

Unto this effect, therefore, he ordered ten or twelve ladders to be made, in all possible haste, so broad that three or four men at once might ascend by them. These being finished, he commanded all the religious men and women whom he had taken prisoners to fix them against the walls of the castle. Thus much he had beforehand threatened the Governor to perform, in case he delivered not the castle. But his answer was: *He would never surrender himself alive.* Captain Morgan was much persuaded that the Governor would not employ his utmost forces, seeing religious women and ecclesiastical persons exposed in the front of the soldiers to the greatest dangers. Thus the ladders, as I have said, were put into the hands of religious persons of both sexes; and these were forced, at the head of the companies, to raise and apply them to the walls. But Captain Morgan was fully deceived in his judgment of this design. For the Governor who acted like a brave and courageous soldier, refused not, in performance of his duty, to use his utmost endeavours to destroy whosoever came near the walls. The religious men and women ceased not to cry unto him and beg of him by all the Saints of Heaven he would deliver the castle, and hereby spare both his and their own lives. But nothing could prevail with the obstinacy and fierceness that had possessed the Governor's mind. Thus many of the religious men and nuns were killed before they could fix the ladders—which at last being done, though with great loss of the said religious people, the Pirates mounted them in great numbers, and with no less valour, having fireballs in their hands, and earthen pots full of powder—all which things, being now at the top of the walls, they kindled and cast in among the Spaniards.

This effort of the Pirates was very great, insomuch as the Spaniards could no longer resist nor defend the castle, which was now entered. Hereupon they all threw down their arms, and craved quarter for their lives. Only the Governor of the city would admit or crave no mercy, but rather killed many of the Pirates with his own hands, and not a few of his own soldiers, because they did not stand to their arms. And, although the Pirates asked him if he would have quarter, yet he constantly answered: *By no means: I had rather die as a valiant soldier than be hanged as a coward.* They endeavoured, as much as they could, to take him prisoner. But he defended himself so obstinately that they were forced to kill him, notwithstanding all the cries and tears of his own wife and daughter, who begged of him upon their knees he would demand quarter and save his life. When the Pirates had possessed themselves of the castle, which was about night, they enclosed therein all the prisoners they had taken, placing the women and men by themselves with some guards upon them. All the wounded were put into a certain apartment by itself, to the intent their own complaints might be the cure of their diseases, for no other was afforded them.

This being done, they fell to eating and drinking after their usual manner—that is to say, committing in both these things all manner of debauchery and excess. These two vices were immediately followed by many insolent actions of rape and adultery committed upon very honest women, as well married as virgins, who being threatened with the sword were constrained to submit their bodies to the violence of these lewd and wicked men. After such manner they delivered themselves up to all sort of debauchery of this kind, that if there had been found only fifty courageous men, they might easily have retaken the city, and killed all the Pirates. The next day, having plundered all they could find, they began to examine some of the prisoners (who had been persuaded by their companions to say they were the richest of the town), charging them severely to discover where they had hidden their riches and goods. But, not being able to extort anything out of them, as they were not the right persons who possessed any wealth, they at last resolved to torture them. This they performed with such cruelty that many of them died upon the rack, or presently after. Soon after, the President of Panama had news brought him of the pillage and ruin of Porto Bello. This intelligence caused him to employ all his care and industry to raise forces, with design to pursue and cast out the Pirates thence. But these cared little for what extraordinary means the President used, as having their ships nigh at hand and being determined to set fire unto the city and retreat. They had now been at Porto Bello fifteen days, in which space of time they had lost many of their men, both by the unhealthiness of the country and the extravagant debaucheries they had committed.

Hereupon they prepared for a departure, carrying on board their ships all the pillage they had gotten. But, before all, they provided the fleet with sufficient victuals for the voyage. While these things were getting ready, Captain Morgan sent an injunction unto the prisoners, that they should pay him a ransom for the city, or else he would by fire consume it to ashes and blow up all the castles into the air. Withal he commanded them to send speedily two persons to seek and procure the sum he demanded, which amounted to 100,000 pieces-of-eight. Unto this effect two men were sent to the President of Panama, who gave him an account of all these tragedies. The President, having now a body of men in a readiness, set forth immediately towards Porto Bello, to encounter the Pirates before their retreat. But these people, hearing of his coming, instead of flying away went out to meet him at a narrow passage through which of necessity he ought to pass. Here they placed an hundred men very well armed, the which at the first encounter put to flight a good party of those of Panama. This accident obliged the President to retire for that time, as not being yet in a posture of strength to proceed any farther. Presently after this encounter, he sent a message unto Captain Morgan, to tell him: *That, in case he departed not suddenly with all his forces from Porto Bello, he ought to expect no quarter for himself nor his companions, when he should take them, as he hoped soon to do.* Captain Morgan, who feared not his threats, as knowing he had a secure retreat in his ships which were nigh at hand, made him answer: *He would not deliver the castles before he had received the contribution-money he had demanded. Which in case it were not paid down, he would certainly burn the whole city, and then leave it, demolishing beforehand the castles and killing the prisoners.*

The Governor of Panama perceived by this answer no means would serve to mollify the hearts of the Pirates, nor reduce them to reason. Hereupon he determined to leave them, as also those of the city, whom he came to relieve, involved in the difficulties of making the best agreement they could with their enemies. Thus in few days more the miserable citizens gathered the contribution wherein they were fined, and brought the entire sum of 100,000 pieces-of-eight unto the Pirates for a ransom of the cruel captivity they were fallen into. But the President of Panama, by these transactions, was brought into an extreme admiration, considering that four-hundred men had been able to take such a great city with so many strong castles, especially seeing they had no pieces of cannon nor other great guns wherewith to raise batteries against them. And, what was more, knowing that the citizens of Porto Bello had always great repute of being good soldiers themselves, and who had never wanted courage in their own defence. This astonishment was so great that it occasioned him, for to be satisfied herein, to send a messenger unto Captain Morgan, desiring him to send him some small pattern of those arms wherewith he had taken with such violence so great a city. Captain Morgan received this messenger very kindly, and treated him with great civility. Which being done, he gave him a pistol and a few small bullets of lead, to carry back unto the President, his master, telling him withal: *He desired him to accept that slender pattern of the arms wherewith he had taken Porto Bello, and keep them for a twelvemonth; after which time he promised to come to Panama and fetch them away.* The Governor of Panama returned the present very soon to Captain Morgan, giving him thanks for the favour of lending him such weapons as he needed not, and withal sent him a ring of gold, with this message: *That he desired him not to give himself the labour of coming to Panama, as he had done to Porto Bello, for he did certify to him, he should not speed so well here as he had done there.*

After these transactions, Captain Morgan (having provided his fleet with all necessaries, and taken with him the best guns of the castles, nailing the rest which he could not carry away) set sail from Porto Bello with all his ships. With these he arrived in few days unto the island of Cuba, where he sought out a place wherein with all quiet and repose he might make the dividend of the spoil they had gotten. They found in ready money 250,000 pieces-of-eight, besides all other merchandizes, as cloth, linen, silks, and other goods. With this rich purchase they sailed again thence unto their common place of rendezvous, Jamaica. Being arrived, they passed here some time in all sorts of vices and debauchery, according to their common manner of doing, spending with huge prodigality what others had gained with no small labour and toil.

9. William Byrd I

letter to Daniel Horsmanden
1690

William Byrd I (1652–1704), father of the better-known William Byrd II (see chapter 10) was born in London in a family of middling circumstances and emigrated to the New World at the age of nineteen, as the heir to his uncle's lands. After briefly joining Nathaniel Bacon's campaign, Byrd shrewdly withdrew when it moved toward outright rebellion, and instead sided with the governor. He rose quickly in the colonial hierarchy to become a member of the House of Burgesses, a colonel in the militia, and ultimately the president of the colonial Council. For his tobacco plantations, he imported hundreds of African slaves, on one occasion putting in an order for 506 in one shipment. From England, he imported indentured servants, asking in one letter for "six, eight, or ten . . . men or lusty boys."

*This voracious appetite for laborers came from a multiplicity of enterprises, for,
besides his commerce in tobacco, Byrd was a fur-trader and general merchant, as
well as a tobacco planter, sending corn and pipe staves to Barbados in return for
slaves, rum, and molasses.*

*In this letter addressed to his brother-in-law, he boasts of his recently acquired
estate of Westover, expresses concern over the indisposition of a genteel lady,
describes an Indian raid, plans to send his son to England, and worries about
where to place his daughters, all in the same tone of a man busy on all possible
frontiers of expansion.*

To Daniel Horsmanden

Virginia, July the 25th, 1690

Dear Sir

I am sorry I could receive but one from you last year, but considering your condition, was forced to excuse you, when I reflect what happiness you proposed to your selfe in the near injoyment of so sweet & beautiful a mistress, but was so unfortunately prevented by one of the most unwellcome distempers that could afflict a lady of youth & beauty, which must bee a sensible affliction to her lover, not onely by prolonging the happy day hee had proposed, but by debarring him from the society of the object hee held most dear & loved as himselfe. I hope this will find you & the (I believe I may call her your) good lady in perfect health, to whom I wish all the happiness this transitory world can afford, & that you meet with none of the thornes, but all the pleasures of matrimony.

My wife & family I thanke God are in good health onely lately I had one killed, two carryed away by the Indians. If the French come not with them wee may bee in hopes of continueing able to indure a small incursion now & then from the Indians alone. However I designe (God willing) to remove downe the river about 20 or 30 miles where I am now building & hope you will send us (according to your promise) yours (with your fair lady's) picture to adorne my new house. I have ordered Will for England & left him in Mr. Perry's care to put him to business, & to let him learn what may bee farther fitt to make him accomplish'd. I doubt not but you will give him good advice. I likewise order'd Mr. Perry to take the girls from Hackny, but how to dispose of them I know not, London being no fitt place for them, & I have no relations in the country. Sister Nutty hath girls enough of her owne. I would bee glad (if you & your lady thinke fitt) that you would take one or both, (unless somewhat else may offer) for some time, & I would willingly pay what you should reasonably desire; I paid the old gentleman £20 per Mr. Perry since I came away.

Pray my service to Sir Charles Tirrell & my Lady. Mr. Jay is (in health) att my new plantation att Westopher where I am now building to looke after affairs there. Please to give my best respects & service to all friends, & accept the same to your selfe & lady with my utmost good wishes from

dear Sir

your oblidged loveing brother & humble servant

WB

Tobacco plantation.

10. Ned (Edward) Ward

from *A Trip to Jamaica*
1698

*Ned Ward (1667–1731), wit, hack writer, author of doggerel verses and scurrilous
pamphlets, launched his career with the publication of A Trip to Jamaica. Based on
an actual voyage to the island, where he had gone in despair of earning his living in
London, only to find things no more encouraging in the New World, it was an
instant popular success and went through six editions in less than a year. Following
Richard Hakluyt, the empire's writers were generally a self-respecting group. Ward
launched his assault on Jamaica with one on authors: "The Condition of an
Author," he suggests, "is much like that of a Strumpet, both exposing our
Reputations to supply our Necessities, till at last we contract such an ill habit, thro'
our Practices, that we are equally troubl'd with an Itch to be always Doing." The
modern empire grew up with the literary profession, as we have several times
noted; Ned Ward here confirms their symbiosis by insulting the one on his way to
insulting the other.*

A Character of JAMAICA.

The Dunghill of the Universe, the Refuse of the whole Creation, the Clippings of the Elements, a shapeless Pile of Rubbish confusd'ly jumbl'd into an Emblem of the *Chaos*, neglected by Omnipotence when he form'd the World into its admirable Order. The Nursery of Heavens Judgments, where the Malignant Seeds of all Pestilence were first gather'd and scatter'd thro' the Regions of the Earth, to Punish Mankind for their Offences. The Place where *Pandora* fill'd her Box, where *Vulcan* Forg'd *Joves* Thunder-bolts, and that *Phaeton*, by his rash misguidance of the Sun, scorched into a Cinder. The Receptacle of Vagabonds, the Sanctuary of Bankrupts, and a Close-stool for the Purges of our Prisons. As Sickly as an Hospital, as Dangerous as the Plague, as Hot as Hell, and as Wicked as the Devil. Subject to Tornadoes, Hurricanes and Earthquakes, as if the Island, like the People, were troubled with the *Dry Belly-Ach*.

Of their Provisions.

The chiefest of their Provisions is *Sea-Turtle*, or *Toad in a Shell*, stew'd in its own Gravy; its lean is as White as a Green-sickness Girl, its Fat of a Calves-turd Colour; and is excellently good to put a Stranger into a Flux, and purge out part of those ill-humours it infallibly Creates. The Belly is call'd *Callipee*, the Back *Callipach*; and is serv'd up to the Table in its own Shell, instead of a Platter. They have *Guanas, Hickeries*, and *Crabs*; the first being an Amphibeous *Serpent*, shap'd like a *Lizard*, but black and larger; the second a *Land-Tortise*, the last needs no Description, but are as numerous as *Frogs* in *England*, and burrow in the Ground like *Rabbets*, so that the whole *Island* may be justly call'd, a *Crab-Warren*. They are Fattest near the *Pallasadoes*, where they will make a Skeleton of a Corps in as little time as a *Tanner* will Flea a Colt, or a *Hound* after Hunting devour a Shoulder of *Mutton*. They have *Beef* without Fat, Lean *Mutton* without Gravy, and *Fowles* as dry as the Udder of an Old Woman, and as tough as a Stake from the Haunches of a Super-anuated *Car-Horse*.

Milk is so plenty, you may buy it for Fifteen Pence a Quart; but Cream so very scarce, that a Firkin of Butter, of their own making, would be so costly a Jewel, that the Richest Man in the Island would be unable to purchase it. They value themselves greatly upon the sweetness of their Pork, which is indeed Lushious, but as flabby as the Flesh of one just risen from a Flux, and ought to be forbid in all hot Countries (as amongst the *Jews*) for the prevention of *Leprosie, Scurvy*, and other Distempers, of which it is a great occasion.

There is very little Veal, and that Lean; for in *England* you may Nurse four Children much cheaper than you can one Calf in *Jamaica*. They have course *Teal*, almost as big as *English Ducks*; and *Muscovy Ducks* as big as *Geese*; But as for their *Geese*, they may be all *Swans*, for I never saw one in the Island.

There are sundry sorts of *Fish*, under *Indian* Names, without Scales, and of a *Serpentine Complection*; they Eat as dry as a *Shed*, and much stronger than stale *Herrings* or *Old Ling*; with *Oyl'd Butter* to the Sauce, as Rank as *Goose-Grease*, improv'd with the Palatable Relish of a stinking *Anchovie*.

They make a rare *Soop* they call *Pepper-Pot*; its an excellent Breakfast for a *Salamander*, or a good preparative for a *Mountebanks Agent*, who Eats Fire one day, that he may get better Victuals the next. Three Spoonfuls so Inflam'd my Mouth, that had I devour'd a Peck of *Horse-Radish*, and Drank after it a Gallon of *Brandy* and *Gunpowder*, (*Dives* like) I could not have been more importunate for a Drop of Water to cool my Tongue.

They greatly abound in a Beautiful Fruit, call'd, a *Cussue*, not unlike an *Apple*, but longer; its soft and very juicy, but so great an Acid, and of a Nature so Restringent, that by Eating of one, it drew up my mouth like a *Hens Fundament*, and made my Palate as Rough, and Tongue as Sore, as if I had been Gargling it with *Allam-Water*: From whence I conjecture, they are a much fitter Fruit to recover *Lost Maiden-heads*, properly apply'd, than to be eaten. Of *Water-Mellons* and *Mas-Mellons* they have plenty; the former is of as cold a quality as a *Cucumber*, and will dissolve in your *Mouth* like *Ice* in a hot *Frying-Pan*, being as *Pleasant* to the *Eater* (and, I believe, as *Wholesome*) as a *Cup* of *Rock-Water* to a Man in a *Hectick Feavour*: The latter are Large and Lushious, but much too watery to be good.

Coco-Nuts, and *Physick-Nuts* are in great esteem amongst the Inhabitants; the former they reckon *Meat*, *Drink*, and *Cloth*, but the Eatable part is secur'd within so strong a *Magazeen*, that it requires a lusty *Carpenter*, well Arm'd with *Ax* and *Handsaw*, to hew a passage to the *Kernel*, and when he has done, it will not recompence his Labour. The latter is big as a *Filbert*, but (like a *Beautiful Woman* well Drest, and *Infectious*) if you venture to Taste, is of ill consequence: Their Shell is Black, and *Japan'd* by Nature, exceeding Art; the Kernel White, and extream Pleasant to the Palat, but of so powerful an Operation, that by taking two, my Guts were Swept as clean, as ever *Tom-T—-á-man* made a *Vault*, or any of the *Black Fraternity* a *Chimney*.

They have *Oranges*, *Lemons*, *Limes*, and several other Fruits, as *Sharp* and *Crabbed* as themselves, not given them as a *Blessing*, but a *Curse*; for Eating so many sower things, Generates a *Corroding Slime* in the Bowels, and is one great occasion of that Fatal and Intolerable, Distemper, *The Dry Belly Ach*; which in a Fortnight, or Three Weeks, takes away the use of their Limbs, that they are forc'd to be led about by *Negro's*. A Man under this Misery, may be said to be the *Scutchion* of the *Island*, the Complection of the Patient being the *Field*, bearing *Or*, charg'd with all the Emblems of Destruction, supported by *Two Devils, Sables*; and *Death* the *Crest Argent*. Many other Fruits there are, that are neither worth Eating, Nameing, or Describing: Some that are never Tasted but in a *Drouth*, and others in a *Famine*.

OF PORT-ROYAL.

It is an Island distinct from the Main of *Jamaica*, tho' before the *Earthquake*, it joyn'd by a Neck of Land to the *Palisados*, but was separated by the Violence of an Inundation (thro' God's Mercy) to prevent the Wickedness of their Metropolis diffusing it self, by Communication, overall the Parts of the Country, and so call that Judgment upon the Whole, which fell more particularly upon the Sinfulest part.

From a Spacious fine Built Town (according to Report) it is now reduc'd, by the Encroachments of the Sea, to a little above a quarter of a Mile in Length, and about half so much the Breadth, having so few remains left of its former splendour, I could think no otherwise, but that every Travellour who had given its Description, made large use of his *License*. The Houses are low, little, and irregular; and if I compare the Best of their Streets in *Port-Royal*, to the Fag-End of *Kent-street*, where the *Broom-Men* Live, I do them more than Justice.

About Ten a Clock in the Morning, their Nostrils are saluted with a *Land Breeze*, which Blowing o'er the Island, searches the bowels of the Mountains, (being always crack'd and full of Vents, by reason of excessive Heat) bringing along with it such *Sulpherous Vapours*, that I have fear'd the whole Island would have burst out into a Flaming *Aetna,* or have stifled us with Suffocating Fumes, like that of melted Mineral and Brimstone.

In the Afternoon, about Four a Clock, they might have the refreshment of a *Sea-Breeze*, but suffering the *Negroes* to carry all their *Nastiness* to *Windward* of the Town, that the Nauseous Effluvias which arise from their stinking Dunghills, are blown in upon them; thus what they might enjoy as a Blessing, they ingratefully pervert by their own ill Management.

They have a Church, 'tis true, but built rather like a *Market-House*; and when the *Flock* were in their *Pens* and the *Pastor* Exalted to over-look his *Sheep*, I took a Survey round me, and saw more variety of *Scare-Crows* than ever was seen at the Feast of *Ugly-Faces*.

Every thing is very Dear, and an Ingenious or an Honest Man may meet with this Encouragement, To spend a Hundred Pounds before he shall get a Penny. *Madera-Wine* and *Bottle-Beer* are Fifteen Pence the Bottle; most *Claret*, Half a Crown; *Rhennish*, Five Shillings; and their best *Canary*, Ten Bits, or Six and Three Pence. They have this pleasure in Drinking, That what they put into their Bellies, they may soon stroak out of their Fingers Ends; for instead of *Exonerating*,[67] they *Fart*; and *Sweat* instead of *Pissing*.

OF THE PEOPLE.

The generality of the Men look as if they had just knock'd off their Feters, and by an unexpected Providence, escap'd the danger of a near Mis-fortune; the dread of which, hath imprinted that in their *Looks*, which they can no more alter than an *Ethiopian* can his *Colour*.

They are all *Colonels, Majors, Captains, Lieutenants*, and *Ensigns*; the two last being held in such disdain, that they are look'd upon as a *Bungling Diver* amongst a Gang of *Expert Pick-Pockets; Pride* being their *Greatness*, and *Impudence* their *Virtue*.

They regard nothing but Money, and value not how they get it; there being no other Felicity to be enjoy'd but purely Riches. They are very Civil to Strangers who bring over considerable Effects; and will try a great many ways to Kill him fairly, for the Lucre of his Cargo: And many have been made Rich by such Windfalls.

---

67. *Exonerating*: disburdening.

A Broken *Apothecary* will make there a Topping *Physician*; a *Barbers Prentice*, a good *Surgeon*; a *Balliffs Follower*, a passable *Lawyer*: and an *English Knave*, a very *Honest Fellow*.

They have so great a veneration for *Religion*, That *Bibles* and *Common-Prayer-Books* are as good a Commodity amongst them, as *Muffs* and *Warming-Pans*.

A little Reputation among the *Women*, goes a great way; and if their Actions be answerable to their Looks, they may vie *Wickedness* with the *Devil*: An *Impudent Air*, being the only *Charms* of their *Countenance*, and a *Lewd Carriage*, the *Study'd Grace* of their *Deportment*. They are such who have been *Scandelous* in *England* to the utmost degree, either *Transported* by the *State*, or led by their *Viscious Inclinations*; where they may be *Wicked* without *Shame*, and *Whore* on without *Punishment*.

They are Stigmatiz'd with *Nick-Names*, which they bear, not with *Patience* only, but with *Pride*; as *Unconscionable Nan, Salt-Beef Peg, Buttock-de-Clink Jenny, etc.* *Swearing, Drinking*, and *Obscene Talk*, are the Principal Qualifications that render them acceptable to *Male Conversation*; and she that wants a perfection in these admirable acquirements, shall be as much Ridicul'd for her *Modesty*, as a *Plain-Dealing Man* amongst a Gang of *Knaves*, for his *Honesty*.

In short, *Virtue* is so *Despis'd*, and all sorts of *Vice Encourag'd* by both *Sexes*, that the Town of *Port-Royal* is the very *Sodom* of the Universe.

FINIS

Chapter 5

Seventeenth-Century Anglo-America: New England and Canada

INTRODUCTION

Long after the first settlers, English people continued to emigrate across the Atlantic; but by the middle of the seventeenth century most were going to settled colonies that already had governments, churches, markets, land distribution patterns, Indian policies, and histories. By the later part of the century, an English emigrant would encounter not just other English emigrants, but creoles; that is, English people native to the colonies. Because migration continued to account for much of the population growth, there is no clear line between generations. But gradually a creole culture developed, with institutions, customs, and sensibilities to which newly arrived colonists had to adapt. This chapter begins with the diary of John Winthrop, who led nearly a thousand people on the so-called Great Migration of 1630; it ends with the diary of Sarah Kemble Knight, who was born in Boston and daydreamed about a London she only encountered in books.

The term "New England" was coined by Captain John Smith in 1616, when settlement still meant Virginia. He explained it as lying between New France and Virginia. By 1640, the New England colonies had already outpaced Virginia in population. (Both, however, would soon be outdistanced by the British Caribbean colonies.) Soon, New England was bordered on the South by New Netherlands, which was seized by the English and renamed New York in 1664. To the North, the English did not seriously rival New France until the founding of the Hudson's Bay Company in 1670, although the Newfoundland Company had built fishing villages in 1610, and as early as 1614 Virginia had sent a military expedition to sack Port Royal.

The boundaries of the New England colonies shifted frequently over the seventeenth century, and differed from the modern New England states. English rulers, including Cromwell, had a habit of issuing conflicting and overlapping charters, and colonies spent a great deal of energy lobbying for recognition in London. Plymouth, in 1620, was the fourth English colony, after Virginia, Newfoundland, and Bermuda; but Plymouth was settled through navigational error, and the colony's land claims never were settled in a charter. Massachusetts Bay, settled in 1629, had superior legality, but its claims conflicted with proprietary grants made to Sir Ferdinando Gorges. Rhode Island, settled by exiles from the Puritan colonies, had to fend off legal claims from Massachusetts Bay, Connecticut, and Plymouth. Hartford and New Haven were for a while independent colonies. New Hampshire became an independent colony in 1679.

Seal of the Massachusetts Bay Company. An Indian is shown saying, "Come Over and Help Us."

Large tracts of New England, including Maine and much of Massachusetts, were in proprietary grants to Gorges and his family; Massachusetts Bay gradually annexed the Gorges grant. It also took over Plymouth, in 1691.

New England was never merely local; it existed only because of the transatlantic trading routes. Plymouth, saddled by heavy debts to its London investors, dealt heavily in the fur trade. (Competition over Indian fur trading is one of the main subtexts of Bradford's rivalry with Morton, in chapter 3.) Other New England colonies exported lumber, naval stores (pitch, turpentine), and fish. The power of London kept the New England economy in an unambiguously dependent relation, shaping it as a province of the empire. Colonists were required to import and export goods only through English ports. Colonists were not allowed to coin their own money, nor to import specie from Britain. Gradually, however, Boston itself became a center for Atlantic shipping, serving the traders and slavers of the Caribbean as well as the mainland colonies. New England carriers and commercial middlemen became increasingly adept at managing the Atlantic world (and evading London control). By the end of the century there were distinct differences of culture between the seaports and the backcountry agricultural towns.

The culture of the entire North Atlantic coast was strongly anchored in southeastern Massachusetts. That was the site of the printing presses (Cambridge, 1639), Harvard College (1637), the courts, the most populous towns, and most of the shipping that connected even the western towns to the imperial center. Even the fabled Acadians, of what is now Nova Scotia, received their supplies from New England traders. Consequently, although English people of all kinds migrated to New England, and although economic motives seem to have prevailed for most, the region's culture was dominated by the Puritan leaders and institutions of Massachusetts Bay, Connecticut, and Plymouth.

Indeed, almost all of the authors in this chapter were Puritans of southeastern Massachusetts. Some of their texts, such as Mary Rowlandson's, could even be considered Puritan polemics. We have relegated the controversies of Puritanism to a separate chapter because theological argument remained a specialized discipline, a literature of its own. New Englanders, Puritan and nonPuritan alike, practiced other kinds of writing as well, many of which linked them to colonists elsewhere or to the English of the mother country.

Most of the genres of this chapter are strikingly similar to autobiography, though autobiography per se was not yet an available form. In journals, diaries, captivity narratives, conversion narratives, and dying confessionals, colonists told stories about their lives. But they always did so for a point; the aim was never to draw attention to the self for its own sake. This fact about the genres of colonial literature says much about a central paradox of Puritan culture: its anxieties about salvation required constant self-examination and self-discipline; yet its attention to self was designed to avoid the interests, pleasures, and distinctions of self. Anne Bradstreet tries to turn her relation into a lesson about the dangers of self. Mary Rowlandson recounts her suffering as a way to forget self. Esther Rodgers speaks only through the mouthpiece of a clergyman, for whom she is an object lesson in the wages of sin. Yet New England was also a commercial culture, increasingly oriented to self-interest. (See the Winthrop-Keayne controversy in chapter 6.) Gradually the Puritan techniques of self-observation took on new meaning; the shift is visible in Knight and Sewall, and by the time of Benjamin Franklin would result in the invention of modern secular autobiography.

This chapter centers on a pair of longer texts, both captivity narratives. The captivity narrative has been called a uniquely American genre. As Radisson's example shows, Canadian captivity narratives exist, and his was probably influenced more by French texts than English ones since English was at best his fourth language. The English colonies, however, made captivity narratives a stock item of the popular press until the nineteenth century. Unlike the French, the English were more engaged in settling than in trading with Indians; the captivity narratives were more popular among them because the genre came to define the racial identities of the settlements. Captor and captive typically remain distinct. For most colonists these stories were the closest thing to novels and romances, which were still morally suspect (though at least one author here, Sarah Knight, had clearly read some). Captivity narratives by Puritans tend to organize their storytelling to emphasize God's providence. Peter Radisson, by contrast, recounts events as happening by chance, human design, or error. These two assumptions about why things happen yield very different stories, as well as very different portraits of Indians. Captor and captive eventually begin to merge in Radisson's tale. Like the *Jesuit Relations*—the annual reports of missionaries in New France that remain our best source for ethnographies of North American Indians—Radisson's narrative strikes the modern reader as more porous to cultural difference; so much so that his own cultural identity often seems hard to locate.

M.W.

Suggested readings: Nicholas Canny and Anthony Pagden, eds., *Colonial Identity in the Atlantic World*. Other captivity narratives can be found in Alden Vaughan and Edward Clark, eds., *Puritans Among the Indians*; Colin Calloway, *North Country Captives*; and Richard Slotkin and James Folsom, eds., *So Dreadfull a Judgment: Puritan Responses to King Philip's War*.

1. John Winthrop

from the journal
1633–48

After arriving in the Massachusetts Bay colony as the leader of what came to be known as the Great Migration (see chapter 3), John Winthrop was repeatedly elected governor. His journal expresses his conception of his public role, recording the events of the colony from political crises to noteworthy weather events. When it was published in the nineteenth century, its editor called it The History of New England. *Winthrop himself appears in the third person, usually as "the governor." Yet it is a very personal record. Often the journal accounts argue vigorously for Winthrop's political views, defending his authority and the high degree of control the Massachusetts government exercised over settlers' lives. "A Democratie," he writes, "is, amongst most civil nations, accounted the meanest and worst form of government." By 1645, resistance to Winthrop's view of authority was so strong that he was impeached, though after he defended himself in a famous speech on liberty (see chapter 6), he was reelected until his death. Given Winthrop's faith in the New England mission, the stakes are high in every episode. The history he records is never purely secular history. When one group of settlers returns to England, God punishes them. In many entries, this search for divine omens, judgments, and confirmations merges imperceptibly with a popular culture of magic and the supernatural.*

[1633: LABOR TROUBLES]

The scarcity of workmen had caused them to raise their wages to an excessive rate, so as a carpenter would have three shillings the day, a laborer two shillings and sixpence, etc.; and accordingly those who had commodities to sell advanced their prices sometime double to that they cost in England, so as it grew to a general complaint, which the court, taking knowledge of, as also of some further evils, which were springing out of the excessive rates of wages, they made an order, that carpenters, masons, etc., should take but two shillings the day, and laborers but eighteen pence, and that no commodity should be sold at above four pence in the shilling more than it cost for ready money in England; oil, wine, etc., and cheese, in regard of the hazard of bringing, etc., [excepted]. The evils which were springing, etc., were: 1. Many spent much time idly, etc., because they could get as much in four days as would keep them a week. 2. They spent much in tobacco and strong waters, etc., which was a great waste to the commonwealth, which, by reason of so many foreign commodities expended, could not have subsisted to this time, but that it was supplied by the cattle and corn, which were sold to new comers at very dear rates, viz., corn at six shillings the bushel, a cow at 20 pounds,—yea, some at 24 pounds, some 26 pounds,—a mare at 35 pounds, an ewe goat at 3 or 4 pounds; and yet many cattle were every year brought out of England, and some from Virginia. Soon after order was taken for prices of commodities, viz., not to exceed the rate of four pence in the shilling above the price in England, except cheese and liquors, etc.

[1639: A TEMPEST]

There was so violent a wind at S. S. E. and S. as the like was not since we came into this land. It began in the evening, and increased till midnight. It overturned some new, strong houses; but the Lord miraculously preserved old, weak cottages. It tare down fences,—people ran out of their houses in the night, etc. There came such a rain withal, as raised the waters at Connecticut twenty feet above their meadows, etc.

The Indians near Aquiday being pawwawing in this tempest, the devil came and fetched away five of them.

[1639: DRAFTING *THE BODY OF LIBERTIES*]

The people had long desired a body of laws, and thought their condition very unsafe, while so much power rested in the discretion of magistrates. Divers attempts had been made at former courts, and the matter referred to some of the magistrates and some of the elders; but still it came to no effect; for, being committed to the care of many, whatsoever was done by some, was still disliked or neglected by others. At last it was referred to Mr. Cotton and Mr. Nathaniel Warde, etc., and each of them framed a model, which were presented to this general court, and by them committed to the governor and deputy and some others to consider of, and so prepare it for the court in the 3d month next. Two great reasons there were, which caused most of the magistrates and some of the elders not to be very forward in this matter. One was, want of sufficient experience of the nature and disposition of the people, considered with the condition of the country and other circumstances, which made them conceive, that such laws would be fittest for us, which should arise pro re nata[1] upon occasions, etc., and so the laws of England and other states grew, and therefore the fundamental laws of England are called customs, consuetudines. 2. For that it would professedly transgress the limits of our charter, which provide, we shall make no laws repugnant to the laws of England, and that we were assured we must do.[2] But to raise up laws by practice and custom had been no transgression; as in our church discipline, and in matters of marriage, to make a law, that marriages should not be solemnized by ministers, is repugnant to the laws of England; but to bring it to a custom by practice for the magistrates to perform it, is no law made repugnant, etc. At length (to satisfy the people) it proceeded, and the two models were digested with divers alterations and additions, and abbreviated and sent to every town, to be considered of first by the magistrates and elders, and then to be published by the constables to all the

---

1. pro re nata: as needed.

2. i.e., published laws would allow London authorities to see and object to Massachusetts practices.

people, that if any man should think fit, that any thing therein ought to be altered, he might acquaint some of the deputies therewith against the next court.[3]

[1640: CURRENCY SHORTAGES]

The scarcity of money made a great change in all commerce. Merchants would sell no wares but for ready money, men could not pay their debts though they had enough, prices of lands and cattle fell soon to the one half and less, yea to a third, and after one fourth part.

[1640: MICE]

About this time there fell out a thing worthy of observation. Mr. Winthrop the younger, one of the magistrates, having many books in a chamber where there was corn of divers sorts, had among them one wherein the Greek testament, the psalms and the common prayer were bound together. He found the common prayer[4] eaten with mice, every leaf of it, and not any of the two other touched, nor any other of his books, though there were above a thousand.

[1641: EMIGRATION WANES]

The parliament of England[5] setting upon a general reformation both of church and state, the Earl of Strafford being beheaded, and the archbishop[6] (our great enemy) and many others of the great officers and judges, bishops and others, imprisoned and called to account, this caused all men to stay in England in expectation of a new world, so as few coming to us, all foreign commodities grew scarce, and our own of no price. Corn would buy nothing: a cow which cost last year 20 pounds might now be bought for 4 or 5 pounds, etc., and many gone out of the country, so as no man could pay his debts, nor the merchants make return into England for their commodities, which occasioned many there to speak evil of us. These straits set our people on work to provide fish, clapboards, plank, etc., and to sow hemp and flax (which prospered very well) and to look out to the West Indies for a trade for cotton. The general court also made orders about payment of debts, setting corn at the wonted price, and payable for all debts which should arise after a time prefixed. They thought fit also to send some chosen men into England, to congratulate the happy success there, and to satisfy our creditors of the true cause why we could not make so current payment now as in former years we had done, and to be ready to make use of any opportunity God should offer for the good of the country here, as also to give any advice, as it should be required, for the settling the right form of church discipline there, but with this caution, that they should not seek supply of our wants in any dishonorable way, as by begging or the like, for we were resolved to wait upon the Lord in the use of all means which were lawful and honorable.

3. Nathaniel Ward's *Body of Liberties* was approved in December 1641.
4. the common prayer: *The Book of Common Prayer,* official prayer book of the Church of England.

5. The parliament of England: the so-called Long Parliament met in 1640 and ruled throughout the English Revolution, executing Charles I in 1649.
6. the archbishop: Archbishop Laud, famed opponent of Puritans.

[1642: BACK MIGRATION]

The sudden fall of land and cattle, and the scarcity of foreign commodities, and money, etc., with the thin access of people from England, put many into an unsettled frame of spirit, so as they concluded there would be no subsisting here, and accordingly they began to hasten away, some to the West Indies, others to the Dutch, at Long Island, etc., (for the governor there invited them by fair offers,) and others back for England. Among others who returned thither, there was one of the magistrates, Mr. Humfrey, and four ministers, and a schoolmaster. These would needs go against all advice, and had a fair and speedy voyage, till they came near England, all which time, three of the ministers, with the schoolmaster, spake reproachfully of the people and of the country, but the wind coming up against them, they were tossed up and down, being in December, so long till their provisions and other necessaries were near spent, and they were forced to strait allowance, yet at length the wind coming fair again, they got into the Sleeve,[7] but then there arose so great a tempest at S. E. as they could bear no sail, and so were out of hope of being saved (being in the night also). Then they humbled themselves before the Lord, and acknowledged God's hand to be justly out against them for speaking evil of this good land and the Lord's people here, etc. Only one of them, Mr. Phillips of Wrentham, in England, had not joined with the rest, but spake well of the people, and of the country; upon this it pleased the Lord to spare their lives, and when they expected every moment to have been dashed upon the rocks, (for they were hard by the Needles,) he turned the wind so as they were carried safe to the Isle of Wight by St. Helen's: yet the Lord followed them on shore. Some were exposed to great straits and found no entertainment, their friends forsaking them. One had a daughter that presently ran mad, and two other of his daughters, being under ten years of age, were discovered to have been often abused by divers lewd persons, and filthiness in his family. The schoolmaster had no sooner hired an house, and gotten in some scholars, but the plague set in, and took away two of his own children.

Others who went to other places, upon like grounds, succeeded no better. They fled for fear of want, and many of them fell into it, even to extremity, as if they had hastened into the misery which they feared and fled from, besides the depriving themselves of the ordinances and church fellowship, and those civil liberties which they enjoyed here; whereas, such as staid in their places, kept their peace and ease, and enjoyed still the blessing of the ordinances, and never tasted of those troubles and miseries, which they heard to have befallen those who departed. Much disputation there was about liberty of removing for outward advantages, and all ways were sought for an open door to get out at; but it is to be feared many crept out at a broken wall. For such as come together into a wilderness, where are nothing but wild beasts and beastlike men, and there confederate together in civil and church estate, whereby they do, implicitly at least, bind themselves to support each other, and all of them that society, whether civil or sacred, whereof they are members, how they can break from this without free consent, is hard to find, so as may satisfy a tender or

---

7. the Sleeve: the English Channel, *La Manche* in French.

good conscience in time of trial. Ask thy conscience, if thou wouldst have plucked up thy stakes, and brought thy family 3000 miles, if thou hadst expected that all, or most, would have forsaken thee there. Ask again, what liberty thou hast towards others, which thou likest not to allow others towards thyself; for if one may go, another may, and so the greater part, and so church and commonwealth may be left destitute in a wilderness, exposed to misery and reproach, and all for thy ease and pleasure, whereas these all, being now thy brethren, as near to thee as the Israelites were to Moses, it were much safer for thee, after his example, to choose rather to suffer affliction with thy brethren, than to enlarge thy ease and pleasure by furthering the occasion of their ruin.

[1644: DEATH FOR ADULTERY]

At this court of assistants one James Britton, a man ill affected both to our church discipline and civil government, and one Mary Latham, a proper young woman about 18 years of age, whose father was a godly man and had brought her up well, were condemned to die for adultery, upon a law formerly made and published in print. It was thus occasioned and discovered. This woman, being rejected by a young man whom she had an affection unto, vowed she would marry the next that came to her, and accordingly, against her friends'[8] minds, she matched with an ancient man who had neither honesty nor ability, and one whom she had no affection unto.

Whereupon, soon after she was married, divers young men solicited her chastity, and drawing her into bad company, and giving her wine and other gifts, easily prevailed with her, and among others this Britton. But God smiting him with a deadly palsy and fearful horror of conscience withal, he could not keep secret, but discovered this, and other the like with other women, and was forced to acknowledge the justice of God in that having often called others fools, etc., for confessing against themselves, he was now forced to do the like. The woman dwelt now in Plymouth patent, and one of the magistrates there, hearing she was detected, etc., sent her to us. Upon her examination, she confessed he did attempt the fact, but did not commit it, and witness was produced that testified (which they both confessed) that in the evening of a day of humiliation through the country for England, etc., a company met at Britton's and there continued drinking sack, etc., till late in the night, and then Britton and the woman were seen upon the ground together, a little from the house. It was reported also that she did frequently abuse her husband, setting a knife to his breast and threatening to kill him, calling him old rogue and cuckold, and said she would make him wear horns as big as a bull. And yet some of the magistrates thought the evidence not sufficient against her, because there were not two direct witnesses; but the jury cast her, and then she confessed the fact, and accused twelve others, whereof two were married men. Five of these were apprehended and committed, (the rest were gone,) but denying it, and there being no other witness against them than the testimony of a condemned person, there could be no proceeding against them. The woman proved

---

8. friend's: family's.

very penitent, and had deep apprehension of the foulness of her sin, and at length attained to hope of pardon by the blood of Christ, and was willing to die in satisfaction to justice. The man also was very much cast down for his sins, but was loth to die, and petitioned the general court for his life, but they would not grant it, though some of the magistrates spake much for it, and questioned the letter, whether adultery was death by God's law now. This Britton had been a professor[9] in England, but coming hither he opposed our church government, etc., and grew dissolute, losing both power and profession of godliness.

[March 21] They were both executed, they both died very penitently, especially the woman, who had some comfortable[10] hope of pardon of her sin, and gave good exhortation to all young maids to be obedient to their parents, and to take heed of evil company, etc.

[1645: WOMEN AND BOOKS]

[April 13] Mr. Hopkins, the governor of Hartford upon Connecticut, came to Boston, and brought his wife with him, (a godly young woman, and of special parts,) who was fallen into a sad infirmity, the loss of her understanding and reason, which had been growing upon her divers years, by occasion of her giving herself wholly to reading and writing, and had written many books. Her husband, being very loving and tender of her, was loath to grieve her; but he saw his error, when it was too late. For if she had attended her household affairs, and such things as belong to women, and not gone out of her way and calling to meddle in such things as are proper for men, whose minds are stronger, etc., she had kept her wits, and might have improved them usefully and honorably in the place God had set her. He brought her to Boston, and left her with her brother, one Mr. Yale,[11] a merchant, to try what means might be had here for her. But no help could be had.

[1645: A SERVANT'S WIT]

The wars in England kept servants from coming to us, so as those we had could not be hired, when their times were out, but upon unreasonable terms, and we found it very difficult to pay their wages to their content, (for money was very scarce). I may upon this occasion report a passage between one of Rowley and his servant. The master, being forced to sell a pair of his oxen to pay his servant his wages, told his servant he could keep him no longer, not knowing how to pay him the next year. The servant answered, he would serve him for more of his cattle. But how shall I do (saith the master) when all my cattle are gone? The servant replied, you shall then serve me, and so you may have your cattle again.[12]

9. professor: believer.
10. comfortable: comforting.

11. one Mr. Yale: father of Elihu Yale, Mrs. Hopkins's nephew, namesake of the university.
12. In the margin Winthrop writes, "insolent."

[1646: EXECUTION OF WILLIAM PLAINE]

Mr. Eaton, the governour of New Haven, wrote to the governour of the Bay, to desire the advice of the magistrates and elders in a special case, which was this: one Plaine of Guilford being discovered to have used some unclean practices, upon examination and testimony, it was found, that being a married man, he had committed sodomy with two persons in England, and that he had corrupted a great part of the youth of Guilford by masturbations, which he had committed, and provoked others to the like above a hundred times; and to some who questioned the lawfulness of such filthy practice, he did insinuate seeds of atheism, questioning whether there was a God, etc. The magistrates and elders (so many as were at hand) did all agree, that he ought to die, and gave divers reasons from the word of God. And indeed it was *horrendum facinus*,[13] and he a monster in human shape, exceeding all human rules and examples that ever had been heard of, and it tended to the frustrating of the ordinance of marriage and the hindering the generation of mankind.

[1648: A WITCH]

At this court one Margaret Jones of Charlestown was indicted and found guilty of witchcraft, and hanged for it. The evidence against her was, 1. that she was found to have such a malignant touch, as many persons, (men, women, and children,) whom she stroked or touched with any affection or displeasure, or, etc., were taken with deafness, or vomiting, or other violent pains or sickness, 2. she practising physic, and her medicines being such things as (by her own confession) were harmless, as aniseed, liquors, etc., yet had extraordinary violent effects, 3. she would use to tell such as would not make use of her physic, that they would never be healed, and accordingly their diseases and hurts continued, with relapse against the ordinary course, and beyond the apprehension of all physicians and surgeons, 4. some things which she foretold came to pass accordingly; other things she could tell of (as secret speeches, etc.) which she had no ordinary means to come to the knowledge of, 5. she had (upon search) an apparent teat in her secret parts as fresh as if it had been newly sucked, and after it had been scanned, upon a forced search, that was withered, and another began on the opposite side, 6. in the prison, in the clear day-light, there was seen in her arms, she sitting on the floor, and her clothes up, etc., a little child, which ran from her into another room, and the officer following it, it was vanished. The like child was seen in two other places, to which she had relation; and one maid that saw it, fell sick upon it, and was cured by the said Margaret, who used means to be employed to that end. Her behavior at her trial was very intemperate, lying notoriously, and railing upon the jury and witnesses, etc., and in the like distemper she died. The same day and hour she was executed, there was a very great tempest at Connecticut, which blew down many trees, etc.

---

13. *horrendum facinus*: a dreadful crime.

[1648: A GHOST SHIP]

There appeared over the harbor at New Haven, in the evening, the form of the keel of a ship with three masts, to which were suddenly added all the tackling and sails, and presently after, upon the top of the poop, a man standing with one hand akimbo under his left side, and in his right hand a sword stretched out toward the sea. Then from the side of the ship which was from the town arose a great smoke, which covered all the ship, and in that smoke she vanished away; but some saw her keel sink into the water. This was seen by many, men and women, and it continued about a quarter of an hour.

2. John Josselyn

from the journal of a voyage to New England 1639

Josselyn (1608?–75) made two voyages to New England, the second in the late 1660s, publishing an account of them in 1674. He is also known as the author of an early study of flora and fauna, called New England's Rarities. *The African woman he describes here would have been one of the first slaves in Massachusetts.*

The Second of *October*, about 9 of the clock in the morning, Mr. *Maverick's* Negro woman came to my chamber window, and in her own Countrey language and tune sang very loud and shril. Going out to her, she used a great deal of respect toward me, and willingly would have expressed her grief in *English*; but I apprehended it by her countenance and deportment, whereupon I repaired to my host, to learn of him the cause, and resolved to intreat him in her behalf, for that I understood before, that she had been a Queen in her own Countrey, and observed a very humble and dutiful garb used towards her by another Negro who was her maid. Mr. *Maverick* was desirous to have a breed of Negroes, and therefore seeing she would not yield by perswasions to company with a Negro young man he had in his house; he commanded him will'd she nill'd she[14] to go to bed to her, which was no sooner done but she kickt him out again. This she took in high disdain beyond her slavery, and this was the cause of her grief.

14. will'd she nill'd she: willy nilly.

3. [Thomas Shepard]

a visit to John Eliot's Indian mission 1646

Converting Indians to Christianity had been one of the constantly reiterated reasons for colonial settlements since the early sixteenth century. The official seal of the Massachusetts Bay colony depicts an Indian saying, "Come Over and Help Us." Yet the Puritan colonies devoted relatively little energy to missions, certainly by comparison with the French in Canada. The most famous exception is John Eliot (1604-90), the "Apostle to the Indians." He published many religious works, primers on Indian language, and popular items such as Dying Speeches of Several Indians. *His most famous (and least read) work is* Mamusse Wunnutupanatamwe Up-Biblum God *(1663), a translation of the Bible into Algonquian. This letter describing his mission settlement was almost certainly written by Thomas Shepard, another leading Puritan divine with a strong interest in Indian conversions (see chapter 3). As with most colonial accounts of Indians, the views and experiences of the Indians can only be inferred.*

Upon November 11, 1646, we came the second time unto the same wigwam of Waaubon, where we found many more Indians met together than the first time we came to them. And having seats provided for us by themselves, and being sat down awhile, we began again with prayer in the English tongue; our beginning this time was with the younger sort of Indian children in catechizing of them, which being the first time of instructing them we thought meet to ask them but only three questions in their own language, that we might not clog their minds or memories with too much at first. The questions asked and answered in the Indian tongue were these three: *1. Question*: who made you and all the world? *Answer*: God. *2. Question*: who do you look should save you and redeem you from sin and hell? *Answer*: Jesus Christ. *3. Question*: how many commandments hath god given you to keep? *Answer*: ten. These questions being propounded to the children severally and one by one, and the answers being short and easy, hence it came to pass that before we went through all, those who were last catechized had more readily learned to answer to them by hearing the same question so oft propounded and answered before by their fellows. And the other Indians who were grown up to more years had perfectly learned them, whom we therefore desired to teach their children again when we were absent, that so when we came again we might see their profiting, the better to encourage them hereunto; we therefore gave something to every child. . . .

Thus having spent some hours with them, we propounded two questions: what do you remember of what was taught you since the last time we were here? After they had spoken one to another for some time, one of them returned this answer, that they did much thank God for our coming, and for what they heard; they were wonderful things unto them.

Do you believe the things that are told you, viz., that God is *musquantum*, i.e., very angry, for the least sin in your thoughts or words or works? They said yes, and hereupon we set forth the terror of God against sinners, and mercy of God to the penitent and to such as sought to know Jesus Christ, and that as sinners should be after death *chechainuppan*, i.e., tormented alive (for we know no other word in the tongue to express extreme torture by), so believers should after death *wowein wicke Jehovah*, i.e., live in all bliss with Jehovah the blessed God, and so we concluded the conference.

Having thus spent the whole afternoon, and night being almost come upon us, considering that the Indians formerly desired to know how to pray and did think that Jesus Christ did not understand Indian language, one of us therefore prepared to pray in their own language, and did so for above a quarter of an hour together, wherein divers of them held up eyes and hands to heaven, all of them (as we understood afterwards) understanding the same; but one of them I cast my eye upon was hanging down his head with his rag before his eyes weeping. At first I feared it was some soreness of his eyes, but lifting up his head again, having wiped his eyes (as not desirous to be seen), I easily perceived his eyes were not sore, yet somewhat red with crying, and so held up his head for a while; yet such was the presence and mighty power of the Lord Jesus on his heart, that he hung down his head again and covered his eyes again and so fell wiping and wiping of them weeping abundantly, continuing thus till prayer was ended, after which he presently turns from us and turns his face to a side and corner of the wigwam, and there falls aweeping more abundantly by himself. Which one of us perceiving, went to him and spake to him encouraging words, at the hearing of which he fell aweeping more and more; so leaving of him, he who spake to him came unto me (being newly gone out of the wigwam) and told me of his tears. So we resolved to go again both of us to him, and speak to him again, and we met him coming out of the wigwam and there we spake again to him, and he there fell into a more abundant renewed weeping, like one deeply and inwardly affected indeed, which forced us also to such bowels[15] of compassion that we could not forbear weeping over him also. And so we parted greatly rejoicing for such sorrowing.

---

15. bowels: internal feeling.

4. John Eliot

Indians and imps
1652

Eliot wrote many pamphlets over the course of his life promoting his missions, especially for an English audience. The following anecdote from one of these tracts, Tears of Repentance, *nicely illustrates the importance of folk magic on both sides of the Puritan-Indian religious exchange; Puritan gravestones, for example, often depicted imps of death.*

A Pawwaw told me, who was of no small note among the Heathen formerly, and also with the best now he hath forsaken his Pawwawing, That after he had been brought by the Word of God to hate the Devil, and to renounce his Imps (which he did publickly) that yet his Imps remained still in him for some months tormenting of his flesh, and troubling of his mind, that he could never be at rest, either sleeping or waking: At length one time when I went down to keep the farthest Lecture about seven miles off, he asked me some Questions, whereof this was one, *viz.*, That if a Pawwaw had his Imps gone from him, what he should have instead to preserve him? Whereunto it was Answered, That if he did beleeve in Christ Jesus, he should have the Spirit of Christ dwelling in him, which is a good and a strong Spirit, and will keep him so safe, that all the Devils in Hell, and Pawwaws on Earth, should not be able to do him any hurt; and that if he did set himself against his Imps, by the strength of God they should all flee away like Muskeetoes: He told me, That he did much desire the Lord, it might be so with him. He further said, That ever since that very time God hath in mercy delivered him from them, he is not troubled with any pain (as formerly) in his Bed, nor dreadful visions of the night, but through the blessing of God, he doth lie down in ease, sleeps quietly, wakes in Peace, and walks in safety, for which he is very glad, and praises God.

5. Michael Wigglesworth

from the diary
1653–55

Michael Wigglesworth is best known today as the popular poet, author of Day of
Doom *(see chapter 8). While he was a tutor at Harvard as a young man, he kept a
diary with unusually intimate confessional passages. Because Wigglesworth is so
wracked in these pages by guilt, shame, and self-castigation, the diary has often
been taken as evidence of Puritanism's most extreme and cartoonish hostility to
pleasure. To be sure, in many passages he regards all sensual pleasure in the world
as sinful. But only recently have scholars begun to consider that Wigglesworth
seems to feel the keenest guilt over erotic attachments to his male pupils, a crime
for which no punishment was thought to be too severe. Most of these passages are
written in a special shorthand code, here represented by italics. Wigglesworth also
describes anxiety about his sexual functioning; he believed he had gonorrhea,
though doctors told him he did not. Partly to relieve himself of both of these
anxieties, he contracted a marriage in the business-like way that was the custom
of the day.*

[FEBRUARY 15, 1653]

Ah Lord I am vile, I desire to abhor my self (o that I could!) before the for these
things. *I find such unresistable torments of carnal lusts or provocation unto
the ejection of seed that I find my self unable to read any thing to inform me
about my distemper because of the prevailing or rising of my lusts. This I have
procured to my self. God hath brought this to my eye this day. Thou hast destroyed
thy self but in me is thy help. Lord let me find help in thee though I have destroyed
my self by my iniquity.*

[FEBRUARY 17, 1653]

*The last night a filthy dream and so pollution escaped me in my sleep for which I
desire to hang down my head with shame and beseech the Lord not to make me
possess the sin of my youth and give me into the hands of my abomination.*

[MARCH 5, 1653]

I still find abundance of pride, and more regarding what man thinks of me than
what gods thoughts are of me. And much distracted thoughts I find arising from too
much doting affection *to some of my pupils one of whom went to Boston with me*

today. I feel no power to love and prize god in my heart, my spirit is so leavend with love to the creature.

[JULY 4–5, 1653]

In the 2 next days I found so much of a spirit of pride and secret joying in some conceived excellence in my self which is too hard for me and I cant prevail over and also so much secret vice and vain thoughts in holy duties and thereby weariness of them and such filthy lust also flowing from my fond affection to my pupils whiles in their presence on the third day after noon that I confess myself an object of God's loathing as my sin is of my own and pray God make it so more to me.

[JANUARY 22, 1655]

I was much carryd away with too much frothiness and love to vanity on thursday and friday having cheerful company in the house with me. *I found myself much overborn with carnal concupiscence, nature being suppressed, for I had not had my afflux in 12 nights. Friday night it came again without any dream that I know of. Yet after it I am still inclined to lust. The Lord help me against it and against discouragement by it and against temptations of another nature and disquietments.*

[MARCH 6, 1655]

I begin to think marriage will be necessary for me (as an ordinance of god appointed to maintain purity which my heart loveth) what ever the event may be. Let me live no longer than I may live honestly good Lord.

[MAY, 1655]

At the time appointed with fear and trembling I came to Rowley to be marryed. The great arguments unto me were, 1: Physicians counsel: 2ly the institution of marryage by god himself for the preservation of purity and chastity, which with most humble and hearty prayers I have begged and still will beg of the Lord. So that I went about the business which god call'd me to attend. And consummated it now is by the will of god May 18, 1655. Oh Lord! let my cry come up unto thee for all the blessings of a marryed estate, A Heart suitable thereto, chastity especially thereby, and life and health if it be thy will. Oh crown thy own ordinance with thy blessing, that it may appear it is not in vain to wait upon thee in the wayes of thy own appointment. *I feel the stirrings and strongly of my former distemper even after the use of marriage the next day which makes me exceeding afraid. I know not how to keep company with my dearest friend but it is with me as formerly in some days already.*

[SEPTEMBER 15, 1655]

God will guide and provide.
He hath done so in troubles as great as these and therefore he can do it and will do it.

In Memoriall of his former mercys received in answer to prayer and off all his goodness hitherto I will erect

A pillar to the prayse of

his grace   EBEN   EZER[16]
                                        September 15   1655

O Dulcis memoria
difficultatis praeteritae!
Olim haec (quae nunc incumbunt
mala, haec inquam)
Meminisse juvabit.
Quae mala nunc affligunt, postea in
Laudem dei, nostramque voluptatem cedent
Quis triumphum caneret, quis spoliis onustus
rederet victor, si numquam dimicaret?

Hitherto the Lord ... *hath holpen me*

some *night pollution escaped me notwithstanding my earnest prayer to the contrary which brought to mind my old sins now too much forgotten (as near as i remember the thoughts that then I had) together with my later sins unto seeming one that had received so many mercies from the Lord. O unthankfulness unthankfulness when shall I get rid of thee.*

16. EBENEZER: from 1 Sam. 7:12.

6. Anne Bradstreet

To My Dear Children

From her own day to the present, Anne Bradstreet (1612?–72) has been the best known colonial poet (see chapter 8). The following testament to her children survives in a manuscript notebook of the 1660s, together with meditations and some of her poems. Though other parts of the notebook are in her own hand, the testament has been copied out by her son, Simon Bradstreet.

This Book by Any yet unread,
  I leave for you when I am dead,
  That being gone, here you may find
What was your living mother's mind.
Make use of what I leave in Love
And God shall blesse you from above.
A. B.

My dear children.

I, knowing by experience that the exhortations of parents take most effect when the speakers leave to speak, and those especially sink deepest which are spoke latest, and being ignorant whether on my death bed I shall have opportunity to speak to any of you, much lesse to All, thought it the best whilst I was able to compose some short matters, (for what else to call them I know not) and bequeath to you, that when I am no more with you, yet I may bee dayly in your remembrance (although that is the least in my aim in what I now do); by that you may gain some spiritual Advantage by my experience. I have not studied in this you read to show my skill, but to declare the Truth, not to sett forth my self, but the Glory of God. If I had minded the former it had been perhaps better pleasing to you, but seeing the last is the best, let it be best pleasing to you.

The method I will observe shall bee this—I will begin with God's dealing with me from my childhood to this Day.

In my young years, about 6 or 7 as I take it, I began to make conscience of my wayes, and what I knew was sinfull—as lying, disobedience to parents, etc.—I avoided it. If at any time I was overtaken with the evills, it was a great Trouble, and I could not be at rest 'till by prayer I had confest it unto God. I was also troubled at the neglect of private Dutyes, though too often tardy that way. I also found much comfort in reading the Scriptures, especially those places I thought most concerned my Condition, and as I grew to have more understanding, so the more solace I took in them.

In a long fitt of sickness which I had on my bed I often comuned with my heart, and made my Suplication to the most High who sett me free from that affliction.

But as I grew up to bee about 14 or 15 I found my heart more carnall, and sitting loose from God; vanity and the follyes of Youth take hold of me.

About 16 the Lord layd his hand sore upon me and smote me with the small pox. When I was in my affliction I besought the Lord, and confessed my pride and Vanity and he was entreated of me, and again restored me. But I rendered not to him according to the benefitt received.

After a short time I changed my Condition and was marryed, and came into this Country, where I found a new World and new manners at which my heart rose. But after I was convinced it was the way of God, I submitted to it and joined to the church, at Boston.

After some time I fell into a lingering sickness like a consumption, together with a lamenesse, which correction I saw the Lord sent to humble and try me and do me Good; and it was not altogether ineffectual. It pleased God to keep me a long time without a child, which was a great grief to me, and cost me many prayers and tears before I obtain one, and after him gave me many more, of whom I now take the care, that as I have brought you into the world, and with great paines, weakness, cares and feares brought you to this, I now travail in birth again of you till Christ be formed in you.

Among all my experiences of gods gracious Dealings with me I have constantly observed this: that he hath never suffered me long to sitt loose from him, but by one affliction or other hath made me look home, and search what was amisse. So usually thus it hath been with me that I have no sooner felt my heart out of order, but I have expected correction for it, which most comonly hath been upon my own person, in sicknesse, weakness, paines, sometimes on my soul in Doubts and feares of Gods displeasure, and my Sincerity towards him. Sometimes he hath smote a child with sickness, sometimes chastened by losses in estate, and these Times (through his great mercy) have been the times of my greatest Getting and Advantage, yea I have found them the Times when the Lord hath manifested the most Love to me. Then have I gone to searching, and have said with David, "Lord, search me and try me, see what wayes of wickedness are in me, and lead me in the way everlasting"; and seldome or never but I have found either some sin I lay under which God would have reformed, or some duty neglected which he would have performed, and by his help I have laid vowes and Bonds upon my Soul to perform his righteous comands.

If at any time you are chastened of God take it as Thankfully and Joyfully as in greatest mercyes. For if yee bee his, yee shall reap the greatest benefitt by it. It hath been no small support to me in times of Darkness when the Almighty hath hid his face from me, that yet I have had abundance of Sweetness and refreshment after affliction and more circumspection in my walking after I have been afflicted. I have been with God like an untoward child, that no longer than the rod has been on my back (or at least in sight) but I have been apt to forgett him and my Self too. Before I was afflicted I went astray, but now I keep thy statutes.

I have had great experience of God's hearing my prayers, and returning comfortable Answers to me, either in granting the thing I prayed for, or else in satisfying my mind without it, and I have been confident it hath been from him, because I have found my heart through his goodness enlarged in Thankfulness to him.

I have often been perplexed that I have not found that constant Joy in my pilgrimage and refreshing which I supposed most of the servants of God have, although he hath not left me altogether without the wittness of his holy spirit who hath oft given me his word and sett to his Seal that it shall bee well with me. I have sometimes tasted of that hidden Manna that the world knowes not, and have sett up my Ebenezer[17] and have resolved with my self that against such a promise, such tastes of sweetness the Gates of Hell shall never prevail. Yet have I many Times sinkings and droopings, and not enjoyed that felicity that sometimes have done. But when I have been in darkness and seen no light, yet have I desired to stay my self upon the Lord, and when I have been in sickness and pain, I have thought if the Lord would but lift up the light of his Countenance upon me, although he ground me to powder it would bee but Light to me, yea oft have I thought were it hell it self and could there find the Love of God toward me, it would bee a Heaven. And could I have been in Heaven without the Love of God, it would have been a hell to me for in Truth it is the absence and presence of God that makes Heaven or Hell.

Many times hath Satan troubled me concerning the verity of the Scriptures, many times by Atheisme how I could know whether there was a God; I never saw any miracles to confirm me, and those which I read of how did [I] know but they were feigned? That there is a God my Reason would soon tell me by the wondrous workes that I see, the vast frame of the Heaven and the Earth, the order of all things night and day, Summer and Winter, Spring and Autumne, the dayly providing for this great household upon the Earth, the preserving and directing of All to its proper End. The consideration of these things would with amazement certainly resolve me that there is an Eternall Being. But how should I know he is such a God as I worship in Trinity, and such a Saviour as I rely upon? Though this hath thousands of Times been suggested to me, yet God hath helped me over. I have argued thus with my self: That there is a God I see; If ever this God hath revealed himself it must bee in his word; and this must bee it or none. Have I not found that operation by it that no humane Invention can work upon the Soul? Hath no Judgments befallen Diverse who have scorned and condemned it? Hath it not been preserved through All Ages maugre[18] all the heathen Tyrants and all of the Enemyes who have opposed it? Is there any story but that which showes the beginnings of Times, and how the world came to bee as wee see? Do wee not know the prophecyes in it fulfilled which could not have been so long foretold by any but God himself?

When I have gott over this Block then have I another putt in my way, and that admitt this bee the true God whom wee worship, and that bee his word, yet why may not the popish Religion bee the right? They have the same God, the same Christ, the same word. They only enterpret it one way, wee another.

This hath sometimes stuck with me, and more it would, by the vain fooleries that are in their Religion, together with their lying miracles, and cruell persecutions of the Saints, which admitt were they as they terme them yet not so to bee dealt withall.[19]

The consideration of these things and many the like would soon turn me to my own Religion again.

17. Ebenezer: see note 16, above.
18. maugre: despite.

19. i.e., even if the Protestant martyrs were heretics as Catholics thought, they were not to be treated as Catholics treated them.

But some new Troubles I have had since the world has been filled with Blasphemy, and Sectaries, and some who have been accounted sincere Christians have been carried away with them, that sometimes I have said, "Is there Faith upon the Earth?" And I have not known what to think. But then I have remembered the words of Christ that so it must bee, and that if it were possible the very elect should bee deceived. Behold saith our Saviour, "I have told you before." That hath stayed my heart, and I can now say, "Return o my Soul to thy Rest, upon this Rock Christ Jesus will I build my faith, and if I perish, I perish." But I know all the powers of Hell shall never prevail against it, I know whom I have trusted, and whom I have believed and that he is able to keep that [which] I have committed to his charge.

Now to the King Imortall, Eternall invisible, the only wise God, bee Honor, and Glory for ever and ever, Amen.

This was written in much sicknesse and weakness, and is very weakly and imperfectly done, but if you can pick any Benefitt out of it, It is the mark which I aimed at.

7. Pierre-Esprit Radisson

The Relation of my Voyage, being in Bondage in the Lands of the Irokoits
1665

Pierre, or Peter, Radisson was at various times in his life French, Indian, and English. He lived in a day when national belonging was more about loyalty to a sovereign than about the birthright of a shared identity with a national people, and his hybrid sense of self may have been typical of many Europeans in the seventeenth-century Atlantic.

Born in St. Malo, in France, he seems to have traveled in Turkey and Italy before going to New France in 1651. There, he was captured by the Iroquois and adopted by an Iroquois family in the place of their recently killed son, as was customary among many Indian tribes. Although he made one attempt to escape, as he relates below, he also rejected a clear opportunity to rejoin the French, returning voluntarily to his Indian village before later changing his mind again, making his way to New Amsterdam (later New York), and back to France. But he was soon back in New France. In the mid-1660s he and his brother began working for the English. They attempted a trading voyage up Hudson's Straits with backing from Boston merchants; when the voyage failed, Radisson went to New England to defend himself. There he met commissioners from King Charles II, who, interested in Radisson's scheme for finding a Northwest passage, escorted him in 1665 to Oxford, where Charles was in retreat from the great London plague.

The Voyages, *a manuscript notebook relating Radisson's journeys in Canada from 1652 to 1664, was written by Radisson in his unique version of English, apparently as preparation for his meeting with Charles II. Radisson's narrative describes one process of acculturation—from French to Iroquois—but it performs another: from French to English. His promotional intent is clear, and, as the later voyages contain some errors of chronology, his reliability has been questioned. Yet the stories are certainly compelling, and existing evidence only corroborates what Radisson says in the selection below. He succeeded in persuading the English king to support his ventures, which eventually resulted in the founding of the Hudson's Bay Company and new imperial rivalry in Canada.*

    Radisson's cultural crossings were by no means over. He continued to work for the English until 1673, but then a dispute with the Hudson's Bay Company prompted him to return to France. For the next ten years he acted as a loyal Frenchman, but returned to the English side in Hudson's Bay in 1684. Nothing is known of him after 1685. To retain the peculiar flavor of Radisson's vivid but tangled writing, we have modernized only where necessary.

The Relation of my Voyage, being in Bondage in the Lands of the Irokoits, which was the next yeare after my coming into Canada, in the yeare 1651, the 24th day of May.

Being persuaded in the morning by two of my comrades to go and recreat ourselves in fowling, I disposed myselfe to keepe them Company; wherfor I cloathed myselfe the lightest way I could possible, that I might be the nimbler and not stay behinde, as much for the prey that I hoped for, as for to escape the danger into which wee have ventered ourselves of an enemy the cruelest that ever was uppon the face of the Earth. It is to bee observed that the french had warre with a wild nation called Iroquoites, who for that time weare soe strong and so to be feared that scarce any body durst stirre out either Cottage or house without being taken or killed, saving that he had nimble limbs to escape their fury; being departed, all three well armed, and unanimiously rather die then abandon one another, notwithstanding these resolutions weare but young mens deboasting; being then in a very litle assurance and lesse security.

    At an offspring of a village of three Rivers we consult together that two should go the watter side, the other in a wood hardby to warne us, for to advertise us if he accidentaly should light [upon] or suspect any Barbars[20] in ambush, we also retreat ourselves to him if we should discover any thing uppon the River. Having comed to the first river, which was a mile distant from our dwellings, wee mett a man who kept cattell, and asked him if he had knowne any appearance of Ennemy, and likewise demanded which way he would advise us to gett better fortune, and what part he spied more danger; he guiding us the best way he could, prohibiting us by no means not to render ourselves att the skirts of the mountains; for, said he, I discovered oftentimes a multitude of people which rose up as it weare of a sudaine from of the Earth, and that doubtless there weare some Enemys that way; which sayings made us looke to ourselves and charge two of our fowling peeces with great shot the one, and the other with small. Priming our pistols, we went where our fancy first lead us, being impossible for us to avoid the destinies of the heavens; no sooner tourned our backs, but my nose fell ableeding without any provocation in the least. Certainly it was a warning for me of a beginning of a yeare and a half of hazards and of miseryes that weare to befall

---

20. Barbars: barbarians, savages.

mee. We did shoot sometime and killed some Duks, which made one of my fellow travellers go no further. I seeing him taking such a resolution, I proferred some words that did not like[21] him, giving him the character of a timourous, childish humor; so this did nothing prevaile with him, to the Contrary that had with him quite another issue then what I hoped for; for offending him with my words he prevailed so much with the others that he persuaded them to doe the same. I lett them goe, laughing them to scorne, beseeching them to helpe me to my fowles, and that I would tell them the discovery of my designes, hoping to kill meat to make us meate att my retourne.

I went my way along the wood some times by the side of the river, where I finde something to shute att, though no considerable quantitie, which made me goe a league off and more, so I could not go in all further then St. Peeter's, which is nine mile from the plantation by reason of the river Ovamasis, which hindered me the passage. I begun'd to think att my retourne how I might transport my fowle. I hide one part in a hollow tree to keep them from the Eagles and other devouring fowles, so as I came backe the same way where before had no bad incounter. Arrived within one halfe a mile where my comrades had left me, I rested awhile by reason that I was looden'd with three geese, tenn ducks, and one crane, with some teales.

After having laid downe my burden upon the grasse, I thought to have heard a noise in the wood by me, which made me to overlook my armes; I found one of my girdle pistols wette. I shott it off and charged it againe, went up to the wood the soffliest I might, to discover and defend myselfe the better against any surprise. After I had gone from tree to tree some 30 paces off I espied nothing; as I came back from out of the wood to an adjacent brooke, I perceived a great number of Ducks; my discovery imbouldened me, and for that there was a litle way to the fort, I determined to shute once more; coming nigh preparing meselfe for to shute, I found another worke: the two young men that I left some tenne houres before heere weare killed. Whether they came after mee, or weare brought thither by the Barbars, I know not. However [they] weare murthered. Looking over them, I knew them albeit quite naked, and their hair standing up, the one being shott through with three boulletts and two blowes of an hatchett on the head, and the other runne thorough in severall places with a sword and smitten with an hatchett. Att the same instance my nose begun'd to bleed, which made me afraid of my life; but with drawing myselfe to the watter side to see if any body followed mee, I espied twenty or thirty heads in a long grasse. Mightily surprized att that view, I must needs passe through the midst of them or tourne backe into the woode. I slipped a boulett uppon the shott and beate the paper into my gunne. I heard a noise, which made me looke on that side; hopeing to save meselfe, perswading myselfe I was not yet perceived by them that weare in the medow, and in the meane while some gunns weare lett off with an horrid cry.

Seeing myselfe compassed round about by a multitude of dogges, or rather devils, that rose from the grasse, rushes and bushes, I shott my gunne, whether unawares or purposly I know not, but I shott with a pistolle confidently, but was seised on all sides by a great number that threw me downe, taking away my arme without giving mee

---

21. like: please.

one blowe; for afterwards I felt no paine att all, onely a great guidinesse in my heade, from whence it comes I doe not remember. In the same time they brought me into the wood, where they shewed me the two heads all bloody. After they consulted together for a while, retired into their boats, which weare four or five miles from thence, and wher I have bin a while before. They laid mee hither, houlding me by the hayre, to the imbarking place; there they began to errect their cottages, which consisted only of some sticks to boyle their meate, whereof they had plenty, but [it] stuncke, which was strange to mee to finde such an alteration so sudaine. They made [me] sitt downe by. After this they searched me and tooke what I had, then stripped me naked, and tyed a rope about my middle, wherin I remained, fearing to persist, in the same posture the rest of the night. After this they removed me, laughing and howling like as many wolves, I knowing not the reason, if not for my skin, that was soe white in respect of theirs. But their gaping did soone cease because of a false alarme, that their scout who stayed behind gave them, saying that the French and the wild Algongins, friends to the French, came with all speed. They presently put out the fire, and tooke hould of the most advantageous passages, and sent 25 men to discover what it meant, who brought certaine tydings of assurance and liberty.

In the meanewhile I was garded by 50 men, who gave me a good part of my cloathes. After kindling a fire againe, they gott theire supper ready, which was sudenly don, for they dresse their meat halfe boyled, mingling some yallowish meale in the broath of that infected stinking meate; so whilst this was adoing they combed my head, and with a filthy grease greased my head, and dashed all over my face with redd paintings. So then, when the meat was ready, they feeded me with their hodpot,[22] forcing me to swallow it in a maner. My heart did so faint at this, that in good deede I should have given freely up the ghost to be freed from their clawes, thinking every moment they would end my life. They perceived that my stomach could not beare such victuals. They tooke some of this stinking meate and boyled it in a cleare watter, then mingled a litle Indian meale put to it, which meale before was tossed amongst bourning sand, and then made in powder betwixt two rocks. I, to shew myselfe cheerfull att this, swallowed downe some of this that seemed to me very unsavoury and clammie by reason of the scume that was upon the meat. Having supped, they untyed mee, and made me lye betwixt them, having one end of one side and one of another, and covered me with a red Coverlet, through which I might have counted the starrs. I slept a sound sleep, for they awaked me uppon the breaking of the day. I dreamed that night that I was with the Jesuits at Quebec drinking beere, which gave me hopes to be free sometimes, and also because I heard those people lived among Dutch people in a place called Menada,[23] and fort of Orang,[24] where without doubt I could drinke beere. I, after this, finding meselfe somewhat altered, and my body more like a devil then anything else, after being so smeared and burst with their filthy meate that I could not digest, but must suffer all patiently.

Finally they seemed to me kinder and kinder, giving me of the best bitts where lesse wormes weare. Then they layd [me] to the watter side, where there weare 7 and 30

22. hodpot: hodgepodge.
23. Menada: Manhattan.

24. fort of Orang: Albany.

boats, for each of them imbark'd himselfe. They tyed me to the barre in a boat, where they tooke at the same instance the heads of those that weare killed the day before, and for to preserve them they cutt off the flesh to the skull and left nothing but skin and haire, putting of it into a litle panne wherein they melt some grease, and gott it dry with hot stones. They spread themselves from off the side of the river a good way, and gathered together againe and made a fearfull noise and shott some gunns off, after which followed a kind of an incondit singing after notes, which was an oudiousom noise. As they weare departing from thence they injoyned silence, and one of the Company, wherein I was, made three shouts, which was answered by the like maner from the whole flocke; which done they tooke their way, singing and leaping, and so past the day in such like. They offered mee meate; but such victuals I reguarded it litle, but could drinke for thirst. My sperit was troubled with infinite deale of thoughts, but all to no purpose for the ease of my sicknesse; sometimes despairing, now againe in some hopes. I allwayes indeavoured to comfort myselfe, though half dead. My resolution was so mastered with feare, that at every stroake of the oares of these inhumans I thought it to be my end.

By sunsett we arrived att the Isles of Richelieu, a place rather for victors than for captives most pleasant. There is to be seen 300 wild Cowes together, a number of Elks and Beavers, an infinit of fowls. There we must make cottages, and for this purpose they imploy all together their wits and art, for 15 of these Islands are drowned in Spring, when the floods begin to rise from the melting of the snow, and that by reason of the lowness of the land. Here they found a place fitt enough for 250 men that their army consisted [of]. They landed mee & shewed mee great kindnesse, saying Chagon, which is as much [as] to say, as I understood afterwards, be cheerfull or merry; but for my part I was both deafe and dumb. Their behaviour made me neverthelesse cheerfull, or att least of a smiling countenance, and constraine my aversion and feare to an assurance, which proved not ill to my thinking; for the young men tooke delight in combing my head, greasing and powdering out a kinde of redd powder, then tying my haire with a redd string of leather like to a coard, which caused my haire to grow longer in a short time.

The day following they prepared themselves to passe the adjacent places and shoote to gett victualls, where we stayed 3 dayes, making great cheere and fires. I more and more getting familiarity with them, that I had the liberty to goe from cottage, having one or two by mee. They untyed mee, and tooke delight to make me speake words of their language, and weare earnest that I should pronounce as they. They tooke care to give me meate as often as I would; they gave me salt that served me all my voyage. They also tooke the paines to put it up safe for mee, not takeing any of it for themselves. There was nothing else but feasting and singing during our abode. I tooke notice that our men decreased, for every night one other boate tooke his way, which persuaded mee that they went to the warrs to gett more booty.

The fourth day, early in the morning, my Brother, viz., he that tooke me, so he called me, embarked me without tying me. He gave me an oare, which I tooke with a good will, and rowed till I sweate againe. They, perceiving, made me give over; not content with that I made a signe of my willingnesse to continue that worke. They consent to my desire, but shewed me how I should row without putting myselfe into a sweat. Our company being considerable hitherto, was now reduced to three score. Mid-day wee came to the River of Richlieu, where we weare not farre gone, but mett a new gang of their people in cottages; they began to hoop and hollow as the first day of my taking. They made me stand upright in the boat, as they themselves, saluting one another with all kindnesse and joy. In this new company there was one that had a minde to doe me mischiefe, but was prevented by him that tooke me. I taking notice of the fellow, I shewed him more friendshipe. I gott some meate roasted for him, and throwing a litle salt and flower over it, which he finding very good tast, gave it to the rest as a rarity, nor did afterwards molest mee.

They tooke a fancy to teach mee to sing; and as I had allready a beginning of their hooping, it was an easy thing for me to learne, our Algonquins making the same noise. They tooke an exceeding delight to heare mee. Often have I sunged in French, to which they gave eares with a deepe silence. We passed that day and night following with litle rest by reason of their joy and mirth. They lead a dance, and tyed my comrades both their heads att the end of a stick and hopt it; this done, every one packt and embarked himselfe, some going one way, some another. Being separated, one of the boats that we mett before comes backe againe and approaches the boat wherein I was; I wondered, a woman of the said company taking hould on my haire, signifying great kindnesse. Shee combs my head with her fingers and tyed my wrist with a bracelett, and sunged. My wish was that shee would proceed in our way. After both companys made a shout wee separated. I was sorry for this woman's departure, for having shewed me such favour att her first aspect, doubtlesse but shee might, if neede required, saved my life.

Our journey was indifferent good, without any delay, which caused us to arrive in a good and pleasant harbour. It was on the side of the sand where our people had any paine scarce to errect their cottages, being that it was a place they had sejourned before. The place round about [was] full of trees. Here they kindled a fire and provided what was necessary for their food. In this place they cutt off my hair in the front and upon the crowne of the head, and turning up the locks of the haire they dab'd mee with some thicke grease. So done, they brought me a looking-glasse. I viewing myselfe all in a pickle, smir'd with redde and black, covered with such a cappe, and locks tyed up with a peece of leather and stunked horridly, I could not but fall in love with myselfe, if not that I had better instructions to shun the sin of pride. So after repasting themselves, they made them ready for the journey with takeing repose that night. This was the time I thought to have escaped, for in vaine, for I being alone feared least I should be apprehended and dealt with more violently. And more-over I was desirous to have seene their country.

Att the sun rising I awaked my brother, telling him by signes it was time to goe. He called the rest, but non would stirre, which made him lye downe againe. I rose and went to the water side, where I walked awhile. If there weare another we might, I dare say, escape out of their sight. Heere I recreated myselfe running a naked swoord into the sand. One of them seeing mee after such an exercise calls mee and shews me his way, which made me more confidence in them. They brought mee a dish full of meate to the water side. I began to eat like a beare.

In the mean time they imbark'd themselves, one of them tooke notice that I had not a knife, brings me his, which I kept the rest of the voyage, without that they had the least feare of me. Being ready to goe, saving my boat that was ammending,[25] which was soone done. The other boats weare not as yett out of sight, and in the way my boat killed a stagg. They made me shoot att it, and not quite dead they runed it thorough with their swoords, and having cutt it in peeces, they devided it, and proceeded on their way. At 3 of the clock in the afternoone we came into a rappid streame, where we weare forced to land and carry our Equipages and boats thorough a dangerous place. Wee had not any encounter that day. Att night where we found cottages ready made, there I cutt wood as the rest with all dilligence. The morning early following we marched without making great noise, or singing as accustomed. Sejourning awhile, we came to a lake 6 leagues wide, about it a very pleasant country imbellished with great forests. That day our wild people killed 2 Bears, one monstrous like for its biggnesse, the other a small one. Wee arrived to a fine sandy bancke, where not long before many Cabbanes weare errected and places made where Prisoners weare tyed.

In this place our wild people sweated after the maner following: first heated stones till they weare redd as fire, then they made a lantherne with small sticks, then stoaring the place with deale[26] trees, saving a place in the middle whereinto they put the stoanes, and covered the place with severall covers, then striped themselves naked, went into it. They made a noise as if the devil weare there; after they being there for an hour they came out of the watter, and then throwing one another into the watter, I thought veryly they weare insensed. It is their usual Custome. Being comed out of this place, they feasted themselves with the two bears turning the outside of the tripes inward not washed. They gave every one his share; as for my part I found them [neither] good, nor savory to the pallet. In the night they heard some shooting, which made them embark themselves speedily. In the mean while they made me lay downe whilst they rowed very hard. I slept securely till the morning, where I found meselfe in great high rushes. There they stayed without noise.

From thence wee proceeded, though not without some feare of an Algonquin army. We went on for some dayes [at] that lake. Att last they endeavoured to retire to the woods, every one carrying his bundle. After a daye's march we came to a litle river where we lay'd that night. The day following we proceeded on our journey, where we mett 2 men, with whome our wild men seemed to be acquainted by some signes. These 2 men began to speake a longe while. After came a company of women, 20 in number, that brought us dry fish and Indian corne. These women loaded themselves, after that we had eaten, like mules with our baggage. We went through a small wood, the way well beaten, until the evening we touched a place for fishing, of 15 Cabbans. There they weare well received but myselfe, who was stroaken by a yong man. He, my keeper, made a signe I should [come] to him againe. I tourning to him instantly, he to me, taking hould of my haire, all the wild men came about us, encouraging with their Cryes and hands, which encouraged me most that none helpt him more than mee.

---

25. i.e., except my boat, which needed repairs.   26. deale: pine.

Wee clawed one another with hands, tooth, and nailes. My adversary being offended I have gotten the best, he kick't me; but my french shoes that they left mee weare harder than his, which made him [give up] that game againe. He tooke me about the wrist, where he found himselfe downe before he was awarre, houlding him upon the ground till some came and putt us asunder. My company seeing mee free, began to cry out, giving me watter to wash me, and then fresh fish to relish me. They encouraged me so much, the one combing my head, the other greasing my haire. There we stayed 2 dayes, where no body durst trouble me.

In the same Cabban that I was, there has bin a wild man wounded with a small shott. I thought I have seen him the day of my taking, which made me feare least I was the one that wounded him. He knowing it to be so had shewed me as much charity as a Christian might have given. Another of his fellowes ([whom] I also wounded) came to me att my first coming there, whom I thought to have come for reveng, contrarywise [he] shewed me a cheerfull countenance; he gave mee a box full of red paintings, calling me his brother. I had not as yett caryed any burden, but meeting with an ould man, gave me a sacke of tobacco of 12 pounds' weight, bearing it uppon my head, as it's their usuall custome. We made severall stayes that day by reason of the severall encounters of their people that came from villages, as warrs, others from fishing and shooting. In that journey our company increased, among others a great many Hurrons that had bin lately taken, and who for the most part are as slaves. We lay'd in the wood because they would not goe into their village in the night time.

The next day we marched into a village where as wee came in sight we heard nothing but outcryes, as from one side as from the other, being a quarter of a mile from the village. They satt downe and I in the midle, where I saw women and men and children with staves and in array, which put me in feare, and instantly stripped me naked. My keeper gave me a signe to be gone as fast as I could drive. In the meane while many of the village came about us, among which a good old woman, and a boy with a hatchet in his hand came near mee. The old woman covered me, and the young man tooke me by the hand and lead me out of the company. The old woman made me step aside from those that weare ready to stricke att mee. There I left the 2 heads of my comrades, and that which comforted me that I escaped the blowes. Then they brought me into their Cottage; there the old woman shewed me kindnesse. Shee gave me to eate. The great terror I had a little before tooke my stomack away from me. I stayed an hour, where a great company of people came to see mee. Heere came a company of old men, having pipes in their mouthes, satt about me.

After smoaking, they lead me into another cabban, where there weare a company all smoaking; they made [me] sitt downe by the fire, which made [me] apprehend they should cast me into the said fire. But it proved otherwise; for the old woman followed mee, speaking aloud, whom they answered with a loud ho, then shee tooke her girdle and about mee shee tyed it, so brought me to her cottage, and made me sitt downe in the same place I was before. Then shee began to dance and sing a while, after [she] brings downe from her box a combe, gives it to a maide that was neare mee, who presently comes to greas and combe my haire, and tooke away the paint that the fellows stuck to my face. Now the old woman getts me some Indian Corne toasted in the fire. I tooke paines to gether it out of the fire; after this shee gave me a blew cover-lett, stokins and shoos, and where with to make me drawers. She looked in my cloathes, and if shee found any lice shee would squeeze them betwixt her teeth, as if they had ben substantiall meate. I lay'd with her son, who tooke me from those of my first takers, and gott at last a great acquaintance with many. I did what I could to gett familiarity with them, yet I suffered no wrong att their hands, taking all freedom, which the old woman inticed me to doe. But still they altered my face where ever I went, and a new dish to satisfy nature.

I tooke all the pleasures imaginable, having a small peece at my command, shooting patriges and squerells, playing most part of the day with my companions. The old woman wished that I would make meselfe more familiar with her 2 daughters, which weare tolerable among such people. They weare accustomed to grease and combe my haire in the morning. I went with them into the wilderness, there they would be gabling which I could not understand. They wanted no company but I was shure to be of the number. I brought all ways some guifts that I received, which I gave to my purse-keeper and refuge, the good old woman. I lived 5 weeks without thinking from whence I came. I learned more of their maners in 6 weeks then if I had bin in france 6 months. Att the end I was troubled in minde, which made her inquire if I was Anjonack, a Huron word. Att this I made as if I weare suported for speaking in a strang language, which shee liked well, calling me by the name of her son who before was killed, Orimha, which signifies ledd or stone, without difference of the words. So that it was my Lordshippe. Shee inquired [of] mee whether I was Asserony, a french. I answering no, saying I was Panugaga, that is, of their nation, for which shee was pleased.

My father feasted 300 men that day. My sisters made me clean for that purpos, and greased my haire. My mother decked me with a new cover and a redd and blew cappe, with 2 necklace of porcelaine. My sisters tyed me with braceletts and garters of the same porcelaine. My brother painted my face, and [put] feathers on my head, and tyed both my locks with porcelaine. My father was liberall to me, giving me a garland instead of my blew cap and a necklace of porcelaine that hung downe to my heels, and a hattchet in my hand. It was hard for me to defend myselfe against any encounter, being so laden with riches. Then my father made a speech shewing many demonstrations of vallor, broak a kettle full of Cagamite[27] with a hattchett. So they sung, as is their usual coustom. They weare waited on by a sort of yong men, bringing downe dishes of meate of Oriniacke,[28] of Castors,[29] and of red deer mingled with some flowers. The order of makeing was thus: the corne being dried between 2 stones into powder, being very thick, putt it into a kettle full of watter, then a quantity of Bear's grease. This banquett being over, they cryed to me Shagon, Orimha, that is, be hearty, stone or ledd. Every one withdrew into his quarters, and so did I.

But to the purpose of my history. As I went to the fields once, where I mett with 3 of my acquaintance, who had a designe for to hunt a great way off, they desired me to goe along. I lett them know in Huron language (for that I knew better then that of the Iroquoits) I was content, desiring them to stay till I acquainted my mother. One of

27. Cagamite: corn mush boiled with meat.
28. Oriniacke: moose.
29. Castors: beaver.

them came along with mee, and gott leave for me of my kindred. My mother gott me presently a sack of meale, 3 paire of shoos, my gun, and tourned backe where the 2 stayed for us. My 2 sisters accompanied me even out of the wildernesse and carried my bundle, where they tooke leave.

We marched on that day through the woods till we came by a lake where we travelled without any rest. I wished I had stayed att home, for we had sad victualls. The next day about noone we came to a River; there we made a skiffe, so litle that we could scarce go into it. I admired their skill in doing of it, for in lesse then 2 hours they cutt the tree and pulled up the Rind, of which they made the boat. We embarked ourselves and went to the lower end of the river, which emptied it selfe into a litle lake of about 2 miles in length and a mile in breadth. We passed this lake into another river broader then the other; there we found a fresh track of a stagge, which made us stay heere a while. It was five of the clock att least when 2 of our men made themselves ready to looke after that beast; the other and I stayed behind. Not long after we saw the stagge crosse the river, which foarding brought him to his ending. So done, they went on their cours, and came backe againe att 10 of the clocke with 3 bears, a castor, and the stagge which was slaine att our sight. How did wee rejoice to see that killed which would make the kettle boyle. After we have eaten, wee slept.

The next day we made trappes for to trapp castors, whilst we weare bussie, one about one thing, one about another. As 3 of us retourned homewards to our cottage we heard a wild man singing. He made us looke to our selves least he should prove an ennemy, but as we have seene him, called to him, who came immediately, telling us that he was in pursuite of a Beare since morning, and that he gave him over, having lost his 2 doggs by the same beare. He came with us to our cottage, where we mett our companion after having killed one beare, 2 staggs, and 2 mountain catts, being 5 in number. Whilst the meat was a boyling that wild man spoake to me the Algonquin language. I wondred to heare this stranger; he tould me that he was taken 2 years agoe; he asked me concerning the 3 rivers and of Quebuck, who wished himselfe there, and I said the same, though I did not intend it. He asked me if I loved the french. I inquired him also if he loved the Algonquins? Marry, quoth he, and so doe I my owne nation. Then replyed he, Brother, cheare up, lett us escape, the 3 rivers are not a farre off. I tould him my 3 comrades would not permitt me, and that they promised my mother to bring me back againe. Then he inquired whether I would live like the Hurrons, who were in bondage, or have my owne liberty with the french, where there was good bread to be eaten. Feare not, quoth he, [we] shall kill them all 3 this night when they will bee a sleepe, which will be an easy matter with their owne hatchetts.

Att last I consented, considering they weare mortall ennemys to my country, that had cutt the throats of so many of my relations, burned and murdered them. I promised him to succour him in his designe. They not understanding our language asked the Algonquin what is that that he said, but tould them some other story, nor did they suspect us in the least. Their belly full, their mind without care, wearyed to the utmost of the formost day's journey, [they] fell a sleepe securely, leaning their armes up and downe without the least danger. Then my wild man pushed me, thinking I was a sleepe. He rises and sitts him downe by the fire, beholding them one after an other, and taking their armes a side, and having the hattchetts in his hand gives me one; to tell the truth I was loathsome to do them mischif that never did me any. Yett for the above said reasons I tooke the hattchet and began the Execution, which was soone done. My fellow comes to him that was nearest to the fire (I dare say he never saw the stroake), and I have done the like to an other, but I hitting him with the edge of the hattchett could not disingage [it] presently, being so deep in his head, [he] rises upon his breast, butt fell back sudainly, making a great noise, which almost waked the third; but my comrade gave him a deadly blow of a hattchet, and presently after I shott him dead.

Then we prepared our selves with all speed, throwing their dead corps, after that the wild man took off their heads, into the watter. We tooke 3 guns, leaving the 4th, their 2 swoords, their hattchetts, their powder and shott, and all their porselaine; we tooke also some meale and meate. I was sorry for to have ben in such an incounter, but too late to repent. Wee tooke our journey that night alongst the river. The break of day we landed on the side of a rock which was smooth. We carryed our boat and equippage into the wood above a hundred paces from the watter side, where we stayed most sadly all that day tormented by the Maringoines;[30] we tourned our boat upside downe, we putt us under it from the raine. The night coming, which was the fitest time to leave that place, we goe without any noise for our safty. Wee travelled 14 nights in that maner in great feare, hearing boats passing by. When we have perceaved any fire, left off rowing, and went by with as litle noise as possible. Att last with many tournings by lande and by watter, wee came to the lake of St. Peeter's.

We landed about 4 of the clock, leaving our skiff in among rushes farr out of the way from those that passed that way and doe us injury. We retired into the wood, where we made a fire some 200 paces from the river. There we roasted some meat and boyled meale; after, we rested ourselves a while from the many labours of the former night.

So, having slept, my companion awaks first, and stirrs me, saying it was high time that we might by day come to our dweling, of which councel I did not approve. [I] tould him the Ennemys commonly weare lurking about the river side, and we should doe very well [to] stay in that place till sunnsett. Then, said he, lett us begon, we [are] passed all feare. Let us shake off the yoake of a company of whelps that killed so many french and black-coats, and so many of my nation. Nay, saith he, Brother, if you come not, I will leave you, and will go through the woods till I shall be over against the french quarters. There I will make a fire for a signe that they may fetch me. I will tell to the Governor that you stayed behind. Take courage, man, says he. With this he tooke his peece and things. Att this I considered how if [I] weare taken att the doore by meere rashnesse; the next, the impossibility I saw to go by myselfe if my comrad would leave me, and perhaps the wind might rise, that I could [only] come to the end of my journey in a long time, and that I should be accounted a coward for not daring to hazard myselfe with him that so much ventured for mee. I resolved to go along through the woods; but the litle constancy that is to be expected in wild men made me feare he should [take] to his heels, which approved his unfortunate advice; for he hath

30. Maringoines: mosquitoes.

lost his life by it, and I in great danger have escaped by the helpe of the Almight. I consent to goe by watter with him.

In a short time wee came to the lake. The watter very calme and cleare. No likly-hood of any storme. We hazarded to the other side of the lake, thinking for more security. After we passed the third part of the lake, I being the foremost, have perceaved as if it weare a black shaddow, which proved a real thing. He at this rises and tells mee that it was a company of buzards, a kinde of geese in that country. We went on, where wee soone perceaved our owne fatall blindnesse, for they weare ennemys. We went back againe towards the lande with all speed to escape the evident danger, but it was too late; for before we could come to the russhes that weare within halfe a league of the waterside we weare tired. Seeing them approaching nigher and nigher, we threw the 3 heads in the watter. They meet with these 3 heads, which makes them to row harder after us, thinking that we had runn away from their country. We weare so neere the lande that we saw the bottom of the watter, but yett too deepe to step in. When those cruel inhumans came within a musquett shott of us, and fearing least the booty should gett a way from them, shott severall times att us, and deadly wounding my comrade, [who] fell dead. I expected such another shott. The litle skiff was pierced in severall places with their shooting, [so] that watter ran in a pace. I defended me selfe with the 2 arms. Att last they environed me with their boats, that tooke me just as I was a sinking. They held up the wild man and threw him into one of their boats and me they brought with all diligence to land. I thought to die without mercy.

They made a great fire and tooke my comrade's heart out, and choped off his head, which they put on an end of a stick and carryed it to one of their boats. They cutt off some of the flesh of that miserable, broyled it and ate it. If he had not ben so desper-ately wounded they had don their best to keepe him alive to make him suffer the more by bourning him with small fires; but being wounded in the chin, and [a] bullet gon through the troat, and another in the shoulder that broake his arme, making him incurable, they burned some parte of his body, and the rest they left there. That was the miserable end of that wretch.

Lett us come now to the beginning of my miseries and calamities that I was to undergo. Whilst they weare bussie about my companion's head, the others tyed me safe and fast in a strang maner; having striped me naked, they tyed me above the elbows behind my back, and then they putt a collar about me, not of porcelaine as before, but a rope wrought about my midle. So [they] brought me in that pickle to the boat. As I was imbarqued they asked mee severall questions. I being not able to answer, gave me great blowes with their fists. [They] then pulled out one of my nailes, and partly untied me.

What displeasure had I, to have seen meselfe taken againe, being almost come to my journey's end, that I must now goe back againe to suffer such torments, as death was to be expected. Having lost all hopes, I resolved alltogether to die, being a folly to think otherwise. I was not the [only] one in the clawes of those wolves. Their company was composed of 150 men. These tooke about Quebucq and other places 2 frenchmen, one french woman, 17 Hurrons, men as [well as] women. They had

Eleven heads which they sayd weare of the Algonquins, and I was the 33rd victim with those cruels.

The wild men that weare Prisners sang their fatal song, which was a mornfull song or noise. The 12 coulours (which weare heads) stood out for a show. We prisoners weare separated, one in one boat, one in an other. As for me, I was put into a boat with a Huron whose fingers weare cutt and bourned, and very [few] amongst them but had the markes of those inhuman devils. They did not permitt me to tarry long with my fellow prisoner, least I should tell him any news, as I imagine, but sent me to another boat, where I remained the rest of the voyage by watter, which proved some-what to my disadvantage.

In this boat there was an old man, who having examined me, I answered him as I could best; tould him how I was adopted by such an one by name, and as I was hunting with my companions that wildman that was killed came to us, and after he had eaten went his way. In the evening [he] came back againe and found us all a sleepe, tooke a hattchett and killed my 3 companions, and awaked me, and so embarked me and brought me to this place. That old man believed me in some measure, which I perceived in him by his kindnesse towards me. But he was not able to protect me from those that [had] a will to doe me mischief. Many slandred me, but I tooke no notice.

Some 4 leagues thence they erected cottages by a small river, very difficult to gett to it, for that there is litle watter on a great sand a league wide. To this very houre I tooke notice how they tyed their captives, though att my owne cost. They planted severall poastes of the bignesse of an arme, then layd us of a length, tyed us to the said poasts far a sunder from one another. Then tyed our knees, our wrists, and elbows, and our hairs directly upon the crowne of our heads, and then cutt 4 barrs of the bignesse of a legge & used thus. They tooke 2 for the necke, puting one of each side, tying the 2 ends together, so that our heads weare fast in a hole like a trappe; like-wayes they did to our leggs. And what tormented us most was the Maringoines and great flyes being in abundance; [we] did all night but puff and blow, that by that means we saved our faces from the sting of those ugly creatures; having no use of our hands, we are cruelly tormented. Our voyage was laborious and most miserable, suffering every night the like misery.

When we came neere our dwellings we mett severall gangs of men to our greatest disadvantage, for we weare forced to sing, and those that came to see us gave porce-laine to those that most did us injury. One cutt off a finger, and another pluck'd out a naile, and putt the end of our fingers into their bourning pipes, & burned severall parts in our bodyes. Some tooke our fingers and of a stick made a thing like a fork, with which [they] gave severall blowes on the back of the hands, which caused our hands to swell, and became att last insensible as dead. Having souffred all these cruel-tyes, which weare nothing to that they make usually souffer their Prisoners, we arrived att last to the place of execution, which is att the coming in to their village, which wheere not [long] before I escaped very neere to be soundly beaten with staves and fists. Now I must think to be no lesse traited by reason of the murder of the 3 men, but the feare of death takes away the feare of blowes.

Nineteen of us prisoners weare brought thither, and 2 left behind with the heads. In this place we had 8 coulours. Who would not shake att the sight of so many men, women, and children armed with all sorte of instruments: staves, hand Irons, heelskins wherein they putt halfe a score bullets? Others had brands, rods of thorne, and all suchlike that their Crueltie could invent to putt their Prisoners to greater torments. Heere, no help, no remedy. We must passe this dangerous passage in our extremity without helpe. He that is the fearfullest, or that is observed to stay the last, getts nothing by it butt more blowes, and putt him to more paine. For the meanest sort of people commonly is more cruell to the fearfullest then to the others that they see more fearfull, being att last to suffer chearfuly and with constancy.

They begun to cry to both sides, we marching one after another, environed with a number of people from all parts to be witnesse to that hidious sight, which seriously may be called the Image of hell in this world. The men sing their fatall song, the women make horrible cryes, the victores cryes of joy, and their wives make acclamations of mirth. In a word, all prepare for the ruine of these poore victimes who are so tyed, having nothing saving only our leggs free, for to advance by litle and litle according [to] the will of him that leades; for as he held us by a long rope, he stayed us to his will, & often he makes us falle, for to shew them cruelty, abusing you so for to give them pleasure and to you more torment.

As our band was great, there was a greater crew of people to see the prisoners, and the report of my taking being now made, and of the death of the 3 men, which afflicted the most part of that nation, great many of which came through a designe of revenge and to molest me more then any other. But it was alltogether otherwise, for among the tumult I perceaved my father & mother with their 2 daughters. The mother pushes in among the Crew directly to mee, and when shee was neere enough, shee clutches hould of my haire as one desperat, calling me often by my name; drawing me out of my ranck, shee putts me into the hands of her husband, who then bid me have courage, conducting me an other way home to his Cabban, when he made me sitt downe. [He] said to me: You senselesse, thou was my son, and thou rendered thyselfe enemy, and thou rendered thyself enemy, thou lovest not thy mother, nor thy father that gave thee thy life, and thou notwithstanding will kill me. Bee merry; Conharrassan, give him to eate. That was the name of one of the sisters. My heart shook with trembling and feare, which tooke away my stomach. Neverthelesse to signifie a bould countenance, knowing well a bould generous minde is allwayes accounted among all sort of nations, especially among wariors, as that nation is very presumptious and haughty. Because of their magnanimity and victories opposing themselves into all dangers and incounters what ever, running over the whole land for to make themselves appeere slaining and killing all they meete in exercising their cruelties, or else shewing mercy to whom they please to give liberty. God gave mee the grace to forgett nothing of my duty, as I tould my father the successe of my voyage in the best tearme I could, and how all things passed, mixturing a litle of their languag with that of the Hurrons, which I learned more fluently than theirs, being longer and more frequently with the Hurrons.

Every one attentively gave ears to me, hoping by this means to save my life. Uppon this heere comes a great number of armed men, enters the Cabban, where finding mee yett tyed with my cords, sitting by my parents, made their addresses to my father, and spak to him very loud. After a while my father made me rise and delivers me into their hands. My mother seeing this, cryes and laments with both my sisters, and I believing in a terrible motion to goe directly on to the place of execution. I must march, I must yeeld wheere force is predominant att the publique place.

I was conducted where I found a good company of those miserable wretches, alltogether beaten with blowes, covered with blood, and bourned. One miserable frenchman, yett breathing, having now ben consumed with blowes of sticks, past so through the hands of this inraged crew, and seeing he could [bear] no more, [they] cutt off his head and threw it into the fire. This was the end of this Execrable wofull body of this miserable.

They made me goe up the scaffold where weare 5 men, 3 women, and 2 children captives, and I made the Eleventh. There weare severall scaffolds nigh one an other, where weare these wretches, who with dolefull singings replenished the heavens with their Cryes. For I can say that an houre before the weather approved very faire, and in an instant the weather changed and rayned Extremely. The most part retired for to avoid this hayle, and now we must expect the full rigour of the weather by the retiration of those perfidious [persons], except one part of the Band of hell who stayed about us for to learn the trade of barbary; for those litle devils seeing themselves all alone, continued [a] thousand inventions of wickednesse. This is nothing strang, seeing that they are brought up, and suck the crueltie from their mother's brest.

I prolong a litle from my purpose of my adventure for to say the torments that I have seen suffred att Coutu, after that they have passed the sallett, att their entering in to the village, and the recounters that they meet ordinarily in the wayes, as above said. They tie the prisoners to a poast by their hands, their backs tourned towards the hangman, who hath a bourning fire of dry wood and rind of trees, which doth not quench easily. They putt into this fire hattchets, swords, and such like instruments of Iron. They take these and quench them on human flesh. They pluck out their nailes for the most part in this sort. They putt a redd coale of fire uppon it, and when it is swolen bite it out with their teeth. After they stop the blood with a brand which by litle and litle drawes the veines the one after another from off the fingers, and when they draw all as much as they can, they cutt it with peeces of redd hott Iron; they squeeze the fingers between 2 stones, and so draw the marrow out of the boanes, and when the flesh is all taken away, they putt it in a dishfull of bourning sand. After they tye your wrist with a corde, putting two for this effect, one drawing him one way, another of another way. If the sinews be not cutt with a stick, putting it through & tourning it, they make them come as fast as they can, and cutt them in the same way as the others. Some others cutt peeces of flesh from all parts of the body & broyle them, gett you to eat it, thrusting them into your mouth, puting into it a stick of fire. They breake your teeth with a stoane or clubbs, and use the handle of a kettle, and upon this do hang 5 or 6 hattchetts, red hott, which they hang about their neck and roast your leggs with brands of fire, and thrusting into it some sticks pointed, wherein they put ledd melted and gunnepowder, and then give it fire like unto artificiall fire,[31]

31. artificial fire: a forge.

and make the patient gather it by the stumps of his remaining fingers. If he cannot sing they make him quack like a henne.

I saw two men tyed to a rope, one att each end, and hang them so all night, throwing red coales att them, or bourning sand, and in such like bourne their feet, leggs, thighs, and breech. The litle ones doe exercise themselves about such cruelties; they deck the bodyes all over with hard straw, putting in the end of this straw, thornes, so leaves them; now & then gives them a litle rest, and sometimes gives them fresh watter and make them repose on fresh leaves. They also give them to eat of the best they have that they come to themselves againe, to give them more torments. Then when they see that the patient can no more take up his haire, they cover his head with a platter made of rind[32] full of bourning sand, and often getts the platter a fire. In the next place they cloath you with a suit made of rind of a tree, and this they make bourne out on your body. They cutt off your stones[33] and the women play with them as with balles. When they see the miserable die, they open him and pluck out his heart; they drink some of his blood, and wash the children's heads with the rest to make them valient. If you have indured all the above said torments patiently and without moanes, and have defied death in singing, then they thrust burning blades all along your boanes, and so ending the tragedie cutt off the head and putt it on the end of a stick and draw his body in quarters which they hawle about their village. Lastly [they] throw him into the watter or leave [him] in the fields to be eaten by the Crowes or doggs.

Now lett me come to our miserable poore captives that stayed all along [in] the raine upon the scaffold to the mercy of 2 or 300 rogues that shott us with litle arrowes, and so drew out our beards and the haire from those that had any. The showre of rayne being over, all come together againe, and having kindled fires began to burne some of those poore wretches. That day they plucked 4 nailes out of my fingers, and made me sing, though I had no mind att that time. I became speechlesse oftentimes; then they gave me watter wherin they boyled a certain herbe that the gunsmiths use to pollish their armes. That liquor brought me to my speech againe. The night being come they made me come downe all naked as I was, & brought [me] to a strang Cottage. I wished heartily it had ben that of my parents. Being come, they tyed me to a poast, where I stayed a full houre without the least molestation.

A woman came there with her boy, inticed him to cutt off one of my fingers with a flint stoan. The boy was not 4 years old. This [boy] takes my finger and begins to worke, but in vaine, because he had not the strength to breake my fingers. So my poore finger escaped, having no other hurt done to it but the flesh cutt round about it. His mother made him suck the very blood that runn from my finger. I had no other torment all that day. Att night I could not sleep for because of the great paine. I did eat a litle, and drunk much watter by reason of a feaver I caught by the cruel torment I suffred.

The next morning I was brought back againe to the scaffold, where there were company enough. They made me sing a new, but my mother came there and made [me] hold my peace, bidding me be cheerfull and that I should not die. Shee brought mee some meate. Her coming comforted me much, but that did not last long; for heare comes severall old people, one of which being on the scaffold, satt him downe

32. rind: bark.   33. stones: testicles.

by me, houlding in his mouth a pewter pipe burning, tooke my thumb and putt it on the burning tobacco, and so smoaked 3 pipes one after another, which made my thumb swell, and the nayle and flesh became as coales. My mother was allwayes by me to comfort me, but said not what I thought. That man having finished his hard worke, but I am sure I felt it harder to suffer it. He trembled, whether for feare or for so much action I cannot tell. My mother tyed my fingers with cloath, and when he was gone shee greased my haire and combed my haire with a wooden comb, fitter to combe a horse's tayle than anything else. Shee goes back againe.

That day they ended many of those poore wretches, slinging some all alive into the midle of a great fire. They burned a frenchwoman; they pulled out her breasts and tooke a child out of her belly, which they broyled and made the mother eat of it; so, in short, [she] died. I was not abused all that day till the night. They bourned the soales of my feet and leggs. A souldier run through my foot a swoord red out of the fire, and plucked severall of my nailes. I stayed in that maner all night. I neither wanted in the meane while meate nor drinke. I was supplied by my mother and sisters. My father alsoe came to see me & tould me I should have courage. That very time there came a litle boy to gnaw with his teeth the end of my fingers. There appears a man to cutt off my thumb, and being about it leaves me instantly & did no harme, for which I was glad. I believe that my father dissuaded him from it.

A while after my father was gon 3 came to the scaffold who swore they would do me a mischiefe, as I thinke, for that he tied his leggs to mine, called for a brand of fire, and layd it between his leggs and mine, and sings: but by good lucke it was out on my side, and did no other effect then bourne my skin, but bourned him to some purpos. In this posture I was to follow him, & being not able to hould mee, draweth mee downe. One of the Company Cutt the rope that held us with his knife, and makes mee goe up againe the scaffold and then went their way.

There I stayed till midday alone. There comes a multitude of people who make me come downe and led mee into a cottage where there weare a number of sixty old men smoaking tobacco. Here they make mee sitt downe among them and stayed about halfe an houre without that they asked who and why I was brought thither, nor did I much care. For the great torments that I souffred, I knew not whether I was dead or alive. And albeit I was in a hott feavor & great pain, I rejoyced att the sight of my brother, that I have not seene since my arrivement. He comes in very sumptuously covered with severall necklaces of porcelaine,[34] & a hattchett in his hand, satt downe by the company and cast an eye on me now and then. Presently and comes in my father with a new and long cover, and a new porcelaine about him, with a hatchett in his hands, like-wise satt downe with the company. He had a calumet of red stoane in his hands, a cake[35] upon his shoulders, that hanged downe his back, and so had the rest of the old men. In that same cake are inclosed all the things in the world, as they tould me often, advertising mee that I should [not] disoblige them in the least nor make them angry, by reason they had in their power the sun, and moone, and the heavans, and consequently all the earth. You must know in this cake there is nothing but tobacco and roots to heale some wounds or sores; some others keepe in it the bones of their deceased

34. porcelaine: wampum.   35. cake: medicine-bag.

friends; most of them wolves' heads, squirrels', or any other beast's head. When there they have any debatement among them they sacrifice to this tobacco, that they throw into the fire, and make smoake, of that they puff out of their pipes; whether for peace or adversity or prosperity or warre, such ceremonies they make very often.

My father, taking his place, lights his pipe & smoaks as the rest. They held great silence. During this they bring 7 prisoners; to wit, 7 women and 2 men, more [than] 10 children from the age of 3 to 12 years, having placed them all by mee, who as yett had my armes tyed. The others all att liberty, being not tyed, which putt me into some despaire least I should pay for all. Awhile after one of the company rises and makes a long speech, now shewing the heavens with his hands, and then the earth, and fire. This good man putt himselfe into a sweate through the earnest discours. Having finished his panigerique, another begins, and also many, one after another.

They gave then liberty to some, butt killed 2 children with hattchetts, and a woman of 50 years old, and threw them out of the cottage (saving onely myselfe) att full liberty. I was left alone for a stake, they contested together [upon] which my father rose and made a speech which lasted above an houre, being naked, having nothing on but his drawers and the cover of his head, and putt himselfe all in a heate. His eyes weare hollow in his head; he appeared to me like mad, and naming often the Algonquins in their language which made me believe he spoake in my behalfe. In that very time comes my mother, with two necklaces of porcelaine, one in her armes, and another about her like a belt. As soone as shee came in shee began to sing and dance, and flings off one of her necklaces in the midle of the place, having made many tourns from one end to the other. Shee takes the other necklace and gives it mee, then goes her way. Then my brother rises and holding his hattchett in his hand sings a military song. Having finished [he] departs. I feared much that he was first to knock me in the head; and happy are those that can escape so well, rather then be bourned. My father rises for a second time and sings; so done, retired himselfe. I thought all their guifts, songs, and speeches should prevaile nothing with mee.

Those that stayed held a councell and spoake one to an other very long, throwing tobacco into the fire, making exclamations. Then the Cottage was open of all sides by those that came to view, some of the company retires, and place was made for them as if they weare Kings. Forty staye about me, and nigh 2000 about my cottage, of men, women, and children. Those that went their way retourned presently. Being sett downe, [they] smoaked againe whilest my father, mother, brother, and sisters weare present. My father sings a while; so done, makes a speech, and taking the porcelaine necklace from off me throws it att the feet of an old man, and cutts the cord that held me, then makes me rise. The joy that I receaved att that time was incomparable, for suddenly all my paines and griefs ceased, not feeling the least paine. He bids me be merry, makes me sing, to which I consented with all my heart. Whilst I did sing they hooped and hollowed on all sides. The old man bid me "ever be cheerful, my son!" Having don, my mother, sisters, and the rest of their friends [sung] and danced.

Then my father takes me by the arme and leads me to his cabban. As we went along nothing was heard but hooping and hollowing on all parts, biding me to take great courage. My mother was not long after me, with the rest of her friends. Now I see myselfe free from death. Their care att this was to give me meate. I have not eaten a bitt all that day, and for the great joy I had conceaved, caused me to have a good stomach, so that I did eat lustily. Then my mother begins to cure my sores and wounds. Then begins my paines anew; for shee cleans my wounds and scrapes them with a knife, and often thrusts a stick in them, and then takes watter in her mouth, and spouts it to make them cleane. The meanwhile my father goes to seeke rootes, and my sister chaws them, and my mother applyes them to my sores as a plaster. The next day the swelling was gone, but worse than before; but in lesse than a fortnight my sores weare healed, saving my feete, that kept [me] more than a whole month in my Cabban. During this time my nailes grewed a pace. I remained onely lame of my midle finger, that they have squeezed between two stoanes. Every one was kind to mee as beforesaid, and [I] wanted[36] no company to be merry with.

I should [be] kept too long to tell you the particulars that befell me during my winter. I was beloved of my Parents as before. My exercise was allwayes a hunting without that any gave me the least injury. My mother kept me most brave, and my sisters tooke great care of mee. Every month I had a white shirt, which my father sent for from the Flemings, who weare not a farr off our village. I could never gett leave to goe along with my brother, who went there very often. Finally, seeing myselfe in the former condition as before, I constituted as long as my father and fortune would permitt mee to live there. Dayly there weare military feasts for the South nations, and others for the Algonquins and for the French. The exclamations, hoopings and cryes, songs and dances, signifies nothing but the murdering and killing, and the intended victory that they will have the next yeare, which is in the beginning of Spring. In those feasts my father heaves up his hattchett against the Algonquins. For this effect [he] makes great preparations for his next incamping. Every night [he] never failes to instruct and encourage the young age to take armes and to reveng the death of so many of their ennemy that lived among the french nation. The desire that I had to make me beloved, for the assurance of my life made me resolve to offer myselfe for to serve, and to take party with them. But I feared much least he should mistrust me touching his advis to my resolution. Neverthelesse I finding him once of a good humour and on the point of honnour encourages his son to break the kettle and take the hattchett and to be gon to the forraigne nations, and that was of courage and of great renowne to see the father of one parte and the son of another part, & that he should not mispraise if he should seperat from him, but that it was the quickest way to make the world tremble, & by that means have liberty everywhere by vanquishing the mortall enemy of his nation; upon this I venture to aske him what I was. [He] presently answers that I was a Iroquoite as himselfe. Lett me revenge, said I, my kindred. I love my brother. Lett me die with him. I would die with you, but you will not because you goe against the French. Lett me a gaine goe with my brother, the prisoners & the heads that I shall bring, to the joy of my mother and sisters, will make me undertake att my retourne to take up the hattchett against those of Quebecq, of the 3 rivers, and Monteroyall in declaring them my name, and that it's I that kills them, and by that you shall know I am your son, worthy to beare that title that you gave me when you adopted me. He sett [up] a great crye, saying, have great courage, son

36. wanted: lacked.

Orimha, thy brother died in the warrs not in the Cabban; he was of a courage not of a woman. I goe to aveng his death. If I die, aveng you mine. That one word was my leave, which made me hope that one day I might escape, having soe great an opportunity; or att least I should have the happinesse to see their country, which I heard so much recommended by the Iroquoites, who brought wondrous stories and the facilitie of killing so many men.

Thus the winter was past in thoughts and preparing for to depart before the melting of the snow, which is very soone in that Country. I began to sett my witts together how I should resolve this my voyage; for my mother opposed against it mightily, saying I should bee lost in the woods, and that I should gett it [put] off till the next yeare. But at last I flattered with her and dissembled; besides, my father had the power in his hands. Shee daring not to deny him any thing because shee was not borne in my father's country, but was taken [when] little in the Huronit's Country. Notwithstanding [she was] well beloved of her husband, having lived together more then fourty years, and in that space brought him 9 children, 4 males and 5 females. Two girls died after a while, and 3 sons killed in the warrs, and one that went 3 years before with a band of 13 men to warre against a fiery nation which is farre beyonde the great lake. The 5th had allready performed 2 voyages with a greate deale of successe. My father was a great Captayne in warrs, having ben Commander in all his times, and distructed many villages of their Ennemy, having killed 19 men with his owne hands, whereof he was marked [on] his right thigh for as many [as] he killed. He should have as many more, but that you must know that the Commander has not amused himselfe to kille, but in the front of his army to encourage his men. If by chance he tooke any prisoners, he calles one of his men and gives him the captives, saying that it's honour enough to command the conquerors, and by his example shews to the yong men that he has the power as much as the honour. He receaved 2 gunn shots and 7 arrows shotts, and was runne through the shoulders with a lance. He was aged 3 score years old, he was talle, and of an excellent witt for a wild man.

[RADISSON RETURNS TO THE INDIAN VILLAGE AFTER THE WAR]

This voyage being ended, albeit I came to this village, twice with feare & terror, the 3d time notwithstanding with joy & contentment. As we came neare the village, a multitude of people came to meete us with great exclamations, and for the most part for my sake, biding me to be cheerfull & qualifying me dodcon, that is, devil, being of great veneration in that country to those that shew any vallour. Being arrived within halfe a league of the village, I shewed a great modesty, as usually warriors use to doe. The whole village prepares to give the scourge to the captives, as you heard before, under which I myselfe was once to undergoe. My mother comes to meet mee, leaping & singing. I was accompanied with both my sisters. Shee takes the woman slave that I had, and would not that any should medle with her. But my brother's prisoner, as the rest of the captives, weare soundly beaten. My mother accepted of my brother's 2 heads. My brother's prisoner was burned the same day, and the day following I received the salary of my booty, which was of porcelaine necklaces, Tourns of beads, pendants, and girdles.

There was but banqueting for a while. The greatest part of both young men & women came to see me, & the women the choicest of meats, and a most dainty and cordiall bit which I goe to tell you; doe not long for it, is the best that is among them. First when the corne is greene they gather so much as need requireth, of which leaves they preserve the biggest leaves for the subject that followes. A dozen more or lesse old women meet together alike, of whome the greatest part want teeth, and seeth not a jott, and their cheeks hange downe like an old hunting-dogg, their eyes full of watter and bloodshott. Each takes an eare of corne and putts in their mouths, which is properly as milke, chawes it, and when their mouths are full, spitts it out in their hands, which possibly they wash not once one yeare; so that their hands are white inside by reason of the grease that they putt to their haire & rubbing of it with the inside of their hands, which keeps them pretty clean, but the outside in the rinknesse of their rinkled hands there is a quarter of an ounze of filth and stinking grease.

And so their hands being full of that mince meate minced with their gumms and [enough] to fill a dish. So they chaw chesnutts; then they mingle this with bear's grease or oyle of flour (in french we call it Tourne Sol) with their hands. So made a mixture, they tye the leaves att one end & make a hodgepot & cover it with the same leaves and tye the upper end so that what is within these leaves becomes a round ball, which they boile in a kettle full of watter or brouth made of meate or fish. So there is the description of the most delicious bitt of the world. I leave you taste of their Salmi gondy, which I hope to tell you in my following discourses of my other voyages in that country, and others that I frequented the space of tenne years.

To make a period of this my litle voyage. After I stayed awhile in this village with all joy & mirth, for feasts, dances, and playes out of meere gladnesse for our small victorious company's happy retourne, so after that their heads had sufficiently danced, they begin to talke [of going] to warre against the hollanders. Most of us are traited againe for the castors we bestowed on them. They resolve unanimously to goe on their designe. Every thing ready, we march along. The next day we arrived in a small brough[37] of the hollanders, where we masters them, without that those beere-bellies had the courage to frowne att us. Whether it was out of hope of lucre or otherwise, we with violence tooke the meate out of their potts, and opening their coubards[38] we take and eat what we [can] gett. For drinking of their wine we weare good fellowes. So much that they fought with swords among themselves without the least offer of any misdeed to me. I drunk more then they, but more soberly, letting them make their quarrells without any notice.

The 4th day we come to the fort of Orange, where we weare very well received, or rather our Castors, every one courting us; and was nothing but prunes and raisins and tobbacco plentifully, and all for ho, ho, which is thanks, adding *nianonnha*, thanke you. We went from house to house. I went into the fort with my brother, and have not yett ben knowne a french. But a french souldier of the fort speaks to me in Iroquois language, & demanded if I was not a stranger, and did veryly believe I was french, for all that I was all dabbled over with painting and greased. I answered him in the same language, that no; and then he speaks in swearing, desiring me how I fell in the hands

37. brough: town.   38. coubards: cupboards.

of those people. And hearing him speake french, amazed, I answered him, for which he rejoyced very much. As he embraces me, he cryes out with such a stirre that I thought him senselesse. He made a shame for all that I was wild but to blush red. I could be no redder than what they painted me before I came there. All came about me, French as well as duch, every one makeing [me] drink out of the bottles, offering me their service; but my time yett was not out, so that I wanted not their service, for the onely rumour of my being a frenchman was enough. The flemish women drawed me by force into their houses, striving who should give, one bread, other meate, to drinke and to eate, and tobacco. I wanted not for those of my nation, Iroquoise, who followed me in a great squadroon through the streets, as if I had bin a monster in nature or a rare thing to be seen.

I went to see the Governor, & [he] talked with me a long time, and tould him the life that I lead, of which he admired. He offred me to buy me from them att what prise so ever, or else should save me, which I accepted not, for severall reasons. The one was for not to be behoulding to them, and the other being loathsome to leave such kind of good people. For then I began to love my new parents that weare so good & so favourable to me. The 3d reason was to watch a better opportunity for to retyre to the french rather than make that long circuit which after I was forced to doe for to retyre to my country more then 2,000 leagues; and being that it was my destiny to discover many wild nations, I would not to strive against destinie. I remitted myselfe to fortune and adventure of time, as a thing ordained by God for his greatest glorie, as I hope it will prove. Our treatis being done, overladend with bootyes abundantly, we putt ourselves in the way that we came to see againe our village, and to passe that winter with our wives, and to eat with them our Cagamitie in peece, hoping that nobody should trouble us during our wintering, and also to Expect or finde our fathers retourning home.

Leaving that place, many cryed to see me among a company of wolves, as that souldier tould me who knowed me the first houre; and the poore man made the tears come to my eyes. The truth is, I found many occasions to retire for to save me, but have not yett souffred enough to have merited my deliverance. In 2 dayes' journey we weare retourned to our cabbans, where every one of us rendered himself to his dearest kindred or master. My sisters weare charged of porcelaine, of which I was shure not to faile, for they weare too liberall to mee and I towards them. I was not 15 dayes retourned, but that nature itselfe reproached me to leade such a life, remembering the sweet behaviour and mildnesse of the french, & considered with meselfe what end should I expect of such a barbarous nation, enemy to God and to man. The great effect that the flemings shewed me, and the litle space was from us there; can I make that journey one day? The great belief that the people had in me should make them not to mistrust me, & by that I should have greater occasion to save me without feare of being pursued.

All these reasons made one deliberat to take a full resolution, without further delay, of saving meselfe to the flemings; for I could be att no safety among such a nation full of reveng. If in case the French & algonquins defeats that troupe of theirs, then what spite they will have will reveng it on my boanes; for where is no law, no faith to undertake to goe to the French. I was once interrupted, nor have I had a desire to venture againe for the second time. I should delight to be broyled as before in pitifull torments. I repented of a good occasion I lett slippe, finding meselfe in the place with offers of many to assist me. But he that is of a good resolution must be of strong hopes of what he undertakes; & if the dangers weare considered which may be found in things of importancy, you ingenious men would become cooks. Finally, without expecting my father's retourne, putting away all feare & apprehension, I constituted to deliver meselfe from their hands at what ever rate it would come too. For this effect I purposed to feign to goe a hunting about the brough; & for to dissemble the better, I cutt long sticks to make handles for a kind of a sword they use, that thereby they might not have the least suspition.

One day I tooke but a simple hattchett & a knife, if occasion presented to cutt some tree, & for to have more defence, if unhappily I should be rencountred, to make them believe that I was lost in the woods. Moreover, as the whole nation tooke me for proud, having allways great care to be guarnished with porcelaine, & that I would fly away like a beggar, a thing very unworthy, in this deliberation I ventured. I inquired my brother if he would keepe me company. I knewed that he never thought, seeing that he was courting of a young woman, who by the report of many was a bastard to a flemish. I had no difficulty to believe, seeing that the colour of her hayre was much more whiter then that of the Iroquoits. Neverthelesse, shee was of a great familie. I left them to their love. In shorte, that without any provision I tooke journey through the forests guided by fortune. No difficulty if I could keepe the highway, which is greatly beatten with the great concours of that people that comes & goes to trade with the flemings; but to avoid all encounters I must prolong a farre off. Soe being assisted by the best hope of the world, I made all diligence in the meene while that my mother nor kindred should mistrust me in the least.

I made my departure att 8 of the clock in the morning the 29th October, 1653. I marched all that journey without eating, but being as accustomed to that, without staying I contined my course att night. Before the breaking of the day I found myselfe uncapable because of my feeblenesse and faintnesse for want of food and repose after such constraint. But the feare of death makes vertu of necessity. The morning commanded me to goe, for it's faire and cold ayre, which [was] somewhat advantageous to keepe [me] more cheerfull. Finally the resolution reterning my courage, att 4 of the clocke att evening, the next daye I arrived in a place full of trees cutt, which made mee looke to myselfe, fearing to approach the habitation, though my designe was such. It is a strange thing that to save this life they abhorre what they wish, & desire which they apprehend. Approaching nigher and nigher untill I perceived an opening that was made by cutting of wood where was one man cutting still wood, I went nearer and called him. [He] incontinently leaves his work & comes to me, thinking I was Iroquoise. I said nothing to him to the contrary. I kept him in that thought, promising him to treat with him all my castors att his house, if he should promise me there should be non of my brother Iroquoise there, by reson we must be liberall to one another. He assured me there was none then there. I tould him that my castors were hidden and that I should goe for them to-morrow. So satisfied [he] leads me to his cabban & setts before me what good cheare he had, not desiring to loose time because the affaire concerned me much. I tould him I was savage, but that I lived awhile among the french, & that I had something valuable to communicate to the governor. That he would give me a peece of paper and Ink and pen. He wondered very much to see that, what he never saw before don by a wildman. He charges himself with my letter, with promise that he should tell it to nobody of my being there, and to retourne the soonest he could possible, having but 2 litle miles to the fort of Orange.

In the meane while of his absence shee shews me good countenance as much as shee could, hoping of a better imaginary profit by me. Shee asked me if we had so much libertie with the french women to lye with them as they; but I had no desire to doe anything, seeing myselfe so insnared att death's door amongst the terrible torments, but must shew a better countenance to a worse game. In the night we heard some wild men singing, which redoubled my torments and apprehension, which inticed me to declare to that woman that my nation would kill [me] because I loved the french and the flemings more than they, and that I resolved hereafter to live with the flemings. Shee perceiving my reason hid me in a corner behind a sack or two of wheat. Nothing was to me but feare. I was scarcely there an houre in the corner, but the flemings came, 4 in number, whereof [one was] that french man [who] had knowne me the first, who presently getts me out & gives me a suite that they brought purposely to disguise me if I chanced to light upon any of the Iroquoits. I tooke leave of my land-lady & landlord, yett [it] grieved me much that I had nothing to bestow upon them but thanks, being that they weare very poore, but not so much as I.

I was conducted to the fort of Orange, where we had no incounter in the way, where I have had the honnour to salute the Governor, who spoake french, and by his speech thought him a french man. The next day he caused an other habit to be given me, with shoos & stokins & also linnen. A minister that was a Jesuit gave me great offer, also a Marchand, to whom I shall ever have infinit obligations, although they weare satisfied when I came to france att Rochel. I stayed 3 days inclosed in the fort & hidden. Many came there to search me, & doubt not but my parents weare of the party. If my father had ben there he would venture hard, & no doubt but was trou-bled att it, & so was my mother, & my parents who loved me as if I weare their owne naturall Son. My poore sisters cryed out & lamented through the town of the flem-ings, as I was tould they called me by my name, for they came there the 3rd day after my flight. Many flemings wondered, & could not perceive how those could love me so well; but the pleasure caused it, as it agrees well with the Roman proverbe, "doe as they doe." I was imbarked by the governor's order; after taking leave, and thanks for all his favours, I was conducted to Menada, a towne faire enough for a new country, where after some 3 weeks I embarked in one of their shipps for holland, where arrived after many boisterous winds and ill weather, and, after some six weeks' sayle and some days, we landed att Amsterdam the 4th of January, 1654. Some days after I imbarked myselfe for france and came to Rochelle well & safe, not without blowing my fingers many times as well as I [had] done before [when] I arrived in holland. I stayed till spring, expecting the transporte of a shippe for new france.

8. Mary Rowlandson

The Sovereignty and Goodness of God 1682

The best-known of all captivity narratives, Mary Rowlandson's story takes place during King Philip's War, fought six years before the book was published. Though a preface to the narrative refers to the war as the "causeless enmity of these barbarians, against the English," the Indians had a long history of grievances. Plymouth Colony officials, seeking to win land rights from the Wampanoag Indians before their rivals in Rhode Island could do so, used strongarm tactics; a Wampanoag sachem died while under arrest in Plymouth. His successor, Metacom (or Metacomet, also known as Philip of Pakanoket), was forced to cede the land, and later was again forced to make a declaration of submission. Finally, King Philip assembled an Indian alliance that launched its first attack in June, 1675. In the following winter a major Indian offensive pushed English forces back all along the Massachusetts frontier, reaching to within ten miles of Boston. The viability of English settlements in New England suddenly seemed in doubt.

During the winter campaign, on February 10, 1676, Indians attacked Lancaster, Massachusetts, wiping out the town and taking several captives. One of them was Mary Rowlandson. Born Mary White in 1636, she had been brought to Massachusetts as a small child with her family, and in 1656 had married the Reverend Joseph Rowlandson in Lancaster. After the war, she and her husband moved to Connecticut, where he died in 1678. It was long thought that her narrative was published posthumously when it appeared in 1682; we now know that she stayed in Connecticut (Lancaster still had not been resettled when her book appeared), remarried, and lived on as Mary Talcott until 1711.

The defeat of the Indian confederation in 1676 turned out to be the end of significant Indian resistance in New England. Philip was shot by an Indian ally of the English in August; his widow and nine-year-old son were sold into slavery in the West Indies. But the English were still struggling with the legacy of the war. Some criticized the colonial leadership for its handling of events. And London was eroding colonial autonomy. Just before the war, in 1674, Charles II had begun a program to administer all of New England and New York under a single royal governor.

In this context Rowlandson offers not just a personal story but an interpretation of the war; she sees it as a warning and judgment from God, one that should call settlers back to the piety of the original Puritan mission. Rowlandson also offers a polemic against "Praying Indians," giving new significance to race as an explanation of the war. Repudiating the language of the Eliot mission, Rowlandson speaks less of heathens and Christians than of Indians and English. Internal evidence suggests that Rowlandson understands the Indian language, but she is at pains to minimize the common ground of the two cultures.

Even the structure of the text makes a polemical point. Rowlandson divides her story into "removes" rather than chapters. As she explains, "It was their usual manner to remove when they had done any mischief." The form of the narrative

*emphasizes the wildness of Indian life, which had always been cited by Europeans
as a ground of the superior land claims of those who settled the land more permanently: in this case, the English. Rowlandson duly notes the sight of English paths,
English houses, and English cattle as she passes by. Clinging to the identity of a
land she left in infancy, she contrasts sharply with Radisson, as well as with other
English. The Indians tease her: "What, will you love Englishmen still?" They
evidently had different experience with other captives; one study shows that over
ten percent of New English captives stayed on with their Indian tribes.*

    The book's full title was The Sovereignty and Goodness of God, Together, with
the Faithfulness of His Promises Displayed; Being a Narrative of the Captivity and
Restauration of Mrs. Mary Rowlandson. *The title may be the work of the anonymous clergyman (probably Increase Mather) who wrote its preface. Yet its emphasis
on God's sovereignty is certainly borne out in some parts of the text. In keeping
with Puritan typology, Rowlandson repeatedly finds her experience foreshadowed
by Biblical events (types). Everything that happens, good or bad, illustrates God's
providence. Nothing is random or merely historical. In some tension with this
theology, however, is Rowlandson's language of mourning, memory, and anger. The
preface states that Rowlandson wrote the narrative not for print, but "to be to her a
Memorandum of God's dealing with her, that she might never forget, but remember
the same, and the several circumstances thereof, all the daies of her life."*

On the tenth of February 1675,[39] came the Indians with great numbers upon
Lancaster: Their first coming was about sun-rising; hearing the noise of some
guns, we looked out; several houses were burning, and the smoke ascending
to heaven. There were five persons taken in one house, the father, and the mother and
a sucking child, they knocked on the head; the other two they took and carried away
alive. There were two others, who being out of their garrison upon some occasion
were set upon; one was knocked on the head, the other escaped: another there was
who running along was shot and wounded, and fell down; he begged of them his life,
promising them money (as they told me) but they would not hearken to him but
knocked him in the head, and stripped him naked, and split open his bowels. Another
seeing many of the Indians about his barn, ventured and went out, but was quickly
shot down. There were three others belonging to the same garrison who were killed;
the Indians getting up upon the roof of the barn, had advantage to shoot down upon
them over their fortification. Thus these murderous wretches went on, burning, and
destroying before them.

    At length they came and beset our own house, and quickly it was the dolefullest day
that ever mine eyes saw. The house stood upon the edge of a hill; some of the Indians
got behind the hill, others into the barn, and others behind any thing that could
shelter them; from all which places they shot against the house, so that the bullets
seemed to fly like hail; and quickly they wounded one man among us, then another,
and then a third. About two hours (according to my observation, in that amazing
time) they had been about the house before they prevailed to fire it (which they did
with flax and hemp, which they brought out of the barn, and there being no defense
about the house, only two flankers[40] at two opposite corners and one of them not

---

39. Before the eighteenth century the new year began on
March 25; the Indian raid took place in 1676 by the modern
calendar.

40. flankers: projecting fortifications.

Spurious portrait of King Philip, engraved a century later by Paul Revere, based on a portrait of a different Indian chief.

finished) they fired it once and one ventured out and quenched it, but they quickly fired again, and that took.

Now is the dreadful hour come, that I have often heard of (in time of war, as it was the case of others) but now mine eyes see it. Some in our house were fighting for their lives, others wallowing in their blood, the house on fire over our heads, and the bloody heathen ready to knock us on the head, if we stirred out. Now might we hear mothers and children crying out for themselves, and one another, Lord, What shall we do? Then I took my children (and one of my sisters, hers) to go forth and leave the house: but as soon as we came to the door and appeared, the Indians shot so thick that the bullets rattled against the house, as if one had taken an handful of stones and threw them, so that we were fain to give back. We had six stout dogs belonging to our garrison, but none of them would stir, though another time, if any Indian had come to the door, they were ready to fly upon him and tear him down. The Lord hereby would make us the more to acknowledge his hand, and to see that our help is always in him. But out we must go, the fire increasing, and coming along behind us, roaring, and the Indians gaping before us with their guns, spears and hatchets to devour us.

No sooner were we out of the house, but my brother-in-law (being before wounded, in defending the house, in or near the throat) fell down dead whereat the Indians scornfully shouted, and holloed, and were presently upon him, stripping off his clothes, the bullets flying thick, one went through my side, and the same (as would seem) through the bowels and hand of my dear child in my arms. One of my elder sister's children, named William, had then his leg broken, which the Indians perceiving, they knocked him on the head. Thus were we butchered by those merciless heathen, standing amazed, with the blood running down to our heels.

My eldest sister being yet in the house, and seeing those woeful sights, the infidels haling mothers one way, and children another, and some wallowing in their blood:

and her elder son telling her that her son William was dead, and myself was wounded, she said, And, Lord, let me die with them; which was no sooner said, but she was struck with a bullet, and fell down dead over the threshold. I hope she is reaping the fruit of her good labors, being faithful to the service of God in her place. In her younger years she lay under much trouble upon spiritual accounts, till it pleased God to make that precious scripture take hold of her heart, 2 Corinthians 12. 9. *And he said unto me, my grace is sufficient for thee.* More than twenty years after I have heard her tell how sweet and comfortable that place was[41] to her.

But to return: the Indians laid hold of us, pulling me one way, and the Children another, and said, Come go along with us; I told them they would kill me: they answered, If I were willing to go along with them, they would not hurt me.

Oh the doleful sight that now was to behold at this house! *Come, behold the works of the Lord, what desolations he has made in the earth.*[42] Of thirty-seven persons who were in this one house, none escaped either present death, or a bitter captivity, save only one, who might say as he, Job 1. 15, *And I only am escaped alone to tell the news.* There were twelve killed, some shot, some stabbed with their spears, some knocked down with their hatchets. When we are in prosperity, oh the little that we think of such dreadful sights, and to see our dear friends, and relations lie bleeding out their heart's blood upon the ground. There was one who was chopped into the head with a hatchet, and stripped naked, and yet was crawling up and down. It is a solemn sight to see so many Christians lying in their blood, some here, and some there, like a company of sheep torn by wolves. All of them stripped naked by a company of hell-hounds, roaring, singing, ranting and insulting, as if they would have torn our very hearts out; yet the Lord by his almighty power preserved a number of us from death, for there were twenty-four of us taken alive and carried captive.

I had often before this said, that if the Indians should come, I should choose rather to be killed by them than be taken alive but when it came to the trial my mind changed; their glittering weapons so daunted my spirit, that I chose rather to go along with those (as I may say) ravenous beasts, than that moment to end my days; and that I may the better declare what happened to me during that grievous captivity, I shall particularly speak of the several removes we had up and down the wilderness.

THE FIRST REMOVE

Now away we must go with those barbarous creatures, with our bodies wounded and bleeding, and our hearts no less than our bodies. About a mile we went that night, up upon a hill within sight of the town, where they intended to lodge. There was hard by[43] a vacant house (deserted by the English before, for fear of the Indians). I asked them whether I might not lodge in the house that night to which they answered, What will you love English men still? This was the dolefullest night that ever my eyes saw. Oh the roaring, and singing and dancing, and yelling of those black creatures in the night, which made the place a lively resemblance of hell. And as

41. i.e., how comforting that passage was.
42. Ps. 46:8.

43. hard by: nearby.

miserable was the waste that was there made, of horses, cattle, sheep, swine, calves, lambs, roasting pigs, and fowl (which they had plundered in the town) some roasting, some lying and burning, and some boiling to feed our merciless enemies; who were joyful enough though we were disconsolate. To add to the dolefulness of the former day, and the dismalness of the present night: my thoughts ran upon my losses and sad bereaved condition. All was gone, my husband gone (at least separated from me, he being in the Bay;[44] and to add to my grief, the Indians told me they would kill him as he came homeward) my children gone, my relations and friends gone, our house and home and all our comforts within doors, and without, all was gone (except my life) and I knew not but the next moment that might go too. There remained nothing to me but one poor wounded babe, and it seemed at present worse than death that it was in such a pitiful condition, bespeaking compassion, and I had no refreshing for it, nor suitable things to revive it. Little do many think what is the savageness and brutishness of this barbarous enemy, aye even those that seem to profess[45] more than others among them, when the English have fallen into their hands.

Those seven that were killed at Lancaster the summer before upon a Sabbath day, and the one that was afterward killed upon a week day, were slain and mangled in a barbarous manner, by One-eyed John, and Marlborough's praying Indians, which Captain Mosely brought to Boston, as the Indians told me.

THE SECOND REMOVE

But now, the next morning, I must turn my back upon the town, and travel with them into the vast and desolate wilderness, I knew not whither. It is not my tongue, or pen can express the sorrows of my heart, and bitterness of my spirit, that I had at this departure: but God was with me, in a wonderful manner, carrying me along, and bearing up my spirit, that it did not quite fail. One of the Indians carried my poor wounded babe upon a horse, it went moaning all along, I shall die, I shall die. I went on foot after it, with sorrow that cannot be expressed. At length I took it off the horse, and carried it in my arms till my strength failed, and I fell down with it: Then they set me upon a horse with my wounded child in my lap, and there being no furniture[46] upon the horse's back, as we were going down a steep hill, we both fell over the horse's head, at which they like inhuman creatures laughed, and rejoiced to see it, though I thought we should there have ended our days, as overcome with so many difficulties. But the Lord renewed my strength still, and carried me along, that I might see more of his power; yea, so much that I could never have thought of, had I not experienced it.

After this it quickly began to snow, and when night came on, they stopped: and now down I must sit in the snow, by a little fire, and a few boughs behind me, with my sick child in my lap; and calling much for water, being now (through the wound) fallen into a violent fever. My own wound also growing so stiff, that I could scarce sit down or rise up; yet so it must be, that I must sit all this cold winter night upon the

44. the Bay: Boston.
45. those that seem to profess: Christianized Indians.
46. furniture: saddle.

cold snowy ground, with my sick child in my arms, looking that every hour would be the last of its life; and having no Christian friend near me, either to comfort or help me. Oh, I may see the wonderful power of God, that my spirit did not utterly sink under my affliction: still the Lord upheld me with his gracious and merciful spirit, and we were both alive to see the light of the next morning.

THE THIRD REMOVE

The morning being come, they prepared to go on their way. One of the Indians got up upon a horse, and they set me up behind him, with my poor sick babe in my lap. A very wearisome and tedious day I had of it; what with my own wound, and my child's being so exceeding sick, and in a lamentable condition with her wound. It may be easily judged what a poor feeble condition we were in, there being not the least crumb of refreshing that came within either of our mouths, from Wednesday night to Saturday night, except only a little cold water. This day in the afternoon, about an hour by sun, we came to the place where they intended, *viz.* an Indian town called Wenimesset, northward of Quabaug. When we were come, Oh the number of pagans (now merciless enemies) that there came about me, that I may say as David, Psalms 27. 13, *I had fainted, unless I had believed*, etc. The next day was the Sabbath: I then remembered how careless I had been of God's holy time, how many Sabbaths I had lost and misspent, and how evilly I had walked in God's sight; which lay so close unto my spirit, that it was easy for me to see how righteous it was with God to cut off the thread of my life, and cast me out of his presence forever. Yet the Lord still showed mercy to me, and upheld me; and as he wounded me with one hand, so he healed me with the other.

This day there came to me one Robert Pepper (a man belonging to Roxbury) who was taken in Captain Beers his fight, and had been now a considerable time with the Indians; and up with them almost as far as Albany, to see King Philip, as he told me, and was now very lately come into these parts. Hearing, I say, that I was in this Indian town, he obtained leave to come and see me. He told me, he himself was wounded in the leg at Captain Beers his fight; and was not able some time to go, but as they carried him, and as he took oaken leaves and laid to his wound, and through the blessing of God he was able to travel again. Then I took oaken leaves and laid to my side, and with the blessing of God it cured me also; yet before the cure was wrought, I may say, as it is in Psalms 38. 5-6. *My wounds stink and are corrupt, I am bowed down greatly, I go mourning all the day long*. I sat much alone with a poor wounded child in my lap, which moaned night and day, having nothing to revive the body, or cheer the spirits of her, but instead of that, sometimes one Indian would come and tell me in one hour, that your master will knock your child in the head, and then a second, and then a third, your master will quickly knock your child in the head.

This was the comfort I had from them, miserable comforters are ye all, as he said.[47] Thus nine days I sat upon my knees, with my babe in my lap, till my flesh was raw

---

47. Job 16:2.

again; my child being even ready to depart this sorrowful world, they bade me carry it out to another wigwam (I suppose because they would not be troubled with such spectacles) whither I went with a very heavy heart, and down I sat with the picture of death in my lap. About two hours in the night, my sweet babe like a lamb departed this life, on Feb. 18, 1675, it being about six years, and five months old. It was nine days from the first wounding, in this miserable condition, without any refreshing of one nature or other, except a little cold water. I cannot but take notice, how at another time I could not bear to be in the room where any dead person was, but now the case is changed; I must and could lie down by my dead babe, side by side all the night after. I have thought since of the wonderful goodness of God to me, in preserving me in the use of my reason and senses, in that distressed time, that I did not use wicked and violent means to end my own miserable life.

In the morning, when they understood that my child was dead they sent for me home to my master's wigwam: (by my master in this writing, must be understood Quinnapin, who was a sagamore,[48] and married King Philip's wife's sister; not that he first took me, but I was sold to him by another Narragansett Indian, who took me when first I came out of the garrison). I went to take up my dead child in my arms to carry it with me, but they bid me let it alone: there was no resisting, but go I must and leave it. When I had been at my master's wigwam, I took the first opportunity I could get, to go look after my dead child: when I came I asked them what they had done with it? Then they told me it was upon the hill: then they went and showed me where it was, where I saw the ground was newly digged, and there they told me they had buried it: there I left that child in the wilderness, and must commit it, and myself also in this wilderness condition, to Him who is above all.

God having taken away this dear child, I went to see my daughter Mary, who was at this same Indian town, at a wigwam not very far off, though we had little liberty or opportunity to see one another. She was about ten years old, and taken from the door at first by a Praying Indian and afterward sold for a gun. When I came in sight, she would fall a-weeping; at which they were provoked, and would not let me come near her, but bade me begone; which was a heart-cutting word to me. I had one child dead, another in the wilderness, I knew not where, the third they would not let me come near to: *Me* (as he said) *have ye bereaved of my children, Joseph is not, and Simeon is not, and ye will take Benjamin also, all these things are against me.*[49]

I could not sit still in this condition, but kept walking from one place to another. And as I was going along, my heart was even overwhelmed with the thoughts of my condition, and that I should have children, and a nation which I knew not ruled over them. Whereupon I earnestly entreated the Lord, that He would consider my low estate, and show me a token for good, and if it were His blessed will, some sign and hope of some relief. And indeed quickly the Lord answered, in some measure, my poor prayers: for as I was going up and down mourning and lamenting my condition, my son came to me, and asked me how I did; I had not seen him before, since the destruction of the town, and I knew not where he was, till I was informed by himself,

---

48. sagamore: chief. 49. Gen. 42:36.

that he was amongst a smaller parcel of Indians, whose place was about six miles off; with tears in his eyes, he asked me whether his sister Sarah was dead; and told me he had seen his sister Mary; and prayed me, that I would not be troubled in reference to himself.

The occasion of his coming to see me at this time, was this: there was, as I said, about six miles from us, a small plantation of Indians, where it seems he had been during his captivity: and at this time, there were some forces of the Indians gathered out of our company, and some also from them (among whom was my son's master) to go to assault and burn Medfield: In this time of the absence of his master, his dame brought him to see me. I took this to be some gracious answer to my earnest and unfeigned desire. The next day, *viz.* to this, the Indians returned from Medfield, all the company, for those that belonged to the other small company, came through the town that now we were at.

But before they came to us, Oh! the outrageous roaring and whooping that there was: They began their din about a mile before they came to us. By their noise and whooping they signified how many they had destroyed (which was at that time twenty-three). Those that were with us at home, were gathered together as soon as they heard the whooping, and every time that the other went over their number, these at home gave a shout, that the very earth rung again: and thus they continued till those that had been upon the expedition were come up to the Sagamore's wigwam; and then, Oh, the hideous insulting and triumphing that there was over some Englishmen's scalps that they had taken (as their manner is) and brought with them.

I cannot but take notice of the wonderful mercy of God to me in those afflictions, in sending me a Bible. One of the Indians that came from Medfield fight, had brought some plunder, came to me, and asked me, if I would have a Bible, he had got one in his basket. I was glad of it, and asked him, whether he thought the Indians would let me read? He answered, Yes: So I took the Bible, and in that melancholy time, it came into my mind to read first the 28th Chapter of Deuteronomy, which I did, and when I had read it, my dark heart wrought on this manner, That there was no mercy for me, that the blessings were gone, and the curses come in their room, and that I had lost my opportunity. But the Lord helped me still to go on reading till I came to Chapter 30 the seven first verses, where I found, there was mercy promised again, if we would return to him by repentance; and though we were scattered from one end of the earth to the other, yet the Lord would gather us together, and turn all those curses upon our enemies. I do not desire to live to forget this scripture, and what comfort it was to me.

Now the Indians began to talk of removing from this place, some one way, and some another. There were now besides myself nine English captives in this place (all of them children, except one woman). I got an opportunity to go and take my leave of them; they being to go one way, and I another, I asked them whether they were earnest with God for deliverance, they told me, they did as they were able, and it was some comfort to me, that the Lord stirred up children to look to Him. The woman *viz.* Goodwife[50] Joslin told me, she should never see me again, and that she could find

---

50. Goodwife: an honorific, like "Mrs.," but lower in rank than "Mistress."

in her heart to run away; I wished her not to run away by any means, for we were near thirty miles from any English town, and she very big with child, and had but one week to reckon; and another child in her arms, two years old, and bad rivers there were to go over, and we were feeble, with our poor and coarse entertainment. I had my Bible with me, I pulled it out, and asked her whether she would read; we opened the Bible and lighted on Psalm 27, in which Psalm we especially took notice of that, *ver. ult., Wait on the Lord, Be of good courage, and he shall strengthen thine heart, wait I say on the Lord.*

THE FOURTH REMOVE

And now I must part with that little company I had. Here I parted from my daughter Mary (whom I never saw again till I saw her in Dorchester, returned from captivity), and from four little cousins and neighbors, some of which I never saw afterward: the Lord only knows the end of them. Amongst them also was that poor woman before mentioned, who came to a sad end, as some of the company told me in my travel: she having much grief upon her spirit, about her miserable condition, being so near her time, she would be often asking the Indians to let her go home; they not being willing to that, and yet vexed with her importunity, gathered a great company together about her, and stripped her naked, and set her in the midst of them; and when they had sung and danced about her (in their hellish manner) as long as they pleased, they knocked her on head, and the child in her arms with her: when they had done that, they made a fire and put them both into it, and told the other children that were with them, that if they attempted to go home, they would serve them in like manner: the children said, she did not shed one tear, but prayed all the while. But to return to my own journey; we travelled about half a day or little more, and came to a desolate place in the wilderness, where there were no wigwams or inhabitants before; we came about the middle of the afternoon to this place, cold and wet, and snowy, and hungry, and weary, and no refreshing, for man, but the cold ground to sit on, and our poor Indian cheer.

Heart-aching thoughts here I had about my poor children, who were scattered up and down among the wild beasts of the forest: my head was light and dizzy (either through hunger or hard lodging, or trouble or all together) my knees feeble, my body raw by sitting double night and day, that I cannot express to man the affliction that lay upon my spirit, but the Lord helped me at that time to express it to himself. I opened my Bible to read, and the Lord brought that precious scripture to me, Jeremiah 31. 16. *Thus saith the Lord, refrain thy voice from weeping, and thine eyes from tears, for thy work shall be rewarded, and they shall come again from the land of the enemy.* This was a sweet cordial to me, when I was ready to faint, many and many a time have I sat down, and wept sweetly over this scripture. At this place we continued about four days.

THE FIFTH REMOVE

The occasion (as I thought) of their moving at this time, was, the English army, it being near and following them: for they went, as if they had gone for their lives, for some considerable way, and then they made a stop, and chose some of their stoutest men, and sent them back to hold the English army in play whilst the rest escaped: and then, like Jehu,[51] they marched on furiously, with their old, and with their young; some carried their old decrepit mothers, some carried one, and some another. Four of them carried a great Indian upon a bier; but going through a thick wood with him, they were hindered, and could make no haste; whereupon they took him upon their backs, and carried him, one at a time, till they came to Baquag River. Upon a Friday, a little after noon we came to this river. When all the company was come up, and were gathered together, I thought to count the number of them, but they were so many, and being somewhat in motion, it was beyond my skill. In this travel, because of my wound, I was somewhat favored in my load; I carried only my knitting work and two quarts of parched meal: being very faint I asked my mistress to give me one spoonful of the meal, but she would not give me a taste. They quickly fell to cutting dry trees, to make rafts to carry them over the river: and soon my turn came to go over: by the advantage of some brush which they had laid upon the raft to sit upon, I did not wet my foot (which many of themselves at the other end were mid-leg deep) which cannot but be acknowledged as a favor of God to my weakened body, it being a very cold time. I was not before acquainted with such kind of doings or dangers. *When thou passeth through the waters I will be with thee, and through the rivers they shall not overflow thee*, Isaiah 43. 2. A certain number of us got over the river that night, but it was the night after the Sabbath before all the company was got over. On the Saturday they boiled an old horse's leg which they had got, and so we drank of the broth, as soon as they thought it was ready, and when it was almost all gone, they filled it up again.

The first week of my being among them, I hardly ate anything; the second week, I found my stomach grow very faint for want of something; and yet it was very hard to get down their filthy trash: but the third week, though I could think how formerly my stomach would turn against this or that, and I could starve and die before I could eat such things, yet they were sweet and savory to my taste. I was at this time knitting a pair of white cotton stockings for my mistress; and had not yet wrought upon a Sabbath day; when the Sabbath came they bade me go to work; I told them it was the Sabbath day, and desired them to let me rest, and told them I would do as much more tomorrow; to which they answered me, they would break my face.

And here I cannot but take notice of the strange providence of God in preserving the heathen: they were many hundreds, old and young, some sick, and some lame, many had papooses at their backs, the greatest number at this time with us, were squaws, and they travelled with all they had, bag and baggage, and yet they got over this river aforesaid; and on Monday they set their wigwams on fire, and away they went: on that very day came the English army after them to this river, and saw the

---

51. like Jehu: see 2 Kings 9:20.

smoke of their wigwams, and yet this river put a stop to them. God did not give them courage or activity to go over after us; we were not ready for so great a mercy as victory and deliverance; if we had been, God would have found out a way for the English to have passed this river, as well as for the Indians with their squaws and children, and all their luggage. *Oh, that my people had hearkened to me, and Israel had walked in my ways, I should soon have subdued their enemies, and turned my hand against their adversaries*, Psalms 81: 13-14.

THE SIXTH REMOVE

On Monday (as I said) they set their wigwams on fire, and went away. It was a cold morning, and before us there was a great brook with ice on it; some waded through it, up to the knees and higher, but others went till they came to a beaver dam, and I amongst them, where through the good providence of God, I did not wet my foot. I went along that day mourning and lamenting, leaving farther my own country, and travelling into the vast and howling wilderness, and I understood something of Lot's wife's temptation, when she looked back:[52] we came that day to a great swamp, by the side of which we took up our lodging that night. When I came to the brow of the hill, that looked toward the swamp, I thought we had been come to a great Indian town (though there were none but our own company). The Indians were as thick as the trees: it seemed as if there had been a thousand hatchets going at once: if one looked before one, there was nothing but Indians, and behind one, nothing but Indians, and so on either hand, I myself in the midst, and no Christian soul near me, and yet how hath the Lord preserved me in safety! Oh the experience that I have had of the goodness of God, to me and mine!

THE SEVENTH REMOVE

After a restless and hungry night there, we had a wearisome time of it the next day. The swamp by which we lay, was, as it were, a deep dungeon, and an exceeding high and steep hill before it. Before I got to the top of the hill, I thought my heart and legs, and all would have broken, and failed me. What through faintness, and soreness of body, it was a grievous day of travel to me. As we went along, I saw a place where English cattle had been: that was comfort to me, such as it was: quickly after that we came to an English path, which so took with me, that I thought I could have freely lain down and died. That day, a little after noon, we came to Squakeag, where the Indians quickly spread themselves over the deserted English fields, gleaning what they could find; some picked up ears of wheat that were crickled[53] down, some found ears of Indian corn, some found ground nuts,[54] and others sheaves of wheat that were frozen together in the shock, and went to threshing of them out. Myself got two ears of Indian corn, and whilst I did but turn my back, one of them was stolen from me, which much troubled me. There came an Indian to them at that time, with a basket of

---

52. Lot's wife: see Gen. 19.
53. crickled: trampled.

54. ground nuts: wild beans.

horse liver. I asked him to give me a piece: What, says he, can you eat horse liver? I told him, I would try, if he would give a piece, which he did, and I laid it on the coals to roast; but before it was half ready they got half of it away from me, so that I was fain to take the rest and eat it as it was, with the blood about my mouth, and yet a savory bit it was to me: *for to the hungry soul, every bitter thing is sweet.*[55] A solemn sight methought it was, to see fields of wheat and Indian corn forsaken and spoiled: and the remainders of them to be food for our merciless enemies. That night we had a mess of wheat for our supper.

THE EIGHTH REMOVE

On the morrow morning we must go over the river, *i.e.* the Connecticut, to meet with King Philip; two canoes full, they had carried over, the next turn I myself was to go; but as my foot was upon the canoe to step in, there was a sudden outcry among them, and I must step back; and instead of going over the river, I must go four or five miles up the river farther northward. Some of the Indians ran one way, and some another. The cause of this rout was, as I thought, their espying some English scouts, who were thereabout. In this travel up the river, about noon the company made a stop, and sat down; some to eat, and others to rest them.

As I sat amongst them, musing of things past, my son Joseph unexpectedly came to me: we asked of each other's welfare, bemoaning our doleful condition, and the change that had come upon us. We had husband and father, and children, and sisters, and friends, and relations, and house, and home, and many comforts of this life: but now we may say, as Job, *Naked came I out of my mother's womb, and naked shall I return: the Lord gave, and the Lord hath taken away, blessed be the name of the Lord.*[56] I asked him whether he would read; he told me, he earnestly desired it. I gave him my Bible, and he lighted upon that comfortable scripture, Psalm 118. 17–18. *I shall not die but live, and declare the works of the Lord: the Lord hath chastened me sore, yet he hath not given me over to death.* Look here, mother (says he), did you read this? And here I may take occasion to mention one principal ground of my setting forth these lines: even as the psalmist says, To declare the works of the Lord, and His wonderful power in carrying us along, preserving us in the wilderness, while under the enemy's hand, and returning of us in safety again, and His goodness in bringing to my hand so many comfortable and suitable scriptures in my distress.

But to return, we travelled on till night; and in the morning, we must go over the river to Philip's crew. When I was in the canoe, I could not but be amazed at the numerous crew of pagans that were on the bank on the other side. When I came ashore, they gathered all about me, I sitting alone in the midst: I observed they asked one another questions, and laughed, and rejoiced over their gains and victories. Then my heart began to fail: and I fell a-weeping which was the first time to my remembrance, that I wept before them. Although I had met with so much affliction, and my heart was many times ready to break, yet could I not shed one tear in their sight: but

---

55. Prov. 27:7.   56. Job 1:21.

rather had been all this while in a maze, and like one astonished: but now I may say as, Psalm 137. 1. *By the rivers of Babylon, there we sat down: yea, we wept when we remembered Zion*. There one of them asked me, why I wept, I could hardly tell what to say: yet I answered, they would kill me: No, said he, none will hurt you. Then came one of them and gave me two spoonfuls of meal to comfort me, and another gave me half a pint of peas; which was more worth than many bushels at another time.

Then I went to see King Philip, he bade me come in and sit down, and asked me whether I would smoke (a usual compliment nowadays amongst saints and sinners) but this no way suited me. For though I had formerly used tobacco, yet I had left it ever since I was first taken. It seems to be a bait, the devil lays to make men lose their precious time: I remember with shame, how formerly, when I had taken two or three pipes, I was presently ready for another, such a bewitching thing it is: but I thank God, he has now given me power over it; surely there are many who may be better employed than to lie sucking a stinking tobacco pipe.

Now the Indians gather their forces to go against Northampton: overnight one went about yelling and hooting to give notice of the design. Whereupon they fell to boiling of ground nuts, and parching of corn (as many as had it) for their provision: and in the morning away they went. During my abode in this place, Philip spake to me to make a shirt for his boy, which I did, for which he gave me a shilling: I offered the money to my master, but he bade me keep it: and with it I bought a piece of horse flesh. Afterwards he asked me to make a cap for his boy, for which he invited me to dinner. I went, and he gave me a pancake, about as big as two fingers; it was made of parched wheat, beaten, and fried in bear's grease, but I thought I never tasted pleasanter meat in my life. There was a squaw who spake to me to make a shirt for her sannup,[57] for which she gave me a piece of bear. Another asked me to knit a pair of stockings, for which she gave me a quart of peas: I boiled my peas and bear together, and invited my master and mistress to dinner, but the proud gossip,[58] because I served them both in one dish, would eat nothing, except one bit that he gave her upon the point of his knife.

Hearing that my son was come to this place, I went to see him, and found him lying flat upon the ground: I asked him how he could sleep so? He answered me, that he was not asleep, but at prayer; and lay so, that they might not observe what he was doing. I pray God he may remember these things now he is returned in safety. At this place (the sun now getting higher) what with the beams and heat of the sun, and the smoke of the wigwams, I thought I should have been blind. I could scarce discern one wigwam from another. There was here one Mary Thurston of Medfield, who seeing how it was with me, lent me a hat to wear: but as soon as I was gone, the squaw (who owned that Mary Thurston) came running after me, and got it away again. Here was the squaw that gave me one spoonful of meal. I put it in my pocket to keep it safe: yet notwithstanding somebody stole it, but put five Indian corns in the room of it: which corns were the greatest provisions I had in my travel for one day.

The Indians returning from Northampton, brought with them some horses, and sheep, and other things which they had taken: I desired them, that they would carry

---

57. sannup: husband.   58. gossip: dame, fellow.

me to Albany, upon one of those horses, and sell me for powder: for so they had sometimes discoursed. I was utterly hopeless of getting home on foot, the way that I came. I could hardly bear to think of the many weary steps I had taken, to come to this place.

THE NINTH REMOVE

But instead of going either to Albany or homeward, we must go five miles up the river, and then go over it. Here we abode a while. Here lived a sorry Indian, who spoke to me to make him a shirt. When I had done it, he would pay me nothing. But he living by the riverside, where I often went to fetch water, I would often be putting of him in mind, and calling for my pay: at last he told me if I would make another shirt, for a papoose not yet born, he would give me a knife, which he did when I had done it. I carried the knife in, and my master asked me to give it him, and I was not a little glad that I had anything that they would accept of, and be pleased with. When we were at this place, my master's maid came home, she had been gone three weeks into the Narragansett country, to fetch corn, where they had stored up some in the ground: she brought home about a peck and a half of corn. This was about the time that their great captain, Naananto, was killed in the Narragansett country. My son being now about a mile from me, I asked liberty to go and see him, they bade me go, and away I went: but quickly lost myself, travelling over hills and through swamps, and could not find the way to him.

And I cannot but admire at the wonderful power and goodness of God to me, in that, though I was gone from home, and met with all sorts of Indians, and those I had no knowledge of, and there being no Christian soul near me; yet not one of them offered the least imaginable miscarriage to me. I turned homeward again, and met with my master, he showed me the way to my son: when I came to him I found him not well: and withall he had a boil on his side, which much troubled him: we bemoaned one another a while, as the Lord helped us, and then I returned again. When I was returned, I found myself as unsatisfied as I was before. I went up and down mourning and lamenting: and my spirit was ready to sink, with the thoughts of my poor children: my son was ill, and I could not but think of his mournful looks, and no Christian friend was near him, to do any office of love for him, either for soul or body. And my poor girl, I knew not where she was, nor whether she was sick, or well, or alive, or dead. I repaired under these thoughts to my Bible (my great comfort in that time) and that scripture came to my hand, *Cast thy burden upon the Lord, and He shall sustain thee*, Psalms 55. 22.

But I was fain to go and look after something to satisfy my hunger, and going among the wigwams, I went into one, and there found a squaw who showed herself very kind to me, and gave me a piece of bear. I put it into my pocket, and came home, but could not find an opportunity to broil it, for fear they would get it from me, and there it lay all that day and night in my stinking pocket. In the morning I went to the same squaw, who had a kettle of ground nuts boiling: I asked her to let me boil my piece of bear in her kettle, which she did, and gave me some ground nuts to eat with it: and I cannot but think how pleasant it was to me. I have sometimes seen bear baked very handsomely among the English, and some like it, but the thought that it was bear, made me tremble: but now that was savory to me that one would think was enough to turn the stomach of a brute creature.

One bitter cold day, I could find no room to sit down before the fire: I went out, and could not tell what to do, but I went into another wigwam, where they were also sitting around the fire, but the squaw laid a skin for me, and bade me sit down, and gave me some ground nuts, and bade me come again: and told me they would buy me, if they were able, and yet these were strangers to me that I never saw before.

THE TENTH REMOVE

That day a small part of the company removed about three-quarters of a mile, intending further the next day. When they came to the place where they intended to lodge, and had pitched their wigwams, being hungry I went again back to the place we were before at, to get something to eat: being encouraged by the squaw's kindness, who bade me come again; when I was there, there came an Indian to look after me, who when he had found me, kicked me all along: I went home and found venison roasting that night, but they would not give me one bit of it. Sometimes I met with favor, and sometimes with nothing but frowns.

THE ELEVENTH REMOVE

The next day in the morning they took their travel, intending a day's journey up the river. I took my load at my back, and quickly we came to wade over the river: and passed over tiresome and wearisome hills. One hill was so steep that I was fain to creep up upon my knees, and to hold by twigs and bushes to keep myself from falling backward. My head also was so light, that I usually reeled as I went; but I hope all these wearisome steps that I have taken, are but a forewarning to me of the heavenly rest. *I know, O Lord, that they judgments are right, and that thou in faithfulness hast afflicted me,* Psalm 119. 75.

THE TWELFTH REMOVE

It was upon a Sabbath day morning, that they prepared for their travel. This morning I asked my master whether he would sell me to my husband; he answered me Nux,[59] which did much rejoice my spirit. My mistress, before we went, was gone to the burial of a papoose, and returning, she found me sitting and reading in my Bible; she snatched it hastily out of my hand, and threw it out of doors; I ran out and caught it up, and put it into my pocket, and never let her see it afterward. Then they packed up their things to be gone, and gave me my load: I complained it was too heavy, whereupon she gave me a slap in the face, and bade me go; I lifted up my heart to God, hoping the redemption was not far off: and the rather because their insolence grew worse and worse.

---

59. Nux: yes.

But the thoughts of my going homeward (for so we bent our course) much cheered my spirit, and made my burden seem light, and almost nothing at all. But (to my amazement and great perplexity) the scale was soon turned: for when we had gone a little way, on a sudden my mistress gives out, she would go no further, but turn back again, and said, I must go back again with her, and she called her sannup, and would have had him gone back also, but he would not, but said, he would go on, and come to us again in three days. My spirit was upon this, I confess, very impatient, and almost outrageous. I thought I could as well have died as went back: I cannot declare the trouble that I was in about it; but yet back again I must go. As soon as I had an opportunity, I took my Bible to read, and that quieting scripture came to my hand, Psalms 46. 10. *Be still, and know that I am God.* Which stilled my spirit for the present: but a sore time of trial, I concluded, I had to go through.

My master being gone, who seemed to me the best friend that I had of an Indian, both in cold and hunger, and quickly so it proved. Down I sat, with my heart as full as it could hold, and yet so hungry that I could not sit neither: but going out to see what I could find, and walking among the trees, I found six acorns, and two chestnuts, which were some refreshment to me. Towards night I gathered me some sticks for my own comfort, that I might not lie a-cold: but when we came to lie down they bade me go out, and lie somewhere else, for they had company (they said) come in more than their own: I told them, I could not tell where to go, they bade me go look; I told them, if I went to another wigwam they would be angry, and send me home again. Then one of the company drew his sword, and told me he would run me through if I did not go presently. Then was I fain to stoop to this rude fellow, and to go out in the night, I knew not whither. Mine eyes have seen that fellow afterwards walking up and down Boston, under the appearance of a friendly Indian, and several others of the like cut.

I went to one wigwam, and they told me they had no room. Then I went to another, and they said the same; at last an old Indian bade me come to him, and his squaw gave me some ground nuts; she gave me also something to lay under my head, and a good fire we had: and through the good providence of God, I had a comfortable lodging that night. In the morning, another Indian bade me come at night, and he would give me six ground nuts, which I did. We were at this place and time about two miles from Connecticut river. We went in the morning to gather ground nuts, to the river, and went back again that night. I went with a good load at my back (for they when they went, though but a little way, would carry all their trumpery with them). I told them the skin was off my back, but I had no other comforting answer from them than this, That it would be no matter if my head were off too.

THE THIRTEENTH REMOVE

Instead of going toward the Bay, which was that I desired, I must go with them five or six miles down the river into a mighty thicket of brush: where we abode almost a fortnight. Here one asked me to make a shirt for her papoose, for which she gave me a mess of broth, which was thickened with meal made of the bark of a tree, and to make it the better, she had put into it about a handful of peas, and a few roasted ground nuts. I had not seen my son a pretty while, and here was an Indian of whom I made inquiry after him, and asked him when he saw him: he answered me, that such a time his master roasted him, and that himself did eat a piece of him, as big as his two fingers, and that he was very good meat: but the Lord upheld my spirit, under this discouragement; and I considered their horrible addictedness to lying, and that there is not one of them that makes the least conscience of speaking of truth. In this place, on a cold night, as I lay by the fire, I removed a stick that kept the heat from me, a squaw moved it down again, at which I looked up, and she threw a handful of ashes in my eyes: I thought I should have been quite blinded, and have never seen more: but lying down, the water run out of my eyes, and carried the dirt with it, that by the morning, I recovered my sight again. Yet upon this, and the like occasions, I hope it is not too much to say with Job, *Have pity upon me, have pity upon me, O ye my friends, for the hand of the Lord has touched me.*[60]

And here I cannot but remember how many times sitting in their wigwams, and musing on things past, I should suddenly leap up and run out, as if I had been at home, forgetting where I was, and what my condition was: but when I was without, and saw nothing but wilderness, and woods, and a company of barbarous heathens, my mind quickly returned to me, which made me think of that, spoken concerning Samson, who said, *I will go out and shake myself as at other times, but he wist not that the Lord was departed from him.*[61] About this time I began to think that all my hopes of restoration would come to nothing. I thought of the English army, and hoped for their coming, and being taken by them, but that failed. I hoped to be carried to Albany, as the Indians had discoursed before, but that failed also. I thought of being sold to my husband, as my master spake, but instead of that, my master himself was gone, and I left behind, so that my spirit was now quite ready to sink.

I asked them to let me go out and pick up some sticks, that I might get alone, and pour out my heart unto the Lord. Then also I took my Bible to read, but I found no comfort here neither, which many times I was wont to find: so easy a thing it is with God to dry up the streams of scripture comfort from us. Yet I can say, that in all my sorrows and afflictions, God did not leave me to have my impatience work towards himself, as if his ways were unrighteous. But I knew that he laid upon me less than I deserved. Afterward, before this doleful time ended with me, I was turning the leaves of my Bible, and the Lord brought to me some scriptures, which did a little revive me, as that Isaiah 55. 8, *For my thoughts are not your thoughts, neither are your ways my ways, saith the Lord.* And also that, Psalms 37. 5, *Commit thy way unto the Lord, trust also in him, and he shall bring it to pass.*

About this time they came yelping from Hadley, where they had killed three Englishmen, and brought one captive with them, *viz.* Thomas Read. They all gathered about the poor man, asking him many questions. I desired also to go and see him; and when I came, he was crying bitterly, supposing they would quickly kill him. Whereupon I asked one of them, whether they intended to kill him; he answered me, they would not: he being a little cheered with that, I asked him about the welfare of my husband, he told me he saw him such a time in the Bay, and he was well, but very

60. Job 19:21.   61. Judg. 16:20.

melancholy. By which I certainly understood (though I suspected it before) that what-soever the Indians told me respecting him was vanity and lies. Some of them told me, he was dead, and they had killed him: some said he was married again, and that the governor wished him to marry; and told him he should have his choice, and that all persuaded I was dead. So like were these barbarous creatures to him who was a liar from the beginning.

As I was sitting once in the wigwam here, Philip's maid came in with the child in her arms, and asked me to give her a piece of my apron, to make a flap for it. I told her I would not: then my mistress bade me give it, but still I said no: the maid told me if I would not give her a piece, she would tear a piece off it: I told her I would tear her coat then, with that my mistress rises up, and takes up a stick big enough to have killed me, and struck at me with it, but I stepped out, and she struck the stick into the mat of the wigwam. But while she was pulling of it out, I ran to the maid and gave her all my apron, and so that storm went over.

Hearing that my son was come to this place, I went to see him, and told him his father was well, but very melancholy: he told me he was as much grieved for his father as for himself; I wondered at his speech, for I thought I had enough upon my spirit in reference to myself, to make me mindless of my husband and everyone else: they being safe among their friends. He told me also, that a while before, his master (together with other Indians) were going to the French for powder; but by the way the Mohawks met with them, and killed four of their company which made the rest turn back again, for which I desired that myself and he may bless the Lord; for it might have been worse with him, had he been sold to the French, than it proved to be in his remaining with the Indians.

I went to see an English youth in this place, one John Gilbert of Springfield. I found him lying without doors, upon the ground; I asked him how he did? He told me he was very sick of a flux, with eating so much blood: they had turned him out of the wigwam, and with him an Indian papoose, almost dead (whose parents had been killed), in a bitter cold day, without fire or clothes: the young man himself had nothing on, but his shirt and waistcoat. This sight was enough to melt a heart of flint. There they lay quiv-ering in the cold, the youth round like a dog; the papoose stretched out, with his eyes and nose and mouth full of dirt, and yet alive, and groaning. I advised John to go and get to some fire: he told me he could not stand, but I persuaded him still, lest he should lie there and die: and with much ado I got him to a fire, and went myself home. As soon as I was got home, his master's daughter came after me, to know what I had done with the Englishman, I told her I had got him to a fire in such a place. Now had I need to pray Paul's prayer, 2 Thessalonians 3.2. *That we may be delivered from unreason-able and wicked men.* For her satisfaction I went along with her, and brought her to him; but before I got home again, it was noised about, that I was running away and getting the English youth, along with me; that as soon as I came in, they began to rant and domineer: asking me where I had been, and what I had been doing? and saying they would knock him on the head: I told them, I had been seeing the English youth, and that I would not run away, they told me I lied, and taking up a hatchet, they came to me, and said they would knock me down if I stirred out again; and so confined me to the wigwam. Now may I say with David, 2 Samuel 24. 14, *I am in a great strait.* If I keep in, I must die with hunger, and if I go out, I must be knocked in head. This distressed condition held that day, and half the next; and then the Lord remembered me, whose mercies are great. Then came an Indian to me with a pair of stockings that were too big for him, and he would have me ravel them out, and knit them fit for him. I showed myself willing, and bade him ask my mistress if I might go along with him a little way; she said yes, I might, but I was not a little refreshed with that news, that I had my liberty again. Then I went along with him, and he gave me some roasted ground nuts, which did again revive my feeble stomach.

Being got out of her sight, I had time and liberty again to look into my Bible: which was my guide by day, and my pillow by night. Now that comfortable scripture presented itself to me, Isaiah 54. 7. *For a small moment have I forsaken thee, but with great mercies will I gather thee.* Thus the Lord carried me along from one time to another, and made good to me this precious promise, and many others. Then my son came to see me, and I asked his master to let him stay a while with me, that I might comb his head, and look over him, for he was almost overcome with lice. He told me, when I had done, that he was very hungry, but I had nothing to relieve him; but bid him go into the wigwams as he went along, and see if he could get anything among them. Which he did, and it seems tarried a little too long; for his master was angry with him, and beat him, and then sold him. Then he came running to tell me he had a new master, and that he had given him some ground nuts already. Then I went along with him to his new master who told me he loved him: and he should not want. So his master carried him away, and I never saw him afterward, till I saw him at Pascataqua in Portsmouth.

That night they bade me go out of the wigwam again: my mistress's papoose was sick, and it died that night, and there was one benefit in it, that there was more room. I went to a wigwam, and they bade me come in, and gave me a skin to lie upon, and a mess of venison and ground nuts, which was a choice dish among them. On the morrow they buried the papoose, and afterward, both morning and evening, there came a company to mourn and howl with her: though I confess, I could not much condole with them. Many sorrowful days I had in this place: often getting alone; *like a crane, or a swallow, so did I chatter: I did mourn as a dove, mine eyes ail with looking upward. Oh, Lord, I am oppressed; undertake for me*, Isaiah 38. 14. I could tell the Lord as Hezekiah, verse 3. *Remember now O Lord, I beseech thee, how I have walked before thee in truth.*[62]

Now had I time to examine all my ways: my conscience did not accuse me of unrighteousness toward one or other: yet I saw how in my walk with God I had been a careless creature. As David said, *Against thee, thee only have I sinned:*[63] and I might say with the poor publican, *God be merciful unto me a sinner.*[64] On the Sabbath days, I could look upon the sun and think how people were going to the house of God, to have their souls refreshed; and then home, and their bodies also: but I was destitute of both; and might say as the poor prodigal, *he would fain have filled his belly with the husks that the swine did eat, and no man gave unto him*, Luke 15. 16. For I must say with him,

62. Isa. 38:3.
63. Ps. 51:4.

64. Luke 18:10-14.

Father I have sinned against heaven, and in thy sight, verse 21. I remembered how on the night before and after the Sabbath, when my family was about me, and relations and neighbors with us, we could pray and sing, and then refresh our bodies with the good creatures of God; and then have a comfortable bed to lie down on: but instead of all this, I had only a little swill for the body, and then like a swine, must lie down on the ground. I cannot express to man the sorrow that lay upon my spirit, the Lord knows it. Yet that comfortable[65] scripture would often come to my mind, *For a small moment have I forsaken thee, but with great mercies will I gather thee.*

THE FOURTEENTH REMOVE

Now must we pack up and be gone from this thicket, bending our course toward the Bay towns, I having nothing to eat by the way this day, but a few crumbs of cake, that an Indian gave my girl the same day we were taken. She gave it me, and I put it in my pocket; there it lay, till it was so moldy (for want of good baking) that one could not tell what it was made of; it fell all to crumbs, and grew so dry and hard, that it was like little flints; and this refreshed me many times, when I was ready to faint. It was in my thoughts when I put it into my mouth, that if ever I returned, I would tell the world what a blessing the Lord gave to such mean food. As we went along, they killed a deer, with a young one in her, they gave me a piece of the fawn, and it was so young and tender, that one might eat the bones as well as the flesh, and yet I thought it very good. When night came on we sat down; it rained, but they quickly got up a bark wigwam, where I lay dry that night. I looked out in the morning, and many of them had lain in the rain all night, I saw by their reeking. Thus the Lord dealt mercifully with me many times, and I fared better than many of them. In the morning they took the blood of the deer, and put it into the paunch, and so boiled it; I could eat nothing of that, though they ate it sweetly. And yet they were so nice[66] in other things, that when I had fetched water, and had put the dish I dipped the water with, into the kettle of water which I brought, they would say, they would knock me down: for they said, it was a sluttish[67] trick.

THE FIFTEENTH REMOVE

We went on our travel. I having got one handful of ground nuts, for my support that day, they gave me my load, and I went on cheerfully (with the thoughts of going homeward) having my burden more on my back than my spirit: we came to Baquag river again that day, near which we abode a few days. Sometimes one of them would give me a pipe, another a little tobacco, another a little salt: which I would change for a little victuals. I cannot but think what a wolfish appetite persons have in a starving condition: for many times when they gave me that which was hot, I was so greedy, that I should burn my mouth, that it would trouble me hours after, and yet I should quickly do the same again. And after I was thoroughly

---

65. comfortable: comforting.
66. nice: fastidious.

67. sluttish: slovenly.

hungry, I was never again satisfied. For though sometimes it fell out, that I got enough, and did eat till I could eat no more, yet I was as unsatisfied as I was when I began. And now could I see that scripture verified (there being many scriptures which we do not take notice of, or understand till we are afflicted) Micah 6. 14. *Thou shalt eat and not be satisfied.* Now I might see more than ever before, the miseries that sin hath brought upon us: many times I should be ready to run out against the heathen, but the scripture would quiet me again, Amos 3. 6, *Shall there be evil in the city, and the Lord hath not done it?* The Lord help me to make a right improvement of His word, and that I might learn that great lesson, Micah 6. 8-9. *He hath showed thee (O Man) what is good, and what doth the Lord require of thee, but to do justly, and love mercy, and walk humbly with they God? Hear ye the rod, and who hath appointed it.*

THE SIXTEENTH REMOVE

We began this remove with wading over Baquag river: the water was up to the knees, and the stream very swift, and so cold that I thought it would have cut me in sunder. I was so weak and feeble, that I reeled as I went along, and thought there I must end my days at last, after my bearing and getting through so many difficulties; the Indians stood laughing to see me staggering along: but in my distress the Lord gave me experience of the truth, and goodness of that promise, Isaiah 43. 2. *when thou passest through the waters, I will be with thee, and through the rivers, they shall not overflow thee.* Then I sat down to put on my stockings and shoes, with the tears running down mine eyes, and many sorrowful thoughts in my heart, but I got up to go along with them. Quickly there came up to us an Indian, who informed them, that I must go to Wachusett to my master, for there was a letter come from the Council to the Sagamores, about redeeming the captives, and that there would be another in fourteen days, and that I must be there ready. My heart was so heavy before that I could scarce speak or go in the path; and yet now so light, that I could run. My strength seemed to come again, and recruit my feeble knees, and aching heart: yet it pleased them to go but one mile that night, and there we stayed two days. In that time came a company of Indians to us, near thirty, all on horseback. My heart skipped within me, thinking they had been Englishmen at the first sight of them, for they were dressed in English apparel, with hats, white neckcloths, and sashes about their waists, and ribbons upon their shoulders: but when they came near, there was a vast difference between the lovely faces of Christians, and the foul looks of these heathens, which much damped my spirit again.

THE SEVENTEENTH REMOVE

A comfortable remove it was to me, because of my hopes. They gave me a pack, and along we went cheerfully; but quickly my will proved more than my strength; having little or no refreshing my strength failed me, and my spirits were almost quite gone. Now may I say with David, Psalm 109. 22-24. *I am poor and needy, and my heart is wounded within me. I am gone like the shadow when it declineth: I am tossed up and down like the locust; my knees are weak through fasting, and my flesh faileth of fatness.* At night we came to an Indian town, and the Indians sat down by a wigwam discoursing, but I was almost spent, and could scarce speak. I laid down my load, and went into the wigwam, and there sat an Indian boiling of horse's feet (they being wont to eat the flesh first, and when the feet were old and dried, and they had nothing else, they would cut off the feet and use them). I asked him to give me a little of his broth, or water they were boiling in; he took a dish, and gave me one spoonful of samp,[68] and bid me take as much of the broth as I would. Then I put some of the hot water to the samp, and drank it up, and my spirit came again. He gave me also a piece of the ruff or ridding of the small guts,[69] and I broiled it on the coals; and now may I say with Jonathan, *See, I pray you, how mine eyes have been enlightened, because I tasted a little of this honey,* 1 Samuel. 14. 29. Now is my spirit revived again; though means be never so inconsiderable, yet if the Lord bestow his blessing upon them, they shall refresh both soul and body.

THE EIGHTEENTH REMOVE

We took up our packs and along we went, but a wearisome day I had of it. As we went along I saw an Englishman stripped naked, and lying dead upon the ground, but knew not who it was. Then we came to another Indian town, where we stayed all night. In this town there were four English children, captives; and one of them my own sister's. I went to see how she did, and she was well, considering her captive condition. I would have tarried that night with her, but they that owned her would not suffer it. Then I went into another wigwam, where they were boiling corn and beans, which was a lovely sight to see, but I could not get a taste thereof. Then I went to another wigwam, where there were two of the English children; the squaw was boiling horse's feet, then she cut me off a little piece, and gave one of the English children a piece also. Being very hungry I had quickly eaten up mine, but the child could not bite it, it was so tough and sinewy, but lay sucking, gnawing, chewing and slobbering of it in the mouth and hand, then I took it of the child, and ate it myself, and savory it was to my taste. Then I may say as Job, 6. 7. *The things that my soul refused to touch, are as my sorrowful meat.* Thus the Lord made that pleasant refreshing, which another time would have been an abomination. Then I went home to my mistress's wigwam; and they told me I disgraced my master with begging, and if I did so any more, they would knock me in the head: I told them, they had as good knock me in the head as starve me to death.

THE NINETEENTH REMOVE

They said, when we went out, that we must travel to Wachusett this day. But a bitter weary day I had of it, travelling now three days together, without resting any day between. At last, after many weary steps, I saw Wachusett hills, but many miles

---

68. samp: porridge.   69. ruff or ridding of the small guts: intestine.

off. Then we came to a great swamp, through which we travelled, up to the knees in mud and water, which was heavy going to one tired before. Being almost spent, I thought I should have sunk down at last, and never gotten out; but I may say, as in Psalm 94. 18, *When my foot slipped, thy mercy, O Lord, held me up*. Going along, having indeed my life, but little spirit, Philip, who was in the company, came up and took me by the hand, and said, Two weeks more and you shall be mistress again. I asked him, if he spake true? He answered, Yes, and quickly you shall come to your master again; who had been gone from us three weeks. After many weary steps we came to Wachusett, where he was: and glad I was to see him. He asked me, When I washed me? I told him not this month, then he fetched me some water himself, and bid me wash, and gave me the glass to see how I looked; and bid his squaw give me something to eat: so she gave me a mess of beans and meat, and a little ground nut cake. I was wonderfully revived with this favor showed me, Psalm 106. 46, *He made them also to be pitied, of all those that carried them captives*.

My master had three squaws, living sometimes with one, and sometimes with another one, this old squaw, at whose wigwam I was, and with whom my master had been those three weeks. Another was Weetamoo, with whom I had lived and served all this while: a severe and proud dame she was, bestowing every day in dressing herself neat as much time as any of the gentry of the land: powdering her hair, and painting her face, going with necklaces, with jewels in her ears, and bracelets upon her hands: when she had dressed herself, her work was to make girdles of wampum and beads. The third squaw was a younger one, by whom he had two papooses. By that time I was refreshed by the old squaw, with whom my master was, Weetamoo's maid came to call me home, at which I fell a-weeping. Then the old squaw told me, to encourage me, that if I wanted victuals, I should come to her, and that I should lie there in her wigwam. Then I went with the maid, and quickly came again and lodged there. The squaw laid a mat under me, and a good rug over me; the first time I had any such kindness showed me. I understood that Weetamoo thought, that if she should let me go and serve with the old squaw, she would be in danger to lose, not only my service, but the redemption pay also. And I was not a little glad to hear this; being by it raised in my hopes, that in God's due time there would be an end of this sorrowful hour. Then in came an Indian, and asked me to knit him three pair of stockings, for which I had a hat, and a silk handkerchief. Then another asked me to make her a shift, for which she gave me an apron.

Then came Tom and Peter,[70] with the second letter from the Council, about the captives. Though they were Indians, I got them by the hand, and burst out into tears; my heart was so full that I could not speak to them; but recovering myself, I asked them how my husband did, and all my friends and acquaintance: They said, They are all very well, but melancholy. They brought me two biscuits, and a pound of tobacco. The tobacco I quickly gave away; when it was all gone, one asked me to give him a pipe of tobacco, I told him it was all gone; then began he to rant and threaten. I told him when my husband came I would give him some: Hang him rogue (says he) I will

---

70. Tom and Peter: Christian Indians acting as mediators.

knock out his brains, if he comes here. And then again, in the same breath they would say, That if there should come an hundred without guns, they would do them no hurt. So unstable and like madmen they were. So that fearing the worst, I durst not send to my husband, though there were some thoughts of his coming to redeem and fetch me, not knowing what might follow. For there was little more trust to them than to the master they served.[71]

When the letter was come, the sagamores met to consult about the captives, and called me to them to enquire how much my husband would give to redeem me. When I came I sat down among them, as I was wont to do, as their manner is: then they bade me stand up, and said, they were the General Court. They bid me speak what I thought he would give. Now knowing that all we had was destroyed by the Indians, I was in a great strait: I thought if I should speak of but a little, it would be slighted, and hinder the matter; if of a great sum, I knew not where it would be procured: yet at a venture, I said twenty pounds, yet desired them to take less; but they would not hear of that, but sent that message to Boston, that for twenty pounds I should be redeemed. It was a Praying Indian that wrote their letter for them.

There was another Praying Indian, who told me, that he had a brother, that would not eat horse; his conscience was so tender and scrupulous (though as large as hell, for the destruction of poor Christians). Then he said, he read that scripture to him, 2 Kings, 6. 25. *There was a famine in Samaria, and behold they besieged it, until an ass's head was sold for fourscore pieces of silver, and the fourth part of a kab of dove's dung, for five pieces of silver.* He expounded this place[72] to his brother, and showed him that it was lawful to eat that in a famine which is not at another time. And now, says he, he will eat horse with any Indian of them all. There was another Praying Indian, who when he had done all the mischief that he could, betrayed his own father into the English hands, thereby to purchase his own life. Another Praying Indian was at Sudbury fight, though, as he deserved, he was afterward hanged for it. There was another Praying Indian, so wicked and cruel, as to wear a string about his neck, strung with Christians' fingers. Another Praying Indian, when they went to Sudbury fight, went with them, and his squaw also with him, with her papoose at her back: before they went to that fight, they got a company together to powwow; the manner was as followeth. There was one that kneeled upon a deerskin, with the company round him in a ring who kneeled, and striking upon the ground with their hands, and with sticks, and muttering or humming with their mouths; beside him who kneeled in the ring, there also stood one with a gun in his hand: then he on the deerskin made a speech, and all manifested assent to it: and so they did many time together. Then they bade him with the gun go out of the ring, which he did, but when he was out, they called him again; but he seemed to make a stand, then they called the more earnestly, till he returned again: then they all sang. Then they gave him two guns, in either hand one: and so he on the deerskin began again; and at the end of every sentence in his speaking, they all assented, humming or muttering with their mouths, and striking upon the ground with their hands. Then they bade him with the two guns go out of

---

71. the master they served: the devil.   72. place: passage.

the ring again; which he did, a little way. Then they called him in again, but he made a stand; so they called him with greater earnestness; but he stood reeling and wavering as if he knew not whither he should stand or fall, or which way to go. Then they called him with exceeding great vehemency, all of them, one and another: after a little while he turned in, staggering as he went, with his arms stretched out, in either hand a gun. As soon as he came in, they all sang and rejoiced exceedingly a while. And then he upon the deerskin, made another speech unto which they all assented in a rejoicing manner: and so they ended their business, and forthwith went to Sudbury-fight.

To my thinking they went without any scruple, but that they should prosper, and gain the victory. And they went out not so rejoicing, but they came home with as great a victory. For they said they had killed two captains, and almost an hundred men. One Englishman they brought along with them: and he said, it was too true, for they had made sad work at Sudbury, as indeed it proved. Yet they came home without that rejoicing and triumphing over their victory, which they were wont to show at other times, but rather like dogs (as they say) which have lost their ears. Yet I could not perceive that it was for their own loss of men: they said, they had not lost above five or six: and I missed none, except in one wigwam. When they went, they acted as if the devil had told them that they should gain the victory: and now they acted, as if the devil had told them they should have a fall. Whether it were so or no, I cannot tell, but so it proved, for quickly they began to fall, and so held on that summer, till they came to utter ruin.

They came home on a Sabbath day, and the powwow that kneeled upon the deerskin came home (I may say, without abuse) as black as the devil. When my master came home, he came to me and bid me make a shirt for his papoose, of a holland-laced pillowbeer.[73] About that time there came an Indian to me and bid me come to his wigwam, at night, and he would give me some pork and ground nuts. Which I did, and as I was eating, another Indian said to me, he seems to be your good friend, but he killed two Englishmen at Sudbury, and there lie their clothes behind you: I looked behind me, and there I saw bloody clothes, with bullet holes in them; yet the Lord suffered not this wretch to do me any hurt; yea, instead of that, he many times refreshed me: five or six times did he and his squaw refresh my feeble carcass. If I went to their wigwam at any time, they would always give me something, and yet they were strangers that I never saw before. Another squaw gave me a piece of fresh pork, and a little salt with it, and lent me her pan to fry it in; and I cannot but remember what a sweet, pleasant and delightful relish that bit had to me, to this day. So little do we prize common mercies when we have them to the full.

The Twentieth Remove

It was their usual manner to remove, when they had done any mischief, lest they should be found out: and so they did at this time. We went about three or four miles, and there they built a great wigwam, big enough to hold an hundred Indians, which

---

73. pillowbeer: pillowcase.

they did in preparation to a great day of dancing. They would say now amongst themselves, that the governor would be so angry for his loss at Sudbury, that he would send no more about the captives, which made me grieve and tremble. My sister being not far from the place where we now were, and hearing that I was here, desired her master to let her come and see me, and he was willing to it, and would go with her: but she being ready before him, told him she would go before, and was come within a mile or two of the place; then he overtook her, and began to rant as if he had been mad; and made her go back again in the rain; so that I never saw her till I saw her in Charlestown. But the Lord requited many of their ill doings, for this Indian her master, was hanged after at Boston.

The Indians now began to come from all quarters, against[74] their merry dancing day. Among some of them came one Goodwife Kettle: I told her my heart was so heavy that it was ready to break: so is mine too, said she, but yet said, I hope we shall hear some good news shortly. I could hear how earnestly my sister desired to see me, and I as earnestly desired to see her: and yet neither of us could get an opportunity. My daughter was also now about a mile off, and I had not seen her in nine or ten weeks, as I had not seen my sister since our first taking. I earnestly desired them to let me go and see them: yea, I entreated, begged, and persuaded them, but to let me see my daughter; and yet so hard-hearted were they, that they would not suffer it. They made use of their tyrannical power whilst they had it: but through the Lord's wonderful mercy, their time was now but short.

On a Sabbath day, the sun being about an hour high in the afternoon, came Mr. John Hoar (the Council permitting him, and his own forward[75] spirit inclining him) together with the two forementioned Indians, Tom and Peter, with their third letter from the Council. When they came near, I was abroad: though I saw them not, they presently called me in, and bade me sit down and not stir. Then they caught up their guns, and away they ran, as if an enemy had been at hand; and the guns went off apace. I manifested some great trouble, and they asked me what was the matter? I told them, I thought they had killed the Englishman (for they had in the meantime informed me that an Englishman was come), they said, No; they shot over his horse, and under, and before his horse; and they pushed him this way and that way, at their pleasure, showing what they could do: then they let them come to their wigwams. I begged of them to let me see the Englishman, but they would not. But there was I fain to sit their pleasure. When they had talked their fill with him, they suffered me to go to him. We asked each other of our welfare, and how my husband did, and all my friends? He told me they were all well, and would be glad to see me. Amongst other things which my husband sent me, there came a pound of tobacco: which I sold for nine shillings in money: for many of the Indians for want of tobacco, smoked hemlock, and ground ivy. It was a great mistake in any, who thought I sent for tobacco: for through the favor of God, that desire was overcome.

I now asked them, whether I should go home with Mr. Hoar? They answered No, one and another of them: and it being night, we lay down with that answer; in the

74. against: preparing for.   75. forward: eager.

morning, Mr. Hoar invited the sagamores to dinner; but when we went to get it ready, we found that they had stolen the greatest part of the provision Mr. Hoar had brought, out of his bags, in the night. And we may see the wonderful power of God, in that one passage, in that when there was such a great number of the Indians together, and so greedy of a little good food; and no English there, but Mr. Hoar and myself: that there they did not knock us in the head, and take what we had: there being not only some provisions, but also trading cloth, a part of the twenty pounds agreed upon: but instead of doing us any mischief, they seemed to be ashamed of the fact, and said, it were some matchit[76] Indian that did it. Oh that we could believe that there is nothing too hard for God! God showed his power over the heathen in this, as he did over the hungry lions when Daniel was cast into the den.

Mr. Hoar called them betime to dinner, but they ate very little, they being so busy in dressing themselves, and getting ready for their dance: which was carried on by eight of them, four men and four squaws; my master and mistress being two. He was dressed in his holland shirt, with great laces sewed at the tail of it, he had his silver buttons, his white stockings, his garters were hung round with shillings, and he had girdles of wampum upon his head and shoulders. She had a kersey coat, and covered with girdles of wampum from the loins upward: her arms from her elbows to her hands were covered with bracelets; there were handfuls of necklaces about her neck, and several sorts of jewels in her ears. She had fine red stockings, and white shoes, her hair powdered and face painted red, that was always before black. And all the dancers were after the same manner. There were two other singing and knocking on a kettle for their music. They kept hopping up and down one after another, with a kettle of water in the midst, standing warm upon some embers, to drink of when they were dry. They held on till it was almost night, throwing out wampum to the standers-by.

At night I asked them again, if I should go home? They all as one said No, except my husband would come for me. When we were lain down, my master went out of the wigwam, and by and by sent in an Indian called James the Printer, who told Mr. Hoar, that my master would let me go home tomorrow, if he would [let] him have one pint of liquors. Then Mr. Hoar called his own Indians, Tom and Peter, and bid them go and see whether he would promise before them three: and if he would, he should have it; which he did, and he had it. Then Philip smelling the business called me to him, and asked me what I would give him, to tell me some good news, and speak a good word for me. I told him, I could not tell what to give him, I would anything I had, and asked him what he would have? He said, two coats and twenty shillings in money, and half a bushel of seed corn, and some tobacco. I thanked him for his love: but I knew the good news as well as the crafty fox.

My master after he had had his drink, quickly came ranting into the wigwam again, and called for Mr. Hoar, drinking to him, and saying, He was a good man: and then again he would say, Hang him, rogue: being almost drunk, he would drink to him, and yet presently say he should be hanged. Then he called for me. I trembled to hear him, yet I was fain to go to him, and he drank to me, showing no incivility. He was

76. matchit: bad.

the first Indian I saw drunk all the while that I was amongst them. At last his squaw ran out, and he after her, around the wigwam, with his money jingling at his knees: but she escaped him: but having an old squaw he ran to her: and so through the Lord's mercy, we were no more troubled that night.

Yet I had not a comfortable night's rest: for I think I can say, I did not sleep for three nights together. The night before the letter came from the council, I could not rest, I was so full of fears and troubles, God many times leaving us most in the dark, when deliverance is nearest: yea, at this time I could not rest night nor day. The next night I was overjoyed, Mr. Hoar being come, and that with such good tidings. The third night I was even swallowed up with the thoughts of things, *viz.* that ever I should go home again; and that I must go, leaving my children behind me in the wilderness; so that sleep was now almost departed from my eyes.

On Tuesday morning they called their General Court (as they call it) to consult and determine, whether I should go home or no: and they all as one man did seemingly consent to it, that I should go home; except Philip, who would not come among them.

But before I go any further, I would take leave to mention a few remarkable passages of providence, which I took special notice of in my afflicted time.

1. Of the fair opportunity lost in the long march, a little after the fort fight, when our English army was so numerous, and in pursuit of the enemy, and so near as to take several and destroy them: and the enemy in such distress for food, that our men might track them by their rooting in the earth for ground nuts, whilst they were flying for their lives. I say, that then our army should want provision, and be forced to leave their pursuit and return homeward: and the very next week the enemy came upon our town, like bears bereft of their whelps, or so many ravenous wolves, rending us and our lambs to death. But what shall I say? God seemed to leave His people to themselves, and order all things for His own holy ends. *Shall there be evil in the city and the Lord hath not done it? They are not grieved for the affliction of Joseph, therefore shall they go captive, with the first that go captive.*[77] It is the Lord's doing, and it should be marvelous in our eyes.

2. I cannot but remember how the Indians derided the slowness, and dullness of the English army, in its setting out. For after the desolations at Lancaster and Medfield, as I went along with them, they asked me when I thought the English army would come after them? I told them I could not tell: It may be they will come in May, said they. Thus did they scoff at us, as if the English would be a quarter of a year getting ready.

3. Which also I have hinted before, when the English army with new supplies were sent forth to pursue after the enemy, and they understanding it, fled before them till they came to Baquag river, where they forthwith went over safely: that that river should be impassable to the English. I can but admire to see the wonderful providence of God in preserving the heathen for further affliction to our poor country. They could go in great numbers over, but the English must stop: God had an overruling hand in all those things.

77. Amos 3:6, 6:6–7.

4. It was thought, if their corn were cut down, they would starve and die with hunger: and all their corn that could be found, was destroyed, and they driven from that little they had in store, into the woods in the midst of winter; and yet how to admiration did the Lord preserve them for his Holy ends, and the destruction of many still amongst the English! Strangely did the Lord provide for them; that I did not see (all the time I was among them) one man, woman, or child, die with hunger.

Though many times they would eat that, that a hog or a dog would hardly touch; yet by that God strengthened them to be a scourge to His people.

The chief and commonest food was ground nuts: they ate also nuts and acorns, artichokes, lily roots, ground beans, and several other weeds and roots, that I know not.

They would pick up old bones, and cut them to pieces at the joints, and if they were full of worms and maggots, they would scald them over the fire to make the vermin come out, and then boil them, and drink up the liquor, and then beat the great ends of them in a mortar, and so eat them. They would eat horse's guts, and ears, and all sorts of wild birds which they could catch: also bear, venison, beaver, tortoise, frogs, squirrels, dogs, skunks, rattlesnakes; yea, the very bark of trees; besides all sorts of creatures, and provision which they plundered from the English. I can but stand in admiration to see the wonderful power of God, in providing for such a vast number of our enemies in the wilderness, where there was nothing to be seen, but from hand to mouth. Many times in a morning, the generality of them would eat up all they had, and yet have some further supply against what they wanted. It is said, Psalm 81. 13–14. *Oh, that my people had hearkened to me, and Israel had walked in my ways, I should soon have subdued their enemies, and turned my hand against their adversaries.* But now our perverse and evil carriages in the sight of the Lord, have so offended Him, that instead of turning His hand against them, the Lord feeds and nourishes them up to be a scourge to the whole land.

5. Another thing that I would observe is, the strange providence of God, in turning things about when the Indians were at the highest, and the English at the lowest. I was with the enemy eleven weeks and five days, and not one week passed without the fury of the enemy, and some desolation by fire and sword upon one place or other. They mourned (with their black faces) for their own losses, yet triumphed and rejoiced in their inhuman, and many times devilish cruelty to the English. They would boast much of their victories; saying, that in two hours time they had destroyed such a captain, and his company at such a place; and such a captain and his company, in such a place; and such a captain and his company in such a place: and boast how many towns they had destroyed, and then scoff, and say, They had done them a good turn, to send them to heaven so soon. Again, they would say, This summer that they would knock all the rogues in the head, or drive them into the sea, or make them fly the country: thinking surely, Agag-like, *The bitterness of death is past.*[78] Now the heathen begin to think all is their own, and the poor Christians' hopes to fail (as to man) and now their eyes are more to God, and their hearts sigh heavenward: and to say in good earnest, *Help Lord, or we perish.*[79] When the Lord had brought His

---

78. I Sam. 15:32.   79. Matt. 8:25.

people to this, that they saw no help in anything but Himself: then He takes the quarrel into His own hand: and though they had made a pit, in their own imaginations, as deep as hell for the Christians that summer, yet the Lord hurled themselves into it. And the Lord had not so many ways before to preserve them, but now He hath as many to destroy them.

But to return again to my going home, where we may see a remarkable change of providence: at first they were all against it, except my husband would come for me; but afterwards they assented to it, and seemed much to rejoice in it; some asked me to send them some bread, others some tobacco, others shaking me by the hand, offering me a hood and scarf to ride in; not one moving hand or tongue against it. Thus hath the Lord answered my poor desire, and the many earnest requests of others put up unto God for me. In my travels an Indian came to me, and told me, if I were willing, he and his squaw would run away, and go home along with me: I told him No: I was not willing to run away, but desired to wait God's time, that I might go home quietly, and without fear. And now God hath granted me my desire.

O the wonderful power of God that I have seen, and the experience that I have had: I have been in the midst of those roaring lions, and savage bears, that feared neither

God, nor man, nor the devil, by night and day, alone and in company: sleeping all sorts together, and yet not one of them ever offered me the least abuse of unchastity to me, in word or action. Though some are ready to say, I speak it for my own credit; but I speak it in the presence of God, and to His glory. God's power is as great now, and as sufficient to save, as when he preserved Daniel in the lions' den; or the three children in the fiery furnace. I may well say as his Psalm 136. 1, *Oh give thanks unto the Lord for he is good, for His mercy endureth forever.* Let the redeemed of the Lord say so, whom He hath redeemed from the hand of the enemy, especially that I should come away in the midst of so many hundreds of enemies quietly and peaceably, and not a dog moving his tongue.

So I took my leave of them, and in coming along my heart melted into tears, more than all the while I was with them, and I was almost swallowed up with the thoughts that ever I should go home again. About the sun going down, Mr. Hoar, and myself, and the two Indians came to Lancaster, and a solemn sight it was to me. There had I lived many comfortable years amongst my relations and neighbors, and now not one Christian to be seen, nor one house left standing. We went on to a farm house that was yet standing, where we lay all night: and a comfortable lodging we had, though nothing but straw to lie on. The Lord preserved us in safety that night, and raised us up again in the morning, and carried us along, that before noon, we came to Concord. Now was I full of joy, and yet not without sorrow: joy to see such a lovely sight, so many Christians together, and some of them my neighbors: there I met with my brother, and my brother-in-law, who asked me, if I knew where his wife was? Poor heart! He had helped to bury her, and knew it not; she being shot down by the house was partly burnt: so that those who were at Boston at the desolation of the town, and came back afterward, and buried the dead, did not know her. Yet I was not without sorrow, to think how many were looking and longing, and my own children amongst the rest, to enjoy that deliverance that I had now received, and I did not know whether ever I should see them again.

Being recruited with food and raiment we went to Boston that day, where I met with my dear husband, but the thoughts of our dear children, one being dead, and the other we could not tell where, abated our comfort each to other. I was not before so much hemmed in with the merciless and cruel heathen, but now as much with pitiful, tender-hearted and compassionate Christians. In that poor, and distressed, and beggarly condition I was received in, I was kindly entertained in several houses: so much love I received from several (some of whom I knew, and others I knew not) that I am not capable to declare it. But the Lord knows them all by name: the Lord reward them sevenfold into their bosoms of His spirituals, for their temporals! The twenty pounds the price of my redemption was raised by some Boston gentlemen, and Mrs. Usher, whose bounty and religious charity, I would not forget to make mention of. Then Mr. Thomas Shepard of Charlestown received us into his house, where we continued eleven weeks; and a father and mother they were to us. And many more tender-hearted friends we met with in that place. We were now in the midst of love, yet not without much and frequent heaviness of heart for our poor children, and other relations, who were still in affliction.

The week following, after my coming in, the governor and Council sent forth to the Indians again; and that not without success; for they brought in my sister, and good-wife Kettle: their not knowing where our children were, was a sore trial to us still, and yet we were not without secret hopes that we should see them again. That which was dead lay heavier upon my spirit, than those which were alive and amongst the heathen; thinking how it suffered with its wounds, and I was in no way able to relieve it; and how it was buried by the heathen in the wilderness from among all Christians. We were hurried up and down in our thoughts, sometimes we should hear a report that they were gone this way, and sometimes that; and that they were come in, in this place or that: we kept enquiring and listening to hear concerning them, but no certain news as yet.

About this time the Council had ordered a day of public thanksgiving: though I thought I had still cause of mourning, and being unsettled in our minds, we thought we would ride toward the eastward, to see if we could hear anything concerning our children. And as we were riding along (God is the wise disposer of all things) between Ipswich and Rowley we met with Mr. William Hubbard, who told us that our son Joseph was come in to Major Waldron's, and another with him, which was my sister's son. I asked him how he knew it? He said, the Major himself told him so. So along we went till we came to Newbury; and their minister being absent, they desired my husband to preach the thanksgiving for them. But he was not willing to stay there that night, but would go over to Salisbury, to hear further, and come again in the morning; which he did, and preached there that day. At night, when he had done, one came and told him that his daughter was come in at Providence: here was mercy on both hands: now hath God fulfilled that precious scripture which was such a comfort to me in my distressed condition. When my heart was ready to sink into the earth (my children being gone I could not tell whither) and my knees trembled under me, and I was walking through the valley of the shadow of death: then the Lord brought, and now has fulfilled that reviving word unto me: *Thus saith the Lord, Refrain thy voice from weeping, and thine eyes from tears, for thy work shall be rewarded, saith the Lord, and they shall come again from the land of the enemy.*[80] Now we were between them, the one on the east, and the other on the west: our son being nearest, we went to him first, to Portsmouth, where we met with him, and with the major also: who told us he had done what he could, but could not redeem him under seven pounds; which the good people thereabouts were pleased to pay. The Lord reward the major, and all the rest, though unknown to me, for their labor of love. My sister's son was redeemed for four pounds, which the Council gave order for the payment of. Having now received one of our children, we hastened toward the other; going back through Newbury, my husband preached there on the Sabbath day: for which they rewarded him many-fold.

On Monday we came to Charlestown, where we heard that the governor of Rhode Island had sent over for our daughter, to take care of her, being now within his jurisdiction: which should not pass without our acknowledgements. But she being nearer Rehoboth than Rhode Island, Mr. Newman went over, and took care of her, and brought her to his own house. And the goodness of God was admirable to us in our low estate, in that he raised up passionate[81] friends on every side to us, when we had nothing to recompense any for their love. The Indians were now gone that way, that it was apprehended dangerous to go to her: but the carts which carried provision to the English army, being guarded, brought her with them to Dorchester, where we received her safe: blessed be the Lord for it, for great is His power, and He can do whatsoever seemeth Him good. Her coming in was after this manner: she was travelling one day with the Indians, with her basket at her back; the company of Indians were got before her, and gone out of sight, all except one squaw; she followed the squaw till night, and then both of them lay down, having nothing over them but the heavens, and under them but the earth. Thus she travelled three days together, not knowing whither she was going: having nothing to eat or drink but water, and green hurtleberries. At last they came into Providence, where she was kindly entertained by several of that town. The Indians often said, that I should never have her under twenty pounds: but now the Lord hath brought her in upon free-cost, and given her to me the second time. The Lord make us a blessing indeed, each to others. Now have I seen that scripture also fulfilled, Deuteronomy 30. 4, 7. *If any of thine be driven out to the outmost parts of heaven, from thence will the Lord thy God gather thee, and from thence will he fetch thee. And the Lord thy God will put all these curses upon thine enemies, and on them which hate thee, which persecuted thee.* Thus hath the Lord brought me and mine out of that horrible pit, and hath set us in the midst of tender-hearted and compassionate Christians. It is the desire of my soul, that we may walk worthy of the mercies received, and which we are receiving.

Our family being now gathered together (those of us that were living) the South Church in Boston hired an house for us: then we removed from Mr. Shepard's, those

---

80. Jer. 31:16.   81. passionate: compassionate.

cordial friends, and went to Boston, where we continued about three-quarters of a year: still the Lord went along with us, and provided graciously for us. I thought it somewhat strange to set up housekeeping with bare walls; but as Solomon says, *Money answers all things,*[82] and that we had through the benevolence of Christian friends, some in this town, and some in that, and others: and some from England, that in a little time we might look, and see the house furnished with love. The Lord hath been exceeding good to us in our low estate, in that when we had neither house nor home, nor other necessaries, the Lord so moved the hearts of these and those towards us, that we wanted neither food, nor raiment for ourselves or ours, Proverbs 18. 24. *There is a friend which sticketh closer than a brother.* And how many such friends have we found, and are now living amongst? And truly such a friend have we found him to be unto us, in whose house we lived, *viz.* Mr. James Whitecomb, a friend unto us near hand, and afar off.

I can remember the time, when I used to sleep quietly without workings in my thoughts, whole nights together, but now it is other ways with me. When all are fast about me, and no eye open, but His who ever waketh, my thoughts are upon things past, upon the awful dispensation of the Lord towards us; upon His wonderful power and might, in carrying of us through so many difficulties, in returning us in safety, and suffering none to hurt us. I remember in the night season, how the other day I was in the midst of thousands of enemies, and nothing but death before me: it is then hard work to persuade myself, that ever I should be satisfied with bread again. But now we are fed with the finest of the wheat, and, as I may say, with honey out of the rock: instead of the husk, we have the fatted calf: the thoughts of these things in the particulars of them, and of the love and goodness of God towards us, make it true of me, what David said of himself, Psalms 6. 6. *I watered my couch with my tears.* Oh! the wonderful power of God that mine eyes have seen, affording matter enough for my thoughts to run in, that when others are sleeping mine are weeping.

I have seen the extreme vanity of this world: one hour I have been in health, and wealth, wanting nothing: but the next hour in sickness and wounds, and death, having nothing but sorrow and affliction.

Before I knew what affliction meant, I was ready sometimes to wish for it. When I lived in prosperity, having the comforts of the world about me, my relations by me, my heart cheerful, and taking little care for anything; and yet seeing many, whom I preferred before myself, under many trials and afflictions, in sickness, weakness, poverty, losses, crosses, and cares of the world, I should be sometimes jealous lest I should not have my portion in this life, and that scripture would come to my mind, Hebrews 12. 6. *For whom the Lord loveth he chasteneth, and scourgeth every son whom he receiveth.* But now I see the Lord had his time to scourge and chasten me. The portion of some is to have their afflictions by drops, now one drop and then another; but the dregs of the cup, the wine of astonishment, like a sweeping rain that leaveth no food, did the Lord prepare to be my portion. Affliction I wanted, and affliction I had, full measure (I thought) pressed down and running over; yet I see, when

82. Eccles. 10:19.

God calls a person to anything, and through never so many difficulties, yet He is fully able to carry them through and make them see, and say they have been gainers thereby. And I hope I can say in some measure, as David did, *It is good for me that I have been afflicted.*[83] The Lord hath showed me the vanity of these outward things. That they are the vanity of vanities, and vexation of spirit; that they are but a shadow, a blast, a bubble, and our whole dependence must be upon Him. If trouble from smaller matters begin to arise in me, I have something at hand to check myself with, and say, why am I troubled? It was but the other day that if I had had the world, I would have given it for my freedom, or to have been a servant to a Christian. I have learned to look beyond present and smaller troubles, and to be quieted under them, as Moses said, Exodus 14. 13. *Stand still and see the salvation of the Lord.*[84]

9. Samuel Sewall

from the diary
1692–1720

Samuel Sewall (1652–1730) was nine when he left England for Massachusetts with his family. After a Harvard education, he became one of the colony's political leaders and eventually chief justice of the colony's superior court. During the Salem witch trials he served as special commissioner; later, he recanted his role in a public confession of error. (See the diary entry for January 14, 1697, below.) He wrote the first tract against slavery in the colonies, The Selling of Joseph *(see chapter 11). But he is probably best known for the diary that he kept, with one gap of eight years, from 1674 to 1729. As a record of intimate life and as a revealing portrait of the author it is without equal in the colonial period. The excerpts from 1720 contain highlights from Sewall's courtship of Madam Winthrop, following the death of his first wife, his failed courtship of the widow Dorothy Denison, his marriage to Abigail Tilly, and her death shortly thereafter. Though Sewall failed in wooing Madam Winthrop, he did remarry in 1722.*

Nov. 6, 1692. Joseph threw a knop of Brass and hit his Sister Betty on the forehead so as to make it bleed and swell; upon which, and for his playing at Prayer-Time, and eating when Return Thanks, I whipd him pretty smartly. When I first went in (call'd by his Grandmother) he sought to shadow and hide himself from me behind the head of the Cradle: which gave me the sorrowfull remembrance of Adam's carriage.

Jan. 14, 1697. Copy of the Bill I put up on the Fast day; giving it to Mr. Willard as he pass'd by, and standing up at the reading of it, and bowing when finished; in the Afternoon.

---

83. Ps. 119:71.

84. The verse continues: "for the Egyptians whom you have seen today, ye shall see them again no more forever."

Samuel Sewall, sensible of the reiterated strokes of God upon himself and family; and being sensible, that as to the Guilt contracted upon the opening of the late commission of Oyer and Terminer at Salem (to which the order for this Day relates) he is, upon many accounts, more concerned than any that he knows of, Desires to take the Blame and shame of it, Asking pardon of men, And especially desiring prayers that God, who has an Unlimited Authority, would pardon that sin and all other his sins; personal and Relative: And according to his infinite Benignity, and Sovereignty, Not Visit the sin of him, or of any other, upon himself or any of his, nor upon the Land: But that He would powerfully defend him against all Temptations to Sin, for the future; and vouchsafe him the efficacious, saving Conduct of his Word and Spirit.

Oct. 19, 1717. Call'd Dr. C. Mather to pray, which he did excellently in the Dining Room, having Suggested good Thoughts to my wife before he went down. After, Mr. Wadsworth pray'd in the Chamber when 'twas suppos'd my wife took little notice. About a quarter of an hour past four, my dear Wife expired in the Afternoon, whereby the Chamber was fill'd with a Flood of Tears. God is teaching me a new Lesson; to live a Widower's Life. Lord help me to Learn; and be a Sun and Shield to me, now so much of my Comfort and Defense are taken away.

Feb. 6, 1718. This morning wandering in my mind whether to live a Single or a Married Life; I had a sweet and very affectionat Meditation Concerning the Lord Jesus; Nothing was to be objected against his Person, Parentage, Relations, Estate, House, Home! Why did I not resolutely, presently close with Him! And I cry'd mightily to God that He would help me so to doe!

March 14, 1718. Deacon Marion comes to me, sits with me a great while in the evening; after a great deal of Discourse about his Courtship—He told [me] the Olivers said they wish'd I would Court their Aunt [Mrs. Winthrop]. I said little, but said twas not five Moneths since I buried my dear Wife. Had said before 'twas hard to know whether best to marry again or no; whom to marry.

Sept. 5, 1720. Going to Son Sewall's I there meet with Madam Winthrop, told her I was glad to meet her there, had not seen her a great while; gave her Mr. Holmes's Sermon.

Sept. 30, 1720. Mr. Colman's Lecture: Daughter Sewall acquaints Madam Winthrop that if she pleas'd to be within at 3. p.m. I would wait on her. She answer'd she would be at home.

Oct. 1, 1720. Satterday, I dine at Mr. Stoddard's: from thence I went to Madam Winthrop's just at 3. Spake to her, saying, my loving wife died so soon and suddenly, 'twas hardly convenient for me to think of Marrying again; however I came to this Resolution, that I would not make my Court to any person without first Consulting with her. Had a pleasant discourse about 7 Single persons sitting in the Fore-seat 7r [September] 29th, viz. Madam Rebekah Dudley, Catharine Winthrop, Bridget Usher, Deliverance Legg, Rebekah Loyd, Lydia Colman, Elizabeth Bellingham. She propounded one and another for me; but none would do, said Mrs. Loyd was about her Age.

Oct. 3, 1720. Waited on Madam Winthrop again; 'twas a little while before she came in. Her daughter Noyes being there alone with me, I said, I hoped my Waiting on her Mother would not be disagreeable to her. She answer'd she should not be against that that might be for her Comfort. I Saluted her, and told her I perceiv'd I must shortly wish her a good Time; (her mother had told me, she was with Child, and within a Moneth or two of her Time). By and by in came Mr. Airs, Chaplain of the Castle, and hang'd up his Hat, which I was a little startled at, it seeming as if he was to lodge there. At last Madam Winthrop came too. After a considerable time, I went up to her and said, if it might not be inconvenient I desired to speak with her. She assented, and spake of going into another Room; but Mr. Airs and Mrs. Noyes presently rose up, and went out, leaving us there alone. Then I usher'd in Discourse from the names in the Fore-seat; at last I pray'd that Katharine [Mrs. Winthrop] might be the person assign'd for me. She instantly took it up in the way of Denyal, as if she had catch'd at an Opportunity to do it, saying she could not do it before she was asked. Said that was her mind unless she should Change it, which she believed she should not; could not leave her Children. I express'd my Sorrow that she should do it so Speedily, pray'd her Consideration, and ask'd her when I should wait on her agen. She setting no time, I mention'd that day Sennight.[85] Gave her Mr. Willard's Fountain open'd with the little print and verses; saying, I hop'd if we did well read that book, we should meet together hereafter, if we did not now. She took the Book, and put it in her Pocket. Took Leave.

Oct. 6, 1720. A little after 6. p.m. I went to Madam Winthrop's. She was not within. I gave Sarah Chickering the Maid 2^s, Juno, who brought in wood, 1^s. Afterward the Nurse came in, I gave her 18^d, having no other small Bill. After awhile Dr. Noyes came in with his Mother; and quickly after his wife came in: They sat talking, I think, till eight a-clock. I said I fear'd I might be some Interruption to their Business: Dr. Noyes reply'd pleasantly: He fear'd they might be an Interruption to me, and went away. Madam seem'd to harp upon the same string. Must take care of her Children; could not leave that House and Neighbourhood where she had dwelt so long. I told her she might doe her children as much or more good by bestowing what she laid out in Hous-keeping, upon them. Said her Son would be of Age the 7th of August. I said it might be inconvenient for her to dwell with her Daughter-in-Law, who must be Mistress of the House. I gave her a piece of Mr. Belcher's Cake and Ginger-Bread wrapped up in a clean sheet of Paper; told her of her Father's kindness to me when Treasurer, and I Constable. My Daughter Judith was gon from me and I was more lonesom—might help to forward one another in our Journey to Canaan.— Mr. Eyre came within the door; I saluted him, ask'd how Mr. Clark did, and he went away. I took leave about 9 aclock. I told [her] I came now to refresh her Memory as to Monday-night; said she had not forgot it. In discourse with her, I ask'd leave to speak with her Sister; I meant to gain Madam Mico's favour to persuade her Sister. She seem'd surpris'd and displeas'd, and said she was in the same condition!

Oct. 10, 1720. In the Evening I visited Madam Winthrop, who treated me with a great deal of Curtesy; Wine, Marmalade. I gave her a News-Letter about the Thanksgiving Proposals, for sake of the verses for David Jeffries. She tells me Dr. Increase Mather visited her this day, in Mr. Hutchinson's Coach.

---

85. Sennight: a week later.

Oct. 11, 1720. I writ a few Lines to Madam Winthrop to this purpose: "Madam, These wait on you with Mr. Mayhew's Sermon, and Account of the state of the Indians on Martha's Vinyard. I thank you for your Unmerited Favours of yesterday; and hope to have the Happiness of Waiting on you to-morrow before Eight a-clock after Noon. I pray God to keep you, and give you a joyfull entrance upon the Two Hundred and twenty ninth year of Christopher Columbus his Discovery; and take Leave, who am, Madam, your humble Servant. S.S.

Oct. 12, 1720. Mrs. Anne Cotton came to door (twas before 8.) said Madam Winthrop was within, directed me into the little Room, where she was full of work behind a Stand; Mrs. Cotton came in and stood. Madam Winthrop pointed to her to set me a Chair. Madam Winthrop's Countenance was much changed from what 'twas on Monday, look'd dark and lowering. At last, the work, (black stuff or Silk) was taken away, I got my Chair in place, had some Converse, but very Cold and indifferent to what 'twas before. Ask'd her to acquit me of Rudeness if I drew off her Glove. Enquiring the reason, I told her twas great odds between handling a dead Goat, and a living Lady. Got it off. I told her I had one Petition to ask of her, that was, that she would take off the Negative she laid on me the third of October; She readily answer'd she could not, and enlarg'd upon it; She told me of it as soon as she could; could not leave her house, children, neighbours, business. I told her she might do som Good to help and support me. Mentioning Mrs. Gookin, Nath, the widow Weld was spoken of; said I had visited Mrs. Denison. I told her Yes! Afterward I said, If after a first and second Vagary she would Accept of me returning, Her Victorious Kindness and Good Will would be very Obliging. She thank'd me for my Book, (Mr. Mayhew's Sermon), But said not a word of the Letter. When she insisted on the Negative, I pray'd there might be no more Thunder and Lightening, I should not sleep all night. I gave her Dr. Preston, The Church's Marriage and the Church's Carriage, which cost me 6s at the Sale. The door standing open, Mr. Airs came in, hung up his Hat, and sat down. After awhile, Madam Winthrop moving, he went out. Jn° Eyre look'd in, I said How do ye, or, your servant Mr. Eyre: but heard no word from him. Sarah fill'd a Glass of Wine, she drank to me, I to her, She sent Juno home with me with a good Lantern, I gave her 6ᵈ and bid her thank her Mistress. In some of our Discourse, I told her I had rather go to the Stone-House adjoining to her, than to come to her against her mind. Told her the reason why I came every other night was lest I should drink too deep draughts of Pleasure. She had talk'd of Canary, her Kisses were to me better than the best Canary. Explain'd the expression Concerning Columbus.

Oct. 13. I tell my Son and daughter Sewall, that the Weather was not so fair as I apprehended.

Oct. 17. In the Evening I visited Madam Winthrop, who Treated me Courteously, but not in Clean Linen as sometimes. She said, she did not know whether I would come again, or no. I ask'd her how she could so impute inconstancy to me. (I had not visited her since Wednesday night being unable to get over the Indisposition received by the Treatment received that night, and *I must* in it seem'd to sound like a made piece of Formality.) Gave her this day's Gazett.

Oct. 19, 1720. Midweek, Visited Madam Winthrop; Sarah told me she was at Mr. Walley's, would not come home till late. I gave her Hannah 3 oranges with her Duty, not knowing whether I should find her or no. Was ready to go home: but said if I knew she was there, I would go thither. Sarah seem'd to speak with pretty good Courage, She would be there. I went and found her there, with Mr. Walley and his wife in the little Room below. At 7 a-clock I mentioned going home; at 8. I put on my Coat, and quickly waited on her home. She found occasion to speak loud to the servant, as if she had a mind to be known. Was Courteous to me; but took occasion to speak pretty earnestly about my keeping a Coach: I said 'twould cost £100 per annum: she said twould cost but £40. . . . Exit. Came away somewhat late.

Oct. 20, 1720. . . . Madam Winthrop not being at Lecture, I went thither first; found her very Serene with her daughter Noyes, Mrs. Dering, and the widow Shipreev sitting at a little Table, she in her arm'd Chair. She drank to me, and I to Mrs. Noyes. After awhile pray'd the favour to speak with her. She took one of the Candles, and went into the best Room, clos'd the shutters, sat down upon the Couch. She told me Madam Usher had been there, and said the Coach must be set on Wheels, and not by Rusting. She spake somthing of my needing a Wigg. Ask'd me what her Sister said to me. I told her, She said, If her Sister were for it, She would not hinder it. But I told her, she did not say she would be glad to have me for her Brother. Said, I shall keep you in the Cold, and asked her if she would be within to morrow night, for we had had but a running Feat. She said she could not tell whether she should, or no. I took Leave. As were drinking at the Governour's, he said: In England the Ladies minded little more than that they might have Money, and Coaches to ride in. I said, And New-England brooks its Name. At which Mr. Dudley smiled. Governor said they were not quite so bad here.

Oct. 21, 1720. Friday, My Son, the Minister, came to me p.m. by appointment and we pray one for another in the Old Chamber; more especially respecting my Courtship. About 6. a-clock I go to Madam Winthrop's; Sarah told me her Mistress was gon out, but did not tell me whither she went. She presently order'd me a Fire; so I went in, having Dr. Sibb's Bowels with me to read. I read the two first Sermons, still no body came in: at last about 9. a-clock Mr. Jnᵒ Eyre came in; I took the opportunity to say to him as I had done to Mrs. Noyes before, that I hoped my Visiting his Mother would not be disagreeable to him; He answered me with much Respect. When twas after 9. a-clock He of himself said he would go and call her, she was but at one of his Brothers: A while after I heard Madam Winthrop's voice, enquiring something about John. After a good while and Clapping the Garden door twice or thrice, she came in. I mentioned something of the lateness; she banter'd me, and said I was later. She receiv'd me Courteously. I ask'd when our proceedings should be made publick: She said They were like to be no more publick than they were already. Offer'd me no Wine that I remember. I rose up at 11 a-clock to come away, saying I would put on my Coat, She offer'd not to help me. I pray'd her that Juno might light me home, she open'd the Shutter, and said twas pretty light abroad; Juno was weary and gon to bed. So I came home by Star-light as well as I could. At my first coming in, I gave Sarah five Shillings. I writ Mr. Eyre his Name in his book with the date October 21. 1720. It cost me 8s. Jehovah jireh![86] Madam told me she had visited M. Mico, Wendell, and Wm Clark of the South [Church].

86. Jehovah jireh: the Lord will provide.

Oct. 22, 1720. Daughter Cooper visited me before my going out of Town, staid till about Sun set. I brought her going near as far as the Orange Tree. Coming back, near Leg's Corner, Little David Jeffries saw me, and looking upon me very lovingly, ask'd me if I was going to see his Grandmother? I said, Not to-night. Gave him a peny, and bid him present my Service to his Grandmother.

Oct. 24, 1720. I went in the Hackny Coach through the Common, stop'd at Madam Winthrop's (had told her I would take my departure from thence). Sarah came to the door with Katee in her Arms: but I did not think to take notice of the Child. Call'd her Mistress. I told her, being encourag'd by David Jeffries loving eyes, and sweet Words, I was come to enquire whether she could find in her heart to leave that House and Neighbourhood, and go and dwell with me at the South-end; I think she said softly, Not yet. I told her It did not ly in my Lands to keep a Coach. If I should, I should be in danger to be brought to keep company with her Neighbour Brooker, (he was a little before sent to prison for Debt). Told her I had an Antipathy against those who would pretend to give themselves; but nothing of their Estate. I would a proportion of my Estate with my self. And I suppos'd she would do so. As to a Perriwig, My best and greatest Friend, I could not possibly have a greater, began to find me with Hair before I was born, and had continued to do so ever since; and I could not find in my heart to go to another. She commended the book I gave her, Dr. Preston, the Church Marriage; quoted him saying 'twas inconvenient keeping out of a Fashion commonly used. I said the Time and Tide did circumscribe my Visit. She gave me a Dram of Black-Cherry Brandy, and gave me a lump of the Sugar that was in it. She wish'd me a good Journy. I pray'd God to keep her, and came away. Had a very pleasant Journy to Salem.

Nov. 4, 1720. Friday, Went again about 7. a-clock; found there Mr. John Walley and his wife: sat discoursing pleasantly. I shew'd them Isaac Moses's [an Indian] Writing. Madam W. serv'd Comfeits to us. After awhile a Table was spread, and Supper was set. I urg'd Mr. Walley to Crave a Blessing; but he put it upon me. About 9. they went away. I ask'd Madam what fashioned Neck-lace I should present her with, She said, None at all. I ask'd her Whereabout we left off last time; mention'd what I had offer'd to give her; Ask'd her what she would give me; She said she could not Change her Condition: She had said so from the beginning; could not be so far from her Children, the Lecture. Quoted the Apostle Paul affirming that a single Life was better than a Married. I answer'd That was for the present Distress. Said she had not pleasure in things of that nature as formerly: I said, you are the fitter to make me a Wife. If she hald in that mind, I must go home and bewail my Rashness in making more haste than good Speed. However, considering the Supper, I desired her to be within next Monday night, if we liv'd so long. Assented. She charg'd me with saying, that she must put away Juno, if she came to me: I utterly deny'd it, it never came in my heart; yet she insisted upon it; saying it came in upon discourse about the Indian woman that obtained her Freedom this Court. About 10. I said I would not disturb the good orders of her House, and came away. She not seeming pleas'd with my Coming away. Spake to her about David Jeffries, had not seen him.

Nov. 7, 1720. My Son pray'd in the Old Chamber. Our time had been taken up by Son and Daughter Cooper's Visit; so that I only read the 130th and 143 Psalm. Twas on the Account of my Courtship. I went to Mad. Winthrop; found her rocking her little Katee in the Cradle. I excus'd my Coming so late (near Eight). She set me an arm'd Chair and Cusheon; and so the Cradle was between her arm'd Chair and mine. Gave her the remnant of my Almonds; She did not eat of them as before; but laid them away; I said I came to enquire whether she had alter'd her mind since Friday, or remained of the same mind still. She said, Thereabouts. I told her I loved her, and was so fond as to think that she loved me: She said had a great respect for me. I told her, I had made her an offer, without asking any advice; she had so many to advise with, that twas a hindrance. The Fire was come to one short Brand besides the Block, which Brand was set up in end; at last it fell to pieces, and no Recruit was made: She gave me a Glass of Wine. I think I repeated again that I would go home and bewail my Rashness in making more haste than good Speed. I would endeavour to contain myself, and not go on to sollicit her to do that which she could not Consent to. Took leave of her. As came down the steps she bid me have a Care. Treated me Courteously. Told her she had enter'd the 4th year of her Widowhood. I had given her the News-Letter before; I did not bid her draw off her Glove as sometime I had done. Her Dress was not so clean as sometime it had been. Jehovah jireh!

Nov. 9, 1720. Dine at Brother Stoddard's: were so kind as to enquire of me if they should invite Madam Winthrop; I answer'd No. Thank'd my Sister Stoddard for her Courtesie; ... She sent her servant home with me with a Lantern. Madam Winthrop's Shutters were open as I pass'd by.

10. Richard Chamberlain

Lithobolia; Or the Stone-Throwing Devil 1698

The following narrative describes, in its inimitable style, what would today be called a poltergeist; lithobolia is a coinage from the Greek, meaning stone-throwing. It makes a fascinating comparison with Puritan witchcraft narratives; it ends benignly, and its author, named only as "R.C.," was not a Puritan. In its mixture of empiricism, popular magic, and learned faith, it resembles many contemporary writings (see, for example, Increase Mather in chapter 7). But its style adds a peculiar flavor of worldly literary gentility to a most otherworldly episode.

Richard Chamberlain was the secretary and intimate friend of George Mason, and thereby hangs a tale. Mason was the descendent of John Mason, to whom the region of present-day New Hampshire had been given as a proprietary grant in 1629. John Mason died in 1635 and the grant, neglected by the Mason family, was settled haphazardly until neighboring Massachusetts asserted its claim on the territory. The Restoration created a more favorable climate for the heirs, and by 1680 George Mason had secured a recognition of his proprietorship. Arriving at the end of 1680, with Chamberlain in tow, he began reserving all unsettled land as his, and collecting small quit-rents on settled lands. The colonists, with the exception of Quakers (such as George Walton, whose house is the scene of the story), resisted,

forcing Mason to return to England for support. Chamberlain was left in charge.
Widely believed to have instigated his close friend's claims, Chamberlain was not
locally popular. Against this troubled background, nowhere mentioned in the text,
the story begins.

Lithobolia: or, the Stone-Throwing Devil. Being an Exact and True Account (by
way of Journal) of the various Actions of Infernal Spirits, or (Devils Incarnate)
Witches, or both; and the great Disturbance and Amazement they gave to George
Waltons Family, at a place call'd Great Island in the Province of New-Hantshire in
New-England; chiefly in Throwing about (by an Invisible hand) Stone, Bricks, and
Brick-bats of all Sizes, with several other things, as Hammers, Mauls, Iron-Crows,
Spits, and other Domestick Utensils, as came into their Hellish Minds, and this for the
space of a Quarter of a Year.
    By R. C. Esq; who was a Sojourner in the same Family
    the whole time, and an Ocular Witness of these Diabolick Inventions.

To the much Honoured R. F. Esq.

To tell strange feats of Daemons, here I am;
Strange, but most true they are, ev'n to a Dram,
Tho' Sadduceans cry, 'tis all a Sham.

Here's Stony Arg'uments of persuasive Dint,
They'l not believe it, told, nor yet in Print:
What should the Reason be? The Devil's in't.

And yet they wish to be convinc'd by Sight,
Assur'd by Apparition of a Sprite;
But Learned Brown doth state[87] the matter right:

Satan will never Instrumental be
Of so much Good, to' Appear to them; for he
Hath them sure by their Infidelity.

But you, my Noble Friend, know better things;
Your Faith, mounted on Religions Wings,
Sets you above the Clouds whence Error springs.

Your Soul reflecting on this lower Sphear,
Of froth and vanity, joys oft to hear
The Sacred Ora'cles, where all Truths appear,

---

87. Learned Brown doth state: Sir Thomas Browne, in *Religio
Medici*.

Which will Conduct out of this Labyrinth of Night,
And lead you to the source of Intellect'ual Light.

Which is the Hearty Prayer of
Your most faithful Humble Servant,
R.C.

Such is the Sceptical Humour of this Age for Incredulity, (not to say Infidelity,) That I wonder they do not take up and profess, in terms, the Pyrrhonian[88] Doctrine of disbelieving their very Senses. For that which I am going to relate happening to cease in the Province of New-Hampshire in America, just upon that Governour's Arrival and Appearance at the Council there,[89] who was informed by my self, and several other Gentlemen of the Council, and other considerable Persons, of the true and certain Reality hereof, yet he continued tenacious in the Opinion that we were all imposed upon by the waggery of some unlucky Boys; which, considering the Circumstances and Passages hereafter mentioned, was altogether impossible.

I have a Wonder to relate; for such (I take it) is so to be termed whatsoever is Praeternatural, and not assignable to, or the effect of, Natural Causes: It is a *Lithobolia*, or Stone-throwing, which happened by Witchcraft (as was supposed) and maliciously perpetrated by an Elderly Woman,[90] a Neighbour suspected, and (I think) formerly detected for such kind of Diabolical Tricks and Practises; and the wicked Instigation did arise upon the account of some small quantity of Land in her Field, which she pretended was unjustly taken into the Land of the Person where the Scene of this Matter lay, and was her Right; she having been often very clamorous about that Affair, and heard to say, with much Bitterness, that her Neighbour (*innuendo*[91] the fore-mentioned Person, his Name George Walton) should never quietly injoy that piece of Ground. Which, as it has confirm'd my self and others in the Opinion that there are such things as Witches, and the Effects of Witchcraft, or at least of the mischievous Actions of Evil Spirits; which some do as little give Credit to, as in the Case of Witches, utterly rejecting both their Operations and their Beings, we having been Eye-Witnesses of this Matter almost every Day for a quarter of a Year together; so it may be a means to rectifie the depraved Judgment and Sentiments of other disbelieving Persons, and absolutely convince them of their Error, if they please to hear, without prejudice, the plain, but most true Narration of it; which was thus.

Some time ago being in America (in His then Majesty's Service) I was lodg'd in the said George Walton's House, a Planter there, and on a Sunday Night [June 11, 1682], about Ten a Clock, many Stones were heard by my self, and the rest of the Family, to be thrown, and (with Noise) hit against the top and all sides of the House, after he the said Walton had been at his Fence-Gate, which was between him and his Neighbour one John Amazeen an Italian,[92] to view it; for it was again, as formerly it had been

---

88. Pyrrhonian: after Pyrrho, Greek skeptical philosopher, c. 300 B.C.
89. Edward Cranfield, first royal governor of New Hampshire, arrived there in October, 1682.
90. Hannah Jones, a neighbor, had quarreled with George Walton. There is no record of her being "detected" in witch-craft, though her mother had been tried for it in 1656 and acquitted.
91. *innuendo*: hinting at.
92. John Amazeen an Italian: "John the Greek," local con-stable, stubborn opponent of Mason and his dues.

(the manner how being unknown) wrung off the Hinges, and cast upon the Ground; and in his being there, and return home with several Persons of (and frequenting) his family and House, about a slight shot distant from the Gate, they were all assaulted with a peal of Stones, (taken, we conceive, from the Rocks hard by the House) and this by unseen Hands or Agents. For by this time I was come down to them, having risen out of my Bed at this strange Alarm of all that were in the House, and do know that they all look'd out as narrowly as I did, or any Person could (it being a bright Moon-light Night), but cou'd make no Discovery. Thereupon, and because there came many Stones, and those pretty great ones, some as big as my Fist, into the Entry or Porch of the House, we withdrew into the next Room to the Porch, no Person having receiv'd any Hurt, (praised be Almighty Providence, for certainly the infernal Agent, constant Enemy to Mankind, had he not been over-ruled, intended no less than Death or Maim) save only that two Youths were lightly hit, one on the Leg, the other on the Thigh, notwithstanding the Stones came so thick, and so forcibly against the sides of so narrow a Room.

Whilst we stood amazed at this Accident, one of the Maidens imagined she saw them come from the Hall, next to that we were in, where searching, (and in the Cellar, down out of the Hall,) and finding no Body, another and my self observed two little Stones in a short space successively to fall on the Floor, coming as from the Ceiling close by us, and we concluded it must necessarily be done by means extraordinary and praeternatural. Coming again into the Room where we first were (next the Porch), we had many of these lapidary Salutations, but unfriendly ones; for, shutting the Door, it was no small Surprise to me to have a good big Stone come with great force and noise (just by my Head) against the Door on the inside; and then shutting the other Door, next the Hall, to have the like Accident; so going out again, upon a necessary Occasion, to have another very near my Body, clattering against the Board-wall of the House; but it was a much greater, to be so near the danger of having my Head broke with a Mall, or great Hammer brushing along the top or roof of the Room from the other end, as I was walking in it, and lighting down by me; but it fell so, that my Landlord had the greatest damage, his Windows (especially those of the first mention'd Room) being with many Stones miserably and strangely batter'd, most of the Stones giving the Blow on the inside, and forcing the Bars, Lead, and hasps of the Casements outwards, and yet falling back (sometimes a Yard or two) into the Room; only one little Stone we took out of the glass of the Window, where it lodg'd its self in the breaking it, in a Hole exactly fit for the Stone.

The Pewter and Brass were frequently pelted, and sometimes thrown down upon the Ground; for the Evil Spirit seemed then to affect variety of Mischief, and diverted himself at this end after he had done so much Execution at the other. So were two Candle-sticks, after many hittings, at last struck off the Table where they stood, and likewise a large Pewter Pot, with the force of these Stones. Some of them were taken up hot, and (it seems) immediately coming out of the Fire; and some (which is not unremarkable) having been laid by me upon the Table along by couples, and numbered, were found missing; that is, two of them, as we return'd immediately to the Table, having turn'd our backs only to visit and view some new Stone-charge or Window-breach; and this Experiment was four or five times repeated, and I still found one or two missing of the Number, which we all mark'd, when I did but just remove the Light from off the Table, and step to the Door, and back again.

After this had continued in all the parts and sides of the first Room (and down the Chimney) for above four hours, I, weary of the Noise, and sleepy, went to Bed, and was no sooner fallen asleep, but was awakened with the unwelcome disturbance of another Battery of a different sort, it issuing with so prodigious a Noise against the thin Board-wall of my Chamber (which was within another) that I could not imagin it less than the fracture and downfall of great part of the Chamber, or at least of the Shelves, Books, Pictures, and other things, placed on that side, and on the Partition-Wall between the Ante-Chamber and the Door of mine. But the Noise immediately bringing up the Company below, they assured me no Mischief of that nature was done, and shewed me the biggest Stone that had as yet been made use of in this unaccountable Accident, weighing eight pound and an half, that had burst open my Chamber Door with a rebound from the Floor, as by the Dent and Bruise in it near the Door I found next Morning, done, probably, to make the greater Noise, and give the more Astonishment, which would sooner be effected by three Motions, and consequently three several Sounds, *viz.* one on the Ground, the next to and on the Door, and the last from it again to the Floor, than if it had been one single Blow upon the Door only; which ('tis probable) wou'd have split the Door, which was not permitted, nor so much as a square of the Glass-Window broken or crack'd (at that time) in all the Chamber.

Glad thereof, and desiring them to leave me, and the Door shut, as it was before, I endeavoured once more to take my Rest, and was once more prevented by the like passage, with another like offensive Weapon, it being a whole Brick that lay in the ante-Chamber Chimney, and used again to the same malicious purpose as before, and in the same manner too, as by the mark in the Floor, whereon was some of the dust of the Brick, broken a little at the end, apparant next Morning, the Brick it self lying just at the Door. However, after I had lain a while, harkning to their Adventures below, I drop'd asleep again, and receiv'd no further Molestation that Night.

In the Morning (*Monday* Morning) I was inform'd by several of the Domesticks of more of the same kind of Trouble; among which the most signal was, the Vanishing of the Spit which stood in the Chimney Corner, and the sudden coming of it again down the same Chimney, sticking of it in a Log that lay in the Fireplace or Hearth; and then being by one of the Family set by on the other side of the Chimney, presently cast out of the Window into the Back-side. Also a pressing-Iron lying on the ledge of the Chimney back, was convey'd invisibly into the Yard. I should think it (too) not unworthy the Relation, that, discoursing then with some of the Family, and others, about what had past, I said, I thought it necessary to take and keep the great Stone, as a Proof and Evidence, for they had taken it down from my Chambers; and so I carried it up, laid it on my Table in my Chamber, and lock'd my Door, and going out upon occasions, and soon returning, I was told by my Landlady that it was, a little while after my going forth, removed again, with a Noise, which they all below heard, and was thrown into the ante-Chamber, and there I found it lying in the middle of it; thereupon I the second time carried it up, and laid it on the Table, and had it in my Custody a long time to show, for the Satisfaction of the Curious.

There were many more Stones thrown about in the House that Morning, and more in the Fields that Day, where the Master of the House was, and the Men at Work. Some more Mr. [Benjamin] Woodbridge, a Minister, and my self, in the Afternoon did see (but could not any Hand throwing them) lighting near, and jumping and tumbling on the Grass: So did one Mrs. Clark, and her Son, and several others; and some of them felt them too. One Person would not be perswaded but that the Boys at Work might throw them, and strait her little Boy standing by her was struck with a Stone on the Back, which caused him to fall a crying, and her (being convinc'd) to carry him away forth-with.

In the Evening, as soon as I had sup'd in the outer Room before mine, I took a little Musical-Instrument, and began to touch it (the Door indeed was then set open for Air), and a good big Stone came rumbling in, and as it were to lead the Dance, but upon a much different account than in the days of Old, and of old fabulous Inchantments, my Musick being none of the best. The Noise of this brought up the Deputy-President's Wife,[93] and many others of the Neighbourhood that were below, who wonder'd to see this Stone followed (as it were) by many others, and a Pewter Spoon among the rest, all which fell strangely into the Room in their Presence, and were taken up by the Company. And beside all this, there was seen by two Youths in the Orchard and Fields, as they said, a black Cat, at the time the Stones were toss'd about, and it was shot at, but missed, by its changing Places, and being immediately at some distance, and then out of sight, as they related: Agreeable to which, it may not be improper to insert, what was observed by two Maids, Grand-Children of Mr. Walton, on the Sunday Night, the beginning of this *Lithoboly*. They did affirm, that as they were standing in the Porch-Chamber Window, they saw, as it were, a Person putting out a Hand out of the Hall Window, as throwing Stones toward the Porch or Entry; and we all know no Person was in the Hall except, at that instant, my self and another, having search'd diligently there, and wondring whence those should come that were about the same time drop'd near us; so far we were from doing it our selves, or seeing any other there to do it.

On *Monday* Night, about the Hour it first began, there were more Stones thrown in the Kitchin, and down the Chimney, one Captain [Walter] Barefoot, of the Council for that Province, being present, with others; and also (as I was going up to Bed) in an upper Chamber, and down those Stairs.

Upon *Tuesday* Night, about Ten, some five or six Stones were severally thrown into the Maid's Chamber near the Kitchin, and the Glass-Windows broke in three new places, and one of the Maids hit as she lay. At the same time was heard by them, and two young Men in the House, an odd, dismal sort of Whistling, and thereupon the Youths ran out, with intent to take the suppos'd Thrower of Stones, if possible; and on the back-side near the Window they heard the Noise (as they said) of something stepping a little way before them, as it were the trampling of a young Colt, as they fancied, but saw nothing; and going on, could discover nothing but that the Noise of the stepping or trampling was ceas'd, and then gone on a little before.

93. the Deputy-President's wife: Mrs. Elias Stileman.

On *Saturday* Morning I found two Stones more on the Stairs; and so some were on Sunday Night convey'd into the Room next the Kitchin.

Upon *Monday* following Mr. Walton going (with his Men) by Water to some other Land, in a place called the Great Bay, and to a House where his Son was placed, they lay there that Night, and the next Morning had this Adventure. As the Men were all at work in the Woods, felling Wood, they were visited with another set of Stones, and they gathered up near upon a Hat-full, and put them between two Trees near adjoining, and returning from carrying Wood, to the Boat, the Hat and its contents (the Stones) were gone, and the Stones were presently after thrown about again, as before; and after search, found that Hat press'd together, and lying under a square piece of Timber at some distance from thence. They had them again at young Walton's House, and half a Brick thrown into a Cradle, out of which his young Child was newly taken up.

Here it may seem most proper to inform the Reader of a parallel passage, (*viz.*) what happened another time to my Landlord in his Boat; wherein going up to the same place (the Great Bay) and loading it with Hay for his use at his own House, about the mid-way in the River (Pascataqua) he found his Boat began to be in a sinking Condition, at which being much surpriz'd, upon search, he discover'd the cause to be the pulling out a Plug or Stopple in the bottom of the Boat, being fixed there for the more convenient letting out of the Rain-Water that might fall into it; a Contrivance and Combination of the old Serpent and the old Woman, or some other Witch or Wizard (in Revenge or innate Enmity) to have drown'd both my good Landlord and his Company.

On *Wednesday*, as they were at work again in the Woods, on a sudden they heard something gingle like Glass, or Metal, among the Trees, as it was falling, and being fallen to the Ground, they knew it to be a Stirrup which Mr. Walton had carried to the Boat, and laid under some Wood; and this being again laid by him in that very Boat, it was again thrown after him. The third time, he having put it upon his Girdle or Belt he wore about his Waste, buckled together before, but at that instant taken off because of the Heat of the Weather, and laid there again buckled, it was fetch'd away, and no more seen. Likewise the Graper, or little Anchor of the Boat, cast over-board, which caus'd the Boat to wind up; so staying and obstructing their Passage. Then the setting-Pole was divers times cast into the River, as they were coming back from the Great Bay, which put them to the trouble of Padling, that is, rowing about for it as often to retrieve it.

Being come to his own House, this Mr. Walton was charg'd again with a fresh Assault in the out-Houses; but we heard of none within doors until Friday after, when, in the Kitchin, were 4 or 5 Stones (one of them hot) taken out of the Fire, as I conceive, and so thrown about. I was then present, being newly come in with Mr. Walton from his middle Field (as he call'd it), where his Servants had been Mowing, and had six or seven of his old troublesome Companions, and I had one fall'n down by me there, and another thin flat Stone hit me on the Thigh with the flat side of it, so as to make me just feel, and to smart a little. In the same Day's Evening, as I was walking out in the Lane by the Field before-mentioned, a great Stone made a rusling Noise in the Stone-Fence between the Field and the Lane, which seem'd to me (as it caus'd me to cast my Eye that way by the Noise) to come out of the Fence, as it were pull'd out from among those Stones loose, but orderly laid close together, as the manner of such Fences in that Country is, and so fell down upon the Ground. Some Persons of Note being then in the Field (whose Names are here under-written) to visit Mr. Walton there, are substantial Witnesses of this same Stonery, both in the Field, and afterward in the House that Night, *viz.* one Mr. Hussey, Son of a Counsellour there. He took up one that having first alighted on the Ground, with rebound from thence hit him on the Heel; and he keeps it to show. And Captain Barefoot, mentioned above, has that which (among other Stones) flew into the Hall a little before Supper; which my self also saw as it first came in at the upper part of the Door into the middle of the Room; and then (tho' a good flat Stone, yet) was seen to rowl over and over, as if trundled, under a Bed in the same Room. In short, these Persons, being wonderously affected with the Strangeness of these Passages, offer'd themselves (desiring me to take them) as Testimonies; I did so, and made a Memorandum, by way of Record, thereof, to this effect. *Viz.*

These Persons under-written do hereby Attest the Truth of their being Eye-Witnesses of at least half a score Stones that Evening thrown invisibly into the Field, and in the Entry of the House, Hall, and one of the Chambers of George Walton's. *Viz.*

SAMUEL JENNINGS, Esq; Governour of West-Jarsey.

WALTER CLARK, Esq; Deputy-Governour of Road-Island.

Mr. ARTHUR COOK.

Mr. MATT. BORDEN of Road-Island.

Mr. OLIVER HOOTON of Barbados, Merchant.

Mr. T. MAUL of Salem in New-England, Merchant.

Captain WALTER BAREFOOT.

Mr. JOHN HUSSEY.

And the Wife of the said Mr. Hussey.[94]

On *Saturday,* [June] 24, One of the Family, at the usual hour at Night, observ'd some few (not above half a dozen) of these natural (or rather unnatural) Weapons to fly into the Kitchin, as formerly; but some of them in an unusual manner lighting gently on him, or coming toward him so easily, as that he took them before they fell to the Ground. I think there was not any thing more that Night remarkable. But as if the malicious Daemon had laid up for Sunday and Monday, then it was that he began (more furiously than formerly) with a great Stone in the Kitchin, and so continued with throwing down the Pewter-Dishes, etc. great part of it all at once coming clattering down, without the stroke of a Stone, little or great, to move it. Then about Midnight this impious Operation not ceasing, but trespassing with a *continuando,*[95] 2 very great Stones, weighing above 30 pound a piece (that used to lye in the Kitchin, in or near the Chimny) were in the former, wonted, rebounding manner, let fly against my Door and Wall in the ante-Chamber, but with some little distance of time. This thundring Noise must needs bring up the Men from below, as before, (I need not say

---

94. All the people on this list, interestingly, were Quakers, with the exception of Barefoot.   95. a *continuando*: a "to be continued."

to wake me) to tell me the Effect, which was the beating down several Pictures, and displacing abundance of things about my Chamber: but the Repetition of this Cannon-Play by these great rumbling Engines, now ready at hand for the purpose, and the like additional disturbance by four Bricks that lay in the outer-Room Chimney (one of which having been so imploy'd the first Sunday Night, as has been said) made me despair of taking Rest, and so forced me to rise from my Bed. Then finding my Door burst open, I also found many Stones, and great pieces of Bricks, to fly in, breaking the Glass-Windows, and a Paper-Light, sometimes inwards, sometimes outwards: So hitting the Door of my Chamber as I came through from the ante-Chamber, lighting very near me as I was fetching the Candlestick, and afterward the Candle being struck out, as I was going to light it again. So a little after, coming up for another Candle, and being at the Stare-foot door, a wooden Mortar with great Noise struck against the Floor, and was just at my Feet, only not touching me, moving from the other end of the Kitchin where it used to lye. And when I came up my self, and two more of the same House, we heard a Whistling, as it were near us in the outer Room, several times. Among the rest of the Tools made use of to disturb us, I found an old Card for dressing Flax in my Chamber.

Now for *Monday* Night, (*June* 26) one of the severest. The disturbance began in the Kitchin with Stones; then as I was at Supper above in the ante-Chamber, the Window near which I sate at Table was broke in 2 or 3 parts of it inwards, and one of the Stones that broke it flew in, and I took it up at the further end of the Room. The manner is observable; for one of the squares was broke into 9 or 10 small square pieces, as if it had been regularly mark'd out into such even squares by a Workman, to the end some of these little pieces might fly in my Face (as they did) and give me a surprize, but without any hurt.

In the mean time it went on in the Kitchin, whither I went down, for Company, all or most of the Family, and a Neighbour, being there; where many Stones (some great ones) came thick and threefold among us, and an old howing Iron,[96] from a Room hard by, where such Utensils lay. Then, as if I had been the design'd Object for that time, most of the Stones that came (the smaller I mean) hit me (sometimes pretty hard) to the number of above 20, near 30, as I remember, and whether I remov'd, sit, or walk'd, I had them, and great ones sometimes lighting gently on me, and in my Hand and Lap as I sate, and falling to the Ground, and sometimes thumping against the Wall, as near as could be to me, without touching me. Then was a Room over the Kitchin infested, that had not been so before, and many Stones greater than usual lumbring there over our Heads, not only to ours, but to the great Disturbance and Affrightment of some Children that lay there. And for Variety, there were sometimes three great, distinct Knocks, sometimes five such sounds as with a great Maul, reiterated divers times.

On *Tuesday* Night (*June* 28) we were quiet; but not so on *Wednesday*, when the Stones were play'd about in the House. And on *Thursday* Morning I found some things that hung on Nails on the Wall in my Chamber, *viz.* a Spherical Sun-Dial, etc. lying on the Ground, as knock'd down by some Brick or Stone in the ante-Chamber.

96. howing Iron: the metal part of a hoe.

But my Landlord had the worst of that Day, tho' he kept the Field, being there invisibly hit above 40 times, as he affirm'd to me, and he receiv'd some shrowd[97] hurtful Blows on the Back, and other Parts, which he much complained of, and said he thought he should have reason to do, even to his dying day; and I observ'd that he did so, he being departed this Life since.

Besides this, Plants of Indian Corn were struck up by the Roots almost, just as if they had been cut with some edged Instrument, whereas *re vera*[98] they were seen to be eradicated, or rooted up with nothing but the very Stones, altho' the injurious Agent was altogether unseen. And a sort of Noise, like that of Snorting and Whistling, was heard near the Men at Work in the Fields many times, many whereof I my self, going thither, and being there, was a Witness of; and parting thence I receiv'd a pretty hard Blow with a Stone on the Calf of my Leg. So it continued that day in two Fields, where they were severally at Work: and my Landlord told me, he often heard likewise a humming Noise in the Air by him, as of a Bullet discharg'd from a Gun; and so said a Servant of his that work'd with him.

Upon *Saturday (July* 1), as I was going to visit my Neighbour Capt. Barefoot, and just at his Door, his Man saw, as well as my self, 3 or 4 Stones fall just by us in the Field, or Close, where the House stands, and not any other Person near us. At Night a great Stone fell in the Kitchin, as I was going to Bed, and the Pewter was thrown down; many Stones flew about, and the Candles by them put out 3 or 4 times, and the Snorting heard; a Negro Maid hit on the Head in the Entry between the Kitchin and Hall with a Porringer from the Kitchin: also the pressing-Iron clattered against the Partition Wall between the Hall and a Chamber beyond it, where I lay, and Mr. Randolph,[99] His Majesty's Officer for the Customs, etc.

Some few Stones we had on *Sunday* Morning, (*July* 2) none at Night. But on *Monday* Morning (the 3*d*) both Mr. Walton, and 5 or 6 with him in the Field, were assaulted with them, and their Ears with the old Snorting and Whistling. In the Afternoon Mr. Walton was hit on the Back with Stones very grievously, as he was in his Boat that lay at a Cove side by his House. It was a very odd prank that was practis'd by the Devil a little while after this. One Night the Cocks of Hay, made the Day before in the Orchard, was spread all abroad, and some of the Hay thrown up into the Trees, and some of it brought into the House, and scatter'd. Two Logs that lay at the Door, laid, one of them by the Chimny in the Kitchin; the other set against the Door of the Room where Mr. Walton then lay, as on purpose to confine him therein: A Form that stood in the Entry (or Porch) was set along by the Fire side, and a joint Stool upon that, with a Napking spread thereon, with two Pewter Pots, and two Candlesticks: A Cheese-Press likewise having a Spit thrust into one of the holes of it, at one end; and at the other end of the Spit hung an Iron Kettle; and a Cheese was taken out, and broke to pieces. Another time, I full well remember 'twas on a Sunday at Night, my Window was all broke with a violent shock of Stones and Brick-bats, which scarce miss'd my self: among these one huge one made its way through the great square or sash of a Casement, and broke a great hole in it, throwing down

---

97. shrowd: sharp.
98. *re vera*: in fact.

99. Edward Randolph, enemy of Puritan Massachusetts, advocated the royal administration of New England.

Books by the way, from the Window to a Picture over-against it, on the other side of the Chamber, and tore a hole quite through it about half a foot long, and the piece of the Cloth hung by a little part of it, on the back-side of the Picture.

After this we were pretty quiet, saving now and then a few Stones march'd about for Exercise, and to keep (as it were) the Diabolical hand in use, till *July* 28, being *Friday,* when about 40 Stones flew about, abroad, and in the House and Orchard, and among the Trees therein, and a Window broke before, was broke again, and one Room where they never used before.

August 1. On *Wednesday* the Window in my ante-Chamber was broke again, and many Stones were plaid about, abroad, and in the House, in the Day-time, and at Night. The same Day in the Morning they tried this Experiment; they did set on the Fire a Pot with Urin, and crooked Pins in it, with design to have it boil, and by that means to give Punishment to the Witch, or Wizard (that might be the wicked Procurer or Contriver of this Stone Affliction) and take off their own; as they had been advised. This was the Effect of it: As the Liquor begun to grow hot, a Stone came and broke the top or mouth of it, and threw it down, and spilt what was in it; which being made good again, another Stone, as the Pot grew hot again, broke the handle off; and being recruited and fill'd the third time, was then with a third Stone quite broke to pieces and split; and so the Operation became frustrate and fruitless.

On *August* 2, two Stones in the Afternoon I heard and saw my self in the House and Orchard; and another Window in the Hall was broke. And as I was entering my own Chamber, a great square of a Casement, being a foot square, was broke, with the Noise as of a big Stone, and pieces of the Glass flew into the Room, but no Stone came in then, or could be found within or without. At Night, as I, with others, were in the Kitchin, many more came in; and one great Stone that lay on a Spinning-Wheel to keep it steady, was thrown to the other side of the Room. Several Neighbours then present were ready to testifie this Matter.

Upon *August* 3, On *Thursday* the Gate between my said Landlord and his Neighbour John Amazeen was taken off again, and thrown into Amazeen's Field, who heard it fall, and averr'd it then made a Noise like a great Gun.

On *Friday* the 4*th*, the Fence against Mr. Walton's Neighbour's Door, (the Woman of whom formerly there was great Suspicion, and thereupon Examination had, as appears upon Record;) this Fence being maliciously pull'd down to let in their Cattel into his Ground; he and his Servants were pelted with above 40 Stones as they went to put it up again; for she had often threatned that he should never injoy his House and Land. Mr. Walton was hit divers times, and all that Day in the Field, as they were Reaping, it ceas'd not, and there fell (by the Mens Computation) above an hundred Stones. A Woman helping to Reap (among the rest) was hit 9 or 10 times, and hurt to that degree, that her left Arm, Hip, Thigh, and Leg, were made black and blue there-with; which she showd to the Woman,[100] Mrs. Walton, and others. Mr. Woodbridge, a Divine, coming to give me a Visit, was hit about the Hip, and one Mr. [George] Jefferys a Merchant, who was with him, on the Leg. A Window in the Kitchin that had been much batter'd before, was now quite broke out, and unwindow'd, no Glass

100. i. e., to Hannah Jones.

or Lead at all being left: a Glass Bottle broke to pieces, and the Pewter Dishes (about 9 of them) thrown down, and bent.

On *Saturday* the *5th*, as they were Reaping in the Field, three Sickles were crack'd and broke by the force of these lapidary Instruments of the Devil, as the Sickles were in the Reapers hands, on purpose (it seems) to obstruct their Labour, and do them Injury and Damage. And very many Stones were cast about that Day; insomuch, that some that assisted at that Harvest-Work, being struck with them, by reason of that Disturbance left the Field, but were follow'd by their invisible Adversaries to the next House.

On *Sunday*, being the *6th*, there fell nothing considerable, nor on *Monday*, (*7th*) save only one of the Children hit with a Stone on the Back. We were quiet to *Tuesday* the *8th*. But on *Wednesday* (*9th*) above 100 Stones (as they verily thought) repeated the Reapers Disquiet in the Corn-Field, whereof some were affirm'd by Mr. Walton to be great ones indeed, near as big as a Man's Head; and Mrs. Walton, his Wife being by Curiosity led thither, with intent also to make some Discovery by the most diligent and vigilant Observation she could use, to obviate the idle Incredulity some inconsiderate Persons might irrationally entertain concerning this venefical[101] Operation; or at least to confirm her own Sentiments and Belief of it. Which she did, but to her Cost; for she received an untoward Blow (with a Stone) on her Shoulder. There were likewise two Sickles bent, crack'd, and disabled with them, beating them violently out of their Hands that held them; and this reiterated three times successively.

After this we injoy'd our former Peace and Quiet, unmolested by these stony Disturbances, that whole month of August, excepting some few times; and the last of all in the Month of September, (the beginning thereof) wherein Mr. Walton himself only (the Original perhaps of this strange Adventure, as has been declared) was the designed concluding Sufferer; who going in his Canoo (or Boat) from the Great Island, where he dwelt, to Portsmouth, to attend the Council, who had taken Cognizance of this Matter, he being Summoned thither, in order to his and the Suspect's Examination, and the Courts taking Order thereabout, he was sadly hit with three pebble Stones as big as ones Fist; one of which broke his Head, which I saw him show to the President of the Council; the others gave him that Pain on the Back, of which (with other like Strokes) he complained then, and afterward to his Death.

Who, that peruses these praeternatural Occurrences, can possibly be so much as Enemy to his own Soul, and irrefutable Reason, as obstinately to oppose himself to, or confusedly fluctuate in, the Opinion and Doctrine of Daemons, or Spirits, and Witches? Certainly he that does so, must do two things more: He must temerariously unhinge, or undermine the Fundamentals of the best Religion in the World; and he must disingenuously quit and abandon that of the Three Theologick Virtues or Graces, to which the great Doctor of the Gentils[102] gave the Precedence, Charity, through his Unchristian and Uncharitable Incredulity.

---

101. venefical: from the Latin *venefica*, a witch.

102. the great Doctor of the Gentils: St. Paul. The reference is to 1 Cor. 13:13.

11. Ned Ward

from *A Trip to New England; With a Character of the Country and People, both English and Indians* 1699

Ned Ward's A Trip to Jamaica *(see chapter 4) was so popular with its London audience that Ward followed it with a sequel about New England. Other imitations were ascribed to him (about trips to Holland and Ireland), but this one appears to be authentic—allowing for Ward's characteristic exaggeration. Like the* Trip to Jamaica, *it testifies to growing popular interest in the English empire following the Glorious Revolution, and a growing metropolitan curiosity about such provincial outlands as Boston.*

Bishops, Bailiffs, and Bastards, were the three Terrible Persecutions which chiefly drove our unhappy Brethren to seek their Fortunes in our Forreign Colonies. One of these Bug-bears, I confess, frighted me from the Blessings of my own dear Native Country; and forc'd me to the Fatigue of a long Voyage, to escape a Scouring.

But whether *Zeal, Debt,* or the sweet Sin of *Procreation,* begot in my Conscience those Fears, which hurried me a great many Leages beyond my *Senses,* I am as unwilling to declare to the World, as a *Romish* Damsel that has lost her *Maiden-head,* is to confess her Frailty to the Priest. . . .

Of BOSTON, *and the* INHABITANTS.

On the *South-west* side of *Massachusetts-Bay,* is *Boston*; whose Name is taken from a Town in *Lincoln-shire*: And is the Metropolis of all *New-England.* The Houses in some parts joyn as in *London.* The *Buildings,* like their *Women,* being *Neat* and *Handsome.* And their *Streets,* like the *Hearts* of the *Male Inhabitants,* are Paved with *Pebble.* . . .

Of the Native ENGLISH *in General.*

The Women (like the Men) are excessive *Smokers*; and have contracted so many ill habits from the *Indians,* that 'tis difficult to find a Woman cleanly enough for a *Cook* to a *Squemish Lady,* or a Man neat enough for a *Vallet* to Sir *Courtly Nice.* I am sure a *Covent-Garden Beau,* or a *Bell-fa* would appear to them much stranger *monsters,* then ever yet were seen in *America.*

They *Smoke* in *Bed*, *Smoke* as they *Nead* their *Bread*, *Smoke* whilst they'r *Cooking* their *Victuals*, *Smoke* at *Prayers*, *Work*, and *Exonoration*, that their Mouths stink as bad as the *Bowl* of a Sailers *Pipe*, which he has funk'd[103] in, without Burning, a whole Voyage to the *Indias*.

Eating, *Drinking*, *Smoking* and *Sleeping*, takes up four parts in five of their Time; and you may divide the remainder into *Religious Excercise*, *Day Labour*, and *Evacuation*. Four Meals a Day, and a good Knap after Dinner, being the Custom of the Country.

Rum, alias *Kill Devil*, is as much ador'd by the *American English*, as a dram of *Brandy* is by an old *Billingsgate*.[104] 'Tis held as the *Comforter* of their *Souls*, the *Preserver* of their *Bodys*, the *Remover* of their *Cares*, and *Promoter* of their *Mirth*; and is a Soveraign Remedy against the *Grumbling* of the *Guts*, a *kibe-heel*,[105] or a *Wounded Conscience*, which are three Epidemical Distempers that afflict the Country.

Their *Industry*, as well as their *Honesty*, deserves equal Observation; for it is practicable amongst them, to go two miles to catch a Horse, and run three Hours after him, to Ride Half a Mile to *Work*, or a Quarter of a Mile to an *Ale-house*.

One Husband-man in *England*, will do more Labour in a Day, than a *New-England* Planter will be at the pains to do in a Week: For to every Hour he spends in his *Grounds*, he will be two at an *Ordinary*.[106]

They have wonderful *Appetites*, and will Eat like *Plough-men*; tho very *Lazy*, and *Plough* like *Gentlemen*: It being no rarity there, to see a Man *Eat* till he *Sweats*, and *Work* till he *Freezes*.

The Women are very *Fruitful*, which shows the Men are *Industrious* in *Bed*, tho' *Idle up*. *Children* and *Servants* are there very Plenty; but *Honest-men* and *Virgins* as scarce as in other places.

Provisions being Plenty, their Marriage-Feasts are very Sumptious. They are sure not to want Company to Celebrate their Nuptials; for its Customary in every Town, for all the Inhabitants to Dine at a Wedding without Invitation: For they value their *Pleasure* at such a rate, and bear such an affection to *Idleness*, that they would run the hazard of *Death* or *Ruin*, rather than let slip so Merry a *Holy-day*.

The *Women*, like Early *Fruits*, are soon *Ripe* and soon *Rotten*. A *Girl* there at Thirteen, thinks herself as well Quallified for a *Husband*, as a forward *Miss* at a Boarding-School, does here at Fifteen for a *Gallant*.

He that Marrys a *New-England* Lass at Sixteen, if she prove a Snappish Gentlewoman, her Husband need not fear she will bite his Nose off; for its ten to one but she hath shed her Teeth, and has done Eating of Crust, before she arrives to that Maturity.

It is usual for the Men to be *Grey* at Thirty; and look as Shrivel'd in the *Face*, as an old *Parchment Indenture* pasted upon a *Barbers Block*. And are such lovers of *Idleness*, that they are desirous of being thought *Old*, to have a better pretence to be *Lazy*.

The Women have done bearing of Children by that time they are Four and Twenty: And she that lives un-Married till she's Twenty Five, may let all the Young Sports-men in the Town give her *Maiden-head* chase without the Danger of a *Timpany*.[107]

---

103. funk'd: smoked.
104. *Billingsgate*: a vulgar person; from the notorious London market.

105. *kibe-heel*: chilblains.
106. *Ordinary*: tavern.
107. *Timpany*: pregnancy.

Notwithstanding their *Sanctity*, they are very *Prophane* in their common *Dialect*. They can neither drive a *Bargain*, nor make a *Jest*, without a Text of Scripture at the end on't.

An *English* Inhabitant having sold a Bottle of *Rum* to an *Indian* (contrary to the Laws of the County) was detected in it; and order'd to be Lash'd. The Fellow brib'd the *Whipster* to use him tenderly; but the *Flog-master* resolving (being a Conscientious Man) to do his Duty Honestly, rather punish'd the Offender with the greater severity, who casting a sorrowful look over his Shoulder, Cry'd out, *the Scripture sayeth, Blessed is the Merciful Man*. The Scourgineer replying, *and it also says, Cursed is he that doeth the work of the Lord Negligently*: And for fear of coming under the *Anathema*, laid him on like an unmerciful *Dog*, till he had given him a thorough Fellow-feeling of his *Cat of Nine-tailes*.[108]

Their Lecture-Days are call'd by some amongst them, *Whore Fair*, from the Levity and Wanton Frollicks of the Young People, who when their Devotion's over, have recourse to the *Ordinaries*, where they plentifully wash away the remembrance of their *Old Sins*, and drink down the fear of a Fine, or the dread of a *Whipping-post*. Then *Uptails-all*[109] and the *Devils* as busie under the *Petticoat*, as a *Juggler* at *Fair*, or a *Whore* at a *Carnival*.

Husking of *Indian-Corn*, is as good sport for the Amorous *Wag-tailes* in *New-England*, as *Maying* amongst us is for our forward Youths and Wenches. For 'tis observ'd, there are more *Bastards* got in that Season, than in all the Year beside; which Occasions some of the looser *Saints* to call it *Rutting Time*.

Many of the Leading *Puritans* may (without Injustice) be thus Characteris'd. They are *Saints* without *Religion*, *Traders* without *Honesty*, *Christians* without *Charity*, *Magistrates* without *Mercy*, *subjects* without *Loyalty*, *Neighbours* without *Amity*, *Faithless Friends, Implacable Enemys*, and *Rich Men* without *Money*.[110]

They all pretend to be driven over by *Persecution*, which their Teachers Roar out against in their Assemblies, with as much bitterness, as a double refin'd *Protestant* can belch forth against the *Whore* of *Babylon*: Yet have they us'd the *Quakers* with such severity, by *Whipping, Hanging*, and other Punishments, forcing them to put to Sea in Vessels without Provision, they flying with Gladness to the Merciless Ocean, as their only Refuge under Heaven, left to escape the *Savage Fury* of their *Unchristian Enemies*, till drove by *Providence* upon *Rhoad-Island* (so call'd from their accidental discovery of it in their Stroling Adventure) which they found full of *Fruits* and *Flowers*, a *Fertile Soil*, and extreamly Pleasant, being the Garden of *America*; where they happily Planted themselves, making great improvements: There Live and Flourish, as the *Righteous*, like a Bay-Tree under the Noses of their *Enemies*.

The *Clergy*, tho' they Live upon the Bounty of their Hearers, are as rediculously *Proud*, as their *Communicants* are shamefully *Ignorant*: For tho' they will not suffer their Unmannerly Flock to worship their Creator with that Reverence and Humility as they ought to do, but tell them 'tis *Popery* to uncover their Heads in the House and Presence of the *Deity*; yet they Oblige every Member to pay an humble respect to the

---

108. *Cat of Nine-tailes*: a kind of whip.
109. *Uptails-all*: "Bottoms up!"

110. without *Money*: New Englanders traded on credit, and faced a chronic shortage of coin.

Parsons Box, when they make their offerings every Sunday, and fling their *Mites* into their *Teachers Treasury*. So that the Haughty *Prelate* exacts more Homage, as due to his own Transcendency, than he will allow to be paid to Heaven or its place of Worship.

If you are not a Member in full Communion with one of their Assemblies, your Progeny is deny'd *Baptism*, for which reason, there are Hundreds amongst them, at Mans Estate, that were never *Christened*.

All *Handicrafts-Men* may live here very well, except a *Pick-pocket*; of all *Artificers* he would find the least Encouragement; for the scarcity of Money would baulk his Tallent.

An Eminent *Planter* came to me for an Ounce of *Venice-treacle*, which I would have sold him for a Shilling; he protested he had liv'd there Fifty Years, and never seen in the whole Term, Ten Pounds in *Silver-Money* of his own; and yet was Rated at a Thousand Pounds, and thought the *Assessors* us'd him kindly: But gave me for my Medicine a Bushel of *Indian-Corn*, vallued at half a Crown, and Vow'd if a Shilling would save his Family from distruction, he knew not how to raise it.

They have a *Charter* for a *Fair* at *Salem*, but it Begins, like *Ingerstone* Market, half an Hour after Eleven a Clock, and Ends half an Hour before Twelve: For I never see any thing in it but by great Accident, and those were *Pumkins*, which were the chief Fruit that supported the *English* at their first settling in these parts. But now they enjoy plenty of good Provisions, *Fish, Flesh* and *Fowl*, and are become as great *Epicures*, as ever Din'd at *Pontack's* Ordinary.

Lobsters and *Cod-fish* are held in such disdain, by reason of their Plenty, 'tis as Scandalous for a poor Man in *Boston* to carry one through the streets, as 'tis for an Alderman in the City of *London*, to be seen walking with a Groatsworth of *Fresh-Herrings*, from *Billings-gate* to his own House.

There were formerly amongst them (as they themselves Report) abundance of *Witches*, and indeed I know not, but there may be as many now, for the Men look still as if they were *Hag-ridden*; and every Stranger, that comes into the Country, shall find they will Deal by him to this Day, as if the *Devil* were in 'em.

Witchcraft they Punish'd with Death, till they had Hang'd the best People in the Country; and Convicted the *Culprit* upon a single Evidence: So that any prejudic'd person, who bore Malice against a Neighbour, had an easie method of removing their Adversary. But since, upon better consideration, they have Mitigated the severity of that unreasonable Law, there has not been one accused of *Witchcraft*, in the whole Country.

Many are the Bug-bear storys reported of these suppos'd *Negromancers*, but few Believ'd, tho' I presume none True, yet all Collected and already Printed, I shall therefore omit the relating of any.

They have one very wholesome Law, which would do mighty well to be in force in *Old-England*; which is a Peculiar method they have of Punishing *Scolds*. If any Turbulent Woman be Troubled with an unruly Member, and uses it to the Defamation of any Body, or disquiet of her Neighbours, upon Complaint, she is order'd to be *Gag'd* and set at her own Door as many Hours as the Magistrates shall think fit, there to be gaiz'd at by all Passengers till the time's expired. Which, to me seems the most

Equitable Law imaginable to Punish more particularly that Member which committed the Offence.

Whipping is a Punishment so Practicable in this Country, upon every slight Offence, that at a Town upon the *Sound*, call'd *New-Haven*, the People do confess, that all the Inhabitants of that Place, above the Age of Fourteen, had been Whip'd for some Misdemeanour or other (except two) the *Minister* and the *Justice*.

12. John Rogers, Jr.

The Declaration and Confession of Esther Rodgers
1701

> *Execution sermons and dying confessions—the latter often printed as cheap broadsides—were among the most popular forms of literature in colonial America. For the clergy, they offered a capital opportunity to combine piety and sensation for a popular audience. In many cases, the confessions say more about the ministers who prepared them than about the convicts who served as the speakers. This narrative comes from* Death the Certain Wages of Sin to the Impenitent *(Boston, 1701), a collection of execution sermons by John Rogers, Jr. (1666–1745). Rogers was the son of a Harvard president, and later supported the Great Awakening. Several other ministers made contributions to* Death the Certain Wages of Sin, *including Nicholas Noyes; here, the preface to Esther Rodgers's narrative is by Samuel Belcher.*

Reader;

   This Serves only to draw the Curtain, that thou mayst behold a Tragick Scene, strangly changed into a Theater of Mercy, *a* Pillar of Salt *Transformed into a Monument of Free Grace; a poor Wretch, entring into Prison a Bloody Malefactor, her Conscience laden with Sins of a Scarlet Die, but there by the Gracious and Powerful, but various workings: first of the Spirit of Bondage, then of Adoption; the space of Eight Months she came forth, Sprinkled, Cleansed, Comforted, a Candidate of Heaven.*

   Whilst she was under Confinement, after she had conceived in her self good Hope of finding Mercy with God, through Christ, she was ready to give a reason of her hope, to such as were Serious and Pious, with Meekness, and much affection. And truly the Reasons and Grounds she went upon were Scriptural, and so able to bear the weight she put upon them; (which Hope the result of her Faith) kept her Company to the last, and failed her not, when she had most need of it. When she walked the dolorous way to the place of her Execution, and approaching near to it, after a little Reluctancy of the Flesh, as soon as she ascended to behold the fatal Tree, her Faith, and courage revived, and she lift up her Feet, and Marched on with an Erected, and Radiant Countenance, as unconcerned with the business of Death, at once out doing all the old Roman Masculine *bravery, and shewing what Grace can do, in, and for the Weaker* Sex; *and this in Presence of a Multitude of Spectators, of whom this Relator was One, and an Admiring Observer: All which is to be Ascribed, Firstly, To the Infinitely Rich, and Free Grace of God; but Ministerially, and Instrumentally to the Labours, Prayers and Endeavours of the Reverend Elders of the Church of* Ipswich, *and many other good Christians there; after her Apprehension in* Newbury *where the Fact was Committed.*

She was Conveyed, (and it was happy for her) that she was Conveyed to the Prison in Ipswich; *where are to be found, (A Nation) Pardon the Expression, Of Sound, Serious and Praying Christians, who made Incessant Prayers to Heaven in her behalf, Praying not only for her, but with her, in their own Houses, joyning & turning their Private Meetings into whole days of Fasting and Prayer; and continuing till the Stars appearing: Yea, by Turns in the Prison also. So turning a* Den of Theives, *(to use* Dr. Wilds *words) into a House of Prayer; and had there been some Thief there, (for I know not who was there) he might Perhaps, with her, been sharer of the benefit. Their Worthy Pastor also, took constant & unwearied pains, Plying the Oar, To waft over her Soul to Heaven; and saw the fruit of all his Labours, and Travels with her, through the Blessing of God, Namely a great & gracious change wrought in her, which she Humbly, Affectionately, and Thankfully acknowledged.*

And now, Let the Great God of Heaven, have all the Praise & Glory of this Action: And let that unhappy Tree; indeed happy in this, that the first that Suffered on it, was (we trust) Fruit Consecrated: But if it be the Will of God, that there may never be Occasion again to make use of it to such Fatal purposes, but only stand as a Buoy, or Seamark, to point out the Rocks and Shelves, where she Shipwrackt her honour; and that all others may HEAR & FEAR, &c. *Which is the Desire and Prayer of,*

Your Servant in the Lord,
SAMUEL BELCHER.

The Declaration & Confession of Esther Rodgers, *Of* Kittery *in the Province of* Main, *in* New England, *Single woman.*

I was born at *Kittery* sometime in May, 1680. At the Age of Thirteen came to live as an Apprentice to Mr. *Joseph Woodbridge* of *Newbury.* Had little or no thoughts of God or Religion, though Living in a Religious Family; was taught to Read, Learned Mr. *Cottons* Catechism, and had frequent opportunities of going to Publick Meetings; but was a careless Observer of Sabbaths, and Hearer of Sermons; no Word that ever I heard or read making any Impression upon my Heart, (as I Remember) Neither did I at all give my self to Secret Prayer, or any other Duty that concerned the Salvation of my Soul. And because I thus neglected God, refused his Counsil, and would not walk in his Ways, therefore he justly gave me up to my own hearts Lusts, and ways of Wickedness.

About the Age of Seventeen, I was left to fall into that foul Sin of Uncleanness, suffering my self to be defiled by a *Negro* Lad living in the same House. After I perceived that I was with Child, I meditated how to prevent coming to Publick Shame; Satan presently setting in with his Temptation, I soon complied and resolved to Murder the Child, if ever I should have one born alive: and continued in my wicked purpose all along, till I had the fatal Opportunity of putting it into Execution. Being delivered of a Living Child, I used means presently to stop the breath of it, and kept it hid in an upper Room, till the Darkness of the Night following, gave advantage for a Private Burial in the Garden.

All this was done in Secret, no person living whatsoever, no not so much as the Father of the child himself was privy to my disposal of it, or knew that I ever had such a Child.

Afterwards reflecting on what I had done, was followed with some Awakening, Frights and Convictions during my abode at Mr. *Woodbridges*, which was about half a year. Yet, never making any serious Address to God for pardon of these my great and hainous Sins. But thence I went to *Piscatequa*, where I lived in a publick House, and soon got over and rid of all my Fears, and even all thoughts thereof, giving my self up to other wicked Company and ways of Evil.

About a year after, I returned to *Newbury* to Mr. *Joseph Woodbridges* again, where my former Sins came fresh to Remembrance, and troubled me a while; which together with other reasons, occasioned my Removal to another place in the Town. But there also I took all Opportunities to follow my old Trade of running out a Nights, or entertaining my Sinful Companions in a back part of the House. And there I fell into the like horrible Pit (as before) *viz.* of Carnal Pollution with the *Negro* man belonging to that House. And being with Child again, I was in as great concern to know how to hide this as the former. Yet did not so soon resolve the Murdering of it, but was continually hurried in my thoughts, and undetermined till the last hour. I went forth to be delivered in the Field, and dropping my Child by the side of a little Pond, (whether alive, or still Born I cannot tell) I covered it over with Dirt and Snow, and speedily returned home again. But being Suspected and Examined, about having had a Child since my going out, made little or no answer (that I remember) till the next Morning. The Child being found by some Neighbours was brought in, & laid before my Face, to my horrible Shame & Terror; under which Confusion I remained during my Confinement at *Newbury*, being about one Month, Thinking only of the punishment I was like to suffer, without any true concernedness as to my Sins against God, or the State of my Immortal Soul; till some time after I came into *Ipswich* Prison; when and where it pleased the Great and Gracious God to work upon my heart, as in the following Relation I have given account of.

A Relation of her Experience, both of some Conviction and Comfort received in the Prison: Communicated to a certain Gentlewoman of the Town, with whom she was very free, before and afterwards.

Taken word for word from her own mouth.

The first time Mr. *Rogers* came to see me; after much other Discourse, he told me of the odiousness of Sin; and that if ever I came to be sensible of it, I should loath it, and not because of my own punishment procured thereby, but because of the Dishonour done to God. Then after he was gone, I began to think that I never loathed Sin so as yet, and was in a dreadful Case indeed; to think what a wretched Condition I had brought my self into, and had dishonoured God: insomuch that I could not Rest, I was so dreadfully harried; and Satan made me believe that it was impossible such a Sinner, should be Saved. And I could not Read, nor Sleep, nor have any Rest night nor day. After a while God made me to think that it was Satans Temptation to keep me from Repentance: But if I could Repent and Believe in the Lord Jesus Christ, I might find mercy, although I was such a Sinner. And although I am such a vile Sinner, I hope God has made me sensible of my sins, he has made me to loath my self, and truly to Repent for Sin. God has made me to see that there is nothing that I can do can save me, but that there is a sufficiency in the Lord Jesus Christ. And I do throw my self at his Feet for mercy, and have hope from his promises. *Let the wicked forsake his way, and the unrighteous man his thoughts, and let him Return to the Lord, for he will have mercy on him: and to our God, for he will abundantly pardon.* And I do so far as I know myself, Repent of my so great sins against so good a God; for that which has been the delight of my Soul, I do now abominably hate! And again 'tis said, *He that confesseth and forsaketh his sin, shall find mercy.* I can truly say, I have confessed my Sins before God and man, and do desire truly to Repent for them. Isa. 1. 18. *Come now let us reason together saith the Lord, though your sins be as scarlet, they shall be white as snow, though they be red like crimson, they shall be as wool.* I hope I have hated the evil of my ways; and do hope to have my Soul washed and cleansed in the Blood of Jesus Christ.

13. Nicholas Noyes

An Essay Against Periwigs
c. 1702

Best known as a leading magistrate in the Salem witch hunt in 1692–93, Nicholas Noyes (1647–1717) was cursed by Sarah Good: "If you take away my life, God give you blood to drink." He was born in Newbury, Massachusetts, and graduated from Harvard before going to Salem as pastor. An ally of Cotton Mather's, he remained a conservative advocate of the New England way. In addition to his sermons, he wrote competent verses in the Puritan metaphysical tradition. The following essay against wigs was preserved in a manuscript copy by Samuel Sewall, who had something of a preoccupation with the subject, though with more acknowledged ambivalence than Noyes. For both men, wigs represent the growing culture—secular or profane—of urbanity.

REASONS AGAINST WEARING OF PERIWIGGS; ESPECIALLY, AGAINST MEN'S WEARING OF PERIWIGGS MADE OF WOMEN'S HAIR, AS THE CUSTOM NOW IS, DEDUCED FROM SCRIPTURE AND REASON.

It removeth one notable Distinction, or means of distinguishing one man from another. For so is a man's own Hair: One man differing from another in Hair; as to Color, thickness, thinness, streightness, curledness. A man with his Hair cut off, and another's put on, looketh not as he did before; especially, if before of Light coloured hair, now dark: or before dark, now Light: before, thin, streight hair; now bushy, and curled, and longer than before; or other the like difference, which is most familiarly made by those that wear perriwigs. So that he that wears a Perriwig doth in effect put on a Vizzard, and disguiseth himself. And the same man ordinarily keepeth diverse Perriwigs differing one from another in length, Colour, Curles, or the like: sometime wearing one, sometimes another: so that such a one is strangely inconsistent with himself; and unlike to day, to what he was yesterday; and so less liable to be known.

Now to affect a Disguise, is not the guise of a good man; but of a bad one. Job 24. 14, 15, 17. It is recorded of Saul and Ahab, and Jeroboam's wife, that they disguised themselves; which gives no Credit to the Cause, if their persons and cases be duely considered. But it may be said, that Jacob disguised himself. And it may be answered, It was with Goat's hair, and not with womens: and he did not cut off his own. But the especial Answer is, that it was in him evidently a particular Lie, and a Cheat, and was fruit of Unbelief, done in Sin, and followed with Sorrow. If it be said that Josiah disguised himself, and went into the Battel, It may be answered, This Instance availeth but little, unless it had succeeded better with him: for it fared with him as it did with

Ahab. And Jehosaphat escaped better in his kingly Equipage, and Royal Apparel. Yet if it be Lawfull for a man to disguise in Battel; Is it therefore in Peace? if upon extraordinary Occasion, is it in Ordinary? But Josiah should not have engaged in that Battel: and disguising himself did not preserve him. 2 Chron. 35. 22 etc. If it be said, One of the Sons of the Prophets disguised himself, 1 Kings, 20. 38. It may be answered, It was on a particular Occasion, and for a short time, and to make him look like a Souldier for an advantage to his Office, that his Reproof might take the more Effect upon a hard-hearted King. It was to make him look unlike himself, and unlike a Prophet, or a Son of a Prophet. But he did not ordinarily goe in a Disguise, as in the case in hand. And supposing it lawfull on extraordinary Occasions; that it is so far from proving it lawfull on Ordinary; that it rather proveth the contrary.

And as for this of Perriwigs, they are many times used for Disguise by the worst of men, as by shaven crownd Popish Priests, Highway Robbers, etc. Dr. Annesly, when by the iniquity of the times, he was forced to abscond, and conceal himself in the day; went abroad in the evening to take the air, and then put on a Perriwigg. When he called for it, he usd to say (as his son-in-law[111] told me) Give me my Rogue; implying that when he had a Perriwigg on, he did not look like himself, nor like an honest man.

2. It removeth one notable visible Distinction of Sex: for so is Hair, as is evident by 1 Cor. 11. 6, 7, 14, 15. And it is obvious to every one, that Men's Hair, and Women's Hair are not ordinarily alike: And if they were, there were no temptation to make Perriwiggs of Women's Hair for Men: and so diverse just prejudices against the Perriwiggs in use, would be removed. Nay men might ordinarily make them of their own Hair; which would yet be less offensive. Whereas now Women are shaven or shorn, and so in that respect are more like Men: being, when shorn, really unlike what they were before, and unlike other modest, and honest Women that would not be shorn or shaven on any tentation. And men putting on their Hair, have hair like Women; and not like Men; as is noted of the Locusts, those Harpyes of Hell: Rev. 9.8. They had Hair as the hair of Women; plainly implying that Men's hair, and Women's hair is not alike.

Now this Transmutation of the visible tokens and Distinctions of Sex, is not lawfull; as is undeniably proved by Deut. 22.5. It is manifest that the hair of Perriwiggs ordinarily, pertains to Women, growing on Women's heads, having been their Glory and Covering for many years; and therefore must needs be unlawfull for Men to wear. And if a Man for this reason; viz. distinction of Sex, might not wear a Woman's Habit; much less might he wear a Woman's Hair. The Words in Deut. 22. 5 are very plain, and very terrible: The Woman shall not wear that which pertaineth to a Man; neither shall a Man put on a Woman's Garment: for all that doe so are abomination to the Lord thy God.

3. It removeth one notable distinction of Age, which is necessary to be known, because of some Duties depending on it.

(1) In respect of Men's selves. The frequent Sight of Gray hairs is a Lecture to men, against Levity, Vanity, and youthful Vagaries and Lusts. It calls for a gracious, grave, and majestical deportment, lest they defile the gray hairs with youthfull folly, and

111. his son-in-law: John Dunton, a bookseller.

Lusts: it puts men in mind of their Mortality; as the Flourishing of the Almond Tree doth of the approaching Summer; Eccles. 12. 5. Whence when gray hairs are removed out of sight; and youthfull ones in stead thereof, in view (as it is oftentimes in the case of Perriwiggs) it hath a natural tendency to make men forget that they stand upon the edge of the Grave, and on the brink of Eternity. Gray Hairs are here and there upon them; and they are not aware of it; Hose. 7. 9. And indeed, how should they be aware of it, when they are removed out of their sight? For, Out of Sight, out of mind; as saith the Proverb.

(2) In respect of Others. Others are obliged to rise up before, and honour the Old man: the demonstrative token of which is his Gray hairs. But strangers to old men cannot so well distinguish of the Age of those they converse with, when youthfull hairs are grafted on a gray head; as is oftimes in the case of Perriwiggs. Are we bound to rise up before the youthfull hair of Girls, and young Women? Levit. 19. 32. Thou shalt rise up before the hoary head, and honour the face of the Old man. It is evident by that Text, that an Old man's face should ordinarily be accompanied with Gray hairs. And when Perriwiggd men are known to be old, tho' they do their utmost to conceal their Age. Yet such Levity and Vanity appears in their affecting youthfull Shows, as renders them contemptible, and is in itself ridiculous. And so the Old man comes to be despised; contrary to the Law of God, and good of human Societies: and the young men led into tentation to this Evil, by Old men's appearing on the Stage without the badge of their Age and Honor; which would chalenge Respect. The Beauty of Old men is the Gray head. Prov. 20. 29.

(3) In respect to God Himself, relating to some of his divine Perfections; particularly, his Majesty and Eternity; which are in some respects shadowed forth in Old men, when they wear their Gray hairs, the Livery of their Old Age: Especially, when a gracious heart is adorned with a gray head: Prov. 16. 31. The hoary head is a Crown of Glory, if it be found in the way of Righteousness. And therefore when God's Majesty and Eternity are set forth in Scripture, it is with white hair, denoting that He is indeed the Ancient of Days; Dan. 7. 9. Rev. 1. 14. His head and his hairs were white like Wool, as white as Snow. It is not therefore meerly good manners, to honor the Old man: but Religion; such a one bearing the image of God in those respects more than they that are younger. Levit. 19. 32. Thou shalt rise up before the hoary head, and honor the face of the Old man, and fear they God; implying that they want the Fear of God, as well as good Manners, that don't rise up before the hoary head. So that when aged persons dissimulate their Age by putting off their Gray hairs, and by putting on youthfull looking hair: they do it, not only in their own wrong, to the loss of some degrees of due honor: but also to the wrong of those they lead into tentation, to despise Old men; which is contrary to the Law of God. Moreover they do wrong to God Himself, whose Fear is promoted by reverence due to Gray hairs.

4. Wearing Perriwigs proceeds many times from a Discontent at GOD's Workmanship. He that likes not his hair because of Color, etc., doth in effect say to his Maker, Why hast thou made me thus? contrary to Rom. 9. 20. Isa. 45. 9. which, were it but to an earthly father, is enough to bring a Wo. Isa. 49.10. Wo to him that saith to his father, What begettest thou, or to the Woman, What hast thou brought forth? For such bring discontent with their hair and Looks, do thereupon affect, and effect to

change it. And altho' they themselves cannot make one hair white or black; yet are so bold with Him that could and did make it of that Color that offends them, suppose white, or black, or red, etc. And this is undeniably a breach of the Tenth Commandment; for a man to be discontent with his own hair, which God made for him, and gave to him: and to covet anothers, which God made for another, and gave to another. To covet another's Hair, is a sin of the same kind with coveting our Neighbour's House, or his wife. For the same Command forbids coveting any thing that is thy Neighbour's: Exod. 20.17.

5. Wearing of Perriwigs evidently marreth the Workmanship of God, and so defaceth his Image. For God and Nature, or God in Nature hath suited man's Complexion and Hair; and in nature they are suited, as Naturalists observe. *Pilorum enim differentia est pro qualitate cutis Animalium*, as Aristotle observed *Lib. de gener.* And this is evident in divers Instances. When the Constitution is hail and flourishing, the Hair is so: and as the Constitution gradually declines and changeth, so doth the Hair. Prov. 20.29. The glory of young men is their strength: but the Beauty of Old men is the Gray head. Therefore it deforms an Old man, to put on him a young person's Hair: as it would deform a young man, to put him on Gray hairs; which is the beauty of old men, not of young. And the Hair, for the most part at least, is coloured and qualified according to natural Causes in the Constitution. Such as is the predominant Element, such is the predominant Temperament, such is the predominant Humor in the Body: and according to that the Flesh and Skin: and according to all these, the Hair, as Physicians know and shew; and is [*blank*] observable to every observing Eye. So that between the Periwigg hair, and the Complexion of him that wears it, there is ordinarily, a manifest Incongruity: so that he that hath Skill in Physiognomy, shall be able to know that this hair could not grow upon that head, no more than Salt-Marsh can grow upon a Hill. And for this reason there is for the most part, an incongruity between a man's hair, and a woman's Complexion: and between a Woman's hair, and a Man's Complexion: The hair of Women being suitable to their soft, moist, cold Constitution: but not to the Masculine hot and dry Constitution. And consequently, in the case in hand, there must needs be an unnatural incongruity between the Complexion, and Hair, when the Complexion and Constitution is Masculine, and the Hair Feminine. Rev. 9. 7, 8. Their faces were as the faces of Men; and they had Hair as the Hair of Women. Now if this were not unnatural and incongruous, and a kind of Monstrosity, to see things so heterogeneous linked together; I see no reason for such description. Note other parts of the Description together with these; Man-faced, Woman-haird, Lion-toothed, Scorpion-taild, Horse-shaped, etc., and it describes such a Medly going to make up a Locust, as we call neither Fish, nor Flesh, nor good red Herring. And what the Poet said of the Mermaid, *Desinet in piscem mulier formosa superne.* And in the case of Periwigs, we may say, *Desinet inque vium mulier formosa superne.* So also to put black hair on the flesh and skin that naturally produceth Red, Yellow, or Light Coloured hair, is unnatural, and incongruous: so likewise to put red hair, or yellow, or Light-colourd, on Flesh and Skin that naturally produceth black. So Youthfull hair, and sunk eyes, deaf ears, wrinkled faces and palsyed heads, etc. are not more suitable, than the Blossoming of Appletrees in Autumn, when the Leaves are falling off. And thus Nature teacheth, that Perriwigs are

undecent and unsuitable on this very score; the Trimming not being suitable to the Cloth, nor the Crop to the Soyl.

6. It seems to be unlawfull, and most foolish and absurd for a Woman to part with her Hair to adorn a Man. And if it be so, it must needs be unlawfull for Men to desire it, and buy it, or beg it, or use it in Perriwigs.

(1) It is a Glory to a Woman to have Long Hair, 1 Cor. 11.15. and therefore a Shame to her to part with it by being shorn, or shaven. 1 Cor. 11.6. Because if it be a Shame to a woman to be shorn or shaven; it is indisputably an Argument taken *ab Absurdo*, and therefore a foolish and absurd thing for a Woman to be shorn or shaven. Which yet is ordinarily done in order to [furnish] perriwigs. But such consult their own Shame.

(2) Her Hair is given her for a Covering to herself, not to another, 1 Cor. 11. 15. So then the End God gave it her for, is perverted. And their brains are exposed to Reproach and Damage who thus uncover their own barns, to thatch others anew; which surely none would doe, unless their own barns were empty; seeing the Recompence is, in stead of well-set hair, to have baldness: which in Scripture is accounted a Curse. Isa. 3.24.

(3) It seems a Disorder in religious Worship, that offends the Angels, for a woman to pray shaven or shorn, 1 Cor. 11. 5, 6, 10, 13. Judge in your selves, is it comely that a Woman pray unto God uncovered? Yet in the sense of that Text and Context, she that is shaven or shorn, prays unto God uncovered, if she prayeth at all to God: for her hair was given to her for a Glory, and for a Covering, as is there manifest. And if by reason of other Covering, men see not their bald Crowns, yet the Angels of God see them; and they cannot be hid from the all-seeing Eye of God, who seeth how ingratefully she hath parted with her Glory, and Covering, which He gave her.

(4) A Woman degrades her self unto the rank and quality of a Beast, when she submits to be shorn as the Beasts are, to cover others with their hair. What a shame is it to women to be content to be made such fools of by men? that when some men's Perriwigs are made of the hair of a Horse's tail, and others of a Goat's beard; that they should voluntarily suffer themselves to be so abused as to part with their hair to make Perriwigs also! And Women's hair and Goat's hair many times goe into the same Perriwigs, as if they were *ejusdem farinae*, or birds of a feather. Nay the woman, of the two, that parted with her hair voluntarily, is more goatish, or at least foolish than the Goat, that parteth with his involuntarily; tho' it be to be so honorably matched as to be hanged Cheek by jowl with a Woman's hair. What a mad World would it be, if women should take the same affection to wearing of Men's beards; as Men do to Women's hair? Would they not be accounted meer Viragos, or virile Houswives? And by the same reason, why should it not be accounted Effeminacy in Men, to covet Women's hair; which is a token of Women's Subjection, when they wear it themselves for a Covering: and to have it cut off, a token of Immodesty. Moreover, what mazed work would it make with Women-kind, if they were bound to supply all Mankind with Perriwig-Stuff? For the Sheep to be dumb before the Shearer, is admired Patience; and yet that is comparatively, no Wonder to this. Because God gave her her Wool for that end. And the Sheep is so subject to Man, that he may at his pleasure cut his Throat, as well as her Wool; and eat her

Flesh, and tan and wear her Skin, as well as her Wool. But God hath not so subjected Women to Men. But as Virgil said of Sheep

Sic vos non vobis vellera fertis Oves

so it may be now said of Women,

Sic vos non vobis mulieres crinificatis.

If the hair of Women be so necessary and usefull, as it is pretended in this Age, for Perriwigs: perhaps the next Age may find a way to spin it, and make Cloth of it. And their Skins well tanned may make good Leather: and at length they will become very profitable Creatures to Men.

7. The Folly and Absurdity of Mens Perriwigging of themselves with Women's Hair, appears in many Particulars.

(1) It is a Shame for a Man to wear long hair; but Perriwigs are usually long Hair. And if Nature teacheth that it is a Shame for a Man to wear long hair tho' his own: Nature must teach that it is much more shamefull to wear Long hair of another body's; and especially of Women's. It was no Shame for Men to wear their own short hair: it must needs therefore be shamefull to part with it for that which it is a Shame for Man to wear; viz. Women's long hair.

(2) Women's hair, when on their own heads, is a token of Subjection: How comes it to cease to be a token of Subjection, when Men wear it? It was made for a token of Subjection in the Wearer; and is no more a token of Superiority in Men: than wearing the Breeches is a token of Subjection in Women. 1 Cor. 11. 3, 4, 5, 6, 7, etc.

(3) To be beholden to another without Cause, is ignominious in a high degree: for the Borrower is Servant to the Lender, at least in some degree. It was an abatement of Solomon's Glory, that it was not genuine, and connatural, as the Lilies' Glory was. Sin exposed Men to this Shame and Misery, to be beholden to some of the Creatures for Clothing and Covering. But in the case of Hair, there is no such need; seeing God and Nature provided for every man hair of his own. In cases of extraordinary Casualty, when the head is left bare, other supply may be made by Perriwigs made of the hair of other Creatures. There is no need to rob Peter, to pay Paul, and to make one bald, that ought to be covered; that another may be covered, that might be conveniently covered some other way.

(4) For a man to pray covered, is absurd and shamefull, and dishonours Christ. But so doe Men when Perriwiged. For the Woman's hair is given for a Covering; and is so to whomsoever wears it in that Length and Abundance, that is usual in Perriwigs: and consequently, such dishonor Christ. 1 Cor. 11. 4.

(5) It is a foolish Exchange, to exchange the Living for the dead. In this case, as well as in others, A living dog is better than a dead Lion. A mean head of Hair living, sweet, lively-coloured and brisk through its constant derivation of its natural juice from the Soil where it first sprung up, is to be prefered before the most flourishing Perriwigg, that is lopped off from the root, and derives no more vital Sap: but is always withering and decaying, and needs artificial Oyle and Perfumes, to keep it from Putrefaction.

(6) A good man would set the more Price upon his own natural Hair because Christ said, The Hairs of your head are all numbred. Mat. 10. 30. And that an hair of their head shall not perish. Luke, 21. 18. That God will have the same Regard to beggd, or borrowd, or bought Perriwigd hair; we have no Security. When the 3 Children were

cast into the fire, not an hair of their head was singed: if they had wore Perriwigs, it had been well if they had escaped so. If Samson had thought to have thatched his shaven crown, and mended his broken Vow with a Perriwigg of Delilah's Hair; though it might have been longer than it was before, and much longer than it was grown to at the time he made the Philistines Sport: I question whether he had had such an extraordinary Assistance, as he had when he pulld down the house on the Philistines heads. If the Baldness of Elisha's head had come by a voluntary shaving of his head, to make room for a Perriwigg made of Women's Hair: the children that laughd at his bald head, might, for ought that I know, have done well enough for all the Bear's. For it had been a ridiculous thing for the old Prophet to have voluntarily laid aside his gray hairs, for to make way for a more florid appearance in a borrowed Dress in some foolish youthfull Woman's hair.

(7) There is manifest Pride, Levity, Vanity, Affectation in Perriwigs. For they are not made in imitation of Mens' Hair, as it naturally groweth. Whereas Art should imitate Nature, where it pretends to mend the accidental defects, or decays of Nature. Let all the World judge, whose perriwigg Locks don't hang in their Eyes, whether the Perriwigg part of Mankind, as to Hair, look like them that go in their own Hair. Whereas the Perriwigs might as easily be made to imitate the honest guise of those Christians that wear their own Hair; if men desired to have them so: and would be less offensive than they are now.

(8) It will not be an easy thing to account with God for so much needless Cost and Expence as is now laid out on Perriwigs. And much more would the Expence be, if the Fashion should prevail among the Generality. Alass, that men should be so prodigal and profuse this way, in an Age so barren and fruitless as to good Works: and when they are so much needed for the maintaining the Government in Order and Honor, and for building Forts, and maintaining Souldiers to defend the Plantation against the Enemys that will take off the Scalp, both Skin and Hair, if we fall into their hands. They that do little or nothing for relieving the Poor; and are backward in maintaining the Worship of God, and make Poverty their Excuse; and yet might bate all the Cost of Perriwigs, as well as the paring of their Nails: Will be found ill Stewards of the Estates which God hath given them.

(9) If all the foregoing Arguments prove no more than that there is an Appearance of Evil in it; yet that is enough to prove that Perriwigs of Women's hair should not be worn by Christian Men: seeing Christians are required to abstain from all Appearance of Evil. Neither should we for so small a Temptation, run the Venture of living in a Course of Sin; and of being Exemplary to others in what is Doubtfull, and, very many good Men think, sinfull: and are offended and grieved at the Sight of Christians that have Faces like Men; and Hair like the Hair of Women: and are especially grieved, when they see Magistrates and Ministers, that are in Reputation for Wisdom, Honor and Office; and ought to be Examples to others in what is Good, are, in their Opinion, become Examples in what is Evil.

14. Sarah Knight

Journal
1704–5

*Sarah Kemble Knight (1666–1727) was born in Boston and lived there until 1714,
when she moved to Connecticut. She was married to Captain Richard Knight, who
died in 1706. But even before his death she was active in making business decisions. In October of 1704 she began a business trip that was to last until March of
the following year; the* Journal *was the result. Sarah Knight is not known to have
written anything else, though she ran a writing school in Boston that Benjamin
Franklin may have attended. Knight's commercial activities probably put her in
close contact with the transatlantic networks of the seaport merchants, and the*
Journal *shows a strong identification with metropolitan literary culture. She imagines fantastic cities based on her reading; in the privacy of her room she composes
witticisms and satiric poetry for her own amusement, but very much in the London
style; and she experiments with different ways of seeing the people she meets as
locals, provincials. The journal becomes her way of being more than merely local
herself. In it she adopts a metropolitan consciousness and measures colonial reality
against urbane standards.*

Monday, Octb'r the second, 1704.—About three o'clock afternoon, I begun
my Journey from Boston to New-Haven; being about two Hundred Mile.
My Kinsman, Capt. Robert Luist, waited on me as farr as Dedham, where I
was to meet the Western post.[112]

I vissitted the Reverd. Mr. Belcher, the Minister of the town, and tarried there till
evening, in hopes the post would come along. But he not coming, I resolved to go to
Billingses where he used to lodge, being 12 miles further. But being ignorant of the
way, Madam Billings, seeing no persuasions of her good spouses or hers could prevail
with me to Lodge there that night, Very kindly went wyth me to the Tavern, where I
hoped to get my guide, And desired the Hostess to inquire of her guests whether any
of them would go with mee. But they being tyed by the Lipps to a pewter engine,
scarcely allowed themselves time to say what clownish

[*Here half a page of the MS. is gone.*]

Pieces of eight, I told her no, I would not be accessary to such extortion.

Then John shan't go, sais shee. No, indeed, shan't hee; And held forth at that rate a
long time, that I began to fear I was got among the Quaking tribe, beleeving not a
Limbertong'd sister among them could out do Madam Hostess.

Upon this, to my no small surprise, son John arrose, and gravely demanded what I

---

112. post: mail rider.

would give him to go with me? Give you, sais I, are you John? Yes, says he, for want of a Better; And behold! this John look't as old as my Host, and perhaps had bin a man in the last Century. Well, Mr. John, sais I, make your demands. Why, half a pss. of eight and a dram, sais John. I agreed, and gave him a Dram (now) in hand to bind the bargain.

My hostess catechis'd John for going so cheep, saying his poor wife would break her heart

[*Here another half page of the MS is gone.*]

His shade on his Horse resembled a Globe on a Gate post. His habitt, Horse and furniture, its looks and goings Incomparably answered the rest.

Thus Jogging on with an easy pace, my Guide telling mee it was dangerous to Ride hard in the Night, which his horse had the sence to avoid,) Hee entertained me with the Adventurs he had passed by late Rideing, and eminent Dangers he had escaped, so that, Remembring the Hero's in Parismus and the Knight of the Oracle,[113] I didn't know but I had mett with a Prince disguis'd.

When we had Ridd about an how'r, wee come into a thick swamp, which by Reason of a great fogg, very much startled mee, it being now very Dark. But nothing dismay'd John: Hee had encountered a thousand and a thousand such Swamps, having a Universall Knowledge in the woods; and readily Answered all my inquiries which were not a few.

In about an how'r, or something more, after we left the Swamp, we come to Billinges, where I was to Lodge. My Guide dismounted and very Complasantly help't me down and shewd the door, signing to me with his hand to Go in; which I Gladly did—But had not gone many steps into the Room, ere I was Interogated by a young Lady I understood afterwards was the Eldest daughter of the family, with these, or words to this purpose, (viz.) Law for mee—what in the world brings You here at this time a night?—I never see a woman on the Rode so Dreadful late, in all the days of my versall life. Who are You? Where are You going? I'm scar'd out of my witts—with much now of the same Kind. I stood aghast, Prepareing to reply, when in comes my Guide. To him Madam turn'd, Roreing out: Lawfull heart, John, is it You?—how de do! Where in the world are you going with this woman? Who is she? John made no Answer but sat down in the corner, fumbled out his black Junk,[114] and saluted that instead of Debb; she then turned agen to mee and fell anew into her silly questions, without asking me to sitt down.

I told her shee treated me very Rudely, and I did not think it my duty to answer her unmannerly Questions. But to get ridd of them, I told her I come there to have the post's company with me to-morrow on my Journey, &c. Miss star'd awhile, drew a chair, bid me sitt, And then run up stairs and putts on two or three Rings, (or else I had not seen them before,) and returning, sett herself just before me, showing the way to Reding, that I might see her Ornaments, perhaps to gain the more respect. But her Granam's new Rung sow,[115] had it appeared, would have affected me as much. I paid honest John with money and dram according to contract, and Dismist him, and

113. Parismus and the Knight of the Oracle: two romances by Emmanuel Forde, from the previous century.

114. black Junk: cheap tobacco.

115. new Rung sow: a pig with a new ring in its snout.

pray'd Miss to shew me where I must Lodge. Shee conducted me to a parlour in a little back Lento,[116] which was almost fill'd with the bedsted, which was so high that I was forced to climb on a chair to gitt up to the wretched bed that lay on it; on which having Stretcht my tired Limbs, and lay'd my head on a Sad-coulourd pillow, I began to think on the transactions of the past day.

Tuesday, October the third, about 8 in the morning, I with the Post proceeded forward without observing any thing remarkable; And about two, afternoon, Arrived at the Post's second stage, where the western Post mett him and exchanged Letters. Here, having called for something to eat, the woman bro't in a Twisted thing like a cable, but something whiter; and laying it on the bord, tugg'd for life to bring it into a capacity to spread; which having with great pains accomplished, shee serv'd in a dish of Pork and Cabage, I suppose the remains of Dinner. The sauce was of a deep Purple, which I tho't was boil'd in her dye Kettle; the bread was Indian, and every thing on the Table service Agreeable to these. I, being hungry, gott a little down; but my stomach was soon cloy'd, and what cabbage I swallowed serv'd me for a Cudd the whole day after.

Having here discharged the Ordnary for self and Guide, (as I understood was the custom,) About Three afternoon went on with my Third Guide, who Rode very hard; and having crossed Providence Ferry, we come to a River which they Generally Ride thro'. But I dare not venture; so the Post got a Ladd and Cannoo to carry me to tother side, and hee rid thro' and Led my horse. The Cannoo was very small and shallow, so that when we were in she seem'd redy to take in water, which greatly terrified mee, and caused me to be very circumspect, sitting with my hands fast on each side, my eyes steady, not daring so much as to lodg my tonge a hair's breadth more on one side of my mouth than tother, nor so much as think on Lott's wife,[117] for a wry thought would have oversett our wherey:[118] But was soon put out of this pain, by feeling the Cannoo on shore, which I as soon almost saluted with my feet; and Rewarding my sculler, again mounted and made the best of our way forwards. The Rode here was very even and the day pleasant, it being now near Sunsett. But the Post told mee we had neer 14 miles to Ride to the next Stage, (where we were to Lodg.) I askt him of the rest of the Rode, foreseeing wee must travail in the night. Hee told mee there was a bad River we were to Ride thro', which was so very fierce a horse could sometimes hardly stem it: But it was but narrow, and wee should soon be over. I cannot express The concern of mind this relation sett me in: no thoughts but those of the dangerous River could entertain my Imagination, and they were as formidable as various, still Tormenting me with blackest Ideas of my Approaching fate—Sometimes seeing my self drowning, otherwhiles drowned, and at the best like a holy Sister Just come out of a Spiritual Bath in dripping Garments.

Now was the Glorious Luminary, with his swift Coursers arrived at his Stage,[119] leaving poor me with the rest of this part of the lower world in darkness, with which *wee* were soon Surrounded. The only Glimering we now had was from the spangled

---

116. Lento: lean-to.
117. Lott's wife: see Gen. 19.
118. wherey: rowboat.

119. the Glorious Luminary, etc.: Knight parodies poetical language for the sun, which in mythology is Apollo's chariot.

Skies, Whose Imperfect Reflections rendered every Object formidable. Each lifeless Trunk, with its shatter'd Limbs, appear'd an Armed Enymie; and every little stump like a Ravenous devourer. Nor could I so much as discern my Guide, when at any distance, which added to the terror.

Thus, absolutely lost in Thought, and dying with the very thoughts of drowning, I come up with the post, who I did not see till even with his Horse: he told me he stopt for mee; and wee Rode on Very deliberatly a few paces, when we entred a Thickett of Trees and Shrubbs, and I perceived by the Horse's going, we were on the descent of a Hill, which, as wee come neerer the bottom, 'twas totaly dark with the Trees that surrounded it. But I knew by the Going of the Horse wee had entred the water, which my Guide told mee was the hazzardous River he had told me of; and hee, Riding up close to my Side, Bid me not fear— we should be over Imediatly. I now ralyed all the Courage I was mistriss of, Knowing that I must either Venture my fate of drowning, or be left like the Children in the wood.[120] So, as the Post bid me, I gave Reins to my Nagg; and sitting as Stedy as Just before in the Cannoo, in a few minutes got safe to the other side, which hee told mee was the Narragansett country.

Here We found great difficulty in Travailing, the way being very narrow, and on each side the Trees and bushes gave us very unpleasant welcomes with their Branches and bow's, which wee could not avoid, it being so exceeding dark. My Guide, as before so now, putt on harder than I, with my weary bones, could follow; so left mee and the way beehind him. Now Returned my distressed aprehensions of the place where I was: the dolesome woods, my Company next to none, Going I knew not whither, and encompassed with Terrifying darkness; The least of which was enough to startle a more Masculine courage. Added to which the Reflections, as in the afternoon of the day that my Call was very Questionable,[121] which till then I had not so Prudently as I ought considered. Now, coming to the foot of a hill, I found great difficulty in ascending; But being got to the Top, was there amply recompenced with the friendly Appearance of the Kind Conductress of the night,[122] Just then Advancing above the Horisontall Line. The Raptures which the Sight of that fair Planett produced in mee, caus'd mee, for the Moment, to forgett my present wearyness and past toils; and Inspir'd me for most of the remaining way with very divirting tho'ts, some of which, with the other Occurances of the day, I reserved to note down when I should come to my Stage. My tho'ts on the sight of the moon were to this purpose:

> Fair Cynthia, all the Homage that I may
> Unto a Creature, unto thee I pay;
> In Lonesome woods to meet so kind a guide,
> To Mee's more worth than all the world beside.
> Some Joy I felt just now, when safe got or'e
> Yon Surly River to this Rugged shore,
> Deeming Rough welcomes from these clownish Trees,

---

120. Children in the wood: in an English ballad, abandoned in the forest by an uncle.
121. My Call was very Questionable: i.e., Knight is doubting the necessity of the journey.
122. Kind Conductress of the night: poetical cliche for the moon, like "Cynthia" in the poem following.

Better than Lodgings with Nereidees.
Yet swelling fears surprise; all dark appears—
Nothing but Light can disipate those fears.
My fainting vitals can't lend strength to say,
But softly whisper, O I wish 'twere day.
The murmer hardly warm'd the Ambient air,
E're thy Bright Aspect rescues from dispair:
Makes the old Hagg her sable mantle loose,
And a Bright Joy do's through my Soul diffuse.
The Boistero's Trees now Lend a Passage Free,
And pleasent prospects thou giv'st light to see.

From hence wee kept on, with more ease than before: the way being smooth and even, the night warm and serene, and the Tall and thick Trees at a distance, especially when the moon glar'd light through the branches, fill'd my Imagination with the pleasent delusion of a Sumpteous citty, fill'd with famous Buildings and churches, with their spiring steeples, Balconies, Galleries and I know not what: Granduers which I had heard of, and which the stories of foreign countries had given me the Idea of.

Here stood a Lofty church—there is a steeple,
And there the Grand Parade—O see the people!
That Famous Castle there, were I but nigh,
To see the mote and Bridg and walls so high—
They'r very fine! sais my deluded eye.

Being thus agreably entertain'd without a thou't of any thing but thoughts themselves, I on a suden was Rous'd from these pleasing Imaginations, by the Post's sounding his horn, which assured mee hee was arrived at the Stage, where we were to Lodge: and that musick was then most musickall and agreeable to mee.

Being come to mr. Havens', I was very civilly Received, and courteously entertained, in a clean comfortable House; and the Good woman was very active in helping off my Riding clothes, and then ask't what I would eat. I told her I had some Chocolett, if shee would prepare it; which with the help of some Milk, and a little clean brass Kettle, she soon effected to my satisfaction. I then betook me to my Apartment, which was a little Room parted from the Kitchen by a single board partition; where, after I had noted the Occurrences of the past day, I went to bed, which, tho' pretty hard, Yet [was] neet and handsome. But I could get no sleep, because of the Clamor of some of the Town topers in next Room, Who were entred into a strong debate concerning the Signifycation of the name of their Country, (viz.) *Narraganset*. One said it was named so by the Indians, because there grew a Brier there, of a prodigious Heighth and bigness, the like hardly ever known, called by the Indians Narragansett; And quotes an Indian of so Barberous a name for his Author, that I could not write it. His Antagonist Replyed no—It was from a Spring it had its name, which hee well knew where it was, which was extreem cold in summer, and as Hott as could be imagined in the winter, which was much resorted to by the natives, and by them called

Narragansett, (Hott and Cold,) and that was the originall of their places name—with a thousand Impertinances not worth notice, which He utter'd with such a Roreing voice and Thundering blows with the fist of wickedness on the Table, that it peirced my very head. I heartily fretted, and wish't 'um tongue tyed; but with as little success as a friend of mine once, who was (as shee said) kept a whole night awake, on a Journey, by a country Lieutenant and a Sergent, Insigne and a Deacon, contriving how to bring a triangle into a Square. They kept calling for tother Gill,[123] which while they were swallowing, was some Intermission; But presently, like Oyle to fire, encreased the flame. I set my Candle on a Chest by the bed side, and setting up, fell to my old way of composing my Resentments, in the following manner:

> I ask thy Aid, O Potent Rum!
> To Charm these wrangling Topers Dum.
> Thou hast their Giddy Brains possest—
> The man confounded with the Beast—
> And I, poor I, can get no rest.
> Intoxicate them with thy fumes:
> O still their Tongues till morning comes!

And I know not but my wishes took effect, for the dispute soon ended with' tother Dram; and so Good night!

Wednesday, October 4th. About four in the morning, we set out for Kingston (for so was the Town called) with a french Docter in our company. Hee and the Post put on very furiously, so that I could not keep up with them, only as now and then they'd stop till they see mee. This Rode was poorly furnished with accommodations for Travellers, so that we were forced to ride 22 miles by the post's account, but neerer thirty by mine, before wee could bait[124] so much as our Horses, which I exceedingly complained of. But the post encourag'd mee, by saying wee should be well accommodated anon at mr. Devills, a few miles further. But I questioned whether we ought to go to the Devil to be helpt out of affliction. However, like the rest of Deluded souls that post to the Infernal denn, Wee made all posible speed to this Devil's Habitation; where alliting, in full assurance of good accommodation, wee were going in. But meeting his two daughters, as I suposed twins, they so neerly resembled each other, both in features and habit, and look't as old as the Divel himselfe, and quite as Ugly, We desired entertainm't, but could hardly get a word out of 'um, till with our Importunity, telling them our necesity, &c. they call'd the old Sophister, who was as sparing of his words as his daughters had bin, and no, or none, was the reply's hee made us to our demands. Hee differed only in this from the old fellow in to'ther Country:[125] hee let us depart. However, I thought it proper to warn poor Travailers to endeavor to Avoid falling into circumstances like ours, which at our next Stage I sat down and did as followeth:

---

123. Gill: a 4-oz. glass, in this case of liquor.   125. the old fellow in to'ther Country: Satan.
124. bait: feed.

May al that dread the cruel fiend of night
Keep on, and not at this curs't Mansion light.
'Tis Hell; 'tis Hell! and Devills here do dwell:
Here dwells the Devill—surely this's Hell.
Nothing but Wants: a drop to cool yo'r Tongue
Cant be procur'd these cruel Fiends among.
Plenty of horrid Grins and looks sevear,
Hunger and thirst, But pitty's bannish'd here—
The Right hand keep, if Hell on Earth you fear!

Thus leaving this habitation of cruelty, we went forward; and arriving at an Ordinary[126] about two mile further, found tollerable accommodation. But our Hostess, being a pretty full mouth'd old creature, entertain'd our fellow travailer, the french Docter, with Inumirable complaints of her bodily infirmities; and whispered to him so lou'd, that all the House had as full a hearing as hee: which was very divirting to the company, (of which there was a great many,) as one might see by their sneering. But poor weary I slipt out to enter my mind in my Journal, and left my Great Landlady with her Talkative Guests to themselves.

From hence we proceeded (about ten forenoon) through the Narragansett country, pretty Leisurely; and about one afternoon come to Paukataug River, which was about two hundred paces over, and now very high, and no way over to to'ther side but this. I dare not venture to Ride thro, my courage at best in such cases but small, And now at the Lowest Ebb, by reason of my weary, very weary, hungry and uneasy Circumstances. So takeing leave of my company, tho' with no little Reluctance, that I could not proceed with them on my Journey, Stop at a little cottage Just by the River, to wait the Waters falling, which the old man that lived there said would be in a little time, and he would conduct me safe over. This little Hutt was one of the wretchedest I ever saw a habitation for human creatures. It was suported with shores enclosed with Clapbords, laid on Lengthways, and so much asunder, that the Light come throu' every where; the doore tyed on with a cord in the place of hinges; The floor the bear earth; no windows but such as the thin covering afforded, nor any furniture but a Bedd with a glass Bottle hanging at the head on't; an earthan cupp, a small pewter Bason, A Board with sticks to stand on, instead of a table, and a block or two in the corner instead of chairs. The family were the old man, his wife and two Children; all and every part being the picture of poverty. Notwithstanding both the Hutt and its Inhabitance were very clean and tydee: to the crossing the Old Proverb, that bare walls make giddy hows-wifes.

I Blest myselfe that I was not one of this miserable crew; and the Impressions their wretchedness formed in me caused mee on the very Spott to say:

Tho' Ill at ease, A stranger and alone,
All my fatigu's shall not extort a grone.
These Indigents have hunger with their ease;

126. Ordinary: inn.

Their best is wors behalfe then my disease.
Their Misirable hutt which Heat and Cold
Alternately without Repulse do hold;
Their Lodgings thyn and hard, their Indian fare,
The mean Apparel which the wretches wear,
And their ten thousand ills which can't be told,
Makes nature er'e 'tis midle age'd look old.
When I reflect, my late fatigues do seem
Only a notion or forgotten Dreem.

I had scarce done thinking, when an Indian-like Animal come to the door, on a creature very much like himselfe, in mien and feature, as well as Ragged cloathing; and having 'litt, makes an Awkerd Scratch with his Indian shoo, and a Nodd, sitts on the block, fumbles out his black Junk, dipps it in the Ashes, and presents it piping hott to his muscheeto's[127] and fell to sucking like a calf, without speaking, for near a quarter of an hower. At length the old man said how do's Sarah do? who I understood was the wretches wife, and Daughter to the old man: he Replyed —as well as can be expected, &c. So I remembred the old say, and suposed I knew Sarah's case. Butt hee being, as I understood, going over the River, as ugly as hee was, I was glad to ask him to show me the way to Saxtons, at Stoningtown; which he promising, I ventur'd over with the old mans assistance; who having rewarded to content, with my Tattertailed guide, I Ridd on very slowly thro' Stoningtown, where the Rode was very Stony and uneven. I asked the fellow, as we went, divers questions of the place and way, &c. I being arrived at my country Saxtons, at Stonington, was very well accommodated both as to victuals and Lodging, the only Good of both I had found since my setting out. Here I heard there was an old man and his Daughter to come that way, bound to N. London; and being now destitute of a Guide, gladly waited for them, being in so good a harbour, and accordingly, Thursday, October the 5th, about 3 in the afternoon, I sat forward with neighbour Polly and Jemima, a Girl about 18 Years old, who hee said he had been to fetch out of the Narragansetts, and said they had Rode thirty miles that day, on a sory lean Jade, with only a Bagg under her for a pillion, which the poor Girl often complain'd was very uneasy.

Wee made Good speed along, which made poor Jemima make many a sow'r face, the mare being a very hard trotter; and after many a hearty and bitter Oh, she at length Low'd out: Lawful Heart father! this bare mare hurts mee Dingeely, I'me direfull sore I vow; with many words to that purpose: poor Child sais Gaffer—she us't to serve your mother so. I don't care how mother us't to do, quoth Jemima, in a pasionate tone. At which the old man Laught, and kik't his Jade o' the side, which made her Jolt ten times harder.

About seven that Evening, we come to New London Ferry: here, by reason of a very high wind, we mett with great difficulty in getting over—the Boat tos't exceedingly, and our Horses capper'd at a very surprizing Rate, and set us all in a fright; especially poor Jemima, who desired her father to say so jack to the Jade, to make her stand. But

---

127. muscheeto's: mustache.

the careless parent, taking no notice of her repeated desires, She Rored out in a Passionate manner: Pray suth father, Are you deaf? Say so Jack to the Jade, I tell you. The Dutiful Parent obey's; saying so Jack, so Jack, as gravely as if hee'd bin to saying Catechise after Young Miss, who with her fright look't of all coullers in the Rain Bow.

Being safely arrived at the house of Mrs. Prentices in N. London, I treated neighbour Polly and daughter for their divirting company, and bid them farewell; and between nine and ten at night waited on the Reverend Mr. Gurdon Saltonstall, minister of the town, who kindly Invited me to Stay that night at his house, where I was very handsomely and plentifully treated and Lodg'd; and made good the Great Character I had before heard concerning him: viz. that hee was the most affable, courteous, Generous and best of men.

Friday, October 6th. I got up very early, in Order to hire somebody to go with mee to New Haven, being in Great parplexity at the thoughts of proceeding alone; which my most hospitable entertainer observing, himselfe went, and soon return'd with a young Gentleman of the town, who he could confide in to Go with mee; and about eight this morning, with Mr. Joshua Wheeler my new Guide, takeing leave of this worthy Gentleman, Wee advanced on towards Seabrook. The Rodes all along this way are very bad, Incumbred with Rocks and mountainos passages, which were very disagreeable to my tired carcass; but we went on with a moderate pace which made the Journy more pleasent. But after about eight miles Rideing, in going over a Bridge under which the River Run very swift, my hors stumbled, and very narrowly 'scaped falling over into the water; which extreemly frightened mee. But through God's Goodness I met with no harm, and mounting agen, in about half a miles Rideing, come to an ordinary, were well entertained by a woman of about seventy and vantage,[128] but of as Sound Intellectuals as one of seventeen. Shee entertain'd Mr. Wheeler with some passages of a Wedding awhile ago at a place hard by, the Brides-Groom being about her Age or something above, Saying his Children was dredfully against their fathers marrying, which shee condemned them extreemly for.

From hence wee went pretty briskly forward, and arriv'd at Saybrook ferry about two of the Clock afternoon; and crossing it, wee call'd at an Inn to Bait, (foreseeing we should not have such another Opportunity till we come to Killingsworth.) Land-lady come in, with her hair about her ears, and hands at full pay scratching. Shee told us shee had some mutton which shee would broil, which I was glad to hear; But I supose forgot to wash her scratchers; in a little time shee brot it in; but it being pickled, and my Guide said it smelt strong of head sause, we left it, and paid sixpence a piece for our Dinners, which was only smell.

So wee putt forward with all speed, and about seven at night come to Killingsworth, and were tollerably well with Travillers fare, and Lodgd there that night.

Saturday, Oct. 7th, we sett out early in the Morning, and being something unaquainted with the way, having ask't it of some wee mett, they told us wee must Ride a mile or two and turne down a Lane on the Right hand; and by their Direction wee Rode on but not Yet comeing to the turning, we mett a Young fellow and ask't him how farr it was to the Lane which turn'd down towards Guilford. Hee said wee must Ride a

128. vantage: more.

little further, and turn down by the Corner of uncle Sams Lott. My Guide vented his Spleen at the Lubber; and we soon after came into the Rode, and keeping still on, without any thing further Remarkabell, about two a clock afternoon we arrived at New Haven, where I was received with all Possible Respects and civility. Here I discharged Mr. Wheeler with a reward to his satisfaction, and took some time to rest after so long and toilsome a Journey; And Inform'd myselfe of the manners and customs of the place, and at the same time employed myselfe in the afair I went there upon.

They are Govern'd by the same Laws as wee in Boston, (or little differing,) thr'out this whole Colony of Connecticot, And much the same way of Church Government, and many of them good, Sociable people, and I hope Religious too: but a little too much Independant in their principalls, and, as I have been told, were formerly in their Zeal very Riggid in their Administrations towards such as their Lawes made Offenders, even to a harmless Kiss or Innocent merriment among Young people. Whipping being a frequent and counted an easy Punishment, about which as other Crimes, the Judges were absolute in their Sentances. They told mee a pleasant story about a pair of Justices in those parts, which I may not omit the relation of.

A negro Slave belonging to a man in the Town, stole a hogs head[129] from his master, and gave or sold it to an Indian, native of the place. The Indian sold it in the neighborhood, and so the theft was found out. Thereupon the Heathen was Seized, and carried to the Justices House to be Examined. But his worship (it seems) was gone into the field, with a Brother in office, to gather in his Pompions.[130] Whither the male-factor is hurried, And Complaint made, and satisfaction in the name of Justice demanded. Their Worships cann't proceed in form without a Bench: whereupon they Order one to be Imediately erected, which, for want of fitter materials, they made with pompions—which being finished, down setts their Worships, and the Malefactor call'd, and by the Senior Justice Interrogated after the following manner. You Indian why did You steal from this man? You sho'dn't do so—it's a Grandy wicked thing to steal. Hol't Hol't, cryes Justice Junior, Brother, You speak negro to him. I'le ask him. You sirrah, why did You steal this man's Hoggshead? Hoggshead? (replys the Indian,) me no stomany.[131] No? says his Worship; and pulling off his hatt, Patted his own head with his hand, sais, Tatapa—You, Tatapa—you; all one this. Hoggshead all one this. Hah! says Netop, now me stomany that. Whereupon the Company fell into a great fitt of Laughter, even to Roreing. Silence is commanded, but to no effect: for they continued perfectly Shouting. Nay, sais his worship, in an angry tone, if it be so, *take mee off the Bench*.

Their Diversions in this part of the Country are on Lecture days and Training days[132] mostly: on the former there is Riding from town to town.

And on training dayes The Youth divert themselves by Shooting at the Target, as they call it, (but it very much resembles a pillory,) where hee that hitts neerest the white has some yards of Red Ribbin presented him, which being tied to his hattband, the two ends streeming down his back, he is Led away in Triumph, with great applause, as the winners of the Olympiack Games. They generally marry very young:

129. hogs head: a barrel.
130. Pompions: pumpkins.
131. stomany: understand.

132. Lecture days and Training days: Thursdays (for religious lectures) and militia drill days.

the males oftener as I am told under twentie than above; they generally make public wedings, and have a way something singular (as they say) in some of them, viz. Just before Joyning hands the Bridgegroom quitts the place, who is soon followed by the Bridesmen, and as it were, dragg'd back to duty—being the reverse to the former practice among us, to steal man's Pride.

There are great plenty of Oysters all along by the sea side, as farr as I Rode in the Collony, and those very good. And they Generally lived very well and comfortably in their famelies. But too Indulgent (especially the farmers) to their slaves: sufering too great familiarity from them, permitting them to sit at Table and eat with them, (as they say to save time,) and into the dish goes the black hoof as freely as the white hand. They told me that there was a farmer lived nere the Town where I lodgd who had some difference with his slave, concerning something the master had promised him and did not punctually perform; which caused some hard words between them; But at length they put the matter to Arbitration and Bound themselves to stand to the award of such as they named—which done, the Arbitrators Having heard the Allegations of both parties, Order the master to pay 40s to black face, and acknowledge his fault. And so the matter ended: the poor master very honestly standing to the award.

There are every where in the Towns as I passed, a Number of Indians the Natives of the Country, and are the most salvage of all the salvages of that kind that I had ever Seen: little or no care taken (as I heard upon enquiry) to make them otherwise. They have in some places Landes of their owne, and Govern'd by Law's of their own making;—they marry many wives and at pleasure put them away, and on the least dislike or fickle humour, on either side, saying *stand away* to one another is a sufficient Divorce. And indeed those uncomely *Stand aways* are too much in Vougue among the English in this (Indulgent Colony) as their Records plentifully prove, and that on very trivial matters, of which some have been told me, but are not proper to be Related by a Female pen, tho some of that foolish sex have had too large a share in the story.

If the natives committ any crime on their own precincts among themselves, the English takes no Cognezens of. But if on the English ground, they are punishable by our Laws. They mourn for their Dead by blacking their faces, and cutting their hair, after an Awkerd and frightfull manner; But can't bear You should mention the names of their dead Relations to them: they trade most for Rum, for which theyd hazzard their very lives; and the English fit them Generally as well, by seasoning it plentifully with water.

They give the title of merchant to every trader; who Rate their Goods according to the time and spetia they pay in: viz. Pay, mony, Pay as mony, and trusting. *Pay* is Grain, Pork, Beef, &c. at the prices sett by the General Court that Year; *mony* is pieces of Eight, Ryalls, or Boston or Bay shillings (as they call them,) or Good hard money, as sometimes silver coin is termed by them; also Wampom, viz Indian beads which serves for change. *Pay as mony* is provisions, as aforesaid one Third cheaper then as the Assembly or General Court sets it; and *Trust* as they and the merchant agree for time.

Now, when the buyer comes to ask for a comodity, sometimes before the merchant answers that he has it, he sais, *is Your pay redy?* Perhaps the Chap Reply's Yes: what do You pay in? say's the merchant. The buyer having answered, then the price is set; as suppose he wants a sixpenny knife, in pay it is 12d—in pay as money eight pence, and hard money its own price, viz. 6d. It seems a very Intricate way of trade and what Lex Mercatoria[133] had not thought of.

Being at a merchants house, in comes a tall country fellow, with his alfogeos[134] full of Tobacco; for they seldom Loose their Cudd, but keep Chewing and Spitting as long as they'r eyes are open,—he advanc't to the midle of the Room, makes an Awkward Nodd, and spitting a Large deal of Aromatick Tincture, he gave a scrape with his shovel like shoo, leaving a small shovel full of dirt on the floor, made a full stop, Hugging his own pretty Body with his hands under his arms, Stood staring rown'd him, like a Catt let out of a Baskett. At last, like the creature Balaam Rode on, he opened his mouth and said: have You any Ribinen for Hatbands to sell I pray? The Questions and Answers about the pay being past, the Ribin is bro't and opened. Bumpkin Simpers, cryes *its confounded Gay I vow*; and beckning to the door, in comes Joan Tawdry, dropping about 50 curtsees, and stands by him: hee shows her the Ribin. *Law, You*, sais shee, *its right Gent,*[135] *You, take it, tis dreadfully pretty.* Then she enquires, *have You any hood silk I pray?* which being brought and bought, *Have You any thred silk to sew it with* says shee, which being accomodated with they Departed. They Generaly stand after they come in a great while speachless, and some-times dont say a word till they are askt what they want, which I Impute to the Awe they stand in of the merchants, who they are constantly almost Indebted too; and must take what they bring without Liberty to choose for themselves; but they serve them as well, making the merchants stay long enough for their pay.

We may Observe here the great necessity and bennifitt both of Education and Conversation; for these people have as Large a portion of mother witt, and sometimes a Larger, than those who have bin brought up in Citties; But for want of emprovements, Render themselves almost Ridiculos, as above. I should be glad if they would leave such follies, and am sure all that Love Clean Houses (at least) would be glad on't too.

They are generaly very plain in their dress, throuout all the Colony, as I saw, and follow one another in their modes; that You may know where they belong, especially the women, meet them where you will. . . .

[NEW YORK]

The Cittie of New York is a pleasant, well compacted place, situated on a Commodius River which is a fine harbour for shipping. The Buildings Brick Generaly, very stately and high, though not altogether like ours in Boston. The Bricks in some of the Houses are of divers Coullers and laid in Checkers, being glazed look very agree-able. The inside of them are neat to admiration, the wooden work, for only the walls are plasterd, and the Sumers and Gist[136] are plained and kept very white scowr'd as so is all the partitions if made of Bords. The fire places have no Jambs (as ours have) But the Backs run flush with the walls, and the Hearth is of Tyles and is as farr out into the Room at the Ends as before the fire, which is Generally Five foot in the Low'r rooms, and the peice over where the mantle tree should be is made as ours with Joyners work, and as I supose is fasten'd to iron rodds inside. The House where the

---

133. Lex Mercatoria: mercantile law.
134. the Spanish Alfogeos: here, cheeks; from Sp. *alforjas*, saddlebags.

135. *Gent*: genteel.
136. Sumers and Gist: lintel and crossbeam.

Vendue[137] was, had Chimmey Corners like ours, and they and the hearths were laid with the finest tile that I ever see, and the stair cases laid all with white tile which is ever clean, and so are the walls of the Kitchen which had a Brick floor. They were making Great preparations to Receive their Governor, Lord Cornbury from the Jerseys, and for that End raised the militia to Gard him on shore to the fort.

They are Generaly of the Church of England and have a New England Gentleman for their minister, and a very fine church set out with all Customary requsites. There are also a Dutch and Divers Conventicles as they call them, viz. Baptist, Quakers, & c. They are not strict in keeping the Sabbath as in Boston and other places where I had bin, But seem to deal with great exactness as farr as I see or Deall with. They are sociable to one another and Curteos and Civill to strangers and fare well in their houses. The English go very fasheonable in their dress. But the Dutch, especially the middling sort, differ from our women, in their habitt go loose, were French muches which are like a Capp and a head band in one, leaving their ears bare, which are sett out with Jewells of a large size and many in number. And their fingers hoop't with Rings, some with large stones in them of many Coullers as were their pendants in their ears, which You should see very old women wear as well as Young.

They have Vendues very frequently and make their Earnings very well by them, for they treat with good Liquor Liberally, and the Customers Drink as Liberally and Generally pay for't as well, by paying for that which they Bidd up Briskly for, after the sack has gone plentifully about, tho' sometimes good penny worths are got there. Their Diversions in the Winter is Riding Sleys about three or four Miles out of Town, where they have Houses of entertainment at a place called the Bowery, and some go to friends Houses who handsomely treat them. Mr. Burroughs cary'd his spouse and Daughter and myself out to one Madame Dowes, a Gentlewoman that lived at a farm House, who gave us a handsome Entertainment of five or six Dishes and choice Beer and metheglin,[138] Cyder, &c. al which she said was the produce of her farm. I believe we mett 50 or 60 slays that day—they fly with great swiftness and some are so furious that they'le turn out of the path for none except a Loaden Cart. Nor do they spare for any diversion the place affords, and sociable to a degree, they'r Tables being as free to their Naybours as to themselves.

Having here transacted the affair I went upon and some other that fell in the way, after about a fortnight's stay there I left New-York with no Little regrett, and Thursday, Dec. 21, set out for New Haven with my Kinsman Trowbridge.

[THE RETURN]

March 3d wee got safe home to Boston, where I found my aged and tender mother and my Dear and only Child in good health with open arms redy to receive me, and my Kind relations and friends flocking in to welcome mee and hear the story of my transactions and travails I having this day bin five months from home and now I cannot fully express my Joy and Satisfaction. But desire sincearly to adore my Great Benefactor for thus graciously carying forth and returning in safety his unworthy handmaid.

---

137. Vendue: sale, market.

138. metheglin: a Welsh spiced drink, like mead.

Chapter 6

Seventeenth-Century Anglo-America:
The Trials of Puritanism

INTRODUCTION

The name "Puritan" began as an insult, and for many it still is. H. L. Mencken defined Puritanism as "the haunting fear that someone, somewhere, may be happy." Arguments about New England Puritanism tend to be more about the later United States, and so it was with Mencken, whose real target was prudery in American culture. On the other side, John Adams's *Dissertation on the Canon and Feudal Laws* (1765) began the tradition of seeing the American Puritans as antiauthoritarian rebels, seekers after religious freedom. United States popular culture keeps this myth alive and well, alongside the apparently contradictory but equally popular view of the Puritans as, in a word, Puritanical.

The term "Puritan" was first applied in the sixteenth century to miscellaneous critics of the Church of England, by Anglican defenders. It had the connotation of purist, or hardliner, and was applied to radicals who complained broadly about corruption in the church. Eventually theological arguments came to polarize English religious culture, culminating in the civil wars of the 1640s and, along the way, the emigration of some Puritans to the West Indian and North Atlantic colonies.

The sharpest debate was about predestination. Unlike modern evangelical Christians, Puritans did not believe that you could be saved by believing in Jesus. They had contempt for this idea, which they called Arminianism (after Jacobus Arminius, a Dutch theologian). Salvation, like everything else, was disposed by God's will. You cannot simply choose your salvation, for only God enables you to do so. His grace is uncoerced, irresistible, and permanent. Sovereignty in all matters is God's; neither the individual's will nor the church's sacraments have the power to save. In the Church of England, however, this view of salvation had begun to give way to a greater emphasis on the individual's acceptance or rejection of grace. William Laud, who became Archbishop of Canterbury in 1633, was avowedly Arminian. To the Puritans, Laud was as bad as the Pope. And to Laud, Puritans were a threat to national peace.

The more Puritans began denouncing the Church of England as intrinsically corrupt, the more the theological debate began to turn on what a true church would be. Since the early days of Elizabeth's reign, many English Protestants had argued that the Anglican church had not gone far enough in rejecting traces of Catholicism, and the hierarchy of bishops came to be a key example as the conflict between the church officials and radicals deepened. In proposing church organizations that would be truer to the spirit of the Apostolic times, Puritans began to reject the basic premise of traditional churches, both Anglican and Catholic: that all residents of a parish should share equally in church membership. Presbyterians introduced different degrees of membership. Congregationalists began forming new churches by voluntary compacts. Some went so far as to say that Christians should remove themselves from the Church of England as a false church; they became known as Separatists, a label often applied to the Puritans at Plymouth. Although most Puritans before the civil wars continued to accept the validity of the Anglican church and the principle of state-established religion, they began to think of churches as differentiating believers from nonbelievers.

Once the inclusiveness of a national church could be questioned, radical questions began opening up. If living within the parish were not enough to bestow rights of membership, what tests could be applied to believers? Who would discipline erring congregations? How could a nation have multiple churches? Should churches be established by government at all? If not, how would they exercise control? Suddenly questions of theology also required a theory of society. The seventeenth century saw an explosion of radical and utopian schemes that was without precedent in human history. Theory could change anything. One result was the English Revolution. Another was Massachusetts.

Most of the leading colonial Puritans were nonseparating Congregationalists: they wanted to form a pure church but without openly renouncing the established church. A church, they believed, was formed by a covenant between God and his elect. Their notion of covenant was inevitably shaped by the contract relations of commerce, but they saw it primarily as modelled on the covenant made between God and Abraham in Genesis 18-19; or more generally on the covenant of grace by which God, in sacrificing Jesus, offered to supersede the old law (the covenant of works). This line of thinking has come to be known as Covenant theology, or federal theology. It justified the exclusionary practices of the churches, which are true churches if they consist not of everyone but of the federated elect. It also inspired the colonial Puritans with the sense of a corporate mission, a joint promise from God.

In the North Atlantic colonies, churches began applying tests of membership, requiring applicants to relate their religious experience. As a result, only a minority in most communities had full privileges of church membership. Since church membership was also a precondition for rights of citizenship, conflict over this system ran deep. There was an irony in conflicts like this one: Puritans in Plymouth and Massachusetts Bay who had been an oppositional minority in England suddenly held power themselves. Their system of church membership had to be reconciled with the conservative practice of maintaining a unified church over the entire colony. Their congregations, without a hierarchy or bishops, had to prevent schism.

In England, however, the rise of Puritanism to power produced a different result. Cromwell's Independents began to consider that different kinds of churches might coexist in the same nation. To the New English, who had crossed the Atlantic in order to purify a church and protect it from error, the novel principle of toleration seemed like a betrayal of the whole Puritan venture, and leading colonists such as Nathaniel Ward returned to England to argue against it. (See selection 5 below.) To their chagrin, the same Roger Williams whom they had banished into the snows now emerged as a leading voice in the English debate.

Almost overnight, the New English had gone from being the vanguard of Puritan experimentation to being a conservative minority on the margin of national history. They certainly did not think they had founded their own nation. As William Hooke reminded his congregation, "There is no Land that claimes our name, but *England*, wee are distinguished from all the Nations in the world by the name of *English*. There is no Potentate breathing, that wee call our dread Soveraigne, but King Charles, nor Lawes of any Land have civilized us but *Englands*; there is no Nation that calls us Countrey-men but the *English*." This feeling led many of the colonists, including leaders such as Henry Vane, to return to England to join in the Puritan victory.

If the New England way began to seem like a minor offshoot of Puritanism during the English Revolution, the Restoration of monarchy and the Church of England in 1660 parted the channels still further. Charles II began centralizing the administration of his empire, putting New England and New York under a royal governor. But by that point the New England way faced crises of its own. The main one turned on whether a believer's covenant with the church was enough to bring membership to the believer's children. God had a covenant with Abraham "and his seed." But did the children, or seed, of the first generation share equally in the covenant? If so, then there was no lasting difference between covenanting congregations and traditional ones. Some New Englanders argued that the act of covenanting had to be renewed by each believer. But this view appeared to weaken the bonds of God's covenant with the body of a people, and drifted toward Arminianism. Puritans were very far from being individualists. In 1662 the issue resulted in the awkward compromise known as the Halfway Covenant, whereby adult children of church members were considered to be "in covenant" and to have some privileges of membership—but not full communion.

Divided by such compromises and isolated from developments at home, New England leaders increasingly insisted that the colonists had lapsed from the original faith. They spoke of declension. Their sermons became jeremiads. As Sacvan Bercovitch argues, however, the New England jeremiad has a twist: it laments the present failures and adversities of New England, but the jeremiad never questions the practicality of the old ideals; paradoxically, present ills reaffirm the old ideals and their long-deferred promise. Samuel Danforth's sermon in this chapter is a classic example; see also Michael Wigglesworth's *God's Controversy with New England*, in chapter 8, for a jeremiad in verse. Ultimately this crisis in the mission of New England would yield a sense of difference between the creoles and the mother country. And as the Danforth sermon illustrates, New England Puritans continued to believe that they were in America not just in the accidental way other people lived in their countries, but for a reason.

This chapter is called "The Trials of Puritanism" partly because Puritanism was self-consciously an experiment, one that was radically adjusted over time through controversies and crises that are only partially represented here. Puritanism was a culture of argument, built on a special role for theoretical discussion and a common culture of logical thought (Ramism) that was sustained in the form of the Puritan sermon, with the enumerated deductions of its *fifthlys* and *sixthlys*. Its principled rejection of customary ways and received wisdom, its view of the world as a constant struggle between the church and Satan, its untroubled confidence that most people, most of the time, are wrong and will be damned—all these guaranteed that Puritan culture would have a history of sectarian conflict. The sects that splintered off in the seventeenth century include Baptists, Quakers, and Gortonists. Nathaniel Ward gives a list of them in *The Simple Cobler*, in selection 5 below. Ironically it is arguable that these splinter groups, not the orthodox Puritans, had the most profound and lasting influence on American religious culture. By allowing more place for the individual soul and its unmediated contact with God, they loosed the centrifugal energies of heterodox opinion.

This chapter is also called "The Trials of Puritanism" because of the importance of trials as an instrument for defining the common culture. The first was that of Anne Hutchinson, who in the eyes of John Winthrop and other leaders came to stand for all the danger of the antinomian tendencies unacknowledged in their own thought. But her banishment was only the beginning. Throughout the century, banishments and executions told the cost of Puritanism's utopian dream of a holy commonwealth, producing outcasts, heretics, and criminals in the course of defining and purging the boundaries of the true Christian community. Many, from Hutchinson to the Salem witches, were women.

Puritanism was also a culture of interpretation. Reading and elaborating the sacred text of the Bible was the solution to every problem. Hermeneutics was considered a science. Puritan preachers became especially skilled at all kinds of allegorical reading. Biblical symbols were thought to be the types that presaged later events, both in the New Testament and in modern history; in this approach, called typology, New England could be understood as Zion, or Canaan. Many thought that the signs of the last times could be read, and that the millenium was at hand. Puritan New Englanders learned to interpret their own history as an illustration of providence, reflecting God's design in the smallest details. (See, for example, Mary Rowlandson's narrative in chapter 5.) This aspect of Puritanism, much more than the learned traditions of argument, tied the clergy directly to a popular culture of religious belief in which celestial omens, monstrous births, and ghosts were as much a part of God's way as the creeds of theologians.

As we saw in chapters 3 and 5, leaders of the American Puritans were writing histories of themselves from the moment they landed. Bradford, Winthrop, Winslow, Johnson, and Danforth—all of whom authored histories of New England—were themselves first-generation immigrants. Later, because so much of the writing of United States history was done by their descendants, the views of these Puritan historians came to dominate the national culture's sense of the past. It is often forgotten that Puritans settled not just New England, but Providence Island (near Nicaragua), Barbados, Virginia, and Newfoundland. Even Oliver Cromwell, unimpressed by New England, looked to the Caribbean for English colonial expansion. It is often a challenge to read the history of Puritanism without simply adopting the histories that they produced about themselves. Especially in the trials by which they produced so many outcasts, one must try to infer the counterhistories that might have been written, the rival points of view that might have been made articulate.

M.W.

Suggested readings: The literature on Puritanism is immense. The classic study is Perry Miller, *The New England Mind* (2 vols.). More accessible starting points might be Edmund Morgan, *Visible Saints*, and Larzer Ziff, *Puritanism in America*. The issue of schism is best treated in Philip Gura, *A Glimpse of Sion's Glory*. On the jeremiad, see Sacvan Bercovitch, *The American Jeremiad*. Important recent studies include Andrew Delbanco, *The Puritan Ordeal*; Janice Knight, *Orthodoxies in Massachusetts*; and Stephen Foster, *The Long Argument*. On Salem, see Stephen Boyer and Paul Nissenbaum, *Salem Possessed*; Karen Karlsen, *The Devil in the Shape of a Woman*; and Bernard Rosenthal, *Salem Story*. On the popular religious culture, see David D. Hall, *Worlds of Wonder, Days of Judgment*.

1.

the Antinomian controversy
1637 and 1644

Puritans had always criticized the Church of England for laboring under a
covenant of works; that is, for teaching that good behavior, ritual attendance, and
the sacraments could bring about salvation. They insisted on a distinction between
justification—God's miraculous attribution of Christ's holiness to the elect—and
sanctification—the holy behavior that, in theory, results from salvation and the
indwelling of the Holy Spirit. Sanctification is evidence of salvation, but does not
cause it. In New England, however, the Puritans were themselves the authorities
who enforced church attendance and good behavior—in short, they insisted on
works. It was perhaps inevitable that they should be accused in the same way of
forgetting the primacy of grace, and of introducing ritual mediations between the
soul and God.

   Anne Marbury (1591-1643) grew up near Boston, England. She married
William Hutchinson, a London merchant, and with him came under the influence
of John Cotton, then preaching in Boston. From him, Anne Hutchinson had
learned a piety of inwardness and an emphasis on the covenant of grace. The
Hutchinsons emigrated in 1634, following Cotton. It is said in her trial that
Hutchinson recoiled at "the meanness of the place" when she arrived (cf. Anne
Bradstreet's narrative in chapter 5). She apparently worked as a midwife and nurse,
and began holding popular discussion and prayer meetings in her home. The
colony's authorities grew alarmed at the size of her following and the public
culture of criticism that grew up around the meetings. Finally, a series of quarrels
and rivalries resulted in her trial. According to Winthrop, she had introduced two
main heresies: "1. That the person of the Holy Ghost dwells in a justified person.
2. That no sanctification can help to evidence to us our justification." But the trial
does not immediately focus on these heresies. It clearly shows the leadership's
anxiety about a woman conducting discussions.

   The examination begins badly for Winthrop. Hutchinson displays a ready intelligence, and repeatedly steps around snares laid for her. Finally, however, she asserts
in passing that a moment of insight came to her as a revelation. Thomas Dudley,
the deputy governor, immediately seizes on the admission: "How! an immediate
revelation!" Hutchinson was excommunicated following a half-hearted recanta-
tion. She moved to Rhode Island, and was later killed by Indians in New York
during an Anglo-Dutch war. A year after her death, John Winthrop's anonymous
pamphlet (once mistakenly attributed to Theodore Weld) rehearsed the whole
episode as a justification of the New England Way and a warning to "opinionists."
Since the pamphlet was published in London, its unusual concluding reference to
Hutchinson as an "American Jesabel" should probably be read as doubly insulting.

Ann Hutchinson

from *The Examination of Mrs. Ann Hutchinson at the court at Newtown* 1637

Mr. Winthrop, governor. Mrs. Hutchinson, you are called here as one of those that have troubled the peace of the commonwealth and the churches here. You are known to be a woman that hath had a great share in the promoting and divulging of those opinions that are causes of this trouble, and to be nearly joined not only in affinity and affection with some of those the court had taken notice of and passed censure upon, but you have spoken divers things as we have been informed very prejudicial to the honour of the churches and ministers thereof. And you have maintained a meeting and an assembly in your house that hath been condemned by the general assembly as a thing not tolerable nor comely in the sight of God nor fitting for your sex. And notwithstanding that was cried down, you have continued the same. Therefore we have thought good to send for you to understand how things are, that if you be in an erroneous way we may reduce you[1] that so you may become a profitable member here among us; otherwise, if you be obstinate in your course, that then the court may take such course that you may trouble us no further. Therefore I would intreat you to express whether you do not hold and assent in practice to those opinions and factions that have been handled in court already, that is to say, whether you do not justify Mr. Wheelwright's sermon and the petition.

Mrs. Hutchinson. I am called here to answer before you but I hear no things laid to my charge.

Gov. I have told you some already and more I can tell you. (*Mrs. H.*) Name one Sir.

Gov. Have I not named some already?

Mrs. H. What have I said or done?

Gov. Why for your doings, this you did harbour and countenance those that are parties in this faction that you have heard of. (*Mrs H.*) That's matter of conscience, Sir.

Gov. Your conscience you must keep or it must be kept for you.

Mrs. H. Must not I then entertain the saints because I must keep my conscience?

Gov. Say that one brother should commit felony or treason and come to his other brother's house, if he knows him guilty and conceals him he is guilty of the same. It is his conscience to entertain him, but if his conscience comes into act in giving counte-

---

1. reduce you: lead you back.

nance and entertainment to him that hath broken the law he is guilty too. So if you do countenance those that are transgressors of the law you are in the same fact.

Mrs. H. What law do they transgress?

Gov. The law of God and of the state.

Mrs. H. In what particular?

Gov. Why in this among the rest, whereas the Lord doth say honour thy father and thy mother.

Mrs. H. Ey Sir in the Lord. (*Gov.*) This honour you have broke in giving countenance to them.

Mrs. H. In entertaining those did I entertain them against any act (for there is the thing) or what God hath appointed?

Gov. You knew that Mr. Wheelwright did preach this sermon and those that countenance him in this do break a law.

Mrs. H. What law have I broken?

Gov. Why the fifth commandment.

Mrs. H. I deny that for he saith in the Lord.

Gov. You have joined with them in the faction.

Mrs. H. In what faction have I joined with them?

Gov. In presenting the petition.[2]

Mrs. H. Suppose I had set my hand to the petition what then? (*Gov.*) You saw that case tried before.

Mrs. H. But I had not my hand to the petition.

Gov. You have councelled them. (*Mrs. H.*) Wherein?

Gov. Why in entertaining them.

Mrs. H. What breach of law is that Sir?

Gov. Why dishonouring of parents.

Mrs. H. But put the case Sir that I do fear the Lord and my parents, may not I entertain them that fear the Lord because my parents will not give me leave?

Gov. If they be the fathers of the commonwealth, and they of another religion, if you entertain them then you dishonour your parents and are justly punishable.

Mrs. H. If I entertain them, as they have dishonoured their parents I do.

Gov. No but you by countenancing them above others put honor upon them.

Mrs. H. I may put honor upon them as the children of God and as they do honor the Lord.

Gov. We do not mean to discourse with those of your sex but only this; you do adhere unto them and do endeavour to set forward this faction and so you do dishonour us.

Mrs. H. I do acknowledge no such thing neither do I think that I ever put any dishonour upon you.

Gov. Why do you keep such a meeting at your house as you do every week upon a set day?

Mrs. H. It is lawful for me so to do, as it is all your practices and can you find a

2. the petition: presented by the Antinomian party to the General Court in March, 1637.

warrant for yourself and condemn me for the same thing? The ground of my taking it up was, when I first came to this land because I did not go to such meetings as those were, it was presently reported that I did not allow of such meetings but held them unlawful and therefore in that regard they said I was proud and did despise all ordinances, upon that a friend came unto me and told me of it and I to prevent such aspersions took it up, but it was in practice before I came therefore I was not the first.

Gov. For this, that you appeal to our practice you need no confutation. If your meeting had answered to the former it had not been offensive, but I will say that there was no meeting of women alone, but your meeting is of another sort for there are sometimes men among you.

Mrs. H. There was never any man with us.

Gov. Well, admit there was no man at your meeting and that you was sorry for it, there is no warrant for your doings, and by what warrant do you continue such a course?

Mrs. H. I conceive there lyes a clear rule in Titus, that the elder women should instruct the younger[3] and then I must have a time wherein I must do it.

Gov. All this I grant you, I grant you a time for it, but what is this to the purpose that you Mrs. Hutchinson must call a company together from their callings to come to be taught of you?

Mrs. H. Will it please you to answer me this and to give me a rule for then I will willingly submit to any truth. If any come to my house to be instructed in the ways of God what rule have I to put them away?

Gov. But suppose that a hundred men come unto you to be instructed will you forbear to instruct them?

Mrs. H. As far as I conceive I cross a rule in it.

Gov. Very well and do you not so here?

Mrs. H. No Sir for my ground is they are men.

Gov. Men and women all is one for that, but suppose that a man should come and say Mrs. Hutchinson I hear that you are a woman that God hath given his grace unto and you have knowledge in the word of God I pray instruct me a little, ought you not to instruct this man?

Mrs. H. I think I may. — Do you think it not lawful for me to teach women and why do you call me to teach the court?

Gov. We do not call you to teach the court but to lay open yourself.

[THOMAS DUDLEY SHARPENS THE ISSUE]

Dep. gov. I would go a little higher with Mrs. Hutchinson. About three years ago we were all in peace. Mrs. Hutchinson from that time she came hath made a disturbance, and some that came over with her in the ship did inform me what she was as soon as she was landed. I being then in place dealt with the pastor and teacher of Boston and desired them to enquire of her, and then I was satisfied that she held

3. Titus 2:3–5.

nothing different from us, but within half a year after, she had vented divers of her strange opinions and had made parties in the country, and at length it comes that Mr. Cotton and Mr. Vane were of her judgment, but Mr. Cotton hath cleared himself that he was not of that mind, but now it appears by this woman's meeting that Mrs. Hutchinson hath so forestalled the minds of many by their resort to her meeting that now she hath a potent party in the country. Now if all these things have endangered us as from that foundation and if she in particular hath disparaged all our ministers in the land that they have preached a covenant of works, and only Mr. Cotton a covenant of grace, why this is not to be suffered, and therefore being driven to the foundation and it being found that Mrs. Hutchinson is she that hath depraved all the ministers and hath been the cause of what is fallen out, why we must take away the foundation and the building will fall.

Mrs. H. I pray Sir prove it that I said they preached nothing but a covenant of works.

Dep. Gov. Nothing but a covenant of works, why a Jesuit may preach truth sometimes.

Mrs. H. Did I ever say they preached a covenant of works then?

Dep. Gov. If they do not preach a covenant of grace clearly, then they preach a covenant of works.

Mrs. H. No Sir, one may preach a covenant of grace more clearly than another, so I said.

[HUTCHINSON MAKES A DAMAGING SLIP]

Mrs. H. If you please to give me leave I shall give you the ground of what I know to be true. Being much troubled to see the falseness of the constitution of the church of England, I had like to have turned separatist; whereupon I kept a day of solemn humiliation and pondering of the thing; this scripture was brought unto me — he that denies Jesus Christ to be come in the flesh is antichrist[4] — This I considered of and in considering found that the papists did not deny him to be come in the flesh, nor we did not deny him — who then was antichrist? Was the Turk antichrist only? The Lord knows that I could not open scripture; he must by his prophetical office open it unto me. So after that being unsatisfied in the thing, the Lord was pleased to bring this scripture out of the Hebrews.[5] He that denies the testament denies the testator, and in this did open unto me and give me to see that those which did not teach the new covenant had the spirit of antichrist, and upon this he did discover the ministry unto me and ever since. I bless the Lord, he hath let me see which was the clear ministry and which the wrong. Since that time I confess I have been more choice and he hath let me to distinguish between the voice of my beloved and the voice of Moses, the voice of John Baptist and the voice of antichrist, for all those voices are spoken of in scripture. Now if you do condemn me for speaking what in my conscience I know to be truth I must commit myself unto the Lord.

---

4. 1 John 2:18.   5. Heb. 9:16.

Mr. Nowell.[6] How do you know that that was the spirit?

Mrs. H. How did Abraham know that it was God that bid him offer his son, being a breach of the sixth commandment?

Dep. Gov. By an immediate voice.

Mrs. H. So to me by an immediate revelation.

Dep. Gov. How! an immediate revelation.

Mrs. H. By the voice of his own spirit to my soul. I will give you another scripture, Jer. 46. 27, 28 — out of which the Lord shewed me what he would do for me and the rest of his servants. — But after he was pleased to reveal himself to me I did presently like Abraham run to Hagar. And after that he did let me see the atheism of my own heart, for which I begged of the Lord that it might not remain in my heart, and being thus, he did shew me this (a twelvemonth after) which I told you of before. Ever since that time I have been confident of what he hath revealed unto me.

[*Obliterated*] another place out of Daniel chap. 7. and he and for us all, wherein he shewed me the sitting of the judgment and the standing of all high and low before the Lord and how thrones and kingdoms were cast down before him. When our teacher came to New-England it was a great trouble unto me, my brother Wheelwright being put by also. I was then much troubled concerning the ministry under which I lived, and then that place in the 30th of Isaiah was brought to my mind. Though the Lord give thee bread of adversity and water of affliction yet shall not thy teachers be removed into corners any more, but thine eyes shall see thy teachers. The Lord giving me this promise and they being gone there was none then left that I was able to hear, and I could not be at rest but I must come hither. Yet that place of Isaiah did much follow me, though the Lord give thee the bread of adversity and water of affliction. This place lying I say upon me then this place in Daniel[7] was brought unto me and did shew me that though I should meet with affliction yet I am the same God that delivered Daniel out of the lion's den, I will also deliver thee. — Therefore I desire you to look to it, for you see this scripture fulfilled this day and therefore I desire you that as you tender the Lord and the church and commonwealth to consider and look what you do. You have power over my body but the Lord Jesus hath power over my body and soul, and assure yourselves thus much, you do as much as in you lies to put the Lord Jesus Christ from you, and if you go on in this course you begin you will bring a curse upon you and your posterity, and the mouth of the Lord hath spoken it.

Dep. Gov. What is the scripture she brings?

Mr. Stoughton.[8] Behold I turn away from you.

Mrs. H. But now having seen him which is invisible I fear not what man can do unto me.

Gov. Daniel was delivered by miracle do you think to be deliver'd so too?

Mrs. H. I do here speak it before the court. I look that the Lord should deliver me by his providence.

Mr. Harlakenden.[9] I may read scripture and the most glorious hypocrite may read them and yet go down to hell.

---

6. Increase Nowell of Charlestown.
7. Dan. 6:4–5.
8. Israel Stoughton of Dorchester.

9. Roger Harlakenden of Cambridge, an assistant in the General Court.

Mrs. H. It may be so.

Mr. Bartholomew.[10] I would remember one word to Mrs. Hutchinson among many others. She knowing that I did know her opinions, being she was at my house at London, she was afraid I conceive or loth to impart herself unto me, but when she came within sight of Boston and looking upon the meanness of the place, I conceive, she uttered these words, if she had not a sure word that England should be destroyed her heart would shake. Now it seemed to me at that time very strange that she should say so.

Mrs. H. I do not remember that I looked upon the meanness of the place nor did it discourage me, because I knew the bounds of my habitation were determined, &c.

Mr. Bartholomew. I speak as a member of the court. I fear that her revelations will deceive.

[Winthrop summarizes]

Gover. The case is altered and will not stand with us now, but I see a marvellous providence of God to bring things to this pass that they are. We have been hearkening about the trial of this thing and now the mercy of God by a providence hath answered our desires and made her to lay open her self and the ground of all these disturbances to be by revelations, for we receive no such [*blank*] made out of the ministry of the word [*blank*] and so one scripture after another, but all this while there is no use of the ministry of the word nor of any clear call of God by his word, but the ground work of her revelations is the immediate revelation of the spirit and not by the ministry of the word, and that is the means by which she hath very much abused the country that they shall look for revelations and are not bound to the ministry of the word, but God will teach them by immediate revelations and this hath been the ground of all these tumults and troubles, and I would that those were all cut off from us that trouble us, for this is the thing that hath been the root of all the mischief.

Court. We all consent with you. . . .

[A final objection]

Mr. Coddington.[11] I do think that you are going to censure therefore I desire to speak a word.

Gov. I pray you speak.

Mr. Coddington. There is one thing objected against the meetings. What if she designed to edify her own family in her own meetings may none else be present?

Gov. If you have nothing else to say but that, it is pity Mr. Coddington that you should interrupt us in proceeding to censure.

Mr. Coddington. I would say more Sir, another thing you lay to her Charge is her speech to the elders. Now I do not see any clear witness against her, and you know it is a rule of the court that no man may be a judge and an accuser too. I do not speak to

10. William Bartholomew, a deputy from Ipswich to the General Court.

11. William Coddington, a deputy from Boston to the General Court.

disparage our elders and their callings, but I do not see any thing that they accuse her of witnessed against her, and therefore I do not see how she should be censured for that. And for the other thing which hath fallen from her occasionally by the spirit of God, you know the spirit of God witnesses with our spirits, and there is no truth in scripture but God bears witness to it by his spirit, therefore I would entreat you to consider whether those things you have alleged against her deserve such censure as you are about to pass, be it to banishment or imprisonment. And again here is nothing proved about the elders, only that she said they did not teach a covenant of grace so clearly as Mr. Cotton did, and that they were in the state of the apostles before the ascension. Why I hope this may not be offensive nor any wrong to them.

Gov. Pass by all that hath been said formerly and her own speeches have been ground enough for us to proceed upon.

Mr. Coddington. I beseech you do not speak so to force things along, for I do not for my own part see any equity in the court in all your proceedings.

John Winthrop

from *A Short Story of the Rise, Reigne, and Ruine of the Antinomians, Familists and Libertines*
1644

THE PREFACE

After we had escaped the cruell hands of persecuting Prelates, and the dangers at Sea, and had prettily well outgrowne our wildernes troubles in our first plantings in New-England; And when our Common-wealth began to be founded, and our Churches sweetely settled in Peace, (God abounding to us in more happy enjoyments then we could have expected:) Lest we should, now, grow secure, our wise God (who seldome suffers his owne, in this their wearysome Pilgrimage to be long without trouble) sent a new storme after us, which proved the sorest tryall that ever befell us since we left our Native soyle.

Which was this, that some going thither from hence full fraught with many unsound and loose opinions, after a time, began to open their packs, and freely vent[12] their wares to any that would be their customers; Multitudes of men and women Church-members and others, having tasted of their Commodities, were eager after them, and were streight infected before they were aware, and some being tainted

---

12. vent: sell.

conveyed the infection to others: and thus that Plague first began amongst us, that had not the wisedome and faithfulnesse of him, that watcheth over his vineyard night and day, by the beames of his Light and Grace cleared and purged the ayre, certainely, we had not beene able to have breathed there comfortably much longer.

[A SIGN FROM GOD]

Then God himselfe was pleased to step in with his casting voice, and bring in his owne vote and suffrage from heaven, by testifying his displeasure against their opinions and practises, as clearly as if he had pointed with his finger, in causing the two fomenting women in the time of the height of the Opinions to produce out of their wombs, as before they had out of their braines, such monstrous births as no Chronicle (I thinke) hardly ever recorded the like. Mistris *Dier* brought forth her birth of a woman child, a fish, a beast, and a fowle, all woven together in one, and without an head.

Mistris *Hutchinson* being big with child, and growing towards the time of her labour, as other women doe, she brought forth not one, (as Mistris Dier did) but (which was more strange to amazement) 30. monstrous births or thereabouts, at once; some of them bigger, some lesser, some of one shape, some of another; few of any perfect shape, none at all of them (as farre as I could ever learne) of humane shape.

And see how the wisdome of God fitted this judgment to her sinne every way, for looke as she had vented mishapen opinions, so she must bring forth deformed monsters; and as about 30. Opinions in number, so many monsters; and as those were publike, and not in a corner mentioned, so this is now come to be knowne and famous over all these Churches, and a great part of the world.

[WINTHROP CONCLUDES]

Here is to been seen the presence of God in his Ordinances, when they are faithfully attended according to his holy will, although not free from human infirmities: This *American Jesabel* kept her strength and reputation, even among the people of God, till the hand of Civill Justice laid hold on her, and then shee began evidently to decline, and the faithfull to bee freed from her forgeries; and now in this last act, when shee might have expected (as most likely shee did) by her seeming repentance of her errors, and confessing her undervaluing of the Ordinances of Magistracy and Ministracy, to have redeemed her reputation in point of sincerity, and yet have made good all her former work, and kept open a back doore to have returned to her vomit again, by her paraphrasticall retractions, and denying any change in her judgment, yet such was the presence and blessing of God in his own Ordinance, that this subtilty of Satan was discovered to her utter shame and confusion, and to the setting at liberty of many godly hearts, that had been captivated by her to that day; and that Church which by her means was brought under much infamy, and neere to dissolution, was hereby sweetly repaired, and a hopefull way of establishment, and her dissembled repentance cleerly detected, God giving her up since the sentence of excommunication, to that hardnesse of heart, as shee is not affected with any remorse, but glories in it, and feares not the vengeance of God, which she lyes under, as if God did work contrary to his own word, and loosed from heaven, while his Church had bound upon earth.

2. John Winthrop and Robert Keayne

the Keayne controversy
1639 and 1653

The Puritan colonies had always been profit ventures, financed by London merchants and the primitive corporations the crown chartered for them. Yet the English emigrants took with them their medieval hostility to commerce, their feudal patterns of land tenure, and their theological hostility to self-interest. The Puritan colonies allocated land by authority, reserved much of it for common use, regulated prices, and restricted consumption on many items. Both Plymouth and Massachusetts experimented with what could easily be called communism. In "Modell of Christian Charity" Winthrop had propounded the theory whereby the collective interest in universal welfare outweighed the profit interests of individuals.

None of this disproves the arguments of Max Weber's classic The Protestant Ethic and the Spirit of Capitalism. *Weber argues that the early modern notions of work and investment grew out of Puritan habits and values—particularly the concept of a vocation in one's labor that makes working significant in itself, independent of consumption. This ethic, which eventually acquired the secular meaning of deferred gratification, was neatly summarized by John Cotton when he urged "diligence in worldly business, and yet deadness to the world."*

In 1639 Robert Keayne, a member of Cotton's church, was summoned to court and charged with overpricing a bag of nails. Other complaints followed, and in the ensuing controversy many tensions and historical contradictions emerged. Fined by the court, Keayne had to wait for his vindication until he wrote his own will. It is a long and rambling document, aptly titled Apologia *in Bernard Bailyn's edition, which is followed here. The selected passage comes as Keayne explains why he has left no public bequest to the colony.*

John Winthrop

from his journal
1639

Mo. 9 (*November*). At a general court holden at Boston, great complaint was made of the oppression used in the country in sale of foreign commodities; and Mr. Robert Keaine, who kept a shop in Boston, was notoriously above others observed and complained of; and, being convented, he was charged with many particulars; in some, for taking above six-pence in the shilling profit; in some above eight-pence; and, in some small things, above two for one; and being hereof convict, (as appears by the records,) he was fined £200, which came thus to pass: The deputies considered, apart, of his fine, and set it at £200, the magistrates agreed but to £100. So, the court being divided, at length it was agreed, that his fine should be £200, but he should pay but £100, and the other should be respited to the further consideration of the next general court. By this means the magistrates and deputies were brought to an accord, which otherwise had not been likely, and so much trouble might have grown, and the offender escaped censure. For the cry of the country was so great against oppression, and some of the elders and magistrates had declared such detestation of the corrupt practice of this man (which was the more observable, because he was wealthy and sold dearer than most other tradesmen, and for that he was of ill report for the like covetous practice in England, that incensed the deputies very much against him). And sure the course was very evil, especial circumstances considered: 1. He being an ancient professor of the gospel: 2. A man of eminent parts: 3. Wealthy, and having but one child: 4. Having come over for conscience' sake, and for the advancement of the gospel here: 5. Having been formerly dealt with and admonished, both by private friends and also by some of the magistrates and elders, and having promised reformation; being a member of a church and commonwealth now in their infancy, and under the curious observation of all churches and civil states in the world. These added much aggravation to his sin in the judgment of all men of understanding. Yet most of the magistrates (though they discerned of the offence clothed with all these circumstances) would have been more moderate in their censure: 1. Because there was no law in force to limit or direct men in point of profit in their trade. 2. Because it is the common practice, in all countries, for men to make use of advantages for raising the prices of their commodities. 3. Because (though he were chiefly aimed at, yet) he was not alone in this fault. 4. Because all men through the country, in sale of cattle, corn, labor, etc., were guilty of the like excess in prices. 5. Because a certain rule could not be found out for an equal rate between buyer and seller, though much labor had been bestowed in it, and divers laws had been made, which, upon experience, were repealed, as being neither safe nor equal. Lastly, and especially, because the law of God appoints no other punishment but double restitution; and, in some cases, as where the offender freely confesseth, and brings his offering, only half added to the principal. After the court had censured him, the church of Boston called him also in question, where (as before he had done in the court) he did, with tears, acknowledge and bewail his covetous and corrupt heart, yet making some excuse for many of the particulars, which were charged upon him, as partly by pretence of ignorance of the true price of some wares, and chiefly by being misled by some false principles, as 1. That, if a man lost in one commodity, he might help himself in the price of another. 2. That if, through want of skill or other occasion, his commodity cost him more than the price of the market in England, he might then sell it for more than the price of the market in New England, etc. These things gave occasion to Mr. Cotton, in his public exercise the next lecture day, to lay open the error of such false principles, and to give some rules of direction in the case.

Some false principles were these:—

1. That a man might sell as dear as he can, and buy as cheap as he can.

2. If a man lose by casualty of sea, etc., in some of his commodities, he may raise the price of the rest.

3. That he may sell as he bought, though he paid too dear, etc., and though the commodity be fallen, etc.

4. That, as a man may take the advantage of his own skill or ability, so he may of another's ignorance or necessity.

5. Where one gives time for payment, he is to take like recompense of one as of another.

The rules for trading were these:—

1. A man may not sell above the current price, i.e., such a price as is usual in the time and place, and as another (who knows the worth of the commodity) would give for it, if he had occasion to use it; as that is called current money, which every man will take, etc.

2. When a man loseth in his commodity for want of skill, etc., he must look at it as his own fault or cross, and therefore must not lay it upon another.

3. Where a man loseth by casualty of sea, or, etc., it is a loss cast upon himself by providence, and he may not ease himself of it by casting it upon another; for so a man should seem to provide against all providences, etc., that he should never lose; but where there is a scarcity of the commodity, there men may raise their price; for now it is a hand of God upon the commodity, and not the person.

4. A man may not ask any more for his commodity than his selling price, as Ephron to Abraham, the land is worth thus much.

Robert Keayne

from his will (*Apologia*)
1653

My former love, cost, and pains both in Old England and here, which I have taken to promote the good of this place, has been answered by divers here with unchristian, uncharitable, and unjust reproaches and slanders since I came hither, as if men had the liberty of their tongues to reproach any that were not beneficial to them. [These attacks came] together with that deep and sharp censure that was laid upon me in the country and carried on with so much bitterness and indignation of some, contrary both to law or any foregoing precedent if I mistake not, and, I am sure, contrary or beyond the quality and desert of the complaints that came against me, which indeed were rather shadows of offense, out of a desire of revenge made great by the aggravations of some to make them heinous and odious than that they were so indeed, and this not in my own judgments only (which may be looked at as partial) but in the judgments of hundreds that have expressed themselves, both then and especially since. Yet by some it was carried on with such violence and pretended zeal as if they had had some of the greatest sins in the world to censure. . . . Had it been in their power or could they have carried it they would not have corrected or reformed but utterly have ruined myself and all that I had, as if no punishment had been sufficient to expiate my offense [of] selling a good bridle for 2 s. that now worse are sold without offense for 3 s., 6 d. nails for 7 d., and 8 d. nails for 10 d. per hundred, which since and to this day are frequently sold by many for a great deal more. And so [it was] in all other things proportionably, as selling gold buttons for two shilling nine pence a dozen that cost above 2 in London and yet were never paid for by them that complained.

These were the great matters in which I had offended, when myself have often seen and heard offenses, complaints, and crimes of a high nature against God and men, such as filthy uncleanness, fornications, drunkenness, fearful oaths, quarreling, mutinies, sabbath breakings, thefts, forgeries, and such like, which hath passed with fines or censures so small or easy as hath not been worth the naming or regarding. These [things] I cannot think upon but with sad thoughts of inequality of such proceedings, which hath been the very cause of tying up my heart and hands from doing such general and public good acts as in my heart I both desired and intended.

[UNJUST CRIES OF OPPRESSION AND EXCESSIVE GAINS]

I did submit to the censure, I paid the fine to the uttermost, which is not nor hath been done by many (nor so earnestly required as mine was) though for certain and not supposed offenses of far higher nature, which I can make good not by hearsay only but in my own knowledge, yea offenses of the same kind. [My own offense] was so greatly aggravated and with such indignation pursued by some, as if no censure could be too great or too severe, as if I had not been worthy to have lived upon the earth. [Such offenses] are not only now common almost in every shop and warehouse but even then and ever since with a higher measure of excess, yea even by some of them that were most zealous and had their hands and tongues deepest in my censure. [At that time] they were buyers, [but since then] they are turned sellers and peddling merchants themselves, so that they are become no offenses now nor worthy questioning nor taking notice of in others. Yet [they cried] oppression and excessive gains, [when] considering the time that they kept the goods bought in their hands before they could or would pay and the quality or rather the business of their pay for kind, yea contrary to their own promises, instead of gains there was apparent loss without any gains to the seller.

The oppression lay justly and truly on the buyer's hand rather than on the seller; but then the country was all buyers and few sellers, though it would not be seen on that side then. For if the lion will say the lamb is a fox, it must be so, the lamb must be content to leave it. But now the country hath got better experience in merchandise, and they have soundly paid for their experience since, so that it is now and was many years ago become a common proverb amongst most buyers that knew those times that my goods and prices were cheap pennyworths in comparison of what hath been taken since and especially [in comparison with] the prices of these times. Yet I have borne this patiently and without disturbance or troubling the Court with any petitions for remission or abatement of the fine, though I have been advised by many friends, yea and some of the same Court, so to do, as if they would be willing to embrace such an occasion to undo what was then done in a hurry and in displeasure, or at least would lessen or mitigate it in a great measure. But I have not been persuaded to it because the more innocently that I suffer, the more patiently have I borne it, leaving my cause therein to the Lord.

3. William Hooke

from *New-Englands Tears for Old-Englands Fears*
1640

The career of William Hooke (1601-78) illustrates vividly the shifting currents of English religious history. An Anglican vicar in Devonshire, he leaned to nonconformity, and fled to New England in 1636. After preaching at Taunton, Massachusetts, and at New Haven, he returned to England in 1656. There, he became domestic chaplain to Oliver Cromwell, and was an influential figure in the later years of the Protectorate. After the Restoration, he lived in obscurity, dying in 1678. While at Taunton, Hooke published two sermons on the state of affairs in England, of which this is the first; the sequel is New-Englands Sence, of Old-England and Irelands Sorrowes, *1645.*

Let us therefore, I beseech you, lay aside the thoughts of all our comforts this day, and let us fasten our eyes upon the calamities of our brethren in old *England*, calamities, at least, imminent calamities dropping, swords that have hung a long time over their heads by a twine thread, judgements long since threatned as foreseene by many of Gods Messengers in the causes, though not foretold by a Spirit prophetically guided; heavy judgements in all probability, when they fall, if they are not fallen already. And not to looke upon the occasions given on the one side or the other, betweene the two Sister Nations: (Sister Nations? ah, the word woundeth,) let us looke this day simply on the event, a sad event in all likelihood, the dividing of a King from his Subjects, and him from them, their mutuall taking up of Armes in opposition and defence; the consequences, even the gloomy and darke consequences thereof, are killing and slaying, and sacking and burning, and robbing, and rifling, cursing and blaspheming, &c.

Wee wonder now and then at the sudden death of a man: alas, you might there see a thousand men not onely healthy, but stout and strong, struck dead in the twinckling of an eye, their breath exhales without so much as, *Lord have mercy upon us*. Death heweth its way thorow a wood of men in a minute of time from the mouth of a murderer, turning a forrest into a Champion[13] suddenly; and when it hath used these to slay their opposites, they are recompenced with the like death themselves. *O, the shrill eare-piercing clangs of the Trumpets, noise of Drums, the animating voyces of Horse Captaines, and Commanders, learned and learning to destroy! There is the undaunted Horse whose neck is clothed with thunder, and the glory of whose nostrills is terrible; how doth hee lye pawing and praunsing in the valley, going forth to meete the armed men? he mocks at feare, swallowing the ground with fierceness and rage, and saying among the trumpets, Ha, Ha, hee smels the battle a far off, the thunder of the Captaines and the shouting.* Here ride some dead men swagging in their deepe saddles; there fall others alive upon their dead Horses; death sends a message to those from the mouth of the Muskets, these it talkes with face to face, and stabs them in the fifth rib: In yonder file there is a man hath his arme struck off from his shoulder, another by him hath lost his leg; here stands a Soldier with halfe a face, there fights another upon his stumps, and at once both kils and is killed; not far off lies a

company wallowing in their sweat and goare; such a man whilst he chargeth his Musket is discharg'd of his life, and falls upon his dead fellow. Every battell of the warriour is with confused noise and garments rouled in blood. In the meanewhile (O formidable!) the infernall fiends follow the Campe to catch after the soules of rude nefarous souldiers (such as are commonly men of that calling) who fight themselves fearlesly into the mouth of hell for revenge, a booty or a little revenue. How thicke and three-fole doe they speed one another to destruction? A day of battell is a day of harvest for the devill. . . .

That which wee are now called unto, is brotherly Compassion, and to doe the part of Jobs friends in my Text, to sit astonished, as at the crying sinnes, so at the feared sorrowes of our Countrymen, for in all probability, their griefe is very great.

To this end, you may think a while upon these particulars.

1. Of our civill relation to that Land, and the Inhabitants therein. There is no Land that claimes our name, but *England*, wee are distinguished from all the Nations in the world by the name of *English*. There is no Potentate breathing, that wee call our dread Soveraigne, but King Charles, nor Lawes of any Land have civilized us but *Englands*; there is no Nation that calls us Countrey-men but the *English*. Brethren! Did wee not there draw in our first breath? Did not the Sunne first shine there upon our heads? Did not that Land first beare us, even that pleasant Island, but for sinne, I would say, that Garden of the Lord, that Paradise?

2. Withall, let us thinke upon our naturall relations to many in that Land. Some of you, I know, have Fathers and Mothers there, some of you have Brethren and Sisters, others of you have Uncles and Aunts there, and near kinsfolke. All these sitting in

---

13. Champion: meadow.

griefe and sorrow, challenge our sympathize; and it is a fearfull sinne to bee voyd of naturall affections: nature wrought in *Abraham*, as well as grace, when his nephew *Lot* was taken captive by the foure Kings.

3. But which is more, let us remember how (for many of us) wee stand in a spirituall relation to many, yea very many in that Land. The same threed of grace is spunne thorow the hearts of all the godly under Heaven. Such a one there is, in thy spirituall Father, hee begot thee in Christ Jesus thorow the Gospell; and there thou hast spirituall Brethren and Sisters and Mothers.

4. John Winthrop

speech to the General Court 1645

In 1645 Winthrop was accused of exceeding his authority as governor. His impeachment brought to a head the long-standing struggle over the balance of power between magistrates and representatives. Following his acquittal, Winthrop delivered the following speech as a way of securing the meaning of his victory. The tension in the speech between the mutuality of contract and hierarchy of authority harks back to his "Modell of Christian Charity," in chapter 3.

I suppose something may be expected from me, upon this charge that is befallen me, which moves me to speak now to you; yet I intend not to intermeddle in the proceedings of the court, or with any of the persons concerned therein. Only I bless God, that I see an issue of this troublesome business. I also acknowledge the justice of the court, and, for mine own part, I am well satisfied, I was publicly charged, and I am publicly and legally acquitted, which is all I did expect or desire. And though this be sufficient for my justification before men, yet not so before the God, who hath seen so much amiss in my dispensations (and even in this affair) as calls me to be humble. For to be publicly and criminally charged in this court, is matter of humiliation, (and I desire to make a right use of it,) notwithstanding I be thus acquitted. If her father had spit in her face, (saith the Lord concerning Miriam,) should she not have been ashamed seven days? Shame had lien upon her, whatever the occasion had been. I am unwilling to stay you from your urgent affairs, yet give me leave (upon this special occasion) to speak a little more to this assembly. It may be of some good use, to inform and rectify the judgments of some of the people, and may prevent such distempers as have arisen amongst us.

The great questions that have troubled the country, are about the authority of the magistrates and the liberty of the people. It is yourselves who have called us to this office, and being called by you, we have our authority from God, in way of an ordinance, such as hath the image of God eminently stamped upon it, the contempt and violation whereof hath been vindicated with examples of divine vengeance. I entreat you to consider, that when you choose magistrates, you take them from among yourselves, men subject to like passions as you are. Therefore when you see infirmities in us, you should reflect upon your own, and that would make you bear the more with us, and not be severe censurers of the failings of your magistrates, when you have continual experience of the like infirmities in yourselves and others. We account him a good servant, who breaks not his covenant. The covenant between you and us is the oath you have taken of us, which is to this purpose, that we shall govern you and judge your causes by the rules of God's laws and our own, according to our best skill. When you agree with a workman to build you a ship or house, etc., he undertakes as well for his skill as for his faithfulness, for it is his profession, and you pay him for both. But when you call one to be a magistrate, he doth not profess nor undertake to have sufficient skill for that office, nor can you furnish him with gifts, etc., therefore you must run the hazard of his skill and ability. But if he fail in faithfulness, which by his oath he is bound unto, that he must answer for. If it fall out that the case be clear to common apprehension, and the rule clear also, if he transgress here, the error is not in the skill, but in the evil of the will: it must be required of him. But if the case be doubtful, or the rule doubtful, to men of such understanding and parts as your magistrates are, if your magistrates should err here, yourselves must bear it.

For the other point concerning liberty, I observe a great mistake in the country about that. There is a twofold liberty, natural (I mean as our nature is now corrupt) and civil or federal. The first is common to man with beasts and other creatures. By this, man, as he stands in relation to man simply, hath liberty to do what he lists; it is a liberty to evil as well as to good. This liberty is incompatible and inconsistent with authority, and cannot endure the least restraint of the most just authority. The exercise and maintaining of this liberty makes men grow more evil, and in time to be worse than brute beasts: *omnes sumus licentia deteriores.* This is that great enemy of truth and peace, that wild beast, which all the ordinances of God are bent against, to restrain and subdue it. The other kind of liberty I call civil or federal, it may also be termed moral, in reference to the covenant between God and man, in the moral law, and the politic covenants and constitutions, amongst men themselves. This liberty is the proper end and object of authority, and cannot subsist without it; and it is a liberty to that only which is good, just, and honest. This liberty you are to stand for, with the hazard (not only of your goods, but) of your lives, if need be. Whatsoever crosseth this, is not authority, but a distemper thereof. This liberty is maintained and exercised in a way of subjection to authority; it is of the same kind of liberty wherewith Christ hath made us free. The woman's own choice makes such a man her husband; yet being so chosen, he is her lord, and she is to be subject to him, yet in a way of liberty, not of bondage; and a true wife accounts her subjection her honor and freedom, and would not think her condition safe and free, but in her subjection to her husband's authority. Such is the liberty of the church under the authority of Christ, her king and husband; his yoke is so easy and sweet to her as a bride's ornaments; and if through frowardness or wantonness, etc., she shake it off, at any time, she is at no rest in her spirit, until she take it up again; and whether her lord smiles upon her, and embraceth her in his arms, or whether he frowns, or rebukes, or smites her, she apprehends the sweetness of his love in all, and is refreshed, supported, and instructed by every such dispensation of his authority over her. On the other side, ye know who they are that complain of this yoke and say, let us break their bands, etc., we will not have this man to rule over us. Even so, brethren, it will be between you and your magistrates. If you stand for your natural corrupt liberties, and will do what is good in your own eyes, you will not endure the least weight of authority, but will murmur, and oppose, and be always striving to shake off that yoke; but if you will be satisfied to enjoy such civil and lawful liberties, such as Christ allows you, then will you quietly and cheerfully submit unto that authority which is set over you, in all the administrations of it, for your good. Wherein, if we fail at any time, we hope we shall be willing (by God's assistance) to hearken to good advice from any of you, or in any other way of God; so shall your liberties be preserved, in upholding the honor and power of authority amongst you.

5. Nathaniel Ward

from *The Simple Cobler of Aggawam in America* 1647

Nathaniel Ward (1578?–1652) went to Massachusetts in 1634, after Laud excommunicated him. He became minister at a town then called by the Indian name Aggawam; it later became Ipswich. He drafted the Body of Liberties, the colony's first published legal code. During the civil wars he returned to England, where he wrote The Simple Cobler to attack the dangerous doctrine of toleration, which was gaining ground among the ranks of the Independents in the army, much to the dismay of the Presbyterians who still dominated Parliament. Despite its learned verbal fireworks, the book went through four editions in the first year. Ward, writing under the persona of Theodore de la Guard (from the Greek for Nathaniel and the French for Ward), poses as a cobbler, and works the shoemaker metaphor throughout the book. It is as self-consciously literary, and as wildly satirical, as anything else written by the Puritans.

Either I am in an Appoplexie, or that man is in a Lethargie, who doth not now sensibly feele God shaking the heavens over his head, and the earth under his feet: The Heavens so, as the Sun begins to turne into darknesse, the Moon into blood, the Starres to fall down to the ground; So that little Light of Comfort or Counsell is left to the sonnes of men: The Earth so, as the foundations are failing, the righteous scarce know where to finde rest, the inhabitants stagger like drunken men: it is in a manner dissolved both in Religions and Relations: And no marvell; for, they have defiled it by transgressing the Lawes, changing the Ordinances, and breaking the Everlasting Covenant. The Truths of God are the Pillars of the world, whereon States and Churches may stand quiet if they will; if they will not, Hee can easily shake them off into delusions, and distractions enough.

Sathan is now in his passions, he feeles his passion approaching; hee loves to fish in royled waters. Though that Dragon cannot sting the vitals of the Elect mortally, yet that Beelzebub can fly-blow their Intellectuals miserably: The finer Religion grows, the finer hee spins his Cobwebs, hee will hold pace with Christ so long as his wits will serve him. Hee sees himselfe beaten out of grosse Idolatries, Heresies, Ceremonies, where the Light breakes forth with power; he will therefore bestirre him to prevaricate Evangelicall Truths, and Ordinances, that if they will needs be walking, yet they shall *laborare varicibus*,[14] and not keep their path, he will put them out of time and place; Assassinating for his Engineers, men of Paracelsian parts; well complexioned for honesty; for, such are fittest to Mountebanke his Chimistry into sicke Churches and weake Judgements.

Nor shall hee need to stretch his strength overmuch in this worke: Too many men having not laid their foundations sure, nor ballasted their Spirits deepe with humility and feare, are prest enough of themselves to evaporate their owne apprehensions. Those that are acquainted with Story know, it hath ever beene so in new Editions of Churches: Such as are least able, are most busie to pudder in the rubbish, and to raise dust in the eyes of more steady Repayrers. Civill Commotions make roome for uncivill practises: Religious mutations, for irreligious opinions: Change of Aire, discovers corrupt bodies; Reformation of Religion, unsound mindes. Hee that hath any well-faced phansy in his Crowne, and doth not vent it now, fears the pride of his owne heart will dub him dunce for ever. Such a one will trouble the whole *Israel* of God with his most untimely births, though he makes the bones of his vanity stick up, to the view and griefe of all that are godly wise. The devill desiers no better sport then to see light heads handle their heels, and fetch their carreers in a time, when the Roofe of Liberty stands open.

The next perplexed Question, with pious and ponderous men, will be: What should bee done for the healing of these comfortlesse exulcerations. I am the unablest adviser of a thousand, the unworthiest of ten thousand; yet I hope I may presume to assert what follows without just offence.

First, such as have given or taken any unfriendly reports of us *New-English*, should doe well to recollect themselves. Wee have beene reputed a Colluvies of wild Opinionists, swarmed into a remote wildernes to find elbow-roome for our phanatick Doctrines and practises: I trust our diligence past, and constant sedulity against such persons and courses, will plead better things for us. I dare take upon me, to bee the Herauld of *New-England* so farre, as to proclaime to the world, in the name of our Colony, that all Familists, Antinomians, Anabaptists, and other Enthusiasts shall have free Liberty to keepe away from us, and such as will come to be gone as fast as they can, the sooner the better.

Secondly, I dare averre, that God doth no where in his word tolerate Christian States, to give Tolerations to such adversaries of his Truth, if they have power in their hands to suppresse them.

Here is lately brought us an Extract of a *Magna Charta*, so called, compiled

---

14. *laborare varicibus*: waste time with trifles.

between the Sub-planters of a *West-Indian* Island;[15] whereof the first Article of constipulation, firmly provides free stable-room and litter for all kinde of consciences, be they never so dirty or jadish; making it actionable, yea, treasonable, to disturbe any man in his Religion, or to discommend it, whatever it be. Wee are very sorry to see such professed prophanenesse in *English* Professors, as industriously to lay their Religious foundations on the ruine of true Religion; which strictly binds every conscience *to contend earnestly for the Truth: to preserve unity of spirit, Faith and Ordinances, to be all like minded, of one accord; every man to take his brother into his Christian care: to stand fast with one spirit, with one mind, striving together for the faith of the Gospel.* and by no meanes to permit Heresies or erronious opinions: But God abhorring such loathsome beverages, hath in his righteous judgement blasted that enterprize, which might otherwise have prospered well, for ought I know; I presume their case is generally knowne ere this.

If the devill might have his free option, I beleeve he would ask nothing else, but liberty to enfranchize all false Religions, and to embondage the true; nor should hee need: It is much to be feared, that laxe Tolerations upon State-pretences and planting necessities, will be the next subtle Stratagem he will spread to distate the Truth of God and supplant the peace of the Churches. Tolerations in things tolerable, exquisitely drawn out by the lines of the Scripture, and pensill of the Spirit, are the sacred favours of Truth, the due latitudes of Love, the faire Compartments of Christian fraternity: but irregular dispensations, dealt forth by the facilities of men, are the frontiers of error, the redoubts of Schisme, the perillous irritaments of carnall and spirituall enmity.

My heart hath naturally detested foure things: The standing of the Apocrypha in the Bible; Forrainers dwelling in my Countrey, to crowd out native Subjects into the corners of the Earth; Alchymized coines; Tolerations of divers Religions, or of one Religion in segregant shapes: He that willingly assents to the last, if he examines his heart by day-light, his conscience will tell him, he is either an Atheist, or an Heretique, or an Hypocrite, or at best a captive to some Lust: Poly-piety is the greatest impiety in the world. True Religion is *Ignis probationis*, which doth *congregare homogenea & segregare heterogenea.*....[16]

He that is willing to tolerate any Religion, or discrepant way of Religion, besides his own, unlesse it be in matters meerly indifferent, either doubts of his own, or is not sincere in it.

He that is willing to tolerate any unsound Opinion, that his own may also be tolerated, though never so sound, will for a need hang Gods Bible at the Devills girdle.

Every Toleration of false Religions, or Opinions hath as many Errours and sins in it, as all the false Religions and Opinions it tolerats, and one sound one more.

That State that will give Liberty of Conscience in matters of Religion, must give Liberty of Conscience and Conversation in their Morall Laws, or else the Fiddle will be out of tune, and some of the strings crack....

Lastly, I dare averre, that it ill becomes Christians any thing well-shod with the preparation of the Gospel, to meditate flight from their deare Countrey upon these

---

16. *West-Indian* Island: Bermuda.

16. *Ignis . . . heterogenea*: testing fire, which combines like things and separates different ones.

disturbances. Stand your grounds ye *Eleazars* and *Shammahs*,[17] stir not a foot so long as you have halfe a foot of ground to stand upon: after one or two such Worthies, a great Victory may be regained, and flying *Israel* may returne to a rich spoile. *Englishmen*, be advised to love *England*, with your hearts and to preserve it by your Prayers. I am bold to say that since the pure Primitive time, the Gospel never thrived so well in any soile on earth, as in the *Brittish*, nor is the like goodnesse of nature, or Cornucopian plenty else-where to be found: if ye lose that Country and finde a better before ye come to Heaven, my Cosmography failes me. I am farre from discouraging any, whom necessity of Conscience or condition thrusts out by head and shoulders: if God calls any into a Wildernesse, Hee will bee no wildernesse to them, *Jer. 2.31.* witnesse his large beneficence to us here beyond expectation.

Ye say, why come not we over to helpe the Lord against the Mighty, in these Sacred battailes?

I answer, many here are diligently observing the counsell of the same Prophet, 22.10. *Weepe not for him that is dead, neither bemoan him; but weep for him that is gone away and shall returne no more to see his Native Country.* Divers make it an Article of our *American* Creed, which a celebrate Divine of *England* hath observed upon *Heb.* 11.9. That no man ought to forsake his owne countrey, but upon extraordinary cause, and when that cause ceaseth, he is bound in conscience to returne if he can: We are looking to him who hath our hopes and seasons in his only wise hand.

In the mean time we desire to bow our knees before the Throne of Grace day and night, that the Lord would be pleased in his tender mercy to still the sad unquietnesse and per-peracute[18] contentions, of that most comfortable and renowned Island, that at length He may have praise in his Churches, and his Churches peace in him, through Jesus Christ.

Should I not keepe promise in speaking a little to Womens fashions, they would take it unkindly: I was loath to pester better matter with such stuffe; I rather thought it meet to let them stand by themselves, like the *Qua Genus* in the Grammer,[19] being Deficients, or Redundants, not to be brought under any Rule: I shall therefore make bold for this once, to borrow a little of their loose tongued Liberty, and misspend a word or two upon their long-wasted, but short-skirted patience: a little use of my stirrup will doe no harme.

> *Ridentem dicere verum, quid prohibet?*[20]
> *Gray Gravity it selfe can well beateam,*
> *That Language be adapted to the Theme.*
> *He that to Parrots speaks, must parrotise:*
> *He that instruct a foole, may act th'unwise.*

It is known more then enough, that I am neither Nigard, nor Cinick, to the due bravery of the true Gentry: if any man mislikes a bullymong drossock[21] more then I,

---

17. *Eleazars* and *Shammahs*: see Neh. 12:42.
18. per-peracute: overly acute.
19. *Qua Genus*: What gender?—a question in elementary grammar lessons.

20. After Horace, *Satires* I.i.24-25: "Ridentem dicere verum Qui vetat": "What's to keep me from telling the truth with a laugh?"
21. bullymong drossock: slovenly woman.

let him take her for his labour: I honour the woman that can honour her selfe with her attire: a good Text alwayes deserves a fair Margent; I am not much offended, if I see a trimme, far trimmer than she that weares it: in a word, whatever Christianity or Civility will allow, I can afford with *London* measure: but when I heare a nugiperous[22] Gentledame inquire what dresse the Queen is in this week: what the nudiustertian[23] fashion of the Court; with egge to be in it in all haste, whatever it be; I look at her as the very gizzard of a trifle, the product of a quarter of a cypher, the epitome of Nothing, fitter to be kickt, if shee were of kickable substance, than either honour'd or humour'd.

To speak moderately, I truly confesse it is beyond the ken of my understanding to conceive, how those women should have any true grace, or valuable vertue, that have so little wit, as to disfigure themselves with such exotick garbes, as not only disman-tles their native lovely lustre, but transclouts them into gantbar-geese, ill-shapen-shotten-shell-fish, Egyptian Hyeroglyphicks, or at the best into French flurts of the pastery, which a proper English woman should scorne with her heels: it is no marvell they weare drailes[24] on the hinder part of their heads, having nothing as it seems in the fore-part, but a few Squirrils brains to help them frisk from one ill-favour'd fashion to another.

> *These whimm' Crown'd shees, these fashion-fansying wits,*
> *Are empty thin brain'd shells, and fidling Kits.*

The very troublers and impoverishers of mankind, I can hardly forbeare to com-mend to the world a saying of a Lady living sometime with the Queen of *Bohemia*, I know not where shee found it, but it is pitty it should be lost.

> *The world is full of care, much like unto a bubble;*
> *Women and care, and care and women, and women and care and trouble.*

The Verses are even enough for such odde pegma's I can make my selfe sick at any time, with comparing the dazling splender wherewith our Gentlewomen were imbell-ished in some former habits, with the gut-foundred goosdom, wherewith they are now surcingled and debauched. Wee have about five or six of them in our Colony: if I see any of them accidentally, I cannot cleanse my phansie of them for a moneth after. I have been a solitary widdower almost twelve yeares, purposed lately to make a step over to my Native Country for a yoke-fellow: but when I consider how women there have tripe-wifed themselves with their cladments, I have no heart to the voyage, least their nauseous shapes and the Sea, should work too sorely upon my stomach. I speak sadly; me thinkes it should breake the hearts of Englishmen, to see so many goodly English-women imprisoned in French Cages, peering out of their hood-holes for some men of mercy to help them with a little wit, and no body relieves them.

---

22. nugiperous: gossipy.
23. nudiustertian: the very newest.

24. drailes: trailing headdresses.

A WORD OF IRELAND:

> *Not of the Nation universally, nor of any man in*
> *it, that hath so much as one haire of Christianity or*
> *Humanity growing on his head or heard, but*
> *onely of the truculent Cut-throats, and*
> *such as shall take up Armes*
> *in their Defence.*

These *Irish* anciently called *Antropophagi*, maneaters: Have a Tradition among them, That when the Devill shewed our Saviour all the Kingdomes of the Earth and their glory, that he would not shew him *Ireland*, but reserved it for himselfe: it is probably true, for he hath kept it ever since for his own peculiar; the old Fox foresaw it would ecclipse the glory of all the rest: he thought it wisdome to keep the land for a Boggards[25] for his unclean spirits imployed in this Hemisphere, and the people, to doe his Son and Heire, I mean the Pope, that service for which *Lewis* the eleventh kept his Barbor *Oliver*,[26] which makes them so blood-thirsty. They are the very Offall of men, Dregges of Mankind, Reproach of Christendome, the Bots that crawle on the Beasts taile I wonder *Rome* it self is not ashamed of them.

I begge upon my hands and knees, that the Expedition against them may be undertaken while the hearts and hands of our Souldiery are hot, to whom I will be bold to say briefly: Happy is he that shall reward them as they have served us, and Cursed be he that shall do that work of the Lord negligently, Cursed be he that holdeth back his Sword from blood: yea, Cursed be he that maketh not his Sword starke drunk with *Irish* blood, that doth not recompence them double for their hellish treachery to the *English*, that maketh them not heaps upon heaps, and their Country a dwelling place for Dragons, an Astonishment to Nations: Let not that eye look for pity, nor that hand to be spared, that pities or spares them, and let him be accursed, that curseth not them bitterly.

---

25. a Boggards: a privy, with a play on bog.

26. *Lewis* the eleventh kept his Barbor *Oliver*: Louis XI sent Oliver to stir up rebellion against the House of Burgundy.

6. Richard Saltonstall

letter to the Boston church
1652

Saltonstall (1610?–94) went to Massachusetts in 1630 with his father, one of the original patentees of the colony. He eventually settled in Ipswich, though several times he returned for substantial intervals to England, where he retained family property. This letter was written during one such sojourn. Saltonstall had always been something of a thorn in the side of Winthrop and the authorities—he supported Robert Child and in 1645 protested the colony's involvement in the slave trade—though he remained an orthodox and respected member of the church.

Reverend and deare friends, whom I unfaynedly love and respect, It doth not a little grieve my spirit to heare what sadd things are reported dayly of your tyranny and persecutions in New England, as that you fyne, whip, and imprison men for their consciences. First, you compell such to come into your assemblyes as you know will not joyne with you in your worship, and when they shew their dislike thereof or witness against it, then you styrre up your magistrates to punish them for such (as you conceyve) their publicke affronts. Truely, friends, this your practice of compelling any in matters of worship to doe that whereof they are not fully persuaded, is to make them sin, for soe the apostle (Rom. 14 and 23) tells us, and many are made hypocrites thereby, conforming in their outward man for feare of punishment. We [who] pray for you and wish you prosperitie every way, hoped the Lord would have given you so much light and love there, that you might have been eyes to God's people here, and not to practice those courses in a wildernes, which you went so farre to prevent. These rigid wayes have layed you very lowe in the hearts of the saynts. I doe assure you I have heard them pray in the publique assemblies that the Lord would give you meeke and humble spirits, not to stryve so much for uniformity as to keepe the unity of the spirit in the bond of peace.

When I was in Holland about the beginning of our warres, I remember some Christians there that then had serious thoughts of planting in New-England, desired me to write to the governor thereof to know if those that differ from you in opinion, yet houlding the same foundation in religion, as Anabaptists, Seekers, Antinomians and the like, might be permitted to live among you, to which I received this short answer from your then governour, Mr. Dudley: God forbid (said he) our love for the truth should be growne soe cold that we should tolerate errours, and when (for satisfaction of myself and others) I desired to know your grounds, he referred me to the books written here between the Presbyterians and Independents, which if that had been sufficient I needed not have sent soe farre to understand the reasons of your practices. I hope you doe not assume to yourselves infallibilitie of judgment, when the most learned of the Apostles confesseth he knew but in parte and sawe but darkely as through a glass, for God is light, and no further than He doth illuminate us can we see, be our partes and learning never so great. Oh that all those who are brethren, though yet they cannot thinke and speake the same things might be of one accord in the Lord. Now the God of patience and consolation grant you to be thus mynded towards one another, after the example of Jesus Christ our blessed Savyor, in whose everlasting arms of protection hee leaves you who will never cease to be your truly and much affectionate friend in the nearest union.

RIC. SALTONSTALL

8. John Cotton

reply to Saltonstall

Honoured and deare Sir,

My brother Wilson and myself do both of us acknowledge your love, as otherwise formerly, so now in the late lines we received from you, that you grieve in spirit to hear dayly complaints against us. It springeth from your compassion of our afflictions therein, wherein we see just cause to desire you may never suffer like injury yourselfe, but may finde others to compassionate and condole with you. For when the complaints you hear of are against our tyranny and persecutions in fining, whipping, and imprisoning men for their consciences, be pleased to understand we look at such complaints as altogether injurious in respect to ourselves, who had no hand or tongue at all to promote either the coming of the persons you ayme at[27] into our assemblyes, or their punishment for their carriage there. Righteous judgment will not take up reports, much less reproaches, against the innocent. The cry of the sins of Sodom was great and loud, and reached up to heaven; yet the righteous God (giving us an example what to do in the like case) he would first go down to see whether their crime were altogether according to the cry, before he would proceede to judgment. Gen. 18. 20, 21. And when he did find the truth of the cry, he did not wrap up all alike promiscuously in judgement, but spared such as he found innocent. We are amongst those whom (if you knew us better) you would account of (as the matron of Abel spake of herself) peacable in Israel, 2 Sam. 20. 19.

Yet neither are we so vast in our indulgence or toleration as to think the men you speak of suffered an unjust censure. For one of them (Obadiah Holmes) being an

27. ayme at: refer to.

excommunicate person himself, out of a church in Plymouth patent, came into this jurisdiction and took upon him to baptize, which I think [he] himself will not say he was compelled here to performe. And he was not ignorant that the rebaptizing of an elder person, and that by a private person out of office and under excommunication, are all of them manifest contestations against the order and government of our churches established (we know) by Gods law, and (he knoweth) by the lawes of the country. And we conceive we may safely appeal to the ingenuity of your owne judgment, whether it would be tolerated in any civil state, for a stranger to come and practise contrary to the known principles of their church estate? As for his whipping, it was more voluntarily chosen by him than inflicted on him. His censure by the court was to have payed (as I know) 30 pounds or else be whipt; in which case, if his suffering of stripes was any worship of God at all, surely it could be accounted no better than will-worship.

The other (Mr. Clarke) was no wiser in that point and his offence was less, so was his fine less, and [he] himself (as I hear) was contented to have it payed for him, whereupon he was released. The imprisonment of either of them was no detriment. I believe they fared neither of them better at home, and I am sure Holmes had not been so well clad of many years before.

But be pleased to consider this point a little further. You think to compell men in matter of worship is to make men sin, according to Rom. 14. 23. If the worship be lawfull in itself, the magistrate compelling him to come to it compelleth him not to sin, but the sin is in his will that needs to be compelled to a christian duty. Josiah compelled all Israel, or (which is all one) made to serve the Lord their God, 2 Chron. 34. 33. yet his act herein was not blamed but recorded amongst his virtuous actions. For a governour to suffer any within his gates to prophane the sabbath, is a sin against the 4th commandment, both in the private householder and in the magistrate; and if he requires them to present themselves before the Lord, the magistrate sinneth not, nor doth the subject sinne so great a sin as if he did refraine to come. If the magistrate connive at his absenting himself from sabbath duties the sin will be greater in the magistrate than can be in the other's passive coming. Naaman's passive going into the house of Rimmon did not violate the peace of his conscience, 2 Kings 5. 18, 19. Bodily presence in a stewes,[28] forced to behold the leudness of whoredomes there committed, is no whoredome at all. No more is it spiritual whoredome to be compelled by force to go to mass.

But (say you) it doth but make men hypocrites, to compell men to conforme the outward man for fear of punishment. If it did so, yet better to be hypocrites than prophane persons. Hypocrites give God part of his due, the outward man, but the prophane person giveth God neither outward nor inward man.

Your prayers for us we thankfully accept, and we hope God hath given us so much light and love (which we think we want) that if our native country were more zealous against horrid blasphemies and heresies than we be, we believe the Lord would look at it as a better improvement of all the great salvations he hath wrought for them than to set open a wide door to all abominations in religion. Do you think the Lord hath

---

28. stewes: brothel.

crowned the state with so many victories that they should suffer so many miscreants to pluck the crown of soveraignty from Christ's head? Some to deny his godhead, some his manhood; some to acknowledge no Christ, nor heaven, nor hell, but what is in a man's self? Some to deny all churches and ordinances, and so to leave Christ no visible kingdome upon earth? And thus Christ by easing England of the yoke of a kingdome shall forfeit his own kingdom among the people of England. Now God forbid, God from heaven forbid, that the people and state of England should so ill requite the Lord Jesus.

You know not, if you thinke we came into this wilderness to practise those courses here which we fled from in England. We believe there is a vast difference between men's inventions and God's institutions; we fled from men's inventions, to which we else should have been compelled; we compell none to men's inventions.

If our ways (rigid ways as you call them) have laid us low in the hearts of God's people, yea and of the saints (as you stile them) we do not believe it is any part of their saintship. Michal had a low esteem of Davids zeal, but he was never a whit lower in the sight of God, nor the higher.

What you wrote out of Holland to our then governor Mr. Dudley, in behalfe of Anabaptists, Antinomians, Seekers, and the like, it seemeth, met with a short answer from him, but zealous; for zeal will not beare such mixtures as coldness or luke-warmeness will, Revel. 2. 2. 14. 15. 20. Neverthelesse, I tell you the truth, we have tolerated in our church some Anabaptists, some Antinomians, and some Seekers, and do so still at this day; though Seekers of all others have least reason to desire tolera-tion in church fellowship. For they that deny all churches and church ordinances since the apostacy of Antichrist, they cannot continue in church fellowship but against their own judgment and conscience; and therefore 4 or 5 of them who openly renounced the church fellowship which they had long enjoyed, the church said amen to their act, and (after serious debate with them till they had nothing to answer) they were removed from their fellowship. Others carry their dissent more privately and inoffen-sively, and so are borne withall in much meekeness.

We are far from arrogating infallibility of judgement to ourselves or affecting uniformity; uniformity God never required, infallibility he never granted us. We content ourselves with unity in the foundation of religion and of church order: Superstructures we suffer to varie; we have learned (through grace) to keep the unity of the spirit in the bond of peace; only we are loth to be blowne up and downe (like chaff) by every winde of new notions.

You see how desirous we are to give you what satisfaction we may to your loving expostulation, which we pray you to accept with the same spirit of love wherewith it is endited.[29] The Lord Jesus guide and keep your heart for ever in the wayes of his truth and peace. So humbly commending our due respect and hearty affection to your worship, we take leave and rest.

29. endited: written.

8. Samuel Danforth

A Brief Recognition of New-Englands Errand into the Wilderness
1671

A classic example of the jeremiad, Danforth's sermon elaborates the New England vision of history as it took shape following the Restoration (1660) and the Half-Way Covenant (1662). It establishes the story of a past golden age of piety, and works to convince the reader that residence in New England is not merely residence in a place, but a mission from God. Danforth was born in Suffolk, England, in 1626, and emigrated with his father in 1634. After graduating from Harvard in 1643, he became an associate of John Eliot in the Indian mission. He also compiled almanacs for several years in the late 1640s, and wrote a treatise on comets as astrological omens. His other major sermon, The Cry of Sodom Inquired Into, appeared in 1674, the year of his death. Like most Puritan sermons, A Brief Recognition has three sections: an explication of an opening text, a statement of general truths ("Doctrine"), and the application ("Use") of those truths for the hearers.

MATTH. 11. 7,8,9.

> *What went ye out into the wilderness to see? A reed*
> *shaken with the wind?*
> *But what went ye out for to see? A man clothed in soft*
> *raiment? behold, they that wear soft clothing, are in*
> *Kings houses.*
> *But what went ye out for to see? A Prophet? yea, I say*
> *unto you, and more than a Prophet.*

These words are our Saviour's *Proem* to his illustrious Encomium of *John* the Baptist. *John* began his Ministry, not in *Jerusalem*, nor in any famous City of *Judea*, but in the *Wilderness*, i.e. in a woody, retired and solitary place, thereby withdrawing himself from the envy and proposterous zeal of such as were addicted to their old Traditions, and also taking the people aside from the noise and tumult of their secular occasions and businesses, which might have obstructed their ready and cheerful attendance unto his Doctrine. The Ministry of *John* at first was entertained by all sorts with singular affection: There *went out to him Jerusalem and all Judea, and all the region round about Jordan*, Mat. 3.5. But after awhile, the people's fervour abated, and *John* being kept under restraint divers months, his authority and esteem began to decay and languish, *John* 5. 35. Wherefore our Saviour, taking occasion from *Johns* Messengers coming to him, after their departure, gives an excellent *Elogie* and Commendation of *John*, to the intent that He might ratifie and confirm his Doctrine and Administration, and revive his Authority and Estimation in the hearts and consciences of the people.

This *Elogie* our Saviour begins with an elegant *Dialogism*, which the Rhetorician calleth *Communication*: gravely deliberating with his Hearers, and seriously enquiring to what purpose they went out into the Wilderness, and what expectation drew them thither. Wherein we have, 1. *The general Question, and main subject of his Inquisition. 2. The particular Enquiries. 3. The Determination of the Question.*

The general Question is, *What went ye out into the Wilderness to see?* He saith not, Whom went ye out to *hear*, but what went ye out to *see*? The phrase agrees to[30] Shows and Stage-plays; plainly arguing that many of those, who seemed well-affected to *John*, and flock'd after him, were *Theatrical* Hearers, *Spectators* rather then *Auditors*; they went not to *hear*, but to *see*, they went to gaze upon a new and strange Spectacle.

This general Question being propounded, the first particular Enquiry is, whether they went to see *A reed shaken with the wind*? The expression is Metaphorical and Proverbial. A reed when the season is calm, lifts up itself and stands upright, but no sooner doth the wind blow upon it, but it shakes and trembles, bends and bows down, and then gets up again: and again it yields and bows, and then lifts up itself again. A notable *Emblem* of light, empty and inconstant persons, who in times of peace and tranquillity, give a fair and plausible Testimony to the Truth; but no sooner do the winds of Temptation blow upon them, and the waves of Troubles roll over them, but they incline and yield to the prevailing Party; but when the Tempest is over, they recover themselves and assert the Truth again. The meaning then of this first Enquiry is, Went ye out into the Wilderness like a light, vain and inconstant man, one that could confess and deny, and deny and confess the same Truth? This Interrogation is to be understood negatively and ironically; *q.d.*[31] Surely ye went not into the desert to behold such a ludicrous and ridiculous sight, *A man like unto a reed shaken with the wind*. Under the negation of the contrary levity, our Saviour sets forth one of *John's* excellencies, *viz.*[32] his eminent *Constancy* in asserting the Truth. The winds of various temptations both on the right hand and on the left, blew upon him, yet he wavered not in his testimony concerning Christ, *He confessed and denied not, but confessed* the truth.

Then the general Question is repeated, *But what went ye out for to see?* and a second particular Enquiry made, Was it to see *a man clothed in soft raiment*? This Interrogation hath also the force of a negation, *q.d.* Surely ye went not into the Wilderness to see a man clothed in silken and costly Apparel. The reason of this is added, *Behold, they that wear soft clothing, are in Kings houses.* Delicate and costly Apparel is to be expected in Princes Courts, and not in wilde Woods and Forrests. Under the negation of *John's* affectation of Courtly delicacy, our Saviour sets forth another of *John's* excellencies, *viz.* his singular *gravity* and *sobriety*, who wore rough garments, and lived on course and mean fare, *Mat.* 3.4. which austere kinde of life

30. agrees to: is appropriate to.
31. *q.d.*: which is to say.
32. *viz.*: namely.

was accommodated to the place and work of his Ministry. *John* Preached in the Wilderness, which was no fit place for silken and soft raiment. His work was to prepare a people for the Lord, by calling them off from worldly pomp and vanities, unto repentance and mourning for sin. His peculiar habit and diet was such as became a penitentiary Preacher.

Thirdly, the generall Question is reiterated, *But what went ye out for to see?* and a third particular Enquiry made, Was it to see *a Prophet?* This Interrogation is to be understood affirmatively, *q.d.* no doubt but it was to see a *Prophet.* Had not *John* been a rare and excellent Minister of God, you would never have gone out of your Cities into the desert to have seen him. Thus our Saviour sets forth another of *John's* admirable excellencies, *viz.* his *Prophetical* Office and Function. *John* was not an ordinary Interpreter of the Law, much less a Teacher of Jewish Tradition, but a *Prophet,* one who by the extraordinary Inspiration of the holy Ghost, made known the Mysteries of Salvation, *Luke 1. 76,77.*

Lastly, our Saviour determines and concludes the Question, He, whom ye went out to see was *more than a Prophet, much more, or abundantly more than a prophet.* This he confirms by his wonted Asseveration, *Yea, I say unto you,* and much more than a Prophet. How was *John* much more than a Prophet? *John* was *Christs Herauld* sent immediately before his face, to proclaim his Coming and Kingdome, and prepare the people for the reception of him by the Baptism of Repentance, *ver. 10.* Hence it follows *ver. 11. Among all that are born of women, there hath not risen a greater Prophet than John. John* was greater then any of the Prophets that were before him, not in respect of his personal graces and virtues, (for who shall perswade us that he excelled *Abraham* in the grace of *Faith,* who was the father of the faithful, or *Moses* in *Meekness,* who was the meekest man on earth, or *David* in *Faithfulness,* who was a man after Gods' own heart, or *Solomon* in *Wisdome,* who was the wisest man that ever was or shall be?) but in respect of the manner of his dispensation. All the *Prophets* foretold Christs Coming, his Sufferings and Glory, but the *Baptist* was his *Harbinger* and *Forerunner,* that bare the Sword before him, Proclaimed his Presence, and made room for him in the hearts of the people. All the *Prophets* saw Christ afar off, but the *Baptist* saw him present, baptized him, and applied the Types to him[33] personally. *Behold the Lamb of God. He saw and bare record that this is the Son of God,* Joh. 1.29,34. *But he that is least in the Kingdome of Heaven, is greater than John.* The least Prophet in the Kingdome of Heaven, *i.e.* the least Minister of the Gospel since Christ's Ascension, is greater than *John,* not in respect of the measure of his personal gifts, nor in respect of the manner of his Calling, but in respect of the *Object* of his Ministry, *Christ on the Throne,* having finished the work of our Redemption, and in respect of the *degree* of the revelation of Christ, which is far more clear and full. *John* shewed Christ in the flesh, and pointed to him with his finger, but the Ministers of the Gospel declare that he hath done and suffered all things necessary to our Salvation, and is risen again and set down at the right hand of God.

---

33. applied the Types to him: recognized that the Scriptures referred to him.

DOCTRINE

Such as have sometime left their pleasant Cities and Habitations to enjoy the pure Worship of God in a Wilderness, are apt in time to abate and cool in their affection thereunto: but then the Lord calls upon them seriously and thoroughly to examine themselves, what it was that drew them into the Wilderness, and to consider that it was not the expectation of ludicrous levity, nor of Courtly pomp and delicacy, but of the free and clear dispensation of the Gospel and Kingdome of God.

This Doctrine consists of two distinct Branches; let me open them severally.[34]

Branch I. *Such as have sometime left their pleasant Cities and Habitations, to enjoy the pure Worship of God in a Wilderness, are apt in time to abate and cool in their affection thereunto.* To what purpose did the Children of *Israel* leave their Cities and Houses in *Egypt*, and go forth into the Wilderness? was it not to *hold a Feast to the Lord*, and to *sacrifice to the God of their fathers*? That was the onely reason, which they gave of their motion to *Pharaoh, Exod.5.1,3.* But how soon did they forget their Errand into the Wilderness, and corrupt themselves in their own Inventions? Within a few months after their coming out of *Egypt, they make a Calf in Horeb, and worship the molten Image, and change their glory into the similitude of an Ox that eateth grass, Psal.*106.19,20. *Exod.*32.7,8. yea for the space of forty years in the Wilderness, while they pretended to Sacrifice to the Lord, they indeed worshipped the Stars and the Host of Heaven, and together with the Lords Tabernacle, carried about with them the Tabernacle of *Moloch, Amos 5.25,26. Acts 7.42,43.* And how did they spend their time in the Wilderness, but in tempting God, and in murmuring against their godly and faithful Teachers and Rulers, *Moses* and *Aaron; Psal.*93.8. To what purpose did the Children of the Captivity upon *Cyrus* his Proclamation, leave their Houses which they had built, and their Vineyards and Oliveyards which they had planted in the Province of *Babylon*, and return to *Judea* and *Jerusalem*, which were now become a Wilderness? was it not that they might build the House of God at *Jerusalem*, and set up the Temple-worship? But how shamefully did they neglect that great and honourable Work for the space of above forty years? They pretended that Gods time was not come to build his House, because of the rubs and obstructions which they met with, whereas all their difficulties and discouragements hindred not their building of stately houses for themselves, *Hag.*1.2,3,4. To what purpose did *Jerusalem* & all *Judea*, & all the region round about *Jordan*, leave their several Cities and Habitations, and flock into the *Wilderness of Judea*? was it not to see that *burning and shining light*, which God had raised up? To hear his heavenly Doctrine, and partake of that new Sacrament, which he administred? O how they were affected with his rare and excellent gifts! with his clear, lively and powerful Ministry! *The Kingdome of Heaven pressed in* upon them *with* a holy *violence, and the violent*, the zealous and affectionate hearers of the Gospel, *took it by force*, Mat.11.12., Luk.16.16. They leapt over all discouragements and impediments, whether outward, as Legal Rites and Ceremonies, or inward, the sense of their own sin and unworthiness, and pressed into

34. severally: separately.

the Kingdome of God, as men rush into a Theatre to see a pleasant Sight, or as Souldiers run into a besieged City, to take the Spoil thereof: but their hot fit is soon over, their affection lasted but for an *hour*, i.e. a short season, *Joh.5.35*.

Reas. 1. Because the *affection* of many to the Ministry of the Gospel and the pure Worship of God, is built upon *temporary* and *transitory* grounds, as the *novelty* and *strangeness of the matter, the rareness and excellency of Ministerial Gifts, the voice of the people, the countenance of great men, and the hope of worldly advantage.* The Jews had lien in ignorance and darkness a long time, being trained up under the superstitious observances of their old Traditions, which were vain, empty and unprofitable Customes, and the Church wanted the gift of Prophecy about four hundred years; and therefore when *John* the *Baptist* arose like a bright and burning light, shining amongst them with admirable gifts of the Spirit, and extraordinary severity and gravity of manners, proclaiming the Coming and Kingdom of the Messias, (which had been oft promised and long expected) and pressing the people to Repentance and good works; O how they admire and reverence him! especially, when grown popular, and countenanced by *Herod* the *Tetrarch*. What sweet affections are kindled! what great expectations are raised! what ravishing joy is conceived! Hoping (as its probable) to make use of his Authority to call off the *Roman* yoke, and recover their Civil Liberties, Riches and Honours. But after a little acquaintance with *John*, (for he was a publick Preacher but a year and half) his Doctrine, Administrations and Prophetical Gifts, grew common and stale things, and of little esteem with them; especially, when they saw their carnal hopes frustrated, the Rulers disaffected, and *Herods* countenance and carriage toward him changed.

Reas. 2. Because *Prejudices* and *Offences* are apt to arise in the hearts of many against the *faithful Dispensers* of the Gospel. The *Pharisees* and *Lawyers* came among others to the Baptism of *John*, but when they hear his sharp reprehensions of their *Viperous* Opinions and Practices, they nauseate[35] his Doctrine, repudiate his Baptism, calumniate his Conversation, *Luke* 7.30. *Herodias* hath an inward grudge and a quarrel against him, because he found fault with her incestuous Marriage, *Mar.6.19.* Yea, that very Age and Generation of the Jews, were like to a company of surly, sullen and froward children, whom no Musick can please; they neither dance after the Pipe, nor make lamentation after the mourner. They inveigh against *John's* austerity, saying that he was transported with diabolical fury, and was an enemy to humane society: and they do as much distaste and abhor *Christ's* gentleness and familiarity, traducing him, as being a sensual and voluptuous person, given to intemperance and luxury, and a Patron and Abettor of looseness and profaneness, *Mat.11.16–19.* Thus doth the frowardness and stubbornness of man, resist and oppose the wisdome and goodness of God, who useth various wayes and instruments to compass poor sinners, but they through their folly and perverseness, frustrate, disanul and abrogate the counsel of God against themselves. The evil spirit that troubled *Saul*, was quieted and allayed by the sweet Melody of *David's* Harp: but the mad and outragious fury that transports men against the Truth and the Ministry thereof, cannot be quieted and allayed by the voice of the Charmers, charm they never so wisely.

---

35. nauseate: become nauseous at.

Branch II. *When men abate and cool in their affection to the pure Worship of God, which they went into the Wilderness to enjoy, the Lord calls upon them seriously and thoroughly to examine themselves, what it was that drew them into the Wilderness, and to consider that it was not the expectation of ludicrous levity, nor of Courtly pomp and delicacy, but of the free and clear dispensation of the Gospel and Kingdome of God.* Our Saviour knowing that the people had lost their first love and singular affection to the revelation of his grace by the Ministry of his Herauld *John*, He is very intense in examining them, what expectation drew them into the Wilderness: He doth not once nor twice, but thrice propound that Question, *What went ye out into the Wilderness to see?* Yea, in particular he enquires whether it were to see a man that was like to *a Reed shaken with the wind?* or whether it were to see *a man clothed like a Courtier*, or whether it were to see a *Prophet*, and then determines the Question, concluding that it was to see a great and excellent Prophet, and that had not they seen rare and admirable things in him, they would never have gone out into the Wilderness unto him.

The Reason is, Because the serious consideration of the inestimable grace and mercy of God in the free and clear dispensation of the Gospel and Kingdome of God, is a special means to convince men of their folly and perverseness in undervaluing the same, and a sanctified remedy to recover their affections thereunto. The Lord fore-seeing the defection of *Israel* after *Moses* his death, commands him to write that Prophetical Song, recorded in *Deut.* 32. as a Testimony against them: wherein the chief remedy, which he prescribes for the prevention and healing of their Apostacy, is their calling to remembrance Gods great and signal love in manifesting himself to them in the Wilderness, in conducting them safely and mercifully and giving them possession of their promised Inheritance, *ver.*7-14. And when *Israel* was apostatized and fallen, the Lord to convince them of their ingratitude and folly, brings to their remembrance his deliverance of them out of *Egypt*, his leading them through the Wilderness for the space of forty years, and not onely giving them possession of their Enemies Land, but also raising up, even of their own Sons, *Prophets*, faithful and eminent Ministers, and of their young men *Nazarites*, who being separated from worldly delights and encumbrances, were Paterns of Purity and Holiness: all which were great and obliging mercies. Yea, the Lord appeals to their own Consciences, whether these his favours were not real and signal, *Amos* 2.10, 11. The Prophet *Jeremiah*, that he might reduce the people from their back-slidings, cries in the ears of *Jerusalem*, with earnestness and boldness declaring unto them, that the Lord remem-bered how well they stood affected towards him, when he first chose them to be his people and espoused them to himself, how they followed him in the Wilderness, and kept close to him in their long and wearisome passage through the uncultured Desert; how they were then consecrated to God, and set apart for his Worship and Service, as the first-fruits are wont to be sequestred and devoted to God: and thereupon expostu-lates with them for their forsaking the Lord, and following after their Idols, *Jer.* 2. 2,3,5,6. Surely our Saviour's *Dialogism* with his Hearers in my Text, is not a meer Rhetorical Elegancy to adorn his Testimony concerning *John*, but a clear and strong conviction of their folly in slighting and despising that which they sometime so highly pretended unto, and a wholesome admonition and direction how to recover their primitive affection to his Doctrine and Administration.

USE

I. Of solemn and serious Enquiry to us all in this general Assembly, Whether we have not in a great measure forgotten our Errand into the Wilderness. You have solemnly professed before God, Angels and Men, that the Cause of your leaving your Country, Kindred and Fathers' houses, and transporting your selves with your Wives, Little Ones and Substance over the vast Ocean into this waste and howling Wilderness, was *your Liberty to walk in the Faith of the Gospel with all good Conscience according to the Order of the Gospel, and your enjoyment of the pure Worship of God according to his Institution, without humane Mixtures and Impositions.* Now let us sadly consider whether our ancient and primitive affections to the Lord Jesus, his glorious Gospel, his pure and Spiritual Worship and the Order of his House, remain, abide and continue firm, constant, entire and inviolate. Our Saviour's reiteration of this Question, *What went ye out into the Wilderness to see?* is no idle repetition, but a sad conviction of our dulness and backwardness to this great duty, and a clear demonstration of the weight and necessity thereof. It may be a grief to us to be put upon such an Inquisition; as it is said of *Peter*, John.21.17. *Peter was grieved, because he said unto him the third time, Lovest thou me?* but the Lord knoweth that a strict and rigid examination of our hearts in this point, is no more than necessary. Wherefore let us call to remembrance the former dayes, and consider whether *it was not then better with us, than it is now.*

In our first and best times the Kingdome of Heaven brake in upon us with a holy violence, and every man pressed into it. What mighty efficacy and power had the clear and faithful dispensation of the Gospel upon your hearts? how affectionately and zealously did you entertain the Kingdome of God? How careful were you, even all sorts, young and old, high and low, to take hold of the opportunities of your Spiritual good and edification? ordering your secular affairs (which were wreathed and twisted together with great variety) so as not to interfere with your general Calling, but that you might *attend upon the Lord without distraction.* How diligent and faithful in preparing your hearts for the reception of the Word, *laying apart all filthiness and superfluity of naughtiness, that you might receive with meekness the ingrossed word, which is able to have your souls; and purging out all malice, guile, hypocrisies, envies, and all evil speakings, and as new-born babies, desiring the sincere milk of the Word, that ye might grow thereby?* How attentive in hearing the everlasting Gospel, *watching daily at the gates of Wisdom, and waiting at the posts of her doors, that ye might finde eternal life, and obtain favour of the Lord?* Gleaning day by day in the field of Gods Ordinances, even among the Sheaves, and gathering up handfuls, which the Lord let fall of purpose for you, and at night going home and beating out what you had gleaned, by Meditation, Repetition, Conference, and therewith feeding your selves and your families. How painful[36] were you in recollecting, repeating and discoursing of what you heard, whetting the Word of God upon the hearts of your Children, Servants and Neighbours? How fervent in Prayer to Almighty God for his divine Blessing upon the Seed sown, that it might take root and fructifie? O what a

---

36. painful: painstaking.

reverent esteem had you in those dayes of Christ's faithful Ambassadors, that declared unto you the Word of Reconciliation! *How beautiful were the feet of them, that preached the Gospel of peace, and brought the glad tidings of Salvation*! you *esteemed them highly in love for their works sake*. Their Persons, Names and Comforts were precious in your eyes; you counted your Selves blessed in the enjoyment of a Pious, Learned and Orthodox Ministry: and though you ate the bread of adversity and drank the water of affliction, yet you rejoyced in this, that your eyes saw your Teachers, they were not removed into corners, and your ears heard a word behinde you, saying, This is the way, walk ye in it, when you turned to the right hand and when you turned to the left, *Isa.* 30.20,21. What earnest and ardent desires had you in those dayes after Communion with Christ in the holy Sacraments? *With desire you desired* to partake of the Seals of the Covenant. You thought your Evidences for Heaven not sure nor authentick, unless the Broad-Seals of the Kingdome were annexed. What solicitude was there in those dayes to *seek the Lord after the right Order?* What searching of the holy Scriptures, what Collations among your Leaders, both in their private Meetings and publick Councils and Synods, to finde out the Order which Christ hath constituted and established in his House? What fervent zeal was there then against Sectaries and Hereticks, and all manner of Heterodoxies? *You could not bear them that were evil*, but tried them that pretended to New Light and Revelations, and found them *liars*. What pious *care* was there of *Sister-Churches*, that those that wanted *Breasts*, might be supplied, and that those that wanted *Peace*, their Dissentions might be healed? What readiness was there in those dayes to call for the help of Neighbour-Elders and Brethren, in case of any Difference or Division that could not be healed at home? What reverence was there then of the Sentence of a Council, as being *decisive* and issuing the Controversie? According to that ancient Proverbial Saying, *They shall surely ask counsel at Abel, and so they ended the matter*, 2 Sam. 20.18. What holy Endeavours were there in those dayes to *propagate* Religion to your Children and Posterity, training them up in the nurture and admonition of the Lord, keeping them under the awe of government, restraining their enormities and extravagancies, charging them to know the God of their fathers, and serve him with a perfect heart and willing minde, and publickly affecting and maintaining their interest in the Lord and in his holy Covenant, and zealously opposing those that denied the same?

And then had the Churches *rest* throughout the several Colonies, and were *edified: and walking in the fear of the Lord, and in the comfort of the holy Ghost, were multiplied*. O how your *Faith* grew exceedingly! you proceeded from faith to faith, from a less to a greater degree and measure, growing up in Him, who is our Head, and receiving abundance of grace and of the gift of righteousness, that you might reign in life by Jesus Christ. O how your *Love and Charity* towards each other abounded! O what comfort of Love! what bowels and mercies! what affectionate care was there one of another! what a holy Sympathy in Crosses and Comforts, weeping with those that wept, and rejoycing with those that rejoyced!

But who is there left among you, that saw these Churches *in their first glory*, and how do you see them now? Are they not in your eyes in comparison thereof, *as nothing? How is the gold become dim! how is the most fine gold changed*! Is not the Temper, Complexion and Countenance of the Churches strangely altered? Doth not a careless, remiss, flat, dry, cold dead frame of spirit, grow in upon us secretly, strongly, prodigiously? They that have Ordinances, are as though they had none; and they that hear the Word, as though they heard it not; and they that pray, as though they prayed not, and they that receive Sacraments, as though they received them not; and they that are exercised in the holy things, using them by the by, as matters of custome and ceremony, so as not to hinder their eager prosecution of other things which their hearts are set upon. Yea and in some particular Congregations amongst us, is there not *in stead of a sweet smell, a stink? and in stead of a girdle, a rent? and in stead of a stomacher,*[37] *a girding with sackcloth? and burning in stead of beauty? yea the Vineyard is all overgrown with thorns, and nettles cover the face thereof, and the stone-wall thereof is broken down*, Prov.24 31. yea, and that which is the most sad and certain sign of calamity approaching, *Iniquity aboundeth, and the love of many waxeth cold*, Mat.24 12. Pride, Contention, Worldliness, Covetousness, Luxury, Drunkenness and Uncleanness break in like a flood upon us, and good men grow cold in their love to God and to one another. If a man be cold in his bed, let them lay on the more clothes, that he may get heat: but we are like to *David* in his old age, *they covered him with clothes, but he gat no heat*, 2 Sam.1.1. The Lord heaps mercies, favours, blessings upon us, and loads us daily with his benefits, but all his love and bounty cannot heat and warm our hearts and affections. Well, the furnace is able to heat and melt the coldest Iron: but how oft hath the Lord cast us into the hot furnace of Affliction and Tribulation, and we have been scorched and burnt, yet not melted, but hardened thereby, *Isa.*63.17. How long hath God kept us in the furnace day after day, month after month, year after year? but all our Afflictions, Crosses, Trials have not been able to keep our hearts in a warm temper.

Now let me freely deliberate with you, what may be the *Causes and Grounds of such decayes and languishings* in our affections to, and estimation of that which we came into the Wilderness to enjoy? Is it because *there is no bread, neither is there any water, and our soul loatheth this light bread?* Numb. 21.5. *Our soul is dried away, and there is nothing at all, besides this Manna, before our eyes*, Numb. 11.6. What, is Manna no bread? Is this Angelical food, light bread, which cannot satisfie, but starves the Soul? Doth our Soul loath the bread of Heaven? The Lord be merciful to us: The full soul loatheth the honey-comb, *Prov. 27.7.*

What then is the cause of our decayes and languishings? Is it because the Spirit of the Lord is straitned and limited in the dispensers of the Gospel, and hence our joyes and comforts are lessened and shortned? *O thou that art named the house of Jacob, is the Spirit of the Lord straitned? are those his doings? Do not my words do good to him that walketh uprightly?* Mic.2.7. Surely it is not for want of fulness in the Spirit of God, that he withholds comforts and blessings from any; neither doth he delight in threatnings and judgments, but his words both promise and perform that which is good and comfortable to them that walk uprightly. The Spirit is able to enlarge it self unto the reviving and cheering of every man's heart; and that should we experience, did not our iniquity put a barre. 2 *Cor.* 6.11,12. *O ye Corinthians, our mouth is open*

37. *stomacher*: an embroidered bodice for men or women.

unto you, our heart is enlarged: Ye are not straitned in us, but ye are straitned in your own bowels. The Spirit of God dilateth and enlargeth the heart of the faithfull Ministry for the good of the people, but many times the people are straitned in their own bowels, and cannot receive such a large portion, as the Lord hath provided for them. *What then is the cause of our coolings, faintings and languishings?* The grand and principal cause is our *Unbelief*: We believe not the Grace and Power of God in Christ. Where is that lively exercise of faith, which ought to be, in our attendance upon the Lord in his holy Ordinances? Christ came to *Nazareth* with his heart full of love and compassion, and his hands full of blessings to bestow upon his old Acquaintance and Neighbours, among whom he had been brought up, but their *Unbelief* restrained his tender mercies, and bound his Omnipotent hands, that he could not do any great or illustrious Miracle amongst them. *Mat.*13.58. *Mark* 6.5,6. *He could do there no mighty work—and he marvelled because of their unbelief.* Unbelief straitens the grace and power of Christ, and straitens the communication of divine favours and special mercies. The word preached profits not, when it is not mixed with faith in them that hear it, *Heb.*4.2. We may pray earnestly, but if we ask not in faith, *how* can we expect to receive anything of the Lord? *Jam.*1.6,7.

But though Unbelief be the principal, yet it is not the sole cause of our decayes and languishings: *Inordinate worldly Cares, predominant Lusts, and malignant Passions and Distempers* stifle and choak the Word, and quench our affections to the Kingdome of God, *Luke* 8.14. The Manna was gathered early in the morning; when the Sun waxed hot, it melted, *Exod.*16. 21; It was a fearful Judgment on *Dathan* and *Abiram*, that the earth opened its mouth and swallowed them up. How many Professors of Religion, are swallowed up alive by earthly affections? Such as escape the *Limepit of Pharisaical Hypocrisie*, fall into the *Coal-pit of Sadducean Atheism and Epicurism*. Pharisaism and Sadduceism do almost divide the Professing World between them. Some split upon the *Rock* of affected ostentation of singular Piety and Holiness, and others are drawn into the *Whirpool*, and perish in the *Gulf* of Sensuality and Luxury.

If any question how seasonable such a Discourse may be upon such a Day, as this; let him consider, *Hag.* 2.10–14. *In the four and twentieth day of the ninth month, in the second year of Darius, came the word of the Lord by Haggai the Prophet, saying, Thus saith the Lord of Hosts, Ask now the Priests concerning the law, saying, If one bear holy flesh in the skirt of his garment, and with his skirt do touch bread, or pottage, or wine, or oyl, or any meat, shall it be holy? And the Priests answered and said, No. Then said Haggai, If one that is unclean by a dead body, touch any of these, shall it be unclean? And the Priests answered and said, It shall be unclean. Then answered Haggai and said, So is this people, and so is this nation before me, saith the Lord; and so is every work of their hands, and that which they offer there is unclean.* It was an high and great day, wherein the Prophet spake these words, and an holy and honourable Work, which the people were employed in. For this day they laid the Foundation of the Lords Temple, *ver.*18. Nevertheless, the Lord saw it necessary this very day to represent and declare unto them, the pollution and uncleanness both of their persons and of their holy Services, that they might be deeply humbled before God, and carry on their present Work more holily and purely. What was their uncleanness? Their eager pursuit of their private Interests, took off their hearts and affections from the affairs of the House of God. It seems they pleased themselves with this, that the Altar stood upon its Bases, and Sacrifices were daily offered thereon, and the building of the Temple was only deferred untill a fit opportunity were afforded, free from disturbance and opposition: and having now gained such a season, they are ready to build the Temple: but the Lord convinceth them out of the Law, that their former negligence was not expiated by their daily Sacrifices, but the guilt thereof rendred both the *Nation* and this *holy and honourable work*, which they were about, *vile and unclean* in the sight of God. And having thus shewn them their spiritual uncleanness, he encourageth them to go on with the work in hand, the building of the Temple, promising them from *this day* to bless them, *ver*.18.

II. Of Exhortation, To excite and stir us all up to attend and prosecute our Errand into the Wilderness. *To what purpose came we into this place, and what expectation drew us hither*? Surely, not the expectation of *Ludicrous Levity*. We came not hither to see *a Reed shaken with the wind*. Then let not us be *Reeds*, light, empty, vain, hollow hearted Professors, shaken with every wind of Temptation: but solid, serious and sober Christians, constant and stedfast in the Profession and Practice of the Truth, *Trees of Righteousness, the planting of the Lord, that he may be glorified*, holding fast the profession of our Faith without wavering.

Alas, there is such variety and diversity of Opinions and Judgements, that we know not what to believe.

Were there not as various and different Opinions touching the Person of Christ, even in the dayes of his flesh? Some said that He was *John the Baptist*, some *Elias*, others *Jeremiah*, or one of the old *Prophets*. Some said he was a gluttonous man, and a wine-bibber, a friend of publicans and sinners: others said He was a *Samaritan*, and had a Devil, yet the Disciples knew what to believe. *Whom say ye that I am? Thou art Christ, the Son of the living God*, Mat.16.15,16. The various heterodox Opinions of the people, serve as a *foil* or tinctured leaf to set off the lustre and beauty of the Orthodox and Apostolical Faith. This is truly commendable, when in such variety and diversity of Apprehensions, you are not byassed by any sinister respects, but discern, embrace and profess the Truth, as it is in Christ Jesus.

But to what purpose came we into the Wilderness, and what expectation drew us hither? Not the expectation of *Courtly Pomp and Delicacy*. We came not hither to see men clothed like *Courtiers*. The affectation of Courtly Pomp and Gallantry, is very unsuitable in a Wilderness. Gorgeous Attire is comely in Princes Courts, if it exceed not the limits of Christian Sobriety: but excess in Kings houses, escapes not divine Vengeance. Zeph.1.8.—*I will punish the Princes and the Kings children, and all such as are clothed with strange Apparel.* The pride and haughtiness of the Ladies of *Zion* in their superfluous Ornaments and stately gestures, brought wrath upon themselves, upon their Husbands, and upon their Children, yea and upon the whole Land, *Isa*.3. 16–26. How much more intolerable and abominable is excess of this kinde in a Wilderness, where we are so far removed from the Riches and Honours of Princes Courts?

To what purpose then came we into the Wilderness, and what expectation drew us hither? Was it not the expectation of the *pure and faithful Dispensation* of the Gospel and Kingdome of God? The times were such that we could not enjoy it in our own Land: and therefore having obtained *Liberty* and a gracious *Patent* from our *Sovereign*, we left our Country, Kindred and Fathers houses, and came into these Wilde Woods and Deserts, where the Lord hath planted us, and made us *dwell in a place of our own, that we might move no more, and that the children of wickedness might afflict not us any more*, 2 Sam.7.10. What is it that *distinguisheth New England* from other Colonies and Plantations in *America*? Not our transportation, over the *Atlantick* Ocean, but the *Ministry* of Gods faithful Prophets, and the fruition of his holy *Ordinances*. Did not the Lord bring *the Philistines from Caphtor, and the Assyrians from Kir*, as well as *Israel from the land of Egypt*? Amos 9.7. But *by a Prophet the Lord brought Israel out of Egypt, and by a Prophet was he preserved*, Hos. 12. 13. What, is the Price and Esteem of Gods Prophets, and their faithful Dispensations, now fallen in our hearts?

The hardships, difficulties and sufferings, which you have exposed your selves unto, that you might dwell in the House of the Lord, and leave your Little Ones under the shadow of the wings of the God of *Israel*, have not been few nor small. And shall we now withdraw our selves and our Little Ones from under those *healing Wings*, and lose that full Reward, which the Lord hath in his heart and hand to bestow upon us? Did we not with *Mary* choose this for our *Part, to sit at Christs feet and hear his word*? and do we now repent of our choice, and prefer the Honours, Pleasures and Profits of the world before it? *You did run well: who doth hinder you, that you should not obey the truth?* Gal.5.7.

Hath the Lord been wanting to us, or failed our expectation? Micah 6.3. *O my people, what have I done unto thee, and wherein have I wearied thee? testifie against me.* Jer. 2.5. *What iniquity have your fathers found in me, that they are gone far from me?* and *ver.*31. *O generation, see ye the word of the Lord: have I been a wilderness unto Israel? a land of darkness?* May not the Lord say unto us, as *Pharaoh* did to *Hadad*, 1 King.11. 22. *What hast thou lacked with me, that behold, thou seekest to go to thine own Country?* Nay, *what could have been done more*, than what the Lord hath done for us? Isa.5.4.

How sadly hath the Lord testified against us, because of our *loss* of our *first love*, and our *remissness* and negligence in his Work? Why hath the Lord smitten us with Blasting and Mildew now seven years together, superadding sometimes severe Drought, sometimes great Tempests, Floods, and sweeping Rains, that leave no food behinde them? Is it not because the Lords House lyeth waste? Temple-work in our Hearts, Families, Churches is shamefully neglected? What should I make mention of *Signes* in the Heavens and in the Earth, *Blazing-Stars, Earthquakes*, dreadful *Thunders* and *Lightnings*, fearful *Burnings*? What meaneth the heat of his great Anger, in calling home so many of his *Ambassadors*? In plucking such burning and shining *Lights* out of the Candlesticks; the principal *Stakes* out of our Hedges; the *Cornerstones* out of our Walls? In removing such faithful *Shepherds* from their Flocks, and breaking down our *defenced Cities, Iron Pillars*, and *Brazen-Walls*? Seemeth it a small thing unto us, that so many of Gods *Prophets* (whose Ministry we came into the Wilderness to enjoy) are taken from us in so short a time? Is it not a Sign that God is making a way for his *Wrath*, when he removes his *Chosen* out of the *Gap*? Doth he not threaten us with a *Famine* of the Word, the *Scattering* of the Flock, the *Breaking* of the Candlesticks, and the turning of the *Songs* of the Temple into *howlings*?

It is high time for us to *remember whence we are fallen, and repent, and do our first works.* Wherefore let us *lift up the hands that hang down, and strengthen the feeble knees, and make straight paths for our feet, lest that which is lame, be turned out of the way, but let it rather be healed,* Heb.12.12, 13. Labour we to redress our Faintings and Swervings, and address our selves to the Work of the Lord. Let us arise and build, and the Lord will be with us, and from this day will he bless us.

Alas, we are feeble and impotent; our hands are withered, and our strength dried up.

Remember the man that had a withered hand: Christ saith unto him, *Stretch forth thy hand; and he stretched it forth; and it was restored whole, like as the other,* Mat.12.13. How could he stretch forth his hand, when it was withered, the Blood and Spirits dried up, and the Nerves and Sinews shrunk up? The Almighty Power of Christ accompanying his Command, enabled the man to stretch forth his withered hand, and in stretching it forth, restored it whole, like as the other. Where the Soveraignty of Christ's Command takes place in the Conscience, there is effectual grace accompanying it to the healing of our Spiritual Feebleness and Impotency, and the enabling of us to perform the duty incumbent on us. Though we have no might, no strength, yet at Christ's Command, make an essay. Where the word of a King is, there is power.

But alas, our Bruise is incurable and our Wound grievous, there is none to repair the Breach, there is no healing Medicine.

The Lord Jesus, the great Physician of *Israel*, hath undertaken the Cure. *I will restore health unto thee, and I will heal thee of thy Wounds, saith the Lord,* Jer. 30.17. No case is to be accounted desperate or incurable, which Christ takes in hand. If he undertake to heal *Jairus* his daughter, he will have her *death* esteemed but a *sleep*, in reference to his power. *She is not dead, but sleepeth,* Mat. 9.24. When Christ came to *Lazarus* his grave, and bade them take away the stone, *Martha* saith, *Lord, by this time he stinketh; for he hath been dead four dayes*: But Christ answereth, *Said I not unto thee, that if thou wouldest believe, thou shouldest see the glory of God?* Joh. 11.40. Let us give glory to God by believing his word, and we shall have real and experimental manifestations of his *glory* for our good and comfort.

But alas, our hearts are sadly prejudiced against the Means and Instruments, by which we might expect that Christ should cure and heal us.

Were not the hearts of *John's Disciples* leavened with carnal emulation and prejudices against *Christ* himself? They would not own him to be the Messias, nor believe their Master's Testimony concerning him: insomuch that the Lord saw it necessary that *John* should decrease and be abased, that *Christ* might encrease and be exalted: and therefore suffered *Herod to shut up John* in Prison, and keep him in durance about twelve months, and at length to cut off his head, *that so these fondlings might be weaned from their Nurse*; and when *John* was dead, his Disciples resort to Jesus, acquaint him with the calamity that befell them, and were perfectly reconciled to him, passing into his school, and becoming his Disciples, *Mat. 14.12.*

But alas, the Times are difficult and perillous; the Wind is stormy, and the Sea tempestous; the Vessel heaves and sits, and tumbles up and down in the rough and boisterous waters, and is in danger to be swallowed up.

Well, remember that the *Lord sitteth upon the flood, yea the Lord sitteth King for ever*, Psal. 29.10. *His way is in the sea, and his path in the great waters, and his footsteps are not known*, Psal. 77.19. *He stilleth the noise of the seas, the noise of their waves, and the tumult of the people*, Psal. 65.7. He saith to the raging Sea, *Peace be still: and the Wind ceaseth, and there is a great calm*, Mark 4.39. Yea, he can enable his people to tread and walk upon the waters. To sail and swim in the waters, is an easie matter; but to walk upon the waters, as upon a pavement, is an act of wonder. *Peter* at Christ's call *came down out of the ship and walked on the water to go to Jesus*, Matth. 14.29. and as long as his Faith held, it upheld him from sinking; when his Faith failed, his body sunk: but he *cried to the Lord, and he stretched forth his hand and caught him, and said unto him, O thou of little faith, wherefore didst thou doubt?*

But what shall we do for bread? The encrease of the field and the labour of the Husbandman fails.

Hear Christ's answer to his Disciples, when they were troubled, because there was but one Loaf in the ship. *O ye of little faith, why reason ye, because you have no bread? perceive ye not yet, neither understand? have ye your heart yet hardened? having eyes, see ye not? and having ears, hear ye not, and do ye not remember?* Mark 8: 17, 18. Mat. 16. 8, 9. Those which have had large and plentiful experience of the grace and power of Christ in providing for their outward Sustenance, and relieving of their Necessities, when ordinary and usual Means have failed, are worthy to be severely reprehended, if afterward they grow anxiously careful and solicitous, because of the defect of outward supplies. In the whole Evangelicall History, I finde not that ever the Lord Jesus did so sharply rebuke his Disciples for anything, as for that fit and pang of Worldly care and solicitude about Bread. Attend we our Errand, upon which Christ sent us into the Wilderness, and he will provide Bread for us. Matth. 6.33. *Seek ye first the Kingdome of God, and his Righteousness, and all these things shall be added unto you.*

But we have many Adversaries, and they have their subtile Machinations and Contrivances, and how soon we may be surprized, we know not.

Our diligent Attention to the Ministry of the Gospel, is a special means, to check and restrain the rage and fury of Adversaries. The people's assiduity in attendance upon Christ's Ministry, was the great obstacle that hindred the execution of the bloody Counsels of the Pharisees. *Luke 19. 47, 48. He taught daily in the Temple, but the chief Priests and the Scribes, and the chief of the people, sought to destroy him, and could not finde what they might do: for all the people were very attentive to hear him.* If the people cleave to the Lord, to his Prophets, and to his Ordinances, it will strike such a fear into the hearts of enemies, that they will be at their wits ends, and not know what to do. However, In this way we have the promise of divine Protection, and Preservation. *Revel. 3. 10. Because thou hast kept the word of my Patience, I also will keep thee from the hour of Temptation, which shall come upon all the world, to try them that dwell upon the earth.* Let us with *Mary* choose this for our Portion, *To sit at Christ's feet and hear his word*; and whosoever complain against us, the Lord Jesus will stand for us, as he did for her, and say, *They have chosen that good part, which shall not be taken away from them*, Luk. 10.42. AMEN.

9. Deodat Lawson

A Brief and True Narrative 1692

This narrative marks the beginning of the famous witch hunt in Salem Village (now Danvers). It narrates the first three weeks of events, in February and March. Its publication, and the sermon Lawson preached on March 24, called Christ's Fidelity the Only Shield against Satan's Malignity, *spurred a more general crisis; the first hanging, in June, was followed by further trials and executions over the summer. Accounts of witches were not uncommon in New England, but the Salem crisis was something new: by the time royal governor Phips ordered a suspension of the trials in October, more than fifty people had, without interrogation, "confessed" to being witches. The Salem proceedings were also unusual for the theme—introduced by Lawson—of Satan's participation as the master conspirator. (For a criticism of the clergy's role, especially Cotton Mather's, see Robert Calef, in selection 10 below. Lawson's narrative should also be compared with Chamberlain's* Lithobolia, *in chapter 5, and Increase Mather's* Illustrious Providences, *in chapter 7.)*

Little is known of Deodat Lawson's life. He was the son of a Puritan minister who was ejected from his pulpit at the Restoration. By 1676 he was in New England; he served as minister to Salem Village and later to Scituate. In 1696, he returned to England, apparently for a visit, and never returned, leading his congregation eventually to replace him. He was still living in England in 1715, apparently back in the ministry.

THE BOOKSELLER TO THE READER.

The ensuing narrative being, a collection of some remarkables, in an affair now upon the stage, made by a credible eyewitness, is now offered unto the reader, only as a taste, of more that may follow in God's time. If the prayers of good people may obtain this favor of God, that the mysterious assaults from hell now made upon so many of our friends may be thoroughly detected and defeated, we suppose the curious will be entertained with as rare a history as perhaps an age has had; whereof this narrative is but a forerunner.

Benjamin Harris

On the nineteenth day of March last I went to Salem Village, and lodged at Nathaniel Ingersoll's near to the minister Mr. P's.[38] house, and presently, after I came into my lodging, Capt. Walcot's daughter Mary came to Lieutenant Ingersoll's and spake to me, but, suddenly after as she stood by the door, was bitten, so that she cried out of her wrist, and looking on it with a candle, we saw apparently the marks of teeth both upper and lower set, on each side of her wrist.

In the beginning of the evening, I went to give Mr. P. a visit. When I was there, his kinswoman, Abigail Williams (about 12 years of age), had a grievous fit; she was at first hurried with violence to and fro in the room (though Mrs. Ingersoll, endeavored to hold her), sometimes making as if she would fly, stretching up her arms as high as she could, and crying *Whist, whist, whist!* several times; presently after she said there was Goodwife N.[39] and said, *Do you not see her? Why there she stands!* And she said Goodwife N. offered her the book, but she was resolved she would not take it, saying often, *I wont, I wont, I wont, take it, I do not know what book it is: I am sure it is none of God's book, it is the devil's book, for ought I know.* After that, she run to the fire, and begun to throw firebrands, about the house; and run against the back, as if she would run up [the] chimney, and, as they said, she had attempted to go into the fire in other fits.

On Lord's day, the twentieth of March, there were sundry of the afflicted persons at meeting, as, Mrs. Pope, and Goodwife Bibber, Abigail Williams, Mary Walcot, Mary Lewis, and Doctor Griggs' maid. There was also at meeting, Goodwife C.[40] (who was afterward examined on suspicion of being a witch): They had several sore fits, in the time of public worship, which did something interrupt me in my first prayer; being so unusual. After psalm was sung, Abigail Williams said to me, *Now stand up, and name your text:* and after it was read, she said, *It is a long text.* In the beginning of sermon, Mrs. Pope, a woman afflicted said to me, *Now there is enough of that.* And in the afternoon, Abigail Williams, upon my referring to my doctrine said to me, *I know no doctrine you had, if you did name one, I have forgot it.*

In sermon time when Goodwife C. was present in the meetinghouse Abigail W. called out, *Look where Goodwife C. sits on the beam suckling her yellow bird betwixt her fingers!* Anne Putnam another girl afflicted said *there was a yellow bird sat on my hat as it hung on the pin in the pulpit:* but those that were by, restrained her from speaking loud about it.

On Monday the 21st of March, the magistrates of Salem appointed to come to examination of Goodwife C. And about twelve of the clock, they went into the meetinghouse, which was thronged with spectators: Mr. Noyes[41] began with a very pertinent and pathetical prayer; and Goodwife C. being called to answer to what was alleged against her, she desired to go to prayer, which was much wondered at, in the presence of so many hundred people: the magistrates told her, they would not admit it; they came not there to hear her pray, but to examine her, in what was alleged against her. The worshipful Mr. Hathorne[42] asked her, *Why she afflicted those children?* She

---

38. Samuel Parris.
39. Rebecca Nurse, seventy-one, mother of eight, later executed as a witch.
40. Martha Corey, later executed.
41. Nicholas Noyes. See chapter 5.
42. John Hathorne of Salem, ancestor of Nathaniel.

said she did not afflict them. He asked her, who did then? She said, *I do not know; how should I know?* The number of the afflicted persons were about that time ten, viz. four married women, Mrs. Pope, Mrs. Putnam, Goodwife Bibber, and an ancient woman, named Goodall, three maids, Mary Walcot, Mercy Lewis, at Thomas Putnam's, and a maid at Dr. Grigg's, there were about three girls from 9 to 12 years of age, each of them, or thereabouts, viz. Elizabeth Parris, Abigail Williams and Ann Putnam; these were most of them at Goodwife C's examination, and did vehemently accuse her in the assembly of afflicting them, by biting, pinching, strangling, etc. And that they did in their fit, see her likeness coming to them, and bringing a book to them, she said, she had no book; they affirmed, she had a yellow bird, that used to suck betwixt her fingers, and being asked about it, if she had any familiar spirit, that attended her, she said, *She had no familiarity with any such thing.* She was a gospel woman: which title she called herself by; and the afflicted persons told her, ah! *She was, a gospel witch.*

Ann Putnam did there affirm, that one day when Lieutenant Fuller was at prayer at her father's house, she saw the shape of Goodwife C. and she thought Goodwife N. praying at the same time to the devil, she was not sure it was Goodwife N. she thought it was; but very sure she saw the shape of Goodwife C. The said C. said, they were poor, distracted, children, and no heed to be given to what they said. Mr. Hathorne and Mr. Noyes replied, it was the judgment of all that were present, they were bewitched, and only she the accused person said, they were distracted.

It was observed several times, that if she did but bite her underlip in time of examination the persons afflicted were bitten on their arms and wrists and produced the marks before the magistrates, ministers and others. And being watched for that, if she did but pinch her fingers, or grasp one hand, hard in another, they were pinched and produced the marks before the magistrates, and spectators. After that, it was observed, that if she did but lean her breast, against the seat, in the meetinghouse (being the bar at which she stood), they were afflicted. Particularly Mrs. Pope complained of grievous torment in her bowels as if they were torn out. She vehemently accused said C. as the instrument, and first threw her muff at her; but that flying not home, she got off her shoe, and hit Goodwife C. on the head with it. After these postures were watched, if said C. did but stir her feet, they were afflicted in their feet, and stamped fearfully. The afflicted persons asked her why she did not go to the company of witches which were before the meetinghouse mustering? Did she not hear the drum beat. They accused her of having familiarity with the devil, in the time of examination, in the shape of a black man whispering in her ear; they affirmed, that her yellow bird, sucked betwixt her fingers in the assembly; and order being given to see if there were any sign, the girl that saw it, said, it was too late now; she had removed a pin, and put it on her head; which was found there sticking upright.

They told her, she had covenanted with the devil for ten years, six of them were gone, and four more to come. She was required by the magistrates to answer that question in the Catechism, *How many persons, be there in the God-Head?* She answered it but oddly, yet was there no great thing to be gathered from it; she denied all that was charged upon her, and said, *They could not prove a witch;* she was that afternoon committed to Salem Prison; and after she was in custody, she did not so appear to them, and afflict them as before.

On Wednesday the 23 of March, I went to Thomas Putnam's, on purpose to see his wife: I found her lying on the bed, having had a sore fit a little before. She spake to me, and said, she was glad to see me; her husband and she, both desired me to pray with her, while she was sensible; which I did, though the apparition said, *I should not go to prayer*. At the first beginning she attended; but after a little time, was taken with a fit: yet continued silent, and seemed to be asleep: when prayer was done, her husband going to her, found her in a fit; he took her off the bed, to set her on his knees; but at first she was so stiff, she could not be bended; but she afterwards set down; but quickly began to strive violently with her arms and legs; she then began to complain of, and as it were to converse personally with, Goodwife N., saying, *Goodwife N. be gone! Be gone! Be gone! are you not ashamed, a woman of your profession, to afflict a poor creature so? what hurt did I ever do you in my life! you have but two years to live, and then the devil will torment your soul, for this your name is blotted out of God's book, and it shall never be put in God's book again, be gone for shame, are you not afraid of that which is coming upon you? I know, I know, what will make you afraid; the wrath of an angry God, I am sure that will make you afraid; be gone, do not torment me, I know what you would have* (we judged she meant, her soul) *but it is out of your reach; it is clothed with the white robes of Christ's righteousness.* After this, she seemed to dispute with the apparition about a particular text of scripture. The apparition seemed to deny it (the woman's eyes being fast closed all this time); she said, *She was sure there was such a text*; and she would tell it; and then the shape would be gone, for said she, *I am sure you cannot stand before that text!* then she was sorely afflicted; her mouth drawn on one side, and her body strained for about a minute, and then said, *I will tell, I will tell; it is, it is, it is!* three or four times, and then was afflicted to hinder her from telling, at last she broke forth and said, *It is the third chapter of the Revelations.* I did something scruple the reading it, and did let my scruple appear, lest Satan should make any superstitious lie to improve the word of the eternal God. However, though not versed in these things, I judged I might do it this once for an experiment. I began to read, and before I had near read through the first verse, she opened her eyes, and was well; this fit continued near half an hour. Her husband and the spectators told me, she had often been so relieved by reading texts that she named, something pertinent to her case; as Isaiah 40:1, Isaiah 49:1, Isaiah 50:1, and several others.

On Thursday the twenty-fourth of March (being in course the lecture day, at the village), Goodwife N. was brought before the magistrates Mr. Hathorne and Mr. Corwin,[43] about ten of the clock, in the forenoon, to be examined in the meeting-house, the Rev. Mr. Hale[44] begun with prayer, and the warrant being read, she was required to give answer, *Why she afflicted those persons?* she pleaded her own innocency with earnestness. Thomas Putnam's wife, Abigail Williams and Thomas Putnam's daughter accused her that she appeared to them, and afflicted them in their fits: but some of the other[s] said, that they had seen her, but knew not that ever she had hurt them; amongst which was Mary Walcot, who was presently after she had so

---

43. Jonathan Corwin of Salem.   44. John Hale of Beverly, Massachusetts.

declared bitten, and cried out of her in the meetinghouse; producing the marks of teeth on her wrist. It was so disposed, that I had not leisure to attend the whole time of examination but both magistrates, and ministers, told me, that the things alleged, by the afflicted, and defences made by her, were much after the same manner, as the former was. And her motions, did produce like effects as to biting, pinching, bruising, tormenting, at their breasts, by her leaning, and when, bended back, were as if their backs was broken. The afflicted persons said, the black man, whispered to her in the assembly, and therefore she could not hear what the magistrates said unto her. They said also that she did then ride by the meetinghouse, behind the black man. Thomas Putnam's wife, had a grievous fit, in the time of examination, to the very great impairing of her strength, and wasting of her spirits, insomuch as she could hardly move hand, or foot, when she was carried out. Others also were there grievously afflicted, so that there was once such a hideous screech and noise (which I heard as I walked, at a little distance from the meetinghouse), as did amaze me, and some that were within, told me the whole assembly was struck with consternation, and they were afraid, that those that sat next to them, were under the influence of witchcraft. This woman also was that day committed to Salem Prison. The magistrates and ministers also did inform me, that they apprehended a child of Sarah G.[45] and examined it, being between 4 and 5 years of age and as to matter of fact, they did unanimously affirm, that when this child, did but cast its eye upon the afflicted persons, they were tormented, and they held her head, and yet so many as her eye could fix upon were afflicted. Which they did several times make careful observation of: the afflicted complained, they had often been bitten by this child, and produced the marks of a small set of teeth, accordingly, this was also committed to Salem Prison, the child looked hale, and well as other children. I saw it at Lieutenant Ingersoll's. After the commitment of Goodwife N. Thomas Putnam's wife was much better, and had no violent fits at all from that 24th of March, to the 5th of April. Some others also said they had not seen her so frequently appear to them, to hurt them.

On the 25th of March (as Captain Stephen Sewall, of Salem, did afterwards inform me), Elizabeth Parris had sore fits, at his house, which much troubled himself, and his wife, so as he told me they were almost discouraged. She related, that the great black man came to her, and told her, if she would be ruled by him, she should have, whatsoever she desired, and go to a golden city. She relating this to Mrs. Sewall, she told the child, it was the devil, and he was a *liar from the beginning*, and bid her tell him so, if he came again: which she did accordingly, at the next coming to her, in her fits.

On the 26th of March, Mr. Hathorne, Mr. Corwin, and Mr. Higginson,[46] were at the prison-keeper's house, to examine the child, and it told them there, it had a little snake that used to suck on the lowest joint of its forefinger; and when they inquired where, pointing to other places, it told them, not there, but there, pointing on the lowest point of the forefinger; where they observed, a deep red spot, about the bigness of a flea bite, they asked who gave it that snake? whether the great black man, it said no, its mother gave it.

---

45. Dorcas, daughter of Sarah Good, who was later executed.   46. John Higginson, Salem minister.

The 31st of March there was a public fast kept at Salem on account of these afflicted persons. And Abigail Williams said, that the witches had a sacrament that day at a house in the village, and that they had red bread and red drink. The first of April, Mercy Lewis, Thomas Putnam's maid, in her fit, said, they did eat red bread like man's flesh, and would have had her eat some: but she would not; but turned away her head, and spit at them, and said, *I will not eat, I will not drink, it is blood*, etc. She said, *That is not the bread of life, that is not the water of life; Christ gives the bread of life, I will have none of it*! This first of April also Mercy Lewis aforesaid saw in her fit a white man and was with him in a glorious place, which had no candles nor sun, yet was full of light and brightness; where was a great multitude in white glittering robes, and they sung the song in the fifth of Revelation the ninth verse, and the 110 Psalm, and the 149 Psalm; and said with herself, *How long shall I stay here! let me be along with you*: She was loath to leave this place, and grieved that she could tarry no longer. This white man hath appeared several times to some of them, and given them notice how long it should be before they had another fit, which was sometimes a day, or day and half, or more or less: it hath fallen out accordingly.

The third of April, the Lord's day, being sacrament day, at the village, Goodwife C. upon Mr. Parris's naming his text, John 6:70, *One of them is a Devil*, the said Goodwife C.[47] went immediately out of the meetinghouse, and flung the door after her violently, to the amazement of the congregation: She was afterward seen by some in their fits, who said, *O Goodwife C. I did not think to see you here*! (and being at their red bread and drink) said to her, *Is this a time to receive the sacrament, you ran away on the Lord's day, and scorned to receive it in the meetinghouse, and, is this a time to receive it? I wonder at you*! This is the sum of what I either saw myself, or did receive information from persons of undoubted reputation and credit.

Remarks of things more than ordinary about the afflicted persons.

1. They are in their fits tempted to be witches, are showed the list of the names of others, and are tortured, because they will not yield to subscribe, or meddle with, or touch the Book, and are promised to have present relief if they would do it.

2. They did in the assembly mutually cure each other, even with a touch of their hand, when strangled, and otherwise tortured; and would endeavor to get to their afflicted, to relieve them.

3. They did also foretell when another's fit was a-coming, and would say, *Look to her*! she will have a fit presently, which fell out accordingly, as many can bear witness, that heard and saw it.

4. That at the same time, when the accused person was present, the afflicted persons saw her likeness in other places of the meetinghouse, suckling her familiar, sometimes in one place and posture, and sometimes in another.

5. That their motions in their fits are preternatural, both as to the manner, which is so strange as a well person could not screw their body into; and as to the violence also it is preternatural being much beyond the ordinary force of the same person when they are in their right mind.

47. Sarah Cloyse, sister of Rebecca Nurse, later executed.

6. The eyes of some of them in their fits are exceeding fast closed, and if you ask a question they can give no answer, and I do believe they cannot hear at that time, yet do they plainly converse with the appearances, as if they did discourse with real persons.

7. They are utterly pressed against any person's praying with them, and told by the appearances, they shall not go to prayer, so Thomas Putnam's wife was told, *I should not pray*; but she said, *I should*: and after I had done, reasoned with the appearance, *Did not I say he should go to prayer.*

8. The aforementioned Mary W. being a little better at ease, the afflicted persons said, *She had signed the book*; and that was the reason she was better. Told me by Edward Putnam.

Remarks concerning the accused.

1. For introduction to the discovery of those that afflicted them, it is reported Mr. Parris's Indian man, and woman,[48] made a cake of rye meal, and the children's water, baked it in the ashes, and gave it to a dog, since which they have discovered, and seen particular persons hurting of them.

2. In time of examination, they seemed little affected, though all the spectators were much grieved to see it.

3. Natural actions in them produced preternatural actions in the afflicted, so that they are their own image without any poppets of wax or otherwise.

4. That they are accused to have a company about 23 or 24 and they did muster in arms, as it seemed to the afflicted persons.

5. Since they were confined, the persons have not been so much afflicted with their appearing to them, biting or pinching of them etc.

6. They are reported by the afflicted persons to keep days of fast and days of thanksgiving, and sacraments; Satan endeavors to transform himself to an angel of light, and to make his kingdom and administrations to resemble those of our Lord Jesus Christ.

7. Satan rages principally amongst the visible subjects of Christ's kingdom and makes use (at least in appearance) of some of them to afflict others; that Christ's kingdom may be divided against itself, and so be weakened.

8. Several things used in England at trial of witches, to the number of 14 or 15 which are wont to pass instead of, or in concurrence with witnesses, at least 6 or 7 of them are found in these accused: see Keble's Statutes.[49]

9. Some of the most solid afflicted persons do affirm the same things concerning seeing the accused out of their fits as well as in them.

10. The witches had a fast, and told one of the afflicted girls, she must not eat, because it was fast day, she said, she would: they told her they would choke her then; which when she did eat, was endeavored.

---

48. Indian man, and woman: Indian here means West Indian. The woman is Tituba, a slave, one of the first women arrested. The two slaves are attempting countermagic, like the pot of urine in *Lithobolia*.

49. Keble's Statutes: Joseph Keble, *An Assistance to Justices of the Peace* (London, 1683).

10. Robert Calef

from *More Wonders of the Invisible World* 1700

In 1693, after the Salem trials were over, a new case sprang up around a girl named Margaret Rule. She received two visits from Robert Calef (1647?–1719), who wrote a manuscript account of what went on in the house. A new controversy ensued, with Cotton Mather denouncing Calef for libel. Calef eventually worked up a compendious book of documents and skeptical reflections on the witchcraft episode. Its title, More Wonders of the Invisible World, *echoed* Wonders of the Invisible World, *the work that Cotton Mather published at the height of the trials, when opinion was in danger of swaying against the clergy and the judges. Mather, anxious and enraged about Calef's manuscript, made sure that no printer in Massachusetts would publish it; the book had to be published in London, where it appeared in 1700. Calef, who presents himself as an objective enquirer, prints both his original account of the visit with Margaret Rule and Mather's reply to that account. About Calef very little is known. A clothier by trade, he left England for America by 1688. In 1707 he moved to Roxbury, where he died in 1719.*

A Letter to Mr. C. M.

Boston, Jan. 11th, 1694.

Mr. Cotton Mather,

R everend Sir, I finding it needful on many accounts, I here present you with the Copy of that Paper, which has been so much Misrepresented, to the End that what shall be found defective or not fairly Represented, if any such shall appear, they may be set right, which Runs thus.

September the 13th, 1693.

In the Evening when the Sun was withdrawn, giving place to Darkness to succeed, I with some others were drawn by curiosity to see Margaret Rule, and so much the rather because it was reported Mr. M——— would be there that Night. Being come to her Fathers House into the Chamber wherein she was in Bed, [I] found her of a healthy countenance of about seventeen Years Old, lying very still, and speaking very little, what she did say seem'd as if she were Lightheaded. Then Mr. M———, Father and Son,[50] came up and others with them, in the whole were about 30 or 40 Persons;

---

50. Increase and Cotton Mather.

they being sat, the Father on a Stool, and the Son upon the Bedside by her, the Son began to question her, Margaret Rule, how do you do? then a pause without any answer. *Question.* What, do there a great many Witches sit upon you? *Answer.* Yes. Q. Do you not know that there is a hard Master? Then she was in a Fit; He laid his hand upon her Face and Nose, but, as he said, without perceiving Breath; then he brush'd her on the Face with his Glove, and rubb'd her Stomach (her breast not covered with the Bed-cloaths) and bid others do so too, and said it eased her, then she revived. Q. Don't you know there is a hard Master? A. Yes. *Reply*; Don't serve that hard Master, you know who. Q. Do you believe? Then again she was in a Fit, and he again rub'd her Breast, etc. (about this time Margaret Perd an attendant assisted him in rubbing of her. The Afflicted spake angerly to her saying don't you meddle with me, and hastily put away her hand) he wrought his Fingers before her Eyes and asked her if she saw the Witches? A. No. Q. Do you believe? A. Yes. Q. Do you believe in you know who? A. Yes. Q. Would you have other people do so too, to believe in you know who? A. Yes. Q. Who is it that Afflicts you? A. I know not, there is a great many of them (about this time the Father question'd if she knew the Spectres? An attendant said, if she did she would not tell; The Son proceeded) Q. You have seen the Black-man, hant you? A. No. *Reply*; I hope you never shall. Q. You have had a Book offered you, hant you? A. No. Q. The brushing of you gives you ease, don't it? A. Yes. She turn'd her selfe and a little Groan'd. Q. Now the Witches Scratch you and Pinch you, and Bite you, don't they? A. Yes. Then he put his hand upon her Breast and Belly, *viz.* on the Cloaths over her, and felt a Living thing, as he said, which moved the Father also to feel, and some others; Q. Don't you feel the Live thing in the Bed? A. No. *Reply*, that is only Fancie. Q. the great company of People increase your Torment, don't they? A. Yes. The People about were desired to withdraw. One Woman said, I am sure I am no Witch, I will not go; so others, so none withdrew. Q. Shall we go to Prayers? Then she lay in a Fit as before. But this time to revive her, they waved a Hat and brushed her Head and Pillow therewith. Q. Shall we go to *Pray*, etc. Spelling the Word. A. Yes. The Father went to Prayer for perhaps half an Hour, chiefly against the Power of the Devil and Witchcraft, and that God would bring out the Afflicters: during Prayer-time, the Son stood by, and when they thought she was in a Fit, rub'd her and brush'd her as before, and beckned to others to do the like; after Prayer he proceeded; Q. You did not hear when we were at Prayer, did you? A. Yes. Q. You don't hear always, you dont hear sometimes past a Word or two, do you? A. No. Then turning him about said, this is just another Mercy Short:[51] Margaret Perd reply'd, she was not like her in her Fits. Q. What does she eat or drink? A. Not eat at all; but drink Rum. Then he admonished the young People to take warning, etc. Saying it was a sad thing to be so Tormented by the Devil and his Instruments. A Young-man present in the habit of a Seaman, reply'd this is the Devil all over. Then the Ministers withdrew. Soon after they were gon the Afflicted desired the Women to be gone, saying, that the Company of the Men was not offensive to her, and having hold of the hand of a Young-man, said to have been

---

51. Mercy Short: subject of Mather's *A Brand Pluck'd out of the Burning.*

her Sweet-heart formerly, who was withdrawing; She pull'd him again into his Seat, saying he should not go to Night.

SEPTEMBER THE 19TH, 1693.

This Night I renew'd my Visit, and found her rather of a fresher Countenance than before, about eight Persons present with her, she was in a Fit Screeming and making a Noise: Three or four Persons rub'd and brush'd her with their hands, they said that the brushing did put them away, if they brush'd or rub'd in the right place; therefore they brush'd and rub'd in several places, and said that when they did it in the right place she could fetch her Breath, and by that they knew. She being come to her self was soon in a merry talking Fit. A Young-man came in and ask'd her how she did? She answered very bad, but at present a little better; he soon told her he must be gon and bid her good Night, at which she seem'd troubled, saying, that she liked his Company, and said she would not have him go till she was well; adding, for I shall Die when you are gon. Then she complained they did not put her on a clean Cap, but let her ly so like a Beast, saying, she should lose her Fellows. She said she wondered any People should be so Wicked as to think she was not Afflicted, but to think she Dissembled. A Young-woman answered Yes, if they were to see you in this merry Fit, they would say you Dissembled indeed; She reply'd, Mr. M——— said this was her laughing time, she must laugh now: She said Mr. M——— had been there this Evening, and she enquired, how long he had been gon? She said, he stay'd alone with her in the room half an Hour, and said that he told her there were some that came for Spies, and to report about Town that she was not Afflicted. That during the said time she had no Fit, that he asked her if she knew how many times he had Prayed for her to Day? And that she answered that she could not tell; and that he replyed he had Prayed for her Nine times to Day; the Attendants said that she was sometimes in a Fit that none could open her Joynts, and that there came an Old Iron-jaw'd Woman and try'd, but could not do it; they likewise said, that her Head could not be moved from the Pillow; I try'd to move her head, and found no more difficulty than another Bodies (and so did others) but was not willing to offend by lifting it up, one being reproved for endeavouring it, they saying angrily you will break her Neck; The Attendants said Mr. M——— would not go to Prayer with her when People were in the Room, as they did one Night, that Night he felt the Live Creature. Margaret Perd and another said they smelt Brimstone; I and others said we did not smell any; then they said they did not know what it was: This Margaret said, she wish'd she had been here when Mr. M——— was here, another Attendant said, if you had been here you might not have been permitted in, for her own Mother was not suffered to be present.

[MATHER REPLIES]

BOSTON, January the 15th, 1694.

Mr. R. C.

Whereas you intimate your desires, that what's not fairly, (I take it for granted you mean truly also,) represented in a Paper you lately sent me, containing a pretended Narrative of a Visit by my Father and self to an Afflicted Young woman, whom we apprehended to be under a Diabolical Possession, might be rectified: I have this to say, as I have often already said, that I do scarcely find any one thing in the whole Paper, whether respecting my Father or self, either fairly or truly represented. Nor can I think that any that know my Parents Circumstances, but must think him deserving a better Character by far, than this Narrative can be thought to give him. When the main design we managed in Visiting the poor Afflicted Creature, was to prevent the Accusations of the Neighbourhood, can it be fairly represented that our design was to draw out such Accusations, which is the representation of the Paper? We have Testimonies of the best Witnesses and in Number not a few, That when we asked Rule whether she thought she knew who Tormented her? the Question was but an Introduction to the Solemn charges which we then largely gave, that she should rather Dye than tell the Names of any whom she might Imagine that she knew. Your Informers have reported the Question, and report nothing of what follows, as essential to the giving of that Question: And can this be termed a piece of fairness? Fair it cannot be, that when Ministers Faithfully and Carefully discharge their Duty to the Miserable in their Flock, little bits, scraps and shreds of their Discourses should be tackt together to make them contemtible, when there shall be no notice of all the Necessary, Seasonable, and Profitable things that occur'd, in those Discourses; And without which, the occasion of the lesser Passages cannot be understood; And yet I am furnished with abundant Evidences, ready to be Sworn, that will possitively prove this part of unfairness, by the above mention'd Narrative, to be done both to my Father and self. Again, it seems not fair or reasonable that I should be expos'd, for which your self (not to say some others) might have expos'd me for, if I had not done, *Viz.* for discouraging so much Company from flocking about the Possest Maid, and yet, as I perswade my self, you cannot but think it to be good advice, to keep much Company from such haunted Chambers; besides the unfairness doth more appear, in that I find nothing repeated of what I said about the advantage, which the Devil takes from too much Observation and Curiosity.

In that several of the Questions in the Paper are so Worded, as to carry in them a presupposal of the things inquired after, to say the best of it is very unfair: But this is not all, the Narrative contains a number of Mistakes and Falshoods; which were they willful and design'd, might justly be termed gross Lies. The representations are far from true, when 'tis affirm'd my Father and self being come into the Room, I began the Discourse; I hope I understand breeding a little better than so: For proof of this, did occasion serve, sundry can depose the contrary.

'Tis no less untrue, that either my Father or self put the Question, how many Witches sit upon you? We always cautiously avoided that expression; It being contrary to our inward belief: All the standers by will (I believe) Swear they did not hear us use it (your Witnesses excepted) and I tremble to think how hardy those woful Creatures must be, to call the Almighty by an Oath, to so false a thing. As false a representation 'tis, that I rub'd Rule's Stomach, her Breast not being covered. The Oath of the nearest Spectators, giving a true account of that matter will prove this to be little less than a gross (if not a doubled) Lie; and to be somewhat plainer, it carries the Face of a Lie contrived on purpose (by them at least, to whom you are beholden for the Narrative) Wickedly and Basely to expose me. For you cannot but know how much this Representation hath contributed, to make People believe a Smutty thing of me; I am far from thinking, but that in your own Conscience you believe, that no indecent Action of that Nature could then be done by me before such observers, had I been so Wicked as to have been inclin'd to what is Base. It looks next to impossible that a reparation should be made me for the wrong done to, I hope, as to any Scandal, an unblemish'd, tho' weak and small Servant of the Church of God.

Nor is what follows a less untruth, that 'twas an Attendant and not my self who said, if Rule knows who Afflicts her, yet she wont tell. I therefore spoke it that I might incourage her to continue in that concealment of all Names whatsoever; to this I am able to furnish my self with the Attestation of Sufficient Oaths. 'Tis as far from true, that my apprehension of the Imp, about Rule, was on her Belly, for the Oaths of the Spectators, and even of those that thought they felt it, can testify that 'twas upon the Pillow, at a distance from her Body. As untrue a Representation is that which follows, Viz. That it was said unto her, that her not Apprehending of that odd palpable, tho' not visible, Mover was from her Fancy, for I endeavoured to perswade her that it might be but Fancy in others, that there was any such thing at all. Witnesses every way sufficient can be produced for this also.

'Tis falsely represented that my Father felt on the Young-woman after the appearance mentioned, for his hand was never near her; Oath can sufficiently vindicate him. 'Tis very untrue that my Father Prayed for perhaps half an Hour, against the power of the Devil and Witchcraft, and that God would bring out the Afflictors. Witnesses of the best Credit, can depose, that his Prayer was not a quarter of an Hour, and that there was no more than about one clause towards the close of the Prayer, which was of this import; And this clause also was guarded with a singular wariness and modesty, Viz. If there were any evil Instruments in this matter God would please to discover them: And that there was more than common reason for that Petition I can satisfie any one that will please to Inquire of me. And strange it is, that a Gentleman that from 18 to 54 hath been an Exemplary Minister of the Gospel; and that besides a station in the Church of God, as considerable as any that his own Country can afford, hath for divers years come off with Honour, in his Application to three Crown'd Heads, and the chiefest Nobility of three Kingdoms, Knows not yet how to make one short Prayer of a quarter of an hour, but in New-England he must be Libell'd for it.

There are divers other down-right mistakes, which you have permitted your self, I would hope not knowingly, and with a Malicious design, to be receiver or Compiler of, which I shall now forbear to Animadvert upon. As for the Appendix of the Narrative I do find myself therein Injuriously treated, for the utmost of your proof for what you say of me, amounts to little more than, viz. Some People told you, that others told them, that such and such things did pass, but you may assure yourself, that

I am not unfurnish'd with Witnesses, that can convict the same. Whereas you would give me to believe the bottom of these your Methods, to be some dissatisfaction about the commonly receiv'd Power of Devils and Witches: I do not only with all freedom offer you the use of any part of my Library, which you may see cause to peruse on that Subject, but also if you and any else, whom you please, will visit me at my Study, yea, or meet me at any other place, less inconvenient than those by you propos'd; I will with all the fairness and calmness in the World dispute the point.

I beg of God that he would bestow as many Blessings on you, as ever on myself, and out of a sincere wish, that you may be made yet more capable of these Blessings, I take this occasion to lay before you the faults (not few nor small ones neither) which the Paper contained, you lately sent me in order to be Examined by me. In case you want a true and full Narrative of my Visit, whereof such an indecent Travesty (to say the best) hath been made, I am not unwilling to communicate it, in mean time must take liberty to say, 'Tis scarcely consistent with Common Civility, much less Christian Charity, to offer the Narrative, now with you, for a true one, till you have a truer, or for a full one, till you have a fuller. Your Sincere (tho Injur'd) Friend and Servant,

C. Mather.

Chapter 7

Science in America: The Seventeenth Century

INTRODUCTION

The development of modern thought in connection with colonization has been a recurrent theme in these introductions, and this connection is particularly evident in the emergence of modern science. If by science one generally understands not only a kind of knowledge but also a way of knowing, both parts of this definition changed fundamentally over the course of the period surveyed in this volume. This change is evident, for instance, in the transformation, over the course of the sixteenth century, in the character of maps. In the fifteenth century, at the start of the age of colonization, a map was not necessarily an accurate rendition of geographical fact. A *mappa-mundi*, or world map, offered an understanding of geography, rather than its exact representation. Theory took precedence over observation. For example, should observation of an area of the globe yield a proportion of land to water that contradicted a cartographer's idea of the world, he might well sketch in an island he thought must exist although no one had actually seen it. For this medieval map-maker, knowledge was a matter of concepts more than of facts. Of course, he did not invent the outlines of the continents or the directions of rivers; he strove to represent the landscape as accurately as he knew it. But accuracy was not as important to him as what he thought of as truth, which descended from geographical and cosmic laws that prevailed no matter what he observed with his limited powers of sight and measurement.

In the sixteenth century, a different kind of map gradually took precedence as sea travel ventured further and further out of sight of any coast. These maps, called portolans or charts, were sketched by sailors and continuously revised to incorporate new information. Portolans had existed earlier but had been considered merely instruments of navigation, while the *mappae-mundi* projected the true nature of the universe. Now, not only seamen but those to whom the seamen reported the stories of their voyages began to picture the globe as it was sketched in the portolans. Mercator's invention of a way to project curved longitudes and latitudes onto a two-dimensional chart sealed the transfer of authority over representations of the world from theory to empirical reality.

This shift of authority signaled a general shift in the basic definition of knowledge, so that it became a matter first of empirical data: an accumulation of observed and verifiable facts. By the late sixteenth and seventeenth centuries, science was based on measurement and experimentation. Francis Bacon, whose interest in colonization illustrates the connection between imperial enterprise and the development of modern

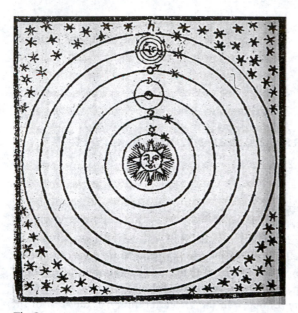

The Copernican system, 1675

science (see his "Of Planta-tions" in chapter 2), is often assigned the role of having codified this new scientific philosophy. Broadly, its estab-lishment was the work of the Royal Society, founded in 1660 but in existence as a group of scholars at least twenty years earlier. One of the first actions of the Royal Society as an institution "for Improving Natural Knowl-edge" was to name two cura-tors of experimentation, one of whom helped Robert Boyle construct his famous air-pump. (The French Académie des Sciences, organized at the end of the seventeenth century, was less exclusively dedicated to experimentation and French science characteristically gave more weight to theory. Until the eighteenth century, the Royal Society was the primary influence on science in the English colonies.)

The new science was a science of practice and also a practical science, whose close relation to actuality was not only a matter of philosophy but of politics. The Royal Society was dedicated to national service, which involved it in building not just the air-pump but the empire. Like the Renaissance mathematician Thomas Hariot who became involved in the fate of the Virginia colony, Boyle was deeply interested in New England, and, out of this engagement, drew up a set of categories for gathering infor-mation to be followed by any exploration party anywhere in the world. Nothing better represents the intrinsic character of seventeenth-century science and its relation to the times than his outline of an empirical investigation that will both increase the sum of knowledge about the world and enable its more efficient colonization. Boyle's "heads" project the list of sciences related to the colonial enterprise: astronomy, navi-gation, cartography, anthropology, natural science (botany, zoology, and minerology).

Two sciences, medicine and linguistics, are left out or invisibly subsumed, perhaps because they require more participation than Boyle envisions for a first survey. But for actually settling foreign territories, medicine and linguistics were essential branches of knowledge and, like the others, through the experience of colonization, became highly experimental. How this worked out in medicine is easy to imagine (the controversy over small-pox innoculation makes it clear), but what it meant for the study of language may be less evident. In fact, the use of language and theories of language changed from the fifteenth to the seventeenth centuries in ways that paralleled contemporary transformations in the conception of knowledge. At the start of the period, language was viewed as a repository of tradition and presumptive reason.

Latin was the language of educated people, connecting their views to transcendent principles. Hobbes, however, denounced metaphorical language as breeding passion and confusion, and Bishop Thomas Sprat, in his 1667 *History of the Royal Society of London,* proposed "a close, naked, natural way of speaking; positive expressions; clear senses, a native easiness; bringing all things as near the mathematical planness" as can be. But plain English took longer to assert itself than objective measurement. When Bacon expanded his *Advancement of Learning* in 1623, he also translated its title into Latin: *De dignitate et augmentis scientiarum.* Newton published the *Principia* in Latin in 1687 and not until 1704—or almost a century after the appearance of the King James Bible—did he publish his *Opticks* in English.

During the seventeenth century, through the new scientific methods applied in conjunction with expanding explorations, Europeans acquired a far more reliable and enabling account of the globe. At the same time, some reports from the field revealed that empirical science, precisely through its reliance on observation, was surprisingly vulnerable to imaginative projections. The careful reports of John Josselyn about the New World's remarkable flora and fauna, and of Increase Mather about some extraordinary events observed in colonial New England, suggest that fact and fantasy can be difficult to distinguish.

M.J.

Suggested readings: The scientific revolution of the seventeenth century has a large literature. Marie Boas, *The Scientific Renaissance, 1450–1630,* offers an overview, as does Alfred Rupert Hall in *From Galileo to Newton.* Treatments of its American manifestation are scattered in these and other works. Perry Miller devotes a chapter of *The New England Mind: From Colony to Province,* "The Experimental Philosophy," to Puritan science, and Daniel J. Boorstin in parts 8 and 9 of *The Americans: The Colonial Experience,* "New World Medicine" and "The Limits of American Science," also looks back to the seventeenth century.

1. John Wilkins

from *A Voyage of Discovery to the Moon* 1638

John Wilkins (1614–72) presided over the meeting of English natural philosophers which decided in 1660 to propose to the King the foundation of a national scientific society. Wilkins became one of its two secretaries. He had earned his membership in the inner circles of English natural philosophy by organizing a group of scientists (which included Robert Boyle) at Wadham, the Oxford college of which he was warden.

The Discovery of a World in the Moon, whose preface is reproduced here, was his first published work. Its rationalism is the more sharply outlined for being applied to the proof of a proposition we now know to be false. But a greater interest lies in the lesson Wilkins draws from the discovery of the New World, that one should never rule out a possibility just because it seems improbable: the universe which opened to admit the new continents remains for him open forever.

That the strangenesse of this opinion is no sufficient reason why it should be rejected, because other certaine truths have beene formerly esteemed ridiculous, and great absurdities entertayned by common consent.

How did the incredulous World gaze at *Columbus* when hee promised to discover another part of the earth, and he could not for a long time by his confidence, or arguments, induce any of the Christian Princes, either to assent unto his opinion, or goe to the charges of an experiment! Now if he who had such good grounds for his assertion, could find no better entertainement among the wiser sort, and upper end of the World; 'tis not likely then that this opinion which I now deliver, shall receive any thing from the men of these daies, especially our vulgar wits, but misbeliefe or derision.

It hath alwaies beene the unhappinesse of new truths in Philosophy, to be derided by those that are ignorant of the causes of things, and rejected by others whose perversenesse ties them to the contrary opinion, men whose envious pride will not allow any new thing for truth which they themselves were not the first inventors of. So that I may justly expect to be accused of a pragmaticall ignorance, and bold ostentation, especially since for this opinion *Xenophanes*,[1] a man whose authority was able to adde some credit to his assertion, could not escape the like censure from others. For *Natales Comes* speaking of that Philosopher, and this his opinion, saith thus: "Some there are who, lest they might seeme to know nothing, will bring up monstrous absurdities in Philosophy, that so afterward they may bee famed for the invention of some-

---

1. *Xenophanes*: Greek philosopher of the sixth century.

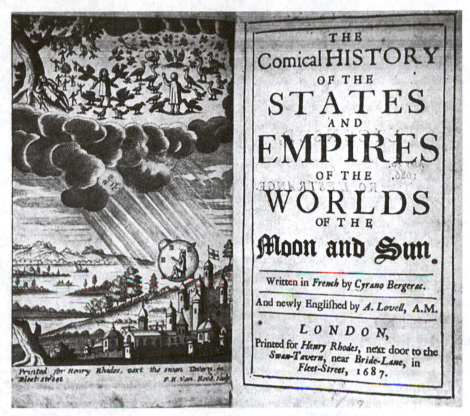

THE
Comical HISTORY
OF THE
STATES
AND
EMPIRES
OF THE
WORLDS
OF THE
𝕸𝖔𝖔𝖓 𝖆𝖓𝖉 𝕾𝖚𝖓.

Written in *French* by *Cyrano Bergerac*.

And newly Englished by *A. Lovell*, A.M.

LONDON,
Printed for *Henry Rhodes*, next door to the
Swan-Tavern, near *Bride-Lane*, in
Fleet-Street, 1 6 8 7.

Frontispiece depicting Cyrano de Bergerac's voyage to the moon, from a 1687 English translation.

what." The same author doth also in another place accuse *Anaxagoras*[2] of folly for the same opinion: "'Tis none of the worst kindes of folly, boldly to affirme one side or other, when a man knows not what to say."

If these men were thus censur'd, I may justly then expect to be derided by most, and to be believed by few or none; especially since this opinion seemes to carry in it so much strangenesse, so much contradiction to the generall consent of others. But however, I am resolved that this shall not be any discouragement, since I know that it is not the common opinion of others that can either adde or detract from the truth. For:

1. Other truths have beene formerly esteemed altogether as ridiculous as this can be.

2. Grosse absurdities have beene entertained by generall opinion. I shall give an instance of each, that so I may the better prepare the Reader to consider things without a prejudice, when hee shall see that the common opposition against this which I affirme cannot any way derogate from its truth.

Other truths have beene formerly accounted as ridiculous as this; I shall specifie that of the Antipodes,[3] which have beene denied and laught at by many wise men and

---

2. *Anaxagoras*: Greek philosopher of the fifth century B.C. .   3. Antipodes: people on the opposite side of the Earth.

great Scholers, such as were *Herodotus*,[4] *St. Austin*,[5] the *Lactantius*,[6] the *Venerable Bede*,[7] *Lucretius* the Poet,[8] *Procopius*,[9] and the voluminous *Abulensis* with others. *Herodotus* counted it so horrible an absurdity, that hee could not forbeare laughing to thinke of it. "I cannot choose but laugh," saith he, "to see so many men venture to describe the earth's compasse, relating those things that are without all sense, as that the Sea flowes about the World, and that the earth it selfe is round as an Orbe."

But this great ignorance is not so much to be admired[10] in him, as in those learneder men of later times, when all sciences began to flourish in the World. Such was Saint *Austin* who censures that relation of the Antipodes to be an incredible fable, and with him agrees the eloquent *Lactantius*. "What," saith he, "are they that thinke there are Antipodes, such as walke with their feet against ours? Doe they speake any likely-hood? Or is there any one so foolish as to believe that there are men whose heeles are higher than their heads? That things which with us do lie on the ground doe hang there? That the Plants and Trees grow downewards, that the haile, and raine, and snow fall upwards to the earth? And doe wee admire the hanging Orchards[11] amongst the seven wonders, whereas here the Philosophers have made the Field and Seas, the Cities and Mountaines hanging? What shall wee thinke," saith hee in *Plutarch*,[12] "that men doe clyng to that place like wormes, or hang by their clawes as Cats, or if wee suppose a man a little beyond the Center, to bee digging with a spade? Is it likely (as it must bee according to this opinion) that the earth which hee loosened, should of it selfe ascend upwards? Or else suppose two men with their middles about the center, the feete of the one being placed where the head of the other is, and so two other men crosse them, yet all these men thus situated according to this opinion should stand upright, and many other such grosse consequences would follow," saith he, "which a false imagination is not able to fancy as possible."

2. Roger Williams

from *A Key into the Language of America* 1643

> Upon arriving in Boston in 1631, Roger Williams (1603–83) was offered a post as minister but refused it because the congregation was not separatist, meaning it did not belong to the group of Puritans who rejected all relations with existing churches. When in 1636 he helped found the colony of Providence on the principle of religious toleration, he had not altered his initial belief in separatist Puritanism.

4. *Herodotus*: Greek historian of the fifth century B.C., often called the "father of history."
5. *St. Austin*: St. Augustine.
6. the *Lactantius*: Latin rhetorician of the third century.
7. the *Venerable Bede*: Anglo-Saxon historian of the seventh and eighth centuries.

8. *Lucretius* the Poet: Latin poet of the first century B.C.
9. *Procopius*: Byzantine historian of the fifth century.
10. admired: marveled at.
11. hanging Orchards: hanging gardens of Babylon.
12. *Plutarch*: Greek biographer of the first century.

*On the contrary, from this belief he deduced a principle of strict separation of
church and state, according to which the state has no right to dictate the personal
convictions or practices of its citizens. The same principle inspired his assertion
that Christians could not morally claim Indian land since the heathen had the same
secular rights as the saved.*

*His interest in native languages and cultures, almost unique among his fellow-
Puritans, flowed from his conviction that, although fatally mistaken about the laws
of heaven, on earth the Indians were men like the Christians. The Key is rare in its
attempt to understand the Indian point of view. It is an instrument of conversation
as well as of conversion. Beginning in the introduction, in which he matches the
names the English give the native Americans with the names they give themselves,
Williams represents relations with the Indians as a dialogue. Colonization, he
believed, should proceed through land purchases and treaties. Still, when the
Pequot Indians resisted being forced from their lands and began to organize other
tribes to do likewise in 1636–37, Williams helped negotiate a treaty between the
English and the Pequots' main ally, the Narragansetts, thus isolating the Pequots
who were exterminated shortly thereafter.*

*A Puritan who maintained the right of Christians to conduct their religious lives
without interference from others, but was for himself utterly uncompromising; an
English colonist and founder of a colony who wanted to treat fairly with the
Indians but intervened against them when they threatened the colonial enterprise;
Roger Williams is exceptionally interesting for the ways he and his career articu-
lated contradictions in Puritan colonization silenced elsewhere, as in William
Bradford's* History, *in chapter 3.*

To my Deare and Welbeloved Friends and Countrey-men, in old and new England

I Present you with a *Key*; I have not heard of the like, yet framed, since it pleased
God to bring that mighty *Continent* of *America* to light: Others of my Country-
men have often, and excellently, and lately written of the *Countrey* (and none that
I know beyond the goodnesse and worth of it.)

This *Key*, respects the *Native Language* of it, and happily may unlocke some
Rarities concerning the *Natives* themselves, not yet discovered.

[To begin with, their names]

First, those of the *English* giving: as *Natives, Salvages, Indians, Wild-men,* (so the
Dutch call them *Wilden) Abergeny men, Pagans, Barbarians, Heathen.*

Secondly, their *Names,* which they give themselves.

I cannot observe, that they ever had (before the comming of the *English, French* or
Dutch amongst them) any *Names* to difference *themselves* from strangers, for they
knew none; but two sorts of *names* they had, and have amongst *themselves.*

First, *generall,* belonging to all *Natives,* as *Ninnuock, Ninnimissinnêwock,
Eniskeetompaéwog,* which signifies *Men, Folke,* or *People.*

Secondly, particular *names,* peculiar to severall *Nations* of them amongst *themselves,* as, *Nanhigganéuck, Massachusêuck, Cawasumsêuck, Cowwesêuck, Quinti-
kéock, Qunnipiêuck, Pequttêog,* etc.

They have often asked mee, why wee call them *Indians, Natives, etc.* And understanding the reason, they will call themselves *Indians*, in opposition to *English*, etc.

[CHAPTER I: OF SALUTATION]

OBSERVATION.

The Natives are of two sorts, (as the English are.) Some more Rude and Clownish, who are not so apt to Salute, but upon *Salutation* resalute lovingly. Others, and the generall, are *sober* and *grave*, and yet chearfull in a meane, and as ready to begin a Salutation as to Resalute, which yet the English generally begin, out of desire to Civilize them.

What cheare Nétop? *is the generall salutation of all English toward them.* Nétop *is friend.*

Netompauog.	*Friends.*

They are exceedingly delighted with Salutations in their own Language.

Neèn, Keèn, Ewò.	*I, you, he.*
Keén ka neen.	*You and I.*
Asco wequássin,	
Asco wequassunnúmmis.	*Good morrow.*
Askuttaaquompsìn?	*How doe you?*
Asnpaumpmaûntam.	*I am very well.*
Taubot paumpmaúntaman.	*I am glad you are well.*
Cowaúnckamish.	*My service to you.*

OBSERVATION.

Acawmenóakit, *Old England*, which is as much as *from the Land on t'other side*: hardly are they brought to believe that that Water is three thousand English mile over, or thereabouts.

Tunnock kuttòme?	*Whither goe you?*
Wékick nittóme.	*To the house.*
Nékick.	*To my house.*
Kékick.	*To your house.*
Tuckowêkin?	*Where dwell you?*
Tuckuttîin?	*Where keep you?*
Matnowetuómeno.	*I have no house.*

OBSERVATION.

Obscure and meane persons amongst them have no Names: *Nullius numeri, &c.* as the Lord Jesus foretells his followers, that their Names should be cast out, *Luk. 6. 22.* as not worthy to be named, *&c.* Againe, because they abhorre to name the dead (Death being the King of Terrours to all naturall men: and though the Natives hold the Soule to live ever, yet not holding a Resurrection, they die, and mourn without Hope.) In that respect I say, if any of their *Sáchims* or neighbours die who were of their names, they lay down those Names as dead.

Nowánnehick nowésuonck.   *I have forgot my Name.*

Which is common amongst some of them, this being one Incivilitie amongst the more rusticall sort, not to call each other by their Names, but Keen, *You*, Ewò, *He, etc.*

Tahéna?	*What is his name?*
Tahossowêtam?	*What is the name of it?*
Tahéttamen?	*What call you this?*
Teáqua?	*What is this?*
Yò néepoush.	*Stay* or *stand here.*
Máttapsh.	*Sit down.*
Noónshem, Nonànum.	*I cannot.*
Tawhitch kuppeeyaúmen?	*What come you for?*
Téaqua kunnaúntamen?	*What doe you fetch?*
Chenock cuppeeyâumis?	*When came you?*
Maish, kitummâyi.	*Just, even now.*
Kitummâyi nippeéam.	*I came just now.*
Yò Commíttamus?	*Is this your Wife?*
Yo cuppáppoos?	*Is this your Child?*
Yó cummúckquachucks?	*Is this your Son?*
Yò cuttaûnis?	*Is this your Daughter?*
Wunnêtu.	*It is a fine Child.*
Tawhitch neepouweéyean?	*Why stand you?*
Pucqúatchick.	*Without dores.*
Tawhítch mat petiteáyean?	*Why come you not in?*
Kukkowêtous.	*I will lodge with you.*
Yò Cówish.	*Do, lodge here.*
Hawúnshech.	*Farewell.*
Chénock wonck cuppeeyeâumen?	*When will you be here againe?*
Nétop tattà.	*My friend I can not tell.*

From these courteous *Salutations* Observe in generall: There is a savour of *civility* and *courtesie* even amongst these wild *Americans*, both amongst *themselves* and towards *strangers*.

More particular:

1. *The Courteous* Pagan *shall condemne*
   Uncourteous Englishmen,
   Who live like Foxes, Beares and Wolves,
   Or Lyon in his Den.

2. *Let none sing* blessings *to their soules,*
   For that they Courteous are:
   The wild Barbarians *with no more*
   Then Nature, goe so farre:

3. *If Natures Sons both* wild *and* tame,
   Humane and Courteous be:
   How ill becomes it Sonnes of God
   To want Humanity?

3. John Josselyn

from *Two Voyages to New England* 1674

John Josselyn's (1610?–92) descriptions of his travels in New England on two occasions, in 1639 and then from 1663 to 1671, offer the most extensive natural history of the region. Josselyn sought to be scientifically accurate, intending his reports for the Royal Society. They are carefully factual, replete with dates, numbers, and measurements, and despite their sometimes fantastic flights, they offer an invaluable glimpse at a landscape and an ecology that was rapidly disappearing as a result of colonial expansion. They also make good reading, infused as they are with the excitement of continually fresh discoveries. Josselyn was a poet of some accomplishment, and his vivid descriptions display considerable literary talent.

[FROM THE *FIRST VOYAGE*: A VISIT TO BOSTON AND ENVIRONS]

Having refreshed myself for a day or two upon *Noddles-Island*,[13] I crossed the Bay in a small boat to *Boston,* which then was rather a Village, than a Town, there being not above Twenty or thirty houses; and presenting my respects to Mr. *Winthorpe* the Governour, and to Mr. *Cotton* the Teacher of *Boston* Church, to whom I delivered from Mr. *Francis Quarles* the poet, the Translation of the 16, 25, 51, 88, 113, and 137. Psalms into *English* Meeter, for his approbation, being civilly treated by all I had occasion to converse with, I returned in the Evening to my lodging.

The Twelfth day of *July,* after I had taken my leave of Mr. *Maverick,* and some other Gentlemen, I took Boat for the Eastern parts of the Countrie, and arrived at *Black point* in the Province of *Main,* which is 150 miles from *Boston,* the Fourteenth day, which makes my voyage 11 weeks and odd dayes.

The Countrey all along as I sailed, being no other than a meer Wilderness, here and there by the Sea-side a few scattered plantations, with as few houses.

About the Tenth of *August,* I hapned to walk into the Woods, not far from the Sea-side, and falling upon a piece of ground over-grown with bushes, called there black Currence, but differing from our Gardent Currence, they being ripe and hanging in

---

13. *Noddles-Island*: East Boston.

lovely bunches; I set up my piece against a stately Oakes, with a resolution to fill my belly, being near half a mile from the house; of a sudden I heard a hollow thumping noise upon the Rocks approaching towards me, which made me presently to recover my piece, which I had no sooner cock'd, than a great and grim over-grown she-Wolf appears, at whom I shot, and finding her Gor-belly stuft with flesh newly taken in, I began presently to suspect that she had fallen foul upon our Goats, which were then valued (our she Goats) at Five pound a Goat; Therefore to make further discovery, I descended (it being low water) upon the Sea sands, with an intent to walk round about a neck of land where the Goats usually kept. I had not gone far before I found the footing of two Wolves, and one Goat betwixt them, whom they had driven into a hollow, betwixt two Rocks, hither I followed their footing, and perceiving by the Crowes, that there was the place of slaughter, I hung my piece upon my back, and upon all four clambered up to the top of the Rock, where I made ready my piece and shot at the dog Wolf, who was feeding upon the remainder of the Goat, which was only the fore shoulders, head and horns, the rest being devoured by the she-Wolf, even to the very hair of the Goat; and it is very observable, that when the Wolves have kill'd a Beast, or a Hog, not a Dog-Wolf amongst them offers to eat any of it, till the she-Wolves have filled their paunches.

The Twenty-fourth of *September,* being Munday about 4 of the clock in the afternoon, a fearful storm of wind began to rage, called a *Hurricane. It is an impetuous wind that goes commonly about the Compass in the space of 24 hours,* it began from the W.N.W. and continued till next morning, the greatest mischief it did us, was the wracking of our Shallop, and the blowing down of many tall Trees, in some places a mile together.

December the Tenth, happened an Eclipse of the Moon at 8 of the clock at night, it continued till after 11 as near as we could guess; in old *England* it began after midnight, and continued till 4 of *the clock in the morning; if Seamen would make observation of the time, either of the beginning or ending of the Eclipse, or total darkness of the Sun and Moon in all places where they happen to be, and confer their observations to some Artist, hereby this longitude of all places might be certainly known, which are now very uncertainly reported to us.*

1639. *May,* which fell out to be extream hot and foggie, about the middle of *May* I kill'd within a stones throw of our house, above four score Snakes, some of them as big as the small of my leg, black of colour, and three yards long, with sharp horn on the tip of their tail two inches in length.

June the Six and twentieth day, very stormie, Lightning and Thunder. I heard now two of the greatest and fearfullest thunderclaps that ever were heard, I am confident. At this time we had some neighboring Gentlemen in our house who came to welcome me into the Countrey; where amongst variety of discourse they told me of a young Lyon (not long before) kill'd at *Piscataway* by an *Indian,* of a *Sea-Serpent* or *Snake,* that lay quoiled up like a Cable upon a Rock at *Cape-Ann;* a Boat passing by with *English* aboard, and two *Indians,* they would have shot the *Serpent,* but the *Indians* diswaded them, saying, that if he were not kill'd outright, they would be all in danger of their lives.

One Mr. *Mittin* related of a *Triton* or *Merman*,[14] which he saw in *Cascobay*, the Gentleman was a great Fouler, and used to goe out with a small Boat or Canow, and fetching a compass about a small Island, (there being many small Islands in the Bay) for the advantage of a shot, was encountred with a *Triton*, who laying his hands upon the side of the Canow, had one of them chopt off with a Hatchet by Mr. *Mittin*, which was in all respects like the hand of a man, the *Triton* presently sunk, dying the water with his purple blood, and was no more seen. The next story was told by Mr. *Foxwell*, now living in the province of *Main*, who having been to the Eastward in a Shallop, as far as *Cape-Ann* a Waggon in his return was overtaken by the night, and fearing to land upon the barbarous shore, he put off a little further to Sea; about midnight they were wakened with a loud voice from the shore, calling upon *Foxwell*, *Foxwell*, come a shore, two or three times: upon the Sands they saw a great fire, and Men and Women hand in hand dancing round about it in a ring, after an hour or two they vanished, and as soon as the day appeared, *Foxwell* puts into a small *Cove*, it being about three quarters floud, and traces along the shore, where he found the footing of Men, Women and Children shod with shoos; and an infinite number of brand-ends thrown up by the water, but neither *Indian* nor *English* could he meet with on the shore, nor in the woods; these with many other stories they told me, the credit whereof I will neither impeach nor inforce, but shall satisfie my self, and I hope the Reader hereof, with the saying of a wise, learned and honourable Knight, *That there are many stranger things in the world, than are to be seen between* London *and* Stanes.

September the Sixth day, one Mr. *John Hickford* the Son of Mr. *Hickford* a Linnen-Draper in *Cheapside*, having been sometime in the province of *Main*, and now determined to return for *England*, sold and kill'd his stock of Cattle and Hoggs, one great Sow he had which he made great account of, but being very fat, and not suspecting that she was with pig, he caused her to be kill'd, and they found 25 pigs within her belly; verifying the old proverb, As fruitful as a white sow. And now we were told of a sow in *Virginia* that brought forth six pigs; their fore-parts Lyons, their hinder-parts hogs. *I have read that at* Bruxels, *Anno 1564. a sow brought forth six pigs, the first whereof (for the last in generating is always in bruit beasts the first brought forth) had the head, face, arms and legs of a man, but the whole trunck of the body from the neck, was of a swine, a sodomitical monster is more like the mother than the father in the organs of the vegetative soul.*

The Three and twentieth, I left *Black-point*, and came to *Richmonds* Island about three leagues to the Eastward, where Mr. *Tralanie* kept a fishing, Mr. *John Winter* a grave and discreet man was his Agent, and imployer of 60 men upon that design.

The Four and twentieth day being *Munday*, I went aboard the *Fellowship* of 100 and 70 Tuns a Flemish bottom, the Master *George Luxon* of *Bittiford* in *Devonshire*, several of my friends came to bid me farewell, among the rest Captain *Thomas Wannerton* who drank to me a pint of kill-devil *alias* Rhum at a draught, at 6 of the clock in the morning we weighed Anchor and set sail for the *Massachusetts-bay*.

14. *Triton* or *Merman*: a sea creature whose human body ends in a fish tail.

The Seven and twentieth day being *Friday,* we Anchored in the afternoon in the *Massachusetts-bay* before *Boston.* Next day I went aboard of Mr. *Hinderson,* Master of a ship of 500 Tuns, and Captain *Jackson* in the *Queen of Bohemia* a privateer, and from thence I went ashore to *Boston,* where I refreshed myself at an Ordinary. Next morning I was invited to a fisherman's house somewhat lower within the *Bay,* and was there by his wife presented with a handful of small Pearl, but none of them bored nor orient. From thence I crost the Bay to *Charles-town,* where at one *Longs* Ordinary I met with Captain *Jackson* and others, walking on the back side we spied a rattle Snake a yard and half long, and as thick in the middle as the small of a man's leg, on the belly yellow, her back spotted with black, russet, yellow and green, placed like scales, at her tail she had a rattle which is nothing but a hollow shelly bussiness joynted, look how many years old she is, so many rattles she hath in her

Josselyn's drawing of jewel weed.

tail, her neck seemed to be no bigger than one Thumb; yet she swallowed a live Chicken, as big as one they give 4 pence for in *England,* presently as we were looking on. In the afternoon I returne to our Ship, being no sooner aboard but we had the sight of an *Indian*-Pinnace sailing by us made of *Birch-bark,* sewed together with the roots of *spruse* and white *Cedar* (drawn out into threads) with a deck, and trimmed with sails top and top gallant very sumptuously.

The Thirtieth day of *September,* I went ashore upon *Noddles*-Islands, where when I was come to Mr. *Mavericks* he would let me go aboard no more, until the Ship was ready to set sail; the next day a grave and sober person described the Monster to me, that was born at *Boston* of one Mrs. *Dyer* a great Sectarie, *the Nine and twentieth of June, it was (it should seem) without a head, but having horns like a Beast, and ears, and scales on a rough skin like a fish called a* Thornback, *legs and claws like a* Hawke, *and in other respects as a Woman-Child.*

[FROM THE SECOND VOYAGE: NEW ENGLAND'S BEASTS OF THE EARTH]

What would you say, if I should tell you that in *Green-land* there are *Does* that have as large horns as *Bucks,* their brow Antlers growing downwards beyond their *Musles,* and broad at the end wherewith they scrape away the snow to the grass, it being impossible for them otherwayes to live in those cold Countries; the head of one of these *Does* was sometime since nailed upon a sign-post in *Charter-house-lane,* and these following verses written upon a board underneath it.

> *Like a* Bucks-*head I stand in open view,*
> *And yet am none; nay, wonder not, 'tis true;*
> *The living Beast that these fair horns did owe*
> *Well known to many, was a* Green-land Doe.
> *The proberb old is here fulfill'd in me,*
> *That every like is not the same you see.*

And for their height since I came into *England* I have read Dr. *Scroderns* his Chymical dispensatory by Dr. *Rowland* where he writes *that when he lived in* Finland *under* Gustavus Horns, *he saw an* Elke, *that was killed and presented to* Gustavus *his Mother, seventeen spans high.* Law you now Sirs of the Gibing crue, if you have any skill in mensuration, tell me what difference there is between Seventeen spans and twelve foot. There are certain transcendentia in every Creature, which are the indelible Characters of God, and which Discover God; There a prudential for you, as *John Rhodes* the Fisherman used to say to his mate, *Kitt Lux.* But to go on with the *Moose;* they are accounted a kind of Deer, and have three *Calves* at a time, which they hide a mile asunder too, as other Deer do, their skins make excellent Coats for Martial men, their sinews which are as big as a man's finger are of perdurable toughness and much used by the *Indians,* the bone that growes upon their heart is an excellent Cordial, their bloud is as thick as an *Asses* or *Bulls* who have the thickest bloud of all others, a man the thinnest. To what age they live I know not, certainly a long time in their proper climate. *Some particular living Creatures cannot live in every particular place or region, especially with the same joy and felicity as it did where it was first bred, for the certain agreement of nature that is between the place and the thing bred in that place: As appeareth by* Elephants, *which being translated or brought out of the Second or Third Climate, though they may live, yet will they never ingender or bring forth young.* So for plants, Birds, &c. Of both these Creatures, some few there are have been brought into *England,* but did not long continue. Sir *R. Baker* in his Chronicle tells us of an *Elephant* in *Henry* the Thirds Raign, which he saith was the first that was ever seen there, which as it seems is an error, unless he restrain it to the *Norman's* time. For Mr. *Speed* writeth that *Claudius Drusus* Emperour of *Rome* brought in the first in his Army; the bones of which digg'd up since are taken for Gyants bones. As for the *Moose* the first that was seen in *England,* was in King

Charles the First Raign; thus much for these magnals amongst the Creatures of God to be wondered at, the next beast to be mentioned is

The *Marouse,* which is somewhat like a *Moose,* but his horns are but small, and himself about the size of a *Stag,* these are the Deer that the flat-footed *Wolves* hunt after.

The *Maccarib* is a Creature not found that ever I heard yet, but upon *Cape-Sable* near to the *French* plantations.

The *Bear* when he goes to mate is a terrible Creature, they bring forth their Cubs in *March,* hunted with doggs they take a Tree where they shoot them, when he is fat he is excellent Venison, which is in *Acorn* time, and in winter, but then there is none dares to attempt to kill him but the *Indian.* He makes his Denn amongst thick Bushes, thrusting here and there store of *Moss,* which being covered with snow and melting in the day time with heat of the Sun, in the night is frozen into a thick coat of Ice; the mouth of his Den is very narrow, here they lye single, never two in a Den all winter. The *Indian* as soon as he finds them, creeps in upon all four, seizes him to the mouth of the Den, where with a club or small hatchet in his right hand he knocks out his brains before he can open his eyes to see his enemy. But sometimes they are too quick for the *Indians,* as one amongst them called black *Robin* lighting upon a male-*Bear* had a piece of his buttock torn off before he could fetch his blow: their grease is very soveraign. One Mr. *Purchase* cured himself of the *Sciatica* with *Bears-grease,* keeping some of it continually in his groine. It is good too for swell'd Cheeks upon cold, for Rupture of the hands in winter, for limbs taken suddenly with *Sciatica, Gout,* or other diseases that cannot stand upright nor go, bed-rid; it must be well chaft in, and the same cloth laid on still; it prevents the shedding of the hair occasioned by the coldness of winters weather; and the yard[15] of a *Bear* which as a *Doggs* or *Foxes* is bonie, is good for to expell Gravel out of the kidneys and bladder, as I was there told by one Mr. *Abraham Philater* a *Jersey-man.*

[THE RETURN]

Now by the merciful providence of the Almighty, having perform'd Two voyages to the North-east parts of the Western-world, I am safely arrived in my Native Countrey; having in part made good the *French* proverb, Travail where thou canst, but dye where thou oughtest, that is, in thine own Countrey.

15. yard: penis.

4. Increase Mather

from *Essay for the Recording of Remarkable Providences*[16] 1684

The Mathers were so powerful in Puritan and New England history that the historian Moses Coit Tyler dubbed them the Mather Dynasty. Increase Mather (1639–1723) was the middle member of the dynasty, son of Richard Mather and father of Cotton Mather. All three represent Puritan orthodoxy, old New England, and principled resistance against the trend to secularism in thought and behavior. It is no paradox to add that Increase Mather and his son Cotton Mather were among the most enlightened natural philosophers of their time, and that in the history of early colonial science, they are among the most important figures.

For Increase Mather as he assembled his Remarkable Providences, *the study of the laws of nature is the study of divine reason. Like any empirical scientist, Mather gathered facts, but he took them as evidence of a transcendent mind. At the same time, trusting to that transcendent mind, Mather was perhaps more prone to accept what he himself could not fully explain than would be a less religious observer. But even when he abandoned strict facticity, within the realm of religious mystery, he still strove for scientific rationality. An instance in the selection here reprinted is his declaration that the devil causes thunderstorms. Many deny this but "An orthodox & rational Man may be of the Opinion" that the devil can fabricate lightning as well as nature can. That phrase is the key to Mather's scientific stance: he is both orthodox and rational.*

There were limits to the alliance Mather forged between orthodoxy and rationality, as his ambivalent participation in the witch trials shows. The mechanism in Remarkable Providences *by which known facts are brought to testify to the existence of the unknown and indeed unknowable, seems to have worked in that case, if not to prove witchcraft, at least to prevent its disproving. The following selection, the fourth chapter of Mather's work, may recall Richard Chamberlain's* Lithobolia *(see chapter 5) and Robert Calef's account of the case of Margaret Rule in his* More Wonders of the Invisible World *(see chapter 6).*

Some Philosophical Meditations. Concerning Antipathies and Sympathies. Of the Loadstone. Of the Nature and Wonderful Effects of Lightning. That Thunder-Storms are often caused by Satan; and sometimes by good Angels. Thunder is the Voice of God, and therefore to be dreaded. All Places in the habitable World are subject to it more or less. No Amulets can preserve men from being hurt thereby. The miserable estate of

---

16. *Providences*: instances of benevolent divine intervention; the foreknowing and beneficent care and government of God.

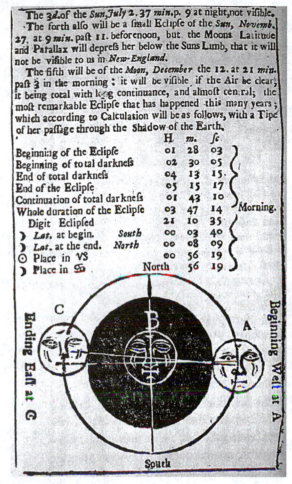

The 3*d.* of the *Sun, July* 2. 37 *min.* p. 9 at night, not visible.
The forth also will be a small Eclipse of the *Sun, Novemb.* 27. at 9 *min.* past 11. before noon, but the Moons Latitude and Parallax will depress her below the Suns Limb, that it will not be visible to us in *New-England.*

The fifth will be of the *Moon, December* the 12. at 21 *min.* past 3 in the morning : it will be visible, if the Air be clear, it being total with long continuance, and almost central; the most remarkable Eclipse that has happened this many years ; which according to Calculation will be as follows, with a Type of her passage through the Shadow of the Earth.

	H.	m.	sc.	
Beginning of the Eclipse	01	28	03	}
Beginning of total darkness	02	30	05	
End of total darkness	04	13	15.	
End of the Eclipse	05	15	17	
Continuation of total darkness	01	43	10	
Whole duration of the Eclipse	03	47	14	} *Morning.*
Digit Eclipsed	21	10	35	
☽ *Lat.* at begin. *South*	00	03	40	
☽ *Lat.* at the end. *North*	00	08	09	}
☉ Place in ♑	00	56	19	
☽ Place in ♋ *North*	56	19		

Diagram of an eclipse, 1703.

Wicked Men upon this account, and the happiness of the Righteous, who may be above all disquieting fears, with respect unto such terrible Accidents.*

Having thus far Related many *Remarkable Providences*, which have hapned in these goings down of the Sun; and some of the particulars, (especially in the last Chapter) being Tragical Stories: The Reader must give me leave upon this occasion a little to divert and re-create my mind, with some Philosophical Meditations; and to conclude with a Theological Improvement thereof. There are Wonders in the Works of Creation as well as Providence, the reason where-of the most knowing amongst Mortals, are not able to comprehend. *Dost thou know the ballancings of the Clouds, the wondrous works of him who is perfect in knowledge?*

I have not yet seen any who give a satisfactory reason of those strange Fountains in *New Spain*, which Ebb and Flow with the Sea, though far from it; and which fall in Rainy Weather, and rise in dry; or concerning that Pit near St. *Bartholmew's* into which if one cast a stone though never so small, it makes a noise as great and terrible as a clap of Thunder. It is no difficult thing to produce a World of Instances, concerning which the usual Answer is, an *occult* Quality is the cause of this strange operation, which is only a Fig-leaf whereby our common Philosophers seek to hide their own ignorance. Nor may we (with *Erastus*) deny that there are marvelous *Sympathies* and *Antipathies* in the natures of things. We know that the Horse does abominate the Camel; the mighty Elephant is afraid of a Mouse: And they say that the Lion, who scorneth to turn his back upon the stoutest Animal, will tremble at the Crowing of a Cock.

Some Men also have strange *Antipathies* in their natures against that sort of Food which others love and live upon. I have read of one that could not endure to eat either

Bread or Flesh. Of another that fell into a Swoonding fit at the smell of a Rose. Others would do the like at the smell of Vineger, or at the sight of an Eel or a Frog. There was a Man that if he did hear the sound of a Bell, he would immediately die away. Another if he did happen to hear any one sweeping a Room, an inexpressible horror would sieze upon him. Another if he heard one whetting a Knife his Gumms would fall a bleeding. Another was not able to behold a Knife that had a sharp point, without being in a strange agony. *Quercetus* speaketh of one that died as he was sitting at the Table, only because an Apple was brought into his sight. There are some who if a Cat accidentally come into the Room, though they neither see it, nor are told of it, will presently be in a Sweat and ready to die away. There was lately one living in *Stow-Market*, that when ever it Thundred would fall into a violent Vomiting, and so continue until the Thunder-storm was over. A Woman had such an *Antipathy* against Cheese that if she did but eat a piece of Bread, cut with a Knife, which a little before had cut Cheese, it would cause a *Deliquium*,[17] yet the same Woman when she was with Child delighted in no meat so much as in Cheese. There was lately (I know not but that he may be living still) a Man that if Pork, or any thing made of Swines flesh were brought into the room, he would fall into a convulsive *Sardonian Laughter*; nor can he for his heart leave as long as that object is before him, so that if it should not be removed, he would certainly laugh himself to death.

It is evident that the peculiar *Antipathies* of some persons are caused by the imaginations of their Parents. There was one that would fall into a *Syncope* if either a Calves-head or a Cabbage were brought near him. There were *navi materni*[18] upon the *Hypocondria*[19] of this person, on his right side there was the form of a Calves head, on his left side a Cabbage imprinted there by the Imagination of his Longing Mother. Most Wonderful is that which *Libavius* and others report, concerning a Man that would be surprized with a *Lipothymy*[20] at the sight of his own Son; nay, upon his approaching near unto him, though he saw him not, for which some assigned this reason, that the Mother when she was with Child, used to feed upon such Meats as were abominable to the Father (concerning the rationality of this conjecture see St. *Kenelm Digby*'s discourse of Bodies, P. 499, 410.) but others said that the Midwife who brought him into the World was a Witch.

Nor are the *Sympathies* in Nature less Wonderful than the *Antipathies*. There is a mutual Friendship between the *Olive tree* and the *Myrtle*. There is a certain Stone called *Pantarbe* which draws Gold unto it. So does the *Adamas* hairs and twigs. The *Sympathy* between the *Load-stone* and *Iron*, which do mutually attract each other, is admirable. There is no Philosopher but Speaketh of this. Some have published whole Treatises (both profitable and pleasant) upon this Argument; In special *Gilbert, Ward, Cabeus, Kepler*, and of late *Kircherus*. I know many Fabulous things have been related concerning the Load-stone by inexperienced Philosophers, and so believed by many others, E. G. that *Onions*, or *Garlick*, or *Ointments* will cause it to lose its vertue. *Johnston*, (and from him Dr. *Browns* in his vulgar Errors) hath truly asserted the contrary. Every one knoweth that the head of a Needle touched therewith will

17. *Deliquium*: failure of the vital powers.
18. *navi materni*: a kind of turnip.
19. *Hypocondria*: part of the abdomen supposed to be the seat of melancholy.
20. *Lipothymy*: fainting, swooning.

continue pointing towards the North Pole: so that the *Magnet* leaveth an impression of its own nature and vertue upon the Needle, causing it to stand pointed as the *Magnet* itself doth. The Loadstone it self is the hardest Iron; and it is a thing known that such Mines are naturally so (notwithstanding the Report of one who saith, that lately in *Devonshire*, Loadstones were found otherwise) posited in the Earth. Just under the Line the Needle lieth Parallel with the Horizon, but Sailing North or South it begins to incline and increase according as it approacheth to either Pole, and would at last endeavour to erect it self, whence some ascribe these strange effects to the North Star, which they suppose to be very magnetical. There is reason to believe that the Earth is the great *Magnet*. Hence (as Mr. *Seller* observes) when a Bar of Iron has stood long in a Window, that end of it which is next to the Earth will have the same vertue which the Load-stone it self has. Some place the first Meridian at the *Azores*, because there the Needle varies not: but the like is to be said of some other parts of the World; yea under the very same Meridian in divers Latitudes there is a great varia- tion as to the pointing of the Needle. *It is affirmed, that between the shore of* Ireland, France, Spain, Guiny, *and the* Azores, *the North point varies towards the East, as some part of the* Azores *it deflecteth not. On the other side of the* Azores, *and this side of the* Equator, *the North point of the Needle wheeleth to the West; so that in the* Lat. 36. *near the shore, the variation is about* 11 gr. *but on the other side of the* Æquator *it is quite otherwise, for in* Brasilía *the South point varies* 12 gr. *unto the West, but Elongating from the Coast of* Brasilia *toward the Shore of* Africa *it varies Eastward, and arriving at the* Cape Delas Aquilas, *it rests in the Meridian and looketh neither way.* Dr. Brown *in* Psudodoxia Epidemica P. 63. *does rationally suppose that the cause of this variation may be the inequality of the Earth variously disposed, and indiffer- ently mixed with the* Sea. *The Needle driveth that way where the greater and most powerful part of the Earth is placed. For whereas on this side of the Isles of* Azores *the Needle varies Eastward, it may be occasioned by that vast Tract, viz.* Europe, Asia *and* Africa, *seated towards the East, and disposing the Needle that way. Sailing further it veers its lilly to the West, and regards that quarter wherein the Land is nearer or greater; and in the same Latitude, as it approacheth the shore augmenteth its variation. Hence at* Rome *there is a less variation (viz. but five degrees) than at* London, *for on the west side of* Rome *are seated the great Continents of* France, Spain, Germany; *but unto* England *there is almost no Earth West, but the whole extent of* Europe *and* Asia *lies Eastward, and therefore at* London *the variation is* 11 Degrees. *Thus also, by reason of the great Continent of* Brasilia, *the Needle deflects towards the Land* 12 Degrees: *but at the Straits of* Magellan, *where the Land is narrowed, and the Sea on the other side, it varies but* 5 or 6. *So because the Cape of* De las Agullas *hath Sea on both sides near it, and other Land remote, and as it were equidistant from it, the Needle conforms to the Meridian. In certain Creeks and Vallies it proveth irregular; the reason whereof may be some vigorous part of the Earth not far distant.* Thus D. *Brown*, whose arguings seem rational.

Some have truly observed of *Crocus Martis* or Steel corroded with Vineger, Sulphur, or otherwise, and after reverberated by Fire, that the Load-stone will not at all attract it: nor will it adhere, but ly therein like Sand. It is likewise certain, that the fire will cause the Load-stone to lose its vertue, inasmuch as its Bituminous Spirits are thereby evaporated. *Porta* (Lib.7. Cap. 7.) saith that he did to his great admiration see a Sulphurous flame brake out of the Load-stone which being dissipated, the Stone lost its attractive vertue. Moreover, the Load-stone by being put into the fire may be caused quite to change its polarity. The truly Noble and Honourable *Robert Boyle*[21] Esq, many of whose excellent Observations and experiments have been advantagious, not only to the *English* Nation but to the Learned World; in his Book of the Usefulness of Experimental, Natural Philosophy, *Page* 15. hath these words; *Taking an Oblong Load-stone, and beating it red hot, I found the attractive faculty in not many minutes, either altogether abolisht, or at least so impaired and weakened, that I was scarce if at all able to discern it. But this hath been observed, though not so faithfully related, by more than one; wherefore I shall add, That by Refrigerating this red hot Load-stone either North or South, I found that I could give its extreams a Polarity (if I may so speak) which they would readily display upon an excited Needle freely placed in æquilibrium: And not only so, but I could by refrigerating the same end, sometimes North, and sometimes South, in a very short time change the Poles of the Load-stone at pleasure, making that which was a quarter of an hour before the North Pole, become the South; and on the contrary, the formerly southern Pole become the northern. And this change was wrought on the Load-stone, not only by cooling it directly North and South, but by cooling it perpendicularly: that end of it which was continuous to the Ground growing the Northern Pole, and so* (according to the Laws Magnetical) *drawing to it the South end; and that which was remotest from the contrary one: As if indeed the Terrestial Globe were as some* Magnetic Philosophers *have supposed it, but a great* Magnet, *since its* effluviums *are able in some cases to impart a magnetic faculty to the Load-stone it self*, Thus far Mr. *Boyle.*

Also D. *Brown* shews, that if we erect a red hot Wire until it cool, then hang it up with Wax and untwisted Silk where the lower end and that which cooled next the Earth does rest, that is the Northern point. And if a Wire be heated only at one end, according as the end is cooled upwards or downwards, it respectively requires a verticity. He also observes, if a Load-stone be made red hot in the fire, it amits the magnetical vigor it had before, and acquireth another from the Earth, in its refrigeration, for that part which cooleth next the Earth will acquire the respect of the North; the experiment whereof he made in a Load-stone of parallelogram or long square figure, wherein only inverting the extreams as it came out of the fire, he altered the Poles or faces thereof at pleasure. Unto some such reason as this, must the wonderful change occasioned by the Lightning in the Compasses of Mr. *Lad*'s Vessel be ascribed: probably the heat of the Lightning caused the Needle to lose its vertue, and the Compass in the Bidikle might stand pointed to the South, and that unhung in the Locker to the West, when they grew cold again, and accordingly continue pointing so ever after.

There is also that which is very mysterious and beyond humane Capacity to comprehend, in Thunder and Lightning. *The Thunder of his Power, who can understand?* Also, *Can any understand the spreadings of the Clouds, or the noise of his Tabernacle?* Hence *Elihu* said (some Interpreters think there was a Thunder-storm at

---

21. *Robert Boyle*: see selection 5 below.

the very instant when those words were spoken) in *Job* 37.5. *He Thundreth marveils.*
It is indeed manifest that these wonderful Meteors are generated out of a Nitrous and
Sulphurous Matter. Hence it is commonly out of dark and thick Clouds that Hail and
coals of Fire break forth, *Psal.* 18. 11, 12. The Scent which the Lightning useth to
leave behind it, in places where it falls, is a sufficient evidence of its being of a
Sulphurous nature. Nay the persons (as well as places) smitten there with have sometimes smelt strong of Brimstone. Two years ago there was a Ship riding at Anchor in a
place in *France*, and a furious Tempest suddenly arising, the Main-Mast was split in
pieces with a Clap of Thunder; the Pendant on the top of the Main-Top-Mast was
burnt to Ashes, twelve Men were beat upon the Deck, five of which lay for dead a
considerable time, no Pulse or Breath being perceived, their Eyes and Teeth Immov-
able, yet had they no visible wound, only an intolerable smell of Brimstone; about half
an hour after by rubbing and forceing open their Mouths, and pouring down some
Cordials, they recovered. At the same time six others were miserably burnt, their flesh
being scorched, yet their Garments not so much as singed; their skin much
discoloured. See Mr. *Burton's* Miracles of Nature, *Page* 181.

Likewise, *August* 23. 1682. A Man walking in the Field near *Darkin* in *England,*
was struck with a Clap of Thunder. One who was near him, ran to take him up, but
found him dead, and his body exceeding hot, and withal smelling so strong of Sulphur
that he was forced to let him ly a considerable time ere he could be removed. It is
reported, that sometimes Thunder and Lightning has been generated out of the
Sulphurous and Bituminous matter which the fiery Mountain *Ætna* hath cast forth.
We know that when there is a mixture of Nitre, Sulphur, and unslaked Lime, Water
will cause fire to break out. And when unto Nitre Brimstone is added, a Report is
caused thereby. And unquestionably, *Nitre* is a special ingredient in the matter of
Thunder and Lightning; This we may gather from the descension of the flame, which
descends not only obliquely but perpendicularly, and that argues it does so not from
any external force, but naturally. Mr. *William Clark* in his natural History of Nitre,
observes that if the quantity of an ounce be put in a fire-shovel, and a live coal put
upon it, the fire-shovel in the bottom will be red hot, and burn through whatever is
under it; which demonstrates that this sort of fire does naturally burn downwards,
when as all other fires do naturally ascend. For this cause *Stella cadens* is rationally
concluded to be a Nitrous Substance; the like is to be affirmed of the Lightning. Hence
also is its terrible and irresistable force. The Nitre in Gunpowder is as the aforesaid
Author expresseth it *Anima Pyrii Pulveris.* Sulphur without *Salt Peter* has no powerful
expulsion with it. The discharging great pieces of Ordnance is fitly called *Artificial
Thundring and Lightning,* since thereby Men do in a moment blow up Houses, beat
down Castles, batter Mountains in pieces. So that there is nothing in nature does so
admirably and Artificially resemble the Thunder and Lightning, both in respect of the
Report, and the terrible, and sudden and amazing execution done thereby: *Flammas
Jovis & sotus imitatur Olympi.*

Hence as those that are shot with a Bullet do not hear the Gun, being struck before
the report cometh to their Ears; so is it usually with them that are Thunder-struck, the
lightning is upon them before the noise is heard. Men commonly tremble at the
dreadful crack when as, if they hear any thing, the danger useth to be past as to that

particular Thunder-clap; though another may come and kill them before they hear it. The Nitre in the Lightning may likewise be esteemed the natural cause of its being of so penetrating and burning a nature. For there is not the like fiery substance in the World again as Nitre is. Many have been of the Opinion that there is a Bolt or Stone descending with the Thunder, but that's a vulgar Error. The *Fulmen* or *Thunder-bolt* is the same with the Lightning, being a Nitro-sulphurious Spirit. It must needs be a more subtile and spiritual body than any Stone is of, that shall penetrate so as these Meteors do. Its true that our Translation reads the words in *Psal. 78.41. He gave their Flocks to hot Thunder-bolts*: But the Original Word Translated *Thunderbolts*, signifieth *Burning Coals*; so that Lightning is thereby intended. *Avicenna* doth indeed say, that he saw a Thunder-bolt which fell at *Corduba* in *Spain*, and that it had a Sulphurous smell, and was like *Armoniac*. It is possible that not only Sulphurous and Bituminous but stony substances may be generated in the Clouds with the Lightning. *George Agricola* writeth that near *Lurgea*, a mass of Iron being fifty pound in weight, fell from the Clouds, which some attempted to make Swords of, but the fire could not melt it, nor hammers bring it into form.

In the Year 1492. At *Ensishemium*, a stone of three hundred pound weight fell from the Clouds, which is kept as a Monument in the Temple there. And in 1581, a Stone came out of the Clouds in *Thuringia*, which was so hot that it could not be touched, with which one might strike fire as with a Flint. There is now to be seen at *Dresden* a Stone which descended out of a Cloud, and is reserved amongst the *Admiranda* belonging to the *Elector* of *Saxony*: some lately living were present at the Fall of that Stone. Again *An.* 1618. In *Bohemia*, a considerable quantity of Brass mettal fell from the Clouds. No longer since than *May* 28. 1677. at a Village near *Hana* in *Germany*, there was a Tempest of Lightning, and a great multitude of stones of a green and partly cærulean colour fell therewith, and a considerable mass of Mineral matter, in tast like *Vitriol*, being pondrous and friable, having also metallick sparks like Gold intermixed. That which is by some called the *Rain-stone* or *Thunder-bolt*, was by the Antients termed *Cerannia*, because of the smell like that of an Horn when put into the fire, which does attend it. Learned *Gesner* (who in respect of his vast Knowledge in the works of God, may be called the *Solomon* of the former age) saith that a Gentleman gave him one of those Stones, supposing it to be a Thunder-bolt, and that it was five digits in length, and three in breadth. This sort of Stone is usually in form like unto an Iron Wedge, and has an hole quite through it. *Joh. de Laet* in his Treatise *de Gemmis Lib. 2. Cap.24*. relates that he saw another of those Stones. *Boetius* (*de Gemmis Lib.2. Cap.261.*) reports that many persons worthy of credit, affirmed that when Houses or Trees had been broken with the Thunder, they did by digging find such Stones in the places where the stroke was given. Nevertheless, that *Fulminus Stones* or *Thunderbolts* do always descend out of the Clouds, when such breaches are made by the Lightning, is (as I said) a *vulgar Error*.

The Effects produced by the Lightning are exceeding marvelous, sometimes Gold, Silver, Brass, Iron has been melted thereby, when the things wherein they have been kept, received no hurt; yea, when the Wax on the Bags which contained them, has not been so much as melted. Liquors have been thereby exhausted out of Vessels, when the Vessels themselves remained untouched: And (which is more wonderful) when the

Cask has been broken by the Lightning, the Wine has remained as it were included in a skin, without being spilt; the reason whereof *Sennerius* supposeth to be, in that the heat of the Lightning did condense the exterior parts of the Wine. It is also a very strange thing, which Histories report concerning *Marcia* (a *Roman Princess*) that the Child in her body was smitten and killed with Lightning, and yet the Mother received no hurt in her own Body. It is hard to give a clear and satisfactory Reason why if a piece of Iron be laid upon the Cask it prevents the Thunder from marring the Wine contained therein, and also keeps Milk from turning. The *Virtuosi* of *France* in their Philosophical Conferences (*vol*.2. P.427.) suppose a Sympathy between Iron and the gross vapors of Thunder and Lightning. They say that which is commonly called the *Thunder-bolt* does sometimes resemble Steel, as it were to shew the correspondence that there is between Iron and Thunder: So that the Air being impregnate by those noisome vapours which are of the same nature with Iron, meeting with some piece of it laid on a Vessel, is joyned to the Iron by Sympathy, the Iron by its attractive vertue receives them, and by its retentive retains them, and by that means prevents the effects. This conjecture is ingenious.

Nor is it easie to give a solid Reason why the Lightning should hurt one creature rather than another. Naturalists observe that it is so. *Feles canes & capras magisillorum obnoxious ictibus observatio sedula dedit* saith *Johnston*.[22] *Bartholinus* conjectures the reason to be the *halitus* in the bodies of those creatures, which are a fit nutriment for the fulminious spirits to prey upon. When fire is set to a train of Gunpowder; it will run accordingly straight or crooked, upwards or downwards as the matter it feeds upon is disposed: So proportionably here: but this is a Subject for ingenious minds further to inquire into. It is moreover difficult to determine how Men are killed therewith, when no visible impression is made upon their Bodies. Some think it is by a meer instantaneous suffocation of their Animal spirits. That poysonful vapours do sometimes attend the Lightning is manifest. *Seneca* saith, that Wine which has been congealed with the Lightning, after it is dissolved, and in appearance returned to its pristine state, it causeth the persons that shall drink of it, either to die or become mad. Naturalists observe, that venemous Creatures being struck with Lightning lose their poyson; the reason of which may be, not only the heat but the venome of those Vapours attracting the poyson to themselves. And that Vapors will kill in a moment is past doubt. In the Philosophical transactions for the year 1665 (P.44.) it is related that seven or eight persons going down Stairs into a Coal-pit, they fell down dead as if they had been shot: There being one of them whose Wife was informed that her Husband was stifled, she went near to him without any inconvenience; but when she went a little further, the Vapors caused her instantly to fall down dead. And it is famously known, concerning the Lake *Avernus* in *Campania*, that if Birds attempt to fly over it, the deadly vapors thereof kill them in a moment. But the Lightning doth more than meerly suffocate with mortiferous vapors. It sometimes penetrates the Brain, and shrivels the Heart and Liver when nothing does appear outwardly. And it does (as Dr. *Goodwin* in his lately published judicious Discourse about the punishment of Sinners in the other World (P. 44) aptly expresseth) *lick up*

---

22. *Feles canes* . . . : careful supervision makes their cats, dogs and goats more obedient than blows.

the vital and animal spirits that run in the Body, when yet the body it self remains unburnt. Those spirits are the *Vinculum*, the tye of Union between the Soul and Body, which the Lightning may consume without so much as singing the body or cloaths there. Nevertheless, upon some it leaveth direful marks, and breaketh their very bones in pieces, and sometimes tears away the flesh from the Bones.

There are some Remarkable Instances confirming this, published in the Philosophical Transactions. Dr. *Wallis* in a Letter written at *Oxford, May* 12, 1666. giving an account of a very sad accident which had then newly hapned there. He saith, that two Schollars of *Wadham* Colledge, being alone in a Boat (without a Waterman) having newly thrust off from shore, at *Medley* to come homewards, standing near the head of the Boat, were presently with a stroke of Thunder or Lightning, both struck off out of the Boat into the Water, the one of them stark dead, in whom though presently taken out of the water (having been by relation scarce a minute in it) there was not discerned any appearance of Life, sense or motion: the other was stuck fast in the Mud (with his feet downwards, and his upper parts above water) like a Post not able to help himself out; but besides a present astonying or numness had no other hurt: but was for the present so disturbed in his Senses that he knew not how he came out of the Boat, nor could remember either Thunder or Lightning that did effect it: and was very feeble and faint upon it (which though presently put into a warm Bed) he had not throughly recovered by the next night; and whither since he have or no, I know not. Others in another Boat, about ten or twenty yards from these (as by their description I estimate) felt a disturbance and shaking in their Boat, and one of them had his Chair struck from under him, and thrown upon him, but had no hurt. These immediately made up to the others, and (some leaping into the Water to them) presently drew them into the Boat or on shore; yet none of them saw these two fall into the water (not looking that way) but heard one of them cry for help presently upon the stroke, and smelt a very strong stinking smell in the Air; which, when I asked him that told it me, what kind of stink? he said, like such a smell, as is perceived upon the striking of Flints together.

He that was dead (when by putting into a warm Bed, and rubbing, and putting strong Waters into his mouth, etc. no Life could be brought into him) was the next morning brought to Town; where among multitudes of others, who came to see; Dr. *Willis*, Dr. *Mellington*, Dr. *Lower*, and my self, with some others, went to view the Corps, where we found no wound at all in the skin; the face and neck swart and black, but not more than might be ordinary, by the setling of the blood: on the right side of the Neck was a little blackish spott about an inch long, and about a quarter of an inch broad at the broadest, and was as if it had been seared with a hot Iron: and as I remember, one somewhat bigger on the left side of the neck below the ear. Streight down the Breast, but towards the left side of it, was a large place, about three quarters of a foot in length, and about two inches in breadth; in some places more, in some less, which was burnt and hard, like Leather burnt with the fire, of a deep blackish red colour, not much unlike the scorched skin of a rosted Pig: and on the forepart of the left Shoulder such another spot about as big as a shilling; but that in the neck was blacker and seemed more seared. From the top of the right shoulder, sloping downwards towards that place in his Breast, was a narrow line of the like scorched skin; as if somewhat had come in there at the neck, and had run down to the breast and there spread broader.

The Buttons of his Dublet were most of them off, which some thought might have been torn off with the blast, getting in at the neck, and then bursting its way out, for which the greatest presumption was (to me) that besides four or five Buttons wanting towards the bottom of the breast, there were about half a dozen together clear off from the bottom of the Collar downwards, and I do not remember that the rest of the buttons did seem to be near worn out, but almost new. The Collar of his Doublet just over the fore-part of the right Shoulder was quite broken asunder, cloth and stiffening, streight and downwards, as if cut or chopt asunder, but with a blunt tool; only the inward linnen or fustian lining of it was whole, by which, and by the view of the ragg'd edges, it seemed manifest to me, that it was from a stroke inward (from without) not outwards from within.

His Hat was strangely torn, not just on the Crown, but on the side of the Hat, and on the Brim. On the side of it was a great hole, more than to put in ones fist through it: some part of it being quite struck away, and from thence divers gashes every way, as if torn or cut with a dull tool, and some of them of a good length, almost quite to the edges of the brim. And besides these, one or two gashes more, which did not communicate with that hole in the side. This also was judged to be by a stroke inwards; not so much from the view of the edges of those Gashes (from which there was scarce any judgement to be made either way) but because the lining was not torn, only ript from the edge of the Hat (where it was sown on) on that side where the hole was made. But his Hat not being found upon his head, but at some distance from him, it did not appear against what part of his head that hole was made.

Another sad disaster hapned *January* 24 1666. When one Mr. *Brooks* of *Hampshire* going from *Winchester* towards his House near *Andover*, in very bad weather, was himself slain by Lightning, and the Horse he rode on under him. For about a Mile from *Winchester* he was found with his face beaten into the Ground, one Leg in the Stirrup, the other in the Horses main; his Cloathes all burnt off his back, not a piece as big as an Hankerchief left intire, and his Hair and all his body singed. With the force that struck him down, his nose was beaten into his face, and his Chin into his Breast; where was a Wound cut almost as low as to his Navil; and his clothes being as aforesaid torn, the pieces were so scattered and consumed, that not enough to fill the crown of a Hat could be found. His Gloves were whole, but his hands in them singed to the Bone. The Hip-bone and Shoulder of his Horse burnt and bruised, and his Saddle torn in little pieces.

Very Remarkable also was that which hapned forty five years ago at another place in *England*, viz. *Withycomb* in *Devonshire*, where on *October* 21. *A.D.* 1638. being Sabbath day, whilest the People were attending the publick Worship of God, a black Cloud coming over the Church, there was suddenly an amazing Clap of Thunder, and with it a Ball of fire came in at the Window, whereby the House was very much damnified, and the People many of them struck down. Some of the Seats in the body of the Church were turned upside down, yet they that sat in them received no hurt. A Gentleman of note there (one Mr. *Hill*) sitting in his Seat by the Chancil, had his head suddenly smitten against the Wall, by which blow he died that night. Another had his

Head cloven, his Skull rent in three pieces, and his Brains thrown upon the Ground whole. The hair of his head through the violence of the blow stuck fast to the Pillar that was near him. A Woman attempting to run out of the Church, had her clothes set on fire; and her flesh on her back torn almost to the very bone. See Mr. *Clarks* Examples *Vol.* 1. *Chap.* 104 P. 501.

It is not Heresie to believe that *Satan* has sometimes a great operation in causing Thunder-storms. I know this is vehemently denied by some. The late Witch-Advocates call it Blasphemy. And an old Council did *Anathematize* the men that are thus perswaded: but by their Favour; An orthodox & rational Man may be of the Opinion, that when the Devil has before him the Vapors and Materials out of which the Thunder and Lightning are generated, his Art is such as that he can bring them into form. If Chymists can make their *aurumfulminans*,[23] what strange things may this *Infernal Chymist* effect? The Holy Scriptures intimate as much as this cometh to In the sacred Story concerning *Job*, we find that Satan did raise a great Wind which blew down the House where *Job's* Children were Feasting. And it is said, *Chap.* 1. *ver.* 16. *That the fire of God fell from Heaven, and burnt up the Sheep and the Servants; This Fire of God* was no doubt Thunder and Lightning; and such as was extraordinary, and is therefore expressed with the Name of God, as is usual amongst the *Hebrews.* Satan had a deep policy in going that way to work, thereby hoping to make *Job* believe God was his Enemy. Mr. *Caryl* (according to his wonted manner) does both wittily and judiciously paraphrase upon the place; *The fire of God* (saith he) *here is conceived to have been some terrible slash of Lightning; and it is the more probable because it is said to fall down from Heaven, that is, out of the Air. There Satan can do mighty things, command much of the Magazine of Heaven, where that dreadful Artillery which makes men tremble, those fiery Meteors, Thunder and Lightning are stored and lodged. Satan let loose by God can do wonders in the Air; He can raise Storms, He can discharge the great Ordnance of Heaven, Thunder and Lightning; and by his Art can make them more terrible and dreadful than they are in their own nature. Satan is said to be the Prince of the Power of the Air,* Eph. 2.2. And we read of the working of Satan with all power and signs, and lying words, 2 *Thess.* 2.9. It is moreover predicted in the Revelation, that Antichrist should *cause fire to come down from Heaven,* Rev. 13.13. Accordingly we read in History, that some of the Popes have by their skill in the black Art, caused Balls of fire to be seen in the Air. So then it is not beyond Satans power to effect such things, if the great God give him leave, without whose leave he cannot blow a Feather: much less raise a Thunder-storm.

And as the Scriptures intimate Satan's Power in the Air to be great, so Histories do abundantly confirm it by remarkable Instances. One of the Scholars of *Empedocles* has testified, that he saw his Master raising Winds and laying them again; and there were once many Witnesses of it, whence they called *Empedocles Clemens Alexandrinus* mentions this as unquestionably true. Our great *Rainold (de libris Apocryphis* Lect. 202.) saith, that we may from *Job* conclude, it was not impossible for *Empedocles* by the Devils aid, to do as has been reported of him. *Dio* relates that

---

23. *aurumfulminans*: fulminate of gold; an explosive precipitate obtained by adding ammonia to a solution of auric chloride; mentioned in Robert Boyle's *New Experiments and Observations*, 1681–82.

when the *Roman* Army in the dayes of the Emperour *Claudius*, pursuing the *Africans*, was in extream danger of perishing by Drought: a Magician undertook to procure water for them, and presently upon his Incantations, an astonishing shower fell. *Jovianus Pontanus* reports, that when King *Ferdinand* besieged the City *Suessa*, all the waters in the Cisterns being dried up, the Citizens had like to have lost their lives by the prevailing Drought. The Popish Priests undertook by Conjuration to obtain Water. The Magical Ceremonies by them observed were most horrid and ridiculous. For they took an Asse, and put the Sacrament of the *Eucharist* into his Mouth, sang Funeral Verses over him, and then buried him alive before the Church doors; as soon as these rites, so pleasing to the Devil were finished, the Heavens began to look black, and the Sea to be agitated with Winds, and anon it rained, and lightned, after a most horrendous manner. *Smetius* in his *Miscellanies*, Lib. 5. Relates that a Girl foolishly imitating the Ceremonies of her Nurse, whom she had sometimes seen raising Tempests, immediately a prodigious Storm of Thunder and Lightning hapned, so as that a Village near *Lipsia* was thereby set on fire; This Relation is mentioned by *Sennertus*, as a thing really true. At some places in *Denmark*, it is a common and a wicked practice to buy Winds, when they are going to Sea. If Satan has so far the power of the Air as to cause Winds, he may cause Storms also. *Livy* reports concerning *Romulus*, that he was by a Tempest of Thunder and Lightning transported no man knew whither, being after that never heard of. *Meurerus (in Comment. Meteorolog.)* speaketh of a Man, that going between *Lipsia* and *Torga*, was suddenly carried out of sight by a Thunder-storm, and never seen more. And the truth of our assertion, seems to be confirmed by one of those sad effects of Lightning mentioned in the precedeing Chapter. For I am informed that when *Matthew Cole* was killed with the Lightning at *North-hampton*, the *Demons* which disturbed his Sister *Ann Cole* (forty miles distant) in *Hartford*, spoke of it; intimating their concurrence in that terrible accident.

The *Jewish Rabbins* affirm, that all great and suddain Destructions are from Satan, the Angel of Death. That he has frequently an hand therein is past doubt. And if the fallen Angels are able (when God shall grant them a Commission) to cause fearful and fatal Thunders, it is much more true concerning the good and holy Angels, 2 *King*. 1. 14, 15. When the Law was given at Mount *Sinai*, there were amazing Thundrings and Lightnings, wherein the great God saw meet to make use of the Ministry of Holy Angels, *Act*. 7.53. *Gal*. 3.19. *Heb*. 2.2. Some think that *Sodom* was destroyed by extraordinary Lightning. Its certain that Holy Angels had an hand in effecting that Desolation, *Gen*. 19.13. We know that one Night the Angel of the Lord smote in the Camp of the *Assyrians* an 185000. It is not improbable, but that those *Assyrians* were killed with Lightning: For it was with respect to that tremendous Providence, that those words were uttered, *Who amongst us shall dwell with the devouring Fire*, Isai. 33.14. Ecclesiastical History informs us that the *Jews* being encouraged by the Apostate *Julian*, were resolved to re-build their Temple; but Lightning from Heaven consumed not only their Work, but all their Tools and Instruments wherewith that cursed Enterprize was to have been carried on, so was their design utterly frustrate. Why might not holy Angels have an hand in that Lightning? There occurs to my mind, a Remarkable Passage mentioned by Dr. *Beard* in his Chapter about the Protection of Holy Angels over them that fear God (*P*. 443.) he saith, that a certain Man travelling between two Woods in a great Tempest of Thunder and Lightening, rode under an Oak to shelter himself, but his Horse would by no means stay under that Oak, but whether his Master would or no, went from that Tree and stayed very quietly under another Tree not far off; he had not been there many Minutes before the first Oak was torn all to fitters[24] with a fearful Clap of Thunder and Lightning. Surely there was the invisible Guardianship of an Holy Angel in that Providence.

But though it be true, that both natural Causes and Angels do many times concurre when Thunder and Lightning, with the awful effects thereof, happen; nevertheless, the supreme cause must not be disacknowledged. The Eternal himself has a mighty hand of providence in such works. He thundreth with the voice of His Excellency. Among the Greeks Thunder was stiled. And the Scripture calls it the *Voice of the Lord. The God of Glory Thundereth. The Voice of the Lord is very powerful, the Voice of the Lord is full of Majesty, the Voice of the Lord breaketh the Cedars, the Voice of the Lord divideth the Flames of Fires*: Lightnings are also said to be the *Arrows of God*, Psal.18.14 upon which account the Children of Men ought to dread the hand of the Highest therein. And the more so that all places in the habitable World are exposed unto Dangers and Destruction by this Artillery of Heaven; though some parts of the Earth are naturally subject thereunto more than others. *Acosta* saith, that it seldom Thunders about *Brasil*; but such Lightnings are frequent there, as make the Night appear brighter than the Noon Day. Travellers report, that there are some Snowy Mountains in *Africa*, on which the Cracks of Thunder are so loud and vehement, as that they are heard fifty Miles off at Sea. In some parts of *Tartaria*, it will both Snow and Thunder at the same time. In the Northern Climates, there use to be vehement Thunders, and Men are often struck dead thereby; In the Province of *Terravara* in *Spain*, grows the Wood for the Cross, to which Superstitious Papists attribute a power to preserve Men from Thunder. So did the *Gentiles* of Old vainly think to secure themselves from Heavens Gun-shot, by carrying those things about them, which they supposed would be as *Amulets* to defend them from all harm. The Tents of the old *Emperors* were made of *Seal-Leather*, because they imagined that the Sea-Calf could not be Thunder-struck. *Tyberius* wore a Crown of Lawrel upon his Head, for that the Philosophers told him that the Lightning could not hurt the Bay Tree. *Rodiginus* affirms the like concerning the Fig-tree. But others declare that they have seen the Laurel smitten and withered with the Lightning: therefore the *Conimbricensian* Philosophers acknowledge this immunity to be fictitious. The like vanity is in their Opinion, who suppose that the Stone by Philosophers called *Brontias* (i.e.) the Thunder-bolt will secure them from harm by Lightning. To conclude, most miserable is the State of all *Christless Sinners*, who know not but that every *Thunder-storm* which comes, may send them to Hell in a moment.

Hi sunt qui trepidant ad omnia fulgurae pallent,
Cum tonat, exanimes primo quoque murmure Caeli.[25]

The Psalmist alludes to a Thunder Storm, when he saith, *The Lord will rain upon the Wicked Snares* (the Lightning cometh suddenly, and taketh Men as Birds in a snare

---

24. fitters: fragments, pieces.

25. These are the ones who tremble and turn pale at every flash of lightning; when it thunders, they are out of their minds at the first rumble from the skies.

before they think of it) *Fire and Brimstone, and a tempest of horrors*, Psal. 11.6. The *Atheism* of *Epicurus* of old, (and of some in these dayes) who taught, that inasmuch as Thunder proceeds from natural causes, it is a childish thing for Men to have an awe upon their hearts when they hear that voice, I say such Atheism is folly and wickedness. For the great God *maketh the way for the Lightning of Thunder*; nor does it ever miss or mistake its way, but alwayes lights where God has appointed it, Job 28.26. He directs the Lightning under the whole Heaven, and unto the ends of the Earth; after it a voice roareth, that they may do whatsoever he commanded them upon the face of the world in the Earth, Job 37.3,12. Yea, and good Men should from this consideration be incited to endeavour that their Garments be kept from defilement, and that they be always walking with God, since they know not but that Death may come upon them suddenly in such a way and by such means as this; As to outward Evils, there is one event to the Righteous and to the Wicked; to him that sacrificeth & to him that sacrificeth not, as is the good so is the sinner. The examples mentioned in the preceding Chapter do confirm it, since divers of those whom the Thunder killed, were good men. And they that are in Christ, and who make it their design to live unto God, need not be dismayed at the most terrifying Thunder-claps, no more than a Child should be afraid when he hears the voice of his loving Father. Notable is that passage related by Mr. *Ambrose*, in his Treatise of Angels (P.265. & by Mr. *Clark, vol.* 1. P. 512.) A prophane Man, who was also a Persecutor of Mr. *Bolton*, riding abroad, it Thundred very dreadfully; at the which the Man greatly trembled; his Wife, who was eminent for Godliness being with him, asked, why he was so much afraid? to whom he replied; are not you afraid to hear these dreadful Thunder claps? no (saith she) not at all, for I know it is the voice of my Heavenly Father; and should a Child be afraid to hear his Fathers voice? At the which the Man was amazed, concluding with himself, these *Puritans* have a divine principle in them, which the World seeth not, that they should have peace and serenity in their Souls when others are filled with dismal fears and horrors. He thereupon went to Mr. *Bolton*, bewailing the wrong he had done him, begging his Pardon and Prayers, and that he would tell him what he must do that so his Soul might be saved: and he became a very godly man everafter. This was an happy Thunder-Storm.

5. Robert Boyle

from *Heads for the Natural History of a Country*
1692

Robert Boyle (1627–91) made a number of important discoveries—for instance the one codified in "Boyle's law" that the volume of a gas varies inversely with the pressure applied to it. But he may have had still more influence on the history of science, as a universally respected presence embodying and defining the emerging scientific way of undogmatic experimentation. This role of shaping the new knowlege is the one he plays in the Heads for the Natural History of a Country *(published posthumously in 1692, but probably written in the 1660s).*

As a founder of the Royal Society, Boyle, on its behalf, drew up a sort of hand-book for explorers. Since the late fifteenth century, knowledge had been pouring into European centers of learning at an unprecedented rate and from places so little known that the avalanche of facts was peculiarly difficult to sort out. Boyle tried to bring some order into this confusion. Explorers carrying his Heads *(meaning head-ings or categories) would bring back their information in better order and more complete. The utilitarian aspect of Boyle's thinking is evident in the questionnaire: every fact he seeks has a use.*

The General Heads for the Natural History of a Country, will respect the Heavens, the Air, the Water, and the Earth. To the first belong the longitude and latitude of the Place, and consequently the length of the longest and shortest days; the climate, parallels, and the visible fixed stars; with the constellations whereto 'tis said to be subject.

Of the Air may be observed its temper, as to heat, dryness and moisture, with the measures of them; its weight, clearness, refractive power, subtilty or grossness, its abounding with, or wanting an esurine salt; its variation according to the several seasons of the year, and the times of the day: How long the several kinds of weather continue; what sorts of meteors the Air most commonly breeds; in what order they are generated; and how long they usually last: To what winds it is liable; whether any of them be stated, ordinary, etc. What diseases are epidemical, that are supposed to arise from the Air: To what other diseases the country is subject, in the production whereof the Air is concerned. What is the usual state of the Air as to the health of the inhabitants; and with what constitutions it agrees better or worse than others. The gravity of the Air is to be learn'd by the barometer.

With regard to the Water are to be considered the sea, its depth, specifick gravity, difference of saltness in different places, the plants, insects, and fishes to be found in it, tides, with respect to the adjacent lands, currents, whirlpools, etc. Rivers, their bigness, course, inundations, taste, subterraneous passages, fruitfulness, etc. lakes, ponds,

Indian corn and blackbird, from The Discovery of New Britaine, *1651.*

springs, and especially mineral waters, their kinds, qualities, virtues, and how examined; the sorts of fishes, their size and goodness, plenty, seasons, ways of breeding, haunts, and the methods of taking them; especially those that are not purely mechanical.

In the Earth may be observed it self, with its inhabitants and productions, as well internal as external; its dimensions, situation, East, West, South, or North; its figure, plains, hills or valleys; their extent, the height of the mountains, either in respect of the neighbouring valleys, or the level of the sea; whether the mountains lie scattered, or in ridges; and whether those run North or South, East or West, etc. What promontories, fiery or smoaking hills, etc. the country has; whether subject to earthquakes or not. Whether the country is coherent, or much broken into islands. What declination the magnetick needle has in several places at the same time; and how much it varies in different times at the same place; whether before hurricanes, the needle loses its direction towards the North; and turns equally to all the points of the compass. The nature of the soil, whether of clay, sand, gravel, etc. its peculiar qualities and productions, as to minerals, vegetables and animals: And how all these are or may be farther improved for the benefit of man.

Under Inhabitants are to be considered both the natives and the strangers who have been long settled there; particularly as to their stature; shape, features, strength, ingenuity, diet, inclinations and customs, that seem not due to education. In the women, their fruitfulness or barrenness, their easy and hard labour, with their exercises and diet; the diseases, with their symptoms, and the diet, air, etc. that influence them.

The external productions are trees, fruits, plants, etc. with the peculiarities observable in them. In what soils, and with what culture they thrive best; with what animals or insects the country abounds, and to what use applied by the inhabitants, as to food, physic, surgery, etc.

By the internal productions of the earth, are here understood things generated in the bowels of it, either to the benefit or hurt of man. Under these are comprehended metals, minerals, stones, precious or common. To examine how the beds of them lie in reference to North or South, etc. What clays and earths are afforded, with their physical or other uses; what coals, salt, or salt-springs, alum, vitriol, sulphur, etc. The number of mines, their situation, depth, signs, waters, damps, quantities of ore, extraneous things, and ways of reducing their ores into metals, etc.

Add to these the enquiries about traditions of all particular things relating to the country, such as are either peculiar to it, or at least uncommon elsewhere.

Enquiries that require learning or skill to answer; with proposals for ways to enable men to give answers to such more difficult enquiries.

To observe the declination of the compass in different longitudes and latitudes; setting down the method by which the observation was made.

To observe the dipping-needle, in the like manner.

To observe the odour, colour, and taste in sea-water; the proportion of its salt in different places; whether in the same sea it be constantly the same; and what are the particularities of that sea-water, where ships cables soonest rot, and where they are best preserved.

To remark, if there be near the South pole a constant current, setting from the South so forcibly, that ships with a stiff gale can hardly make way against it; and near the North, a current forcibly carrying ships towards the pole; or if this motion reciprocate once in half a year.

To observe what subterraneous passages there are, whereby seas communicate with one another.

What effect the winds have upon the seas; and how far from the surface they agitate the waters.

The ebbings and flowings, with the age of the moon when the neap and spring-tides happen; to what height it ebbs and flows at these times upon the coast, or the islands far off in the sea; and if it flow there differently from the tides near the main land; and how much sooner it begins on one side than another.

To mark narrowly the way of coming into particular creeks and harbours; with their bearings and distances from the neighbouring places.

To sound all along at coming in; and to mark the depths and shallows near the shore, or farther off from the coast, as also near shelves or banks.

To mark in the sounding not only the depth, but all the grounds, whether clayie, sandy or ouzy, etc. To mark whether the sea always rises towards the shore, unless accidentally hindered. How the bottom of the sea differs from the surface of the earth; with the stones and minerals to be found there.

To take notice of the winds, their changes, or set times of blowing, and in what longitude and latitude, especially the trade-winds; upon what coast the trade-winds are most frequent; and by what signs they may be foreseen.

To observe and record all extraordinary meteors, lightnings, thunders, and their effects, *Ignes fatui*,[26] comets, etc. marking the places of their appearing and disappearing.

To examine the weights of the several waters that occur, both near the upper and lower part of the sea; the power ascribed to the sea of throwing up Amber, ambergrise, etc. and its shining in the night.

---

26. *Ignes fatui*: literally, foolish fire. A hovering, phosphorescent light caused by spontaneous combustion of inflammable gases from the decay of organic matter.

6.

three selections about smallpox

Smallpox was among the most dreaded diseases in the sometimes pestilential colonies. In seventeenth- and eighteenth-century Europe, smallpox was a common childhood disease and therefore, while many died of it, the general level of immunity was high. The native Americans had never been exposed to smallpox, however, and its ravages among them were catastrophic. Meanwhile, in the absence of crowded conditions and large cities, the incidence of the disease fell off and ceased to be a common event. European settlers thus began to lose their immunities until a series of sudden raging epidemics suggested that they could become almost as vulnerable as the Indians. It was in this cont ext, in 1677, that the Brief Rule *was written, one of the earliest attempts to educate a public in medical measures.*

In 1714, Cotton Mather read a letter in the Transactions of the Royal Society of London *describing the process of inoculation as a general phenomenon, whereby a mild case of a disease seemed to produce immunity. When an epidemic broke out in Boston in 1721, Mather urged the physician Zabdiel Boylston (1679–1766) to develop a program of inoculation. Against strong medical opposition, Boylston inoculated several hundred Bostonians and the results were decisive: the chances of dying from the disease were nine times those of dying from inoculation. As the technique and therefore the odds improved, inoculation became almost a common colonial practice, only later copied in Europe where the conservative medical profession had greater control.*

One of those who had denounced Boylston and Mather in 1721 was James Franklin, editor of the New England Courant *and brother of Benjamin Franklin. At the time, the younger Franklin went along with the campaign of calumny, which makes his belated endorsement of inoculation below the more significant.*

Thomas Thacher

A Brief Rule to Guide the Common-People of New-England How To Order Themselves and Theirs in the Small Pocks, or Measels
1678

The *Small Pox* (whose nature and cure the *Measels* follow) is a disease in the blood, endeavouring to recover a new form and state.

2. This nature attempts — 1. By Separation of the impure from the pure, thrusting it out from the Veins to the Flesh. — 2. By driving out the impure from the Flesh to the Skin.

3. The first Separation is done in the first four Days by a Feverish boiling (Ebullition) of the Blood, laying down the impurities in the Fleshy parts which kindly effected the Feverish tumult is calmed.

4. The second Separation from the Flesh to the Skin, or *Superficies* is done through the rest of the time of the disease.

5. There are several Errors in ordering these sick ones in both these Operations of Nature which prove very dangerous and commonly deadly either by overmuch hastening Nature beyond its own pace, or in hindering of it from its own vigorous operation.

6. The Separation by Ebullition in the Feverish heat is over heightned by too much Clothes, too hot a room, hot *Cordials*, as *Diascordium*, *Gascons powder* and such like, for hence come *Phrenzies*, dangerous excessive sweats, or flowing of the Pocks into one overspreading sore, vulgarly called the Flux.

7. The same Separation is overmuch hindred by preposterous cooling that Feverish boiling heat, by *blood letting, Glysters*: enema. *Vomits, purging,* or *cooling medicines.* For though these many times hasten the coming forth of the *Pox,* yet they take away that supply which should keep out till they are ripe, wherefore they sink in again to the deadly danger of the sick.

8. If a *Phrensie* happen, or through a *Plethorie* (that is fulness of blood) the Circulation of the blood be hindred, and thereupon the whole mass of blood choaked up, then either let blood, or see that their diet, or medicines be not altogether cooling, but let them in no wise be heating, therefore let him lye no otherwise covered in his bed then he was wont in his health: His Chamber not made hot with fire if the weather be temperate, let him drink small Beer only warm'd with a Tost, let him sup up thin *Water-gruel,* or *Water-pottage* made only of Indian Flower and Water, instead of *Oatmeal*: Let him eat *boild Apples*: But I would not advise at this time any medicines besides. By this means that excessive *Ebullition* (or boiling of his blood) will by degrees abate, and the Symptoms cease; if not, but the blood be so inraged that it will admit of no delay, then either let blood (if Age will bear it) or else give some notably cooling medicine, or refresh him with more free Air.

9. But if the boiling of the blood be weak and dull that there is cause to fear it is not able to work a Separation, as its wont to be in such as have been let blood, or are fat, or Flegmatick, or brought low by some other sickness or labour of the (*Gonorrhea*) running of the Reins, or some other Evacuation: In such Cases, *Cordials* must drive them out, or they must die.

10. In time of driving out the *Pocks* from the Flesh, here care must be had that the *Postules* keep out in a right measure till they have attain'd their end without going in again for that is deadly.

11. In this time take heed when the *Pustules* appear whilst not yet ripe, least by too much heat there arise a new *Ebullition* (or Feverish boiling) for this troubles the driving out, or brings back the separated parts in the blood, or the Fleshy parts overheated are disabled from a right suppuration, or lastly the temper of the blood and tone of the Flesh is so perverted that it cannot overcome and digest the matter driving out.

12. Yet on the other hand the breaking out must not be hindred, by exposing the sick unto the cold. The degree of heat must be such as is natural agrees with the temper of the Fleshy parts: That which exceeds or falls is dangerous: Therefore the season of the year, Age of the sick, and their manner of life here require a discreet and different Consideration, requiring the Counsel of an expert Physician.

13. But if by any error a new *Ebullition* ariseth, the same art must be used to allay it as is before exprest.

14. If the *Pustules* go in and a flux of the belly follows (for else there is no such danger) *Cordials* are to be used, yet moderate and not too often for fear of new *Ebullition*.

15. If much spitting (*Ptyalismus*) follow you may hope all will go well, therefore by no means hinder it: Only with warm small Beer let their mouths be washed.

16. When the *Pustles* are dryed and fallen, purge well, especially if it be in *Autumn*.

17. As soon as this disease appears by its signs, let the sick abstain from Flesh and Wine, and open Air, let him use small Beer warmed with a Tost for his ordinary drink, and moderately when he desires it. For Food use *Water-gruel*, *Water-pottage*, and other things having no manifest hot quality, easy of digestion, boild Apples, and Milk sometimes for change, but the coldness taken off. Let the use of his bed be according to the season of the year, and the multitude of the *Pocks*, or as sound persons are wont. In Summer let him rise according to custom, yet so as to be defended both from heat and cold in Excess, the disease will be the sooner over and less troublesome, for being kept in bed nourisheth the Feverish heat and makes the *Pocks* break out with a painful inflamation.

18. In a colder season and breaking forth of a multitude of *Pustules*, forcing the sick to keep his bed, let him be covered according to his custom in health, a moderate fire in the Winter being kindled in his Chamber, Morning and Evening: neither need he keep his Arms always in bed, or ly still in the same place, or fear least he should sweat which is very dangerous especially to youth.

19. Before the fourth Day use no medicines to drive out, nor be too strict with the sick; for by how much the more gently the *Pustules* do grow, by so much the fuller and perfecter will the Separation be.

20. On the fourth Day a gentle *Cordial* may help once given.

21. From that time a small draught of warm Milk (not hot) a little dy'd with *Saffron* may be given Morning and Evening till the *Pustules* are come to their due greatness and ripeness.

22. When the *Pustules* begin to dry and crust, lest the rotten vapours strike inward, which sometimes causeth sudden Death; take Morning and Evening some temperate *Cordial* as four or five spoonfuls of *Malago Wine* tinged with a little *Saffron*.

23. When the *Pustules* are dryed and fallen off, purge once and again, especially in the *Autumn Pocks*.

24. Beware of anointing with *Oils*, *Fats*, *Ointments*, and such defensives, for keeping the corrupted matter in the *Pustules* from drying up; by the moisture, they fret deeper into the Flesh, and so make the more deep Scarrs.

25. The young and lively Men that are brought to a plentiful sweat in this sickness, about the eighth Day the sweat drops of it self, by no means afterwards to be drawn

out again the sick thereupon feels most troublesome, distrest and anguish, and then makes abundance of water, and so dyes.

26. Few young Men and strong thus handled escape, except they fall into abundance of spitting or plentiful bleeding at the Nose.

27. Signs discovering the Assault at first are beating pain in the Head, Forehead, and temples, pain in the Back, great sleepiness, glistring of the Eyes, shining glimmerings seem before them, itching of them also, with tears flowing of themselves, itching of the Nose, short breath, dry Cough, oft sneezing, hoarseness, heat, redness, and sense of pricking over the whole Body, terrors in the sleep, sorrow and restlessness, beating of the heart, *Urine* sometimes as in health, sometime filthy from great *Ebullition*, and all this or many of these with a Feverish distemper.

28. *Signs warning of the probable Event. If they break forth easily, quickly, and soon come to ripening, if the Symptoms be gentle, the Fever mild and after the breaking forth it abate; if the voice be free, breathing easy; especially if the Pox be red, white, distinct, soft, few, round, sharp top'd, only without and not in the Inward parts; if there be large bleeding at the Nose. These signs are hopeful.*

29. *But such signs are doubtful, when they difficultly appear, when they sink in again when they are black, blewish, green, hard, all in one, if the Fever abate not with their breaking forth, if there be swooning, difficulty of breathing, great thirst, quinsey, great unquietness, and it is very dangerous, if there be join'd with it some other malignant Fever, called by some the pestilential Pox: The* Spotted Fever *is oft joined with it.*

30. *Deadly Signs if the* Flux *of the* Belly *happen, when they are broke forth, if the* Urine *be bloody, or black, or the* Ordure *of that Colour; Or if the pure blood be cast out by the Belly or Gums: These signs are for the most part deadly.*

These things have I written Candid Reader, *not to inform the Learned* Physician *that hath much more cause to understand what pertains to this disease than I, but to give some light to those that have not such Advantages, leaving the difficulty of this disease to the* Physicians Art, Wisdom, *&* Faithfulness, *for the right managing of them in the whole course of the disease tends both to the* Patients *safety, and the* Physicians *desired success in his Administrations: For in vain is the* Physicians Art *imployed, if they are not under a* Regular Regiment. *I am, tho' no* Physician, *yet a well-wisher to the sick: And therefore intreating the Lord to turn our hearts, and stay His Hand. I am*

A Friend, Reader to thy Welfare, 21 d. 11 m. 1677-8.

Thomas Thacher

Cotton Mather

letter to Hans Sloane
1722

March 10, 1722

So considerable a part of mankind fearfully perishing by the smallpox, and many more of us grievously suffering by that miserable distemper, you will allow me to entertain you with a few more communications, and write you (I think it's) a fourth letter upon it.

The distemper has lately visited and ransacked the city of Boston, and in little more than half a year, of more than five thousand persons that have undergone it, near nine hundred have died. But how many lives might have been saved if our unhappy physicians had not poisoned and bewitched our people with a blind rage, that has appeared very like a satanic possession, against the method of relief and safety in the way of the *Smallpox Inoculated*.

I prevailed with one physician (and for it I have had bloody attempts made upon my life by some of our energumens) to introduce the practise. And the experiment has been made upon almost three hundred objects in our neighborhood, young and old (from one year to seventy) weak and strong, male and female, white and black, in mid-summer, in autumn, in winter; and it succeeds to admiration.

I cannot learn that anyone has died of it, tho' the experiment has been made under various and marvellous disadvantages. Five or six have died *upon* it, or after it, but from other diseases or accidents, chiefly from having taken the infection in the common way, by inspiration, before it could be given them in this way of transplantation. However, at present I need say no more of this, having already given you some report of our proceedings in it.

To them who are under the inoculation of the smallpox, we commonly give a vomit in the time of their decumbiture,[27] a day or two before the expected eruption. One of our patients, not vomiting so freely as he would have done, thrust a finger or two into his throat, which fetched up what was to be discharged from his uneasy stomach. He had but a few of the smallpox, and the pustules were sufficiently of the distinct sort, as it uses to be where they have the smallpox inoculated. But the fingers that had been thus employed proved as full as they could hold, and of the confluent sort, which he now thought his whole body would have been, if he had not in this way prevented it.

Your Dr. Leigh, in his *Natural History of Lancashire*, counts it an occurrence worth relating, that there were some cats known to catch the smallpox, and pass

27. decumbiture: lying down in bed because of illness.

regularly through the state of it, and then to die. We have had among us the very same occurrence.

It was generally observed, and complained, that the pigeon-houses of the city continued unfruitful, and the pigeons did not hatch or lay as they used to do, all the while that the smallpox was in its epidemical progress. And it is very strongly affirmed, that our dunghill-fowl felt much of the like effect upon them. We have so many among us who have been visited with the plague in other countries many years ago, and who have never been arrested with it, tho' they have been exposed as much as any other people to it, that it now begins to obtain a belief with us, that they who have had the plague will never have the smallpox after it.

I will add but one thing more. For succor under the smallpox, where life is in danger, after all the methods and medicines that our Sydenham and others rely upon, I can assure you we have yet found nothing so sure as this. Procure for the patient as early as may be, by epispastics, a plentiful discharge at the handwrists or ankles, or both (I say, *as early as may be!*) and keep them running till the danger is over. When the venom of the smallpox makes an evident and violent invasion on the nobler parts, this discharge *does wonderfully.* I am sorry it was so late before we fell into this way; but it has constantly prospered. I know not that it has once miscarried, since we came into it.

Benjamin Franklin

from the *Autobiography*, Part III
1788

In 1736 I lost one of my Sons a fine Boy of 4 Years old, by the Small Pox taken in the common way. I long regretted bitterly & still regret that I had not given it to him by Inoculation; This I mention for the Sake of Parents, who omit that Operation on the Supposition that they should never forgive themselves if a Child died under it; my Example showing that the Regret may be the same either way, and that therefore the safer should be chosen.

Chapter 8

Poetry: The Seventeenth Century

INTRODUCTION

The unity of poetry as a special kind of discourse—it all has line breaks—can sometimes lead one to forget how different are the contexts in which poetry appears. In Thomas Morton's *New English Canaan* (see chapter 3), poetry brings Morton's men and the Plymouth Pilgrims to the brink of violence. The settlers at Mount Wollaston, preparing for a maypole celebration, quite naturally had "a poem in readiness made." True, it was a bit "Enigmaticall." The Puritans didn't appreciate the riddle, thought Morton, because they lacked the knowledge of classical literature to decode it; he gives a lesson in literary criticism to show how little they knew. And true, the accompanying song was performed by the company in a somewhat "Bacchanalian" manner, with the singers not only inviting Indian women to join them but playing at Jupiter and Ganymede among themselves. The Puritans "distasted" such sport. William Bradford, for his part, wrote that Morton "to show his poetry composed sundry rhymes and verses, some tending to lasciviousness." Or, Bradford writes laconically, "worse practices."

The showdown at Mount Wollaston involved a conflict between two ideas of poetry. Morton's, a synthesis of popular forms such as riddles and songs with learned classical traditions, was profoundly secular, drawing frankly on pagan themes, music, and dance. It could not have been more suited to rile the Plymouth Puritans. Perhaps Morton expected the Puritans to have no love of poetry at all. They were, after all, iconoclasts, famously hostile both to the pleasures of the senses and to manmade symbols. Artifice was not to be valued as an end in itself. "If therefore the verses are not always so smooth and elegant as some may desire or expect," John Cotton wrote some years later in his preface to *The Whole Book of Psalmes*, "let them consider that God's Altar needs not our polishings." Yet as this chapter shows, Puritans cultivated poetry for their own purposes, ranging from devotional meditation to public narrative. They even loved riddles and anagrams; "Ah! old must dye!" (below) is only one of the better known examples of what seems to have been a popular pastime. So distinguished is the poetry of such Puritan authors as Anne Bradstreet and Edward Taylor that many readers will be surprised to learn that not all colonial poets were Puritans. Yet the conflict between rival aesthetics continued throughout the period.

New World verse in English may be dated from John Rastell's *New Interlude*, in chapter 2. English voyages of exploration regularly produced commendatory verses, such as a 1563 poem for a voyage by Thomas Stutely:

Now Stuteley hoist thy sail,
Thy wished land to finde:
And never doo regard vain talke,
For wurds they are but winde.

Throughout the sixteenth and seventeenth centuries, poems on American subjects typically appeared as dedicatory verses in narratives of exploration, treatises on geography, or promotional tracts on plantation. John Smith's *Generall History* (1624), for example, carried ten dedicatory verses, each by a different author. Many are routine. But some authors, notably Ben Jonson, could make dedicatory verse more interesting than the books they launched.

In the same years, cheaply printed popular ballads not only addressed a wider audience than learned poetry; they debated the attractions of the colonies somewhat more freely. Examples can be found in this chapter both for and against settlement, in ballad rhymes meant to be sung to well-known tunes (see selections 3 and 5 below).

Learned poetry of Britain also began to draw on the language of the New World for poetic purposes. As the selection from Spenser's *Faerie Queene* shows, America could signify worlds of imagination. English works such as Shakespeare's *The Tempest* and Milton's *Paradise Lost* use the same device, albeit to very different ends. These poetic Americas may seem at times to have little to do with the literal one. When John Donne writes of America in 1598 as:

That unripe side of earth, that heavy clime
That gives us man up now, like *Adams* time

he creates a mythic Indian. Toward the end of the seventeenth century, the poet and playwright John Dryden would turn that Indian into the noble savage. Such poeticisms, however, are far from irrelevant to the colonial world. They helped to shape the terms in which the English saw themselves as civilized, and became part of the repertoire of both imperial discourse and a nascent opposition to empire. Andrew Marvell's "Bermudas" seems deliberately suspended between poetic and nonpoetic traditions of New World writing; it presents an elegant song of invitation to settlement, but it frames that song as the utterance of English voyagers splashily rowing their way to shore while nature listens. In the poem, the song anticipates colonization. The singers never quite arrive.

The close relation between poetry and the New World that Marvell plays with was well established in the conventions of both learned and popular poetry by the time that verse came to be written in the colonies themselves. In Roger Williams's 1643 *Key into the Language of America*, for example, a tension is already visible between the Indians as described in the prose sections and the poeticized Indians who appear in the verses that Williams inserts at the end of each chapter. (A sample may be seen in chapter 7.) *A Key into the Language of America* is a treatise on Indian language. But Williams, interestingly, does not describe Indian song as poetry. He makes no attempt to translate it in verse form—though he does sometimes ventriloquize his own speeches, figuratively, as those of Indians.

Not until more than a century later would the English begin to turn the oral performances of Indian song or myth into versified texts. Nineteenth-century ethnographers took down many texts, some of which may record versions of oral tradition reaching back before the English arrived. (A selection of them may be found in the Library of America's *American Poetry: The Nineteenth Century*.) Yet there is considerable evidence that colonization was altering Indian ritual and performance from an early date. (See, for example, David Brainerd's journal in chapter 9.) Later transcriptions should not be taken as the product of Indian tribes, as though Indians lived outside of history. A performance context for traditional song, moreover, is very different from a textual context for poetry.

Colonists themselves had widely differing contexts for verse. Some, like George Alsop, wrote for publication in London, which remained the center of prestigious poetic culture. Some of the most interesting colonial poetry, however, was written not for publication at all, but for devotional exercises. Edward Taylor's meditations, composed to prepare himself for the sacrament of the Lord's Supper, remained unpublished and unknown until the twentieth century. Anne Bradstreet's intimate poetry, for which she is now best known, was published only after her death, and differs dramatically from the public poetry she prepared for circulation. Even the public poems were printed without her consent.

The devotional verse of Bradstreet and Taylor is somewhat belated, influenced less by the British poets of their own day than by those of the early seventeenth century: Donne, Herbert, Quarles, and other poets of what has come to be known as the metaphysical school. The metaphysical poets are known for ingenuity and concentration of metaphor, which they use to intensify the inwardness of experience in intimate contexts—both in amorous poetry, richly sexualized by Donne, and in devotional poetry, which Herbert and others carried to new levels of mysticism. Neither Bradstreet nor Taylor would have countenanced the sensuality of Donne's aesthetic. The primacy of figurative language in their poetry was supported more by Puritan traditions of Biblical exegesis and typology. But Bradstreet also sustains those conventions in amorous verse, where she draws on the pagan imagery of classical literature. And Taylor folds the metaphysical eros of poetic language directly into his mystical meditations.

Other colonial poets wrote in private, intimate forms for less theological reasons. Henry Kelsey and Sarah Knight (see chapter 5) turn to verse out of a sense of isolation in colonial settings. At the opposite extreme was Michael Wigglesworth, one of the few writers in this chapter who wrote for publication in the colonial press itself. His ponderous and apocalyptic *Day of Doom* was a bestseller, and entered oral tradition through memorization. The New England press had begun to produce a number of popular verse forms, such as the poems that filled many almanacs. The most important popular form in the colonies was the elegy, the form directly defined by the ever-present colonial concern with death. (A 1710 example by Benjamin Tompson can be found in chapter 14.) The elegy usually commemorates an individual; but New

England elegies typically turn the work of mourning into a caution against self, a memento mori, and a reaffirmation of collective mission. More than any other form, the elegy stands in between the intimate, devotional tradition of manuscript verse and the authoritative rhetoric of public poetry.

M.W.

Suggested readings: The Puritans, especially Bradstreet and Taylor, have been the subject of specialized studies, and often appear in such general works as Roy Harvey Pearce's *The Continuity of American Poetry*. But there has never been a systematic treatment of colonial verse. The literature may be sampled directly in Harrison Meserole's anthology, *Seventeenth-Century American Poetry*.

1. Edmund Spenser

from *The Faerie Queene,* Book II
1590

Spenser (1552?–99) began his most famous work in 1579, publishing the first part in 1590 and the final three books in 1596. The poem tries to manufacture a British mythology, using a deliberately archaic style (i's instead of j's, for example) to conjure a sense of the past. Yet Spenser was very much a man of present politics and the emergent culture of empire. While composing The Faerie Queene *he was involved in English efforts to colonize Ireland, which, in his* View of the Present State of Ireland, *he calls "a savage nation." Spenser's analogy between the New World and the moon can be compared to that of John Wilkins in chapter 7.*

I

Right well I wote[1] most mighty Soueraine,
That all this famous antique history,
Of some th'aboundance of an idle braine
Will iudged be, and painted forgery,
Rather then matter of iust memory,
Sith[2] none, that breatheth liuing aire, does know,
Where is that happy land of Faery,
Which I so much do vaunt, yet no where show,
But vouch antiquities, which no body can know.

2

But let that man with better sence aduize,
That of the world least part to vs is red:
And dayly how through hardy enterprize,
Many great Regions are discouered,
Which to late age were neuer mentioned.
Who euer heard of th'Indian *Peru?*
Or who in venturous vessell measured
The *Amazons* huge riuer now found trew?
Or fruitfullest *Virginia* who did euer vew?

---

1. wote: know.   2. sith: since.

3

Yet all these were, when no man did them know:
Yet haue from wisest ages hidden beene:
And later times things more vnknowne shall show.
Why then should witlesse man so much misweene[3]
That nothing is, but that which he hath seene?
What if within the Moones faire shining spheare?
What if in euery other starre vnseene
Of other worldes he happily should heare?
He wonder would much more: yet such to some appeare.

2. Robert Hayman

verses on Newfoundland
1628

*Hayman (1575–1629) seems to have gone to Newfoundland around 1618, staying
there until his death. In 1628 he published* Quodlibets, *a book of epigrams in
imitation of Ben Jonson and others. All 367 epigrams in the book were written in
Newfoundland, and many describe it, though others are on topics of more
common European interest.*

*To a worthy Friend, who often objects the coldnesse of the Winter in Newfound-
Land, and may serve for all those who have the like conceit.*

You say that you would live in Newfound-land,
Did not this one thing your conceit withstand;
You feare the *Winters* cold, sharp, piercing ayre.
They love it best, that have once wintered there.
Winter is there, short, wholesome, constant, cleare,
Not thicke, unwholesome, shuffling, as 'tis here.

A Skeltonicall continued ryme, in praise of my New-found-Land.

Although in cloathes, company, buildings faire,
With England, New-found-land cannot compare:
Did some know what contentment I found there,
Always enough, most times somewhat to spare,

3. misweene: think wrongly.

With little paines, lesse toyle, and lesser care,
Exempt from taxings, il newes, Lawing, feare,
If cleane, and warme, no matter what you weare,
Healthy, and wealthy, if men carefull are,
With much—much more, then I will now declare,
(I say) if some wise men knew what this were,
(I doe beleeve) they'd live no other where.

3. Anonymous

A West-Country Man's Voyage to New England
c. 1632

*The earliest source for this popular ballad is a songbook of 1661, but it was almost
certainly composed before 1635, when Boston replaced Dorchester as the main
Massachusetts town. The song is written in a caricatured regional dialect (e.g.,
"che" for "I"); west country men were stereotypically unlettered oafs. Rather
unusually for a printed text, it ridicules the promotional literature of planting, as
well as such Puritan innovations as secular marriage rites.*

My Masters give audience, and listen to me,
And streight che will tell you where che have be:
Che have been in New-England, but now cham come o'er,
Itch do think they shal catch me go thither no more.

Before che went o'er Lord how Voke did tell
How vishes did grow, and how birds did dwell
All one among t'other, in the wood and the water,
Che thought had been true, but che find no such matter.

When first che did land che mazed me quite,
And 'twas of all daies on a Satterday night,
Che wondred to see the strong buildings were there,
'Twas all like the standing at Bartholmew Fair.

Well, that night che slept till near Prayer time,
Next morning che wondred to hear no Bells chime,
And when che had ask'd the reason, che found
'Twas because they had never a Bell in the Town.

At last being warned to Church to repair,
Where che did think certain che'd sho'd hear some prayer,
But the Parson there no such matter did teach,
They scorn'd to pray, they were all able to preach.

The virst thing they did, a Zalm they did sing,
I pluckt out my Zalm book, which with me did bring,
Che was troubled to seek him,[4] 'cause they call him by name,
But they had got a new Song to the tune of the same.

When Sermon was done was a child to baptize
About sixteen years old, as volk did surmize,
And no Godfather nor Godmother, yet 'twas quiet and still,
The Priest durst not cross him for fear of his ill will.

A Sirra, quoth I, and to dinner che went,
And gave the Lord thanks for what he had sent;
Next day was a wedding, the brideman my friend,
He kindly invites me, so thither I wend.

But this, above all, to me wonder did bring,
To see a Magistrate marry, and had ne'r a ring;
Che thought they would call me the woman to give,
But che think he stole her, for he askt no man leave.

Now this was new Dorchester as they told me,
A Town very famous in all that Country;
They said 'twas new building, I grant it was true,
Yet methinks old Dorchester as fine as the new.

Che staid there among them till che was weary at heart,
At length there came shipping, che got leave to depart:
But when all was ended che was coming away,
Che had threescore shillings for swearing to pay.[5]

But when che saw that, an oath more che swore,
Che would stay no more longer to swear on the score:
Che bid farewell to those Fowlers and Fishers,
So God bless old England and all his well wishers.

---

4. him: i.e., it, the psalm.   5. i.e., fines for swearing.

4. George Herbert

from "The Church Militant"
1633

Herbert (1593–1633) is known mainly as a devoutly meditative poet. In this passage he shows a strong, if ambivalent, national consciousness. The selection comes from "The Church Militant," the long final poem of The Temple, *Herbert's only book of poetry, published just after his death in 1633. The poem traces a link between empire and religion from antiquity to the modern age, with the italicized couplet acting as a refrain, punctuating Herbert's history of the world. Compare this version of the* translatio imperii *theme with Bishop Berkeley's, in chapter 14.*

Religion stands on tip-toe in our land,
Readie to passe to the *American* strand.
When height of malice, and prodigious lusts,
Impudent sinning, witchcrafts, and distrusts
(The marks of future bane) shall fill our cup
Unto the brimme, and make our measure up;
When *Seine* shall swallow *Tiber*, and the *Thames*
By letting in them both, pollutes her streams:[6]
When *Italie* of us shall have her will,
And all her calender of sinnes fulfill;
Whereby one may fortell, what sinnes next yeare
Shall both in *France* and *England* domineer:
Then shall Religion to *America* flee:
They[7] have their times of Gospel, ev'n as we.
My God, thou dost prepare for them a way
By carrying first their gold from them away:
For gold and grace did never yet agree:
Religion alwaies sides with povertie.
We think we rob them, but we think amisse:
We are more poore, and they more rich by this.
Thou wilt revenge their quarrell, making grace
To pay our debts, and leave our ancient place
To go to them, while that which now their nation
But lends to us, shall be our desolation.

---

6. When *Seine*, etc.: a reference to the influence of France and Rome over the English court.

7. They: i.e., native Americans.

Yet as the Church shall thither westward flie,
So Sinne shall trace and dog her instantly:
They have their period also and set times
Both for their vertuous actions and their crimes.
And where of old the Empire and the Arts
Usher'd the Gospel ever in mens hearts,
Spain hath done one; when Arts perform the other,
The Church shall come, & Sinne the Church shall smother:
That when they have accomplished their round,
And met in th' east their first and ancient sound,[8]
Judgement may meet them both & search them round.
Thus do both lights, as well in Church as Sunne,
Light one another, and together runne.
Thus also Sinne and Darknesse follow still
The Church and Sunne with all their power and skill.
But as the Sunne still goes both west and east;
So also did the Church by going west
Still eastward go; because it drew more neare
To time and place, where judgement shall appeare.
How deare to me, O God, thy counsels are!
         Who may with thee compare?

5. Anonymous

A Friendly Invitation to a New Plantation ["The Zealous Puritan"] 1638

> *Popular ballads also supported the Puritans. This text survives from a collection of 1662, where it was called "The Zealous Puritan." But it is very likely the poem that was registered for publication in 1638 under the title given here, which is more appropriate to the poem.*

My Brethren all attend,
And list to my relation:
This is the day, mark what I say,
Tends to your renovation;
Stay not among the Wicked,
Lest that with them you perish,
But let us to *New-England* go
And the Pagan People cherish;

Then for the truths sake come along, come along,
Leave this place of Superstition:
Were it not for we, that the Brethren be,
You would sink into Perdition.

There you may teach our hymns,
Without the Laws controulment:
We need not fear, the Bishops there,
Nor Spiritual-Courts inroulment;
Nay, the Surplice shall not fright us,
Nor superstitious blindness;
Nor scandals rise, when we disguise,
And our Sisters kiss in kindness;
      Then for the truths sake, &c.

For Company I fear not,
There goes my Cosin *Hannah*,
And *Ruben*, so persuades to go
My Cosin *Joyce, Susanna.*
With *Abigail* and *Faith*,
And *Ruth*, no doubt, comes after;
And *Sarah* kind, will not stay behind,
My Cosin *Constance* Daughter;
      Then for the truths sake, &c.

Tom Tyler is prepared,
And th' Smith as black as coal;
Ralph Cobler too with us will go,
For he regards his soul;
The Weaver, honest *Simon*,
With *Prudence, Jacob's* Daughter,
And *Sarah*, she, and *Barbary*,
Professeth to come after;
      Then for the truths sake, &c.

When we, that are elected,
Arrive in that fair Country,
Even by our faith, as the Brethren saith,
We will not fear our entry;
The Psalms shall be our Musick,
Our time spent in expounding,
Which in our zeal we will reveal
To the Brethrens joy abounding;
      Then for the truths sake, &c.

6. Anonymous

New England's Annoyances
c. 1642

This ballad, unlike the previous ones, derives from the American side of the Atlantic. It long survived in oral tradition, though stanza 14 suggests that it dates from the period of intensifying religious conflict, probably near the beginning of the English Civil Wars. Its humor interestingly blends self-parody and partisan promotion. One scholar calls it "America's first folk song."

1

New England's annoyances you that would know them,
Pray ponder these verses which briefly doth show them.
The place where we live is a wilderness wood,
Where grass is much wanting that's fruitful and good.

2

From the end of November till three months are gone,
The ground is all frozen as hard as a stone,
Our mountains and hills and vallies below,
Being commonly covered with ice and with snow.

3

And when the north-wester with violence blows,
Then every man pulls his cap over his nose;
But if any's so hardy and will it withstand,
He forfeits a finger, a foot, or a hand.

4

When the ground opens we then take the hoe,
And make the ground ready to plant and to sow;
Our corn being planted and seed being sown,
The worms destroy much before it is grown.

5

While it is growing much spoil there is made,
By birds and by squirrels that pluck up the blade;
Even when it is grown to full corn in the ear,
It's apt to be spoil'd by hog, racoon, and deer.

6

Our money's soon counted, for we have just none,
All that we brought with us is wasted and gone.
We buy and sell nothing but upon exchange,
Which makes all our dealings uncertain and strange.

7

And now our garments begin to grow thin,
And wool is much wanted to card and to spin;
If we can get a garment to cover without,
Our innermost garment is clout upon clout.[8]

8

Our clothes we brought with us are apt to be torn,
They need to be clouted before they are worn,
For clouting our garments does injure us nothing:
Clouts double are warmer than single whole clothing.

9

If flesh meat be wanting to fill up our dish,
We have carrots and pumpkins and turnips and fish;
And when we have a mind for a delicate dish,
We repair to the clam banks, and there we catch fish.

10

Instead of pottage and puddings and custards and pies,
Our pumpkins and parsnips are common supplies;
We have pumpkin at morning and pumpkin at noon;
If it was not for pumpkins we should be undone.

8. clout: patch.

11

If barley be wanting to make into malt,
We must be contented and think it no fault;
For we can make liquor to sweeten our lips,
Of pumpkins and parsnips and walnut tree chips.

12

And of our green corn-stalks we make our best beer,
We put it in barrels to drink all the year:
Yet I am as healthy, I verily think,
Who make the spring-water my commonest drink.

13

And we have a Cov'nant one with another,
Which makes a division 'twixt brother and brother:
For some are rejected, and others made Saints,
Of those that are equal in virtues and wants.

14

For such like annoyance we've many mad fellows
Find fault with our apples before they are mellow;[9]
And they are for England, they will not stay here,
But meet with a lion in shunning a bear.

15

Now while some are going let others be coming,
For while liquor is boiling it must have a scumming;
But we will not blame them, for birds of a feather,
By seeking their fellows are flocking together.

16

But you who the Lord intends hither to bring,
Forsake not the honey for fear of the sting;
But bring both a quiet and contented mind,
And all needful blessing you surely shall find.

9. mellow: ripe.

7.

from *The Whole Booke of Psalmes Faithfully Translated into English Metre*
1640

Commonly known as The Bay Psalm Book, *this translation was the first English book printed in the New World. (The American Spanish press, of course, was a century older.) According to Cotton Mather, it was the work of the "chief Divines" of the colony, including his grandfather Richard Mather, but much controversy has surrounded its exact authorship. The 23rd psalm has been attributed to John Cotton, along with the preface, which is an important treatise on the theology and practice of church music. These versions were made to be sung, as "The West-Country Man's Voyage" illustrates. As poetry,* The Bay Psalm Book *has been much ridiculed. One specialist calls Psalm 137 "the most atrocious piece in the whole volume." The importance of this and other psalms to colonial poets can be seen below in chapter 14, where three other renditions of Psalm 137 are gathered, or in Benjamin Franklin's* Autobiography *(see chapter 10), in which Franklin and his friends compose versions of Psalm 18.*

PSALME 23

A PSALM OF DAVID

    The Lord to me a shepherd is,
        want therefore shall not I.
2   He in the folds of tender grass,
        doth cause me down to lie:
    To waters calm me gently leads
3   Restore my soul doth he:
    he doth in paths of righteousness:
        for his name's sake lead me.
4   Yea though in valley of death's shade
        I walk, none ill I'll fear:
    because thou are with me, thy rod,
        and staff my comfort are.
5   For me a table thou has spread,
        in presence of my foes:
    thou dost anoint my head with oil.
        my cup it overflows.

6   Goodness & mercy surely shall
                all my days follow me:
        and in the Lord's house I shall dwell
                so long as days shall be.

PSALME 137

        The rivers on of Babilon
                there when wee did sit downe:
        yea even then wee mourned, when
                wee remembered Sion.
2   Our Harps wee did hang it amid,
                upon the willow tree.
3   Because there they that us away
                led in captivitee,
        Requir'd of us a song, & thus
                askt mirth: us waste who laid,
        sing us among a Sions song,
                unto us then they said.
4   The lords song sing can wee? being
5   in strangers land. Then let
        loose her skill my right hand, if I
                Jerusalem forget.
6   Let cleave my tongue my pallate on,
                if minde thee doe not I:
        if chiefe joyes or'e I prize not more
                Jerusalem my joy.
7   Remember Lord, Edoms sons word,
                unto the ground said they,
        it rase, it rase, when as it was
                Jerusalem her day.
8   Blest shall hee bee, that payeth thee,
                daughter of Babilon,
        whom must be waste: that which thou hast
                rewarded us upon.
9   O happie hee shall surely bee
                that taketh up, that eke
        thy little ones against the stones
                doth into pieces breake.

8. Anonymous

Ah! Old Must Dye
1645

*This poem was sent anonymously to Thomas Dudley while he was governor of
Massachusetts; its title is an anagram of his name—a favorite kind of wit among
Puritan writers.*

A death's head on your hand you neede not weare,
A dying head you on your shoulders beare.
You neede not one to mind you, you must dye,
You in your name may spell mortalitye.
Younge men may dye, but old men, these dye must,
'Twill not be long before you turne to dust.
Before you turne to dust! ah! must! old! dye!
What shall younge doe, when old in dust doe lye?
When old in dust lye, what N. England doe?
When old in dust doe lye, it's best dye too.

9. Andrew Marvell

Bermudas
1653

Marvell (1621–78) may have drawn on firsthand accounts of Bermuda by the Puritan John Oxenbridge, who had twice been to Bermuda to escape church authorities. Marvell lodged with Oxenbridge in 1653, when he is thought to have written the poem. He also seems to have known Captain Smith's General History. *Author of several tributes to Oliver Cromwell, Marvell became tutor to Cromwell's ward William Dutton in the same year. Cromwell at the time was much interested in the West Indies, forming his so-called Western Design, which would result in 1654 with the military expedition that in 1655 conquered Jamaica.*

Where the remote Bermudas ride
In the ocean's bosom unespied,
From a small boat, that rowed along,
The listening winds received this song.
          'What should we do but sing his praise
That led us through the watery maze,
Unto an isle so long unknown,
And yet far kinder than our own?
Where he the huge sea-monsters wracks,
That lift the deep upon their backs,
He lands us on a grassy stage,
Safe from the storms, and prelate's rage.
He gave us this eternal spring,
Which here enamels everything,
And sends the fowl to us in care,
On daily visits through the air.
He hangs in shades the orange bright,
Like golden lamps in a green night,
And does in the pom'granates close
Jewels more rich than Ormus[10] shows.
He makes the figs our mouths to meet,
And throws the melons at our feet,
But apples[11] plants of such a price,

10. Ormus: Hormuz, on the Persian gulf.   11. apples: pineapples.

No tree could ever bear them twice.
With cedars, chosen by his hand,
From Lebanon, he stores the land,
And makes the hollow seas, that roar,
Proclaim the ambergris on shore.[12]
He cast (of which we rather boast)
The gospel's pearl upon our coast,
And in these rocks for us did frame
A temple, where to sound his name.
Oh let our voice his praise exalt,
Till it arrive at heaven's vault:
Which thence (perhaps) rebounding, may
Echo beyond the Mexique Bay.'
     Thus sung they, in the English boat,
An holy and a cheerful note,
And all the way, to guide their chime,
With falling oars they kept the time.

10. George Alsop

The Author to his Book
1666

*George Alsop (1638–80?) went to Maryland as an indentured servant in 1658. An
ardent royalist, he exulted in the news of Cromwell's death, which came just as he
departed England. A few years later, after a serious illness, he was back in England,
where monarchy had been restored. He published his only book, A Character of
the Province of Maryland, in 1666. The principal modern edition bowdlerized the
text for its racy style, entirely omitting this prefatory verse. The poem can be
compared with Bradstreet's "The Author to her Book" in selection 11 below.*

When first *Apollo* got my brain with Childe,
He made large promise never to beguile,
But like an honest Father, he would keep
Whatever Issue from my Brain did creep:
With that I gave consent, and up he threw
Me on a Bench, and strangely he did do;
Then every week he daily came to see
How his new Physick still did work with me.

12. ambergris on shore: ambergris is a secretion of the sperm
whale, highly valued in making perfume. The English settlers
of Bermuda had in fact discovered a large amount of ambergris on the shore.

And when he did perceive he'd don the feat,
Like an unworthy man he made retreat,
Left me in desolation, and where none
Compassionated when they heard me groan.
What could he judge the Parish then would think,
To see me fair, his Brat as black as Ink?
If they had eyes, they'd swear I were no Nun,
But got with Child by some black *Africk* Son,
And so condemn me for my Fornication,
To beat them Hemp to stifle half the Nation.
Well, since 'tis so, I'le alter this base Fate,
And lay his Bastard at some Noble's Gate;
Withdraw my self from Beadles,[13] and from such,
Who would give twelve pence I were in their clutch:
Then, who can tell? this Child which I do hide,
May be in time a Small-beer Col'nel *Pride*.[14]
But while I talk, my business it is dumb,
I must lay double-clothes unto thy Bum,
Then lap thee warm, and to the world commit
The Bastard Off-spring of a New-born wit.
Farewel poor Brat, thou in a monstrous World,
In swadling bands, thus up and down art hurl'd;
There to receive what Destiny doth contrive,
Either to perish, or be sav'd alive.
Good Fate protect thee from a Criticks power,
For if he comes, thou'rt gon in half an hour,
Stifl'd and blasted, 'tis their usual way,
To make that Night, which is as bright as Day.
For if they once but wring, and skrew their mouth,
Cock up their Hats, and set the point Du-South,
Armes all a kimbo, and with belly strut,
As if they had *Parnassus* in their gut:
These are the Symtomes of the murthering fall
Of my poor Infant, and his burial.
Say he should miss thee, and some ign'rant Asse
Should find thee out, as he along doth pass,
It were all one, he'd look into thy Tayle,
To see if thou wert Feminine or Male;[15]
When he'd half starv'd thee, for to satisfie
His peeping Ign'rance, he'd then let thee lie;

---

13. Beadles: church officers who enforced the laws against poverty, vagrancy, and bastardy.
14. Col'nel *Pride*: a royalist hero who barred some seventy members of Parliament from entering the House of Commons in 1648.
15. Feminine or Male: a play on the literary distinction between masculine and feminine rhymes.

And vow by's wit he ne're could understand,
The Heathen dresses of another Land:
Well, 'tis no matter, wherever such as he
Knows one grain, more then his simplicity.
Now, how the pulses of my Senses beat,
To think the rigid Fortune thou wilt meet;
Asses and captious Fools, not six in ten
Of thy Spectators will be real men,
To Umpire up the badness of the Cause,
And screen my weakness from the rav'nous Laws,
Of those that will undoubted sit to see
How they might blast this new-born Infancy:
If they should burn him, they'd conclude hereafter,
'Twere too good death for him to dye a Martyr:
And if they let him live, they think it will
Be but a means for to encourage ill,
And bring in time some strange *Antipod'ans*,[16]
A thousand Leagues beyond *Philippians*,[17]
To storm our Wits; therefore he must not rest,
But shall be hang'd, for all he has been prest:[18]
Thus they conclude.—My Genius comforts give,
In Resurrection he will surely live.

Trafique is Earth's great Atlas 1666

The Character of the Province of Maryland *ends each chapter with an untitled verse; the following paean to commerce stands at the end of chapter 4, "Upon Trafique." Its theme was to become a favorite in the poetry of the next century. Atlas, in Greek mythology, was the Titan employed in supporting the heavens above his head.*

Trafique is Earth's great *Atlas*, that supports
The pay of Armies, and the height of Courts,
And makes Mechanicks live, that else would die
Meer starving Martyrs to their penury:
None but the Merchant of this thing can boast,
He, like the Bee, comes loaden from each Coast,
And to all Kingdoms, as within a Hive,
Stows up those Riches that doth make them thrive:
Be thrifty, *Mary-Land*, keep what thou hast in store,
And each years Trafique to thy self get more.

---

16. *Antipod'ans*: those who live on the opposite side of the world (the antipodes).
17. *Philippians*: the Philippines.

18. prest: a pun on the instrument of torture and the instrument of printing.

11. Anne Bradstreet

Bradstreet (1612?–72) belonged to the elite of the Massachusetts Bay Colony; both her father and her husband were governors of the colony. She was born in England; her father served as steward to the earl of Lincoln, and she seems to have read widely in the estate's library. Around 1628, she married Simon Bradstreet, with whom she emigrated in 1630, on the same ship to which Winthrop preached "A Modell of Christian Charity." The Bradstreets lived in present-day Cambridge before moving to Ipswich, and then again to Andover.

By her own account, given in chapter 5, she had mixed feelings about emigration, and the early poems show a keen identification with European literary culture. In 1650 her brother-in-law John Woodbridge carried some of her poems to England and had them published there as The Tenth Muse, Lately Sprung up in America. *Woodbridge's preface, anticipating that readers would be shocked to read something written by a woman, offered a testimonial: "It is the work of a woman, honoured, and esteemed where she lives, for her gracious demeanour, her eminent parts, her pious conversation, her courteous disposition, her exact diligence in her place, and discrete managing of her family occasions, and more than so, these poems are the fruit but of some few hours, curtailed from her sleep and other refreshments."*

In the first lines of the Prologue, Bradstreet seems to cede epic and public themes to men, accepting minor status as a woman writer. In the context of The Tenth Muse, *this gesture may be a feint, as the poems that follow treat exactly of such subjects. They include "The Four Monarchies" and "A Dialogue between Old England and New." Bradstreet wrote "The Author to her Book" and "Contemplations" for an intended second edition of her poems. When the book was finally published in 1678, six years after her death, the editor included the other lyrics below as well.*

Prologue
1650

1

To sing of Wars, of Captaines, and of Kings,
Of Cities founded, Common-wealths begun,
For my mean Pen, are too superiour things,
And how they all, or each, their dates have run:
Let Poets, and Historians set these forth,
My obscure Verse, shal not so dim their worth.

2

But when my wondring eyes, and envious heart,
Great *Bartas*[19] sugar'd lines doe but read o're;
Foole, I doe grudge, the Muses did not part
'Twixt him and me, that over-fluent store;
A *Bartas* can doe what a *Bartas* wil,
But simple I, according to my skill.

3

From School-boye's tongue, no Rhethorick we expect,
Nor yet a sweet Consort, from broken strings,
Nor perfect beauty, where's a maine defect.
My foolish, broken, blemish'd Muse so sings;
And this to mend, alas, no Art is able,
'Cause Nature made it so irreparable.

4

Nor can I, like that fluent sweet tongu'd *Greek*[20]
Who lisp'd at first, speake afterwards more plaine.
By Art, he gladly found what he did seeke,
A full requitall of his striving paine:
Art can doe much, but this maxime's most sure,
A weake or wounded braine admits no cure.

5

I am obnoxious to each carping tongue,
Who sayes, my hand a needle better fits.
A Poet's Pen, all scorne I should thus wrong;
For such despight they cast on female wits:
If what I doe prove well, it wo'nt advance,
They'l say its stolen, or else, it was by chance.

6

But sure the antick *Greeks* were far more milde,
Else of our Sex, why feigned they those nine,[21]
And poesy made, *Calliope's* owne childe?
So 'mongst the rest, they plac'd the Arts divine.
But this weake knot they will full soone untye,
The *Greeks* did nought, but play the foole and lye.

19. *Great Bartas*: Guillaume Du Bartas (1544–99), whose massive poem *La Sepmaine du Creation* was translated by Joshua Sylvester as *The Divine Weekes and Workes*.

20. that fluent sweet tongu'd *Greek*: Demosthenes (384–322 B.C.), Greek orator who trained his speech by putting pebbles in his mouth.

21. those nine: the muses.

7

Let *Greeks* be *Greeks*, and Women what they are,
Men have precedency, and still excell.
It is but vaine, unjustly to wage war.
Men can doe best, and Women know it well;
Preheminence in each, and all is yours,
Yet grant some small acknowledgement of ours.

8

And oh, ye high flown quils, that soare the skies,
And ever with your prey, still catch your praise,
If e're you daigne these lowly lines, your eyes
Give wholsome Parsley wreath, I ask no Bayes:[22]
This meane and unrefined stuffe of mine,
Will make your glistering gold but more to shine.

The Author to her Book

Thou ill-form'd offspring of my feeble brain,
Who after birth did'st by my side remain,
Till snatcht from thence by friends, less wise then true
Who thee abroad, expos'd to publick view,
Made thee in raggs,[23] halting to th' press to trudge,
Where errors were not lessened (all may judg).
At thy return my blushing was not small,
My rambling brat (in print) should mother call.
I cast thee by as one unfit for light,
Thy Visage was so irksome in my sight.
Yet being mine own, at length affection would
Thy blemishes amend, if so I could.

22. Bayes: the bay, or laurel wreath, the sign of victory.

23. raggs: paper was made from rags until the nineteenth century.

I wash'd thy face, but more defects I saw,
And rubbing off a spot, still made a flaw.
I stretcht thy joynts to make thee even feet,[24]
Yet still thou run'st more hobling then is meet;
In better dress to trim thee was my mind,
But nought save home-spun Cloth, i' th' house I find.
In this array, 'mongst Vulgars mayst thou roam,
In Criticks hands, beware thou dost not come;
And take thy way where yet thou are not known,
If for thy Father askt, say, thou hadst none:
And for thy Mother, she alas is poor,
Which caus'd her thus to send thee out of door.

Contemplations

Sometime now past in the Autumnal Tide,
When *Phoebus*[25] wanted but one hour to bed,
The trees all richly clad, yet void of pride,
Were gilded o're by his rich golden head.
Their leaves & fruits seem'd painted, but was true
Of green, of red, of yellow, mixed hew.
Rapt were my sences at this delectable view.

2

I wist not what to wish, yet sure thought I,
If so much excellence abide below;
How excellent is he that dwells on high?
Whose power and beauty by his works we know.
Sure he is goodness, wisdome, glory, light,
That hath this under world so richly dight:[26]
More Heaven then Earth was here, no winter & no night.

3

Then on a stately Oak I cast mine Eye,
Whose ruffling top the Clouds seem'd to aspire.
How long since thou wast in thine Infancy?
Thy strength, and stature, more thy years admire.
Hath hundred winters past since thou wast born?
Or thousand since thou brakest thy shell of horn?
If so, all these as nought, Eternity doth scorn.

24. feet: a pun on metrical feet.
25. *Phoebus*: Apollo, the sun.

26. dight: decorated.

4

Then higher on the glistering Sun I gaz'd
Whose beams was shaded by the leavie Tree.
The more I look'd, the more I grew amaz'd,
And softly said, what glory's like to thee?
Soul of this world, this Universes Eye,
No wonder, some made thee a Deity:
Had I not better known, (alas) the same had I.

5

Thou as a Bridegroom from thy Chamber rushes,
And as a strong man, joyes to run a race.
The morn doth usher thee, with smiles & blushes.
The Earth reflects her glances in thy face.
Birds, insects, Animals with Vegative,
Thy heat from death and dulness doth revive:
And in the darksome womb of fruitful nature dive.

6

Thy swift Annual, and diurnal Course,
Thy daily streight, and yearly oblique path,
Thy pleasing fervor, and thy scorching force,
All mortals here the feeling knowledg hath.
Thy presence makes it day, thy absence night,
Quaternal Seasons caused by thy might:
Hail Creature, full of sweetness, beauty & delight.

7

Art thou so full of glory, that no Eye
Hath strength, thy shining Rayes once to behold?
And is thy splendid Throne erect so high
As to approach it, can no earthly mould?
How full of glory then must thy Creator be?
Who gave this bright light luster unto thee:
Admir'd, ador'd for ever, be that Majesty.

8

Silent alone, where none or[27] saw, or heard,
In pathless paths I led my wandring feet,

27. or: either.

My humble Eyes to lofty Skyes I rear'd
To sing some Song, my mazed Muse thought meet.
My great Creator I would magnifie,
That nature had, thus decked liberally:
But Ah, and Ah, again, my imbecility!

9

I heard the merry grashopper then sing,
The black clad Cricket, bear a second part,
They kept one tune, and played on the same string,
Seeming to glory in their little Art.
Shall Creatures abject, thus their voices raise?
And in their kind resound their makers praise:
Whilst I as mute, can warble forth no higher layes?

10

When present times look back to Ages past,
And men in being fancy those are dead,[28]
It makes things gone perpetually to last,
And calls back moneths and years that long since fled.
It makes a man more aged in conceit,[29]
Than was *Methuselah*, or's grand-sire great:
While of their persons & their acts his mind doth treat.

11

Sometimes in *Eden* fair, he seems to be,
Sees glorious *Adam* there made Lord of all,
Fancyes the Apple, dangle on the Tree,
That turn'd his Sovereign to a naked thral.
Who like a miscreant's driven from that place,
To get his bread with pain, and sweat of face:
A penalty impos'd on his backsliding Race.

12

Here sits our Grandame in retired place,
And in her lap, her bloody *Cain* new born,
The weeping Imp oft looks her in the face,
Bewails his unknown hap, and fate forlorn;

---

28. i.e., and living men imagine those of the past.   29. conceit: thought.

His Mother sighs, to think of Paradise,
And how she lost her bliss, to be more wise,
Believing him that was, and is, Father of lyes.

13

Here *Cain* and *Abel* come to sacrifice.
Fruits of the Earth, and Fatlings each do bring.
On *Abel's* gift the fire descends from Skies,
But no such sign on false *Cain's* offering;
With sullen hateful looks he goes his wayes.
Hath thousand thoughts to end his brothers dayes,
Upon whose blood his future good he hopes to raise.

14

There *Abel* keeps his sheep, no ill he thinks.
His brother comes, then acts his fratricide,
The Virgin Earth, of blood her first draught drinks.
But since that time she often hath been cloy'd.
The wretch with gastly face and dreadful mind,
Thinks each he sees will serve him in his kind,
Though none on Earth but kindred near then could he find.

15

Who fancyes not his looks now at the Barr,
His face like death, his heart with horror fraught,
Nor Male-factor ever felt like warr,
When deep dispair, with wish of life hath fought,
Branded with guilt, and crusht with treble woes,
A Vagabond to Land of *Nod* he goes,
A City builds, that wals might him secure from foes.

16

Who thinks not oft upon the Fathers ages,
Their long descent, how nephews sons they saw,
The starry observations of those Sages,
And how their precepts to their sons were law,
How Adam sigh'd to see his Progeny,
Cloath'd all in his black sinfull Livery,
Who neither guilt, nor yet the punishment could fly?

17

Our life compare we with their length of dayes:
Who to the tenth of theirs doth now arrive?
And though thus short, we shorten many wayes,
Living so little while we are alive;
In eating, drinking, sleeping, vain delight
So unawares comes on perpetual night,
And puts all pleasures vain unto eternal flight.

18

When I behold the heavens as in their prime,
And then the earth (though old) stil clad in green,
The stones and trees, insensible of time,
Nor age nor wrinkle on their front are seen,
If winter come, and greeness then do fade,
A Spring returns, and they more youthfull made;
But Man grows old, lies down, remains where once he's laid.

19

By birth more noble than those creatures all,
Yet seems by nature and by custome curs'd,
No sooner born, but grief and care makes fall
That state obliterate he had at first:
Nor youth, nor strength, nor wisdom spring again
Nor habitations long their names retain,
But in oblivion to the final day remain.

20

Shall I then praise the heavens, the trees, the earth
Because their beauty and their strength last longer
Shall I wish there, or never to had birth,
Because they're bigger, & their bodyes stronger?
Nay, they shall darken, perish, fade and dye,
And when unmade, so ever shall they lye,
But man was made for endless immortality.

21

Under the cooling shadow of a stately Elm
Close sate I by a goodly Rivers side,
Where gliding streams the Rocks did overwhelm;
A lonely place, with pleasures dignifi'd.

I once that lov'd the shady woods so well,
Now thought the rivers did the trees excel,
And if the sun would ever shine, there would I dwell.

22

While on the stealing stream I fixt mine eye,
Which to the long'd for Ocean held its course,
I markt, nor crooks, nor rubs that there did lye
Could hinder ought, but still augment its force.
O happy Flood, quoth I, that holds thy race
Till thou arrive at thy beloved place,
Nor is it rocks or shoals that can obstruct thy pace.

23

Nor is't enough, that thou alone may'st slide,
But hundred brooks in thy cleer waves do meet,
So hand in hand along with thee they glide
To *Thetis* house,[30] where all imbrace and greet:
Thou Emblem true, of what I count the best,
O could I lead my Rivolets to rest,
So may we press to that vast mansion, ever blest.

24

Ye Fish which in this liquid Region 'bide,
That for each season, have your habitation,
Now salt, now fresh where you think best to glide
To unknown coasts to give a visitation,
In Lakes and ponds, you leave your numerous fry,
So nature taught, and yet you know not why,
You watry folk that know not your felicity.

25

Look how the wantons frisk to task the air,
Then to the colder bottome streight they dive,
Eftsoon to *Neptun's* glassie Hall repair
To see what trade they great ones there do drive,
Who forrage o're the spacious sea-green field,
And take the trembling prey before it yield,
Whose armour is their scales, their spreading fins their shield.

30. *Thetis* house: the sea.

26

While musing thus with contemplation fed,
And thousand fancies buzzing in my brain,
The sweet-tongu'd Philomel[31] percht ore my head,
And chanted forth a most melodious strain
Which rapt me so with wonder and delight,
I judg'd my hearing better than my sight,
And wisht me wings with her a while to take my flight.

27

O merry Bird (said I) that fears no snares,
That neither toyles nor hoards up in thy barn,
Feels no sad thoughts, nor cruciating cares
To gain more good, or shun what might thee harm
Thy cloaths ne're wear, thy meat is every where,
Thy bed a bough, thy drink the water cleer,
Reminds[32] not what is past, nor whats to come dost fear.

28

The dawning morn with songs thou dost prevent,[33]
Sets hundred notes unto thy feathered crew,
So each one tunes his pretty instrument,
And warbling out the old, begin anew,
And thus they pass their youth in summer season,
Then follow thee into a better Region,
Where winter's never felt by that sweet airy legion.

29

Man at the best a creature frail and vain,
In knowledg ignorant, in strength but weak,
Subject to sorrows, losses, sickness, pain,
Each storm his state, his mind, his body break,
From some of these he never finds cessation,
But day or night, within, without, vexation,
Troubles from foes, from friends, from dearest, near'st Relation.

31. Philomel: a nightingale.
32. Reminds: remembers.

33. prevent: anticipate.

30

And yet this sinfull creature, frail and vain,
This lump of wretchedness, of sin and sorrow,
This weather-beaten vessel wrackt with pain,
Joyes not in hope of an eternal morrow;
Nor all his losses, crosses and vexation,
In weight, in frequency and long duration
Can make him deeply groan for that divine Translation.

31

The Mariner that on smooth waves doth glide,
Sings merrily, and steers his Barque with ease,
As if he had command of wind and tide,
And now becomes great Master of the seas;
But suddenly a storm spoiles all the sport,
And makes him long for a more quiet port,
Which 'gainst all adverse winds may serve for fort.

32

So he that faileth in this world of pleasure,
Feeding on sweets, that never bit of th' sowre,
That's full of friends, of honour and of treasure,
Fond fool, he takes this earth ev'n for heav'ns bower.
But sad affliction comes & makes him see
Here's neither honour, wealth, or safety;
Only above is found all with security.

33

O Time the fatal wrack of mortal things,
That draws oblivions curtains over kings,
Their sumptuous monuments, men know them not,
Their names without a Record are forgot,
Their parts, their ports, their pomp's all laid in th' dust
Nor wit nor gold, nor buildings scape times rust;
But he whose name is grav'd in the white stone[34]
Shall last and shine when all of these are gone.

34. See Rev. 2:17.

Here followes some verses upon the burning of our House, July 10th, 1666

<small>COPYED OUT OF A LOOSE PAPER</small>

In silent night when rest I took,
For sorrow near I did not look,
I waken'd was with thundring noise
And Piteous shreiks of dreadfull voice.
That fearfull sound of fire and fire,
Let no man know is my Desire.

I, starting up, the light did spye,
And to my God my heart did cry
To strengthen me in my Distresse
And not to leave me succourlesse.
Then coming out beheld a space,
The flame consume my dwelling place.

And, when I could no longer look,
I blest his Name that gave and took,
That layd my goods now in the dust:
Yea so it was, and so 'twas just.
It was his own: it was not mine;
Far be it that I should repine.

He might of All justly bereft,
But yet sufficient for us left.
When by the Ruines oft I past,
My sorrowing eyes aside did cast,
And here and there the places spye
Where oft I sate, and long did lye.

Here stood that Trunk, and there that chest;
There lay that store I counted best:
My pleasant things in ashes lye,
And them behold no more shall I.
Under thy roof no guest shall sitt,
Nor at thy Table eat a bitt.

No pleasant tale shall 'ere be told,
Nor things recounted done of old.
No Candle 'ere shall shine in Thee,
Nor bridegroom's voice ere heard shall bee.
In silence ever shalt thou lye;
Adeiu, Adeiu; All's vanity.

Then streight I 'gin my heart to chide,
And did they wealth on earth abide?
Didst fix thy hope on mouldring dust,
The arm of flesh didst make thy trust?
Raise up thy thoughts above the skye
That dunghill mists away may flie.

Thou hast an house on high erect,
Fram'd by that mighty Architect,
With glory richly furnished,
Stands permanent though this bee fled.
It's purchased, and paid for too
By him who hath enough to doe.

A Prise so vast as is unknown,
Yet, by his Gift, is made thine own.
Ther's wealth enough, I need no more;
Farewell my Pelf, farewell my Store.
The world no longer let me Love,
My hope and Treasure lyes Above.

Before the Birth of one of her Children

All things within this fading world hath end,
Adversity doth still our joyes attend.
No tyes so strong, no friends so clear and sweet,
But with deaths parting blow is sure to meet.
The sentence past is most irrevocable,
A common thing, yet oh inevitable.
How soon, my Dear, death may my steps attend,
How soon't may be thy Lot to lose thy friend,
We both are ignorant, yet love bids me
These farewell lines to recommend to thee,
That when that knot's unty'd that made us one,
I may seem thine, who in effect am none.
And if I see not half my dayes that's due,
What nature would, God grant to yours and you.
The many faults that well you know I have,
Let be interr'd in my oblivious grave.
If any worth or virtue were in me,
Let that live freshly in thy memory.
And when thou feel'st no grief, as I no harms,
Yet love thy dead, who long lay in thine arms.
And when thy loss shall be repaid with gains
Look to my little babes my dear remains.
And if thou love thy self, or loved'st me
These O protect from step Dames injury.
And if chance to thine eyes shall bring this verse,
With some sad sighs honour my absent Herse;
And kiss this paper for thy loves dear sake,
Who with salt tears this last Farewel did take.

To my Dear and loving Husband

If ever two were one, then surely we.
If ever man were lov'd by wife, then thee.
If ever wife was happy in a man,
Compare with me ye women if you can.
I prize thy love more than whole Mines of gold,
Or all the riches that the East doth hold.
My love is such that Rivers cannot quench,
Nor ought but love from thee, give recompence.
Thy love is such I can no way repay.
The heavens reward thee manifold I pray.
Then while we live, in love let's so persever,
That when we live no more, we may live ever.

A Letter to her Husband, absent upon Publick employment

As loving Hind that (Hartless) wants her Deer,
Scuds through the woods and Fern with harkning ear,
Perplext, in every bush & nook doth pry,
Her dearest Deer, might answer ear or eye;
So doth my anxious soul, which now doth miss,
A dearer Dear (far dearer Heart) than this.
Still wait with doubts, & hopes, and failing eye,
His voice to hear, or person to discry.
Or as the pensive Dove doth all alone
(On withered bough) most uncouthly bemoan
The absence of her Love, and loving Mate,
Whose loss hath made her so unfortunate:
Ev'n thus doe I, with many a deep sad groan
Bewail my turtle true, who now is gone,
His presence and his safe return, still wooes,
With thousand doleful sighs & mournfull Cooes.
Or as the loving Mullet, that true Fish,
Her fellow lost, nor joy nor life do wish,
But lanches on that shore, there for to dye,
Where she her captive husband doth espy.

Mine being gone, I lead a joyless life.
I have a loving peer, yet seem no wife.
But worst of all, to him can't steer my course,
I here, he there, alas, both kept by force.
Return my Dear, my joy, my only Love,
Unto thy Hinde, thy Mullet and thy Dove,
Who neither joyes in pasture, house nor streams.
The substance gone, O me, these are but dreams.
Together at one Tree, oh let us brouze,
And like two Turtles, roost within one house,
And like the Mullets in one River glide,
Let's still remain but one, till death divide.
> *Thy loving Love and Dearest Dear,*
> *At home, abroad, and every where.*

12. Michael Wigglesworth

Born in Yorkshire, Michael Wigglesworth (1631–1705) arrived in Massachusetts with his parents in 1638. The family later settled at New Haven. Wigglesworth attended Harvard and served as tutor there before becoming pastor at Malden, Massachusetts. Selections from his diary may be found in chapter 5. Sickly, he was described by Cotton Mather as "a feeble, little shadow of a man." But his 1662 poem "The Day of Doom," stretching to 224 stanzas, became a bestseller, easily the most popular English American poem. Many New Englanders are said to have recited it from memory until the twentieth century.

"God's Controversy with New-England" is a versified example of a jeremiad, common among New England sermons. The jeremiad laments the corruption of the present day community and its decline from a better (largely invented) past. It does so not to question the wisdom of the original mission, or to imagine that its sense of promise may have been illusory, but to reinvigorate the sense of a divine mandate for the future—one that is only more urgent for being deferred.

God's Controversy with New-England

WRITTEN IN THE TIME OF THE GREAT DROUGHT ANNO 1662
BY A LOVER OF NEW-ENGLAND'S PROSPERITY

Isaiah, 5. 4.—What could have been done more to my vineyard, that I have not done in it? wherefore, when I looked that it should bring forth grapes, brought it forth wilde grapes?

THE AUTHOR'S REQUEST UNTO THE READER

Good christian Reader judge me not
          As too censorious,
For pointing at those faults of thine
          Which are notorious.
For if those faults be none of thine
          I do not thee accuse:
But if they be, to hear thy faults
          Why shouldest thou refuse?

I blame not thee to spare my self:
          But first at home begin,
And judge my self, before that I
          Reproove another's sin.
Nor is it I that thee reproove;
          Let God himself be heard,
Whose awfull providence's voice
          No man may disregard.

Quod Deus omnipotens regali voce minatur,
Quod tibi proclamant uno simul ore prophetae
Quodq' ego cum lachrymis testor de numinis ira,
Tu leve comentu ne ducas, Lector Amice.[35]

NEW-ENGLAND PLANTED, PROSPERED, DECLINING, THREATNED, PUNISHED

Beyond the great Atlantick flood
          There is a region vast,
A country where no English foot
          In former ages past:
A waste and howling wilderness,
          Where none inhabited
But hellish fiends, and brutish men
          That Devils worshiped.

This region was in darkness plac't
          Far off from heavens light,
Amidst the shaddows of grim death
          And of Eternal night.

---

35. What God Omnipotent tells you with a ruler's voice,
What the prophets proclaim unto you with one mouth, And
what I with many tears testify in wrath, You may not consider
lightly, Dear Reader.

For there the Sun of righteousness
      Had never made to shine
The light of his sweet countenance,
      And grace which is divine:

Until the time drew nigh wherein
      The glorious Lord of hostes
Was pleasd to lead his armies forth
      Into those forrein coastes.
At whose approach the darkness sad
      Soon vanished away,
And all the shaddows of the night
      Were turnd to lightsome day.
The dark and dismal western woods
      (The Devils den whilere)
Beheld such glorious Gospel-shine,
      As none beheld more cleave.
Where sathan had his scepter sway'd
      For many generations,
The King of Kings set up his throne
      To rule amongst the nations.

The stubborn he in pieces brake,
      Like vessels made of clay:
And those that sought his peoples hurt
      He turned to decay.
Those curst Amalekites,[36] that first
      Lift up their hand on high
To fight against God's Israel,
      Were ruin'd fearfully.

Thy terrours on the Heathen folk,
      O Great Jehovah, fell:
The fame of thy great acts, o Lord,
      Did all the nations quell.
Some hid themselves for fear of thee
      In forrests wide and great:
Some to thy people croutching came,
      For favour to entreat.

Some were desirous to be taught
      The knowledge of thy wayes,
And being taught, did soon accord
      Therein to spend their dayes.

36. See Gen. 36.

Thus were the fierce and barbarous
            Brought to civility,
And those that liv'd like beasts (or worse)
            To live religiously.

O happiest of dayes wherein
            The blind received sight,
And those that had no eyes before
            Were made to see the light!
The wilderness hereat rejoyc't,
            The woods for joy did sing,
The vallys and the little hills
            Thy praises ecchoing.
Here was the hiding place, which thou,
            Jehovah, didst provide
For thy redeemed ones, and where
            Thou didst thy jewels hide
In per'lous times, and saddest dayes
            Of sack-cloth and of blood,
When th' overflowing scourge did pass
            Through Europe, like a flood.

While almost all the world beside
            Lay weltring in their gore:
We, only we, enjoyd such peace
            As none enjoyd before.
No forrein foeman did us fray,
            Nor threat'ned us with warrs:
We had no enemyes at home,
            Nor no domestick jarrs.

The Lord had made (such was his grace)
            For us a Covenant
Both with the men, and with the beasts,
            That in this desart haunt:
So that through places wilde and waste
            A single man, disarm'd,
Might journey many hundred miles,
            And not at all be harm'd.

Amidst the solitary woods
            Poor travellers might sleep
As free from danger as at home,
            Though no man watch did keep.

Thus were we priviledg'd with peace,
     Beyond what others were.
Truth, Mercy, Peace, with Righteousness,
     Took up their dwelling here.

Our Governour was of our selves,
     And all his Bretheren,
For wisdom and true piety,
     Select, and chosen men.
Who, Ruling in the fear of God,
     The righteous cause maintained,
And all injurious violence,
     And wickedness, restrained.
Our temp'rall blessings did abound:
     But spirituall good things
Much more abounded, to the praise
     Of that great King of Kings.
God's throne was here set up; here was
     His tabernacle pight:[37]
This was the place, and these the folk
     In whom he took delight.

Our morning starrs shone all day long:
     Their beams gave forth such light,
As did the noon-day sun abash,
     And 's glory dazle quite.
Our day continued many yeers,
     And had no night at all:
Yea many thought the light would last,
     And be perpetuall.

Such, O New-England, was thy first,
     Such was thy best estate:
But, Loe! a strange and suddain change
     My courage did amate.[38]
The brightest of our morning starrs
     Did wholly disappeare:
And those that tarried behind
     With sack-cloth covered were.

Moreover, I beheld and saw
     Our welkin[39] overkest,

37. pight: pitched.
38. amate: daunt.

39. welkin: sky.

And dismal clouds for sun-shine late
      O'respread from east to west.
The air became tempestuous;
      The wilderness gan quake:
And from above with awfull voice
      Th' Almighty thundring spake.

      Are these the men that erst at my command
      Forsook their ancient seats and native soile,
      To follow me into a desart land,
      Contemning all the travell[40] and the toile,
      Whose love was such to purest ordinances
As made them set at nought their fair inheritances?

      Are these the men that prized libertee
      To walk with God according to their light,
      To be as good as he would have them bee,
      To serve and worship him with all their might,
      Before the pleasures which a fruitfull field,
And Country flowing-full of all good things, could yield?

      Are these the folk whom from the brittish Iles,
      Through the stern billows of the watry main,
      I safely led so many thousand miles,
      As if their journey had been through a plain?
      Whom having from all enemies protected,
And through so many deaths and dangers well directed,

      I brought and planted on the Western shore,
      Where nought but bruits and salvage wights[41] did swarm
      (Untaught, untrain'd, untam'd by Vertue's lore)
      That sought their blood, yet could not do them harm?
      My fury's flaile them thresht, my fatall broom
Did sweep them hence, to make my people Elbow-room.

      Are these the men whose gates with peace I crown'd,
      To whom for bulwarks I Salvation gave,
      Whilst all things else with rattling tumults sound,
      And mortall frayes send thousands to the grave?
      Whilst their own brethren bloody hands embrewed[42]
In brothers blood, and Fields with carcases bestrewed?

---

40. travell: travail.
41. bruits and salvage wights: brutes and savage beings.
42. embrewed: imbrued.

Is this the people blest with bounteous store,
By land and sea full richly clad and fed,
Whom plenty's self stands waiting still before,
And powreth out their cups well tempered?
For whose dear sake an howling wildernes
I lately turned into a fruitfull paradeis?

Are these the people in whose hemisphere
Such bright-beam'd, glist'ring, sun-like starrs I placed,
As by their influence did all things cheere,
As by their light blind ignorance defaced,
As errours into lurking holes did fray,
As turn'd the late dark night into a lightsome day?

Are these the folk to whom I milked out
And sweetnes stream'd from Consolations brest;
Whose soules I fed and strengthened throughout
With finest spirituall food most finely drest?
On whom I rained living bread from Heaven,
Withouten Errour's bane, or Superstition's leaven?

With whom I made a Covenant of peace,
And unto whom I did most firmly plight
My faithfulness, If whilst I live I cease
To be their Guide, their God, their full delight;
Since them with cords of love to me I drew,
Enwrapping in my grace such as should them ensew.

Are these the men, that now mine eyes behold,
Concerning whom I thought, and whilome spake,
First Heaven shall pass away together scrold,[43]
Ere they my lawes and righteous wayes forsake,
Or that they slack to runn their heavenly race?
Are these the same? or are some others come in place?

If these be they, how is it that I find
In stead of holyness Carnality,
In stead of heavenly frames an Earthly mind,
For burning zeal luke-warm Indifferency,
For flaming Love, key-cold Dead-heartedness,
For temperance (in meat, and drinke, and cloaths) excess?

43. pass away together scrold: roll up like a scroll.

Whence cometh it, that Pride, and Luxurie
Debate, Deceit, Contention and Strife,
False-dealing, Covetousness, Hypocrisie
(With such like Crimes) amongst them are so rife,
That one of them doth over-reach another?
And that an honest man can hardly trust his Brother?

How is it, that Security, and Sloth,
Amongst the best are Common to be found?
That grosser sinns, in stead of Graces growth,
Amongst the many more and more abound?
I hate dissembling shews of Holiness.
Or practise as you talk, or never more profess.[44]

Judge not, vain world, that all are hypocrites
That do profess more holiness then thou:
All foster not dissembling, guilefull sprites,
Nor love their lusts, though very many do.
Some sin through want of care and constant watch,
Some with the sick converse, till they the sickness catch.

Some, that maintain a reall root of grace,
Are overgrown with many noysome weeds,
Whose heart, that those no longer may take place,
The benefit of due correction needs.
And such as these however gone astray
I shall by stripes reduce into a better way.

Moreover some there be that still retain
Their ancient vigour and sincerity;
Whom both their own, and others sins, constrain
To sigh, and mourn, and weep, and wail, and cry:
And for their sakes I have forborn to powre
My wrath upon Revolters to this present houre.

To praying Saints I always have respect,
And tender love, and pittiful regard:
Nor will I now in any wise neglect
Their love and faithfull service to reward;
Although I deal with others for their folly,
And turn their mirth to tears that have been too too jolly.

44. Or . . . or: Either . . . or.

For thinke not, O Backsliders, in your heart,
That I shall still your evill manners beare:
Your sinns me press as sheaves do load a cart,
And therefore I will plague you for this geare
  Except you seriously, and soon, repent,
Ile not delay your pain and heavy punishment.

And who be those themselves that yonder shew?
The seed of such as name my dreadful Name!
On whom whilere compassions skirt I threw
Whilest in their blood they were, to hide their shame!
  Whom my preventing love did neer me take!
Whom for mine own I mark't, lest they should me forsake!

I look't that such as these to vertue's Lore
(Though none but they) would have Enclin'd their ear:
That they at least mine image should have bore,
And sanctify'd my name with awfull fear.
  Let pagan's Bratts pursue their lusts, whose meed
Is Death: For christians children are an holy seed.

But hear O Heavens! Let Earth amazed stand;
Ye Mountaines melt, and Hills come flowing down:
Let horror seize upon both Sea and Land;
Let Natures self be cast into a stown.
  I children nourisht, nurtur'd and upheld:
But they against a tender Father have rebell'd.

What could have been by me performed more?
Or wherein fell I short of your desire?
Had you but askt, I would have op't my store,
And given what lawfull wishes could require.
  For all this bounteous cost I lookt to see
Heaven-reaching-hearts, and thoughts, Meekness, Humility.

But lo, a sensuall Heart all void of grace,
An Iron neck, a proud presumptuous Hand;
A self-conceited, stiff, stout, stubborn Race,
That fears no threats, submitts to no command:
  Self-will'd, perverse, such as can beare no yoke;
A Generation even ripe for vengeance stroke.

Such were that Carnall Brood of Israelites
That Josua and the Elders did ensue,

Who growing like the cursed Cananites
Upon themselves my heavy judgments drew.
Such also was that fleshy Generation,
Whom I o'rewhelmed by waters deadly inundation.

They darker light, and lesser meanes misused;
They had not such Examples them to warn:
You clearer Rules, and Precepts, have abused,
And dreadfull monuments of others harm.
My gospel's glorious light you do not prize:
My Gospel's endless, boundless grace you clean despize.

My painfull[45] messengers you disrespect,
Who toile and sweat and sweale[46] themselves away,
Yet nought at all with you can take effect,
Who hurrie headlong to your own decay.
In vain the Founder melts, and taketh pains:
Bellows and Lead's consum'd, but still your dross remains.

What should I do with such a stiff-neckt race?
How shall I ease me of such Foes as they?
What shall befall despizers of my Grace?
I'le surely beare their Candle-stick away,
And Lamps put out. Their glorious noon-day light
I'le quickly turn into a dark Egyptian night.

Oft have I charg'd you by my Ministers
To gird your selves with sack cloth, and repent.
Oft have I warnd you by my Messengers;
That so you might my wrathfull ire prevent:
But who among you hath this warning taken?
Who hath his Crooked wayes, and wicked works forsaken?

Yea many grow to more and more excess;
More light and loose, more Carnall and prophane.
The sins of Sodom, Pride, and Wantonness,
Among the multitude spring up amain.
Are these the fruits of pious Education,
To run with greater speed and Courage to Damnation?

If here and there some two, or three, shall steere
A wiser Course, then their Companions do,

---

45. painfull: painstaking.   46. sweale: melt.

You make a mock of such; and scoff, and jeere
    Becaus they will not be so bad as you.
    Such is the Generation that succeeds
The men, whose eyes have seen my great and awfull deeds.

    Now therefore hearken and encline your ear,
    In judgment I will henceforth with you plead;
    And if by that you will not learn to fear,
    But still go on a sensuall life to lead:
    I'le strike at once an All-Consuming stroke;
Nor cries nor tears shall then my fierce intent revoke.

Thus ceast his Dreadful-threatning voice
    The High and lofty-One.
The Heavens stood still Appal'd thereat;
    The Earth beneath did groane.
Soon after I beheld and saw
    A mortall dart come flying:
I lookt again, and quickly saw
    Some fainting, others dying.

The Heavens more began to lowre,
    The welkin Blacker grew:
And all things seemed to forebode
    Sad changes to ensew.
From that day forward hath the Lord
    Apparently contended
With us in Anger, and in Wrath:
    But we have not amended.

Our healthfull dayes are at an end,
    And sicknesses come on
From yeer to yeer, becaus our hearts
    Away from God are gone.
New-England, where for many years
    You scarcely heard a cough,
And where Physicians had no work,
    Now finds them work enough.

Now colds and coughs, Rhewms, and sore-throats,
    Do more and more abound:
Now Agues sore and Feavers strong
    In every place are found.
How many houses have we seen
    Last Autumn, and this spring,

Wherein the healthful were too few
    To help the languishing.

One wave another followeth,
    And one disease begins
Before another cease, becaus
    We turn not from our sins.
We stopp our ear against reproof,
    And hearken not to God:
God stops his ear against our prayer,
    And takes not off his rod.

Our fruitful seasons have been turnd
    Of late to barrenness,
Sometimes through great and parching drought,
    Sometimes through rain's excess.
Yea now the pastures and corn fields
    For want of rain do languish:
The cattell mourn, and hearts of men
    Are fill'd with fear and anguish.

The clouds are often gathered,
    As if we should have rain:
But for our great unworthiness
    Are scattered again.
We pray and fast, and make fair shewes,
    As if we meant to turn:
But whilest we turn not, God goes on
    Our fields and fruits to burn.

And burnt are all things in such sort,
    That nothing now appears,
But what may wound our hearts with grief,
    And draw foorth floods of teares.
All things a famine do presage
    In that extremity,
As if both men, and also beasts,
    Should soon be done to dy.

This O New-England hast thou got
    By riot, and excess:
This hast thou brought upon thy self
    By pride and wantonness.
Thus must thy worldlyness be whipt.
    They, that too much do crave,

Provoke the Lord to take away
      Such blessings as they have.

We have been also threatened
      With worser things then these:
And God can bring them on us still,
      To morrow if he please.
For if his mercy be abus'd,
      Which holpe us at our need
And mov'd his heart to pitty us,
      We shall be plagu'd indeed.

Beware, O sinful Land, beware;
      And do not think it strange
That sorer judgements are at hand,
      Unless thou quickly change.
Or God, or thou, must quickly change;
      Or else thou art undon:
Wrath cannot cease, if sin remain,
      Where judgment is begun.

Ah dear New-England! dearest land to me;
Which unto God hast hitherto been dear,
And mayst be still more dear than formerlie,
If to his voice thou wilt incline thine ear.

Consider wel and wisely what the rod,
Wherewith thou art from yeer to yeer chastized,
Instructeth thee. Repent, and turn to God,
Who wil not have his nurture be despized.

Thou still hast in thee many praying saints,
Of great account, and precious with the Lord,
Who dayly powre out unto him their plaints,
And strive to please him both in deed and word.

Cheer on, sweet souls, my heart is with you all,
And shall be with you, maugre[47] sathan's might:
And whereso'ere this body be a Thrall,[48]
Still in New-England shall be my delight.

---

47. maugre: despite.   48. Thrall: servant.

A Song of Emptiness

To Fill Up The Empty Pages Following. Vanity of Vanities.

Vain, frail, short liv'd, and miserable Man,
Learn what thou art when thine estate is best:
A restless Wave o'th' troubled Ocean,
A Dream, a lifeless Picture finely drest.

A Wind, a Flower, a Vapour, and a Bubble,
A Wheel that stands not still, a trembling Reed,
A rolling Stone, dry Dust, light Chaff, and Stubble,
A Shadow of Something, but nought indeed.

Learn what deceitful Toyes, and empty things,
This World, and all its best Enjoyments bee.
Out of the Earth no true Contentment springs,
But all things here are vexing Vanitee.

For what is *Beauty,* but a fading Flower?
Or what is *Pleasure,* but the Devils bait,
Whereby he catcheth whom he would devour,
And multitudes of Souls doth ruinate?

And what are *Friends* but mortal men, as we?
Whom Death from us may quickly separate;
Or else their hearts may quite estranged be,
And all their love be turned into hate.

And what are *Riches* to be doted on?
Uncertain, fickle, and ensnaring things;
They draw Men's Souls into Perdition,
And when most needed, take them to their wings.

Ah foolish Man! that sets his heart upon
Such empty Shadows, such wild Fowl as these,
That being gotten will be quickly gone,
And whilst they stay increase but his disease.

As in a Dropsie, drinking draughts begets,
The more he drinks, the more he still requires:
So on this World whoso affection sets,
His Wealth's encrease encreaseth his desires.

O happy Man, whose portion is above,
Where Floods, where Flames, where Foes cannot bereave him,
Most wretched man, that fixed hath his love
Upon this World, that surely will deceive him!

For, what is *Honour*? What is *Sov'raignty*,
Whereto mens hearts so restlesly aspire?
Whom have they Crowned with Felicity?
When did they ever satisfie desire?

The Ear of Man with hearing is not fill'd:
To see new sights still coveteth the Eye:
The craving Stomack though it may be still'd,
Yet craves again without a new supply.

All Earthly things, man's Cravings answer not,
Whose little heart would all the World contain,
(If all the World should fall to one man's Lot)
And notwithstanding empty still remain.

The *Eastern Conquerour*[49] was said to weep,
When he the *Indian* Ocean did view,
To see his Conquest bounded by the Deep,
And no more Worlds remaining to subdue.

Who would that man in his Enjoyments bless,
Or envy him, or covet his estate,
Whose gettings do augment his greediness,
And make his wishes more intemperate?

Such is the wonted and the common guise
Of those on Earth that bear the greatest Sway:
If with a few the case be otherwise
They seek a Kingdom that abides for ay.

Moreover they, of all the Sons of men,
That Rule, and are in highest places set,
Are most inclin'd to scorn their Bretheren
And God himself (without great grace) forget.

49. *Eastern Conqueror*: Alexander the Great.

For as the Sun doth blind the gazer's eyes,
That for a time they nought discern aright:
So Honour doth befool and blind the Wise,
And their own Lustre 'reaves them of their sight.

Great are their Dangers, manifold their Cares;
Thro' which, whilst others Sleep, they scarcely Nap:
And yet are oft surprized unawares,
And fall unweeting into Envies Trap!

The mean Mechanick finds his kindly rest,
All void of fear Sleepeth the Country-Clown,[50]
When greatest Princes often are distrest,
And cannot Sleep upon their Beds of Down.
Could *Strength* or *Valour* men Immortalize,
Could *Wealth* or *Honour* keep them from decay,
There were some cause the same to Idolize,
And give the lye to that which I do say.

But neither can such things themselves endure
Without the hazard of a Change one hour,
Nor such as trust in them can they secure
From dismal dayes, or Death's prevailing pow'r.

If *Beauty* could the beautiful defend
From Death's dominion, than fair *Absalom*
Had not been brought to such a shameful end:
But fair and foul unto the Grave must come.

If *Wealth* or *Scepters* could Immortal make,
Then wealthy *Crœsus,* wherefore art thou dead?
If *Warlike force,* which makes the World to quake,
Then why is *Julius Caesar* perished?

Where are the *Scipio's* Thunder-bolts of War?
Renowned *Pompey, Caesar* Enemie?
Stout *Hannibal, Rome's* Terror known so far?
Great *Alexander,* what's become of thee?

If *Gifts* and *Bribes* Death's favour might but win,
If *Power,* if force, or *Threatnings* might it fray,
All these, and more, had still surviving been:
But all are gone, for Death will have no Nay.

---

50. Country-Clown: rustic man.

Such is this World with all her Pomp and Glory,
Such are the men whom worldly eyes admire:
Cut down by Time, and now become a Story,
That we might after better things aspire.

Go boast thy self of what thy heart enjoyes,
Vain Man! triumph in all thy worldly Bliss:
Thy best enjoyments are but Trash and Toyes:
Delight thy self in that which worthless is.
Omnia praetereunt praeter amare deum.[51]

13. John Milton

from *Paradise Lost*
1674

Echoes of New World writing abound in Paradise Lost, *which among other things repeatedly calls Eden "this new world." In the following passage from book 9 [ll. 1084 ff.], Adam and Eve discover their shame after the fall; Adam is speaking to Eve. Milton draws on images of both East and West India.*

        O might I here
In solitude live savage, in some glade
Obscur'd, where highest Woods impenetrable
To Star or Sun-light, spread thir umbrage[52] broad,
And brown as Evening: Cover me ye Pines,
Ye Cedars, with innumerable boughs
Hide me, where I may never see them more.
But let us now, as in bad plight, devise
What best may for the present serve to hide
The Parts of each from other, that seem most
To shame obnoxious, and unseemliest seen,
Some Tree whose broad smooth Leaves together sew'd,
And girded on our loins, may cover round
Those middle parts, that this new comer, Shame,
There sit not, and reproach us as unclean.
        So counsell'd hee, and both together went
Into the thickest Wood, there soon they chose

---

51. All things pass save love of God.   52. umbrage: shade.

Adam and Eve, illustrated by de Bry for Hariot's Briefe and True Report, *where it appears without comment.*

The Figtree, not that kind for Fruit renown'd,
But such as at this day to *Indians* known
In *Malabar* or *Decan* spreads her Arms
Branching so broad and long, that in the ground
The bended Twigs take root, and Daughters grow
About the Mother Tree, a Pillar'd shade
High overarch't, and echoing Walks between;
There oft the *Indian* Herdsman shunning heat
Shelters in cool, and tends his pasturing Herds
At Loopholes cut through thickest shade: Those Leaves
They gather'd, broad as *Amazonian* Targe,
And with what skill they had, together sew'd,
To gird thir waist, vain Covering if to hide
Thir guilt and dreaded shame; O how unlike
To that first naked Glory. Such of late
Columbus found th' *American* so girt
With feather'd Cincture, naked else and wild
Among the Trees on Isles and woody Shores.

14. Edward Taylor

from *Sacramental Meditations*
First Series

*Edward Taylor (1644–1729) emigrated from England in 1668. He studied at
Harvard, becoming friends with Increase Mather as well as Samuel Sewall, with
whom he shared a room. In 1671 he moved to the frontier town of Westfield,
Massachusetts, to serve as pastor; he would remain there for over half a century,
until his death in 1729. Taylor instructed his heirs not to publish the writings he
left behind, and his poetry lay unknown until 1937, when it was discovered in his
manuscripts, which by then were held by the Yale University library. Most of the
poems are in two long series of "Sacramental Meditations." Taylor composed these
poems as meditative exercises preparatory to the communion, which following the
Half-Way Covenant of 1662 was still considered a privilege of the elect, not open
to all baptized church members. Taylor defended this orthodox understanding of
the Lord's Supper against the more public and evangelical conception of his
neighbor Solomon Stoddard. The meditations derive much of their intensity from
this theological background, and from Taylor's sense of sacramental mystery.
Taylor's meditations comb the Bible for analogies (called types) for the communion, often drawing imagery from the Song of Solomon. His theology allowed a
richly erotic and violent language of the body. Remote from centers of literary
culture, Taylor wrote in an archaic style heavily influenced by English poets of his
youth, such as George Herbert and Francis Quarles. But he also had in his library
one book of colonial poetry: the 1678 edition of Anne Bradstreet.*

Meditation One

What Love is this of thine, that Cannot bee
     In thine Infinity, O Lord, Confinde,
Unless it in thy very Person see
     Infinity and Finity Conjoyn'd?
     What! hath thy Godhead, as not satisfi'de,
     Marri'de our Manhood, making it its Bride?

Oh, Matchless Love! Filling Heaven to the brim!
     O'rerunning it: all running o're beside
This World! Nay, Overflowing Hell, wherein
     For thine Elect, there rose a mighty Tide!
     That there our Veans might through thy Person bleed,
     To quench those flames, that else would on us feed.

Oh! that thy love might overflow my Heart!
>   To fire the same with Love: for Love I would.
But oh! my streight'ned Breast! my Lifeless Sparke!
>   My Fireless Flame! What Chilly Love, and Cold?
>   In measure small! In Manner Chilly! See!
>   Lord, blow the Coal: Thy Love Enflame in mee.

The Reflexion

CANTICLES 2:1: I AM THE ROSE OF SHARON.

Lord, art thou at the Table Head above
>   Meat, Med'cine, Sweetness, sparkling Beautys, to
Enamour Souls with Flaming Flakes of Love,
>   And not my Trencher, nor my Cup o'reflow?
>   Ben't I a bidden guest? Oh! sweat mine Eye:
>   O'reflow with Teares: Oh! draw thy fountains dry.

Shall I not smell thy sweet, oh! Sharons Rose?
>   Shall not mine Eye salute thy Beauty? Why?
Shall thy sweet leaves their Beautious sweets upclose?
>   As halfe ashamde my sight should on them ly?
>   Woe's me! For this my sighs shall be in grain,
>   Offer'd on Sorrows Altar for the same.

Had not my Soule's, thy Conduit, Pipes stopt bin
>   With mud, what Ravishment would'st thou Convay?
Let Graces Golden Spade dig till the Spring
>   Of tears arise, and cleare this filth away.
>   Lord, let thy Spirit raise my sighings till
>   These Pipes my soule do with thy sweetness fill.

Earth once was Paradise of Heaven below,
>   Till inkefac'd sin had it with poyson stockt;
And Chast this Paradise away into
>   Heav'ns upmost Loft, and it in Glory Lockt.
>   But thou, sweet Lord, hast with thy golden Key
>   Unlockt the Doore, and made, a golden day.

Once at thy Feast, I saw thee Pearle-like stand
>   'Tween Heaven and Earth, where Heavens Bright glory all
In streams fell on thee, as a floodgate and,
>   Like Sun Beams through thee on the World to Fall.
>   Oh! sugar sweet then! my Deare sweet Lord, I see
>   Saints Heaven-lost Happiness restor'd by thee.

Shall Heaven and Earth's bright Glory all up lie,
>Like Sun Beams bundled in the sun, in thee?
Dost thou sit Rose at Table Head, where I
>Do sit, and Carv'st no morsell sweet for mee?
>So much before, so little now! Sprindge,[53] Lord,
>Thy Rosie Leaves, and me their Glee afford.

Shall not thy Rose my Garden fresh perfume?
>Shall not thy Beauty my dull Heart assaile?
Shall not thy golden gleams run through this gloom?
>Shall my black Velvet Mask thy fair Face Vaile?
>Pass o're my Faults: shine forth, bright sun; arise!
>Enthrone thy Rosy-selfe within mine Eyes.

Meditation Eight

JOH. 6. 51. I AM THE LIVING BREAD

I kening[54] through Astronomy Divine
>The Worlds bright Battlement, wherein I spy
A Golden Path my Pensill cannot line
>From that bright Throne unto my Threshold ly.
>And while my puzzled thoughts about it pore
>I finde the Bread of Life in't at my doore.

When that this Bird of Paradise put in
>This Wicker Cage (my Corps) to tweedle praise
Had peckt the Fruite forbid: and so did fling
>Away its Food; and lost its golden dayes,
>It fell into Celestiall Famine sore,
>And never could attain a morsell more.

Alas! alas! Poore Bird, what wilt thou doe?
>This Creatures field no food for Souls e're gave:
And if thou knock at Angells dores, they show
>An Empty Barrell: they no soul bread have.
>Alas! Poore Bird, the Worlds White Loafe is done,
>And cannot yield thee here the smallest Crumb.

---

53. Sprindge: spread.   54. kening: kenning, discovering.

In this sad state, Gods Tender Bowells[55] run
>Out streams of Grace: And he to end all strife,
The Purest Wheate in Heaven, his deare-dear Son
>Grinds, and kneads up into this Bread of Life:
>Which Bread of Life from Heaven down came and stands
>Disht on thy Table up by Angells Hands.

Did God mould up this Bread in Heaven, and bake,
>Which from his Table came, and to thine goeth?
Doth he bespeake thee thus: This Soule Bread take;
>Come, Eate thy fill of this, thy Gods White Loafe?
>Its Food too fine for Angells; yet come, take
>And Eate thy fill! Its Heavens Sugar Cake.

What Grace is this knead in this Loafe? This thing
>Souls are but petty things it to admire.
Yee Angells, help: This fill would to the brim
>Heav'ns whelm'd-down[56] Chrystall meele Bowle, yea and higher.
>This Bread of Life dropt in thy mouth doth Cry:
>Eate, Eate me, Soul, and thou shalt never dy.

Meditation Thirty-Nine

1 JOH. 2. 1. IF ANY MAN SIN, WE HAVE AN ADVOCATE

My Sin! my Sin, My God, these Cursed Dregs,
>Green, Yellow, Blew streakt Poyson hellish, ranck,
Bubs[57] hatcht in natures nest on Serpents Eggs,
>Yelp, Cherp and Cry; they set my Soule a Cramp.
>I frown, Chide, strik and fight them, mourn and Cry
>To Conquour them, but cannot them destroy.

I cannot kill nor Coop them up: my Curb
>'S less than a Snaffle in their mouth: my Rains
They as a twine thrid,[58] snap: by hell they're spurd:
>And load my Soule with swagging loads of pains.
>Black Imps, young Divells, snap, bite, drag to bring
>And pick mee headlong hells dread Whirle Poole in.

Lord, hold thy hand: for handle mee thou may'st
>In Wrath: but, oh, a twinckling Ray of hope

---

55. Bowells: in this period, the organ of sympathy.
56. whelm'd-down: overturned.

57. Bubs: pustules.
58. thrid: thread.

Methinks I spie thou graciously display'st.
        There is an Advocate: a doore is ope.
        Sin's poyson swell my heart would till it burst,
        Did not a hope hence creep in't thus, and nurse't.

Joy, joy, Gods Son's the Sinners Advocate
        Doth plead the Sinner guiltless, and a Saint.
But yet Atturnies pleas spring from the State
        The Case is in: if bad its bad in plaint.
        My Papers do contain no pleas that do
        Secure mee from, but knock me down to, woe.

I have no plea mine Advocate to give:
        What now? He'l anvill Arguments greate Store
Out of his Flesh and Blood to make thee live.
        O Deare bought Arguments: Good pleas therefore.
        Nails made of heavenly Steel, more Choice than gold
        Drove home, Well Clencht, eternally will hold.

Oh! Dear bought Plea, Deare Lord, what buy't so deare?
        What with thy blood purchase thy plea for me?
Take Argument out of thy Grave t'appeare
        And plead my Case with, me from Guilt to free.
        These maule both Sins, and Divells, and amaze
        Both Saints, and Angells; Wreath their mouths with praise.

What shall I doe, my Lord? what do, that I
        May have thee plead my Case? I fee thee will
With Faith, Repentance, and obediently
        Thy Service gainst Satanick Sins fulfill.
        I'l fight thy fields while Live I do, although
        I should be hackt in pieces by thy foe.

Make me thy Friend, Lord, be my Surety: I
        Will be thy Client, be my Advocate:
My Sins make thine, thy Pleas make mine hereby.
        Thou wilt mee save, I will thee Celebrate.
        Thou'lt kill my Sins that cut my heart within:
        And my rough Feet shall thy smooth praises sing.

Meditation Forty-Nine

MATTHEW 25: 21: ENTER THOU INTO THE JOY OF THY LORD.

Lord, do away my Motes and Mountains great.
     My nut is vitiate. Its kirnell rots:
Come, kill the Worm, that doth its kirnell eate,
     And strike thy sparkes within my tinderbox.
     Drill through my metall heart an hole, wherein
     With graces Cotters to thyself it pin.

A Lock of Steel upon my Soule, whose key
     The serpent keeps, I feare, doth lock my doore:
O pick 't: and through the key-hole make thy way,
     And enter in, and let thy joyes run o're.
     My Wards are rusty. Oyle them till they trig
     Before thy golden key: thy Oyle makes glib.

Take out the Splinters of the World that stick
     Do in my heart. Friends, Honours, Riches, and
The Shivers in't of Hell whose venoms quick
     And firy, make it swoln and ranckling stand.
     These wound and kill: those shackle strongly to
     Poore knobs of Clay, my heart. Hence sorrows grow.

Cleanse, and enlarge my kask: It is too small:
     And tartariz'd with worldly dregs dri'de in't.
It's bad mouth'd too: and though thy joyes do Call
     That boundless are, it ever doth them stint.
     Make me thy Chrystall Caske: those wines in't tun
     That in the Rivers of thy joyes do run.

Lord, make me, though suck't through a straw or Quill,
     Tast of the Rivers of thy joyes, some drop.
'Twill sweeten me: and all my Love distill
     Into thy glass; and me for joy make hop.
     'Twill turn my water into wine, and fill
     My Harp with Songs my Masters joyes distill.

Sacramental Meditations
Second Series

Meditation Seventy-Six

PHILIPPIANS 3: 21: WHO SHALL CHANGE OUR VILE BODY, THAT IT MAY BE
FASHIONED LIKE UNTO HIS GLORIOUS BODY . . .

Will yee be neighbourly, ye Angells bright?
      Then lend mee your Admiring Facultie:
Wonders presented stand, above my might,
      That call from mee the highest Extasie.
      If you deny mee this, my pimping Soule,
      These Wonders pins up in an Auger hole.

If my Rush Candle on its wick-ware flame
      Of Ignis lambens,[59] Oh! bright garb indeed:
What then, when Flakes of flaming Glory train
      From thy bright glorious bulk to 'ray my weed.
      What, my vile Body like thy Glorious, Form'd?
      What Wonder here? My body thus adorn'd!

What, shall mine hempen harle[60] move in thy Loome
      Into a web (an harden[61] web indeed),
Be made its Makers Tent Cloth? I presume.
      Within these Curtains Grace keeps Hall, and breeds:
      But shall my harden-hangings ever ware
      A bright bright glory like thy body faire?

Meethinks thy smile doth make thy Footstoole so
      Spread its green carpet 'fore thy feet for joy,
And Bryers climb thereup, bright roses blow
      Out in sweet reechs to meet thee in the sky:
      And makes the sportive Starrs play Hide-and-Seek.
      And on thy bodies Glory peeping keep.

And shall not I (whose form transformed shall be,
      To be shap'te like thy glorious body, Lord,

59. Ignis lambens: licking flame.   61. harden: a pun. Hards are inferior flax.
60. harle: drawn-out flax or hemp.

That Angells bright, as gaster'd,[62] gaze at mee
      To see such Glory on my dresser board),
      Transported be hereat for very joy,
      Whose intrest lies herein, and gloriously?

What, shall the frosty Rhime upon my locks
      Congeale my braine with Chilly dews, whereby
My Phansie is benumbd: and put in Stocks,
      And thaws not into steams of reeching joy?
      Oh! strange Ingratitude! Let not this Frame
      Abide, Lord, in mee. Fire mee with thy flame.

Lord, let thy Glorious Body send such rayes
      Into my Soule, as ravish shall my heart,
That Thoughts how thy bright Glory out shall blaze
      Upon my body, may such Rayes thee dart.
      My Tunes shall dance then on these Rayes, and Caper
      Unto thy Praise: when Glory lights my Taper.

Upon a Spider Catching a Fly

Thou sorrow, venom Elfe:
      Is this thy play,
To spin a web out of thyselfe
      To Catch a Fly?
          For why?

I saw a pettish wasp
      Fall foule therein:
Whom yet thy Whorle pins[63] did not clasp
      Lest he should fling
          His sting.

But as afraid, remote
      Didst stand hereat,
And with thy little fingers stroke
      And gently tap
          His back.

62. gaster'd: aghast.

63. Whorle pins: cotter pins connecting parts of a spinning wheel.

Thus gently him didst treate
       Lest he should pet,
And in a froppish,[64] waspish heate
       Should greatly fret
           Thy net.

Whereas the silly Fly,
       Caught by its leg,
Thou by the throate took'st hastily,
       And 'hinde the head
           Bite Dead.

This goes to pot, that not
       Nature doth call.
Strive not above what strength hath got,
       Lest in the brawle
           Thou fall.

This Frey seems thus to us:
       Hells Spider gets
His intrails spun to whip Cords thus,
       And wove to nets,
           And sets.

To tangle Adams race
       In's stratagems
To their Destructions, Spoil'd, made base
       By venom things,
           Damn'd Sins.

But mighty, Gracious Lord,
       Communicate
Thy Grace to breake the Cord; afford
       Us Glorys Gate
           And State.

We'l Nightingaile sing like,
       When pearcht on high
In Glories Cage, thy glory, bright:
       And thankfully,
           For joy.

64. froppish: fretful.

Huswifery

Make me, O Lord, thy Spin[n]ing Wheele compleate;
     Thy Holy Worde my Distaff make for mee.
Make mine Affections they Swift Flyers neate,
       And make my Soule thy holy Spoole to bee.
       My Conversation make to be thy Reele.
       And reele the yarn thereon spun of thy Wheele.

Make me thy Loome then, knit therein this Twine:
       And make thy Holy Spirit, Lord, winde quills:
Then weave the Web thyselfe. The yarn is fine.
       Thine Ordinances make my Fulling Mills.[65]
       Then dy the same in Heavenly Colours Choice,
       All pinkt[66] with Varnish't Flowers of Paradise.

Then cloath therewith mine Understanding, Will,
       Affections, Judgment, Conscience, Memory;
My Words, and Actions, that their shine may fill
       My wayes with glory and thee glorify.
       Then mine apparell shall display before yee
       That I am Cloathd in Holy robes for glory.

The Ebb and Flow

When first thou on me, Lord, wrought'st thy Sweet Print,[67]
       My heart was made thy tinder box.
       My 'ffections were thy tinder in't:
          Where fell thy Sparkes by drops.
Those holy Sparks of Heavenly Fire that came
Did ever catch and often out would flame.

But now my Heart is made they Censar trim,
       Full of the golden Altars fire,
       To offer up Sweet Incense in
          Unto thyselfe intire:

65. Fulling Mills: for cleaning cloth.
66. pinkt: adorned.
                67. Print: image.

I finde my tinder scarce thy sparks can feel
That drop out from thy Holy flint and Steel.

Hence doubts out bud for feare thy fire in mee
      'S a mocking Ignis Fatuus,
    Or lest thine Altars fire out bee,
        It's hid in ashes thus.
Yet when the bellows of thy Spirit blow
Away mine ashes, then they fire doth glow.

15. Henry Kelsey

Now Reader Read for I am well assur'd 1693

> *Henry Kelsey, born in London around 1670, went to Canada in 1684 as an apprentice for the Hudson's Bay Company. There he ranged widely, carrying mail, negotiating with Indians, and exploring territory. On one notable journey of 1690-92, he was the first white man to see the prairies. Caught up in English-French wars and rivalries, he spent some time as a prisoner of war before returning to London briefly in 1695. From then until his retirement in 1722 he went back and forth between London and Canada, eventually serving as governor of the Hudson's Bay Company. Among his writings are a Cree dictionary, notes on Indian beliefs, and journals of several travels. The poem below is the verse preface to his journal for the 1690-92 trip. He died in England, sometime between 1724 and 1730.*

Now Reader Read for I am well assur'd
Thou dost not know the hardships I endur'd
In this same desert where Ever that I have been
Nor wilt thou me believe without that thou had seen
the Emynent Dangers that did often me attend
But still I lived in hopes that once it would amend
And makes me free from hunger & from Cold
Likewise many other things which I cannot here unfold
For many times I have often been oppresst
With fears & Cares that I could not take my rest
Because I was alone & no friend could find
And once that in my travels I was left behind
Which struck fear & terror into me
But still I was resolved this same Country for to see
Although through many dangers I did pass
Hoped still to undergo them at the Last

Now Considering that it was my dismal fate
For to repent I thought it now to late
Trusting still unto my masters Consideration
Hoping they will Except[68] of this my small Relation
Which here I have pend & still will Justifie
Concerning of those Indians & their Country
If this wont do farewell to all as I may say
And for my living i'll seek some other way
In sixteen hundred & ninety'th year
I set forth as plainly may appear
Through Gods assistance for to understand
The natives language & to see their land
And for my masters interest I did soon
Sett from the house the twealth of June
Then up the River I with heavy heart
Did take my way & from all English part
To live amongst the Natives of this place
If god permits me for one two years space
The Inland Country of Good report hath been
By Indians but by English yet not seen
Therefore I on my Journey did not stay
But making all the hast I could upon our way
Gott on the borders of the stone Indian Country
I took possession on the tenth Instant[69] July
And for my masters I speaking for them all
This neck of land I deerings point did call
Distance from hence by Judgement at the lest
From the house six hundred miles southwest
Through Rivers which run strong with falls
thirty three Carriages[70] five lakes in all
The ground begins for to be dry with wood
Poplo & birch with ashs thats very good
For the Natives of that place which knows
No use of Better than their wooden Bows
According to the use & custom of this place
In September I brought those Natives to a peace
But I had no sooner from those Natives turnd my back
Some of the home Indians came upon their track
And for old grudges & their minds to fill
Came up with them Six tents of which they kill'd
This ill news kept secrett was from me
Nor none of those home Indians did I see

68. Except: i.e., accept.
69. Instant: past, most recent.

70. Carriages: portages.

Untill that they their murder all had done
And the Chief acter was he thats called the Sun
So far I have spoken concerning of the spoil
And now will give account of that same Country soile
Which hither part is very thick of wood
Affords small nutts with little cherryes very good
Thus it continues till you leave the woods behind
And then you have beast of severall kind
The one is a black Buffillo great
Another is an outgrown Bear which is good meat
His skin to gett I have used all the ways I can
He is mans food & he makes food of man
His hide they would not me it preserve
But said it was a god & they should Starve
This plain affords nothing but Beast & grass
And over it in three days time we past
getting unto the woods on the other side
It being about forty sixe miles wide
This wood is poplo ridges with small ponds of water
there is beavour in abundance but no Otter
with plains & ridges in the Country throughout
Their Enemies many whom they cannot rout
But now of late they hunt their Enemies
And with our English guns do make them flie
At deerings point after the frost
I set up their a Certain Cross
In token of my being there
Cut out on it the date of year
And Likewise for to veryfie the same
added to it my master sir Edward deerings name
So having no more to trouble you withall I am
Sir you most obedient & faithful Servant at Command

                                        Henry Kelsey

THREE

THE EIGHTEENTH CENTURY

Chapter 9

Religion in the Enlightenment

INTRODUCTION

The English colonies of America had different religious cultures from their earliest founding: Congregationalism in New England, the Anglican church in New York, the South, and the West Indies. Catholics claimed a foothold in Maryland, Baptists in Rhode Island, Presbyterians in New Jersey, Pennsylvania, and North Carolina, Quakers in Pennsylvania and New Jersey. Dissenting sects sprang up in all areas. Some new immigrants brought religious systems with them, such as Lutherans and Moravians in Pennsylvania. Others, notably African slaves, brought religious backgrounds that splintered or went underground in the colonies, making their influence felt indirectly. By the end of the eighteenth century Methodism would be a growing force, along with evangelical strands in the more established denominations. A synagogue had appeared in Bridgetown, Barbados, in the middle of the seventeenth century; another followed in New York.

Despite the variety of denominations, in most colonies the basic principle of establishmentarianism went unchallenged until the Revolutionary period. (As late as 1840, Henry Thoreau could cause a stir by refusing to pay his church tax.) In Congregationalist New England as well as the Anglican South, the church was territorial, embracing all who lived in its vicinity. It was supported by public revenue and had public disciplinary powers. And its ceremonies were central events in public culture. Nonestablished churches lived in its shadow. (There were exceptions, such as New Jersey, where no church managed to dominate long enough to secure state establishment.) Toleration, outside of Rhode Island, was sharply limited; even the forward-thinking Pennsylvania barred Catholics and Jews from public life.

In practice, colonial culture seems to have been much less thoroughly religious than its official institutions. Despite a rash of revivals near midcentury, church attendance was hardly universal. Few areas could boast even fifty percent attendance among eligible adults. In New York City the figure does not seem to have exceeded fifteen percent; even in Puritan Boston, Samuel Mather claimed in 1780 that "not one sixth" came to church. Crevecoeur remarked that "religious indifference is imperceptibly disseminated from one end of the country to the other." Indifference to the church, however, did not often lead to an articulate secularism. Nonreligion left little record. An avowed atheist was hard to find in colonial America.

Enlightenment thought in the colonies seldom took the anticlerical cast that it had in Catholic Europe (in Voltaire, for example). On the contrary, the clergy were often

Contemporary cartoon of the evangelist George Whitefield.

in the vanguard of the Enlightenment. Cotton Mather's enthusiasm for the Royal Society had many echoes, largely because the new rationality was so conspicuously associated with the unnaturally pious Newton and with Locke the evangelist. John Locke's 1695 defense of religion was called *The Reasonableness of Christianity*; the assumptions behind his title marked a radical shift in paradigms. The idea of a rational religion imperceptibly took deep hold throughout the colonies. Against the strong objections of Jonathan Edwards, the Puritan emphasis on the sovereignty of God yielded to a more rational and benevolent God. Edwards, the greatest defender of Calvinist orthodoxy in the eighteenth century, had himself read Newton and Locke devotedly as a teenager, and had tried brilliantly to square as much of Calvinist orthodoxy as possible with Lockean psychology, Newtonian physics, and the English school of deductive philosophy. To his dying day, Edwards never saw science and theology as separate. Not until after the Revolution did piety and rationalism polarize. Even then, the antiChristian Paine remained religious, and the divines who attacked him so bitterly used—or tried to use—arguments of rational demonstration.

The general drift of religion in the eighteenth-century colonies was toward voluntarism and subjectivism. People began to choose salvation, and to feel it once they had chosen it. Religion gradually became less central to public order and more central to the distinctive experience of the individual. Emotion, which for Puritans was at best a circumstantial sign of election, came to be the true mode of religious conversion. Arminianism became less of a heresy and more the unnamed assumptions of evangelical and liberal religion. Calvinism and Deism lost out equally in this shift, replaced by a culture of sentiment that would allow a new, indigenous version of Christianity to take root in the popular culture of the early nineteenth century.

Much of the historical debate about eighteenth-century religion has to do with its influence on politics, particularly on the Revolution. In his "Dissertation on the Canon and Feudal Laws," John Adams opined that the struggles against authority in religion and in politics were essentially the same. Many modern historians have followed a similar line of thought, arguing that the revivalists and dissenters fuelled the antiauthoritarian mood of the Revolution. Henry May, in a celebrated study of the Enlightenment, claimed that there was "an antinomian, anti-rationalist, revivalist element in most American radicalism." But others disagree, pointing out that most of the midcentury revivalists were not themselves antiauthoritarian. Certainly the political sermon came to be an important genre, contributing much to the emerging culture of public opinion; ironically, it did so partly because of establishmentarianism, which meant that preachers were speaking at public events, such as elections, and on state-decreed days of fasting or thanksgiving.

The Christianizing of the Indians, meanwhile, had begun to have unexpected results. One was the appearance of literate Indian clergy. Samson Occom's sermon—ironically an execution sermon for the hanging of a fellow Indian—was the first publication by a Native American author in English. Less visible to whites, and certainly less acceptable to them, were changes in Native American religion that resulted from the Protestant missions. David Brainerd, a missionary to the Indians, records in his journal an encounter with an Indian who has become a kind of counter-missionary, a revivalist promoting what he considers the true, old Indian religion.

The fragmentation of religious culture among the slaves, often enforced by owners, has led historian Jon Butler to speak of an "African spiritual holocaust." African religions were nowhere preserved as entire or systematic religious cultures—though slaves held onto some religious practices, such as the ring shout, a ritual dance derived from West Africa. In some places new forms of magical-religious culture developed. (There is evidence of Obeah, or voodoo, from the early eighteenth century.) Some African beliefs—such as a distinction between the big me, or the ordinary self, and the little me, an ecstatic inner soul—have in the views of some scholars deeply influenced American Christianity as a whole. Mostly because of the owners' fears of resistance, however, very little was done to Christianize slaves before about 1760, and African-American Christianity was still emerging at the end of the century.

M.W.

Suggested readings: Jon Butler, *Awash in a Sea of Faith: Christianizing the American People*; Henry F. May, *The Enlightenment in America*; and Patricia Bonomi, *Under the Cope of Heaven: Religion, Society, and Politics in Colonial America*.

1. Jonathan Edwards

[Of Being]
1721

Jonathan Edwards (1703–1758), was both precociously modern and traditional.
He had a thorough comprehension of Locke's Essay Concerning Human
Understanding *by his early teens, and read Newton at Yale, where he graduated in*
1720, at the age of 16. Yet he saw his world only in terms of the sacred history of
God's work of redemption; secular history remained empty to him, to such a
degree that the historian Peter Gay called him "the last medieval American."

   Born in Connecticut, Edwards was the son, grandson, and great-grandson of
Protestant ministers. After leaving Yale, he joined his grandfather, Solomon
Stoddard, as pastor in Northampton, Massachusetts. Not long after, he acquired
his first slave. In 1734 and 1735, Edwards was the center of an enthusiastic revival
in Northampton. He published a report of the revival in 1737, as A Faithful
Narrative of the Surprising Work of God. *More revivals followed, especially in the*
period from 1740 to 1744. These events have come to be known as the Great
Awakening. Some scholars rate the awakening as the most important event in colo-
nial America before the imperial crisis of the 1760s. Others question whether it
was an event at all; the term, which was not coined until a century later, vaguely
applies to revivals widely scattered in time and place. (See Franklin's autobiog-
raphy, below, for a sketch of the most famous revival preacher, the Anglican
George Whitefield.)

   At any rate, Edwards was an ambivalent evangelist because he was an unam-
bivalent Calvinist. His grandfather Stoddard had made a number of innovations at
Northampton, including open communion—occasioning a debate with his more
orthodox neighbor, Edward Taylor. After Stoddard's death, however, Edwards
came to regard the policy as a mistake. He tried to return to older ways, including
tests of conversion before admission to communion. The congregation—already
unhappy over Edwards's stern disciplinary response to some some young men who
read "bad" (pornographic) books—rebelled, and in 1750 Edwards was forced to
leave his pulpit. He accepted a post in Stockbridge as missionary to the Indians and
pastor to the local church. It was here that he wrote his major works, including
Freedom of the Will *(1754),* The Nature of True Virtue *(1755), and* Original Sin
(1758). In January of 1758, Edwards began serving as the president of the College
of New Jersey (later Princeton); in March, he died from a smallpox inoculation.

   "Of Being," an early fragment, was written while Edwards was pursuing his
master's degree at Yale. It shows the rigor, precision, and ambition of his thinking,
as he tries to make a philosopher's vocabulary demonstrate the sovereignty of God.
The calmly rational style is more typical of Edwards's work than is the sulphuric
rhetoric of his more famous sermon, "Sinners in the Hands of an Angry God."

That there should absolutely be nothing at all is utterly impossible. The mind can never, let it stretch its conceptions ever so much, bring itself to conceive of a state of perfect nothing. It puts the mind into mere convulsion and confusion to endeavor to think of such a state, and it contradicts the very nature of the soul to think that it should be; and it is the greatest contradiction, and the aggregate of all contradictions, to say that there should not be. 'Tis true we can't so distinctly show the Contradiction by words, because we cannot talk about it without speaking horrid nonsense and contradicting ourselves at every word, and because *nothing* is that whereby we distinctly show other particular contradictions. But here we are run up to our first principle, and have no other to explain the nothingness or not being of nothing by. Indeed, we can mean nothing else by *nothing* but a state of absolute contradiction. And if any man thinks that he can think well enough how there should be nothing, I'll engage that what he means by *nothing* is as much something as anything that ever he thought of in his life; and I believe that if he knew what nothing was it would be intuitively evident to him that it could not be. So that we see it is necessary some being should eternally be. And 'tis a more palpable contradiction still to say that there must be being somewhere, and not otherwhere; for the words *absolute nothing* and *where* contradict each other. And besides, it gives as great a shock to the mind to think of pure nothing in any one place, as it does to think of it in all; and it is self-evident that there can be nothing in one place as well as in another, and so if there can be in one, there can be in all. So that we see this necessary, eternal being must be infinite and omnipresent.

(Place this as a lemma[1] where it suits best, and let it be more fully demonstr[ated]:) This infinite and omnipresent being cannot be solid. Let us see how contradictory it is to say that an infinite being is solid; for solidity surely is nothing but resistance to other solidities.

Space is this necessary, eternal, infinite and omnipresent being. We find that we can with ease conceive how all other beings should not be. We can remove them out of our minds, and place some other in the room of them; but space is the very thing that we can never remove and conceive of its not being. If a man would imagine space anywhere to be divided, so as there should be nothing between the divided parts, there remains space between notwithstanding, and so the man contradicts himself. And it is self-evident, I believe, to every man, that space is necessary, eternal, infinite and omnipresent. But I had as good speak plain: I have already said as much as that space is God. And it is indeed clear to me, that all the space there is not proper to body, all the space there is without the bounds of the creation, all the space there was before the creation, is God himself, and nobody would in the least stick at it, if it were not because of the gross conceptions that we have of space.

And how doth it grate upon the mind, to think that something should be from all eternity, and nothing all the while be conscious of it. Let us suppose, to illustrate it, that the world had a being from all eternity, and had many great changes and wonderful revolutions, and all the while nothing knew; there was no knowledge in the

---

1. lemma: a prefatory statement of an argument or theme.

universe of any such thing. How is it possible to bring the mind to imagine? Yea, it is really impossible it should be, that anything should be, and nothing know it. Then you'll say, if it be so, it is because nothing has any existence anywhere else but in consciousness; no, certainly nowhere else, but either in created or uncreated consciousness.

Supposing there were another universe only of bodies, created at a great distance from this, created in excellent order and harmonious motions, and a beautiful variety; and there was no created intelligence in it, nothing but senseless bodies. Nothing but God knew anything of it. I demand in what respect this world has a being, but only in the divine consciousness. Certainly in no respect. There would be figures and magnitudes, and motions and proportions—but where? Where else, but in the Almighty's knowledge. How is it possible there should? Then you'll say: For the same reason, in a room close shut up, that nobody sees nor hears nothing in it, there is nothing any other way than in God's knowledge. I answer: Created beings are conscious of the effects of what is in the room; for perhaps there is not one leaf of a tree, nor spire of grass, but what has effects all over the universe, and will have to the end of eternity. But any otherwise, there is nothing in a room shut up, but only in God's consciousness. How can anything be there any other way? This will appear to be truly so to anyone that thinks of it with the whole united strength of his mind. Let us suppose for illustration this impossibility, that all the spirits in the universe to be for a time deprived of their consciousness, and God's consciousness at the same time to be intermitted. I say, the universe for that time would cease to be, of itself; and not only, as we speak, because the Almighty could not attend to uphold the world, but because God knew nothing of it. 'Tis our foolish imagination that will not suffer us to see. We fancy there may be figures and magnitudes, relations and properties, without anyone's knowing of it. But it is our imagination hurts us. We don't know what figures and properties are.

Our imagination makes us fancy we see shapes and colors and magnitudes though nobody is there to behold it. But to help our imagination let us thus state the case: Let us suppose the world deprived of every ray of light, so that there should not be the least glimmering of light in the universe. Now all will own that in such a case, the universe would be immediately really deprived of all its colors. One part of the universe is no more red, or blue, or green, or yellow, or black, or white, or light, or dark, or transparent or opaque than another. There would be no visible distinction between the world and the rest of the incomprehensible void—yea, there would be no difference in these respects between the world and the infinite void. That is, any part of that void would really be as light and as dark, as white and as black, as red and green, as blue and as brown, as transparent and as opaque as any part of the universe. Or, as there would be in such case no difference between the world and nothing in these respects, so there would be no difference between one part of the world and another. All, in these respects, is alike confounded with and indistinguishable from infinite emptiness.

At the same time, also let us suppose the universe to be altogether deprived of motion, and all parts of it to be at perfect rest (the former supposition is indeed included in this, but we distinguish them for better clearness). Then the universe would not differ from the void in this respect; there will be no more motion in one than the other. Then also solidity would cease. All that we mean or can be meant by solidity is resistance—resistance to touch, the resistance of some parts of space. This is all the knowledge we get of solidity by our senses, and, I am sure, all that we can get any other way. But solidity shall be shown to be nothing else more fully hereafter. But there can be no resistance if there is no motion. One body cannot resist another when there is perfect rest amongst them. But you'll say, though there is not actually resistance, yet there is potential existence, that is, such and such parts of space would resist upon occasion. But this is all I would have: that there is no solidity now; not but that God would cause there to be an occasion. And if there is no solidity, there is no extension, for extension is the extendedness of the solidity. Then all figure and magnitude and proportion immediately ceases.

Put both these suppositions together—that is, deprive the world of light and motion—and the case would stand thus with the world: there would be neither white nor black, neither blue nor brown, bright nor shaded, pellucid nor opaque; no noise or sound, neither heat nor cold, neither fluid nor wet nor dry, hard nor soft, nor solidity, nor extension, nor figure, nor magnitude, nor proportion; nor body, nor spirit. What then is become of the universe? Certainly, it exists nowhere but in the divine mind. This will be abundantly clearer to one after having read what I have to say further of solidity, etc. So that we see that a world without motion can exist nowhere else but in the mind, either infinite or finite.

Corollary. It follows from hence, that those beings which have knowledge and consciousness are the only proper and real and substantial beings, inasmuch as the being of other things is only by these. From hence we may see the gross mistake of those who think material things the most substantial beings, and spirits more like a shadow; whereas spirits only are properly substance.

A state of absolute nothing is a state of absolute contradiction. Absolute nothing is the aggregate of all the absurd contradictions in the world, a state wherein there is neither body, nor spirit, nor space: neither empty space nor full space, neither little nor great, narrow nor broad, neither infinitely great space nor finite space, nor a mathematical point; neither up nor down, neither north nor south (I don't mean as it is with respect to the body of the earth or some other great body, but no contrary points nor positions nor directions); no such thing as either here or there, this way and that way, or only one way. When we go about to form an idea of perfect nothing we must shut out all of these things. We must shut out of our minds both space that has something in it, and space that has nothing in it. We must not allow ourselves to think of the least part of space, never so small, nor must we suffer our thoughts to take sanctuary in a mathematical point. When we go to expel body out of our thoughts, we must be sure not to leave empty space in the room of it; and when we go to expel emptiness from our thoughts we must not think to squeeze it out by anything close, hard and solid, but we must think of the same that the sleeping rocks dream of; and not till then shall we get a complete idea of nothing.

A state of nothing is a state wherein every proposition in Euclid is not true, nor any of those self-evident maxims by which they are demonstrated; and all other eternal truths are neither true nor false.

When we go to inquire whether or no there can be absolutely nothing we speak nonsense. In inquiring, the stating of the question is nonsense, because we make a disjunction where there is none. *Either* being *or* absolute nothing is no disjunction, no more than whether a triangle is a triangle or not a triangle. There is no other way, but only for there to be existence; there is no such thing as absolute nothing. There is such a thing as nothing with respect to this ink and paper. There is such a thing as nothing with respect to you and me. There is such a thing as nothing with respect to this globe of earth, and with respect to this created universe. There is another way besides these things having existence. But there is no such thing as nothing with respect to entity or being, absolutely considered. And we don't know what we say, if we say we think it possible in itself that there should not be entity.

2. Jonathan Edwards

Personal Narrative
c. 1739

The following story is a conversion narrative rather than a modern autobiography. In it, Edwards inventories the evidences of his own salvation. As a loyal Calvinist, Edwards believed that it is never possible to know that one were saved; election is God's alone, and too great a sense of confidence on the subject would be sinful and delusional. Puritan theology required permanent self-doubt. However, since sanctification by grace can be presumed to have some effects in the soul, salvation leaves traces. Since Edwards inclined to a conservative understanding of church membership, limiting communion to the certified elect, he saw the examination of such traces as important not only for the individual, but for the elders of the congregation as well. The conversion narrative is a public act of self-trial.

Edwards's conversion narrative goes far beyond the usual examples of the genre in several key respects. It depicts a rich inner life of affect, looking forward slightly to the Treatise Concerning Religious Affections *(1746), in which Edwards considers carefully how twelve different emotions can be tested to see if they are evidences of salvation. The "Personal Narrative" also rings with the language of the sublime. Edwards embraces a sentiment of annihilation and abjection in relation to the infinite and omnipotent God. He treasures the oxymoron of God's sweet severity, taking from it both pain and pleasure. This sense of the sublime, in something close to the sense that Kant would later give it, allows Edwards also to have a perverse pleasure in exactly those aspects of the world that are most terrifying, especially thunderstorms. Thus the "Personal Narrative" contains some of the earliest appreciations of nature in the modern mode, contrasting with the treatment of "wilderness" in Bradford or Danforth.*

I had a variety of concerns and exercises about my soul from my childhood; but had two more remarkable seasons of awakening, before I met with that change, by which I was brought to those new dispositions, and that new sense of things, that I have since had. The first time was when I was a boy, some years before I went to college, at a time of remarkable awakening in my father's congregation. I was then very much affected for many months, and concerned about the things of religion, and my soul's salvation; and was abundant in duties. I used to pray five times a day in secret, and to spend much time in religious talk with other boys; and used to meet with them to pray together. I experienced I know not what kind of delight in religion. My mind was much engaged in it, and had much self-righteous pleasure; and it was my delight to abound in religious duties. I, with some of my schoolmates joined together, and built a booth in a swamp, in a very secret and retired place, for a place of prayer. And besides, I had particular secret places of my own in the woods, where I used to retire by myself; and used to be from time to time much affected. My affections seemed to be lively and easily moved, and I seemed to be in my element, when engaged in religious duties. And I am ready to think, many are deceived with such affections, and such a kind of delight, as I then had in religion, and mistake it for grace.

But in process of time, my convictions and affections wore off; and I entirely lost all those affections and delights, and left off secret prayer, at least as to any constant performance of it; and returned like a dog to his vomit, and went on in ways of sin. Indeed, I was at some times very uneasy, especially towards the latter part of the time of my being at college. Till it pleased God, in my last year at college, at a time when I was in the midst of many uneasy thoughts about the state of my soul, to seize me with a pleurisy; in which he brought me nigh to the grave, and shook me over the pit of hell.

But yet, it was not long after my recovery, before I fell again into my old ways of sin. But God would not suffer me to go on with any quietness; but I had great and violent inward struggles: till after many conflicts with wicked inclinations, and repeated resolutions, and bonds that I laid myself under by a kind of vows to God, I was brought wholly to break off all former wicked ways, and all ways of known outward sin; and to apply myself to seek my salvation, and practice the duties of religion: but without that kind of affection and delight, that I had formerly experienced. My concern now wrought more by inward struggles and conflicts, and self-reflections. I made seeking my salvation the main business of my life. But yet it seems to me, I sought after a miserable manner: which has made me sometimes since to question, whether ever it issued in that which was saving; being ready to doubt, whether such miserable seeking was ever succeeded. But yet I was brought to seek salvation, in a manner that I never was before. I felt a spirit to part with all things in the world, for an interest in Christ. My concern continued and prevailed, with many exercising things and inward struggles; but yet it never seemed to be proper to express my concern that I had, by the name of terror.

From my childhood up, my mind had been wont to be full of objections against the doctrine of God's sovereignty, in choosing whom he would to eternal life, and rejecting whom he pleased; leaving them eternally to perish, and be everlastingly tormented in hell. It used to appear like a horrible doctrine to me. But I remember the time very well, when I seemed to be convinced, and fully satisfied, as to this sovereignty of God, and his justice in thus eternally disposing of men, according to his sovereign pleasure. But never could give an account, how, or by what means, I was thus convinced; not in the least imagining, in the time of it, nor a long time after, that there was any extraordinary influence of God's Spirit in it: but only that now I saw further, and my reason apprehended the justice and reasonableness of it. However, my mind rested in it; and it put an end to all those cavils and objections, that I had till then abode with me, all the preceding part of my life. And there has been a wonderful alteration in my mind, with respect to the doctrine of God's sovereignty, from that day to this; so that I scarce ever have found so much as the rising of an objection against God's sovereignty, in the most absolute sense, in showing mercy on whom he will show mercy, and hardening and eternally damning whom he will. God's absolute sovereignty, and justice, with respect to salvation and damnation, is what my mind seems to rest assured of, as much as of anything that I see with my eyes; at least it is so at times. But I have oftentimes since that first conviction, had quite another kind of sense of God's sovereignty, than I had then. I have often since, not only had a conviction, but a *delightful* conviction. The doctrine of God's sovereignty has very often appeared, an exceeding pleasant, bright and sweet doctrine to me: and absolute sovereignty is what I love to ascribe to God. But my first conviction was not with this.

The first that I remember that ever I found anything of that sort of inward, sweet delight in God and divine things, that I have lived much in since, was on reading those words, 1 Tim. 1:17. *Now unto the King eternal, immortal, invisible, the only wise God, be honor and glory forever and ever, Amen.* As I read the words, there came into my soul, and was as it were diffused through it, a sense of the glory of the Divine Being; a new sense, quite different from anything I ever experienced before. Never any words of Scripture seemed to me as these words did. I thought with myself, how excellent a Being that was; and how happy I should be, if I might enjoy that God, and be wrapped up to God in heaven, and be as it were swallowed up in him. I kept saying, and as it were singing over these words of Scripture to myself; and went to prayer, to pray to God that I might enjoy him; and prayed in a manner quite different from what I used to do; with a new sort of affection. But it never came into my thought, that there was anything spiritual, or of a saving nature in this.

From about that time, I began to have a new kind of apprehensions and ideas of Christ, and the work of redemption, and the glorious way of salvation by him. I had an inward, sweet sense of these things, that at times came into my heart; and my soul was led away in pleasant views and contemplations of them. And my mind was greatly engaged, to spend my time in reading and meditating on Christ; and the beauty and excellency of his person, and the lovely way of salvation, by free grace in him. I found no books so delightful to me, as those that treated of these subjects. Those words, Cant. 2:1, used to be abundantly with me: *I am the rose of Sharon, the lily of the valleys.* The words seemed to me sweetly to represent, the loveliness and beauty of Jesus Christ. And the whole Book of Canticles used to be pleasant to me; and I used to be much in reading it, about that time. And found, from time to time, an inward sweetness, that used, as it were, to carry me away in my contemplations; in what I know not how to express otherwise, than by a calm, sweet abstraction of soul from all the concerns of this world; and a kind of vision, or fixed ideas and imaginations, of being alone in the mountains, or some solitary wilderness, far from all mankind, sweetly conversing with Christ, and wrapped and swallowed up in God.

The sense I had of divine things, would often of a sudden as it were, kindle up a sweet burning in my heart; an ardor of my soul, that I know not how to express.

Not long after I first began to experience these things, I gave an account to my father, of some things that had passed in my mind. I was pretty much affected by the discourse we had together. And when the discourse was ended, I walked abroad alone, in a solitary place in my father's pasture, for contemplation. And as I was walking there, and looked up on the sky and clouds; there came into my mind, a sweet sense of the glorious majesty and grace of God, that I know not how to express. I seemed to see them both in a sweet conjunction: majesty and meekness joined together: it was a sweet and gentle, and holy majesty; and also a majestic meekness; an awful sweetness; a high, and great, and holy gentleness.

After this my sense of divine things gradually increased, and became more and more lively, and had more of that inward sweetness. The appearance of everything was altered: there seemed to be, as it were, a calm, sweet cast, or appearance of divine glory, in almost everything. God's excellency, his wisdom, his purity and love, seemed to appear in everything; in the sun, moon and stars; in the clouds, and blue sky; in the grass, flowers, trees; in the water, and all nature; which used greatly to fix my mind. I often used to sit and view the moon, for a long time; and so in the daytime, spent much time in viewing the clouds and sky, to behold the sweet glory of God in these things: in the meantime, singing forth with a low voice, my contemplations of the Creator and Redeemer. And scarce anything, among all the works of nature, was so sweet to me as thunder and lightning. Formerly, nothing had been so terrible to me. I used to be a person uncommonly terrified with thunder: and it used to strike me with terror, when I saw a thunderstorm rising. But now, on the contrary, it rejoiced me. I felt God at the first appearance of a thunderstorm. And used to take the opportunity at such times, to fix myself to view the clouds, and see the lightnings play, and hear the majestic and awful voice of God's thunder: which oftentimes was exceeding entertaining, leading me to sweet contemplations of my great and glorious God. And while I viewed, used to spend my time, as it always seemed natural to me, to sing or chant forth my meditations; to speak my thoughts in soliloquies, and speak with a singing voice.

I felt then a great satisfaction as to my good estate. But that did not content me. I had vehement longings of soul after God and Christ, and after more holiness; wherewith my heart seemed to be full, and ready to break: which often brought to my mind, the words of the Psalmist, Ps. 119:28, *My soul breaketh for the longing it hath*. I often felt a mourning and lamenting in my heart, that I had not turned to God sooner, that I might have had more time to grow in grace. My mind was greatly fixed on divine things; I was almost perpetually in the contemplation of them. Spent most of my time in thinking of divine things, year after year. And used to spend abundance of my time, in walking alone in the woods, and solitary places, for meditation, soliloquy and prayer, and converse with God. And it was always my manner, at such times, to sing forth my contemplations. And was almost constantly in ejaculatory prayer, wherever I was. Prayer seemed to be natural to me; as the breath, by which the inward burnings of my heart had vent. The delights which I now felt in things of religion, were of an exceeding different kind, from those forementioned, that I had when I was a boy. They were totally of another kind; and what I then had no more notion or idea of, than one born blind has of pleasant and beautiful colors. They were of a more inward, pure, soul-animating and refreshing nature. Those former delights, never reached the heart; and did not arise from any sight of the divine excellency of the things of God; or any taste of the soul-satisfying, and life-giving good, there is in them.

My sense of divine things seemed gradually to increase, till I went to preach at New York; which was about a year and a half after they began. While I was there, I felt them, very sensibly, in a much higher degree, than I had done before. My longings after God and holiness, were much increased. Pure and humble, holy and heavenly Christianity, appeared exceeding amiable to me. I felt in me a burning desire to be in everything a complete Christian; and conformed to the blessed image of Christ: and that I might live in all things, according to the pure, sweet and blessed rules of the gospel. I had an eager thirsting after progress in these things. My longings after it, put me upon pursuing and pressing after them. It was my continual strife day and night, and constant inquiry, how I should *be* more holy, and *live* more holily, and more becoming a child of God, and disciple of Christ. I sought an increase of grace and holiness, and that I might live an holy life, with vastly more earnestness, than ever I sought grace, before I had it. I used to be continually examining myself, and studying and contriving for likely ways and means, how I should live holily, with far greater diligence and earnestness, than ever I pursued anything in my life: but with too great a dependence on my own strength; which afterwards proved a great damage to me. My experience had not then taught me, as it has done since, my extreme feebleness and impotence, every manner of way; and the innumerable and bottomless depths of secret corruption and deceit, that there was in my heart. However, I went on with my eager pursuit after more holiness; and sweet conformity to Christ.

The heaven I desired was a heaven of holiness; to be with God, and to spend my eternity in divine love, and holy communion with Christ. My mind was very much taken up with contemplations on heaven, and the enjoyments of those there; and living there in perfect holiness, humility and love. And it used at that time to appear a great part of the happiness of heaven, that there the saints could express their love to Christ. It appeared to me a great clog and hindrance and burden to me, that what I felt within, I could not express to God, and give vent to, as I desired. The inward ardor of my soul, seemed to be hindered and pent up, and could not freely flame out as it would. I used often to think, how in heaven, this sweet principle should freely and fully vent and express itself. Heaven appeared to me exceeding delightful as a world of love. It appeared to me, that all happiness consisted in living in pure, humble, heavenly, divine love.

I remember the thoughts I used then to have of holiness. I remember I then said sometimes to myself, I do certainly know that I love holiness, such as the gospel prescribes. It appeared to me, there was nothing in it but what was ravishingly lovely. It appeared to me, to be the highest beauty and amiableness, above all other beauties: that it was a *divine* beauty; far purer than anything here upon earth; and that everything else, was like mire, filth and defilement, in comparison of it.

Holiness, as I then wrote down some of my contemplations on it, appeared to me to be of a sweet, pleasant, charming, serene, calm nature. It seemed to me, it brought an inexpressible purity, brightness, peacefulness and ravishment to the soul: and that it made the soul like a field or garden of God, with all manner of pleasant flowers; that is all pleasant, delightful and undisturbed; enjoying a sweet calm, and the gently vivifying beams of the sun. The soul of a true Christian, as I then wrote my meditations, appeared like such a little white flower, as we see in the spring of the year; low and humble on the ground, opening its bosom, to receive the pleasant beams of the sun's glory; rejoicing as it were, in a calm rapture; diffusing around a sweet fragrancy; standing peacefully and lovingly, in the midst of other flowers round about; all in like manner opening their bosoms, to drink in the light of the sun.

There was no part of creature-holiness, that I then, and at other times, had so great a sense of the loveliness of, as humility, brokenness of heart and poverty of spirit: and there was nothing that I had such a spirit to long for. My heart as it were panted after this, to lie low before God, and in the dust; that I might be nothing, and that God might be all; that I might become as a little child.

While I was there at New York, I sometimes was much affected with reflections on my past life, considering how late it was, before I began to be truly religious; and how wickedly I had lived till then: and once so as to weep abundantly, and for a considerable time together.

On January 12, 1723, I made a solemn dedication of myself to God, and wrote it down; giving up myself, and all that I had to God; to be for the future in no respect my own; to act as one that had no right to himself, in any respect. And solemnly vowed to take God for my whole portion and felicity; looking on nothing else as any part of my happiness, nor acting as if it were: and his law for the constant rule of my obedience: engaging to fight with all my might, against the world, the flesh and the devil, to the end of my life. But have reason to be infinitely humbled, when I consider, how much I have failed of answering my obligation.

I had then abundance of sweet religious conversation in the family where I lived, with Mr. John Smith, and his pious mother. My heart was knit in affection to those, in whom were appearances of true piety; and I could bear the thoughts of no other companions, but such as were holy, and the disciples of the blessed Jesus.

I had great longings for the advancement of Christ's kingdom in the world. My secret prayer used to be in great part taken up in praying for it. If I heard the least hint of any thing that happened in any part of the world, that appeared to me, in some respect or other, to have a favorable aspect on the interest of Christ's kingdom, my soul eagerly catched at it; and it would much animate and refresh me. I used to be earnest to read public newsletters, mainly for that end; to see if I could not find some news favorable to the interest of religion in the world.

I very frequently used to retire into a solitary place, on the banks of Hudson's River, at some distance from the city, for contemplation on divine things, and secret converse with God; and had many sweet hours there. Sometimes Mr. Smith and I walked there together, to converse of the things of God; and our conversation used much to turn on the advancement of Christ's kingdom in the world, and the glorious things that God would accomplish for his church in the latter days.

I had then, and at other times, the greatest delight in the holy Scriptures, of any book whatsoever. Oftentimes in reading it, every word seemed to touch my heart. I felt an harmony between something in my heart, and those sweet and powerful words.

I seemed often to see so much light, exhibited by every sentence, and such a refreshing ravishing food communicated, that I could not get along in reading. Used oftentimes to dwell long on one sentence, to see the wonders contained in it; and yet almost every sentence seemed to be full of wonders.

I came away from New York in the month of April 1723, and had a most bitter parting with Madam Smith and her son. My heart seemed to sink within me, at leaving the family and city, where I had enjoyed so many sweet and pleasant days. I went from New York to Wethersfield by water. As I sailed away, I kept sight of the city as long as I could; and when I was out of sight of it, it would affect me much to look that way, with a kind of melancholy mixed with sweetness. However, that night after this sorrowful parting, I was greatly comforted in God at Westchester, where we went ashore to lodge: and had a pleasant time of it all the voyage to Saybrook. It was sweet to me to think of meeting dear Christians in heaven, where we should never part more. At Saybrook we went ashore to lodge on Saturday, and there kept sabbath; where I had a sweet and refreshing season, walking alone in the fields.

After I came home to Windsor, remained much in a like frame of my mind, as I had been in at New York; but only sometimes felt my heart ready to sink, with the thoughts of my friends at New York. And my refuge and support was in contemplations on the heavenly state; as I find in my Diary of May 1, 1723. It was my comfort to think of that state, where there is fullness of joy; where reigns heavenly, sweet, calm and delightful love, without alloy; where there are continually the dearest expressions of this love; where is the enjoyment of the persons loved, without ever parting; where these persons that appear so lovely in this world, will really be inexpressibly more lovely, and full of love to us. And how sweetly will the mutual lovers join together to sing the praises of God and the Lamb! How full will it fill us with joy, to think, that this enjoyment, these sweet exercises will never cease or come to an end; but will last to all eternity!

Continued much in the same frame in the general, that I had been in at New York, till I went to New Haven, to live there as tutor of the College; having one special season of uncommon sweetness: particularly once at Bolton, in a journey from Boston, walking out alone in the fields. After I went to New Haven, I sunk in religion; my mind being diverted from my eager and violent pursuits after holiness, by some affairs that greatly perplexed and distracted my mind.

In September 1725, I was taken ill at New Haven; and endeavoring to go home to Windsor, was so ill at the North Village, that I could go no further: where I lay sick for about a quarter of a year. And in this sickness, God was pleased to visit me again with the sweet influences of his Spirit. My mind was greatly engaged there on divine, pleasant contemplations, and longings of soul. I observed that those who watched with me, would often be looking out for the morning, and seemed to wish for it; which brought to my mind those words of the Psalmist, which my soul with sweetness made its own language, *My soul waiteth for the Lord more than they that watch for the morning: I say, more than they that watch for the morning.* And when the light of the morning came, and the beams of the sun came in at the windows, it refreshed my soul from one morning to another. It seemed to me to be some image of the sweet light of God's glory.

I remember, about that time, I used greatly to long for the conversion of some that I was concerned with. It seemed to me, I could gladly honor them, and with delight be a servant to them, and lie at their feet, if they were but truly holy.

But some time after this, I was again greatly diverted in my mind, with some temporal concerns, that exceedingly took up my thoughts, greatly to the wounding of my soul: and went on through various exercises, that it would be tedious to relate, that gave me much more experience of my own heart, than ever I had before.

Since I came to this town [Northampton], I have often had sweet complacency in God in views of his glorious perfections, and the excellency of Jesus Christ. God has appeared to me, a glorious and lovely Being, chiefly on the account of his holiness. The holiness of God has always appeared to me the most lovely of all his attributes. The doctrines of God's absolute sovereignty, and free grace, in showing mercy to whom he would show mercy; and man's absolute dependence on the operations of God's Holy Spirit, have very often appeared to me as sweet and glorious doctrines. These doctrines have been much my delight. God's sovereignty has ever appeared to me, as great part of his glory. It has often been sweet to me to go to God, and adore him as a sovereign God, and ask sovereign mercy of him.

I have loved the doctrines of the gospel: they have been to my soul like green pastures. The gospel has seemed to me to be the richest treasure; the treasure that I have most desired, and longed that it might dwell richly in me. The way of salvation by Christ, has appeared in a general way, glorious and excellent, and most pleasant and beautiful. It has often seemed to me, that it would in a great measure spoil heaven, to receive it in any other way. That text has often been affecting and delightful to me, Is. 32:2, *A man shall be an hiding place from the wind, and a covert from the tempest; as rivers of water in a dry place, as the shadow of a great rock in a weary land.*

It has often appeared sweet to me, to be united to Christ; to have him for my head, and to be a member of his body: and also to have Christ for my teacher and prophet. I very often think with sweetness and longings and pantings of soul, of being a little child, taking hold of Christ, to be led by him through the wilderness of this world. That text, Matt. 18, at the beginning, has often been sweet to me: *Except ye be converted, and become as little children, ye shall not enter into the kingdom of heaven.* I love to think of coming to Christ, to receive salvation of him, poor in spirit, and quite empty of self; humbly exalting him alone; cut entirely off from my own root, and to grow into, and out of Christ: to have God in Christ to be all in all; and to live by faith on the Son of God, a life of humble, unfeigned confidence in him. That Scripture has often been sweet to me, Ps. 115:1, *Not unto us, O Lord, not unto us, but unto thy name give glory, for thy mercy, and for thy truth's sake.* And those words of Christ, Luke 10:21, *In that hour Jesus rejoiced in spirit, and said, I thank thee, O Father, Lord of heaven and earth, that thou hast hid these things from the wise and prudent, and hast revealed them unto babes: even so, Father; for so it seemed good in thy sight.* That sovereignty of God that Christ rejoiced in, seemed to me to be worthy to be rejoiced in; and that rejoicing of Christ, seemed to me to show the excellency of Christ, and the Spirit that he was of.

Sometimes only mentioning a single word, causes my heart to burn within me: or only seeing the name of Christ, or the name of some attribute of God. And God has appeared glorious to me, on account of the Trinity. It has made me have exalting thoughts of God, that he subsists in three persons; Father, Son, and Holy Ghost.

The sweetest joys of delights I have experienced, have not been those that have arisen from a hope of my own good estate; but in a direct view of the glorious things of the gospel. When I enjoy this sweetness, it seems to carry me above the thoughts of my own safe estate. It seems at such times a loss that I cannot bear, to take off my eye from the glorious, pleasant object I behold without me, to turn my eye in upon myself, and my own good estate.

My heart has been much on the advancement of Christ's kingdom in the world. The histories of the past advancement of Christ's kingdom, have been sweet to me. When I have read histories of past ages, the pleasantest thing in all my reading has been, to read of the kingdom of Christ being promoted. And when I have expected in my reading, to come to any such thing, I have lotted upon it[2] all the way as I read. And my mind has been much entertained and delighted, with the Scripture promises and prophecies, of the future glorious advancement of Christ's kingdom on earth.

I have sometimes had a sense of the excellent fullness of Christ, and his meetness and suitableness as a Savior; whereby he has appeared to me, far above all, the chief of ten thousands. And his blood and atonement has appeared sweet, and his righteousness sweet; which is always accompanied with an ardency of spirit, and inward strugglings and breathings and groanings, that cannot be uttered, to be emptied of myself, and swallowed up in Christ.

Once, as I rid out into the woods for my health, anno 1737; and having lit from my horse in a retired place, as my manner commonly has been, to walk for divine contemplation and prayer; I had a view, that for me was extraordinary, of the glory of the Son of God; as mediator between God and man; and his wonderful, great, full, pure and sweet grace and love, and meek and gentle condescension. This grace, that appeared to me so calm and sweet, appeared great above the heavens. The person of Christ appeared ineffably excellent, with an excellency great enough to swallow up all thought and conception. Which continued, as near as I can judge, about an hour; which kept me, the bigger part of the time, in a flood of tears, and weeping aloud. I felt withal, an ardency of soul to be, what I know not otherwise how to express, than to be emptied and annihilated; to lie in the dust, and to be full of Christ alone; to love him with a holy and pure love; to trust in him; to live upon him; to serve and follow him, and to be totally wrapped up in the fullness of Christ; and to be perfectly sanctified and made pure, with a divine and heavenly purity. I have several other times, and views very much of the same nature, and that have had the same effects.

I have many times had a sense of the glory of the third person in the Trinity, in his office of sanctifier; in his holy operations communicating divine light and life to the soul. God in the communications of his Holy Spirit, has appeared as an infinite fountain of divine glory and sweetness; being full and sufficient to fill and satisfy the soul:

---

2. lotted upon it: counted upon it.

pouring forth itself in sweet communications, like the sun in its glory, sweetly and pleasantly diffusing light and Life. I have sometimes had an affecting sense of the excellency of the Word of God, as a Word of life; as the light of life; a sweet, excellent, life-giving Word: accompanied with a thirsting after that Word, that it might dwell richly in my heart.

I have often since I lived in this town, had very affecting views of my own sinfulness and vileness; very frequently so as to hold me in a kind of loud weeping, sometimes for a considerable time together: so that I have often been forced to shut myself up. I have had a vastly greater sense of my own wickedness, and the badness of my heart, since my conversion, than ever I had before. It has often appeared to me, that if God should mark iniquity against me, I should appear the very worst of all mankind; of all that have been since the beginning of the world to this time: and that I should have by far the lowest place in hell. When others that have come to talk with me about their soul concerns, have expressed the sense they have had of their own wickedness, by saying that it seemed to them, that they were as bad as the devil himself; I thought their expressions seemed exceeding faint and feeble, to represent my wickedness. I thought I should wonder, that they should content themselves with such expressions as these, if I had any reason to imagine, that their sin bore any proportion to mine. It seemed to me, I should wonder at myself, if I should express *my* wickedness in such feeble terms as they did.

My wickedness, as I am in myself, has long appeared to me perfectly ineffable, and infinitely swallowing up all thought and imagination; like an infinite deluge, or infinite mountains over my head. I know not how to express better, what my sins appear to me to be, than by heaping infinite upon infinite, and multiplying infinite by infinite. I go about very often, for this many years, with these expressions in my mind, and in my mouth, "Infinite upon Infinite. Infinite upon Infinite!" When I look into my heart, and take a view of my wickedness, it looks like an abyss infinitely deeper than hell. And it appears to me, that were it not for free grace, exalted and raised up to the infinite height of all the fullness and glory of the great Jehovah, and the arm of his power and grace stretched forth, in all the majesty of his power, and in all the glory of his sovereignty; I should appear sunk down in my sins infinitely below hell itself, far beyond sight of everything, but the piercing eye of God's grace, that can pierce even down to such a depth, and to the bottom of such an abyss.

And yet, I ben't in the least inclined to think, that I have a greater conviction of sin than ordinary. It seems to me, my conviction of sin is exceeding small, and faint. It appears to me enough to amaze me, that I have no more sense of my sin. I know certainly, that I have very little sense of my sinfulness. That my sins appear to me so great, don't seem to me to be, because I have so much more conviction of sin than other Christians, but because I am so much worse, and have so much more wickedness to be convinced of. When I have had these turns of weeping and crying for my sins, I thought I knew in the time of it, that my repentance was nothing to my sin.

I have greatly longed of late, for a broken heart, and to lie low before God. And when I ask for humility of God, I can't bear the thoughts of being no more humble, than other Christians. It seems to me, that though their degrees of humility may be suitable for them; yet it would be a vile self-exaltation in me, not to be the lowest in humility of all mankind. Others speak of their longing to be humbled to the dust. Though that may be a proper expression for them, I always think for myself, that I ought to be humbled down below hell. 'Tis an expression that it has long been natural for me to use in prayer to God. I ought to lie infinitely low before God.

It is affecting to me to think, how ignorant I was, when I was a young Christian, of the bottomless, infinite depths of wickedness, pride, hypocrisy and deceit left in my heart.

I have vastly a greater sense, of my universal, exceeding dependence on God's grace and strength, and mere good pleasure, of late, than I used formerly to have; and have experienced more of an abhorrence of my own righteousness. The thought of any comfort or joy, arising in me, on any consideration, or reflection on my own amiableness, or any of my performances or experiences, or any goodness of heart or life, is nauseous and detestable to me. And yet I am greatly afflicted with a proud and self-righteous spirit; much more sensibly, than I used to be formerly. I see that serpent rising and putting forth its head, continually, everywhere, all around me.

Though it seems to me, that in some respects I was a far better Christian, for two or three years after my first conversion, than I am now; and lived in a more constant delight and pleasure: yet of late years, I have had a more full and constant sense of the absolute sovereignty of God, and a delight in that sovereignty; and have had more of a sense of the glory of Christ, as a mediator, as revealed in the gospel.

On one Saturday night in particular, had a particular discovery of the excellency of the gospel of Christ, above all other doctrines; so that I could not but say to myself; "This is my chosen light, my chosen doctrine": and of Christ, "This is my chosen prophet." It appeared to me to be sweet beyond all expression, to follow Christ, and to be taught and enlightened and instructed by him; to learn of him, and live to him.

Another Saturday night, January 1739, had such a sense, how sweet and blessed a thing it was, to walk in the way of duty, to do that which was right and meet to be done, and agreeable to the holy mind of God; that it caused me to break forth into a kind of a loud weeping, which held me some time; so that I was forced to shut myself up, and fasten the doors. I could not but as it were cry out, "How happy are they which do that which is right in the sight of God! They are blessed indeed, they are the happy ones!" I had at the same time, a very affecting sense, how meet and suitable it was that God should govern the world, and order all things according to his own pleasure; and I rejoiced in it, that God reigned, and that his will was done.

3. Jonathan Edwards

Sinners in the Hands of an Angry God
1741

Undoubtedly Edwards's most famous work, Sinners in the Hands of an Angry God *is atypical for its rhetorical appeal to the audience. Preached at the height of the second wave of revivals, it spares no imaginative device: "The bow of God's wrath is bent, and the arrow made ready on the string, and justice bends the arrow at your heart, and strains the bow, and it is nothing but the mere pleasure of God, and that of an angry God, without any promise or obligation at all, that keeps the arrow one moment from being made drunk with your blood." This language was not intended, as some modern readers might assume, to scare the audience into being saved. Edwards did not think that it was in the hearer's power to will or choose salvation; that depended on the arbitrary will of God. Edwards's aim is to jar his audience out of a confidence in their own salvation, whether they believe or not. Many in New England had come to view the Covenant of Grace as a standing offer, one that God was obliged to make good for those who accepted its terms. Edwards insists that God is "without any promise or obligation at all." Grace is unmerited, unconstrained, and unknowable. The force with which Edwards makes this old-fashioned and familiar theological point reminds us that secular ratio-nalism had begun to shape the surrounding environment. Edwards has to wipe away any notion of a pastoral or contractual God; he has to cause his hearers not to expect the "reasonableness" of Christianity. Some of his most sublime language is reserved for defamiliarizing the world, making strange the assumption that busi-ness should go on as usual, that life could ever be lived unreflectively, that a safe and comfortable happiness is all that the soul could dream. The familiar Calvinist theology in Edwards's hands takes on a potent antiworldliness in an increasingly worldly context; arguing against any faith in the individual self, he has to argue more loudly than his Puritan ancestors ever had.*

DEUT. 32:35. THEIR FOOT SHALL SLIDE IN DUE TIME.

In this verse is threatened the vengeance of God on the wicked unbelieving Israelites, that were God's visible people, and lived under means of grace; and that, notwithstanding all God's wonderful works that he had wrought towards that people, yet remained, as is expressed, v. 28, void of counsel, having no understanding in them; and that, under all the cultivations of heaven, brought forth bitter and poiso-nous fruit; as in the two verses next preceding the text.

The expression that I have chosen for my text, *Their foot shall slide in due time,* seems to imply the following things, relating to the punishment and destruction that these wicked Israelites were exposed to.

1. That they were *always* exposed to destruction, as one that stands or walks in slippery places is always exposed to fall. This is implied in the manner of their destruction's coming upon them, being represented by their foot's sliding. The same is expressed, Ps. 73:18, "Surely thou didst set them in slippery places; thou castedst them down into destruction."

2. It implies that they were always exposed to *sudden* unexpected destruction. As he that walks in slippery places is every moment liable to fall; he can't foresee one moment whether he shall stand or fall the next; and when he does fall, he falls at once, without warning. Which is also expressed in that, Ps.73:18-19, "Surely thou didst set them in slippery places; thou castedst them down into destruction. How are they brought into desolation as in a moment?"

3. Another thing implied is that they are liable to fall *of themselves*, without being thrown down by the hand of another. As he that stands or walks on slippery ground, needs nothing but his own weight to throw him down.

4. That the reason why they are not fallen already, and don't fall now, is only that God's appointed time is not come. For it is said, that when that due time, or appointed time comes, "their foot shall slide." Then they shall be left to fall as they are inclined by their own weight. God won't hold them up in these slippery places any longer, but will let them go; and then, at that very instant, they shall fall into destruction; as he that stands in such slippery declining ground on the edge of a pit that he can't stand alone, when he is let go he immediately falls and is lost.

The observation from the words that I would now insist upon is this,

[DOCTRINE]

There is nothing that keeps wicked men, at any one moment, out of hell,
but the mere pleasure of God.

By the mere pleasure of God, I mean his sovereign pleasure, his arbitrary will, restrained by no obligation, hindered by no manner of difficulty, any more than if nothing else but God's mere will had in the least degree, or in any respect whatsoever, any hand in the preservation of wicked men one moment.

The truth of this observation may appear by the following considerations.

I. There is no want of *power* in God to cast wicked men into hell at any moment. Men's hands can't be strong when God rises up: the strongest have no power to resist him, nor can any deliver out of his hands.

He is not only able to cast wicked men into hell, but he can most *easily* do it. Sometimes an earthly prince meets with a great deal of difficulty to subdue a rebel, that has found means to fortify himself, and has made himself strong by the numbers of his followers. But it is not so with God. There is no fortress that is any defense from the power of God. Though hand join in hand, and vast multitudes of God's enemies combine and associate themselves, they are easily broken in pieces: they are as great heaps of light chaff before the whirlwind; or large quantities of dry stubble before devouring flames. We find it easy to tread on and crush a worm that we see crawling on the earth; so 'tis easy for us to cut or singe a slender thread that anything hangs by; thus easy is it for God when he pleases to cast his enemies down to hell. What are we, that we should think to stand before him, at whose rebuke the earth trembles, and before whom the rocks are thrown down?

II. They *deserve* to be cast into hell; so that divine justice never stands in the way, it makes no objection against God's using his power at any moment to destroy them. Yea, on the contrary, justice calls aloud for an infinite punishment of their sins. Divine justice says of the tree that brings forth such grapes of Sodom, "Cut it down, why cumbreth it the ground," Luke 13:7. The sword of divine justice is every moment brandished over their heads, and 'tis nothing but the hand of arbitrary mercy, and God's mere will, that holds it back.

III. They are *already* under a sentence of condemnation to hell. They don't only justly deserve to be cast down thither; but the sentence of the law of God, that eternal and immutable rule of righteousness that God has fixed between him and mankind, is gone out against them, and stands against them; so that they are bound over already to hell. John 3:18, "He that believeth not is condemned already." So that every unconverted man properly belongs to hell; that is his place; from thence he is. John 8:23, "Ye are from beneath." And thither he is bound; 'tis the place that justice, and God's Word, and the sentence of his unchangeable law assigns to him.

IV. They are now the objects of that very *same* anger and wrath of God that is expressed in the torments of hell: and the reason why they don't go down to hell at each moment, is not because God, in whose power they are, is not then very angry with them; as angry as he is with many of those miserable creatures that he is now tormenting in hell, and do there feel and bear the fierceness of his wrath. Yea, God is a great deal more angry with great numbers that are now on earth, yea, doubtless with many that are now in this congregation, that it may be are at ease and quiet, than he is with many of those that are now in the flames of hell.

So that it is not because God is unmindful of their wickedness, and don't resent it, that he don't let loose his hand and cut them off. God is not altogether such an one as themselves, though they may imagine him to be so. The wrath of God burns against them, their damnation don't slumber, the pit is prepared, the fire is made ready, the furnace is now hot, ready to receive them, the flames do now rage and glow. The glittering sword is whet, and held over them, and the pit hath opened her mouth under them.

V. The *devil* stands ready to fall upon them and seize them as his own, at what moment God shall permit him. They belong to him; he has their souls in his possession, and under his dominion. The Scripture represents them as his "goods," Luke 11:21. The devils watch them; they are ever by them, at their right hand; they stand waiting for them, like greedy hungry lions that see their prey, and expect to have it, but are for the present kept back; if God should withdraw his hand, by which they are restrained, they would in one moment fly upon their poor souls. The old serpent is gaping for them; hell opens its mouth wide to receive them; and if God should permit it, they would be hastily swallowed up and lost.

VI. There are in the souls of wicked men those hellish *principles* reigning, that would presently kindle and flame out into hellfire, if it were not for God's restraints.

There is laid in the very nature of carnal men a foundation for the torments of hell: there are those corrupt principles, in reigning power in them, and in full possession of them, that are seeds of hellfire. These principles are active and powerful, and exceeding violent in their nature, and if it were not for the restraining hand of God upon them, they would soon break out, they would flame out after the same manner as the same corruptions, the same enmity does in the hearts of damned souls, and would beget the same torments in 'em as they do in them. The souls of the wicked are in Scripture compared to the troubled sea, Is. 57:20. For the present God restrains their wickedness by his mighty power, as he does the raging waves of the troubled sea, saying, "Hitherto shalt thou come, and no further"; but if God should withdraw that restraining power, it would soon carry all afore it. Sin is the ruin and misery of the soul; it is destructive in its nature; and if God should leave it without restraint, there would need nothing else to make the soul perfectly miserable. The corruption of the heart of man is a thing that is immoderate and boundless in its fury; and while wicked men live here, it is like fire pent up by God's restraints, whenas if it were let loose it would set on fire the course of nature; and as the heart is now a sink of sin, so, if sin was not restrained, it would immediately turn the soul into a fiery oven, or a furnace of fire and brimstone.

VII. It is no security to wicked men for one moment, that there are no *visible means of death* at hand. 'Tis no security to a natural man, that he is now in health, and that he don't see which way he should now immediately go out of the world by any accident, and that there is no visible danger in any respect in his circumstances. The manifold and continual experience of the world in all ages, shows that this is no evidence that a man is not on the very brink of eternity, and that the next step won't be into another world. The unseen, unthought of ways and means of persons going suddenly out of the world are innumerable and inconceivable. Unconverted men walk over the pit of hell on a rotten covering, and there are innumerable places in this covering so weak that they won't bear their weight, and these places are not seen. The arrows of death fly unseen at noonday; the sharpest sight can't discern them. God has so many different unsearchable ways of taking wicked men out of the world and sending 'em to hell, that there is nothing to make it appear that God had need to be at the expense of a miracle, or go out of the ordinary course of his providence, to destroy any wicked man, at any moment. All the means that there are of sinners going out of the world, are so in God's hands, and so universally absolutely subject to his power and determination, that it don't depend at all less on the mere will of God, whether sinners shall at any moment go to hell, than if means were never made use of, or at all concerned in the case.

VIII. Natural men's prudence and care to preserve their own lives, or the care of others to preserve them, don't secure 'em a moment. This divine providence and universal experience does also bear testimony to. There is this clear evidence that men's own wisdom is no security to them from death; that if it were otherwise we should see some difference between the wise and politic men of the world, and others, with regard to their liableness to early and unexpected death; but how is it in fact? Eccles. 2:16, "How dieth the wise man? as the fool."

IX. All wicked men's pains and contrivance they use to escape hell, while they continue to reject Christ, and so remain wicked men, don't secure 'em from hell one moment. Almost every natural man that hears of hell, flatters himself that he shall escape it; he depends upon himself for his own security; he flatters himself in what he has done, in what he is now doing, or what he intends to do; everyone lays out matters in his own mind how he shall avoid damnation, and flatters himself that he contrives well for himself, and that his schemes won't fail. They hear indeed that there are but few saved, and that the bigger part of men that have died heretofore are gone to hell; but each one imagines that he lays out matters better for his own escape than others have done: he don't intend to come to that place of torment; he says within himself, that he intends to take care that shall be effectual, and to order matters so for himself as not to fail.

But the foolish children of men do miserably delude themselves in their own schemes, and in their confidence in their own strength and wisdom; they trust to nothing but a shadow. The bigger part of those that heretofore have lived under the same means of grace, and are now dead, are undoubtedly gone to hell: and it was not because they were not as wise as those that are now alive: it was not because they did not lay out matters as well for themselves to secure their own escape. If it were so, that we could come to speak with them, and could inquire of them, one by one, whether they expected when alive, and when they used to hear about hell, ever to be the subjects of that misery, we doubtless should hear one and another reply, "No, I never intended to come here; I had laid out matters otherwise in my mind; I thought I should contrive well for myself; I thought my scheme good; I intended to take effectual care; but it came upon me unexpected; I did not look for it at that time, and in that manner; it came as a thief; death outwitted me; God's wrath was too quick for me. O my cursed foolishness! I was flattering myself, and pleasing myself with vain dreams of what I would do hereafter, and when I was saying peace and safety, then sudden destruction came upon me."

X. God has laid himself under *no obligation* by any promise to keep any natural man out of hell one moment. God certainly has made no promises either of eternal life, or of any deliverance or preservation from eternal death, but what are contained in the covenant of grace, the promises that are given in Christ, in whom all the promises are yea and amen. But surely they have no interest in the promises of the covenant of grace that are not the children of the covenant, and that don't believe in any of the promises of the covenant, and have no interest in the *mediator* of the covenant.

So that whatever some have imagined and pretended about promises made to natural men's earnest seeking and knocking, 'tis plain and manifest that whatever pains a natural man takes in religion, whatever prayers he makes, till he believes in Christ, God is under no manner of obligation to keep him a *moment* from eternal destruction.

So that thus it is, that natural men are held in the hand of God over the pit of hell; they have deserved the fiery pit, and are already sentenced to it; and God is dreadfully provoked, his anger is as great towards them as to those that are actually suffering the executions of the fierceness of his wrath in hell, and they have done nothing in the least to appease or abate that anger, neither is God in the least bound by any promise to hold 'em up one moment; the devil is waiting for them, hell is gaping for them, the flames gather and flash about them, and would fain lay hold on them, and swallow them up; the fire pent up in their own hearts is struggling to break out; and they have no interest in any mediator, there are no means within reach that can be any security to them. In short, they have no refuge, nothing to take hold of, all that preserves them every moment is the mere arbitrary will, and uncovenanted unobliged forbearance of an incensed God.

APPLICATION.

The use may be of *awakening* to unconverted persons in this congregation. This that you have heard is the case of every one of you that are out of Christ. That world of misery, that lake of burning brimstone is extended abroad under you. *There* is the dreadful pit of the glowing flames of the wrath of God; there is hell's wide gaping mouth open; and you have nothing to stand upon, nor anything to take hold of: there is nothing between you and hell but the air; 'tis only the power and mere pleasure of God that holds you up.

You probably are not sensible of this; you find you are kept out of hell, but don't see the hand of God in it, but look at other things, as the good state of your bodily constitution, your care of your own life, and the means you use for your own preservation. But indeed these things are nothing; if God should withdraw his hand, they would avail no more to keep you from falling, than the thin air to hold up a person that is suspended in it.

Your wickedness makes you as it were heavy as lead, and to tend downwards with great weight and pressure towards hell; and if God should let you go, you would immediately sink and swiftly descend and plunge into the bottomless gulf, and your healthy constitution, and your own care and prudence, and best contrivance, and all your righteousness, would have no more influence to uphold you and keep you out of hell, than a spider's web would have to stop a falling rock. Were it not that so is the sovereign pleasure of God, the earth would not bear you one moment; for you are a burden to it; the creation groans with you; the creature is made subject to the bondage of your corruption, not willingly; the sun don't willingly shine upon you to give you light to serve sin and Satan; the earth don't willingly yield her increase to satisfy your lusts; nor is it willingly a stage for your wickedness to be acted upon; the air don't willingly serve you for breath to maintain the flame of life in your vitals, while you spend your life in the service of God's enemies. God's creatures are good, and were made for men to serve God with, and don't willingly subserve to any other purpose, and groan when they are abused to purposes so directly contrary to their nature and end. And the world would spew you out, were it not for the sovereign hand of him who hath subjected it in hope. There are the black clouds of God's wrath now hanging directly over your heads, full of the dreadful storm, and big with thunder; and were it not for the restraining hand of God it would immediately burst forth upon you. The sovereign pleasure of God for the present stays his rough wind; otherwise it would come with fury, and your destruction would come like a whirlwind, and you would be like the chaff of the summer threshing floor.

The wrath of God is like great waters that are dammed for the present; they increase more and more, and rise higher and higher, till an outlet is given, and the longer the stream is stopped, the more rapid and mighty is its course, when once it is let loose. 'Tis true, that judgment against your evil works has not been executed hitherto; the floods of God's vengeance have been withheld; but your guilt in the meantime is constantly increasing, and you are every day treasuring up more wrath; the waters are continually rising and waxing more and more mighty; and there is nothing but the mere pleasure of God that holds the waters back that are unwilling to be stopped, and press hard to go forward; if God should only withdraw his hand from the floodgate, it would immediately fly open, and the fiery floods of the fierceness and wrath of God would rush forth with inconceivable fury, and would come upon you with omnipotent power; and if your strength were ten thousand times greater than it is, yea ten thousand times greater than the strength of the stoutest, sturdiest devil in hell, it would be nothing to withstand or endure it.

The bow of God's wrath is bent, and the arrow made ready on the string, and justice bends the arrow at your heart, and strains the bow, and it is nothing but the mere pleasure of God, and that of an angry God, without any promise or obligation at all, that keeps the arrow one moment from being made drunk with your blood.

Thus are all you that never passed under a great change of heart, by the mighty power of the Spirit of God upon your souls; all that were never born again, and made new creatures, and raised from being dead in sin, to a state of new, and before altogether unexperienced light and life (however you may have reformed your life in many things, and may have had religious affections, and may keep up a form of religion in your families and closets, and in the house of God, and may be strict in it), you are thus in the hands of an angry God; 'tis nothing but his mere pleasure that keeps you from being this moment swallowed up in everlasting destruction.

However unconvinced you may now be of the truth of what you hear, by and by you will be fully convinced of it. Those that are gone from being in the like circumstances with you, see that it was so with them; for destruction came suddenly upon most of them, when they expected nothing of it, and while they were saying, "Peace and safety": now they see, that those things that they depended on for peace and safety, were nothing but thin air and empty shadows.

The God that holds you over the pit of hell, much as one holds a spider, or some loathsome insect, over the fire, abhors you, and is dreadfully provoked; his wrath towards you burns like fire; he looks upon you as worthy of nothing else, but to be cast into the fire; he is of purer eyes than to bear to have you in his sight; you are ten thousand times so abominable in his eyes as the most hateful venomous serpent is in ours. You have offended him infinitely more than ever a stubborn rebel did his prince: and yet 'tis nothing but his hand that holds you from falling into the fire every moment: 'tis to be ascribed to nothing else, that you did not go to hell the last night; that you was suffered to awake again in this world, after you closed your eyes to sleep: and there is no other reason to be given why you have not dropped into hell since you arose in the morning, but that God's hand has held you up: there is no other reason to be given why you han't gone to hell since you have sat here in the house of God, provoking his pure eyes by your sinful wicked manner of attending his solemn worship: yea, there is nothing else that is to be given as a reason why you don't this very moment drop down into hell.

O sinner! Consider the fearful danger you are in: 'tis a great furnace of wrath, a wide and bottomless pit, full of the fire of wrath, that you are held over in the hand of that God, whose wrath is provoked and incensed as much against you as against many of the damned in hell: you hang by a slender thread, with the flames of divine wrath flashing about it, and ready every moment to singe it, and burn it asunder; and you have no interest in any mediator, and nothing to lay hold of to save yourself, nothing to keep off the flames of wrath, nothing of your own, nothing that you ever have done, nothing that you can do, to induce God to spare you one moment.

And consider here more particularly several things concerning that wrath that you are in such danger of.

First. *Whose* wrath it is: it is the wrath of the infinite God. If it were only the wrath of man, though it were of the most potent prince, it would be comparatively little to be regarded. The wrath of kings is very much dreaded, especially of absolute monarchs, that have the possessions and lives of their subjects wholly in their power, to be disposed of at their mere will. Prov. 20:2, "The fear of a king is as the roaring of a lion: whoso provoketh him to anger, sinneth against his own soul." The subject that very much enrages an arbitary prince, is liable to suffer the most extreme torments, that human art can invent or human power can inflict. But the greatest earthly potentates, in their greatest majesty and strength, and when clothed in their greatest terrors, are but feeble despicable worms of the dust, in comparison of the great and almighty Creator and King of heaven and earth: it is but little that they can do, when most enraged, and when they have exerted the utmost of their fury. All the kings of the earth before God are as grasshoppers, they are nothing and less than nothing: both their love and their hatred is to be despised. The wrath of the great King of Kings is as much more terrible than theirs, as his majesty is greater. Luke 12:4–5, "And I say unto you my friends, be not afraid of them that kill the body, and after that have no more that they can do: but I will forewarn you whom ye shall fear; fear him, which after he hath killed, hath power to cast into hell; yea I say unto you, fear him."

Second. 'Tis the *fierceness* of his wrath that you are exposed to. We often read of the *fury* of God; as in Is. 59:18, "According to their deeds, accordingly he will repay fury to his adversaries." So Is. 66:15, "For behold, the Lord will come with fire, and with chariots like a whirlwind, to render his anger with fury, and his rebukes with flames of fire." And so in many other places. So we read of God's *fierceness.* Rev. 19:15, there we read of "the winepress of the fierceness and wrath of almighty God." The words are exceeding terrible: if it had only been said, "the wrath of God," the words would have implied that which is infinitely dreadful: but 'tis not only said so, but "the fierceness and wrath of God": the fury of God! the fierceness of Jehovah! Oh how dreadful must that be! Who can utter or conceive what such expressions carry in them! But it is not only said so, but "the fierceness and wrath of *almighty God.*" As though there would be a very great manifestation of his almighty power, in what the fierceness of his wrath should inflict, as though omnipotence should be as it were enraged, and exerted, as men are wont to exert their strength in the fierceness of their wrath. Oh! then what will be the consequence! What will become of the poor worm that shall suffer it! Whose hands can be strong? and whose heart endure? To what a dreadful, inexpressible, inconceivable depth of misery must the poor creature be sunk, who shall be the subject of this!

Consider this, you that are here present, that yet remain in an unregenerate state. That God will execute the fierceness of his anger, implies that he will inflict wrath without any pity: when God beholds the ineffable extremity of your case, and sees your torment to be so vastly disproportioned to your strength, and sees how your poor soul is crushed and sinks down, as it were into an infinite gloom, he will have no compassion upon you, he will not forbear the executions of his wrath, or in the least lighten his hand; there shall be no moderation or mercy, nor will God then at all stay his rough wind; he will have no regard to your welfare, nor be at all careful lest you should suffer too much, in any other sense than only that you shall not suffer beyond what strict justice requires: nothing shall be withheld, because it's so hard for you to bear. Ezek. 8:18, "Therefore will I also deal in fury; mine eye shall not spare, neither will I have pity; and though they cry in mine ears with a loud voice, yet I will not hear them." Now God stands ready to pity you; this is a day of mercy; you may cry now with some encouragement of obtaining mercy: but when once the day of mercy is past, your most lamentable and dolorous cries and shrieks will be in vain; you will be wholly lost and thrown away of God as to any regard to your welfare; God will have no other use to put you to but only to suffer misery; you shall be continued in being to no other end; for you will be a vessel of wrath fitted to destruction; and there will be no other use of this vessel but only to be filled full of wrath: God will be so far from pitying you when you cry to him, that 'tis said he will only laugh and mock, Prov. 1:25–32.

How awful are those words, Is. 63:3, which are the words of the great God, "I will tread them in mine anger, and will trample them in my fury, and their blood shall be sprinkled upon my garments, and I will stain all my raiment." 'Tis perhaps impossible to conceive of words that carry in them greater manifestations of these three things, viz. contempt, and hatred, and fierceness of indignation. If you cry to God to pity you, he will be so far from pitying you in your doleful case, or showing you the least regard or favor, that instead of that he'll only tread you under foot: and though he will know that you can't bear the weight of omnipotence treading upon you, yet he won't regard that, but he will crush you under his feet without mercy; he'll crush out your blood, and make it fly, and it shall be sprinkled on his garments, so as to stain all his raiment. He will not only hate you, but he will have you in the utmost contempt; no place shall be thought fit for you, but under his feet, to be trodden down as the mire of the streets.

Third. The misery you are exposed to is that which God will inflict to that end, that he might show what that wrath of Jehovah is. God hath had it on his heart to show to angels and men, both how excellent his love is, and also how terrible his wrath is. Sometimes earthly kings have a mind to show how terrible *their* wrath is, by the extreme punishments they would execute on those that provoke 'em. Nebuchadnezzar, that mighty and haughty monarch of the Chaldean empire, was willing to show *his* wrath, when enraged with Shadrach, Meshach, and Abednego; and accordingly gave order that the burning fiery furnace should be yet seven times hotter than it was before; doubtless it was raised to the utmost degree of fierceness that human art could raise it: but the great God is also willing to show *his wrath*, and magnify his awful majesty and mighty power in the extreme sufferings of his enemies. Rom. 9:22, "What if God, willing to show *his* wrath, and to make his power known, endured with much long-suffering the vessels of wrath fitted to destruction?" And seeing this is his design, and what he has determined, to show how terrible the unmixed, unrestrained wrath, the fury and fierceness of Jehovah is, he will do it to effect. There will be something accomplished and brought to pass, that will be dreadful with a witness. When the great and angry God hath risen up and executed his awful vengeance on the poor sinner; and the wretch is actually suffering the infinite weight and power of his indignation, then will God call upon the whole universe to behold that awful majesty, and mighty power that is to be seen in it. Is. 33:12–14, "And the people shall be as the burning of lime, as thorns cut up shall they be burnt in the fire. Hear ye that are far off what I have done; and ye that are near acknowledge my might. The sinners in Zion are afraid, fearfulness hath surprised the hypocrites. Who among us shall dwell with the devouring fire? who among us shall dwell with everlasting burnings?"

Thus it will be with you that are in an unconverted state, if you continue in it; the infinite might, and majesty and terribleness of the omnipotent God shall be magnified upon you, in the ineffable strength of your torments: you shall be tormented in the presence of the holy angels, and in the presence of the Lamb; and when you shall be in this state of suffering, the glorious inhabitants of heaven shall go forth and look on the awful spectacle, that they may see what the wrath and fierceness of the Almighty is, and when they have seen it, they will fall down and adore that great power and majesty. Is. 66:23-24, "And it shall come to pass, that from one new moon to another, and from one sabbath to another, shall all flesh come to worship before me, saith the Lord; and they shall go forth and look upon the carcasses of the men that have transgressed against me; for their worm shall not die, neither shall their fire be quenched, and they shall be an abhorring unto all flesh."

Fourth. '*Tis everlasting* wrath. It would be dreadful to suffer this fierceness and wrath of almighty God one moment; but you must suffer it to all eternity: there will be no end to this exquisite horrible misery: when you look forward, you shall see a long forever, a boundless duration before you, which will swallow up your thoughts and amaze your soul; and you will absolutely despair of ever having any deliverance, any end, any mitigation, any rest at all; you will know certainly that you must wear out long ages, millions of millions of ages, in wrestling and conflicting with this almighty merciless vengeance; and then when you have so done, when so many ages have actually been spent by you in this manner, you will know that all is but a point to what remains. So that your punishment will indeed be infinite. Oh who can express what the state of a soul in such circumstances is! All that we can possibly say about it, gives but a very feeble faint representation of it; 'tis inexpressible and inconceivable: for "who knows the power of God's anger?" [Ps. 90:11].

How dreadful is the state of those that are daily and hourly in danger of this great wrath, and infinite misery! But this is the dismal case of every soul in this congregation, that has not been born again, however moral and strict, sober and religious they may otherwise be. Oh that you would consider it, whether you be young or old. There is reason to think, that there are many in this congregation now hearing this discourse, that will actually be the subjects of this very misery to all eternity. We know not who they are, or in what seats they sit, or what thoughts they now have: it may be they are now at ease, and hear all these things without much disturbance, and are now flattering themselves that they are not the persons, promising themselves that they shall escape. If we knew that there was one person, and but one, in the whole congregation that was to be the subject of this misery, what an awful thing would it be to think of! If we knew who it was, what an awful sight would it be to see such a person! How might all the rest of the congregation lift up a lamentable and bitter cry over him! But alas! instead of one, how many is it likely will remember this discourse in hell? And it would be a wonder if some that are now present, should not be in hell in a very short time, before this year is out. And it would be no wonder if some person that now sits here in some seat of this meetinghouse in health, and quiet and secure, should be there before tomorrow morning. Those of you that finally continue in a natural condition, that shall keep out of hell longest, will be there in a little time! your damnation don't slumber; it will come swiftly, and in all probability very suddenly upon many of you. You have reason to wonder, that you are not already in hell. 'Tis doubtless the case of some that heretofore you have seen and known, that never deserved hell more than you, and that heretofore appeared as likely to have been now alive as you: their case is past all hope; they are crying in extreme misery and perfect despair; but here you are in the land of the living, and in the house of God, and have an opportunity to obtain salvation. What would not those poor damned, hopeless souls give for one day's such opportunity as you now enjoy!

And now you have an extraordinary opportunity, a day wherein Christ has flung the door of mercy wide open, and stands in the door calling and crying with a loud voice to poor sinners; a day wherein many are flocking to him, and pressing into the kingdom of God; many are daily coming from the east, west, north and south; many that were very lately in the same miserable condition that you are in, are in now an happy state, with their hearts filled with love to him that has loved them and washed them from their sins in his own blood, and rejoicing in hope of the glory of God. How awful is it to be left behind at such a day! To see so many others feasting, while you are pining and perishing! To see so many rejoicing and singing for joy of heart, while you have cause to mourn for sorrow of heart, and howl for vexation of spirit! How can you rest one moment in such a condition? Are not your souls as precious as the souls of the people at Suffield,[3] where they are flocking from day to day to Christ?

Are there not many here that have lived *long* in the world, that are not to this day born again, and so are aliens from the commonwealth of Israel, and have done nothing ever since they have lived, but treasure up wrath against the day of wrath? Oh sirs, your case in an especial manner is extremely dangerous; your guilt and hardness of heart is extremely great. Don't you see how generally persons of your years are passed over and left, in the present remarkable and wonderful dispensation of God's mercy? You had need to consider yourselves, and wake thoroughly out of sleep; you cannot bear the fierceness and wrath of the infinite God.

And you that are *young men*, and *young women*, will you neglect this precious season that you now enjoy, when so many others of your age are renouncing all

---

3. The next neighboring town. [Edwards's note.]

youthful vanities, and flocking to Christ? You especially have now an extraordinary opportunity; but if you neglect it, it will soon be with you as it is with those persons that spent away all the precious days of youth in sin, and are now come to such a dreadful pass in blindness and hardness.

And you *children* that are unconverted, don't you know that you are going down to hell, to bear the dreadful wrath of that God that is now angry with you every day, and every night? Will you be content to be the children of the devil, when so many other children in the land are converted, and are become the holy and happy children of the King of Kings?

And let everyone that is yet out of Christ, and hanging over the pit of hell, whether they be old men and women, or middle aged, or young people, or little children, now hearken to the loud calls of God's Word and providence. This acceptable year of the Lord, that is a day of such great favor to some, will doubtless be a day of as remarkable vengeance to others. Men's hearts harden, and their guilt increases apace at such a day as this, if they neglect their souls: and never was there so great danger of such persons being given up to hardness of heart, and blindness of mind. God seems now to be hastily gathering in his elect in all parts of the land; and probably the bigger part of adult persons that ever shall be saved, will be brought in now in a little time, and that it will be as it was on that great outpouring of the Spirit upon the Jews in the apostles' days, the election will obtain, and the rest will be blinded. If this should be the case with you, you will eternally curse this day, and will curse the day that ever you was born, to see such a season of the pouring out of God's Spirit; and will wish that you had died and gone to hell before you had seen it. Now undoubtedly it is, as it was in the days of John the Baptist: the ax is in an extraordinary manner laid at the root of the trees, that every tree that brings not forth good fruit, may be hewn down, and cast into the fire.

Therefore let everyone that is out of Christ, now awake and fly from the wrath to come. The wrath of almighty God is now undoubtedly hanging over great part of this congregation: let everyone fly out of Sodom: "Haste and escape for your lives, look not behind you, escape to the mountain, lest you be consumed" [Gen. 19:17].

4. Jonathan Edwards

"Concerning the Nature of the Will," from *Freedom of the Will* 1754

Arminianism—the idea that the individual had a choice of salvation, that one's will made the difference—had always been the bête noire of the Puritans. (See chapter 6.) Arminian thinking received an unexpected boost as voluntary relations became more important in the social world. The psychology of John Locke, which had been such a formative influence on the young Edwards, laid the groundwork for an equation of freedom with the exercise of the will. When Edwards turned to a philosophical consideration of the will during his rustication at Stockbridge, therefore, he was not fighting ancient theologians; he was fighting all of modern liberal culture. In this opening section to his great treatise, Edwards lays out what he sees as the core issue: the Lockean distinction between desire and will. It would be hard to imagine modern culture without this distinction—concepts of addiction, for example, would make no sense without it. Yet Edwards, never shy of a tough argument, decides to pitch his battle against Arminianism on this point.

It may possibly be thought, that there is no great need of going about to define or describe the Will; this word being generally as well understood as any other words we can use to explain it: and so perhaps it would be, had not philosophers, metaphysicians and polemic divines brought the matter into obscurity by the things they have said of it. But since it is so, I think it may be of some use, and will tend to the greater clearness in the following discourse, to say a few things concerning it.

And therefore I observe, that the Will (without any metaphysical refining) is plainly, that by which the mind chooses anything. The faculty of the Will is that faculty or power or principle of mind by which it is capable of choosing: an act of the will is the same as an act of choosing or choice.

If any think 'tis a more perfect definition of the Will, to say, that it is that by which the soul either chooses or refuses; I am content with it: though I think that 'tis enough to say, it's that by which the soul chooses: for in every act of Will whatsoever, the mind chooses one thing rather than another; it chooses something rather than the contrary, or rather than the want or nonexistence of that thing. So in every act of refusal, the mind chooses the absence of the thing refused; the positive and the negative are set before the mind for its choice, and it chooses the negative; and the mind's making its choice in that case is properly the act of the Will: the Will's determining between the two is a voluntary determining; but that is the same thing as making a choice. So that whatever names we call the act of the Will by—choosing, refusing,

approving, disapproving, liking, disliking, embracing, rejecting, determining, directing, commanding, forbidding, inclining or being averse, a being pleased or displeased
with—all may be reduced to this of choosing. For the soul to act voluntarily, is ever-
more to act electively.

Mr. Locke says,[4] "The Will signifies nothing but a power or ability to prefer or
choose." And in the foregoing page says, "The word 'preferring' seems best to express
the act of volition"; but adds, that "it does it not precisely; for (says he) though a man
would prefer flying to walking, yet who can say he ever wills it?" But the instance he
mentions don't prove that there is anything else in "willing" but merely "preferring":
for it should be considered what is the next and immediate object of the Will, with
respect to a man's walking, or any other external action; which is not his being
removed from one place to another; on the earth, or through the air; these are remoter
objects of preference; but such or such an immediate exertion of himself. The thing
nextly chosen or preferred when a man wills to walk, is not his being removed to such
a place where he would be, but such an exertion and motion of his legs and feet, etc.
in order to it. And his willing such an alteration in his body in the present moment, is
nothing else but his choosing or preferring such an alteration in his body at such a
moment, or his liking it better than the forbearance of it. And God has so made and
established the human nature, the soul being united to a body in proper state, that the
soul preferring or choosing such an immediate exertion or alteration of the body, such
an alteration instantaneously follows. There is nothing else in the actings of my mind,
that I am conscious of while I walk, but only my preferring or choosing, through
successive moments, that there should be such alterations of my external sensations
and motions; together with a concurring habitual expectation that it will be so; having
ever found by experience, that on such an immediate preference, such sensations and
motions do actually instantaneously, and constantly arise. But it is not so in the case
of flying: though a man may be said remotely to choose or prefer flying; yet he don't
choose or prefer, incline to or desire, under circumstances in view, any immediate
exertion of the members of his body in order to it; because he has no expectation that
he should obtain the desired end by any such exertion; and he don't prefer or incline
to any bodily exertion or effort under this apprehended circumstance, of its being
wholly in vain. So that if we carefully distinguish the proper objects of the several acts
of the Will, it will not appear by this, and suchlike instances, that there is any difference between volition and preference; or that a man's choosing, liking best, or being
best pleased with a thing, are not the same with his willing that thing; as they seem to
be according to those general and more natural notions of men, according to which
language is formed. Thus an act of the Will is commonly expressed by its pleasing a
man to do thus or thus; and a man's doing as he wills, and doing as he pleases, are the
same thing in common speech.

Mr. Locke says, "the Will is perfectly distinguished from Desire; which in the very
same action may have a quite contrary tendency from that which our Wills set us
upon. A man (says he) whom I cannot deny, may oblige me to use persuasions to

---

4. Mr. Locke says: John Locke, in *An Essay Concerning
Human Understanding.*

another, which, at the same time I am speaking, I may wish may not prevail on him. In this case 'tis plain the Will and Desire run counter." I don't suppose, that Will and Desire are words of precisely the same signification: Will seems to be a word of a more general signification, extending to things present and absent. Desire respects something absent. I may prefer my present situation and posture, suppose sitting still, or having my eyes open, and so may will it. But yet I can't think they are so entirely distinct, that they can ever be properly said to run counter. A man never, in any instance, wills anything contrary to his desires, or desires anything contrary to his Will. The forementioned instance, which Mr. Locke produces, don't prove that he ever does. He may, on some consideration or other, will to utter speeches which have a tendency to persuade another, and still may desire that they may not persuade him: but yet his Will and Desire don't run counter at all. The thing which he wills, the very same he desires; and he don't will a thing, and desire the contrary in any particular. In this instance, it is not carefully observed, what is the thing willed, and what is the thing desired: if it were, it would be found that Will and Desire don't clash in the least. The thing willed on some consideration, is to utter such words; and certainly, the same consideration so influences him, that he don't desire the contrary; all things considered, he chooses to utter such words, and don't desire not to utter 'em. And so as to the thing which Mr. Locke speaks of as desired, viz. that the words, though they tend to persuade, should not be effectual to that end, his Will is not contrary to this; he don't will that they should be effectual, but rather wills that they should not, as he desires. In order to prove that the Will and Desire may run counter, it should be shown that they may be contrary one to the other in the same thing, or with respect to the very same object of Will or Desire: but here the objects are two; and in each, taken by themselves, the Will and Desire agree. And 'tis no wonder that they should not agree in different things, however little distinguished they are in their nature. The Will may not agree with the Will, nor Desire agree with Desire, in different things. As in this very instance which Mr. Locke mentions, a person may, on some consideration, desire to use persuasions, and at the same time may desire they may not prevail; but yet nobody will say, that Desire runs counter to Desire; or that this proves that Desire is perfectly a distinct thing from Desire. The like might be observed of the other instance Mr. Locke produces, of a man's desiring to be eased of pain, etc.

But not to dwell any longer on this, whether Desire and Will, and whether Preference and Violation be precisely the same thing or no; yet, I trust it will be allowed by all, that in every act of Will there is an act of choice; that in every volition there is a preference, or a prevailing inclination of the soul, whereby the soul, at that instant, is out of a state of perfect indifference, with respect to the direct object of the volition. So that in every act, or going forth of the Will, there is some preponderation of the mind or inclination, one way rather than another; and the soul had rather *have* or *do* one thing than another, or than not to have or do that thing; and that there, where there is absolutely no preferring or choosing, but a perfect continuing equilibrium, there is no volition.

5. Jonathan Edwards

"Of Self-Love," from *The Nature of True Virtue* 1755

Like arguments against Arminianism, the old Puritan hostility toward the self was acquiring new relevance in the eighteenth century; the pursuit of self-interest was increasingly being seen as morally legitimate, tending in the long run to virtue and public welfare. "Private vices, public benefits," Mandeville had written in 1714. In this changing context of market culture Edwards returns to consider whether an attachment to private interest could be said to motivate virtue. His answer involves the classic Lockean psychology of associations of ideas, and reflects as well his undying confidence that a moral world created by God must be the same as a moral world governed by natural universal laws.

Many assert that all love arises from self-love. In order to determine this point, it should be clearly determined what is meant by self-love. Self-love, I think, is generally defined "a man's love of his own happiness"; which is short, and may be thought very plain: but in reality is an ambiguous definition, as the expression his own, is equivocal, and liable to be taken in two very different senses. For a man's own happiness may either be taken universally, for all the happiness or pleasure of which the mind is in any regard the subject, or whatever is grateful and pleasing to men: or it may be taken for the pleasure a man takes in his own proper, private, and separate good. And so self-love may be taken two ways:

1. It may be taken for the same as his loving whatsoever is pleasing to him. Which comes only to this, that self-love is a man's liking, and being suited and pleased in that which he likes, and which pleases him; or, that it is a man's loving what he loves. For whatever a man loves, that thing is grateful and pleasing to him, whether that be his own peculiar happiness, or the happiness of others. And if this be all that they mean by self-love, no wonder they suppose that all love may be resolved into self-love. For it is undoubtedly true, that whatever a man loves, his love may be resolved into his loving what he loves. If by self-love is meant nothing else but a man's loving what is grateful or pleasing to him, and being averse to what is disagreeable, this is calling that self-love, which is only a general capacity of loving or hating; or a capacity of being either pleased or displeased; which is the same thing as a man's having a faculty of will. For if nothing could be either pleasing or displeasing, agreeable or disagreeable to a man, then he could incline to nothing, and will nothing. But if he is capable of having inclination, will and choice, then what he inclines to and chooses, is grateful to him, whatever that be; whether it be his own private good, the good of his neigh-

bours, or the glory of God. And so far as it is grateful or pleasing to him, so far it is a part of his pleasure, good, or happiness.

But if this be what is meant by self-love, there is an impropriety and absurdity even in the putting of the question, Whether all our love, or our love to each particular object of our love, does not arise from self-love? For that would be the same as to enquire, Whether the reason why our love is fixed on such and such particular objects, is not, that we have a capacity of loving some things? This may be a general reason why men love or hate any thing at all; and therein differ from stones and trees, which love nothing and hate nothing. But it can never be a reason why men's love is placed on such and such objects. That a man in general loves and is pleased with happiness, or has a capacity of enjoying happiness, cannot be the reason why such and such things become his happiness: as for instance, why the good of his neighbour, or the happiness and glory of God, is grateful and pleasing to him, and so becomes a part of his happiness.

Or if what they mean who say that all love comes from self-love, be not that our loving such and such particular persons and things arises from our love to happiness in general, but from a love to our own happiness, which consists in these objects; so, the reason why we love benevolence to our friends or neighbours is because we love our happiness, consisting in their happiness, which we take pleasure in: still the notion is absurd. For here the effect is made the cause of that of which it is the effect: our happiness, consisting in the happiness of the person beloved, is made the cause of our love to that person. Whereas the truth plainly is, that our love to the person is the cause of our delighting, or being happy in his happiness. How comes our happiness to consist in the happiness of such as we love, but by our hearts being first united to them in affection, so that we as it were look on them as ourselves, and so on their happiness as our own? Men who have benevolence to others have pleasure when they see others' happiness, because seeing their happiness gratifies some inclination that was in their hearts before. They before inclined to their happiness; which was by benevolence or goodwill; and therefore, when they see their happiness, their inclination is suited, and they are pleased. But the being of inclinations and appetites is prior to any pleasure in gratifying these appetites.

2. Self-love, as the phrase is used in common speech, most commonly signifies a man's regard to his confined private self, or love to himself with respect to his private interest.

By private interest I mean that which most immediately consists in those pleasures, or pains, that are personal. For there is a comfort, and a grief, that some have in others' pleasures or pains; which are in others originally, but are derived to them, or in some measure become theirs, by virtue of a benevolent union of heart with others. And there are other pleasures and pains that are originally our own, and not what we have by such a participation with others. Which consist in perceptions agreeable or contrary to certain personal inclinations implanted in our nature; such as the sensitive appetites and aversions. Such also is the disposition or the determination of the mind to be pleased with external beauty, and with all inferior, secondary beauty, consisting in uniformity, proportion, etc. whether in things external or internal, and to dislike the contrary deformity. Such also is the natural disposition in men to be pleased in a perception of their being the objects of the honour and love of others, and displeased with others' hatred and contempt. For pleasures and uneasiness of this kind are doubtless as much owing to an immediate determination of the mind by a fixed law of our nature, as any of the pleasures or pains of external sense. And these pleasures are properly of the private and personal kind; being not by any participation of the happiness or sorrow of others, through benevolence. It is evidently mere self-love that appears in this disposition. It is easy to see that a man's love to himself will make him love love to himself, and hate hatred to himself. And as God has constituted our nature, self-love is exercised in no one disposition more than in this. Men probably are capable of much more pleasure and pain through this determination of the mind, than by any other personal inclination or aversion whatsoever. Though perhaps we do not so very often see instances of extreme suffering by this means as by some others, yet we often see evidences of men's dreading the contempt of others more than death; and by such instances may conceive something what men would suffer if universally hated and despised; and may reasonably infer something of the greatness of the misery that would arise under a sense of universal abhorrence, in a great view of intelligent being in general, or in a clear view of the Deity, as incomprehensibly and immensely great, so that all other beings are as nothing and vanity—together with a sense of his immediate continual presence, and an infinite concern with him and dependence upon him—and living constantly in the midst of most clear and strong evidences and manifestations of his hatred and contempt. These things may be sufficient to explain what I mean by private interest; in regard to which self-love, most properly so called, is immediately exercised.

And here I would observe, that if we take self-love in this sense, so love to some others may truly be the effect of self-love; i.e. according to the common method and order which is maintained in the laws of nature. For no created thing has power to produce an effect any otherwise than by virtue of the laws of nature. Thus that a man should love those who are of his party, and who are warmly engaged on his side, and promote his interest, is the natural consequence of a private self-love. Indeed there is no metaphysical necessity in the nature of things, that because a man loves himself and regards his own interest, he therefore should love those that love him and promote his interest, i.e. to suppose it to be otherwise implies no contradiction. It will not follow from any absolute metaphysical necessity, that because bodies have solidity, cohesion, and gravitation towards the centre of the earth, therefore a weight suspended on the beam of a balance should have greater power to counterbalance a weight on the other side, when at a distance from the fulcrum, than when it is near. It implies no contradiction that it should be otherwise; but only as it contradicts that beautiful proportion and harmony, which the Author of Nature observes in the laws of nature he has established. Neither is there any absolute necessity, that because there is an internal mutual attraction of the parts of the earth, or any other sphere, whereby the whole becomes one solid coherent body, therefore other bodies that are around it should also be attracted by it, and those that are nearest be attracted most. But according to the order and proportion generally observed in the laws of nature, one of these effects is connected with the other, so that it is justly looked upon as the same power of attraction in the globe of the earth, which draws bodies about the earth towards its centre, with that which attracts the parts of the earth themselves one to another; only exerted under different circumstances. By a like order of nature, a man's love to those who love him, is no more than a certain expression or effect of self-love. No other principle is needful in order to the effect, if nothing intervenes to countervail the natural tendency of self-love. Therefore there is no more true virtue in a man thus loving his friends merely from self-love, than there is in self-love itself, the principle from whence it proceeds. So a man being disposed to hate those that hate him, or to resent injuries done him, arises from self-love, in like manner as loving those that love us, and being thankful for kindness shown us.

But it is said by some, that it is apparent there is some other principle concerned in exciting the passions of gratitude and anger besides self-love, viz. a moral sense, or sense of moral beauty and deformity, determining the minds of all mankind to approve of, and be pleased with virtue, and to disapprove of vice, and behold it with displicence;[5] and that their seeing or supposing this moral beauty or deformity in the kindness of a benefactor, or opposition of an adversary, is the occasion of these affections of gratitude or anger. Otherwise, why are not these affections excited in us towards inanimate things that do us good or hurt? Why do not we experience gratitude to a garden, or fruitful field? And why are we not angry with a tempest, or blasting mildew, or an overflowing stream? We are very differently affected towards those that do us good from the virtue of generosity, or hurt us from the vice of envy and malice, than towards things that hurt or help us, which are destitute of reason and will. Concerning this I would make several remarks.

1. Those who thus argue, that gratitude and anger cannot proceed from self-love, might argue in the same way, and with equal reason, that neither can these affections arise from love to others: which is contrary to their own scheme. They say that the reason why we are affected with gratitude and anger towards men, rather than things without life, is moral sense: which they say is the effect of that principle of benevolence or love to others, or love to the public, which is naturally in the hearts of all mankind. But now, I might say, according to their own way of arguing, gratitude and anger cannot arise from love to others, or love to the public, or any sense of mind that is the fruit of public affection. For how differently are we affected towards those who do good or hurt to the public from understanding and will, and public motive, from what we are towards such inanimate things as the sun and the clouds, that do good to the public by enlightening and enlivening beams and refreshing showers; or mildew, and an overflowing stream, that does hurt to the public by destroying the fruits of the earth? Yea, if such a kind of argument be good, it will prove that gratitude and anger cannot arise from the united influence of self-love and public love, or moral sense arising from public affection. For if so, why are we not affected towards inanimate things that are beneficial or injurious both to us and the public, in the same manner as to them that are profitable or hurtful to both on choice and design, and from benevolence or malice?

---

5. displicence: displeasure.

2. On the supposition, that men love those who love them, and are angry with those who hate them, from the natural influence of self-love; it is not at all strange that the Author of Nature, who observes order, uniformity, and harmony in establishing its laws, should so order, that it should be natural for self-love to cause the mind to be affected differently towards exceedingly different objects; and that it should cause our heart to extend itself in one manner towards inanimate things, which gratify self-love without sense or will, and in another manner towards beings which we look upon as having understanding and will, like ourselves, and exerting these faculties in our favour, and promoting our interest from love to us. No wonder, seeing we love ourselves, that it should be natural to us to extend something of that same kind of love which we have for ourselves, to them who are the same kind of beings as ourselves, and comply with the inclinations of our self-love, by expressing the same sort of love towards us.

3. If we should allow that to be universal, that in gratitude and anger there is the exercise of some kind of moral sense—as it is granted there is something that may be so called—all the moral sense that is essential to those affections, is a sense of *Desert*; which is to be referred to that sense of justice before spoken of, consisting in an appre-hension of that secondary kind of beauty that lies in uniformity and proportion; which solves all the difficulty in the objection. Others' love and kindness to us, or their ill-will and injuriousness, appear to us to deserve our love or our resentment. Or in other words, it seems to us no other than just, that as they love us and do us good, we also should love them and do them good. And so it seems just, that when others' hearts oppose us, and they from their hearts do us hurt, our hearts should oppose them, and that we should desire themselves may suffer in like manner as we have suffered, i.e. there appears to us to be a natural agreement, proportion, and adjust-ment between these things; which is indeed a kind of moral sense, or sense of beauty in moral things. But, as was before shown, it is a moral sense of a secondary kind, and is entirely different from a sense or relish of the original essential beauty of true virtue; and may be without any principle of true virtue in the heart. Therefore, doubtless, it is a great mistake in any to suppose, that the moral sense which appears and is exercised in a sense of desert, is the same thing as a love of virtue, or a disposition and determi-nation of mind to be pleased with true virtuous beauty, consisting in public benevo-lence. Which may be further confirmed if it be considered, that even with respect to a sense of justice or desert, consisting in uniformity, and agreement between others' actions towards us and our actions towards them, in a way of well-doing or of ill-doing, it is not absolutely necessary to the being of these passions of gratitude and anger, that there should be any notion of justice in them, in any public or general view of things: as will appear by what shall be next observed.

4. Those authors who hold that the moral sense which is natural to all mankind, consists in a natural relish of the beauty of virtue, and so arises from a principle of true virtue implanted by nature in the hearts of all, hold that true virtue consists in public benevolence. Therefore, if the affections of gratitude and anger necessarily imply such a moral sense as they suppose, then these affections imply some delight in the public good, and an aversion of the mind to public evil. And if so, then every time a man feels anger for opposition, or gratitude for any favour, there must be at least a

supposition of a tendency to public injury in that opposition, and a tendency to public benefit in the favour that excites his gratitude. But how far is this from being true? For instance: a ship's crew enter into a conspiracy against the master, to murder him, and run away with the ship, and turn pirates: but before they bring their matters to ripeness for execution, one of them repents, and opens the whole design; whereupon the rest are apprehended and brought to justice. The crew are enraged with him who has betrayed them, and earnestly seek opportunity to revenge themselves upon him. And for an instance of gratitude; a gang of robbers that have long infested the neighbouring country, have a particular house whither they resort, and where they meet from time to time to divide their booty, and hold their consultations for carrying on their pernicious designs. The magistrates and officers of the country, after many fruitless endeavours to discover their secret place of resort, at length are well-informed where it is, and are prepared with sufficient force to surprise them, and seize them all at the place of rendezvous, at an hour appointed when they understand they will all be there. A little before the arrival of the appointed hour, while the officers with their bands are approaching, some person is so kind to these robbers, as to give them notice of their danger, so as just to give them opportunity to escape. They are thankful to him, and give him a handful of money for his kindness. Now in such instances I think it is plain, that there is no supposition of a public injury in that which is the occasion of their anger; yea, they know the contrary. Nor is there any supposition of public good in that which excites their gratitude; neither has public benevolence, or more sense, consisting in a determination to approve of what is for the public good, any influence at all in the affair. And though there be some affection, besides a sense of uniformity and proportion, that has influence in such anger and gratitude, it is not public affection or benevolence, but private affection; yea, that affection which is to the highest degree private, consisting in a man's love of his own person.

5. The passion of anger, in particular, seems to have been unluckily chosen as a medium to prove a sense and determination to delight in virtue, consisting in benevolence natural to all mankind. For if that moral sense which is exercised in anger, were that which arose from a benevolent temper of heart, being no other than a sense of relish of the beauty of benevolence, one would think a disposition to anger should increase at least in some proportion, as a man had more of a sweet, benign, and benevolent temper: which seems contrary to experience, which shows that the less men have of benevolence, and the more they have of a contrary temper, the more are they disposed to anger and deep resentment of injuries.

And though gratitude be that which many speak of as a certain noble principle of virtue, which God has implanted in the hearts of all mankind; and though it be true there is a gratitude that is truly virtuous: and the want of gratitude, or an ungrateful temper, is truly vicious, and argues an abominable depravity of heart; yet I think, what has been observed may serve to convince such as impartially consider it, not only that not all anger, or hating those which hate us, but also that not all gratitude, or loving those which love us, arises from a truly virtuous benevolence of heart.

Another sort of affections which may be properly referred to self-love as its source, and which might be expected to be the fruit of it, according to the general analogy of nature's laws, is that of affections to such as are near to us by the ties of nature. Such are those of whose beings we have been the occasion, in which we have a very peculiar propriety, and whose circumstances, even from the beginning of their existence, many ways lead them to a high esteem of us, and to treat us with great dependence, submission and compliance. These the constitution of the world makes to be united in interest, and accordingly to act as one, in innumerable affairs, with a communion in each other's affections, desires, cares, friendships, enmities, and pursuits. As to the opinion of those who ascribe the natural affection there is between parents and children to a particular instinct of nature, I shall take notice of it afterwards.

And as men may love persons and things from self-love, so may their love to qualities and characters arise from the same source. Some represent this, as though there were need of a great degree of metaphysical refining to make it out, that men approve of others from self-love, whom they hear of at a distance, or read of in history, or see represented on the stage, from whom they expect no profit or advantage. But perhaps it is not considered, that what we approve of in the first place is the character; and from the character we approve the person. And is it a strange thing, that men should from self-love like a temper or character, which in its nature and tendency falls in with the nature and tendency of self-love; and which we know by experience and self-evidence, without metaphysical refining, in the general tends to men's pleasure and benefit? And on the contrary, is it strange that any should dislike what they see tends to men's pain and misery? Is there need of a great degree of subtlety and abstraction to make it out, that a child, who has heard and seen much of what is calculated strongly to fix an idea of the pernicious, deadly nature of the rattlesnake, should have an aversion to that species from self-love; so as to have a degree of this aversion and disgust excited by seeing even the picture of that animal? And that from the same self-love it should be pleased with a lively representation of some pleasant fruit of which it has often tasted the sweetness? Or with the image of some bird, which it has always been told is innocent, and with whose pleasant singing it has often been entertained? Yet the child neither fears being bitten by the picture of the snake, nor expects to eat of the painted fruit, or to hear the figure of the bird sing. I suppose none will think it difficult to allow, that such an approbation or disgust of a child may be accounted for from its natural delight in the pleasure, of taste and hearing, and its aversion to pain and death, through self-love, together with the habitual connection of these agreeable or terrible ideas with the form and qualities of these objects, the ideas of which are impressed on the mind of the child by their images.

And where is the difficulty of allowing, that a person may hate the general character of a spiteful and malicious man, for the like reason as he hates the general nature of a serpent; knowing from reason, instruction and experience, that malice in men is pernicious to mankind, as well as spite or poison in a serpent? And if a man may from self-love disapprove the vices of malice, envy, and others of that sort, which naturally tend to the hurt of mankind, why may he not from the same principle approve the contrary virtues of meekness, peaceableness, benevolence, charity, generosity, justice, and the social virtues in general; which he as easily and clearly knows, naturally tend to the good of mankind? It is undoubtedly true, that some have a love to these virtues from a higher principle. But yet I think it as certainly true, that there is generally in mankind a sort of approbation of them, which arises from self-love.

Besides what has been already said, the same thing further appears from this; that men commonly are most affected towards, and most highly approve, those virtues which agree with their interest most, according to their various conditions in life. We see that persons of low condition are especially enamoured with a condescending, accessible, affable temper in the great; not only in those whose condescension has been exercised towards themselves; but they will be peculiarly taken with such a character when they have accounts of it from others, or when they meet with it in history, or even in romance. The poor will most highly approve and commend liberality. The weaker sex, who especially need assistance and protection, will peculiarly esteem and applaud fortitude and generosity in those of the other sex, of whom they read or hear, or which they have represented to them on a stage.

I think it plain from what has been observed, that as men may approve and be disposed to commend a benevolent temper from self-love; so the higher the degree of benevolence is, the more may they approve of it. This will account for some kind of approbation, from this principle, even of love to enemies, viz. as a man loving his enemies is an evidence of a high degree of benevolence of temper; the degree of it appearing from the obstacles it overcomes. And it may be here observed, that the consideration of the tendency and influence of self-love may show, how men in general may approve of justice from another ground, besides that approbation of the secondary beauty there is in uniformity and proportion, which is natural to all. Men, from their infancy, see the necessity of it, not only that it is necessary for others or for human society; but they find the necessity of it for themselves, in instances that continually occur; which tends to prejudice them in its favour, and to fix an habitual approbation of it from self-love.

Again, that forementioned approbation of justice and desert, arising from a sense of the beauty of natural agreement and proportion, will have a kind of reflex, and indirect influence to cause men to approve benevolence, and disapprove malice; as men see that he who hates and injures others deserves to be hated and punished, and that he who is benevolent, and loves others and does them good, deserves himself also to be loved and rewarded by others, as they see the natural congruity or agreement, and mutual adaptness of these things. And having always seen this, malevolence becomes habitually connected in the mind with the idea of being hated and punished, which is disagreeable to self-love; and the idea of benevolence is habitually connected and associated with the idea of being loved and rewarded by others, which is grateful to self-love. And by virtue of this association of ideas, benevolence itself becomes grateful, and the contrary displeasing.

Some vices may become in a degree odious by the influence of self-love, through an habitual connection of ideas of contempt with it; contempt being what self-love abhors. So it may often be with drunkenness, gluttony, sottishness, cowardice, sloth, niggardliness. The idea of contempt becomes associated with the idea of such vices, both because we are used to observe that these things are commonly objects of contempt, and also find that they excite contempt in ourselves. Some of them appear marks of littleness, i.e. of small abilities, and weakness of mind, and insufficiency for any considerable effects among mankind. By others, men's influence is contracted into a narrow sphere, and by such means persons become of less importance, and more insignificant. And things of little importance are naturally little accounted of. And some of these ill qualities are such as mankind find it their interest to treat with contempt, as they are very hurtful to human society. There are no particular moral virtues whatsoever, but what in some or other of these ways, and most of them in several, come to have some kind of approbation from self-love, without the influence of a truly virtuous principle; nor any particular vices, but what, by the same means, meet with some disapprobation.

This kind of approbation and dislike, through the joint influence of self-love and association of ideas, is in many vastly heightened by education. This is the means of a strong, close, and almost irrefragable association, in innumerable instances of ideas, which have no connection any other way than by education; and is the means of greatly strengthening that association or connection which persons are led into by other means: as any one would be convinced, perhaps more effectually than in most other ways, if they had opportunity of any considerable acquaintance with American savages and their children.

6. David Brainerd

from the journal
1745

> While at Yale, David Brainerd (1718–47) came under the influence of the more antinomian strand of the revivals, the so-called New Light party. Apparently anti-authoritarian in spirit, he was cited for disrespect and expelled from the college. In 1742 he became a missionary to the Indians. The mission left no great impact, and Brainerd died not long thereafter, at the home of his mentor Jonathan Edwards. But during his mission he had kept a journal which Edwards published in 1749, together with a biographical sketch that offered Brainerd as a saint. The last entry here offers a rare glimpse at the hybrid transformation of native religion in response to Christian missionaries. As critic Larzer Ziff has pointed out, Brainerd's fascinated horror at the Indian revivalist no doubt owes to the native conjurer's being, in effect, a mirror image of Brainerd himself.

September 19. Visited an Indian town called Juniata, situate on an island in Susquehanna. Was much discouraged with the temper and behavior of the Indians here, although they appeared friendly when I was with them the last spring, and then gave me encouragement to come and see them again: But they now seemed resolved to retain their pagan notions and persist in their idolatrous practices.

September 20. Visited the Indians again at Juniata island, and found them almost universally very busy in making preparations for a great sacrifice and dance. Had no opportunity to get them together in order to discourse with them about Christianity, by reason of their being so much engaged about their sacrifice. My spirits were much sunk with a prospect so very discouraging and especially seeing I had now no interpreter but a pagan, who was as much attached to idolatry as any of them (my own interpreter having left me the day before, being obliged to attend upon some important business otherwise, and knowing that he could neither speak nor understand the language of these Indians), so that I was under the greatest disadvantage imaginable; however, I attempted to discourse privately with some of them, but without any appearance of success: notwithstanding, I still tarried with them.

In the evening they met together, near a hundred of them, and danced round a large fire, having prepared ten fat deer for the sacrifice, the fat of whose inwards they burnt in the fire while they were dancing, and sometimes raised the flame to a prodigious height, at the same time yelling and shouting in such a manner that they might easily have been heard two miles or more.

They continued their sacred dance all night, or near the matter; after which they ate the flesh of the sacrifice, and so retired each one to his lodging.

I enjoyed little satisfaction this night, being entirely alone on the island (as to any Christian company), and in the midst of this idolatrous revel; and having walked to and fro till body and mind were pained and much oppressed, I at length crept into a little crib made for corn, and there slept on the poles.

Lord's Day, September 21. Spent the day with the Indians on the island. As soon as they were well up in the morning, I attempted to instruct them, and labored for that purpose to get them together, but quickly found they had something else to do; for near noon they gathered together all their powwows (or conjurers) and set about half a dozen of them to playing their juggling tricks, and acting their frantic distracted postures, in order to find out why they were then so sickly upon the island, numbers of them being at that time disordered with a fever and bloody flux. In this exercise they were engaged for several hours, making all the wild, ridiculous, and distracted motions imaginable; sometimes singing, sometimes howling, sometimes extending their hands to the utmost stretch, spreading all their fingers; and seemed to push with them as if they designed to fright something away, or at least keep it off at arms end; sometimes stroking their faces with their hands, then spurting water as fine as mist; sometimes setting flat on the earth, then bowing down their faces to the ground; wringing their sides, as if in pain and anguish; twisting their faces, turning up their eyes, grunting, puffing, etc.

Their monstrous actions tended to excite ideas of horror, and seemed to have something in them (as I thought) peculiarly suited to raise the devil, if he could be raised by anything odd, ridiculous, and frightful. Some of them, I could observe, were much more fervent and devout in the business than others, and seemed to chant, peep, and mutter with a great degree of warmth and vigor, as if determined to awaken and engage the powers below. I sat at a small distance, not more than thirty feet from them (though undiscovered), with my Bible in my hand, resolving if possible to spoil their sport and prevent their receiving any answers from the infernal world, and there viewed the whole scene. They continued their hideous charms and incantations for more than three hours, until they had all wearied themselves out, although they had in that space of time taken sundry intervals of rest, and at length broke up, I apprehended, without receiving any answer at all.

After they had done powwowing, I attempted to discourse with them about Christianity; but they soon scattered and gave me no opportunity for anything of that nature. A view of these things, while I was entirely alone in the wilderness, destitute of the society of anyone that so much as "named the name of Christ" [II Tim. 2 : 19], greatly sunk my spirits, gave me the most gloomy turn of mind imaginable, almost stripped me of all resolution and hope respecting further attempts for propagating the Gospel and converting the pagans, and rendered this the most burdensome and disagreeable Sabbath that ever I saw. But nothing, I can truly say, sunk and distressed me like the loss of my hope respecting their conversion. This concern appeared so great, and seemed to be so much my own, that I seemed to have nothing to do on earth if this failed: And a prospect of the greatest success in the saving conversion of souls under Gospel light would have done little or nothing towards compensating for the loss of my hope in this respect; and my spirits now were so damped and depressed that I had no heart nor power to make any further attempts among them for that purpose, and could not possibly recover my hope, resolution, and courage, by the utmost of my endeavors.

The Indians of this island can many of them understand the English language considerably well, having formerly lived in some part of Maryland among or near the white people, but are very vicious, drunken, and profane, although not so savage as those who have less acquaintance with the English. Their customs in divers respects differ from those of other Indians upon this river. They don't bury their dead in a common form, but let their flesh consume above ground in close cribs made for that purpose; and at the end of the year, or perhaps sometimes a longer space of time, they take the bones, when the flesh is all consumed, and wash and scrape them, and afterwards bury them with some ceremony. Their method of charming or conjuring over the sick seems somewhat different from that of other Indians, though for substance the same: And the whole of it, among these and others, perhaps is an imitation of what seems, by Naaman's expression (II Kgs. 5 : 11), to have been the custom of the ancient heathens. For it seems chiefly to consist in their "striking their hands over the diseased," repeatedly stroking of them, and "calling upon their gods," excepting the spurting of water like a mist, and some other frantic ceremonies common to the other conjurations I have already mentioned.

When I was in these parts in May last, I had an opportunity of learning many of the notions and customs of the Indians, as well as of observing many of their practices: I then travelling more than an hundred and thirty miles upon the river above the English settlements; and having in that journey a view of some persons of seven or eight distinct tribes, speaking so many different languages. But of all the sights I ever saw among them, or indeed anywhere else, none appeared so frightful or so near akin to what is usually imagined of infernal powers; none ever excited such images of terror in my mind, as the appearance of one who was a devout and zealous reformer, or rather restorer, of what he supposed was the ancient religion of the Indians. He made his appearance in his pontifical garb, which was a coat of bears' skins, dressed with the hair on, and hanging down to his toes, a pair of bearskin stockings, and a great wooden face, painted the one half black, the other tawny, about the color of an Indian's skin, with an extravagant mouth, cut very much away: the face fastened to a bearskin cap which was drawn over his head. He advanced toward me with the instrument in his hand that he used for music in his idolatrous worship, which was a dry tortoiseshell, with some corn in it, and the neck of it drawn on to a piece of wood, which made a very convenient handle. As he came forward he beat his tune with the rattle, and danced with all his might, but did not suffer any part of his body, not so much as his fingers, to be seen: And no man would have guessed by his appearance and actions that he could have been a human creature, if they had not had some intimation of it otherways. When he came near me I could not but shrink away from him, although it was then noonday, and I knew who it was, his appearance and gestures were so prodigiously frightful! He had a house consecrated to religious uses, with divers images cut out upon the several parts of it. I went in and found the ground beat almost as hard as a rock with their frequent dancing in it. I discoursed with him about Christianity, and some of my discourse he seemed to like; but some of it he disliked entirely. He told me that God had taught him his religion, and that he never would turn from it, but wanted to find some that would join heartily with him in it; for the Indians, he said, were grown very degenerate and corrupt. He had thoughts, he said, of leaving all his friends and travelling abroad, in order to find some that would join with him; for he believed God had some good people somewhere that felt as he did. He had not always, he said, felt as he now did, but had formerly been like the rest of the Indians, until about four or five years before that time: Then, he said, his heart was very much distressed, so that he could not live among the Indians, but got away into the woods and lived alone for some months. At length, he says, God comforted his heart and showed him what he should do; and since that time he had known God and tried to serve him; and loved all men, be they who they would, so as he never did before. He treated me with uncommon courtesy, and seemed to be hearty in it. And I was told by the Indians that he opposed their drinking strong liquor with all his power; and if at any time he could not dissuade them from it, by all he could say, he would leave them and go crying into the woods. It was manifest he had a set of religious notions that he had looked into for himself, and not taken for granted upon bare tradition; and he relished or disrelished whatever was spoken of a religious nature, according as it either agreed or disagreed with his standard. And while I was discoursing he would sometimes say, "Now that I like: so God has taught me," etc. And some of his sentiments seemed very just. Yet he utterly denied the being of a devil, and declared there was no such a creature known among the Indians of old times, whose religion he supposed he was attempting to revive. He likewise told me that departed souls all went southward, and that the difference between the good and bad was this: that the former were admitted into a beautiful town with spiritual walls, or walls agreeable to the nature of souls; and that the latter would forever hover round those walls, and in vain attempt to get in. He seemed to be sincere, honest and conscientious in his own way, and according to his own religious notions, which was more than I ever saw in any other pagan: And I perceived he was looked upon and derided amongst most of the Indians as a precise zealot that made a needless noise about religious matters. But I must say, there was something in his temper and disposition that looked more like true religion than anything I ever observed amongst other heathens.

But alas! how deplorable is the state of the Indians upon this river! The brief representation I have here given of their notions and manners is sufficient to show that they are "led captive by Satan at his will" [II Tim. 2 : 26] in the most eminent manner: and, methinks, might likewise be sufficient to excite the compassion and engage the prayers of pious souls for these their fellow men, who sit in "the regions of the shadow of death" [Matt. 4 : 16].

7. Samson Occom

A Sermon Preached by Samson Occom 1772

In 1771 a Christian Indian named Moses Paul was expelled from a bar in New Haven for being drunk and disorderly. Swearing revenge, he killed the next person to come out the door, a white man. Paul repented before his execution, and decided to make good use of the occasion: he sent for Samson Occom (1723–92). Occom was already the most famous preacher among the Christian Indians, having made a much publicized tour of England a few years earlier to raise money for the Indian Charity School begun by Eleazar Wheelock (now Dartmouth College). Occom responded with an execution sermon, long a popular genre, especially well received in New Haven because Paul's was the first hanging in twenty years. When Occom published it in 1772 he became the first Indian author to publish in English.

"I was born a heathen and raised up in heathenism," Occom writes in a 1768 autobiographical sketch. A Mohegan, he began studying English after being stirred by missionaries at the age of sixteen. Ordained in 1759, he spent most of the following years promoting Wheelock's missions. After returning from his two-year tour of England, he quarrelled with Wheelock over the dwindling extension of charity to Indian students. Much of the rest of his life was occupied with failed schemes to resettle Christian Indians on lands further west. His only other published work is the Collection of Hymns and Spiritual Songs *(1774).*

In the sermon Occom faces a difficult task. He addresses three audiences, each marked in a different section of the sermon: whites, Indians, and Moses Paul himself. The handling of the tension, even incoherence, between these audiences is something of a rhetorical feat. How would each section have sounded to the other audiences?

The sacred words that I have chosen to speak from, upon this undesirable occasion are found written in the Epistle of St. Paul to the ROMANS, VI. 23. For the Wages of Sin is Death, but the Gift of God is Eternal Life through Jesus Christ our Lord.

Death is called the king of terrors, and it ought to be the subject of every man and woman's thoughts daily; because it is that unto which they are liable every moment of their lives: And therefore it cannot be unreasonable to think, speak and hear of it at any time, and especially on this mournful occasion; for we must all come to it, how soon we cannot tell; whether we are prepared or not prepared, ready or not ready, whether death is welcome or not welcome, we must feel the force of it: Whether we concern ourselves with death or not, it will concern itself with us. Seeing that this is the case with every one of us, what manner of persons ought we to be in all holy conversation and godliness; how ought men to exert themselves in preparation for death, continually; for they know not what a day or an hour may bring forth, with respect to them. But alas! according to the appearance of mankind in general; death is the least thought of. They go on from day to day as if they were to live here forever, as if this was the only life. They contrive, rack their inventions, disturb their rest, and even hazard their lives in all manner of dangers, both by sea and land; yea, they leave no stone unturned that they may live in the world, and at the same time have little or no contrivance to die well. God and their souls are neglected, and heaven and eternal happiness are disregarded; Christ and his religion are despised—yet most of these very men intend to be happy when they come to die, not considering that there must be great preparation in order to die well. Yea there is none so fit to live as those that are fit to die; those that are not fit to die are not fit to live. Life and death are nearly connected; we generally own that it is a great and solemn thing to die. If this be true, then it is a great and solemn thing to live, for as we live so we shall die. But I say again, how do mankind realize these things? They are busy about the things of this world as if there was no death before them. Dr. Watts[6] pictures them out to the life in his psalms:

> See the vain race of mortals move,
>   Like shadows o'er the plain,
> They rage and strive, desire and love,
>   But all the noise is vain.
>
> Some walk in honour's gaudy show,
>   Some dig for golden ore,
> They toil for heirs they know not who,
>   And strait are seen no more.

But on the other hand, life is the most precious thing, and ought to be the most desired by all rational creatures. It ought to be prized above all things; yet there is nothing so abused and despised as life, and nothing so neglected: I mean eternal life is shamefully disregarded by men in general, and eternal death is chosen rather than life. This is the general complaint of the Bible from the beginning to the end. As long as Christ is neglected, life is refused, as long as sin is cherished, death is chosen. And this seems to be the woful case of mankind of all nations, according to their appearance in these days: For it is too plain to be denied, that vice and immorality, and floods of iniquity are abounding every where amongst all nations, and all orders and ranks of men, and in every sect of people. Yea there is a great agreement and harmony among all nations, and from the highest to the lowest to practice sin and iniquity; and the

---

6. *Dr. Watts*: Isaac Watts (1674–1748), English hymn writer.

pure religion of Jesus Christ is turned out of doors, and is dying without; or, in other words, the Lord Jesus Christ is turned out of doors by men in general, and even by his professed people. "He Came to his own, and his own received him not."[7] But the devil is admitted, he has free access to the houses and hearts of the children of men: Thus life is refused and death is chosen.

But in further speaking upon our text by divine assistance, I shall consider these two general propositions.

I. That sin is the cause of all the miseries that befall the children of men, both as to their bodies and souls, for time and eternity.

II. That eternal life and happiness is the gift of God through Jesus Christ our Lord.

In speaking to the first proposition, I shall first consider the nature of sin; and secondly I shall consider the consequences of sin or the wages of sin, which is death. First then, we are to describe the nature of sin.

Sin is the transgression of the law:—This is the scripture definition of sin.—Now the law of God being holy, just and good; sin must be altogether unholy, unjust and evil. If I was to define sin, I should call it a contrariety to God; and as such it must be the vilest thing in the world; it is full of all evil; it is the evil of evils; the only evil in which dwells no good thing; and it is most destructive to God's creation, wherever it takes effect. It was sin that transformed the very angels in heaven, into devils; and it was sin that caused hell to be made. If it had not been for sin, there never would have been such a thing as hell or devil, death or misery.

And if sin is such a thing as we have just described, it must be worse than the devils in hell itself.—Sin is full of deadly poison; it is full of malignity and hatred against God; against all his divine perfections and attributes, against his wisdom, against his power, against his holiness and goodness, against his mercy and justice, against his law and gospel; yea against his very being and existence. Were it in the power of sin, it would even dethrone God, and set itself on the throne.

When Christ the Son of the Most High came down from the glorious world above, into this wretched world of sin and sorrow, to seek and to save that which was lost, sin or sinners rose up against him, as soon as he entered our world, and pursued him with hellish malice, night and day, for above thirty years together, till they killed him.

Further, sin is against the Holy Ghost; it opposes all its good and holy operations upon the children of men. When, and wherever there is the out pouring of the Spirit of God, upon the children of men, in a way of conviction and conversion; sin will immediately prompt the devil and his children to rise up against it, and they will oppose the work with all their power, and in every shape. And if open opposition will not do, the devil will mimic the work and thus prevent the good effect.

Thus we find by the scripture accounts, that whenever God raises up men, and uses them as instruments of conviction and conversion, the devil and his instruments will rise up to destroy both the reformers and the reformed. Thus it had been from the early days of christianity to this day. We have found it so in our day. In the time of the outpouring of the Spirit of God in these colonies, to the conviction and reformation of many; immediately sin and the devil influenced numbers to rise up against the good

7. John 1:11.

work of God, calling it a delusion, and work of the devil. And thus sin also opposes every motion of the Spirit of God, in the heart of every christian; this makes a warfare in the soul.

2. I shall endeavour to show the sad consequences or effects of sin upon the children of men.

Sin has poisoned them, and made them distracted or fools. The psalmist says, The fool hath said in his heart, there is no God.[8] And Solomon, through his proverbs, calls ungodly sinners fools; and their sin he calls their folly and foolishness.[9] The apostle James says, But the tongue can no man tame, it is an unruly evil, full of deadly poison.[10] It is the heart that is in the first place full of deadly poison. The tongue is only an interpreter of the heart. Sin has vitiated the whole man, both soul and body; all the powers are corrupted; it has turned the minds of men against all good, towards all evil. So poisoned are they according to the prophet, Isa. v. 20. "Wo unto them that call evil good and good evil; that put darkness for light, and light for darkness; that put bitter for sweet, and sweet for bitter." And Christ Jesus saith in John 3. 19, 20. "And this is the condemnation, that light has come into the world, and men have loved darkness rather than light, because their deeds were evil. For every one that doeth evil, hateth the light, neither cometh to the light lest his deeds should be reproved." Sin hath stupified mankind, they are now ignorant of God their Maker; neither do they enquire after him. And they are ignorant of themselves, they know not what is good for them, neither do they understand their danger; and they have no fear of God before their eyes.

Further, sin hath blinded their eyes, so that they cannot discern spiritual things: neither do they see the way that they should go, and they are as deaf as adders, so that they cannot hear the joyful sound of the gospel that brings glad tidings of peace and pardon to sinners of mankind. Neither do they regard the charmer charming never so wisely.—Not only so, but sin has made man proud, though he has nothing to be proud of; for he has lost his excellency, his beauty and happiness; he is a bankrupt and is excommunicated from God; he was turned out of paradise by God himself, and became a vagabond in God's world, and as such he has no right or title to the least crumb of mercy, in the world: Yet he is proud, he is haughty, and exalts himself above God, though he is wretched and miserable, and poor and blind and naked. He glories in his shame. Sin has made him beastly and devilish; yea, he is sunk beneath the beasts, and is worse than the ravenous beasts of the wilderness. He is become ill-natured, cruel and murderous; he is contentious and quarrelsome. I said he is worse than the ravenous beasts, for wolves and bears don't devour their own kind, but man does; yea, we have numberless instances of women killing their own children; such women I think are worse than she-tygers.

Sin has made man dishonest, and deceitful, so that he goes about cheating and defrauding and deceiving his fellow-men in the world: Yea, he has become a cheat himself, he goes about in vain shew; we do not know where to find man. Sometimes we find as an angel of God; and at other times we find as a devil, even one and the

8. Ps. 14:1.
9. Prov. 12:23, 14:8, 14:24, 15:2.

10. James 3:8.

same man. Sin has made a man a liar even from the womb; so there is no believing nor trusting him. The royal psalmist says, "The wicked are estranged from the womb, they go astray as soon as they are born, speaking lies."[11] His language is also corrupted. Whereas he had a pure and holy language, in his innocency, to adore and praise God his Maker, he now curses and swears, and profanes, the holy name of God, and curses and damns his fellow creatures. In a word, man is a most unruly and ungovernable creature, and is become as the wild ass's colt, and is harder to tame than any of God's creatures in this world.—In short, man is worse than all the creatures in this lower world, his propensity is to evil and that continually; he is more like the devil than any creature we can think of: And I think it is not going beyond the word of God, to say man is the most devilish creature in the world. Christ said to his disciples, One of you is a devil; to the Jews he said, Ye are of your father the devil, and the lusts of your father ye will do. Thus every unconverted soul is a child of the devil, sin has made them so.

We have given some few hints of the nature of sin, and the effects of sin on mankind.

We shall in the next place consider the wages or the reward of sin, which is death.

Sin is the cause of all the miseries that attend poor sinful man, which will finally bring him to death, death temporal and eternal. I shall first consider his temporal death.

His temporal death then begins as soon as he is born. Though it seems to us that he is just beginning to live, yet in fact he is just entered into a state of death: St. Paul says, "Wherefore, as by one man sin entered into the world, and death by sin; and so death passed upon all men, for that all have sinned."[12] Man is surrounded with ten thousand instruments of death, and is liable to death every moment of his life; a thousand diseases await him on every side continually; the sentence of death has pass'd upon them as soon as they are born; yea they are struck with death as soon as they breathe. And it seems all the enjoyments of men in this world are also poisoned with sin; for God said to Adam after he had sinned, "Cursed is the ground for thy sake, in sorrow shalt thou eat of it all the days of thy life."[13] By this we plainly see that every thing that grows out of the ground is cursed, and all creatures that God hath made for man are cursed also; and whatever God curses is a cursed thing indeed. Thus death and destruction is in all the enjoyments of men in this life, every enjoyment in this world is liable to misfortune in a thousand ways, both by sea and land.

How many ships, that have been loaded with the choicest treasures of the earth have been swallowed up in the ocean, many times just before they enter their desired haven. And vast treasures have been consumed by fire on the land, &c.—And the fruits of the earth are liable to many judgments. And the dearest and nearest enjoyments of men are generally balanced with equal sorrow and grief.—A man and his wife who have lived together in happiness for many years; that have comforted each other in various changes of life, must at last be separated; one or the other must be taken away first by death, and then the poor survivor is drowned in tears, in sorrow,

11. Ps. 58:3.
12. Rom. 5:12.
13. Gen. 3:17.

mourning and grief. And when a child or children are taken away by death, the bereaved parents are bowed down with sorrow and deep mourning. When Joseph was sold by his brethren unto the Ishmaelites, they took his coat and rolled it in blood, and carried it to their father, and the good old patriarch knew it to be Joseph's coat, and he concluded that his dear Joseph was devoured by evil beasts; and he was plunged all over in sorrow and bitter mourning, and he refused to be comforted. And so when tender parents are taken away by death, the children are left comfortless. All this is the sad effects of sin—These are the wages of sin.

And secondly we are to consider man's spiritual death, while he is here in this world. We find it thus written in the word of God, "And the Lord God commanded the man, saying of every tree of the garden thou mayst freely eat: but of the tree of knowledge of good and evil, thou shalt not eat of it, for in the day thou eatest thereof thou shalt surely die."[14] And yet he did eat of it, and so he and all his posterity are but dead men. And St. Paul to the Ephesians saith, "You hath he quickened who were dead in trespasses and sins."[15]—The great Mr. Henry[16] says, in this place, that unregenerate souls are dead in trespasses and sins. All those who are in their sins, are dead in sins; yea, in trespasses and sins; and which may signify all sorts of sins, habitual and actual; sins of heart and life. Sin is the death of the soul. Wherever that prevails, there is a privation of all spiritual life. Sinners are dead in state, being destitute of the principles and powers of spiritual life; and cut off from God, the fountain of life: and they are dead in law, as a condemned malefactor is said to be a dead man. Now a dead man, in a natural sense, is unactive, and is of no service to the living; there is no correspondence between the dead and the living: There is no agreement or union between them, no fellowship at all between the dead and the living. A dead man is altogether ignorant of the intercourse among the living:—Just so it is with men that are spiritually dead; they have no agreeable activity. Their activity in sin, is their deadness and inactivity towards God. They are of no service to God; and they have no correspondence with heaven; and there is no agreement or fellowship between them and the living God; and they are totally ignorant of the agreeable and sweet intercourse there is between God and his children here below: and they are ignorant, and know nothing of that blessed fellowship and union there is among the saints here below. They are ready to say indeed, behold how they love one another! But they know nothing of that love, that the children of God enjoy. As sin is in opposition to God; so sinners are at enmity against God; there is no manner of agreement between them.

Let us consider further. God is a living God, he is all life, the fountain of life; and a sinner is a dead soul; there is nothing but death in him. And now judge ye, what agreement can there be between them! God is a holy and pure God, and a sinner is an unholy and filthy creature;—God is a righteous Being, and a sinner is an unrighteous creature; God is light, and a sinner is darkness itself, &c. Further, what agreement can there be between God and a liar, a thief, a drunkard, a swearer, a profane creature, a whoremonger, an adulterer, an idolater, &c. No one that has any sense, dare say that there is any agreement. Further, as sinners are dead to God, as such, they have no

14. Gen. 2:16–17.
15. Eph. 2:1.

16. great Mr. Henry: Matthew Henry (1662–1714), author of a commentary on the Bible.

delight in God, and godliness; they have no taste for the religion of Jesus Christ: they have no pleasure in the holy exercise of religion. Prayer is no pleasant work with them; or if they have any pleasure in it, it is not out of love to God, but out of self-love, like the Pharisees of old; they loved to pray in open view of men, that they might have praise from them. And perhaps, they were not careful to pray in secret. These were dead souls, they were unholy, rotten hypocrites, and so all their prayers and religious exercises were cold, dead, and abominable services to God. Indeed they are dead to all the duties that God requires of them: they are dead to the holy bible; to all the laws, commands, and precepts thereof; and to the ordinances of the gospel of the Lord Jesus Christ. When they read the book of God, it is like an old almanack to them, a dead book. But it is because they are dead, and as such, all their services are against God, even their best services are an abomination unto God; yea, sinners are so dead in sin, that the threatnings of God don't move them. All the thunderings and lightnings of Mount-Sinai don't stir them. All the curses of the law are out against them; yea, every time they read these curses in the bible, they are cursing them to their faces, and to their very eyes; yet they are unconcern'd, and go on in sin without fear. And lastly here, sin has so stupified the sinner, that he will not believe his own senses, he won't believe his own eyes, nor his own ears, he reads the book of God, but he does not believe what he reads. And he hears of God, and heaven, and eternal happiness, and of hell and eternal misery; but he believes none of these things; he goes on, as if there were no God, nor heaven and happiness; neither has he any fear of hell and eternal torments; and he sees his fellow-men dropping away daily on every side, yet he goes on carelessly in sin, as if he never was to die. And if he at any time thinks of dying, he hardly believes his own thoughts.——Death is at a great distance, so far off, that he dont concern himself about it, so as to prepare for it. God mournfully complains of his people, that they dont consider;—O that they were wise, that they understood this, that they would consider their latter end.

The next thing I shall consider, is the actual death of the body, or separation between soul and body. At the cessation of natural life, there is no more joy or sorrow; no more hope nor fear, as to the body; no more contrivance and carrying on of business; no more merchandizing and trading; no more farming; no more buying and selling; no more building of any kind, no more contrivance at all to live in the world; no more honor nor reproach; no more praise; no more good report, nor evil report; no more learning of any trades, arts or sciences in the world; no more sinful pleasures, they are all at an end; recreations, visiting, tavern-hunting, musick and dancing, chambering and carousing, playing at dice and cards, or any game whatsoever; cursing and swearing, and profaning the holy name of God, drunkeness, fighting, debauchery, lying and cheating, in this world must cease forever: Not only so, but they must bid an eternal farewell to all the world; bid farewell to all their beloved sins and pleasures; and the places and possessions that knew them once, shall know them no more forever. And further, they must bid adieu to all sacred and divine things. They are obliged to leave the bible, and all the ordinances thereof; and to bid farewell to preachers, and all sermons, and all christian people, and christian conversation; they must bid a long farewell to sabbaths and seasons, and opportunities of worship; yea an eternal farewell to all mercy and all hope; an eternal farewell to God the Father, Son and Holy Ghost, and adieu to heaven and all happiness, to saints and all the inhabitants of the upper world. At your leisure please to read the destruction of Babylon; you will find it written in the 18th of the Revelations.

On the other hand, the poor departed soul must take up its lodging in sorrow, wo and misery, in the lake that burns with fire and brimstone, were the worm dieth not and the fire is not quenched; where a multitude of frightful deformed devils dwell, and the damned ghosts of Adam's race; where darkness, horror and despair reigns, or where hope never comes, and where poor guilty naked souls will be tormented with exquisite torments, even the wrath of the Almighty poured out upon the damned souls; the smoke of their torments ascending up forever and ever; their mouths and nostrils streaming forth with living fire; and hellish groans, cries and shrieks all around them, and merciless devils upbraiding them for their folly and madness, and tormenting them incessantly. And there they must endure the most unsatiable, fruitless desire, and the most overwhelming shame and confusion and the most horrible fear, and the most doleful sorrow, and the most racking despair. When they cast their flaming eyes to heaven, with Dives in torments, they behold an angry GOD, whose eyes are as a flaming fire, and they are struck with ten thousand darts of pain; and the sight of the happiness of the saints above, adds to their pains and aggravates their misery. And when they reflect upon their past folly and madness in neglecting the great salvation in their day, it will pierce them with ten thousand inconceivable torments; it will as it were enkindle their hell afresh; and it will cause them to curse themselves bitterly, and curse the day in which they were born, and curse their parents that were the instruments of their being in the world; yea, they will curse, bitterly curse, and wish that very GOD that gave them their being to be in the same condition with them in hell torments. This is what is called the second death and it is the last death, and an eternal death to a guilty soul.

And O eternity, eternity, eternity! Who can measure it? Who can count the years thereof? Arithmetic must fail, the thoughts of men and angels are drowned in it; how shall we describe eternity? To what shall we compare it? Were it possible to employ a fly to carry off this globe by the small particles thereof, and to carry them to such a distance that it would return once in *ten thousand* years for another particle, and so continue till it has carried off all this globe, and framed them together in some unknown space, till it has made just such a world as this is: After all, eternity would remain the same unexhausted duration. This must be the unavoidable portion of all impenitent sinners, let them be who they will, great or small, honorable or ignoble, rich or poor, bond or free. Negroes, Indians, English, or of what nation soever; all that die in their sins must go to hell together; for the wages of sin is death.

The next thing that I was to consider is this:

That eternal life and happiness is the free gift of God through Jesus Christ our Lord.

Under this proposition I shall now endeavour to show that this life and happiness is.

The life that is mentioned in our text is a spiritual life, it is the life of the soul; from sin to holiness, from darkness to light, a translation from the kingdom and dominion of satan, to the kingdom of God's grace. In other words, it is being restored to the image of God and delivered from the image of satan. And this life consists in union of the soul to God, and communion with God; a real participation of the divine nature, or in the Apostle's words, is a Christ formed within us; I live says he, yet not I but Christ liveth in me.[17] And the Apostle John saith God is love and he that dwelleth in love, dwelleth in God, and God in him.[18] This is the life of the soul. It is called emphatically life, because it is a life that shall never have a period, a stable, a permanent, and unchangeable life, called in the scriptures everlasting life, or life eternal. And the happiness of this life consists in communion with God, or in the spiritual enjoyment of God. As much as a soul enjoys of God in this life, just so much of life and happiness he enjoys or possesses; yea, just so much of heaven he enjoys. A true christian, desires no other heaven but the enjoyment of God; a full and perfect enjoyment of God, is a full and perfect heaven and happiness to a gracious soul.—Further, this life is called eternal life because God has planted a living principle in the soul; and whereas he was dead before, now he is made alive unto God; there is an active principle within him towards God, he now moves towards God in his religious devotions and exercises; is daily comfortably and sweetly walking with God, in all his ordinances and commands; his delight is in the ways of God; he breathes towards God, a living breath, in praises, prayers, adorations and thanksgivings; his prayers are now heard in the heavens, and his praises delight the ears of the Almighty, and his thanksgivings are accepted, so alive is he now to God, that it is his meat and drink, yea more than his meat and drink, to do the will of his heavenly Father. It is his delight, his happiness and pleasure to serve God. He does not drag himself to his duties now, but he does them out of choice, and with alacrity of soul. Yea, so alive is he to God, that he gives up himself and all that he has entirely to God, to be for him and no other; his whole aim is to glorify God, in all things, whether by life or death, all the same to him.

We have a bright example of this in St. Paul. After he was converted, he was all alive to God; he regarded not his life but was willing to spend and be spent in the service of his God; he was hated, revil'd, despised, laughed at, and called all manner of evil names; was scourged, stoned and imprisoned; and all could not stop his activity towards God. He would boldly and courageously go on in preaching the gospel of the Lord Jesus Christ, to poor lost and undone sinners; he would do the work God set him about, in spite of all opposition he met with either from men or devils, earth or hell; come death or come life, none of these things moved him, because he was alive unto God. Though he suffered hunger and thirst, cold and heat, poverty and nakedness by day and by night, by sea, and by land, and was in danger always; yet he would serve God amidst all these dangers. Read his amazing account in 2 Cor. 11. 23, and on.

Another instance of marvellous love towards God, we have in Daniel. When there was a proclamation of prohibition, sent by the king to all his subjects forbidding them to call upon their gods for 30 days; which was done by envious men, that they might find occasion against Daniel the servant of the most high God; yet he having the life of God in his soul regarded not the king's decree, but made his petition to his God, as often as he used to do though death was threatened to the disobedient. But he feared not the hell they had prepared; for it seems, the den resembled hell, and the lions represented the devils. And when he was actually cast into the lions den, the ravenous

17. Gal. 2:20.   18. John 4:16.

beasts became meek and innocent as lambs, before the prophet, because he was alive unto God; the spirit of the Most High was in him, and the lions were afraid before him. Thus it was with Daniel and Paul; they went through fire and water, as the common saying is, because they had eternal life in their souls in an eminent manner; and they regarded not this life for the cause and glory of God. And thus it has been in all ages with true Christians. Many of the fore-fathers of the English, in this country, had this life and are gone the same way, that the holy Prophets and Apostles went. Many of them went through all manner of sufferings for God; and a great number of them are gone home to heaven, in chariots of fire. I have seen the place in London, called Smithfield, where numbers were burnt to death for the religion of Jesus Christ. And there is the same life in true christians now in these days; and if there should persecutions arise in our day, I verily believe, true christians would suffer with the same spirit and temper of mind, as those did, who suffered in days past.—This is the life which our text speaks of.

We proceed in the next place to show, that this life, which we have described, is the free gift of God, through Jesus Christ our Lord.

Sinners have forfeited all mercy into the hands of divine justice and have merited hell and damnation to themselves; for the wages of sin is everlasting death, but heaven and happiness is a free gift; it comes by favor; and all merit is excluded; and especially if we consider that we are fallen sinful creatures, and there is nothing in us that can recommend us to the favour of God; and we can do nothing that is agreeable and acceptable to God; and the mercies we enjoy in this life are altogether from the pure mercy of God; we are unequal to them. Good old Jacob cried out, under the sense of his unworthiness, "I am less than the least of all thy mercies,"[19] and we have nothing to give unto God; if we essay to give all the service that we are capable of, we should give him nothing but what was his own, and when we give up ourselves unto God, both soul and body, we give him nothing; for we were his before; he had a right to do with us as he pleased, either to throw us into hell, or to save us.—There is nothing that we can call our own, but our sins; and who is he that dares to say, I expect to have heaven for my sins? for our text says, that the wages of sin is death. If we are thus unequal and unworthy of the least mercy in this life, how much more are we unworthy of eternal life? Yet God can find it in his heart to give it. And it is altogether unmerited; it is a free gift to undeserving and hell deserving sinners of mankind: it is altogether of God's sovereign good pleasure to give it. It is of free grace and sovereign mercy, and from the unbounded goodness of God; he was self-moved to it. And it is said that this life is given in and through our Lord Jesus Christ. It could not be given in any other way, but in and through the death and suffering of the Lord Jesus Christ; Christ himself is the gift, and he is the christian's life. "For God so loved the world that he gave his only begotten Son, that whosoever believed in him should not perish but have everlasting life."[20] The word says further, "For by grace ye are saved, through faith, and that not of yourselves it is the gift of God."[21] This is given through Jesus Christ our Lord; it is Christ that purchased it with his own blood; he prepared it

19. Gen. 32:10.   21. Eph. 2:8.
20. John 3:16.

with his divine and almighty power; and by the same power, and by the influence of his spirit, he prepares us for it; and his divine grace preserves us to it. In a word, he is all in all in our eternal salvation; all this is the free gift of God.

I have now gone through what I proposed from my text. And I shall now make some application of the whole.

First to the criminal in particular; and then to the auditory in general.

My poor unhappy Brother MOSES,

As it was your own desire that I should preach to you this last discourse, so I shall speak plainly to you.—You are the bone of my bone, and flesh of my flesh. You are an Indian, a despised creature, but you have despised yourself; yea you have despised God more; you have trodden under foot his authority; you have despised his commands and precepts; And now as God says, be sure your sins will find you out. And now, poor Moses, your sins have found you out, and they have overtaken you this day; the day of your death is now come; the king of terrors is at hand; you have but a very few moments to breathe in this world.—The just law of man, and the holy laws of Jehovah, call aloud for the destruction of your mortal life; God says, "Whoso sheddeth man's blood by man shall his blood be shed." This is the ancient decree of heaven, and it is to be executed by man; nor have you the least gleam of hope of escape, for the unalterable sentence is past: The terrible day of execution is come; the unwelcome guard is about you; and the fatal instruments of death are now made ready; your coffin and your grave, your last lodging are open ready to receive you.

Alas! poor Moses, now you know by sad, by woful experience, the living truth of our text, that the wages of sin is death. You have been already dead; yea, twice dead: By nature spiritually dead. And since the awful sentence of death has been passed upon you, you have been dead to all the pleasures of this life; or all the pleasures, lawful or unlawful, have been dead to you: And death, which is the wages of sin, is standing even on this side of your grave ready to put a final period to your mortal life; and just beyond the grave, eternal death awaits your poor soul, and devils are ready to drag your miserable soul down to their bottomless den, where everlasting wo and horror reigns; the place is filled with doleful shrieks, howls and groans of the damned. Oh! to what a miserable, forlorn, and wretched condition has your extravagance folly and wickedness brought you! i.e. if you die in your sins. And O! what manner of repentance ought you to manifest! How ought your heart to bleed for what you have done! How ought you to prostrate your soul before a bleeding God! And under self-condemnation, cry out ah Lord, ah Lord, what have I done?—Whatever partiality, injustice and error there may be among the judges of the earth, remember that you have deserved a thousand deaths, and a thousand hells, by reason of your sins, at the hands of a holy God. Should God come out against you in strict justice, alas! what could you say for yourself; for you have been brought up under the bright sunshine, and plain, and loud sound of the gospel; and you have had a good education; you can read and write well; and God has given you a good natural understanding: And therefore your sins are so much more aggravated. You have not sinned in such an ignorant manner as others have done; but you have sinned with both your eyes open as it were, under the light even the glorious light of the gospel of the Lord Jesus Christ.—You have sinned against the light of your own conscience, against your knowledge and understanding; you have sinned against the pure and holy laws of God, the just laws of men; you have sinned against heaven and earth; you have sinned against all the mercies and goodness of God; you have sinned against the whole bible, against the Old and New-Testament; you have sinned against the blood of Christ, which is the blood of the everlasting covenant. O poor Moses, see what you have done! And now repent, repent, I say again repent; see how the blood you shed cries against you, and the avenger of blood is at your heels. O fly, fly, to the blood of the Lamb of God for the pardon of all your aggravated sins.

But let us now turn to a more pleasant theme.—Though you have been a great sinner, a heaven-daring sinner; yet hark and hear the joyful sound from heaven, even from the King of kings, and Lord of lords; that the gift of God is eternal life, through Jesus Christ our Lord. It is the free gift offered to the greatest sinners, and upon their true repentance towards God and faith in the Lord Jesus Christ they shall be welcome to the life they have spoken of: it is offered upon free terms. He that hath no money may come; he that hath no righteousness, no goodness may come, the call is to poor undone sinners; the call is not to the righteous, but sinners calling them to repentance. Hear the voice of the Son of the Most High God, Come unto me all ye that labor and are heavy laden, and I will give you rest. This is a call, a gracious call to you poor Moses, under your present burden and distresses. And Christ alone has a right to call sinners to himself. It would be presumption for a mightly angel to call a poor sinner in this manner; and were it possible for you to apply to all God's creatures, they would with one voice tell you, that it was not in them to help you. Go to all the means of grace, they would prove miserable helps without Christ himself. Yea, apply to all the ministers of the gospel in the world, they would all say, that it was not in them, but would only prove as indexes, to point out to you, the Lord Jesus Christ, the only Saviour of sinners of mankind. Yea, go to all the angels in heaven they would do the same. Yea, go to God the Father himself without Christ, he could not help you, to speak after the manner of men, he would also point to the Lord Jesus Christ, and say this is my beloved Son, in whom I am well pleased hear ye him. Thus you see, poor Moses, that there is none in heaven, or earth, that can help you, but Christ; he alone has power to save, and to give life.—God the eternal Father appointed him, chose him, authorized and fully commissioned him to save sinners. He came down from heaven into this lower world, and became as one of us, and stood in our room. He was the second Adam. And as God demanded correct obedience of the first Adam; the second fulfil'd it; and as the first sinned and incurred the wrath and anger of God, the second endured it; he suffered in our room. As he became sin for us, he was a man of sorrows, and acquainted with grief; all our stripes were laid upon him; yea, he was finally condemned, because we were under condemnation; and at last was executed and put to death, for our sins; was lifted up between the heavens and the earth, and was crucified on the accursed tree; his blessed hands and feet were fastened there; there he died a shameful and ignominious death; There he finished the great work of our redemption: There his hearts blood was shed for our cleansing: There he fully satisfied the divine justice of God, for penitent, believing sinners, though they have been the chief of sinners.—O Moses! this is good news to you in this last day of your life; here is a crucified Saviour at hand for your sins; his blessed hands are outstretched, all in a gore of blood for you. This is the only Saviour, an Almighty Saviour, just such as you stand in infinite and perishing need of. O, poor Moses! hear the dying prayer of a gracious Saviour on the accursed tree. Father forgive them for they know not what they do. This was a prayer for his enemies and murderers; and it is for you, if you will now only repent and believe in him. O, why will you die eternally, poor Moses, since Christ has died for sinners? Why will you go to hell from beneath a bleeding Saviour as it were? This is the day of your execution, yet it is the accepted time, it is the day of salvation if you will now believe in the Lord Jesus Christ. Must Christ follow you into the prison by his servants and there intreat you to accept of eternal life, and will you refuse it? Must he follow you even to the gallows, and there beseech of you to accept of him, and will you refuse him? Shall he be crucified hard by your gallows, as it were, and will you regard him not? O poor Moses, now believe on the Lord Jesus Christ with all your heart, and thou shalt be saved eternally. Come just as you are, with all your sins and abominations, with all your filthiness, with all your blood-guiltiness, with all your condemnation, and lay hold of the hope set before you this day. This is the last day of salvation with your soul; you will be beyond the bounds of mercy in a few minutes more. O what a joyful day would it be if you would now openly believe in and receive the Lord Jesus Christ; it would be the beginning of heavenly days with your poor soul; instead of a melancholy day, it would be a wedding day to your soul: It would cause the very angels in heaven to rejoice, and the saints on earth to be glad; it would cause the angels to come down from the realms above, and wait hovering about your gallows, ready to convey your soul to the heavenly mansions. There to taste the possession of eternal glory and happiness, and join the heavenly choirs in singing the songs of Moses and the Lamb: There to set down forever with Abraham, Isaac and Jacob in the kingdom of God's glory; and your shame and guilt shall be forever banished from the place, and all sorrow and fear forever fly away, and tears be wiped from your face; and there shall you forever admire the astonishing and amazing and infinite mercy of God in Christ Jesus, in pardoning such a monstrous sinner as you have been; there you will claim the highest note of praise, for the riches of free grace in Christ Jesus. But if you will not except[22] of a Saviour so freely offered to you in this last day of your life, you must this

---

22. except: accept.

very day bid a farewell to God the Father Son and holy Ghost, to heaven and all the saints and angels that are there; and you must bid all the saints in this lower world an eternal farewell, and even the whole world. And so I must leave you in the hands of God; and I must turn to the whole auditory.

Sirs.—We may plainly see, from what we have heard, and from the miserable object before us, into what a doleful condition sin has brought mankind, even into a state of death and misery. We are by nature as certainly under the sentence of death from God, as this miserable man is by the just determination of man; for we are all dying creatures, and we are, or ought to be sensible of it; and this is the dreadful fruit of sin. O let us then fly from all appearance of sin; let us fight against it with all our might; let us repent and turn to God, and believe on the Lord Jesus Christ, that we may live for ever: Let us all prepare for death, for we know not how soon, nor how suddenly we may be called out of the world.

Permit me in particular, reverend gentlemen and fathers in Israel, to speak a few words to you, though I am very sensible that I need to be taught the first principles of the oracles of God, by the least of you. But since the Providence of God has so ordered it, that I must speak here on this occasion, I beg that you would not be offended nor be angry with me.

God has raised you up from among your brethren, and has qualified and authorized you to do his great work; and you are the servants of the Most High God, and ministers of the Lord Jesus Christ; you are Christ's ambassadors; you are called shepherds, watchmen overseers, or bishops, and you are rulers of the temples of God, or of the assemblies of God's people; you are God's angels, and as such you have nothing to do but to wait on God, and to do the work the Lord Jesus Christ your blessed Lord and Master has set you about, not fearing the face of any man, nor seeking to please men, but your Master. You are to declare the whole counsel of God, and to give a portion to every soul in due season; as a physician gives a portion to his patients, according to their diseases, so you are to give a portion to every soul in due season according to their spiritual maladies: Whether it be agreeable or not agreeable to them, you must give it to them; whether they will love you or hate you for it, you must do your work. Your work is to encounter sin and satan; this was the very end of the coming of Christ into the world, and the end of his death and sufferings; it was to make an end of sin and to destroy the works of the devil. And this is your work still, you are to fight the battles of the Lord. Therefore combine together, and be as terrible as an army with banners; attack this monster sin in all its shapes and windings, and lift up your voices as trumpets and not spare, call aloud, call your people to arms against this common enemy of mankind, that sin may not be their ruin. Call upon all orders ranks and degrees of people, to rise up against sin and satan. Arm your selves with fervent prayer continually, this is a terrible weapon against the kingdom of satan. And preach the death and sufferings, and the resurrection of Jesus Christ; for nothing is so destructive to the kingdom of the devil as this is. But what need I speak any more! Let us all attend, and hear the great Apostle of the Gentiles speak unto us in Eph. 6 ch. from the tenth verse and onward. Finally my bretheren, be strong in the Lord, and in the power of his might; put on the whole armour of God, that ye may be able to stand against the wiles of the devil. For we wrestle not against flesh and blood, but against principalities, against powers, against the rulers of darkness of this world, against spiritual wickedness in high places. Wherefore take unto you the whole armour of God, that ye may be able to stand in the evil day, and having done all, to stand. Stand therefore, having your loins girt about with truth, and having on the breast-plate of righteousness; And your feet shod with the preparation of the gospel of peace: Above all, taking the shield of faith, wherewith ye shall be able to quench all the fiery darts of the wicked: And take the helmet of salvation, and the sword of the spirit, which is the word of God: Praying always with all prayer and supplication in the spirit, and watching therunto with all perservance, and supplication for all saints.

I shall now address myself to the Indians, my brethren and kindred according to the flesh.

My poor Kindred,

You see the woful consequences of sin, by seeing this our poor miserable countryman now before us, who is to die this day for his sins and great wickedness. And it was the sin of drunkenness that has brought this destruction and untimely death upon him. There is a dreadful wo denounced from the Almighty against drunkards; and it is this sin, this abominable, this beastly and accursed sin of drunkenness, that has stript us of every desirable comfort in this life; by this we are poor miserable and wretched; by this sin we have no name nor credit in the world among polite nations; for this sin we are despised in the world, and it is all right and just, for we despise ourselves more; and if we don't regard ourselves, who will regard us? And it is for our sins and especially for that accursed, that most devilish sin of drunkenness that we suffer every day. For the love of strong drink we spend all that we have, and every thing we can get. By this sin we can't have comfortable houses, nor any thing comfortable in our houses; neither food nor raiment, nor decent utensils. We are obliged to put up with any sort of shelter just to screen us from the severity of the weather, and we go about with very mean, ragged and dirty clothes, almost naked. And we are half-starved, for the most of the time oblidged to pick up any thing to eat. And our poor children are suffering every day for want of the necessaries of life; they are very often crying for want of food, and we have nothing to give them; and in the cold weather they are shivering and crying, being pinched with cold. All this for the love of strong drink. And this is not all the misery and evil we bring on ourselves in this world; but when we are intoxicated with strong drink we drown our rational powers, by which we are distinguished from the brutal creation; we unman ourselves, and bring ourselves not only level with the beasts of the field, but seven degrees beneath them; yea we bring ourselves level with the devils; I don't know but we make ourselves worse than devils, for I never heard of drunken devils.

My poor kindred, do consider what a dreadful abominable sin drunkenness is. God made us men, and we chuse to be beasts and devils, God made us rational creatures, and we chuse to be fools. Do consider further, and behold a drunkard and see how he looks when he has drowned his reason; how deformed and shameful does he appear? He disfigures every part of him, both soul and body, which was made after the Image of God. He appears with awful deformity, and his whole visage is disfigured; if he attempts to speak he cannot bring out his words distinct, so as to be understood; if he walks he reels and staggers to and fro, and tumbles down. And see how he behaves, he is now laughing, and then he is crying, he is singing, and the next minute he is mourning, and is all love with every one, and anon he is raging and for fighting, and killing all before him, even the nearest and dearest relations and friends: Yea, nothing it too bad for a drunken man to do. He will do that which he would not do for the world, in his right mind; he may lie with his own sister or daughter as Lot did.

Further, when a person is drunk, he is just good for nothing in the world; he is of no service to himself, to his family, to his neighbours, or his country; and how much more unfit is he to serve God: Yet we are just fit for the service of the devil.

Again, a man in drunkenness is in all manner of dangers, he may be killed by his fellow-men, by wild beasts, and tame beasts; he may fall into the fire, into the water, or into a ditch; or he may fall down as he walks along, and break his bones or his neck; and he may cut himself with edge-tools. Further if he has any money or any thing valuable, he may lose it all, or may be robbed, or he may make a foolish bargain and be cheated out of all he has.

I believe you know the truth of what I have just now said, many of you by sad experience; yet you will go on still in your drunkenness. Though you have been cheated over and over again, and you have lost your substance by drunkenness, yet you will venture to go on in this most destructive sin. O fools, when will ye be wise?—We all know the truth of what I have been saying, by what we have seen and heard of drunken deaths. How many have been drowned in our rivers, and how many frozen to death in the winter season! yet drunkards go on without fear and consideration: Alas, alas! What will become of all such drunkards? Without doubt they must all go to hell, except they truly repent and turn to God. Drunkeness is so common amongst us, that even our young men, (and what is still more shocking) *young women* are not ashamed to get drunk. Our young men will get drunk as soon as they will eat when they are hungry.—It is generally esteemed among men more abominable for a woman to be drunk than a man; and yet there is nothing more common amongst us than female drunkards. Women ought to be more modest than men; the holy scriptures recommend modesty to women in particular;—But drunken women have no modesty at all. It is more intolerable for a woman to get drunk, if we consider further, that she is in great danger of falling into the hands of the sons of Belial, or wicked men and being shamefully treated by them.

And here I cannot but observe, we find in sacred writ, a wo denounced against men who put their bottles to their neighbours mouth to make them drunk, that they may see their nakedness: And no doubt there are such devilish men now in our days, as there were in the days of old.

And to conclude, Consider my poor kindred, you that are drunkards, into what a miserable condition you have brought yourselves. There is a dreadful wo thundering against you every day, and the Lord says, That drunkards shall not inherit the kingdom of heaven.

And now let me exhort you all to break off from your drunkenness, by a gospel repentance, and believe on the Lord Jesus and you shall be saved. Take warning by this doleful sight before us, and by all the dreadful judgments that have befallen poor drunkards. O let us all reform our lives, and live as becomes dying creatures, in time to come. Let us be persuaded that we are accountable creatures of God, and we must be called to an account in a few days. You that have been careless all your days, now awake to righteousness, and be concerned for your poor never-dying souls. Fight against all sins, and especially the sin that easily besets you, and behave in time to come as becomes rational creatures; and above all things receive and believe on the Lord Jesus Christ, and you shall have eternal life; and when you come to die, your souls will be received into heaven, there to be with the Lord Jesus in eternal happiness, with all the saints in glory: Which God of his infinite mercy grant, through Jesus Christ our Lord.—AMEN.

8. Elizabeth Ashbridge

from *Some Account of the Fore-Part of the Life of Elizabeth Ashbridge*
1774

> *Elizabeth Ashbridge (1713–55) was born in Cheshire, England, ran away from home to marry at the age of fourteen, was widowed five months later, and three years after that arrived in New York as an indentured servant. Three years later she bought out the rest of her term and remarried. In the course of this second marriage, she became a Quaker, much to her husband's chagrin. Widowed a second time, she married a third and settled in a Quaker community in Goshen, Pennsylvania, until again setting off on a visit to England, where she died aged forty-two. Her account of her life accentuates the picaresque, and although she writes ostensibly from the perspective of her spiritual conversion, her piety does not quite repress a certain pride in having surmounted so many dramatic tribulations.*
>
> *The biography just sketched suggests one good reason for her pride: as a woman, however committed she might be to a Franklinesque ambition, she could never have sufficient control of her life to pursue directly any program of her own. In her struggle to achieve a Quaker life, Ashbridge describes confronting, along with her own weaknesses, the strong opposition of her husband as well as of a world that denies women especially what she precisely seeks: the power to work out her own salvation, to speak for herself. Yet Elizabeth Ashbridge became a well-known preacher, speaking not only for herself but for others. The general scarcity of texts by women in this collection is a context to bear in mind when reading Ashbridge's Account, whose existence is itself unusually significant.*

My life being attended with many uncommon occurrences, some of which I brought upon myself, which I believe were for my good, I have therefore thought proper to make some remarks on the dealings of Divine Goodness with me. . . . I most earnestly desire that whosoever reads the following lines may take warning and shun the evils that through the deceitfulness of Satan I have been drawn into. . . .

In nine weeks from the time I left Dublin we arrived at New York, viz. on the 15 of the 7th month, 1732. Now those to whom I had been instrumental to preserve life proved treacherous to me.—I was a stranger in a strange land.

The captain got an indenture and demanded of me to sign it, at the same time threatening me if I refused it. I told him I could find means to satisfy him for my passage without being bound, but he told me I might take my choice: either to sign that or have the other in force which I signed in Ireland. I therefore in a fright signed the latter, and though there was no magistrate present it proved sufficient to make me a servant for four years. In two weeks time I was sold, and were it possible to convey in characters a scene of the sufferings of my servitude, it would affect the most stony heart with pity for a young creature who had been so tenderly brought up. For though my father had no great estate yet he lived well, and I had been used to little but the school, though it had been better for me now if I had been brought up to greater hardships.

For a while I was pretty well used, but in a little time the scale turned, which was occasioned by a difference between my master and me, wherein I was innocent; but from that time he set himself against me, and was so inhuman that he would not suffer me to have clothes to be decent in, making me to go barefoot in the snowy weather, and to be employed in the meanest drudgery, wherein I suffered the utmost hardships that my body was able to bear, and which the rest of my troubles had like to have been my ruin to all eternity, had not Almighty God interposed. My master would seem to be a religious man, often taking the Sacrament, so called, and used to pray every night in his family, except when his prayer book was lost, for he never prayed without it as I remember, but the difference was of such a kind, that I was sick of his religion. For though I had but little myself, I had an idea what sort of people they should be who professed much. But at length the enemy[23] by his insinuations made me believe there was no such a thing as religion, and that the convictions I had felt in my youth were nothing more than the prejudice of education, which convictions were at times so strong that I have gone and fallen on the ground, crying for mercy. But now I began to be hardened and for some months don't remember I felt any such thing, so that I was ready to conclude there was no God, and that all was priestcraft, I having a different opinion of those sort of men than what I had in my youth. And what corroborated with my atheistical opinion was this: my master's house used to be a place of great resort for the clergy, which gave me an opportunity of making my remarks on them; for sometimes those that came out of the country used to lodge there, and their evening diversions often was playing at cards and singing, and in a few moments after, praying and singing psalms to Almighty God. But I thought, if there be a God, he must be a pure Being and will not hear the prayers of polluted lips; for he hath in an abundant manner shown mercy to me, as will be shown in the sequel, which did not suffer me to doubt in this manner any longer. For when my feet were near the bottomless pit, he plucked me back.

I had to one woman and no other discovered the occasion of this difference, and the nature of it, which two years before had happened betwixt my master and me, and by that means he heard of it, and though he knew it to be true, he sent for the town

23. the enemy: Satan.

whipper to correct me for it, and upon his appearing, I was called in and ordered to strip, without asking whether I deserved it or not, at which my heart was ready to burst, for I could as freely have given up my life as suffer such ignominy. And I then said, If there be a God, be graciously pleased to look down on one of the most unhappy creatures, and plead my cause, for thou knowest what I have said is the truth, and had it not been from a principle more noble than he was capable of, I would have told it before his wife. Then fixing my eyes on the barbarous man, in a flood of tears, I said to him, "Sir, if you have no pity on me, yet for my father's sake spare me from this shame" (for before this he had heard of my father several ways), "and if you think I deserve such punishment, do it yourself." He then took a turn about the room and bid the whipper go about his business, so I came off without a blow, which I thought something remarkable.

I now began to think my credit was gone, for they said several things of me which (I bless God) were not true; and here I suffered so much cruelty that I knew not how to bear it, and the enemy immediately came in and put me in a way how to get rid of it all, by tempting me to end my miserable life, which I joined with, and for that purpose went into the garret in order to hang myself, at which time I was convinced there was a God, for as my feet entered the place, horror seized me to that degree that I trembled much, and while I stood in amazement, it seemed as though I heard a voice say, "There is a hell beyond the grave," at which I was greatly astonished and convinced of an Almighty Power, to whom I prayed, saying, "God be merciful and enable me to bear whatsoever thou of thy providence shall bring or suffer to come upon me for my disobedience." I then went downstairs, but let none know what I had been about.

Soon after this I had a dream, and though some may ridicule dreams, yet this seems very significant to me; therefore I shall mention it.—I thought somebody knocked at the door, which when I had opened there stood a grave woman, holding in her right hand an oil lamp burning, who with a solid countenance fixed her eyes on me and said, "I am sent to tell thee, that if thou wilt return to the Lord thy God, he will have mercy on thee, and thy lamp shall not be put out in obscure darkness"; upon which the light flamed from the lamp in a very radiant manner and the vision left me. But oh! alas, I did not give up to join with the heavenly vision, as I think I may call it; for, after all this, I was near being caught in another snare, which if I had, would probably have been my ruin, from which I was also preferred.[24]

I was accounted a fine singer and dancer, in which I took great delight, and once falling in company with some of the stage players, then at New York, they took a great fancy to me, as they said, and persuaded me to become an actress amongst them, and they would find means to get me from my servitude, and that I should live like a lady. The proposal took with me, and I used much pains to qualify myself for the stage, by reading plays, even when I should have slept; but after all this I found a stop in my mind, when I came to consider what my father would think when he heard of it, who had not only forgiven my disobedience in marriage, but had sent for me home, though my proud heart would not suffer me to return in so mean a condition I was then in, but rather chose bondage.

24. preferred: saved.

When I had served three years, I bought the remainder of my time, and got a genteel maintenance by my needle; but alas! I was not sufficiently punished by my former servitude but got into another, and that for life; for a few months after this, I married a young man, who fell in love with me for my dancing—-a poor motive for a man to choose a wife, or a woman to choose a husband.

As to my part I fell in love for nothing I saw in him, and it seems unaccountable that I, who had refused several offers, both in this country and in Ireland, should at last marry a man I had no value for.

In a week after we were married, my husband, who was a schoolmaster, removed from New York, and took me along with him to New England, and settled at a place called Westerley, in Rhode Island government. With respect to religion, he was much like myself, without any; for when he was in drink he would use the worst of oaths. I don't mention this to expose my husband, but to show the effect it had upon me, for I now saw myself ruined, as I thought, being joined to a man I had no love for, and who was a pattern of no good to me. I therefore began to think we were like two joining hands and going to destruction, which made me conclude that if I was not forsaken of God, to alter my course of life. But to love the Divine Being, and not to love my husband, I saw was an inconfidency,[25] and seemed impossible; therefore I requested, with tears, that my affections might increase towards my husband, and I can say in truth that my love was sincere to him. I now resolved to do my duty towards God, and expecting that I must come to the knowledge of it by reading the Scriptures, I read them with a strong resolution of following their directions; but the more I read the more uneasy I grew, especially about baptism, for although I had reason to believe I was sprinkled in my infancy, because at the age of fourteen I passed under the bishop's hands for confirmation, as it is called, yet I could not find any precedent for that practice, and upon reading where it is said, he that believes and is baptized, etc., I observed that belief went before baptism, which I was not capable of when I was sprinkled, at which I grew very uneasy, and living in a neighborhood that were mostly Seventh Day Baptists, I conversed with them, and at length thinking it to be really my duty, I was baptized by one of their teachers, but did not join strictly with them, though I began to think the seventh-day the true sabbath, and for some time kept it as such. My husband did not yet oppose me, for he saw I grew more affectionate to him,

25. inconfidency: unfaithfulness.

but I did not yet leave off singing and dancing so much, but I could divert him whenever he desired it.

Soon after this my husband and I concluded to go for England, and for that purpose went to Boston, where we found a ship bound for Liverpool, and agreed for our passage, expecting to sail in two weeks. But my time was not yet come, for there came one called a gentleman, who hired the ship to carry him and his attendants to Philadelphia and to take no other passengers. There being no other ship near sailing, we for that time gave it over.

We stayed several weeks at Boston, and I remained still dissatisfied as to religion, though I had reformed my conduct so as to be accounted by those that knew me a sober woman. But that was not sufficient; for even then I expected to find the sweets of such a change, and though several thought me religious, I dared not to think myself so, and what to do to be so, I seemed still an utter stranger to. I used to converse with people of all societies, as opportunity offered, and, like many others, had got a deal of head knowledge, and several societies thought me of their opinion, but I joined strictly with none, resolving never to leave searching till I found the TRUTH. This was in the 22d year of my age.

While we were at Boston, I went one day to the Quakers' meeting, not expecting to find what I wanted, but from a motive of curiosity. At this meeting there was a woman spoke, at which I was a little surprised, for I had never heard one before. I looked on her with pity for her ignorance, and in contempt of her practice said to myself, "I am sure you're a fool, for if ever I should turn Quaker, which will never be, I could not be a preacher." In these and such like thoughts I sat while she was speaking. After she had done, there stood up a man, which I could better bear; he spoke well, as I thought, from good Joshua's resolutions, viz., "As for me and my house we will serve the Lord." After a time of silence he went to prayer, which was attended with something so awful and affecting that I was reduced to tears, yet a stranger to the cause.

Soon after this we left Boston, for my husband was given to ramble, which was very disagreeable to me; but I must submit. We went to Rhode Island, where he hired a place to keep a school. This place was mostly inhabited with Presbyterians, where I soon got acquainted with some of the most religious amongst them; for though I was poor, I was favored with respect amongst people of the best credit and had frequent discourses with them, but the more I was acquainted with their principles, the worse I liked them, so that I remained dissatisfied, and the old enemy of my happiness, knowing I was resolved to abandon him, assaulted me afresh and laid a bait with which I had like to have been caught. For one day having been abroad, at my return home, I found the people, at whose house we had taken a room, had left some flax in an apartment through which I went to my own, at sight of which I was tempted to steal some to make some thread; and I went and took a small bunch in my hand, at which I was smote with remorse and immediately laid it down, saying, "Lord help me from such a vile act as this." But the twisting serpent did not leave me yet, his assaults were so strong and prevalent that I took it into my room; when I came there horror seized me, and bursting into tears, I cried, "O God of mercy; enable me to resist this temptation," which he of his mercy did, and gave me power to say, "I will regard thy convictions." So I carried it back, and returning to my room, I was so filled with thanksgiving to God, and rapt into such a frame as I have not words to express, neither can any guess but those who have resisted temptation and tasted of the same sweet peace by experience. . . .

I loved to go to meetings, but did not like to be seen to go on weekdays, and therefore to shun it used to go from my school through the woods to them. But notwithstanding all my care, the neighbors that were not Friends soon began to revile, calling me Quaker, saying they supposed I intended to be a fool and turn preacher. I then received the same censure that I, a little above a year before, had passed on one of the handmaids of the Lord at Boston; and so weak was I, alas, I could not bear the reproach, and in order to change their opinions got in to greater excess in apparel than I had freedom to wear for some time before I became acquainted with Friends. In this condition I continued till my husband came, and then began the trial of my faith. Before he reached me, he heard I was turned Quaker, at which he stamped, saying, "I had rather have heard she had been dead, well as I love her, for if so all my comfort is gone." He then came to me, and had not seen me for four months; I got up and met him, saying, "My dear, I am glad to see thee," at which he fell in a great passion, and said, "The devil THEE thee, don't THEE me." I used all the mild means I could to pacify him, and at length got him fit to go and speak to my relations; but he was alarmed, and as soon as he got alone he said, "So I see your Quaker relations have made you one." I told him they had not, which was true, nor had I ever told them how it was with me. But he would have it that I was one, and therefore should not stay amongst them, and having found a place to his mind, hired it, and came directly back to fetch me, and in one afternoon walked near thirty miles to keep me from meeting, the next day being the first-day, and on the morrow took me to the aforesaid place, hired lodgings at a Church-man's house, who was one of the wardens and a bitter enemy to Friends, and would tell me a great deal of ridiculous stuff. But my judgment was too clearly convinced to believe. I still did not appear like a Friend, but they all believed I was one. When my husband and him used to be making their diversions and revilings, I used to sit in silence; but now and then an involuntary sigh would break from me, at which he would say to my husband, "There, did not I tell you your wife was a Quaker, and she will be a preacher soon," upon which my husband once in a great rage came up to me, and striking his hand over me said, "You had better be hanged on that day." I then, Peter like, in a panic denied my being a Quaker, at which great horror seized upon me, and continued for near three months, so that I again feared that by denying the Lord who bought me the heavens were shut against me; for great darkness surrounded me, and I was again plunged in despair.

I used to walk much alone in the woods, where no eye saw, or ear heard me, and there lamented my miserable condition, and have often gone from morning till night without breaking my fast, with which I was brought so low that my life was a burden to me. The devil seemed to vaunt [that although] the sins [of] my youth were forgiven, yet now he was sure of me, for that I had committed the unpardonable sin, and hell would inevitably be my portion, and my torments would be greater than if I had hanged myself at the first.

In this doleful condition I had now to bewail my misery, and even in the night, when I could not sleep, under the painful distress of my mind. And if my husband perceived me weeping he used to revile me for it. At last, when he and his friends thought themselves too weak to overset me, though I feared it was already done, he went to the priest at Chester to advise what to do with me. This man knew I was a member of the Church, for I had shown him my certificate. His advice was to take me out of Pennsylvania and find some place where there was no Quakers, and there my opinion would wear off. To this my husband agreed, saying he did not care where he went, if he could but restore me to that liveliness of temper I was naturally of, and to that Church of which I was a member. I, on my part, had no spirit to oppose their proposals, neither much cared where I was; for I seemed to have nothing to hope for, but daily expected to be made a spectacle of Divine Wrath, and I was possessed it would be by thunder.

The time of removal came, and I was not suffered to bid my relations farewell. My husband was poor and kept no horse, so I must travel on foot. We came to Wilmington, fifteen miles thence to Philadelphia, by water; here he took me to a tavern, where I soon became a spectacle and discourse of the company. My husband told them his wife was turned Quaker, and that he designed, if possible, to find out some place where there was none. Oh, thought I, I was once in condition of deserving that name, but now it was over with me. Oh, that I might, from a true hope, once more have an opportunity to confess to the TRUTH, though sure of all manner of cruelties, yet I would not regard it. These were my concerns while he was entertaining the company with my story, in which he told them that I had been a good dancer, but now he could neither get me to dance nor sing; upon which one of the company starts up, saying, "I'll go fetch my fiddle and we'll have a dance," at which my husband was pleased. The fiddle came, the sight of which put me in a sad condition, for fear, if I refused, my husband would be in a great passion. However I took up this resolution not to comply, whatever might be the consequence. He came to me and took me by the hand, saying, "Come, my dear, shake off that gloom, let's have a civil dance; you would now and then, when you were a good Church-woman and that is better than a stiff Quaker." I, trembling, desired to be excused. But he insisted on it, and knowing his temper to be exceeding choleric, I durst not say much, but would not consent. He then pulled me round the room till tears affected my eyes, at sight of which the musician stopped, and said, "I'll play no more, let your wife alone," of which I was glad. There was also a man in company who came from Freehold, in West Jersey, who said, "I see your wife is a Quaker, but if you'll take my advice, you need not go so far (for my husband designed to go to Staten Island); come and live amongst us and we'll soon cure her from her Quakerism, and we want both a school-master and mistress." To which he agreed, and a happy turn it was for me, as will be seen by and by, and the wonderful turn of Providence, who had not yet abandoned me, but raised a glimmering hope and afforded the answer of peace in refusing to dance, for which I was more rejoiced than if I were made a mistress of much riches; and in floods of tears, said, "Lord, I dread to ask, and yet without thy gracious pardon I am miserable; I therefore fall down before thy throne, imploring mercy at thy hand. O Lord, once more I beseech thee try my obedience, and then whatsoever thou commands, I will obey, and not fear to confess thee before men." Thus was my soul engaged before God in sincerity, and he of his tender mercy heard my cries, and in me has shown that he delights not in the death of a sinner, for he again set my soul at liberty and I could praise him. . . .

Now the unwearied adversary[26] found out another scheme, and with it assaulted me so strong that I thought all I had gone through was happiness, viz. the reformation of my husband, which also I had too much reason to doubt, for it fell out according to my fears, and he grew worse here, and took to drinking, so that it seemed as though my life was to be a continual scene of sorrow; and most earnestly I prayed to Almighty God, to endue me with patience to bear my afflictions and submit to his providence, which I can say in truth I did without murmuring, or ever uttering an unsavory expression, to the best of my knowledge, except once when my husband coming home a little in drink, in which frame he was very fractious, and finding me at work by a candle, came to me, put it out, and fetching me a box on the ear said, "You don't earn your light," which unkind usage——for he had not struck me of two years before—went hard with me, and I uttered these rash expressions, "Thou art a vile man," and was a little angry, but soon recovered and was sorry for it. He struck me again, which I received without so much as a word in return, and [he] went on in a distracted manner, uttering several rash expressions that bespoke despair, as that he now believed he was predestined to damnation, and he did not care how soon God would strike him dead and the like. I durst say but little, but at length I broke out in these words, "Lord look down on my afflictions, and deliver me by some means or other." I was answered I should soon be, and so I was, but in such a manner as I verily believed it would have killed me.

In a little time he went to Burlington, where he got in drink and enlisted for a common soldier to go to Cuba, anno dom. 1740. I had drank many bitter cups, but this seemed to exceed them all; for indeed my very senses seemed shaken. I now a thousand times blamed myself for making such an undevised request, fearing I had displeased God by it, and though he had granted it, it was in displeasure and suffered to be in this manner to punish me. But I can say I never desired his death more than my own, nay not so much. I have since had cause to believe his mind was benefited by the undertaking, which hope makes up for all I have suffered from him, being informed that he did in the army what he could not do at home, viz. suffer for the testimony of TRUTH. When they came to an engagement, he refused to fight, for which he was whipped and brought before the general, who asked him why he enlisted, if he would not fight. "I did it," said he, "in a drunken frolic, when the devil had the better of me, but my judgment is convinced that I ought not, neither will I, whatever I suffer. I have but one life and you may take that if you please, but I'll never take up arms." They used him with much cruelty to make him yield, but could not, by means whereof he was so disabled that the general sent him to the hospital at Chelsea, near London, where in nine months he died, and I hope made a good end, for which I prayed both night and day, till I heard of his death.

---

26. unwearied adversary: Satan.

Thus I thought it my duty to say what I could in his favor, as I have been obliged to say so much of his hard usage to me, all which I hope did me good, and although he was so bad yet had several good properties, and I never thought him the worst of men. He was one I loved, and had he let religion have its perfect work, I should have thought myself happy in the lowest state of life; and I have cause to bless God, who enabled me in the station of a wife to do my duty, and now a widow, to submit to his will, always believing everything he doth to be right. May he in all stations of life so preserve me by the arm of Divine Power that I may never forget his tender mercies to me, the remembrance whereof doth often bow down my soul in humility before his throne, saying, Lord, what was I, that thou should'st have revealed to my soul the knowledge of the TRUTH, and done so much for me, who deserved thy displeasure rather. But in me thou hast shown thy long-suffering and tender mercy. May Thou, O God, be glorified, and I abased, for it is thy own works that praise thee, and, of a truth, to the humble soul makest everything sweet.

9. Benjamin Franklin

two revisions of Job

Legendary as a man of the world, Benjamin Franklin (1706–90) was a child of Puritan Boston. Apprenticed to his printer brother, Franklin ran away to Philadelphia, where he became established as a printer and, eventually, local leader. By 1748 he was able to retire from the printing house. The ultimate creole intellectual, Franklin left in 1757 for what turned out to be nearly twenty years in London as an agent for Pennsylvania and other colonies. He returned just before the Continental Congress, which then sent him as emissary to France during the Revolution. Not until 1785 did he settle again in Philadelphia, just in time for the Constitutional Convention. A true polymath of the Enlightenment style, he distinguished himself on both sides of the Atlantic by researches in natural science as well as politics and literature; samples of his work will be found in every remaining chapter of this anthology.

While still a teenager in Boston, as he tells us in the Autobiography, *he was converted to deism by some Christian polemics that, he thought, quoted stronger arguments for deism than they could muster against it. While in London in 1725, he wrote a pamphlet called* Dissertation on Liberty and Necessity, Pleasure and Pain; *from its deistic stance it touches on many of the key issues of Edwards's theology. Another deistic manuscript from 1728 anticipates Paine's belief in multiple worlds. Franklin soon repudiated his youthful writings—though not their substance. In a completely typical moment he writes: "I began to suspect that this Doctrine tho' it might be true, was not very useful." For the rest of his life Franklin moved carefully in a Christian culture, but perhaps shows his distance from Christianity nowhere more than when he adopts its texts and its language. In his plan for "The Art of Virtue" in the* Autobiography, *for example, he defines humility thus: "Imitate Jesus and Socrates." Aside from the irony about humility, this gesture demonstrates that for Franklin there was no sacred text.*

Revisions of the Bible were something of a favorite pastime for Franklin, as the widely separate dates of these examples demonstrate. The first was written as filler

for his newspaper, The Pennsylvania Gazette; "The Levée" was a bagatelle
produced while Franklin was emissary to France and himself awaiting audiences at
Versailles. In it, Franklin seems to arouse sympathy for the devil. Though Franklin
does not dispute Christians in these sketches, he shows the radical paradigm shift
from the world of his childhood simply by treating the Bible as subject to history, a
text like others. Everything comes down to politics.

from the *Pennsylvania Gazette* 1734

By being too nice in the Choice of the little Pieces sent me by my Correspondents to be printed, I had almost discouraged them from writing to me any more. For the Time to come, and that my Paper may become still more generally agreeable, I have resolved not to regard my own Humour so much in what I print; and thereupon I give my Readers the two following Letters.

Mr. *Franklin*,

You gave us in your last a melancholy Account of Human Life, in the Meditation upon that Subject. The gloomy and splenetick Part of your Readers like it much; but as for me, I do not love to see the dark Side of Things; and besides, I do not think such Reflections upon Life altogether just. The World is a very good World, and if we behave our selves well, we shall doubtless do very well in it. I never thought even *Job* in the right, when he repin'd that the Days of a Man are *few* and *full of Trouble*; for certainly both these Things cannot be together just Causes of Complaint; if our Days are full of Trouble, the fewer of 'em the better. But as for the Author of the Meditation above-mention'd, besides what he says in common with *Job*, he seems to complain in several respects very weakly, and without the least shadow of Reason; in particular, That he cannot be alive now, and ten Years ago, and ten Years hence, at the same time: With very little Variation, as you shall see, his elegant Expressions will serve for a Child who laments that he cannot eat his Cake and have his Cake.

All the few days we live are full of Vanity; and our choicest Pleasures sprinkled with bitterness:

All the few Cakes we have are puffed up with Yeast; and the nicest Gingerbread is spotted with Flyshits!

The time that's past is vanish'd like a dream; and that which is to come is not yet at all:

The Cakes that we have eaten are no more to be seen; and those which are to come are not yet baked.

The present we are in stays but for a moment, and then flies away, and returns no more:

The present Mouthful is chewed but a little while, and then is swallowed down, and comes up no more.

Already we are dead to the years we have liv'd; and shall never live them over again:

Already we have digested the Cakes we have eaten, and shall never eat them over again.

But the longer we live, the shorter is our life; and in the end we become a little lump of clay.

And the more we eat, the less is the Piece remaining; and in the end the whole will become Sir-reverence!

O vain, and miserable world! how sadly true is all this story!

O vain and miserable Cake-shop! &c.

Away with all such insignificant Meditations. I am for taking *Solomon's* Advice, *eating Bread with Joy, and drinking Wine with a merry Heart.* Let us rejoice and bless God, that we are neither Oysters, Hogs, nor Dray-Horses; and not stand repining that He has not made us Angels; lest we be found unworthy of that share of Happiness He has thought fit to allow us.

I am, Yours, &c.

S. M.

SIR,

Seeing a very *melancholy* Piece in your Paper of last Week, asking your Pardon, I think we have enough of that Humour in the World already, without your Addition: I have therefore written the following few Lines in order to palliate it. And as that may be very acceptable to some of your Readers, this may to some others, if you think fit to give it a Place in your next.

I am, Yours, &c.

J. Anonymous.

Most happy are we, the sons of men, above all other creatures, who are born to behold the glorious rays of the sun, and to enjoy the pleasant fruits of the earth.

With what pleasure did our parents first receive us, first to hear us cry, then to see us smile, and afterwards to behold us growing up and thriving in the world.

By their good examples and a vertuous education, they put us in the right path to happiness, as all good parents do;

Then we, by making a right use of that share of reason with which God hath endued us, spend our days in gaining and enjoying the blessings of life, which are innumerable.

If we meet with crosses and disappointments, they are but as sowr sauce to the sweet meats we enjoy, and the one hath not a right relish without the other.

As time passes away, it carries our past pains with it, and returns no more; and the longer we live the fewer misfortunes we have to go through.

If death takes us off in the heighth of our prosperity, it takes us from the pains which may ensue.

And a great blessing attends old age, for by that we are naturally wean'd from the pleasures of youth, and a more solid pleasure takes place, The thoughts of our having so far escaped all the hazards that attend mankind, and a contemplation on all our former good actions.

And if we have done all the good we could, we have done all that we ought, and death is no terror to a good man.

And after we are far declined, with hearty praises and thanks we recommend our soul to God, the eternal Being from whom we received it.

Then comes the grave, and the sweet sleep of death, pleasant as a bed to a weary traveller after a long journey.

The Levée
1779

In the first chapter of Job we have an account of a transaction said to have arisen in the court, or at the *levée*, of the best of all possible princes, or of governments by a single person, viz. that of God himself.

At this *levée*, in which the sons of God were assembled, Satan also appeared.

It is probable the writer of that ancient book took his idea of this *levée* from those of the eastern monarchs of the age he lived in.

It is to this day usual at the *levées* of princes, to have persons assembled who are enemies to each other, who seek to obtain favor by whispering calumny and detraction, and thereby ruining those that distinguish themselves by their virtue and merit. And kings frequently ask a familiar question or two, of every one in the circle, merely to show their benignity. These circumstances are particularly exemplified in this relation.

If a modern king, for instance, finds a person in the circle who has not lately been there, he naturally asks him how he has passed his time since he last had the pleasure of seeing him? the gentleman perhaps replies that he has been in the country to view his estates, and visit some friends. Thus Satan being asked whence he cometh? answers, "From going to and fro in the earth, and walking up and down in it." And being further asked, whether he had considered the uprightness and fidelity of the prince's servant Job, he immediately displays all the malignance of the designing courtier, by answering with another question: "Doth Job serve God for naught? Hast thou not given him immense wealth, and protected him in the possession of it? Deprive him of that, and he will curse thee to thy face." In modern phrase, Take away his places[27] and his pensions, and your Majesty will soon find him in the opposition.

This whisper against Job had its effect. He was delivered into the power of his adversary, who deprived him of his fortune, destroyed his family, and completely ruined him.

The book of Job is called by divines a sacred poem, and, with the rest of the Holy Scriptures, is understood to be written for our instruction.

What then is the instruction to be gathered from this supposed transaction?

Trust not a single person with the government of your state. For if the Deity himself, being the monarch may for a time give way to calumny, and suffer it to operate the destruction of the best of subjects; what mischief may you not expect from such power in a mere man, though the best of men, from whom the truth is often industriously hidden, and to whom falsehood is often presented in its place, by artful, interested, and malicious courtiers?

And be cautious in trusting him even with limited powers, lest sooner or later he sap and destroy those limits, and render himself absolute.

For by the disposal of places, he attaches to himself all the placeholders, with their

27. places: government positions.

numerous connexions, and also all the expecters and hopers of places, which will form a strong party in promoting his views. By various political engagements for the interest of neighbouring states or princes, he procures their aid in establishing his own personal power. So that, through the hopes of emolument in one part of his subjects, and the fear of his resentment in the other, all opposition falls before him.

10. Benjamin Franklin

letter to Ezra Stiles
1790

Ezra Stiles, grandson of Edward Taylor, was president of Yale College, bastion of Congregational theology. He had written Franklin on January 28, asking his views "concerning Jesus of Nazareth." The "Gov'r Yale" of whom Franklin speaks is Elihu Yale, the nabob and governor of the East India Company who had contributed to the college in exchange for its being named after him.

REVEREND AND DEAR SIR,

Philad^a, March 9. 1790.

I received your kind Letter of Jan'y 28, and am glad you have at length received the portrait of Gov'r Yale from his Family, and deposited it in the College Library. He was a great and good Man, and had the Merit of doing infinite Service to your Country by his Munificence to that Institution. The Honour you propose doing me by placing mine in the same Room with his, is much too great for my Deserts; but you always had a Partiality for me, and to that it must be ascribed. I am however too much obliged to Yale College, the first learned Society that took Notice of me and adorned me with its Honours, to refuse a Request that comes from it thro' so esteemed a Friend. But I do not think any one of the Portraits you mention, as in my Possession, worthy of the Place and Company you propose to place it in. You have an excellent Artist lately arrived. If he will undertake to make one for you, I shall cheerfully pay the Expense; but he must not delay setting about it, or I may slip thro' his fingers, for I am now in my eighty-fifth year, and very infirm.

I send with this a very learned Work, as it seems to me, on the antient Samaritan Coins, lately printed in Spain, and at least curious for the Beauty of the Impression. Please to accept it for your College Library. I have subscribed for the Encyclopaedia now printing here, with the Intention of presenting it to the College. I shall probably depart before the Work is finished, but shall leave Directions for its Continuance to the End. With this you will receive some of the first numbers.

You desire to know something of my Religion. It is the first time I have been questioned upon it. But I cannot take your Curiosity amiss, and shall endeavour in a few Words to gratify it. Here is my Creed. I believe in one God, Creator of the Universe.

That he governs it by his Providence. That he ought to be worshipped. That the most acceptable Service we render to him is doing good to his other Children. That the soul of Man is immortal, and will be treated with Justice in another Life respecting its Conduct in this. These I take to be the fundamental Principles of all sound Religion, and I regard them as you do in whatever Sect I meet with them.

As to Jesus of Nazareth, my Opinion of whom you particularly desire, I think the System of Morals and his Religion, as he left them to us, the best the World ever saw or is likely to see; but I apprehend it has received various corrupting Changes, and I have, with most of the present Dissenters in England, some Doubts as to his Divinity; tho' it is a question I do not dogmatize upon, having never studied it, and think it needless to busy myself with it now, when I expect soon an Opportunity of knowing the Truth with less Trouble. I see no harm, however, in its being believed, if that Belief has the good Consequence, as probably it has, of making his Doctrines more respected and better observed; especially as I do not perceive, that the Supreme takes it amiss, by distinguishing the Unbelievers in his Government of the World with any peculiar Marks of his Displeasure.

I shall only add, respecting myself, that, having experienced the Goodness of that Being in conducting me prosperously thro' a long life, I have no doubt of its Continuance in the next, though without the smallest Conceit of meriting such Goodness. My Sentiments on this Head you will see in the Copy of an old Letter enclosed, which I wrote in answer to one from a zealous Religionist, whom I had relieved in a paralytic case by electricity, and who, being afraid I should grow proud upon it, sent me his serious though rather impertinent Caution. I send you also the Copy of another Letter, which will shew something of my Disposition relating to Religion. With great and sincere Esteem and Affection, I am, Your obliged old Friend and most obedient humble Servant

P. S. Had not your College some Present of Books from the King of France? Please to let me know, if you had an Expectation given you of more, and the Nature of that Expectation? I have a Reason for the Enquiry.

I confide, that you will not expose me to Criticism and censure by publishing any part of this Communication to you. I have ever let others enjoy their religious Sentiments, without reflecting on them for those that appeared to me unsupportable and even absurd. All Sects here, and we have a great Variety, have experienced my good will in assisting them with Subscriptions for building their new Places of Worship; and, as I have never opposed any of their Doctrines, I hope to go out of the World in Peace with them all.

11. Thomas Paine

from *The Age of Reason*
1794

Like Benjamin Franklin's, but less happily, the life of Thomas Paine (1737–1809) charts the course of historic upheavals in the Atlantic world. The son of an English corsetmaker, Paine was in London lobbying Parliament on behalf of excise collectors when he met Benjamin Franklin. Franklin persuaded Paine to move to Philadelphia. Arriving in 1774, he threw himself into colonial politics, writing the famous Common Sense *in 1776, broaching for the first time in public the idea of independence. During the Revolution he wrote sixteen pamphlets under the title* The American Crisis *(see chapter 11). After the war, the state of New York presented him with a farm at New Rochelle, where Paine worked on the design of an iron bridge. In 1787 he began travelling to Europe to promote his bridge and, for good measure, world revolution on the American model. His* The Rights of Man *appeared in 1791 as a response to Edmund Burke's* Reflections on the Revolution in France. *Banished as a traitor in England, he was briefly embraced by France, until he was jailed there during the Reign of Terror (1793). The Age of Reason was written in prison. Finally released at the request of the new American ambassador, James Monroe, Paine was convinced that the previous ambassador had connived at his imprisonment. He returned to America in 1802, but Federalist hostility to the* The Rights of Man *and vengeful Christian attacks on* The Age of Reason *left him ostracized. He was accused of every sin: drunkenness, adultery, atheism. When he died at New Rochelle, burial in the local churchyard was refused.*

TO MY FELLOW CITIZENS OF THE UNITED STATES OF AMERICA.

I put the following work under your protection. It contains my opinion upon religion. You will do me the justice to remember, that I have always strenuously supported the right of every man to his own opinion, however different that opinion might be to mine. He who denies to another this right, makes a slave of himself to his present opinion, because he precludes himself the right of changing it.

The most formidable weapon against errors of every kind is reason. I have never used any other, and I trust I never shall.

Your affectionate friend and fellow-citizen,

THOMAS PAINE.

Paris, 8th Pluvôise.
Second year of the French Republic, one and indivisible.
January 27th, O.S. 1794.

[PAINE'S PROFESSION OF FAITH]

It has been my intention, for several years past, to publish my thoughts upon religion. I am well aware of the difficulties that attend the subject, and from that consideration, had reserved it to a more advanced period of life. I intended it to be the last offering I should make to my fellow-citizens of all nations, and that at a time when the purity of the motive that induced me to it could not admit of a question, even by those who might disapprove the work. The circumstance that has now taken place in France of the total abolition of the whole national order of priesthood, and of everything appertaining to compulsive systems of religion, and compulsive articles of faith, has not only precipitated my intention, but rendered a work of this kind exceedingly necessary, lest in the general wreck of superstition, of false systems of government and false theology, we lose sight of morality, of humanity and of the theology that is true.

As several of my colleagues, and others of my fellow-citizens of France, have given me the example of making their voluntary and individual profession of faith, I also will make mine; and I do this with all that sincerity and frankness with which the mind of man communicates with itself.

I believe in one God, and no more; and I hope for happiness beyond this life.

I believe in the equality of man; and I believe that religious duties consist in doing justice, loving mercy, and endeavoring to make our fellow-creatures happy.

But, lest it should be supposed that I believe many other things in addition to these, I shall, in the progress of this work, declare the things I do not believe, and my reasons for not believing them.

I do not believe in the creed professed by the Jewish Church, by the Roman Church, by the Greek Church, by the Turkish Church, by the Protestant Church, nor by any church that I know of. My own mind is my own church.

All national institutions of churches, whether Jewish, Christian or Turkish, appear to me no other than human inventions, set up to terrify and enslave mankind, and monopolize power and profit.

I do not mean by this declaration to condemn those who believe otherwise; they have the same right to their belief as I have to mine. But it is necessary to the happiness of man that he be mentally faithful to himself. Infidelity does not consist in believing, or in disbelieving; it consists in professing to believe what he does not believe.

It is impossible to calculate the moral mischief, if I may so express it, that mental lying has produced in society. When a man has so far corrupted and prostituted the chastity of his mind as to subscribe his professional belief to things he does not believe he has prepared himself for the commission of every other crime.

He takes up the trade of a priest for the sake of gain, and in order to qualify himself for that trade he begins with a perjury. Can we conceive any thing more destructive to morality than this?

Soon after I had published the pamphlet "Common Sense," in America, I saw the exceeding probability that a revolution in the system of government would be followed by a revolution in the system of religion. The adulterous connection of church and state, wherever it has taken place, whether Jewish, Christian or Turkish, has so effectually prohibited by pains and penalties every discussion upon established creeds, and upon first principles of religion, that until the system of government should be changed, those subjects could not be brought fairly and openly before the world; but that whenever this should be done, a revolution in the system of religion would follow. Human inventions and priestcraft would be detected; and man would return to the pure, unmixed and unadulterated belief of one God, and no more.

[CONCERNING MISSIONS AND REVELATIONS]

Every national church or religion has established itself by pretending some special mission from God, communicated to certain individuals. The Jews have their Moses; the Christians their Jesus Christ, their apostles and saints; and the Turks their Mahomet, as if the way to God was not open to every man alike.

Each of those churches show certain books, which they call *revelation*, or the Word of God. The Jews say that their Word of God was given by God to Moses, face to face; the Christians say that their Word of God came by divine inspiration; and the Turks say that their Word of God (the Koran) was brought by an angel from heaven. Each of those churches accuses the other of unbelief; and for my own part, I disbelieve them all.

As it is necessary to affix right ideas to words, I will, before I proceed further into the subject, offer some observations on the word *revelation*. Revelation, when applied to religion, means something communicated *immediately* from God to man.

No one will deny or dispute the power of the Almighty to make such a communication, if He pleases. But admitting, for the sake of a case, that something has been revealed to a certain person, and not revealed to any other person, it is revelation to that person only. When he tells it to a second person, a second to a third, a third to a fourth, and so on, it ceases to be a revelation to all those persons. It is revelation to the first person only, and *hearsay* to every other, and consequently they are not obliged to believe it.

It is a contradiction in terms and ideas, to call anything a revelation that comes to us at second-hand, either verbally or in writing. Revelation is necessarily limited to the first communication—after this it is only an account of something which that person says was a revelation made to him; and though he may find himself obliged to believe it, it cannot be incumbent on me to believe it in the same manner; for it was not a revelation made to *me*, and I have only his word for it that it was made to him. When Moses told the children of Israel that he received the two tables of the commandments from the hands of God, they were not obliged to believe him, because they had no other authority for it than his telling them so; and I have no other authority for it than some historian telling me so. The commandments carry no internal evidence of divinity with them; they contain some good moral precepts, such as any man qualified to be a lawgiver, or a legislator, could produce himself, without having recourse to supernatural intervention.[28]

28. It is, however, necessary to except the declaration which says that God *visits the sins of the fathers upon the children*; it is contrary to every principle of moral justice. [Paine's note.]

When I am told that the Koran was written in heaven and brought to Mahomet by an angel, the account comes too near the same kind of hearsay evidence and second-hand authority as the former. I did not see the angel myself and, therefore, I have a right not to believe it.

When also I am told that a woman called the Virgin Mary, said, or gave out, that she was with child without any cohabitation with a man, and that her betrothed husband, Joseph, said that an angel told him so, I have a right to believe them or not; such a circumstance required a much stronger evidence than their bare word for it; but we have not even this—for neither Joseph nor Mary wrote any such matter themselves; it is only reported by others that *they said so*—it is hearsay upon hearsay, and I do not choose to rest my belief upon such evidence.

It is, however, not difficult to account for the credit that was given to the story of Jesus Christ being the Son of God. He was born at a time when the heathen mythology had still some fashion and repute in the world, and that mythology had prepared the people for the belief of such a story. Almost all the extraordinary men that lived under the heathen mythology were reputed to be the sons of some of their gods. It was not a new thing, at that time, to believe a man to have been celestially begotten; the intercourse of gods with women was then a matter of familiar opinion.

Their Jupiter, according to their accounts, had cohabited with hundreds: the story, therefore, had nothing in it either new, wonderful or obscene; it was conformable to the opinions that then prevailed among the people called Gentiles, or Mythologists, and it was those people only that believed it.

The Jews, who had kept strictly to the belief of one God, and no more, and who had always rejected the heathen mythology, never credited the story.

It is curious to observe how the theory of what is called the Christian Church sprung out of the tail of the heathen mythology. A direct incorporation took place in the first instance, by making the reputed founder to be celestially begotten. The trinity of gods that then followed was no other than a reduction of the former plurality, which was about twenty or thirty thousand; the statue of Mary succeeded the statue of Diana of Ephesus; the deification of heroes changed into the canonization of saints; the Mythologists had gods for everything; the Christian Mythologists had saints for everything; the Church became as crowded with the one as the Pantheon had been with the other, and Rome was the place of both. The Christian theory is little else than the idolatry of the ancient Mythologists, accommodated to the purposes of power and revenue; and it yet remains to reason and philosophy to abolish the amphibious fraud.

[ON JESUS CHRIST]

Nothing that is here said can apply, even with the most distant disrespect, to the real character of Jesus Christ. He was a virtuous and an amiable man. The morality that he preached and practised was of the most benevolent kind; and though similar systems of morality had been preached by Confucius, and by some of the Greek philosophers, many years before; by the Quakers since; and by many good men in all ages, it has not been exceeded by any.

Jesus Christ wrote no account of himself, of his birth, parentage, or anything else; not a line of what is called the New Testament is of his own writing. The history of him is altogether the work of other people; and as to the account given of his resurrection and ascension, it was the necessary counterpart to the story of his birth. His historians, having brought him into the world in a supernatural manner, were obliged to take him out again in the same manner, or the first part of the story must have fallen to the ground.

The wretched contrivance with which this latter part is told exceeds every thing that went before it. The first part, that of the miraculous conception, was not a thing that admitted of publicity; and therefore the tellers of this part of the story had this advantage, that though they might not be credited, they could not be detected. They could not be expected to prove it, because it was not one of those things that admitted of proof, and it was impossible that the person of whom it was told could prove it himself.

But the resurrection of a dead person from the grave, and his ascension through the air, is a thing very different as to the evidence it admits of, to the invisible conception of a child in the womb. The resurrection and ascension, supposing them to have taken place, admitted of public and ocular demonstration, like that of the ascension of a balloon, or the sun at noon-day, to all Jerusalem at least.

A thing which everybody is required to believe requires that the proof and evidence of it should be equal to all, and universal; and as the public visibility of this last related act was the only evidence that could give sanction to the former part, the whole of it falls to the ground, because that evidence never was given. Instead of this, a small number of persons, not more than eight or nine, are introduced as proxies for the whole world to say they saw it, and all the rest of the world are called upon to believe it. But it appears that Thomas did not believe the resurrection, and, as they say, would not believe without having ocular and manual demonstration himself. *So neither will I*, and the reason is equally as good for me, and for every other person, as for Thomas.

It is in vain to attempt to palliate or disguise this matter. The story, so far as relates to the supernatural part, has every mark of fraud and imposition stamped upon the face of it. Who were the authors of it is as impossible for us now to know, as it is for us to be assured that the books in which the account is related were written by the persons whose names they bear; the best surviving evidence we now have respecting this affair is the Jews. They are regularly descended from the people who lived in the times this resurrection and ascension is said to have happened, and they say, *it is not true*. It has long appeared to me a strange inconsistency to cite the Jews as a proof of the truth of the story. It is just the same as if a man were to say, I will prove the truth of what I have told you by producing the people who say it is false.

That such a person as Jesus Christ existed, and that he was crucified, which was the mode of execution at that day, are historical relations strictly within the limits of probability. He preached most excellent morality and the equality of man; but he preached also against the corruptions and avarice of the Jewish priests, and this brought upon him the hatred and vengeance of the whole order of priesthood.

The accusation which those priests brought against him was that of sedition and conspiracy against the Roman government, to which the Jews were then subject and tributary; and it is not improbable that the Roman government might have some secret apprehensions of the effects of his doctrine, as well as the Jewish priests; neither is it improbable that Jesus Christ had in contemplation the delivery of the Jewish nation from the bondage of the Romans. Between the two, however, this virtuous reformer and revolutionist lost his life.

[Christianism and Pantheism]

My father being of the Quaker profession, it was my good fortune to have an exceedingly good moral education, and a tolerable stock of useful learning. Though I went to the grammar school,[29] I did not learn Latin, not only because I had no inclination to learn languages, but because of the objection the Quakers have against the books in which the language is taught. But this did not prevent me from being acquainted with the subjects of all the Latin books used in the school.

The natural bent of my mind was to science. I had some turn, and I believe some talent, for poetry; but this I rather repressed than encouraged, as leading too much into the field of imagination. As soon as I was able I purchased a pair of globes, and attended the philosophical lectures of Martin and Ferguson, and became afterward acquainted with Dr. Bevis, of the society called the Royal Society, then living in the Temple, and an excellent astronomer.

I had no disposition for what is called politics. It presented to my mind no other idea than as contained in the word Jockeyship. When, therefore, I turned my thoughts toward matter of government I had to form a system for myself that accorded with the moral and philosophic principles in which I have been educated. I saw, or at least I thought I saw, a vast scene opening itself to the world in the affairs of America, and it appeared to me that unless the Americans changed the plan they were pursuing with respect to the government of England, and declared themselves independent, they would not only involve themselves in a multiplicity of new difficulties, but shut out the prospect that was then offering itself to mankind through their means. It was from these motives that I published the work known by the name of "Common Sense," which was the first work I ever did publish; and so far as I can judge of myself, I believe I should never have been known in the world as an author on any subject whatever had it not been for the affairs of America. I wrote "Common Sense" the latter end of the year 1775, and published it the first of January, 1776. Independence was declared the fourth of July following.

Any person who has made observations on the state and progress of the human mind by observing his own cannot but have observed that there are two distinct classes of what are called thoughts—those that we produce in ourselves by reflection and the act of thinking, and those that bolt into the mind of their own accord. I have always made it a rule to treat these voluntary visitors with civility, taking care to examine, as well as I was able, if they were worth entertaining, and it is from them I

29. The same school, Thetford in Norfolk that the present Counsellor Mingay went to and under the same master. [Paine's note.]

have acquired almost all the knowledge that I have. As to the learning that any person gains from school education, it serves only, like a small capital, to put him in a way of beginning learning for himself afterward.

Every person of learning is finally his own teacher, the reason of which is that principles, being a distinct quality to circumstances, cannot be impressed upon the memory; their place of mental residence is the understanding and they are never so lasting as when they begin by conception. Thus much for the introductory part.

From the time I was capable of conceiving an idea and acting upon it by reflection, I either doubted the truth of the Christian system or thought it to be a strange affair; I scarcely knew which it was, but I well remember, when about seven or eight years of age, hearing a sermon read by a relation of mine, who was a great devotee of the Church, upon the subject of what is called *redemption by the death of the Son of God.*

After the sermon was ended, I went into the garden, and as I was going down the garden steps (for I perfectly recollect the spot) I revolted at the recollection of what I had heard, and thought to myself that it was making God Almighty act like a passionate man who killed His son when He could not revenge Himself in any other way, and, as I was sure a man would be hanged who did such a thing, I could not see for what purpose they preached such sermons.

This was not one of that kind of thoughts that had anything in it of childish levity; it was to me a serious reflection, arising from the idea I had that God was too good to do such an action, and also too almighty to be under any necessity of doing it. I believe in the same manner at this moment; and I moreover believe that any system of religion that has anything in it that shocks the mind of a child cannot be a true system.

It seems as if parents of the Christian profession were ashamed to tell their children anything about the principles of their religion. They sometimes instruct them in morals and talk to them of the goodness of what they call Providence, for the Christian mythology has five deities—there is God the Father, God the Son, God the Holy Ghost, the God Providence and the Goddess Nature. But the Christian story of God the Father putting His son to death, or employing people to do it (for that is the plain language of the story) cannot be told by a parent to a child; and to tell him that it was done to make mankind happier and better is making the story still worse—as if mankind could be improved by the example of murder; and to tell him that all this is a mystery is only making an excuse for the incredibility of it.

How different is this to the pure and simple profession of Deism! The true Deist has but one Deity, and his religion consists in contemplating the power, wisdom and benignity of the Deity in His works, and in endeavoring to imitate Him in everything moral, scientifical and mechanical.

The religion that approaches the nearest of all others to true Deism, in the moral and benign part therof, is that professed by the Quakers; but they have contracted themselves too much by leaving the works of God out of their system. Though I reverence their philanthropy, I cannot help smiling at the conceit that if the taste of a Quaker could have been consulted at the Creation what a silent and drab-colored Creation it would have been! Not a flower would have blossomed its gayeties, nor a bird been permitted to sing.

Quitting these reflections, I proceed to other matters. After I had made myself master of the use of the globes and of the orrery,[30] and conceived an idea of the infinity of space, and the eternal divisibility of matter, and obtained at least a general knowledge of what is called natural philosophy, I began to compare, or, as I have before said, to confront the eternal evidence those things afford with the Christian system of faith.

Though it is not a direct article of the Christian system, that this world that we inhabit is the whole of the habitable creation, yet it is so worked up therewith, from what is called the Mosaic account of the Creation, the story of Eve and the apple, and the counterpart of that story, the death of the Son of God, that to believe otherwise, that is, to believe that God created a plurality of worlds, at least as numerous as what we call stars, renders the Christian system of faith at once little and ridiculous, and scatters it in the mind like feathers in the air. The two beliefs cannot be held together in the same mind, and he who thinks that he believes both has thought but little of either.

Though the belief of a plurality of worlds was familiar to the ancients, it is only within the last three centuries that the extent and dimensions of this globe that we inhabit have been ascertained. Several vessels following the tract of the ocean have sailed entirely around the world, as a man may march in a circle and come round by the contrary side of the circle to the spot he set out from.

The circular dimensions of our world, in the widest part, as a man would measure the widest round of an apple or ball, is only twenty-five thousand and twenty English miles, reckoning sixty-nine miles and a half to an equatorial degree, and may be sailed round in the space of about three years.[31]

A world of this extent may, at first thought, appear to us to be great; but if we compare it with the immensity of space in which it is suspended, like a bubble or balloon in the air, it is infinitely less in proportion than the smallest grain of sand is to the size of the world, or the finest particle of dew to the whole ocean, and is therefore but small; and, as will be hereafter shown, is only one of a system of worlds of which the universal creation is composed.

It is not difficult to gain some faint idea of the immensity of space in which this and all other worlds are suspended if we follow a progression of ideas. When we think of the size or dimensions of a room our ideas limit themselves to the walls, and there they stop; but when our eye or our imagination darts into space, that is, when it looks upward into what we call the open air, we cannot conceive any walls or boundaries it can have, and if for the sake of resting our ideas we suppose a boundary, the question immediately renews itself, and asks what is beyond that boundary? —and in the same manner, what is beyond the next boundary? And so on till the fatigued imagination returns and says, *There is no end.* Certainly, then, the Creator was not pent for room

---

30. As this book may fall into the hands of persons who do not know what an orrery is, it is for their information I add this note, as the name gives no idea of the uses of the thing. The orrery has its name from the person who invented it. It is a machinery of clock-work, representing the universe in miniature, and in which the revolution of the earth round itself and round the sun, the revolution of the moon round the earth, the revolution of the planets round the sun, their rela- tive distances from the sun, as the center of the whole system, their relative distances from each other and their different magnitudes, are represented as they really exist in what we call the heavens. [Paine's note.]

31. Allowing a ship to sail, on an average, three miles in an hour, she would sail entirely round the world in less than one year, if she could sail in a direct circle; but she is obliged to follow the course of the ocean. [Paine's note.]

when He made this world no larger than it is, and we have to seek the reason in something else.

If we take a survey of our own world, or rather of this of which the Creator has given us the use as our portion of the immense system of creation, we find every part of it—the earth, the waters, and the air that surrounds it—filled, and, as it were, crowded with life, down from the largest animals that we know of to the smallest insects the naked eye can behold, and from thence to others still smaller, and totally invisible without the assistance of the microscope. Every tree, every plant, every leaf serves not only as a habitation but as a world to some numerous race, till animal existence becomes so exceedingly refined that the effluvia of a blade of grass would be food for thousands.

Since, then, no part of our earth is left unoccupied, why is it to be supposed that the immensity of space is a naked void, lying in eternal waste? There is room for millions of worlds as large or larger than ours, and each of them millions of miles apart from each other. Having now arrived at this point, if we carry our ideas only one thought further, we shall see, perhaps, the true reason, at least a very good reason for our happiness, why the Creator, instead of making one immense world extending over an immense quantity of space, has preferred dividing that quantity of matter into several distinct and separate worlds, which we call planets, of which our earth is one. But before I explain my ideas upon this subject, it is necessary (not for the sake of those who already know, but for those who do not) to show what the system of the universe is. . . .

Chapter 10

Histories

INTRODUCTION

In 1764, just when the English had established themselves as the major power in North America through the Treaty of Paris, Edward Gibbon was nonetheless moved by the sight of Roman ruins to write a history of the decline and fall of empire. Gibbon, who later served as commissioner of trade and plantations, feared that what had happened to the Romans could happen to the British, so that the English empire would in its turn fall prey to the mutability of power. Already in the sixteenth century, Spenser had written several cantos of *The Faerie Queene* on mutability, in which he concluded that change was the ultimate force shaping the universe. The idea that the world is in constant flux was certainly appropriate to the start of the European imperial epoch. Over the sixteenth and seventeenth centuries, scientific thinking shifted from seeking to define the stable forms and qualities of the physical universe to studying the laws of its motion. Newton replaced Aristotle. Motion and change came to be seen as fundamental to the universe, and historical process as fundamental to civilization. By Gibbon's time, the definition of civilization as the product of history, and of history as unceasing and unending change, had become central concepts in the self-definition of Europe as a modern civilization.

Aristotle had defined man as a social animal, one who lived in society. For most of the writers surveyed in this chapter, man is a historical animal who lives in a progressing society, in constant pursuit of his own improvement. In other words, people are as interested, or more, in creating a better future as in rationalizing their present situation. With varying degrees of skepticism, these writers see the course of history advancing human happiness. More common than Gibbon's anxiety is the optimistic view expressed in George Berkeley's famous verse, "Westward the course of empire takes its way," which identifies the conquest of England's New World empire with an infinite global destiny.

In this chapter, a preoccupation with history, motion, and progress brings together an otherwise disparate collection of texts representing a wide variety of genres: in addition to more or less conventional historical narratives, the table of contents lists travel reports and journals, part of a novel, a diary, an autobiography, an almanac, a memoir, a magazine essay. All these texts have in common a consciousness that they and their authors, whatever their local or personal concerns, figure in a larger narrative. Their stories move forward, carried not only by their own momentum, but by that of the colonial enterprise. It is important here to distinguish between this sense of transcendent meaning and the one that infuses providential and sacred histories of the seventeenth century, some of which appear in chapter 3. For all their frequent invocations of Christianity, the histories in this chapter are secular. Their ultimate concern is not God but man. Franklin offers a definitive account of this shift in the *Autobiography*, when he recounts how he came to see that the rules of conduct set down in scripture should be followed, not because scripture said so, but because they made life better and easier.

The notion that history is a narrative of change lent human beings the power, collectively, to create their world; it also greatly enhanced the sense of power of individuals. Franklin's autobiography sketches a

"The Brave Old Hendrick," a Mohawk chief, c. 1740.

single man's career, but its importance has been vastly enlarged by his participation in the construction of a new world. Franklin, in his exemplary autobiography (along with Stephen Burroughs in his cautionary memoirs and William Byrd in his diary), implies that his life has universal relevance. Yet the notion of an autobiography, a memoir, or a diary connotes a distinctive and delimited individuality. Because the autobiographer has helped make the history of his time, however, he is a public as well as a private person, and can claim representative status. There is nothing exceptionally American in this claim. At the same time as Franklin was writing his *Autobiography*, Rousseau, in his *Confessions*, depicted himself as both unique and archetypal.

Europeans and Euro-Americans, viewing history as the crucible of self-definition, systematically denied historical capability to the native Americans and to Africans. A recurrent motif of colonial self-justification is the denial that the previous inhabitants ever possessed their territories, since they had failed to build upon them anything the colonists could recognize as civilizations. As Nathaniel Ames explained this failure, its first step lay in not having a sense of history: "The Ignorant Natives for Want of Letters have forgot their Stock; and know not from whence they came, or how, or when they arrived here, or what has happened since." The enslaved Africans, having been moved across the globe and given fundamental tasks in the appropriation of new territories, were nevertheless declared incompetent for progress.

The narratives written or related by slaves and former slaves nevertheless revolve around themes of mobility and change. The freedom denied is repeatedly defined as freedom of movement and of self-creation over time. Olaudah Equiano, slave to a West Indies ship captain, lived a parody of the basic principles that defined individual identity in England and Europe by travelling all over the world while in bondage and engaging in commerce with a skill and perseverance that Franklin could not have improved on, in the hope of buying a self. As Equiano daily enacts the identity others deny him, the grotesque contradiction of slavery becomes blatant. When he finally achieves his freedom, one of his first plans is a voyage "to see Old England once more," thus retrospectively refuting white society's assertion of his non-being: the past he reclaims, of travel and commercial engagement with foreign markets, establishes that he was always the man he is now; that he could never have been other than a traveller in history.

There were some who demurred from the rush to history. Jonathan Swift expressed his scathing opinion of empire-building, travel, and historical progress in *Gulliver's Travels*; this Tory view being that also of Peter Oliver, who was not impressed by American aspirations to build a new world. Finally, another voice demurs, the oldest of those heard in this chapter, that of "the Indian God, Moiship." Having created Cape Cod, as this Indian legend has it, not over time but through a set of discrete, definitive acts, when Europeans arrived, Moiship "left New England and has never been heard of since."

M.J.

Suggested readings: Jay Fliegelman, in *Prodigals and Pilgrims: The American Revolution Against Patriarchal Authority, 1750–1800*, provides a historical and cultural context, while describing a transformation in the definition of the colonial family, with broad ideological implications. William Andrews, in *To Tell a Free Story: The First Century of Afro-American Autobiography, 1760–1865*, and Philip D. Curtin, in a collection of African texts, *Africa Remembered: Narratives by West Africans from the Era of the Slave Trade*, represent slavery as an individual and personal experience. Roy Harvey Pearce was one of the first to take European-Indian relations as a focus for analyzing American culture, in *Savagism and Civilization: A Study of the Indian and the American Mind*. Laurel Thatcher Ulrich's *Good Wives: Image and Reality in the Lives of Women in Northern New England, 1650–1750* is a corrective to the conventional histories.

1. Joseph Addison

The Spectator, No. 69
1711

The Tatler *and the* Spectator *were periodicals edited and in large part written by two prominent members of the London world of letters, Richard Steele and Joseph Addison (1672–1719). Steele launched the enterprise with the* Tatler *(1709–11), in which he wrote essays on a wide and topical variety of cultural and moral subjects. Addison joined Steele in producing the* Spectator *(1711–12). Often humorous and always witty, the essays of both periodicals were nonetheless seriously committed to an emerging Whig ethic of political moderation, sensible economy, cultural propriety, and civic-mindedness. They also had a pedagogical thrust, for instance urging the education of upper-middle class women, or demonstrating a less ornamented but clearer prose style (much admired and copied by Benjamin Franklin), or a mode of argumentation that tempered rhetorical sophistication with common sense.*

As is clear from Addison's ringing encomium to empire in the essay below, Addison and Steele were strong partisans of the rise of the mercantile and financial class. Addison recalls Hakluyt, urging colonization forward and wholeheartedly committing his pen to its service.

Saturday, May 19, 1711

Hic segetes, illic veniunt felicius uvæ: Arborei foetus alibi, atque injussa virescunt Gramina. Nonne vides, croceos ut Tmolus odores, India mittit ebur, molles sua thura Sabæi? At Chalybes nudi ferrum, virosaque Pontus Castorea, Eliadum palmas Epirus equarum? Continuo has leges æternaque foedera certis Imposuit Natura locis . . .

Vir.[1]

There is no Place in the Town which I so much love to frequent as the *Royal-Exchange.* It gives me a secret Satisfaction, and, in some measure, gratifies my Vanity, as I am an *Englishman,* to see so rich an Assembly of Country-men and Foreigners consulting together upon the private Business of Mankind, and making this

---

1. This Ground with *Bacchus,* that with *Ceres* suits:
That other loads the Trees with happy Fruits.
A fourth with Grass, unbidden, decks the Ground:
Thus *Tmolus* is with yellow Saffron crown'd:
India, black Ebon and white Ivory bears:
And soft *Idume* weeps her od'rous Tears.
Thus *Pontus* sends her Beaver Stones from far;
And naked *Spanyards* temper Steel for War.
Epirus for th' *Elean* Chariot breeds,
(In hopes of Palms,) a Race of running Steeds.
This is the Orig'nal Contract; these the Laws
Impos'd by Nature, and by Nature's Cause, On sundry Places.
Virgil, *Georgics,* I. 54–61, in Dryden's translation.

Metropolis a kind of *Emporium* for the whole Earth. I must confess I look upon High-Change to be a great Council, in which all considerable Nations have their Representatives. Factors[2] in the Trading World are what Ambassadors are in the Politick World; they negotiate Affairs, conclude Treaties, and maintain a good Correspondence between those wealthy Societies of Men that are divided from one another by Seas and Oceans, or live on the different Extremities of a Continent. I have often been pleased to hear Disputes adjusted between an Inhabitant of *Japan* and an Alderman of *London,* or to see a Subject of the *Great Mogul* entering into a League with one of the *Czar* of *Muscovy.* I am infinitely delighted in mixing with these several Ministers of Commerce, as they are distinguished by their different Walks and different Languages: Sometimes I am justled among a Body of *Armenians:* Sometimes I am lost in a Crowd of *Jews,* and sometimes make one in a Groupe of *Dutch-men.* I am a *Dane, Swede,* or *French-Man* at different times, or rather fancy my self like the old Philosopher, who upon being asked what Country-man he was, replied, That he was a Citizen of the World.

Though I very frequently visit this busie Multitude of People, I am known to no Body there but my Friend, Sir ANDREW, who often smiles upon me as he sees me bustling in the Croud, but at the same time connives at my Presence without taking any further notice of me. There is indeed a Merchant of *Egypt,* who just knows me by sight, having formerly remitted me some Mony to *Grand Cairo;* but as I am not versed in the Modern *Coptick,* our Conferences go no further than a Bow and a Grimace.

This grand Scene of Business gives me an infinite Variety of solid and substantial Entertainments. As I am a great Lover of Mankind, my Heart naturally overflows with Pleasure at the sight of a prosperous and happy Multitude, insomuch that at many publick Solemnities I cannot forbear expressing my Joy with Tears that have stolen down my Cheeks. For this reason I am wonderfully delighted to see such a Body of Men thriving in their own private Fortunes, and at the same time promoting the Publick Stock; or in other Words, raising Estates for their own Families, by bringing into their Country whatever is wanting, and carrying out of it whatever is superfluous.

Nature seems to have taken a particular Care to disseminate her Blessings among the different Regions of the World, with an Eye to this mutual Intercourse and Traffick among Mankind, that the Natives of the several Parts of the Globe might have a kind of Dependance upon one another, and be united together by their common Interest. Almost every *Degree* produces something peculiar to it. The Food often grows in one Country, and the Sauce in another. The Fruits of *Portugal* are corrected by the Products of *Barbadoes:* The Infusion of a *China* Plant sweetned with the Pith of an *Indian* Cane: The *Philippick* Islands give a Flavour to our *European* Bowls. The single Dress of a Woman of Quality is often the Product of an hundred Climates. The Muff and the Fan come together from the different Ends of the Earth. The Scarf is sent from the Torrid Zone, and the Tippet from beneath the Pole. The Brocade Petticoat rises out of the Mines of *Peru,* and the Diamond Necklace out of the Bowels of *Indostan.*

2. Factors: agents.

If we consider our own Country in its natural Prospect, without any of the Benefits and Advantages of Commerce, what a barren uncomfortable Spot of Earth falls to our Share! Natural Historians tell us, that no Fruit grows originally among us, besides Hips and Haws, Acorns and Pig-Nutts, with other Delicacies of the like Nature; That our Climate of it self, and without the Assistances of Art, can make no further Advances towards a Plumb than to a Sloe, and carries an Apple to no greater a Perfection than a Crab: That our Melons, our Peaches, our Figs, our Apricots, and Cherries, are Strangers among us, imported in different Ages, and naturalized in our *English* Gardens; and that they would all degenerate and fall away into the Trash of our own Country, if they were wholly neglected by the Planter, and left to the Mercy of our Sun and Soil. Nor has Traffick more enriched our Vegetable World, than it has improved the whole Face of Nature among us. Our Ships are laden with the Harvest of every Climate: Our Tables are stored with Spices, and Oils, and Wines: Our Rooms are filled with Pyramids of *China,* and adorned with the Workmanship of *Japan:* Our Morning's-Draught comes to us from the remotest Corners of the Earth: We repair our Bodies by the Drugs of *America,* and repose our selves under *Indian* Canopies. My Friend Sir ANDREW calls the Vineyards of *France* our Gardens; the Spice-Islands our Hot-Beds; the *Persians* our Silk-Weavers, and the *Chinese* our Potters. Nature indeed furnishes us with the bare Necessaries of Life, but Traffick gives us a great Variety of what is Useful, and at the same time supplies us with every thing that is Convenient and Ornamental. Nor is it the least part of this our Happiness, that whilst we enjoy the remotest Products of the North and South, we are free from those Extremities of Weather which give them Birth; That our Eyes are refreshed with the green Fields of *Britain,* at the same time that our Palates are feasted with Fruits that rise between the Tropicks.

For these Reasons there are not more useful Members in a Commonwealth than Merchants. They knit Mankind together in a mutual Intercourse of good Offices, distribute the Gifts of Nature, find Work for the Poor, add Wealth to the Rich, and Magnificence to the Great. Our *English* Merchant converts the Tin of his own Country into Gold, and exchanges his Wooll for Rubies. The *Mahometans* are cloathed in our *British* Manufacture, and the Inhabitants of the Frozen Zone warmed with the Fleeces of our Sheep.

When I have been upon the *Change,* I have often fancied one of our old Kings standing in Person, where he is represented in Effigy, and looking down upon the wealthy Concourse of People with which that Place is every Day filled. In this Case, how would he be surprized to hear all the Languages of *Europe* spoken in this little Spot of his former Dominions, and to see so many private Men, who in his Time would have been the Vassals of some powerful Baron, Negotiating like Princes for greater Sums of Mony than were formerly to be met with in the Royal Treasury! Trade, without enlarging the *British* Territories, has given us a kind of additional Empire: It has multiplied the Number of the Rich, made our Landed Estates infinitely more Valuable than they were formerly, and added to them an Accession of other Estates as Valuable as the Lands themselves.

2. Daniel Defoe

from *Robinson Crusoe*
1719

One of the first modern English novels, The Life and Strange Surprizing
Adventures of Robinson Crusoe, *by Daniel Defoe (1660–1731), demonstrates the
way national identity and, by extension, the identity of individual members of a
nation fulfill themselves in the acquisition of an empire. Robinson Crusoe is a
typical Englishman who has been repeatedly driven to ship out on far-flung
voyages by an obscure but irresistible sense of destiny. Shipwrecked alone on an
"un-inhabited Island on the Coast of America," Crusoe at once sets to reconsti-
tuting a proper English life, orderly, hard-working, pious. He builds a cabin, puts
in a garden, then another farther away, takes possession of the island, and finally
completes his empire by acquiring a bondservant, when he rescues a native from
being eaten by his cannibal enemies. Like Columbus baptizing San Salvador,
Crusoe begins by naming his new possession. The Indian is henceforth to be
"Friday" after the day of his rebirth under English auspices, while Crusoe at last
achieves the full measure of his English imperial being by becoming "Master."
With three components—an Englishman, a new world, and a naked savage—
Defoe put together the basic narrative of European colonization.*

*There is a fourth component subsumed in Crusoe: his tools and the gun with
which he rescues the naked savage from his fellows. For an Englishman is by definition not naked, and his dress features not only breeches and waistcoats but tech-
nology—knives, hammers, and rifles. In the first passage below, Crusoe ponders
the store of useful items he has been able to salvage from the wrecked ship, and
concludes that he was unlikely to have rebuilt his world without them; to save him,
Providence saved the instruments of civilization. Else he would have died as an
Englishman, even if he had lived as a savage.*

*As there is a complicating component in Defoe's colonial narrative, there is a
complication as well in its ideology. While never doubting the superiority of his
Christian civilization, Crusoe is less certain about the rights this gives him over the
uncivilized. Below, he muses in terms that recall Roger Williams (see chapter 7)
whether he has the right to appoint himself judge of the savages, who may possess
worldly rights for all their benighted souls. Such scruples are inspired by Crusoe's
Protestant faith as well as by his English nationalism: the savages had, besides their
souls which only Providence had the right to act upon, a national being whose
integrity other nations were bound to respect. These speculations do not prevent
Crusoe a few pages later from taking possession body and soul of "my man Friday."
His scruples are not, however, inconsequential; Defoe's exploration of the possible
error of some colonial ways participates in the same self-examination as the*
Spectator *eight years earlier, in retelling the story of a perfidious Englishman and his
Indian victim (see chapter 13).*

[Crusoe manages to salvage a considerable store of useful items]

Then it occurred to me again, how well I was furnished for my subsistence, and what would have been my case if it had not happened (which was a hundred thousand to one) that the ship floated from the place where she first struck, and was driven so near to the shore, that I had time to get all these things out of her; what would have been my case, if I had been to have lived in the condition in which I at first came on shore, without necessaries of life, or necessaries to supply and procure them? Particularly, said I aloud (though to myself), what should I have done without a gun, without ammunition, without any tools to make anything, or to work with, without clothes, bedding, a tent, or any manner of covering?

[Finding that "savages" visit his island, Crusoe plans for a fight]

I was satisfied I might securely wait till I saw any of their boats coming; and might then, even before they would be ready to come on shore, convey myself, unseen, into some thickets of trees, in one of which there was a hollow large enough to conceal me entirely; and there I might sit and observe all their bloody doings, and take my full aim at their heads, when they were so close together, as that it would be next to impossible that I should miss my shot, or that I could fail wounding three or four of them at the first shot. In this place, then, I resolved to fix my design; and, accordingly, I prepared two muskets and my ordinary fowling-piece. The two muskets I loaded with a brace of slugs each, and four or five smaller bullets, about the size of pistol-bullets; and the fowling-piece I loaded with near a handful of swan-shot, of the largest size: I also loaded my pistols with about four bullets each; and in this posture, well provided with ammunition for a second and third charge, I prepared myself for my expedition.

After I had thus laid the scheme of my design, and, in my imagination, put it in practice, I continually made my tour every morning up to the top of the hill, which was from my castle, as I called it, about three miles, or more, to see if I could observe any boats upon the sea, coming near the island, or standing over towards it: but I began to tire of this hard duty, after I had, for two or three months, constantly kept my watch, but came always back without any discovery: there having not in all that time, been the least appearance, not only on and near the shore, but on the whole ocean, so far as my eyes or glasses could reach every way.

As long as I kept my daily tour to the hill to look out, so long also I kept up the vigor of my design, and my spirits seemed to be all the while in a suitable form for so outrageous an execution as the killing twenty or thirty naked savages, for an offence, which I had not at all entered into discussion of in my thoughts, any further than my passions were at first fired by the horror I conceived at the unnatural custom[3] of the people of that country; who, it seems, had been suffered by Providence, in his wise disposition of the world, to have no other guide than that of their own abominable and vitiated passions; and, consequently, were left, and perhaps had been so for some ages, to act such horrid things, and receive such dreadful customs, as nothing but

---

3. unnatural custom: cannibalism.

nature, entirely abandoned by Heaven, and actuated by some hellish degeneracy, could have run them into. But now, when, as I have said, I began to be weary of the fruitless excursion, which I had made so long and so far every morning in vain, so my opinion of the action itself began to alter; and I began, with cooler and calmer thoughts, to consider what I was going to engage in: what authority or call I had to pretend to be judge and executioner upon these men as criminals, whom Heaven had thought fit, for so many ages, to suffer, unpunished, to go on, and to be, as it were, the executioners of his judgments one upon another. How far these people were offenders against me, and what right I had to engage in the quarrel of that blood which they shed promiscuously one upon another, I debated this very often with myself, thus: How do I know what God himself judges in this particular case? It is certain these people do not commit this as a crime; it is not against their own consciences reproving, or their light reproaching them; they do not know it to be an offence, and then commit it in defiance of divine justice, as we do in almost all the sins we commit. They think it no more a crime to kill a captive taken in war, than we do to kill an ox; nor to eat human flesh, than we do to eat mutton.

When I considered this a little, it followed necessarily that I was certainly in the wrong in it; that these people were not murderers in the sense that I had before condemned them in my thoughts, any more than those Christians were murderers who often put to death the prisoners taken in battle; or more frequently, upon many occasions put whole troops of men to the sword, without giving quarter, though they threw down their arms and submitted. In the next place, it occurred to me, that although the usage they gave one another was thus brutish and inhuman, yet it was really nothing to me; these people had done me no injury: that if they attempted me, or I saw it necessary, for my immediate preservation, to fall upon them, something might be said for it; but that I was yet out of their power, and they really had no knowledge of me, and consequently no design upon me; and therefore it could not be just for me to fall upon them: that this would justify the conduct of the Spaniards in all their barbarities practised in America, where they destroyed millions of these people: who, however they were idolaters and barbarians, and had several bloody and barbarous rites in their customs, such as sacrificing human bodies to their idols, were yet, as to the Spaniards, very innocent people; and that the rooting them out of the country is spoken of with the utmost abhorrence and detestation by even the Spaniards themselves at this time, and by all other Christian nations in Europe, as a mere butchery, a bloody and unnatural piece of cruelty, unjustifiable either to God or man, and for which the very name of a Spaniard is reckoned to be frightful and terrible to all people of humanity, or of Christian compassion,—as if the kingdom of Spain were particularly eminent for the produce of a race of men who were without principles of tenderness, or the common bowels of pity to the miserable, which is reckoned to be a mark of generous temper in the mind.

These considerations really put me to a pause, and to a kind of a full stop; and I began, by little and little, to be off my design, and to conclude I had taken wrong measures in my resolutions to attack the savages; and that it was not my business to meddle with them, unless they first attacked me; and that it was my business, if possible, to prevent; but that if I were discovered and attacked by them, I knew my duty. On the other hand, I argued with myself, that this really was the way not to deliver myself, but entirely to ruin and destroy myself; for unless I was sure to kill every one that not only should be on shore at that time, but that should ever come on shore afterwards, if but one of them escaped to tell their country-people what had happened, they would come over again by thousands to revenge the death of their fellows, and I should only bring upon myself a certain destruction, which at present, I had no manner of occasion for. Upon the whole, I concluded, that neither in principle nor in policy I ought, one way or other, to concern myself in this affair: that my business was, by all possible means, to conceal myself from them, and not to leave the least signal to them to guess by that there were any living creatures upon the island, I mean of human shape. Religion joined in with this prudential resolution, and I was convinced now, many ways, that I was perfectly out of my duty when I was laying all my bloody schemes for the destruction of innocent creatures, I mean innocent as to me. As to the crimes they were guilty of towards one another, I had nothing to do with them; they were national, and I ought to leave them to the justice of God, who is the governor of nations, and knows how, by national punishments, to make a just retribution for national offences, and to bring public judgments upon those who offend in a public manner, by such ways as best please him. This appeared so clear to me now, that nothing was a greater satisfaction to me than that I had not been suffered to do a thing which I now saw so much reason to believe would have been no less a sin than that of wilful murder, if I had committed it; and I gave most humble thanks on my knees to God, that had thus delivered me from blood-guiltiness; beseeching him to grant me the protection of his providence, that I might not fall into the hands of the barbarians, or that I might not lay my hands upon them, unless I had a more clear call from Heaven to do it, in defence of my own life.

[CRUSOE RESCUES A PRISONER FROM THE CANNIBAL FEAST]

He was a comely, handsome fellow, perfectly well made, with straight, strong limbs, not too large, tall, and well-shaped, and, as I reckon, about twenty-six years of age. He had a very good countenance, not a fierce and surly aspect; but seemed to have something very manly in his face; and yet he had all the sweetness and softness of an European in his countenance too, especially when he smiled. His hair was long and black, not curled like wool; his forehead very high and large; and a great vivacity and sparkling sharpness in his eyes. The color of his skin was not quite black, but very tawny; and yet not an ugly, yellow, nauseous tawny, as the Brazilians and Virginians, and other natives of America are, but of a bright kind of a dun olive-color, that had in it something very agreeable, though not very easy to describe. His face was round and plump; his nose small, not flat like the Negroes; a very good mouth, thin lips, and his fine teeth well set, and as white as ivory.

After he had slumbered, rather than slept, about half an hour he awoke again, and came out of the cave to me, for I had been milking my goats, which I had in the enclosure just by; when he espied me, he came running to me, laying himself down again upon the ground, with all the possible signs of an humble, thankful disposition, making a great many antic gestures to show it. At last, he lays his head flat upon the ground, close to my foot, and sets my foot upon his head, as he had done before; and after this made all the signs to me of subjection, servitude, and submission imaginable, to let me know he would serve me as long as he lived. I understood him in many things, and let him know I was very well pleased with him. In a little time I began to speak to him and teach him to speak to me; and, first, I let him know his name should be FRIDAY, which was the day I saved his life: I called him so for the memory of the time, I likewise taught him to say Master; and then let him know that was to be my name: I likewise taught him to say Yes and No, and to know the meaning of them. I gave him some milk in an earthen pot, and let him see me drink it before him, and sop my bread in it; and gave him a cake of bread to do the like, which he quickly complied with, and made signs that it was very good for him. I kept there with him all that night; but as soon as it was day, I beckoned to him to come with me, and let him know I would give him some clothes: at which he seemed very glad, for he was stark naked. As we went by the place where he had buried the two men, he pointed exactly to the place, and showed me the marks that he had made to find them again, making signs to me that we should dig them up again, and eat them. At this I appeared very angry, expressed my abhorrence of it, made as if I would vomit at the thoughts of it, and beckoned with my hand to him to come away, which he did immediately, with great submission. I then led him up to the top of the hill, to see if his enemies were gone; and pulling out my glass, I looked, and saw plainly the place where they had been, but no appearance of them or their canoes: so that it was plain that they were gone, and had left their two comrades behind them, without any search after them.

But I was not content with this discovery; but having now more courage, and consequently more curiosity, I took my man Friday with me, giving him the sword in his hand, with the bow and arrows at his back, which I found he could use very dexterously, making him carry one gun for me, and I two for myself; and away we marched to the place where these creatures had been, for I had a mind now to get some fuller intelligence of them. When I came to the place, my very blood ran chill in my veins, and my heart sunk within me, at the horror of the spectacle: indeed it was a dreadful sight, at least it was so to me, though Friday made nothing of it. The place was covered with human bones, the ground dyed with their blood, and great pieces of flesh, left here and there, half-eaten, mangled, and scorched; and, in short, all the tokens of the triumphant feast they had been making there, after a victory over their enemies. I saw three skulls, five hands, and the bones of three or four legs and feet, and abundance of other parts of the bodies; and Friday, by his signs, made me understand that they brought over four prisoners to feast upon; that three of them were eaten up, and that he, pointing to himself, was the fourth; that there had been a great battle between them and their next king, whose subjects, it seems, he had been one of, and that they had taken a great number of prisoners; all which were carried to several places by those who had taken them in the fight, in order to feast upon them, as was done here by these wretches upon those they brought hither.

I caused Friday to gather up all the skulls, bones, flesh, and whatever remained, and lay them together in a heap, and make a great fire upon it, and burn them all to ashes. I found Friday had still a hankering stomach after some of the flesh, and was still a cannibal in his nature; but I discovered so much abhorrence, at the very thoughts of it, and at the least appearance of it, that he durst not discover it; for I had, by some means, let him know that I would kill him if he offered it.

When he had done this, we came back to our castle; and there I fell to work for my man Friday: and, first of all, I gave him a pair of linen drawers, which I had out of the poor gunner's chest I mentioned which I found in the wreck; and which, with a little alteration, fitted him very well, and then I made him a jerkin of goat's skin, as well as my skill would allow (for I was now grown a tolerable good tailor); and I gave him a cap, which I made of hare's skin, very convenient and fashionable enough; and thus he was clothed for the present, tolerably well, and was mighty well pleased to see himself almost as well clothed as his master. It is true, he went awkwardly in those clothes at first; wearing the drawers was very awkward to him, and the sleeves of the waistcoat galled his shoulders, and the inside of his arms; but after a little easing them where he complained they hurt him, and using himself to them, he took to them at length very well.

The next day after I came home to my hutch with him, I began to consider where I should lodge him; and that I might do well for him, and yet be perfectly easy myself, made a little tent for him in the vacant place between my two fortifications, in the inside of the last and in the outside of the first. As there was a door or entrance there into my cave, I made a formal framed doorcase, and a door to it of boards, and set it up in the passage, a little within the entrance; and causing the door to open in the inside, I barred it up in the night, taking in my ladders too; so that Friday could no way come at me in the inside of my innermost wall, without making so much noise in getting over that it must needs waken me: for my first wall had now a complete roof over it of long poles, covering all my tent, and leaning up to the side of the hill; which was again laid across with smaller sticks, instead of laths, and then thatched over a great thickness with the rice-straw, which was strong, like reeds: and at the hole or place which was left to go in or out by the ladder, I had placed a kind of trap door, which, if it had been attempted on the outside, would not have opened at all, but would have fallen down, and made a great noise: as to weapons, I took them all into my side every night. But I needed none of all this precaution; for never man had a more faithful, loving, sincere servant than Friday was to me; without passions, sullenness, or designs, perfectly obliged and engaged—his very affections were tied to me, like those of a child to a father; and I dare say, he would have sacrificed his life for the saving mine upon any occasion whatsoever: the many testimonies he gave me of this put it out of doubt, and soon convinced me that I needed to use no precautions, as to my safety on his account.

This frequently gave me occasion to observe, and that with wonder, that however it had pleased God, in his providence, and in the government of the works of his hands, to take from so great a part of the world of his creatures the best uses to which their faculties and the powers of their souls are adapted, yet that he has bestowed upon them the same powers, the same reason, the same affections, the same sentiments of kindness and obligation, the same passions and resentments of wrongs, the same sense of gratitude, sincerity, fidelity, and all the capacities of doing good, and receiving good, that he has given to us; and that when he pleases to offer them occasions of exerting these, they are as ready, nay, more ready, to apply them to the right uses for which they were bestowed, than we are. This made me very melancholy sometimes, in reflecting, as the several occasions presented, how mean a use we make of all these, even though we have these powers enlightened by the great lamp of instruction, the Spirit of God, and by the knowledge of his word added to our understanding; and why it has pleased God to hide the like saving knowledge from so many millions of souls, who, if I might judge by this poor savage, would make a much better use of it than we did. From hence, I sometimes was led too far, to invade the sovereignty of Providence, and as it were arraign the justice of so arbitrary a disposition of things, that should hide that light from some, and reveal it to others, and yet expect a like duty from both; but I shut it up, and checked my thoughts with this conclusion; first, That we did not know by what light and law these should be condemned: but that as God was necessarily, and, by the nature of his being, infinitely holy and just, so it could not be, but that if these creatures were all sentenced to absence from Himself, it was on account of sinning against that light which, as the scripture says, was a law to themselves, and by such rules as their consciences would acknowledge to be just, tho' the foundation was not discovered to us: and (2d) that still as we are all the clay in the hand of the potter, no vessel could say to Him, Why has Thou formed me thus?

But to return to my new companion: I was greatly delighted with him, and made it my business to teach him every thing that was proper to make him useful, handy, and helpful; but especially to make him speak, and understand when I spake, and he was the aptest schollar that ever was, and particularly was so merry, so constantly diligent, and so pleased, when he cou'd but understand me, or make me understand him, that it was very pleasant to me to talk to him; and now my life began to be so easy, that I began to say to my self, that could I but have been safe from more savages, I cared not if I was never to remove from the place while I lived.

After I had been two or three days returned to my castle I thought that, in order to bring Friday off from his horrid way of feeding, and from the relish of a cannibal's stomach, I ought to let him taste other flesh; so I took him out with me one morning to the woods. I went indeed intending to kill a kid out of my own flock, and bring him home and dress it; but as I was going, I saw a she goat lying down in the shade, and two young kids sitting by her. I catched hold of Friday. 'Hold,' says I, 'stand still,' and made signs to him not to stir; immediately I presented my piece, shot and killed one of the kids. The poor creature, who had at a distance seen me kill the savage his enemy, but did not know or could imagine how it was done, was sensibly surprized, trembled and shook and looks so amazed that I thought he would have sunk down. He did not see the kid I shot at, or perceive I had killed it, but ripped up his wastcoat to feel if he was not wounded, and as I found, presently thought I was resolved to kill him; for he came and kneeled down to me, and embraceing my knees, said a great many things I did not understand; but I could easily see that the meaning was to pray me not to kill him.

I soon found a way to convince him that I would do him no harm, and taking him by the hand, laughed at him, and pointed to the kid which I had killed, beckoned to him to run and fetch it, which he did; and while he was wondering and looking to see how the creature was killed, I loaded my gun again, and by and by saw a great fowl like a hawk sit upon a tree within shot; so to let Friday understand a little what I would do, I called him to me again, pointed at the fowl, which was indeed a parrot, tho' I thought it had been a hawk; I say, pointing to the parrot, and to my gun, and to the ground under the parrot, to let him see I would make it fall, I made him understand that I would shoot and kill that bird; accordingly I fired and bad him look, and immediately he saw the parrot fall, he stood like one frighted again, notwithstanding all I had said to him; and I found he was the more amazed because he did not see me put any thing into the gun; but thought that there must be some wonderful fund of death and destruction in that thing, able to kill man, beast, bird, or any thing near or far off, and the astonishment this created in him was such as could not wear off for a long time; and I believe, if I would have let him, he would have worshipped me and my gun. As for the gun itself, he would not so much as touch it for several days after; but he would speak to it, and talk to it, as if it had answered him, when he was by himself; which, as I afterwards learned of him, was to desire it not to kill him. Well, after his astonishment was a little over at this, I pointed to him to run and fetch the bird I had shot, which he did, but stayed some time; for the parrot, not being quite dead, had fluttered away a good distance from the place where she fell: however, he found her, took her up, and brought her to me; and as I had perceived his ignorance about the gun before, I took this advantage to charge the gun again, and not to let him see me do it, that I might be ready for any other mark that might present; but nothing more offered at that time; so I brought home the kid [i.e., his goat], and the same evening I took the skin off, and cut it out as well as I could; and having a pot fit for that purpose, I boiled or stewed some of the flesh, and made some very good broth. After I had begun to eat some, I gave some to my man, who seemed very glad of it, and liked it very well; but that which was strangest to him, was to see me eat salt with it. He made a sign to me that the salt was not good to eat; and putting a little into his mouth, he seemed to nauseate it, and would spit and sputter at it, washing his mouth with fresh water after it; on the other hand, I took some meat into my mouth without salt, and I pretended to spit and sputter for want of salt, as fast as he had done at the salt; but it would not do; he would never care for salt with his meat or in his broth; at least, not for a great while, and then but very little.

Having thus fed him with boiled meat and broth, I was resolved to feast him the next day with roasting a piece of the kid: this I did, by hanging it before the fire on a string, as I had seen many people do in England, setting two poles up, one on each side of the fire, and one across on the top, and tying the string to the cross-stick, letting the meat turn continually. This, Friday admired very much: but when he came to taste the flesh, he took so many ways to tell me how well he liked it, that I could not but understand him; and at last he told me, as well as he could, he would never eat man's flesh any more, which I was very glad to hear.

The next day I set him to work to beating some corn out, and sifting it in the manner I used to do, as I observed before; and he soon understood how to do it as well as I, especially after he had seen what the meaning of it was, and that it was to make bread of it: for after that I let him see me make my bread, and bake it too; and in a little time Friday was able to do all the work for me, as well as I could do it myself.

I began now to consider, that having two mouths to feed instead of one, I must provide more ground for my harvest, and plant a larger quantity of corn than I used to do: so I marked out a larger piece of land, and began the fence in the same manner as before, in which Friday worked not only very willingly and very hard, but did it very cheerfully: and I told him what it was for; that it was for corn to make more bread, because he was now with me, and that I might have enough for him and myself too. He appeared very sensible of that part, and let me know that he thought I had much more labor upon me on his account than I had for myself; and that he would work the harder for me, if I would tell him what to do.

This was the pleasantest year of all the life I led in this place. Friday began to talk pretty well, and understand the names of almost everything I had occasion to call for, and of every place I had to send him to, and talked a great deal to me; so that, in short, I now began to have some use for my tongue again, which, indeed, I had very little occasion for before, that is to say, about speech. Besides the pleasure of talking to him, I had a singular satisfaction in the fellow himself, his simple unfeigned honesty appeared to me more and more every day, and I began really to love the creature; and on his side, I believe he loved me more than it was possible for him ever to love any thing before.

3. Charles Brockden Brown

"Robinson Crusoe," from *The Literary Magazine* 1804

Charles Brockden Brown (1771–1810) was five years old when the War for Independence began and thus represents the first generation of United States writers. Born into a Quaker family in Philadelphia, and heir to a tradition combining idealism with a commitment to commerce, Brown became one of the first professional writers of the new nation and engaged in a wide variety of literary enterprises. Although, as the author of Wieland *(1798) and* Edgar Huntly *(1799), he is known today almost exclusively as a novelist (see chapter 13 for his comments on the novel), he was an all-around man of letters and wrote numerous essays for literary magazines. His enthusiasm for* Robinson Crusoe *is a little unexpected, in that Brown's own novels are complicated psychological dramas, while the hero of Defoe's story seldom takes time for introspection. On the other hand, Brown's constant theme is the encounter of civilized men and women with the wild unknown, as he himself reminds us here. His subject is not the psyche in the abstract but in confrontation with the concrete realities of the colonial enterprise.*

I received this book, as a present, when a child of ten years old, and read it with all the raptures which it usually affords to children. Twenty years have since elapsed, and during that time, it has laid quietly in my book-case. Numberless times have I run over my books in search of something to beguile a lonely hour. "Robinson Crusoe," have I said, as my eye glanced over it, "that's stale. I have ransacked the bowels of that long ago. Besides, it is a tale only fit for children." Now, however, [on a stormy evening with nothing else to read] I began my task with desperate resolution; but very soon did I discover sufficient reasons for continuing it in the book itself. Every thing was new to me. Either the particulars had been entirely forgotten, or they appeared to me in a light entirely new, and suggested reflections which had never before occurred, and which, indeed, could not possibly occur to the raw and unexperienced imagination of a child. I never read a work which appeared before me robed in so much novelty and singularity as this work now wears. I know of none, whose plan is, in any degree, similar to it, and which has more importance and dignity. I no longer see in it, the petty adventures of a shipwrecked man, the recreations of a boyish fancy; but the workings of a mind, left to absolute and unaccustomed solitude; and a picture of the events by which the race of man is dispersed over the world, by which desert regions are colonized, and the foundations laid of new and civilized communities.

4. Jonathan Swift

from *Gulliver's Travels*
1726

> *Jonathan Swift (1667–1745), the English satirist of many facets of the emerging modern world, took a dim view as well of empire building. Gulliver's Travels (Travels into Several Remote Nations of the World) was published in 1726. Its hero undertakes four voyages of which the last is to Houyhnhnmland where horses rule and human beings are a degenerate species called Yahoos. Enlightened by the Houyhnhnms, Gulliver becomes skeptical of the ways of his own world. Upon his return to England, he is reluctant to give the secretary of state a report of his travels, despite knowing full well that "whatever Lands are discovered by a Subject, belong to the Crown." In the first place, he doubts "whether our Conquests in the Countries I treat of, would be as easy as those of Ferdinando Cortez over the naked Americans."*

But, I had another Reason which made me less forward to enlarge his Majesty's Dominions by my Discoveries: To say the Truth, I had conceived a few Scruples with relation to the distributive Justice of Princes upon those Occasions. For Instance, A Crew of Pyrates are driven by a Storm they know not whither; at length a Boy discovers Land from the Top-mast; they go on Shore to rob and plunder; they see an harmless People, are entertained with Kindness, they give the Country a new Name, they take formal Possession of it for the King, they set up a rotton Plank or a Stone for a Memorial, they murder two or three Dozen of the Natives, bring away a Couple more by Force for a Sample, return home, and get their Pardon. Here commences a new Dominion acquired with a Title by *Divine Right*. Ships are sent with the first Opportunity; the Natives driven out or destroyed, their Princes tortured to discover their Gold; a free Licence given to all Acts of Inhumanity and Lust; the Earth reeking with the Blood of its Inhabitants: And this execrable Crew of Butchers employed in so pious an Expedition, is a *modern Colony* sent to convert and civilize an idolatrous and barbarous People.

5. William Byrd II

from the *History of the Dividing Line Betwixt Virginia and North Carolina* and the *Secret History* 1728

William Byrd II (1674–1744), son of a wealthy Virginia planter, was educated in England, returning to the colonies at his father's death in 1704 to take his place in the Southern colonial oligarchy. He was its ideal type: a gentleman of cultivated tastes whose house, Westover, was one of the finest in the English manor style characteristic of Virginia's golden age; an ambitious planter who inherited 26,000 acres and left an estate of 179,000; a stern master to his slaves and a witty courtier to the ladies; an amateur of letters with one of the finest libraries in the colonies, a knowledge of Greek, Latin, and Hebrew, and a witty style in a variety of genres, personal letters, satires, character sketches, light verse, and, notably, the two histories he wrote following a journey walking the boundary line between Virginia and North Carolina.

In 1728, Byrd represented Virginia on a surveying expedition to settle a territorial dispute between Virginia and North Carolina. He kept two journals, one to be made public, the other secret, for the eyes of like-minded friends. While in the secret journal, Byrd caricatures his colleagues—"Firebrand," "Meanwell," "Dr. Humdrum," he being "Steddy,"—his sharpest satire is of the Scotch-Irish settlers living along the disputed boundary. The historian Kenneth Lockridge has suggested that the "line" run by "Steddy" "was ultimately a social line. On one side was a social order emanating in its essence from men like himself. On the other, was the social chaos of 'lubberland.'" The contrast in the matching entries below between serious report and lampoon likewise expresses a sense of rightful social distinctions. Both histories, as they describe bringing order into the wilderness, not only argue for hierarchy but also embody it. Neither history was published during Byrd's life. The History *appeared in 1841 but the* Secret History *not until 1929.*

Despite being so long unpublished, the Histories *have acquired an important place in the American literary tradition where, looking back, they provide an excellent example of eighteenth-century Anglophile belles lettres (see introduction to chapter 13) and can be seen to anticipate nineteenth-century humor.*

The History

March 9

The Surveyors enter'd Early upon their Business this Morning, and ran the Line thro' Mr. Eyland's Plantation, as far as the Banks of North River. They passt over it in the Periauga,[4] and landed in Gibbs' Marsh, which was a mile in

---

4. Periauga: dug-out canoe.

Breadth, and tolerably firm. They trudg'd thro' this Marsh without much difficulty as far as the High Land, which promis'd more Fertility than any they had seen in these Parts. But this firm Land lasted not long before they came upon the dreadful Pocoson they had been threaten'd with. Nor did they find it one Jot better than it had been painted to them. The Beavers and Otters had render'd it quite impassable for any Creature but themselves.

Our poor Fellows had much ado to drag their Legs after them in this Quagmire, but disdaining to be baulkt, they cou'd hardly be persuaded from pressing forward by the Surveyors, who found it absolutely Necessary to make a Traverse in the Deepest Place, to prevent their Sticking fast in the Mire, and becoming a Certain Prey to the Turkey-Buzzards.

This Horrible Day's Work Ended two Miles to the Northward of Mr. Merchant's Plantation, divided from N W River by a Narrow Swamp, which is causway'd over. We took up our Quarters in the open Field, not far from the House, correcting, by a Fire as large as a Roman-Funeral-Pile, the Aguish Exhalations arising from the Sunken Grounds that Surrounded us.

The Secret History

March 9

In the Morning we walk't with the Surveyors to the Line, which cut thro' Eyland's Plantation, & came to the Banks of North River. Hither the Girls above mention'd attended us, but an Old Woman came along with them for the Security of their Vertue. Others rose out of their Sick Beds to see such Raritys as we were. One of our Periaugas sat the Surveyors & 5 Men over North River. They landed in a miry Marsh, which led to a very deep Pocoson. Here they met with Bever Dams & Otter holes, which it was not practicable to pass in a direct Line, tho' the Men offer'd to do it with great Alacrity: But the Surveyors were contented to make a Traverse. While they were struggling with these difficultys, we Commissioners went in State in the other Periauga to N. W. River, and row'd up as high as Mr Merchants. He lives near half a mile from the River having a Causway leading thro' a filthy Swamp to his Plantation. I encampt in his Pasture with the Men, tho' the other Commissioners endulg'd themselves so far as to ly in the House. But it seems they broke the Rules of Hospitality, by several gross Freedoms they offer'd to take with our Landlord's Sister. She was indeed a pretty Girl, and therefore it was prudent to send her out of harm's Way. I was the more concern'd at this unhandsome Behaviour, because the People were extremely Civil to us, & deserv'd a better Treatment. The Surveyors came to us at Night, very much Jaded with their dirty work, and Orion Slept so Sound that he had been burn't in his Blanket, if the Centry had not been kinder to him than he deserv'd.

The History

March 10

The Sabbath happen'd very opportunely to give some ease to our jaded People, who rested religiously from every work, but that of cooking the Kettle. We observed very few corn-fields in our Walks, and those very small, which sem'd the Stranger, to us, because we could see no other Tokens of Husbandry or Improvement. But, upon further Inquiry, we were given to understand People only made Corn for themselves and not for their Stocks, which know very well how to get their own Living.

Both Cattle and Hogs ramble in the Neighbouring Marshes and Swamps, where they maintain themselves the whole Winter long, and are not fetch'd home till the Spring. Thus these Indolent Wretches, during one half of the Year, lose the Advantage of the Milk of their cattle, as well as their Dung, and many of the poor Creatures perish in the Mire, into the Bargain, by this ill Management.

Some, who pique themselves more upon Industry than their Neighbours, will, now and then, in compliment to their Cattle, cut down a Tree whose Limbs are loaden with the Moss aforemention'd. The trouble wou'd be too great to Climb the Tree in order to gather this Provender, but the Shortest way (which in this Country is always counted the best) is to fell it, just like the Lazy Indians, who do the same by such Trees as bear fruit, and so make one Harvest for all. By this bad Husbandry Milk is so Scarce, in the Winter Season, that were a Big-belly'd Woman to long for it, She would lose her Longing. And, in truth, I believe this is often the Case, and at the same time a very good reason why so many People in this Province are markt with a Custard Complexion.

The only Business here is raising of Hogs, which is manag'd with the least Trouble, and affords the Diet they are most fond of. The Truth of it is the Inhabitants of N Carolina devour so much Swine's flesh, that it fills them full of gross Humours. For want too of a constant Supply of Salt, they are commonly obliged to eat it Fresh, and that begets the highest taint of Scurvy. Thus, whenever a Severe Cold happens to Constitutions thus Vitiated, tis apt to improve into the Yaws, called there very justly the country-Distemper. This has all the Symptoms of the Pox, with this Aggravation, that no Preparation of Mercury will touch it. First it seizes the Throat, next the Palate, and lastly shews its spite to the poor Nose, of which tis apt in a small time treacherously to undermine the Foundation.

This Calamity is so common and familiar here, that it ceases to be a Scandal, and in the disputes that happen about Beauty, the Noses have in some Companies much ado to carry it. Nay, tis said that once, after three good Pork years, a Motion had like to have been made in the House of Burgesses, that a Man with a Nose shou'd be incapable of holding any Place of Profit in the Province; which Extraordinary Motion could never have been intended without Some Hopes of a Majority.

THE SECRET HISTORY

March 10

This being Sunday we rested the Men & Surveyors, tho' we cou'd not celebrate the Sabbath as we ought for want of our Chaplain. I had a Letter from him informing me that all was well, both Soul & Body, under his Care. Capt Wilkins went home to make his wife a Visit, and brought me a Bottle of Milk, which was better than a Bottle of Tokay. Firebrand took all Occasions to set Orion above Astrolabe, which there was no reason for, but because he had the Honour to be recommended by him. I halted as bad as old Jacob, without having wrestled with any thing like an Angel.

The Men were concern'd at it, and had observ'd so much of Firebrand's sweet

Temper, that they swore they wou'd make the best of their way home if it pleas'd God to disable me from proceeding on the Business. But I walk't about as much as I cou'd, & thereby made my Hips very pliable. We found Capt Willis Wilson here, whose Errand was to buy Pork, which is the Staple Commodity of North Carolina, & which with Pitch & Tar makes up the whole of their Traffick. The Truth of it is, these People live so much upon Swine's flesh, that it don't only encline them to the Yaws, & consequently to the downfall of their Noses, but makes them likewise extremely hoggish in their Temper, & many of them seem to Grunt rather than Speak in their ordinary conversation.

THE HISTORY

March 12

Every thing had been so soakt with the Rain, that we were oblig'd to lie by a good Part of the Morning and dry them. However, that time was not lost, because it gave the Surveyors an Opportunity of Platting off their Work, and taking the Course of the River. It likewise helpt to recruit the Spirits of the Men, who had been a little harass'd with Yesterday's March. Notwithstanding all this, we crosst the River before Noon, and advanc'd our Line 3 Miles. It was not possible to make more of it, by reason good Part of the way was either Marsh or Pocoson. The Line cut two or three Plantations, leaving Part of them in Virginia, and part of them in Carolina. This was a Case that happen'd frequently, to the great Inconvenience of the Owners, who were therefore oblig'd to take out two Patents and Pay for a new Survey in each Government.

In the Evening we took up our Quarters in Mr. Ballance's Pasture, a little above the Bridge built over N W River. There we discharg'd the two Periaugas, which in truth had been very Servicable in transporting us over the Many Waters in that Dirty and Difficult Part of our Business.

Our Landlord had a tolerable good House and Clean Furniture, and yet we cou'd not be tempted to lodge in it. We chose rather to lye in the open Field, for fear of growing too tender. A clear Sky, spangled with Stars, was our Canopy, which being the last thing we saw before we fell asleep gave us Magnificent Dreams. The Truth of it is, we took so much pleasure in that natural kind of Lodging, that I think at the foot of the Account Mankind are great Losers by the Luxury of Feather-Beds and warm apartments.

The curiosity of beholding so new and withal so Sweet a Method of encamping, brought one of the Senators of N Carolina to make us a Mid-night Visit. But he was so very Clamorous in his Commendations of it, that the Centinel, not seeing his Quality, either thro' his habit or Behaviour, had like to have treated him roughly.

After excusing the Unseasonableness of his Visit, and letting us know he was a Parliament Man, he swore he was so taken with our Lodging, that he would set Fire to his House as soon as he got Home, and teach his Wife and Children to lie, like us, in the open field.

THE SECRET HISTORY

March 12

Complaint was made to Me this Morning, that the Men belonging to the Periauga, had stole our People's Meat while they Slept. This provoked me to treat them a la

Dragon, that is to swear at them furiously; & by the good Grace of my Oaths, I might have past for an Officer in his Majesty's Guards. I was the more out of Humour, because it disappointed us in our early March, it being a standing Order to boil the Pot over Night, that we might not be hinder'd in the Morning. This Accident, & Necessity of drying our Bed-Cloaths kept us from decamping til near 12 a Clock. By this delay the Surveyors found time to plot off their Work, and to observe the Course of the River. Then they past it over against Northern's Creek, the Mouth of which was very near our Line. But the Commissioners made the best of their way to the Bridge, and going ashoar walkt to M[r] Ballance's Plantation. I retir'd early to our Camp at some distance from the House, while my Collegues tarry'd within Doors, & refresh't themselves with a Cheerful Bowl. In the Gaiety of their Hearts, they invited a Tallow-faced Wench that had sprain'd her Wrist to drink with them, and when they had rais'd her in good Humour, they examined all her hidden Charms, and play'd a great many gay Pranks. While Firebrand who had the most Curiosity, was ranging over her sweet Person, he pick't off several Scabs as big as Nipples, the Consequence of eating too much Pork. The poor Damsel was disabled from making any resistance by the Lameness of her Hand; all she cou'd do, was, to sit stil, & make the Fashionable Exclamation of the Country, Flesh a live & tear it, & by what I can understand she never spake so properly in her Life. One of the Representatives of N. Carolina made a Midnight Visit to encamping, brought one of the Senators of N Carolina to make us a Midnight Visit. But he was so very Clamorous in his Commendations of it, that the Centinel, not seeing his Quality, either thro' his habit or Behaviour, had like to have treated him roughly.

After excusing the Unseasonableness of his Visit, and letting us know he was a Parliament Man, he swore he was so taken with our Lodging, that he would set Fire to his House as soon as he got Home, and teach his Wife and Children to lie, like us, in the open field.

THE HISTORY

March 14

Before nine of the Clock this Morning, the Provisions, Bedding and other Necessaries, were made up into Packs for the Men to carry on their Shoulders into the Dismal.[5] They were victuall'd for 8 days at full Allowance, Nobody doubting but that wou'd be abundantly Sufficient to carry them thro' that Inhospitable Place; nor Indeed was it possible for the Poor Fellows to Stagger under more. As it was, their Loads weigh'd from 60 to 70 Pounds, in just Proportion to the Strength of those who were to bear them.

Twou'd have been unconscionable to have Saddled them with Burthens heavier than that, when they were to lugg them thro' a filthy Bogg, which was hardly practicable with no Burthen at all.

Besides this Luggage at their Backs, they were oblig'd to measure the distance, mark the Trees, and clear the way for the Surveyors every Step they went. It was really a Pleasure to see with how much Cheerfulness they undertook, and with how much

---

5. the Dismal: the great Dismal Swamp, hitherto uncharted.

Spirit they went thro' all this Drudgery. For their Greater Safety, the Commissioners took care to furnish them with Peruvian-Bark, Rhubarb and Hipocoacanah, in case they might happen, in that wet Journey, to be taken with fevers or Fluxes.

Altho' there was no need for Example to inflame Persons already so cheerful, yet to enter the People with better grace, the Author and two more of the Commissioners accompanied them half a Mile into the Dismal. The Skirts of it were thinly Planted with Dwarf Reeds and Gall-Bushes, but when we got into the Dismal itself, we found the Reeds grew there much taller and closer, and, to mend the matter was so interlac'd with bamo-briars, that there was no scuffling thro' them without the help of Pioneers. At the same time, we found the Ground moist and trembling under our feet like a Quagmire, insomuch that it was an easy Matter to run a Ten-Foot-Pole up to the Head in it, without exerting any uncommon Strength to do it.

Two of the Men, whose Burthens were the least cumbersome, had orders to march before, with their Tomahawks, and clear the way, in order to make an Opening for the Surveyors. By their Assistance we made a Shift to push the Line half a Mile in 3 Hours, and then reacht a small piece of firm Land, about 100 Yards wide, Standing up above the rest like an Island. Here the people were glad to lay down their Loads and take a little refreshment, while the happy man, whose lot it was to carry the Jugg of Rum, began already, like Aesop's Bread-Carriers to find it grow a good deal lighter.

After reposing about an Hour, the Commissioners recommended Vigour and Constancy to their Fellow-Travellers, by whom they were answer'd with 3 Cheerful Huzzas, in Token of Obedience. This Ceremony was no sooner but they took up their Burthens and attended the Motion of the Surveyors, who, tho' they workt with all their might, could reach but one Mile farther, the same obstacles still attending them which they had met with in the Morning.

However small this distance may seem to such as are us'd to travel at their Ease, yet our Poor Men, who were oblig'd to work with an unwieldy Load at their Backs, had reason to think it a long way; Especially in a Bogg where they had no firm Footing, but every Step made a deep Impression, which was instantly fill'd with Water. At the same time they were labouring with their Hands to cut down the Reeds, which were Ten-feet high, their Legs were hampered with the Bryars. Besides, the Weather happen'd to be very warm, and the tallness of the Reeds kept off every Friendly Breeze from coming to refresh them. And, indeed, it was a little provoking to hear the Wind whistling among the Branches of the White Cedars, which grew here and there amongst the Reeds, and at the same time not have the Comfort to feel the least Breath of it.

In the mean time the 3 Commissioners return'd out of the Dismal the same way they went in, and having join'd their Brethren, proceeded that Night as far as Mr. Wilson's.

This worthy Person lives within sight of the Dismal, in the Skirts whereof his Stocks range and Maintain themselves all the Winter, and yet he knew as little of it as he did of Terra Australis Incognita. He told us a Canterbury Tale of a North Briton, whose Curiosity Spurr'd him a long way into this great Desert, as he call'd it, near 20 Years ago, but he having no Compass, nor seeing the Sun for several Days Together, wander'd about till he was almost famisht; but at last he bethought himself of a Secret his Countrymen make use of to Pilot themselves in a Dark day.

He took a fat Louse out of his Collar, and expos'd it to the open day on a Piece of White Paper, which he brought along with him for his Journal. The poor Insect having no Eye-lids, turn'd himself about till he found the Darkest Part of the Heavens, and so made the best of his way towards the North. By this Direction he Sterr'd himself Safe out, and gave such a frightful account of the Monsters he saw, and the Distresses he underwent, that no mortall Since has been hardy enough to go upon the like dangerous Discovery.

THE SECRET HISTORY

March 14

This Morning early the Men began to make up the Packs they were to carry on their Shoulders into the Dismal. They were victual'd for 8 Days, which was judg'd sufficient for the Service. Those Provisions with the Blankets & other Necessaries loaded the Men with a Burthen of 50 or 60^{lb} for Each. Orion helpt most of all to make these Loads so heavy, by taking his Bed, and several changes of Raiment, not forgeting a Suit for Sundays along with him. This was a little unmercifull, which with his peevish Temper made him no Favorite. We fixt them out about ten in the Morning, & then Meanwell, Puzzlecause, & I went along with them, resolving to enter them fairly into this dreadful Swamp, which no body before ever had either the Courage or Curiosity to pass. But Firebrand & Shoebrush chose rather to toast their Noses over a good Fire, & Spare their dear Persons. After a March of 2 Miles thro' very bad way, the Men sweating under their Burthens, we arriv'd at the Edge of the Dismal, where the Surveyors had left off the Night before. Here Steddy thought proper to encourage the Men by a short harangue to this effect. "Gentlemen, we are at last arriv'd at this dreadfull place, which til now has been thought unpassable. Tho' I make no doubt but you will convince every Body, that there is no difficulty which may not be conquer'd by Spirit & constancy. You have hitherto behaved with so much Vigour, that the most I can desire of you, is to persevere unto the End; I protest to You the only reason we don't Share in Your Fatigue, is, the fear of adding to Your Burthens, (which are but too heavy already,) while we are Sure we can add nothing to your Resolution. I shall say no more, but only pray the Almighty to prosper your Undertaking, & grant we may meet on the other Side in perfect Health & Safety." The Men took this Speech very kindly, and answer'd it in the most cheerful manner, with 3 Huzzas. Immediately we enter'd the Dismal, 2 Men clearing the way before the Surveyors, to enable them to take their Sight. The Reeds which grew about 12 feet high, were so thick, & so interlaced with Bamboe-Briars, that our Pioneers were forc't to open a Passage. The Ground, if I may properly call it so, was so Spungy, that the Prints of our Feet were instantly fill'd with Water. Amongst the Reeds here & there stood a white Cedar, commonly mistaken for Juniper. Of this Sort was the Soil for about half a Mile together, after which we came to a piece of high land about 100 Yards in Breadth. We were above 2 Hours scuffling thro' the Reeds to this Place, where we refresh't the poor Men. Then we took leave, recommending both them & the Surveyors to Providence. We funish'd Astrolabe with Bark & other Medicines, for any of the People, that might happen to be Sick, not forgetting 3 Kinds of Rattle-Snake Root made into Doses in case of Need. It was 4 a

Clock before we return'd to our Quarters, where we found our Collegues under some Apprehension that we were gone with the People quite thro' the Dismal. During my Absence Firebrand was so very carefull in sending away the Baggage, that he forgot the Candles. When we had settled Accounts with our Landlord, we rode away to Capt Wilson's, who treated us with Pork upon Pork. He was a great Lover of Conversation, & rather than it shou'd drop, he wou'd repeat the same Story over & over. Firebrand chose rather to litter the Floor, than lye with the Parson, & since he cou'd not have the best Bed, he sullenly wou'd have none at all. However it broil'd upon his Stomach so much, that he swore anough in the Night, to bring the Devil into the Room had not the Chaplain been there.

The History

November 6

All the Land we Travell'd over this day, and the day before, that is to say from the river Irvin to Sable Creek, is exceedingly rich, both on the Virginia Side of the Line, and that of Carolina. Besides whole Forests of Canes, that adorn the Banks of the River and Creeks thereabouts, the fertility of the Soil throws out such a Quantity of Winter Grass, that Horses and Cattle might keep themselves in Heart all the cold Season without the help of any Fodder. Nor have the low Grounds only this advantage, but likewise the Higher Land, and particularly that which we call the Highland Pond, which is two miles broad, and of a length unknown.

I question not but there are 30,000 Acres at least, lying Altogether, as fertile as the Lands were said to be about Babylon, which yielded, if Herodotus tells us right, an Increase of no less than 2 or 300 for one. But this hath the Advantage of being a higher and consequently a much healthier, Situation than that. So that a Colony of 1000 families might, with the help of Moderate Industry, pass their time very happily there.

Besides grazing and Tillage, which would abundantly compensate their Labour, they might plant Vineyards upon the Hills, in which Situation the richest Wines are always produc'd.

They might also propagate white Mulberry Trees, which thrive exceedingly in this climate, in order to the feeding of silk-worms, and making of Raw Silk.

They might too produce Hemp, Flax and Cotton, in what quantity they pleas'd, not only for their own use, but likewise for Sale. Then they might raise very plentiful Orchards, of both Peaches and Apples, which contribute as much as any Fruit to the Luxury of Life. There is no Soil or Climate will yield better Rice than this, which is a Grain of prodigious Increase, and of very wholesome Nourishment. In short every thing will grow plentifully here to supply either the Wants of Wantonness of Man.

Nor can I so much as wish that the more tender Vegetables might grow here, such as Orange, Lemon, and Olive Trees, because then we shou'd lose the much greater benefit of the brisk North-West Winds, which purge the Air, and sweep away all the Malignant Fevers, which hover over countries that are always warm.

The Soil wou'd also want the advantages of Frost, and Snow, which by their Nitrous Particles contribute not a little to its Fertility. Besides the Inhabitants wou'd be depriv'd of the Variety and Sweet Vicissitude of the Season, which is much more delightful than one dull and Constant Succession of Warm Weather, diversify'd only by Rain and Sun Shine.

There is also another convenience, that happens to this country by cold weather—it destroys a great Number of Snakes, and other Venomous Reptiles, and troublesome Insects, or at least lays them to Sleep for Several Months, which otherwise would annoy us the whole year round, & multiply beyond all Enduring.

Though Oranges and Lemons are desirable Fruits, and Useful enough in many Cases, yet, when the Want of them is Supply'd by others more useful, we have no cause to complain.

There is no climate that produces every thing, since the Deluge Wrencht the Poles of the World out of their Place, nor is it fit it shou'd be so, because it is the Mutual Supply one country receives from another, which creates a mutual Traffic and Intercourse amongst men. And in Truth, were it not for the correspondence, in order to make up for each other's Wants, the Wars betwixt Bordering Nations, like those of the Indians and other barbarous People, wou'd be perpetual and irreconcileable.

The Secret History

November 6

We sat not out til near 12, & past over very uneven Ground, tho' our Comfort was that it was open and clear of Bushes. We avoided crossing the Dan twice, by going round the Bent of it. About 3 we past by Mount Pleasant, and proceeded along the River Side to Sable Creek, which we crost, and encampt a little beyond it near the Banks of the Dan. The Horses fared Sumptuously here upon Canes & Grass. Hamilton wounded a Buck, which made him turn upon the Dogs, & even pursue them 40 Yards with great Fury. But he got away from us, chusing rather to give the Wolves a Supper, than to more cruel Man. However our other Gunners had better Fortune, in killing a Doe & 2 year-old Cubb. Thus Providence supply'd us every day with Food sufficient for us, making the Barren Wilderness a Theater of Plenty. The Wind blew very cold, and produced a hard Frost. Our Journey this day did not exceed 5 Miles, great part of which in Complement to my Horse, I perform'd on Foot, notwithstanding the way was Mountainous, and the Leaves that cover'd the Hills as slippery as Ice.

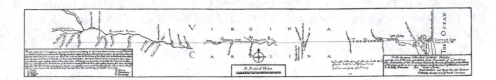

6. Dr. Alexander Hamilton

from *Itinerarium*
1744

Dr. Alexander Hamilton (1712–56) arrived in Maryland from Scotland as a young man, married well, and became a successful physician and one of the most distinguished men of the colony. This journal of a four-month journey from Annapolis, Maryland, to York, Maine, and back is an excellent example of eighteenth-century belles lettres (see the introduction to chapter 13). Witty, urbane, sophisticated in its cultural and social judgments, the Itinerarium *displays the high polish that colonial culture could achieve as well as the relatively well-established state of the colonies in general. The prosperous and populous coastal settlements are here clearly more cultivated than they were forty years earlier when Sarah Knight (see chapter 5) made a similar journey, passing from town to town through semiwilderness. Hamilton never leaves civilization. He travels with relative ease and stays at comfortable inns along with a remarkable variety of travellers brought together by a thriving commerce that Hamilton identifies as the basic principle uniting the colonies.*

Die Mercurii Trigessimo Memsis Maii Inchoatum Anno MDCCXLIV[6]
Annapolis, Wednesday, May 30th.—

I set out from *Annapolis* in *Maryland,* upon Wednesday the 30th of May at eleven o'clock in the morning; contrary winds and bad weather prevented my intended passage over Chesapeak Bay; so taking the Patapscoe road, I proposed going by the way of Bohemia to Newtown upon Chester, a very circumflex course, but as the journey was intended only for health and recreation, I was indifferent whether I took the nearest or the farthest route, having likewise a desire to see that part of the country. I was in seeming bad order at my first setting out, being suspicious that one of my horses was lame; but he performed well, and beyond my expectation. I travelled but twenty-six miles this day; there was a cloudy sky, and an appearance of rain. Some miles from town I met Mr. H———t going to Annapolis. He returned with me to his own house, where I was well entertained and had one night's lodging and a country dinner.

Friday, June 8th.— I read Montaigne's *Essays* in the forenoon, which is a strange medley of subjects, and particularly entertaining.

I dined at a tavern with a very mixed company of different nations and religions. There were Scots, English, Dutch, Germans, and Irish; there were Roman Catholicks,

---

6. *Die Mercurii,* etc.: On the thirtieth day of the month of Mercury (May), beginning in the year 1744.

Churchmen, Presbyterians, Quakers, Newlightmen, Methodists, Seventhdaymen, Moravians, Anabaptists, and one Jew. The whole company consisted of twenty-five, planted round an oblong table, in a great hall well stocked with flies.

The company divided into committees in conversation; the prevailing topick was politicks, and conjectures of a French war. A knot of Quakers there talked only about selling of flour and the low price it bore; they touched a little upon religion, and high words arose among some of the sectaries, but their blood was not hot enough to quarrel, or, to speak in the canting phrase, their zeal wanted fervency.

This landscape from the Columbian Magazine *of 1788 shows the view from Bushongo tavern, along the road to Baltimore.*

A gentleman that sat next me proposed a number of questions concerning Maryland, understanding I had come from thence. In my replies I was reserved, pretending to know little of the matter, as being a person whose business did not lie in the way of history and politicks.

In the afternoon I went to see some ships that lay in the river. Among the rest were three vessels a-fitting out for privateers,—a ship, a sloop, and a schooner. The ship was a large vessel, very high and full-rigged; one Captain Mackey intended to command her upon the cruise. At six o'clock I went to the coffee-house and drank a dish of coffee with Mr. H———l.

After staying there an hour or two, I was introduced by Dr. Phineas Bond into the Governour's Club, a society of gentlemen that meet at a tavern every night, and converse on various subjects. The Governour gives them his presence once a week, which is generally upon Wednesday, so that I did not see him there. Our conversation was entertaining; the subject was the English poets and some of the foreign writers, particularly Cervantes, author of Don Quixote, whom we loaded with eulogiums due to his character.

At eleven o'clock I left this club and went to my lodging.

Saturday, June 16th.—At the entry of this bay is a little craggy island about one or two miles long called Coney Island. Before I came to New York Ferry, I rid a bye way where, in seven miles' riding, I had 24 gates to open. Dromo, being about 20 paces before me, stopped at a house where, when I came up, I found him discoursing a negroe girl who spoke Dutch to him. "Dis de way to York?" says Dromo. "Yaw, dat is Yarikee," said the wench, pointing to the steeples. "What devil you say?" replys Dromo. "Yaw, mynheer," said the wench. "Damme you, what you say?" said Dromo again. "Yaw, yaw," said the girl. "You a damn black bitch," said Dromo and so rid on. The road here for several miles is planted thick upon each side with rows of cherry trees, like hedges, and the lots of land are mostly inclosed with stone fences.

Tuesday, June 19th.—At breakfast with my landlady I found two strange gentlemen that had come from Jamaica. They had just such cloudy countenances as are commonly wore the morning after a debauch in drinking. Our conversation was a medley, but the chief subject we went upon was the difference of climate in the American Provinces, with relation to the influence they had upon human bodies. I gave them as just an account as I could of Maryland, the air and temperature of that Province, and the distempers incident to the people there. I could not help suspecting that there were some physicians in the company by the tenour of the discourse, but could not understand for certain that any one there besides myself was a professed physician.

One gentleman there that came from Curaçao told us that in a month's time he had known either thirty or forty souls buried, which, in his opinion, was a great number for the small neighbourhood where he lived. I could scarce help laughing out at this speech, and was just going to tell him that I did not think it was customary to bury souls anywhere but in Ireland; but I restrained my tongue, having no mind to pick a quarrel for the sake of a joke.

We dined at Todd's, with seven in company, upon veal, beefsteaks, green pease, and raspberries for a dessert. There talking of a certain free negro in Jamaica, who was a man of estate, good sense, and education, the fore-mentioned gentleman who had entertained us in the morning about burying of souls, gravely asked if that negro's parents were not whites, for he was sure that nothing good could come of the whole generation of blacks.

Afternoon I drank tea with Mrs. Boswall, having, to pass away time, read some of the journal of proceedings against the conspirators at New York.[7] At night I went to a tavern fronting the Albany coffee-house along with Doctor Colchoun, where I heard a tolerable *concerto* of musick, performed by one violin and two German flutes. The violin was by far the best I had heard played since I came to America. It was handled by one Mr. H—d.

Wednesday, June 20th.— I dined this day at Todd's, where I met with one Mr. M——ls, a minister at Shrewsbury in the Jerseys, who had formerly been for some years minister at Albany. I made an agreement to go to Albany with him the first opportunity that offered. I inquired accordingly at the coffeehouse for the Albany sloops, but I found none ready to go.

I got acquainted with one Mr. Weemse, a merchant of Jamaica, my countryman and fellow lodger at Mrs. Hogg's. He had come here for his health, being afflicted with the rheumatism. He had much of the gentleman in him, was good-natured, but fickle; for he determined to go to Albany and Boston in company with me; but, sleeping upon it, changed his mind. He drank too hard, whence I imagined his rheumatism proceeded more than from the intemperate of the Jamaica air.

Monday, July 9th.—I waited upon Mr. Bayard this morning, and had letters of credit drawn upon Mr. Lechmere at Boston. I dined with Mr. M——s and other company at Todd's, and went to tarry this night at the inn where my horses were, in order to set out to-morrow morning betimes on my journey for Boston. We heard news this day of an English vessel, laden with ammunition and bound for New England, being taken on the coast. I spent the evening at Waghorn's, where we had

7. conspirators at New York: see selection 7 below.

Mr. Wendall's company, who entertained us as before. We had among us this night our old friend Major Spratt, who now and then gave us an extempore rhyme. I retired to bed at twelve o'clock.

The people of New York, at the first appearance of a stranger, are seemingly civil and courteous, but this civility and complaisance soon relaxes if he be not either highly recommended or a good toaper. To drink stoutly with the Hungarian Club, who are all bumper men, is the readiest way for a stranger to recommend himself, and a set among them are very fond of making a stranger drunk. To talk bawdy and to have a knack at punning passes among some there for good sterling wit. Governour Clinton himself is a jolly toaper and gives good example, and for that one quality is esteemed among these dons.

Sunday, August 12th.—I went this day, with Mr. Hughes and Peach, to Hooper's meeting, dined at Laughton's, and went again to meeting in the afternoon, where I saw Mrs. Blackater and her two daughters in a glaring dress.

This day I was taken notice of in passing the street by a lady who inquired of Mr. Hughes concerning me. "Lord!" said she, "what strange mortal is that?" "'T is the flower of the Maryland beaux," said Hughes. "Good God!" said the belle, "does that figure come from Maryland?" "Madam," said Hughes, "he is a Maryland physician." "O Jesus! a physician! deuce take such oddlooking physicians." I desired Hughes when he told me of this conference to give my humble service to the lady, and tell her that it gave me vast pleasure to think that anything particular about my person could so attract her resplendent eyes as to make her take notice of me in such a singular manner, and that I intended to wait upon her that she might entertain her opticks with my oddity, and I mine with her unparalleled charms.

I took a walk on the Long Wharf after sermon, and spent the evening very agreeably with Mr. Lightfoot and some other gentlemen at his lodging. Our discourse began upon philosophy, and concluded in a smutty strain.

Wednesday, September 12th.—I was waked this morning before sunrise with a strange bawling and hollowing without doors. It was the landlord ordering his negroes, with an imperious and exalted voice. In his orders the known term or epithet of *son of a bitch* was often repeated.

I came downstairs, and found one Mr. White, a Philadelphian, and the loggerheaded fellow that supped with us last night ordering some tea for breakfast. Mr. Mason, among other judicious questions, asked me how cheeses sold in Maryland. I told him I understood nothing of that kind of merchandise, but if he wanted to know the price of cathartics and emetics there, I could inform him. He asked me what sort of commodities these were. I replied that it was a particular kind of truck which I dealt in. When our tea was made it was such abominable stuff that I could not drink of it, but drank a porringer of milk. . . .

In this itineration I compleated, by land and water together, a course of 1624 miles. The northern parts I found in general much better settled than the southern. As to politeness and humanity they are much alike, except in the great towns, where the inhabitants are more civilized, especially at Boston.

Finis

7. Daniel Horsmanden

from *Journal of the Proceedings Against the Conspirators, at New York in 1741*
1744

Daniel Horsmanden (1691–1778), the nephew of William Byrd and a lawyer emigrated from England, presided over the trial that was the climax of the "New York conspiracy." In 1741, a series of unexplained fires, coinciding with robberies, aroused suspicions of a criminal conspiracy to burn down Manhattan. From this it was an evident next step to seek the culprits among the city's more than 2,000 slaves. Accusations mushroomed, rumors proliferated, and eventually 13 blacks were burned at the stake and 16 hanged; 4 whites convicted of acting as fences and possibly instigators were also hanged, and 70 blacks and 7 whites were deported. Many at the time questioned part or all of the proceedings; Cadwallader Colden compared the episode to the Salem witch trials and called it a "Bloody Tragedy." What is certain is that fear of a slave rising haunted white society and inspired both the extravagances of the conspiracy charge and the ferocity of the punishments.

At the trial, a lawyer named John Smith argued what would become a classic defense of slavery, that the slaves were better off "than the poor of most Christian countries" and that they themselves had been "amid the continual plunder, cruelty, and rapine of their native countries." He saw a proof that they did not rise up for good cause in the fact that many of the accused leaders of the conspiracy came from the households of the colonial aristocracy, Roosevelts, DeLanceys, Jays, Livingstons, where they were known to be "indulged." The excerpts below are particularly illuminating of the logic through which slavery induced ever-harsher treatment of the slaves.

[THE LAWYER JOHN SMITH SUMS UP THE PROCEEDINGS]

Thus, gentlemen, I have distinguished the several points of the evidence against the prisoners, and have repeated the substance of what each witness has said to each point, and shall leave it to you to determine whether the prisoners are guilty or not. I have endeavoured to lay no more weight upon any part of the evidence, than it will well bear; and I hope I have not urged any consequence which the fact proved will not fairly warrant.

Gentlemen, the prisoners have been indulged with the same kind of trial as is due to free men, though they might have been proceeded against in a more summary and less favourable way. The negro evidence, in the manner in which it has been produced is warranted by the act of assembly that has been read to you; the law requires no oath to be administered to them, and indeed it would seem to be a profanation of it, to administer it to a

Heathen in the legal form. You have seen that the court has put them under the most solemn caution, that their small knowledge of religion can render them capable of. The being and perfections of an Almighty, all knowing, and just God, and the terrors of an eternal world, have been plainly laid before them, and strongly pressed upon them. Unless they were professed Christians, and had taken upon them the bonds and obligations of that religion, their word, with the cautions that have been used, I suppose will be thought by you, as satisfactory as any oath that could have been devised. But, gentlemen, the court has no power to administer an oath, but in the common form, and if Pagan negroes could not be received as witnesses against each other, without an oath in legal form, it is easy to perceive that the greatest villanies would often pass with impunity.

Before I conclude, I cannot help observing to you, gentlemen, that by divers parts of the evidence, it appears that this horrid scene of iniquity has been chiefly contrived and promoted at meetings of negroes in great numbers on Sundays. This instructive circumstance may teach us many lessons, both of reproof and caution, which I only hint at, and shall leave the deduction of the particulars to every one's reflection.

Gentlemen, the monstrous ingratitude of this black tribe, is what exceedingly aggravates their guilt. Their slavery among us is generally softened with great indulgence; they live without care, and are commonly better fed and clothed, and put to less labour, than the poor of most Christian countries. They are indeed slaves, but under the protection of the law, none can hurt them with impunity: they are really more happy in this place, than in the midst of the continual plunder, cruelty, and rapine of their native countries; but notwithstanding all the kindness and tenderness with which they have been treated amongst us, yet this is the second attempt of the same kind, that this brutish and bloody species of mankind have made within one age. [This refers to a previous rising in 1712.] That justice that was provoked by former fires, and the innocent blood that was spilt in your streets, should have been a perpetual terror to the negroes that survived the vengeance of that day, and should have been a warning to all that had come after them. But I fear, gentlemen, that we shall never be quite safe, till that wicked race are under more restraint, or their number greatly reduced within this city. But I shall not insist further, but refer you, gentlemen, to the direction of the court; and if the evidence against these prisoners proves sufficient in your judgment to convict them, I make no doubt but you will bring in a verdict accordingly, and do what in you lies to rid this country of some of the vilest creatures in it.

Then the jury were charged, and a constable was sworn to attend them as usual; and they withdrew; and being soon returned, found the prisoners guilty of both indictments.

The prisoners were asked, what they had to offer in arrest of judgment, why they should not receive sentence of death? and they offering nothing but repetitions of protestations of their innocence; the third justice proceeded to sentence, as followeth:

Quack and Cuffee, the criminals at the bar,

You both now stand convicted of one of the most horrid and detestable pieces of villainy, that ever satan instilled into the heart of human creatures to put in practice; ye, and the rest of your colour, though you are called slaves in this country; yet are you all far, from the condition of other slaves in other countries; nay, your lot is superior to that of thousands of white people. You are furnished with all the necessaries of life, meat, drink, and clothing, without care, in a much better manner than you could provide for yourselves, were you at liberty; as the miserable condition of many free people here of your complexion might abundantly convince you. What then could prompt you to undertake so vile, so wicked, so monstrous, so execrable and hellish a scheme, as to murder and destroy your own masters and benefactors? nay, to destroy root and branch, all the white people of this place, and to lay the whole town in ashes.

I know not which is the more astonishing, the extreme folly, or wickedness, of so base and shocking a conspiracy; for as to any view of liberty or government you could propose to yourselves, upon the success of burning the city, robbing, butchering, and destroying the inhabitants; what could it be expected to end in, in the account of any rational and considerate person among you, but your own destruction? And as the wickedness of it, you might well have reflected, you that have sense, that there is a God above, who has always a clear view of all your actions, who sees into the utmost recesses of the heart, and knoweth all your thoughts; shall he not, do ye think, for all this bring you into judgment, at that final and great day of account, the day of judgment, when the most secret treachery will be disclosed, and laid open to the view, and every one will be rewarded according to their deeds, and their use of that degree of reason which God-Almighty has entrusted them with.

Ye that were for destroying us without mercy, ye abject wretches, the outcasts of the nations of the earth, are treated here with tenderness and humanity; and, I wish I could not say, with too great indulgence also; for you have grown wanton with excess of liberty, and your idleness has proved your ruin, having given you the opportunities of forming this villainous and detestable conspiracy; a scheme compounded of the blackest and foulest vices, treachery, blood-thirstiness, and ingratitude. But be not deceived, God Almighty only can and will proportion punishments to men's offences; ye that have shewn no mercy here, and have been for destroying all about ye, and involving them in one general massacre and ruin, what hopes can ye have of mercy in the other world? For shall not the judge of all the earth do right? Let me in compassion advise ye then; there are but a few moments between ye and eternity; ye ought therefore seriously to lay to heart these things; earnestly and sorrowfully to bewail your monstrous and crying sins, in this your extremity; and if ye would reasonably entertain any hopes of mercy at the hands of God, ye must shew mercy here yourselves, and make what amends ye can before ye leave us, for the mischief you have already done, by preventing any more being done. Do not flatter yourselves, for the same measure which you give us here, will be measured to you again in the other world; ye must confess your whole guilt, as to the offences of which ye stand convicted, and for which ye will presently receive judgment; ye must discover the whole scene of iniquity which has been contrived in this monstrous confederacy, the chief authors and actors, and all and every [one of] the parties concerned, aiding and assisting therein, that by your means a full stop may be put to this horrible and devilish undertaking. And these are the only means left ye to shew mercy; and the only reasonable ground ye can go upon, to entertain any hopes of mercy at the hands of God, before whose judgment seat ye are so soon to appear.

Ye cannot be so stupid, surely, as to imagine, that when ye leave this world, when your souls put off these bodies of clay, ye shall become like the beasts that perish, that your spirits shall only vanish into the soft air and cease to be. No, your souls are immortal, they will live forever, either to be eternally happy, or eternally miserable in the other world, where you are now going.

If ye sincerely and in earnest repent you of your abominable sins, and implore the divine assistance at this critical juncture, in working out the great and momentous article of the salvation of your souls; upon your making all the amends, and giving all the satisfaction which is in each of your powers, by a full and complete discovery of the conspiracy, and of the several persons concerned in it, as I have observed to ye before, then and only upon these conditions can ye reasonably expect mercy at the hands of God Almighty for your poor, wretched and miserable souls.

Here ye must have justice, for the justice of human laws has at length overtaken ye, and we ought to be very thankful, and esteem it a most merciful and wondrous act of Province, that your treacheries and villanies have been discovered; that your plot and contrivances, your hidden works of darkness have been brought to light, and stopped in their career; that in the same net which you have hid so privly for others your own feet are taken: that the same mischief which you have contrived for others, and have in part executed, is at length fallen upon your own pates, whereby the sentence which I am now to pronounce will be justified against ye; which is,

That you and each of you be carried from hence to the place from whence you came, and from thence to the place of execution, where you and each of you shall be chained to a stake, and burnt to death; and the lord have mercy upon your poor, wretched souls.

Ordered, that the execution of the said Quack and Cuffee be on Saturday the 30th of this instant, between the hours of one and seven o'clock in the afternoon of the same day.

8. Nathaniel Ames II

A Thought Upon the Past, Present, and Future of British America
1758

The enthusiastic author of this summation of the wonders of North America was, as his major occupation, the writer and publisher of an almanac, Poor Richard's *chief competition,* The Astronomical Diary and Almanack, *which appeared regularly from 1725 to 1763. Nathaniel Ames II (1708–64) was an intellectually distinguished eccentric who here projects a rosy view of the colonial project complete with bracing beginning in Bradford's "howling wilderness" and European expansion "to the Western Ocean."*

America is a subject which daily becomes more and more interesting:—I shall therefore fill these Pages with a Word upon its Past, Present and Future State. I. First of its Past State: Time has cast a Shade upon this Scene.—Since the Creation innumerable Accidents have happened here, the bare mention of which would create Wonder and Surprize; but they are all lost in Oblivion: The ignorant Natives for Want of Letters have forgot their Stock; and know not from whence they came, or how, or when they arrived here, or what has happened since:—Who can tell what wonderful Changes have happen'd by the mighty Operations of Nature, such as Deluges, Vulcanoes, Earthquakes, &c.!—Or whether great tracts of Land were not absorbed into those vast Lakes or Inland Seas which occupy so much Space to the West of us.—But to leave the Natural, and come to the Political State: We know how the *French* have erected a Line of Forts from the *Ohio* to *Nova Scotia,* including all the inestimable Country to the West of us, into their exorbitant Claim.—This, with infinite Justice, the *English* resented, & in this Cause our Blood has been spill'd: Which brings to our Consideration,

II. Secondly, The Present State of NORTH AMERICA.—A Writer upon this present Time says, "The Parts of *North America* which may be claimed by *Great Britain* or *France* are of as much Worth as either Kingdom.—That fertile Country to the West of the Appalachian Mountains (a String of 8 or 900 Miles in Length,) between *Canada* and the *Mississippi,* is of larger Extent than all *France, Germany* and *Poland;* and all well provided with Rivers, a very fine wholesome Air, a rich Soil, capable of producing Food and Physick, and all Things necessary for the Conveniency and Delight of Life: In fine, the Garden of the World!"—Time was we might have been possess'd of it: At this Time two mighty Kings contend for this inestimable Prize:—Their respective Claims are to be measured by the Length of their Swords.—The Poet says, The Gods and Opportunity ride Post; that you must take her by the Forelock being Bald Behind.—Have we not too fondly depended upon our Numbers?—Sir *Francis Bacon* says, "The Wolf careth not how many the Sheep be:" But Numbers well spirited, with the Blessing of Heaven will do Wonders, when by military Skill and Discipline, the Commanders can actuate (as by one Soul) the most numerous bodies of arm'd People:—Our Numbers will not avail till the Colonies are united; for whilst divided, the strength of the Inhabitants is broken like the petty Kingdoms in *Africa.* —If we do not join Heart and Hand in the common Cause against our exulting Foes, but fall to disputing among ourselves, it may really happen as the Governour of *Pennsylvania* told his Assembly, "We shall have no Priviledge to dispute about, nor Country to dispute in."—

III. Thirdly, of the Future State of NORTH AMERICA—Here we find a vast Stock of proper Materials for the Art and Ingenuity of Man to work upon:—Treasures of immense Worth; conceal'd from the poor ignorant aboriginal Natives! The

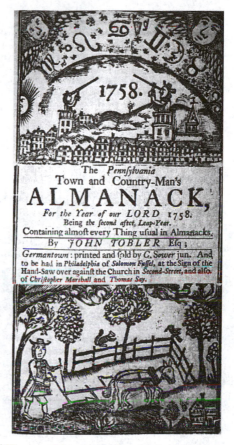

Curious have observ'd, that the Progress of Humane Literature (like the Sun) is from the East to the West; thus has it travelled thro' *Asia* and *Europe,* and now is arrived at the Eastern Shore of *America.* As the Coelestial Light of the Gospel was directed here by the Finger of GOD, it will doubtless, finally drive the long! long! Night of Heathenish Darkness from *America:*—So Arts and Sciences will change the Face of Nature in their Tour from Hence over the Appalachian Mountains to the Western Ocean; and as they march thro' the vast Desert, the Residence of Wild Beasts will be broken up, and their obscene Howl cease for ever;—Instead of which the Stones and Trees will dance together at the Music of *Orpheus,*—the Rocks will disclose their hidden Gems,—and the inestimable Treasures of Gold & Silver be broken up. Huge Mountains of Iron Ore are already discovered; and vast Stores are reserved for future Generations: This Metal more useful than Gold and Silver, will imploy Millions of Hands, not only to form the martial Sword, and peaceful Share, alternately; but an Infinity of Utensils improved in the Exercise of Art, and Handicraft amongst Men. Nature thro' all her Works has stamp'd Authority on this Law, namely, "That all fit Matter shall be improved to its best Purposes."—Shall not then those vast Quarries, that teem with mechanic Stone,—those for Structure be piled into great Cities,—and those for Sculpture into Statues to perpetuate the Honor of renowned Heroes; even those who shall NOW save their Country.—O! Ye unborn Inhabitants of America! Should this Page escape its destin'd Conflagration at the Year's End, and these Alphabetical Letters remain legible,—when your Eyes behold the Sun after he has rolled the Seasons round for two or three Centuries more, you will know that in Anno Domini 1758, we dream'd of your Times.

9.

newspaper advertisements for runaway slaves

Whereas *Cambridge, a Negro Man belonging to* James Oliver *of Boston doth absent himself sometimes from his Master: SAID NEGRO PLAYS WELL UPON A FLUTE, AND NOT SO WELL ON A VIOLIN. This is to desire all Masters and Heads of Families not to suffer said Negro to come into their Houses to teach their Prentices or Servants to play, nor on any other Accounts. All Masters of Vessels are also forbid to have anything to do with him on any Account, as they may answer it in the Law. N. B. Said Negro is to be sold: Enquire of said* Oliver.

[*Boston Evening Post,* October 24, 1743]

Ran away from his Master *Eleazer Tyng, Esq. at* Dunstable, *on the 26th May past, a Negro Man Serrant Call'd Robbin, almost of the complexion of an Indian, short thick square shoulder'd Fellow, a very short neck, and thick legs, about 28 Years old, talks good English, can read and write, and plays on the Fiddle; he was born at* Dunstable *and it is thought he has been entic'd to enlist into the service, or to go to* Philadelphia: *Had on when he went away, a strip'd cotton and Linnen blue and white Jacket, red Breeches with Brass Buttons, blue Yarn Stockings, a fine Shirt, and took another of a meaner Sort, a red Cap, a Beaver Hat with a mourning Weed in it, and sometimes wears a Wig. Whoever will apprehend said Negro and secure him, so that his Master may have him again, or bring him to the Ware-House of Messiers* Alford *and* Tyng, *in* Boston, *shall have a reward of* Ten Pounds, *old Tenor, and all reasonable Charges.*

N. B. And all Masters of Vessels or others are hereby cautioned against harbouring, concealing or carrying off said Servant, on Penalty of the Law.

[*New York Gazette Revived in the Weekly Post-Boy,* July 18, 1748]

Run away from the subscriber on Monday, the 20th of this instant, a mulatto slave named David Gratenread; he is an arch fellow, very well known by most people, plays the fiddle extremely well, has a wide mouth, a little piece bit out of one of his ears, has a large bump upon one of his shins, about 37 years of age, 5 ft

6 or 7 inches high, and may perhaps change his name and pretend to pass as a free man; he carried with him a new brown cloth waistcoat lappelled, lined with white taminy, and yellow gilt buttons, a new pair of buckskin breeches, gold-laced hat, a fine Holland shirt, brown cut wig, and several old clothes that I cannot remember, except an old lappelled kersey waistcoat. I believe he carried his fiddle with him. . . . Whoever apprehends the said runaway, and brings him to me, or commits him to any goal, so that I get him again, shall have five pounds reward if taken in this colony, if out thereof ten pounds.

Richard King
[*Virginia Gazette*, May 14, 1767]

10. Ukawsaw Gronniosaw (James Albert)

from *A Narrative of The Most Remarkable Particulars in the Life of James Albert Ukawsaw Gronniosaw, an African Prince*
1770

> The Narrative of Ukawsaw Gronniosaw is subtitled "As Related by Himself" and thus belongs to the group of slave narratives written with the assistance of white transcribers and editors. Gronniosaw's was "taken from his own mouth, and committed to paper by the elegant pen of a young lady," which probably accounts for at least some of its expressions of piety. Gronniosaw's tale was nonetheless an important source and example for the later writings of Olaudah Equiano (see selection 16 below) and Ottobah Cugoano (see chapter 11).
>
> The excerpts here describe Gronniosaw's enslavement when those with whom he has travelled to the African coast betray him; his master subsequently willing him "ten pounds and my freedom," the second episode tells of the African's first encounter with Christian society as a free man.

[Enslavement in Africa and America]

I was now more than a thousand miles from home, without a friend, or means to procure one. Soon after I came to the merchant's house, I heard the drums beat remarkably loud, and the trumpets blow. The persons accustomed to this employ are obliged to go on a very high structure, appointed for that purpose, that the sound may be heard at a great distance. They are higher than the steeples in England. I was mightily pleased with sounds so entirely new to me, and was very inquisitive to know the cause of this rejoicing, and asked many questions concerning it. I was answered that it was meant as a compliment to me, because I was grandson to the King of Bournou.

This account gave me a secret pleasure, but I was not suffered long to enjoy this satisfaction; for in the evening of the same day, two of the merchant's sons, boys about my own age, came running to me, and told me that the next day I was to die, for the king intended to behead me. I replied, that I was sure it could not be true, for I came there to play with them, and to see houses walk upon the water with wings to them, and to see the white folks; but I was soon informed that their king imagined I was sent by my father as a spy, and would make such discoveries at my return home as would enable them to make war with great advantage to ourselves; and for these reasons he had resolved that I should never return to my native country. When I heard this, I suffered misery that cannot be described. I wished a thousand times that I had never left my friends and country. But still the Almighty was pleased to work miracles for me.

The morning I was to die, I was washed, and all my gold ornaments made bright and shining, and then carried to the palace, where the king was to behead me himself, as is the custom of the place. He was seated, upon a throne at the top of an exceeding large yard, or court, which you must go through to enter the palace. It is as wide and spacious as a large field in England. I had a lane of lifeguards to go through, which I guessed to be about three hundred paces.

I was conducted by my friend, the merchant, about half way up, then he durst proceed no farther. I went up to the king alone. I advanced with an undaunted courage, and it pleased God to melt the heart of the king, who sat with his cimeter[8] in his hand ready to behead me; yet, being himself so affected, he dropped it out of his hand, and took me upon his knees, and wept over me. I put my right hand round his neck, and pressed him to my heart. He set me down and blessed me, and added, that he would not kill me, that I should not go home, but be sold for a slave. I was then conducted back again to the merchant's house.

The next day he took me on board a French brig; but the captain did not choose to buy me. He said I was too small; so the merchant took me home with him again.

The partner, whom I have spoken of as my enemy, was very angry to see me return, and again proposed putting an end to my life; for he represented to the other that I should bring them into troubles and difficulties, and that I was so little that no person would buy me. The merchant's resolution began to waver, and I was indeed afraid that I should be put to death. But, however, he said he would try me once more.

A few days after, a Dutch ship came into the harbour, and they carried me on board, in hopes that the captain would purchase me. As they went, I heard them agree, that if they could not sell me then, they would throw me overboard. I was in extreme agony when I heard this, and as soon as ever I saw the Dutch captain, I ran to him, and put my arms round him, and said, 'Father, save me,' for I knew that if he did not buy me I should be treated very ill, or possibly murdered. And though he did not understand my language, yet it pleased the Almighty to influence him in my behalf, and he bought me for two yards of check, which is of more value there than in England.

8. cimeter: scimitar.

When I left my dear mother, I had a large quantity of gold about me, as is the custom of our country. It was made into rings, and they were linked one into another, and formed into a kind of chain, and so put round my neck, and arms, and legs, and a large piece hanging at one ear, almost in the shape of a pear. I found all this troublesome, and was glad when my new master took it from me. I was now washed, and clothed in the Dutch or English manner. My master grew very fond of me, and I loved him exceedingly. I watched every look, was always ready when he wanted me, and endeavoured to convince him by every action that my only pleasure was to serve him well. I have since thought that he must have been a serious man. His actions corresponded very well with such a character. He used to read prayers in public to the ship's crew every Sabbath day; and when I first saw him read, I was never so surprised in my life, as when I saw the book talk to my master, for I thought it did, as I observed him to look upon it, and move his lips. I wished it would do so with me. As soon as my master had done reading, I followed him to the place where he put the book, being mightily delighted with it, and when nobody saw me, I opened it, and put my ear down close upon it, in great hopes that it would say something to me; but I was very sorry, and greatly disappointed, when I found that it would not speak. This thought immediately presented itself to me, that every body and every thing despised me because I was black.

I was exceedingly sea-sick at first; but when I became more accustomed to the sea, it wore off. My master's ship was bound for Barbadoes. When we arrived there, he thought fit to speak of me to several gentlemen of his acquaintance, and one of them expressed a particular desire to see me. He had a great mind to buy me; but the captain could not immediately be prevailed upon to part with me. However, as the gentleman seemed very solicitous, he at length let me go, and I was sold for fifty dollars (*four-and-sixpenny pieces in English.*) My new master's name was Vanhorn, a young gentleman. His home was in New England, in the city of New York, to which place he took me with him. He dressed me in his livery, and was very good to me. My chief business was to wait at table and tea, and clean knives, and I had a very easy place; but the servants used to curse and swear surprisingly, which I learned faster than anything; indeed, it was almost the first English I could speak. If any of them affronted me, I was sure to call upon God to damn them immediately; but I was broken off it all at once, occasioned by the correction of an old black servant that lived in the family. One day I had just cleaned the knives for dinner, when one of the maids took one to cut bread and butter with; at which I was very angry, and immediately called upon God to damn her, when this old black man told me that I must not say so. I asked him why? He replied that there was a wicked man called the devil, who lived in hell, and would take all who said these words, and put them into the fire, and burn them. This terrified me greatly, and I was entirely broken off swearing.

Soon after this, as I was placing the china for tea, my mistress came into the room just as the maid had been cleaning it, and the girl had unfortunately sprinkled the wainscot with the mop, at which my mistress was very angry. The girl very foolishly answered her again, which made her worse, and she called upon God to damn her. I was vastly concerned to hear this, as she was a fine young lady, and was very good to me, insomuch that I could not help speaking to her; 'Madam,' said I, 'you must not say so.' 'Why?' said she. 'Because there is a black man called the devil, that lives in hell, and he will put you into the fire and burn you, and I shall be very sorry for that.' 'Who told you this?' replied my lady. 'Old Ned,' said I. 'Very well,' was all her answer; but she told my master of it, and he ordered that old Ned should be tied up and whipped, and he was never suffered to come into the kitchen with the rest of the servants afterwards. My mistress was not angry with me, but rather diverted with my simplicity, and by way of talk, she repeated what I had said to many of her acquaintances that visited her; and among the rest, Mr. Freelandhouse, a very gracious, good minister, heard it, who took a great deal of notice of me, and desired my master to part with me to him. He would not hear of it at first, but being greatly persuaded, he let me go, and Mr. Freelandhouse gave fifty pounds for me. He took me home with him, and made me kneel down, and put my two hands together, and prayed for me, and every night and morning he did the same. I could not make out what he did this for, nor the meaning of it, nor what they spoke to when they talked. I thought it comical, but I liked it very well.

After I had been a little while with my new master, I grew more familiar, and asked him the meaning of prayer. (I could hardly speak English to be understood.) He took great pains with me, and made me understand that he prayed to God, who lived in heaven; that he was my Father and best Friend. I told him that this must be a mistake, that my father lived at Bournou, and that I wanted very much to see him, and likewise my dear mother and sister, and I wished he would be so good as to send me home to them; and I added all that I could think of to induce him to convey me back. I appeared in great trouble, and my good master was so affected, that the tears ran down his face. He told me that God was a great and good Spirit, that he created all the world, and every person and thing in it, in Ethiopia, Africa, and America, and everywhere. I was delighted when I heard this. 'There,' said I, 'I always thought so when I lived at home. Now if I had wings like an eagle, I would fly to tell my dear mother that God is greater than the sun, moon, and stars, and that they were made by him.' I was exceedingly pleased with this information of my master's, because it corresponded so well with my own opinion. I thought, now if I could but get home, I should be wiser than all my country-folks, my grandfather, or father, or mother, or any of them. But though I was somewhat enlightened by this information of my master's, yet I had no other knowledge of God but that he was a good Spirit, and created every body, and every thing. I never was sensible in myself, nor had any one ever told me, that he would punish the wicked and love the just. I was only glad that I had been told there was a God, because I had always thought so.

My dear kind master grew very fond of me, as was his lady. She put me to school, but I was uneasy at that, and did not like to go; but my master and mistress, in the gentlest terms, requested me to learn, and persuaded me to attend my school without any anger at all; so that at last I began to like it better, and learnt to read pretty well. My schoolmaster was a good man, and was very indulgent to me; his name was Vanosdore. I was in this state when, one Sunday, I heard my master preach from these words out of the Revelation (i.7); 'Behold, he cometh in the clouds, and every eye shall see him, and they that pierced him.' These words affected me excessively. I was in great agony, because I thought my master directed them to me only; and I fancied that he observed me with unusual earnestness. I was farther confirmed in this belief, as I looked round the church and could see no one person besides myself in such grief and distress as I was. I began to think that my master hated me, and was very desirous to go home to my own country; for I thought that if God did come, as he said, he would certainly be most angry with *me*, as I did not know what he was, nor had ever heard of him before.

I went home in great trouble, but said nothing to anybody. I was somewhat afraid of my master; for I thought he disliked me. The next text I heard him preach from was, 'Follow peace with all men, and holiness, without which no man shall see the Lord.' (Heb. xii. 14.) He preached the law so severely, that it made me tremble. He said that God would judge the whole world, Ethiopia, Asia, Africa, and everywhere. I was now excessively perplexed, and undetermined what to do, as I had now reason to believe that my situation would be equally bad, to go as to stay. I kept these thoughts to myself, and said nothing to any person whatever.

[CHRISTIAN ENGLAND]

I never knew how to set a proper value on money. If I had but a little meat and drink to supply the present necessities of life, I never wished for more; and when I had any, I always gave it where I saw an object in distress. If it was not for my dear wife and children, I should pay as little regard to money now as I did at that time. I continued some time with Mr. Dunscum as his servant, and he was very kind to me. But I had a vast inclination to visit England, and wished continually that it would please Providence to make a clear way for me to see this island. I entertained a notion that if I could get to England, I should never more experience either cruelty or ingratitude; so that I was very desirous to get among Christians. I knew Mr. Whitfield[9] very well. I had often heard him preach at New York. In this disposition I enlisted in the 28th regiment of foot, who were designed for Martinico, in the late war. We went in Admiral Pocock's fleet from New York to Barbadoes, and from thence to Martinico. When that was taken, we proceeded to the Havannah, and took that place likewise. There I got discharged. I was at that time worth about thirty pounds, but I never regarded money in the least. I would not tarry for my prize-money, lest I should lose my chance of going to England. I went with the Spanish prisoners to Spain, and came to Old England with the English prisoners. I cannot describe my joy when we arrived within sight of Portsmouth. But I was astonished, when we landed, to hear the inhabitants of that place curse and swear, and be otherwise profane. I expected to find nothing but goodness, gentleness, and meekness in this Christian land, and I suffered great perplexity of mind at seeing so much wickedness.

I inquired if any serious Christian people resided there, and the woman I made the inquiry of answered me in the affirmative, and added that she was one of them. I was heartily glad to hear her say so. I thought I could give her my whole heart. She kept a public house. I deposited with her all the money that I had not an immediate occasion

---

9. Mr. Whitfield: George Whitefield, eighteenth-century evangelist who had his greatest success in the colonies where he greatly impressed the young Benjamin Franklin (see selec- tion 11 below) and was an important agent of the Great Awakening.

for, as I thought it would be safer with her. I gave her twenty-five guineas, six of which I desired her to lay out to the best advantage, in buying me some shirts, a hat, and some other necessaries. I made her a present of a very handsome large looking glass that I brought with me from Martinico, in order to recompense her for the trouble I had given her. I must do this woman the justice to acknowledge that she did lay out some little for my use, but the nineteen guineas, and part of the six guineas, with my watch, she would not return, but denied that I ever gave them to her.

I soon perceived that I had got amongst bad people, who defrauded me of money and watch, and that all my promised happiness was blasted. I had no friend but God, and I prayed to him earnestly. I could scarcely believe it possible that the place where so many eminent Christians had lived and preached could abound with so much wickedness and deceit. I thought it worse than Sodom, considering the great advantage they possessed. I cried like a child, and that almost continually. At length God heard my prayers, and raised me up a friend indeed.

This publican had a brother who lived on Portsmouth Common, whose wife was a very serious, good woman. When she heard of the treatment I had met with, she came and inquired into my real situation, and was greatly troubled at the ill usage I had received, and she took me home to her own house. I now began to rejoice, and my prayer was turned into praise. She made use of all the arguments in her power to prevail upon her who had wronged me to return my watch and money, but it was to no purpose, as she had given me no receipt, and I had nothing to show for it; so that I could not demand it. My good friend was excessively angry with her, and obliged her to give me back four guineas, which she said she gave me out of charity, though, in fact, it was my own, and a great deal more. She would have employed other means to oblige her to give up my money, but I would not suffer her. 'Let it go,' said I; 'my God is in heaven.' I did not mind my loss in the least. All that grieved me was that I had been disappointed in finding some Christian friends, with whom I hoped to enjoy a little sweet and comfortable society.

I thought the best method that I could take now was to go to London, and find out Mr. Whitfield, who was the only living soul that I knew in England, and get him to direct me how to procure a living without being troublesome to any person. I took leave of my Christian friends at Portsmouth, and went in the stage to London. A creditable tradesman in the city, who went up with me in the stage, offered to show me the way to Mr. Whitfield's tabernacle, knowing that I was a perfect stranger. I thought it very kind, and accepted his offer; but he obliged me to give him half-a-crown for going with me, and likewise insisted on my giving him five shillings more for conducting me to Dr. Gifford's meeting.

I began now to entertain a very different idea of the inhabitants of England to what I had figured to myself before I came among them. Mr. Whitfield received me very friendly, was heartily glad to see me, and directed me to a proper place to board and lodge, in Petticoat-lane, till he could think of some way to settle me in, and paid for my lodging, and all my expenses. The morning after I came to my new lodgings, as I was at breakfast with the gentlewoman of the house, I heard the noise of some looms over our heads, and upon inquiring what it was, she told me that a person was weaving silk. I expressed a great desire to see it, and asked if I might. She told me that she would go up with me, for she was sure that I should be very welcome; and she was as good as her word. As soon as we entered the room, the person that was weaving looked about and smiled upon us, and I loved her from that moment. She asked me many questions, and I, in return, talked a great deal to her. I found that she was a member of Mr. Allen's meeting, and I began to entertain a good opinion of her, though I was almost afraid to indulge this inclination, lest she should prove like the rest that I had met with, at Portsmouth, &c., and which had almost given me a dislike to all white women. But after a short acquaintance, I had the happiness to find that she was very different, and quite sincere, and I was not without hopes that she entertained some esteem for me. We often went together to hear Dr. Gifford. As I had always a propensity to relieve every object in distress as far as I was able, I used to give to all that complained to me, sometimes half a guinea at a time, as I did not understand the real value of it. But this good woman took great pains to correct and advise me in that and many other respects.

11. Benjamin Franklin

Autobiography, Part I
1771

Franklin's writings ranged from newspaper columns to humorous essays written in a wide variety of voices, to an almanac to political tracts to reports of scientific experiments to letters, so that he not only covered the spectrum of colonial letters, he personally expanded it considerably. He wrote the Autobiography *in three parts, the first in 1771 and thus before the Revolution but at the height of colonial society, the second in 1784 at the successful conclusion of the War for Independence, and the third in 1788 immediately after the drafting of the Constitution. The first part (reprinted here in full) was written, therefore, not by Franklin the quintessential American, as he has come down in the historical and literary traditions, but by a colonial Franklin who sees himself in a primary relation to England, being for extended periods at home there. The young man making his way in the world of this first part is an unusually enterprising Englishman for whom the colonies provide an exceptional opportunity; his metamorphosis into a representative young American fulfilling a characteristic destiny of upward mobility will happen retrospectively, in the later parts of the* Autobiography *and especially in the eyes of future readers. Only the second and third parts were written for publication.*

Although ostensibly autobiographical, Franklin's account of his life is not confessional like Rousseau's, but exemplary on the model of Pilgrim's Progress, *only with worldly success as the destination. Unlike Rousseau, who opens his* Confessions *by describing how he came to have a certain peculiar erotic taste, Franklin mentions sex seldom, treats his marriage like a business transaction, and fails to explain how he has come to be addressing this book to an illegitimate son. This reticence has been criticized by readers who found the exemplary young hero's relentless optimism and pragmatism shallow and opportunistic.*

But the life proposed in the Autobiography *is probably no more intended to be taken as complete or realistic than the idealized and expurgated account it offers of Franklin's own life. Read as an allegory of the individual in the New World, this tale of an improbably rational and cheerful young man reveals a more complex vision of life by insisting that to succeed one has to be unremittingly disciplined, hard-working and single-minded, and by acknowledging that even then, success requires manipulation, dissimulation and even on occasion outright lies.*

The importance of the Autobiography *in the American literary tradition lies in its style as well as in its content, for Franklin here demonstrates a way of writing prose that has become the national ideal. "Smooth, clear and short," his sentences and paragraphs combine the heritage of the Puritan "plain style" with the simplified but elegant prose of eighteenth-century Whig writers, notably Addison and Steele.*

PART ONE

Twyford,[10] at the Bishop
of St Asaph's
1771.

Dear Son,[11]

I have ever had a Pleasure in obtaining any little Anecdotes of my Ancestors. You may remember the Enquiries I made among the Remains of my Relations when you were with me in England; and the Journey I took for that purpose. Now imagining it may be equally agreable to you to know the Circumstances of *my* Life, many of which you are yet unacquainted with; and expecting a Weeks uninterrupted Leisure in my present Country Retirement, I sit down to write them for you. To which I have besides some other Inducements. Having emerg'd from the Poverty & Obscurity in which I was born & bred, to a State of Affluence & some Degree of Reputation in the World, and having gone so far thro' Life with a considerable Share of Felicity, the conducing Means I made use of, which, with the Blessing of God, so well succeeded, my Posterity may like to know, as they may find some of them suitable to their own Situations, & therefore fit to be imitated.—That Felicity, when I reflected on it, has induc'd me sometimes to say, that were it offer'd to my Choice, I should have no Objection to a Repetition of the same Life from its Beginning, only asking the Advantage Authors have in a second Edition to correct some Faults of the first. So would I if I might, besides correcting the Faults, change some sinister Accidents & Events of it for others more favourable, but tho' this were deny'd, I should still accept the Offer. However, since such a Repetition is not to be expected, the Thing most like living one's Life over again, seems to be a *Recollection* of that Life; and to make that Recollection as durable as possible, the putting it down in Writing.—Hereby, too, I shall indulge the Inclination so natural in old Men, to be talking of themselves and their own past Actions, and I shall indulge it, without being troublesome to others who thro' respect to Age might think themselves oblig'd to give me a Hearing, since

---

10. Twyford: the country estate of Jonathan Shipley, bishop of Asaph, located near Winchester, England.

11. Dear Son: William Temple Franklin, Franklin's illegitimate son, was then governor of New Jersey. He would side with England in the Revolution, and become permanently estranged from his father.

this may be read or not as any one pleases. And lastly, (I may as well confess it, since my Denial of it will be believ'd by no body) perhaps I shall a good deal gratify my own *Vanity*. Indeed I scarce ever heard or saw the introductory Words, *Without Vanity I may say,* &c. but some vain thing immediately follow'd. Most People dislike Vanity in others whatever Share they have of it themselves, but I give it fair Quarter wherever I meet with it, being persuaded that it is often productive of Good to the Possessor & to others that are within his Sphere of Action: And therefore in many Cases it would not be quite absurd if a Man were to thank God for his Vanity among the other Comforts of Life.

And now I speak of thanking God, I desire with all Humility to acknowledge, that I owe the mention'd Happiness of my past Life to his kind Providence, which led me to the Means I us'd & gave them Success.—My Belief of This, induces me to *hope,* tho' I must not *presume,* that the same Goodness will still be exercis'd towards me in continuing that Happiness, or in enabling me to bear a fatal Reverso, which I may experience as others have done, the Complexion of my future Fortune being known to him only: and in whose Power it is to bless to us even our Afflictions.

The Notes one of my Uncles (who had the same kind of Curiosity in collecting Family Anecdotes) once put into my Hands, furnish'd me with several Particulars, relating to our Ancestors. From those Notes I learnt that the Family had liv'd in the same Village, Ecton in Northamptonshire, for 300 Years, & how much longer he knew not, (perhaps from the Time when the Name *Franklin* that before was the Name of an Order of People, was assum'd by them for a Surname, when others took Surnames all over the Kingdom.—) on a Freehold of about 30 Acres, aided by the Smith's Business which had continued in the Family till his Time, the eldest Son being always bred to that Business. A Custom which he & my Father both followed as to their eldest Sons.—When I search'd the Register at Ecton, I found an Account of their Births, Marriages and Burials, from the Year 1555 only, there being no Register kept in that Parish at any time preceding.—By that Register I perceiv'd that I was the youngest Son of the youngest Son for 5 Generations back. My Grandfather Thomas, who was born in 1598, lived at Ecton till he grew too old to follow Business longer, when he went to live with his Son John, a Dyer at Banbury in Oxfordshire, with whom my Father serv'd an Apprenticeship. There my Grandfather died and lies buried. We saw his Gravestone in 1758. His eldest Son Thomas liv'd in the House at Ecton, and left it with the Land to his only Child, a Daughter, who with her Husband, one Fisher of Wellingborough sold it to Mr Isted, now Lord of the Manor there. My Grandfather had 4 Sons that grew up, viz. Thomas, John, Benjamin and Josiah. I will give you what Account I can of them at this distance from my Papers, and if those are not lost in my Absence, you will among them find many more Particulars. Thomas was bred a Smith under his Father, but being ingenious, and encourag'd in Learning (as all his Brothers like wise werre,) by an Esquire Palmer then the principal Gentleman in that Parish, he qualify'd himself for the Business of Scrivener, became a considerable Man in the County Affairs, was a chief Mover of all publick Spirited Undertakings, for the County or Town of Northampton & his own Village, of which many Instances were told us at Ecton and he was much taken Notice of and patroniz'd by the then Lord Halifax. He died in 1702 Jan. 6. old Stile, just 4 Years to a Day before I was born. The Account we receiv'd of his Life & Character from some old People at Ecton, I remember struck you as something extraordinary from its Similarity to what you knew of mine. Had he died on the same Day, you said one might have suppos'd a Transmigration.—John was bred a Dyer, I believe of Woollens. Benjamin, was bred a Silk Dyer, serving an Apprenticeship at London. He was an ingenious Man, I remember him well, for when I was a Boy he came over to my Father in Boston, and lived in the House with us some Years. He lived to a great Age. His Grandson Samuel Franklin now lives in Boston. He left behind him two Quarto Volumes, M.S. of his own Poetry, consisting of little occasional Pieces address'd to his Friends and Relations, of which the following sent to me, is a Specimen.

Sent to My Name upon a Report
of his Inclination to Martial affaires
7 July 1710

Beleeve me Ben. It is a Dangerous Trade
The Sword has Many Marr'd as well as Made
By it doe many fall Not Many Rise
Makes Many poor few Rich and fewer Wise
Fills Towns with Ruin, fields with blood beside
Tis Sloths Maintainer, And the Shield of pride
Fair Citties Rich to Day, in plenty flow
War fills with want, Tomorrow, & with woe
Ruin'd Estates, The Nurse of Vice, broke limbs & scarss
Are the Effects of Desolating Warrs

Sent to B. F. in N. E. 15 July 1710

B   e to thy parents an Obedient Son
E   ach Day let Duty constantly be Done
N   ever give Way to sloth or lust or pride
I   f free you'd be from Thousand Ills beside
A   bove all Ills be sure Avoide the shelfe
M   ans Danger lyes in Satan sin and selfe
I   n vertue Learning Wisdome progress Make
N   ere shrink at Suffering for thy saviours sake
F   raud and all Falshood in thy Dealings Flee
R   eligious Always in thy station be
A   dore the Maker of thy Inward part
N   ow's the Accepted time, Give him thy Heart
K   eep a Good Consceince 'tis a constant Frind
L   ike Judge and Witness This Thy Acts Attend
I   n Heart with bended knee Alone Adore
N   one but the Three in One Forevermore.

He had form'd a Shorthand of his own, which he taught me, but never practicing it I have now forgot it. I was nam'd after this Uncle, there being a particular Affection between him and my Father. He was very pious, a great Attender of Sermons of the best Preachers, which he took down in his Shorthand and had with him many Volumes of them. —He was also much of a Politician, too much perhaps for his Station. There fell lately into my Hands in London a Collection he had made of all the principal Pamphlets relating to Publick Affairs from 1641 to 1717. Many of the Volumes are wanting, as appears by the Numbering, but there still remains 8 Vols. Folio, and 24 in 4to & 8vo.—A Dealer in old Books met with them, and knowing me by my sometimes buying of him, he brought them to me. It seems my Uncle must have left them here when he went to America, which was above 50 Years since. There are many of his Notes in the Margins.

This obscure Family of ours was early in the Reformation, and continu'd Protestants thro' the Reign of Queen Mary, when they were sometimes in Danger of Trouble on Account of their Zeal against Popery. They had got an English Bible, & to conceal & secure it, it was fastned open with Tapes under & within the Frame of a Joint Stool. When my Great Great Grandfather read in it to his Family, he turn'd up the Joint Stool upon his Knees, turning over the Leaves then under the Tapes. One of the Children stood at the Door to give Notice if he saw the Apparitor coming, who was an Officer of the Spiritual Court. In that Case the Stool was turn'd down again upon its feet, when the Bible remain'd conceal'd under it as before. This Anecdote I had from my Uncle Benjamin.—The Family continu'd all of the Church of England till about the End of Charles the 2ds Reign, when some of the Ministers that had been outed for Nonconformity, holding Conventicles in Northamptonshire, Benjamin & Josiah adher'd to them, and so continu'd all their Lives. The rest of the Family remain'd with the Episcopal Church.

Josiah, my Father, married young, and carried his Wife with three Children unto New England, about 1682. The Conventicles having been forbidden by Law, & frequently disturbed, induced some considerable Men of his Acquaintance to remove to that Country, and he was prevail'd with to accompany them thither, where they expected to enjoy their Mode of Religion with Freedom.—By the same Wife he had 4 children more born there, and by a second Wife ten more, in all 17, of which I remember 13 sitting at one time at his Table, who all grew up to be Men & Women, and married;—I was the youngest Son and the youngest Child but two, & was born in Boston, N. England.

My Mother the 2d Wife was Abiah Folger, a Daughter of Peter Folger, one of the first Settlers of New England, of whom honourable mention is made by Cotton Mather, in his Church History of that Country, (entitled Magnalia Christi Americana) as a *godly learned Englishman*, if I remember the Words rightly.—I have heard that he wrote sundry small occasional Pieces, but only one of them was printed which I saw now many Years since. It was written in 1675, in the homespun Verse of that Time & People, and address'd to those then concern'd in the Government there. It was in favour of Liberty of Conscience, & in behalf of the Baptists, Quakers, & other Sectaries, that had been under Persecution; ascribing the Indian Wars & other

Distresses, that had befallen the Country to that Persecution, as so many Judgments of God, to punish so heinous an Offence; and exhorting a Repeal of those uncharitable Laws. The whole appear'd to me as written with a good deal of Decent Plainness & manly Freedom. The six last concluding Lines I remember, tho' I have forgotten the two first of the Stanza, but the Purport of them was that his Censures proceeded from *Goodwill,* & therefore he would be known as the Author,

> because to be a Libeller, (says he)
>   I hate it with my Heart.
> From Sherburne Town[12] where now I dwell,
>   My Name I do put here,
> Without Offence, your real Friend,
>   It is Peter Folgier.

My elder Brothers were all put Apprentices to different Trades. I was put to the Grammar School at Eight Years of Age, my Father intending to devote me as the Tithe of his Sons to the Service of the Church. My early Readiness in learning to read (which must have been very early, as I do not remember when I could not read) and the Opinion of all his Friends that I should certainly make a good Scholar, encourag'd him in this Purpose of his. My Uncle Benjamin too approv'd of it, and propos'd to give me all his Shorthand Volumes of Sermons I suppose as a Stock to set up with, if I would learn his Character. I continu'd however at the Grammar School not quite one Year, tho' in that time I had risen gradually from the Middle of the Class of that Year to be the Head of it, and farther was remov'd into the next Class above it, in order to go with that into the third at the End of the Year. But my Father in the mean time, from a View of the Expence of a College Education which, having so large a Family, he could not well afford, and the mean Living many so educated were afterwards able to obtain, Reasons that he gave to his Friends in my Hearing, altered his first Intention, took me from the Grammar School, and sent me to a School for Writing & Arithmetic kept by a then famous Man, Mr Geo. Brownell, very successful in his Profession generally, and that by mild encouraging Methods. Under him I acquired fair Writing pretty soon, but I fail'd in the Arithmetic, & made no Progress in it.—At Ten Years old, I was taken home to assist my Father in his Business, which was that of a Tallow Chandler and Sope-Boiler. A Business he was not bred to, but had assumed on his Arrival in New England & on finding his Dying Trade would not maintain his Family, being in little Request. Accordingly I was employed in cutting Wick for the Candles, filling the Dipping Mold, & the Molds for cast Candles, attending the Shop, going of Errands, &c.—I dislik'd the Trade and had a strong Inclination for the Sea; but my Father declar'd against it; however, living near the Water, I was much in and about it, learnt early to swim well, & to manage Boats, and when in a Boat or Canoe with other Boys I was commonly allow'd to govern, especially in any case of Difficulty; and upon other Occasions I was generally a Leader among the Boys, and

---

12. In the Island of Nantucket. [Franklin's note.]

sometimes led them into Scrapes, of which I will mention one Instance, as it shows an early projecting public Spirit, tho' not then justly conducted. There was a Salt Marsh that bounded part of the Mill Pond, on the Edge of which at Highwater, we us'd to stand to fish for Minews. By much Trampling, we had made it a mere Quagmire. My Proposal was to build a Wharf there fit for us to stand upon, and I show'd my Comrades a large Heap of Stones which were intended for a new House near the Marsh, and which would very well suit our Purpose. Accordingly in the Evening when the Workmen were gone, I assembled a Number of my Playfellows, and working with them diligently like so many Emmets, sometimes two or three to a Stone, we brought them all away and built our little Wharff.—The next Morning the Workmen were surpriz'd at Missing the Stones; which were found in our Wharff; Enquiry was made after the Removers; we were discovered & complain'd of; several of us were corrected by our Fathers; and tho' I pleaded the Usefulness of the Work, mine convinc'd me that nothing was useful which was not honest.—

I think you may like to know something of his Person & Character. He had an excellent Constitution of Body, was of middle Stature, but well set and very strong. He was ingenious, could draw prettily, was skill'd a little in Music and had a clear pleasing Voice, so that when he play'd Psalm Tunes on his Violin & sung withal as he some times did in an Evening after the Business of the Day was over, it was extreamly agreable to hear. He had a mechanical Genius too, and on occasion was very handy in the Use of other Tradesmen's Tools. But his great Excellence lay in a sound Understanding, and solid Judgment in prudential Matters, both in private & publick Affairs. In the latter indeed he was never employed, the numerous Family he had to educate & the Straitness of his Circumstances, keeping him close to his Trade, but I remember well his being frequently visited by leading People, who consulted him for his Opinion on Affairs of the Town or of the Church he belong'd to & show'd a good deal of Respect for his Judgment and Advice. He was also much consulted by private Persons about their Affairs when any Difficulty occur'd, & frequently chosen an Arbitrator between contending Parties.—At his Table he lik'd to have as often as he could, some sensible Friend or Neighbour, to converse with, and always took care to start some ingenious or useful Topic for Discourse, which might tend to improve the Minds of his Children. By this means he turn'd our Attention to what was good, just, & prudent in the Conduct of Life; and little or no Notice was ever taken of what related to the Victuals on the Table, whether it was well or ill drest, in or out of season, of good or bad flavour, preferable or inferior to this or that other thing of the kind; so that I was bro't up in such a perfect Inattention to those Matters as to be quite Indifferent what kind of Food was set before me; and so unobservant of it, that to this Day, if I am ask'd I can scarce tell, a few Hours after Dinner, what I din'd upon.—This has been a Convenience to me in travelling, where my Companions have been sometimes very unhappy for want of a suitable Gratification of their more delicate because better instructed Tastes and Appetites.—

My Mother had likewise an excellent Constitution. She suckled all her 10 Children. I never knew either my Father or Mother to have any Sickness but that of which they dy'd, he at 89 & she at 85 Years of age. They lie buried together at Boston, where I some Years since plac'd a Marble stone over their Grave with this Inscription

Josiah Franklin
And Abiah his Wife
Lie here interred.
They lived lovingly together in Wedlock
Fifty-five Years.—
Without an Estate or any gainful Employment,
By constant Labour and Industry,
With God's Blessing,
They maintained a large Family
Comfortably;
And brought up thirteen Children,
And seven Grandchildren
Reputably.
From this Instance, Reader,
Be encouraged to Diligence in thy Calling,
And distrust not Providence.
He was a pious & prudent Man,
She a discreet and virtuous Woman.
Their youngest Son,
In filial Regard to their Memory,
Places this Stone.
J. F. born 1655—Died 1744. Ætat 89
A. F. born 1667—died 1752—-85

By my rambling Digressions I perceive my self to be grown old. I us'd to write more methodically.—But one does not dress for private Company as for a publick Ball. 'Tis perhaps only Negligence.—

To return. I continu'd thus employ'd in my Father's Business for two Years, that is till I was 12 Years old; and my Brother John, who was bred to that Business having left my Father, married and set up for himself at Rhodeisland, there was all Appearance that I was destin'd to supply his Place and be a Tallow Chandler. But my Dislike to the Trade continuing, my Father was under Apprehensions that if he did not find one for me more agreable, I should break away and get to Sea, as his Son Josiah had done to his great Vexation. He therefore sometimes took me to walk with him, and see Joiners, Bricklayers, Turners, Braziers, &c. at their Work, that he might observe my Inclination, & endeavour to fix it on some Trade or other on Land.—It has ever since been a Pleasure to me to see good Workmen handle their Tools; and it has been useful to me, having learnt so much by it, as to be able to do little Jobs my self in my House, when a Workman could not readily be got; & to construct little Machines for my Experiments while the Intention of making the Experiment was fresh & warm in my Mind. My Father at last fix'd upon the Cutler's Trade, and my Uncle Benjamin's Son Samuel who was bred to that Business in London being about that time establish'd in Boston, I was sent to be with him some time on liking. But his Expectations of a Fee with me displeasing my Father, I was taken home again.—

From a Child I was fond of Reading, and all the little Money that came into my Hands was ever laid out in Books. Pleas'd with the Pilgrim's Progress, my first Collection was of John Bunyan's Works, in separate little Volumes. I afterwards sold them to enable me to buy R. Burton's Historical Collections; they were small Chapmen's Books and cheap, 40 or 50 in all.—My Father's little Library consisted chiefly of Books in polemic Divinity, most of which I read, and have since often regretted, that at a time when I had such a Thirst for Knowledge, more proper Books had not fallen in my Way, since it was now resolv'd I should not be a Clergyman. Plutarch's Lives there was, in which I read abundantly, and I still think that time spent to great Advantage. There was also a Book of Defoe's called an Essay on Projects and another of Dr Mather's call'd Essays to do Good, which perhaps gave me a Turn of Thinking that had an Influence on some of the principal future Events of my Life.

This Bookish Inclination at length determin'd my Father to make me a Printer, tho' he had already one Son, (James) of that Profession. In 1717 my Brother James return'd from England with a Press & Letters to set up his Business in Boston. I lik'd it much better than that of my Father, but still had a Hankering for the Sea.—To prevent the apprehended Effect of such an Inclination, my Father was impatient to have me bound to my Brother. I stood out some time, but at last was persuaded and signed the Indentures, when I was yet but 12 Years old.—I was to serve as an Apprentice till I was 21 Years of Age, only I was to be allow'd Journeyman's Wages during the last Year. In a little time I made great Proficiency in the Business, and became a useful Hand to my Brother. I now had Access to better Books. An Acquaintance with the Apprentices of Booksellers, enabled me sometimes to borrow a small one, which I was careful to return soon & clean. Often I sat up in my Room reading the greatest Part of the Night, when the Book was borrow'd in the Evening & to be return'd early in the Morning lest it should be miss'd or wanted.—And after some time an ingenious Tradesman who had a pretty Collection of Books, & who frequented our Printing House, took Notice of me, invited me to his Library, & very kindly lent me such Books as I chose to read. I now took a Fancy to Poetry, and made some little Pieces. My Brother, thinking it might turn to account encourag'd me, & put me on composing two occasional Ballads. One was called the *Light House Tragedy*, & contain'd an Account of the drowning of Capt. Worthilake with his Two Daughters; the other was a Sailor Song on the Taking of *Teach* or Blackbeard the Pirate. They were wretched Stuff, in the Grubstreet Ballad Stile, and when they were printed he sent me about the Town to sell them. The first sold wonderfully, the Event being recent, having made a great Noise. This flatter'd my Vanity. But my Father discourag'd me, by ridiculing my Performances, and telling me Verse-makers were generally Beggars; so I escap'd being a Poet, most probably a very bad one. But as Prose Writing has been a great Use to me in the Course of my Life, and was a principal Means of my Advancement, I shall tell you how in such a Situation I acquir'd what little Ability I have in that Way.

There was another Bookish Lad in the Town, John Collins by Name, with whom I was intimately acquainted. We sometimes disputed, and very fond we were of Argument, & very desirous of confuting one another. Which disputacious Turn, by the way, is apt to become a very bad Habit, making People often extreamly disagreable in Company, by the Contradiction that is necessary to bring it into Practice, & thence, besides souring & spoiling the Conversation, is productive of Disgusts & perhaps Enmities where you may have occasion for Friendship. I had caught it by reading my Father's Books of Dispute about Religion. Persons of good Sense, I have since observ'd, seldom fall into it, except Lawyers, University Men, and Men of all Sorts that have been bred at Edinborough. A Question was once some how or other started between Collins & me, of the Propriety of educating the Female Sex in Learning, & their Abilities for Study. He was of Opinion that it was improper; & that they were naturally unequal to it. I took the contrary Side, perhaps a little for Dispute sake. He was naturally more eloquent, had a ready Plenty of Words, and sometimes as I thought bore me down more by his Fluency than by the Strength of his Reasons. As we parted without settling the Point, & were not to see one another again for some time, I sat down to put my Arguments in Writing, which I copied fair & sent to him. He answer'd & I reply'd. Three or four Letters of a Side had pass'd, when my Father happen'd to find my Papers, and read them. Without entring into the Discussion, he took occasion to talk to me about the Manner of my Writing, observ'd that tho' I had the Advantage of my Antagonist in correct Spelling & pointing (which I ow'd to the Printing House) I fell far short in elegance of Expression, in Method and in Perspicuity, of which he convinc'd me by several Instances. I saw the Justice of his Remarks, & thence grew more attentive to the *Manner* in Writing, and determin'd to endeavour at Improvement.—

About this time I met with an odd Volume of the Spectator. I had never before seen any of them. I bought it, read it over and over, and was much delighted with it. I thought the Writing excellent, & wish'd if possible to imitate it. With that View, I took some of the Papers, & making short Hints of the Sentiment in each Sentence, laid them by a few Days, and then without looking at the Book, try'd to compleat the Papers again, by expressing each hinted Sentiment at length & as fully as it had been express'd before, in any suitable Words that should come to hand.

Then I compar'd my Spectator with the Original, discover'd some of my Faults & corrected them. But I found I wanted a Stock of Words or a Readiness in recollecting & using them, which I thought I should have acquir'd before that time, if I had gone on making Verses, since the continual Occasion for Words of the same Import but of different Length, to suit the Measure, or of different Sound for the Rhyme, would have laid me under a constant Necessity of searching for Variety, and also have tended to fix that Variety in my Mind, & make me Master of it. Therefore I took some of the Tales & turn'd them into Verse: And after a time, when I had pretty well forgotten the Prose, turn'd them back again. I also sometimes jumbled my Collections of Hints into Confusion, and after some Weeks, endeavour'd to reduce them into the best Order, before I began to form the full Sentences & compleat the Paper. This was to teach me Method in the Arrangement of Thoughts. By comparing my Work afterwards with the original, I discover'd many faults and amended them; but I sometimes had the Pleasure of Fancying that in certain Particulars of small Import, I had been lucky enough to improve the Method or the Language and this encourag'd me to think I might possibly in time come to be a tolerable English Writer, of which I was extreamly ambitious.

My Time for these Exercises & for Reading, was at Night after Work, or before Work began in the Morning; or on Sundays, when I contrived to be in the Printing House alone, evading as much as I could the common Attendance on publick Worship, which my Father used to exact of me when I was under his Care:—And which indeed I still thought a Duty; tho' I could not, as it seemed to me, afford the Time to practise it.

When about 16 Years of Age, I happen'd to meet with a Book written by one Tryon, recommending a Vegetable Diet. I determined to go into it. My Brother being yet unmarried, did not keep House, but boarded himself & his Apprentices in another Family. My refusing to eat Flesh occasioned an Inconveniency, and I was frequently chid for my singularity. I made my self acquainted with Tryon's Manner of preparing some of his Dishes, such as Boiling Potatoes, or Rice, making Hasty Pudding, & a few others, and then propos'd to my Brother, that if he would give me Weekly half the Money he paid for my Board, I would board my self. He instantly agreed to it, and presently found that I could save half what he paid me. This was an additional Fund for buying Books: But I had another Advantage in it. My Brother and the rest going from the Printing House to their Meals, I remain'd there alone, and dispatching presently my light Repast, (which often was no more than a Bisket or a Slice of Bread, a Handful of Raisins or a Tart from the Pastry Cook's, and a Glass of Water) had the rest of the Time till their Return, for Study, in which I made the greater Progress from that greater Clearness of Head & quicker Apprehension which usually attend Temperance in Eating & Drinking. And now it was that being on some Occasion made asham'd of my Ignorance in Figures, which I had twice fail'd in learning when at School, I took Cocker's Book of Arithmetick, & went thro' the whole by my self with great Ease.—I also read Seller's & Sturmy's Books of Navigation, & became acquainted with the little Geometry they contain, but never proceeded far in that Science.—And I read about this Time Locke on Human Understanding and the Art of Thinking by Messrs du Port Royal.

While I was intent on improving my Language, I met with an English Grammar (I think it was Greenwood's) at the End of which there were two little Sketches of the Arts of Rhetoric and Logic, the latter finishing with a Specimen of a Dispute in the Socratic Method. And soon after I procur'd Xenophon's Memorable Things of Socrates, wherein there are many Instances of the same Method. I was charm'd with it, adopted it, dropt my abrupt Contradiction, and positive Argumentation, and put on the humble Enquirer & Doubter. And being then, from reading Shaftsbury & Collins, become a real Doubter in many Points of our Religious Doctrine, I found this Method safest for my self & very embarassing to those against whom I used it, therefore I took a Delight in it, practis'd it continually & grew very artful & expert in drawing People even of superior Knowledge into Concessions the Consequences of which they did not foresee, entangling them in Difficulties out of which they could not extricate themselves, and so obtaining Victories that neither my self nor my Cause always deserved.—I continu'd this Method some few Years, but gradually left it, retaining only the Habit of expressing my self in Terms of modest Diffidence, never using when I advance any thing that may possibly be disputed, the Words, *Certainly*, *undoubtedly*, or any others that give the Air of Positiveness to an Opinion; but rather say, *I conceive,* or *I apprehend* a Thing to be so or so, *It appears to me,* or *I should think it so or so for such & such Reasons,* or *I imagine* it to be so, or *it is so if I am not mistaken.*—This Habit I believe has been of great Advantage to me, when I have had occasion to inculcate my Opinions & persuade Men into Measures that I have been from time to time engag'd in promoting.—And as the chief Ends of Conversation are to *inform,* or to be *informed,* to *please* or to *persuade,* I wish well meaning sensible Men would not lessen their Power of doing Good by a Positive assuming Manner that seldom fails to disgust, tends to create Opposition, and to defeat every one of those Purposes for which Speech was given us, to wit, giving or receiving Information, or Pleasure: For If you would *inform,* a positive dogmatical Manner in advancing your Sentiments, may provoke Contradiction & prevent a candid Attention. If you wish Information & Improvement from the Knowledge of others and yet at the same time express your self as firmly fix'd in your present Opinions, modest sensible Men, who do not love Disputation, will probably leave you undisturb'd in the Possession of your Error; and by such a Manner you can seldom hope to recommend your self in *pleasing* your Hearers, or to persuade those whose Concurrence you desire.—Pope says, judiciously,

> *Men should be taught as if you taught them not,*
> *And things unknown propos'd as things forgot,—*

farther recommending it to us,

> *To speak tho' sure, with seeming Diffidence.*

And he might have couple'd with this Line that which he has coupled with another, I think less properly,

> *For want of Modesty is want of Sense.*

If you ask why *less properly,* I must repeat the Lines;

> "Immodest Words admit of *no* Defence;
> "*For* Want of Modesty is Want of Sense."

Now is not *Want of Sense,* (where a Man is so unfortunate as to want it) some Apology for his *Want of Modesty?* and would not the Lines stand more justly thus?

> Immodest Words admit *but this* Defence,
> That Want of Modesty is Want of Sense.

This however I should submit to better Judgments.—

My Brother had in 1720 or 21, begun to print a Newspaper. It was the second that appear'd in America, & was called *The New England Courant.* The only one before it, was *the Boston News Letter.* I remember his being dissuaded by some of his Friends from the Undertaking, as not likely to succeed, one Newspaper being in their Judgment enough for America.—At this time 1771 there are not less than five & twenty.—He went on however with the Undertaking, and after having work'd in composing the Types & printing off the Sheets I was employ'd to carry the Papers thro' the Streets to the Customers.—He had some ingenious Men among his Friends who amus'd themselves by writing little Pieces for this Paper, which gain'd it Credit, & made it more in Demand; and these Gentlemen often visited us.—Hearing their Conversations, and their Accounts of the Approbation their Papers were receiv'd with, I was excited to try my Hand among them. But being still a Boy, & suspecting that my Brother would object to printing any Thing of mine in his Paper if he knew it to be mine, I contriv'd to disguise my Hand, & writing an anonymous Paper I put it in at Night under the Door of the Printing House. It was found in the Morning & communicated to his Writing Friends when they call'd in as Usual. They read it, commented on it in my Hearing, and I had the exquisite Pleasure, of finding it met with their Approbation, and that in their different Guesses at the Author none were named but Men of some Character among us for Learning & Ingenuity.—I suppose now that I was rather lucky in my Judges: And that perhaps they were not really so very good ones as I then esteem'd them. Encourag'd however by this, I wrote and convey'd in the same Way to the Press several more Papers, which were equally approv'd, and I kept my Secret till my small Fund of Sense for such Performances was pretty well exhausted, & then I discovered[13] it; when I began to be considered a little more by my Brother's Acquaintance, and in a manner that did not quite please him, as he thought, probably with reason, that it tended to make me too vain. And perhaps this might be one Occasion of the Differences that we began to have about this Time. Tho' a Brother, he considered himself as my Master, & me as his Apprentice; and accordingly expected the same Services from me as he would from another; while I thought he demean'd me too much in some he requir'd of me, who from a Brother expected more Indulgence. Our Disputes were often brought before our Father, and I fancy I was either generally in the right, or else a better Pleader, because the Judgment was generally in my favour: But my Brother was passionate & had often beaten me, which I took extreamly amiss; and thinking my Apprenticeship very tedious, I was continually wishing for some Opportunity of shortening it, which at length offered in a manner unexpected.

One of the Pieces in our News-Paper, on some political Point which I have now forgotten, gave Offence to the Assembly. He was taken up, censur'd and imprison'd for a Month by the Speaker's Warrant, I suppose because he would not discover his Author. I too was taken up & examin'd before the Council; but tho' I did not give them any Satisfaction, they contented themselves with admonishing me, and dismiss'd me; considering me perhaps as an Apprentice who was bound to keep his Master's Secrets. During my Brother's Confinement, which I resented a good deal, notwithstanding our private Differences, I had the Management of the Paper, and I made bold to give our Rulers some Rubs in it, which my Brother took very kindly, while others began to consider me in an unfavourable Light, as a young Genius that had a Turn for

---

13. discovered: revealed.

Libelling & Satyr. My Brother's Discharge was accompany'd with an Order of the House, (a very odd one) *that James Franklin should no longer print the Paper called the New England Courant.* There was a Consultation held in our Printing House among his Friends what he should do in this Case. Some propos'd to evade the Order by changing the Name of the Paper; but my Brother seeing Inconveniences in that, it was finally concluded on as a better Way, to let it be printed for the future under the Name of *Benjamin Franklin.* And to avoid the Censure of the Assembly that might fall on him, as still printing it by his Apprentice, the Contrivance was, that my old Indenture should be return'd to me with a full Discharge on the Back of it, to be shown on Occasion; but to secure to him the Benefit of my Service I was to sign new Indentures for the Remainder of the Term, which were to be kept private. A very flimsy Scheme it was, but however it was immediately executed, and the Paper went on accordingly under my Name for several Months. At length a fresh Difference arising between my Brother and me, I took upon me to assert my Freedom, presuming that he would not venture to produce the new Indentures. It was not fair in me to take this Advantage, and this I therefore reckon one of the first Errata of my Life: But the Unfairness of it weigh'd little with me, when under the Impressions of Resentment, for the Blows his Passion too often urg'd him to bestow upon me. Tho' He was otherwise not an ill-natur'd Man: Perhaps I was too saucy & provoking.—

When he found I would leave him, he took care to prevent my getting Employment in any other Printing-House of the Town, by going round & speaking to every Master, who accordingly refus'd to give me Work. I then thought of going to New York as the nearest Place where there was a Printer: and I was the rather inclin'd to leave Boston, when I reflected that I had already made my self a little obnoxious, to the governing Party; & from the arbitrary Proceedings of the Assembly in my Brother's Case it was likely I might if I stay'd soon bring my self into Scrapes; and farther that my indiscrete Disputations about Religion began to make me pointed at with Horror by good People, as an Infidel or Atheist; I determin'd on the Point: but my Father now siding with my Brother, I was sensible that if I attempted to go openly, Means would be used to prevent me. My Friend Collins therefore undertook to manage a little for me. He agreed with the Captain of a New York Sloop for my Passage, under the Notion of my being a young Acquaintance of his that had got a naughty Girl with Child, whose Friends would compel me to marry her, and therefore I could not appear or come away publickly. So I sold some of my Books to raise a little Money, Was taken on board privately, and as we had a fair Wind, in three Days I found my self in New York near 300 Miles from home, a Boy of but 17, without the least Recommendation to or Knowledge of any Person in the Place, and with very little Money in my Pocket.

My Inclinations for the Sea, were by this time worne out, or I might now have gratify'd them.—But having a Trade, & supposing my self a pretty good Workman, I offer'd my Service to the Printer of the Place, old Mr W^m. Bradford.—He could give me no Employment, having little to do, and Help enough already: But, says he, my Son at Philadelphia has lately lost his principal Hand, Aquila Rose, by Death. If you go thither I believe he may employ you.—Philadelphia was 100 Miles farther. I set out, however, in a Boat for Amboy; leaving my Chest and Things to follow me round by Sea. In crossing the Bay we met with a Squall that tore our rotten Sails to pieces, prevented our getting into the Kill, and drove us upon Long Island. In our Way a drunken Dutchman, who was a Passenger too, fell overboard; when he was sinking I reach'd thro' the Water to his shock Pate & drew him up so that we got him in again.—His Ducking sober'd him a little, & he went to sleep, taking first out of his Pocket a Book which he desir'd I would dry for him. It prov'd to be my old favourite Author Bunyan's Pilgrim's Progress in Dutch, finely printed on good Paper with copper Cuts, a Dress better than I had ever seen it wear in its own Language. I have since found that it has been translated into most of the Languages of Europe, and suppose it has been more generally read than any other Book except perhaps the Bible.—Honest John was the first that I know of who mix'd Narration & Dialogue, a Method of Writing very engaging to the Reader, who in the most interesting Parts finds himself as it were brought into the Company, & present at the Discourse. De foe in his Cruso, his Moll Flanders, Religious Courtship, Family Instructor, & other Pieces, has imitated it with Success. And Richardson has done the same in his Pamela, &c.

When we drew near the Island we found it was at a Place where there could be no Landing, there being a great Surff on the stony Beach. So we dropt Anchor & swung round towards the Shore. Some People came down to the Water Edge & hallow'd to us, as we did to them. But the Wind was so high & the Surff so loud, that we could not hear so as to understand each other. There were Canoes on the Shore, & we made Signs & hallow'd that they should fetch us, but they either did not understand us, or thought it impracticable. So they went away, and Night coming on, we had no Remedy but to wait till the Wind should abate, and in the mean time the Boatman & I concluded to sleep if we could, and so crouded into the Scuttle with the Dutchman who was still wet, and the Spray beating over the Head of our Boat, leak'd thro' to us, so that we were soon almost as wet as he. In this Manner we lay all Night with very little Rest. But the Wind abating the next Day, we made a Shift to reach Amboy before Night, having been 30 Hours on the Water without Victuals, or any Drink but a Bottle of filthy Rum:—The Water we sail'd on being salt.

In the Evening I found my self very feverish, & went ill to Bed. But having read somewhere that cold Water drank plentifully was good for a Fever, I follow'd the Prescription, sweat plentifully most of the Night, my Fever left me, and in the Morning crossing the Ferry, proceeded on my Journey, on foot, having 50 Miles to Burlington, where I was told I should find Boats that would carry me the rest of the Way to Philadelphia.

It rain'd very hard all the Day, I was thoroughly soak'd, and by Noon a good deal tir'd, so I stopt at a poor Inn, where I staid all Night, beginning now to wish I had never left home. I cut so miserable a Figure too, that I found by the Questions ask'd me I was suspected to be some runaway Servant, and in danger of being taken up on that Suspicion.—However I proceeded the next Day, and got in the Evening to an Inn within 8 or 10 Miles of Burlington, kept by one Dr Brown.

He entred into Conversation with me while I took some Refreshment, and finding I had read a little, became very sociable and friendly. Our Acquaintance continu'd as long as he liv'd. He had been, I imagine, an itinerant Doctor, for there was no Town in England, or Country in Europe, of which he could not give a very particular Account. He had some Letters, & was ingenious, but much of an Unbeliever, & wickedly undertook some Years after to travesty the Bible in doggrel Verse as Cotton had done Virgil.—By this means he set many of the Facts in a very ridiculous Light, & might have hurt weak minds if his Work had been publish'd:—but it never was.—At his House I lay that Night, and the next Morning reach'd Burlington.—But had the Mortification to find that the regular Boats were gone, a little before my coming, and no other expected to go till Tuesday, this being Saturday. Wherefore I return'd to an old Woman in the Town of whom I had bought Gingerbread to eat on the Water, & ask'd her Advice; she invited me to lodge at her House till a Passage by Water should offer; & being tired with my foot Travelling, I accepted the Invitation. She understanding I was a Printer, would have had me stay at that Town & follow my Business, being ignorant of the Stock necessary to begin with. She was very hospitable, gave me a Dinner of Ox Cheek with great Goodwill, accepting only of a Pot of Ale in return. And I tho't my self fix'd till Tuesday should come. However walking in the Evening by the Side of the River a Boat came by, which I found was going towards Philadelphia, with several People in her. They took me in, and as there was no Wind, we row'd all the Way; and about Midnight not having yet seen the City, some of the Company were confident we must have pass'd it, and would row no farther, the others knew not where we were, so we put towards the Shore, got into a Creek, landed near an old Fence with the Rails of which we made a Fire, the Night being cold, in October, and there we remain'd till Daylight. Then one of the Company knew the Place to be Cooper's Creek a little above Philadelphia, which we saw as soon as we got out of the Creek, and arriv'd there about 8 or 9 a Clock, on the Sunday morning, and landed at the Market street Wharff.—

I have been the more particular in this Description of my Journey, & shall be so of my first Entry into that City, that you may in your Mind compare such unlikely Beginning with the Figure I have since made there. I was in my working Dress, my best Cloaths being to come round by Sea. I was dirty from my Journey; my Pockets were stuff'd out with Shirts & Stockings; I knew no Soul, nor where to look for Lodging. I was fatigu'd with Travelling, Rowing & Want of Rest. I was very hungry, and my whole Stock of Cash consisted of a Dutch Dollar and about a Shilling in Copper. The latter I gave the People of the Boat for my Passage, who at first refus'd it on Account of my Rowing; but I insisted on their taking it, a Man being sometimes more generous when he has but a little Money than when he has plenty, perhaps thro' Fear of being thought to have but little. Then I walk'd up the Street, gazing about, till near the Market House I met a Boy with Bread. I had made many a Meal on Bread, & inquiring where he got it, I went immediately to the Baker's he directed me to in second Street; and ask'd for Bisket, intending such as we had in Boston, but they it seems were not made in Philadelphia, then I ask'd for a threepenny Loaf, and was told they had none such: so not considering or knowing the Difference of Money & the greater Cheapness nor the Names of his Bread, I bad him give me three pennyworth of any sort. He gave me accordingly three great Puffy Rolls. I was surpriz'd at the Quantity, but took it, and having no Room in my Pockets, walk'd off, with a Roll under each Arm, & eating the other. Thus I went up Market Street as far as fourth Street, passing by the Door of Mr Read, my future Wife's Father, when she standing at the Door saw me, & thought I made as I certainly did a most awkward ridiculous Appearance. Then I turn'd and went down Chestnut Street and part of Walnut Street, eating my Roll all the Way, and coming round found my self again at Market street Wharff, near the Boat I came in, to which I went for a Draught of the River Water, and being fill'd with one of my Rolls, gave the other two to a Woman & her Child that came down the River in the Boat with us and were waiting to go farther. Thus refresh'd I walk'd again up the Street, which by this time had many clean dress'd People in it who were all walking the same Way; I join'd them, and thereby was led into the great Meeting House of the Quakers near the Market. I sat down among them, and after looking round a while & hearing nothing said, being very drowzy thro' Labour & want of Rest the preceding Night, I fell fast asleep, and continu'd so till the Meeting broke up, when one was kind enough to rouse me. This was therefore the first House I was in or slept in, in Philadelphia.—

Walking again down towards the River, & looking in the Faces of People, I met a young Quaker Man whose Countenance I lik'd, and accosting him requested he would tell me where a Stranger could get Lodging. We were then near the Sign of the Three Mariners. Here, says he, is one Place that entertains Strangers, but it is not a reputable House; if thee wilt walk with me, I'll show thee a better. He brought me to the Crooked Billet in Water-Street. Here I got a Dinner. And while I was eating it, several sly Questions were ask'd me, as it seem'd to be suspected from my youth & Appearance, that I might be some Runaway. After Dinner my Sleepiness return'd: and being shown to a Bed, I lay down without undressing, and slept till Six in the Evening; was call'd to Supper; went to Bed again very early and slept soundly till the next Morning. Then I made my self as tidy as I could, and went to Andrew Bradford the Printer's.—I found in the Shop the old Man his Father, whom I had seen at New York, and who travelling on horse back had got to Philadelphia before me.—He introduc'd me to his son, who receiv'd me civilly, gave me a Breakfast, but told me he did not at present want a Hand, being lately supply'd with one. But there was another Printer in town lately set up, one Keimer, who perhaps might employ me; if not, I should be welcome to lodge at his House, & he would give me a little Work to do now & then till fuller Business should offer.

The old Gentleman said, he would go with me to the new Printer: And when we found him, Neighbour, says Bradford, I have brought to see you a young Man of your Business, perhaps you may want such a One. He ask'd me a few Questions, put a Composing Stick in my Hand to see how I work'd, and then said he would employ me soon, tho' he had just then nothing for me to do. And taking old Bradford whom he had never seen before, to be one of the Towns People that had a Good Will for him, enter'd into a Conversation on his present Undertaking & Prospects; while Bradford not discovering that he was the other Printer's Father; on Keimer's Saying he expected soon to get the greatest Part of the Business into his own Hands, drew him on by artful Questions and starting little Doubts, to explain all his Views, what Interest he rely'd on & in what manner he intended to proceed.—I who stood by & heard all, saw immediately that one of them was a crafty old Sophister, and the other a mere Novice. Bradford left me with Keimer, who was greatly surpriz'd when I told him who the old Man was.

Keimer's Printing House I found, consisted of an old shatter'd Press, and one small worn-out Fount of English, which he was then using himself, composing in it an Elegy on Aquila Rose before-mentioned, an ingenious young Man of excellent Character much respected in the Town, Clerk of the Assembly, & a pretty Poet. Keimer made Verses, too, but very indifferently.—He could not be said to write them, for his Manner was to compose them in the Types directly out of his Head; so there being no Copy, but one Pair of Cases, and the Elegy likely to require all the Letter, no one could help him.—I endeavour'd to put his Press (which he had not yet us'd, & of which he understood nothing) into Order fit to be work'd with; & promising to come & print off his Elegy as soon as he should have got it ready, I return'd to Bradford's who gave me a little Job to do for the present, & there I lodged & dieted. A few Days after Keimer sent for me to print off the Elegy. And now he had got another Pair of Cases, and a Pamphlet to reprint, on which he set me to work.—

These two Printers I found poorly qualified for their Business. Bradford had not been bred to it, & was very illiterate; and Keimer tho' something of a Scholar, was a mere Compositor, knowing nothing of Presswork. He had been one of the French Prophets and could act their enthusiastic Agitations. At this time he did not profess any particular Religion, but something of all on occasion; was very ignorant of the World, & had, as I afterwards found, a good deal of the Knave in his Composition. He did not like my Lodging at Bradford's while I work'd with him. He had a House indeed, but without Furniture, so he could not lodge me: But he got me a Lodging at Mr Read's before-mentioned, who was the Owner of his House. And my Chest & Clothes being come by this time, I made rather a more respectable Appearance in the Eyes of Miss Read, than I had done when she first happen'd to see me eating my Roll in the Street.—

I began now to have some Acquaintance among the young People of the Town, that were Lovers of Reading with whom I spent my Evenings very pleasantly and gaining Money by my Industry & Frugality, I lived very agreably, forgetting Boston as much as I could, and not desiring that any there should know where I resided except my Friend Collins who was in my Secret, & kept it when I wrote to him.—At length an Incident happened that sent me back again much sooner than I had intended.—

I had a Brother-in-law, Robert Holmes, Master of a Sloop, that traded between Boston and Delaware. He being at New Castle 40 Miles below Philadelphia, heard there of me, and wrote me a Letter, mentioning the Concern of my Friends[14] in Boston at my abrupt Departure, assuring me of their Goodwill to me, and that every thing would be accommodated to my Mind if I would return, to which he exhorted me very earnestly.—I wrote an Answer to his Letter, thank'd him for his Advice, but stated my Reasons for quitting Boston fully, & in such a Light as to convince him I was not so wrong as he had apprehended.—Sir William Keith Governor of the Province, was then at New Castle, and Capt. Holmes happening to be in Company with him when my Letter came to hand, spoke to him of me, and show'd him the Letter. The Governor read it, and seem'd surpriz'd when he was told my Age. He said I appear'd a young Man of promising Parts, and therefore should be encouraged: The Printers at Philadelphia were wretched ones, and if I would set up there, he made no doubt I should succeed; for his Part, he would procure me the publick Business, & do me every

14. Friends: family.

other Service in his Power. This my Brother-in-Law afterwards told me in Boston. But I knew as yet nothing of it; when one Day Keimer and I being at Work together near the Window, we saw the Governor and another Gentleman (which prov'd to be Col. French, of New Castle) finely dress'd, come directly across the Street to our House, & heard them at the Door. Keimer ran down immediately, thinking it a Visit to him. But the Governor enquir'd for me, came up, & with a Condescension[15] & Politeness I had been quite unus'd to, made me many Compliments, desired to be acquainted with me, blam'd me kindly for not having made my self known to him when I first came to the Place, and would have me away with him to the Tavern where he was going with Col. French to taste as he said some excellent Madeira. I was not a little surpriz'd, and Keimer star'd like a Pig poison'd. I went however with the Governor & Col. French, to a Tavern the Corner of Third Street, and over the Madeira he propos'd my Setting up my Business, laid beforre me the Probabilities of Success, & both he & Col French, assur'd me I should have their Interest & Influence in procuring the Publick Business of both Governments. On my doubting whether my Father would assist me in it, Sir William said he would give me a Letter to him, in which he would state the Advantages, —and he did not doubt of prevailing with him. So it was concluded I should return to Boston in the first Vessel with the Governor's Letter recommending me to my Father. In the mean time the Intention was to be kept secret, and I went on working with Keimer as usual, the Governor sending for me now & then to dine with him, a very great Honour I thought it, and conversing with me in the most affable, familiar, & friendly manner imaginable. About the End of April 1724 a little Vessel offer'd for Boston. I took Leave of Keimer as going to see my Friends. The Governor gave me an ample Letter, saying many flattering things of me to my Father, and strongly recommending the Project of my setting up at Philadelphia, as a Thing that must make my Fortune.—We struck on a Shoal in going down the Bay & sprung a Leak, we had a blustring time at Sea, and were oblig'd to pump almost continually, at which I took my Turn.—We arriv'd safe however at Boston in about a Fortnight.—I had been absent Seven Months and my Friends had heard nothing of me, for my Br. Holmes was not yet return'd; and had not written about me. My unexpected Appearance surpriz'd the Family; all were however very glad to see me and made me Welcome, except my Brother. I went to see him at his Printing-House: I was better dress'd than ever while in his Service, having a genteel new Suit from Head to foot, a Watch, and my Pockets lin'd with near Five Pounds Sterling in Silver. He receiv'd me not very frankly, look'd me all over, and turn'd to his Work again. The Journey-Men were inquisitive where I had been, what sort of a Country it was, and how I lik'd it? I prais'd it much, & the happy Life I led in it; expressing strongly my Intention of returning to it; and one of them asking what kind of Money we had there, I produc'd a handful of Silver, and spread it before them, which was a kind of Raree-Show they had not been us'd to, Paper being the Money of Boston. Then I took an Opportunity of letting them see my Watch: and lastly, (my Brother still glum & sullen) I gave them a Piece of Eight to drink & took my Leave.—This Visit of mine offended him extreamly.

---

15. Condescension: generosity.

For when my Mother some time after spoke to him of a Reconciliation, & of her Wishes to see us on good Terms together, & that we might live for the future as Brothers, he said, I had insulted him in such a Manner before his People that he could never forget or forgive it.—In this however he was mistaken.—

My Father receiv'd the Governor's Letter with some apparent Surprize; but said little of it to me for some Days; when Capt. Homes returning, he show'd it to him, ask'd if he knew Keith, and what kind of a Man he was: Adding his Opinion that he must be of small Discretion, to think of setting a Boy up in Business who wanted yet 3 Years of being at Man's Estate. Homes said what he could in favor of the Project; but my Father was clear in the Impropriety of it; and at last gave a flat Denial to it. Then he wrote a civil Letter to Sir William thanking him for the Patronage he had so kindly offered me, but declining to assist me as yet in Setting up, I being in his Opinion too young to be trusted with the Management of a Business so important; & for which the Preparation must be so expensive.—

My Friend & Companion Collins, who was a Clerk at the Post-Office, pleas'd with the Account I gave him of my new Country, determin'd to go thither also:—And while I waited for my Fathers Determination, he set out before me by Land to Rhode Island, leaving his Books which were a pretty Collection of Mathematicks & Natural Philosophy, to come with mine & me to New York where he propos'd to wait for me. My Father, tho' he did not approve Sir William's Proposition was yet pleas'd that I had been able to obtain so advantageous a Character from a Person of such Note where I had resided, and that I had been so industrious & careful as to equip my self so handsomely in so short a time: therefore seeing no Prospect of an Accommodation between my Brother & me, he gave his Consent to my Returning again to Philadelphia, advis'd me to behave respectfully to the People there, endeavour to obtain the general Esteem, & avoid lampooning & libelling to which he thought I had too much Inclination;—telling me, that by steady Industry and a prudent Parsimony, I might save enough by the time I was One and Twenty to set me up, & that if I came near the Matter he would help me out with the Rest.—This was all I could obtain, except some small Gifts as Tokens of his & my Mother's Love, when I embark'd again for New-York, now with their Approbation & their Blessing.—

The Sloop putting in at Newport, Rhode Island, I visited my Brother John, who had been married & settled there some Years. He received me very affectionately, for he always lov'd me.—A Friend of his, one Vernon, having some Money due to him in Pensilvania, about 35 Pounds Currency, desired I would receive it for him, and keep it till I had his Directions what to remit it in. Accordingly he gave me an Order.—This afterwards occasion'd me a good deal of Uneasiness.—At Newport we took in a Number of Passengers for New York: Among which were two young Women, Companions, and a grave, sensible Matron-like Quaker-Woman with her Attendants.—I had shown an obliging Readiness to do her some little Services which impress'd her I suppose with a degree of Good-will towards me.—Therefore when she saw a daily growing Familiarity between me & the two Young Women, which they appear'd to encourage, she took me aside & said, Young Man, I am concern'd for thee, as thou has no Friend with thee, and seems not to know much of the World, or of the Snares Youth is expos'd to; depend upon it those are very bad Women, I can see it in all their

Actions, and if thee art not upon thy Guard, they will draw thee into some Danger: they are Strangers to thee,—and I advise thee in a friendly Concern for thy Welfare, to have no Acquaintance with them.—As I seem'd at first not to think so ill of them as she did, she mention'd some Things she had observ'd & heard that had escap'd my Notice; but now convinc'd me she was right. I thank'd her for her kind Advice, and promis'd to follow it.—When we arriv'd at New York, they told me where they liv'd, & invited me to come and see them: but I avoided it. And it was well I did: For the next Day, the Captain miss'd a Silver Spoon & some other Things that had been taken out of his Cabbin, and knowing that these were a Couple of Strumpets, he got a Warrant to search their Lodgings, found the stolen Goods, and had the Thieves punish'd.—So tho' we had escap'd a sunken Rock which we scrap'd upon in the Passage, I thought this Escape of rather more Importance to me. At New York I found my Friend Collins, who had arriv'd there some Time before me. We had been intimate from Children, and had read the same Books together. But he had the Advantage of more time for Reading, & Studying and a wonderful Genius for Mathematical Learning in which he far outstript me. While I liv'd in Boston most of my Hours of Leisure for Conversation were spent with him, & he continu'd a sober as well as an industrious Lad; was much respected for his Learning by several of the Clergy & other Gentlemen, & seem'd to promise making a good Figure in Life: but during my Absence he had acquir'd a Habit of Sotting with Brandy; and I found by his own Account & what I heard from others, that he had been drunk every day since his Arrival at New York, & behav'd very oddly. He had gam'd too and lost his Money, so that I was oblig'd to discharge his Lodgings, & defray his Expences to and at Philadelphia:—Which prov'd extreamly inconvenient to me.—The then Governor of N York, Burnet, Son of Bishop Burnet hearing from the Captain that a young Man, one of his Passengers, had a great many Books, desired he would bring me to see him. I waited upon him accordingly, and should have taken Collins with me but that he was not sober. The Governor treated me with great Civility, show'd me his Library, which was a very large one, & we had a good deal of Conversation about Books & Authors. This was the second Governor who had done me the Honour to take Notice of me, which to a poor Boy like me was very pleasing.—We proceeded to Philadelphia. I received on the Way Vernon's Money, without which we could hardly have finish'd our Journey.—Collins wish'd to be employ'd in some Counting House; but whether they discover'd his Dramming by his Breath, or by his Behaviour, tho' he had some Recommendations, he met with no Success in any Application, and continu'd Lodging & Boarding at the same House with me & at my Expence. Knowing I had that Money of Vernon's he was continually borrowing of me, still promising Repayment as soon as he should be in Business. At length he had got so much of it, that I was distress'd to think what I should do, in case of being call'd on to remit it.—His Drinking continu'd, about which we sometimes quarrel'd, for when a little intoxicated he was very fractious. Once in a Boat on the Delaware with some other young Men, he refused to row in his Turn: I will be row'd home, says he. We will not row you, says I. You must says he, or stay all Night on the Water, just as you please. The others said, Let us row; What signifies it? But my Mind being soured with his other Conduct, I continu'd to refuse. So he swore he would make me row, or throw me overboard; and coming along stepping on the Thwarts towards me, when he came up & struck at me, I clapt my Hand under his Crutch, and rising pitch'd him head-foremost into the River. I knew he was a good Swimmer, and so was under little Concern about him; but before he could get round to lay hold of the Boat, we had with a few Strokes pull'd her out of his Reach.—And ever when he drew near the Boat, we ask'd if he would row, striking a few Strokes to slide her away from him.— He was ready to die with Vexation, & obstinately would not promise to row; however seeing him at last beginning to tire, we lifted him in; and brought him home dripping wet in the Evening. We hardly exchang'd a civil Word afterwards; and a West India Captain who had a Commission to procure a Tutor for the Sons of a Gentleman at Barbadoes, happening to meet with him, agreed to carry him thither. He left me then, promising to remit me the first Money he should receive in order to discharge the Debt. But I never heard of him after.—The Breaking into this Money of Vernon's was one of the first great Errata[16] of my Life. And this Affair show'd that my Father was not much out in his Judgment when he suppos'd me too Young to manage Business of Importance. But Sir William, on reading his Letter, said he was too prudent. There was great Difference in Persons, and Discretion did not always accompany Years, nor was Youth always without it. And since he will not set you up, says he, I will do it my self. Give me an Inventory of the Things necessary to be had from England, and I will send for them. You shall repay me when you are able; I am resolv'd to have a good Printer here, and I am sure you must succeed. This was spoken with such an Appearance of Cordiality, that I had not the least doubt of his meaning what he said.—I had hitherto kept the Proposition of my Setting up a Secret in Philadelphia, & I still kept it. Had it been known that I depended on the Governor, probably some Friend that knew him better would have advis'd me not to rely on him, as I afterwards heard it as his known Character to be liberal of Promises which he never meant to keep.—Yet unsolicited as he was by me, how could I think his generous Offers insincere? I believ'd him one of the best Men in the World.—

I presented him an Inventory of a little Printing House, amounting by my Computation to about £100 Sterling. He lik'd it, but ask'd me if my being on the Spot in England to chuse the Types & see that every thing was good of the kind, might not be of some Advantage. Then, says he, when there, you may make Acquaintances & establish Correspondencies in the Bookselling, & Stationary Way. I agreed that this might be advantageous. Then says he, get yourself ready to go with Annis; which was the annual Ship, and the only one at that Time usually passing between London and Philadelphia. But it would be some Months before Annis sail'd, so I continu'd working with Keimer, fretting about the Money Collins had got from me, and in daily Apprehensions of being call'd upon by Vernon, which however did not happen for some Years after.—

I believe I have omitted mentioning that in my first Voyage from Boston, being becalm'd off Block Island, our People set about catching Cod & hawl'd up a great many. Hitherto I had stuck to my Resolution of not eating animal Food; and on this

16. Errata: Latin for errors, used also for a printer's correction slip.

Occasion, I consider'd with my Master Tryon, the taking every Fish as a kind of unpro-vok'd Murder, since none of them had or ever could do us any Injury that might justify the Slaughter.—All this seem'd very reasonable.—But I had formerly been a great Lover of Fish, & when this came hot out of the Frying Pan, it smelt admirably well. I balanc'd some time between Principle & Inclination: till I recollected, that when the Fish were opened, I saw smaller Fish taken out of their Stomachs:—Then, thought I, if you eat one another, I don't see why we mayn't eat you. So I din'd upon Cod very heartily and continu'd to eat with other People, returning only now & then occasion-ally to a vegetable Diet. So convenient a thing it is to be a *reasonable Creature,* since it enables one to find or make a Reason for every thing one has a mind to do.—

Keimer & I liv'd on a pretty good familiar Footing & agreed tolerably well: for he suspected nothing of my Setting up. He retain'd a great deal of his old Enthusiasms, and lov'd an Argumentation. We therefore had many Disputations. I us'd to work him so with my Socratic Method, and had trapann'd him so often by Questions apparently so distant from any Point we had in hand, and yet by degrees led to the Point, and brought him into Difficulties & Contradictions, that at last he grew ridiculously cautious, and would hardly answer me the most common Question, without asking first, *What do you intend to infer from that?* However it gave him so high an Opinion of my Abilities in the Confuting Way, that he seriously propos'd my being his Colleague in a Project he had of setting up a new Sect. He was to preach the Doctrines, and I was to confound all Opponents. When he came to explain with me upon the Doctrines, I found several Conundrums which I objected to, unless I might have my Way a little too, and introduce some of mine. Keimer wore his Beard at full Length, because somewhere in the Mosaic Law it is said, *thou shalt not mar the Corners of thy Beard.* He likewise kept the seventh day Sabbath; and these two Points were Essentials with him.—I dislik'd both, but agreed to admit them upon Condition of his adopting the Doctrine of using no animal Food. I doubt, says he, my Constitu-tion will not bear that. I assur'd him it would, & that he would be the better for it. He was usually a great Glutton, and I promis'd myself some Diversion in half-starving him. He agreed to try the Practice if I would keep him Company. I did so and we held it for three Months. We had our Victuals dress'd and brought to us regularly by a Woman in the Neighbourhood, who had from me a List of 40 Dishes to be prepar'd for us at different times, in all which there was neither Fish Flesh nor Fowl, and the Whim suited me the better at this time from the Cheapness of it, not costing us above 18^d Sterling each, per Week.—I have since kept several Lents most strictly, Leaving the common Diet for that, and that for the common, abruptly, without the least Inconvenience: So that I think there is little in the Advice of making those Changes by easy Graduations.—I went on pleasantly, but Poor Keimer suffer'd grievously, tir'd of the Project, long'd for the Flesh Pots of Egypt, and order'd a roast Pig; He invited me & two Women Friends to dine with him, but it being brought too soon upon table, he could not resist the Temptation, and ate it all up before we came.—

I had made some Courtship during this time to Miss Read, I had a great Respect & Affection for her, and had some Reason to believe she had the same for me: but as I was about to take a long Voyage, and we were both very young, only a little above 18. it was thought most prudent by her Mother to prevent our going too far at present, as a Marriage if it was to take place would be more convenient after my Return, when I should be as I expected set up in my Business. Perhaps too she thought my Expectations not so well founded as I imagined them to be.—

My chief Acquaintances at this time were, Charles Osborne, Joseph Watson, & James Ralph; All Lovers of Reading. The two first were Clerks to an eminent Scrivener or Conveyancer in the Town, Charles Brogden; the other was Clerk to a Merchant. Watson was a pious sensible young Man, of great Integrity.—The others rather more lax in their Principles of Religion, particularly Ralph, who as well as Collins had been unsettled by me, for which they both made me suffer.—Osborne was sensible, candid, frank, sincere, and affectionate to his Friends; but in litterary Matters too fond of Criticising. Ralph, was ingenious, genteel in his Manners, & extreamly eloquent; I think I never knew a prettier Talker.— Both of them great Admirers of Poetry, and began to try their Hands in little Pieces. Many pleasant Walks we four had together, on Sundays into the Woods near Skuylkill, where we read to one another & conferr'd on what we read. Ralph was inclin'd to pursue the Study of Poetry, not doubting but he might become eminent in it and make his Fortune by it, alledging that the best Poets must when they first began to write, make as many Faults as he did.— Osborne dissuaded him, assur'd him he had no Genius for Poetry, & advis'd him to think of nothing beyond the Business he was bred to; that in the mercantile way tho' he had no Stock, he might by his Diligence & Punctuality recommend himself to Employment as a Factor, and in time acquire wherewith to trade on his own Account. I approv'd the amusing one's Self with Poetry now & then, so far as to improve one's Language, but no farther. On this it was propos'd that we should each of us at our next Meeting produce a Piece of our own Composing, in order to improve by our mutual Observations, Criticisms & Corrections. As Language & Expression was what we had in View, we excluded all Considerations of Invention, by agreeing that the Task should be a Version of the 18th Psalm, which describes the Descent of a Deity. When the Time of our Meeting drew nigh, Ralph call'd on me first, & let me know his Piece was ready. I told him I had been busy, & having little Inclination had done nothing.—He then show'd me his Piece for my Opinion; and I much approv'd it, as it appear'd to me to have great Merit. Now, says he, Osborne never will allow the least merit in any thing of mine, but makes 1000 Criticisms out of mere Envy. He is not so jealous of you. I wish therefore you would take this Piece, & produce it as yours. I will pretend not to have had time, & so produce nothing: We shall then see what he will say to it.—It was agreed, and I immediately transcrib'd it that it might appear in my own hand. We met. Watson's Performance was read: there were some Beauties in it: but many Defects. Osborne's was read: It was much better. Ralph did it Justice, remark'd some Faults, but applauded the Beauties. He himself had nothing to produce. I was backward, seem'd desirous of being excus'd, had not had sufficient Time to correct; &c. but no Excuse could be admitted, produce I must. It was read and repeated; Watson and Osborne gave up the Contest; and join'd in applauding it immoderately. Ralph only made some Criticisms & propos'd some Amendments, but I defended my Text. Osborne was against Ralph, & told him he was no better a Critic than Poet; so he dropt the Argument. As they two went home together, Osborne express'd himself still more strongly in favour of what he thought my Production, having restrain'd himself before as he said, lest I should think it Flattery. But who would have imagin'd, says he, that Franklin had been capable of such a Performance; such Painting, such Force! such Fire! he has even improv'd the Original! In his common Conversation, he seems to have no Choice of Words; he hesitates and blunders; and yet, good God, how he writes!—When we next met, Ralph discover'd the Trick we had plaid him, and Osborne was a little laught at. This Transaction fix'd Ralph in his Resolution of becoming a Poet. I did all I could to dissuade him from it, but He continu'd scribbling Verses, till *Pope* cur'd him.[17]—He became however a pretty good Prose Writer. More of him hereafter. But as I may not have occasion again to mention the other two, I shall just remark here, that Watson died in my Arms a few Years after, much lamented, being the best of our Set. Osborne went to the West Indies, where he became an eminent Lawyer & made Money, but died young. He and I had made a serious Agreement, that the one who happen'd first to die, should if possible make a friendly Visit to the other, and acquaint him how he found things in that separate State. But he never fulfill'd his Promise.

The Governor, seeming to like my Company, had me frequently to his House; & his Setting me up was always mention'd as a fix'd thing. I was to take with me Letters recommendatory to a Number of his Friends, besides the Letter of Credit, to furnish me with the necessary Money for purchasing the Press & Types, Paper, &c. For these Letters I was appointed to call at different times, when they were to be ready, but a future time was still named.—Thus we went on till the Ship whose Departure too had been several times postponed was on the Point of sailing. Then when I call'd to take my Leave & receive the Letters, his Secretary, Dr Bard, came out to me and said the Governor was extreamly busy, in writing, but would be down at Newcastle before the Ship, & there the Letters would be delivered to me.

Ralph, tho' married & having one Child, had determined to accompany me in this Voyage. It was thought he intended to establish a Correspondence, & obtain Goods to sell on Commission. But I found afterwards, that thro' some Discontent with his Wifes Relations, he purposed to leave her on their Hands, & never return again.— Having taken leave of my Friends, & interchang'd some Promises with Miss Read, I left Philadelphia in the Ship, which anchor'd at Newcastle. The Governor was there. But when I went to his Lodging, the Secretary came to me from him with the civillest Message in the World, that he could not then see me being engag'd in Business of the utmost Importance, but should send the Letters to me on board, wish'd me heartily a good Voyage and a speedy Return, &c. I return'd on board, a little puzzled, but still not doubting.—

Mr Andrew Hamilton, a famous Lawyer of Philadelphia, had taken Passage in the same Ship for himself and Son: and with Mr Denham a Quaker Merchant, & Messrs Onion & Russel Masters of an Iron Work in Maryland, had engag'd the Great Cabin; so that Ralph and I were forc'd to take up with a Birth in the Steerage:—And none on board knowing us, were considered as ordinary Persons.—But Mr Hamilton & his Son (it was James, since Governor) return'd from New Castle to Philadelphia, the

---

17. till *Pope* cured him: Alexander Pope mocked Ralph in his satire of contemporary piety, *The Dunciad:* "Silence, ye wolves! while Ralph to Cynthia howls, / And makes night hideous—Answer him, ye owls!" III, ll. 165–66.

Father being recall'd by a great Fee to plead for a seized Ship.—And just before we sail'd Col. French coming on board, & showing me great Respect, I was more taken Notice of, and with my Friend Ralph invited by the other Gentlemen to come into the Cabin, there being now Room. Accordingly we remov'd thither.

Understanding that Col. French had brought on board the Governor's Dispatches, I ask'd the Captain for those Letters that were to be under my Care. He said all were put into the Bag together; and he could not then come at them; but before we landed in England, I should have an Opportunity of picking them out. So I was satisfy'd for the present, and we proceeded on our Voyage. We had a sociable Company in the Cabin, and lived uncommonly well, having the Addition of all Mr Hamilton's Stores, who had laid in plentifully. In this Passage Mr Denham contracted a Friendship for me that continued during his Life. The Voyage was otherwise not a pleasant one, as we had a great deal of bad Weather.—

When we came into the Channel, the Captain kept his Word with me, & gave me an Opportunity of examining the Bag for the Governor's Letters. I found none upon which my Name was put, as under my Care; I pick'd out 6 or 7 that by the Handwriting I thought might be the promis'd Letters, especially as one of them was directed to Basket the King's Printer, and another to some Stationer. We arriv'd in London the 24th of December, 1724.—I waited upon the Stationer who came first in my Way, delivering the Letter as from Gov. Keith. I don't know such a Person, says he: but opening the Letter, O, this is from Riddlesden; I have lately found him to be a compleat Rascal, and I will have nothing to do with him, nor receive any Letters from him. So putting the Letter into my Hand, he turn'd on his Heel & left me to serve some Customer.—I was surprized to find these were not the Governor's Letters. And after recollecting and comparing Circumstances, I began to doubt his Sincerity.—I found my Friend Denham, and opened the whole Affair to him. He let me into Keith's Character, told me there was not the least Probability that he had written any Letters for me, that no one who knew him had the smallest Dependance on him, and he laught at the Notion of the Governor's giving me a Letter of Credit, having as he said no Credit to give.—On my expressing some Concern about what I should do: He advis'd me to endeavour getting some Employment in the Way of my Business. Among the Printers here, says he, you will improve yourself; and when you return to America, you will set up to greater Advantage.—

We both of us happen'd to know, as well as the Stationer, that Riddlesden the Attorney, was a very Knave. He had half ruin'd Miss Read's Father by drawing him in to be bound for him. By his Letter it appear'd, there was a secret Scheme on foot to the Prejudice of Hamilton, (Suppos'd to be then coming over with us,) and that Keith was concern'd in it with Riddlesden. Denham, who was a Friend of Hamilton's, thought he ought to be acquainted with it. So when he arriv'd in England, which was soon after, partly from Resentment & Ill-Will to Keith & Riddlesden, & partly from Good Will to him: I waited on him, and gave him the Letter. He thank'd me cordially, the Information being of Importance to him. And from that time he became my Friend, greatly to my Advantage afterwards on many Occasions.

But what shall we think of a Governor's playing such pitiful Tricks, & imposing so grossly on a poor ignorant Boy! It was a Habit he had acquired. He wish'd to please every body; and having little to give, he gave Expectations.—He was otherwise an ingenious sensible Man, a pretty good Writer, & a good Governor for the People, tho' not for his Constituents the Proprietaries, whose Instructions he sometimes disregarded.—Several of our best Laws were of his Planning, and pass'd during his Administration.—

Ralph and I were inseparable Companions. We took Lodgings together in Little Britain at 3/6 per Week, as much as we could then afford.—He found some Relations, but they were poor & unable to assist him. He now let me know his Intentions of remaining in London, and that he never meant to return to Philadelphia.—He had brought no Money with him, the whole he could muster having been expended in paying his Passage.—I had 15 Pistoles: So he borrowed occasionally of me, to subsist while he was looking out for Business.—He first endeavoured to get into the Playhouse, believing himself qualify'd for an Actor; but Wilkes, to whom he apply'd, advis'd him candidly not to think of that Employment, as it was impossible he should succeed in it.—Then he propos'd to Roberts, a Publisher in Paternoster Row, to write for him a Weekly Paper like the Spectator, on certain Conditions, which Roberts did not approve. Then he endeavour'd to get Employment as a Hackney Writer to copy for the Stationers & Lawyers about the Temple: but could find no Vacancy.—

I immediately got into Work at Palmer's then a famous Printing House in Bartholomew Close; and here I continu'd near a Year. I was pretty diligent; but spent with Ralph a good deal of my Earnings in going to Plays & other Places of Amusement. We had together consum'd all my Pistoles, and now just rubb'd on from hand to mouth. He seem'd quite to forget his Wife & Child, and I by degrees my Engagements with Miss Read, to whom I never wrote more than one Letter, & that was to let her know I was not likely soon to return. This was another of the great Errata of my Life, which I should wish to correct if I were to live it over again.—In fact, by our Expences, I was constantly kept unable to pay my Passage.

At Palmer's I was employ'd in Composing for the second Edition of Woollaston's Religion of Nature. Some of his Reasonings not appearing to me well-founded, I wrote a little metaphysical Piece, in which I made Remarks on them. It was entitled, *A Dissertation on Liberty & Necessity, Pleasure and Pain.*—I inscrib'd it to my Friend Ralph.—I printed a small Number. It occasion'd my being more consider'd by Mr Palmer, as a young Man of some Ingenuity, tho' he seriously expostulated with me upon the Principles of my Pamphlet which to him appear'd abominable. My printing this Pamphlet was another Erratum.

While I lodg'd in Little Britain I made an Acquaintance with one Wilcox a Bookseller, whose Shop was at the next Door. He had an immense Collection of second-hand Books. Circulating Libraries were not then in Use; but we agreed that on certain reasonable Terms which I have now forgotten, I might take, read & return any of his Books. This I esteem'd a great Advantage, & I made as much Use of it as I could.—

My Pamphlet by some means falling into the Hands of one Lyons, a Surgeon, Author of a Book intituled *The Infallibility of Human Judgment,* it occasioned an Acquaintance between us; he took great Notice of me, call'd on me often, to converse on these Subjects, carried me to the Horns a pale Ale-House in [   ] Lane,

Cheapside, and introduc'd me to Dr Mandevile,[18] Author of the Fable of the Bees who had a Club there, of which he was the Soul, being a most facetious entertaining Companion. Lyons too introduc'd me to Dr Pemberton, at Batson's Coffee House, who promis'd to give me an Opportunity some time or other of seeing Sir Isaac Newton, of which I was extreamly desirous; but this never happened.

I had brought over a few Curiosities among which the principal was a Purse made of the Asbestos, which purifies by Fire. Sir Hans Sloane heard of it, came to see me, and invited me to his House in Bloomsbury Square; where he show'd me all his Curiosities, and persuaded me to let him add that to the Number, for which he paid me handsomely.—

In our House there lodg'd a young Woman; a Millener, who I think had a Shop in the Cloisters. She had been genteelly bred; was sensible & lively, and of most pleasing Conversation.—Ralph read Plays to her in the Evenings, they grew intimate, she took another Lodging, and he follow'd her. They liv'd together some time, but he being still out of Business, & her Income not sufficient to maintain them with her Child, he took a Resolution of going from London, to try for a Country School, which he thought himself well qualify'd to undertake, as he wrote an excellent Hand, & was a Master of Arithmetic & Accounts.—This however he deem'd a Business below him, & confident of future better Fortune when he should be unwilling to have it known that he once was so meanly employ'd, he chang'd his Name, & did me the Honour to assume mine.—For I soon after had a Letter from him, acquainting me, that he was settled in a small Village in Berkshire, I think it was, where he taught reading & writing to 10 or a dozen Boys at 6 pence each per Week, recommending Mrs T. to my Care, and desiring me to write to him directing for Mr Franklin Schoolmaster at such a Place. He continu'd to write frequently, sending me large Specimens of an Epic Poem, which he was then composing, and desiring my Remarks & Corrections.—These I gave him from time to time, but endeavour'd rather to discourage his Proceeding. One of Young's Satires was then just publish'd. I copy'd & sent him a great Part of it, which set in a strong Light the Folly of pursuing the Muses with any Hope of Advancement by them. All was in vain. Sheets of the Poem continu'd to come by every Post. In the mean time Mrs T. having on his Account lost her Friends & Business, was often in Distresses, & us'd to send for me, and borrow what I could spare to help her out of them. I grew fond of her Company, and being at this time under no Religious Restraints, & presuming on my Importance to her, I attempted Familiarities, (another Erratum) which she repuls'd with a proper Resentment, and acquainted him with my Behaviour. This made a Breach between us, & when he return'd again to London, he let me know he thought I had cancel'd all the Obligations he had been under to me.— So I found I was never to expect his Repaying me what I lent to him or advanc'd for him. This was however not then of much Consequence, as he was totally unable.— And in the Loss of his Friendship I found my self reliev'd from a Burthen. I now began to think of getting a little Money beforehand; and expecting better Work, I left

---

18. Dr Mandevile: Bernard de Mandeville, author of *The Fable of the Bees: or Private Vices, Public Benefits* (1714). His thesis that social benefits come not from altruism but from the pursuit of self-interest must have been attractive to Franklin, as it was to Adam Smith (see chapter 11).

Palmer's to work at Watt's near Lincoln's Inn Fields, a still greater Printing House. Here I continu'd all the rest of my Stay in London.

At my first Admission into this Printing House, I took to working at Press, imagining I felt a Want of the Bodily Exercise I had been us'd to in America, where Presswork is mix'd with Composing. I drank only Water; the other Workmen, near 50 in Number, were great Guzzlers of Beer. On occasion I carried up & down Stairs a large Form of Types in each hand, when others carried but one in both Hands. They wonder'd to see from this & several Instances that the Water-American as they call'd me was *stronger* than themselves who drunk *strong* Beer. We had an Alehouse Boy who attended always in the House to supply the Workmen. My Companion at the Press, drank every day a Pint before Breakfast, a Pint at Breakfast with his Bread and Cheese; a Pint between Breakfast and Dinner; a Pint at Dinner; a Pint in the Afternoon about Six o'clock, and another when he had done his Day's-Work. I thought it a detestable Custom.—But it was necessary, he suppos'd, to drink *strong* Beer that he might be *strong* to labour. I endeavour'd to convince him that the Bodily Strength afforded by Beer could only be in proportion to the Grain or Flour of the Barley dissolved in the Water of which it was made; that there was more Flour in a Pennyworth of Bread, and therefore if he would eat that with a Pint of Water, it would give him more Strength than a Quart of Beer.—He drank on however, & had 4 or 5 Shillings to pay out of his Wages every Saturday Night for that muddling Liquor; an Expence I was free from.—And thus these poor Devils keep themselves always under.

Watts after some Weeks desiring to have me in the Composing-Room, I left the Pressmen. A new *Bienvenu* or Sum for Drink, being 5/, was demanded of me by the Compostors. I thought it an Imposition, as I had paid below. The Master thought so too, and forbad my Paying it. I stood out two or three Weeks, was accordingly considered as an Excommunicate, and had so many little Pieces of private Mischief done me, by mixing my Sorts, transposing my Pages, breaking my Matter, &c. &c. if I were ever so little out of the Room, & all ascrib'd to the Chapel Ghost, which they said ever haunted those not regularly admitted, that notwithstanding the Master's Protection, I found myself oblig'd to comply and pay the Money; convinc'd of the Folly of being on ill Terms with those one is to live with continually. I was now on a fair Footing with them, and soon acquir'd considerable Influence. I propos'd some reasonable Alterations in their Chapel Laws,[19] and carried them against all Opposition. From my Example a great Part of them, left their muddling Breakfast of Beer & Bread & Cheese, finding they could with me be supply'd from a neighbouring House with a large Porringer of hot Water-gruel, sprinkled with Pepper, crumb'd with Bread, & a Bit of Butter in it, for the Price of a Pint of Beer, viz, three halfpence. This was a more comfortable as well as cheaper Breakfast, & kept their Heads clearer.—Those who continu'd sotting with Beer all day, were often, by not paying, out of Credit at the Alehouse, and us'd to make Interest with me to get Beer, *their Light*, as they phras'd it, *being out*. I watch'd the Pay table on Saturday Night, & collected what I stood engag'd for them, having to pay some times near Thirty Shillings a Week on

---

19. A Printing House is always called a Chappel by the Workmen. [Franklin's note.]

their Accounts.—This, and my being esteem'd a pretty good Riggite, that is a jocular verbal Satyrist, supported my Consequence in the Society.—My constant Attendance, (I never making a St. Monday), recommended me to the Master; and my uncommon Quickness at Composing, occasion'd my being put upon all Work of Dispatch which was generally better paid. So I went on now very agreably.—

My Lodging in Little Britain being too remote, I found another in Duke-street opposite to the Romish Chapel. It was two pair of Stairs backwards at an Italian Warehouse. A Widow Lady kept the House; she had a Daughter & a Maid Servant, and a Journey-man who attended the Warehouse, but lodg'd abroad.—After sending to enquire my Character at the House where I last lodg'd, she agreed to take me in at the same Rate 3/6 per Week, cheaper as she said from the Protection she expected in having a Man lodge in the House. She was a Widow, an elderly Woman, had been bred a Protestant, being a Clergyman's Daughter, but was converted to the Catholic Religion by her Husband, whose Memory she much revered, had lived much among People of Distinction, and knew a 1000 Anecdotes of them as far back as the Times of Charles the second. She was lame in her Knees with the Gout, and therefore seldom stirr'd out of her Room, so sometimes wanted Company; and hers was so highly amusing to me; that I was sure to spend an Evening with her whenever she desired it. Our Supper was only half an Anchovy each, on a very little Strip of Bread & Butter, and half a Pint of Ale between us.—But the Entertainment was in her Conversation. My always keeping good Hours, and giving little Trouble in the Family, made her unwilling to part with me; so that when I talk'd of a Lodging I had heard of, nearer my Business, for 2/ a Week, which, intent as I now was on saving Money, made some Difference; she bid me not think of it, for she would abate me two Shillings a Week for the future, so I remain'd with her at 1/6 as long as I staid in London.—

In a Garret of her House there lived a Maiden Lady of 70 in the most retired Manner, of whom my Landlady gave me this Account, that she was a Roman-Catholic, had been sent abroad when young & lodg'd in a Nunnery with an Intent of becoming a Nun: but the Country not agreeing with her, she return'd to England, where there being no Nunnery, she had vow'd to lead the Life of a Nun as near as might be done in those Circumstances: Accordingly She had given all her Estate to charitable Uses, reserving only Twelve Pounds a Year to live on, and out of this Sum she still gave a great deal in Charity, living her self on Watergruel only, & using no Fire but to boil it.—She had lived many Years in that Garret, being permitted to remain there gratis by successive catholic Tenants of the House below, as they deem'd it a Blessing to have her there. A Priest visited her, to confess her every Day. I have ask'd her, says my Landlady, how she, as she liv'd, could possibly find so much Employment for a Confessor? O, says she, it is impossible to avoid *vain Thoughts*. I was permitted once to visit her: She was chearful & polite, & convers'd pleasantly. The Room was clean, but had no other Furniture than a Matras, a Table with a Crucifix & Book, a Stool, which she gave me to sit on, and a Picture over the Chimney of St. *Veronica*, displaying her Handkerchief with the miraculous Figure of Christ's bleeding Face on it, which she explain'd to me with great Seriousness. She look'd pale, but was never sick, and I give it as another Instance on how small an Income Life & Health may be supported.—

At Watts's Printinghouse I contracted an Acquaintance with an ingenious young Man, one Wygate, who having wealthy Relations, had been better educated than most Printers, was a tolerable Latinist, spoke French, & lov'd Reading. I taught him, & a Friend of his, to swim, at twice going into the River, & they soon became good Swimmers. They introduc'd me to some Gentlemen from the Country who went to Chelsea by Water to see the College and Don Saltero's Curiosities. In our Return, at the Request of the Company, whose Curiosity Wygate had excited, I stript & leapt into the River, & swam from near Chelsea to Blackfryars, performing on the Way many Feats of Activity both upon & under Water, that surpriz'd & pleas'd those to whom they were Novelties.—I had from a Child been ever delighted with this Exercise, had studied & practis'd all Thevenot's Motions & Positions, added some of my own, aiming at the graceful & easy, as well as the Useful.—All these I took this Occasion of exhibiting to the Company, & was much flatter'd by their Admiration.— And Wygate, who was desirous of becoming a Master, grew more & more attach'd to me, on that account, as well as from the Similarity of our Studies. He at length propos'd to me travelling all over Europe together, supporting ourselves every where by working at our Business. I was once inclin'd to it. But mentioning it to my good Friend Mr Denham, with whom I often spent an Hour, when I had Leisure. He dissuaded me from it; advising me to think only of returning to Pensilvania, which he was now about to do.—

I must record one Trait of this good Man's Character. He had formerly been in Business at Bristol, but fail'd in Debt to a Number of People, compounded and went to America. There, by a close Application to Business as a Merchant, he acquir'd a plentiful Fortune in a few Years. Returning to England in the Ship with me, He invited his old Creditors to an Entertainment, at which he thank'd them for the easy Composition they had favour'd him with, & when they expected nothing but the Treat, every Man at the first Remove, found under his Plate an Order on a Banker for the full Amount of the unpaid Remainder with Interest.

He now told me he was about to return to Philadelphia, and should carry over a great Quantity of Goods in order to open a Store there: He propos'd to take me over as his Clerk, to keep his Books (in which he would instruct me) copy his Letters, and attend the Store. He added, that as soon as I should be acquainted with mercantile Business he would promote me by sending me with a Cargo of Flour & Bread &c to the West Indies, and procure me Commissions from others; which would be profitable, & if I manag'd well, would establish me handsomely. The Thing pleas'd me, for I was grown tired of London, remember'd with Pleasure the happy Months I had spent in Pennsylvania, and wish'd again to see it. Therefore I immediately agreed, on the Terms of Fifty Pounds a Year Pennsylvania Money; less indeed than my then present Gettings as a Compostor, but affording a better Prospect.—

I now took Leave of Printing, as I thought for ever, and was daily employ'd in my new Business; going about with Mr Denham among the Tradesmen, to purchase various Articles, & see them pack'd up, doing Errands, calling upon Workmen to dispatch, &c. and when all was on board, I had a few Days Leisure. On one of these Days I was to my Surprize sent for by a great Man I knew only by Name, a Sir William Wyndham and I waited upon him. He had heard by some means or other of my Swimming from Chelsey to Blackfryars, and of my teaching Wygate and another young Man to swim in a few Hours. He had two Sons about to set out on their Travels; he wish'd to have them first taught Swimming; and propos'd to gratify me handsomely if I would teach them.—They were not yet come to Town and my Stay was uncertain, so I could not undertake it. But from this Incident I thought it likely, that if I were to remain in England and open a Swimming School, I might get a good deal of Money.—And it struck me so strongly, that had the Overture been sooner made me, probably I should not so soon have returned to America.—After Many Years, you & I had something of more Importance to do with one of these Sons of Sir William Wyndham, become Earl of Egremont, which I shall mention in its Place.—

Thus I spent about 18 Months in London. Most Part of the Time, I work'd hard at my Business, & spent but little upon my self except in seeing Plays, & in Books.—My Friend Ralph had kept me poor. He owed me about 27 Pounds; which I was now never likely to receive; a great Sum out of my small Earnings. I lov'd him notwithstanding, for he had many amiable Qualities.—tho' I had by no means improv'd my Fortune.—But I had pick'd up some very ingenious Acquaintance whose Conversation was of great Advantage to me, and I had read considerably.

We sail'd from Gravesend on the 23d of July 1726.—For The Incidents of the Voyage, I refer you to my Journal, where you will find them all minutely related. Perhaps the most important Part of that Journal is the *Plan* to be found in it which I formed at Sea, for regulating my future Conduct in Life. It is the more remarkable, as being form'd when I was so young, and yet being pretty faithfully adhered to quite thro' to old Age.—We landed in Philadelphia the 11th of October, where I found sundry Alterations. Keith was no longer Governor, being superceded by Major Gordon: I met him walking the Streets as a common Citizen. He seem'd a little asham'd at seeing me, but pass'd without saying any thing. I should have been as much asham'd at seeing Miss Read, had not her Friends despairing with Reason of my Return, after the Receipt of my Letter, persuaded her to marry another, one Rogers, a Potter, which was done in my Absence. With him however she was never happy, and soon parted from him, refusing to cohabit with him, or bear his Name It being now said that he had another Wife. He was a worthless Fellow tho' an excellent Workman which was the Temptation to her Friends. He got into Debt, and ran away in 1727 or 28, went to the West Indies, and died there. Keimer had got a better House, a Shop well supply'd with Stationary, plenty of new Types, a number of Hands tho' none good, and seem'd to have a great deal of Business.

Mr Denham took a Store in Water Street, where we open'd our Goods. I attended the Business diligently, studied Accounts, and grew in a little Time expert at selling.— We lodg'd and boarded together, he counsell'd me as a Father, having a sincere Regard for me: I respected & lov'd him: and we might have gone on together very happily: But in the Beginning of Feb.y 1726/7 when I had just pass'd my 21st Year, we both were taken ill. My Distemper was a Pleurisy, which very nearly carried me off:—I suffered a good deal, gave up the Point in my own mind, & was rather disappointed when I found my self recovering; regretting in some degree that I must now sometime or other have all that disagreable Work to do over again.—I forget what his

Distemper was. It held him a long time, and at length carried him off. He left me a small Legacy in a nuncupative Will, as a Token of his Kindness for me, and he left me once more to the wide World. For the Store was taken into the Care of his Executors, and my Employment under him ended:—My Brother-in-law Homes, being now at Philadelphia, advis'd my Return to my Business. And Keimer tempted me with an Offer of large Wages by the Year to come & take the Management of his Printing-House that he might better attend his Stationer's Shop.—I had heard a bad Character of him in London, from his Wife & her Friends, & was not fond of having any more to do with him. I try'd for farther Employment as a Merchant's Clerk; but not readily meeting with any, I clos'd again with Keimer.—

I found in *his* House these Hands; Hugh Meredith a Welsh-Pensilvanian, 30 Years of Age, bred to Country Work: honest, sensible, had a great deal of solid Observation, was something of a Reader, but given to drink:—Stephen Potts, a young Country Man of full Age, bred to the Same:—of uncommon natural Parts, & great Wit & Humour, but a little idle.—These he had agreed with at extream low Wages, per Week, to be rais'd a Shilling every 3 Months, as they would deserve by improving in their Business, & the Expectation of these high Wages to come on hereafter was what he had drawn them in with.—Meredith was to work at Press, Potts at Bookbinding, which he by Agreement, was to teach them, tho' he knew neither one nor t'other. John ——— a wild Irishman brought up to no Business, whose Service for 4 Years Keimer had purchas'd from the Captain of a Ship. He too was to be made a Pressman. George Webb, an Oxford Scholar, whose Time for 4 Years he had likewise bought, intending him for a Compositor: of whom more presently. And David Harry, a Country Boy, whom he had taken Apprentice. I soon perceiv'd that the Intention of engaging me at Wages so much higher than he had been us'd to give, was to have these raw cheap Hands form'd thro' me, and as soon as I had instructed them, then, they being all articled to him, he should be able to do without me.—I went on however, very chearfully; put his Printing House in Order, which had been in great Confusion, and brought his Hands by degrees to mind their Business and to do it better.

It was an odd Thing to find an Oxford Scholar in the Situation of a bought Servant. He was not more than 18 Years of Age, & gave me this Account of himself; that he was born in Gloucester, educated at a Grammar School there, had been distinguish'd among the Scholars for some apparent Superiority in performing his Part when they exhibited Plays; belong'd to the Witty Club there, and had written some Pieces in Prose & Verse which were printed in the Gloucester Newspapers.—Thence he was sent to Oxford; there he continu'd about a Year, but not well-satisfy'd, wishing of all things to see London & become a Player. At length receiving his Quarterly Allowance of 15 Guineas, instead of discharging his Debts, he walk'd out of Town, hid his Gown in a Furz Bush, and footed it to London, where having no Friend to advise him, he fell into bad Company, soon spent his Guineas, found no means of being introduc'd among the Players, grew necessitous, pawn'd his Cloaths & wanted Bread. Walking the Street very hungry, & not knowing what to do with himself, a Crimp's Bill was put into his Hand, offering immediate Entertainment & Encouragement to such as would bind themselves to serve in America. He went directly, sign'd the Indentures, was put into the Ship & came over; never writing a Line to acquaint his Friends what was become of him. He was lively, witty, good-natur'd and a pleasant Companion; but idle, thoughtless & imprudent to the last Degree.

John the Irishman soon ran away. With the rest I began to live very agreably; for they all respected me, the more as they found Keimer incapable of instructing them, and that from me they learnt something daily. We never work'd on a Saturday, that being Keimer's Sabbath. So I had two Days for Reading. My Acquaintance with ingenious People in the Town, increased. Keimer himself treated me with great Civility & apparent Regard; and nothing now made me uneasy but my Debt to Vernon, which I was yet unable to pay being hitherto but a poor Oeconomist.—He however kindly made no Demand of it.

Our Printing-House often wanted Sorts, and there was no Letter Founder in America. I had seen Types cast at James's in London, but without much Attention to the Manner: However I now contriv'd a Mould, made use of the Letters we had, as Puncheons, struck the Matrices in Lead, and thus supply'd in a pretty tolerable way all Deficiencies. I also engrav'd several Things on occasion. I made the Ink, I was Warehouse-man & every thing, in short quite a Factotum.

But however serviceable I might be, I found that my Services became every Day of less Importance, as the other Hands improv'd in the Business. And when Keimer paid my second Quarter's Wages, he let me know that he felt them too heavy, and thought I should make an Abatement. He grew by degrees less civil, put on more of the Master, frequently found Fault, was captious and seem'd ready for an Out-breaking. I went on nevertheless with a good deal of Patience, thinking that his incumber'd Circumstances were partly the Cause. At length a Trifle snapt our Connexion. For a great Noise happening near the Courthouse, I put my Head out of the Window to see what was the Matter. Keimer being in the Street look'd up & saw me, call'd out to me in a loud Voice and angry tone to mind my Business, adding some reproachful Words, that nettled me the more for their Publicity, all the Neighbours who were looking out on the same Occasion being Witnesses how I was treated. He came up immediately into the Printing-House, continu'd the Quarrel, high Words pass'd on both Sides, he gave me the Quarter's Warning we had stipulated, expressing a Wish that he had not been oblig'd to so long a Warning: I told him his Wish was unnecessary for I would leave him that Instant; and so taking my Hat walk'd out of Doors; desiring Meredith whom I saw below to take care of some Things I left, & bring them to my Lodging.—

Meredith came accordingly in the Evening, when we talk'd my Affair over. He had conceiv'd a great Regard for me, & was very unwilling that I should leave the House while he remain'd in it. He dissuaded me from returning to my native Country which I began to think of. He reminded me that Keimer was in debt for all he possess'd, that his Creditors began to be uneasy, that he kept his Shop miserably, sold often without Profit for ready Money, and often trusted without keeping Account. That he must therefore fail; which would make a Vacancy I might profit of.—I objected my Want of Money. He then let me know, that his Father had a high Opinion of me, and from some Discourse that had pass'd between them, he was sure would advance Money to set us up, if I would enter into Partnership with him.—My Time, says he, will be out with Keimer in the Spring. By that time we may have our Press & Types in from London:—I am sensible I am no Workman. If you like it, Your Skill in the Business shall be set against the Stock I furnish; and we will share the Profits equally.—The Proposal was agreable, and I consented. His Father was in Town, and approv'd of it, the more as he saw I had great Influence with his Son, had prevail'd on him to abstain long from Dramdrinking, and he hop'd might break him of that wretched Habit entirely, when we came to be so closely connected. I gave an Inventory to the Father, who carry'd it to a Merchant; the Things were sent for; the Secret was to be kept till they should arrive, and in the mean time I was to get Work if I could at the other Printing House.—But I found no Vacancy there, and so remain'd idle a few Days, when Keimer, on a Prospect of being employ'd to print some Paper-money, in New Jersey, which would require Cuts & various Types that I only could supply, and apprehending Bradford might engage me & get the Jobb from him, sent me a very civil Message, that old Friends should not part for a few Words the Effect of sudden Passion, and wishing me to return. Meredith persuaded me to comply, as it would give more Opportunity for his Improvement under my daily Instructions.—So I return'd, and we went on more smoothly than for some time before.—The New Jersey Job was obtain'd. I contriv'd a Copper-Plate Press for it, the first that had been seen in the Country.—I cut several Ornaments and Checks for the Bills. We went together to Burlington, where I executed the Whole to Satisfaction, & he received so large a Sum for the Work, as to be enabled thereby to keep his Head much longer above Water.—

At Burlington I made an Acquaintance with many principal People of the Province. Several of them had been appointed by the Assembly a Committee to attend the Press, and take Care that no more Bills were printed than the Law directed. They were therefore by Turns constantly with us, and generally he who attended brought with him a Friend or two for Company. My Mind having been much more improv'd by Reading than Keimer's, I suppose it was for that Reason my Conversation seem'd to be more valu'd. They had me to their Houses, introduc'd me to their Friends and show'd me much Civility, while he, tho' the Master, was a little neglected. In truth he was an odd Fish, ignorant of common Life, fond of rudely opposing receiv'd Opinions, slovenly to extream dirtiness, enthusiastic in some Points of Religion, and a little Knavish withal. We continu'd there near 3 Months, and by that time I could reckon among my acquired Friends, Judge Allen, Samuel Bustill, the Secretary of the Province, Isaac Pearson, Joseph Cooper & several of the Smiths, Members of Assembly, and Isaac Decow the Surveyor General. The latter was a shrewd sagacious old Man, who told me that he began for himself when young by wheeling Clay for the Brickmakers, learnt to write after he was of Age, carry'd the Chain for Surveyors, who taught him Surveying, and he had now by his Industry acquir'd a good Estate; and says he, I foresee, that you will soon work this Man out of his Business & make a Fortune in it at Philadelphia. He had not then the least Intimation of my Intention to set up there or any where.—These Friends were afterwards of great Use to me, as I occasionally was to some of them.—They all continued their Regard for me as long as they lived.—

Before I enter upon my public Appearance in Business, it may be well to let you know the then State of my Mind, with regard to my Principles and Morals, that you may see how far those influenc'd the future Events of my Life. My Parent's had early given me religious Impressions, and brought me through my Childhood piously in the Dissenting Way. But I was scarce 15 when, after doubting by turns of several Points as

I found them disputed in the different Books I read, I began to doubt of Revelation it self. Some Books against Deism fell into my Hands; they were said to be the Substance of Sermons preached at Boyle's Lectures. It happened that they wrought an Effect on me quite contrary to what was intended by them: For the Arguments of the Deists which were quoted to be refuted, appeared to me much Stronger than the Refutations. In short I soon became a thorough Deist. My Arguments perverted some others, particularly Collins & Ralph: but each of them having afterwards wrong'd me greatly without the least Compunction, and recollecting Keith's Conduct towards me, (who was another Freethinker) and my own towards Vernon & Miss Read which at Times gave me great Trouble, I began to suspect that this Doctrine tho' it might be true, was not very useful.—My London Pamphlet, which had for its Motto those Lines of Dryden

> —*Whatever is, is right*
> *Tho' purblind Man / Sees but a Part of*
> *The Chain, the nearest Link,*
> *His Eyes not carrying to the equal Beam,*
> *That poizes all, above.*

And from the Attributes of God, his infinite Wisdom, Goodness & Power concluded that nothing could possibly be wrong in the World, & that Vice & Virtue were empty Distinctions, no such Things existing: appear'd now not so clever a Performance as I once thought it; and I doubted whether some Error had not insinuated itself unperceiv'd, into my Argument, so as to infect all that follow'd, as is common in metaphysical Reasonings.—I grew convinc'd that *Truth, Sincerity & Integrity* in Dealings between Man & Man, were of the utmost Importance to the Felicity of Life, and I form'd written Resolutions, (which still remain in my Journal Book) to practise them ever while I lived. Revelation had indeed no weight with me as such; but I entertain'd an Opinion, that tho' certain Actions might not be bad *because* they were forbidden by it, or good *because* it commanded them; yet probably those Actions might be forbidden *because* they were bad for us, or commanded *because* they were beneficial to us, in their own Natures, all the Circumstances of things considered. And this Persuasion, with the kind hand of Providence, or some guardian Angel, or accidental favourable Circumstances & Situations, or all together, preserved me (thro' this dangerous Time of Youth & the hazardous Situations I was sometimes in among Strangers, remote from the Eye & Advice of my Father,) without any *wilful* gross Immorality or Injustice that might have been expected from my Want of Religion.—I say *wilful*, because the Instances I have mentioned, had something of *Necessity* in them, from my Youth, Inexperience, & the Knavery of others.—I had therefore a tolerable Character to begin the World with, I valued it properly, & determin'd to preserve it.—

We had not been long return'd to Philadelphia, before the New Types arriv'd from London.—We settled with Keimer, & left him by his Consent before he heard of it.— We found a House to hire near the Market, and took it. To lessen the Rent, (which was then but 24£ a Year tho' I have since known it let for 70) We took in Thomas Godfrey a Glazier, & his Family, who were to pay a considerable Part of it to us, and we to board with them. We had scarce opened our Letters & put our Press in Order, before George House, an Acquaintance of mine, brought a Countryman to us; whom he had met in the Street enquiring for a Printer. All our Cash was now expended in the Variety of Particulars we had been obliged to procure, & this Countryman's Five Shillings, being our First Fruits & coming so seasonably, gave me more Pleasure than any Crown I have since earn'd; and from the Gratitude I felt towards House, has made me often more ready than perhaps I should otherwise have been to assist young Beginners.—

There are Croakers in every Country always boding its Ruin. Such a one then lived in Philadelphia, a Person of Note, an elderly Man, with a wise Look and very grave Manner of Speaking. His Name was Samuel Mickle. This Gentleman, a Stranger to me, stopt one Day at my Door, and ask'd me if I was the young Man who had lately opened a new Printing-house: Being answer'd in the Affirmative; He said he was sorry for me; because it was an expensive Undertaking, & the Expence would be lost, for Philadelphia was a sinking Place, the People already half Bankrupts or near being so; all Appearances of the contrary such as new Buildings & the Rise of Rents, being to his certain Knowledge fallacious, for they were in fact among the Things that would soon ruin us. And he gave me such a Detail of Misfortunes now existing or that were soon to exist, that he left me half-melancholy. Had I known him before I engag'd in this Business, probably I never should have done it.—This Man continu'd to live in this decaying Place, & to declaim in the same Strain, refusing for many Years to buy a House there, because all was going to Destruction, and at last I had the Pleasure of seeing him give five times as much for one as he might have bought it for when he first began his Croaking.—

I should have mention'd before, that in the Autumn of the preceding Year, I had form'd most of my ingenious Acquaintance into a Club, for mutual Improvement, which we call'd the Junto. We met on Friday Evenings. The Rules I drew up, requir'd that every Member in his Turn should produce one or more Queries on any Point of Morals, Politics or Natural Philosophy, to be discuss'd by the Company, and once in three Months produce and read an Essay of his own Writing on any Subject he pleased. Our Debates were to be under the Direction of a President, and to be conducted in the sincere Spirit of Enquiry after Truth, without fondness for Dispute, or Desire of Victory; and to prevent Warmth, all Expressions of Positiveness in Opinion, or of direct Contradiction, were after some time made contraband & prohibited under small pecuniary Penalties. The first Members were, Joseph Brientnal, a Copyer of Deeds for the Scriveners; a good-natur'd friendly middle-ag'd Man, a great Lover of Poetry, reading all he could meet with, & writing some that was toler- able; very ingenious in many little Nicknackeries, & of sensible Conversation. Thomas Godfrey, a self-taught Mathematician, great in his Way, & afterwards Inventor of what is now call'd Hadley's Quadrant. But he knew little out of his way, and was not a pleasing Companion, as like most Great Mathematicians I have met with, he expected unusual Precision in every thing said, or was forever denying or distin- guishing upon Trifles, to the Disturbance of all Conversation.—He soon left us. Nicholas Scull, a Surveyor, afterwards Surveyor-General, Who lov'd Books, & some- times made a few Verses. William Parsons, bred a Shoemaker, but loving Reading, had acquir'd a considerable Share of Mathematics, which he first studied with a View to

Astrology that he afterwards laught at. He also became Surveyor General.—William Maugridge, a Joiner, & a most exquisite Mechanic, & a solid sensible Man. Hugh Meredith, Stephen Potts, & George Webb, I have Characteris'd before. Robert Grace, a young Gentleman of some Fortune, generous, lively & witty, a Lover of Punning and of his Friends. And William Coleman, then a Merchant's Clerk, about my Age, who had the coolest clearest Head, the best Heart, and the exactest Morals, of almost any Man I ever met with. He became afterwards a Merchant of great Note, and one of our Provincial Judges: Our Friendship continued without Interruption to his Death, upwards of 40 Years. And the Club continu'd almost as long and was the best School of Philosophy, Morals & Politics that then existed in the Province; for our Queries which were read the Week preceding their Discussion, put us on reading with Attention upon the several Subjects, that we might speak more to the purpose: and here too we acquired better Habits of Conversation, every thing being studied in our Rules which might prevent our disgusting each other. From hence the long Continuance of the Club, which I shall have frequent Occasion to speak farther of hereafter; But my giving this Account of it here, is to show something of the Interest I had, every one of these exerting themselves in recommending Business to us.—Brientnal particularly procur'd us from the Quakers, the Printing 40 Sheets of their History, the rest being to be done by Keimer: and upon this we work'd exceeding hard, for the Price was low. It was a Folio, Pro Patria Size, in Pica with Long Primer Notes. I comps'd of it a Sheet a Day, and Meredith work'd it off at Press. It was often 11 at Night and sometimes later, before I had finish'd my Distribution[20] for the next days Work: For the little Jobbs sent in by our other Friends now & then put us back. But so determin'd I was to continue doing a Sheet a Day of the Folio, that one Night when having impos'd my Forms, I thought my Days Work over, one of them by accident was broken and two Pages reduc'd to Pie,[21] I immediately distributed & compos'd it over again before I went to bed. And this Industry visible to our Neighbours began to give us Character and Credit; particularly I was told, that mention being made of the new Printing Office at the Merchants Every-night-Club, the general Opinion was that it must fail, there being already two Printers in the Place, Keimer & Bradford; but Doctor Baird (whom you and I saw many Years after at his native Place, St. Andrews in Scotland) gave a contrary Opinion; for the Industry of that Franklin, says he, is superior to any thing I ever saw of the kind: I see him still at work when I go home from Club; and he is at Work again before his Neighbours are out of bed. This struck the rest, and we soon after had Offers from one of them to supply us with Stationary. But as yet we did not chuse to engage in Shop Business.

I mention this Industry the more particularly and the more freely, tho' it seems to be talking in my own Praise, that those of my Posterity who shall read it, may know the Use of that Virtue, when they see its Effects in my Favour throughout this Relation.—

George Webb, who had found a Friend that lent him wherewith to purchase his Time of Keimer, now came to offer himself as a Journeyman to us. We could not then imploy him, but I foolishly let him know, as a Secret, that I soon intended to begin a

20. Distribution: returning the letters to their cases after printing.   21. i.e., two pages already set were spilled.

Newspaper, & might then have Work for him.—My Hopes of Success as I told him were founded on this, that the then only Newspaper, printed by Bradford was a paltry thing, wretchedly manag'd, no way entertaining; and yet was profitable to him.—I therefore thought a good Paper could scarcely fail of good Encouragement. I requested Webb not to mention it, but he told it to Keimer, who immediately, to be beforehand with me, published Proposals for Printing one himself,—on which Webb was to be employ'd.—I resented this, and to counteract them, as I could not yet begin our Paper, I wrote several Pieces of Entertainment for Bradford's Paper, under the Title of the Busy Body which Breintnal continu'd some Months. By this means the Attention of the Publick was fix'd on that Paper, & Keimers Proposals which we burlesqu'd & ridicul'd, were disregarded. He began his Paper however, and after carrying it on three Quarters of a Year, with at most only 90 Subscribers, he offer'd it to me for a Trifle, & I having been ready some time to go on with it, took it in hand directly and it prov'd in a few Years extreamly profitable to me.—

I perceive that I am apt to speak in the singular Number, though our Partnership still continu'd. The Reason may be, that in fact the whole Management of the Business lay upon me. Meredith was no Compositor, a poor Pressman, & seldom sober. My Friends lamented my Connection with him, but I was to make the best of it.

Our first Papers made a quite different Appearance from any before in the Province, a better Type & better printed: but some spirited Remarks of my Writing on the Dispute then going on between Governor Burnet and the Massachusetts Assembly, struck the principal People, occasion'd the Paper & the Manager of it to be much talk'd of, & in a few Weeks brought them all to be our Subscribers. Their Example was follow'd by many, and our Number went on growing continually.—This was one of the first good Effects of my having learnt a little to scribble.—Another was, that the leading Men, seeing a News Paper now in the hands of one who could also handle a Pen, thought it convenient to oblige & encourage me.—Bradford still printed the Votes & Laws & other Publick Business. He had printed an Address of the House to the Governor in a coarse blundering manner; We reprinted it elegantly & correctly, and sent one to every Member. They were sensible of the Difference, it strengthen'd the Hands of our Friends in the House, and they voted us their Printers for the Year ensuing.

Among my Friends in the House I must not forget Mr Hamilton before mentioned, who was then returned from England & had a Seat in it. He interested himself for me strongly in that Instance, as he did in many others afterwards, continuing his Patronage till his Death. Mr Vernon about this time put me in mind of the Debt I ow'd him:—but did not press me.—I wrote him an ingenuous Letter of Acknowledgements, crav'd his Forbearance a little longer which he allow'd me, & as soon as I was able I paid the Principal with Interest & many Thanks.—So that *Erratum* was in some degree corrected.—

But now another Difficulty came upon me, which I had never the least Reason to expect. Mr. Meredith's Father, who was to have paid for our Printing House according to the Expectations given me, was able to advance only one Hundred Pounds, Currency, which had been paid, & a Hundred more was due to the Merchant; who grew impatient & su'd us all. We gave Bail, but saw that if the Money could not be rais'd in time, the Suit must come to a Judgment & Execution, & our hopeful

Prospects must with us be ruined, as the Press & Letters must be sold for Payment, perhaps at half-Price.—In this Distress two true Friends whose Kindness I have never forgotten nor ever shall forget while I can remember any thing, came to me separately unknown to each other, and without any Application from me, offering each of them to advance me all the Money that should be necessary to enable me to take the whole Business upon my self if that should be practicable, but they did not like my continuing the Partnership with Meredith, who as they said was often seen drunk in the Streets, & playing at low Games in Alehouses, much to our Discredit. These two Friends were *William Coleman* & *Robert Grace*. I told them I could not propose a Separation while any Prospect remain'd of the Merediths fulfilling their Part of our Agreement. Because I thought my self under great Obligations to them for what they had done & would do if they could. But if they finally fail'd in their Performance, & our Partnership must be dissolv'd, I should then think myself at Liberty to accept the Assistance of my Friends. Thus the matter rested for some time. When I said to my Partner, perhaps your Father is dissatisfied at the Part you have undertaken in this Affair of ours, and is unwilling to advance for you & me what he would for you alone: If that is the Case, tell me, and I will resign the whole to you & go about my Business. No—says he, my Father has really been disappointed and is really unable; and I am unwilling to distress him farther. I see this is a Business I am not fit for. I was bred a Farmer, and it was a Folly in me to come to Town & put my self at 30 Years of Age an Apprentice to learn a new Trade. Many of our Welsh People are going to settle in North Carolina where Land is cheap: I am inclin'd to go with them, & follow my old Employment. You may find Friends to assist you. If you will take the Debts of the Company upon you, return to my Father the hundred Pound he has advanc'd, pay my little personal Debts, and give me Thirty Pounds & a new Saddle, I will relinquish the Partnership & leave the whole in your Hands. I agreed to this Proposal. It was drawn up in Writing, sign'd & seal'd immediately. I gave him what he demanded & he went soon after to Carolina; from whence he sent me next Year two long Letters, containing the best Account that had been given of that Country, the Climate, Soil, Husbandry, &c. for in those Matters he was very judicious. I printed them in the Papers, and they gave grate Satisfaction to the Publick.

As soon as he was gone, I recurr'd to my two Friends; and because I would not give an unkind Preference to either, I took half what each had offered & I wanted, of one, & half of the other; paid off the Company Debts, and went on with the Business in my own Name, advertising that the Partnership was dissolved. I think this was in or about the Year 1729.—

About this Time there was a Cry among the People for more Paper-Money, only 15,000£ being extant in the Province & that soon to be sunk. The wealthy Inhabitants oppos'd any Addition, being against all Paper Currency, from an Apprehension that it would depreciate as it had done in New England to the Prejudice of all Creditors.— We had discuss'd this Point in our Junto, where I was on the Side of an Addition, being persuaded that the first small Sum struck in 1723 had done much good, by increasing the Trade Employment, & Number of Inhabitants in the Province, since I now saw all the old Houses inhabited, & many new ones building, where as I remember'd well, that when I first walk'd about the Streets of Philadelphia, eating my Roll, I saw most of the Houses in Walnut street between Second & Front streets with Bills on their Doors, to be let; and many likewise in Chestnut Street, & other Streets; which made me then think the Inhabitants of the City were one after another deserting it.— Our Debates possess'd me so fully of the Subject, that I wrote and printed an anonymous Pamphlet on it, entitled, *The Nature & Necessity of a Paper Currency.* It was well receiv'd by the common People in general; but the Rich Men dislik'd it; for it increas'd and strengthen'd the Clamour for more Money; and they happening to have no Writers among them that were able to answer it, their Opposition slacken'd, & the Point was carried by a Majority in the House. My Friends there, who conceiv'd I had been of some Service, thought fit to reward me, by employing me in printing the Money, a very profitable Jobb, and a great Help to me.—This was another Advantage gain'd by my being able to write. The Utility of this Currency became by Time and Experience so evident, as never afterwards to be much disputed, so that it grew soon to 55000£ and in 1739 to 80,000£ since which it arose during War to upwards of 350,000£. Trade, Building & Inhabitants all the while increasing. Tho' I now think there are Limits beyond which the Quantity may be hurtful.—

I soon after obtain'd, thro' my Friend Hamilton, the Printing of the NewCastle Paper Money, another profitable Jobb, as I then thought it; small Things appearing great to those in small Circumstances. And these to me were really great Advantages, as they were great Encouragements.—He procured me also the Printing of the Laws and Votes of that Government which continu'd in my Hands as long as I follow'd the Business.—

I now open'd a little Stationer's Shop. I had in it Blanks of all Sorts the correctest that ever appear'd among us, being assisted in that by my Friend Brientnal; I had also Paper, Parchment, Chapmen's Books, &c. One Whitemash a Compositor I had known in London, an excellent Workman now came to me & work'd with me constantly & diligently, and I took an Apprentice the Son of Aquila Rose. I began now gradually to pay off the Debt I was under for the Printing-House.—In order to secure my Credit and Character as a Tradesmen, I took care not only to be in *Reality* Industrious & frugal, but to avoid all *Appearances* of the Contrary. I drest plainly; I was seen at no Places of idle Diversion; I never went out a-fishing or shooting; a Book, indeed, sometimes debauch'd me from my Work; but that was seldom, snug, & gave no Scandal: and to show that I was not above my Business, I sometimes brought home the Paper I purchas'd at the Stores, thro' the Streets on a Wheelbarrow. Thus being esteem'd an industrious thriving young Man, and paying duly for what I bought, the Merchants who imported Stationary solicited my Custom, others propos'd supplying me with Books, & I went on swimmingly.—In the mean time Keimer's Credit & Business declining daily, he was at last forc'd to sell his Printing-house to satisfy his Creditors. He went to Barbadoes, & there lived some Years, in very poor Circumstances.

His Apprentice David Harry, whom I had instructed while I work'd with him, set up in his Place at Philadelphia having bought his Materials. I was at first apprehensive of a powerful Rival in Harry, as his Friends were very able, & had a good deal of Interest. I therefore propos'd a Partnership to him; which he, fortunately for me, rejected with Scorn. He was very proud, dress'd like a Gentleman, liv'd expensively, took much Diversion & Pleasure abroad, ran in debt, & neglected his Business, upon which all Business left him; and finding nothing to do, he follow'd Keimer to Barbadoes; taking the Printinghouse with him. There this Apprentice employ'd his former Master as a Journeyman. They quarrel'd often. Harry went continually behind-hand, and at length was forc'd to sell his Types, and return to his Country Work in Pensilvania. The Person that bought them, employ'd Keimer to use them, but in a few years he died. There remain'd now no Competitor with me at Philadelphia, but the old one, Bradford, who was rich & easy, did a little Printing now & then by straggling Hands, but was not very anxious about the Business. However, as he kept the Post Office, it was imagined he had better Opportunities of obtaining News, his Paper was thought a better Distributer of Advertisements than mine, & therefore had many more, which was a profitable thing to him & a Disadvantage to me. For tho' I did indeed receive & send Papers by the Post, yet the publick Opinion was otherwise; for what I did send was by Bribing the Riders who took them privately: Bradford being unkind enough to forbid it: which occasion'd some Resentment on my Part; and I thought so meanly of him for it, that when I afterwards came into his Situation, I took care never to imitate it.

I had hitherto continu'd to board with Godfrey who lived in Part of my House with his Wife & Children, & had one Side of the Shop for his Glazier's Business, tho' he work'd little, being always absorb'd in his Mathematics.—Mrs Godfrey projected a Match for me with a Relation's Daughter, took Opportunities of bringing us often together, till a serious Courtship on my Part ensu'd the Girl being in herself very deserving. The old Folks encourag'd me by continual Invitations to Supper, & by leaving us together, till at length it was time to explain. Mrs Godfrey manag'd our little Treaty. I let her know that I expected as much Money with their Daughter as would pay off my Remaining Debt for the Printing-house, which I believe was not then above a Hundred Pounds. She brought me Word they had no such Sum to spare. I said they might mortgage their House in the Loan Office.—The Answer to this after some Days was, that they did not approve the Match; that on Enquiry of Bradford they had been inform'd the Printing Business was not a profitable one, the Types would soon be worn out & more wanted, that S. Keimer & D. Harry had fail'd one after the other, and I should probably soon follow them; and therefore I was forbidden the House, & the Daughter shut up.—Whether this was a real Change of Sentiment, or only Artifice, on a Supposition of our being too far engag'd in Affection to retract, & therefore that we should steal a Marriage, which would leave them at Liberty to give or withold what they pleas'd, I know not: But I suspected the latter, resented it, and went no more. Mrs Godfrey brought me afterwards some more favourable Accounts of their Disposition, & would have drawn me on again: But I declared absolutely my Resolution to have nothing more to do with that Family. This was resented by the Godfreys, we differ'd, and they removed, leaving me the whole House, and I resolved to take no more Inmates. But this Affair having turn'd my Thoughts to Marriage, I look'd round me, and made Overtures of Acquaintance in other Places; but soon found that the Business of a Printer being generally thought a poor one, I was not to expect Money with a Wife unless with such a one, as I should not otherwise think agreable.—In the mean time, that hard-to-be-govern'd Passion of Youth, had hurried me frequently into Intrigues with low Women that fell in my Way, which were attended with some Expence & great Inconvenience, besides a continual Risque to my Health by a Distemper which of all Things I dreaded, tho' by great good Luck I escaped it.

A friendly Correspondence as Neighbours & old Acquaintances, had continued between me & Mrs Read's Family who all had a Regard for me from the time of my first Lodging in their House. I was often invited there and consulted in their Affairs, wherein I sometimes was of Service.—I pity'd poor Miss Read's unfortunate Situation, who was generally dejected, seldom chearful, and avoided Company. I consider'd my Giddiness & Inconstancy when in London as in a great degree the Cause of her Unhappiness; tho' the Mother was good enough to think the Fault more her own than mine, as she had prevented our Marrying before I went thither, and persuaded the other Match in my Absence. Our mutual Affection was revived, but there were now great Objections to our Union. That Match was indeed look'd upon as invalid, a preceding Wife being said to be living in England; but this could not easily be prov'd, because of the Distance &c. And tho' there was a Report of his Death, it was not certain. Then, tho' it should be true, he had left many Debts which his Successor might be call'd upon to pay. We ventured however, over all these Difficulties, and I took her to Wife Sept. 1. 1730. None of the Inconveniencies happened that we had apprehended, she prov'd a good & faithful Helpmate, assisted me much by attending the Shop, we throve together, and have ever mutually endeavour'd to make each other happy.—Thus I corrected that great *Erratum* as well as I could.

About this Time our Club meeting, not at a Tavern, but in a little Room of Mr Grace's set apart for that Purpose; a Proposition was made by me, that since our Books were often referr'd to in our Disquisitions upon the Queries, it might be convenient to us to have them all together where we met, that upon Occasion they might be consulted; and By thus clubbing our Books to a common Library, we should, while we lik'd to keep them together, have each of us the Advantage of using the Books of all the other Members, which would be nearly as beneficial as if each owned the whole. It was lik'd and agreed to, & we fill'd one End of the Room with such Books as we could best spare. The Number was not so great as we expected; and tho' they had been of great Use, yet some Inconveniencies occurring for want of due Care of them, the Collection after about a Year was separated, & each took his Books home again.

And now I set on foot my first Project of a public Nature, that for a Subscription Library. I drew up the Proposals, got them put into Form by our great Scrivener Brockden, and by the help of my Friends in the Junto, procur'd Fifty Subscribers of 40/ each to begin with & 10/ a Year for 50 Years, the Term our Company was to continue. We afterwards obtain'd a Charter, the Company being increas'd to 100. This was the Mother of all the N American Subscription Libraries now so numerous. It is become a great thing itself, & continually increasing.—These Libraries have improv'd the general Conversation of the Americans, made the common Tradesmen & Farmers as intelligent as most Gentlemen from other Countries, and perhaps have contributed in some degree to the Stand so generally made throughout the Colonies in Defence of their Privileges.—

Mem°.

Thus far was written with the Intention express'd in the Beginning and therefore contains several little family Anecdotes of no Importance to others. What follows was written many Years after in compliance with the Advice contain'd in these Letters, and accordingly intended for the Publick. The Affairs of the Revolution occasion'd the Interruption.

[FROM PART TWO, "THE ART OF VIRTUE," 1784]

In the various Enumerations of the moral Virtues I had met with in my Reading, I found the Catalogue more or less numerous, as different Writers included more or fewer Ideas under the same Name. Temperance, for Example, was by some confin'd to Eating & Drinking, while by others it was extended to mean the moderating every other Pleasure, Appetite, Inclination or Passion, bodily or mental, even to our Avarice & Ambition. I propos'd to myself, for the sake of Clearness, to use rather more Names with fewer Ideas annex'd to each, than a few Names with more Ideas; and I included under Thirteen Names of Virtues all that at that time occurr'd to me as necessary or desirable, and annex'd to each a short Precept, which fully express'd the Extent I gave to its Meaning.—

These Names of Virtues with their Precepts were
        I. TEMPERANCE.
Eat not to Dulness
Drink not to Elevation.
        2. SILENCE.
Speak not but what may benefit others or your self. Avoid trifling Conversation.
        3. ORDER.
Let all your Things have their Places. Let each Part of your Business have its Time.
        4. RESOLUTION.
Resolve to perform what you ought. Perform without fail what you resolve.
        5. FRUGALITY.
Make no Expence but to do good to others or yourself: i.e. Waste nothing.
        6. INDUSTRY.
Lose no Time.—Be always employ'd in something useful.—Cut off all unnecessary Actions.—
        7. SINCERITY.
Use no hurtful Deceit.
Think innocently and justly; and, if you speak; speak accordingly.
        8. JUSTICE.
Wrong none, by doing Injuries or omitting the Benefits that are your Duty.
        9. MODERATION.
Avoid Extreams. Forbear resenting Injuries so much as you think they deserve.
        10. CLEANLINESS.
Tolerate no Uncleanness in Body, Cloaths or Habitation.—
        11.TRANQUILITY.
Be not disturbed at Trifles, or at Accidents common or unavoidable.
        12. CHASTITY.
Rarely use Venery but for Health or Offspring; Never to Dulness, Weakness, or the Injury of your own or another's Peace or Reputation.—
        13. HUMILITY.
Imitate Jesus and Socrates.—

My intention being to acquire the *Habitude* of all these Virtues, I judg'd it would be well not to distract my Attention by attempting the whole at once, but to fix it on one of them at a time, and when I should be Master of that, then to proceed to another, and so on till I should have gone thro' the thirteen. And as the previous Acquisition of some might facilitate the Acquisition of certain others, I arrang'd them with that View as they stand above. *Temperance* first, as it tends to procure that Coolness & Clearness of Head, which is so necessary where constant Vigilance was to be kept up, and Guard maintained, against the unremitting Attraction of ancient Habits, and the Force of perpetual Temptations. This being acquir'd & establish'd, *Silence* would be more easy, and my Desire being to gain Knowledge at the same time that I improv'd in Virtue, and considering that in Conversation it was obtain'd rather by the Use of the Ears than of the Tongue, & therefore wishing to break a Habit I was getting into of Prattling, Punning & Joking, which only made me acceptable to trifling Company, I gave *Silence* the second Place. This, and the next, *Order*, I expected would allow me more Time for attending to my Project and my Studies; RESOLUTION once become habitual, would keep me firm in my Endeavours to obtain all the subsequent Virtues; *Frugality* & *Industry*, by freeing me from my remaining Debt, & producing Affluence & Independance would make more easy the Practice of *Sincerity* and *Justice*, &c. &c. Conceiving then that agreeable to the Advice of Pythagoras in his Golden Verses,[22] daily Examination would be necessary, I contriv'd the following Method for conducting that Examination.

I made a little Book in which I allotted a Page for each of the Virtues. I rul'd each Page with red Ink so as to have seven Columns, one for each Day of the Week, marking each Column with a Letter for the Day. I cross'd these Columns with thirteen red Lines, marking the Beginning of each Line with the first Letter of one of the Virtues, on which Line & in its proper Column I might mark by a little black Spot every Fault I found upon Examination, to have been committed respecting that Virtue upon that Day.

I determined to give a Week's strict Attention to each of the Virtues successively. Thus in the first Week my great Guard was to avoid every the least Offence against Temperance, leaving the other Virtues to their ordinary Chance, only marking every Evening the Faults of the Day. Thus if in the first Week I could keep my first Line marked T clear of Spots, I suppos'd the Habit of that Virtue so much strengthen'd and its opposite weaken'd, that I might venture extending my Attention to include the next, and for the following Week keep both Lines clear of Spots. Proceeding thus to the last, I could go thro' a Course compleat in Thirteen Weeks, and four Courses in a Year.—And like him who having a Garden to weed, does not attempt to eradicate all the bad Herbs at once, which would exceed his Reach and his Strength, but works on

---

22. *Let not the stealing God of Sleep surprize,*
Nor creep in Slumbers on thy weary Eyes,
Ere ev'ry Action of the former Day,
Strictly thou dost, and righteously *survey.*
With Rev'rence at thy own Tribunal stand,
And answer justly to thy own Demand.
Where have I been? In what have I transgrest?
What Good or Ill has this Day's Life exprest?
Where have I fail'd in what I ought to do?

In what to GOD, to Man, or to myself I owe?
Inquire severe whate'er from first to last,
From Morning's Dawn till Ev'nings Gloom has past.
If Evil were thy Deeds, repenting mourn,
And let thy Soul with strong Remorse be torn:
If Good, the Good with Peace of Mind repay,
And to thy secret Self with Pleasure say,
Rejoice, my Heart, for all went well to Day. [Franklin's note.]

one of the Beds at a time, & having accomplish'd the first proceeds to a second; so I should have, (I hoped) the encouraging Pleasure of seeing on my Pages the Progress I made in Virtue, by clearing successively my Lines of their Spots, till in the End by a Number of Courses, I should be happy in viewing a clean Book after a thirteen Weeks daily Examination. . . .

The Precept of *Order* requiring that *every Part of my Business should have its allotted Time*, one Page in my little Book contain'd the following Scheme of Employment for the Twenty-four Hours of a natural Day,

The Morning Ques-tion, What Good shall I do this Day?	5	Rise, wash, and address *Powerful Goodness;* contrive Day's Business and take the Resolution of the Day; prosecute the present Study: and breakfast?—
	6	
	7	
	8	
	9	Work.
	10	
	11	
	12	Read, or overlook my Accounts, and dine.
	1	
	2	Work.
	3	
	4	
	5	
	6	Put Things in their Places, Supper, Musick, or Diversion, or Conversation, Examination of the Day.
	7	
Evening Question, What Good have I done to day?	8	
	9	
	10	Sleep.—
	11	
	12	
	1	
	2	
	3	
	4	

I enter'd upon the Execution of this Plan for Self Examination, and continu'd it with occasional Intermissions for some time. I was surpriz'd to find myself so much fuller of Faults than I had imagined, but I had the Satisfaction of seeing them diminish.

12. Peter Oliver

from *Origin and Progress of the American Rebellion*
1776

Peter Oliver (1713–91) was a loyalist in the Revolution and an Englishman all his life. Born into a distinguished Boston family, he went from Harvard to a life of wealth and culture based on various successful business ventures. He was a judge in the colonial administration and an eloquent opposer of all moves toward independence. A Tory in manners, culture, and politics, he never wavered in his understanding of the English settlements in America as overseas extensions of England; in 1776, he left permanently for England.

His account of what he insists on calling a "rebellion" and not a "revolution" not only presents another side of the story, it projects another view of the winners (see his portrait of Franklin), and offers a reasonable defense of positions not always well represented in the inevitably nationalist historical tradition.

London March 1st. 1781.

Sir!

The Revolt of *North America*, from their Allegiance to & Connection with the Parent State, seems to be as striking a Phaenomenon, in the political World, as hath appeared for many Ages past; & perhaps it is a *singular* one. For, by adverting to the historick Page, we shall find no Revolt of Colonies, whether under the *Roman* or any other State, but what originated from severe Oppressions, derived from the supreme Head of the State, or from those whom he had entrusted as his Substitutes to be Governors of his Provinces. In such Cases, the Elasticity of human Nature hath been exerted, to throw off the Burdens which the Subject hath groaned under; & in most of the Instances which are recorded in History, human Nature will still justify those Efforts.

But for a Colony, which had been nursed, in its Infancy, with the most tender Care & Attention; which had been indulged with every Gratification that the most froward Child could wish for; which had even bestowed upon it such Liberality, which its Infancy & Youth could not *think* to ask for; which had been repeatedly saved from impending Destruction, sometimes by an Aid unsought—at other times by Assistance granted to them from their own repeated humble Supplications; for such Colonies to plunge into an unnatural Rebellion, & in the Reign of a Sovereign, too, whose publick Virtues had announced him to be the Father of his Country, & whose private Virtues had distinguished him as an Ornament of the human Species—this surely, to an attentive Mind, must strike with some Degree of Astonishment; & such a Mind would anxiously wish for a Veil to throw over the Nakedness of human Nature. . . .

A contemporary political cartoon: Poor old England struggles to control his colonies.

[TROOPS ORDERED TO BOSTON]

But the Time was approaching, which promised some Degree of Protection to those who wished for the Restoration of Government. Two Regiments were ordered from *Hallifax*. This brought the ruling Powers into a Dilemma; some of them trembled at the Rod, others bullyed, hectored, & swore that they would kill them, as they landed & passed through the Streets; & actually proposed Methods of firing at them from the Windows of the Houses. Many People expected a Fracas; but when the Hour of Attack approached, the Novelty of a military Parade served but to amuse a vast Rabble; & even some of the Leaders of the Faction, went out & saluted the commanding Officer on his Arrival Sept. 28, 1768. The Streets, & the Doors & Windows of the Houses, were crouded with Spectators to view the Procession. It happened, that a Lady was standing at her Door to enjoy her Share of it. At that Time, a Man passing by her, who had but just before hectored and bullyed, in her presence, that the Troops should never land, & that he would fight up to his Knees in Blood to prevent it: he, seeing her eye the Parade, spake thus to her, "What do you stand there for? I would not look at them." She replied, "You are a very pretty Fellow! You said that you would fight up to your Knees in Blood, to destroy them, & you are now afraid to *look* at them."

The next Thing was, to provide the Troops with Quarters. The Town of *Boston* refused. Had they been requested to furnish them with Halters,[23] the Request would have been instantaneously complied with. These would have given the Inhabitants a full Swing at their wonted Riot. The Governor was now obliged to provide the Quarters himself, in the only Places where he could quarter them; one of which places

23. Halters: nooses.

was *Faneuil Hall*, the celebrated School for *Catalines*, & of Sedition. This was a great Shock to them. It was a Prophanation of their *Sanctum Sanctorum*. It must not be forgiven. They accordingly exorted their selves to pick Quarrells with the Soldiers; they insulted & abused them.

Colo. *Dalrymple*, who was the first Officer in Command, was very prudent; & very strict in his Orders to the Troops, to bear the Insults, & not return them; & perhaps, Troops were never fortified with more Patience, or more obedient to Command. They cloathed themselves with Patience although the Dress did not become such an Order of Men so well as their old military Garb. But the new Dress soon grew thread bare & useless. Persons were imployed to provoke them, in Order to give Pretence for their Removal.

A famous Bruiser was pitched upon for the Attack. He began with a Soldier, who was quite in Peace; the Soldier reasoned with him, & asked him, "why he abused an innocent inoffensive Man?" But Reason was of no avail against a determined Insult. The Soldier was determined not to resent. The Man challenged him to fight: the Soldier replied, "that his Officer had given him Orders to the contrary." At the last, the Man gave such an Affront as not only a Soldier, but even human Nature could not bear. He beat his Antagonist in such a Manner, which rather more than satisfied him. At that Juncture, Colo. *Dalrymple* stepped in, & ordered the Soldier off for Punishment, for Breach of Orders; but some, even of the Faction, who were present at the beginning of the Affray, pleaded in behalf of the Soldier; that the provocation was beyond a bearing; & so saved him from the Halbords.

The Presence of two british Regiments was, at that Time a Restraint upon Riots; & the Faction could not, by all their Stratagems, effectuate the Removal of them, untill the Year 1770, when Capt. Preston's Guard fired upon the Mob & killed 5 of them;[24] as will be more particularly related when we arrive at that memorable Æra; untill that Time, although the Interval was but short, yet it was observable, that the Town of Boston had not been so free from Disorders for several Years past. Before, there was no safety for Persons in walking the Streets at Nights, free of Insults. Now, it was the Reverse. The Soldiers were under so good Discipline; that they were peculiarly civil, when unmolested; & seemed rather to chuse to give Protection than Offence.

It is never prudent to lose Time if it can be saved. The Faction left no Stone unturned, either in this Province, or by constant Correspondence with the neighbouring Provinces, to discourage the importation of british Manufactures. Some of the Merchants had already imported vast Quantities of them. They chose to monopolize, for there had been many of the Petty Shopkeepers, who formerly purchased of them, had turned Merchants theirselves, & imported their own Goods. The Merchants in *England* were so fond of getting rid of their Goods, that they gave a Credit to any who asked for it, & to many who had no Estates at all; which they were soon convinced of, either by losing all, or a great Part of their Debts. It was therefore the Art of the great Traders to ruin the lesser ones, & engross the whole of the Business to theirselves; both which they, in some Degree, effectuated; & notwithstanding of their solemn Promises & Subscriptions, they imported Goods enough for the Demand for them. Their little, low mercantile Arts would have shocked a modest Mind unversed

24. Oliver refers to the 1770 "Boston Massacre."

in such Chicanery. The Ladies too were so zealous for the Good of their Country, that they agreed to drink no Tea, except the Stock of it which they had by them; or in Case of Sickness. Indeed, they were cautious enough to lay in large Stocks before they promised; & they could be sick just as suited their Convenience or Inclination. Chocolate & Coffee were to be substituted for Tea; & it was really diverting, to see a Circle of Ladies about a Tea Table, & a Chocolate or Coffee Pot in the midst of it filled with Tea, one chusing a Dish of Chocolate, & another a Cup of Coffee. Such a Finesse would not only be a laughable Scene to a Spectator, but it must be a Fund of Mirth to theirselves, who framed such an evasive Conceit.

As to the other Evasion of Sickness; there were many who could not afford to purchase a Quantity of Tea in Stock. They, poor Souls! were forced to take Turns to be sick, & invite their Acquaintance to visit them; & so the Sickness went on by Rotation. There were others who could afford to keep a large Stock by them; & one of them, who was very warm in her Love to her Country & to Tea, declared that she would not drink any, after her present Stock was expended; being asked, "what Stock of it she possessed"? Replied, "She had but one Chest in all"; & doubtless, if she had outlived her Stock, she would have been admitted into her Sexe's Hospital of Invalids.

The Clergy also, were faithfull Laborers in their Master's Vineyard; not only those who had worked hard from the beginning of the Day, but those who entred at the eleventh Hour. One of these pious Men, who had just came reeking hot from the publick Worship, seeing the Rabble breaking the Windows of one who had dared openly to be an Importer; he made an Halt in the Crowd, with this Exclamation, "see how those Boys fight for us."

The Garretts now were crowded with the Rabble, in full Divan, with a Clergyman to præside; whose Part was to declaim on Politicks & Sedition, instead of propagating that Gospel of Peace, which, upon their entring into holy Orders, they had solemnly sworn to its divine Author to spend their Lives in inculcating. But they, pious Men, had learned of the aforementioned Smuggler, *to tuck the false Manifest in their Sleeve,* when the Oath was administred to them. Gracious God! Is it possible, that Men, who had so solemnly devoted themselves to thy Service, could act with such Duplicity as to disgrace even human Nature itself? Yes! it is possible, & the *New England* Clergy will be everlasting Monuments of the Disgrace.

In one of those Night Garret Meetings, the entire Structure of the *Babel* of Confusion was very near to Destruction. The serpentine Dr. Cooper præsided. The Crowd of factious Senators was great. Their Weight sunk the Floor; & they sunk with it—no very great Damage was done. Had the *Parson,* like *Samson,* grasped the Pillars & been buried in the Ruins with his gaping *Philistines,* he would have reared a Monument to his Fame which perhaps would have prevented the present Rebellion, or, in such Case, he might possibly have been buried in Oblivion, instead of surviving to commit such atrocious Acts as will perpetuate his Name with indelible Infamy.

Thus, by nocturnal Meetings, Mr. *Samuel Adams's* Psalm-singing Myrmidons; Comittees of Correspondence throughout the Province; Emissaries from one Colony to another upon the Continent; non-Importation Agreements; the Ladies' new invented chymical Process, of transmuting Chocolate & Coffee into Tea; together with many other Arts, learn'd in the Schools of Folly, Madness and Rebellion, they so far accomplished their Purposes, as to intimidate the Parliament of *Great Britain* into a partial Repeal of their late Act, *of Duties upon Paper, Glass, Painters Colours & Tea;* the *Tea* Part of the Act was left unrepealed. This, the Colonies, for the present, acquiesced in. The *Inch* was given to them, and they well knew, from their former Success at rioting, that they could take the *Ell* when it best suited them. The *Tea* grew scarce, & they were not averse to an Opening for a new importation, to stock theirselves with that & with such an enormous Quantity of English Goods, as might create a Debt to the english Merchants, to insure new Allies to theirselves; & such a Debt, which many of the Importers never designed to pay. They always had their Geniusses, who (by the *Mob Whistle*, as horrid as the *Iroquois Yell* which always tingled in the Ears of every one who had once heared it) could fabricate the Structure of Rebellion from a single Straw. These were always ready for their Work; & it will not be long before the Ædiface is erected, & such a one that the Exertions of *Great Britain* could scarcely prostrate.

I had forgot to mention one of the *Tea Substitutes*. It was a Vegetable, which the *Labradore Coast* abounds with, & which grows plenteously in the Eastern Parts of the *Massachusetts Bay*. It is a plant of an aromatick Flavor. This, the Clergy recommended: the Physicians, prudently, did not advise against it; & the People drank it— but the Fashion of drinking it, like all other Fashions, soon was changed—it brought on Disorders in Health; & among the rest a *Vertigo*, as fatal as that which they had brought upon theirselves with Respect to Liberty; & had they continued in the Use of *that*, as long as they had in their Reveries about the *other*, *Great Britain* would have had but few Colonists to contend with. Perhaps it would have been more eligible for them to have died that Way than by the Sword, & the Pestilence which was the consequent upon it: this would have saved them from the accumulated Guilt of Murder, Treason & Rebellion.

[Benjamin Franklin]

Dr. *Benjamin Franklin* was a Native of *Boston* in the *Massachusetts Bay*. He was born in 1706, of very reputable Parents. His Father was a capital Tallow Chandler, & a worthy honest Man. His Brother also was a Man held in very good esteem. The Doctor himself was what is called a *Printers Devil*, but, by a Climax in Reputation, he reversed the Phrase, & taught us to read it backward, as Witches do the Lords Prayer. He worked at the Business of the Press untill he went to *England*, & continued in *London* for about two Years, to perfect himself in the Art, & black as the Art was before, he made it much blacker, by forcing the Press often to speak the Thing that was not. He published a Libel in *Boston*, for which he was obliged to quit. He fled to *Rhode Island*, the Asylum for those who had done what they ought not to have done—from thence he went to *Philadelphia*, & settled in the printing Business. The *Philadelphia* News Paper was published by him; & the Almanacks of *Poor Richard*, which he annually struck off, were interlaced with many usefull Observations in Agriculture & other Sciences.

Dr. *Franklin* (pardon the Expression) was cursed with a full Share of Understanding; he was a Man of Genius, but of so unprincipled an Heart, that the Merit of all his political & philosophical Disquisitions can never atone for the Mischiefs which he plunged Society into, by the Perversion of his Genius. He had such an Insight into human Nature, that he insinuated himself into various publick Departments in the Province of *Pennsilvania,* & at last arrived to the Office of one of the Post Masters in *America,* a Place worth 4 or £500. Sterling p Year. He was now released from the necessary Cares for a moderate Support; & was at Leisure to indulge in what might first strike his Fancy. He invented a Fire Stove, to warm Rooms in the northern Climates, & at the same Time to save Fuel; he succeeded: but, at the same Time, they were so destructive of Health that they fell into Disuse. He also invented a Chamber Urn contrived to make the Flame descend instead of rising from the Fire: upon which a young Clergyman of a poetical Turn, made the following Lines, vizt.

> Like a *Newton*, sublimely he soar'd
>   To a Summit before unattain'd,
> New Regions of Science explor'd,
>   And the Palm of Philosophy gain'd.
>
> With a Spark that he caught from the Skies
>   He display'd an unparalell'd Wonder,
> And we saw, with Delight & Surprize,
>   That his Rod would defend us from Thunder.
>
> Oh! had he been Wise to pursue
>   The Track for his Talents design'd,
> What a Tribute of Praise had been due
>   To the Teacher & Friend of Mankind?
>
> But, to covet political Fame
>   Was in him a degrading Ambition,
> A Spark that from *Lucifer* came,
>   And kindled the Blaze of Sedition.
>
> Let Candor then write on his Urn,
>   Here lies the renowned Inventor,
> Whose Flame to the Skies ought to burn,
>   But, inverted, descends to the Centre.

Agreeable to the Hint given in the above Lines, the Doctor had made some new Experiments in Electricity, which drew the Attention of the Literate, as well as of the great Vulgar & the Small. The Eclat, which was spread from some new Phaenomena he had discovered in this Science, introduced him into some of the first Company in *England,* whither he came, soon after he struck out these new Scenes. Men of Science gave their Attention, and others, of no ignoble Degree, gaped with a foolish Face of Praise; & it was this Circumstance, lucky for him, but unlucky for *Great Britain* & her Colonies, which gave such a Shock to Government, & brought on such Convulsions, as the english Constitution will not be cured of in one Century, if ever.

By this Introduction, he grew into Importance with the Leaders of the Opposition in *England*. They found him to be usefull to them, in their Attempts, to subvert the Foundations of Government, & they caught at every Circumstance that Chance threw in their Way. They knew him to be as void of every Principle as theirselves, & each of them play'd into the others Hands. The Doctor play'd his Card well, & procured the Agency of some of the Colonies; & the lower House of *Massachusetts* Assembly chose him for theirs. I have seen Letters from him to the latter, inciting them to a Revolt, at the same Time when he enjoyed the above lucrative Office from the Crown; but he was so abandoned to an utter Insensibility of Virtue or Honor, that he would not stick at any Villainy to gratifye his Pride.

When the Stamp Act was on the Tapis, he encouraged the passing of it; & procured, for one of his Friends, the Appointment of a Stamp Master. He procured the Government of *New Jersies* for his Son; who hath behaved with a spirited Fidelity to his Sovereign to this Day. But his unnatural Treatment of this Son will fix upon him an indelible Reproach; for when the Son was about to imbark for his Government, he was in Arrears £100 Sterling, & could not leave *England* without discharging them. The Father refused to assist him, & a private Gentleman, out of Compassion, lent him the Mony—and this Son afterwards was harrassed for his Loyalty & kept in a Gaol as a Prisoner in *Connecticut*, where he suffered greatly his self & where he lost his Lady, through Hardships. All this he underwent, whilst his humane Father had the Control of the Congress, & never attempted his Release. This fixes a Character which a Savage would blush at. Whilst he was in *England*, he travelled from one manufacturing Town to another, spreading Sedition as he went, & prognosticating the Independance of *America*; & notwithstanding all the Civilities he met with here, & the Bounties of the Crown, he afterwards boasted, in an intercepted Letter to his american Friends, of humbling *this huckstering Nation*, as he politely & gratefully termed them. Surely! his patriotick Friends in *England* must have Souls callous to every virtuous Feeling, to support a Man, whose every Exertion tends to the Ruin of his Country.

After the Destruction of Lieut. Govr. *Hutchinson's* House in 1765, Dr. *Franklin* maintained a familiar literary Correspondence with him, & condemned the Opposition of the Faction to him. Yet this very Man, a Traitor to his Friend as well as to his Country, set another abandoned Man to filch, from a Gentleman's File of Letters, left in his Custody by a deceased Brother, a Number of confidential ones wrote by Mr. *Hutchinson* to that Brother, which did Honor to the Writer; & had they been attended to by Government, would in all Probability have put a Stop to the present Rebellion. This base Theft brought on a Duel between the Thief & the Proprietor of the Letters. The Latter nearly lost his Life, being unacquainted with the Sword; but fought upon the false Principle of Honor, because he must fight; & carried off those Marks in his Back which Swordsmen pronounced of the murderous Kind. Upon a hearing of the State of this Transaction, before the King and Council, Dr. *Franklin*, with the Effrontery of that Countenance where Virtue could never raise a Blush, took the Theft upon himself; & was discarded by every Man who felt any Regard to Propriety of Character. It may, with strict Justice, be said of the Doctor, what *Churchill* says of his Hero in the Duellist,

> —of Virtue,
> Not one dull, dim Spark in his Soul,
> Vice, glorious Vice, possess'd the whole;
> And in her Service truly warm,
> He was in Sin, most Uniform.

Pride is Dr. *Franklin's* ruling Passion, & from this Source may be traced all the Actions of his Life. He had a Contempt of Religion, of Mankind, & even of those whom he had duped; & had he viewed the Subject in a moral Light, he would have contemned hisself. Had *Churchill* drawn his Character, instead of saying, as he did of his Hero,

And shove his Savior from the Wall. He would have changed his Phrase into—*and shove his Savior, God & All*.

He is now caressed at that perfidious Court, where it would have been Thought; further Instructions were not necessary; untill this Adept in the Science of Perfidy appeared, like a blazing Meteor, & has taught them, that all their former Knowledge was but the first Rudiments of their Grammar; & has qualified them for *Professors* in that Art which they were too well acquainted with before. This Hatred to the english Nation is so rivetted that it is no Breach of Charity to suppose, that when he makes his Exit:

> Such, in those Moments as in all the past
> *Ye Gods! let Britain sink!* will be his last.

13. Edward Gibbon

from *Decline and Fall of the Roman Empire* 1776

Edward Gibbon (1737–94) formed his project of writing the history of the decline and fall of the Roman empire when he was a young man serving in the army in Italy and was deeply moved by the sight of the ruins of the Capitol. The first volume appeared in 1776 to immediate acclaim and controversy, especially over its assertion that the emergence of Christianity had been detrimental to Rome. He saw in the eclipse of the Roman empire the doom of civilization which is always vulnerable to barbarity and feared a similar fate for Europe.

It is the duty of a patriot to prefer and promote the exclusive interest and glory of his native country: but a philosopher may be permitted to enlarge his views, and to consider Europe as one great republic, whose various inhabitants have attained almost the same level of politeness and cultivation. The balance of power will continue to fluctuate, and the prosperity of our own, or the neighboring kingdoms, may be alternately exalted or depressed; but these partial events cannot essentially injure our general state of happiness, the system of arts, and laws, and manners, which so advantageously distinguish, above the rest of mankind, the Europeans and their colonies. The savage nations of the globe are the common enemies of civilized society; and we may inquire, with anxious curiosity, whether Europe is still threatened with a repetition of those calamities, which formerly oppressed the arms and institutions of Rome.

14. William Robertson

from *The History of America*
1777

> *The development of America needs to be seen in the context of the growth of a global European and more specifically English empire even after 1776. A year after the English colonies had announced their separate status, this very popular and influential history of America quite matter-of-factly cast it as part of the history of Europe. For William Robertson (1721–93), America derived its meaning from its refraction of the meanings of Europe, from the way the New World carried the evolution of the old forward, from the revelations it afforded about universal human traits and dilemmas (Robertson's account of the New World's aboriginal societies was a particular source of the History's popularity), and from its status as England's most successful plantation. The passages below open the book by looking back to the beginning of history, or indeed its two beginnings, first with the Creation, then secondly and to more effect with Trade. God created Man, Man created Commerce, and Commerce created America.*

The progress of men, in discovering and peopling the various parts of the earth, has been extremely slow. Several ages elapsed before they removed far from those mild and fertile regions in which they were originally placed by their Creator. The occasion of their first general dispersion is known; but we are unacquainted with the course of their migrations, or the time when they took possession of the different countries which they now inhabit. Neither history nor tradition furnishes such information concerning these remote events, as enables us to trace, with any certainty, the operations of the human race in the infancy of society.

We may conclude, however, that all the early migrations of mankind were made by land. The ocean which surrounds the habitable earth, as well as the various arms of the sea which separate one region from another, though destined to facilitate the communication between distant countries, seem, at first view, to be formed to check the progress of man, and to mark the bounds of that portion of the globe to which nature had confined him. It was long, we may believe, before men attempted to pass these formidable barriers, and became so skilful and adventurous as to commit themselves to the mercy of the winds and waves, or to quit their native shores in quest of remote and unknown regions.

Navigation and shipbuilding are arts so nice[25] and complicated, that they require the ingenuity, as well as experience, of many successive ages to bring them to any degree of perfection. From the raft or canoe, which first served to carry a savage over the river that obstructed him in the chase, to the construction of a vessel capable of conveying a numerous crew with safety to a distant coast, the progress in improvement is immense. Many efforts would be made, many experiments would be tried, and much labour as well as invention would be employed, before men could accomplish this arduous and important undertaking. The rude and imperfect state in which navigation is still found among all nations which are not considerably civilized, corresponds with this account of its progress, and demonstrates that in early times the art was not so far improved as to enable men to undertake distant voyages, or to attempt remote discoveries.

As soon, however, as the art of navigation became known, a new species of correspondence among men took place. It is from this era that we must date the commencement of such an intercourse between nations as deserves the appellation of commerce. Men are, indeed, far advanced in improvement before commerce becomes an object of great importance to them. They must even have made some considerable progress towards civilization, before they acquire the idea of property, and ascertain it so perfectly as to be acquainted with the most simple of all contracts, that of exchanging by barter one rude commodity for another. But as soon as this important right is established, and every individual feels that he has an exclusive title to possess or to alienate whatever he has acquired by his own labour and dexterity, the wants and ingenuity of his nature suggest to him a new method of increasing his acquisitions and enjoyments, by disposing of what is superfluous in his own stores, in order to procure what is necessary or desirable in those of other men. Thus a commercial intercourse begins, and is carried on among the members of the same community. By degrees, they discover that neighbouring tribes possess what they themselves want, and enjoy comforts of which they wish to partake. In the same mode, and upon the same principles, that domestic traffic is carried on within the society, an external commerce is established with other tribes or nations. Their mutual interest and mutual wants render this intercourse desirable, and imperceptibly introduce the maxims and laws which facilitate its progress and render it secure. But no very extensive commerce can take place between contiguous provinces, whose soil and climate being nearly the same yield similar productions. Remote countries cannot convey their commodities, by land, to those places where on account of their rarity they are desired, and become valuable. It is to navigation that men are indebted for the power of transporting the superfluous stock of one part of the earth to supply the wants of another. The luxuries and blessings of a particular climate are no longer confined to itself alone, but the enjoyment of them is communicated to the most distant regions.

In proportion as the knowledge of the advantages derived from navigation and commerce continued to spread, the intercourse among nations extended. The ambition of conquest, or the necessity of procuring new settlements, were no longer the

25. nice: exact.

sole motives of visiting distant lands. The desire of gain became a new incentive to activity, roused adventurers, and sent them forth upon long voyages, in search of countries whose products or wants might increase that circulation which nourishes and gives vigour to commerce. Trade proved a great source of discovery: it opened unknown seas, it penetrated into new regions, and contributed more than any other cause to bring men acquainted with the situation, the nature, and commodities of the different parts of the globe.

15. John Filson

The Adventures of Daniel Boon
1784

> *Daniel Boone was essentially illiterate, and his account of his life and adventures was almost certainly written by John Filson (1747–88), probably on the basis of direct conversations. Filson was a land speculator who had acquired thousands of acres in the new territory of Kentucky and was seeking settlers. His book,* Kentucke, *to which* The Adventures of Daniel Boon *was appended, was frankly promotional, as indeed is the story of Daniel Boone. But this last evoked a response that went far beyond land sales, for it promoted the whole of western expansion and a new concept of the nation defined in that imperial image.*

Curiosity is natural to the soul of man, and interesting objects have a powerful influence on our affections. Let these influencing powers actuate, by the permission or disposal of Providence, from selfish or social views, yet in time the mysterious will of Heaven is unfolded, and we behold our conduct, from whatsoever motives excited, operating to answer the important designs of heaven. Thus we behold Kentucke, lately an howling wilderness, the habitation of savages and wild beasts, become a fruitful field; this region, so favourably distinguished by nature, now become the habitation of civilization, at a period unparalelled in history, in the midst of a raging war, and under all the disadvantages of emigration to a country so remote from the inhabited parts of the continent. Here; where the hand of violence shed the blood of the innocent; where the horrid yells of savages, and the groans of the distressed, sounded in our ears, we now hear the praises and adorations of our Creator; where wretched wigwams stood, the miserable abodes of savages, we behold the foundations of cities laid, that, in all probability, will rival the glory of the greatest upon earth. And we view Kentucke situated on the fertile banks of the great Ohio, rising from obscurity to shine with splendor, equal to any other of the stars of the American hemisphere.

The settling of this region well deserves a place in history. Most of the memorable events I have myself been exercised in; and, for the satisfaction of the public, will briefly relate the circumstances of my adventures, and scenes of life, from my first movement to this country until this day.

It was on the first of May, in the year 1769, that I resigned my domestic happiness for a time, and left my family and peacable habitation on the Yadkin River, in North-Carolina, to wander through the wilderness of America, in quest of the country of Kentucke, in company with John Finley, John Stewart, Joseph Holden, James Monay, and William Cool. We proceeded successfully, and after a long and fatiguing journey through a mountainous wilderness, in a westward direction, on the seventh day of June following, we found ourselves on Red-River, where John Finley had formerly been trading with the Indians, and, from the top of an eminence, saw with pleasure the beautiful level of Kentucke. Here let me observe, that for some time we had experienced the most uncomfortable weather as a prelibation[26] of our future sufferings. At this place we encamped, and made a shelter to defend us from the inclement season, and began to hunt and reconnoitre the country. We found everywhere abundance of wild beasts of all sorts, through this vast forest. The buffaloes were more frequent than I have seen cattle in the settlements, browzing on the leaves of the cane, or croping the herbage on those extensive plains, fearless, because ignorant, of the violence of man. Sometimes we saw hundreds in a drove, and the numbers about the salt springs were amazing. In this forest, the habitation of beasts of every kind natural to America, we practiced hunting with great success until the twenty-second day of December following.

This day John Stewart and I had a pleasing ramble, but fortune changed the scene in the close of it. We had passed through a great forest, on which stood myriads of trees, some gay with blossoms, others rich with fruits. Nature was here a series of wonders, and a fund of delight. Here she displayed her ingenuity and industry in a variety of flowers and fruits, beautifully coloured, elegantly shaped, and charmingly flavoured; and we were diverted with innumerable animals presenting themselves perpetually to our view.—In the decline of the day, near Kentucke river, as we ascended the brow of a small hill, a number of Indians rushed out of a thick cane-brake upon us, and made us prisoners. The time of our sorrow was now arrived, and the scene fully opened. The Indians plundered us of what we had, and kept us in confinement seven days, treating us with common savage usage. During this time we discovered no uneasiness or desire to escape, which made them less suspicious of us; but in the dead of night, as we lay in a thick cane brake by a large fire, when sleep had locked up their senses, my situation not disposing me for rest, I touched my companion and gently awoke him. We improved this favorable opportunity, and departed, leaving them to take their rest, and speedily directed our course towards our old camp, but found it plundered, and the company dispersed and gone home. About this time my brother, Squire Boon, with another adventurer, who came to explore the country shortly after us, was wandering through the forest, determined to find me, if possible, and accidentally found our camp. Notwithstanding the unfortunate circumstances of our company, and our dangerous situation, as surrounded with hostile savages, our meeting so fortunately in the wilderness made us reciprocally sensible of the utmost satisfaction. So much does friendship triumph over misfortune, that sorrows and sufferings vanish at the meeting not only of real friends, but of the most distant acquaintances, and substitutes happiness in their room.

26. prelibation: foretaste.

Soon after this, my companion in captivity, John Stewart, was killed by the savages, and the man that came with my brother returned home by himself. We were then in a dangerous, helpless situation, exposed daily to perils and death amongst savages and wild beasts, not a white man in the country but ourselves.

Thus situated, many hundred miles from our families in the howling wilderness, I believe few would have equally enjoyed the happiness we experienced. I often observed to my brother, You see now how little nature requires to be satisfied. Felicity, the companion of content, is rather found in our own breasts than in the enjoyment of external things: And I firmly believe it requires but a little philosophy to make a man happy in whatsoever state he is. This consists in a full resignation to the will of Providence; and a resigned soul finds pleasure in a path strewed with briars and thorns.

We continued not in a state of indolence, but hunted every day, and prepared a little cottage to defend us from the Winter storms. We remained there undisturbed during the Winter; and on the first day of May, 1770, my brother returned home to the settlement by himself, for a new recruit of horses and ammunition, leaving me by myself, without bread, salt or sugar, without company of my fellow creatures, or even a horse or dog. I confess I never before was under greater necessity of exercising philosophy and fortitude. A few days I passed uncomfortably. The idea of a beloved wife and family, and their anxiety upon the account of my absence and exposed situation, made sensible impressions on my heart. A thousand dreadful apprehensions presented themselves to my view, and had undoubtedly disposed me to melancholy, if further indulged.

One day I undertook a tour through the country, and the diversity and beauties of nature I met with in this charming season, expelled every gloomy and vexatious thought. Just at the close of day the gentle gales retired, and left the place to the disposal of a profound calm. Not a breeze shook the most tremulous leaf. I had gained the summit of a commanding ridge, and, looking round with astonishing delight, beheld the ample plains, the beauteous tracts below. On the other hand, I surveyed the famous river Ohio that rolled in silent dignity, marking the western boundary of Kentucke with inconceivable grandeur. At a vast distance I beheld the mountains lift their venerable brows, and penetrate the clouds. All things were still. I kindled a fire near a fountain of sweet water, and feasted on the loin of a buck, which a few hours before I had killed. The sullen shades of night soon overspread the whole hemisphere, and the earth seemed to gasp after the hovering moisture. My roving excursion this day had fatigued my body, and diverted my imagination. I laid me down to sleep, and I awoke not until the sun had chased away the night. I continued this tour, and in a few days explored a considerable part of the country, each day equally pleased as the first. I returned again to my old camp, which was not disturbed in my absence. I did not confine my lodging to it, but often reposed in thick cane-brakes, to avoid the savages, who, I believe, often visited my camp, but fortunately for me, in my absence. In this situation I was constantly exposed to danger, and death. How unhappy such a situation for a man tormented with fear, which is vain if no danger comes, and if it does, only augments the pain. It was my happiness to be destitute of this afflicting passion, with which I had the greatest reason to be affected. The prowling wolves diverted my nocturnal hours with perpetual howlings; and the various species of animals in this vast forest, in the daytime, were continually in my view.

Thus I was surrounded with plenty in the midst of want. I was happy in the midst of dangers and inconveniences. In such a diversity it was impossible I should be disposed to melancholy. No populous city, with all the varieties of commerce and stately structures, could afford so much pleasure to my mind, as the beauties of nature I found here.

Thus, through an uninterrupted scene of sylvan pleasures, I spent the time until the 27th day of July following, when my brother, to my great felicity, met me, according to appointment, at our old camp. Shortly after, we left this place, not thinking it safe to stay there longer, and proceeded to Cumberland river, reconnoitring that part of the country until March, 1771, and giving names to the different waters.

Soon after, I returned home to my family with a determination to bring them as soon as possible to live in Kentucke, which I esteemed a second paradise, at the risk of my life and fortune.

I returned safe to my old habitation, and found my family in happy circumstances. I sold my farm on the Yadkin, and what goods we could not carry with us; and on the twenty-fifth day of September, 1773, bade a farewell to our friends, and proceeded on our journey to Kentucke, in company with five families more, and forty men that joined us in Powel's Valley, which is one hundred and fifty miles from the now settled parts of Kentucke. This promising beginning was soon overcast with a cloud of adversity; for upon the tenth day of October, the rear of our company was attacked by a number of Indians, who killed six, and wounded one man. Of these my eldest son was one that fell in the action. Though we defended ourselves, and repulsed the enemy, yet this unhappy affair scattered our cattle, brought us into extreme difficulty, and so discouraged the whole company, that we retreated forty miles, to the settlement on Clench river. We had passed over two mountains, viz. Powels and Walden's, and were approaching Cumberland mountain when this adverse fortune overtook us. These mountains are in the wilderness, as we pass from the old settlements in Virginia to Kentucke, are ranged in S. west and N. east direction, are of a great length and breadth, and not far distant from each other. Over these, nature hath formed passes, that are less difficult than might be expected from a view of such huge piles. The aspect of these cliffs is so wild and horrid, that it is impossible to behold them without terror. The spectator is apt to imagine that nature had formerly suffered some violent convulsion; and that these are the dismembered remains of the dreadful shock; the ruins, not of Persepolis or Palmyra, but of the world!

I remained with my family on Clench until the sixth of June, 1774, when I and one Michael Stoner were solicited by Governor Dunmore, of Virginia, to go to the Falls of the Ohio, to conduct into the settlement a number of surveyors that had been sent thither by him some months before; this country having about this time drawn the attention of many adventurers. We immediately complied with the Governor's request, and conducted in the surveyors, compleating a tour of eight hundred miles, through many difficulties, in sixty-two days.

Soon after I returned home, I was ordered to take the command of three garrisons during the campaign, which Governor Dunmore carried on against the Shawanese Indians: After the conclusion of which, the Militia was discharged from each garrison, and I being relieved from my post, was solicited by a number of North-Carolina gentlemen, that were about purchasing the lands lying on the S. side of Kentucke River, from the Cherokee Indians, to attend their treaty at Wataga, in March, 1775, to negotiate with them, and, mention the boundaries of the purchase. This I accepted, and at the request of the same gentlemen, undertook to mark out a road in the best passage from the settlement through the wilderness to Kentucke, with such assistance as I thought necessary to employ for such an important undertaking.

I soon began this work, having collected a number of enterprising men, well armed. We proceeded with all possible expedition until we came within fifteen miles of where Boonsborough now stands, and where we were fired upon by a party of Indians that killed two, and wounded two of our number; yet, although surprised and taken at a disadvantage, we stood our ground. This was on the twentieth of March, 1775. Three days after, we were fired upon again, and had two men killed, and three wounded. Afterwards we proceeded on to Kentucke river without opposition; and on the first day of April began to erect the fort of Boonsborough at a salt lick, about sixty yards from the river, on the S. side.

On the fourth day, the Indians killed one of our men.—We were busily employed in building this fort, until the fourteenth day of June following, without any farther opposition from the Indians; and having finished the works, I returned to my family, on Clench.

In a short time, I proceeded to remove my family from Clench to this garrison; where we arrived safe without any other difficulties than such as are common to this passage, my wife and daughter being the first white women that ever stood on the banks of Kentucke river.

On the twenty-fourth day of December following we had one man killed, and one wounded, by the Indians, who seemed determined to persecute us for erecting this fortification.

On the fourteenth day of July, 1776, two of Col. Calaway's daughters, and one of mine, were taken prisoners near the fort. I immediately pursued the Indians, with only eight men, and on the sixteenth overtook them, killed two of the party, and recovered the girls. The same day on which this attempt was made, the Indians divided themselves into different parties, and attacked several forts, which were shortly before this time erected, doing a great deal of mischief. This was extremely distressing to the new settlers. The innocent husbandman was shot down, while busy cultivating the soil for his family's supply. Most of the cattle around the stations were destroyed. They continued their hostilities in this manner until the fifteenth of April, 1777, when they attacked Boonsborough with a party of above one hundred in number, killed one man, and wounded four—Their loss in this attack was not certainly known to us.

On the fourth day of July following, a party of about two hundred Indians attacked Boonsborough, killed one man, and wounded two. They besieged us forty-eight hours; during which time seven of them were killed, and at last, finding themselves not likely to prevail, they raised the siege, and departed.

The Indians had disposed their warriors in different parties at this time, and attacked the different garrisons to prevent their assisting each other, and did much injury to the distressed inhabitants.

On the nineteenth day of this month, Col. Logan's fort was besieged by a party of about two hundred Indians. During this dreadful siege they did a great deal of mischief, distressed the garrison, in which were only fifteen men, killed two, and wounded one. The enemies loss was uncertain, from the common practice which the Indians have of carrying off their dead in time of battle. Col. Harrod's fort was then defended by only sixty-five men, and Boonsborough by twenty-two, there being no more forts or white men in the country, except at the Falls, a considerable distance from these, and all taken collectively, were but a handful to the numerous warriors that were every where dispersed through the country, intent upon doing all the mischief that savage barbarity could invent. Thus we passed through a scene of sufferings that exceeds description.

On the twenty-fifth of this month a reinforcement of forty-five men arrived from North-Carolina, and about the twentieth of August following, Col. Bowman arrived with one hundred men from Virginia. Now we began to strengthen, and from hence, for the space of six weeks, we had skirmishes with Indians, in one quarter or other, almost every day.

The savages now learned the superiority of the Long Knife, as they call the Virginians, by experience; being out-generalled in almost every battle. Our affairs began to wear a new aspect, and the enemy, not daring to venture on open war, practiced secret mischief at times.

On the first day of January, 1778, I went with a party of thirty men to the Blue Licks, on Licking River, to make salt for the different garrisons in the country.

On the seventh day of February, as I was hunting, to procure meat for the company, I met with a party of one hundred and two Indians, and two Frenchmen, on their march against Boonsborough, that place being particularly the object of the enemy.

They pursued, and took me; and brought me on the eighth day to the Licks, where twenty-seven of my party were, three of them having previously returned home with the salt. I knowing it was impossible for them to escape, capitulated with the enemy, and, at a distance in their view, gave notice to my men of their situation, with orders not to resist, but surrender themselves captives.

The generous usage the Indians had promised before in my capitulation, was afterwards fully complied with, and we proceeded with them as prisoners to old Chelicothe, the principal Indian town, on Little Miami, where we arrived, after an uncomfortable journey, in very severe weather, on the eighteenth day of February, and received as good treatment as prisoners could expect from savages—On the tenth day of March following, I, and ten of my men, were conducted by forty Indians to Detroit, where we arrived the thirtieth day, and were treated by Governor Hamilton, the British commander at that post, with great humanity.

During our travels, the Indians entertained me well; and their affection for me was so great, that they utterly refused to leave me there with the others, although the Governor offered them one hundred pounds Sterling for me, on purpose to give me a parole to go home. Several English gentlemen there, being sensible of my adverse fortune, and touched with human sympathy, generously offered a friendly supply for my wants, which I refused, with many thanks for their kindness; adding, that I never expected it would be in my power to recompense such unmerited generosity.

The Indians left my men in captivity with the British at Detroit, and on the tenth day of April brought me towards Old Chelicothe, where we arrived on the twenty-fifth day of the same month. This was a long and fatiguing march, through an exceeding fertile country, remarkable for fine springs and streams of water. At Chelicothe I spent my time as comfortably as I could expect; was adopted, according to their custom, into a family where I became a son, and had a great share in the affection of my new parents, brothers, sisters, and friends. I was exceedingly familiar and friendly with them, always appearing as chearful and satisfied as possible, and they put great confidence in me. I often went a hunting with them, and frequently gained their applause for my activity at our shooting-matches. I was careful not to exceed many of them in shooting; for no people are more envious than they in this sport. I could observe, in their countenances and gestures, the greatest expressions of joy when they exceeded me; and, when the reverse happened, of envy. The Shawanese king took great notice of me, and treated me with profound respect, and entire friendship, often entrusting me to hunt at my liberty. I frequently returned with the spoils of the woods, and as often presented some of what I had taken to him, expressive of duty to my sovereign. My food and lodging was, in common, with them, not so good indeed as I could desire, but necessity made every thing acceptable.

I now began to meditate an escape, and carefully avoided their suspicions, continuing with them at Old Chelicothe until the first day of June following, and then was taken by them to the salt springs on Sciotha, and kept there, making salt, ten days. During this time I hunted some for them, and found the land, for a great extent about this river, to exceed the soil of Kentucke, if possible, and remarkably well watered.

When I returned to Chelicothe, alarmed to see four hundred and fifty Indians, of their choicest warriors, painted and armed in a fearful manner, ready to march against Boonsborough, I determined to escape the first opportunity.

On the sixteenth, before sun-rise, I departed in the most secret manner, and arrived at Boonsborough on the twentieth, after a journey of one hundred and sixty miles; during which, I had but one meal.

I found our fortress in a bad state of defence, but we proceeded immediately to repair our flanks, strengthen our gates and posterns, and form double bastions, which we compleated in ten days. In this time we daily expected the arrival of the Indian army; and at length, one of my fellow prisoners, escaping from them, arrived, informing us that the enemy had an account of my departure, and postponed their expedition three weeks.—The Indians had spies out viewing our movements, and were greatly alarmed with our increase in number and fortifications. The Grand Councils of the nations were held frequently, and with more deliberation than usual. They evidently saw the approaching hour when the Long Knife would dispossess them of their desirable habitations; and anxiously concerned for futurity, determined utterly to extirpate the whites out of Kentucke. We were not intimidated by their movements, but frequently gave them proofs of our courage.

About the first of August, I made an incursion into the Indian country, with a party of nineteen men, in order to surprise a small town up Sciotha, called Paint-Creek-Town. We advanced within four miles thereof, where we met a party of thirty Indians, on their march against Boonsborough, intending to join the others from Chelicothe. A smart fight ensued betwixt us for some time: At length the savages gave way, and fled.

We had no loss on our side: The enemy had one killed, and two wounded. We took from them three horses, and all their baggage; and being informed, by two of our number that went to their town, that the Indians had entirely evacuated it, we proceeded no further, and returned with all possible expedition to assist our garrison against the other party. We passed by them on the sixth day, and on the seventh, we arrived safe at Boonsborough.

On the eighth, the Indian army arrived, being four hundred and forty-four in number, commanded by Capt. Duquesne, eleven other Frenchmen, and some of their own chiefs, and marched up within view of our fort, with British and French colours flying; and having sent a summons to me, in his Britannick Majesty's name, to surrender the fort, I requested two days consideration, which was granted.

It was now a critical period with us.—We were a small number in the garrison:—A powerful army before our walls, whose appearance proclaimed inevitable death, fearfully painted, and marking their footsteps with desolation. Death was preferable to captivity; and if taken by storm, we must inevitably be devoted to destruction. In this situation we concluded to maintain our garrison, if possible. We immediately proceeded to collect what we could of our horses, and other cattle, and bring them through the posterns into the fort: And in the evening of the ninth, I returned answer, that we were determined to defend our fort while a man was living—Now, said I to their commander, who stood attentively hearing my sentiments, We laugh at all your formidable preparations: But thank you for giving us notice and time to provide for our defence. Your efforts will not prevail; for our gates shall for ever deny you admittance.—Whether this answer affected their courage, or not, I cannot tell; but, contrary to our expectations, they formed a scheme to deceive us, declaring it was their orders, from Governor Hamilton, to take us captives, and not to destroy us; but if nine of us would come out, and treat with them, they would immediately withdraw their forces from our walls and return home peaceably. This sounded grateful in our ears; and we agreed to the proposal.

We held the treaty within sixty yards of the garrison, on purpose to divert them from a breach of honour, as we could not avoid suspicions of the savages. In this situation the articles were formally agreed to, and signed; and the Indians told us it was customary with them, on such occasions, for two Indians to shake hands with every white-man in the treaty, as an evidence of entire friendship. We agreed to this also, but were soon convinced their policy was to take us prisoners.—They immediately grappled us; but, although surrounded by hundreds of savages, we extricated ourselves from them, and escaped all safe into the garrison, except one that was wounded, through a heavy fire from their army. They immediately attacked us on every side, and a constant heavy fire ensued between us day and night for the space of nine days.

In this time the enemy began to undermine our fort, which was situated sixty yards from Kentucke river. They began at the water-mark, and proceeded in the bank some distance, which we understood by their making the water muddy with the clay; and we immediately proceeded to disappoint their design, by cutting a trench a-cross their subterranean passage. The enemy discovering our counter-mine, by the clay we threw out of the fort, desisted from that stratagem: And experience now fully convincing them that neither their power nor policy could effect their purpose, on the twentieth day of August they raised the siege, and departed.

During this dreadful siege, which threatened death in every form, we had two men killed, and four wounded, besides a number of cattle. We killed of the enemy thirty-seven, and wounded a great number. After they were gone, we picked up one hundred and twenty-five pounds weight of bullets, besides what stuck in the logs of our fort; which certainly is a great proof of their industry. Soon after this, I went into the settlement, and nothing worthy of a place in this account passed in my affairs for some time.

During my absence from Kentucke, Col. Bowman carried on an expedition against the Shawanese, at Old Chelicothe, with one hundred and sixty men, in July, 1779. Here they arrived undiscovered, and a battle ensued, which lasted until ten o'clock, A.M. when Col. Bowman, finding he could not succeed at this time, retreated about thirty miles. The Indians, in the mean time, collecting all their forces, pursued and overtook him, when a smart fight continued near two hours, not to the advantage of Col. Bowman's party.

Col. Harrod proposed to mount a number of horse, and furiously to rush upon the savages, who at this time fought with remarkable fury. This desperate step had a happy effect, broke their line of battle, and the savages fled on all sides. In these two battles we had nine killed, and one wounded. The enemy's loss uncertain, only two scalps being taken.

On the twenty-second day of June, 1780, a large party of Indians and Canadians, about six hundred in number, commanded by Col. Bird, attacked Riddle's and Martin's stations, at the Forks of Licking River, with six pieces of artillery. They carried this expedition so secretly, that the unwary inhabitants did not discover them, until they fired upon the forts; and, not being prepared to oppose them, were obliged to surrender themselves miserable captives to barbarous savages, who immediately after tomahawked one man and two women, and loaded all the others with heavy baggage, forcing them along toward their towns, able or unable to march. Such as were weak and faint by the way, they tomahawked. The tender women, and helpless children, fell victims to their cruelty. This, and the savage treatment they received afterwards, is shocking to humanity, and too barbarous to relate.

The hostile disposition of the savages, and their allies, caused General Clark, the commandant at the Falls at the Ohio, immediately to begin an expedition with his own regiment, and the armed force of the country, against Pecaway, the principal town of the Shawanese, on a branch of Great Miami, which he finished with great success, took seventeen scalps, and burnt the town to ashes, with the loss of seventeen men.

About this time I returned to Kentucke with my family; and here, to avoid an enquiry into my conduct, the reader being before informed of my bringing my family to Kentucke, I am under the necessity of informing him that, during my captivity with the Indians, my wife, who despaired of ever seeing me again, expecting the Indians had put a period to my life, oppressed with the distresses of the country, and bereaved of me, her only happiness, had, before I returned, transported my family and goods, on horses, through the wilderness, amidst a multitude of dangers, to her father's house, in North-Carolina.

Shortly after the troubles at Boonsborough, I went to them, and lived peaceably there until this time. The history of my going home, and returning with my family, forms a series of difficulties, an account of which would swell a volume, and being foreign to my purpose, I shall purposely omit them.

I settled my family in Boonsborough once more; and shortly after, on the sixth day of October, 1780, I went in company with my brother to the Blue Licks; and, on our return home, we were fired upon by a party of Indians. They shot him, and pursued me, by the scent of their dog, three miles; but I killed the dog, and escaped. The Winter soon came on, and was very severe, which confined the Indians to their wigwams.

The severity of this Winter caused great difficulties in Kentucke. The enemy had destroyed most of the corn, the Summer before. This necessary article was scarce, and dear; and the inhabitants lived chiefly on the flesh of buffaloes. The circumstances of many were very lamentable: However, being a hardy race of people, and accustomed to difficulties and necessities, they were wonderfully supported through all their sufferings, until the ensuing Fall, when we received abundance from the fertile soil.

Towards Spring, we were frequently harassed by Indians; and, in May, 1782, a party assaulted Ashton's station, killed one man, and took a Negro prisoner. Capt. Ashton, with twenty-five men, pursued, and overtook the savages, and a smart fight ensued, which lasted two hours; but they being superior in number, obliged Captain Ashton's party to retreat, with the loss of eight killed, and four mortally wounded; their brave commander himself being numbered among the dead.

The Indians continued their hostilities; and, about the tenth of August following, two boys were taken from Major Hoy's station. This party was pursued by Capt. Holder and seventeen men, who were also defeated, with the loss of four men killed, and one wounded. Our affairs became more and more alarming. Several stations which had lately been erected in the country were continually infested with savages, stealing their horses and killing the men at every opportunity. In a field, near Lexington, an Indian shot a man, and running to scalp him, was himself shot from the fort, and fell dead upon his enemy.

Every day we experienced recent mischiefs. The barbarous savage nations of Shawanese, Cherokees, Wyandots, Tawas, Delawares, and several others near Detroit, united in a war against us and assembled their choicest warriors at old Chelicothe, to go on the expedition, in order to destroy us, and entirely depopulate the country. Their savage minds were inflamed to mischief by two abandoned men, Captains McKee and Girty. Miami rivers, Old Chelicothe, Pecaway, New Chelicothe, Will's Towns, and Chelicothe, burnt them all to ashes, entirely destroyed their corn, and other fruits, and every where spread a scene of desolation in the country. In this expedition we took seven prisoners and five scalps, with the loss of only four men, two of whom were accidentally killed by our own army.

This campaign in some measure damped the spirits of the Indians, and made them sensible of our superiority. Their connections were dissolved, their armies scattered, and a future invasion put entirely out of their power; yet they continued to practice mischief secretly upon the inhabitants, in the exposed parts of the country.

In October following, a party made an excursion into that district called the Crab Orchard, and one of them, being advanced some distance before the others, boldly entered the house of a poor defenceless family, in which was only a Negro man, a woman and her children, terrified with the apprehensions of immediate death. The savage, perceiving their defenceless situation, without offering violence to the family attempted to captivate the Negro, who, happily proved an over-match for him, threw him on the ground, and, in the struggle, the mother of the children drew an ax from a corner of the cottage, and cut his head off, while her little daughter shut the door. The savages instantly appeared, and applied their tomahawks to the door. An old rusty gun-barrel, without a lock, lay in a corner, which the mother put through a small crevice, and the savages, perceiving it, fled. In the mean time, the alarm spread through the neighbourhood; the armed men collected immediately, and pursued the savages into the wilderness. Thus Providence, by the means of this Negro, saved the whole of the poor family from destruction. From that time, until the happy return of peace between the United States and Great-Britain, the Indians did us no mischief. Finding the great king beyond the water disappointed in his expectations, and conscious of the importance of the Long Knife, and their own wretchedness, some of the nations immediately desired peace; to which, at present, they seem universally disposed, and are sending ambassadors to General Clark, at the Falls of the Ohio, with the minutes of their Councils; a specimen of which, in the minutes of the Piankashaw Council, is subjoined.

To conclude, I can now say that I have verified the saying of an old Indian who signed Col. Henderson's deed. Taking me by the hand, at the delivery thereof, Brother, says he, we have given you a fine land, but I believe you will have much trouble in settling it.—My footsteps have often been marked with blood, and therefore I can truly subscribe to its original name. Two darling sons, and a brother, have I lost by savage hands, which have also taken from me forty valuable horses, and abundance of cattle. Many dark and sleepless nights have I been a companion for owls, separated from the chearful society of men, scorched by the Summer's sun, and pinched by the Winter's cold, an instrument ordained to settle the wilderness. But now the scene is changed: Peace crowns the sylvan shade.

What thanks, what ardent and ceaseless thanks are due to that all-superintending Providence which has turned a cruel war into peace, brought order out of confusion, made the fierce savages placid, and turned away their hostile weapons from our country! May the same Almighty Goodness banish the accursed monster, war, from all lands, with her hated associates, rapine and insatiable ambition. Let peace, descending from her native heaven, bid her olives spring amidst the joyful nations; and plenty, in league with commerce, scatter blessings from her copious hand.

This account of my adventures will inform the reader of the most remarkable events of this country.—I now live in peace and safety, enjoying the sweets of liberty, and the bounties of Providence, with my once fellow-sufferers, in this delightful country, which I have seen purchased with a vast expence of blood and treasure, delighting in the prospect of its being, in a short time, one of the most opulent and powerful states on the continent of North-America; which, with the love and gratitude of my country-men, I esteem a sufficient reward for all my toil and dangers.

DANIEL BOON

Fayette county, Kentucke.

16. Olaudah Equiano (Gustavus Vassa)

from *The Interesting Narrative of the Life of Olaudah Equiano or Gustavus Vassa the African* 1789

"The fundamental problem confronting anyone interested in studying black views of bondage," John Blassingame has explained, "is that the slave had few opportunities to tell what it meant to be a chattel." The few narratives that do exist, exceptional achievements against exceptional obstacles, are thus all the more precious. The Interesting Narrative of Olaudah Equiano (1745?–97) is one of the most valuable of this group. It is the life story of a man born in Benin, Africa, in the Ibo tribe who, kidnapped at the age of eleven, survived the infamous middle passage to arrive a slave in Barbados. His story was not typical, for he managed to acquire an education and even eventually to purchase his freedom from his last master, a Quaker merchant. Free, he went back to England and thereafter, through several further displacements, committed himself to abolitionist efforts.

His Narrative was an immediate success, going through eight editions in the first five years after its publication. Elegantly written, it is virtually unique in several ways: for its three-continent-wide view of colonial history; for its account of life in Africa before colonization and slavery; and for its political analysis of the relation between the expanding mercantile economy and the slave-trade.

Equiano's account of the slave auction at Barbados recalls Richard Ligon's in chapter 4.

[THE SLAVE SHIP]

The first object that saluted my eyes when I arrived on the coast was the sea, and a slave ship, which was then riding at anchor, and waiting for its cargo. These filled me with astonishment, that was soon converted into terror, which I am yet at a loss to describe, and much more the then feelings of my mind when I was carried on board. I was immediately handled and tossed up to see if I was sound, by some of the crew; and I was now persuaded that I had got into a world of bad spirits, and that they were going to kill me. Their complexions too, differing so much from ours, their long hair, and the language they spoke, which was very different from any I had ever heard, united to confirm me in this belief. Indeed such were the horrors of my views and fears at the moment, that if ten thousand worlds had been my own, I would have freely parted with them all to have exchanged my condition with the meanest slave in my own country. When I looked round the ship too, and saw a large furnace or copper boiling and a multitude of black people, of every description, chained together, every one of their countenances expressing dejection and sorrow, I no longer doubted of my fate; and, quite overpowered with horror and anguish, I fell motionless on the deck, and fainted. When I recovered a little, I found some black people about me, who I believed were some of those who brought me on board, and had been receiving their pay: they talked to me in order to cheer me, but all in vain. I asked them if we were not to be eaten by those white men with horrible looks, red faces, and long hair. They told me I was not: and one of the crew brought me a small portion of spirituous liquor in a wine glass; but, being afraid of him, I would not take it out of his hand. One of the blacks therefore took it from him and gave it to me, and I took a little down my palate, which, instead of reviving me, as they thought it would, threw me into the greatest consternation at the strange feeling it produced, having never tasted any such liquor before.

Soon after this the blacks who brought me on board went off, and left me abandoned to despair. I now saw myself deprived of all chance of returning to my native country, or even the least glimpse of gaining the shore, which I now considered as friendly; and I even wished for my former slavery, in preference to my present situation, which was filled with horrors of every kind, still heightened by my ignorance of what I was to undergo.

[Barbados]

At last we came in sight of the island of Barbadoes, at which the whites on board gave a great shout, and made many signs of joy to us. We did not know what to think of this, but as the vessel drew nearer we plainly saw the harbour, and other ships of different kinds and sizes; and we soon anchored amongst them off Bridge Town. Many merchants and planters now came on board, though it was in the evening. They put us in separate parcels, and examined us attentively. They also made us jump, and pointed to the land, signifying we were to go there. We thought by this we should be beaten by these ugly men, as they appeared to us; and, when soon after we were all put down under the deck again, there was much dread and trembling among us, and nothing but bitter cries to be heard all the night from these apprehensions, insomuch that at last the white people got some old slaves from the land to pacify us. They told us we were not to be eaten, but to work, and were soon to go on land, where we should see many of our country people. This report eased us much; and, sure enough, soon after we landed, there came to us Africans of all languages.

We were conducted immediately to the merchant's yard, where we were all pent up together like so many sheep in a fold, without regard to sex or age. As every object was new to me, every thing I saw filled me with surprise. What struck me first was that the houses were built with bricks in stories, and were in every other respect different from those I had seen in Africa; but I was still more astonished at seeing people on horseback. I did not know what this could mean; and indeed I thought these people full of nothing but magical arts. While I was in this astonishment one of my fellow prisoners spoke to a countryman of his about the horses, who said they were the same kind they had in their country. I understood them, though they were from a distant part of Africa, and I thought it odd I had not seen any horses there; but afterwards, when I came to converse with different Africans, I found they had many horses amongst them, and much larger than those I then saw.

We were not many days in the merchants' custody before we were sold after the usual manner, which is this:—On a signal given, such as the beat of a drum, the buyers rush at once into the yard where the slaves are confined, and make choice of that parcel they like best. The noise and clamour with which this is attended, and the eagerness visible in the countenances of the buyers, serve not a little to increase the apprehensions of the terrified Africans, who may well be supposed to consider them the ministers of that destruction to which they think themselves devoted. In this manner, without scruple, are relations and friends separated, most of them never to see each other again. I remember in the vessel in which I was brought over in, in the man's apartment, there were several brothers, who, in the sale, were sold in different lots; and it was very moving on this occasion to see their distress and hear their cries at parting. O, ye nominal Christians! might not an African ask you, "learned you this from your God, who says unto you, Do unto all men as you would men should do unto you? Is it not enough that we are torn from our country and friends, to toil for your luxury and lust of gain? Must every tender feeling be likewise sacrificed to your avarice? Are the dearest friends and relations now rendered more dear by their separation from the rest of their kindred, still to be parted from each other, and thus prevented from cheering the gloom of slavery, with the small comfort of being together, and mingling their sufferings and sorrows? Why are parents to lose their children, brothers their sisters, or husbands their wives? Surely this is a new refinement in cruelty, which, while it has no advantage to atone for it, thus aggravates distress, and adds fresh horrors even to the wretchedness of slavery."

[VIRGINIA]

I now totally lost the small remains of comfort I had enjoyed in conversing with my countrymen; the women, too, who used to wash and take care of me, were all gone different ways, and I never saw one of them afterwards.

I stayed in this island for a few days; I believe it could not be above a fortnight; when I and some few more slaves, who from very much fretting were not saleable among the rest, were shipped off in a sloop for North America. On the passage we were better treated than when coming from Africa, and we had plenty of rice and fat pork. We were landed up a river a good way from the sea, about Virginia county, where we saw few of our native Africans, and not one soul who could talk to me. I was a few weeks weeding grass and gathering stones in a plantation; and at last all my companions were distributed different ways, and only myself was left. I was now exceedingly miserable, and thought myself worse off than any of the rest of my companions; for they could talk to each other, but I had no person to speak to that I could understand. In this state I was constantly grieving and pining, and wishing for death rather than any thing else. While I was in this plantation the gentleman to whom I supposed the estate belonged being unwell, I was one day sent for to his dwelling-house to fan him. When I came into the room where he was, I was very much affrighted at some things I saw, and the more so, as I had seen a black woman slave as I came through the house, who was cooking the dinner, and the poor creature was cruelly loaded with various kinds of iron machines; she had one particularly on her head, which locked her mouth so fast that she could scarcely speak, and could not eat or drink. I was much astonished and shocked at this contrivance, which I afterwards learned was called the iron muzzle. Soon after I had a fan put into my hand, to fan the gentleman while he slept; and so I did indeed with great fear. While he was fast asleep I indulged myself a great deal in looking about the room, which to me appeared very fine and curious. The first object that engaged my attention was a watch, which hung on the chimney, and was going. I was quite surprised at the noise it made, and was afraid it would tell the gentleman any thing I might do amiss: and when I immediately after observed a picture hanging in the room, which appeared constantly to look at me, I was still more affrighted, having never seen such things as these before. At one time I thought it was something relative to magic; and not seeing it move, I thought it might be some way the whites had to keep their great men when they died, and offer them libations, as we used to do to our friendly spirits. In this state of anxiety I remained till my master awoke, when I was dismissed out of the room, to my no small satisfaction and relief; for I thought that these people were all made up of wonders. In this place I was called JACOB; but on board the African Snow, I was called MICHAEL.

I had been some time in this miserable, forlorn, and much dejected state, without any one to talk to, which made my life a burden, when the kind and unknown hand of the Creator, who in every deed leads the blind in a way they know not, now began to appear to my comfort; for one day the captain of a merchant ship, called the "Industrious Bee," came on some business to my master's house. This gentleman, whose name was Michael Henry Pascal, was a lieutenant in the royal navy, but now commanded this trading ship, which was somewhere in the confines of the county many miles off. While he was at my master's house it happened that he saw me, and liked me so well that he made a purchase of me. I think I have often heard him say he gave thirty or forty pounds sterling for me; the exact sum I do not now remember. However he meant me for a present to some of his friends in England: and I was sent accordingly from the house of my then master, one Mr. Campbell, to the place where the ship lay. I was conducted on horseback by an elderly black man, a mode of travelling which appeared very odd to me. When I arrived, I was carried on board a fine large ship, loaded with tobacco, &c. and just ready to sail for England. I now thought my condition much mended; having sails to lie on, and plenty of good victuals to eat; and every body on board used me very kindly, quite contrary to what I had seen of any white people before; I therefore began to think that they were not all of the same disposition. A few days after I was on board we sailed for England. I was still at a loss to conjecture my destiny. By this time, however I could smatter a little imperfect English, and I wanted to know as well I could where we were going. Some of the people of the ship used to tell me they were going to carry me back to my own country, and this made me very happy. I was quite rejoiced at the idea of going back; and thought if I should get home what wonders I should have to tell. But I was reserved for another fate, and was soon undeceived when we came within sight of the English coast.

While I was on board of this ship my captain and master named me GUSTAVUS VASSA. I at that time began to understand him a little, and refused to be called so, and told him, as well as I could, that I would be called JACOB; but he said I should not, and still called me Gustavus. And when I refused to answer to my new name, which at first I did, it gained me many a cuff; so at length I submitted, and by it I have been known ever since. The ship had a very long passage; and on that account we had very short allowance of provisions; having towards the last only one pound and a half of bread per week, and about the same quantity of meat, and one quart of water a-day. We spoke with only one vessel during the voyage, and but once caught a few fishes. In our extremity the captain and people told me in jest they would kill and eat me, but I thought them in earnest, and was depressed beyond measure, expecting every moment to be my last. While I was in this situation one evening they caught a large shark, and got it on board. This rejoiced my heart exceedingly, as I thought it would serve the people to eat instead of their eating me; but very soon, to my astonishment, they cut off a small part of the tail, and tossed the rest over the side. This increased my consternation; and I did not know what to think of these white people, though I very much feared they intended to kill and eat me.

There was on board the ship a young lad, who had never been at sea before, about four or five years older than myself; his name was Richard Baker. He was a native of America, had received an excellent education, and was of a most amiable temper. Soon after I went on board he shewed me a great deal of partiality and attention, and in return I grew very fond of him. We at length became inseparable; and, for the space of two years, he was of great use to me, and was my constant companion and instructor. Although this dear youth had many slaves of his own, yet he and I have gone through many sufferings together on shipboard; and have many nights lain in each other's bosoms, when in great distress. Thus such a friendship was cemented between us, as we cherished till his death, which, to my very grief, happened in the year 1759, when he was up the Archipelago, on board his Majesty's ship the Preston: an event which I never ceased to regret, as I lost at once a kind interpreter, an agreeable companion, and a faithful friend; who at the age of fifteen, discovered a mind superior to prejudice, being not ashamed to notice, to associate with, and to be the friend and instructor of one who was ignorant, a stranger, and a slave! My master had lodged in his mother's house in America: he respected him very much, and made him always eat with him in the cabin. He used often to tell him jocularly that he would kill and eat me. Sometimes he used to say to me—the black people were not good to eat, and ask me if we did not eat people in my country. I said "No:" then he said he would first kill Dick, as he always called him, and afterwards me. Though this hearing relieved my mind a little as to myself, I was alarmed for Dick, and whenever he was called I used to be very much afraid he was to be killed; and I would peep and watch to see if they were going to kill him; nor was I free from this consternation till we made the land. . . .

I had often seen my master and Dick employed in reading; and I had a great curiosity to talk to the books, as I thought they did; and so to learn how all things had a beginning. For that purpose I have often taken up a book, and talked to it, and then put my ears to it, when alone, in hopes it would answer me; and I have been very much concerned when I found it remaining silent.

[PROFITS OF SLAVERY]

I had the good fortune to please my master in every department in which he employed me; and there was scarcely any part of his business, or household affairs, in which I was not occasionally engaged. I often supplied the place of a clerk, in receiving and delivering cargoes to the ships, in tending stores, and delivering goods; and, besides this, I used to shave and dress my master, when convenient, and take care of his horse; and when it was necessary, which was very often, I worked likewise on board of his different vessels. By these means I became very useful to my master, and saved him, as he used to acknowledge, above a hundred pounds a year. Nor did he scruple to say I was of more advantage to him than any of his clerks; tho' their usual wages in the West-Indies are from sixty to a hundred pounds current a year.

I have sometimes heard it asserted that a negro cannot earn his master the first cost; but nothing can be further from the truth. I suppose nine tenths of the mechanics throughout the West-Indies are negro slaves; and I well know the coopers among them earn two dollars a-day; the carpenters the same, and oftentimes more; also the masons, smiths, and fishermen, &c. and I have known many slaves whose masters would not take a thousand pounds current for them. But surely this assertion refutes itself: for, if it be true, why do the planters and merchants pay such a price for slaves? And, above all, why do those, who make this assertion, exclaim the most loudly against the abolition of the slave trade? So much are men blinded, and to such inconsistent arguments are they driven by mistaken interest! I grant, indeed, that slaves are sometimes, by half-feeding, half-clothing, over-working, and stripes, reduced so low, that they are turned out as unfit for service, and left to perish in the woods, or to expire on a dunghill.

[PROFITS OF ABOLITION]

As the inhuman traffic of slavery is to be taken into the consideration of the British legislature, I doubt not, if a system of commerce was established in Africa, the demand for manufactures will most rapidly augment, as the native inhabitants will insensibly adopt the British fashions, manners, customs, &c. In proportion to the civilization, so will be the consumption of British manufactures.

The wear and tear of a continent, nearly twice as large as Europe, and rich in vegetable and mineral productions, is much easier conceived than calculated.

A case in point. It cost the Aborigines of Britain little or nothing in clothing, &c. The difference between their forefathers and the present generation, in point of consumption, is literally infinite. The supposition is most obvious.—It will be equally immense in Africa.—The same cause, viz. civilization, will ever have the same effect.

It is trading upon safe grounds. A commercial intercourse with Africa opens an inexhaustible source of wealth to the manufacturing interests of Great Britain; and to all which the slave-trade is an objection.

If I am not misinformed, the manufacturing interest is equal, if not superior, to the landed interest, as to the value, for reasons which will soon appear. The abolition of slavery, so diabolical, will give a most rapid extension of manufactures, which is totally and diametrically opposite to what some interested people assert.

The manufactures of this country must and will, in the nature and reason of things, have a full and constant employ, by supplying the African markets.

Population, the bowels, and surface of Africa, abound in valuable and useful returns; the hidden treasures of centuries will be brought to light and into circulation. Industry, enterprise, and mining, will have their full scope, proportionably as they civilize. In a word, it lays open an endless field of commerce to the British manufacturers and merchant adventurers. The manufacturing interest and the general interests are synonimous. The abolition of slavery would be in reality an universal good.

17. Noah Webster

"The Story of Columbus," from *The Little Reader's Assistant*
1791

Noah Webster (1758–1843), was the author of the classic American Dictionary of the English Language, *published for the first time in 1828. The selection below comes from a book he wrote toward the beginning of his career as a codifier and promulgator of what he insisted was an American linguistic culture, no doubt rooted in England's, but becoming increasingly distinct. His first effort to define and promote this culture was* The American Spelling Book *(1785), the "blue-backed speller" that, through 400 editions producing more than 100 million copies, effectively founded a national educational tradition. The Little Readers Assistant followed in 1791, with the additional ambition of teaching morals as well as letters. A short sketch of the life of John Smith ends, "What a hero was Capt. Smith! How many Turks and Indians did he slay! How often was he upon the brink of death, and how bravely did he encounter every danger. Such a man affords a noble example for all to follow, when they resolve to be good and brave." The life of Columbus also offers a noble example and a first lesson in the emerging national mythology.*

About three hundred years ago, this country was not known to the people in Europe. Indians only lived here, and the face of the earth was covered with woods. Columbus, a learned and brave man, believed he might find land by sailing from Europe westward across the ocean; he requested several kings to let him have ships and men to go on a voyage for this purpose, some of whom refused to encourage him, because they thought his scheme wild and foolish. But at last the king and queen of Spain were persuaded to assist Columbus, and they furnished him with three ships and ninety men. He sailed from Spain on the third day of August, in the year of our Lord one thousand four hundred and ninety two, and proceeded westward. When he had been out about three weeks, his men began to grow uneasy, for fear they should not find land, and never be able to return against the trade winds. Columbus kept their spirits alive as long as he could; but finally they threatened to throw him overboard, if he would not return to Spain immediately. Columbus then promised, if they would consent to continue the course three days longer, and they did not in that time discover land, he would then return to Spain. This promise appeased the murmurs of his seamen, and they proceeded on their voyage. On the morning of the third day, a man at mast-head cried out, *Land!* Joy seized every heart at this unexpected cry; every man cordially embraced his fellow, and all thanked their brave commander for his resolution and perseverance. Columbus received the glad news with the calmness of a hero; he smiled and welcomed his men to a new world.

The land first discovered was one of the Bahama Islands, south-east of Georgia. Columbus afterwards discovered some of the West-India Islands, and returned to Spain, where he was received with joy and wonder.

He afterwards made another voyage to America and made further discoveries; but unfortunate man! Some of his countrymen grew jealous of his rising fame, spread false reports about him and his designs and thus prevailed upon the king of Spain to strip him of his authority. Accordingly his power was taken from him and given to his enemies, and the great, the amiable Columbus was sent to Spain in irons. He was afterwards released and sent to America again, cast away upon an Island among savages, and there he was suffered to remain a year; he was then taken and carried to Spain, and after wandering about, neglected and forlorn for many months, he died. Thus it is sometimes the fate of the best men to receive the worst treatment.

One little story about Columbus must not be forgotten. When he was first returning to Spain, after he had discovered this country, there arose a violent storm, and he was in danger of being swallowed up in the sea; in which case all his discoveries would have been lost to the world. His courage and coolness did not forsake him in the hour of danger; he wrote a short account of his voyage, wrapped the paper in an oiled cloth, enclosed it in a cake of wax, to keep it dry, put it in an empty cask, and threw it overboard, so that if his ships had been lost in the storm, the cask might possibly have been taken up by other vessels and his discoveries thus have been preserved.

How noble and brave was the whole conduct of Columbus! What a glorious discovery did he make! a continent, many thousand miles in length, containing millions of acres of rich land, and numberless rivers abounding with fish. This is the goodly land which we inherit, and where we may enjoy plenty with peace and freedom. Let every child in America learn to speak the praises of the great Columbus.

18. William Baylies

the legend of Moiship, or Maushop 1793

While the English, as compared to the Spanish and French, showed a striking lack of interest in Indian culture, there were exceptions, like Roger Williams (see chapter 7). By the end of the colonial era there were others. In 1786, when New England had been not only colonized but nationalized by the European invaders, a physician and state senator named William Baylies visited Gay Head, which had become a center for surviving Indian tribes in the area. He heard the legend of Moiship (probably in English) and recorded it, eventually publishing it in the journal of the American Academy of Arts and Sciences in 1793.

In former times, the Indian God, Moiship, resided in this part of the island; and made the crater, described above, his principal seat. To keep up his fires, he pulled up the largest trees by the roots; on which, to satisfy his hunger, he broiled the whale, and the great fish of the sea, throwing out the refuse sufficient to cover several acres. He did not consume all himself; but with a benevolent hand, often supplied them with food ready cooked. To facilitate the catching these fish, he threw many large stones, at proper distances, into the sea, on which he might walk with greater ease to himself. This is now called the Devil's bridge. On a time, an offering was made to him of all the tobacco on Martha's Vineyard, which having smoked, he knocked the snuff out of his pipe, which formed Nantucket. When the Christian religion took place in the island, he told them, as light had come among them, and he belonged to the kingdom of darkness, he must take his leave; which, to their great sorrow, he accordingly did; and has never been heard of since.

MICO CHLUCCO the LONG WARIOR or *KING of the SIMINOLES*

19. Stephen Burroughs

from *Memoirs of the Notorious Stephen Burroughs* 1798

Robert Frost wrote a Preface for a 1924 edition of the Memoirs of Stephen
Burroughs *(1765–1840) and suggested the reader might place this book "On the
same shelf with Benjamin Franklin and Jonathan Edwards." Franklin and Edwards
represent "what we have been as a young nation," Frost explained. And
"Burroughs comes in reassuringly when there is question of our not unprincipled
wickedness. . . ." For Burroughs demonstrates the existence, already at the beginning of national history, of a "sophisticated wickedness, the kind that knows its
grounds and can twinkle." Burroughs inhabits a moral universe, he just runs afoul
of its laws. Then again, its laws run afoul of him, for Burroughs always has his
reasons.*

*He was no ruffian, but came from a respected family in Hanover, New
Hampshire, his father being town pastor. The son early showed his bent for crimes
of all kinds; he was variously sought and arrested for theft, fraud, rape, and coun-
terfeiting. The Memoirs retrace a life's path strewn with the debris of colonial
proprieties. For all its "twinkle," Burrough's narrative of the criminal underside of
colonial life on the one hand, and the harsh workings of colonial justice on the
other, is also often quite grim.*

"Full well I know you; deep, too deep engrav'd
On memory's tablet your rude horrors live."

In relating the facts of my life to you, I shall endeavor to give as simple an account
of them as I am able, without coloring or darkening any circumstances; although
the relation of many matters will give me a degree and kind of pain, which only
they who feel can describe. I have often lamented my neglect of keeping minutes of the
occurrences of my life, from time to time, when they were fresh in my memory, and
alive to my feelings; the disadvantage of which I now feel, when I come to run over in
my mind the chain which has connected the events together. Many circumstances are
entirely lost, and many more so obscurely remembered, that I shall not even attempt
to give them a place in this account. Not to trouble you with any more prefatory
remarks, I will proceed to the relation.

I am the only son of a clergyman, living in Hanover, in the state of New Hampshire;
and, were any to expect merit from their parentage, I might justly look for that merit.
But I am so far a republican, that I consider a man's merit to rest entirely with himself,
without any regard to family, blood, or connection. My father being a Presbyterian by

principle, I was educated in all the rigor of that order, which illy suited my volatile, impatient temper of mind; this being the case, my first entrance on the stage of life, was by no means the most agreeable. My thirst for amusement was insatiable, and as in my situation, the only dependence for that gratification was entirely within myself, I sought it in pestering others, especially those who were my superiors in age, and in making them appear in a ludicrous situation, so as to raise the laugh at their expense, and partake of the general diversion, which such a matter created. My success in those undertakings was so great, that I became the terror of the people where I lived, and all were very unanimous in declaring, that Stephen Burroughs was the worst boy in town; and those who could get him whipt were most worthy of esteem. Their attempts to bring on my back a flagellation were often very successful, for my heedless temper seldom studied for a retreat, when I was fairly in danger; however, the repeated application of this birchen medicine never cured my pursuit of fun.

[IN AN EARLY ESCAPADE, A FRIEND OVERCOMES HIS SCRUPLES AGAINST COUNTERFEITING]

"From what I have observed, I believe you will readily agree with me, that I am right in prosecuting my present plan, if I can make it evident, that no danger of injury will arise to any one from it, and that by it, many will be made better. Money, of itself, is of no consequence, only as we, by mutual agreement, annex to it a nominal value, as the representation of property. Anything else might answer the same purpose, equally with silver and gold, should mankind only agree to consider it as such, and carry that agreement into execution in their dealings with each other. We find this verified in fact, by those bills of credit which are in circulation through the world. Those bills, simply, are good for nothing; but the moment mankind agree to put a value on them, as representing property, they become of as great consequence as silver and gold, and no one is injured by receiving a small insignificant piece of paper for an hundred bushels of what, when mankind stamp that value upon it, by agreeing to receive it for that amount. Therefore, we find the only thing necessary to make a matter valuable is to induce the world to deem it so; and let that esteem be raised by any means whatever, yet the value is the same, and no one becomes injured by receiving it at the valuation. Hence, we find the world putting an enormous value upon certain stones, which intrinsically are of no use, as for instance, the diamond, the carbuncle, etc. These stones cannot be made use of in any pursuit of life. They will not serve for food, for raiment, or for any instrument of any kind whatever; therefore, of what real use can they be? Their scarcity, and certain peculiarities, have induced mankind to esteem them; and this esteem stamps a value upon them, so that they pass from one to another as the representation of property; hence, the holders of them always have a valuable possession, and probably always will have, which they at any time can exchange for property of more immediate consequence to their support. Had I the art of making diamonds, do you suppose I should transgress the laws of equity in putting that art into practice? except I should fill the world with them, so as to destroy their scarcity, and hence depreciate their value in the hands of others. To put this art into practice, so as to enrich myself, and not destroy that due proportion between representative property and real property, is doing myself a favor, and injuring none. Gold and silver are made use of for convenience, to transact our business of barter and exchange with each other, as the representation of property, it being less cumbersome, and more easy to communicate from one to another, than real property of any kind: hence, when there is a due proportion of representative property, business can be transacted to the greatest advantage, and with the greatest ease. And when the public experience a scarcity or redundancy, they of course suffer an inconveniency: therefore, that person who contributes his mite to keep the balance between these two species of property justly poised, is a blessing to himself, and to the community of which he is a member. That an undue scarcity of cash now prevails, is a truth too obvious for me to attempt to prove. Your own observation will convince you of it. Hence, whoever contributes, really, to increase the quantity of cash, does not only himself, but likewise the community, an essential benefit."

[BURROUGHS IS SENTENCED TO A TERM ON A PRISON ISLAND]

When I first came on to this island, there were in all only sixteen prisoners. The principal part of them were kept at work in the blacksmith's shop. The remainder did little or nothing. Our provision was one pound of bread and three-fourths of a pound of meat per day.

The officers who were in commission here, were of the following description, viz. First, Major Perkins, a man of about six feet high, well proportioned, and strong built; possessed with care, fidelity, and great attention to his duty, as a military character. He was a man of sentiment and feeling. His courage was unimpeachable, having tried it myself as thoroughly as was necessary to learn that circumstance. Notwithstanding his personal courage, he stood in such fear of his superiors in society, that he could not always maintain such a state of independency as to act himself. His military education had taught him obedience to his superiors, and he now maintained that principle with a degree of mechanical exactness. Major Perkins had a family living on the island with him. This family consisted of Mrs. Perkins, whose amiable and compassionate conduct has left the most grateful feelings in my heart, and a number of children, how many I do not recollect.

Lieutenant Treat was a man about five feet ten inches in height, trim built, and slender; more fond of appearing in the fashion, with regard to his dress, the cock of his hat, etc., than he was to raise the garrison to the highest pitch of military fame. There was nothing very positive in his character. He was by no means a bad man, and as for his goodness, it did not appear with such eclat as to place him in a very conspicuous situation in society.

Ensign Burbeck may be described by comparing him to a petulant boy, of about fourteen years old, who had never been taught or restrained by parental authority. He was more fond of his dogs than of any other society; playing with them by the day together.

Immediately after my confinement on this island, I began to look about, to see whether a possibility for escaping remained. I viewed the building in which I was confined. It was made of brick, the walls of which were five feet thick, laid in cement, which was much harder than the brick themselves. I searched every corner for a spot upon which I could work without detection, our room being searched every day, to see whether the prisoners had made any attempt to break away. I at length hit upon a place. There was a chimney at one end of the room, grated in a very strong manner, about twelve feet above its funnel, which was sufficiently large for a man to go up. About three feet above the mantlepiece of this fireplace, I concluded to begin my operation. Here I could work, and not have my labors discovered, unless very critical search was made up the chimney. I had not been at work long before I had made a beginning of a hole sufficiently large to crawl through; I then took a board, and blacking it like the chimney-back, made it of the proper size, and put it into the hole, so that the strictest search could produce no discovery. The prisoners in the room with me were seven in number. These prisoners were all turned out to work about sunrise, when the doors of the prison were again shut, and not opened until 12 o'clock, when the prisoners came from work, and continued half an hour: they were then taken back again to work, and there remained until sunset. Therefore, I had as much as sixteen hours in the twenty-four, in which I could work upon this brick wall, which work I continued, with the most unremitting attention.

The labor was incredible! I could, in the first place, work only with a large nail, rubbing away the brick gradually, not daring to make the least noise, lest the sentries, who stood round the prison, should overhear me at work, and thereby become discovered. One night I rubbed the brick so hard, as to be overheard by the sentry, standing on the other side of the wall. The alarm was immediately given, and the guard and officers rushed into the room to detect us in our operations. Fortunately, I overheard the sentry tell the sergeant of the guard, that Burroughs was playing the devil in the jail. The sergeant ran to inform the officers, and I had but just time to put my board in its place, and set down to greasing my shoes, when the officers entered, and with a great degree of sternness, inquired where I had been at work? I told them that I had been rubbing some hard soot off the chimney and grinding it fine to mix with the grease, and put on to my shoes. They laughed at my nicety about my shoes, that I should wish for sleek shining shoes in this situation. Major Perkins knowing my inattentiveness to dress, could not so readily believe that blacking my shoes was the only object in view; he therefore made a very strict search for some other matter, which should account for the noise the sentry had heard: but, after a fruitless pursuit of such an object, they gave over their search, concluding that one among the thousand strange whims which marked my character, had prompted me to set about blacking my shoes, at that time.

After they were gone, I felt as strong a disposition to laugh at them, for the deception under which they were laboring, as they did whilst present to laugh at me, for the whim of greasing and blacking my shoes. This temporary check was of the utmost importance in my further prosecution of this business. It made me more careful for the future, not to pursue my labors with too much impatient impetuosity, a failing I ever was subject to.

The prisoners in the room were merry on the occasion of my turning the suspicion of the officers so entirely from the real object to another very foreign from it. They thought it a manifestation of ability. In fine, I had gained such an ascendency over the prisoners, that they implicitly gave up to my opinion in all our little matters: and more particularly, when any contention arose among them, I generally succeeded in amicably terminating the difficulty without their proceeding to blows.

My conduct towards all, I determined should be marked with the strictest impartiality. I not only satisfied my own mind in the business, but likewise took the greatest pains to show them, that I meant to be an impartial friend towards all parties. When they fell into disputes and bickerings, I would address them to the following purport, viz. "Gentlemen" (even the convicts were fond of good words, and would listen when I called them gentlemen much sooner than when I addressed them by a less elevated epithet), "our situation you are all sensible is very miserable; do the best we can, it will not be tolerable; but when, in addition to slavery, we render our society hateful and irksome to each other, by falling into broils and wrangles, it then becomes a hell indeed, and answers the strongest wish of our inveterate foes. I know there are many circumstances calculated to harass and sour your minds; to render you peevish and petulant; to make you at variance with the whole race of mankind: but to indulge these feelings only renders your case worse rather than better; it gratifies your enemies and serves every purpose which they could desire; therefore, as wise men, I expect you will act with prudence, with regard to your own comfort and to the views of those who wish you ill." Even the convicts had reason sufficient to hear these arguments with attention, and they generally practiced according to this direction; so strong is that principle in all men to listen to the voice of friendship.

I determined to be more careful in prosecuting my labor on the wall for the future, and check that impatience which often hurried me on beyond the dictates of prudence. I now wrought with the greatest caution, and made slow but sure advances. After I had been employed in this business about a week, I found I could work to greater advantage if I had a small iron crow; therefore, I ordered one of the prisoners, who wrought in the shop, to make me one about a foot long, and sharp at one end. This he found an opportunity to do, undiscovered by the overseer, and brought it to me. I found that with this crow I could pry off half a brick at a time without the least noise, after I had worn a hole with my nail, sufficiently large to thrust in my crow. The rubbish which I took out of the wall I put every night into a tub, standing in our room for necessary occasions, and this was emptied by one of the prisoners every morning into the water.

After I had labored with unceasing assiduity for two months, I found one night, after I had pried away a brick, that I could run my arm out of the prison into the open air. This circumstance made my heart leap with joy. After such a length of labor, to find my toils crowned with apparent success, gave me a tone of pleasure of which you can have no idea.

Upon examination, I found the breach through the wall was just below a covered way, so that it would remain unseen in the daytime, unless discovered by some accident. I had measured the height of the covered way by a geometrical operation, not being permitted to come near it: and this was done with an instrument made by my penknife; that penknife which had done me such excellent service in Northampton jail.

When the prisoners saw my measurement was exact, their idea of my profound knowledge was greatly raised; and they appeared to entertain the most sanguine assurance, that their liberty was certain when their operations were directed under my auspices.

After I had found the hole through the wall was entirely secreted by the covered way, I proceeded to make it sufficiently large to pass through.

After all this was accomplished, one difficulty still remained. The sentry standing on the covered way would undoubtedly hear us in going out at this hole; and moreover, if we should be so fortunate as to get, unheard, into the covered way, yet we must come out of that within five feet of the place where he stood, and therefore could not prevent a discovery.

Under these circumstances, we found it necessary to lie quiet until some rainy night should remove the sentry from his stand on the covered way, to some place of shelter. This was generally the case when the weather was foul or uncomfortable, unless some special cause should detain him to this particular spot. I recollect, that soon after the officers had found me blacking my shoes with soot, the sentinels kept their post, invariably, on the covered way, in every kind of weather; but they had, by this time, become more at ease in their feelings, and consequently would, at such time, retire into an alley leading through the bombproof.

We did not wait many days for the happy moment, before we heard the sentry leave his station on the covered way, and enter the alley, for shelter from the rain. About 11 o'clock at night, I made the necessary arrangements for the expedition. The island being in a circular form, I ordered seven men to go round it to the south, whilst I went round to the north. The reason why I did this was of the following nature, viz. There was a wharf on the western shore of this island, where the boats were kept, and a sentry placed over them. It was necessary, after we had escaped out of the bombproof, to procure a boat, in order to transport ourselves off the island; and as there were none, except what were immediately under the eye of the sentry, the only alternative which remained, was to make the sentry a prisoner, and carry him off with us. As this was a business in which some nicety of conduct was necessary, I chose to trust no one to execute it but myself; and therefore, ordered the seven prisoners round the island, a different way from what I went myself, and directed them to advance to within fifteen rods of the sentinel, and make a noise sufficient to attract his attention towards them. This would bring the sentry between me and the other seven prisoners; and when he was turned towards them, I should be at his back.

Having made these arrangements, all the prisoners silently crawled out of the hole, following them myself as soon as I saw they all had passed without any accident. We all met at the spot appointed. I told the men to be cautious, not to be in a hurry; not to be in any perturbation; but to proceed leisurely and considerately to the spot appointed. I told them to be five minutes in getting to the spot. I then left them. I hastened round, and arrived as near to the sentry as I thought prudent, about one minute and a half before I heard the noise from the other men. At the noise, the sentry turned and hailed, "Who comes there?" No answer was made. Immediately on seeing the attention of the sentry turned from me, I arose from my position flat on the ground, and advanced as near as twenty feet, and lay down again. Immediately the noise from the seven men was again renewed; and the sentry's attention was fixed to the object of the noise. He again hailed in a very peremptory manner, cocked his gun, and made ready to fire. By this time I had arisen from the ground, and advanced to within about eight feet of the sentry, when I heard the piece cock, and saw him present it! I immediately darted at him, seized him in an instant, and clapped my hand over his mouth, to prevent him from making a noise, which should alarm the other soldiers on guard. When I first laid hold of him, he started, and attempted to get from me, making a noise through his nose as though very much terrified: crying "eh! eh! eh!" I told him that the least noise from him should produce instant death; that I would rip his guts out the first moment he proved refractory. After I had sufficiently terrified him, I took my hand from his mouth, and told him that no harm should befall him, so long as he behaved in a peaceable manner. I took his gun and cartridge-box from him. The other prisoners now coming up, we all went into the barge, carrying ten oars, and put off.

It was now about half an hour past twelve at night, it being extremely dark and rainy, and nothing to steer by, except mere conjecture. We were ignorant of the time of tide, whether it was ebbing or flowing, and consequently could not tell which way we drifted: however, we determined to row until we came to some land. I set myself in the stern sheets, steering the boat; Richards, the sentry, set in the bottom of the boat, between my legs. The gun with the fixed bayonet lay by me, and the cartridge-box hanging by my side. The other men were at their oars, rowing the boat. We had proceeded about far enough, as we judged, to be in the middle of the channel, between the island and Dorchester, whither we meant to direct our course.

It was now demanded of me, by one of the men who sat forward rowing the boat, what I meant to do with Richards? As I did not know where we should in fact land, I was undetermined in my own mind what I should do with him when I came to land, and gave an answer to that amount. The person asking this question, looking upon his escape as certain, began to put on airs of consequence, and answered me in a sarcastic manner, "Well, Captain Burroughs, as you have had the command until you do not know what to do, it is best for some other person to take it, who does know what to do"; and then turning himself to Richards, continued his discourse, "and as for you, Mr. Richards, you'll please to walk overboard, that we may not, after this, hear any of your tales told to your brother swads.[27] If you walk over without fuss, it is well, if not, you shall be thrown over, tied neck and heels."

When I heard this insolent treatment and dastardly language, I could hardly conceive what it meant. Unprovokedly to throw Richards into the water, was a manifestation of a language of the heart, which appeared to me so unnatural, that I could not believe the person using it, to be serious. Yet I could not conceive any propriety in using it in any other light. Richards himself was terrified. He began to supplicate me in the most moving terms, to save him from the destruction which was ready to fall upon him. His entreaties made such an impression upon my mind, that I should have given him my assistance, if I had been opposed by every man in the boat: however I did not yet believe he was in that degree of danger which he appeared to apprehend; but was soon undeceived by the three forward hands shipping their oars and coming aft.

I endeavored to expostulate, but to no effect. I saw they were resolutely bent on their diabolical purpose! I saw the disposition of the infernals pictured in their opera-

27. swads: soldiers.

tions. I let go the helm, started up, and swore by the Almighty, that I'd send the first to hell who dared lay a hand on Richards. The poor fellow, at this time, lay in the bottom of the boat trembling with agony, and crying in the most piteous manner. The blood flew quick through my veins. The plaintive cries of Richards vibrated upon my heart, and braced every nerve. At this moment the first villain who had proposed this infernal plan, laid hold of me by the shoulder to prevent my interposing between Richards and the others, who were about throwing him overboard.

When I found his hand griping my shoulder, I immediately reached my arm over his back, caught him by the waistband of his breeches and dashed him to the bottom of the boat. The moment of my laying hold of him, I determined to throw him into the sea, and why I did not, I have never since been able to tell. After I had thrown him into the bottom of the boat, I caught the gun on which was a bayonet fixed; this I brought to a charge and made a push at the man nearest me, who drew back, took his seat at the oar, when all again was quiet.

We continued rowing until we struck fast on the ground, but could see no land. We left the boat and waded about until we discovered the shore. When we came to the land, we could not determine on what place we had fallen. We were soon satisfied, however, by the drum on the Castle beating the long-roll, and immediately after, beating to arms. We heard the alarm in that direction which plainly pointed out, that we were somewhere near Dorchester Point. We saw the Castle in an uproar, and all the signals of alarm which are usually made on such occasions.

After we had found where we were, the three men who engaged in throwing Richards overboard, left us, and went away together. I then told Richards that he might go where he pleased; that he must be sensible I had saved his life, even at the risk of my own; therefore, the dictates of gratitude would teach him a line of conduct which would not militate against my escape. This he promised in the most solemn manner. He was warm in his expressions of gratitude towards me. I believed him sincere. He departed.

In this transaction, I enjoyed a sensation of pleasure very exquisite. To receive the tribute of a grateful heart, flowing from a stream of sincerity, was a circumstance, which in a measure counterbalanced many evils, which I had experienced. We had all lost our shoes in the mud, in getting to dry land; therefore, had to travel barefooted. It was the space of an hour and a half after we had landed, before we found the way off this point of land; the night being extremely dark, and we all strangers to the ground.

After we had found the road, I told the four men who were with me, that the better way would be to separate, and every man shift for himself. This observation struck a damp upon all who were with me. They entreated me to tarry with them until the night following, when they could have a better chance of getting clear of the country without detection; they feared falling into the hands of their pursuers if I left them. They felt a certainty of escape if I remained with them. My compassion was moved, and I acted directly contrary from what I knew was according to a system of prudence. We agreed to remain all together until the next night.

The day began to dawn, and we found it necessary to look after some place, to which we could retire from the observation of the inhabitants; all the men, except myself, being dressed in the uniform of the Castle, and of course, would be noticed by the first observer. Some proposed retiring into a swamp, and secreting ourselves in its dark recesses; some proposed the plan of going into the first grove of woods, and climbing up to the top of some trees, and securing ourselves that way. To these proposals I made the following reply: it is likely, that as soon as daylight has fairly appeared, the inhabitants of the country will be alarmed; and warm pursuit will be made after us; and every place, where the inhabitants will think it likely that we should hide, will be searched by them in the most critical manner. No places will be sought more thoroughly than thick swamps and high bushy trees; therefore, it will be our best way to hide where the people will not look after us, if such a place may be found. For my own part, I had rather take my chance, under present circumstances, in the open field than in a swamp or at the top of a tree.

The objects of the swamp and woods were immediately relinquished, and they all seemed content to leave the matter to my judgment entirely. We travelled on with rapidity about one mile further, and then came into a little thicket of houses, and a barn standing immediately on the road among them; this barn we all entered and found two mows of hay. I ascended one mow, and having taken up the hay by flakes, near the side of the barn, to the depth of six feet, three of us went down, and the hay fell back into its former situation, covering us entirely over at the same time. I had ordered the other two to go on to the other mow, and do as they had seen me. They accordingly went, and I supposed all secure.

Not long after this, there came a number of women into the barn to milk the cows. Soon after, I heard children round the barn, as though they were in pursuit of something with a dog. I soon found that a skunk was their object under the barn. However, when the women had finished milking their cows, the children were all ordered into the house, this day being Sunday.

To my astonishment and surprise, the two men who had gone to the other mow, now came over where I was, and told me, they could not find a place to hide; "and indeed," said they, "we do not like to be so far off, for it appears to us, that we shall be taken if we are!" How I felt under this situation you will readily conceive, by supposing yourself in my place, and people expected into the barn every minute to fodder their cattle! I jumped out of my place, told them to lie down in a moment, covered them over with hay, and returned into my place, just as the young men came into the barn to take care of their cattle. They came on to the mow where we were lying, and took the hay from it for their cows; but made no discovery: and yet, notwithstanding all this, one of our men, by the name of Burrel, whom I had covered over with hay, was asleep before the young men went out of the barn, and snored so loud, as to be heard; but the men did not know what noise it was, nor where it came from.

Immediately after these men had left the barn, I again jumped out of my hole, went to Burrel, who had uncovered his head entirely, waked him, and expostulated with him in the severest terms. "This is the consequence," said I, "of attending to your request of remaining with you. Your own heedless disposition, not only exposes yourself to be found, but likewise involves me in the same danger. Is it a matter of such indifference to you whether you are again taken, that you can tamely and calmly fall asleep at the moment when you are surrounded with danger? If no regard to your own safety will influence you on this occasion, yet, I should suppose you might pay some attention to my welfare, seeing it was by your earnest entreaty I continued with you, being influenced by no other motive than compassion towards you. If nothing else will answer, I will have recourse to the means which are in my power; and if I find you asleep again, I will positively put you to death; and this I think will be entirely just, if no other measure will answer to ensure my safety." I was of opinion this threat would answer the purpose, for which it was intended, viz. that fear would operate upon him so strongly, as to prevent his sleeping in such a situation for the future.

We lay quiet all the forenoon, without any accident: during this time, I endeavored to make some arrangement in my own mind for my future conduct. I concluded that I should be able to reach the state of Rhode Island by the next morning, when I should be no longer obliged to travel under cover of the night; when I could again mix with society, without viewing them as my open and declared enemies.

We heard the various bells ringing at Dorchester meetinghouses for the exercises of the day. The forenoon meeting was finished, and the first bell for the exercises of the afternoon was ringing, when a number of men came into the barn to put a horse into the chaise, standing on the barnfloor. The streets were full of people going to the meetinghouse. A number of children came likewise into the barn with the men, and climbed on to the mow where we lay secreted, looking for hens' nests. At this moment Burrel began again to snore, which brought the children immediately to the spot where he lay, and his head being uncovered, they saw it, and cried out, "Daddy, daddy, here's the skunk! here's the skunk!" It hardly appeared credible to the old gentleman that a skunk should be on the haymow; he therefore manifested some doubt as to his children's report, but they were determined he should believe them, and affirmed it again with warmth, "it certainly is a skunk, daddy, for it has got ears."

The peculiar manner in which this was uttered, made the people, on the barnfloor, think something uncommon was there. They accordingly ascended the mow to the number of eight or nine, in order to satisfy themselves concerning this matter. By this time Burrel awaking, saw he was discovered, and began to pull the hay over his head. Those who were on the mow saw it, and were now convinced, that the children in fact had seen something that had ears. They took the pitchfork and moved the hay, which lay over these two men, and immediately saw that they were convicts, escaped the preceding night from the Castle.

The barn was instantly filled with people from the street, on the alarm's being given of these men. Through the whole scene, from the first opening of the barn by the men, who were about putting the horse into the chaise, till this time, my feelings were of the keenest kind. When I had succeeded with all my plans for escape thus far, when I had endured with so much patience, a course of such incredible labor, as what I performed in breaking through the bombproof; when I had furthermore, overcome the difficulties of making the sentry a prisoner, of preserving him from death, of finding the land we sought, through the thickest shades of night, and the uncertainty of being drifted out of our course by adverse tides; and then by a retrograde course of incidents, to be deprived of the object to which all these labors were directed, was a prospect which filled my mind with the keenest anxiety, and kept my fears in a perpetual state of alarm.

Burrel was a man of great stupidity, and I feared his senseless conduct more than anything else. You will wonder at my continuing with him! I wonder at it myself. My weak side was an inconsiderate compassion. I did continue with him, and too late I saw my error. However, I acted the foolish part in another respect, viz. by not taking him into the hole with me, where I could have kept him perpetually under my eye. He was very disagreeable, and the object of being freed from a momentary inconvenience was so powerful on my mind, at that time, that for this paltry consideration, I lost my liberty for more than two years.

I heard the children around the haymow with the utmost pain. I heard Burrel's snoring with indignation and horror! I now almost gave myself over for lost! But what were my sensations when the people ascended the mow and discovered these two convicts, plainly seeing who they were by their dress.

However, all hope of escape was not lost. I thought it yet possible to remain undiscovered, if the two convicts behaved with any prudence, seeing we were so far under the hay. The question was asked, "what had become of the other prisoners who had made their escape?" Burrel answered, that he should not tell, "but if they were anywhere in that barn, they are right down there," pointing with his finger to the spot where we in fact were. With this information, they began the search again, pitching the hay from the spot, till they came down to the place where we had been secreted. The feeble twig upon which my last hopes remained was now broken, and I sunk into a state of despair. All my fond hopes were lost in a moment, and I found myself only fallen into a state of greater wretchedness, in the room of being liberated from my former misery.

"Is this the reward," said I to the inhabitants, "for saving one of your number, but a short time since, from the devouring jaws of death, ready to swallow him up? But a little time since, he stood in need of my pity. I granted him that compassion which nature has taught me to show. I now stand in need of your pity; will you not grant what you, in a like situation, would request? Remember that this world is a state of revolution. You may yet see the time in which you will want the exercise of compassion, even from me, however improbable the present appearance. You would then lament not having shown that compassion which you would stand in need of yourselves. You can hardly imagine that my escape can produce any injury to you. I shall leave you, and shall never return to a place where I might be in danger of confinement. You who are parents, may have children in my situation; would not your hearts yearn with compassion towards a child in my condition? Would not you feel the most earnest desire, that some breast, softened by the tender emotions of compassion, would say unto your child, go—enjoy the blessing which nature bestows; wanton in the streams of liberty, and celebrate the day of jubilee? Would not the strong emotions of gratitude fire your heart, towards such a benevolent part of creation? Would not such a compassionate action appear to you more lovely than the beauties of the morning; more glorious than the sun in his majesty? This, surely you would say, is a narration of Deity; a spark of the fire of love, manifested by nature's God in the daily dispensations of his providence to man."

All my entreaties were to no effect. The minds of people were so fortified against every observation which I made, that the ideas of pity or compassion were shut entirely out. They knew not my feelings, therefore could not judge with regard to that conduct which I thought they ought to exercise towards me. They had never been in my situation, hence could not view it in its proper light.

We were all carried to a public house, and kept there until a guard came from the island and conducted us back again. Immediately upon our landing upon the island, I was ordered into irons. This was a circumstance proving the ideas existing here, of my being the soul of every enterprise; and indeed they had pretty good evidence to found their opinion upon, considering that I was the only person remaining in the room out of which we escaped, through the day, without being turned into the shop to work; and their recollecting the circumstance, likewise, of blacking my shoes with soot, in order to account for the noise which the sentry had formerly heard; the reason of the noise being now more clearly understood than formerly.

The next morning we were all summoned, with great pomp and ceremony, before the three officers, sitting as a court-martial, and there heard an enumeration of the crimes laid to our charge, which amounted to five in number, viz. first, breaking the jail; second, carrying the sentry from his post; third, taking the arms and ammunition of the garrison and carrying them away; fourth, taking the boat belonging to the garrison, and carrying it off the island; fifth, and lastly, deserting from our state of confinement. Of all these crimes we were found guilty, and received sentence of thirty-nine stripes for each, with the cat-o'ninetails, amounting in all to one hundred and ninety-five lashes; we however obtained a remission of ninety-five, and received one hundred only, the next day at sunsetting.

Chapter 11

The Literature of Politics

INTRODUCTION

The title of this chapter may be difficult to read aloud because it requires emphasizing both "literature" and "politics." In the texts selected here the literary and the political are equally active considerations. "Literature," in eighteenth-century Anglo-America, was broadening its meaning along with its public. "Politics" was undergoing a transformation largely in response to the expanding literary public. The "literature of politics" thus consists of writings that address political issues, in an era when political issues were themselves shaped by emerging modes of writing and publishing.

This chapter therefore unfolds something like a mobius strip, with both its themes—literature and politics—continually uppermost. If this sounds like complicated travelling, it may be easier to envision in the company of Benjamin Franklin, whose many literary innovations were inspired by a desire to create a new polity for new times. Indeed, Franklin did not just travel the mobius strip of literary politics and political literature, he was one of its chief engineers in the English colonies.

In the *Autobiography* (see chapter 10), Franklin describes his self-education as laying the ground for his rise in society. The account of how his first few savings went for a copy of *Pilgrim's Progress* not only identifies the narrative of Franklin's life with the great Protestant allegory, incorporating its guiding principles; as importantly, the anecdote carries the lesson that a *book* is a wise first investment in upward mobility. He who would be rich, let him first read, is a motto inscribed everywhere in the *Autobiography*, in the story it tells, the advice it proffers, and in its very existence; or rather, ". . . let him first read *and write*." For Franklin seems to have begun his career in self-improvement by improving his writing style, acquiring, after Bunyan's epic, a collection from the *Spectator* so that he could practice imitating the essays of the English journalists Addison and Steele.

Franklin had rejected his father's trade in candle- and soap-making and, instead, followed his older brother into the commerce of printing and newspaper publishing. In 1775, there were thirty-eight newspapers being published in the thirteen colonies. Franklin's advocacy of writing as the means to advancement reflected his general sense that the world was changing in the way both represented and fomented by newspapers. He is often cited as a founder of public institutions—libraries, fire companies, a system of street cleaning, and a post office. The creation of these institutions projects a much expanded definition of social life as more than a realm of

personal encounters and common pursuits. A post office extends the business of individuals communicating with one another into an impersonal traffic. Its goal is communication itself—not just the transportation of information from one place to another, but its general circulation throughout the community. The existence of a post office implies a social geography outside the personal perimeters of private correspondents. And when private correspondents communicate through a post office, they not only exchange information but also participate in its general circulation: they act publically as well as privately. They define themselves as persons in epistolary contact with their peers, and also as members of a letter-writing public. Eighteenth-century Philadelphia, as well as Boston, New York, London, and Paris, increasingly lived and worked through such publics—newspaper-reading publics, letter-writing publics, and political publics.

A luxuriance of forms and kinds of writing served these publics, consolidating and empowering them. Besides newspapers, which themselves are vehicles for a remarkable display of genres, this was also the age of the pamphlet. Paper-bound and sold for one to two shillings apiece, they could be as thick as eighty pages, though most were from ten to fifty. Short, cheap books, as easy to produce as to acquire as to read, made the whole range of colonial thinking—including sermons, philosophical essays, speeches, collections of letters as well as political treatises—accessible to persons across the social spectrum. Between 1750 and 1776, more than 400 pamphlets were published on the single issue of relations to England (including Thomas Paine's *Common Sense* and *American Crisis*); by 1783, 1,500 had appeared. And besides pamphlets there were broadsides, novels, compilations of reports and documents, books of advice, almanacs, manuals, collections of essays and sermons, and books of poetry.

For all this, neither the public realms of literature nor of politics were universally accessible; status and economics closed them to many. Indeed, the Junto, a club Franklin organized to discuss and influence public life in Philadelphia, was secret. But Franklin was not being unusually contradictory in devoting himself to the creation of a self-ruling public polity while, at the same time, developing ways of overruling it. Some version of this divided attitude is at the center of virtually all the political writings of the period.

Perhaps the most famous document in the literature surrounding the drawing up of the Constitution, *The Federalist #10,* "To Break and Control the Violence of Faction," written by James Madison, takes great pains to exonerate republican government from the charge of democracy. A large republic, argues Madison, distances elected representatives from their constituencies, which are in consequence prevented from exerting a direct influence on the government. On the other side of this dispute, those who argued for a democratic republic closer to its constituents, generally stipulated that "the manners, sentiments, and interests" of those represented "should be similar." Dissimilarity (religious, cultural, racial, ethnic, or economic) makes a representative government unworkable for *both* federalists and anti-federalists. The former want a republic that transcends "heterogenous and discordant principles," the latter, one that excludes them.

The literature of politics contains many texts protesting the illogic of a public realm closed to whole sections of society. Abigail Adams and Judith Sargent Murray point out the contradiction in denying to women rights ostensibly inalienable. Slavery and the slave trade, as George Mason, Franklin, and Ottobah Cugoano argue, would appear to invalidate the whole notion of a republic. William Manning, showing "How the Few and Many Differ in Their Ideas of Interest," observes that the "Many," who labor for wages, have always been ruled and overruled by the "Few" men of property, and that this has not changed with the Revolution. Crèvecoeur sees the Revolution itself becoming another demonstration that "the innocent class are always the victims of the few."

Before the Revolution, Crèvecoeur had imagined the English colonies as a democratic paradise, and the idyllic vision of a self-sufficient tiller of the soil he described in "What is an American?" has since become a national myth. His *Letters from an American Farmer,* however, oppose independence. The demand for independence is often depicted as an unfolding necessity, an event the colonies moved toward logically and inexorably. It was, in fact, as historians keep repeating, harshly contested. John Adams, who had no reason to exaggerate the fragility of popular support, estimated that fully a third of the colonists were opposed to declaring independence. Many colonists, even members of groups reputed to be the backbone of the Revolution, like the yeomen, were adamantly against it. The tenant farmers of upstate New York, as well as the hill farmers of the South, for instance, feared the local tyranny of wealthy landowners too much to want to see them constituted an independent authority. Crèvecoeur's despair at the reappearance, in the New World, of power relations he had thought left behind in the Old offers an argument against the Revolution from a democratic standpoint, and suggests that the identification of the Loyalist with a disgruntled English aristocrat is too simple.

It is truer, perhaps, to look at the dominant disputes of the period as, in general, disagreements about how to manage the emergence of a modern world. Bernard Bailyn found that the two sides in the dispute over independence cited essentially the same arguments based on the same texts. The question was how to construct a legitimate authority for a newly self-possessed and self-governing population. A major source of arguments for the pro-independence colonists were English libertarians, notably John Trenchard and Thomas Gordon, authors of *Cato's Letters*, which crossed over to the colonies virtually upon publication beginning in 1720. The debate over the colonies' treatment raged on both sides of the Atlantic. The war for American independence was a broadly significant moment in the development of a new kind of social and political community in the West generally, a community in which the printing press had transformed the conduct and even the nature of politics.

M.J.

Suggested readings: Bernard Bailyn's *Ideological Origins of the American Revolution* is an authoritative introduction to the key issues and terms of late-eighteenth-century colonial politics. J.G.A. Pocock's *The Machiavellian Moment: Florentine Political Thought and the Atlantic Republican Tradition* traces the evolution of republican ideology to its culminating point in colonial and Revolutionary America. Linda Kerber focuses on women for a similar investigation in *Women of the Republic: Intellect and Ideology in Revolutionary America*, while Winthrop Jordan, in *White Over Black: American Attitudes Toward the Negro, 1550–1812*, writes the history of racism. Garry Wills's *Inventing America: Jefferson's Declaration of Independence* is a close reading informed by the historical and cultural context.

1. Samuel Sewall

The Selling of Joseph
1700

Slavery was not a feature of southern plantation society only; it existed also in the northern colonies (see chapter 10 and Daniel Horsmanden's Journal). The first slaves were Indians, but by the end of the seventeenth century most were Africans working as agricultural laborers, sometimes as highly skilled artisans, and as house servants. There is no record of controversy over this state of affairs until 1700, when Sewall, in The Selling of Joseph, *produced the first antislavery text in the colonies.*

Sewall was a judge and indeed one of those who, in 1692, presided over the Salem witch trials. (See his diary in chapter 5.) It was in his juridical capacity that he received the appeal of a slave named Adam against his master, whom Adam accused of reneging on a promise of manumission. Sewall took the occasion to issue a public appeal for an end to slavery itself. Adam's master, John Saffin (1626–1710), a judge of the same court, responded with his own text, A Brief and Candid Answer to a late Printed Sheet, Entitled, The Selling of Joseph.

Sewall's text invokes the Bible against human bondage: "Joseph was rightfully no more a Slave to his Brethren, than they were to him: and they had no more Authority to Sell him, than they had to Slay him." As for secular reasons to end slavery, "Caveat Emptor!" Buyer beware: the presence of enslaved Africans everywhere in the white community corrupts its morals and stunts its growth. Saffin granted that the slaves were "the Creatures of God," but so inferior to their masters as to be naturally their servants, and if their servants, then as legitimately their bond-servants, following the example of Abraham. Moreover, economic and social necessity both counseled maintenance, first because the masters could not afford to emancipate their slaves and "so lose all they money they cost," and second, because free, the Africans would have to be sent out of the country immediately "or else the remedy would be worse than the Disease." The debate over slavery would pursue just these arguments all the way up to Emancipation.

Forasmuch as Liberty *is in real value next unto* Life: *None ought to part with it themselves, or deprive others of it, but upon most mature Consideration.*

The Numerousness of Slaves at this day in the Province, and the Uneasiness of them under their Slavery, hath put many upon thinking whether the Foundation of it be firmly and well laid; so as to sustain the Vast Weight that is built upon it. It is most certain that all Men, as they are the Sons of *Adam*, are Coheirs; and have equal Right unto Liberty, and all other outward Comforts of Life. GOD *hath given the Earth unto the Sons of* Adam, Psal 115.16. *And hath made of One Blood, all Nations of Men, for to dwell on all the face of the Earth, and hath determined the Times before appointed, and the bounds of their habitation: That they should seek the Lord. Forasmuch then as we are the Offspring of GOD &c.* Act 17.26, 27, 29. Now although the Title given by the last ADAM, doth infinitely better Mens Estates, respecting GOD and themselves; and grants them a most beneficial and inviolable Lease under the Broad Seal of Heaven, who were before only Tenants at Will: Yet through the Indulgence of GOD to our First Parents after the Fall, the outward Estate of all and every of their Children, remains the same, as to one another. So that Originally, and Naturally, there is no such thing as Slavery. *Joseph* was rightfully no more a Slave to his Brethren, than they were to him: and they had no more Authority to *Sell* him, than they had to *Slay* him. And if *they* had nothing to do to Sell him; the *Ishmaelites* bargaining with them, and paying down Twenty pieces of Silver, could not make a Title. Neither could *Potiphar* have any better Interest in him than the *Ishmaelites* had. *Gen.* 37.20, 27, 28. For he that shall in this case plead *Alteration of Property*, seems to have forfeited a great part of his own claim to Humanity. There is no proportion between Twenty Pieces of Silver, and LIBERTY. The Commodity it self is the Claimer. If *Arabian* Gold be imported in any quantities, most are afraid to meddle with it, though they might have it at easy rates; lest if it should have been wrongfully taken from the Owners, it should kindle a fire to the Consumption of their whole Estate. 'Tis pity there should be more Caution used in buying a Horse, or a little lifeless dust; than there is in purchasing Men and Women: Whenas they are the Offspring of GOD, and their Liberty is, . . . *Auro pretiosior Omni.* And seeing GOD hath said, *He that Stealeth a Man and Selleth him, or if he be found in his hand, he shall surely be put to Death.* Exod. 21.16. This Law being of Everlasting Equity, wherein Man Stealing is ranked amongst the most atrocious of Capital Crimes: What louder Cry can there be made of that Celebrated Warning, CAVEAT EMPTOR!

And all things considered, it would conduce more to the Welfare of the Province, to have White Servants for a Term of Years, than to have Slaves for Life. Few can endure to hear of a Negro's being made free; and indeed they can seldom use their freedom well; yet their continual aspiring after their forbidden Liberty, renders them Unwilling Servants. And there is such a disparity in their Conditions, Colour & Hair, that they can never embody[1] with us, and grow up into orderly Families, to the Peopling of the Land: but still remain in our Body Politick as a kind of extravasat[2] Blood. As many Negro men as there are among us, so many empty places there are in our Train Bands, and the places taken up of Men that might make Husbands for our Daughters. And the Sons and Daughters of *New England* would become more like *Jacob*, and *Rachel*, if this Slavery were thrust quite out of doors. Moreover it is too well known what Temptations Masters are under, to connive at the Fornication of their Slaves; lest they should be obliged to find them Wives, or pay their Fines. It seems to be practically pleaded that they might be Lawless; 'tis thought much of, that the Law should have Satisfaction for their Thefts, and other Immoralities; by which means, *Holiness to the Lord*, is more rarely engraven upon this sort of Servitude. It is likewise most lamentable to think, how in taking Negros out of *Africa*, and Selling of them here, That

---

1. embody: procreate.   2. extravasat: outside its proper vessel.

which GOD has joyned together men do boldly rend asunder; Men from their Country, Husbands from their Wives, Parents from their Children. How horrible is the Uncleanness, Mortality, if not Murder, that the Ships are guilty of that bring great Crouds of these miserable Men, and Women. Methinks, when we are bemoaning the barbarous Usage of our Friends and Kinsfolk in *Africa*: it might not be unseasonable to enquire whether we are not culpable in forcing the *Africans* to become Slaves amongst our selves. And it may be a question whether all the Benefit received by *Negro* Slaves, will balance the Accompt of Cash laid out upon them; and for the Redemption of our own enslaved Friends out of *Africa*. Besides all the Persons and Estates that have perished there.

Obj. 1. *These Blackamores are of the Posterity of* Cham, *and therefore are under the Curse of Slavery.* Gen. 9.25, 26, 27.

Answ. Of all Offices, one would not begg this; *viz.* Uncall'd for, to be an Executioner of the Vindictive Wrath of God; the extent and duration of which is to us uncertain. If this ever was a Commission; How do we know but that it is long since out of Date? Many have found it to their Cost, that a Prophetical Denunciation of Judgment against a Person or People, would not warrant them to inflict that evil. If it would, *Hazael* might justify himself in all he did against his Master, and the *Israelites*, from 2 *Kings* 8.10, 12.

But it is possible that by cursory reading, this Text may have been mistaken. For *Canaan* is the Person Cursed three times over, without the mentioning of *Cham*. Good Expositors suppose the Curse entaild on him, and that this Prophesie was accomplished in the Extirpation of the *Canaanites*, and in the Servitude of the *Gibeonites*. *Vide Pareum.*[3] Whereas the Blackmores are not descended of *Canaan*, but of *Cush*. Psal. 68.31. *Princes shall come out of Egypt Ethiopia shall soon stretch out her hands unto God.* Under which Names, all *Africa* may be comprehended; and their Promised Conversion ought to be prayed for. *Jer.* 13.23. *Can the Ethiopian change his skin?* This shows that Black Men are the Posterity of *Cush:* Who time out of mind have been distinguished by their Colour. And for want of the true, *Ovid* assigns a fabulous cause of it.

> *Sanguine tum credunt in*
> *corpora summa vocato*
> *Æthiopum populos nigrum*
> *traxisse colorem.*[4] Metamorph. lib. 2.

Obj. 2. *The* Nigers *are brought out of a Pagan Country, into places where the Gospel is Preached.*

Answ. Evil must not be done, that good may come of it. The extraordinary and comprehensive Benefit accruing to the Church of God, and to *Joseph* personally, did not rectify his brethrens Sale of him.

---

3. *Vide Pareum*: See Pareus. David Pareus, a seventeenth-century Protestant theologian.
4. "It was then, as men think, that the peoples of Ethiopia became black-skinned since the blood was drawn to the surface of their bodies by the heat." Ovid, from the myth of Phaeton.

Obj. 3. *The Africans* have *Wars one with another: Our Ships bring lawful Captives taken in those Wars.*

Answ. For ought is known, their Wars are much such as were between *Jacob's* Sons and their Brother *Joseph*. If they be between Town and Town; Provincial, or National: Every War is upon one side Unjust. An Unlawful War can't make lawful Captives. And by Receiving, we are in danger to promote, and partake in their Barbarous Cruelties. I am sure, if some Gentlemen should go down to the *Brewsters* to take the Air, and Fish: And a stronger party from *Hull* should Surprise them, and Sell them for Slaves to a Ship outward bound: they would think themselves unjustly dealt with; both by Sellers and Buyers. And yet 'tis to be feared, we have no other kind of Title to our *Nigers*. *Therefore all things whatsoever ye would that men should do to you, do ye even so to them: for this is the Law and the Prophets.* Matt. 7.12.

Obj. 4. Abraham *had Servants bought with his Money, and born in his House.*

Answ. Until the Circumstances of *Abraham's* purchase be recorded, no Argument can be drawn from it. In the mean time, Charity obliges us to conclude, that He knew it was lawful and good.

It is Observable that the *Israelites* were strictly forbidden the buying, or selling one another for Slaves. *Levit.* 25.39,46. *Jer.* 34.8. . . . 22. And GOD gaged His Blessing in lieu of any loss they might conceipt they suffered thereby. *Deut.* 15.18. And since the partition Wall is broken down, inordinate Self love should likewise be demolished. GOD expects that Christians should be of a more Ingenuous and benign frame of spirit. Christians should carry it to all the World, as the *Israelites* were to carry it one towards another. And for men obstinately to persist in holding their Neighbours and Brethren under the Rigor of perpetual Bondage, seems to be no proper way of gaining Assurance that God has given them Spiritual Freedom. Our Blessed Saviour has altered the Measures of the ancient Love-Song, and set it to a most Excellent New Tune, which all ought to be ambitious of Learning. *Matt.* 5. 43, 44. *John* 13.34. These *Ethiopians*, as black as they are; seeing they are the Sons and Daughters of the First *Adam*, the Brethren and Sisters of the Last ADAM, and the Offspring of GOD; They ought to be treated with a Respect agreeable.

Servitus perfecta voluntaria, inter Christianum & Christianum, ex parte servi patientis saepe est licita quia est necessaria: sed ex parte domini agentis, & procurando & exercendo, vix potest esse licita: quia non convenit regulae illi generali: Quaecunque volueritis ut faciant vobis homines, ita & vos facite eis. Matt. 7.12.

Perfecta servitus poenae, non potest jure locum habere, nisi ex delicto gravi quod ultimum supplicium aliquo modo meretur: quia Libertas ex naturali aestimatione proxime accedit ad vitam ipsam, & eidem a multis praeferri solet.[5]

Ames. Cas. Consc. Lib. 5. Cap. 23. Thes. 2, 3. *BOSTON* of the *Massachusets*; Printed by *Bartholomew Green*, and *John Allen*, June, 24th. 1700.

---

5. *Servitus perfecta,* etc.: Perfect servitude, so it be voluntary, is on the submissive servants' part often lawful between Christian and Christian because indeed it is necessary: but on the Master's part who is the agent, in procuring and exercising the authority, it is scarce lawful; in respect, if he wants that general Canon, What you would have men do unto you, even so do unto them; *Perfecta servitus,* etc.: Perfect servitude, by way of punishment, can have no place by right, unless for some heinous offence, which might deserve in some measure the ultimate punishment since liberty according to natural reason comes closest to life itself and is apt by many to be preferred to it.

2. John Saffin

A Brief and Candid Answer
1701

That Honourable and Learned Gentleman, the Author of a Sheet, Entituled, *The Selling of Joseph, A* Memorial, seems from thence to draw this conclusion, that because the Sons of *Jacob* did very ill in selling their Brother *Joseph* to the *Ishmaelites,* who were Heathens, therefore it is utterly unlawful to Buy and Sell Negroes, though among Christians; which Conclusion I presume is not well drawn from the Premises, nor is the case parallel; for it was unlawful for the *Israelites* to Sell their Brethren upon any account, or pretence whatsoever during life. But it was not unlawful for the Seed of *Abraham* to have Bond men, and Bond women either born in their House, or bought with their Money, as it is written of *Abraham, Gen. 14. 14. & 21 .10. & Exod.* 21. 16. & *Levit.* 25. 44. 45, 46 *v.* After the giving of the Law: And in *Josh.* 9. 23. That famous Example of the *Gibeonites* is a sufficient proof where there no other.

To speak a little to the Gentlemans first Assertion: *That none ought to part with their Liberty themselves, or deprive others of it but upon mature consideration;* a prudent exception, in which he grants, that upon some consideration a man may be deprived of his Liberty. And then presently in his next Position or Assertion he denies it, *viz.: It is most certain, that all men as they are the Sons of* Adam *are Coheirs, and have equal right to Liberty, and all other Comforts of Life,* which he would prove out of *Psal.* 115. 16. *The Earth hath he given to the Children of Men.* True, but what is all this to the purpose, to prove that all men have equal right to Liberty, and all outward comforts of this life; which Position seems to invert the Order that God hath set in the World, who hath Ordained different degrees and orders of men, some to be High and Honourable, some to be Low and Despicable; some to be Monarchs, Kings, Princes and Governours, Masters and Commanders, others to be Subjects, and to be Commanded; Servants of sundry sorts and degrees, bound to obey; yea, some to be born Slaves, and so to remain during their lives, as hath been proved. Otherwise there would be a meer parity among men, contrary to that of the Apostle, I *Cor.* 12 *from the* 13 *to the* 26 *verse,* where he sets forth (by way of comparison) the different sorts and offices of the Members of the Body, indigitating that they are all of use, but not equal, and of like dignity. So God hath set different Orders and Degrees of Men in the World, both in Church and Common weal. Now, if this Position of parity should be true, it would then follow that the ordinary Course of Divine Providence of God in the World should be wrong, and unjust, (which we must not dare to think, much less to affirm) and all the sacred Rules,

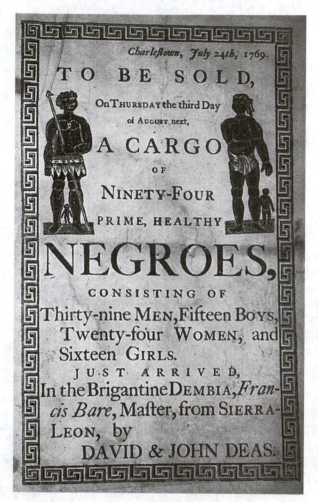

Precepts and Commands of the Almighty which he hath given the Son of Men to observe and keep in their respective Places, Orders and Degrees, would be to no purpose; which unaccountably derogate from the Divine Wisdom of the most High, who hath made nothing in vain, but hath Holy Ends in all his Dispensations to the Children of men.

In the next place, this worthy Gentleman makes a large Discourse concerning the Utility and Conveniency to keep the one, and inconveniency of the other; respecting white and black Servants, which conduceth most to the welfare and benefit of this Province: which he concludes to be white men, who are in many respects to be preferred before Blacks; who doubts that? doth it therefore follow, that it is altogether unlawful for Christians to buy and keep Negro Servants (for this is the Thesis) but that those that have them ought in Conscience to set them free, and so lose all the money they cost (for we must not live in any known sin) this seems to be his opinion; but it is a Question whether it ever was the Gentleman's practice? But if he could perswade the General Assembly to make an Act, That all that have Negroes, and do set them free, shall be Reimbursed out of the Publick Treasury, and that there shall be no more Negroes brought into the Country; 'tis probable there would be more of his opinion; yet he would find it a hard task to bring the Country to consent thereto; for then the Negroes must be all sent out of the Country, or else the remedy would be worse than the Disease; and it is to be feared that those Negroes that are free, if there be not some strict course taken with them by Authority, they will be a plague to this Country.

Again, If it should be unlawful to deprive them that are lawful Captives, or Bondmen of their Liberty for Life being Heathens; it seems to be more unlawful to deprive our Brethren, of our own or other Christian Nations of the Liberty, (though but for a time) by binding them to Serve some Seven, Ten, Fifteen, and some Twenty Years, which oft times proves for their whole Life, as many have been; which in effect is the same in Nature, though different in the time, yet this was allow'd among the *Jews* by the Law of God; and is the constant practice of our own and other Christian Nations in the World: the which our Author by his Dogmatical Assertions doth condemn as Irreligious; which is Diametrically contrary to the Rules and Precepts which God hath given the diversity of men to observe in their respective Stations, Callings, and Conditions of Life, as hath been observed.

And to illustrate his Assertion our Author brings in by way of Comparison the Law of God against man Stealing, on pain of Death: Intimating thereby, that Buying and Selling of Negro's is a breach of that Law, and so deserves Death: A severe Sentence: But herein he begs the Question with a *Caveat Emptor*. For, in that very Chapter there is a Dispensation to the People of *Israel*, to have Bond men, Women and Children, even of their own Nation in some case; and Rules given therein to be observed concerning them; Verse the 4*th*. And in the before cited place, *Levit*. 25.44, 45, 46. Though the *Israelites* were forbidden (ordinarily) to make Bond men and Women of their own Nation, but of Strangers they might: the words run thus, verse 44. *Both thy Bond men, and thy Bond maids which thou shalt have shall be of the Heathen, that are round about you: of them shall you Buy Bond men and Bond maids*, &c. See also, I *Cor*. 12.13. Whether we be Bond or Free, which shows that in the times of the New Testament, there were Bond men also, &c.

In fine, The sum of this long Haurange, is no other, than to compare the Buying and Selling of Negro's unto the Stealing of Men, and the Selling of *Joseph* by his Brethren, which bears no proportion therewith, nor is there any congruiety therein, as appears by the foregoing Texts.

Our Author doth further proceed to answer some Objections of his own framing, which he supposes some might raise.

Object. I. *That these Blackamores are of the Posterity of* Cham, *and therefore under the Curse of Slavery*. Gen. 9.25, 26, 27. The which the Gentleman seems to deny, saying, *they ware the Seed of Canaan that were Cursed, &c.*

Answ. Whether they were so or not, we shall not dispute: this may suffice, that not only the seed of *Cham* or *Canaan*, but any lawful Captives of other Heathen Nations may be made Bond men as hath been proved.

Obj. 2. *That the Negroes are brought out of Pagan Countreys into places where the Gospel is Preached*. To which he Replies, *that we must not doe Evil that Good may come of it*.

Ans. To which we answer, That it is no Evil thing to bring them out of their own Heathenish Country, where they may have the Knowledge of the True God, be Converted and Eternally saved.

Obj. 3. *The Africans have Wars one with another; our Ships bring lawful Captives taken in those Wars*.

To which our Author answers Conjecturally, and Doubtfully, *for ought we know*, that which may or may not be; which is insignificant, and proves nothing. He also compares the Negroes Wars, one Nation with another, with the Wars between *Joseph* and his Brethren. But where doth he read of any such War? We read indeed of a

Domestick Quarrel they had with him, they envyed and hated *Joseph;* but by what is Recorded, he was meerly passive and meek as a Lamb. This Gentleman farther adds, *That there is not any War but is unjust on one side, &c.* Be it so, what doth that signify: We read of lawful Captives taken in the Wars, and lawful to be Bought and Sold without contracting the guilt of the *Agressors;* for which we have the example of *Abraham* before quoted; but if we must stay while both parties Warring are in the right, there would be no lawful Captives at all to be Bought; which seems to be rediculous to imagine, and contrary to the tenour of Scripture, and all Humane Histories on that subject.

Obj. 4. *Abraham had Servants bought with his Money, and born in his House. Gen.* 14.14. To which our worthy Author answers, *until the Circumstances of Abraham's purchase be recorded, no Argument can be drawn from it.*

Ans. To which we Reply, this is also Dogmatical, and proves nothing. He farther adds, *In the mean time Charity Obliges us to conclude, that he knew it was lawful and good.* Here the gentleman yields the case; for if we are in Charity bound to believe *Abrahams* practice, in buying and keeping *Slaves* in his house to be lawful and good: then it follows, that our Imitation of him in this his Moral Action, is as warrantable as that of his Faith; *who is the Father of all them that believe. Rom.* 4.16.

In the close of all, Our Author Quotes two more places of Scripture, *viz.; Levit.* 25.46, and *Jer.* 34, from the 8. to the 22. *v.* To prove that the people of Israel were strictly forbidden the Buying and Selling one another for *Slaves:* who questions that? and what is that to the case in hand? What a strange piece of Logick is this? 'Tis unlawful for Christians to Buy and Sell one another for slaves. *Ergo,* It is unlawful to Buy and Sell Negroes that are lawful Captiv'd Heathens.

And after a Serious Exhortation to us all to Love one another according to the Command of Christ. *Math.* 5.43, 44. This worthy Gentleman concludes with this Assertion, *That these Ethiopeans as Black as they are, seeing they are the Sons and Daughters of the first* Adam; *the Brethren and Sisters of the Second* Adam, *and the Offspring of God; we ought to treat them with a respect agreeable.*

Ans. We grant it for a certain and undeniable verity, That all Mankind are the Sons and Daughters of *Adam,* and the Creatures of God: But it doth not therefore follow that we are bound to love and respect all men alike; this under favour we must take leave to deny; we ought in charity, if we see our Neighbour in want, to relieve them in a regular way, but we are not bound to give them so much of our Estates, as to make them equal with our selves, because they are our Brethren, the Sons of *Adam,* no, not our own natural Kinsmen: We are Exhorted *to do good unto all, but especially to them who are of the Houshold of Faith, Gal.* 6.10. And we are to love, honour and respect all men according to the gift of God that is in them: I may love my Servant well, but my Son better; Charity begins at home, it would be a violation of common prudence, and a breach of good manners, to treat a Prince like a Peasant. And this worthy Gentleman would deem himself much neglected, if we should show him no more Defference than to an ordinary Porter: And therefore these florid expressions, the Sons and Daughters of the First *Adam,* the Brethren and Sisters of the Second *Adam,* and the Offspring of God, seem to be misapplied to import and insinuate, that we ought to tender Pagan Negroes with all love, kindness, and equal respect as to the best of men.

By all which it doth evidently appear both by Scripture and Reason, the practice of the People of God in all Ages, both before and after the giving of the Law, and in the times of the Gospel, that there were Bond men, Women and Children commonly kept by holy and good men, and improved in Service; and therefore by the Command of God, *Lev. 25, 44,* and their venerable Example, we may keep Bond men, and use them in our Service still; yet with all candour, moderation and Christian prudence, according to their state and condition consonant to the Word of God.

The Negroes Character.

Cowardly and cruel are those Blacks *Innate,*
Prone to Revenge, Imp of inveterate hate.
He that exasperates them, soon espies
Mischief and Murder in their very eyes.
Libidinous, Deceitful, False and Rude,
The spume Issue of Ingratitude.
The Premises consider'd, all may tell,
How near good Joseph *they are parallel.*

3. John Trenchard and Thomas Gordon

Cato's Letters, no. 106, "Of plantations and colonies"
1722

From 1720 to 1724, John Trenchard (1662–1723) and Thomas Gordon (?–1750), writing together as "Cato," produced a series of letters in the Whig London Journal *which were very widely read in the colonies as well. Their pseudonym refers to a Roman censor whose attacks on corruption and decadence became legendary. The first letters of the English "Cato" denounced the scandalous mismanagement of the South Sea Company. (Edward Gibbon's grandfather was involved and ruined in the Company's failure, perhaps contributing to the grandson's pessimism regarding the empire's future.) Trenchard and Gordon were staunch republicans, favoring a role for monarchy as the guardian against corruption. Their notion of the good empire centers its activities on commerce, offering an extended market and opportunities for investment and growth. In the colonies, this view was taken as an argument for equal treatment of colonists who were Englishmen investing abroad and enriching not only themselves but the country.*

Cato's view of colonial relations is distinctly Machiavellian: "It is not to be hoped, in the corrupt State of human Nature, that any Nation will be subject to another any longer than it finds its own Account in it, and cannot help itself." ("Nation" here indicates only a coherent and self-sufficient social group with no

*necessary political identity. "Country" is the word they would use to mean what
we mean by "nation.")*

   *From this principle of self-interest, Trenchard and Gordon derive two corol-
laries. The first is that the mother country must do everything it can to prevent the
colonies from developing self-sufficiency, especially in the area of manufacturing;
the second is that this policy needs to be carried out "by gentle and insensible
Methods" or it will lead to rebellion. Even, they go so far as to suggest, should the
colonies become so well established that a sort of equality seems indicated,
following the "Example of Merchants and Shopkeepers," it were best to accede to
it. In 1722, Cato already envisions the Commonwealth.*

Saturday, December 8, 1722.
Of Plantations and Colonies.

S<small>IR</small>,

   I Intend, in this Letter, to give my Opinion about Plantations; a Subject which seems
to me to be understood but by few, and little Use is made of it where it is. It is most
certain, that the Riches of a Nation consist in the Number of its Inhabitants, when
those Inhabitants are usually employed, and no more of them live upon the Industry
of others (like Drones in a Hive) than are necessary to preserve the Economy of the
Whole: For the rest, such as Gamesters, Cheats, Thieves, Sharpers, and Abbey-
Lubbers, with some of their Betters, waste and destroy the publick Wealth, without
adding any thing to it. Therefore, if any Nation drive either by Violence, or by ill
Usage and Distress, any of its Subjects out of their Country, or send any of them out
in foolish Wars, or useless Expeditions, or for any other Causes, which do not return
more Advantage than bring Loss, they so far enervate their State, and let out Part of
their best Heart's Blood.

   Now, in many Instances, Men add more to the publick Stock by being out of their
Country, than in it; as Ambassadors, publick Ministers, and their Retinues, who
transact the Affairs of a Nation; Merchants and Tradesmen, who carry on its Traffick;
Soldiers, in necessary Wars; and sometimes Travellers, who teach us the Customs,
Manners and Policies, of distant Countries, whereby we may regulate and improve our
own. All, or most of these, return to us again with Advantage. But, in other Instances,
a Man leaves his Country, never, or very rarely to return again; and then the State will
suffer Loss, if the Person so leaving it be not employed Abroad in such Industry, in
raising such Commodities, or in performing such Services, as will return more Benefit
to his native Country, than they suffer Prejudice by losing an useful Member.

   This is often done by planting Colonies, which are of Two Sorts: One to keep
conquered Countries in Subjection, and to prevent the Necessity of constant Standing
Armies: a Policy which the *Romans* practised, till their Conquests grew too numerous,
the conquered Countries too distant, and their Empire too unwieldy to be managed by
their native Force only; and then they became the Slaves of those whom they
conquered. This Policy for many Ages, we ourselves used in *Ireland*, till the Fashion of
our Neighbours, and the Wisdom of modern Ages, taught us the Use of Armies: And I
wish that those who come after us may never learn all their Uses. I must confess, that I
am not wise enough to enter into all the Policy made use of formerly in governing that

Country; and shall in proper Time communicate my Doubts, in hopes to receive better Information. In the mean time, I cannot but persuade myself, that when our Superiors are at leisure from greater Affairs, it may be possible to offer them a Proposition more honourable to the Crown, more advantageous to each Kingdom, and to the particular Members of them, and vastly more conducive to the Power of the whole *British* Empire, than the doubtful State which they are now in. But as this is not the Purpose of my present Letter, I shall proceed to consider the Nature of the other Sort of Colonies.

The other Sort of Colonies are for Trade, and intended to encrease the Wealth and Power of the native Kingdom; which they will abundantly do if managed prudently, and put and kept under a proper Regulation. No Nation has, or ever had, all the Materials of Commerce within itself: No Climate produces all Commodities; and yet it is the Interest, Pleasure, or Convenience, of every People, to use or trade in most or all of them; and rather to raise them themselves, than to purchase them from others, unless in some Instances, when they change their own Commodities for them, and employ as many or more People at Home in that Exchange, such as would lose their Employment by purchasing them from Abroad. Now, Colonies planted in proper Climates, and kept to their proper Business, undoubtedly do this; and particularly many of our own Colonies in the *West Indies* employ ten times their own Number in *Old England*, by sending them from hence Provisions, Manufactures, Utensils for themselves and their Slaves, by Navigation, working up the Commodities that they send us, by retaining and exporting them afterwards, and in returning again to us Silver and Gold, and Materials for new Manufactures; and our Northern Colonies do, or may if encouraged, supply us with Timber, Hemp, Iron, and other Metals, and indeed with most or all the Materials of Navigation, and our Neighbours too, through our Hands; and by that Means settle a solid Naval Power in *Great Britain*, not precarious, and subject to Disappointments, and the Caprices of our Neighbours; which Management would make us soon Masters of most of the Trade of the World.

I would not suggest so distant a Thought, as that any of our Colonies, when they grow stronger, should ever attempt to wean themselves from us; however, I think too much Care cannot be taken to prevent it, and to preserve their Dependences upon their Mother-Country. It is not to be hoped, in the corrupt State of human Nature, that any Nation will be subject to another any longer than it finds its own Account in it, and cannot help itself. Every Man's first Thought will be for himself, and his own Interest; and he will not be long to seek for Arguments to justify his being so, when he knows how to attain what he proposes. Men will think it hard to work, toil, and run Hazards, for the Advantage of others, any longer than they find their own Interest in it, and especially for those who use them ill: All Nature points out that Course. No Creatures suck the Teats of their Dams longer than they can draw Milk from thence, or can provide themselves with better Food: Nor will any Country continue their Subjection to another, only because their Great-Grandmothers were acquainted.

This is the Course of human Affairs; and all wise States will always have it before their Eyes. They will well consider therefore how to preserve the Advantages arising from Colonies, and avoid the Evils. And I conceive, that there can be but two Ways in Nature to hinder them from throwing off their Dependence; one to keep it out of their Power, and the other out of their Will. The first must be by Force; and the latter by using them well, and keeping them employed in such Productions, and making such Manufactures, as will support themselves and Families comfortably, and procure them Wealth too, or at least not prejudice their Mother-Country.

Force can never be used effectually to answer the End, without destroying the Colonies themselves. Liberty and Encouragement are necessary to carry People thither, and to keep them together when they were there; and Violence will hinder both. Any Body of Troops considerable enough to awe them, and keep them in Subjection, under the Direction too of a needy Governor, often sent thither to make his Fortune, and at such a Distance from any Application for Redress, will soon put an end to all Planting, and leave the Country to the Soldiers alone; and if it did not, would eat up all the Profit of the Colony. For this Reason, arbitrary Countries have not been equally successful in planting Colonies with free ones; and what they have done in that kind has, either been by Force, at a vast Expence, or by departing from the Nature of their Government, and giving such Privileges to Planters as were denied to their other Subjects. And I dare say, that a few prudent Laws, and a little prudent Conduct, would soon give us far the greatest Share of the Riches of all *America*, perhaps drive many of other Nations out of it, or into our Colonies, for Shelter.

If Violence, or Methods tending to Violence, be not used to prevent it, our Northern Colonies must constantly encrease in People, Wealth, and Power. Men living in healthy Climates, paying easy or no Taxes, not molested with Wars, must vastly encrease by natural Generation; besides that vast Numbers every Day flow thither from our own Dominions, and from other Parts of *Europe*, because they have there ready Employment, and Lands given to them for Tilling; insomuch that I am told they have doubled their Inhabitants since the Revolution,[6] and in less than a Century must become powerful States; and the more powerful they grow, still the more People will flock thither. And there are so many Exigences in all States, so many foreign Wars, and domestick Disturbances, that these Colonies can never want Opportunities, if they watch for them, to do what they shall find their Interest to do; and therefore we ought to take all the Precautions in our Power, that it shall never be their Interest to act against that of their native Country; an Evil which can no otherwise be averted than by keeping them fully employed in such Trades as will encrease their own, as well as our Wealth; for it is much to be feared, if we do not find Employment for them, they may find it for us.

No two Nations, no two Bodies of Men, or scarce two single Men, can long continue in Friendship, without having some Cement of their Union; and where Relation, Acquaintance, or mutual Pleasures are wanting, mutual Interests alone can bind it: But when those Interests separate, each Side must assuredly pursue their own. The Interest of Colonies is often to gain Independency; and is always so when they no longer want Protection, and when they can employ themselves more advantageously than in supplying Materials of Traffick to others: And the Interest of the Mother-Country is always to keep them dependent, and so employed; and it requires all their Address to do it; and it is certainly more easily and effectually done by gentle and insensible Methods than by Power alone.

6. Revolution: the Glorious Revolution of 1689.

Men will always think that they have a Right to Air, Earth, and Water, a Right to employ themselves for their own Support, to live by their own Labours, to apply the Gifts of God to their own Benefit; and, in order to it, to make the best of their Soil, and to work up their own Product: And when this cannot be done without Detriment to their Mother-Country, there can be but one fair, honest, and indeed effectual Way to prevent it; which is, to divert them upon other Employments as advantageous to themselves, and more so to their Employers; that is, in raising such Growth, and making such Manufactures, as will not prejudice their own, or at least in no Degree equal to the Advantage which they bring: And when such Commodities are raised or made, they ought to be taken off their Hands, and the People ought not to be forced to find out other Markets by Stealth, or to throw themselves upon new Protectors. Whilst People have full Employment, and can maintain themselves comfortably in a Way which they have been used to, they will never seek after a new one, especially when they meet Encouragement in one, and are discountenanced in the other.

As without this Conduct Colonies must be mischievous to their Mother-Country, for the Reasons before given, so with it the greatest Part of the Wealth which they acquire centers there; for all their Productions are so many Augmentations of our Power and Riches, as they are Returns of the People's Labour, the Rewards of Merchants, or Increase of Navigation; without which all who are sent Abroad are a dead Loss to their Country, and as useless as if really dead; and worse than so, if they become Enemies: for we can send no Commodities to them, unless they have others to exchange for them, and such as we find our Interest in taking.

As to our Southern Plantations, we are in this respect upon a tolerable Foot already; for the Productions there are of so different a Nature from our own, that they can never interfere with us; and the Climates are so unhealthy, that no more People will go or continue there than are necessary to raise the Commodities which we want; and consequently they can never be dangerous to us: But our Northern Colonies are healthy Climates, and can raise all or most of the Commodities, which our own Country produces. They constantly encrease in People, and will constantly encrease; and, without the former Precautions, must, by the natural Course of human Affairs, interfere with most Branches of our Trade, work up our best Manufactures, and at last grow too powerful and unruly to be governed for our Interest only: And therefore, since the Way lies open to us to prevent so much Mischief, to do so much Good, and add so much Wealth and Power to *Great Britain,* by making those Countries the Magazines of our naval Stores,[7] I hope we shall not lose all these Advantages, in Compliment to the Interests of a few private Gentlemen, or even to a few Countries.

We have had a Specimen of this wise Conduct in prohibiting the *Irish* Cattle, which were formerly brought to *England* lean, in Exchange for our Commodities, and fatted here; but are now killed and sent Abroad directly from *Ireland:* And so we lose the whole Carriage and Merchants Advantage, and the Vent of the Commodities sent to purchase them. And lately we have made such another prudent Law, to prevent the importing their Woollen Manufacture; which has put them upon wearing none of

---

7. naval Stores: shipbuilding supplies.

ours, making all or most of their own Cloth themselves; exporting great Quantities of all Sorts by stealth, and the greater Part of their Wool to rival Nations; and, by such Means it is that we are beholden to the Plague in *France*, to their *Mississippi* Company, and their total Loss of Credit, that we have not lost a great Part of that Manufacture. It is true, we have made some notable Provision to hedge in the Cuckoo, and to make all the People of that Kingdom execute a Law, which it is every Man's Interest there not to execute; and it is executed accordingly.

I shall sometime hereafter consider that Kingdom in relation to the Interest of *Great Britain;* and shall say at present only, that it is too powerful to be treated only as a Colony; and that if we design to continue them Friends, the best Way to do it is, to imitate the Example of Merchants and Shopkeepers; that is, when their Apprentices are acquainted with their Trade and their Customers, and are out of their Time, to take them into Partnership, rather than let them set up for themselves in their Neighbourhood.

4. William Livingston

Liberty of the Press
1752

Whig lawyer, man of letters and poet, William Livingston (1723–90) modelled his journal The Independent Reflector *(1752–53) on Addison and Steele's* Spectator. *The essay "Liberty of the Press," which appeared in* The Independent Reflector, *expresses the classic moderate position proper to one born into the New York land-owning aristocracy, and in the process of building an important legal career in the predominantly mercantile middle-class colonies. On the one hand, he rejoices in the power of a free press to restrict "arbitrary Governments." On the other hand, with as much emphasis, he cautions against unbridled freedom: "the Liberty of the Press, is always to be restricted from becoming a Prejudice to the public weal." A free press, for Livingston, is a balancing act: "A Printer ought not to publish every Thing that is offered him; but what is conducive of general Utility, he should not refuse, be the Author a Christian, Jew, Turk or Infidel." This liberal rather than libertarian view of the press grants rights over it to both individuals and the community.*

Individuals can abuse the liberty of the press as readily as governments can suppress it. Livingston's vision of the ideal society served by a responsible free press is a community of self-regulating individuals of economic substance and cultural authority, rational beings reasonably concerned for the general welfare. It is an important precondition of this civil society—composed of civic-minded publics in which the self-regulating individuals have voluntarily gathered for the common good of themselves and one another—that class conflict be muted by the enlightened dominance of the more affluent and educated. Livingston's essay demonstrates that at mid-century the English colonies can be addressed as a community of gentlemen and merchants.

OF THE USE, ABUSE, AND LIBERTY OF THE PRESS

—Arts in my Train,
And azure-mantled Science, swift we spread
A sounding Pinion.—

Thomson, *Liberty*

Whether the Art of PRINTING has been of greater Service or Detriment to the World, has frequently been made the Subject of fruitless Controversy. The best Things have been perverted to serve the vilest Purposes, their being therefore subject to Abuse, is an illogical Argument against their Utility. Before the Invention of the Press, the Progress of Knowledge was slow, because the Methods of diffusing it were laborious and expensive. The shortest Production was too costly to its Author; and unless the Writer had an opulent Fortune, or rich Patrons to pay off his *Amanuenses,* he was driven to the Necessity of retailing his Compositions. To arrive at Fame and literary Glory, was not in the Power of every great Genius; and doubtless Posterity has lost the Sentiments of many eminent Men, which might have been equally useful and important, with the Writings of those, who make the brightest Appearance in the Annals of Fame. It is otherwise since the Discovery of the Art of *Printing.* The most inferior Genius, however impoverished, can spread his Thoughts thro' a Kingdom. The Public has the Advantage of the Sentiments of all its Individuals. Thro' the Press, Writers of every Character and Genius, may promulge their Opinions; and all conspire to rear and support the Republic of Letters. The Patriot can by this Means, diffuse his salutary Principles thro' the Breasts of his Countrymen, interpose his friendly Advice unasked, warn them against approaching Danger, unite them against the Arm of despotic Power, and perhaps, at the Expence of but a few Sheets of Paper, save the State from impending Destruction. The Divine is not confined within the narrow Limits of his parochial Duties, but may preach in his Writings to the whole World. Like Powers in Mechanics, he does as it were, multiply himself: For at the Instant he Visits the Sick of his own Parish, he is perhaps consoling Hundreds against the Fears of Death, in foreign Nations and different Languages, and preaching to many Thousands at the same Time. And surely his Pleasure must equal his Labours, when he reflects, that his pastoral Care extends thro' the whole christian-iz'd World; that however thin and secluded his particular Parish may be, yet that several Nations are within the Sphere of his Influence; that he shall even live after his Death, and Thousands whom he never saw, be his Crown of rejoicing at the great Day of Judgment. Such also are the Advantages of *Printing,* to the Philosopher, the Moralist, the Lawyer, and Men of every other Profession and Character, whose Sentiments may be diffused with the greatest Ease and Dispatch, and comparatively speaking at a trifling Expence. In short, as the glorious Luminary of the Heavens, darts its Rays with incredible Velocity, to the most distant Confines of our System, so the Press, as from one common Center, diffuses the bright Beams of Knowledge, with prodigious Dispatch, thro' the vast Extent of the civilized World.

Secrecy, is another Advantage, which an Author had not before the Art of *Printing* was discovered. As long as Power may be perverted, from the original Design of its

This title page for The American Magazine *shows a view of Boston, with improbable Indians. Note the Long Wharf.*

being lodged with the Magistrate, for protecting the Innocent and punishing the Guilty, so long it will be necessary to conceal the Author who remarks it, from the Malice of the Officer guilty of so pernicious a Perversion; and by Means of this Art he may write undiscovered, as it is impossible to detect him by the Types of the Press.

It must indeed be confessed, that this useful Discovery has, like many others, been prostituted to serve the basest Ends. This great Means of Knowledge, this grand Security of civil Liberty, has been the Tool of arbitrary Power, Popery, Bigotry, Superstition, Profaneness, and even of Ignorance itself. The Press groans under the Weight of the most horrid Impieties, the most ruinous and destructive Principles in Religion and Politics, the idlest Romances, the most contemptible Fustian, Slander and Impotence. But to shut up the Press because it has been abused, would be like burning our Bibles and proscribing Religion, because its Doctrines have been disobeyed and misrepresented; or like throwing off all Law and Restraint, and sinking into a State of Nature, because the over-grown Power of the civil Ruler, abusing his Trust, has sacrificed the Lives and Properties of his Subjects, to lawless and tyrannical Sway. The horrid Practices of NERO, would by no Means have been a sufficient Reason for the

Destruction of the Roman Polity. Nor had it been less than Madness in the *English* Nation, to have dissolved the Bonds of our Constitution, and sunk into Anarchy and Confusion, even tho' CHARLES I and JAMES II had provoked the just Resentment of an injured and oppressed People. Such a Condition would have been worse than that of SYRACUSE, under the most unlimited Despotism. The Truth is, the Tyrant should in such Case be deposed, but the State should survive him; and rather than live without Law, without Society, and the innumerable Blessings it includes, better would it be, to suffer with only a distant Hope of Redress, the ungoverned Sway of the most arbitrary Monarch the World ever saw.

The wide Influence of the Press is so dangerous to arbitrary Governments, that in some of them it is shut up, and in others greatly restrained. The Liberty of complaining, of carrying that Complaint to the Throne itself, and of breathing the Sighs of an afflicted, oppressed Nation, has too great a Tendency to produce a Revolution to be suffered in despotic Governments. No Press is tolerated in the *Ottoman* Empire. Power supported without Right, cannot bear, and therefore will not submit itself to a public Examination. Knowledge inspires a Love of Liberty,—and Liberty in the People, is incompatable with the Security of an arbitrary Legislator. To the same Causes are to be ascribed, the Restrictions on the Press in Roman Catholic Countries: Notwithstanding which, the Grand Segnior surpasses the Pope in Policy, which is not the only Proof of his Holiness's Fallibility. That Hierarchy which supports itself by keeping the People in Ignorance, and inhibiting its Devotees the Use of the Bible, oppugns its own Principles, by admitting the Use of the Press; which, as it affords the Opportunity of diffusing Knowledge and Truth thro' the World, must, by inevitable Consequence, equally spread abroad a Contempt of his *Holiness*, and the Worship, Discipline and Doctrines of his Church. Neither the Amours of HENRY VIII which to asperse Protestantism, the Papists ascribe as its Origin, nor any other natural Cause, had so happy [a] Tendency to destroy the Power of the See of *Rome,* as the Liberty of the Press. Popery and Slavery could not stand before true Religion and Liberty; and as the Press was the Instrument of both, the Rights of St. PETER's Chair were no sooner publicly contested, than despised and diminished.

No Nation in *Europe,* is more jealous of the *Liberty of the Press* than the *English,* nor is there a People, among whom it is so grossly abused. With us, the most unbounded Licentiousness prevails. We are so besotted with the Love of Liberty, that running into Extreams, we even tolerate those Things which naturally tend to its Subversion. And what is still more surprizing, an Author justly chargeable with Principles destructive of our Constitution, with Doctrines the most abject and slavish, may proceed even with inveterate Malice, to vilify, burlesque and deny our greatest Immunities and Privileges, and shall yet be suffered to justify himself under the unrestrainable Rights of the Press. An Absurdity grossly stupid and mischievous. What! sap the Constitution, disturb the public Tranquility, and ruin the State, and yet plead a Right to such Liberty derived from the Law of that State! The *Liberty of the Press,* like Civil Liberty, is talked of by many, and understood but by few; the latter is taken by Multitudes, for an irrefrainable Licence of acting at Pleasure; an equal Unrestraint in Writing, is often argued from the former, but both are false and equally dangerous to our Constitution. Civil Liberty is built upon a Surrender of so much of our natural

Liberty, as is necessary for the good Ends of Government; and the Liberty of the Press, is always to be restricted from becoming a Prejudice to the public Weal. The Design of entering into a State of Society, is to promote and secure the Happiness of its Individuals. Whatever tends to this End, is politically lawful, and no State can permit any Practice detrimental to the public Tranquility, but in direct Opposition to its fundamental Principles. Agreeable to this Doctrine I lay it down as a Rule, that when the Press is prejudicial to the public Weal, it is abused: and that the Prohibition of printing any Thing, not repugnant to the Prosperity of the State, is an unjustifiable and tyrannical Usurpation.

If, on the one Hand, we suppose any broader Foundation for the *Liberty of the Press,* it will become more destructive of public Peace, than if it were wholly shut up: And a Freedom of publishing what is not prejudicial to the general Good, must be allowed; because, what can do no Harm can be no Evil, and there can be no Punishment without a Transgression. Besides, a Promotion of the public Welfare, of which the Press is often an Instrument, should be so far from suffering Discouragements, that as it is a political Virtue, it merits rather the Rewards than the Frowns of the Magistrate. Thus the Press will have all that Liberty which is due to it, and never be checked, but where its being unrestricted will prove an Evil, and therefore only where it ought to be checked. Liberty and Science may then spread their Wings, and take the most unbounded Flights. But should Tyranny erect its formidable Head, and extend its Iron Scepter, the Nation may publish, and any private Person represent the general Calamity with Impunity. Does Corruption or Venality prevail, the Patriot is at Liberty to inveigh and suppress it. The boldest Criminal lies open to Censure and Satire, and any Man may expose and detect him. The Divine may put Vice at a Stand; every Attack upon the publick Welfare may be reprehended, and every destructive Scheme baffled and exposed; for all Men are free in that Way, to defeat every Project that is detrimental to the Public. This Privilege is a great One, and we should all conspire to maintain it. This is the true LIBERTY OF THE PRESS, for which Englishmen ought to contend. Such a Liberty can never be dangerous, either to the Public, or their Ruler; but on the contrary may often be necessary. What a certain great Politician said of the Freedom of Speech, is so applicable to that of the Press, that I cannot omit its Insertion. "The more," says he, "Men express of their Hate and Resentment, perhaps the less they retain, and sometimes they vent the Whole that Way: But these Passions, where they are smothered, will be apt to fester, to grow venemous, and to discharge themselves by a more dangerous Organ than the Mouth, even by an armed and vindictive Hand. Less dangerous is a railing Mouth, than a Heart filled and inflamed with Bitterness and Curses; and more terrible to a Prince, ought to be the secret Execrations of his People, than their open Revilings, or, than even the Assaults of his Enemies."

All those who oppose the Freedom I have contended for,—a Liberty of promoting the common Good of Society, and of publishing any Thing else not repugnant thereto,—are Enemies to the Common Wealth; and many will fall under this Character, who are as ready to cry out for the *Liberty of the Press* as the warmest Patriot. Of this the various Orders that obtain amongst Men, furnish sufficient Examples: I shall instance but in two.

Never does a Writer of Genius and Spirit appear, unshackled with blind Prejudices and little Attachments to Party. A Writer who exposes the Roguery of Ecclesiastics, and displays the Beauty of genuine unadulterated Christianity, but he gives as it were Birth to a swarm of impotent Scribblers, who arrogate to themselves an Authority from God, to anathemize and deliver him over to the Devil; and the sooner to compleat his Doom, will invoke the secular Arm for Assistance. Strange that they should have a Power from God, to consign a Man over to eternal Torments, and yet be restrained by that very God, from illuminating his Understanding by Fire and Faggot, unless at the good Pleasure of the Magistrate! Such as these I call Enemies, both to the Press and the Public, tho' the former groans under the Burden of their Nonsense, Superstition and Bigotry.

The Press is for ever in the Mouths of Printers, and one would imagine, that as they live by its Liberty, they would understand its true Limits, and endeavour to preserve its rightful Extent. But the Truth is, there is scarce one in Twenty of them; that knows the one or aims at the other.

A Printer ought not to publish every Thing that is offered him; but what is conducive of general Utility, he should not refuse, be the Author a Christian, Jew, Turk or Infidel. Such Refusal is an immediate Abridgement of the Freedom of the Press. When on the other Hand, he prostitutes his Art by the Publication of any Thing injurious to his Country, it is criminal,—It is high Treason against the State. The usual Alarm rung in such Cases, the common Cry of an Attack upon the LIBERTY OF THE PRESS, is groundless and trifling. The Press neither has, nor can have such a Liberty, and whenever it is assumed, the Printer should be punished. Private Interest indeed has, with many of them, such irresistible Charms, and the general Good is so feeble a Motive, that the only Liberty they know and wish for, is of publishing every Thing with Impunity for which they are paid. I could name a Printer, so attached to his private Interest, that for the sake of advancing it, set up a Press, deserted his Religion, made himself the Tool of a Party he despised, privately contemned and vilified his own Correspondents, published the most infamous Falsehoods against others, slandered half the People of his Country, promised afterwards to desist, broke that Promise, continued the Publication of his Lies, Forgeries and Misrepresentations; and to compleat his Malignity, obstinately refused to print the Answers or Vindications of the Persons he had abused; and yet even this Wretch, had the Impudence to talk of the *Liberty of the Press*. God forbid! that every Printer should deserve so infamous a Character. There are among them, Men of Sense, Ingenuity, and rational Lovers of Liberty, for which the greater Part are less solicitous than the Generality of other Men, as a Confinement of the Press to its true Limits, is more frequently opposed to their private Advantage. It would be easy to enumerate a Variety of others, equally Pretenders to a Regard for the *Liberty of the Press*, and as evidently Enemies to the *Press* and the *Public*: But I shall reserve the farther Consideration of this Subject for a following Year, when the Conduct of Bigots and their Adherents, will, probably, supply me with some necessary Remarks.

5. Thomas Pownall

from *The Administration of the Colonies of America*
1764

Colonial administration was a tradition for Thomas Pownall (1722–1805), whose grandfather had been deputy governor of Bombay. The grandson looked west instead, arriving in the New World in 1753 as secretary to the governor of New York. He stayed three years, during which he established his credentials in American colonization. Although most of his subsequent career was spent on English soil, he was briefly governor of Massachusetts, in which post he was much appreciated by the colonists. His major work, from which a brief excerpt is reprinted, is The Administration of the Colonies, *whose success was measured by six editions from 1764 to 1777. Like Trenchard and Gordon but without their reluctance, Pownall here imagines a great English Commonwealth, "A grand Marine Dominion consisting of our Possessions in the Atlantic and in America united into a one Empire, in a one Center, where the Seat of Government is."*

In the first uncultur'd ages of Europe, when men sought nothing but to possess, and to secure possession, the power of the *sword* was the predominant spirit of the world; it was that, which formed the Roman empire; and it was the same, which, in the declension of that empire, divided again the nations into the several governments formed upon the ruins of it.

When men afterward, from leisure, began to exercise the powers of their minds in (what is called) learning; religion, the only learning at that time, led them to a concern for their spiritual interests, and consequently led them under their spiritual guides. The power of *religion* would hence as naturally predominate and rule, and did actually become the ruling spirit of the policy of Europe. It was this spirit, which, for many ages formed, and gave away kingdoms; this which created the anointed Lords over them, or again excommunicated and execrated these sovereigns; this that united and allied the various nations, or plung'd them into war and bloodshed; this, that formed the ballance of the power of the whole, and actuated the second grand scene of Europe's history.

But since the people of Europe have formed their communication with the commerce of Asia; have been, for some ages past, settling on all sides of the Atlantic Ocean, and in America, have been possessing every seat and channel of commerce, and have planted and raised that to an interest which has taken root;—since they now feel the powers which derive from this, and are extending it to, and combining it with others; the spirit of *commerce* will become that predominant power, which will form the general policy, and rule the powers of Europe: and hence a grand commercial interest, the basis of a great commercial dominion, under the present site and circumstances of the world, will be formed and arise. The rise and forming of this commercial interest is what precisely constitutes the present crisis.

The European possessions and interests in the Atlantic and in America lye under various forms, in plantations of sugar, tobacco, rice, and indigo, in farms of tillage and pasture, in fisheries, Indian hunts, forests, naval stores, and mines; each different site produces some special matter of supply necessary to one part of that food and raiment become requisite to the present state of the world; but is, as to its own local power of produce, totally destitute of some other equally necessary branch of supply. The various nature of the lands and seas lying in every degree and aspect of climate, and the special produce and vegetation that is peculiar to each, forms this local limited capacity of produce. At the same time that nature has thus confined and limited the produce of each individual site to one, or at most to few branches of supply, at the same time hath she extended the necessities of each to many branches beyond what its own produce can supply. The West India islands produce sugar, melosses, cotton, &c. they want the materials for building and mechanics, and many of the necessaries of food and raiment: The lumber, hides, the fish, flour, provisions, live-stock, and horses, produced in the northern colonies on the continent, must supply the islands with these requisites. On the other hand, the sugar and melosses of the sugar islands is become a necessary intermediate branch of the North American trade and fisheries. The produce of the British sugar islands cannot supply both Great Britain and North America with the necessary quantity; this makes the melosses of the foreign sugar islands also neces-sary to the present state of the North American trade. Without Spanish silver, become necessary to the circulation of the British American trade, and even to their internal course of sale and purchase, not only great part of that circulation must cease to flow, but the means of purchasing the manufactures of Great Britain would be equally circumscribed: Without the British supplies, the Spanish settlements would be scarce able to carry on their culture, and would be in great distress.

The ordinary course of the labour and generation of the negroes in the West India islands makes a constant external supply of these subjects necessary, and this connects the trade of Africa with the West Indies; the furr and Indian trade, and the European goods necessary to the Indian, are what form the Indian connection.—I do not enter into a particular detail of all the reciprocations of those wants and supplies, nor into a proof of the necessary interconnections arising from thence; I only mark out the general *traits* of these, in order to explain what I mean when I say, that by the limita-tion of the capacities and extent of the necessities of each, all are interwoven into a necessary intercourse of supplies, and all indissolubly bound in an union and commu-nion of *one general composite interest* of the whole of the Spanish, French, Dutch,

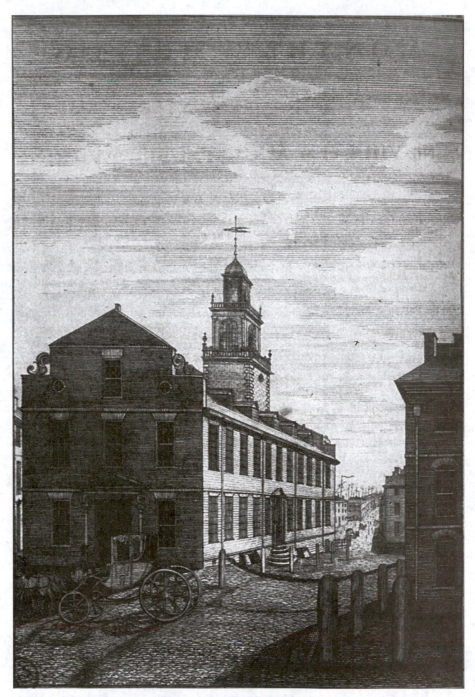

"S.W. View of the State-House, in Boston," *from the* Massachusetts Magazine, *1791.*

Danish, and British settlements. This is the *natural state* of the European possessions in the Atlantic and in America; this general communion is that natural interest under which, and by which, they must subsist.

On the contrary, the spirit of policy, by which the mother countries send out and on which they establish colonies, being to confine the trade of their respective colonies solely to their own special intercourse, and to hold them incommunicable of all other intercourse or commerce, the *artificial or political state* of these colonies becomes distinct from that which is above described as their natural state.—The political state is that which policy labours to establish by a principle of repulsion; the natural one is that state under which they actually exist and move by a general, common, and mutual principle of attraction. This one general interest thus distinct must have some one general tendency or direction distinct also, and peculiar to its own system. There must be some center of these composite movements, some lead that will predominate and govern in this general interest—That particular branch of business and its connections in this general commercial interest, which is most extensive, necessary, and permanent, settles and commands the market; and those merchants who actuate this branch must acquire an ascendency, and will take the lead of this interest. This lead will predominate throughout the general intercourse, will dissolve the effect of all artificial connections which government would create, and form the natural connections under which these interests actually exist,—will supersede all particular laws and customs, and operate by those which the nature and actual circumstances of the several interests require.

This lead is the foundation of a commercial dominion, which, whether we attend to it or not, will be formed: whether this idea may be thought real or visionary is of no consequence as to the existence and procession of this power, for the interest, which is the basis of it, is already formed;—yet it would become the wisdom, and is the duty of those who govern us, to profit of, to possess, and to take the lead of it already formed and arising fast into dominion; it is our duty so to interweave those nascent powers into, and to combine their influence with, the same interests which actuate our own government; so to connect and combine the operations of our trade with this interest, as to partake of its influence and to build on its power. Although this interest may be, as above described, different and even distinct from the peculiar interests of the mother countries, yet it cannot become independent, it must, and will fall under the dominion of *some* of the potentates of Europe. The great question at this crisis is, and the great struggle will be, which of the states of Europe shall be in those circumstances, and will have the vigour and wisdom so to profit of those circumstances, as to take this interest under its dominion, and to unite it to its government. This lead seemed at the beginning of the late war to oscillate between the English and French, and it was in this war that the dominion also hath been disputed. The lead is now in our hands, we have such connection in its influence, that, whenever it becomes the foundation of a dominion, that dominion must be ours.

It is therefore the duty of those who govern us, to carry forward this state of things to the weaving of this lead into our system, that Great Britain may be no more considered *as the kingdom of this Isle only, with many appendages of provinces, colonies, settlements, and other extraneous parts,* but as A GRAND MARINE DOMINION

CONSISTING OF OUR POSSESSIONS IN THE ATLANTIC AND IN AMERICA UNITED INTO A ONE EMPIRE, IN A ONE CENTER, WHERE THE SEAT OF GOVERNMENT IS.

The center of power, instead of remaining fixed as it now is in Great Britain, will, as the magnitude of the power and interest of the Colonies increases, be drawn out from the island, by the same laws of nature analogous in all cases, by which the center of gravity in the solar system, now near the surface of the sun, would, by an encrease of the quantity of matter in the planets, be drawn out beyond that surface. Knowing therefore the laws of nature, shall we like true philosophers follow, where that system leads, to form one general system of dominion by an union of Great Britain and her Colonies, fixing, while it may be so fixed, the common center in Great Britain, or shall we without ever seeing that such center must be formed by an inter-communion of the powers of all the territories as parts of the dominions of Great Britain, like true modern policitians, and from our own narrow temporary ideas of a local center, labour to keep that center in Great Britain by force against encreasing powers, which will, finally, by an overbalance heave that center itself out of its place? Such measures would be almost as wise and his who standing in a scale should thrust his stick up against the beam to prevent it from descending, while his own weight brought it the faster down. That policy which shall ever attempt to connect the Colonies to Great Britain *by power,* will in that very instant connect them *to one another in policy.*

[FAIR AND EVEN GENEROUS TREATMENT OF THE COLONIES WILL PAY OFF]

Were some such arrangements taken for a revision and further establishment of the laws of trade, upon the principle of extending the British general commerce, by encouraging the trade of the Colonies, in subordination to, and in coincidence therewith, the trade of the Colonies would be administered by that true spirit from whence it rose, and by which it acts; and the true application of the benefits which arise to a mother country from its Colonies would be made. Under this spirit of administration, the government, as I said above, could not be too watchful to carry its laws of trade into effectual execution.—But under the present state of those laws, and that trade, there is great danger that any severity of execution, which should prove effectual in the cases of the importation into the Colonies of foreign European and East-India goods, might force the Americans to trade for their imports, upon terms, on which the trade could not support itself, and therefore become in the event a means to bring on the necessity of these Americans manufacturing for themselves. Nothing does at present, with that active and acute people, prevent their going into manufactures, except the proportionate dearness of labour, as referred to the terms on which they can import; but encrease the price of their imports to a certain degree, let the extent of their settlements, either by policy from home or invasion of Indians abroad, be confined, and let their foreign trade and navigation be, in some measure suppressed;—their paper-currency limited within too narrow bounds, and the exclusion of that trade which hath usually supplied them with silver-money too severely insisted upon;—this proportion of the price of labour will much sooner cease to be an object of objection to manufacturing there, than is commonly apprehended.

Boston's South Battery, before 1765.

The winters in that climate are long and severe; during which season no labour can be done without doors. That application therefore of their servants labour, to manufactures for home consumption, which under any other circumstances would be too dear for the product created by it, becomes, under these circumstances, all clear gains. And if the Colonists cannot on one hand purchase foreign manufactures at any reasonable price, or have not money to purchase with, and there are, on the other, many hands idle which used to be employed in navigation, and all these, as well as the husbandmen, want employment; these circumstances will soon overbalance the difference of the rate of labour in Europe and in America.

And if the Colonies, under any future state of administration, which they see unequal to the management of their affairs, *once come to feel their own strength in this way*, their independence on government, at least on the administration of government, will not be an event so remote as our leaders may think, which yet nothing but such false policy can bring on. For, on the contrary, put their governments and laws on a true and constitutional basis, regulate their money, their revenue, and their trade, and do not check their settlements, they must ever depend on the trade of the mother country for their supplies, they will never establish manufactures, their hands being elsewhere employed, and the merchants being always able to import such on terms[8] that must ruin the manufacturer. Unable to subsist without, or to unite against the mother country, they must always remain subordinate to it, in all the transactions of their commerce, in all the operation of their laws, in every act of their government:—The several Colonies, no longer considered as demesnes of the crown, mere appendages to the realm, will thus become united therein, members and parts of the realm, as essential parts of a one organized whole, *the commercial dominion of Great Britain*. THE TAKING LEADING MEASURES TO THE FORMING OF WHICH, OUGHT, AT THIS JUNCTURE, TO BE THE GREAT OBJECT OF GOVERNMENT.

8. This is a fact too well known and understood to need any particular proof—but if need were, the writer of these papers could demonstrate this from the prices of wool, hemp, and flax, and the labour of carding, dressing, spinning, weaving, &c. in North America, compared with the prices of the same articles of produce and labour in Britain. It is therefore an idle vaunt in the Americans, when they talk of setting up manufactures *for trade*; but it would be equally injudicious in government here to force any measure that may render the manufacturing for *home consumption* an object of prudence, or even of pique in the Americans. And yet after all, should any thing of this sort extend itself to a degree that interfered with the exports of Great Britain to the Colonies—the same duties of an excise which lie upon the manufactures of Great Britain, levied upon those of America, would soon restore the balance. This consideration, one might imagine, would induce those who are prudent in America, to advise the rest to moderation in their opposition. [Pownal's note.]

6.

two popular broadsides

Broadsides were the lowliest of colonial publications, sheets printed only on one side on cheap paper, hawked in the streets, and not intended to be preserved, although often they were. Their contents ranged from ballads to political disquisitions, and their public was sometimes just barely literate. Yet broadsides were an important part of the colonial writing scene, representing not so much dissent— although they could do so—as the non-official way of letters and politics both.

In the two broadsides reprinted here, voices by tradition mostly silent ostensibly take it upon themselves to address the public. The first voice pretends to be a chimney sweep, the type itself of the lowly: engaged in proverbially dirty work, poorly educated, and poor. Yet he can "reed and rite," and were he to find himself a magistrate, he suggests, he might do rather better, and certainly fairer, than his betters. The second piece represents women, who customarily neither fight nor write. They can do both, this sheet offers: provide aid and succor for the brave soldiers at the front, and also be important allies in the field of print—witness this broadside.

"To the printur of the Penselvaney Kronical" Philadelphia 1772

mr Godard
i was Caled into a gentelmans hous tother day to sweep his Chimlees and wen i got to the top of won of them i sung my favrit song thare are sweepers in hi life as well as in low but wen i came amost doun i herd two or 3 Pepel tauking sofly in the rume i kep myself quiet behinde my Blancket and lissend and herd them tauk about the Elekshon and thay menshond sum gentelmens names who they said had bene the cheef hands in makeng sum very bad laus and amung the rest that that upreses the chimlee sweepers and fixes thare wagges i wunderd that such grate Men wold dabe thare hands with us and speshily won of thare sqires i wunder wy he shold bare any il wil aganste us as we ware nither printurs nor stele makers nor iorn masters and if he ever blakd his close aganste owr blanckets by goin in a hury by us it was nun of owr fauts and more than all that my master who i alwas pay 3 Shilens a day to for my vurk tels me we ware unlawFuly used for that as owr cumunetee was not gustlee rePresented now master printur i understand you are a favrit with him if you can use your influnce to ingage with him to change with me this next Elekshon for won yere he wil be more experencd in owr way and wil not take it upon him to setel Pepels

wagges and i promes you tho i can reed and rite i wil do no harm in his plase such as makin yure exises and yure stamps nor medel with yure dogs nor thro away yure munny in the mud and may be i now and then may speke wen any boddy says any thing about sweeps or so and tho we must continnu to ware the stamp of the beste on owr forheds yet if things go on so i am afrade we shall next be burnt in the forhed with the stamp of the devell G-d forgiv me for sayin so

so no more at presant from yure humble Sarvant to comand

Terence sweep

Philad.a October 1st 1772

"The Sentiments of an American Woman" Philadelphia 1780

On the commencement of actual war, the Women of America manifested a firm resolution to contribute as much as could depend on them, to the deliverance of their country. Animated by the purest patriotism, they are sensible of sorrow at this day, in not offering more than barren wishes for the success of so glorious a Revolution. They aspire to render themselves more really useful; and this sentiment is universal from the north to the south of the Thirteen United States. Our ambition is kindled by the fame of those heroines of antiquity, who have rendered their sex illustrious, and have proved to the universe, that, if the weakness of our Constitution, if opinion and manners did not forbid us to march to glory by the same paths as the Men, we should at least equal, and sometimes surpass them in our love for the public good. I glory in all that which my sex has done great and commendable. I call to mind with enthusiasm and with admiration, all those acts of courage, of constancy and patriotism, which history has transmitted to us: The people favoured by Heaven, preserved from destruction by the virtues, the zeal and the resolution of Deborah, of Judith, of Esther: The fortitude of the mother of the Macchabees, in giving up her sons to die before her eyes: Rome saved from the fury of a victorious enemy by the efforts of Volumnia, and other Roman Ladies: So many famous sieges where the Women have been seen forgeting the weakness of their sex, building new walls, digging trenches with their feeble hands, furnishing arms to their defenders, they themselves darting the missile weapons on the enemy, resigning the ornaments of their apparel, and their fortune, to fill the public treasury, and to hasten the deliverance of their country; burying themselves under its ruins; throwing themselves into the flames rather than submit to the disgrace of humiliation before a proud enemy.

Born for liberty, disdaining to bear the irons of a tyrannic Government, we associate ourselves to the grandeur of those Sovereigns, cherished and revered, who have held with so much splendour the scepter of the greatest States, The Batildas, the Elizabeths, the Maries, the Catharines, who have extended the empire of liberty, and contented to reign by sweetness and justice, have broken the chains of slavery, forged

by tyrants in the times of ignorance and barbarity. The
Spanish Women, do they not
make, at this moment, the
most patriotic sacrifices, to
encrease the means of victory
in the hands of their Sovereign.
He is a friend to the French
Nation. They are our allies.
We call to mind, doubly interested, that it was a French
Maid who kindled up amongst
her fellow-citizens, the flame
of patriotism buried under
long misfortunes: It was the
Maid of Orleans who drove
from the kingdom of France
the ancestors of those same
British, whose odious yoke we
have just shaken off; and
whom it is necessary that we
drive from this Continent.

"Bunker's Hill, or America's Head Dress." This London cartoon parodies women's coiffures as much as the Revolution.

But I must limit myself to
the recollection of this small
number of achievements. Who
knows if persons disposed to censure, and sometimes too severely with regard to us,
may not disapprove our appearing acquainted even with the actions of which our sex
boasts? We are at least certain, that he cannot be a good citizen who will not applaud
our efforts for the relief of the armies which defend our lives, our possessions, our
liberty? The situation of our soldiery has been represented to me; the evils inseparable
from war, and the firm and generous spirit which has enabled them to support these.
But it has been said, that they may apprehend, that, in the course of a long war, the
view of their distresses may be lost, and their services be forgotten. Forgotten! never; I
can answer in the name of all my sex. Brave Americans, your disinterestedness, your
courage, and your constancy will always be dear to America, as long as she shall
preserve her virtue.

We know that at a distance from the theatre of war, if we enjoy any tranquility, it is
the fruit of your watchings, your labours, your dangers. If I live happy in the midst of
my family; if my husband cultivates his field, and reaps his harvest in peace; if,
surrounded with my children, I myself nourish the youngest, and press it to my
bosom, without being affraid of seeing myself separated from it, by a ferocious enemy;
if the house in which we dwell; if our barns, our orchards are safe at the present time
from the hands of those incendiaries, it is to you that we owe it. And shall we hesitate
to evidence to you our gratitude? Shall we hesitate to wear a cloathing more simple;
hair dressed less elegant, while at the price of this small privation, we shall deserve

your benedictions. Who, amongst us, will not renounce with the highest pleasure, those vain ornaments, when she shall consider that the valiant defenders of America will be able to draw some advantage from the money which she may have laid out in these; that they will be better defended from the rigours of the seasons, that after their painful toils, they will receive some extraordinary and unexpected relief; that these presents will perhaps be valued by them at a greater price, when they will have it in their power to say: *This is the offering of the Ladies.* The time is arrived to display the same sentiments which animated us at the beginning of the Revolution, when we renounced the use of teas, however agreeable to our taste, rather than receive them from our persecutors; when we made it appear to them that we placed former necessaries in the rank of superfluities, when our liberty was interested; when our republican and laborious hands spun the flax, prepared the linen intended for the use of our soldiers; when exiles and fugitives we supported with courage all the evils which are the concomitants of war. Let us not lose a moment; let us be engaged to offer the homage of our gratitude at the altar of military valour, and you, our brave deliverers, while mercenary slaves combat to cause you to share with them, the irons with which they are loaded, receive with a free hand our offering, the purest which can be presented to your virtue,

By an American Woman.

7. Benjamin Franklin

An Edict by the King of Prussia
1773

Franklin addressed this satire anonymously to an English newspaper while himself living in London as a colonial agent.

For the Public Advertiser.

The SUBJECT of the following Article of

FOREIGN INTELLIGENCE

being exceeding EXTRAORDINARY, is the Reason of its being separated from the usual Articles of *Foreign News.*

Dantzick, September 5.

We have long wondered here at the Supineness of the English Nation, under the Prussian Impositions upon its Trade entering our Port. We did not till lately know the *Claims,* antient and modern, that hang over that Nation, and therefore could not suspect that it might submit to those Impositions from a Sense of *Duty,* or from Principles of *Equity.* The following *Edict,* just made public, may, if serious, throw some Light upon this Matter.

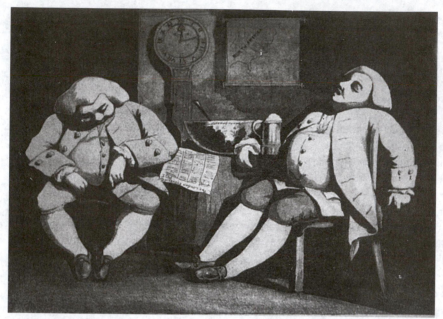

"A Pair of Politicians waiting for the Extraordinary Gazette." A map of North America hangs in the background.

'FREDERICK, by the Grace of God, King of *Prussia*, &c. &c. &c. to all present and to come, HEALTH. The Peace now enjoyed throughout our Dominions, having afforded us Leisure to apply ourselves to the Regulation of Commerce, the Improvement of our Finances, and at the same Time the easing our *Domestic Subjects* in their Taxes: For these Causes, and other good Considerations us thereunto moving, We hereby make known, that after having deliberated these Affairs in our Council, present our dear Brothers, and other great Officers of the State, Members of the same, WE, of our certain Knowledge, full Power and Authority Royal, have made and issued this present Edict, viz.

'WHEREAS it is well known to all the World, that the first German Settlements made in the Island of *Britain*, were by Colonies of People, Subjects to our renowned Ducal Ancestors, and drawn from *their* Dominions, under the Conduct of *Hengist, Horsa, Hella, Uffa, Cerdicus, Ida,* and others; and that the said Colonies have flourished under the Protection of our august House, for Ages past, have never been *emancipated* therefrom, and yet have hitherto yielded little Profit to the same. And whereas We Ourself have in the last War fought for and defended the said Colonies against the Power of *France*, and thereby enabled them to make Conquests from the said Power in *America*, for which we have not yet received adequate Compensation. And whereas it is just and expedient that a Revenue should be raised from the said Colonies in *Britain* towards our Indemnification; and that those who are Descendants of our antient Subjects, and thence still owe us due Obedience, should contribute to the replenishing of our Royal Coffers, as they must have done had their

Ancestors remained in the Territories now to us appertaining: WE do therefore hereby ordain and command, That from and after the Date of these Presents, there shall be levied and paid to our Officers of the Customs, on all Goods, Wares and Merchandizes, and on all Grain and other Produce of the Earth exported from the said Island of *Britain,* and on all Goods of whatever Kind imported into the same, a *Duty* of *Four and an Half* per Cent. *ad Valorem,* for the Use of us and our Successors.—And that the said Duty may more effectually be collected, We do hereby ordain, that all Ships or Vessels bound from *Great Britain* to any other Part of the World, or from any other Part of the World to *Great Britain,* shall in their respective Voyages touch at our Port of KONINGSBERG, there to be unladen, searched, and charged with the said Duties.

'AND WHEREAS there have been from Time to Time discovered in the said Island of *Great Britain* by our Colonists there, many Mines or Beds of Iron Stone; and sundry Subjects of our antient Dominion, skilful in converting the said Stone into Metal, have in Times past transported themselves thither, carrying with them and communicating that Art; and the Inhabitants of the said Island, *presuming* that they had a natural Right to make the best Use they could of the natural Productions of their Country for their own Benefit, have not only built Furnaces for smelting the said Stone into Iron, but have erected Plating Forges, Slitting Mills, and Steel Furnaces, for the more convenient manufacturing of the same, thereby endangering a Diminution of the said Manufacture in our antient Dominion. We *do therefore* hereby farther ordain, that from and after the Date hereof, no Mill or other Engine for Slitting or Rolling of Iron, or any Plating Forge to work with a Tilt-Hammer, or any Furnace for making Steel, shall be erected or continued in the said Island of *Great Britain:* And the Lord Lieutenant of every County in the said Island is hereby commanded, on Information of any such Erection within his County, to order and by Force to cause the same to be abated and destroyed, as he shall answer the Neglect thereof to Us at his Peril.—But We are nevertheless graciously pleased to permit the Inhabitants of the said Island to transport their Iron into *Prussia,* there to be manufactured, and to them returned, they paying our Prussian Subjects for the Workmanship, with all the Costs of Commission, Freight and Risque coming and returning, any Thing herein contained to the contrary notwithstanding.

'WE do not however think fit to extend this our Indulgence to the Article of *Wool,* but meaning to encourage not only the manufacturing of woollen Cloth, but also the raising of Wool in our antient Dominions, and to prevent *both,* as much as may be, in our said Island, We do hereby absolutely forbid the Transportation of Wool from thence even to the Mother Country *Prussia;* and that those Islanders may be farther and more effectually restrained in making any Advantage of their own Wool in the Way of Manufacture, We command that none shall be carried *out of one County into another,* nor shall any Worsted-Bay, or Woollen-Yarn, Cloth, Says, Bays, Kerseys, Serges, Frizes, Druggets, Cloth-Serges, Shalloons, or any other Drapery Stuffs, or Woollen Manufactures whatsoever, made up or mixt with Wool in any of the said Counties, be carried into any other County, or be Water-borne even across the smallest River or Creek, on Penalty of Forfeiture of the same, together with the Boats, Carriages, Horses, &c. that shall be employed in removing them. *Nevertheless* Our loving Subjects there are hereby permitted, (if they think proper) to use all their Wool as *Manure for the Improvement of their Lands.*

'AND WHEREAS the Art and Mystery of making *Hats* hath arrived at great Perfection in *Prussia,* and the making of Hats by our remote Subjects ought to be as much as possible restrained. And forasmuch as the Islanders before-mentioned, being in Possession of Wool, Beaver, and other Furs, have *presumptuously* conceived they had a Right to make some Advantage thereof, by manufacturing the same into Hats, to the Prejudice of our domestic Manufacture, We do therefore hereby strictly command and ordain, that no Hats or Felts whatsoever, dyed or undyed, finished or unfinished, shall be loaden or put into or upon any Vessel, Cart, Carriage or Horse, to be transported or conveyed *out of one County* in the said Island *into another County,* or to *any other Place whatsoever,* by any Person or Persons whatsoever, on Pain of forfeiting the same, with a Penalty of *Five Hundred Pounds* Sterling for every Offence. Nor shall any Hat-maker in any of the said Counties employ more than two Apprentices, on Penalty of *Five Pounds* Sterling per Month: We intending hereby that such Hat-makers, being so restrained both in the Production and Sale of their Commodity, may find no Advantage in continuing their Business.—But lest the said Islanders should suffer Inconveniency by the Want of Hats, We are farther graciously pleased to permit them to send their Beaver Furs to *Prussia;* and We also permit Hats made thereof to be exported from *Prussia* to *Britain,* the People thus favoured to pay all Costs and Charges of Manufacturing, Interest, Commission to Our Merchants, Insurance and Freight going and returning, as in the Case of Iron.

'And lastly, Being willing farther to favour Our said Colonies in *Britain,* We do hereby also ordain and command, that all the Thieves, Highway and Street-Robbers, House-breakers, Forgerers, Murderers, So—tes, and Villains of every Denomination, who have forfeited their Lives to the Law in *Prussia,* but whom We, in Our great Clemency, do not think fit here to hang, shall be emptied out of our Gaols into the said Island of *Great Britain for the* BETTER PEOPLING *of that Country.*

'We flatter Ourselves that these Our Royal Regulations and Commands will be thought *just* and *reasonable* by Our much-favoured Colonists in *England,* the said Regulations being copied from their own Statutes of 10 and 11 Will. III. C. 10.—5 Geo. II. C. 22.—23 Geo. II. C. 29.—4 Geo. I. C. II. and from other equitable Laws made by their Parliaments, or from Instructions given by their Princes, or from Resolutions of both Houses entered into for the GOOD *Government* of their own Colonies in *Ireland* and *America.*

'And all Persons in the said Island are hereby cautioned not to oppose in any wise the Execution of this Our Edict, or any Part thereof, such Opposition being HIGH TREASON, of which all who are *suspected* shall be transported in Fetters from *Britain* to *Prussia,* there to be tried and executed according to the *Prussian Law.*

'Such is our Pleasure.

'Given at *Potsdam* this twenty-fifth Day of the Month of
    August, One Thousand Seven Hundred and Seventy.
    three, and in the Thirty-third Year of our Reign.
'By the KING in his Council.

'RECHTMÆSSIG, Secr.'

Some take this Edict to be merely one of the King's *Jeux d'Esprit*: Others suppose it serious, and that he means a Quarrel with England: But all here think the Assertion it concludes with, "that these Regulations are copied from Acts of the English Parliament respecting their Colonies," a very *injurious* one: it being impossible to believe, that a People distinguished for their *Love of Liberty*, a Nation so *wise*, so *liberal in its Sentiments*, so *just and equitable* towards its *Neighbours*, should, from mean and *injudicious* Views of *petty immediate Profit*, treat *its own Children* in a Manner so *arbitrary* and TYRANNICAL!

8. Samuel Johnson

from *Taxation no Tyranny: An Answer to the Resolutions and Address of the American Congress*
1775

Samuel Johnson (1709–84), conservative wit, master of elegant prose and brilliant talk, particularly disliked Americans and, as his friend James Boswell sometimes warned the unwary, was prone to fits of anger at the mere mention of the colonies. The passage below from his essay Taxation no Tyranny *touches upon a point of indisputable contradiction.*

We are told, that the subjection of Americans may tend to the diminution of our own liberties: an event, which none but very perspicacious politicians are able to foresee. If slavery be thus fatally contagious, how is it that we hear the loudest yelps for liberty among the drivers of negroes?

9. Edmund Burke

from *Speech of Edmund Burke, Esq. on Moving His Resolutions for Conciliation with the Colonies*
1775

From a belief that inequality was the natural state of nature and society both, Edmund Burke (1729–97) deduced that government should both secure the property and rights of the powerful and allow everyone the greatest liberty possible to pursue their own improvement. His speech for "Conciliation with the Colonies" embodies both parts of this principle. The colonists were Englishmen committed to the exercise of their traditional liberties. These had proven their value over a long history leading to the establishment of a great empire. The growing affluence of the American colonies, redounding to England, was proving the benefits of freedom once again, and it would be dangerously contradictory to deny the colonists the privileges whose exercise had made them successful. On the contrary, England and the empire should welcome its overseas subjects with gratitude for their contributions to the common enrichment and prestige. On the English side of the growing conflict with the colonies, influential writings by prestigious figures like Trenchard and Gordon, Pownall, and Burke argued to the end for a transformation in colonial relations.

The proposition is Peace. Not Peace through the medium of War; not Peace to be hunted through the labyrinth of intricate and endless negociations; not Peace to arise out of universal discord, fomented, from principle, in all parts of the Empire; not Peace to depend on the Juridical Determination of perplexing questions; or the precise marking the shadowy boundaries of a complex Government. It is simple Peace; sought in its natural course, and its ordinary haunts.—It is Peace sought in the Spirit of Peace; and laid in principles purely pacific. I propose, by removing the Ground of the difference, and by restoring the *former unsuspecting confidence of the Colonies in the Mother Country,* to give permanent satisfaction to your people; and (far from a scheme of ruling by discord) to reconcile them to each other in the same act, and by the bond of the very same interest, which reconciles them to British Government. . . .

I have in my hand two accounts; one a comparative state of the export trade of England to its Colonies, as it stood in the year 1704, and as it stood in the year 1772. . . . Our general trade has been greatly augmented; and augmented more or less in almost every part to which it ever extended; but with this material difference; that of the Six Millions which in the beginning of the century constituted the whole mass of our export commerce, the Colony trade was but one-twelfth part; it is now (as a part of Sixteen Millions) considerably more than a third of the whole. This is the relative proportion of the importance of the Colonies at these two periods; and all reasoning concerning our mode of treating them must have this proportion as its basis; or it is a reasoning weak, rotten, and sophistical. . . .

This growth of our national prosperity has happened within the short period of the Life of man. It has happened within Sixty-eight years. There are those alive whose memory might touch the two extremities. [Here Burke offers the example of Lord Bathurst, imagining him addressed by a predicting angel thus:] 'Young man, There is America—which at this day serves for little more than to amuse you with stories of savage men, and uncouth manners; yet shall, before you taste of death, shew itself equal to the whole of that commerce which now attracts the envy of the world. Whatever England has been growing to by a progressive increase of improvement, brought in by varieties of people, by succession of civilizing conquests and civilizing settlements in a series of Seventeen Hundred years, you shall see as much added to her by America in the course of a single life!' If this state of his country had been foretold to him, would it not require all the sanguine credulity of youth, and all the fervid glow of enthusiasm, to make him believe it? Fortunate man, he has lived to see it! Fortunate indeed, if he lives to see nothing that shall vary the prospect and cloud the setting of his day! . . .

Perhaps, Sir, I am mistaken in my idea of an Empire, as distinguished from a single State or Kingdom. But my idea of it is this; that an Empire is the aggregate of many States, under one common head; whether this head be a monarch, or a presiding republic. It does, in such constitutions, frequently happen (and nothing but the dismal, cold, dead uniformity of servitude can prevent its happening) that the subordinate parts have many local privileges and immunities. Between these privileges, and the supreme common authority, the line may be extremely nice. Of course disputes, often too, very bitter disputes, and much ill blood, will arise. But though every privilege is an exemption (in the case) from the ordinary exercise of the supreme authority, it is no denial of it. The claim of a privilege seems rather, *ex vi termini,* to imply a superior power. For to talk of the privileges of a State or of a person, who has no superior, is hardly any better than speaking nonsense. Now, in such unfortunate quarrels, among the component parts of a great political union of communities, I can scarcely conceive of anything more compleatly imprudent, than for the Head of the Empire to insist, that, if any privilege is pleaded against his will, or his acts, that his whole authority is denied; instantly to proclaim rebellion, to beat to arms, and to put the offending provinces under the ban. Will not this, Sir, very soon teach the provinces to make no distinctions on their part? Will it not teach them that the Government, against which a claim of Liberty is tantamount to high-treason, is a Government to which submission is equivalent to slavery? It may not always be quite convenient to impress dependent communities with such an idea. . . .

In this situation, let us seriously and coolly ponder. What is it we have got by all our menaces, which have been many and ferocious? What advantage have we derived from the penal laws we have passed, and which, for the time, have been severe and numerous? What advances have we made towards our object, by the sending of a force, which, by land and sea, is no contemptible strength? Has the disorder abated?

Nothing less.—When I see things in this situation, after such confident hopes, bold promises, and active exertions, I cannot, for my life, avoid a suspicion, that the plan itself is not correctly right.

If then the removal of the causes of this spirit of American Liberty be, for the greater part, or rather entirely, impracticable; if the ideas of Criminal Process be inapplicable, or, if applicable, are in the highest degree inexpedient, what way yet remains? No way is open, but the third and last—to comply with the American Spirit as necessary; or, if you please, to submit to it, as a necessary Evil. . . . My idea therefore, without considering whether we yield as a matter of right, or grant as matter of favour, is *to admit the people of our Colonies into an interest in the constitution;* and, by recording that admission in the Journals of Parliament, to give them as strong an assurance as the nature of the thing will admit, that we mean for ever to adhere to that solemn declaration of systematic indulgence. . . . Let us get an American revenue as we have got an American empire. English privileges have made it all that it is; English privileges alone will make it all it can be.

10. Abigail Adams

letter to John Adams
1776

This famous letter written by Abigail Adams (1744–1818) to her husband on the eve of the Revolution is best known for a passage she inserted as if in afterthought: "and by the way . . . Remember the Ladies." Because of her social position, Abigail Adams's advocacy of more rights for women demanded respect. But, in the event, women did not get independence, and in the next century they were forced to conduct their own "Rebellion." Abigail Adams's letter is notable both for the strength of its protest and for a certain equivocation in its demands. Some wise men have willingly abandoned the role of master to women to become their friends, she writes, implying her husband has followed this happy course. However, having invoked the model of friendship, she stops short of claiming equality; in her last sentence, she calls on right-thinking men to imitate "the Supreem Being" in making use of their power for women's happiness.

March 31, 1776

I wish you would ever write me a Letter half as long as I write you; and tell me if you may where your Fleet are gone? What sort of Defence Virginia can make against our common Enemy? Whether it is so situated as to make an able Defence? Are not the Gentery Lords and the common people vassals, are they not like the uncivilized Natives Brittain represents us to be? I hope their Riffel Men who have shewen themselves very savage and even Blood thirsty; are not a specimen of the Generality of the people.

Female soldier, from a contemporary broadside.

I am willing to allow the Colony great merit for having produced a Washington but they have been shamefully duped by a Dunmore.

I have sometimes been ready to think that the passion for Liberty cannot be Eaquelly Strong in the Breasts of those who have been accustomed to deprive their fellow Creatures of theirs. Of this I am certain that it is not founded upon that generous and christian principal of doing to others as we would that others should do unto us.

Do not you want to see Boston; I am fearfull of the small pox, or I should have been in before this time. I got Mr. Crane to go to our House and see what state it was in. I find it has been occupied by one of the Doctors of a Regiment, very dirty, but no other damage has been done to it. The few things which were left in it are all gone. Cranch has the key which he never delivered up. I have wrote to him for it and am determined to get it cleand as soon as possible and shut it up. I look upon it a new acquisition of property, a property which one month ago I did not value at a single Shilling, and could with pleasure have seen it in flames.

The Town in General is left in a better state than we expected, more oweing to a percipitate flight than any Regard to the inhabitants, tho some individuals discovered a sense of honour and justice and have left the rent of the Houses in which they were, for the owners and the furniture unhurt, or if damaged sufficient to make it good.

Others have committed abominable Ravages. The Mansion House of your President is safe and the furniture unhurt whilst both the House and Furniture of the Solisiter General have fallen a prey to their own merciless party. Surely the very Fiends feel a Reverential awe for Virtue and patriotism, whilst they Detest the paricide and traitor.

I feel very differently at the approach of spring to what I did a month ago. We knew not then whether we could plant or sow with safety, whether when we had toild we could reap the fruits of our own industery, whether we could rest in our own Cottages, or whether we should not be driven from the sea coasts to seek shelter in the wilderness, but now we feel as if we might sit under our own vine and eat the good of the land.

I feel a gaieti de Coar[9] to which before I was a stranger. I think the Sun looks brighter, the Birds sing more melodiously, and Nature puts on a more chearfull countanance. We feel a temporary peace, and the poor fugitives are returning to their deserted habitations.

Tho we felicitate ourselves, we sympathize with those who are trembling least the Lot of Boston should be theirs. But they cannot be in similar circumstances unless pusilanimity and cowardise should take possession of them. They have time and warning given them to see the Evil and shun it. (I long to hear that you have declared an independancy—and by the way in the new Code of Laws which I suppose it will be necessary for you to make I desire you would Remember the Ladies, and be more generous and favourable to them than your ancestors.) Do not put such unlimited power into the hands of the Husbands. Remember all Men would be tyrants if they could. (If perticuliar care and attention is not paid to the Laidies we are determined to foment a Rebelion, and will not hold ourselves bound by any Laws in which we have no voice, or Representation.)

That your Sex are Naturally Tyrannical is a Truth so thoroughly established as to admit of no dispute, but such of you as wish to be happy willingly give up the harsh title of Master for the more tender and endearing one of Friend. Why then, not put it out of the power of the vicious and the Lawless to use us with cruelty and indignity with impunity. Men of Sense in all Ages abhor those customs which treat us only as the vassals of your Sex. Regard us then as Beings placed by providence under your protection and in immitation of the Supreem Being make use of that power only for our happiness.

11. Adam Smith

from *The Wealth of Nations*
1776

1776 was a big year in words as well as in deeds. The Wealth of Nations, *the classic text of private enterprise and the market economy, appeared that year (along with the first volume of Edward Gibbon's* History of the Decline and Fall of the Roman Empire). *In the sections below, Adam Smith (1723–90) demonstrates the complexity of his analysis, which, countrary to some later representations, does not advocate giving the market or its masters either a free hand or the final say on their conduct, let alone on the national economy in general. It is altogether possible, according to Smith, that policies good for shopkeepers will be bad for the nation, even for a nation of shopkeepers.*

Nonetheless, suggesting that a peaceful separation of the colonies from England would be to the advantage of both by opening the future to unrestricted commerce, Smith expresses his ongoing belief in the beneficent potential of "the mercantile system" whose triumph has been, in his view, the best thing to come from the discovery of America.

---

9. gaieti de Coar: gaiety of heart.

[EMPIRE AND COMMERCE]

To found a great empire for the sole purpose of raising up a people of customers, may at first sight appear a project fit only for a nation of shopkeepers. It is, however, a project altogether unfit for a nation of shopkeepers; but extremely fit for a nation whose government is influenced by shopkeepers. Such statesmen, and such statesmen only, are capable of fancying that they will find some advantage in employing the blood and treasure of their fellow-citizens, to found and maintain such an empire. Say to a shopkeeper, Buy me a good estate, and I shall always buy my clothes at your shop, even though I should pay somewhat dearer than what I can have them for at other shops; and you will not find him very forward to embrace your proposal. But should any other person buy you such an estate, the shopkeeper would be much obliged to your benefactor if he would enjoin you to buy all your clothes at his shop. England purchased for some of her subjects, who found themselves uneasy at home, a great estate in a distant country. The price, indeed, was very small, and instead of thirty years purchase, the ordinary price of land in the present times, it amounted to little more than the expence of the different equipments which made the first discovery, reconnoitred the coast, and took a fictitious possession of the country. The land was good and of great extent, and the cultivators having plenty of good ground to work upon, and being for some time at liberty to sell their produce where they pleased, became in the course of little more than thirty or forty years (between 1620 and 1660) so numerous and thriving a people, that the shopkeepers and other traders of England wished to secure to themselves the monopoly of their custom. Without pretending, therefore, that they had paid any part, either of the original purchase-money, or of the subsequent expence of improvement, they petitioned the parliament that the cultivators of America might for the future be confined to their shop; first, for buying all the goods which they wanted from Europe; and, secondly, for selling all such parts of their own produce as those traders might find it convenient to buy. For they did not find it convenient to buy every part of it. Some parts of it imported into England might have interfered with some of the trades which they themselves carried on at home. Those particular parts of it, therefore, they were willing that the colonists should sell where they could; the farther off the better; and upon that account proposed that their market should be confined to the countries south of Cape Finisterre. A clause in the famous act of navigation established this truly shopkeeper proposal into a law.

The maintenance of this monopoly has hitherto been the principal, or more properly perhaps the sole end and purpose of the dominion which Great Britain assumes over her colonies. In the exclusive trade, it is supposed, consists the great advantage of provinces, which have never yet afforded either revenue or military force for the support of the civil government, or the defence of the mother country. The monopoly is the principal badge of their dependency, and it is the sole fruit which has hitherto been gathered from that dependency. Whatever expence Great Britain has hitherto laid out in maintaining this dependency, has really been laid out in order to support this monopoly. The expence of the ordinary peace establishment of the colonies amounted, before the commencement of the present disturbances, to the pay of twenty regiments of foot; to the expence of the artillery, stores, and extraordinary provisions with which it was necessary to supply them; and to the expence of a very considerable naval force which was constantly kept up, in order to guard, from the smuggling vessels of other nations, the immense coast of North America, and that of our West Indian islands. The whole expence of this peace establishment was a charge upon the revenue of Great Britain, and was, at the same time, the smallest part of what the dominion of the colonies has cost the mother country. If we would know the amount of the whole, we must add to the annual expence of this peace establishment the interest of the sums which, in consequence of her considering her colonies as provinces subject to her dominion, Great Britain has upon different occasions laid out upon their defence. We must add to it, in particular, the whole expence of the late war, and a great part of that of the war which preceded it. The late war was altogether a colony quarrel, and the whole expence of it, in whatever part of the world it may have been laid out, whether in Germany or the East Indies, ought justly to be stated to the account of the colonies. It amounted to more than ninety millions sterling, including not only the new debt which was contracted, but the two shillings in the pound additional land tax, and the sums which were every year borrowed from the sinking fund. The Spanish war which began in 1739, was principally a colony quarrel. Its principal object was to prevent the search of the colony ships which carried on a contraband trade with the Spanish main. This whole expence is, in reality, a bounty which has been given in order to support a monopoly. The pretended purpose of it was to encourage the manufactures, and to increase the commerce of Great Britain. But its real effect has been to raise the rate of mercantile profit, and to enable our merchants to turn into a branch of trade, of which the returns are more slow and distant than those of the greater part of other trades, a greater proportion of their capital than they otherwise would have done; two events which if a bounty could have prevented, it might perhaps have been very well worth while to give such a bounty.

Under the present system of management, therefore, Great Britain derives nothing but loss from the dominion which she assumes over her colonies.

To propose that Great Britain should voluntarily give up all authority over her colonies, and leave them to elect their own magistrates, to enact their own laws, and to make peace and war as they might think proper, would be to propose such a measure as never was, and never will be adopted, by any nation in the world. No nation ever voluntarily gave up the dominion of any province, how troublesome soever it might be to govern it, and how small soever the revenue which it afforded might be in proportion to the expence which it occasioned. Such sacrifices, though they might frequently be agreeable to the interest, are always mortifying to the pride of every nation, and what is perhaps of still greater consequence, they are always contrary to the private interest of the governing part of it, who would thereby be deprived of the disposal of many places of trust and profit, of many opportunities of acquiring wealth and distinction, which the possession of the most turbulent, and, to the great body of the people, the most unprofitable province seldom fails to afford. The most visionary enthusiast would scarce be capable of proposing such a measure, with any serious hopes at least of its ever being adopted. If it was adopted, however, Great Britain would not only be immediately freed from the whole annual expence of the peace establishment of the colonies, but might settle with them such a treaty of commerce as would effectually secure to her a free trade, more advantageous to the great body of the people, though less so to the merchants, than the monopoly which she at present enjoys. By thus parting good friends, the natural affection of the colonies to the mother country, which, perhaps, our late dissensions have well nigh extinguished, would quickly revive. It might dispose them not only to respect, for whole centuries together, that treaty of commerce which they had concluded with us at parting, but to favour us in war as well as in trade, and, instead of turbulent and factious subjects, to become our most faithful, affectionate, and generous allies; and the same sort of parental affection on the one side, and filial respect on the other, might revive between Great Britain and her colonies, which used to subsist between those of ancient Greece and the mother city from which they descended.

[MEANWHILE THE OLD WORLD HAS BEEN TRANSFORMED BY THE EMERGENCE OF THE NEW]

The discovery of America, and that of a passage to the East Indies by the Cape of Good Hope, are the two greatest and most important events recorded in the history of mankind. Their consequences have already been very great: but, in the short period of between two and three centuries which has elapsed since these discoveries were made, it is impossible that the whole extent of their consequences can have been seen. What benefits, or what misfortunes to mankind may hereafter result from those great events, no human wisdom can foresee. By uniting, in some measure, the most distant parts of the world, by enabling them to relieve one another's wants, to increase one another's enjoyments, and to encourage one another's industry, their general tendency would seem to be beneficial. To the natives, however, both of the East and West Indies, all the commercial benefits which can have resulted from those events have been sunk and lost in the dreadful misfortunes which they have occasioned. These misfortunes, however, seem to have arisen rather from accident than from any thing in the nature of those events themselves. At the particular time when these discoveries were made, the superiority of force happened to be so great on the side of the Europeans, that they were enabled to commit with impunity every sort of injustice in those remote countries. Hereafter, perhaps, the natives of those countries may grow stronger, or those of Europe may grow weaker, and the inhabitants of all the different quarters of the world may arrive at that equality of courage and force which, by inspiring mutual fear, can alone overawe the injustice of independent nations into some sort of respect for the rights of one another. But nothing seems more likely to establish this equality of force than that mutual communication of knowledge and of all sorts of improvements which an extensive commerce from all countries to all countries naturally, or orather necessarily, carries along with it. And one of the principal effects of those discoveries has been to raise the mercantile system to a degree of splendour and glory which it could never otherwise have attained to.

12. Thomas Jefferson

A Declaration by the Representatives of the United States of America
1776

For his epitaph, Thomas Jefferson (1743–1826) wished, along with his founding of the University of Virginia, to have cited two of his writings, the first being the Declaration of Independence. *The text reprinted here is his draft, which was revised somewhat before being issued. The words in italic are those which were changed, and the changes appear in small print.*

The Declaration, *by which the English colonies announced their decision to separate from England, was a quintessentially English document. Its author was an English thinker thinking on foreign soil. The intellectual and ideological tradition most frequently identified as such, in the making of the American mind, is the body of Puritan doctrines brought from England to justify and organize the building of a different kind of society in the New World. However, the philosophical and political Enlightenment was just as influential. English Puritanism framed the reasons for Massachusetts; here English and European natural rights political philosophy justifies American independence.*

Subsequent developments have tended to obscure two aspects of Jefferson's version of the Declaration *in particular. The first is its secularism, which reflects Jefferson's conviction that religion ought not to enter the realm of politics. Religion is mentioned twice in the draft, first in the claim that "nature's God" entitles the colonists to full equality with England, and a second time in the accusation that the English king has behaved worse than an "infidel." In the full phrase, "the laws of nature and of nature's God," grammatical form places nature and its God on equal footing: the laws of nature and the laws of God agree. This is orthodox deism; Jefferson's God is an impersonal deity expressed not as will or desire but through the workings of natural laws. In this connection, it is significant that the second piece of writing Jefferson wanted inscribed on his tombstone was the* Statute of Virginia for Religious Freedom *(1786).*

Another aspect of the Declaration *that later history has made especially difficult to decipher is its stance on slavery. Historians continue to debate the meaning of the paragraph (removed in revision) attacking the King for imposing upon the colonies the "piratical warfare" of the slave trade. Jefferson offers a three-part indictment. First, the king began the slave trade. Second, he insisted on continuing it. The third part, however, makes it clear that the first two do not imply that the colonies mean to cast off slavery along with English oppression. For the culminating offense is that the King has been "exciting those very people to rise in arms among us."*

The irresolvable ambiguity of this paragraph, rejecting slavery while defending the slave order, is of its time, being inspired, at once and inextricably, by the ideals of an emerging modern liberalism and the desire for state power. Combining these or juggling them, Jefferson's passage focusses on the trade in slaves. The market,

not the plantation, is the area of contention, the area in which independence is to
be won—independence meaning, among other things, exclusive power over the
plantation.

When in the course of human events it becomes necessary for one people to dissolve the political bands which have connected them with another, and to assume among powers of the earth the separate & equal station to which the laws of nature and of nature's God entitle them, a decent respect to the opinions of mankind requires that they should declare the causes which impel them to the separation.

We hold these truths to be self-evident: that all men are created equal; that they are endowed by their creator with *inherent and* inalienable rights; that among these certain are life, liberty, & the pursuit of happiness: that to secure these rights, govern-ments are instituted among men, deriving their just powers from the consent of the governed; that whenever any form of government becomes destructive of these ends, it is the right of the people to alter or abolish it, & to institute new government, laying it's foundation on such principles, & organizing it's powers in such form, as to them shall seem most likely to effect their safety & happiness. Prudence indeed will dictate that governments long established should not be changed for light & transient causes; and accordingly all experience hath shown that mankind are more disposed to suffer while evils are sufferable, than to right themselves by abolishing the forms to which they are accustomed. But when a long train of abuses & usurpations *begun at a distin-guished period and* pursuing invariably the same object, evinces a design to reduce them under absolute despotism, it is their right, it is their duty to throw off such government, & to provide new guards for their future security. Such has been the patient sufferance of these colonies; & such is now the necessity which constrains them to *expunge* their former systems of government. The history of the present king of Great Britain is a history of *unremitting* injuries & usurpations, *among which appears no solitary fact to contradict the uniform tenor of the rest but all have* in direct object the establishment of an absolute tyranny over these states. To prove this let facts by submitted to a candid world *for the truth of which we pledge a faith yet unsullied by falsehood.*

He has refused his assent to laws the most wholesome & necessary for the public good.

He has forbidden his governors to pass laws of immediate & pressing importance, unless suspended in their operation till his assent should be obtained; & when so suspended, he has utterly neglected to attend to them.

He has refused to pass other laws for the accommodation of large districts of people, unless those people would relinquish the right of representation in the legisla-ture, a right inestimable to them, & formidable to tyrants only.

He has called together legislative bodies at places unusual, uncomfortable,and distant from the depository of their public records, for the sole purpose of fatiguing them into compliance with his measures.

He has dissolved representative houses repeatedly *& continually* for opposing with manly firmness his invasions on the rights of the people.

certain

alter
repeated
all having

He has refused for a long time after such dissolutions to cause others to be elected, whereby the legislative powers, incapable of annihilation, have returned to the people at large for their exercise, the state remaining in the meantime exposed to all the dangers of invasion from without & convulsions within.

He has endeavored to prevent the population of these states; for that purpose obstructing the laws for naturalization of foreigners, refusing to pass others to encourage their migrations hither, & raising the conditions of new appropriations of lands.

obstructed / by

He has *suffered* the administration of justice *totally to cease in some of these states* refusing his assent to laws for establishing judiciary powers.

He has made *our* judges dependant on his will alone, for the tenure of their offices, & the amount & paiment of their salaries.

He has erected a multitude of new offices *by a self assumed power* and sent hither swarms of new officers to harass our people and eat out their substance.

He has kept among us in times of peace standing armies *and ships of war* without the consent of our legislatures.

He has affected to render the military independant of, & superior to the civil power.

He has combined with others to subject us to a jurisdiction foreign to our constitutions & unacknowledged by our laws, giving his assent to their acts of pretended legislation for quartering large bodies of armed troops among us; for protecting them by a mock-trial from punishment for any murders which they should commit on the inhabitants of these states; for cutting off our trade with all parts of the world; for

in many cases

imposing taxes on us without our consent; for depriving us [ ] of the benefits of trial by jury; for transporting us beyond seas to be tried for pretended offences; for abolishing the free system of English laws in a neighboring province, establishing therein an arbitrary government, and enlarging it's boundaries, so as to render it at once an

colonies

example and fit instrument for introducing the same absolute rule into these *states*; for taking away our charters, abolishing our most valuable laws, and altering fundamentally the forms of our governments; for suspending our own legislatures, & declaring themselves invested with power to legislate for us in all cases whatsoever.

by declaring us out of his protection, and waging war against us.

He has abdicated government here *withdrawing his governors, and declaring us out of his allegiance & protection.*

He has plundered our seas, ravaged our coasts, burnt our towns, & destroyed the lives of our people.

He is at this time transporting large armies of foreign mercenaries to compleat the works of death, desolation & tyranny already begun with circumstances of cruelty

scarcely paralelled in the most barbarous ages, & totally

and perfidy [ ] unworthy the head of a civilized nation.

He has constrained our fellow citizens taken captive on the high seas to bear arms against their country, to become the executioners of their friends & brethren, or to fall themselves by their hands.

excited domestic insurrection among us, & has

He has [ ] endeavored to bring on the inhabitants of our frontiers the merciless Indian savages, whose known rule of warfare is an undistinguished destruction of all ages, sexes, & conditions *of existence.*

He has incited treasonable insurrections of our fellow-citizens, with the allurements of forfeiture & confiscation of our property.

He has waged cruel war against human nature itself, violating it's most sacred rights of life and liberty in the persons of a distant people who never offended him, captivating & carrying them into slavery in another hemisphere, or to incur miserable death in their transportation thither. This piratical warfare, the opprobium of IN-FIDEL powers, is the warfare of the CHRISTIAN king of Great Britain. Determined to keep open a market where MEN should be bought & sold, he has prostituted his negative for

"The Bloody Massacre," engraved by Paul Revere in 1770.

suppressing every legislative attempt to prohibit or to restrain this execrable commerce. And that this assemblage of horrors might want no fact of distinguished die, he is now exciting those very people to rise in arms among us, and to purchase that liberty of which he has deprived them, by murdering the people on whom he also obtruded them: thus paying off former crimes committed against the LIBERTIES of one people, with crimes which he urges them to commit against the LIVES of another.

In every stage of these oppressions we have petitioned for redress in the most humble terms: our repeated petitions have been answered only by repeated injuries.

A prince whose character is thus marked by every act which may define a tyrant is unfit to be the ruler of a [ ] people *who mean to be free. Future ages will scarcely* **free** *believe that the hardiness of one man adventured, within the short compass of twelve years only, to lay a foundation so broad & so undisguised for tyranny over a people fostered & fixed in principles of freedom.*

Nor have we been wanting in attentions to our British brethren. We have warned them from time to time of attempts by their legislature to extend *a jurisdiction over* **an unwarrantable** *these our states.* We have reminded them of the circumstances of our emigration & **us** settlement here, *no one of which could warrant so strange a pretension: that these were effected at the expense of our own blood & treasure, unassisted by the wealth or the strength of Great Britain: that in constituting indeed our several forms of government, we had adopted one common king, thereby laying a foundation for perpetual league & amity with them: but that submission to their parliament was no part of our constitution, nor ever in idea, if history may be credited: and,* we [ ] appealed to their **have / and we have conjured them by /** native justice and magnanimity *as well as to* the ties of our common kindred to **would** disavow these usurpations which *were likely to* interrupt our connection and corre- **inevitably** spondence. They too have been deaf to the voice of justice & of consanguinity, *and when occasions have been given them, by the regular course of their laws, of removing* *from their councils the disturbers of our harmony, they have, by their free election, re-established them in power. At this very time too they are permitting their chief magistrate to send over not only soldiers of our common blood, but Scotch & foreign mercenaries to invade & destroy us. These facts have given the last stab to agonizing affection, and manly spirit bids us to renounce forever these unfeeling brethren. We must endeavor to forget our former love for them, and hold them as we hold the rest of mankind, enemies in war, in peace friends. We might have been a free and a great people together; but a communication of grandeur & of freedom it seems is below their dignity. Be it so, since they will have it. The road to happiness & to glory is open to us too. We will tread it apart from them, and* acquiesce in the necessity which denounces our *eternal* separation [ ]!

We must therefore

and hold them as we hold the rest of mankind, enemies in war, in peace friends.

We therefore the representatives of the United States of America in General Congress assembled do in the name & by authority of the good people of these *states reject & renounce all allegiance & subjection to the kings of Great Britain & all others who may hereafter claim by, through or under them: we utterly dissolve all political connection which may heretofore have subsisted between us & the people or parliament of Great Britain: & finally we do assert & declare these colonies to be free & independent states,* & that as free & independent states, they have full power to levy war, conclude peace, contract alliances, establish commerce, & to do all other acts & things which independent states may of right do.

And for the support of this declaration we mutually pledge to each other our lives, our fortunes, & our sacred honor.

We therefore the representatives of the United States of America in General Congress assembled, appealing to the supreme judge of the world for the rectitude of our intentions, do in the name, & by the authority of the good people of these colonies, solemnly publish & declare that these united colonies are & of right ought to be free & independent states; that they are absolved from all allegiance to the British crown, and that all political connection between them & the state of Great Britain is, & ought to be, totally dissolved; & that as free & independent states they have full power to levy war, conclude peace, contract alliances, establish commerce & to do all other acts & things which independant states may of right do.

And for the support of this declaration, with a firm reliance on the protection of divine providence we mutually pledge to each other our lives, our fortunes, & our sacred honor.

The Declaration thus signed on the 4th, on paper was engrossed on parchment, & signed again on the 2d. of August.

13. Thomas Jefferson

Notes on the State of Virginia, Query 19
1781

In chapter 12, we reprint the longest entry in Jefferson's Notes on the State of Virginia, *the account of America's natural environmnent. The* Notes *were written on demand, in response to a questionnaire which dictated the Queries. The brevity of the answer to Query 19, in contrast to the length of that to Query 6 on the topic of "mines and other subterraneous riches; its trees, plants, fruits, etc.," makes clear, before one starts reading, Jefferson's lack of enthusiasm for "manufactures, commerce, interior and exterior trade." His personal situation as a prominent member of the Virginia plantation aristocracy (owner of several plantations totalling about 10,000 acres and worked by nearly 200 slaves) does not sufficiently explain this stance, since the plantations, which produced cash crops, involved Jefferson as much with commerce as with agriculture. Rather, on the evidence of his immediate passage in the text from the question of commerce and manufacturing to a discussion of the social organization they imply, Jefferson's preference for agriculture appears to depend as much on what it prevents as on what it produces: agriculture needs to be the occupation of the majority in order to prevent the rise of social classes. Far from representing himself or Virginia in this Query, he projects "labour in the earth" in the ideal image of its practice in Pennsylvania or Massachusetts: one farmer, one farm.*

The present state of manufactures, commerce, interior and exterior trade?

We never had an interior trade of any importance. Our exterior commerce has suffered very much from the beginning of the present contest. During this time we have manufactured within our families the most necessary articles of cloathing. Those of cotton will bear some comparison with the same kinds of manufacture in Europe; but those of wool, flax and hemp are very coarse, unsightly, and unpleasant: and such is our attachment to agriculture, and such our preference for foreign manufactures, that be it wise or unwise, our people will certainly return as soon as they can, to the raising raw materials, and exchanging them for finer manufactures than they are able to execute themselves.

The political œconomists of Europe have established it as a principle that every state should endeavour to manufacture for itself: and this principle, like many others, we transfer to America, without calculating the difference of circumstance which should often produce a difference of result. In Europe the lands are either cultivated, or locked up against the cultivator. Manufacture must therefore be resorted to of necessity not of choice, to support the surplus of their people. But we have an immensity of land courting the industry of the husbandman. Is it best then that all our citizens should be employed in its improvement, or that one half should be called off from that to exercise manufactures and handicraft arts for the other? Those who labour in the earth are the chosen people of God, if ever he had a chosen people, whose breasts he has made his peculiar deposit for substantial and genuine virtue. It is the focus in which he keeps alive that sacred fire, which otherwise might escape from the face of the earth. Corruption of morals in the mass of cultivators is a phænomenon of which no age nor nation has furnished an example. It is the mark set on those, who not looking up to heaven, to their own soil and industry, as does the husbandman, for their subsistance, depend for it on the casualties and caprice of customers. Dependance begets subservience and venality, suffocates the germ of virtue, and prepares fit tools for the designs of ambition. This, the natural progress and consequence of the arts, has sometimes perhaps been retarded by accidental circumstances: but, generally speaking, the proportion which the aggregate of the other classes of citizens bears in any state to that of its husbandmen, is the proportion of its unsound to its healthy parts, and is a good-enough barometer whereby to measure its degree of corruption. While we have land to labour then, let us never wish to see our citizens occupied at a work-bench, or twirling a distaff. Carpenters, masons, smiths, are wanting in husbandry: but, for the general operations of manufacture, let our work-shops remain in Europe. It is better to carry provisions and materials to workmen there, than bring them to the provisions and materials, and with them their manners and principles. The loss by the transportation of commodities across the Atlantic will be made up in happiness and permanence of government. The mobs of great cities add just so much to the support of pure government, as sores do to the strength of the human body. It is the manners and spirit of a people which preserve a republic in vigour. A degeneracy in these is a canker which soon eats to the heart of its laws and constitution.

14. Thomas Paine

An Occasional Letter on the Female Sex
1775

By his own description, Paine's concept of the republic was shaped less by political theories than by "moral and philosophical principles" (see chapter 9 and The Age of Reason), developed in the context of a life lived more often among the low born than the high. His republicanism differed significantly thereby from the combination of universal rights and social hierarchy envisioned by Jefferson, and from Franklin's open meritocracy. Paine represents the small minority among the Revolutionaries who believed themselves to be building a more or less egalitarian society. One implication of his rejection of social hierarchy is the advocacy of the rights of women, set out in this letter.

O Woman! lovely Woman!
Nature made thee to temper man,
We had been Brutes without you.
                              Otway.

If we take a survey of ages and of countries, we shall find the women, almost—without exception—at all times and in all places, adored and oppressed. Man, who has never neglected an opportunity of exerting his power, in paying homage to their beauty, has always availed himself of their weakness. He has been at once their tyrant and their slave.

Nature herself, in forming beings so susceptible and tender, appears to have been more attentive to their charms than to their happiness. Continually surrounded with griefs and fears, the women more than share all our miseries, and are besides subjected to ills which are peculiarly their own. They cannot be the means of life without exposing themselves to the loss of it; every revolution which they undergo, alters their health, and threatens their existence. Cruel distempers attack their beauty—and the hour, which confirms their release from those, is perhaps the most melancholy of their lives. It robs them of the most essential characteristic of their sex. They can then only hope for protection from the humiliating claims of pity, or the feeble voice of gratitude.

Society, instead of alleviating their condition, is to them the source of new miseries. More than one half of the globe is covered with savages; and among all these people women are completely wretched. Man, in a state of barbarity, equally cruel and indolent, active by necessity, but naturally inclined to repose, is acquainted with little more than the physical effects of love; and, having none of those moral ideas which only can soften the empire of force, he is led to consider it as his supreme law, subjecting to his despotism those whom reason had made his equal, but whose imbecility betrayed them to his strength. "Nothing" (says Professor Miller, speaking of the women of barbarous nations) "can exceed the dependence and subjection in which they are kept, or the toil and drudgery which they are obliged to undergo. The husband, when he is not engaged in some warlike exercise, indulges himself in idleness, and devolves upon his wife the whole burden of his domestic affairs. He disdains to assist her in any of those servile employments. She sleeps in a different bed, and is seldom permitted to have any conversation or correspondence with him."

The women among the Indians of America are what the Helots were among the Spartans, a vanquished people, obliged to toil for their conquerors. Hence on the banks of the Oroonoko, we have seen mothers slaying their daughters out of compassion, and smothering them in the hour of their birth. They consider this barbarous pity as a virtue.

> "The men (says Commodore Byron, in his account of the inhabitants of South-America) exercise a most despotic authority over their wives, whom they consider in the same view they do any other part of their property, and dispose of them accordingly: Even their common treatment of them is cruel; for though the toil and hazard of procuring food lies entirely on the women, yet they are not suffered to touch any part of it till the husband is satisfied; and then he assigns them their portion, which is generally very scanty, and such as he has not a stomach for himself."

Among the nations of the East we find another kind of despotism and dominion prevail—the Seraglio, and the domestic servitude of woman, authorised by the manners and established by the laws. In Turkey, in Persia, in India, in Japan, and over the vast empire of China, one half of the human species is oppressed by the other.

The excess of oppression in those countries springs from the excess of love.

All Asia is covered with prisons, where beauty in bondage waits the caprices of a master. The multitude of women there assembled have no will, no inclinations but his: Their triumphs are only for a moment; and their rivalry, their hate, and their animosities, continue till death. There the lovely sex are obliged to repay even their servitude with the most tender affections; or, what is still more mortifying, with the counterfeit of an affection, which they do not feel: There the most gloomy tyranny has subjected them to creatures, who, being of neither sex, are a dishonour to both: There, in short, their education tends only to debase them; their virtues are forced; their very pleasures are involuntary and joyless; and after an existence of a few years—till the bloom of youth is over—their period of neglect commences, which is long and dreadful. In the temperate latitude where the climates, giving less ardour to passion, leave more confidence in virtue, the women have not been deprived of their liberty, but a severe legislation has, at all times, kept them in a state of dependence. One while, they were confined to their own apartments, and debarred at once from business and amusement; at other times, a tedious guardianship defrauded their hearts, and insulted their understandings. Affronted in one country by polygamy, which gives them their rivals for their inseparable companions; inslaved in another by indissoluble ties, which often join the gentle to the rude, and sensibility to brutality: Even in countries where they may be esteemed most happy, constrained in their desires in the disposal of their goods, robbed of freedom of will by the laws, the slaves of opinion, which rules them with absolute sway, and construes the slightest appearances into guilt; surrounded on all sides by judges, who are at once tyrants and their seducers, and who, after having prepared their faults, punish every lapse with dishonour—nay, usurp the right of degrading them on suspicion! Who does not feel for the tender sex? Yet such, I am sorry to say, is the lot of woman over the whole earth. Man with regard to them, in all climates, and in all ages, has been either an insensible husband or an oppressor; but they have sometimes experienced the cold and deliberate oppression of pride, and sometimes the violent and terrible tyranny of jealousy. When they are not beloved they are nothing; and, when they are, they are tormented. They have almost equal cause to be afraid of indifference and of love. Over three quarters of the globe nature has placed them between contempt and misery.

"The melting desires, or the fiery passions," says Professor Ferguson, "which in one climate take place between the sexes, are, in another, changed into a sober consideration, or a patience of mutual disgust. This change is remarked in crossing the Mediterranean, in following the course of the Mississippi, in ascending the mountains of Caucasus, and in passing from the Alps and the Pyrenees to the shores of the Baltic.

"The burning ardours and torturing jealousies of the Seraglio and Harem, which have reigned so long in Asia and Africa, and which, in the southern parts of Europe, have scarcely given way to the differences of religion and civil establishments, are found, however, with an abatement of heat in the climate, to be more easily changed, in one latitude, into a temporary passion, which engrosses the mind without infeebling it, and which excites to romantic atchievments. By a farther progress to the north it is changed into a spirit of gallantry, which employs the wit and fancy more than the heart, which prefers intrigue to enjoyment, and substitutes affection and vanity where sentiment and desire have failed. As it departs from the sun, the same passion is farther composed into a habit of domestic connection, or frozen into a state of insensibility, under which the sexes at freedom scarcely choose to unite their society."

Even among people where beauty received the highest homage, we find men who would deprive the sex of every kind of reputation: "The most virtuous woman," says a celebrated Greek, "is she who is least talked of." That morose man, while he imposes duties upon women, would deprive them of the sweets of public esteem, and in exacting virtues from them, would make it a crime to aspire at honour.

If a woman were to defend the cause of her sex, she might address him in the following manner:

"How great is your injustice? If we have an equal right with you to virtue, why should we not have an equal right to praise? The public esteem ought to wait upon merit. Our duties are different from yours, but they are not therefore less difficult to fulfil, or of less consequence to society: They are the fountains of your felicity, and the sweetness of life. We are wives and mothers. 'Tis we who form the union and the cordiality of families: 'Tis we who soften that savage rudeness which considers every-thing as due to force, and which would involve man with man in eternal war. We cultivate in you that humanity which makes you feel for the misfortunes of others, and our tears forewarn you of your own danger. Nay, you cannot be ignorant that we have need of courage not less than you: More feeble in ourselves, we have perhaps more trials to encounter. Nature assails us with sorrow, law and custom press us with constraint, and sensibility and virtue alarm us with their continual conflict. Sometimes also the name of citizen demands from us the tribute of fortitude. When you offer your blood to the State think that it is ours. In giving it our sons and our husbands we give more than ourselves. You can only die on the field of battle, but we have the misfortune to survive those whom we love most. Alas! while your ambitious vanity is unceasingly labouring to cover the earth with statues, with monuments, and with inscriptions to eternize, if possible, your names, and give yourselves an existence, when this body is no more, why must we be condemned to live and to die unknown? Would that the grave and eternal forgetfulness should be our lot. Be not our tyrants in all: Permit our names to be sometimes pronounced beyond the narrow circle in which we live: Permit friendship, or at least love, to inscribe its emblems on the tomb where our ashes repose; and deny us not that public esteem which, after the esteem of one's self, is the sweetest reward of well doing."

All men, however, it must be owned, have not been equally unjust to their fair companions. In some countries public honours have been paid to women. Art has erected them monuments. Eloquence has celebrated their virtues, and History has collected whatever could adorn their character.

15. Thomas Paine

The American Crisis, #1
1776

The first of the thirteen essays that make up The American Crisis *(three more were appended) was written late in 1776 as the initial push of the colonial army under George Washington appeared to have been halted. The remarkable achievement of this essay is to project, in the face of British troops, not an outraged English colonist but an American fighting for the freedom of his country. Invoking the example of frontiersmen fighting the Indians for the land, Paine creates by this analogy the American with whose coming the colonial era closes. The English and the Indians are henceforth invaders, and America belongs to Americans who are neither, but a new race altogether.*

December 19, 1776

These are the times that try men's souls: The summer soldier and the sunshine patriot will, in this crisis, shrink from the service of his country; but he that stands it NOW, deserves the love and thanks of man and woman. Tyranny, like hell, is not easily conquered; yet we have this consolation with us, that the harder the conflict, the more glorious the triumph. What we obtain too cheap, we esteem too lightly:—'Tis dearness only that gives every thing its value. Heaven knows how to set a proper price upon its goods; and it would be strange indeed, if so celestial an article as FREEDOM should not be highly rated. Britain, with an army to enforce her tyranny, has declared, that she has a right (*not only to* TAX) but "*to* BIND *us in* ALL CASES WHAT-SOEVER," and if being *bound in that manner* is not slavery, then is there not such a thing as slavery upon earth. Even the expression is impious, for so unlimited a power can belong only to GOD.

Whether the Independence of the Continent was declared too soon, or delayed too long, I will not now enter into as an argument; my own simple opinion is, that had it been eight months earlier, it would have been much better. We did not make a proper use of last winter, neither could we, while we were in a dependent state. However, the fault, if it were one, was all our own; we have none to blame but ourselves.[10] But no great deal is lost yet; all that Howe has been doing for this month past is rather a ravage than a conquest, which the spirit of the Jersies a year ago would have quickly repulsed, and which time and a little resolution will soon recover.

I have as little superstition in me as any man living, but my secret opinion has ever been, and still is, that GOD almighty will not give up a people to military destruction, or leave them unsupportedly to perish, who had so earnestly and so repeatedly sought to avoid the calamities of war, by every decent method which wisdom could invent. Neither have I so much of the infidel in me, as to suppose, that HE has relinquished the government of the world, and given us up to the care of devils; and as I do not, I cannot see on what grounds the king of Britain can look up to heaven for help against us: A common murderer, a highwayman, or a housebreaker, has as good a pretence as he.

'Tis surprising to see how rapidly a panic will sometimes run through a country. All nations and ages have been subject to them: Britain has trembled like an ague at the report of a French fleet of flat bottomed boats; and in the fourteenth century the whole English army, after ravaging the kingdom of France, was driven back like men petrified with fear; and this brave exploit was performed by a few broken forces collected and headed by a woman, Joan of Arc. Would, that Heaven might inspire some Jersey maid to spirit up her countrymen, and save her fair fellow-sufferers from ravage and ravishment! Yet panics, in some cases, have their uses; they produce as much good as hurt. Their duration is always short; the mind soon grows thro' them, and acquires a firmer habit than before. But their peculiar advantage is, that they are the touchstones of sincerity and hypocrisy, and bring things and men to light, which might otherwise have lain for ever undiscovered. In fact, they have the same effect on

---

10. "The present winter" (meaning the last) "is worth an age, if rightly employed, but if lost, or neglected, the whole Continent will partake of the evil; and there is no punishment that man does not deserve, be he who, or what, or where he will, that may be the means of sacrificing a season so precious and useful." [Paine's note.]

secret traitors, which an imaginary apparition would upon a private murderer. They sift out the hidden thoughts of man, and hold them up in public to the world. Many a disguised Tory has lately shewn his head, that shall penitentially solemnize with curses the day on which Howe arrived upon the Delaware.

As I was with the troops at fort Lee, and marched with them to the edge of Pennsylvania, I am well acquainted with many circumstances, which those, who lived at a distance, know but little or nothing of. Our situation there was exceedingly cramped, the place being on a narrow neck of land between the North river and the Hackensack. Our force was inconsiderable, being not one fourth so great as Howe could bring against us. We had no army at hand to have relieved the garrison, had we shut ourselves up and stood on the defence. Our ammunition, light artillery, and the best part of our stores, had been removed upon the apprehension that Howe would endeavour to penetrate the Jersies, in which case fort Lee could be of no use to us; for it must occur to every thinking man, whether in the army or not, that these kind of field forts are only for temporary purposes, and last in use no longer than the enemy directs his force against the particular object, which such forts are raised to defend. Such was our situation and condition at fort Lee on the morning of the 20th of November, when an officer arrived with information, that the enemy with 200 boats had landed about seven or eight miles above: Major General Green, who commanded the garrison, immediately ordered them under arms, and sent express to his Excellency General Washington at the town of Hackensack, distant by the way of the ferry six miles. Our first object was to secure the bridge over the Hackensack, which laid up the river between the enemy and us, about six miles from us and three from them. General Washington arrived in about three quarters of an hour, and marched at the head of the troops towards the bridge, which place I expected we should have a brush for; however they did not chuse to dispute it with us, and the greatest part of our troops went over the bridge, the rest over the ferry, except some which passed at a mill on a small creek, between the bridge and the ferry, and made their way through some marshy grounds up to the town of Hackensack, and there passed the river. We brought off as much baggage as the waggons could contain, the rest was lost. The simple object was to bring off the garrison, and to march them on till they could be strengthened by the Jersey or Pennsylvania militia, so as to be enabled to make a stand. We staid four days at Newark, collected in our outposts with some of the Jersey militia, and marched out twice to meet the enemy on information of their being advancing, though our numbers were greatly inferiour to theirs. Howe, in my little opinion, committed a great error in generalship, in not throwing a body of forces off from Staaten Island through Amboy, by which means he might have seized all our stores at Brunswick, and intercepted our march into Pennsylvania: But, if we believe the power of hell to be limited, we must likewise believe that their agents are under some providential controul.

I shall not now attempt to give all the particulars of our retreat to the Delaware; suffice it for the present to say, that both officers and men, though greatly harassed and fatigued, frequently without rest, covering, or provision, the inevitable consequences of a long retreat, bore it with a manly and a martial spirit. All their wishes were one, which was, that the country would turn out and help them to drive the enemy back. Voltaire has remarked, that king William never appeared to full advantage but in difficulties and in action; the same remark may be made on General Washington, for the character fits him. There is a natural firmness in some minds which cannot be unlocked by triffles, but which, when unlocked, discovers a cabinet of fortitude; and I reckon it among those kind of public blessings, which we do not immediately see, that GOD hath blest him with uninterrupted health, and given him a mind that can even flourish upon care.

I shall conclude this paper with some miscellaneous remarks on the state of our affairs; and shall begin with asking the following question, Why is it that the enemy hath left the New-England provinces, and made these middle ones the seat of war? The answer is easy: New-England is not infested with Tories, and we are. I have been tender in raising the cry against these men, and used numberless arguments to shew them their danger, but it will not do to sacrifice a world to either their folly or their baseness. The period is now arrived, in which either they or we must change our sentiments, or one or both must fall. And what is a Tory? Good GOD! what is he? I should not be afraid to go with a hundred Whigs against a thousand Tories, were they to attempt to get into arms. Every Tory is a coward, for a servile, slavish, self-interested fear is the foundation of Toryism; and a man under such influence, though he may be cruel, never can be brave.

But before the line of irrecoverable separation be drawn between us, let us reason the matter together: Your conduct is an invitation to the enemy, yet not one in a thousand of you has heart enough to join him. Howe is as much deceived by you as the American cause is injured by you. He expects you will all take up arms, and flock to his standard with muskets on your shoulders. Your opinions are of no use to him, unless you support him personally; for 'tis soldiers, and not Tories, that he wants.

I once felt all that kind of anger, which a man ought to feel, against the mean principles that are held by the Tories: A noted one, who kept a tavern at Amboy, was standing at his door, with as pretty a child in his hand, about eight or nine years old, as most I ever saw, and after speaking his mind as freely as he thought was prudent, finished with this unfatherly expression, *"Well! give me peace in my day."* Not a man lives on the Continent but fully believes that a seperation must some time or other finally take place, and a generous parent would have said, *"If there must be trouble, let it be in my day, that my child may have peace;"* and this single reflection, well applied, is sufficient to awaken every man to duty. Not a place upon earth might be so happy as America. Her situation is remote from all the wrangling world, and she has nothing to do but to trade with them. A man may easily distinguish in himself between temper and principle, and I am as confident, as I am that GOD governs the world, that America will never be happy till she gets clear of foreign dominion. Wars, without ceasing, will break out till that period arrives, and the Continent must in the end be conqueror; for, though the flame of liberty may sometimes cease to shine, the coal never can expire.

America did not, nor does not, want force; but she wanted a proper application of that force. Wisdom is not the purchase of a day, and it is no wonder that we should err at first sitting off. From an excess of tenderness, we were unwilling to raise an army, and trusted our cause to the temporary defence of a well meaning militia. A summer's experience has now taught us better; yet with those troops, while they were collected, we were able to set bounds to the progress of the enemy, and, thank GOD! they are again assembling. I always considered a militia as the best troops in the world for a sudden exertion, but they will not do for a long campaign. Howe, it is probable, will make an attempt on this city; should he fail on this side the Delaware, he is ruined; if he succeeds, our cause is not ruined. He stakes all on his side against a part of ours; admitting he succeeds, the consequence will be, that armies from both ends of the Continent will march to assist their suffering friends in the middle States; for he cannot go every where, it is impossible. I consider Howe as the greatest enemy the Tories have; he is bringing a war into their country, which, had it not been for him and partly for themselves, they had been clear of. Should he now be expelled, I wish, with all the devotion of a Christian, that the names of Whig and Tory may never more be mentioned; but should the Tories give him encouragement to come, or assistance if he come, I as sincerely wish that our next year's arms may expell them from the Continent, and the Congress appropriate their possessions to the relief of those who have suffered in well doing. A single successful battle next year will settle the whole. America could carry on a two years war by the confiscation of the property of disaffected persons, and be made happy by their expulsion. Say not that this is revenge, call it rather the soft resentment of a suffering people, who, having no object in view but the GOOD of ALL, have staked their OWN ALL upon a seemingly doubtful event. Yet it is folly to argue against determined hardness; eloquence may strike the ear, and the language of sorrow draw forth the tear of compassion, but nothing can reach the heart that is steeled with prejudice.

Quitting this class of men, I turn with the warm ardour of a friend to those who have nobly stood, and are yet determined to stand the matter out: I call not upon a few, but upon all; not on THIS State or THAT State, but on EVERY State; up and help us; lay your shoulders to the wheel; better have too much force than too little, when so great an object is at stake. Let it be told to the future world, that in the depth of winter, when nothing but hope and virtue could survive, that the city and the country, alarmed at one common danger, came forth to meet and to repulse it. Say not, that thousands are gone, turn out your tens of thousands; throw not the burthen of the day upon Providence, but *"shew your faith by your works,"* that GOD may bless you. It matters not where you live, or what rank of life you hold, the evil or the blessing will reach you all. The far and the near, the home counties and the back, the rich and the poor, shall suffer or rejoice alike. The heart that feels not now, is dead: The blood of his children shall curse his cowardice, who shrinks back at a time when a little might have saved the whole, and made *them* happy. I love the man that can smile in trouble, that can gather strength from distress, and grow brave by reflection. 'Tis the business of little minds to shrink; but he whose heart is firm, and whose conscience approves his conduct, will pursue his principles unto death. My own line of reasoning is to myself as strait and clear as a ray of light. Not all the treasures of the world, so far as I believe, could have induced me to support an offensive war, for I think it murder; but if a thief break into my house, burn and destroy my property, and kill or threaten to kill me, or those that are in it, and to *"bind me in all cases whatsoever,"* to his absolute will, am I to suffer it? What signifies it to me, whether he who does it, is a king or a common man; my countryman or not my countryman? whether it is done by an individual villain, or an army of them? If we reason to the root of things we shall find no difference; neither can any just cause be assigned why we should punish in the one case, and pardon in the other. Let them call me rebel, and welcome, I feel no concern from it; but I should suffer the misery of devils, were I to make a whore of my soul by swearing allegiance to one, whose character is that of a sottish, stupid, stubborn, worthless, brutish man. I conceive likewise a horrid idea in receiving mercy from a being, who at the last day shall be shrieking to the rocks and mountains to cover him, and fleeing with terror from the orphan, the widow and the slain of America.

There are cases which cannot be overdone by language, and this is one. There are persons too who see not the full extent of the evil that threatens them; they solace themselves with hopes that the enemy, if they succeed, will be merciful. It is the madness of folly to expect mercy from those who have refused to do justice; and even mercy, where conquest is the object, is only a trick of war: The cunning of the fox is as murderous as the violence of the wolfe; and we ought to guard equally against both. Howe's first object is partly by threats and partly by promises, to terrify or seduce the people to deliver up their arms, and receive mercy. The ministry recommended the same plan to Gage, and this is what the Tories call making their peace; *"a peace which passeth all understanding"* indeed! A peace which would be the immediate forerunner of a worse ruin than any we have yet thought of. Ye men of Pennsylvania, do reason upon those things! Were the back counties to give up their arms, they would fall an easy prey to the Indians, who are all armed: This perhaps is what some Tories would not be sorry for. Were the home counties to deliver up their arms, they would be exposed to the resentment of the back counties, who would then have it in their power to chastise their defection at pleasure. And were any one State to give up its arms, THAT State must be garrisoned by all Howe's army of Britons and Hessians to preserve it from the anger of the rest. Mutual fear is a principal link in the chain of mutual love, and woe be to that State that breaks the compact. Howe is mercifully inviting you to barbarous destruction, and men must be either rogues or fools that will not see it. I dwell not upon the vapours of imagination; I bring reason to your ears; and in language, as plain as A, B, C, hold up truth to your eyes.

I thank GOD that I fear not. I see no real cause for fear. I know our situation well, and can see the way out of it. While our army was collected, Howe dared not risk a battle, and it is no credit to him that he decamped from the White Plains, and waited a mean opportunity to ravage the defenceless Jersies; but it is great credit to us, that, with an handful of men, we sustained an orderly retreat for near an hundred miles, brought off our ammunition, all our field-pieces, the greatest part of our stores, and had four rivers to pass. None can say that our retreat was precipitate, for we were near three weeks in performing it, that the country might have time to come in. Twice we marched back to meet the enemy and remained out till dark. The sign of fear was not seen in our camp, and had not some of the cowardly and disaffected inhabitants spread false alarms thro' the country, the Jersies had never been ravaged. Once more we are again collected and collecting; our new army at both ends of the Continent is recruiting fast, and we shall be able to open the next campaign with sixty thousand men, well armed and cloathed. This is our situation, and who will may know it. By perseverance and fortitude we have the prospect of a glorious issue; by cowardice and submission, the sad choice of a variety of evils—a ravaged country—a depopulated city—habitations without safety, and slavery without hope—our homes turned into barracks and baudy-houses for Hessians, and a future race to provide for whose fathers we shall doubt of. Look on this picture, and weep over it!—and if there yet remains one thoughtless wretch who believes it not, let him suffer it unlamented.

16. Judith Sargent Murray

On the Equality of the Sexes
1779

Because as a girl she had been permitted to attend her brother's lessons, Judith Sargent Murray (1751–1820) was unusually well educated for a woman of her time. Her feminist manifesto, the first in American writing, reveals her sophistication in the philosophy and rhetoric of the Enlightenment. She claims for women the same universal potential for individual growth and distinction as men, recognizing differences among individuals but not groups. She propounds a classic liberal argument foreshadowing Mary Wollstonecraft (whose Vindication of the Rights of Women *was published thirteen years later), refusing any notion that women are innately different in their mental capacities and attributes. She thus disagrees with other feminists who argue for the rights of women on the ground that their different qualities and contributions deserve equal social and political status. Where differences exist, Murray strives to explain them away. If women gossip more than men, for instance, this is, for her, testimony to women's powers of imagination having been deformed by the constraints of a conventional female existence. What she wants for women is the opportunity men have to be each one an individual.*

That minds are not alike, full well I know,
This truth each day's experience will show;
To heights surprising some great spirits soar,
With inborn strength mysterious depths explore;
Their eager gaze surveys the path of light,
Confessed it stood to Newton's piercing sight.
   Deep science, like a bashful maid retires,
And but the *ardent* breast her worth inspires;
By perserverance the coy fair is won.
And Genius, led by Study, wears the crown.
   But some there are who wish not to improve,
Who never can the path of knowledge love,
Whose soul's almost with the dull body one,
With anxious care each mental pleasure shun;
Weak is the leveled, enervated mind,
And but while here to vegetate designed.
The torpid spirit mingling with its clod,
Can scarcely boast its origin from God;
Stupidly dull—they move progressing on—
They eat, and drink, and all their work is done.

While others, emulous of sweet applause,
Industrious seek for each event a cause,
Tracing the hidden springs whence knowledge flows,
Which nature all in beauteous order shows.
   Yet cannot I their sentiments imbibe,
Who this distinction to the sex ascribe,
As if a woman's form must needs enroll,
A weak, a servile, an inferior soul;
And that the guise of man must still proclaim,
Greatness of mind, and him, to be the same:
Yet as the hours revolve fair proofs arise,
Which the bright wreath of growing fame supplies;
And in past times some men have *sunk* so *low*,
That female records nothing *less* can show.
But imbecility is still confined,
And by the lordly sex to us consigned;
They rob us of the power t' improve,
And then declare we only trifles love;
Yet haste the era, when the world shall know,
That such distinctions only dwell below;
The soul unfettered, to no sex confined,
Was for the abodes of cloudless day designed.
   Meantime we emulate their manly fires,
Though erudition all their thoughts inspires,
Yet nature with *equality* imparts,
And *noble passions*, swell e'en *female hearts*.

Is it upon mature consideration we adopt the idea that nature is thus partial in her distributions? Is it indeed a fact that she hath yielded to one-half of the human species so unquestionable a mental superiority? I know that to both sexes elevated understandings, and the reverse, are common. But, suffer me to ask in what the minds of females are so notoriously deficient or unequal. May not the intellectual powers be ranged under these four heads—imagination, reason, memory and judgment? The province of imagination hath long since been surrendered up to us, and we have been crowned undoubted sovereigns of the regions of fancy. Invention is perhaps the most arduous effort of the mind; this branch of imagination hath been particularly ceded to us, and we have been time out of mind invested with that creative faculty. Observe the variety of fashions (here I bar the contemptuous smile) which distinguish and adorn the female world; how continually are they changing, insomuch that they almost render the wise man's assertion problematical, and we are ready to say, *there is something new under the sun*. Now what a playfulness, what an exuberance of fancy, what strength of inventive imagination, doth this continual variation discover? Again, it hath been observed that if the turpitude of the conduct of our sex hath been ever so enormous, so extremely ready are we, that the very first thought presents us with an apology so plausible as to produce our actions even in an amiable light. Another instance of our creative powers is our talent for slander; how ingenious are we at inventive scandal! what a formidable story can we in a moment fabricate merely from the force of a prolific imagination! how many reputations, in the fertile brain of a female, have been utterly despoiled! how industrious are we at improving a hint! suspicion how easily do we convert into conviction, and conviction, embellished by the power of eloquence, stalks abroad to the surprise and confusion of unsuspecting innocence. Perhaps it will be asked if I furnish these facts as instances of excellency in our sex. Certainly not; but as proofs of a creative faculty, of a lively imagination. Assuredly, great activity of mind is thereby discovered, and was this activity properly directed, what beneficial effects would follow. Is the needle and kitchen sufficient to employ the operations of a soul thus organized? I should conceive not. Nay, it is a truth that those very departments leave the intelligent principle vacant, and at liberty for speculation. Are we deficient in reason? we can only reason from what we know, and if an opportunity of acquiring knowledge hath been denied us, the inferiority of our sex cannot fairly be deduced from thence.

Memory, I believe, will be allowed us in common, since every one's experience must testify that a loquacious old woman is as frequently met with as a communicative old man; their subjects are alike drawn from the fund of other times, and the transactions of their youth or of maturer life entertain, or perhaps fatigue you, in the evening of their lives. "But our judgment is not so strong—we do not distinguish so well."—Yet it may be questioned, from what doth this superiority, in this determining faculty of the soul, proceed? May we not trace its source in the difference of education, and continued advantages? Will it be said that the judgment of a male of two years old is more sage than that of a female's of the same age? I believe the reverse is generally observed to be true. But from that period what partiality! how is the one exalted, and the other depressed, by the contrary modes of education which are adopted! the one is taught to aspire, and the other is early confined and limited. As their years increase, the sister must be wholly domesticated, while the brother is led by the hand through all the flowery paths of science. Grant that their minds are by nature equal, yet who shall wonder at the *apparent* superiority, if indeed custom becomes *second nature*; nay, if it taketh place of nature, and that it doth the experience of each day will evince. At length arrived at womanhood, the uncultivated fair one feels a void, which the employments allotted her are by no means capable of filling. What can she do? to books she may not apply; or if she doth, *to those only of the novel kind*, lest she merit the appellation of a *learned lady*; and what ideas have been affixed to this term, the observation of many can testify. Fashion, scandal, and sometimes what is still more reprehensible, are then called in to her relief; and who can say to what lengths the liberties she takes may proceed.

Meantime she herself is most unhappy; she feels the want of a cultivated mind. Is she single, she in vain seeks to fill up time from sexual employments or amusements. Is she united to a person whose soul nature made equal to her own, education hath set him so far above her that in those entertainments which are productive of such rational felicity, she is not qualified to accompany him. She experiences a mortifying consciousness of inferiority, which embitters every enjoyment. Doth the person to whom her adverse fate hath consigned her possess a mind incapable of improvement, she is equally wretched, in being so closely connected with an individual whom she cannot but despise. Now, was she permitted the same instructors as her brother (with an eye however to their particular departments), for the employment of a rational mind an ample field would be opened. In astronomy she might catch a glimpse of the immensity of the Deity, and thence she would form amazing conceptions of the august and supreme Intelligence. In geography she would admire Jehovah in the midst of his benevolence: thus adapting this globe to the various wants and amusements of its inhabitants. In natural philosophy she would adore the infinite majesty of heaven, clothed in condescension; and as she traversed the reptile world, she would hail the goodness of a creating God. A mind thus filled would have little room for the trifles with which our sex are, with too much justice, accused of amusing themselves; and they would thus be rendered fit companions for those, who should one day wear them as their crown. Fashions, in their variety, would then give place to conjectures which might perhaps conduce to the improvement of the literary world; and there would be no leisure for slander or detraction. Reputation would not then be blasted, but serious speculations would occupy the lively imaginations of the sex. Unnecessary visits would be precluded, and that custom would only be indulged by way of relaxation, or to answer the demands of consanguinity and friendship. Females would become discreet, their judgments would be invigorated, and their partners for life being circumspectly chosen, an unhappy Hymen would then be as rare as is now the reverse.

Will it be urged that those acquirements would supersede our domestic duties? I answer that every requisite in female economy is easily attained; and, with truth I can add, that when once attained, they require no further *mental attention*. Nay, while we are pursuing the needle or the superintendency of the family, I repeat that our minds are at full liberty for reflection; that imagination may exert itself in full vigor; and that if a just foundation is early laid, our ideas will then be worthy of rational beings. If we were industrious, we might easily find time to arrange them upon paper, or should avocations press too hard for such an indulgence, the hours allotted for conversation would at least become more refined and rational. Should it still be vociferated, "Your domestic employments are sufficient"—I would calmly ask, is it reasonable that a candidate for immortality, for the joys of heaven, an intelligent being, who is to spend an eternity in contemplating the works of Deity, should at present be so degraded as to be allowed no other ideas than those which are suggested by the mechanism of a pudding or the sewing the seams of a garment? Pity that all such censurers of female improvement do not go one step further and deny their future existence; to be consistent they surely ought.

Yes, ye lordly, ye haughty sex, our souls are by nature *equal* to yours; the same breath of God animates, enlivens, and invigorates us; and that we are not fallen lower than yourselves, let those witness who have greatly towered above the various discouragements by which they have been so heavily oppressed; and though I am unacquainted with the list of celebrated characters on either side, yet from the observations I have made in the contracted circle in which I have moved, I dare confidently believe, that from the commencement of time to the present day, there hath been as many females, as males, who, by the *mere force of natural powers*, have merited the crown of applause; who, *thus unassisted,* have seized the wreath of fame. I know there are who assert, that as the animal powers of the one sex are superior, of course their mental faculties also must be stronger; thus attributing strength of mind to the transient organization of this earth-born tenement. But if this reasoning is just, man must be content to yield the palm to many of the brute creation, since by not a few of his brethren of the field, he is far surpassed in bodily strength. Moreover, was this argument admitted, it would prove too much, for ocular demonstration evinceth, that there are many robust masculine ladies, and effeminate gentlemen. Yet I fancy that Mr. Pope, though clogged with an enervated body, and distinguished by a diminutive stature, could nevertheless lay claim to greatness of soul; and perhaps there are many other instances which might be adduced to combat so unphilosophical an opinion. Do we not often see, that when the clay-built tabernacle is well nigh dissolved, when it is just ready to mingle with the parent soil, the immortal inhabitant aspires to, and even attaineth heights the most sublime, and which were before wholly unexplored. Besides, were we to grant that animal strength proved anything, taking into consideration the accustomed impartiality of nature, we should be induced to imagine that she had invested the female mind with superior strength as an equivalent for the bodily powers of man. But waving this however palpable advantage, for *equality only,* we wish to contend.

I am aware that there are many passages in the sacred oracles which seem to give the advantage to the other sex; but I consider all these as wholly metaphorical. Thus David was a man after God's own heart, yet see him enervated by his licentious passions! behold him following Uriah to the death, and shew me wherein could consist the immaculate Being's complacency. Listen to the curses which Job bestoweth upon the day of his nativity, and tell me where is his perfection, where his patience—*literally* it existed not. David and Job were types of him who was to come; and the superiority of man, as exhibited in scripture, being also emblematical, all arguments deduced from thence, of course fall to the ground. The exquisite delicacy of the female mind proclaimeth the exactness of its texture, while its nice sense of honor announceth its innate, its native grandeur. And indeed, in one respect, the preeminence seems to be tacitly allowed us, for after an education which limits and confines, and employments and recreations which naturally tend to enervate the body and debilitate the mind; after we have from early youth been adorned with ribbons and other gewgaws, dressed out like the ancient victims previous to a sacrifice, being taught by the care of our parents in collecting the most showy materials that the ornamenting our exterior ought to be the principal object of our attention; after, I say, fifteen years thus spent, we are introduced into the world, amid the united adulation of every beholder.

Praise is sweet to the soul; we are immediately intoxicated by large draughts of flattery, which, being plentifully administered, is to the pride of our hearts the most acceptable incense. It is expected that with the other sex we should commence immediate war, and that we should triumph over the machinations of the most artful. We must be constantly upon our guard; prudence and discretion must be our characteristics; and we must rise superior to, and obtain a complete victory over those who have been long adding to the native strength of their minds by an unremitted study of men and books, and who have, moreover, conceived from the loose characters which they have seen portrayed in the extensive variety of their reading, a most contemptible opinion of the sex. Thus unequal, we are, notwithstanding, forced to the combat, and the infamy which is consequent upon the smallest deviation in our conduct, proclaims the high idea which was formed of our native strength; and thus, indirectly at least, is the preference acknowledged to be our due. And if we are allowed an equality of acquirement, let serious studies equally employ our minds, and we will bid our souls arise to equal strength. We will meet upon even ground, the despot man; we will rush with alacrity to the combat, and, crowned by success, we shall then answer the exalted expectations which are formed.

Though sensibility, soft compassion, and gentle commiseration are inmates in the female bosom, yet against every deep-laid art, altogether fearless of the event, we will set them in array; for assuredly the wreath of victory will encircle the spotless brow. If we meet an equal, a sensible friend, we will reward him with the hand of amity, and through life we will be assiduous to promote his happiness; but from every deep-laid scheme for our ruin, retiring·into ourselves, amid the flowery paths of science, we will indulge in all the refined and sentimental pleasures of contemplation. And should it still be urged that the studies thus insisted upon would interfere with our more peculiar department, I must further reply that *early hours,* and close application, will do wonders; and to her who is from the first dawn of reason taught to fill up time rationally, both the requisites will be easy. I grant that niggard fortune is too generally unfriendly to the mind, and that much of that valuable treasure, time, is necessarily expended upon the wants of the body; but it should be remembered, that in embarrassed circumstances our companions have as little leisure for literary improvement as is afforded to us; for most certainly their provident care is at least as requisite as our exertions. Nay, we have even more leisure for sedentary pleasures, as our avocations are more retired, much less laborious, and, as hath been observed, by no means require that avidity of attention which is proper to the employments of the other sex. In high life, or, in other words, where the parties are in possession of affluence, the objection respecting time is wholly obviated, and of course falls to the ground; and it may also be repeated that many of those hours which are at present swallowed up in fashion and scandal might be redeemed, were we habituated to useful reflections.

But in one respect, O ye arbiters of our fate! we confess that the superiority is undubitably yours; you are by nature formed for our protectors; we pretend not to vie with you in bodily strength; upon this point we will never contend for victory. Shield us then, we beseech you, from external evils, and in return we will transact *your* domestic affairs. Yes, *your,* for are you not equally interested in those matters with ourselves? Is not the elegancy of neatness as agreeable to your sight as to ours, is not the well favored viand equally delightful to your taste; and doth not your sense of hearing suffer as much from the discordant sounds prevalent in an ill regulated family, produced by the voices of children and many *et ceteras?*

Constantia.[11]

11. Constantia: Murray's pen name.

17. Ottobah Cugoano (John Stuart)

from *Thoughts and Sentiments on the Evil and Wicked Traffic of the Slavery and Commerce of the Human Species*
1787

Ottobah Cugoano's experience as a slave was in no way typical, since, for one thing, it ended. Born in what is now Ghana, Cugoano was enslaved in 1770 but by 1788 was living in England as a free man, a servant in the household of the painter Cosway. Like Ukawsaw Gronniosaw and Olaudah Equiano, Cugoano devoted his freedom to arguing the case against slavery. Here he offers a set of proposals culminating in a double argument that recurs throughout the literature by former slaves: by putting an end to slavery, the English will profit not just in virtue but in cash. Promising through freedom ten times the profits of slavery, Cugoano, for all his invocation of Christianity, seems to have few illusions about the motive forces of European society.

And now that blessings may come instead of a curse, and that many beneficent purposes of good might speedily arise and flow from it, and be more readily promoted: I would hereby presume to offer the following considerations, as some outlines of a general reformation which ought to be established and carried on. And first, I would propose, that there ought to be days of mourning and fasting appointed, to make enquiry into that great and pre-eminent evil for many years past carried on against the Heathen nations, and the horrible iniquity of making merchandize of us, and cruelly enslaving the poor Africans: and that you might seek grace and repentance, and find mercy and forgiveness before God Omnipotent; and that he may give you wisdom and understanding to devise what ought to be done.

Secondly, I would propose that a total abolition of slavery should be made and proclaimed; and that an universal emancipation of slaves should begin from the date thereof, and be carried on in the following manner: That a proclamation should be caused to be made, setting forth the Antichristian unlawfulness of the slavery and commerce of the human species; and that it should be sent to all the courts and nations in Europe, to require their advice and assistance, and as they may find it unlawful to carry it on, let them whosoever will join to prohibit it. And if such a proclamation be found advisable to the British legislature, let them publish it, and cause it to be published, throughout all the British empire, to hinder and prohibit all men under their government to traffic either in buying or selling men; and, to prevent it, a penalty might be made against it of one thousand pounds, for any man either to buy or sell another man. And that it should require all slave-holders, upon the immediate information thereof, to mitigate the labour of their slaves to that of a lawful servitude, without tortures or oppression; and that they should not hinder, but cause and procure some suitable meand of instruction for them in the knowledge of the Christian religion. And agreeable to the late *royal Proclamation, for the Encouragement of Piety and Virtue, and for the preventing and punishing of Vice, Profaneness and Immorality*; that by no means, under any pretence whatsoever, either for themselves or their masters, the slaves under their subjection should not be suffered to work on the Sabbath days, unless it be such works as necessity and mercy may require. But that those days, as well as some other hours selected for the purpose, should be appropriated for the time of their instruction; and that if any of their owners should not provide such suitable instructors for them, that those slaves should be taken away from them and given to others who would maintain and instruct them for their labour.

And that it should be made known to the slaves, that who had been above seven years in the islands or elsewhere, if they had obtained any competent degree of knowledge of the Christian religion, and the laws of civilization, and had behaved themselves honestly and decently, that they should immediately become free; and that their owners should give them reasonable wages and maintenance for their labour, and not cause them to go away unless they could find some suitable employment elsewhere. And accordingly, from the date of their arrival to seven years, as they arrive at some suitable progress in knowledge, and behaved themselves honestly, that they should be getting free in the course of that time, and at the end of seven years to let every honest man and woman become free; for in the course of that time, they would have sufficiently paid their owners by their labour, both for their first purpose, and for the expenses attending their education. By being thus instructed in the course of seven years, they would become tractable and obedient, useful labourers, dutiful servants and good subjects; and Christian men might have the honor and happiness to see many of them vieing with themselves to praise the God of their salvation. And it might be another necessary duty for Christians, in the course of that time, to make enquiry concerning some of their friends and relations in Africa: and if they found any intelligent persons amongst them, to give them as good education as they could, and find out a way of recourse to their friends; that as soon as they had made any progress in useful learning and the knowledge of the Christian religion, they might be sent back to Africa, to be made useful there as soon, and as many of them as could be made fit for instructing others. The rest would become useful residentors in the colonies; where there might be employment enough given to all free people, with suitable wages according to their usefulness, in the improvement of land; and the more encouragement that could be given to agriculture, and every other branch of useful industry, would thereby encrease the number of the inhabitants; without which any country, however blessed by nature, must continue poor.

And, thirdly, I would propose, that a fleet of some ships of war should be immediately sent to the coast of Africa, and particularly where the slave trade is carried on, with faithful men to direct that none should be brought from the coast of Africa without their own consent and the approbation of their friends, and to intercept all merchant ships that were bringing them away, until such a scrutiny was made, whatever nation they belonged to. And I would suppose, if Great-Britain was to do any thing of this kind, that it would meet with the general approbation and assistance of other Christian nations; but whether it did or not, it could be very lawfully done at all the British forts and settlements on the coast of Africa; and particular remonstrances could be given to all the rest, to warn them of the consequences of such an evil and enormous wicked traffic as is now carried on. The Dutch have some crocodile settlers at the Cape, that should be called to a particular account for their murders and inhuman babarities. But all the present governors of the British forts and factories should be dismissed, and faithful and good men appointed in their room; and those forts and factories, which at present are a den of thieves, might be turned into shepherd's tents, and have good shepherds sent to call the flocks to feed beside them. Then would doors of hospitality in abundance be opened in Africa to supply the weary travellers, and that immense abundance which they are enriched with, might be diffused afar; but the character of the inhabitants on the west coast of Africa, and the rich produce of their country, have been too long misrepresented by avaricious plunderers and merchants who deal in slaves; and if that country was not annually ravished and laid waste, there might be a very considerable and profitable trade carried on with the Africans.

And, should the noble Britons, who have often supported their own liberties with their lives and fortunes, extend their philanthropy to abolish the slavery and oppression of the Africans, they might have settlements and many kingdoms united in a friendly alliance with themselves, which might be made greatly to their own advantage, as well as they might have the happiness of being useful to promoting the prosperity and felicity of others, who have been cruelly injured and wrongfully dealt with. Were the Africans to be dealt with in a friendly manner, and kind instructions to be administered unto them, as by degrees they became to love learning, there would be nothing in their power, but what they would wish to render their service in return for the means of improving their understanding; and the present British factories, and other settlements, might be enlarged to a very great extent. And as Great-Britain has been remarkable for ages past, for encouraging arts and sciences, and may now be put in competition with any nation in the known world, if they would take compassion on the inhabitants of the coast of Guinea, and to make use of such means as would be needful to enlighten their minds in the knowledge of Christianity, their virtue, in this respect, would have its own reward. And as the Africans became refined and established in light and knowledge, they would imitate their noble British friends, to improve their lands, and make use of that industry as the nature of their country might require, and to supply those that would trade with them, with such productions as the nature of their climate would produce; and, in every respect, the fair Britons would have the preference with them to a very great extent; and, in another respect, they would become a kind of first ornament to Great-Britain for her tender and compassionate care of such a set of distressed poor ignorant people.

And were the noble Britons, and their august Sovereign, to cause protection and encouragement to be given to those Africans, they might expect in a short time, if need required it, to receive from thence great supplies of men in a lawful way, either for industry or defence; and of other things in abundance from so great a source, where every thing is luxurious and plenty, if not laid waste by barbarity and gross ignorance.

Due encouragement being given to so great, so just, and such a noble undertaking, would soon bring more revenue in a righteous way to the British nation, than ten times its share in all the profits that slavery can produce;[12] and such a laudable example would inspire every generous and enterprizing mind to imitate so great and worthy a nation, for establishing religion, justice, and equity to the Africans, and, in doing this, would be held in the highest esteem by all men, and be admired by all the world.

18. George Mason and James Madison

from the Virginia ratification debate 1788

This debate took place during the course of Virginia's ratification of the Constitution. George Mason (1725–92) was a Virginia planter who came out of retirement in 1775 to join in the preparations for national independence. One of his first and most important contributions was a Declaration of Rights which Jefferson drew on for the first part of his own Declaration; it eventually became the core of the Bill of Rights. Ultimately, Mason refused to sign the Constitution because of its compromises on two key issues: the slave trade, which was to be continued for twenty years, and the tariff. The position he takes here is essentially the same as Jefferson's in the struck paragraph of the Declaration of Independence: Mason recalls that opposition to the slave trade was one of the grounds upon which the colonies separated from England, while at the same time complaining that the Constitution fails to provide "security for the property of that kind which we have already." Like Jefferson, Mason was opposed not only to the slave trade but to the institution of slavery, but nonetheless was concerned for its orderly conduct.

James Madison (1751–1836), in his response, sums up the compromise that brought slavery into the new nation: "Great as the evil is, a dismemberment of the Union would be worse." Refuting Mason's accusation that the proposed Government would retain the power to impede the profitable pursuit of the slave economy or even effectively to free the slaves by taxing them beyond their masters' means, Madison vindicates his own model of relations between business and government: the government must have the power to levy reasonable taxes on everyone and to protect private property universally. The Constitution prohibits taxes that could amount to prohibition, and it offers the planters a new security through a fugitive slave law. Paraphrasing the argument of the deep South planters in a language that almost eclipses the fact that the "property . . . possessed . . . purchased, or otherwise acquired" is composed of human beings, Madison might be seen projecting the next stage in the debate over slavery, which would focus on its domestic perpetuation.

12. A gentleman of my acquaintance told me that, if ever he hears tell of any thing of this kind taking place, he has a plan in contemplation, which would, in some equitable manner, produce from one million to fifteen millions stereling to the British government annually, as it might be required; of which a due proportion of that revenue would be paid by the Africans; and that it would prevent all smuggling and illicit traffic; in a great measure, prevent running into debt, long imprisonment, and all unlawful bankruptcies; effectually prevent all dishonesty and swindling, and almost put an end to all robbery, fraud and theft. [Cugoano's note.]

Mr. *George Mason,*—Mr. Chairman.—This is a fatal section, which has created more dangers than any other.—The first clause, allows the importation of slaves for twenty years. Under the royal Government, this evil was looked upon as a great oppression, and many attempts were made to prevent it; but the interest of the African merchants prevented its prohibition. No sooner did the revolution take place, than it was thought of. It was one of the great causes of our separation from Great-Britain. Its exclusion has been a principal object of this State, and most of the States in the Union. The augmentation of slaves weakens the States; and such a trade is diabolical in itself, and disgraceful to mankind. Yet by this Constitution it is continued for twenty years. As much as I value an union of all the States, I would not admit the Southern States into the Union, unless they agreed to the discontinuance of this disgraceful trade, because it would bring weakness and not strength to the Union. And though this infamous traffic be continued, we have no security for the property of that kind which we have already. There is no clause in this Constitution to secure it; for they may lay such a tax as will amount to manumission. And should the Government be amended, still this detestable kind of commerce cannot be discontinued till after the expiration of twenty years.—For the fifth article, which provides for amendments, expressly excepts this clause. I have ever looked upon this as a most disgraceful thing to America. I cannot express my detestation of it. Yet they have not secured us the property of the slaves we have already. So that "They have done what they ought not to have done, and have left undone what they ought to have done."

Mr. *Madison,*—Mr. Chairman.—I should conceive this clause to be impolitic, if it were one of those things which could be excluded without encountering greater evils.—The Southern States would not have entered into the Union of America, without the temporary permission of that trade. And if they were excluded from the Union, the consequences might be dreadful to them and to us. We are not in a worse situation than before. That traffic is prohibited by our laws, and we may continue the prohibition. The Union in general is not in a worse situation. Under the articles of Confederation, it might be continued forever: But by this clause an end may be put to it after twenty years. There is therefore an amelioration of our circumstances. A tax may be laid in the mean time; but it is limited, otherwise Congress might lay such a tax as would amount to a prohibition. From the mode of representation and taxation, Congress cannot lay such a tax on slaves as will amount to manumission. Another clause secures us that property which we now possess. At present, if any slave elopes to any of those States where slaves are free, he becomes emancipated by their laws. For the laws of the States are uncharitable to one another in this respect. But in this Constitution, "No person held to service, or labor, in one State, under the laws thereof, escaping into another, shall in consequence of any law or regulation therein, be discharged from such service or labor; but shall be delivered up on claim of the party to whom such service or labour may be due."—This clause was expressly inserted to enable owners of slaves to reclaim them. This is a better security than any that now exists. No power is given to the General Government to interpose with respect to the property in slaves now held by the States. The taxation of this State being equal only to its representation, such a tax cannot be laid as he supposes. They cannot prevent the importation of slaves for twenty years; but after that period they can. The Gentlemen from South-Carolina and Georgia argued in this manner:—"We have now liberty to import this species of property, and much of the property now possessed, has been purchased, or otherwise acquired, in contemplation of improving it by the assistance of imported slaves. What would be the consequence of hindering us from it? The slaves of Virginia would rise in value, and we would be obliged to go to your markets." I need not expatiate on this subject. Great as the evil is, a dismemberment of the Union would be worse. If those States should disunite from the other States, for not indulging them in the temporary continuance of this traffic, they might solicit and obtain aid from foreign powers.

19. James Madison

The Federalist, #10
1787

James Madison (1751–1836) differed from his fellow Virginian Thomas Jefferson in his more favorable view of trade and commerce. A moderate supporter of unified commercial and monetary policies, he was thus also of the Federalist party, backing the Constitution against those who worried that it granted too much power to the national government. When Alexander Hamilton undertook a campaign of letters to be published in New York newspapers arguing for ratification of the Constitution in that key state, he enlisted Madison's help. Along with John Jay, Madison and Hamilton produced eighty-five letters between October 1787 and August 1788. The letters were published anonymously, signed "Publius," and collected as The Federalist. *Among the Federalist papers, which together comprise one of the most important texts of American political theory, the tenth, written by Madison, is perhaps the most frequently consulted today.*

At the center of its argument is a distinction familiar to eighteenth-century political discussion between "republic," or a government by enlightened, disinterested men seeking the best for the whole community, and "democracy," which implied the participation of all the members of a society, including those whose lack of property and of education deprived them, according to their betters, of a transcending sense of the general welfare. The common wisdom was that republics had to be small, so that the representatives of the community could speak for the whole and the governed would accept the rule of the whole even when individually thwarted. Republican representatives governed on behalf of the populace, which trusted them to know its interests better than it did itself. Athens and Rome were the great exemplary republics, small in population and land and ruled by a still smaller minority of the best and brightest.

The great fear of many of the debaters over the Constitution—and one reason for resisting federalism—was that the federated colonies constituted too numerous and diverse a society for republican government, which would soon degenerate into democracy. The innovative point of Madison's argument in Federalist #10 *is that, on the contrary, republics work best with large populations and over broad territories. The distance from his constituency that the country's size requires frees the representative to take a larger view. Rather than just embodying the demands*

of this or that "faction" (a word that generally means class), the elected representa-
tive, far from home, comes to identify equally with the function of government as
such; he becomes free not to represent his constituency if he judges it better. No
argument for ratification could have been more powerful than this exposition of
the mechanism by which representative government in the United States was
limited in its responsiveness to the general population, and could only become
more so as the country developed.

To the People of the State of New-York

Among the numerous advantages promised by a well constructed Union, none deserves to be more accurately developed than its tendency to break and control the violence of faction. The friend of popular governments, never finds himself so much alarmed for their character and fate, as when he contemplates their propensity to this dangerous vice. He will not fail therefore to set a due value on any plan which, without violating the principles to which he is attached, provides a proper cure for it. The instability, injustice and confusion introduced into the public councils, have in truth been the mortal diseases under which popular governments have every where perished; as they continue to be the favorite and fruitful topics from which the adversaries to liberty derive their most specious declamations. The valuable improvements made by the American Constitutions on the popular models, both ancient and modern, cannot certainly be too much admired; but it would be an unwarrantable partiality, to contend that they have as effectually obviated the danger on this side as was wished and expected. Complaints are every where heard from our most considerate and virtuous citizens, equally the friends of public and private faith, and of public and personal liberty; that our governments are too unstable; that the public good is disregarded in the conflicts of rival parties; and that measures are too often decided, not according to the rules of justice, and the rights of the minor party; but by the superior force of an interested and over-bearing majority. However anxiously we may wish that these complaints had no foundation, the evidence of known facts will not permit us to deny that they are in some degree true. It will be found indeed, on a candid review of our situation, that some of the distresses under which we labor, have been erroneously charged on the operation of our governments; but it will be found, at the same time, that other causes will not alone account for many of our heaviest misfortunes; and particularly, for that prevailing and increasing distrust of public engagements, and alarm for private rights, which are echoed from one end of the continent to the other. These must be chiefly, if not wholly, effects of the unsteadiness and injustice, with which a factious spirit has tainted our public administration.

By a faction I understand a number of citizens, whether amounting to a majority or minority of the whole, who are united and actuated by some common impulse of passion, or of interest, adverse to the rights of other citizens, or to the permanent and aggregate interests of the community.

There are two methods of curing the mischiefs of faction: the one, by removing its causes; the other, by controling its effects.

There are again two methods of removing the causes of faction: the one by destroying the liberty which is essential to its existence; the other, by giving to every citizen the same opinions, the same passions, and the same interests.

It could never be more truly said than of the first remedy, that it is worse than the disease. Liberty is to faction, what air is to fire, an aliment without which it instantly expires. But it could not be a less folly to abolish liberty, which is essential to political life, because it nourishes faction, than it would be to wish the annihilation of air, which is essential to animal life, because it imparts to fire its destructive agency.

The second expedient is as impracticable, as the first would be unwise. As long as the reason of man continues fallible, and he is at liberty to exercise it, different opinions will be formed. As long as the connection subsists between his reason and his self-love, his opinions and his passions will have a reciprocal influence on each other; and the former will be objects to which the latter will attach themselves. The diversity in the faculties of men from which the rights of property originate, is not less an insuperable obstacle to a uniformity of interests. The protection of these faculties is the first object of Government. From the protection of different and unequal faculties of acquiring property, the possession of different degrees and kinds of property immediately results: and from the influence of these on the sentiments and views of the respective proprietors, ensues a division of the society into different interests and parties.

The latent causes of faction are thus sown in the nature of man; and we see them every where brought into different degrees of activity, according to the different circumstances of civil society. A zeal for different opinions concerning religion, concerning Government, and many other points, as well of speculation as of practice; an attachment to different leaders ambitiously contending for pre-eminence and power; or to persons of other descriptions whose fortunes have been interesting to the human passions, have in turn divided mankind into parties, inflamed them with mutual animosity, and rendered them much more disposed to vex and oppress each other, than to co-operate for their common good. So strong is this propensity of mankind to fall into mutual animosities, that where no substantial occasion presents itself, the most frivolous and fanciful distinctions have been sufficient to kindle their unfriendly passions, and excite their most violent conflicts. But the most common and durable source of factions, has been the various and unequal distribution of property. Those who hold, and those who are without property, have ever formed distinct interests in society. Those who are creditors, and those who are debtors, fall under a like discrimination. A landed interest, a manufacturing interest, a mercantile interest, a monied interest, with many lesser interests, grow up of necessity in civilized nations, and divide them into different classes, actuated by different sentiments and views. The regulation of these various and interfering interests forms the principal task of modern Legislation, and involves the spirit of party and faction in the necessary and ordinary operations of Government.

No man is allowed to be a judge in his own cause; because his interest would certainly bias his judgment, and, not improbably, corrupt his integrity. With equal, nay with greater reason, a body of men, are unfit to be both judges and parties, at the same time; yet, what are many of the most important acts of legislation, but so many judicial determinations, not indeed concerning the rights of single persons, but concerning the rights of large bodies of citizens; and what are the different classes of legislators, but advocates and parties to the causes which they determine? Is a law proposed concerning private debts? It is a question to which the creditors are parties on one side, and the debtors on the other. Justice ought to hold the balance between them. Yet the parties are and must be themselves the judges; and the most numerous party, or, in other words, the most powerful faction must be expected to prevail. Shall domestic manufactures be encouraged, and in what degree, by restrictions on foreign manufactures? are questions which would be differently decided by the landed and the manufacturing classes; and probably by neither, with a sole regard to justice and the public good. The apportionment of taxes on the various descriptions of property, is an act which seems to require the most exact impartiality; yet there is perhaps no legislative act in which greater opportunity and temptation are given to a predominant party, to trample on the rules of justice. Every shilling with which they over-burden the inferior number, is a shilling saved to their own pockets.

It is in vain to say, that enlightened statesmen will be able to adjust these clashing interests, and render them all subservient to the public good. Enlightened statesmen will not always be at the helm: Nor, in many cases, can such an adjustment be made at all, without taking into view indirect and remote considerations, which will rarely prevail over the immediate interest which one party may find in disregarding the rights of another, or the good of the whole.

The inference to which we are brought, is, that the *causes* of faction cannot be removed; and that relief is only to be sought in the means of controling its *effects*.

If a faction consists of less than a majority, relief is supplied by the republican principle, which enables the majority to defeat its sinister views by regular vote: It may clog the administration, it may convulse the society; but it will be unable to execute and mask its violence under the forms of the Constitution. When a majority is included in a faction, the form of popular government on the other hand enables it to sacrifice to its ruling passion or interest, both the public good and the rights of other citizens. To secure the public good, and private rights, against the danger of such a faction, and at the same time to preserve the spirit and the form of popular government, is then the great object to which our enquiries are directed: Let me add that it is the great desideratum, by which alone this form of government can be rescued from the opprobrium under which it has so long labored, and be recommended to the esteem and adoption of mankind.

By what means is this object attainable? Evidently by one of two only. Either the existence of the same passion or interest in a majority at the same time, must be prevented; or the majority, having such co-existent passion or interest, must be rendered, by their number and local situation, unable to concert and carry into effect schemes of oppression. If the impulse and the opportunity be suffered to coincide, we well know that neither moral nor religious motives can be relied on as an adequate control. They are not found to be such on the injustice and violence of individuals, and lose their efficacy in proportion to the number combined together; that is, in proportion as their efficacy becomes needful.

From this view of the subject, it may be concluded, that a pure Democracy, by which I mean, a Society, consisting of a small number of citizens, who assemble and administer the Government in person, can admit of no cure for the mischiefs of faction. A common passion or interest will, in almost every case, be felt by a majority of the whole; a communication and concert results from the form of Government itself; and there is nothing to check the inducements to sacrifice the weaker party, or an obnoxious individual. Hence it is, that such Democracies have ever been spectacles of turbulence and contention; have ever been found incompatible with personal security, or the rights of property; and have in general been as short in their lives, as they have been violent in their deaths. Theoretic politicians, who have patronized this species of Government, have erroneously supposed, that by reducing mankind to a perfect equality in their political rights, they would, at the same time, be perfectly equalized and assimilated in their possessions, their opinions, and their passions.

A Republic, by which I mean a Government in which the scheme of representation takes place, opens a different prospect, and promises the cure for which we are seeking. Let us examine the points in which it varies from pure Democracy, and we shall comprehend both the nature of the cure, and the efficacy which it must derive from the Union.

The two great points of difference between a Democracy and a Republic are, first, the delegation of the Government, in the latter, to a small number of citizens elected by the rest: secondly, the greater number of citizens, and greater sphere of country, over which the latter may be extended.

The effect of the first difference is, on the one hand to refine and enlarge the public views, by passing them through the medium of a chosen body of citizens, whose wisdom may best discern the true interest of their country, and whose patriotism and love of justice, will be least likely to sacrifice it to temporary or partial considerations. Under such a regulation, it may well happen that the public voice pronounced by the representatives of the people, will be more consonant to the public good, than if pronounced by the people themselves convened for the purpose. On the other hand, the effect may be inverted. Men of factious tempers, of local prejudices, or of sinister designs, may by intrigue, by corruption or by other means, first obtain the suffrages, and then betray the interests of the people. The question resulting is, whether small or extensive Republics are most favorable to the election of proper guardians of the public weal; and it is clearly decided in favor of the latter by two obvious considerations.

In the first place it is to be remarked that however small the Republic may be, the Representatives must be raised to a certain number, in order to guard against the cabals of a few; and that however large it may be, they must be limited to a certain number, in order to guard against the confusion of a multitude. Hence the number of Representatives in the two cases, not being in proportion to that of the Constituents, and being proportionally greatest in the small Republic, it follows, that if the proportion of fit characters, be not less, in the large than in the small Republic, the former will present a greater option, and consequently a greater probability of a fit choice.

In the next place, as each Representative will be chosen by a greater number of citizens in the large than in the small Republic, it will be more difficult for unworthy candidates to practise with success the vicious arts, by which elections are too often carried; and the suffrages of the people being more free, will be more likely to centre on men who possess the most attractive merit, and the most diffusive and established characters.

It must be confessed, that in this, as in most other cases, there is a mean, on both sides of which inconveniencies will be found to lie. By enlarging too much the number of electors, you render the representative too little acquainted with all their local circumstances and lesser interests; as by reducing it too much, you render him unduly attached to these, and too little fit to comprehend and pursue great and national objects. The Federal Constitution forms a happy combination in this respect; the great and aggregate interests being referred to the national, the local and particular, to the state legislatures.

The other point of difference is, the greater number of citizens and extent of territory which may be brought within the compass of Republican, than of Democratic Government; and it is this circumstance principally which renders factious combinations less to be dreaded in the former, than in the latter. The smaller the society, the fewer probably will be the distinct parties and interests composing it; the fewer the distinct parties and interests, the more frequently will a majority be found of the same party; and the smaller the number of individuals composing a majority, and the smaller the compass within which they are placed, the more easily will they concert and execute their plans of oppression. Extend the sphere, and you take in a greater variety of parties and interests; you make it less probable that a majority of the whole will have a common motive to invade the rights of other citizens; or if such a common motive exists, it will be more difficult for all who feel it to discover their own strength, and to act in unison with each other. Besides other impediments, it may be remarked, that where there is a consciousness of unjust or dishonorable purposes, communication is always checked by distrust, in proportion to the number whose concurrence is necessary.

Hence it clearly appears, that the same advantage, which a Republic has over a Democracy, in controling the effects of faction, is enjoyed by a large over a small Republic—is enjoyed by the Union over the States composing it. Does this advantage consist in the substitution of Representatives, whose enlightened views and virtuous sentiments render them superior to local prejudices, and to schemes of injustice? It will not be denied, that the Representation of the Union will be most likely to possess these requisite endowments. Does it consist in the greater security afforded by a greater variety of parties, against the event of any one party being able to outnumber and oppress the rest? In an equal degree does the encreased variety of parties, comprised within the Union, encrease this security. Does it, in fine, consist in the greater obstacles opposed to the concert and accomplishment of the secret wishes of an unjust and interested majority? Here, again, the extent of the Union gives it the most palpable advantage.

The influence of factious leaders may kindle a flame within their particular States, but will be unable to spread a general conflagration through the other States: a religious sect, may degenerate into a political faction in a part of the Confederacy; but the variety of sects dispersed over the entire face of it, must secure the national Councils against any danger from that source: a rage for paper money, for an abolition of debts, for an equal division of property, or for any other improper or wicked project, will be less apt to pervade the whole body of the Union, than a particular member of it; in the same proportion as such a malady is more likely to taint a particular county or district, than an entire State.

In the extent and proper structure of the Union, therefore, we behold a Republican remedy for the diseases most incident to Republican Government. And according to the degree of pleasure and pride, we feel in being Republicans, ought to be our zeal in cherishing the spirit, and supporting the character of Federalists.

20. Benjamin Franklin

Sidi Mehemet Ibrahim on the Slave Trade
1790

*Looking over the texts dealing with slavery included in this chapter, one can see a
characteristic approach emerging. From Samuel Sewall beginning the American
attack on slavery in* The Selling of Joseph; *to Thomas Jefferson, whose discussion
of slavery in his draft of the* Declaration of Independence *is more specifically about
the slave trade; to Ottobah Cugoano's proposition (Olaudah Equiano makes the
same suggestion) that England could reap greater profits by trading with Africans
than by enslaving them; to the debate over slavery in the ratification of the
Constitution, which was a debate over the slave trade; to Benjamin Franklin's
satiric attack in "Sidi Mehemet Ibrahim on the Slave Trade," slavery is represented
first and fundamentally in terms of trade; that is, no doubt reflecting the world
view of a mercantile century, as a matter of commerce. It may help to distinguish
this view of slavery to compare it with Harriet Beecher Stowe's in the next century.
For her and for most nineteenth-century abolitionists, the evil lay in the violation
of the integrity of personhood, of the realm of personal identity and domestic relations by commerce. The earlier writers seem to define the problem rather as the
violation of commerce, slavery destroying the beneficence of trade.*

*Here Franklin satirizes all the commonly cited rationales for slavery, ranging
from financial to cultural and racial, ending up, in the Divan's Resolution, with a
remarkably close paraphrase of the conclusion of the Mason-Madison debate.*

To the editor of the federal gazette

Sir,   March 23d, 1790.

Reading last night in your excellent Paper the speech of Mr. Jackson in Congress
against their meddling with the Affair of Slavery, or attempting to mend the Condition
of the Slaves, it put me in mind of a similar One made about 100 Years since by Sidi
Mehemet Ibrahim, a member of the Divan of Algiers, which may be seen in Martin's
Account of his Consulship, anno 1687. It was against granting the Petition of the Sect
called *Erika*, or Purists, who pray'd for the Abolition of Piracy and Slavery as being
unjust. Mr. Jackson does not quote it; perhaps he has not seen it. If, therefore, some of
its Reasonings are to be found in his eloquent Speech, it may only show that men's
Interests and Intellects operate and are operated on with surprising similarity in all
Countries and Climates, when under similar Circumstances. The African's Speech, as
translated, is as follows.

"Allah Bismillah, &c.
God is great, and Mahomet is his Prophet.

"Have these *Erika* considered the Consequences of granting their Petition? If we cease our Cruises against the Christians, how shall we be furnished with the Commodities their Countries produce, and which are so necessary for us? If we forbear to make Slaves of their People, who in this hot Climate are to cultivate our Lands? Who are to perform the common Labours of our City, and in our Families? Must we not then be our own Slaves? And is there not more Compassion and more Favour due to us as Mussulmen, than to these Christian Dogs? We have now above 50,000 Slaves in and near Algiers. This Number, if not kept up by fresh Supplies, will soon diminish, and be gradually annihilated. If we then cease taking and plundering the Infidel Ships, and making Slaves of the Seamen and Passengers, our Lands will become of no Value for want of Cultivation; the Rents of Houses in the City will sink one half; and the Revenues of Government arising from its Share of Prizes be totally destroy'd! And for what? To gratify the whims of a whimsical Sect, who would have us, not only forbear making more Slaves, but even to manumit those we have.

"But who is to idemnify their Masters for the Loss? Will the State do it? Is our Treasury sufficient? Will the *Erika* do it? Can they do it? Or would they, to do what they think Justice to the Slaves, do a greater Injustice to the Owners? And if we set our Slaves free, what is to be done with them? Few of them will return to their Countries; they know too well the greater Hardships they must there be subject to; they will not embrace our holy Religion; they will not adopt our Manners; our People will not pollute themselves by intermarrying with them. Must we maintain them as Beggars in our Streets, or suffer our Properties to be the Prey of their Pillage? For Men long accustom'd to Slavery will not work for a Livelihood when not compell'd. And what is there so pitiable in their present Condition? Were they not Slaves in their own Countries?

"Are not Spain, Portugal, France, and the Italian states govern'd by Despots, who hold all their Subjects in Slavery, without Exception? Even England treats its Sailors as Slaves; for they are, whenever the Government pleases, seiz'd, and confin'd in Ships of War, condemn'd not only to work, but to fight, for small Wages, or a mere Subsistence, not better than our Slaves are allow'd by us. Is their Condition then made worse by their falling into our Hands? No; they have only exchanged one Slavery for another, and I may say a better; for here they are brought into a Land where the Sun of Islamism gives forth its Light, and shines in full Splendor, and they have an Opportunity of making themselves acquainted with the true Doctrine, and thereby saving their immortal Souls. Those who remain at home have not that Happiness. Sending the Slaves home then would be sending them out of Light into Darkness.

"I repeat the Question, What is to be done with them? I have heard it suggested, that they may be planted in the Wilderness, where there is plenty of Land for them to subsist on, and where they may flourish as a free State; but they are, I doubt, too little dispos'd to labour without Compulsion, as well as too ignorant to establish a good government, and the wild Arabs would soon molest and destroy or again enslave them. While serving us, we take care to provide them with every thing, and they are treated with Humanity. The Labourers in their own Country are, as I am well informed, worse fed, lodged, and cloathed. The Condition of most of them is therefore already mended, and requires no further Improvement. Here their Lives are in

Safety. They are not liable to be impress'd for Soldiers, and forc'd to cut one another's Christian Throats, as in the Wars of their own Countries. If some of the religious mad Bigots, who now teaze us with their silly Petitions, have in a Fit of blind Zeal freed their Slaves, it was not Generosity, it was not Humanity, that mov'd them to the Action; it was from the conscious Burthen of a Load of Sins, and Hope, from the supposed Merits of so good a Work, to be excus'd Damnation.

"How grossly are they mistaken in imagining Slavery to be disallow'd by the Alcoran! Are not the two Precepts, to quote no more, '*Masters, treat your Slaves with kindness; Slaves, serve your Masters with Cheerfulness and Fidelity,*' clear Proofs to the contrary? Nor can the Plundering of Infidels be in that sacred Book forbidden, since it is well known from it, that God has given the World, and all that it contains, to his faithful Mussulmen, who are to enjoy it of Right as fast as they conquer it. Let us then hear no more of this detestable Proposition, the Manumission of Christian Slaves, the Adoption of which would, by depreciating our Lands and Houses, and thereby depriving so many good Citizens of their Properties, create universal Discontent, and provoke Insurrections, to the endangering of Government and producing general Confusion. I have therefore no doubt, but this wise Council will prefer the Comfort and Happiness of a whole Nation of true Believers to the Whim of a few *Erika*, and dismiss their Petition."

The Result was, as Martin tells us, that the Divan came to this Resolution; "The Doctrine, that Plundering and Enslaving the Christians is unjust, is at best *problematical;* but that it is the Interest of this State to continue the Practice, is clear; therefore let the Petition be rejected."

And it was rejected accordingly.

And since like Motives are apt to produce in the Minds of Men like Opinions and Resolutions, may we not, Mr. Brown, venture to predict, from this Account, that the Petitions to the Parliament of England for abolishing the Slave-Trade, to say nothing of other Legislatures, and the Debates upon them, will have a similar Conclusion? I am, Sir, your constant Reader and humble Servant,

HISTORICUS

21. William Manning

from *The Key of Liberty*
1799

> The full title of The Key of Liberty *continues,* Showing the Causes Why a Free Government Has Always Failed and a Remedy against It. Addressed to the Republicans, Farmers, Mechanics, and Laborers in America by a Laborer. *The second part of this subtitle is important and unusual. For, besides Thomas Paine, there are virtually no writers in this collection who could sign themselves "a Laborer." Benjamin Franklin began as one, but, rejecting his father's trade of*

candle-making as well as all other trades but printing, he at once entered the
company of political men and writers, even before his early retirement. William
Manning (1747–1814), a Massachusetts farmer self-educated to the extent reflected
in the efficient, if sometimes awkward prose of this essay, did not aspire to
Franklinesque ascent. Franklin, having early seen that the freedom of the press
belongs to the man who owns it, set about owning a press. Manning exposes this
fundamental truth about capitalist society from the perspective of the majority for
whom Franklin's strategy is not an option.

Manning's idiom of the few and the many is common in the period. During the
drafting of the Constitution, *for instance, Alexander Hamilton had explained that*
"All communities divide themselves into the few and the many." The few were
"rich and well-born," the many, poor, uneducated, and thus unfit to govern them-
selves. In a just and efficient American republic, the few will have to govern.
Manning here proposes a rare counterargument.

To all the Republicans, Farmers, Mechanics, and Labourers in America your Candid attention is Requested to the Sentiments of a Labourer

[Introduction]

Learning & Knowledge are essential to the preservation of Liberty & unless we
have more of it among us we Cannot Support our Liberties Long.

I am not a Man of Learning myself for I never had the advantage of six months schooling in my life. I am no traveller for I never was 50 Miles from where I was born in any direction, & I am no great reader of ancient history for I always followed hard labour for a living. But I always thought it My duty to search into & see for myself in all matter that concerned me as a member of society, & when the war began between Britain and America I was in the prime of Life & highly taken up with Liberty and a free Government. I saw almost the first blood that was shed in Concord fighting & scores of men dead, dying & wounded in the Cause of Liberty, which caused serious sensations in my mind.

But I believed then & still believe it is a good cause which we ought to defend to the very last, & I have been a Constant Reader of public Newspapers & closely attended to men & measures ever since, through the war, through the operation of paper money, framing Constitutions, making & constructing Laws, & seeing what selfish & contracted ideas of interests would influence the best picked men & bodies of men.

I have often thought it was impossible ever to support a free Government, but firmly believing it to the best sort & the only one approved of by heaven it was my unwearied study & prayers to the almighty for many years to find out the real cause & a remedy and I have for many years been satisfied in my own mind what the causes are & what would in a great measure prove a remedy provided it was carried into effect.

But I had no thoughts of publishing my sentiments on it until the adoption of the British treaty[13] in the manner it has been done. But seeing the unwearied pains and the

13. British treaty: the treaty signed in 1794 was popularly regarded as sacrificing other interests to those of merchants and shipowners.

unjustifiable measures taken by large numbers of all orders of men who get a living without labour in Elections & many other things to injure the interests of the Labourer & deprive us of the privilege of a free government, I came to a resolution (although I have neither learning nor leisure for the purpose) to improve on my Constitutional Right & give you my sentiments on what the causes are & a remedy.

In doing which I must study brevity throughout the whole and but just touch on many things on which volumes might be written, but hope I shall do it so as to be understood, and as I have no room for compliments & shall often make observations on sundry orders of men & their conduct, I beg leave once for all to observe that I am far from thinking any orders of men who live without Labour are entirely needless or that they are all chargeable with blame. But on the contrary I firmly believe that there is a large number in all orders who are true friends to Liberty & that it is from them that Liberty always has & always will receive its principal support. But I also believe that a large majority of them are actuated by very different principles. Also as I am not furnished with Documents & other information that would be useful I may represent Some things different from what they really are & so desire that they may be taken only as my Opinion & believed no further than they appear Evident.

A Description of Mankind and Necessity of Government

To search into & know ourselves is of the greatest importance, & the want of it is the cause of the greatest evils suffered in Society. If we knew what alterations might be made in our Minds and Conduct by alterations in our Education, age, Circumstances, & Conditions in this Life, we should be vastly less censorious on others for their conduct, & more cautious of trusting them when there was no need of it.

Men are born & grow up in this world with a vast variety of capacities, strengths & abilities both of Body and Mind, & have strongly implanted within them numerous passions & lusts continually urging them to fraud, violence & acts of injustice toward one another. He has implanted in him a sense of Right & Wrong, so that if he would always follow the dictates of Conscience & consider the advantages of Society & mutual assistance he would need no other Law or Government. Yet as he is sentenced by the just decrees of heaven to hard Labour for a Living in this world, & has so strongly implanted in him a desire of Self Support, Self Love, Self Conceit, Self Importance, & Self aggrandisement, that it engrosses all his care and attention so that he can see nothing beyond Self—for Self (as once described by a Divine) is like an object placed before the eye that hinders the sight of every thing beyond.

This Selfishness may be discerned in all persons, let their conditions in life be what they will, & it operates so powerfully as to disqualify them from judging impartially in their own cause, & a person's being raised to stations of high Honour and trust doth not clear him from this selfishness. But on the contrary it is a solemn truth that the higher a Man is raised in stations of honour, power and trust, the greater are his temptations to do wrong and gratify those selfish principles. Give a man honour & he wants more. Give him power & he wants more. Give him money & he wants more. In short he is never easy, but the more he has the more he wants.

The most comprehensive description of Man I ever saw was by a writer as followeth: —Viz— Man is a being made up of Self Love seeking his own happiness to the misery of all around him, who would damn a world to save himself from temporal or other punishment, & he who denies this to be his real character is ignorant of himself, or else is more than a man.

Many persons were they to hear such a description of themselves would cry out as Hazael did, 'what, is thy Servant a Dog?'[14] etc. But if they should once get into the circumstances he was in, & have the power & temptations he had, they would prove themselves to be just such a Dog as he did. Haman is another striking evidence of the depravity & pride of the human heart, for though he could boast of the highest preferments in the greatest kingdom on Earth, the poor Devil exclaimed 'all this avails me nothing so long as Mordecai refuses to bow the knee.'

From this disposition of Man or the depravity of the human heart, arises not only the advantage but the absolute necessity of Civil government—without it Mankind would be continually at war with their own species, stealing, robbing, fighting with & killing one another. This all Nations on Earth have been convinced of, and have established it in some form or other, & their sole aim in doing it is their safety & happiness. But for want of wisdom or some plan to curb the ambition & govern those to whom they give their power, they have often been brought to suffer as Much under their governments as they would without any—and it still remains uncertain whether any such plan can be found out or not.

Shows how the Few & Many Differ in their Interests in [the Government's] operation

In the sweat of thy face shall though get thy bread until thou return to the ground, is the irreversible sentence of Heaven on Man for his rebellion. To be sentenced to hard Labour during life is very unpleasant to human Nature. There is a great aversion to it perceivable in all men—yet it is absolutely necessary that a large majority of the world should labour, or we could not subsist. For Labour is the sole parent of all property—the land yieldeth nothing without it, & there is no food, clothing, shelter, vessel or other necessary of life but what costs Labour & is generally esteemed valuable according to the Labour it costs. Therefore no person can possess property without labouring, unless he get it by force or craft, fraud or fortune out of the earnings of others.

But from the great variety of capacities, strength & abilities of men there always was, & always will be, a very unequal distribution of property in the world. Many are so rich that they can live without Labour. Also the merchant, physician, lawyer & divine, the philosopher and school master, the Judicial & Executive Officers, & many others who could honestly get a living without bodily labours. As all these professions require a considerable expense of time & property to qualify themselves therefore, & as no person after qualifying himself & making a pick on a profession by which he means to live, can have it dishonourable or unproductive, so all these professions naturally unite

14. Hazael: II Kings 8:13.

in their schemes to make their callings as honourable & lucrative as possible. Also as ease & rest from Labour are reasoned among the greatest pleasures of Life, pursued by all with the greatest avidity & when attained at once creates a sense of superiority; & as pride & ostentation are natural to the human heart; these orders of men generally associate together and look down with too much contempt on those that Labour.

On the other hand the Labourer being conscious that it is Labour that supports the whole, & that the more there is that live without Labour & the higher they live or the greater their salaries & fees are, so much the harder he must work, or the shorter he must live, this makes the Labourer watch the others with a jealous eye & often has reason to complain of real impositions. But before I proceed to show how the few & many differ in money matters I will give a short description of what Money is.

Money is not property of itself but only the Representative of property. Silver & Gold are not so valuable as Iron & Steel for real use, but receive all their value from the use that is made of them as a medium of trade. Money is simply this—a thing of lighter carriage than property that has an established value set upon it either by law or general Consent. For Instance if a dollar or a piece of paper, or a chip, would pass throughout a nation or the world for a bushel of corn or any other property to the value of said corn, then it would be the representative of so much property.

Also Money is a thing that will go where it will fetch the most as naturally as water runs down hill, for the possessor will give it where it will fetch the most. Also when there is an addition to the quantity or an extraordinary use of barter & credit in commerce, the prices of property will rise. On the other hand if Credit is ruined & the medium made scarcer, the price of all kinds of property will fall in proportion. Here lies the great scuffle between the few & the many. As the interests & incomes of the few lies chiefly in money at interest, rents, salaries, & fees that are fixed on the nominal value of money, they are interested in having money scarce & the price of labour and production as low as possible. For instance, if the prices of labour and production should fall one half, it would be just the same to the few as if their rents, fees & salaries were doubled, all of which they would get out of the many. Besides, the fall of Labour and production and scarcity of money always brings the many Into distress & compels them into a state of dependence on the few for favours & assistance in a thousand ways.

On the other hand, if the many could raise the price of Labour etc. one half & have the money circulate freely, they could pay their debts, eat & drink & enjoy the good of their labour without being dependent on the few for assistance. Also high prices operate as a bounty on industry & economy. An industrious & prudent man may presently lay up something against time of need when prices are high; but if a person leaves off work & lives high when prices are up, his money or property will last him but a little while.

But the greatest danger the Many are under in these money matters are from the Judicial & Executive Officers, especially so as their incomes for a living are almost wholly gotten from the follies and and distress of the Many, & they being governed by the same selfish principles as other men are. They are the Most interested in the distress of the many of any in the Nation. The scarcer money is & the greater the distress of the many, the better for them. It not only doubles the nominal sum of their pay, but doubles & triples their business, & the many are obliged to come to them cap in hand & beg for mercy, patience & forbearance.

This gratifies both their pride and covetousness, when on the other hand when money is plenty & rises high they have little or nothing to do. This is the Reason why they ought to be kept entirely from the Legislative Body, & unless there can be wisdom enough in the People to keep the three Departments of Government entirely separate, a free Government can't be supported. For in all these conceived difference of interests, it is just the business and duty of the Legislative Body to determine what is Justice or what is Right & Wrong; & the duty of every individual in the nation to regulate his conduct according to their decisions. And if the Many were always fully & fairly represented in the Legislative Body, they never would be oppressed or find fault so as to trouble the Government, but would always be zealous to support it.

The Reasons why a free Government has always failed is from the unreasonable demands & desires of the few. They can't bear to be on a level with their fellow creatures, or submit to the determinations of a Legislature where (as they call it) the Swinish Multitude[15] are fairly represented, but sicken at the idea & are ever hankering & striving after Monarchy or Aristocracy where the people have nothing to do in matters of government but to support the few in luxury & idleness.

For those & many other reasons, a large majority of those that live without Labour are ever opposed to the principles & operation of a free Government, and though the whole of them do not amount to one eighth part of the people, yet by their combinations, arts & schemes have always made out to destroy it sooner or later.

[ON LEARNING]

Learning is of the greatest importance to the support of a free government, & to prevent this the few are always crying up the advantages of costly colleges, national academies & grammar schools, in order to make places for men to live without work, & so strengthen their party. But are always opposed to cheap schools and woman schools, the only or principle means by which learning is spread among the Many.

[ON KNOWLEDGE]

The greatest & best means of obtaining the knowledge necessary for a free man to have, is by Liberty of the Press, or public Newspapers. To counteract and destroy this privilege the few spare no pains to make them as costly as possible & to contradict everything in them that favours the interests of the Many, putting Darkness for Light, & Light for Darkness, falsehood for truth, & truth for falsehood, etc.

[ON MERCHANTS]

The merchants have organized themselves & have their Chambers of Commerce & correspondence from one end of the Continent to the other. Although they are in

---

15. Swinish Multitude: from Edmund Burke, *Reflections on the Revolution in France* (1790): "Learning will be cast into the mire and trodden down under the hoofs of a swinish multitude."

many respects a great advantage to the Many, by making vent for our produce & furnishing us with necessaries & conveniences from other countries, yet if we should be drawn into a war by their adventures we should pay very dear for all the advantages we receive from them. Besides, foreign trade not well regulated is the most dangerous to the interest of the Many of any thing we have to fear. Our money may be all carried off from among us for that which will do us no good.

Foreign manufactories may be cheapest at first cost but not in the long run. Merchants may grow rich on the ruins of our mechanics & manufactories, & bring us into as bad a condition as we were in 1786, for they look only to their own interests. It is evident that a large part of the merchants were in favor of the British treaty and fond of carrying on a trade with that sinking Nation, which trade leaves a balance against America of more than 4 million dollars annually, which will ruin us in a few years unless it is stopped.

Chapter 12

Science in America: The Eighteenth Century

INTRODUCTION

One of the major figures in colonial science was a London merchant who made his counting house the hub of transatlantic scientific communication by receiving letters, reports, and samples of American flora and fauna, and passing them along to scientists all over England and the continent. The importance of this merchant, Peter Collinson, points to the main enterprise of colonial science, which in the eighteenth century was still mostly concerned with gathering information about the new lands. The New World had been from the first an object of enormous scientific interest. By the early eighteenth century, American-born or permanent settlers had taken over the roles of collector, surveyor, and explorer. Through Collinson, John Bartram, a farmer and botanist living outside Philadelphia, received a royal pension to collect seeds and plants. Benjamin Franklin carried over a few boxes of these on a trip to London. Jared Eliot, Thomas Jefferson, Cadwallader Colden, John Logan, John Mitchell—virtually all educated farmers in the colonies engaged in some form of botanical research—sent their findings to Europe. At one point, Jefferson dispatched an entire elk to the Count de Buffon in Paris.

Natural history and historians dominated the scientific scene. A natural historian, Logan, brought the first copy of Newton's *Principia Mathematica* to America in 1708, and the learned community followed the major trends of English and European science. Yet, while American natural philosophy was Newtonian the way all English science was, the *Principia* was not a frequent reference. When Franklin tried in the middle of the century to establish the American Philosophical Society as an equivalent to the Royal Society and the French Académie des Sciences, his co-organizer was John Bartram; they planned it by drawing up the list of natural historians.

This resident group would claim a distinct and perhaps superior knowledge derived from its experience on the ground. In 1781–82, as the war for independence waxed and waned around him, Jefferson found occasion to refute Buffon's thesis that nature in the New World, having degenerated for want of cultivation, was inferior to Europe's. Buffon was the authoritative author of the first systematic natural history. Still, with all due respect, Jefferson reported that his own collected samples showed American plants and animals were, in fact, somewhat bigger than their European counterparts, and also more fertile. The possession modern science takes of its worlds is perhaps the most complete of all the forms of taking possession. Jefferson, devoting many more pages to the exposition of Buffon's errors than to any other single subject

in the *Notes*, claims the New World on the ground not just of history, as in the *Declaration*, but of knowledge. In the world constituted by Bacon's dictum that "knowledge itself is power," Jefferson's history gives him rights over America, but his knowledge gives him America itself.

It is important to note that Jefferson does not dispute Buffon's theoretical principle that cultivation improves nature, but only his measurements and calculations—his facts. A few years later, writing to the Reverend James Madison, Jefferson reported irritably that Jan Ingenhouse, a Dutch physiologist, was proposing that "*light* promotes vegetation"; this, in Jefferson's opinion, was another example of a current "rage of drawing general conclusions from partial and equivocal observation." In his view, general ideas were to be avoided until they became virtual facts. "It is always better to have no ideas, than false ones," he declared, "to believe nothing, than to believe what is wrong."

Of course, neither an interest in natural history nor the view that science should be based entirely on facts was exclusively American. We have already traced empiricism to sixteenth- and seventeenth-century England in the work of Francis Bacon and the Royal Society (see chapter 7); in the eighteenth century, John Locke was its preeminent exponent. But the empirical philosophy of science was like Puritanism: an idea that transplanted so well to America, it became characteristically American. There is, of course, a relation between empirical science and Puritanism, and the example of Jonathan Edwards makes it explicit. Though he was probably no more than eleven when he wrote out his observations of insects, Edwards was already the ideal American scientist when he wrote that the phenomenon he described was not to be taken "as an hypothesis, but as a plain fact, which my own eyes have witnessed, and which every one's senses may make him as certain of as of anything else."

While there does appear to be something characteristically American, therefore, in Jefferson's skepticism about theoretical reasoning, the fact that he was living in France when he learned of Ingenhouse's theory probably inspired him to be especially severe. For in Paris, in the 1780s, Jefferson would have been an empiricist not only through preference but also by assignment. A heated dispute over the usefulness of theory divided French philosophy. Franklin's experiments in electricity were cited by the antitheory party as proving the superiority of unprejudiced experimentation.

Moreover, that Franklin had gone from showing that lightning was electricity, to constructing a lighting rod for the protection of peoples' houses, provided a parable of the science of practice resulting in both provable and practical knowledge. Thus America's way of science was defined in Paris and London as well as in Philadelphia—in the case of Franklin, perhaps more in Paris than in Philadelphia.

For despite his reputation among French natural philosophers (the eighteenth-century term for scientists) as one who scorned systems, Franklin's experiments and, indeed, his inventions, did flow from theoretical premises. His letters to European and English correspondents reveal an ambitiously speculative mind. And while he certainly produced plenty of instruments and devices, these involved elaborate theorizing. The lightning rod is a prime example. The work on electricity it implements, Franklin's most famous, projects an entire metaphysics. Yet even as he assiduously sought recognition for this work, he also participated fully in the promotion of his image as a man more interested in stoves than in theories. (One of his stoves, the Pennsylvania fireplace, seems to have worked only in theory, proving inefficient and possibly dangerous in practice.)

It is true that Franklin's work was unusual in colonial science, so that although he misrepresented himself, he did not misrepresent his American colleagues. Nonetheless, the oddity of his assuming a persona that belied his work, but through which he offered himself as a representative of American science, may be instructive. The implication that the characterization of an especially pragmatic American science was both real *and* a fabrication, can highlight the way such characterizations are all more or less invented.

—M.J.

Suggested reading: The standard text is Brooke Hindle's *The Pursuit of Science in Revolutionary America, 1735–1789*. Daniel Boorstin's discussions in *The Americans: The Colonial Experience* (see reading suggestions for chapter 7) cover the eighteenth century as well. Three books by I. B. Cohen measure the interest of this period in the evolution of American science and thought: *Franklin and Newton, Benjamin Franklin's Science*, and *Science and the Founding Fathers: Science in the Political Thought of Jefferson, Franklin, Adams and Madison*.

1. Cotton Mather

from *The Christian Philosopher* 1721

The youngest of the Mather Dynasty, Cotton Mather (1663–1728) is also the best-known today. Our concern with him here is as a natural philosopher rather than as a theologian, though it is not really possible to separate these two sides of his thinking. What has been said of his father's joining of orthodoxy and rationality (see chapter 7) can be repeated here as a gloss on the title of his collection of scientific essays, The Christian Philosopher, *for by "philosopher" he means "natural philosopher"—in today's idiom, "scientist."*

The Christian Philosopher *shows the range of Mather's interests, which extended to areas beyond the natural sciences to include what would today be called chemistry and, in the essay reprinted below, physics. The last is an exposition of Newtonian science. One of Mather's proudest achievements was his election to the Royal Society.*

ESSAY XVII. *Of the* AIR.

The *Air* of our Atmosphere, in which we breathe, is a diaphanous, compressible, dilatable *Fluid*; a Body covering the Earth and the Sea, to a great height above the highest Mountains: in this, among other things, differing from the *Æther*, that it refracts the Rays of the Moon, and other Luminaries.

There seem to be three different sorts of *Corpuscles*, whereof the *Air* is composed. There are such as are carried up into the *Air* from other Bodies, as *Vapours* exhaled by the *Sun's Heat*, or by subterraneous. There may be also a more subtile kind, mixed with our *Air*, emitted from the *Heavenly Bodies*, and from the *Magnetick Steams* of the Globe on which we sojourn. But there may be a third sort of Particles, which may most properly merit the Name of *Aerial*; as being the distinguishing Parts of the Air, taken in the stricter sense of the Term. These Particles have an *Elasticity* in them; are springy; resemble the *Spring* of a *Watch*. *Elasticity* is an essential Property of the *Air*, and it is thought no other *Fluid* has any thing of it, but only so far as it participates of *Air*, or has *Air* contain'd in the Pores of it. Our *Air* abounds with Particles of such a nature, that in case they be bent, or press'd by the Weight of the incumbent part of the *Atmosphere*, or of any other Body, they endeavour to free themselves from that Pressure, by bearing against the Bodies that keep them under it; and as soon as the Removal of these Bodies gives them way, they expand the whole parcel of *Air* which they composed.

Dr. *Hook* thinks the Air to be little else than a Tincture or Solution of terrestrial and aqueous Particles, dissolved in, and agitated by the *Æther*, and to have something *saline* in their Nature.

Mr. *Boyle* found, that one and the same Portion of Air may take up 52,000 times the Space it doth at another time. He found, that the same Quantity of Air, by only having the Pressure of the Atmosphere taken off in the *Pneumatick Engine*, and without increasing the Spring with any adventitious Heat, would possess above 13,000 times its natural Dimensions. Dr. *Gregory* proceeds, That accordingly a Globe of *Air*, of one Inch diameter, would at the Distance of the Semidiameter of the Earth from the Earth, fill all the Planetary Regions as far as, and much beyond the Sphere of *Saturn*. Admirable Rarefaction!

The *Weight of Air* was discover'd first by *Galilæus*, who finding that *Water* could not by pumping be raised any higher than 34 or 35 Foot, concluded that the old Notion of an infinite *Fuga Vacui* would never do; and so fell to thinking on the Counterbalance of *the Weight of the Air*. *Torricellius* afterwards pursued and improved the Thought, and as a further Proof of *the Weight of the Air*, invented that which we call *the Torricellian Experiment*.

Mr. *Boyle* found by repeated Experiments, that the Weight of *Air* to *Water* is as 1 to 1000.

Dr. *Halley* rather determines the *Specifick Gravity* of Air to Water, to be about 1 to 800. *Mercury* is to Air as 10,800 to 1. And so, a Cylinder of *Air*, of 900 Feet, is equal to an Inch of *Mercury*.

We will, with Dr. *Wainwright*, suppose a cubical Foot of *Water* to weigh 76 Pounds *Troy* Weight. The Compass of a Foot square upon the Superficies of our Bodies, must sustain a Quantity of *Air*, equal to 2660 Pounds Weight. If the Superficies of a Man's Body contains fifteen square Feet, which is pretty near the Truth, he would sustain a Weight equal to 39,900 Pounds *Troy*:[1] standard system of weights used for precious metals and precious stones which is above thirteen *Tun*. The difference between the greatest and the least Pressure of the *Air* upon our Bodies, is equal to 3982 Pounds *Troy*. On which the Doctor says, 'No wonder then we suffer in our Health by Changes of Weather; 'tis surprizing that every such Change does not entirely break the Frame of our Bodies to pieces, and be the constant Harbinger of sudden Death.'

My God, it is because I have obtained Help from thee, that I continue to this Day!

Sir *Isaac Newton* thinks *true and permanent Air* to be made by Fermentation and Rarefaction of Bodies, that are of a very fixed Nature. And it is plain, those Particles *fly* and *avoid* one another with the greatest Force *at a distance*, which when they are *very near*, do *attract* and *adhere* to one another with the greatest Violence.

The Particles of *true and permanent Air*, being extracted from the densest and most fixed Bodies, will be more dense and crass than those of *Vapour*, and from hence, it's likely, may be heavier than those; and the Parts of an *humid Atmosphere* may be lighter than those of a *dry* one, as in fact they appear to be. He thinks therefore, that the Rarefaction and Condensation of the Air cannot be accounted for from the *Spring*, or Elastick Forms of the Particles, without a Supposition, that they are endued with

---

1. Pounds *Troy*: standard system of weights used for precious metals and precious stones.

some *Centrifugal* Force or Power, by which they *fly* and *avoid* one another, and the dense Bodies, from whence they are extracted.

This may be the cause for *Filtration*, and the Ascent of Water in small capillary Tubes, to a much greater height, than the Surface of the Water in the open Vessel, in which they are placed. The Air within the Tubes is much rarer than in more open Spaces, and by that means not pressing so much on the Surface of the Water within the Tubes, as without.

It is admirable to consider the Necessity of *Air* to the whole *animal* World; how soon the *vital Flame* does languish and expire, if *Air* be withheld from it! Even the Inhabitants of the Water cannot live without the Use of it. It is evident that the *Air*, at the least that part of it which is the Aliment of *Fire*, and the Fuel of the *vital Flame* in Animals, easily penetrates the Body of Water exposed to it, and with a wondrous Insinuation diffuses itself thro every part of it. Put Fishes into a Vessel of a narrow mouth, full of Water, they will continue to live and swim there whole Months and Years. But if with any Covering you stop the Vessel, so as to exclude the *Air*, or interrupt the Communication of it with the Water, they will suddenly be suffocated; which was an Experiment often made by *Rondeletius*. The *Insects* rather need more *Air* than other Creatures, having more *Air-Vessels* for their Bulk, and many Orifices on each side of their Bodies for the Admission of *Air*, which if you stop with Oil or Honey, they presently die, and revive no more. *Pliny* knew not the reason of his own Observation; *Oleo illito Insecta omnia exanimantur:*[2] Yea, *Malpighius* has discovered and demonstrated, that the *Plants* themselves have a kind of Respiration, being furnished with a Plenty of Vessels for the Derivation of *Air* to all their Parts. Dr. *Hulse*, and Mr. *Ray*, and others, have now also render'd it very evident, That the *Fœtus* in the Womb does receive a measure of *Air* from the maternal Blood, by the *Placenta Uterina*, or the *Cotyledons*. When this Communication is broken off, what is it that now, to preserve the Life of the Animal, speedily raises the *Lungs*, and fetches into them an abundance of *Air*, which causes a sudden and mighty Accension in the Blood, for the Maintenance whereof a far greater Quantity of Air is requisite? Certainly some intelligent Being must now interpose, to put the Diaphragm, and all the Muscles that serve to Respiration, into their Motion!

My God, I know thee! And now, as our ingenious *Waller* sings;

Thus wing'd with Praise, we penetrate the Sky,
Teach Clouds and Stars to praise Him as we fly.
For that He reigns, all Creatures should rejoice,
And we with Songs supply their want of Voice.
Angels and we, assisted by this Art,
May sing together, tho we dwell apart.

'The *Syrians* worshipped the *Air* as a *God*. I will worship Him that created it.
I will give Thanks to the Glorious God, for the Benefits with which the *Air* is

---

2. Having been smeared with olive oil, all the insects die.

replenished by his Bounty. It was long since called the *Paranymph*, by which the Espousal and Communion between *Heaven* and *Earth* is carried on.

I *breathe* in the *Favours* of God continually. An ungrateful Wretch, if I do not *breathe out* his *Praises*!

How justly might the Great God fill the Air with invisible *Arrows* of Death, and such deleterious *Miasms*, and pestilential *Poisons*, as might suffer the *Unholy* and *Unthankful* to *breathe* no longer in it!

2. Jonathan Edwards

letter on spiders
1723

Edwards was among those who died as a result of being inoculated in the smallpox experiments described in chapter 7. His participation in the experiment dramatizes the commitment to scientific inquiry already noted among the leading Puritan think-ers. For Edwards, in the generation after Cotton Mather, was perhaps the most important theologian of the group. Like his colleagues, he was a rationalist who believed that God communicates with human beings by instilling them with ideas.

This letter (probably written when Edwards was eleven years old) reveals—the better for its naivete—the faith in observation and fact-gathering that, following Bacon and Locke, defines the science of eighteenth-century Anglo-America. It was addressed to Judge Paul Dudley, Fellow of the Royal Society of London.

Windsor, Oct. 31, 1723

Sir:

In the postscript of your letter to my father you manifest a willingness to receive anything else that he has observed in nature worthy of remark; that which is the subject of the following lines by him was thought to be such: he has laid it upon me to write the account, I having had advantage to make more full observations. If you think, Sir, that they are not worthy the taking notice of, with greatness and goodness overlook and conceal. They are some things that I have happily seen of the wondrous and curious works of the spider. Although everything pertaining to this insect is admirable, yet there are some phenomena relating to them more particularly wonderful.

Everybody that is used to the country knows of their marching in the air from one tree to another, sometimes at the distance of five or six rods, though they are wholly destitute of wings: nor can one go out in a dewy morning at the latter end of August and beginning of September but he shall see multitudes of webs reaching from one tree and shrub to another; which webs are commonly thought to be made in the night because they appear only in the morning by reason of the dew that hangs on them, whereas they never work in the night, they love to lie still when the air is dark and moist; but these webs may be seen well enough in the daytime by an observing eye, by their reflection of the sunbeams; especially late in the afternoon may those webs that are between the eye, and that part of the horizon that is under the sun, be seen very plainly, being advantageously posited to reflect the rays, and the spiders themselves may be very often seen traveling in the air from one stage to another amongst the trees in a very unaccountable manner.

But, Sir, I have often seen that which is yet more astonishing. In a very calm serene day in the forementioned time of year, standing at some distance between the end of an house or some other opaque body, so as just to hide the disk of the sun and keep off his dazzling rays, and looking along close by the side of it, I have seen vast multitudes of little shining webs and glistening strings, brightly reflecting the sunbeams, and some of them of a great length, and at such a height that one would think that they were tacked to the vault of the heavens, and would be burnt like tow in the sun, making a very pleasing as well as surprising appearance. It is wonderful at what a distance these webs may plainly be seen in such a position to the sunbeams, which are so fine that they cannot be seen in another position, though held near to the eye; some that are at a great distance appear (it cannot be otherwise) several thousands of times as big as they ought: They doubtless appear under as great an angle as a body of a foot diameter ought to do at such a distance; so greatly doth coruscation increase the apparent bigness of bodies at a distance, as is observed in the fixed stars. But that which is most astonishing is that very often there appears at the end of these webs, spiders sailing in the air with them, doubtless with abundance of pleasure, though not with so much as I have beheld them and shewed them to others. And since I have seen these things I have been very conversant with spiders. Resolving if possible to find out the mysteries of these their amazing works, and pursuing my observations, I discovered one wonder after another till I have been so happy as very frequently to see their whole manner of working; which is thus:

When a spider would go from one tree or branch to another, or would recreate himself by sailing or floating in the air, he first lets himself down a little way from the twig he stands on by a web, as in Fig. 1; and then taking hold of it by his forefeet as in Fig. 2, and then separates or loosens the part of the web *cd* from the part *bc* by which he hangs; which part of the web *cd*, being thus loosened, will by the motion of the air be carried out towards *e*, which will by the sufferance of the spider be drawn [out] of his tail with infinite ease by the moving air, to what length the spider pleases, as in Fig. 3: And if the further end of the web *de*, as it is running out and moving to and fro, happens to catch by a shrub or the branch of a tree, the spider immediately feels it and fixes the hither end of it, *d*, to the web *bc*, and goes over as by a bridge by the web *de*. Every particular of this, Sir, my eyes have innumerable times made me sure of, saving that I never could distinctly see how they separated the part of the web *cd* (Fig. 2) from the part *bc*, whether it be done by biting of it off or how, because so small a piece of so fine a web is altogether imperceptible amongst the spider's legs, and because the spider is so very quick and dexterous in doing of it all. But I have seen that it is done, though I have not seen how they do it. For this, Sir, I can see: that the web *bc* (Fig. 3) is separated, and not joined to the spider's tail, while the web *de* is drawing out.

Now, Sir, it is certain that these webs, when they first come from the spider, are so rare a substance that they are lighter than the air, because they will immediately ascend in a calm air, and never descend except driven by a wind: and 'tis as certain that what swims and ascends in the air is lighter than the air, as that what ascends and swims in water is lighter than that: So that if we should suppose any such time wherein the air is perfectly calm, this web is so easily drawn out of the spider's tail, that barely the levity of it is sufficient to carry it out to any length. But at least its levity, or ascending inclination, together with so much motion as the air is never without, will well suffice for this. Wherefore, if it be so that the end of the web *de* (Fig. 3) catches by no tree nor other body till it be drawn out so long that its levity shall be so great as to be more than equal to the gravity of the spider, or so that the web and the spider taken together shall be lighter than such a quantity of air as takes up equal space, then according to the universally acknowledged laws of nature the web and the spider together will ascend and not descend in the air. As when a man [is] at the bottom of the water, if he has hold of a piece of timber so great that the wood's tendency upwards is greater than the man's tendency downwards, he

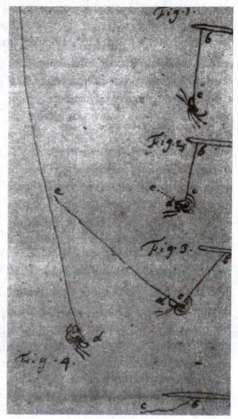

The Spider's Trajectory. (Edwards's sketch)

together with the wood will ascend to the surface of the water. Therefore, when the spider perceives that the web *de* is long enough to bear him up by its ascending force (which force the spider feels by its drawing of him towards *e*), he lets go his hold of the web *bc* (Fig. 4) and, holding by the web *de*, ascends and floats in the air with it. If there be not web more than enough just to equal with its levity the gravity of the spider, the spider together with the web will hang *in equilibrio*, neither ascending nor descending, otherwise than as the air moves; but if there be so much web that its ascending tendency, or rather the buoying force of the air upon it, shall be greater than the descending tendency of the spider, they will ascend till the air is so thin, till they together are just of an equal weight with so much air. But if the web be so short as not to counterpoise the weight of the spider, the web and spider will fall till they come to the ground.

And this very way, Sir, I have multitudes of times seen spiders mount away into the air with a vast train of this silver web before them from a stick in mine hand; for if the spider be disturbed upon the stick by shaking of it he will presently in this manner leave it. Their way of working may very distinctly be seen if they are held up in the sun, in a calm day, against a dark door or anything that is black.

And this, Sir, is the way of spiders' working. This is the way of their going from one thing to another at a distance, and this is the way of their flying in the air. And although I can say I am certain of it, I don't desire that the truth of it should be received upon my word, though I could bring others to testify to it to whom I have shewn it, and who have looked on with admiration: But everyone's eyes who will take the pains to observe will make them equally sure of it; only those who would make experiment must take notice that it is not every sort of spider that is a flying spider, for those spiders that keep in houses are a quite different sort, as also those that keep in the ground, and those that keep in swamps upon the ground amongst the bogs, and those that keep in hollow trees and rotten logs; but those spiders that keep on branches of trees and shrubs are the flying spiders. They delight most in walnut trees, and are that sort of spiders that make those curious, network, polygonal webs that are so frequently to be seen in the latter end of the year. There are more of this sort of spider by far than of any other.

Corol. 1. Hence the wisdom of the Creator in providing of the spider with that wonderful liquor with which their bottle tail is filled, that may so easily be drawn out so exceeding fine, and being in this way exposed to the air will so immediately convert to a dry substance that shall be so very rare as to be lighter than the air, and will so excellently serve to all their purposes.

Corol. 2. Hence the exuberant goodness of the Creator, who hath not only provided for all the necessities, but also for the pleasure and recreation of all sorts of creatures, even the insects.

But yet, Sir, I am assured that the chief end of this faculty that is given them is not their recreation but their destruction, because their destruction is unavoidably the constant effect of it; and we find nothing that is the continual effect of nature but what is the end of the means by which it is brought to pass: but it is impossible but that the greatest part of the spiders upon the land should every year be swept into the ocean. For these spiders never fly except the weather be fair and the atmosphere dry, but the atmosphere is never clear and dry, neither in this nor any other continent, only when the wind blows from the midland parts, and consequently towards the sea; as here in New England, the fair weather is only when the wind is westerly, the land being on that side and the ocean on the easterly. I scarcely ever have seen any of these spiders flying but when they have been hastening directly towards the sea. And the time of their flying being so long, even from about the middle of August, every sunshiny day till about the end of October (though their chief time, as was observed before, is the latter end of August and beginning of September). And they, never flying from the sea but always towards it, must get there at last. And it seems unreasonable to think that they have sense to stop themselves when they come near the sea, for then we should see hundreds of times more spiders on the seashore than anywhere else. When they are once carried over the water their webs grow damp and moist and lose their levity and their wings fail them, and let them down into the water.

The same also holds true of other sorts of flying insects, for at those times that I have viewed the spiders with their webs in the air there has also appeared vast multitudes of flies at a great height, and all flying the same way with the spiders and webs, direct to the ocean. And even such as butterflies, millers, and moths, which keep in the grass at this time of year, I have seen vastly higher than the tops of the highest trees, all going the same way. These I have seen towards evening, right overhead, and without a screen to defend my eye from the sunbeams, which I used to think were seeking a warmer climate. The reason of their flying at that time of year I take to be because the ground and trees and grass, the places of their residence in summer, begin to be chill and uncomfortable. Therefore when the sun shines pretty warm they leave them, and mount up into the air and expand their wings to the sun, and flying for nothing but their own ease and comfort, they suffer themselves to go that way that they can go with the greatest ease, and so where the wind pleases: and it being warmth they fly for, they never fly against the wind nor sidewise to it, they find it cold and laborious; they therefore seem to use their wings but just so much as to bear them up, and suffer themselves to go with the wind. So that it must necessarily be that almost all aerial insects, and spiders which live upon them and are made up of them, are at the end of the year swept away into the sea and buried in the ocean, and leave nothing behind them but their eggs for a new stock the next year.

Corol. 1. Hence there is reason to admire at the wisdom of the Creator, and to be convinced that it is exercised about such little things in this wonderful contrivance of annually carrying off and burying the corruption and nauseousness of the air, of which flying insects are little collections, in the bottom of the ocean where it will do no harm; and especially the strange way of bringing this about in spiders, which are collections of these collections, their food being flying insects, flies being the poison of the air, and spiders are the poison of flies collected together. And what great inconveniences should we labor under if it were not so, for spiders and flies are such exceedingly multiplying creatures, that if they only slept or lay benumbed in winter, and were raised again in the spring, which is commonly thought, it would not be many years before we should be plagued with as vast numbers as Egypt was. And if they died ultimately in winter, they by the renewed heat of the sun would presently again be dissipated into the nauseous vapors of which they are made up, and so would be of no use or benefit in that in which now they are so very serviceable and which is the chief end of their creation.

Corol. 2. The wisdom of the Creator is also admirable in so nicely and mathematically adjusting their plastic nature, that notwithstanding their destruction by this means and the multitudes that are eaten by birds, that they do not decrease and so by little and little come to nothing; and in so adjusting their destruction to their multiplication they do neither increase, but taking one year with another, there is always an equal number of them.

These, Sir, are the observations I have had opportunity to make on the wonders that are to be seen in the most despicable of animals. Although these things appear for the main very certain to me, yet, Sir, I submit it all to your better judgment, and deeper insight. I humbly beg to be pardoned for running the venture, though an utter stranger, of troubling you with so prolix an account of that which I am altogether uncertain whether you will esteem worthy of the time and pains of reading. Pardon me if I thought it might at least give you occasion to make better observations on these wondrous animals, that should be worthy of communicating to the learned world, from whose glistening webs so much of the wisdom of the Creator shines.

Pardon, Sir, your most obedient humble servant,

Jonathan Edwards

3. Jared Eliot

from *Essays Upon Field Husbandry in New England*
1760

*Jared Eliot (1685–1763) was a physician, a natural philosopher who investigated
the properties of iron, and an experimental farmer interested in hardier grains,
better methods of fertilizing, and especially in the culture of silkworms—in short, a
gentleman and a scholar, eighteenth-century style. A leading member of the
community of colonial natural philosophers whose observations and collections of
samples continued the exploration of the New World, Eliot in his* Essays *exempli-
fies the fusion of everyday practice, experiment, and philosophical speculation that
characterized colonial science. His motto might well have been the Dutch proverb
he cites, "That something is always good for something."*

*Notable also in this selection is Eliot's advocacy of a plain and simple prose
which, as he demonstrates, nonetheless retains a place for the display of learning
(for instance about ancient Rome); learning not pompously paraded but still
evident, marking a gentleman, albeit one who wishes to be read and understood by
a broad public.*

[FROM THE FIRST ESSAY]

I began last *March* to Drein another Meadow of Forty Acres, up in *Guilford*
Woods; this was a shaking Meadow; A Man standing upon it might shake the
Ground several Rods round him. It seemed to be only a strong sward of Grass
Roots laid over a soft Mud of the consistence of Pancake Batter: There was not abundance of Bushes in it, but abundance of Cramberry Vines, and a great burthen of poor
wild Grass: The Meadow was deemed so poor that none would take it up. I was pitied
as being about to waste a great deal of Money; but they comforted themselves that if I
spent it unprofitably, others that stood in need of it would get it: They are now of
another opinion.

At the only Out-let of this Meadow, there was Fall sufficient, but very Rocky; we
must dig four or five Foot deep to get the Advantage of it.

In *March* when I went up to make the Out-let Drein there was such a torrent of
Water that we could do nothing; I ordered therefore a Tree to be cut down across the
Brook, and prepared Flitches[3] instead of Plank which we set aslant, the upper end

---

3. Flitches: a lengthwise strip from the outer part of a tree-
trunk.

resting upon the Staddle that was fallen across the Brook, laid them as close as we could, and stopped the Chinks and large Chasms with top Tow[4] by which means we shut the Water into the Meadow, then wro't[5] at the Trench or main Drein in the Day, and let it out at Night, till it was in a good measure accomplished. When I ordered the top Tow to be carried, the Men wondred what it was designed for, but when they saw how useful it was in making a cheap Dam they were pleased with it. I put them in mind of the *Dutch* Proverb, who say of things that are very mean, *That something is always good for something.*

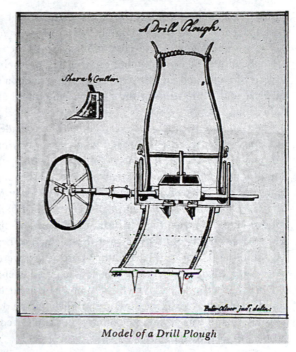

Model of a Drill Plough

[FROM THE SECOND ESSAY]

As to the increasing Scarcity of Wheat, one Reason may be the illicit Trade carried on with the Enemy; but the principal Reason, I suppose to be what follows, *viz.* When our fore-Fathers settled here, they entered a Land which probably never had been Ploughed since the Creation; the Land being new they depended upon the natural Fertility of the Ground, which served their purpose very well, and when they had worn out one piece they cleared another, without any concern to amend their Land, except a little helped by the Fold and Cart-dung, whereas in *England* they would think a Man a bad Husband[6] if he should pretend to sow Wheat on Land without any Dressing.

Sometimes they dress their Land with Lime, Chalk, Soot; sometimes with Rags, Hogs and Cattles Hair, Horn-shavings and Ashes, and with various other sorts of manure; by which means they have fine Crops of Wheat upon Land which hath been Improved more than a Thousand Years; for they reckon Twenty Bushels to the Acre but a middling Crop.

Our Lands being thus worn out, I suppose to be one Reason why so many are inclined to Remove to new Places that they may raise Wheat: As also that they may have more Room, thinking that we live too thick.

Now whether I have assigned the true Reasons or Causes of the present Difficulties under which many parts of the Country suffer, is submitted to the censure of the judi-

4. Tow: the coarse and broken fibers of hemp or flax.
5. wro't: worked.

6. Husband: farmer.

cious Reader, the matters of Fact are certain, whatever becomes of the Reasons assigned: *For if all Men cannot judge, yet all Men can feel.*

Every observing reader of History must have taken notice of the account given of great Numbers of People living on and having their Subsistance from very small parcels of Land, and mighty Armies are raised from a small Territory, which is to the surprize and admiration of the Reader; which will afford a great variety of useful Reflections.

The Children of Israel were very Numerous considering the smallness of the Land of *Canaan*, as will appear by the List given in to King *David*, consequent upon his Command to have the People Numbered: More particularly what will shew the Populousness of that Land, is what we read, 2 Chron. 13.3. *And Abijah set the battle in array, with an Army of valiant Men of War, even four hundred thousand chosen Men: Jeroboam also set the battle in array against him with eight hundred thousand chosen Men.* It is true, their Militia was formed as ours, of the Body of the People, from Sixteen Years old to Sixty, yet this seemed to be a collection of only their best Men and the flower of their Military Force; they were *chosen Men, Men of Valour,* neither old Men, sick Persons, nor new married Men, who were exempted by Law, Cowards or Cripples; of which there must be great Numbers, besides Women and Children, who have Mouths to Eat, tho' they had neither hands nor strength to Fight. This holy Land was an Inland Country, not supported by Trade, but supplied by the Product of their own Land.

[FROM THE FIFTH ESSAY]

In this Essay, I design to shew how Land may be tilled, and the Dung so applied as that a little Dung shall extend as far, and do as much to promote and produce a Crop of Corn, as six Times so much Dung applied in the Common Way. The old worn out Land is to be tilled in such a Manner that affords a Prospect, that the same Land in two or three Years, shall produce Crops without Dung, or any Sort of Manure, in some Measure agreeable to the Method of the excellent and truly learned Mr. *Tull,*[7] a Summary of whose Principles or Doctrine, I here present to the Reader in his own Words.

"The only Way we have to inrich the Earth, is to divide it into many Parts, by Manure or by Tillage, or by both: This is called *Pulveration.* The Salt of Dung divide or pulverize the Soil by *Fermentation,* Tillage by the Attrition or *Contusion* of Instruments, of which the Plough is the Chief. The Superficies or Surfaces of those divided Parts of the Earth, is the Artificial Pasture of Plants, and affords the Vegetable Pabulum to such Roots as come into contact with it. There is no Way to exhaust the Earth of this Pabulum, but by the Roots of the Plants, and Plants are now proved to extend their Roots more than was formerly thought they did. Division is infinite, and the more Parts the Soil is divided into, the more of that Superficies or vegetable

---

7. Mr. *Tull:* Jethro Tull, a seventeenth-century Englishman whose lifelong experiments in agriculture were published in *The New Horse-Houghing Husbandry* (1731). The book aroused controversy but was much admired and followed by enlightened farmers in the colonies. He also invented a plow and a seed drill which became ubiquitous.

Pasture must it have, and more of those Benefits which descend from the Atmosphere will it receive. Therefore if the Earth be divided, if it be by Tillage, it answers the same End as if it had been performed by Dung."

In the fore-cited Passage, Mr. *Tull* has had but little Regard to the Capacity of his Reader: Nor will it be much better understood than if it had been wrote in an unknown Tongue, there being so many Words used by him which common Farmers do not understand; and therefore that Book has not been so useful as otherwise it might have been. That excellent Writer seems to me to have entered deeper into the true Principles of Husbandry, than any Author I have ever read. Had he taken Pains to accommodate himself to the Unlearned, his Book would have been much more useful than now it is.

I am very sensible, that the low Stile, the Plainness and Simplicity of these Essays, has exposed them to the Centure of those who do not well consider for whom they are intended and written.

It is much easier to let the Pen run forward in a pompous Parade of Learning, than to bring it into such subjection as to convey and communicate important Truths in such Words as shall be understood, and to use such Plainness and Simplicity as will bring all down to the Level of the most inferior Capacity.

4. Benjamin Franklin

Of Lightning, and the Method (Now Used in America) of Securing Buildings and Persons from Its Mischievous Effects
1767

Franklin became interested in the phenomenon of electricity in 1743 when reports of electrical experiments in France and Germany began to proliferate in international journals. In 1749, the ever-helpful Peter Collinson sent a glass tube in current use in Europe, and Franklin began the series of experiments that won him international fame. He reported on these in a set of letters gathered, in 1751, into a book, Experiments and Observations on Electricity *which suggested the terminology of negative and positive charges that became standard. In the event, his theory—that there exists a single electrical fluid, with negative electricity resulting from a deficiency in this fluid— was mistaken. But his terms stuck.*

His electrical experiments with lightning was so dramatic it has passed into folklore. Franklin was not the first to declare lightning an electrical discharge, but he was the first to do something about it. The letter reprinted here sets out the theory and practice of the lightning rod, a particularly welcome invention in the colonies, where houses were generally built of wood. The precision of Franklin's account represents not only his desire that it be usable as a blueprint but his immersion in experimentation and its exactitude. This selection may recall Increase Mather's discussion of lightning in chapter 7.

Experiments made in electricity first gave philosophers a suspicion that the matter of lightning was the same with the electric matter. Experiments afterwards made on lightning obtained from the clouds by pointed rods, received into bottles, and subjected to every trial, have since proved this suspicion to be perfectly well founded; and that whatever properties we find in electricity, are also the properties of lightning.

This matter of lightning, or of electricity, is an extream subtile fluid, penetrating other bodies, and subsisting in them, equally diffused.

When by any operation of art or nature, there happens to be a greater proportion of this fluid in one body than in another, the body which has most, will communicate to that which has least, till the proportion becomes equal; provided the distance between them be not too great; or, if it is too great, till there be proper conductors to convey it from one to the other.

If the communications be through the air without any conductor, a bright light is seen between the bodies, and a sound is heard. In our small experiments we call this light and sound the electric spark and snap; but in the great operations of nature, the light is what we call *lightning*, and the sound (produced at the same time, tho' generally arriving later at our ears than the light does to our eyes) is, with its echoes, called *thunder*.

If the communication of this fluid is by a conductor, it may be without either light or sound, the subtle fluid passing in the substance of the conductor.

If the conductor be good and of sufficient bigness, the fluid passes through it without hurting it. If otherwise, it is damaged or destroyed.

All metals, and water, are good conductors.—Other bodies may become conductors by having some quantity of water in them, as wood, and other materials used in building, but not having much water in them, they are not good conductors, and therefore are often damaged in the operation.

Glass, wax, silk, wool, hair, feathers, and even wood, perfectly dry are non-conductors: that is, they resist instead of facilitating the passage of this subtle fluid.

When this fluid has an opportunity of passing through two conductors, one good, and sufficient, as of metal, the other not so good, it passes in the best, and will follow it in any direction.

The distance at which a body charged with this fluid will discharge itself suddenly, striking through the air into another body that is not charged, or not so highly charg'd, is different according to the quantity of the fluid, the dimensions and form of the bodies themselves, and the state of the air between them.—This distance, whatever it happens to be between any two bodies, is called their *striking distance*, as till they come within that distance of each other, no stroke will be made.

The clouds have often more of this fluid in proportion than the earth; in which case as soon as they come near enough (that is, within the striking distance) or meet with a conductor, the fluid quits them and strikes into the earth. A cloud fully charged with this fluid, if so high as to be beyond the striking distance from the earth, passes quietly without making noise or giving light; unless it meets with other clouds that have less.

Tall trees, and lofty buildings, as the towers and spires of churches, become sometimes conductors between the clouds and the earth; but not being good ones, that is,

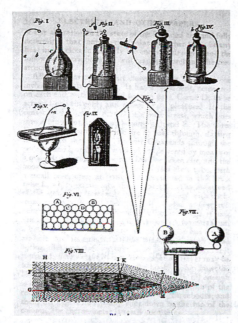

Illustration from Franklin's Experiments and Observations on Electricity.

not conveying the fluid freely, they are often damaged.

Buildings that have their roofs covered with lead, or other metal, and spouts of metal continued from the roof into the ground to carry off the water, are never hurt by lightning, as whenever it falls on such a building, it passes in the metals and not in the walls.

When other buildings happen to be within the striking distance from such clouds, the fluid passes in the walls whether of wood, brick or stone, quitting the walls only when it can find better conductors near them, as metal rods, bolts, and hinges of windows or doors, gilding on wainscot, or frames of pictures; the silvering on the backs of looking-glasses; the wires for bells; and the bodies of animals, as containing watry fluids. And in passing thro' the house it follows the direction of these conductors, taking as many in its way as can assist it in its passage, whether in a strait or crooked line, leaping from one to the other, if not far distant from each other, only rending the wall in the spaces where these partial good conductors are too distant from each other.

An iron rod being placed on the outside of a building, from the highest part continued down into the moist earth, in any direction strait or crooked, following the form of the roof or other parts of the building, will receive the lightning at its upper end, attracting it so as to prevent its striking any other part; and, affording it a good conveyance into the earth, will prevent its damaging any part of the building.

A small quantity of metal is found able to conduct a great quantity of this fluid. A wire no bigger than a goose quill, has been known to conduct (with safety to the building as far as the wire was continued) a quantity of lightning that did prodigious damage both above and below it; and probably larger rods are not necessary, tho' it is common in America, to make them of half an inch, some of three quarters, or an inch diameter.

The rod may be fastened to the wall, chimney, &c. with staples of iron.—The lightning will not leave the rod (a good conductor) to pass into the wall (a bad conductor), through those staples.—It would rather, if any were in the wall, pass out of it into the rod to get more readily by that conductor into the earth.

If the building be very large and extensive, two or more rods may be placed at different parts, for greater security.

Small ragged parts of clouds suspended in the air between the great body of clouds and the earth (like leaf gold in electrical experiments), often serve as partial conductors for the lightning, which proceeds from one of them to another, and by their help comes within the striking distance to the earth or a building. It therefore strikes through those conductors a building that would otherwise be out of the striking distance.

Long sharp points communicating with the earth, and presented to such parts of clouds, drawing silently from them the fluid they are charged with, they are then attracted to the cloud, and may leave the distance so great as to be beyond the reach of striking.

It is therefore that we elevate the upper end of the rod six or eight feet above the highest part of the building, tapering it gradually to a fine sharp point, which is gilt to prevent its rusting.

Thus the pointed rod either prevents a stroke from the cloud, or, if a stroke is made, conducts it to the earth with safety to the building.

The lower end of the rod should enter the earth so deep as to come at the moist part, perhaps two or three feet; and if bent when under the surface so as to go in a horizontal line six or eight feet from the wall, and then bent again downwards three or four feet, it will prevent damage to any of the stones of the foundation.

A person apprehensive of danger from lightning, happening during the time of thunder to be in a house not so secured, will do well to avoid sitting near the chimney, near a looking glass, or any gilt pictures or wainscot; the safest place is in the middle of the room, (so it be not under a metal lustre suspended by a chain) sitting in one chair and laying the feet up in another. It is still safer to bring two or three mattrasses or beds into the middle of the room, and folding them up double, place the chair upon them; for they not being so good conductors as the walls, the lightning will not chuse an interrupted course through the air of the room and the bedding, when it can go thro' a continued better conductor the wall. But where it can be had, a hamock or swinging bed, suspended by silk cords equally distant from the walls on every side, and from the cieling and floor above and below, affords the safest situation a person can have in any room whatever; and what indeed may be deemed quite free from danger of any stroke by lightning.

Paris, Sept. 1767

B. F.

5. Thomas Jefferson

from *Notes on the State of Virginia*, Query 6
1781

Notes on the State of Virginia *was written in answer to a French questionnaire circulated to all the colonies to aid France in its decision whether to support the Revolution. Disposed to back any development that would tend to weaken England, the French king nonetheless wanted assurances that the new American nation would be an advantageous ally. One advantage would lie in significant amounts of natural resources, hence the question about "mines and other subterraneous riches [and] trees, plants, fruits, etc."*

It is not surprising, therefore, to find Jefferson answering at length and as persuasively as possible. But one part of his response to Query 6 may be puzzling when read out of context: the long refutation of the Count de Buffon's "theory of the tendency of nature to belittle her productions on this side of the Atlantic." Buffon, who was in the process of inventing natural history as a field of knowledge, was enormously influential, and in Europe his theory was widely accepted. For one thing, it tended to justify colonization both coming and going: the new continents were inferior to Europe and therefore fit to be her subjects, but the New World could improve under cultivation and therefore colonization would do it good. Jefferson, wishing instead to justify independence from the Old World, wound up arguing the independent worthiness of the continent before the coming of the white men, almost as if he were not one of them. In this regard, he dramatizes the phenomenon of identification with the continent itself that attended its appropriation by the former Europeans, now "Americans."

Query 6 cites directly the passage from Buffon's Natural History *to which Jefferson particularly objected. The selection below omits the first part of the Query, with is descriptions of Virginia's "mines and other subterraneous riches; its trees, plants, fruits, etc."*

ANIMALS

Our quadrupeds have been mostly described by Linnæus and Mons. de Buffon. Of these the Mammoth, or big buffalo, as called by the Indians, must certainly have been the largest. Their tradition is, that he was carnivorous, and still exists in the northern parts of America. A delegation of warriors from the Delaware tribe having visited the governor of Virginia, during the present revolution, on matters of business, after these had been discussed and settled in council, the governor asked them some questions relative to their country, and, among others, what they knew or had heard of the animal whose bones were found at the Saltlicks, on the Ohio. Their chief speaker immediately put himself into an attitude of oratory, and with a pomp suited to what he conceived the elevation of his subject, informed him that it was a tradition handed down from their fathers, 'That in ancient times a herd of these tremendous animals came to the Big-bone licks, and began an universal destruction of the bear, deer, elks, buffaloes, and other animals, which had been created for the use of the Indians: that the Great Man above, looking down and seeing this, was so enraged that he seized his lightning, descended on the earth, seated himself on a neighbouring mountain, on a rock, of which his seat and the print of his feet are still to be seen, and hurled his bolts among them till the whole were slaughtered, except the big bull, who presenting his forehead to the shafts, shook them off as they fell; but missing one at length, it wounded him in the side; whereon, springing round, he bounded over the Ohio, over the Wabash, the Illinois, and finally over the great lakes, where he is living at this day.' It is well known that on the Ohio, and in many parts of America further north, tusks, grinders, and skeletons of unparalleled magnitude, are found in great numbers, some lying on the surface of the earth, and some a little below it. A Mr. Stanley, taken prisoner by the Indians near the mouth of the Tanissee, relates, that, after being transferred through several tribes, from one to another, he was at length carried over the mountains west of the Missouri to a river which runs westwardly; that these bones abounded there; and that the natives described to him the animal to which they belonged as still existing in the northern parts of their country; from which description he judged it to be an elephant. Bones of the same kind have been lately found, some feet below the surface of the earth, in salines opened on the North Holston, a branch of the Tanissee, about the latitude of 36 1/2°. North. From the accounts published in Europe, I suppose it to be decided, that these are of the same kind with those found in Siberia. Instances are mentioned of like animal remains found in the more southern climates of both hemispheres; but they are either so loosely mentioned as to leave a doubt of the fact, so inaccurately described as not to authorize the classing them with the great northern bones, or so rare as to found a suspicion that they have been carried thither as curiosities from more northern regions. So that on the whole there seem to be no certain vestiges of the existence of this animal further south than the salines last mentioned. It is remarkable that the tusks and skeletons have been ascribed by the naturalists of Europe to the elephant, while the grinders have been given to the hippopotamus, or river-horse. Yet it is acknowledged, that the tusks and skeletons are much larger than those of the elephant, and the grinders many times greater than those of the hippopotamus, and essentially different in form. Wherever these grinders are found, there also we find the tusks and skeleton; but no skeleton of the hippopotamus nor grinders of the elephant. It will not be said that the hippopotamus and elephant came always to the same spot, the former to deposit his grinders, and the latter his tusks and skeleton. For what became of the parts not deposited there? We must agree then that these remains belong to each other, that they are of one and the same animal, that this was not a hippopotamus, because the hippopotamus had no tusks nor such a frame, and because the grinders differ in their size as well as in the number and form of their points. That it was not an elephant, I think ascertained by proofs equally decisive. I will not avail myself of the authority of the celebrated [8]anatomist, who, from an examination of the form and structure of the

---

8. Hunter. [This and subsequent notes are Jefferson's.]

tusks, has declared they were essentially different from those of the elephant; because another [9]anatomist, equally celebrated, has declared, on a like examination, that they are precisely the same. Between two such authorities I will suppose this circumstance equivocal. But, I. The skeleton of the mammoth (for so the incognitum has been called) bespeaks an animal of five or six times the cubic volume of the elephant, as Mons. de Buffon has admitted. 2. The grinders are five times as large, are square, and the grinding surface studded with four or five rows of blunt points: whereas those of the elephant are broad and thin, and their grinding surface flat. 3. I have never heard an instance, and suppose there has been none, of the grinder of an elephant being found in America. 4. From the known temperature and constitution of the elephant he could never have existed in those regions where the remains of the mammoth have been found. The elephant is a native only of the torrid zone and its vicinities: if, with the assistance of warm apartments and warm clothing, he has been preserved in life in the temperate climates of Europe, it has only been for a small portion of what would have been his natural period, and no instance of his multiplication in them has ever been known. But no bones of the mammoth, as I have before observed, have been ever found further south than the salines of the Holston, and they have been found as far north as the Arctic circle. Those, therefore, who are of opinion that the elephant and mammoth are the same, must believe, 1. That the elephant known to us can exist and multiply in the frozen zone; or, 2. That an internal fire may once have warmed those regions, and since abandoned them, of which, however, the globe exhibits no unequivocal indications; or, 3. That the obliquity of the ecliptic, when these elephants lived, was so great as to include within the tropics all those regions in which the bones are found; the tropics being, as is before observed, the natural limits of habitation for the elephant. But if it be admitted that this obliquity has really decreased, and we adopt the highest rate of decrease yet pretended, that is, of one minute in a century, to transfer the northern tropic to the Arctic circle, would carry the existence of these supposed elephants 250,000 years back; a period far beyond our conception of the duration of animal bones left exposed to the open air, as these are in many instances. Besides, though these regions would then be supposed within the tropics, yet their winters would have been too severe for the sensibility of the elephant. They would have had too but one day and one night in the year, a circumstance to which we have no reason to suppose the nature of the elephant fitted. However, it has been demonstrated, that, if a variation of obliquity in the ecliptic takes place at all, it is vibratory, and never exceeds the limits of 9 degrees, which is not sufficient to bring these bones within the tropics. One of these hypotheses, or some other equally voluntary and inadmissible to cautious philosophy, must be adopted to support the opinion that these are the bones of the elephant. For my own part, I find it easier to believe that an animal may have existed, resembling the elephant in his tusks, and general anatomy, while his nature was in other respects extremely different. From the 30th degree of South latitude to the 30th of North, are nearly the limits which nature has fixed for the existence and multiplication of the elephant known to us. Proceeding thence northwardly to 36 1/2 degrees, we enter those assigned to the mammoth. The further

9. D'Aubenton.

we advance North, the more their vestiges multiply as far as the earth has been explored in that direction; and it is as probable as otherwise, that this progression continues to the pole itself, if land extends so far. The center of the Frozen zone then may be the Achmé of their vigour, as that of the Torrid is of the elephant. Thus nature seems to have drawn a belt of separation between these two tremendous animals, whose breadth indeed is not precisely known, though at present we may suppose it about 6 1/2 degrees of latitude; to have assigned to the elephant the regions South of these confines, and those North to the mammoth, founding the constitution of the one in her extreme of heat, and that of the other in the extreme of cold. When the Creator has therefore separated their nature as far as the extent of the scale of animal life allowed to this planet would permit, it seems perverse to declare it the same, from a partial resemblance of their tusks and bones. But to whatever animal we ascribe these remains, it is certain such a one has existed in America, and that it has been the largest of all terrestrial beings. It should have sufficed to have rescued the earth it inhabited, and the atmosphere it breathed, from the imputation of impotence in the conception and nourishment of animal life on a large scale: to have stifled, in its birth, the opinion of a writer, the most learned too of all others in the science of animal history, that nature is less active, less energetic on one side of the globe than she is on the other. As if both sides were not warmed by the same genial sun; as if a soil of the same chemical composition, was less capable of elaboration into animal nutriment; as if the fruits and grains from that soil and sun, yielded a less rich chyle, gave less extension to the solids and fluids of the body, or produced sooner in the cartilages, membranes, and fibres, that rigidity which restrains all further extension, and terminates animal growth. The truth is, that a Pigmy and a Patagonian, a Mouse and a Mammoth, derive their dimensions from the same nutritive juices. The difference of increment depends on circumstances unsearchable to beings with our capacities. Every race of animals seems to have received from their Maker certain laws of extension at the time of their formation. Their elaborative organs were formed to produce this, while proper obstacles were opposed to its further progress. Below these limits they cannot fall, nor rise above them. What intermediate station they shall take may depend on soil, on climate, on food, on a careful choice of breeders. But all the manna of heaven would never raise the Mouse to the bulk of the Mammoth.

The opinion advanced by the Count de Buffon, [xviii. 100–156.] is 1. That the animals common both to the old and new world, are smaller in the latter. 2. That those peculiar to the new, are on a smaller scale. 3. That those which have been domesticated in both, have degenerated in America: and 4. That on the whole it exhibits fewer species. And the reason he thinks is, that the heats of America are less; that more waters are spread over its surface by nature, and fewer of these drained off by the hand of man. In other words, that *heat* is friendly, and *moisture* adverse to the production and developement of large quadrupeds. I will not meet this hypothesis on its first doubtful ground, whether the climate of America be comparatively more humid? Because we are not furnished with observations sufficient to decide this question. And though, till it be decided, we are as free to deny, as others are to affirm the fact, yet for a moment let it be supposed. The hypothesis, after this supposition, proceeds to another; that *moisture* is unfriendly to animal growth. The truth of this is inscrutable to us by reasonings a priori. Nature has hidden from us her modus agendi. Our only appeal on such questions is to experience; and I think that experience is against the supposition. It is by the assistance of *heat* and *moisture* that vegetables are elaborated from the elements of earth, air, water, and fire. We accordingly see the more humid climates produce the greater quantity of vegetables. Vegetables are mediately or immediately the food of every animal: and in proportion to the quantity of food, we see animals not only multiplied in their numbers, but improved in their bulk, as far as the laws of their nature will admit. Of this opinion is the Count de Buffon himself in another part of his work: [viii. 134.] 'In general it appears that a slightly cold climate is better for our cattle than a hot one and that they grow heavier and larger in proportion to a country's humidity and the abundance of its pastures. The oxen of Denmark, of Podolie, of the Ukraine and of Tartary which is inhabited by Calmoques, are the largest of all.' Here then a race of animals, and one of the largest too, has been increased in its dimensions by *cold* and *moisture*, in direct opposition to the hypothesis, which supposes that these two circumstances diminish animal bulk, and that it is their contraries *heat* and *dryness* which enlarge it. But when we appeal to experience, we are not to rest satisfied with a single fact. Let us therefore try our question on more general ground. Let us take two portions of the earth, Europe and America for instance, sufficiently extensive to give operation to general causes; let us consider the circumstances peculiar to each, and observe their effect on animal nature. America, running through the torrid as well as temperate zone, has more *heat*, collectively taken, than Europe. But Europe, according to our hypothesis, is the *dryest*. They are equally adapted then to animal productions; each being endowed with one of those causes which befriend animal growth, and with one which opposes it. If it be thought unequal to compare Europe with America, which is so much larger, I answer, not more so than to compare America with the whole world. Besides, the purpose of the comparison is to try an hypothesis, which makes the size of animals depend on the *heat* and *moisture* of climate. If therefore we take a region, so extensive as to comprehend a sensible distinction of climate, and so extensive too as that local accidents, or the intercourse of animals on its borders, may not materially affect the size of those in its interior parts, we shall comply with those conditions which the hypothesis may reasonably demand. The objection would be the weaker in the present case, because any intercourse of animals which may take place on the confines of Europe and Asia, is to the advantage of the former, Asia producing certainly larger animals than Europe. Let us then take a comparative view of the Quadrupeds of Europe and America, presenting them to the eye in three different tables, in one of which shall be enumerated those found in both countries; in a second those found in one only; in a third those which have been domesticated in both. To facilitate the comparison, let those of each table be arranged in gradation according to their sizes, from the greatest to the smallest, so far as their sizes can be conjectured. The weights of the large animals shall be expressed in the English avoirdupoise pound and its decimals: those of the smaller in the ounce and its decimals. Those which are marked thus *, are actual weights of particular subjects, deemed among the largest of their species. Those marked thus †, are furnished by judicious persons, well acquainted with the species, and saying, from conjecture only, what the largest individual they had seen would probably have weighed. The other weights are taken from Messrs. Buffon and D'Aubenton, and are of such subjects as came casually to their hands for dissection. This circumstance must be remembered where their weights and mine stand opposed: the latter being stated, not to produce a conclusion in favour of the American species, but to justify a suspension of opinion until we are better informed, and a suspicion in the mean time that there is no uniform difference in favour of either; which is all I pretend.

A COMPARATIVE VIEW OF THE QUADRUPEDS OF EUROPE AND OF AMERICA.

I. ABORIGINALS OF BOTH.

	Europe. lb.	America. lb.
Mammoth		
Buffalo. Bison		*1800
White bear. Ours blanc		
Caribou. Renne		
Bear. Ours	153.7	*410
Elk. Elan. Original, palmated		
Red deer. Cerf	288.8	*273
Fallow deer. Daim	167.8	
Wolf. Loup	69.8	
Roe. Chevreuil	56.7	
Glutton. Glouton. Carcajou		
Wild cat. Chat sauvage		†30
Lynx. Loup cervier	25.	
Beaver. Castor	18.5	*45
Badger. Blaireau	13.6	
Red Fox. Renard	13.5	
Grey Fox. Isatis		
Otter. Loutre	8.9	†12
Monax. Marmotte	6.5	
Vison. Fouine	2.8	
Hedgehog. Herisson	2.2	
Martin. Marte	1.9	†6
	oz.	oz.
Water rat. Rat d'eau	7.5	
Wesel. Belette	2.2	
Flying squirrel. Polatouche	2.2	†4
Shrew mouse. Musaraigne	1.	

II. Aboriginals of one only.

Europe.	lb.	America.	lb.
Sanglier. Wild boar	280.	Tapir	534.
Mouflon. Wild sheep	56.	Elk, round horned	†450.
Bouquetin. Wild goat		Puma	
Lievre. Hare	7.6	Jaguar	218.
Lapin. Rabbet	3.4	Cabiai	109.
Putois. Polecat	3.3	Tamanoir	109.
Genette	3.1	Tamandua	65.4

	oz.		
Desman. Muskrat		Cougar of N. Amer.	75.
Ecureuil. Squirrel	12.	Cougar of S. Amer.	59.4
Hermine. Ermin	8.2	Ocelot	
Rat. Rat	7.5	Pecari	46.3
Loirs	3.1	Jaguaret	43.6
Lerot. Dormouse	1.8	Alco	
Taupe. Mole	1.2	Lama	
Hamster	.9	Paco	
Zisel		Paca	32.7
Leming		Serval	
Souris. Mouse	.6	Sloth. Unau	27 1/4
		Saricovienne	
		Kincajou	
		Tatou Kabassou	21.8
		Urson. Urchin	
		Raccoon. Raton	16.5
		Coati	
		Coendou	16.3
		Sloth. Aï	13.
		Sapajou Ouarini	
		Sapajou Coaita	9.8
		Tatou Encubert	
		Tatou Apar	
		Tatou Cachica	7.
		Little Coendou	6.5
		Opossum. Sarigue	
		Tapeti	
		Margay	
		Crabier	
		Agouti	4.2
		Sapajou Saï	3.5
		Tatou Cirquinçon	

Tatou Tatouate	3.3
Mouffette Squash	
Mouffette Chinche	
Mouffette Conepate.	
Scunk	
Mouffette. Zorilla	
Whabus. Hare. Rabbet	
Aperea	
Akouchi	
Ondatra. Muskrat	
Pilori	
Great grey squirrel	†2.7
Fox squirrel of Virginia	†2.625
Surikate	2.
Mink	†2.
Sapajou. Sajou	1.8
Indian pig. Cochon	
d'Inde	1.6
Sapajou. Saïmiri	1.5
Phalanger	
Coquallin	
Lesser grey squirrel	†1.5
Black squirrel	†1.5
Red squirrel	10. oz.
Sagoin Saki	
Sagoin Pinche	
Sagoin Tamarin	
Sagoin Ouistiti	4.4 oz.
Sagoin Marikine	
Sagoin Mico	
Cayopollin	
Fourmillier	
Marmose	
Sarigue of Cayenne	
Tucan	
Red mole	
Ground squirrel	4. oz.

III. Domesticated in both.

	Europe.	America.
	lb.	lb.
Cow	763.	*2500
Horse		*1366
Ass		
Hog		*1200
Sheep		*125
Goat		*80
Dog	67.6	
Cat	7.	

I have not inserted in the first table the Phoca nor leather-winged bat, because the one living half the year in the water, and the other being a winged animal, the individuals of each species may visit both continents.

Of the animals in the 1st table Mons. de Buffon himself informs us, [XXVII. 130. XXX. 213.] that the beaver, the otter, and shrew mouse, though of the same species, are larger in America than Europe. This should therefore have corrected the generality of his expressions XVIII. 145. and elsewhere, that the animals common to the two countries, are considerably less in America than in Europe, 'and this without exception.' He tells us too, [Quadrup. VIII. 334. edit. Paris, 1777] that on examining a bear from America, he remarked no difference, 'in the form of this American bear compared to the European.' But adds from Bartram's journal, that an American bear weighed 400 lb. English, equal to 367 lb. French: whereas we find the European bear examined by Mons. D'Aubenton, [XVII. 82.] weighed but 141 lb. French. That the palmated Elk is larger in America than Europe we are informed by Kalm, [I. 233. Lond. 1772.] a Naturalist who visited the former by public appointment for the express purpose of examining the subjects of Natural history. In this fact Pennant [Ib. 233.] concurs with him. [Barrington's Miscellanies.] The same Kalm tells us that the Black Moose, or Renne of America, [I. xxvii.] is as high as a tall horse; and Catesby, that it is about the bigness of a middle sized ox. The same account of their size has been given me by many who have seen them. [XXIV. 162.] But Mons. D'Aubenton says that the Renne of Europe is but about the size of a Red-deer.

The wesel is larger in America than in Europe, [XV. 42.] as may be seen by comparing its dimensions as reported by Mons. D'Aubenton and Kalm. The latter tells us, that the lynx, badger, red fox, and flying squirrel, are the *same* in America as in Europe: [I. 359. I. 48. 221. 251. II. 52.] by which expression I understand, they are the same in all material circumstances, in size as well as others: for if they were smaller, they would differ from the European. Our grey fox is, by Catesby's account, [II. 78.] little different in size and shape from the European fox. I presume he means the red fox of Europe, [I. 220.] as does Kalm, where he says, that in size 'they do not quite come up to our foxes.' For proceeding next to the red fox of America, he says 'they are entirely the same with the European sort.' Which shews he had in view one European sort only, which was the red. So that the result of their testimony is, that the

American grey fox is somewhat less than the European red; [XXVII. 63. XIV. 119. Harris, II.387. Buffon. Quad. IX. 1.] which is equally true of the grey fox of Europe, as may be seen by comparing the measures of the Count de Buffon and Mons. D'Aubenton. The white bear of America is as large as that of Europe. The bones of the Mammoth which have been found in America, are as large as those found in the old world. It may be asked, why I insert the Mammoth, as if it still existed? I ask in return, why I should omit it, as if it did not exist? Such is the œconomy of nature, that no instance can be produced of her having permitted any one race of her animals to become extinct; of her having formed any link in her great work so weak as to be broken. To add to this, the traditionary testimony of the Indians, that this animal still exists in the northern and western parts of America, would be adding the light of a taper to that of the meridian sun. Those parts still remain in their aboriginal state, unexplored and undisturbed by us, or by others for us. He may as well exist there now, as he did formerly where we find his bones. If he be a carnivorous animal, as some Anatomists have conjectured, and the Indians affirm, his early retirement may be accounted for from the general destruction of the wild game by the Indians, which commences in the first instant of their connection with us, for the purpose of purchasing matchcoats, hatchets, and fire locks, with their skins. There remain then the buffalo, red deer, fallow deer, wolf, roe, glutton, wild cat, monax, vison, hedge-hog, martin, and water rat, of the comparative sizes of which we have not sufficient testimony. It does not appear that Messrs. de Buffon and D'Aubenton have measured, weighed, or seen those of America. It is said of some of them, by some travellers, that they are smaller than the European. But who were these travellers? Have they not been men of a very different description from those who have laid open to us the other three quarters of the world? Was natural history the object of their travels? Did they measure or weigh the animals they speak of? or did they not judge of them by sight, or perhaps even from report only? Were they acquainted with the animals of their own country, with which they undertake to compare them? Have they not been so ignorant as often to mistake the species? A true answer to these questions would probably lighten their authority, so as to render it insufficient for the foundation of an hypothesis. How unripe we yet are, for an accurate comparison of the animals of the two countries, will appear from the work of Mons. de Buffon. The ideas we should have formed of the sizes of some animals, from the information he had received at his first publications concerning them, are very different from what his subsequent communications give us. And indeed his candour in this can never be too much praised. One sentence of his book must do him immortal honour. [Quad. IX. 158.] 'I like as much a person who frees me from an error as one who teaches me a truth because a corrected error is a truth.' He seems to have thought the Cabiai he first examined wanted little of its full growth. [XXV. 184.] 'It was not yet entirely mature.' Yet he weighed but 46 1/2 lb. and he found afterwards, [Quad. IX. 132.] that these animals, when full grown, weigh 100 lb. [XIX. 2.] He had supposed, from the exami-nation of a jaguar, said to be two years old, which weighed but 16 lb. 12 oz. that, when he should have acquired his full growth, he would not be larger than a middle sized dog.

But a subsequent account raises his weight to 200 lb. [Quad. IX. 41.] Further information will, doubtless, produce further corrections. The wonder is, not that there is yet something in this great work to correct, but that there is so little. The result of this view then is, that of 26 quadrupeds common to both countries, 7 are said to be larger in America, 7 of equal size, and 12 not sufficiently examined. So that the first table impeaches the first member of the assertion, that of the animals common to both countries, the American are smallest, 'and this without exception.' It shews it not just, in all the latitude in which its author has advanced it, and probably not to such a degree as to found a distinction between the two countries.

Proceeding to the second table, which arranges the animals found in one of the two countries only, Mons. de Buffon observes, that the tapir, the elephant of America, is but of the size of a small cow. To preserve our comparison, I will add that the wild boar, the elephant of Europe, is little more than half that size. I have made an elk with round or cylindrical horns, an animal of America, and peculiar to it; because I have seen many of them myself, and more of their horns; and because I can say, from the best information, that, in Virginia, this kind of elk has abounded much, and still exists in smaller numbers; and I could never learn that the palmated kind had been seen here at all. I suppose this confined to the more Northern latitudes.[10] I have made our hare or rabbet peculiar, believing it to be different from both the European animals of those denominations, and calling it therefore by its Algonquin name Whabus, to keep it distinct from these. [Kalm II. 340.I.82.] Kalm is of the same opinion. I have enumerated the squirrels according to our own knowledge, derived from daily sight of them, because I am not able to reconcile with that the European appellations and descriptions. I have heard of other species, but they have never come within my own notice. These, I think, are the only instances in which I have departed from the authority of Mons. de Buffon in the construction of this table. I take him for my ground work, because I think him the best informed of any Naturalist who has ever written. The result is, that there are 18 quadrupeds peculiar to Europe; more than four times as

---

10. The descriptions of Theodat, Denys and La Hontan, cited by Mons. de Buffon under the article Elan, authorize the supposition, that the flat-horned elk is found in the northern parts of America. It has not however extended to our latitudes. On the other hand, I could never learn that the round-horned elk has been seen further North than the Hudson's river. This agrees with the former elk in its general character, being, like that, when compared with a deer, very much larger, its ears longer, broader, and thicker in proportion, its hair much longer, neck and tail shorter, having a dewlap before the breast (caruncula gutturalis Linnæi) a white spot often, if not always; of a foot diameter, on the hinder part of the buttocks round the tail; its gait a trot, and attended with a rattling of the hoofs: but distinguished from that decisively by its horns, which are not palmated, but round and pointed. This is the animal described by Catesby as the Cervus major Americanus, the Stag of America, le Cerf de l'Amerique. But it differs from the Cervus as totally, as does the palmated elk from the dama. And in fact it seems to stand in the same relation to the palmated elk, as the red deer does to the fallow. It has abounded in Virginia, has been seen, within my knowledge, on the Eastern side of the Blue ridge since the year 1765, is now common beyond those mountains, has been often brought to us and tamed, and their horns are in the hands of many. I should designate it as the 'Alces Americanus cornibus teretibus.' It were to be wished, that Naturalists, who are acquainted with the renne and elk of Europe, and who may hereafter visit the northern parts of America, would examine well the animals called there by the names of grey and black moose, caribou, orignal, and elk. Mons. de Buffon has done what could be done from the materials in his hands, towards clearing up the confusion introduced by the loose application of these names among the animals they are meant to designate. He reduces the whole to the renne and flat-horned elk. From all the information I have been able to collect, I strongly suspect they will be found to contain three, if not four distinct species of animals. I have seen skins of a moose, and of the caribou: they differ more from each other, and from that of the round-horned elk, than I ever saw two skins differ which belonged to different individuals of any wild species. These differences are in the colour, length, and coarseness of the hair, and in the size, texture, and marks of the skin. Perhaps it will be found that there is, 1. the moose, black and grey, the former being said to be the male, and the latter the female. 2. The caribou or renne. 3. The flat-horned elk, or orignal. 4. The round-horned elk. Should this last, though possessing so nearly the characters of the elk, be found to be the same with the Cerf d'Ardennes or Brandhirtz of Germany, still there will remain the three species first enumerated.

many, to wit 74, peculiar to America; that the[11] first of these 74 weighs more than the whole column of Europeans; and consequently this second table disproves the second member of the assertion, that the animals peculiar to the new world are on a smaller scale, so far as that assertion relied on European animals for support: and it is in full opposition to the theory which makes the animal volume to depend on the circumstances of *heat* and *moisture*.

The IIId. table comprehends those quadrupeds only which are domestic in both countries. That some of these, in some parts of America, have become less than their original stock, is doubtless true; and the reason is very obvious. In a thinly peopled country, the spontaneous productions of the forests and waste fields are sufficient to support indifferently the domestic animals of the farmer, with a very little aid from him in the severest and scarcest season. He therefore finds it more convenient to receive them from the hand of nature in that indifferent state, than to keep up their size by a care and nourishment which would cost him much labour. If, on this low fare, these animals dwindle, it is no more than they do in those parts of Europe where the poverty of the soil, or poverty of the owner, reduces them to the same scanty subsistance. It is the uniform effect of one and the same cause, whether acting on this or that side of the globe. It would be erring therefore against that rule of philosophy, which teaches us to ascribe like effects to like causes, should we impute this diminution of size in America to any imbecility or want of uniformity in the operations of nature. It may be affirmed with truth that, in those countries, and with those individuals of America, where necessity or curiosity has produced equal attention as in Europe to the nourishment of animals, the horses, cattle, sheep, and hogs of the one continent are as large as those of the other. There are particular instances, well attested, where individuals of this country have imported good breeders from England, and have improved their size by care in the course of some years. To make a fair comparison between the two countries, it will not answer to bring together animals of what might be deemed the middle or ordinary size of their species; because an error in judging of that middle or ordinary size would vary the result of the comparison. Thus Monsieur D'Aubenton considers a horse of 4 feet 5 inches high and 400 lb. weight French, equal to 4 feet 8.6 inches and 436 lb. English, [VII. 432.] as a middle sized horse. Such a one is deemed a small horse in America. The extremes must therefore be resorted to. The same anatomist dissected a horse of 5 feet 9 inches height, French measure, equal to 6 feet 1.7 English. This is near 6 inches higher than any horse I have seen: [VII. 474.] and could it be supposed that I had seen the largest horses in America, the conclusion would be, that ours have diminished, or that we have bred from a smaller stock. In Connecticut and Rhode-Island, where the climate is favorable to the production of grass, bullocks have been slaughtered which weighed 2500, 2200, and 2100 lb. nett; and those of 1800 lb. have been frequent. I have seen a

---

11. The Tapir is the largest of the animals peculiar to America. I collect his weight thus. Mons. de Buffon says, XXIII. 274. that he is of the size of a Zebu, or a small cow. He gives us the measures of a Zebu, ib. 94. as taken by himself, viz. 5 feet 7 inches from the muzzle to the root of the tail, and 5 feet 1 inch circumference behind the fore legs. A bull, measuring in the same way 6 feet 9 inches and 5 feet 2 inches, weighed 600 lb. VIII. 153. The Zebu then, and of course the Tapir, would weigh about 500 lb. But one individual of every species of European peculiars would probably weigh less than 400 lb. These are French measures and weights.

[12]hog weigh 1050 lb. after the blood, bowels, and hair had been taken from him. Before he was killed an attempt was made to weigh him with a pair of steel-yards, graduated to 1200 lb. but he weighed more. Yet this hog was probably not within fifty generations of the European stock. I am well informed of another which weighed 1100 lb. gross. Asses have been still more neglected than any other domestic animal in America. They are neither fed nor housed in the most rigorous season of the year. Yet they are larger than those measured by Mons. D'Aubenton, of 3 feet 7 1/4 inches, 3 feet 4 inches, and 3 feet 2 1/2 inches, the latter weighing only 215.8 lb. [VIII. 48. 35. 66.] These sizes, I suppose, have been produced by the same negligence in Europe, which has produced a like diminution here. Where care has been taken of them on that side of the water, they have been raised to a size bordering on that of the horse; not by the *heat* and *dryness* of the climate, but by good food and shelter. Goats have been also much neglected in America. Yet they are very prolific here, bearing twice or three times a year, and from one to five kids at a birth. [XVIII. 96.] Mons. de Buffon has been sensible of a difference in this circumstance in favour of America. But what are their greatest weights I cannot say. A large sheep here weighs 100 lb. [IX. 41.] I observe Mons. D'Aubenton calls a ram of 62 lb. one of the middle size. But to say what are the extremes of growth in these and the other domestic animals of America, would require information of which no one individual is possessed. The weights actually known and stated in the third table preceding will suffice to shew, that we may conclude, on probable grounds, that, with equal food and care, the climate of America will preserve the races of domestic animals as large as the European stock from which they are derived; and consequently that the third member of Mons. de Buffon's assertion, that the domestic animals are subject to degeneration from the climate of America, is as probably wrong as the first and second were certainly so.

That the last part of it is erroneous, which affirms that the species of American quadrupeds are comparatively few, is evident from the tables taken all together. By these it appears that there are an hundred species aboriginal of America. [XXX. 219.] Mons. de Buffon supposes about double that number existing on the whole earth. Of these Europe, Asia, and Africa, furnish suppose 126; that is, the 26 common to Europe and America, and about 100 which are not in America at all. The American species then are to those of the rest of the earth, as 100 to 126, or 4 to 5. But the residue of the earth being double the extent of America, the exact proportion would have been but as 4 to 8.

Hitherto I have considered this hypothesis as applied to brute animals only, and not in its extension to the man of America, whether aboriginal or transplanted. It is the opinion of Mons. de Buffon that the former furnishes no exception to it. [XVIII. 146.] 'In this New World, therefore, there is some combination of elements and other physical causes, something that opposes the amplification of animated Nature. There are obstacles to the development and perhaps to the formation of large germs. Even those which, from the kindly influences of another climate, have acquired their complete form and expansion, shrink and diminish under a niggardly sky and an unprolific land, thinly peopled with wandering savages, who, instead of using this territory as a

---

12. In Williamsburg, April, 1769.

master, had no property or empire; and having subjected neither the animals nor the elements, nor conquered the seas, nor directed the motions of rivers, nor cultivated the earth, held only the first rank among animated beings, and existed as creatures of no consideration in Nature, a kind of weak automatons, incapable of improving or fecunding her intentions. She treated them rather like a stepmother than a parent, by denying them the invigorating sentiment of love, and the strong desire of multiplying their species.

For, though the American savage be nearly of the same stature with men in polished societies, yet this is not a sufficient exception to the general contraction of animated Nature throughout the whole Continent. In the savage, the organs of generation are small and feeble. He has no hair, no beard, no ardour for the female. Though nimbler than the European, because more accustomed to running, his strength is not so great. His sensations are less acute; and yet he is more cowardly and timid. He has no vivacity, no activity of mind. The activity of the body is not so much an exercise or spontaneous motion, as a necessary action produced by want. Destroy his appetite for victuals and drink, and you will at once annihilate the active principle of all his movements; he remains, in stupid repose, on his limbs or couch for whole days. It is easy to discover the cause of the scattered life of savages, and of their estrangement from society. They have been refused the most precious spark of Nature's fire. They have no ardour for women, and, of course, no love of mankind. Unacquainted with the most lively and most tender of all attachments, their other sensations of this nature are cold and languid. Their love to parents and children is extremely weak. The bonds of the most intimate of all societies, that of the same family, are feeble; and one family has no attachment to another. Hence no union, no republic, no social state, can take place among the morality of their manners. Their heart is frozen, their society cold, their empire cruel. They regard their females as servants destined to labour, or as beasts of burden, whom they load unmercifully with the produce of their hunting, and oblige, without pity or gratitude, to perform labours which often exceed their strength. They have few children, and pay little attention to them. Every thing must be referred to the first cause: They are indifferent, because they are weak; and this indifference to the sex is the original stain which disgraces Nature, prevents her from expanding, and, by destroying the germs of life, cuts the root of society.

Hence man makes no exception to what has been advanced. Nature by denying him the faculty of love, has abused and untracted him more than any other animal.'

An afflicting picture indeed, which, for the honor of human nature, I am glad to believe has no original. Of the Indian of South America I know nothing; for I would not honor with the appellation of knowledge, what I derive from the fables published of them. These I believe to be just as true as the fables of Æsop. This belief is founded on what I have seen of man, white, red, and black, and what has been written of him by authors, enlightened themselves, and writing amidst an enlightened people. The Indian of North America being more within our reach, I can speak of him somewhat from my own knowledge, but more from the information of others better acquainted with him, and on whose truth and judgment I can rely. From these sources I am able to say, in contradiction to this representation, that he is neither more defective in ardor, nor more impotent with his female, than the white reduced to the same diet and exercise: that he is brave, when an enterprize depends on bravery; education with him making the point of honor consist in the destruction of an enemy by stratagem, and in the preservation of his own person free from injury; or perhaps this is nature; while it is education which teaches us to honor force more than finesse: that he will defend himself against an host of enemies, always chusing to be killed, rather than to surrender, though it be to the whites, who he knows will treat him well: that in other situations also he meets death with more deliberation, and endures tortures with a firmness unknown almost to religious enthusiasm with us: that he is affectionate to his children, careful of them, and indulgent in the extreme: that his affections comprehend his other connections, weakening, as with us, from circle to circle, as they recede from the center: that his friendships are strong and faithful to the uttermost extremity: that his sensibility is keen, even the warriors weeping most bitterly on the loss of their children, though in general they endeavour to appear superior to human events: that his vivacity and activity of mind is equal to ours in the same situation; hence his eagerness for hunting, and for games of chance. The women are submitted to unjust drudgery. This I believe is the case with every barbarous people. With such, force is law. The stronger sex therefore imposes on the weaker. It is civilization alone which replaces women in the enjoyment of their natural equality. That first teaches us to subdue the selfish passions, and to respect those rights in others which we value in ourselves. Were we in equal barbarism, our females would be equal drudges. The man with them is less strong than with us, but their woman stronger than ours; and both for the same obvious reason; because our man and their woman is habituated to labour, and formed by it. With both races the sex which is indulged with ease is least athletic. An Indian man is small in the hand and wrist for the same reason for which a sailor is large and strong in the arms and shoulders, and a porter in the legs and thighs.—They raise fewer children than we do. The causes of this are to be found, not in a difference of nature, but of circumstance. The women very frequently attending the men in their parties of war and of hunting, child-bearing becomes extremely inconvenient to them. It is said, therefore, that they have learnt the practice of procuring abortion by the use of some vegetable; and that it even extends to prevent conception for a considerable time after. During these parties they are exposed to numerous hazards, to excessive exertions, to the greatest extremities of hunger. Even at their homes the nation depends for food, through a certain part of every year, on the gleanings of the forest: that is, they experience a famine once in every year. With all animals, if the female be badly fed, or not fed at all, her young perish: and if both male and female be reduced to like want, generation becomes less active, less productive. To the obstacles then of want and hazard, which nature has opposed to the multiplication of wild animals, for the purpose of restraining their numbers within certain bounds, those of labour and of voluntary abortion are added with the Indian. No wonder then if they multiply less than we do. Where food is regularly supplied, a single farm will shew more of cattle, than a whole country of forests can of buffaloes. The same Indian women, when married to white traders, who feed them and their children plentifully and regularly, who exempt them from excessive drudgery, who keep them stationary and unexposed to accident, produce and raise as many children as the white women. Instances are known, under these circumstances, of their rearing a dozen children. An inhuman practice once prevailed in this country of making slaves of the Indians. It is a fact well known with us, that the Indian women so enslaved produced and raised as numerous families as either the whites or blacks among whom they lived.—It has been said, that Indians have less hair than the whites, except on the head. But this is a fact of which fair proof can scarcely be had. With them it is disgraceful to be hairy on the body. They say it likens them to hogs. They therefore pluck the hair as fast as it appears. But the traders who marry their women, and prevail on them to discontinue this practice, say, that nature is the same with them as with the whites. Nor, if the fact be true, is the consequence necessary which has been drawn from it. Negroes have notoriously less hair than the whites; yet they are more ardent. But if cold and moisture be the agents of nature for diminishing the races of animals, how comes she all at once to suspend their operation as to the physical man of the new world, whom the Count acknowledges to be 'just about the same physical stature as a man of our world,' and to let loose their influence on his moral faculties? How has this 'combination of the elements and other physical causes, so contrary to the enlargement of animal nature in this new world, [XVIII.145.] these obstacles to the developement and formation of great germs,' been arrested and suspended, so as to permit the human body to acquire its just dimensions, and by what inconceivable process has their action been directed on his mind alone? To judge of the truth of this, to form a just estimate of their genius and mental powers, more facts are wanting, and great allowance to be made for those circumstances of their situation which call for a display of particular talents only. This done, we shall probably find that they are formed in mind as well as in body, on the same module with the Homo sapiens Europæus.'[13] The principles of their society forbidding all compulsion, they are to be led to duty and to enterprize by personal influence and persuasion. Hence eloquence in council, bravery and address in war, become the foundations of all consequence with them. To these acquirements all their faculties are directed. Of their bravery and address in war we have multiplied proofs, because we have been the subjects on which they were exercised. Of their eminence in oratory we have fewer examples, because it is displayed chiefly in their own councils. Some, however, we have of very superior lustre. I may challenge the whole orations of Demosthenes and Cicero, and of any more eminent orator, if Europe has furnished more eminent, to produce a single passage, superior to the speech of Logan, a Mingo chief, to Lord Dunmore, when governor of this state. And, as a testimony of their talents in this line, I beg leave to introduce it, first stating the incidents necessary for understanding it. In the spring of the year 1774, a robbery and murder were committed on an inhabitant of the fron-tiers of Virginia, by two Indians of the Shawanee tribe. The neighbouring whites, according to their custom, undertook to punish this outrage in a summary way. Col. Cresap, a man infamous for the many murders he had committed on those much-injured people, collected a party, and proceeded down the Kanhaway in quest of vengeance. Unfortunately a canoe of women and children, with one man only, was seen coming from the opposite shore, unarmed, and unsuspecting an hostile attack from the whites. Cresap and his party concealed themselves on the bank of the river,

13. Linn. Syst. Definition of a Man.

and the moment the canoe reached the shore, singled out their objects, and, at one fire, killed every person in it. This happened to be the family of Logan, who had long been distinguished as a friend of the whites. This unworthy return provoked his vengeance. He accordingly signalized himself in the war which ensued. In the autumn of the same year, a decisive battle was fought at the mouth of the Great Kanhaway, between the collected forces of the Shawanees, Mingoes, and Delawares, and a detachment of the Virginia militia. The Indians were defeated, and sued for peace. Logan however disdained to be seen among the suppliants. But, lest the sincerity of a treaty should be distrusted, from which so distinguished a chief absented himself, he sent by a messenger the following speech to be delivered to Lord Dunmore.

'I appeal to any white man to say, if ever he entered Logan's cabin hungry, and he gave him not meat; if ever he came cold and naked, and he clothed him not. During the course of the last long and bloody war, Logan remained idle in his cabin, an advocate for peace. Such was my love for the whites, that my countrymen pointed as they passed, and said, 'Logan is the friend of white men.' I had even thought to have lived with you, but for the injuries of one man. Col. Cresap, the last spring, in cold blood, and unprovoked, murdered all the relations of Logan, not sparing even my women and children. There runs not a drop of my blood in the veins of any living creature. This called on me for revenge. I have sought it: I have killed many: I have fully glutted my vengeance. For my country, I rejoice at the beams of peace. But do not harbour a thought that mine is the joy of fear. Logan never felt fear. He will not turn on his heel to save his life. Who is there to mourn for Logan?—Not one.'

Before we condemn the Indians of this continent as wanting genius, we must consider that letters have not yet been introduced among them. Were we to compare them in their present state with the Europeans North of the Alps, when the Roman arms and arts first crossed those mountains, the comparison would be unequal, because, at that time, those parts of Europe were swarming with numbers; because numbers produce emulation, and multiply the chances of improvement, and one improvement begets another. Yet I may safely ask, How many good poets, how many able mathematicians, how many great inventors in arts or sciences, had Europe North of the Alps then produced? And it was sixteen centuries after this before a Newton could be formed. I do not mean to deny, that there are varieties in the race of man, distinguished by their powers both of body and mind. I believe there are, as I see to be the case in the races of other animals. I only mean to suggest a doubt, whether the bulk and faculties of animals depend on the side of the Atlantic on which their food happens to grow, or which furnishes the elements of which they are compounded? Whether nature has enlisted herself as a Cis or Trans-Atlantic partisan? I am induced to suspect, there has been more eloquence than sound reasoning displayed in support of this theory; that it is one of those cases where the judgment has been seduced by a glowing pen: and whilst I render every tribute of honor and esteem to the celebrated Zoologist, who has added, and is still adding, so many precious things to the treasures of science, I must doubt whether in this instance he has not cherished error also, by lending her for a moment his vivid imagination and bewitching language.

So far the Count de Buffon has carried this new theory of the tendency of nature to belittle her productions on this side the Atlantic. Its application to the race of whites, transplanted from Europe, remained for the Abbé Raynal 'It is surprising that America has not yet produced a good poet, an able mathematician, a man of genius in even one art or one science.' 7. Hist. Philos. p. 92. ed. Maestricht. 1774. 'America has not yet produced one good poet'. When we shall have existed as a people as long as the Greeks did before they produced a Homer, the Romans a Virgil, the French a Racine and Voltaire, the English a Shakespeare and Milton, should this reproach be still true, we will enquire from what unfriendly causes it has proceeded, that the other countries of Europe and quarters of the earth shall not have inscribed any name in the roll of poets. But neither has America produced 'one able mathematician, one man of genius in a single art or a single science.' In war we have produced a Washington, whose memory will be adored while liberty shall have votaries, whose name will triumph over time, and will in future ages assume its just station among the most celebrated worthies of the world, when that wretched philosophy shall be forgotten which would have arranged him among the degeneracies of nature. In physics we have produced a Franklin, than whom no one of the present age has made more important discoveries, nor has enriched philosophy with more, or more ingenious solutions of the phænomena of nature. We have supposed Mr. Rittenhouse second to no astronomer living: that in genius he must be the first, because he is self-taught. As an artist he has exhibited as great a proof of mechanical genius as the world has ever produced. He has not indeed made a world; but he has by imitation approached nearer its Maker than any man who has lived from the creation to this day[14]. As in philosophy and war, so in government, in oratory, in painting, in the plastic art, we might shew that America, though but a child of yesterday, has already given hopeful proofs of genius, as well of the nobler kinds, which arouse the best feelings of man, which call him into action, which substantiate his freedom, and conduct him to happiness, as of the subordinate, which serve to amuse him only. We therefore suppose, that this reproach is as unjust as it is unkind; and that, of the geniuses which adorn the present age, America contributes its full share. For comparing it with those countries, where genius is most cultivated, where are the most excellent models for art, and scaffoldings for the attainment of science, as France and England for instance, we calculate thus. The United States contain three millions of inhabitants; France twenty millions; and the British islands ten. We produce a Washington, a Franklin, a Rittenhouse. France then should have half a dozen in each of these lines, and Great-Britain half that number, equally eminent. It may be true, that France has: we are but just becoming acquainted with her, and our acquaintance so far gives us high ideas of the genius of her inhabitants. It would be injuring too many of them to name particularly a Voltaire, a Buffon, the constellation of Encyclopedists, the Abbé Raynal himself, etc. etc. We therefore have reason to believe she can produce her full quota of genius. The present war having so long cut off all communication with Great Britain, we are not able to make a fair estimate of the state of science in that country. The spirit in which she wages war is the only sample before our eyes, and that does not seem the legitimate offspring either of science or of civilization. The sun of her glory is

14. There are various ways of keeping truth out of sight. Mr. Rittenhouse's model of the planetary system has the plagiary appellation of an Orrery; and the quadrant invented by Godfrey, an American also, and with the aid of which the European nations traverse the globe, is called Hadley's quadrant.

fast descending to the horizon. Her philosophy has crossed the Channel, her freedom the Atlantic, and herself seems passing to that awful dissolution, whose issue is not given human foresight to scan.[15]

Having given a sketch of our minerals, vegetables, and quadrupeds, and being led by a proud theory to make a comparison of the latter with those of Europe, and to extend it to the Man of America, both aboriginal and emigrant, I will proceed to the remaining articles comprehended under the present query.

Between ninety and an hundred of our birds have been described by Catesby. His drawings are better as to form and attitude, than colouring, which is generally too high. They are the following.

[An uncommented list follows, omitted here.]

To this catalogue of our indigenous animals, I will add a short account of an anomaly of nature, taking place sometimes in the race of negroes brought from Africa, who, though black themselves, have in rare instances, white children, called Albinos. I have known four of these myself, and have faithful accounts of three others. The circumstances in which all the individuals agree are these. They are of a pallid cadaverous white, untinged with red, without any coloured spots or seams; their hair of the same kind of white, short, coarse, and curled as is that of the negro; all of them well formed, strong, healthy, perfect in their senses, except that of sight, and born of parents who had no mixture of white blood. Three of these Albinos were sisters, having two other full sisters, who were black. The youngest of the three was killed by lightning, at twelve years of age. The eldest died at about 27 years of age, in child-bed, with her second child. The middle one is now alive in health, and has issue, as the eldest had, by a black man, which issue was black. They are uncommonly shrewd, quick in their apprehensions and in reply. Their eyes are in a perpetual tremulous vibration, very weak, and much affected by the sun: but they see better in the night than we do. They are of the property of Col. Skipwith, of Cumberland. The fourth is a negro woman, whose parents came from Guinea, and had three other children, who were of their own colour. She is freckled, her eye-sight so weak that she is obliged to wear a bonnet in the summer; but it is better in the night than day. She had an Albino child by a black man. It died at the age of a few weeks. These were the property of Col. Carter, of Albemarle. A sixth instance is a woman of the property of a Mr. Butler, near Petersburgh. She is stout and robust, has issue a daughter, jet black, by a black man. I am not informed as to her eye sight. The seventh instance is of a male

15. In a later edition of the Abbé Raynal's work, he has withdrawn his censure from that part of the new world inhabited by the Federo-Americans; but has left it still on the other parts. North America has always been more accessible to strangers than South. If he was mistaken then as to the former, he may be so as to the latter. The glimmerings which reach us from South America enable us only to see that its inhabitants are held under the accumulated pressure of slavery, superstition, and ignorance. Whenever they shall be able to rise under this weight, and to shew themselves to the rest of the world, they will probably shew they are like the rest of the world. We have not yet sufficient evidence that there are more *lakes* and *fogs* in South America than in other parts of the earth. As little do we know what would be their operation on the mind of man. That country has been visited by Spaniards and Portugueze chiefly, and almost exclusively. These, going from a country of the old world remarkably dry in its soil and climate, fancied there were more lakes and fogs in South America than in Europe. An inhabitant of Ireland, Sweden, or Finland, would have formed the contrary opinion. Had South America then been discovered and seated by a people from a fenny country, it would probably have been represented as much drier than the old world. A patient pursuit of facts, and cautious combination and comparison of them, is the drudgery to which man is subjected by his Maker, if he wishes to attain sure knowledge.

belonging to a Mr. Lee, of Cumberland. His eyes are tremulous and weak. He is tall of stature, and now advanced in years. He is the only male of the Albinos which have come within my information. Whatever be the cause of the disease in the skin, or in its colouring matter, which produces this change, it seems more incident to the female than male sex. To these I may add the mention of a negro man within my own knowledge, born black, and of black parents; on whose chin, when a boy, a white spot appeared. This continued to increase till he became a man, by which time it had extended over his chin, lips, one cheek, the under jaw and neck on that side. It is of the Albino white, without any mixture of red, and has for several years been stationary. He is robust and healthy, and the change of colour was not accompanied with any sensible disease, either general or topical.

Of our fish and insects there has been nothing like a full description or collection. More of them are described in Catesby than in any other work. Many also are to be found in Sir Hans Sloane's Jamaica, as being common to that and this country. The honey-bee is not a native of our continent. Marcgrave indeed mentions a species of honey-bee in Brasil. But this has no sting, and is therefore different from the one we have, which resembles perfectly that of Europe. The Indians concur with us in the tradition that it was brought from Europe; but when, and by whom, we know not. The bees have generally extended themselves into the country, a little in advance of the white settlers. The Indians therefore call them the white man's fly, and consider their approach as indicating the approach of the settlements of the whites. A question here occurs, How far northwardly have these insects been found? That they are unknown in Lapland, I infer from Scheffer's information, that the Laplanders eat the pine bark, prepared in a certain way, instead of those things sweetened with sugar. 'Hoc comedunt pro rebus saccharo conditis.' Scheff. Lapp. c. 18. Certainly, if they had honey, it would be a better substitute for sugar than any preparation of the pine bark. Kalm tells us the honey bee cannot live through the winter in Canada. [I. 126.] They furnish then an additional proof of the remarkable fact first observed by the Count de Buffon, and which has thrown such a blaze of light on the field of natural history, that no animals are found in both continents, but those which are able to bear the cold of those regions where they probably join.

6. William Bartram

from *Travels through North and South Carolina, Georgia, East and West Florida*
1791

The son of John Bartram, (botanist, horticulturalist, agricultural experimenter, and one of the central figures in colonial natural philosophy), William Bartram (1739–1823) went into the family business, though at first with little success. He undertook the four-year voyage described in his Travels *in order to flee his creditors and in the hope of finally establishing himself. The journey yielded a wealth of intriguing and delightful observations, but things did not go well on his return in 1777. The Revolution complicated getting the manuscript published, and it was not until 1791 that a partial transcription appeared, while the complete manuscript waited another 150 years.*

The reception of the partial work was heartening, though mainly in Europe, where nine pirated editions testified to its popularity. American reviewers found the narrative excessively romantic. Bartram's greatest success came in the next century, when the Travels *was taken up by the Romantic poets, especially by Coleridge, who described Bartram's tale of his travels as "a series of poems." His drawings both for the* Travels *and elsewhere were admired by everyone: Bartram made natural science into art. The selections below give a sense of his rather ornate lyricism. This does not prevent him from seeing the violence and even the brutality of nature, captured in the account of the epic battle of the crocodiles.*

[FROM THE INTRODUCTION]

The attention of a traveller should be particularly turned, in the first place, to the various works of Nature, to mark the distinctions of the climates he may explore, and to offer such useful observations on the different productions as may occur. Men and manners undoubtedly hold the first rank—whatever may contribute to our existence is also of equal importance, whether it be found in the animal or vegetable kingdoms; neither are the various articles, which tend to promote the happiness and convenience of mankind, to be disregarded. How far the writer of the following sheets has succeeded in furnishing information on these subjects, the reader will be capable of determining. From the advantages the journalist enjoyed under his father John Bartram, botanist to the king of Great-Britain, and fellow of the Royal Society, it is hoped that his labours will present new as well as useful information to the botanist and zoologist.

This world, as a glorious apartment of the boundless palace of the sovereign Creator, is furnished with an infinite variety of animated scenes, inexpressibly beautiful and pleasing, equally free to the inspection and enjoyment of all his creatures.

Perhaps there is not any part of creation, within the reach of our observations, which exhibits a more glorious display of the Almighty hand, than the vegetable world. Such a variety of pleasing scenes, ever changing, throughout the seasons, arising from various causes and assigned each to the purpose and use determined.

[FROM PART ONE, CHAPTER FIVE]

Having completed my Hortus Siccus, and made up my collections of seeds and growing roots, the fruits of my late western tour, and sent them to Charleston, to be forwarded to Europe, I spent the remaining part of this season in botanical excursions to the low countries, between Carolina and East Florida, and collected seeds, roots, and specimens, making drawings of such curious subjects as could not be preserved in their native state of excellence.

During this recess from the high road of my travels, having obtained the use of a neat light cypress canoe, at Broughton Island, a plantation, the property of the Hon. Henry Laurens, Esq. where I stored myself with necessaries, for the voyage, and resolved upon a trip up the Alatamaha.

I ascended this beautiful river, on whose fruitful banks the generous and true sons of liberty securely dwell, fifty miles above the white settlements.

How gently flow thy peaceful floods, O Alatamaha! How sublimely rise to view, on thy elevated shores, yon Magnolian groves, from whose tops the surrounding expanse is perfumed, by clouds of incense, blended with the exhaling balm of the Liquid-amber, and odours continually arising from circumambient aromatic groves of Illicium, Myrica, Laurus, and Bignonia.

When wearied, with working my canoe against the impetuous current (which becomes stronger by reason of the mighty floods of the river, with collected force, pressing through the first hilly ascents, where the shores on each side the river present to view rocky cliffs rising above the surface of the water, in nearly flat horizontal masses, washed smooth by the descending floods, and which appear to be a composition, or concrete, of sandy lime-stone) I resigned my bark to the friendly current, reserving to myself the control of the helm. My progress was rendered delightful by the sylvan elegance of the groves, chearful meadows, and high distant forests, which in grand order presented themselves to view. The winding banks of the river, and the high projecting promontories, unfolded fresh scenes of grandeur and sublimity. The deep forests and distant hills re-echoed the chearing social lowings of domestic herds. The air was filled with the loud and shrill whooping of the wary sharp-sighted crane. Behold, on yon decayed, defoliated Cypress tree, the solitary wood-pelican, dejectedly perched upon its utmost elevated spire; he there, like an ancient venerable sage, sets himself up as a mark of derision, for the safety of his kindred tribes. The crying-bird, another faithful guardian, screaming in the gloomy thickets, warns the feathered tribes of approaching peril; and the plumage of the swift sailing squadrons of Spanish curlews (white as the immaculate robe of innocence) gleam in the cerulean skies.

Thus secure and tranquil, and meditating on the marvellous scenes of primitive nature, as yet unmodified by the hand of man, I gently descended the peaceful stream, on whose polished surface were depicted the mutable shadows from its pensile banks;

Alligator, Alligator mississippiensis. *(Bartram's drawing and label.)*

whilst myriads of finny inhabitants sported in its pellucid floods. . . .

O peaceful Alatamaha! gentle by nature! how thou art ruffled! thy wavy surface disfigures every object, presenting them obscurely to the sight, and they at length totally disappear, whilst the furious winds and sweeping rains bend the lofty groves, and prostrate the quaking grass, driving the affrighted creatures to their dens and caverns.

The tempest now relaxes, its impetus is spent, and a calm serenity gradually takes place; by noon they break away, the blue sky appears, the fulgid sun-beams spread abroad their animating light, and the steady western wind resumes his peaceful reign. The waters are purified, the waves subside, and the beautiful river regains its native calmness: so it is with the varied and mutable scenes of human events on the stream of life. The higher powers and affections of the soul are so blended and connected with the inferior passions, that the most painful feelings are excited in the mind when the latter are crossed: thus in the moral system, which we have planned for our conduct, as a ladder whereby to mount to the summit of terrestrial glory and happiness, and from whence we perhaps meditated our flight to heaven itself, at the very moment when we vainly imagine ourselves to have attained its point, some unforeseen accident intervenes, and surprises us; the chain is violently shaken, we quit our hold and fall: the well contrived system at once becomes a chaos; every idea of happiness recedes; the splendour of glory darkens, and at length totally disappears; every pleasing object is defaced, all is deranged, and the flattering scene passes quite away, a gloomy cloud pervades the understanding, and when we see our progress retarded, and our best intentions frustrated, we are apt to deviate from the admonitions and convictions of virtue, to shut our eyes upon our guide and protector, doubt of his power, and despair of his assistance. But let us wait and rely on our God, who in due time will shine forth in brightness, dissipate the envious cloud, and reveal to us how finite and circumscribed is human power, when assuming to itself independent wisdom.

[FROM PART TWO, CHAPTER FIVE: THE ALLIGATORS]

The evening was temperately cool and calm. The crocodiles began to roar and appear in uncommon numbers along the shores and in the river. I fixed my camp in an open plain, near the utmost projection of the promontory, under the shelter of a large Live Oak, which stood on the highest part of the ground and but a few yards from my boat. From this open, high situation, I had a free prospect of the river, which was a matter of no trivial consideration to me, having good reason to dread the subtle attacks of the alligators, who were crouding about my harbour. Having collected a good quantity of wood for the purpose of keeping up a light and smoke during the night, I began to think of preparing my supper, when, upon examining my stores, I found but a scanty provision, I thereupon determined, as the most expeditious way of supplying my necessities, to take my bob and try for some trout. About one hundred yards above my harbour, began a cove or bay of the river, out of which opened a large lagoon. The mouth or entrance from the river to it was narrow, but the waters soon after spread and formed a little lake, extending into the marshes, its entrance and shores with in I observed to be verged with floating lawns of the Pistia and Nymphea and other aquatic plants; these I knew were excellent haunts for trout.

Spotted Turtle, Clemmys guttata; *Milk snake* Lampropeltis triangulum. *(Bartram's drawing and label.)*

The verges and islets of the lagoon were elegantly embellished with flowering plants and shrubs; the laughing coots with wings half spread were tripping over the little coves and hiding themselves in the tufts of grass; young broods of the painted summer teal, skimming the still surface of the waters, and following the watchful parent unconscious of danger, were frequently surprised by the voracious trout, and he in turn, as often by the subtle, greedy alligator. Behold him rushing forth from the flags and reeds. His enormous body swells. His plaited tail brandished high, floats upon the lake. The waters like a cataract descend from his opening jaws. Clouds of smoke issue from his dilated nostrils. The earth trembles with his thunder. When immediately from the opposite coast of the lagoon, emerges from the deep his rival champion. They suddenly dart upon each other. The boiling surface of the lake marks their rapid course, and a terrific conflict commences. They now sink to the bottom folded together in horrid wreaths. The water becomes thick and discoloured. Again they rise, their jaws clap together, re-echoing through the deep surrounding forests. Again they sink, when the contest ends at the muddy bottom of the lake, and the vanquished makes a hazardous escape, hiding himself in the muddy turbulent waters and sedge on a distant shore. The proud victor exulting returns to the place of action. The shores and forests resound his dreadful roar, together with the triumphing shouts of the plaited tribes around, witnesses of the horrid combat.

My apprehensions were highly alarmed after being a spectator of so dreadful a battle; it was obvious that every delay would but tend to encrease my dangers and difficulties, as the sun was near setting, and the alligators gathered around my harbour from all quarters; from these considerations I concluded to be expeditious in my trip to the lagoon, in order to take some fish. Not thinking it prudent to take my fusee with me, lest I might lose it overboard in case of a battle, which I had every reason to dread before my return, I therefore furnished myself with a club for my defence, went on board, and penetrating the first line of those which surrounded my harbour, they gave way; but being pursued by several very large ones, I kept strictly on the watch, and paddled with all my might towards the entrance of the lagoon, hoping to be shel-

American Lotus or Water Chinquapin seed vessel,
Nelumbo lutea; *Snail* Triodopsis albolabris; *Black root,*
Prerocaulon undulatum. *(Bartram's drawing and label.)*

tered there from the multitude of my assailants; but ere I had half-way reached the place, I was attacked on all sides, several endeavouring to overset the canoe. My situation now became precarious to the last degree: two very large ones attacked me closely, at the same instant, rushing up with their heads and part of their bodies above the water, roaring terribly and belching floods of water over me. They struck their jaws together so close to my ears, as almost to stun me, and I expected every moment to be dragged out of the boat and instantly devoured, but I applied my weapons so effectually about me, though at random, that I was so successful as to beat them off a little; when, finding that they designed to renew the battle, I made for the shore, as the only means left me for my preservation, for, by keeping close to it, I should have my enemies on one side of me only, whereas I was before surrounded by them, and there was a probability, if pushed to the last extremity, of saving myself, by jumping out of the canoe on shore, as it is easy to outwalk them on land, although comparatively as swift as lightning in the water. I found this last expedient alone could fully answer my expectations, for as soon as I gained the shore they drew off and kept aloof. This was a happy relief, as my confidence was, in some degree, recovered by it. On recollecting myself, I discovered that I had almost reached the entrance of the lagoon, and determined to venture in, if possible to take a few fish and then return to my harbour, while day-light continued; for I could now, with caution and resolution, make my way with safety along shore, and indeed there was no other way to regain my camp, without leaving my boat and making my retreat through the marshes and reeds, which, if I could even effect, would have been in a manner throwing myself away, for then there would have been no hopes of ever recovering my bark, and returning in safety to any settlements of men. I accordingly proceeded and made good my entrance into the lagoon, though not without opposition from the alligators, who formed a line across the entrance, but did not pursue me into it, nor was I molested by any there, though there were some very large ones in a cove at the upper end. I soon caught more trout than I had present occasion for, and the air was too hot and sultry to admit of their being kept for many hours, even though salted or barbecued.

I now prepared for my return to camp, which I succeeded in with but little trouble, by keeping close to the shore, yet I was opposed upon re-entering the river out of the lagoon, and pursued near to my landing (though not closely attacked) particularly by an old daring one, about twelve feet in length, who kept close after me, and when I stepped on shore and turned about, in order to draw up my canoe, he rushed up near my feet and lay there for some time, looking me in the face, his head and shoulders out of water; I resolved he should pay for his temerity, and having a heavy load in my

Warmouth ("Great Yellow Bream"), Chaenobryttus coronarius. *(Bartram's drawing and label.)*

fusee, I ran to my camp, and returning with my piece, found him with his foot on the gunwale of the boat, in search of fish, on my coming up he withdrew sullenly and slowly into the water, but soon returned and placed himself in his former position, looking at me and seeming neither fearful or any way disturbed. I soon dispatched him by lodging the contents of my gun in his head, and then proceeded to cleanse and prepare my fish for supper, and accordingly took them out of the boat, laid them down on the sand close to the water, and began to scale them, when, raising my head, I saw before me, through the clear water, the head and shoulders of a very large alligator, moving slowly towards me; I instantly stepped back, when, with a sweep of his tail, he brushed off several of my fish. It was certainly most providential that I looked up at that instant, as the monster would probably, in less than a minute, have seized and dragged me into the river. This incredible boldness of the animal disturbed me greatly, supposing there could now be no reasonable safety for me during the night, but by keeping continually on the watch; I therefore, as soon as I had prepared the fish, proceeded to secure myself and effects in the best manner I could: in the first place, I hauled my bark upon the shore, almost clear out of the water, to prevent their oversetting or sinking her, after this every moveable was taken out and carried to my camp, which was but a few yards off; then ranging some dry wood in such order as was the most convenient, cleared the ground round about it, that there might be no impediment in my way, in case of an attack in the night, either from the water or the land; for I discovered by this time, that this small isthmus, from its remote situation and fruitfulness, was resorted to by bears and wolves. Having prepared myself in the best manner I could, I charged my gun and proceeded to reconnoitre my camp and the adjacent grounds; when I discovered that the peninsula and grove, at the distance of about two hundred yards from my encampment, on the land side, were invested by a Cypress swamp, covered with water, which below was joined to the shore of the little lake, and above to the marshes surrounding the lagoon, so that I was confined to an islet exceedingly circumscribed, and I found there was no other retreat for me, in case of an attack, but by either ascending one of the large Oaks, or pushing off with my boat.

It was by this time dusk, and the alligators had nearly ceased their roar, when I was again alarmed by a tumultuous noise that seemed to be in my harbour, and therefore engaged my immediate attention. Returning to my camp I found it undisturbed, and then continued on to the extreme point of the promontory, where I saw a scene, new and surprising, which at first threw my senses into such a tumult, that it was some time before I could comprehend what was the matter; however, I soon accounted for the prodigious assemblage of crocodiles at this place, which exceeded every thing of the kind I had ever heard of.

How shall I express myself so as to convey an adequate idea of it to the reader, and at the same time avoid raising suspicions of my want of veracity. Should I say, that the river (in this place) from shore to shore, and perhaps near half a mile above and below me, appeared to be one solid bank of fish, of various kinds, pushing through this narrow pass of St. Juans into the little lake, on their return down the river, and that the alligators were in such incredible numbers, and so close together from shore to shore, that it would have been easy to have walked across on their heads, had the animals been harmless. What expressions can sufficiently declare the shocking scene that for some minutes continued, whilst this mighty army of fish were forcing

Timber Rattlesnake, Crotalus horridus. *(Bartram's drawing and label.)*

the pass? During this attempt, thousands, I may say hundreds of thousands of them were caught and swallowed by the devouring alligators. I have seen an alligator take up out of the water several great fish at a time, and just squeeze them betwixt his jaws, while the tails of the great trout flapped about his eyes and lips, ere he had swallowed them. The horrid noise of their closing jaws, their plunging amidst the broken banks of fish, and rising with their prey some feet upright above the water, the floods of water and blood rushing out of their mouths, and the clouds of vapour issuing from their wide nostrils, were truly frightful. This scene continued at intervals during the night, as the fish came to the pass. After this sight, shocking and tremendous as it was, I found myself somewhat easier and more reconciled to my situation, being convinced that their extraordinary assemblage here, was owing to this annual feast of fish, and that they were so well employed in their own element, that I had little occasion to fear their paying me a visit.

It being now almost night, I returned to my camp, where I had left my fish broiling, and my kettle of rice stewing, and having with me, oil, pepper and salt, and excellent oranges hanging in abundance over my head (a valuable substitute for vinegar) I sat down and regaled myself chearfully; having finished my repast, I rekindled my fire for light, and whilst I was revising the notes of my past day's journey, I was suddenly roused with a noise behind me toward the main land; I sprang up on my feet, and listening, I distinctly heard some creature wading in the water of the isthmus; I seized my gun and went cautiously from my camp, directing my steps towards the noise; when I had advanced about thirty yards, I halted behind a coppice of Orange trees, and soon perceived two very large bears, which had made their way through the water, and had landed in the grove, about one hundred yards distance from me, and were advancing towards me. I waited until they were within thirty yards of me, they there began to snuff and look towards my camp, I snapped my piece, but it flashed, on which they both turned about and galloped off, plunging through the water and swamp, never halting as I suppose, until they reached fast land, as I could hear them leaping and plunging a long time; they did not presume to return again, nor was I molested by any other creature, except being occasionally awakened by the whooping of owls, screaming of bitterns, or the wood-rats running amongst the leaves. . . .

I beheld a great number of hillocks or small pyramids, resembling hay cocks, ranged like an encampment along the banks, they stood fifteen or twenty yards distant from the water, on a high marsh, about four feet perpendicular above the water; I knew them to be the nests of the crocodile, having had a description of them before, and now expected a furious and general attack, as I saw several large crocodiles swimming abreast of these buildings. These nests being so great a curiosity to me, I was determined at all events immediately to land and examine them. Accordingly I ran my bark on shore at one of their landing places, which was a sort of nick or little dock, from which ascended a sloping path or road up to

Bobolink or Ricebird, Dolichonyz oryzivorus; *Rice*, Oryza sativa; *Immature Yellow Rat or Chicken Snake*, Elaphe quadrivittata; *Green Tree Frog*, Hyla cinerea. *(Bartram's drawing and label.)*

the edge of the meadow, where their nests were, most of them were deserted, and the great thick whitish egg-shells lay broken and scattered upon the ground round about them.

The nests or hillocks are of the form of an obtuse cone, four feet high and four or five feet in diameter at their bases; they are constructed with mud, grass and herbage: at first they lay a floor of this kind of tempered mortar on the ground, upon which they deposit a layer of eggs, and upon this a stratum of mortar seven or eight inches in thickness, and then another layer of eggs, and in this manner one stratum upon another, nearly to the top: I believe they commonly lay from one to two hundred eggs in a nest: these are hatched I suppose by the heat of the sun, and perhaps the vegetable substances mixed with the earth, being acted upon by the sun, may cause a small degree of fermentation, and so increase the heat in those hillocks. The ground for several acres about these nests shewed evident marks of a continual resort of alligators; the grass was every where beaten down, hardly a blade or straw was left standing; whereas, all about, at a distance, it was five or six feet high, and as thick as it could grow together. The female, as I imagine, carefully watches her own nest of eggs until they are all hatched, or perhaps while she is attending her own brood, she takes under her care and protection, as many as she can get at one time, either from her own particular nest or others: but certain it is, that the young are not left to shift for themselves, having had frequent opportunities of seeing the female alligator, leading about the shores her train of young ones, just like a hen does her brood of chickens, and she is equally assiduous and courageous in defending the young, which are under their care, and providing for their subsistence; and when she is basking

Snapping Turtle, Chelydrida serpentina. *(Bartram's drawing and label.)*

upon the warm banks, with her brood around her, you may hear the young ones continually whining and barking, like young puppies. I believe but few of a brood live to the years of full growth and magnitude, as the old feed on the young as long as they can make prey of them.

The alligator when full grown is a very large and terrible creature, and of prodigious strength, activity and swiftness in the water. I have seen them twenty feet in length, and some are supposed to be twenty-two or twenty-three feet; their body is as large as that of a horse; their shape exactly resembles that of a lizard, except their tail, which is flat or cuniform, being compressed on each side, and gradually diminishing from the abdomen to the extremity, which, with the whole body is covered with horny plates or squamae, impenetrable when on the body of the live animal, even to a rifle ball, except about their head and just behind their fore-legs or arms, where it is said they are only vulnerable. The head of a full grown one is about three feet, and the mouth opens nearly the same length, the eyes are small in proportion and seem sunk deep in the head, by means of the prominency of the brows; the nostrils are large, inflated and prominent on the top, so that the head in the water, resembles, at a distance, a great chunk of wood floating about. Only the upper jaw moves, which they raise almost perpendicular, so as to form a right angle with the lower one. In the fore part of the upper jaw, on each side, just under the nostrils, are two very large, thick, strong teeth or tusks, not very sharp, but rather the shape of a cone, these are as white as the finest polished ivory, and are not covered by any skin or lips, and always in sight, which gives the creature a frightful appearance; in the lower jaw are holes opposite to these teeth, to receive them; when they clap their jaws together it causes a surprising noise, like that which is made by forcing a heavy plank with violence upon the ground, and may be heard at a great distance.

But what is yet more surprising to a stranger, is the incredible loud and terrifying roar, which they are capable of making, especially in the spring season, their breeding time; it most resembles very heavy distant thunder, not only shaking the air and waters, but causing the earth to tremble; and when hundreds and thousands are roaring at the same time, you can scarcely be persuaded, but that the whole globe is violently and dangerously agitated.

An old champion, who is perhaps absolute sovereign of a little lake or lagoon (when fifty less than himself are obliged to content themselves with swelling and roaring in little coves round about) darts forth from the reedy coverts all at once, on the surface of the waters, in a right line; at first seemingly as rapid as lightning, but gradually more slowly until he arrives at the center of the lake, when he stops; he now swells himself by drawing in wind and water through his mouth, which causes a loud sonorous rattling in the throat for near a minute, but it is immediately forced out again through his mouth and nostrils, with a loud noise, brandishing his tail in the air, and the vapour ascending from his nostrils like smoke. At other times, when swollen to an extent ready to burst, his head and tail lifted up, he spins or twirls round on the surface of the water. He acts his part like an Indian chief when rehearsing his feats of war, and then retiring, the exhibition is continued by others who dare to step forth, and strive to excel each other, to gain the attention of the favourite female.

Having gratified my curiosity at this general breeding place and nursery of crocodiles, I continued my voyage up the river without being greatly disturbed by them: in my way I observed islets or floating fields of the bright green Pistia, decorated with other amphibious plants, as Senecio Jacobea, Persicaria amphibia, Coreopsis bidens, Hydrocotile fluitans, and many others of less note.

Chapter 13

Belles Lettres

INTRODUCTION

The emergence of a literature of belles lettres in Anglo-America reflected the success of the colonies: it meant there now existed a community of settlers who took settling the New World enough for granted not to write about it. Instead of histories, they wrote essays in which style mattered as much as content and sometimes more; they even wrote essays about essay-writing. In these literary pursuits, they did continue to reflect upon their location, but not as any sort of wilderness. Culturally the New World was quite comparable to the Old, they claimed; in fact, when one allowed for the difference in size, the communities of the cultivated in England and its colonies were no different. The belletrists would crown the colonizing mission by building Londons on the Chesapeake, the Hudson, and the Schuylkill.

"Belles lettres," a literary mode that originated in seventeenth-century France, signified writing in the style and service of cultivated society. The English mostly kept the French term but on occasion translated it as "polite letters." Belles lettres denotes a linguistic self-consciousness testifying to the superior education of both writer and reader, who come together more through literature than through life. Or rather, they meet in a world reconstructed by literature, for belles lettres makes life literary, adding an aesthetic dimension to morality.

The concerns addressed by belles lettres are not those of how to earn a living but of how to live well. They are the concerns of a relatively affluent and homogeneous community. If eighteenth-century literary society was thus rather exclusive in regard to class, it was more receptive to women, who appear for the first time not just as individuals but as a group. The group of women who participated in the belletristic culture was itself exclusive, the educated and wealthy daughters and wives of the colonial upper-class. But if they gained admittance through their class, it was not altogether despite their sex, for one of the implications of separating literature from life was, in the context of a middle-class society where women represented sensibility, to give a feminine cast to literature. The literary salons that characterize the eighteenth-century world of letters in France and England were literary homes run by women mostly for men; however, these women also wrote. In the colonies, Elizabeth Graeme Fergusson held the most important salon, and the group of women she gathered around her—Susanna Wright, Annis Boudinot Stockton, and Hannah Griffits—all were recognized writers in a world of letters that was itself a novelty.

The exclusiveness of the belles lettres community was reflected in the fact that much

of its literary output circulated only in manuscript. Among the most distinguished of the unpublished writings are those of William Byrd II, whose two *Histories* appear in chapter 10. While the *Secret Diary* featured in this chapter was never meant for publication, it abundantly reveals its author's literary self-consciousness and ambition. His days routinely began with reading "a chapter in Hebrew and some Greek in Lucian," or Thucydides or Homer; sometimes he read Latin in the afternoon, and he wrote voluminously. Byrd's entries report the details of physical life, his fraught relations with his wife and with the other inhabitants of his plantation including his slaves; they record business transactions, new acquisitions for his wardrobe, the weather, the list of visitors, and—on the same fundamental level of the everyday—his literary pursuits. The *Diary* is a unique document of belletrist culture for its exposition of how its members' literary notions informed their lives, of who they were when they were at home.

Dr. Alexander Hamilton, on the other hand, kept a diary of life at his club. His *Itinerarium* appears in chapter 10 and is itself a work of belles lettres. Hamilton's major contribution to the genre, however, was the organization of the Tuesday Club. In England, clubs were a major feature of the society of belles lettres, masculine versions of the salons. Like the salons, they were ambiguously connected to eighteenth-century society; or rather they embodied its ambiguity. By having to be organized, they testified to the break-up of aristocratic tradition; but their exclusivity was a modern fortress defending them against an increasingly intrusive public. The clever conversations and the humorous anecdotes reported in Hamilton's *History of the Ancient and Honorable Tuesday Club* turn on mockery, on a mock rendition of the world outside the Club seen as ridiculously serious. Humor effects a distance from those too busy to laugh.

Benjamin Franklin's secret Junto was perhaps the most exclusive of all the clubs; its hand-picked members included a shoemaker, a joiner, a copyist, a surveyor, a clerk, and one "Gentleman of some Fortune." Instead of displaying itself, the Junto met clandestinely to pursue "mutual Improvement" and plot the public welfare. Paper currency, a lending library and a fire department were all Junto projects. Yet this secret doing-good shared one goal with the upper-class clubs. Both in the colonies and in England, the aristocracy of manners and letters that the clubs assembled was a would-be aristocracy. The Junto was out to create an equally powerful cultivated middle class, an aristocracy of merit. Addison and Steele were purveyors of elite learning and style to a newly emerged elite. Franklin consciously followed their example to the same end.

In 1809, Fisher Ames reported that a question was arousing exceptional passion in intellectual circles. He paraphrased it scornfully: "Whether in point of intellect we are equal to Europeans, or only a race of degenerate creoles?" His answer was that the new nation would never boast works of genius so long as a relative social equality prevailed. If Ames's contempt for the popular mind seems aberrant, it is worth recalling the repeated stipulations in *The Federalist* that the United States was to be a republic and not a democracy; for these express a like anxiety about popular rule. Politically, this anxiety led to advocating a strong central government resting on a system of representation designed as much to prevent voter influence as to enable it. The more or less stable outcome was a republic that balanced protecting wealth and privilege with guaranteeing basic rights to all citizens. In the absence of structures or schemes to achieve this balance in the literary realm, America in literature has been, almost from the first, two nations.

M.J.

Suggested reading: David Shields's "British-American Belles Lettres," in *The Cambridge History of American Literature: Volume 1: 1590–1820*, offers an overall survey of colonial belles lettres. Kenneth Silverman's *Cultural History of the American Revolution* treats the literature of belles lettres in the general cultural context. Cathy Davidson's *Revolution and the Word: The Rise of the Novel in America* studies the controversial literature of the novel, as does Steven Watts in *The Romance of Real Life: Charles Brockden Brown and the Origins of American Culture*. Two more specialized studies are Robert Ferguson's *Law and Letters in American Culture* and Joseph A. Leo Lemay's *Men of Letters in Colonial Maryland*.

1. William Byrd II

from *The Secret Diary* and *The London Diary* 1709–12; 1717–21

Byrd evidently liked writing in secret. His Secret History of the Dividing Line appears in chapter 10. Below are excerpts from personal diaries kept in coded short-hand, the first at Westover in Virginia and the second while Byrd was living in London. They offer a rare view of daily life in the plantation society, and a relatively unreconstructed account of the private life of a thoroughly successful colonist.

How did a colonial aristocrat organize his days on the plantation? Byrd's began with self-cultivation: culture before agriculture. The Diary, a mirror he held up to himself, reveals a highly educated man who read Greek, Hebrew, and Latin, kept up with the contemporary literary scene, and was himself a stylish writer: the gentleman as a man of letters.

At the same time, this man of letters was also master of hundreds of slaves and thousands of acres, and the Diary contradicts any legend that Virginia's aristocrats cultivated themselves in genteel leisure. As frequently as Byrd reads Lucian before breakfast, he checks out his estates before dinner, and as regularly as he "dances my dance" for exercise (no one has been able to learn exactly what this entails), he hands out punishments, including severe beatings, for what he judges to be derelictions of duty and incursions on plantation profits.

The entries below cover three major themes in the Diary: literature, plantation management, and sex. The first entry, from 1711, presents a standard day filled with occupations that recur throughout the Diary. Until he retires for the day, forgetting his prayers, Byrd, conferring, overseeing, negotiating, rules his fiefdom with essentially unlimited authority. In the second entry (1712), Byrd inadvertently reveals the way the institution of slavery permeates the domestic life of the masters as well as the slaves; and the third appears here because it follows directly in the Diary, and therefore represents the succession of days and what life was like at Westover when not much was happening.

The final two entries were written in London where Byrd had gone in 1714 to deal with financial matters and also to continue his suit for the governorship. In the fourth (1718), Byrd goes about a gentleman's daily routine in the capital, its intense sociability, a theater for political alliances and economic deals. The final entry (1719) is one of many in which Byrd keeps account of his sexual accomplishments.

I rose at 3 o'clock and read a chapter in Hebrew and some Greek in Lucian. I said my prayers and ate boiled milk for breakfast. I danced my dance. I ordered the sloop to be unloaded. Redskin Peter pretended to be sick and I put a [branding-iron] on the place he complained of and put the [bit] upon him. The boy called the Doc was sent from Falling Creek with a swollen thigh. My sick people were better, thank God Almighty. I received a courteous letter from the Governor by Tom, who brought no news. I ate boiled pork for dinner. Mr. Mumford came down after dinner and told me all was well at Appomattox. When he had got some victuals we took a walk to see the people load the sloop and afterwards about the plantation. In the evening G-r-l came and let me know things were well at Falling Creek. He brought me a letter from Tom Turpin in which he agreed to stay with me for £25 a year. I ate some roast beef for supper. I neglected to say my prayers, but had good health, good thoughts, and good humor, thank God.

I rose about 7 o'clock and read a chapter in Hebrew but no Greek because Mr. G-r-l was here and I wished to talk with him. I ate boiled milk for breakfast and danced my dance. I reprimanded him for drawing so many notes on me. However I told him if he would let me know his debts I would pay them provided he would let a mulatto of mine that is his apprentice come to work at Falling Creek the last two years of his service, which he agreed. I had a terrible quarrel with my wife concerning Jenny that I took away from her when she was beating her with the tongs. She lifted up her hands to strike me but forbore to do it. She gave me abundance of bad words and endeavored to strangle herself, but I believe in jest only. However after acting a mad woman a long time she was passive again. I ate some roast beef for dinner. In the afternoon Mr. G-r-l went away and I took a walk about the plantation. At night we drank some cider by way of reconciliation and I read nothing. I said my prayers and had good health, good thoughts, and good humor, thank God Almighty. I sent Tom to Williamsburg with some fish to the Governor and my sister Custis. My daughter was indisposed with a small fever.

I rose about 7 o'clock and read a chapter in Hebrew and some Greek in Lucian. I said my prayers and ate some boiled milk for breakfast. My daughter was better this morning, thank God. I beat Billy Wilkins for telling a lie. I settled some accounts and read some Latin and then read some news till dinner and then ate some roast beef for dinner. In the afternoon I read more news and then more Latin. I danced my dance and in the evening took a walk about the plantation and my wife with me. In the evening Tom returned from Williamsburg with letters from several persons containing some public [rumors] concerning the Duke of Marlborough being removed from all his places of honor and profit and that it was talked that he was also put into the Tower. I read nothing but said my prayers and had good health, good thoughts, and good humor, thank God Almighty.

I rose about 8 o'clock and read a chapter in Hebrew and some Greek in Homer. I said my prayers, and had boiled milk for breakfast. The weather was clear and warm, the wind west. About 10 o'clock came my Aunt Sherard and stayed about half an hour. About eleven I went to my Lord Percival's and he was out; then to Mr. G-n-y and stayed with him quarter of an hour; then to Colonel Blakiston's but he was out. Then to my Lord Orrery's where I drank some chocolate and stayed about an hour. Then I went to my Lord Islay's about some of his gimcracks and came home about 1 o'clock and wrote a letter till two and then went to my Lord Orrery's to dinner and my Lord Windsor and my Lord Islay dined there and I ate some pigeon pie. After dinner we drank Burgundy till six, and then went to Will's Coffeehouse, and from thence I went to the play, and from thence to Mrs. U-m-s where I ate a jelly and stayed till twelve, and then walked home and neglected my prayers, for which God forgive me.

I rose about 7 o'clock and read a chapter in Hebrew and some Greek in Lucian. I said my prayers, and had milk for breakfast. The weather was warm and cloudy, the wind southwest. I washed my feet and wrote a letter till 11 o'clock and then I went to visit Mr. V-n-n but he was from home. Then to the Cockpit to the Council office and then to Mrs. Southwell's and sat with her till 1 o'clock and then I went to Mrs. U-m-s and stayed there half an hour, and then walked home and ate a roast chicken for dinner barely done. After dinner I put several things in order and took a nap till five and then I went to Mrs. Pierson's, but she was from home; then to Mrs. Blakiston's and sat with her about half an hour, and then to Mrs. B-r-n where I drank some milk coffee, and then to Will's, where I drank a dish of chocolate and then went to Mother Smith's, where I supped with Betty G-r-n-r and then we went to bed and I rogered her two times very powerfully.

2. Richard Steele

The Spectator, No. 11
1711

As he explains in the essay, Richard Steele (1672–1729) read the story of Inkle and Yarico in Richard Ligon's True and Exact History of the Island of Barbados *(see chapter 4). The historian Peter Hulme has traced the tale's subsequent career, beginning with its 1734 translation into verse, followed by three more poetic versions in only four years, a play, and then an avalanche of poems, stories, plays, and paintings.*

Most of those who retold "Inkle and Yarico" after Steele treated the fate of the heroine as a study in the evils of slavery. Steele, by presenting the story as a lesson in the politics of romance rather than of empire, stresses the theme of love betrayed. But he too is wholly sympathetic to the loving Indian girl and critical of the perfidious Englishman. Yet Steele was no less a supporter of the Empire than his co-editor Joseph Addison (see chapter 10). Spectator No.11 does not impugn colonization itself. By deploring immorality in the pursuit of empire, it might even be read as a vindication of conquests like the one in which Inkle participates, suggesting that they need not be unethical, if only the conquerors behave with integrity. Still, the story of Inkle and Yarico offers a rare perspective on English imperial fervor, suggesting that, despite patriotic rhetoric and talk of a civilizing mission, the empire builders did not always enjoy a perfectly clear conscience. (See Robinson Crusoe *in chapter 10 for a similar instance.)*

Dat veniam corvis, vexat censura columbas.[1]—Juv.

Arietta is visited by all Persons of both Sexes, who may have any Pretence to Wit and Gallantry. She is in that time of Life which is neither affected with the Follies of Youth or Infirmities of Age; and her Conversation is so mixed with Gaiety and Prudence, that she is agreeable both to the Young and the Old. Her Behaviour is very frank, without being in the least blameable; and as she is out of the Tract of any amorous or ambitious Pursuits of her own, her Visitants entertain her with Accounts of themselves very freely, whether they concern their Passions or their Interests. I made her a Visit this Afternoon, having been formerly introduced to the Honour of her Acquaintance, by my friend *Will. Honeycomb*, who has prevailed upon her to admit me sometimes into her Assembly, as a civil, inoffensive Man. I found her accompanied with one Person only, a Common-Place Talker, who, upon my Entrance, rose, and after a very slight Civility sat down again; then turning to *Arietta*, pursued his Discourse, which I found was upon the old Topick, of Constancy in Love. He went on with great Facility in repeating what he talks every Day of his Life; and, with the Ornaments of insignificant Laughs and Gestures, enforced his Arguments by Quotations out of Plays and Songs, which allude to the Perjuries of the Fair, and the general Levity of Women. Methought he strove to shine more than ordinarily in his Talkative Way, that he might insult my Silence, and distinguish himself before a Woman of *Arietta*'s Taste and Understanding. She had often an Inclination to interrupt him, but could find no Opportunity, 'till the Larum ceased of its self; which it did not 'till he had repeated and murdered the celebrated Story of the *Ephesian* Matron.[2]

Arietta seemed to regard this Piece of Raillery as an Outrage done to her Sex; as indeed I have always observed that Women, whether out of a nicer Regard to their Honour, or what other Reason I cannot tell, are more sensibly touched with those general Aspersions, which are cast upon their Sex, than Men are by what is said of theirs.

When she had a little recovered her self from the serious Anger she was in, she replied in the following manner.

Sir, when I consider, how perfectly new all you have said on this Subject is, and that the Story you have given us is not quite two thousand Years Old, I cannot but think it a Piece of Presumption to dispute with you: But your Quotations put me in Mind of the Fable of the Lion and the Man. The Man walking with that noble Animal, showed him, in the Ostentation of Human Superiority, a Sign of a Man killing a Lion. Upon which the Lion said very justly, *We Lions are none of us Painters, else we could show a hundred Men killed by Lions, for one Lion killed by a Man.* You Men are Writers, and can represent us Women as Unbecoming as you please in your Works, while we are unable to return the Injury. You have twice or thrice observed in your Discourse, that Hypocrisy is the very Foundation of our Education; and that an Ability to dissemble our affections, is a professed Part of our Breeding. These, and such other Reflections, are sprinkled up and down the Writings of all Ages, by Authors, who

---

1. You ensure the dove yet pardon the perverted raven.

2. Story of the *Ephesian* Matron: while mourning over her husband's corpse, she meets and marries a seductive stranger.

leave behind them Memorials of their Resentment against the Scorn of particular Women, in Invectives against the whole Sex. Such a Writer, I doubt not, was the celebrated *Petronius*, who invented the pleasant Aggravations of the Frailty of the *Ephesian* Lady; but when we consider this Question between the Sexes, which has been either a Point of Dispute or Raillery ever since there were Men and Women, let us take Facts from plain People, and from such as have not either Ambition or Capacity to embellish their Narrations with any Beauties of Imagination. I was the other Day amusing myself with *Ligon's* Account of *Barbadoes*; and, in Answer to your well-wrought Tale, I will give you (as it dwells upon my Memory) out of that honest Traveller, in his fifty fifth page, the History of *Inkle* and *Yarico*.

Mr. *Thomas Inkle* of *London*, aged twenty Years, embarked in the *Downs*, on the good Ship called the *Achilles*, bound for the *West Indies*, on the 16th of June 1647, in order to improve his Fortune by Trade and Merchandize. Our Adventurer was the third Son of an eminent Citizen, who had taken particular Care to instill into his Mind an early Love of Gain, by making him a perfect Master of Numbers, and consequently giving him a quick View of Loss and Advantage, and preventing the natural Impulses of his Passions, by Prepossession towards his Interests. With a Mind thus turned, young *Inkle* had a Person every way agreeable, a ruddy Vigour in his Countenance, Strength in his Limbs, with Ringlets of fair Hair loosely flowing on his Shoulders. It happened, in the Course of the Voyage, that the *Achilles*, in some Distress, put into a Creek on the Main of *America*, in search of Provisions: The Youth, who is the Hero of my Story, among others, went ashore on this Occasion. From their first Landing they were observed by a Party of *Indians*, who hid themselves in the Woods for that Purpose. The *English* unadvisedly marched a great distance from the Shore into the Country, and were intercepted by the Natives, who slew the greatest Number of them. Our Adventurer escaped among others, by flying into a Forest. Upon his coming into a remote and pathless Part of the Wood, he threw himself tired and breathless on a little Hillock, when an *Indian* Maid rushed from a Thicket behind him: After the first Surprize, they appeared mutually agreeable to each other. If the *European* was highly charmed with the Limbs, Features, and wild Graces of the Naked *American*; the *American* was no less taken with the Dress, Complexion, and Shape of an *European*, covered from Head to Foot. The *Indian* grew immediately enamoured of him, and consequently sollicitous for his Preservation: She therefore conveyed him to a Cave, where she gave him a Delicious Repast of Fruits, and led him to a Stream to slake his Thirst. In the midst of these good Offices, she would sometimes play with his Hair, and delight in the Opposition of its Colour to that of her Fingers: Then open his Bosome, then laugh at him for covering it. She was, it seems, a Person of Distinction, for she every day came to him in a different Dress, of the most beautiful Shells, Bugles, and Bredes. She likewise brought him a great many Spoils, which her other Lovers had presented to her; so that his Cave was richly adorned with all the spotted Skins of Beasts, and most Party-coloured Feathers of Fowls, which that World afforded. To make his Confinement more tolerable, she would carry him in the Dusk of the Evening, or by the favour of Moon-light, to unfrequented Groves, and Solitudes, and show him where to lye down in Safety, and sleep amidst the Falls of Waters, and Melody of Nightingales. Her Part was to watch and hold him in her

Arms, for fear of her Country-men, and wake on Occasions to consult his Safety. In this manner did the Lovers pass away their Time, till they had learn'd a Language of their own, in which the Voyager communicated to his Mistress, how happy he should be to have her in his Country, where she should be Cloathed in such Silks as his Wastecoat was made of, and be carried in Houses drawn by Horses, without being exposed to Wind or Weather. All this he promised her the Enjoyment of, without such Fears and Alarms as they were there tormented with. In this tender Correspondence these Lovers lived for several Months, when *Yarico*, instructed by her Lover, discovered a Vessel on the Coast, to which she made Signals, and in the Night, with the utmost Joy and Satisfaction accompanied him to a Ships-Crew of his Country-Men, bound for *Barbadoes*. When a Vessel from the Main arrives in that Island, it seems the Planters

Inkle and Yarico, engraved for Abbé Raynal's Histoire des Deux Indes, *1780.*

come down to the Shoar, where there is an immediate Market of the *Indians* and other Slaves, as with us of Horses and Oxen.

To be short, Mr. *Thomas Inkle*, now coming into *English* Territories, began seriously to reflect upon his loss of Time, and to weigh with himself how many Days Interest of his Mony he had lost during his Stay with *Yarico*. This Thought made the Young Man very pensive, and careful what Account he should be able to give his Friends of his Voyage. Upon which Considerations, the prudent and frugal young Man sold *Yarico* to a *Barbadian* Merchant; notwithstanding that the poor Girl, to incline him to commiserate her Condition, told him that she was with Child by him: But he only made use of that Information, to rise in his Demands upon the Purchaser.

I was so touch'd with this Story, (which I think should be always a Counterpart to the *Ephesian* Matron) that I left the Room with Tears in my Eyes; which a Woman of *Arietta's* good Sense, did, I am sure, take for greater Applause, than any Compliments I could make her.

R.

3. Dr. Alexander Hamilton

from *The History of the Ancient and Honorable Tuesday Club*
1745–56

> *Hamilton organized the Tuesday Club of Annapolis, Maryland, in 1745 as a place where the most distinguished men of the colony might gather for good talk and excellent company. As the Club's secretary, self-dubbed "Loquacious Scribble," Hamilton kept a continual record of its activities and conversations. While they testify to the existence of an established and class-conscious aristocracy, Hamilton's records seem also to reflect a certain nervousness about its members' status: the opening distinction between a true Club and other forms of association, as well as the first sentence of the second selection, almost inviting censure from "People of a Low and gross taste," project a defensiveness that other evidence suggests guards two areas of vulnerability. The first would be the area of relations with the middling classes of the colonies, whose acquiescence in such recently acquired aristocratic distinction is at times uncertain; the second lies in the opposite direction, in the Tuesday Club's relations with its London equivalents who probably need to be reassured that, although colonial, the Club members are not therefore provincial.*

OF CLUBS IN GENERAL, AND THEIR ANTIQUITY.

By *Clubs* I mean those societies, which generally meet of an evening, either at some tavern or private house, to converse, or look at one another, smoke a pipe, drink a toast, be politic or dull, lively or frolicksome, to philosophize or triffle, argue or debate, talk over Religion, News, Scandal or bawdy, or spend the time in any other Sort of Clubical amusement. Out of this definition I expressly exclude, all your card matches and meetings, those properly belonging to the celebrated modern assemblies called Routs and Drums which are many degrees Inferior to Clubs, as being less ancient.

It has been observed by some ancient philosophers, particularly one Sir Isaac Newton, that there exists a certain affection or fellow feeling, between all bodies in nature, by which they have a strong tendency, to approach, one towards another, to Join, and even to Incorporate, and that a perfect antipathy is never, a partial one seldom to be met with; This has been called by these Philosophers, the power of attraction, which we find prevails and governs very much, among men and other Animals, and occasions that great propensity in human nature, to unite and form into Clubs.

MR ATTORNEY WOUDBE APPEARS IN CLUB, TRIAL OF JONATHAN GROG ESQR, HIS CONDEMNATION AND SENTENCE, NEW SONG INTRODUCED BY HIS HONOR THE PRESIDENT, CONGRATULATORY PYNDARIC ODE BY THE POET LAUREAT.

People of a Low and gross taste, are often offended at a Serious manner of Jesting, either in Conversation or writing; what I mean by a Serious manner of Jesting, is running a Course of Ridicule, on Subjects, that are esteemed to be of a Serious and Solemn nature; for this reason, I doubt not, but many low and Gross Critics, will Condemn me, for presuming to Jest upon Subjects of this nature, (according to their profound estimation) and particularly our Solemn and grave professors of the Law, who esteem their Science, (as they call it, tho' I rather think it an art) the quintessence of human reason, and their Judicial Proceedings, thereon founded very Grand, Solemn & Sublime, in all its parts. It is true, that I have in various places of this Important and Solemn history, especially in giving an account of the Club trials, represented that Science, and its professors, the Gentlemen of the long robe in no favorable light, for which I have no other apology to make, than that I take our Law (especially our Common law) proceedings to be *Seria mixta Jocis*;[3] *Seria*, in so far, as the Intention of them is pretended to be the Securing of right and property, and *Mixta Jocis*, as they are many times Crouded & overloaded, with such triffling distinctions, such minute punc- tillios and forms, far fetched definitions, distorted reasonings and prolix tautologies, as would make any reasonable man, who is not a party Interrested or concerned in this profitable, extravagant, and expensive ocupation, split his midriff with Laughter.

The Profound Doctors of this profounder profession, may, if they please think me an Ignorant puppy, and, that I prate in this manner, because I know nothing of the matter, and apply to me the Scurvey proverb of *Ne Sutor ultra Crepidam*,[4]—'Tis very true, my Learned friends, I never trowbled my head about any such Intricate and Subtile Studies, but Call me what you please, Ignorant or dull, I hope I am only so in Law, and not In fact, as you know, by your own wise maxims, a man may be dead in Law, and not in fact, I hope I have natural reason Sufficient to form a Judgement of the perfections and Imperfections, The Integrity & the flaws, breaks or botches of this Slippery Craft, however deep and learned it's foundations or props may be, and I may safely aver, and have the Concurrence of many Candid Judges, that our modes and Proceedings in Law, (common Law I still mean) are more founded upon national Custom, than upon Reason; and, That national Custom (especially the custom of conquering nations, for from them our Common Law took it's original) is always founded on Reason, I believe, few discerning men will allow; it being rather estab- lished on the will and pleasure of the Conquerors, which Sort of reason, may seem reasonable to them, but absurd to all the world besides, (I beg pardon for Introducing here such Clubical terms, as *reasonable Reason*, and *Reason absurd*, but had I time I could quote many Common law terms to support me here).

Besides, If we Grant that *Reason Simpliciter*, as Reason, is common to all mankind, (and I think my Philosophy tells me this is true) then, the Common Law, if founded on reason as they say, would be common to all nations, but should this fundamental reason, on which this bulky fabric stands, be any other reason, but Common reason, or, in plainer words, Common Sense, I would not give a farthing, for either the Edifice or it's prop; Since we know then that this Common law is not universal, and that it is

---

3. *Seria mixta Jocis*: serious matters mixed with jokes.

4. *Ne Sutor ultra Crepidam*: let the cobbler not judge beyond shoes. Valerius Maximus 8.12.3.

founded on Custom, there must necessarily be many absurdities in it, and all the Reason its professors can brag of, is to reduce these absurdities to some Show of reason; hence, many Learned arguments have been devised, to establish the equity and reasonableness of the Law of Combats, and the manner of old, of determining Right and Wrong, by dint of blows and hard knocks, to place on a Rational foundation, Trials by fire and water ordeal, and the discovery of witches by their floating or sinking in a pond or river, abundance of Learned treatises have been wrote, concerning the law of duels, and how in proper form and methods, men might Cut one another's throats, to solder up Crack'd honor, and separate truth from falshood, which learned tracts, and arguments, In times past had their value and Character, and were looked upon, as a very Rational method of procedure, tho' now obselete, and thrust out of doors, and I am afraid, our Common law is still stuffed with numberless absurdities, owing their birth to the same Gothic original, not withstanding the wisdom of the Legislature of late has Cleared it of that Barbarous Jargon of old obselete Norman French, and dog latin, of which many Grave and ponderous volumes may be seen at this day, printed in a fine black Character, and it is to be wished that some Great Genius, would scour away the Rubbish of Silly reasons which abound in these vast books, such for example, as that of a Certain Grave Judge, who gives this reason, why a father cannot Inherit his Son's Lands, vizt: *Quia terra gravis est et non potest ascendere;*[5] but these fooleries would Surely be much sooner exploded, and share the same fate with the Codes, concerning Single Combat and duels, were it not, that they serve to Inrich the professors of this Cunning Science, and render the profits thereof more extensive, a method being hereby Ingeniously Contrived, whereby to baffle mathematical demonstration, and keep a man waiting twenty or thirty years, squandering his money & fooling away his life, before it can be determined that twice two makes four.

Let no rash Critic therefore Censure the methods of proceeding in these our Club Trials, or pronounce them absurd or nonsensical, since they have so great a pattern, as the Courts of Common Law to Copy from, nor let any find fault with our Clubical punishments, of a Condemned Criminal, should he be Sentenced to *sing a Song*, to expiate his trespass, since, had we time or room here, we could produce proceedings and punishments alike absurd, in our Grave and Solemn Courts of Judicatory.

---

5. Because land is heavy and cannot ascend.

4. Benjamin Franklin

Speech of Miss Polly Baker
1747

In the three selections that follow, Franklin demonstrates a remarkable literary range. To create Polly Baker, he develops a voice that not only characterizes her humorously but permits her to speak with humor, while making readers aware that the narrator advocates neither her argument nor even her triumphant opportunism. Applauding her gumption, rather, he takes a stance typical of the satirist who generally does not project an ideal of his or her own: Franklin here mocks conventional sexual piety without positively endorsing its violation.

"Father Abraham's Speech" originally appeared as the preface to Franklin's 1758 almanac, Poor Richard Improved. *It has been popular ever since, perhaps because it digests so many aphorisms from Poor Richard's Almanac. Although it has often been reprinted as "The Way to Wealth," "Father Abraham's Speech" is the more appropriate title: the essay is far from simple instructions for getting rich. Both Father Abraham and Poor Richard are fictitious personæ, and the elaborate framing device of the sketch has less to do with economics than with fame, vanity, and quotation.*

"The Ephemera," written and printed as one of a series of "Bagatelles" while Franklin was living in France, represents him in his least familiar guise, as an abstract thinker posing basic philosophical questions. Life is short, we say, but we don't mean it, or not as Franklin represents it here. What if we did take seriously phrases like "here today, gone tomorrow"?

The SPEECH *of Miss* Polly Baker, *before a Court of Judicature, at* Connecticut *in* New England, *where she was prosecuted the fifth Time for having a Bastard Child; which influenced the Court to dispense with her Punishment, and induced one of her Judges to marry her the next Day.*

May it please the Honourable Bench to indulge me a few Words: I am a poor unhappy Woman; who have no Money to Fee Lawyers to plead for me, being hard put to it to get a tolerable Living. I shall not trouble your Honours with long Speeches; for I have not the presumption to expect, that you may, by any Means, be prevailed on to deviate in your Sentence from the Law, in my Favour. All I humbly hope is, that your Honours would charitably move the Governor's Goodness on my Behalf, that my Fine may be remitted. This is the Fifth Time, Gentlemen, that I have been dragg'd before your Courts on the same Account; twice I have paid heavy Fines, and twice have been brought to public Punishment, for want of Money to pay those Fines. This may have been agreeable to the Laws; I do not dispute it: But since Laws are sometimes unreasonable in themselves, and therefore repealed; and others bear too hard on the Subject in particular Circumstances; and therefore there is left a Power somewhere to dispense with the Execution of them; I take the Liberty to say, that I think this Law, by which I am punished, is both unreasonable in itself, and particularly severe with regard to me, who have always lived an inoffensive Life in the Neighbourhood where I was born, and defy my Enemies (if I have any) to say I ever wrong'd Man, Woman, or Child. Abstracted from the Law, I cannot conceive (may it please your Honours) what the Nature of my Offence is. I have brought Five fine Children into the World, at the Risque of my Life: I have maintained them well by my own Industry, without burthening the Township, and could have done it better, if it had not been for the heavy Charges and Fines I have paid. Can it be a Crime (in the Nature of Things I mean) to add to the Number of the King's Subjects, in a new Country that really wants People? I own I should think it rather a Praise worthy, than a Punishable Action. I have debauch'd no other Woman's Husband, nor inticed any innocent Youth: These Things I never was charged with; nor has any one the least cause of Complaint against me, unless, perhaps the Minister, or the Justice, because I have had Children without being Married, by which they have miss'd a Wedding Fee. But, can even this be a Fault of mine? I appeal to your Honours. You are pleased to allow I don't want Sense; but I must be stupid to the last Degree, not to prefer the honourable State of Wedlock, to the Condition I have lived in. I always was, and still am, willing to enter into it; I doubt not my Behaving well in it, having all the Industry, Frugality, Fertility, and Skill in Oeconomy, appertaining to a good Wife's Character. I defy any Person to say I ever Refused an Offer of that Sort: On the contrary, I readily Consented to the only Proposal of Marriage that ever was made me, which was when I was a Virgin; but too easily confiding in the Person's Sincerity that made it, I unhappily lost my own Honour, by trusting to his; for he got me with Child, and then forsook me: That very Person you all know; he is now become a Magistrate of this County; and I had hopes he would have appeared this Day on the Bench, and have endeavoured to moderate the Court in my Favour; then I should have scorn'd to have mention'd it; but I must Complain of it as unjust and unequal, that my Betrayer and Undoer, the first Cause of all my Faults and Miscarriages (if they must be deemed such) should be advanced to Honour and Power, in the same Government that punishes my Misfortunes with Stripes and Infamy. I shall be told, 'tis like, that were there no Act of Assembly in the Case, the Precepts of Religion are violated by my Transgressions. If mine, then, is a religious Offence, leave it, Gentlemen, to religious Punishments. You have already excluded me from all the Comforts of your Church Communion: Is not that sufficient? You believe I have offended Heaven, and must suffer eternal Fire: Will not that be sufficient? What need is there, then, of your additional Fines and Whippings? I own, I do not think as you do; for, if I thought, what you call a Sin, was really such, I would not presumptuously commit it. But how can it be believed, that Heaven is angry at my having Children, when, to the little done by me towards it, God has been pleased to add his divine Skill and admirable Workmanship in the Formation of their Bodies, and crown'd it by furnishing them with rational and immortal Souls? Forgive me Gentlemen, if I talk a little extravagantly on these Matters; I am no Divine: But if you, great Men,[6] must be making Laws, do not turn natural and useful Actions into Crimes, by your Prohibitions. Reflect a little on the horrid Consequences of this Law in particular: What Numbers of procur'd Abortions! and how many distress'd Mothers have been driven, by the Terror of Punishment and public Shame, to imbrue, contrary to Nature, their own trembling Hands in the Blood of their helpless Offspring! Nature would have induc'd them to nurse it up with a Parent's Fondness. 'Tis the Law therefore, 'tis the Law itself that is guilty of all these Barbarities and Murders. Repeal it then, Gentlemen; let it be expung'd for ever from your Books: And on the other hand, take into your wise Consideration, the great and growing Number of Batchelors in the Country, many of whom, from the mean Fear of the Expence of a Family, have never sincerely and honourably Courted a Woman in their Lives; and by their Manner of Living, leave unproduced (which I think is little better than Murder) Hundreds of their Posterity to the Thousandth Generation. Is not theirs a greater Offense against the Public Good, than mine? Compel them then, by a Law, either to Marry, or pay double the Fine of Fornication every Year. What must poor young Women do, whom Custom has forbid to sollicit the Men, and who cannot force themselves upon Husbands, when the Laws take no Care to provide them any, and yet severely punish if they do their Duty without them? Yes, Gentlemen, I venture to call it a Duty; 'tis the Duty of the first and great Command of Nature, and of Nature's God, *Increase and multiply*: A Duty, from the steady Performance of which nothing has ever been able to deter me; but for it's Sake, I have hazarded the Loss of the public Esteem, and frequently incurr'd public Disgrace and Punishment; and therefore ought, in my humble Opinion, instead of a Whipping, to have a Statue erected to my Memory.

5. Benjamin Franklin

Father Abraham's Speech
1758

Courteous Reader,

I have heard that nothing gives an Author so great Pleasure, as to find his Works respectfully quoted by other learned Authors. This Pleasure I have seldome enjoyed; for tho' I have been, if I may say it without Vanity, an *Eminent Author* of Almanacks annuyally now a full Quarter of a Century, my Brother Authors in the same Way, for what Reason I know not, have ever been very sparing in their Applauses; and no other Author has taken the least Notice of me, so that did not my

---

6. Turning to some Gentlemen of the Assembly, then in Court. [Franklin's note.]

Writings produce me some solid *Pudding,* the great Deficiency of *Praise* would have quite discouraged me.

I concluded at length, that the People were the best Judges of my Merit; for they buy my Works; and besides, in my Rambles, where I am not personally known, I have frequently heard one or other of my Adages repeated, with, *as Poor Richard says,* at the End on't; this gave me some Satisfaction, as it showed not only that my Instructions were regarded, but discovered likewise some Respect for my Authority; and I own, that to encourage the Practice of remembering and repeating those wise Sentences, I have sometimes *quoted myself* with great Gravity.

The figure of the zodiac, from Poor Richard's Almanac.

Judge then how much I must have been gratified by an Incident I am going to relate to you. I stopt my Horse lately where a great Number of People were collected at a Vendue of Merchant Goods. The Hour of Sale not being come, they were conversing on the Badness of the Times, and one of the Company call'd to a plain clean old Man, with white Locks, *Pray, Father* Abraham, *what think you of the Times? Won't these heavy Taxes quite ruin the Country? How shall we be ever able to pay them? What would you advise us to?*—Father *Abraham* stood up, and reply'd, If you'd have my Advice, I'll give it you in short, for a *Word to the Wise is enough,* and *many Words won't fill a Bushel,* as *Poor Richard says.* They join'd in desiring him to speak his Mind, and gathering round him, he proceeded as follows;

"Friends, says he, and Neighbours, the Taxes are indeed very heavy, and if those laid on by the Government were the only Ones we had to pay, we might more easily discharge them; but we have many others, and much more grievous to some of us. We are taxed twice as much by our *Idleness,* three times as much by our *Pride,* and four times as much by our *Folly,* and from these Taxes the Commissioners cannot ease or deliver us by allowing an Abatement. However let us hearken to good Advice, and something may be done for us; *God helps them that help themselves,* as *Poor Richard* says, in his Almanack of 1733.

It would be thought a hard Government that should tax its People one tenth Part of their *Time,* to be employed in its Service. But Idleness taxes many of us much more, if we reckon all that is spent in absolute *Sloth,* or doing of nothing, with that which is spent in idle Employments or Amusements, that amount to nothing. *Sloth,* by bringing on Diseases, absolutely shortens Life. *Sloth, like Rust, consumes faster than Labour wears, while the used Key is always bright,* as *Poor Richard* says. But *dost thou love Life, then do not squander Time, for that's the Stuff Life is made of,* as *Poor Richard* says. —How much more than is necessary do we spend in Sleep! forgetting that *The sleeping Fox catches no Poultry,* and that *there will be sleeping enough in the Grave,* as *Poor Richard* says. If Time be of all Things the most precious, *wasting Time* must be, as *Poor Richard* says, *the greatest Prodigality,* since, as he elsewhere tells us, *Lost*

Time is never found again; and what we call *Time-enough, always proves little enough:* Let us then up and be doing, and doing to the Purpose; so by Diligence shall we do more with less Perplexity. *Sloth makes all Things difficult, but Industry all easy,* as *Poor Richard* says; and *He that riseth late, must trot all Day, and shall scarce overtake his Business at Night.* While *Laziness travels so slowly, that Poverty soon overtakes him,* as we read in *Poor Richard,* who adds, *Drive Business, let not that drive thee; and Early to Bed, and early to rise, makes a Man healthy, wealthy and wise.*

So what signifies *wishing and hoping* for better Times. We may make these Times better if we bestir ourselves. *Industry need not wish,* as *Poor Richard* says, and *He that lives upon Hope will die fasting. There are no Gains, without Pains;* then *Help Hands, for I have no Lands,* or if I have, they are smartly taxed. And, as *Poor Richard* likewise observes *He that hath a Trade hath an Estate,* and *He that hath a Calling hath an Office of Profit and Honour;* but then the *Trade* must be worked at, and the *Calling* well followed, or neither the *Estate,* nor the *Office,* will enable us to pay our Taxes. —If we are industrious we shall never starve; for, as *Poor Richard* says, *At the working Man's House* Hunger *looks in, but dares not enter.* Nor will the Bailiff or the Constable enter, for *Industry pays Debts, while Despair encreaseth them,* says *Poor Richard.* —What though you have found no Treasure, nor has any rich Relation left you a Legacy, *Diligence is the Mother of Good-luck,* as *Poor Richard* says, *and God gives all Things to Industry.* Then *plough deep, while Sluggards sleep, and you shall have Corn to sell and to keep,* says *Poor Dick.* Work while it is called To-day, for you know not how much you may be hindered To-morrow, which makes *Poor Richard* say, *One To-day is worth two Tomorrows;* and farther, *Have you somewhat to do Tomorrow, do it Today.* If you were a Servant, would you not be ashamed that a good Master should catch you idle? Are you then your own Master, *be ashamed to catch yourself idle,* as *Poor Dick* says. When there is so much to be done for yourself, your Family, your Country, and your gracious King, be up by Peep of Day; *Let not the Sun look down and say, Inglorious here he lies.* Handle your Tools without Mittens; remember that *the Cat in Gloves catches no Mice,* as *Poor Richard* says. 'Tis true there is much to be done, and perhaps you are weak handed, but stick to it steadily, and you will see great Effects, for *constant Dropping wears away Stones,* and by *Diligence and Patience the Mouse ate in two the Cable;* and *little Strokes fell great Oaks,* as *Poor Richard* says in his Almanack, the Year I cannot just now remember.

Methinks I hear some of you say, *Must a Man afford himself no Leisure?*—I will tell thee, my Friend, what *Poor Richard* says, *Employ the Time well if thou meanest to gain Leisure; and, since thou art not sure of a Minute, throw not away an Hour.* Leisure, is Time for doing something useful; this Leisure the diligent Man will obtain, but the lazy Man never; so that, as *Poor Richard* says, *a Life of Leisure and a Life of Laziness are two Things.* Do you imagine that Sloth will afford you more Comfort than Labour? No, for as *Poor Richard* says, *Trouble springs from Idleness, and grievous Toil from needless Ease. Many without Labour, would live by their* WITS *only, but they break for want of Stock.* Whereas Industry gives Comfort, and Plenty, and Respect: *Fly Pleasures, and they'll follow you. The diligent Spinner has a large Shift;* and *now I have a Sheep and a Cow, every Body bids me Good morrow;* all which is well said by *Poor Richard.*

But with our Industry, we must likewise be steady, *settled* and *careful,* and oversee our own Affairs *with our own Eyes,* and not trust too much to others; for, as *Poor Richard* says,

> *I never saw an oft removed Tree,*
> *Nor yet an oft removed Family,*
> *That throve so well as those that settled be.*

And again, *Three Removes is as bad as a Fire;* and again, *Keep thy Shop, and thy Shop will keep thee;* and again, *If you would have your Business done, go; If not, send.* And again,

> *He that by the Plough would thrive,*
> *Himself must either hold or drive.*

And again, *The Eye of a Master will do more Work than both his Hands;* and again, *Want of Care does us more Damage than Want of Knowledge;* and again, *Not to oversee Workmen, is to leave them your Purse open.* Trusting too much to others Care is the Ruin of many; for, as the *Almanack* says, *In the Affairs of this World, Men are saved, not by Faith, but by the Want of it;* but a Man's own Care is profitable; for, saith *Poor Dick, Learning is to the Studious, and Riches to the Careful,* as well as *Power to the Bold, and Heaven to the Virtuous.* And farther, *If you would have a faithful Servant, and one that you like, serve yourself.* And again, he adviseth to Circumspection and Care, even in the smallest Matters, because sometimes *a little Neglect may breed great Mischief,* adding, *For want of a Nail the Shoe was lost; for want of a Shoe the Horse was lost; and for want of a Horse the Rider was lost,* being overtaken and slain by the Enemy, all for want of Care about a Horse-shoe Nail.

So much for Industry, my Friends, and Attention to one's own Business; but to these we must add *Frugality,* if we would make our *Industry* more certainly successful. A Man may, if he knows not how to save as he gets, *keep his Nose all his Life to the Grindstone,* and die not worth a *Groat* at last. A *fat Kitchen makes a lean Will,* as *Poor Richard* says; and,

> *Many Estates are spent in the Getting,*
> *Since Women for Tea forsook Spinning and Knitting,*
> *And Men for Punch forsook Hewing and Splitting.*

If you would be wealthy, says he, in another Almanack, *think of Saving as well as of Getting:* The *Indies have not made* Spain *rich, because her* Outgoes *are greater than her* Incomes. Away then with your expensive Follies, and you will not have so much Cause to complain of hard Times, heavy Taxes, and chargeable Families; for, as *Poor Dick* says,

> *Women and Wine, Game and Deceit,*
> *Make the Wealth small, and the Wants great.*

And farther, *What maintains one Vice, would bring up two Children.* You may think perhaps, That a *little* Tea, or a *little* Punch now and then, Diet a *little* more costly, Clothes a *little* finer, and a *little* Entertainment now and then, can be no *great* Matter; but remember what *Poor Richard* says, *Many a* Little *makes a Mickle;* and farther, *Beware of little* Expences; *a small Leak will sink a great Ship;* and again, *Who Dainties love, shall Beggars prove;* and moreover, *Fools make Feasts, and wise Men eat them.*

Here you are all got together at this Vendue of *Fineries and Knicknacks*. You call them *Goods,* but if you do not take Care, they will prove *Evils* to some of you. You expect they will be sold *cheap,* and perhaps they may for less than they cost; but if you have no Occasion for them, they must be *dear* to you. Remember what *Poor Richard* says, *Buy what thou hast no Need of, and ere long thou shalt sell thy Necessaries.* And again, *At a great Pennyworth pause a while:* He means, that perhaps the Cheapness is *apparent* only, and not *real;* or the Bargain, by straitning thee in thy Business, may do thee more Harm than Good. For in another Place he says, *Many have been ruined by buying good Pennyworths.* Again, *Poor Richard* says, 'Tis *foolish to lay out Money in a Purchase of Repentance;* and yet this Folly is practised every Day at Vendues, for want of minding the Almanack. *Wise Men,* as *Poor Dick* says, *learn by others Harms, Fools scarcely by their own;* but, *Felix quem faciunt aliena Pericula cautum.* Many a one, for the Sake of Finery on the Back, have gone with a hungry Belly, and half starved their Families; *Silks and Sattins, Scarlet and Velvets,* as *Poor Richard* says, *put out the Kitchen Fire.* These are not the *Necessaries* of Life; they can scarcely be called the *Conveniencies,* and yet only because they look pretty, how many *want* to *have* them. The *artificial* Wants of Mankind thus become more numerous than the *natural;* and, as *Poor Dick* says, *For one* poor *Person, there are an hundred* indigent. By these, and other Extravagancies, the Genteel are reduced to Poverty, and forced to borrow of those whom they formerly despised, but who through *Industry* and *Frugality,* have maintained their Standing; in which Case it appears plainly, that a *Ploughman on his Legs is higher than a Gentleman on his Knees,* as *Poor Richard* says. Perhaps they have had a small Estate left them, which they knew not the Getting of; they think *'tis Day, and will never be Night;* that a little to be spent out of *so* much, is not worth minding; *(a Child and a Fool,* as *Poor Richard* says, *imagine* Twenty Shillings *and* Twenty Years *can never be spent)* but, *always taking out of the Meal-tub, and never putting in, soon comes to the Bottom;* then, as *Poor Dick* says, *When the Well's dry, they know the Worth of Water.* But this they might have known before, if they had taken his Advice; *If you would know the Value of Money, go and try to borrow some;* for, *he that goes a borrowing goes a sorrowing;* and indeed so does he that lends to such People, when he goes *to get it in again.*—*Poor Dick* farther advises, and says,

> *Fond* Pride of Dress, is *sure a very Curse;*
> *E'er* Fancy *you consult, consult your Purse.*

And again, *Pride is as loud a Beggar as* Want, *and a great deal more saucy.* When you have bought one fine Thing you must buy ten more, that your Appearance may be all of a Piece; but *Poor Dick* says, 'Tis *easier to* suppress *the first Desire, than* to satisfy *all that follow it.* And 'tis as truly Folly for the Poor to ape the Rich, as for the Frog to swell, in order to equal the Ox.

> *Great Estates may venture more,*
> *But little Boats should keep near Shore.*

'Tis however a Folly soon punished; for *Pride that dines on Vanity, sups on Contempt,* as *Poor Richard* says. And in another Place, *Pride breakfasted with Plenty, dined with Poverty, and supped with Infamy.* And after all, of what Use is this *Pride of Appearance,* for which so much is risked, so much is suffered? It cannot promote

Health, or ease Pain; it makes no Increase of Merit in the Person, it creates Envy, it hastens Misfortune.

> *What is a Butterfly? At best*
> *He's but a Caterpillar drest.*
> *The gaudy Fop's his Picture just,*

as *Poor Richard* says.

But what Madness must it be to *run in Debt* for these Superfluities! We are offered, by the Terms of this Vendue, *Six Months Credit*; and that perhaps has induced some of us to attend it, because we cannot spare the ready Money, and hope now to be fine without it. But, ah, think what you do when you run in Debt; *You give to another Power over your Liberty.* If you cannot pay at the Time, you will be ashamed to see your Creditor; you will be in Fear when you speak to him; you will make poor pitiful sneaking Excuses, and by Degrees come to lose your Veracity, and sink into base downright lying; for, as *Poor Richard* says, *The second Vice is Lying, the first is running in Debt.* And again, to the same Purpose, *Lying rides upon Debts Back.* Whereas a freeborn *Englishman* ought not to be ashamed or afraid to see or speak to any Man living. But Poverty often deprives a Man of all Spirit and Virtue: *'Tis hard for an empty Bag to stand upright,* as *Poor Richard* truly says. What would you think of that Prince, or that Government, who should issue an Edict forbidding you to dress like a Gentleman or a Gentlewoman, on Pain of Imprisonment or Servitude? Would you not say, that you are free, have a Right to dress as you please, and that such an Edict would be a Breach of your Privileges, and such a Government tyrannical? And yet you are about to put yourself under that Tyranny when you run in Debt for such Dress! Your Creditor has Authority at his Pleasure to deprive you of your Liberty, by confining you in Goal for Life, or to sell you for a Servant, if you should not be able to pay him! When you have got your Bargain, you may, perhaps, think little of Payment; but *Creditors, Poor Richard* tells us, *have better Memories than Debtors;* and in another Place says, *Creditors are a superstitious Sect, great Observers of set Days and Times.* The Day comes round before you are aware, and the Demand is made before you are prepared to satisfy it. Or if you bear your Debt in Mind, the Term which at first seemed so long, will, as it lessens, appear extreamly short. *Time* will seem to have added Wings to his Heels as well as Shoulders. *Those have a short Lent,* saith *Poor Richard, who owe Money to be paid at Easter.* Then since, as he says, *The Borrower is a Slave to the Lender, and the Debtor to the Creditor,* disdain the Chain, preserve your Freedom; and maintain your Independency: Be *industrious* and *free*; be *frugal* and *free.* At present, perhaps, you may think yourself in thriving Circumstances, and that you can bear a little Extravagance without Injury; but,

> *For Age and Want, save while you may;*
> *No Morning Sun lasts a whole Day,*

as *Poor Richard* says. —Gain may be temporary, and uncertain, but ever while you live, Expence is constant and certain; and *'tis easier to build two Chimnies than to keep one in Fuel,* as *Poor Richard* says. So *rather go to Bed supperless than rise in Debt.*

> *Get what you can, and what you get hold;*
> *'Tis the Stone that will turn all your Lead into Gold,*

as *Poor Richard* says. And when you have got the Philosopher's Stone, sure you will no longer complain of bad Times, or the Difficulty of paying Taxes.

This Doctrine, my Friends, is *Reason and Wisdom;* but after all, do not depend too much upon your own *Industry, and Frugality, and Prudence,* though excellent Things, for they may all be blasted without the Blessing of Heaven; and therefore ask that Blessing humbly, and be not uncharitable to those that at present seem to want it, but comfort and help them. Remember *Job* suffered, and was afterwards prosperous.

And now to conclude, *Experience keeps a dear School, but Fools will learn in no other, and scarce in that;* for it is true, *we may give Advice, but we cannot give Conduct,* as *Poor Richard* says: However, remember this, *They that won't be counselled, can't be helped,* as *Poor Richard* says: And farther, That if *you will not hear Reason, she'll surely rap your Knuckles."*

Thus the old Gentleman ended his Harangue. The People heard it, and approved the Doctrine, and immediately practised the contrary, just as if it had been a common Sermon; for the Vendue opened, and they began to buy extravagantly, notwithstanding all his Cautions, and their own Fear of Taxes.—I found the good Man had thoroughly studied my Almanacks, and digested all I had dropt on those Topicks during the Course of Five-and-twenty Years. The frequent Mention he made of me must have tired any one else, but my Vanity was wonderfully delighted with it, though I was conscious that not a tenth Part of the Wisdom was my own which he ascribed to me, but rather the *Gleanings* I had made of the Sense of all Ages and Nations. However, I resolved to be the better for the Echo of it; and though I had at first determined to buy Stuff for a new Coat, I went away resolved to wear my old One a little longer. *Reader,* if thou wilt do the same, thy Profit will be as great as mine.

I am, as ever,

Thine to serve thee,

Richard Saunders.

July 7, 1757.

6. Benjamin Franklin

The Ephemera
1778

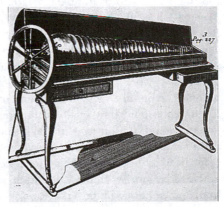

The glass harmonica, an instrument invented by Franklin. Both Mozart and Beethoven wrote music for it.

Passy Sept 20, 1778

You may remember, my dear Friend, that when we lately spent that happy Day in the delightful Garden and sweet Society of the Moulin Joli, I stopt a little in one of our Walks, and staid some time behind the Company. We had been shewn numberless Skeletons of a kind of little Fly, called an Ephemere all whose successive Generations we were told were bred and expired within the Day. I happen'd to see a living Company of them on a Leaf, who appear'd to be engag'd in Conversation.—You know I understand all the inferior Animal Tongues: my too great Application to the Study of them is the best Excuse I can give for the little Progress I have made in your charming Language. I listened thro' Curiosity to the Discourse of these little Creatures, but as they in their national Vivacity spoke three or four together, I could make but little of their Discourse. I found, however, by some broken Expressions that I caught now & then, they were disputing warmly the Merit of two foreign Musicians, one a *Cousin*, the other a *Musketo*; in which Dispute they spent their time seemingly as regardless of the Shortness of Life, as if they had been Sure of living a Month. Happy People! thought I, you live certainly under a wise, just and mild Government; since you have no public Grievances to complain of, nor any Subject of Contention but the Perfection or Imperfection of foreign Music. I turned from them to an old grey-headed one, who was single on another Leaf, & talking to himself. Being amus'd with his Soliloquy, I have put it down in writing in hopes it will likewise amuse her to whom I am So much indebted for the most pleasing of all Amusements, her delicious Company and her heavenly Harmony.

"It was, says he, the Opinion of learned Philosophers of our Race, who lived and flourished long before my time, that this vast World, the *Moulin Joli*, could not itself subsist more than 18 Hours; and I think there was some Foundation for that Opinion, since by the apparent Motion of the great Luminary that gives Life to all Nature, and which in my time has evidently declin'd considerably towards the Ocean at the End of our Earth, it must then finish its Course, be extinguish'd in the Waters that surround us, and leave the World in Cold and Darkness, necessarily producing universal Death and Destruction. I have lived seven of these Hours; a great Age; being no less than 420 minutes of Time. How very few of us continue So long.—I have seen Generations born, flourish and expire. My present Friends are the Children and Grandchildren of the Friends of my Youth, who are now, alas, no more! And I must soon follow them; for by the Course of Nature, tho' still in Health, I cannot expect to live above 7 or 8 Minutes longer. What now avails all my Toil and Labour in amassing Honey-Dew on this Leaf, which I cannot live to enjoy! What the political Struggles I have been engag'd in for the Good of my Compatriotes, Inhabitants of this Bush, or my philosophical Studies for the Benefit of our Race in general! For in Politics *what can Laws do without Morals*. Our present Race of Ephemeres will in a Course of Minutes, become corrupt like those of other and older Bushes, and consequently as wretched. And in Philosophy how small our Progress! Alas, *Art is long and Life is short*!—My Friends would comfort me with the Idea of a Name they Say I shall leave behind me; and they tell me I have *lived long enough, to Nature and to Glory*;—But what will Fame be to an Ephemere who no longer exists? And what will become of all History in the 18th Hour, when the World itself, even the whole *Moulin Joli* shall come to its End, and be buried in universal Ruin?—To me, after all my eager Pursuits, no solid Pleasures now remain, but the Reflection of a long Life spent in meaning well, the sensible Conversation of a few good Lady-Ephemeres, and now and then a kind Smile and a Tune from the ever-amiable BRILLANTE."

7. Thomas Jefferson

from *Notes on the State of Virginia,* Query 4
1781

The description of Virginia's mountains starts out firmly prosaic by referring the questioner to maps. Then things begin to escalate, and shortly Jefferson is writing one of the classic texts of the American sublime: the description of the Blue Ridge pass, "one of the most stupendous scenes in nature." This is writing as literature and as participation in the transatlantic literary world, in which the notion of the sublime—classically defined by Edmund Burke as an intense emotion rising to the point of terror before overwhelming and possibly life-threatening natural elements—was a favored artistic strategy as well as philosophical trope.

A *notice of its* Mountains?

For the particular geography of our mountains I must refer to Fry and Jefferson's map of Virginia; and to Evans's analysis of his map of America for a more philosophical view of them than is to be found in any other work. It is worthy notice, that our mountains are not solitary and scattered confusedly over the face of the country; but that they commence at about 150 miles from the sea-coast, are disposed in ridges one behind another, running nearly parallel with the sea-coast, though rather approaching it as they advance north-eastwardly. To the south-west, as the tract of country between the sea-coast and the Mississipi becomes narrower, the mountains converge into a single ridge, which, as it approaches the Gulph of Mexico, subsides into plain country, and gives rise to some of the waters of that Gulph, and particularly to a river called the Apalachicola, probably from the Apalachies, an Indian nation formerly residing on it. Hence the mountains giving rise to that river, and seen from its various parts, were called the Apalachian mountains, being in fact the end or termination only of the great ridges passing through the continent. European geographers however extended the name northwardly as far as the mountains extended; some giving it, after their separation into different ridges, to the Blue ridge, others to the North mountain, others to the Alleghaney, others to the Laurel ridge, as may be seen in their different maps. But the fact I believe is, that none of these ridges were ever known by that name to the inhabitants, either native or emigrant, but as they saw them so called in European maps. In the same direction generally are the veins of lime-stone, coal and other minerals hitherto discovered: and so range the falls of our great rivers. But the courses of the great rivers are at right angles with these. James and Patowmac penetrate through all the ridges of mountains eastward of the Alleghaney; that is broken by no water-course. It is in fact the spine of the country between the Atlantic on one side, and the

Mississipi and St. Laurence on the other. The passage of the Patowmac through the Blue ridge is perhaps one of the most stupendous scenes in nature. You stand on a very high point of land. On your right comes up the Shenandoah, having ranged along the foot of the mountain an hundred miles to seek a vent. On your left approaches the Patowmac, in quest of a passage also. In the moment of their junction they rush together against the mountain, rend it asunder, and pass off to the sea. The first glance of this scene hurries our senses into the opinion, that this earth has been created in time, that the mountains were formed first, that the rivers began to flow afterwards, that in this place particularly they have been dammed up by the Blue ridge of mountains, and have formed an ocean which filled the whole valley; that continuing to rise they have at length broken over at this spot, and have torn the mountain down from its summit to its base. The piles of rock on each hand, but particularly on the Shenandoah, the evident marks of their disrupture and avulsion from their beds by the most powerful agents of nature, corroborate the impression. But the distant finishing which nature has given to the picture is of a very different character. It is a true contrast to the fore-ground. It is as placid and delightful, as that is wild and tremendous. For the mountain being cloven asunder, she presents to your eye, through the cleft, a small catch of smooth blue horizon, at an infinite distance in the plain country, inviting you, as it were, from the riot and tumult roaring around, to pass through the breach and participate of the calm below. Here the eye ultimately composes itself; and that way too the road happens actually to lead. You cross the Patowmac above the junction, pass along its side through the base of the mountain for three miles, its terrible precipices hanging in fragments over you, and within about 20 miles reach Frederic town and the fine country round that. This scene is worth a voyage across the Atlantic. Yet here, as in the neighbourhood of the natural bridge, are people who have passed their lives within half a dozen miles, and have never been to survey these monuments of a war between rivers and mountains, which must have shaken the earth itself to its center.—The height of our mountains has not yet been estimated with any degree of exactness. The Alleghaney being the great ridge which divides the waters of the Atlantic from those of the Missisipi, its summit is doubtless more elevated above the ocean than that of any other mountain. But its relative height, compared with the base on which it stands, is not so great as that of some others, the country rising behind the successive ridges like the steps of stairs. The mountains of the Blue ridge, and of these the Peaks of Otter, are thought to be of a greater height, measured from their base, than any others in our country, and perhaps in North America. From data, which may found a tolerable conjecture, we suppose the highest peak to be about 4000 feet perpendicular, which is not a fifth part of the height of the mountains of South America, nor one third of the height which would be necessary in our latitude to preserve ice in the open air unmelted through the year. The ridge of mountains next beyond the Blue ridge, called by us the North mountain, is of the greatest extent; for which reason they were named by the Indians the Endless mountains.

A substance supposed to be Pumice, found floating on the Missisipi, has induced a conjecture, that there is a volcano on some of its waters: and as these are mostly known to their sources, except the Missouri, our expectations of verifying the conjecture would of course be led to the mountains which divide the waters of the Mexican Gulph from those of the South Sea; but no volcano having ever yet been known at such a distance from the sea, we must rather suppose that this floating substance has been erroneously deemed Pumice.

8. J. Hector St. John de Crèvecoeur

from *Letters from an American Farmer* 1782

Creator of the "American farmer" as neither "Russian boor" nor "Hungarian peasant," but "humble planter," "tiller of the soil," and "cultivator of the earth"; the first and possibly the most successful promulgator of the myth of the American yeoman lost his farm to hostile neighbors and was driven back to the Old World because of his Loyalist sympathies. This apparent paradox points toward the complicated political situation in which the Revolution unfolded and particularly the anxious question of who (what group in the colonies) would replace English authority. J. Hector St. John de Crèvecoeur (1735–1813), in Letter XII, "Distresses of a Frontier Man," sets out his fear that the local rich will oppress their poor neighbours and that, nationally, a government controlled by the wealthy and powerful will recreate European iniquities.

Letters from an American Farmer is not autobiographical, although its very successful creation of a persona has often misled readers into thinking it was. The name J. Hector St. John de Crèvecoeur Americanized Michel Guillaume Jean de Crèvecoeur, who, born in Normandy into the petty nobility, arrived in Canada at the age of nineteen armed with a solid Jesuit education to serve under General Montcalm. The Letters are written in the prose of eighteenth-century belles lettres, rising to sublime moments and rich in self-conscious sentiment. The introductory first letter opens with this sentence whose elegant form quite disproves its modest content: "Who would have thought that because I received you with hospitality and kindness, you should imagine me capable of writing with propriety and perspecuity?"

The idyllic life of Crèvecoeur's typical American, Farmer John, embodies ideals and an optimism that the Revolution shattered for his author. Crèvecoeur explains his reluctance to join the uprising in Letter XII. That he more easily imagines his way of life surviving in the Indian wilderness than among the revolted English colonists, measures the extent of the domestic conflict accompanying the war.

[FROM LETTER II, "ON THE SITUATION, FEELINGS, AND PLEASURES OF AN AMERICAN FARMER"]

As you are the first enlightened European[7] I had ever the pleasure of being acquainted with, you will not be surprised that I should, according to your earnest desire and my promise, appear anxious of preserving your friendship

---

7. the first enlightened European: Crèvecoeur addressed the *Letters* to the Abbé Raynal, author of the *Histoire philoso-* *phique et politique des établissements des Européens dans les deux Indes.*

A newly cleared American farm, from Patrick Campbell, Travels in the Interior Inhabited Parts of North America *(Edinburgh, 1793). The figure on the left is a white settler. The others are Indians.*

and correspondence. By your accounts, I observe a material difference subsists between your husbandry, modes, and customs and ours; everything is local; could we enjoy the advantages of the English farmer, we should be much happier, indeed, but this wish, like many others, implies a contradiction; and could the English farmer have some of those privileges we possess, they would be the first of their class in the world. Good and evil, I see, are to be found in all societies, and it is in vain to seek for any spot where those ingredients are not mixed. I therefore rest satisfied and thank God that my lot is to be an American farmer instead of a Russian boor or an Hungarian peasant. I thank you kindly for the idea, however dreadful, which you have given me of their lot and condition; your observations have confirmed me in the justness of my ideas, and I am happier now than I thought myself before. It is strange that misery, when viewed in others, should become to us a sort of real good, though I am far from rejoicing to hear that there are in the world men so thoroughly wretched; they are no doubt as harmless, industrious, and willing to work as we are. Hard is their fate to be thus condemned to a slavery worse than that of our Negroes. Yet when young, I entertained some thoughts of selling my farm. I thought it afforded but a dull repetition of the same labours and pleasures. I thought the former tedious and heavy, the latter few and insipid; but when I came to consider myself as divested of my farm, I then found the world so wide, and every place so full, that I began to fear lest there would be no room for me. My farm, my house, my barn, presented to my imagination objects from which I adduced quite new ideas; they were more forcible than before. Why should not I find myself happy, said I, where my father was before? He left me no good books, it is true; he gave me no other education than the art of reading and writing;

but he left me a good farm and his experience; he left me free from debts, and no kind of difficulties to struggle with. I married, and this perfectly reconciled me to my situation; my wife rendered my house all at once cheerful and pleasing; it no longer appeared gloomy and solitary as before; when I went to work in my fields, I worked with more alacrity and sprightliness; I felt that I did not work for myself alone, and this encouraged me much. My wife would often come with her knitting in her hand and sit under the shady tree, praising the straightness of my furrows and the docility of my horses; this swelled my heart and made everything light and pleasant, and I regretted that I had not married before.

I felt myself happy in my new situation, and where is that station which can confer a more substantial system of felicity than that of an American farmer possessing freedom of action, freedom of thoughts, ruled by a mode of government which requires but little from us? I owe nothing but a peppercorn to my country, a small tribute to my king, with loyalty and due respect; I know no other landlord than the lord of all land, to whom I owe the most sincere gratitude. My father left me three hundred and seventy-one acres of land, forty-seven of which are good timothy meadow; an excellent orchard; a good house; and a substantial barn. It is my duty to think how happy I am that he lived to build and to pay for all these improvements; what are the labours which I have to undergo, what are my fatigues, when compared to his, who had everything to do, from the first tree he felled to the finishing of his house? Every year I kill from 1,500 to 2,000 weight of pork, 1,200 of beef, half a dozen of good wethers in harvest; of fowls my wife has always a great stock; what can I wish more? My Negroes are tolerably faithful and healthy; by a long series of industry and honest dealings, my father left behind him the name of a good man; I have but to tread his paths to be happy and a good man like him. I know enough of the law to regulate my little concerns with propriety, nor do I dread its power; these are the grand outlines of my situation, but as I can feel much more than I am able to express, I hardly know how to proceed.

When my first son was born, the whole train of my ideas was suddenly altered; never was there a charm that acted so quickly and powerfully; I ceased to ramble in imagination through the wide world; my excursions since have not exceeded the bounds of my farm, and all my principal pleasures are now centred within its scanty limits; but at the same time, there is not an operation belonging to it in which I do not find some food for useful reflections. This is the reason, I suppose, that when you were here, you used, in your refined style, to denominate me the farmer of feelings; how rude must those feelings be in him who daily holds the axe or the plough, how much more refined on the contrary those of the European, whose mind is improved by education, example, books, and by every acquired advantage! Those feelings, however, I will delineate as well as I can, agreeably to your earnest request.

When I contemplate my wife, by my fireside, while she either spins, knits, darns, or suckles our child, I cannot describe the various emotions of love, of gratitude, of conscious pride, which thrill in my heart and often overflow in involuntary tears. I feel the necessity, the sweet pleasure, of acting my part, the part of an husband and father, with an attention and propriety which may entitle me to my good fortune. It is true these pleasing images vanish with the smoke of my pipe, but though they disappear from my mind, the impression they have made on my heart is indelible. When I play with the infant, my warm imagination runs forward and eagerly anticipates his future temper and constitution. I would willingly open the book of fate and know in which page his destiny is delineated. Alas! Where is the father who in those moments of paternal ecstasy can delineate one half of the thoughts which dilate his heart? I am sure I cannot; then again, I fear for the health of those who are become so dear to me, and in their sicknesses I severely pay for the joys I experienced while they were well. Whenever I go abroad, it is always involuntary. I never return home without feeling some pleasing emotion, which I often suppress as useless and foolish. The instant I enter on my own land, the bright idea of property, of exclusive right, of independence, exalt my mind. Precious soil, I say to myself, by what singular custom of law is it that thou wast made to constitute the riches of the freeholder? What should we American farmers be without the distinct possession of that soil? It feeds, it clothes us; from it we draw even a great exuberancy, our best meat, our richest drink; the very honey of our bees comes from this privileged spot. No wonder we should thus cherish its possession; no wonder that so many Europeans who have never been able to say that such portion of land was theirs cross the Atlantic to realize that happiness. This formerly rude soil has been converted by my father into a pleasant farm, and in return, it has established all our rights; on it is founded our rank, our freedom, our power as citizens, our importance as inhabitants of such a district. These images, I must confess, I always behold with pleasure and extend them as far as my imagination can reach; for this is what may be called the true and the only philosophy of an American farmer.

[FROM LETTER XII, "DISTRESSES OF A FRONTIER MAN"]

I wish for a change of place; the hour is come at last, that I must fly from my house and abandon my farm! But what course shall I steer, inclosed as I am? The climate best adapted to my present situation and humour would be the polar regions, where six months day and six months night divide the dull year: nay, a simple Aurora Borealis would suffice me, and greatly refresh my eyes, fatigued now by so many disagreeable objects. The severity of those climates, that great gloom, where melancholy dwells, would be perfectly analagous to the turn of my mind. Oh, could I remove my plantation to the shores of the Oby, willingly would I dwell in the hut of a Samoyede; with chearfulness would I go and bury myself in the cavern of a Laplander. Could I but carry my family along with me, I would winter at Pello, or Tobolsky, in order to enjoy the peace and innocence of that country. But let me arrive under the pole, or reach the antipodes, I never can leave behind me the remembrance of the dreadful scenes to which I have been a witness; therefore never can I be happy! Happy, why would I mention that sweet, that enchanting word? Once happiness was our portion; now it is gone from us, and I am afraid not to be enjoyed again by the present generation! Which ever way I look, nothing but the most frightful precipices present themselves to my view, in which hundreds of my friends and acquaintances have already perished: of all animals that live on the surface of this planet, what is man when no longer connected with society; or when he finds himself surrounded by a convulsed and a half dissolved one? ... As a member of a large society which extends to many parts of the world, my connection with it is too distant to be as strong as that which binds me to the inferior division in the midst of which I live. I am told that the great nation, of which we are a part, is just, wise, and free, beyond any other on earth, within its own insular boundaries; but not always so to its distant conquests: I shall not repeat all I have heard, because I cannot believe half of it. As a citizen of a smaller society, I find that any kind of opposition to its now prevailing sentiments, immediately begets hatred: how easily do men pass from loving, to hating and cursing one another! I am a lover of peace, what must I do? I am divided between the respect I feel for the ancient connection, and the fear of innovations, with the consequence of which I am not well acquainted; as they are embraced by my own countrymen. I am conscious that I was happy before this unfortunate Revolution. I feel that I am no longer so; therefore I regret the change. This is the only mode of reasoning adapted to persons in my situation. If I attach myself to the Mother Country, which is 3000 miles from me, I become what is called an enemy to my own region; if I follow the rest of my countrymen, I become opposed to our ancient masters: both extremes appear equally dangerous to a person of so little weight and consequence as I am, whose energy and example are of no avail.

As to the argument on which the dispute is founded, I know little about it. Much has been said and written on both sides, but who has a judgement capacious and clear enough to decide? The great moving principles which actuate both parties are much hid from vulgar eyes, like mine; nothing but the plausible and the probable are offered to our contemplation. The innocent class are always the victim of the few; they are in all countries and at all times the inferior agents, on which the popular phantom is erected; they clamour, and must toil, and bleed, and are always sure of meeting with oppression and rebuke. It is for the sake of the great leaders on both sides, that so much blood must be spilt; that of the people is counted as nothing. Great events are not achieved for us, though it is *by* us that they are principally accomplished; by the arms, the sweat, the lives of the people. Books tell me so much that they inform me of nothing. Sophistry, the bane of freemen, launches forth in all her deceiving attire! After all, most men reason from passions; and shall such an ignorant individual as I am decide, and say this side is right, that side is wrong? Sentiment and feeling are the only guides I know. Alas, how should I unravel an argument, in which reason herself hath given way to brutality and bloodshed! What then must I do? I ask the wisest lawyers, the ablest casuists, the warmest patriots; for I mean honestly. Great Source of wisdom! inspire me with light sufficient to guide my benighted steps out of this intricate maze! Shall I discard all my ancient principles, shall I renounce that name, that nation which I held once so respectable? I feel the powerful attraction; the sentiments they inspired grew with my earliest knowledge, and were grafted upon the first rudiments of my education. On the other hand, shall I arm myself against that country where I first drew breath, against the playmates of my youth, my bosom friends, my acquaintance?—the idea makes me shudder! Must I be called a parricide, a traitor, a villain, lose the esteem of all those whom I love, to preserve my own; be shunned like a rattlesnake, or be pointed at like a bear? I have neither heroism nor magnanimity enough to make so great a sacrifice. Here I am tied, I am fastened by numerous strings, nor do I repine at the pressure they cause; ignorant as I am, I can pervade the utmost extent of the calamities which have already overtaken our poor afflicted country. I can see the great and accumulated ruin yet extending itself as far as the theatre of war has reached; I hear the groans of thousands of families now ruined and desolated by our aggressors. I cannot count the multitude of orphans this war has made; nor ascertain the immensity of blood we have lost. Some have asked, whether it was a crime to resist; to repel some parts of this evil.

Others have asserted, that a resistance so general makes pardon unattainable, and repentance useless; and dividing the crime among so many, renders it imperceptible. What one party calls meritorious, the other denominates flagitious. These opinions vary, contract, or expand, like the events of the war on which they are founded. What can an insignificant man do in the midst of these jarring contradictory parties, equally hostile to persons situated as I am? And after all who will be the really guilty?—Those most certainly who fail of success. Our fate, the fate of thousands, is then necessarily involved in the dark wheel of fortune. Why then so many useless reasonings; we are the sport of fate. Farewell education, principles, love of our country, farewell; all are become useless to the generality of us: he who governs himself according to what he calls his principles, may be punished either by one party or the other, for those very principles. He who proceeds without principle, as chance, timidity, or self-preservation directs, will not perhaps fare better; but he will be less blamed. What are *we* in the great scale of events, we poor defenseless frontier inhabitants? What is it to the gazing world, whether we breathe or whether we die? Whatever virtue, whatever merit and disinterestedness we may exhibit in our secluded retreats, of what avail? We are like the pismires destroyed by the plough; whose destruction prevents not the future crop. Self-preservation, therefore, the rule of nature seems to be the best rule of conduct; what good can we do by vain resistance, by useless efforts? The cool, the distant spectator, placed in safety, may arraign me for ingratitude, may bring forth the principles of Solon or Montesquieu; he may look on me as wilfully guilty; he may call me by the most opprobrious names. Secure from personal danger, his warm imagination, undisturbed by the least agitation of the heart, will expatiate freely on this grand question; and will consider this extended field, but as exhibiting the double scene, of attack and defence. To him the object becomes abstracted, the intermediate glares, the perspective distance and a variety of opinions unimpaired by affections, presents to his mind but one set of ideas. Here he proclaims the high guilt of the one, and there the right of the other; but let him come and reside with us one single month, let him pass with us through all the successive hours of necessary toil, terror and affright, let him watch with us, his musket in his hand, through tedious, sleepless nights, his imagination furrowed by the keen chissel of every passion; let his wife and his children become exposed to the most dreadful hazards of death; let the existence of his property depend on a single spark, blown by the breath of an enemy; let him tremble with us in our fields, shudder at the rustling of every leaf; let his heart, the seat of the most affecting passions, be powerfully wrung by hearing the melancholy end of his relations and friends; let him trace on the map the progress of these desolations; let his alarmed imagination predict to him the night, the dreadful night when it may be his turn to perish, as so many have perished before. Observe then, whether the man will not get the better of the citizen, whether his political maxims will not vanish! Yes, he will cease to glow so warmly with the glory of the metropolis; all his wishes will be turned toward the preservation of his family!

[DESPAIRING OF LIFE AMONG THE ENGLISH, HE ENVISIONS LIVING AS AN AMERICAN FARMER AMONG THE INDIANS]

You may therefore, by means of anticipation, behold me under the Wigwham; I am so well acquainted with the principal manners of these people, that I entertain not the least apprehension from them. I rely more securely on their strong hospitality, than on the witnessed compacts of many Europeans. As soon as possible after my arrival, I design to build myself a wigwham, after the same manner and size with the rest, in order to avoid being thought singular, or giving occasion for any railleries; though these people are seldom guilty of such European follies. I shall erect it hard by the lands which they propose to allot me, and will endeavour that my wife, my children, and myself may be adopted soon after our arrival. Thus becoming truly inhabitants of their village, we shall immediately occupy that rank within the pale of their society, which will afford us all the amends we can possibly expect for the loss we have met with by the convulsions of our own. According to their customs we shall likewise receive names from them, by which we shall always be known. My youngest children shall learn to swim, and to shoot with the bow, that they may acquire such talents as will necessarily raise them into some degree of esteem among the Indian lads of their own age; the rest of us must hunt with the hunters. I have been for several years an expert marksman; but I dread lest the imperceptible charm of Indian education, may seize my younger children, and give them such a propensity to that mode of life, as may preclude their returning to the manners and customs of their parents. I have but one remedy to prevent this great evil; and that is, to employ them in the labour of the fields, as much as I can; I am even resolved to make their daily subsistence depend altogether on it. As long as we keep ourselves busy in tilling the earth, there is no fear of any of us becoming wild; it is the chase and the food it procures, that have this strange effect. Excuse a simile—those hogs which range in the woods, and to whom grain is given once a week, preserve their former degree of tameness; but if, on the contrary, they are reduced to live on ground nuts, and on what they can get, they soon become wild and fierce.

For my part, I can plough, sow, and hunt, as occasion may require; but my wife, deprived of wool, and flax, will have no room for industry; what is she then to do? like the other squaws, she must cook for us the nasaump, the ninchickè, and such other preparations of corn as are customary among these people. She must learn to bake squashes and pumpkins under the ashes; to slice and smoke the meat of our own killing, in order to preserve it; she must chearfully adopt the manners and customs of her neighbours, in their dress, deportment, conduct, and internal œconomy, in all respects. Surely if we can have fortitude enough to quit all we have, to remove so far, and to associate with people so different from us; these necessary compliances are but part of the scheme. The change of garments, when those they carry with them are worne out, will not be the least of my wife's and daughter's concerns: though I am in hopes that self-love will invent some sort of reparation. Perhaps you would not believe that there are in the woods looking-glasses, and paint of every colour; and that the inhabitants take as much pains to adorn their faces and their bodies, to fix their bracelets of silver, and plait their hair, as our forefathers the Picts used to do in the time of the Romans. Not that I would wish to see either my wife or daughter adopt those savage customs; we can live in great peace and harmony with them without descending to every article; the interruption of trade hath, I hope, suspended this mode of dress. My wife understands inoculation perfectly well, she inoculated all our children one after another, and has successfully performed the operation on several scores of people, who, scattered here and there through our woods, were too far removed from all medical assistance. If we can persuade but one family to submit to it, and it succeeds, we shall then be as happy as our situation will admit of; it will raise her into some degree of consideration, for whoever is useful in any society will always be respected. If we are so fortunate as to carry one family through a disorder, which is the plague among these people, I trust to the force of example, we shall then become truly necessary, valued, and beloved; we indeed owe every kind office to a society of men who so readily offer to assist us into their social partnership, and to extend to my family the shelter of their village, the strength of their adoption, and even the dignity of their names. God grant us a prosperous beginning, we may then hope to be of more service to them than even missionaries who have been sent to preach to them a Gospel they cannot understand.

As to religion, our mode of worship will not suffer much by this removal from a cultivated country, into the bosom of the woods; for it cannot be much simpler than that which we have followed here these many years: and I will with as much care as I can, redouble my attention, and twice a week, retrace to them the great outlines of their duty to God and to man. I will read and expound to them some part of the decalogue, which is the method I have pursued ever since I married.

Half a dozen of acres on the shores of——, the soil of which I know well, will yield us a great abundance of all we want; I will make it a point to give the overplus to such Indians as shall be most unfortunate in their huntings; I will persuade them, if I can, to till a little more land than they do, and not to trust so much to the produce of the chase. To encourage them still farther, I will give a quirn to every six families; I have built many for our poor back settlers, it being often the want of mills which prevents them from raising grain. As I am a carpenter, I can build my own plough, and can be of great service to many of them; my example alone, may rouse the industry of some, and serve to direct others in their labours. The difficulties of the language will soon be removed; in my evening conversations, I will endeavour to make them regulate the trade of their village in such a manner as that those pests of the continent, those Indian traders, may not come within a certain distance; and there they shall be obliged to transact their business before the old people. I am in hopes that the constant respect which is paid to the elders, and shame, may prevent the young hunters from infringing this regulation. The son of——, will soon be made acquainted with our schemes, and I trust that the power of love, and the strong attachment he professes for my daughter, may bring him along with us: he will make an excellent hunter; young and vigorous, he will equal in dexterity the stoutest man in the village. Had it not been for this fortunate circumstance, there would have been the greatest danger; for however I respect the simple, the inoffensive society of these people in their villages, the strongest prejudices would make me abhor any alliance with them in blood: disagreeable no doubt, to nature's intentions which have strongly divided us by so many indelible characters. In the days of our sickness, we shall have recourse to their medical knowledge, which is well calculated for the simple diseases to which they are subject. Thus shall we metamorphose ourselves, from neat, decent, opulent planters, surrounded with every conveniency which our external labour and internal industry could give, into a still simpler people divested of every thing beside hope, food, and the raiment of the woods: abandoning the large framed house, to dwell under the wigwham; and the featherbed, to lie on the matt, or bear's skin. There shall we sleep undisturbed by fruitful dreams and apprehensions; rest and peace of mind will make us the most ample amends for what we shall leave behind. These blessings cannot be purchased too dear; too long have we been deprived of them. I would chearfully go even to the Mississippi, to find that repose to which we have been so long strangers. My heart sometimes seems tired with beating, it wants rest like my eye-lids, which feel oppressed with so many watchings.

9. Benjamin Franklin

Remarks Concerning the Savages of North-America
1783

This essay was written and printed in France, where Franklin lived from 1776 to 1785, representing the United States in a series of negotiations for French support against Britain. At Passy, where he established himself, Franklin set up a small press, as if the possibility of printing were a necessity of life or, perhaps, as self-advertisement of the sort described in the Autobiography.

The essay addresses a European audience, and thus the exceptionally respectful treatment of Indians in "Remarks Concerning the Savages of North-America" may be inspired partly by a desire to represent America generally at its most impressive. Under similar circumstances, Jefferson declared Indian oratory equal to Greek (see chapter 12). Still, the opening sentence of Franklin's essay, dismissing the term "savage," recalls Montaigne's defense of cannibals and seems written in explicit defiance of Franklin's New England ancestors.

S avages we call them, because their manners differ from ours, which we think the Perfection of Civility; they think the same of theirs.

Perhaps if we could examine the manners of different Nations with Impartiality, we should find no People so rude as to be without any Rules of Politeness; nor any so polite as not to have some remains of Rudeness.

The Indians giving a talk to Colonel Bouquet, 1766. The scene is an event in Pontiac's uprising in 1764.

The Indian Men, when young, are Hunters and Warriors; when old, Counsellors; for all their Government is by the Counsel or Advice of the Sages; there is no Force, there are no Prisons, no Officers to compel Obedience, or inflict Punishment. Hence they generally study Oratory; the best Speaker having the most Influence. The Indian Women till the Ground, dress the Food, nurse and bring up the Children, and preserve and hand down to Posterity the Memory of Public Transactions. These Employments of Men and Women are accounted natural and honorable. Having few Artificial Wants, they have abundance of Leisure for Improvement by Conversation. Our laborious manner of Life compared with theirs, they esteem slavish and base; and the Learning on which we value ourselves; they regard as frivolous and useless. An Instance of this occurred at the Treaty of Lancaster in Pennsylvania, Anno 1744, between the Government of Virginia & the Six Nations. After the principal Business was settled, the Commissioners from Virginia acquainted the Indians by a Speech, that there was at Williamsburg a College with a Fund for Educating Indian Youth, and that if the Chiefs of the Six-Nations would send down half a dozen of their Sons to that College, the Government would take Care that they should be well provided for, and instructed in all the Learning of the white People. It is one of the Indian Rules of Politeness not to answer a public Proposition the same day that it is made; they think it would be treating it as a light Matter; and that they show it Respect by taking time to consider it, as of a Matter important. They therefore deferred their Answer till the day following; when their Speaker began by expressing their deep Sense of the Kindness of the Virginia Government, in making them that Offer; for we know, says he, that you highly esteem the kind of Learning taught in those Colleges, and that the Maintenance of our Young Men while with you, would be very expensive to you. We are convinced therefore that you mean to do us good by your Proposal, and we thank you heartily. But you who are wise must know, that different Nations have different Conceptions of things; and you will therefore not take it amiss, if our Ideas of this Kind of Education happen not to be the same with yours. We have had some Experience of it: Several of our Young People were formerly brought up at the Colleges of the Northern Provinces; they were instructed in all your Sciences; but when they came back to us, they were bad Runners, ignorant of every means of living in the Woods, unable to bear either Cold or Hunger, knew neither how to build a Cabin, take a Deer, or kill an Enemy, spoke our Language imperfectly; were therefore neither fit for Hunters, Warriors, or Counsellors; they were totally good for nothing. We are however not the less obliged by your kind Offer, tho' we decline accepting it; and to show our grateful Sense of it, if the Gentlemen of Virginia will send us a dozen of their Sons, we will take great Care of their Education, instruct them in all we know, and make *Men* of them.

Having frequent Occasions to hold public Councils, they have acquired great Order and Decency in conducting them. The old Men sit in the foremost Ranks, the Warriors in the next, and the Women and Children in the hindmost. The Business of the Women is to take exact notice of what passes, imprint it in their Memories, for they have no Writing, and communicate it to their Children. They are the Records of the Council, and they preserve Tradition of the Stipulations in Treaties a hundred Years back, which when we compare with our Writings we always find exact. He that would speak, rises. The rest observe a profound Silence. When he has finished and sits down, they leave him five or six Minutes to recollect, that if he has omitted any thing he intended to say, or has any thing to add, he may rise again and deliver it. To interrupt another, even in common Conversation, is reckoned highly indecent. How different this is from the Conduct of a polite British House of Commons, where scarce a Day passes without some Confusion that makes the Speaker hoarse in calling *to order*; and how different from the mode of Conversation in many polite Companies of Europe, where if you do not deliver your Sentence with great Rapidity, you are cut off in the middle of it by the impatient Loquacity of those you converse with, & never suffer'd to finish it.

The Politeness of these Savages in Conversation is indeed carried to excess, since it does not permit them to contradict, or deny the Truth of what is asserted in their Presence. By this means they indeed avoid Disputes, but then it becomes difficult to know their Minds, or what Impression you make upon them. The Missionaries who have attempted to convert them to Christianity, all complain of this as one of the great Difficulties of their Mission. The Indians hear with Patience the Truths of the Gospel explained to them, and give their usual Tokens of Assent and Approbation: you would think they were convinced. No such Matter. It is mere Civility.

A Suedish Minister having assembled the Chiefs of the Sasquehanah Indians, made a Sermon to them, acquainting them with the principal historical Facts on which our Religion is founded, such as the Fall of our first Parents by Eating an Apple, the Coming of Christ to repair the Mischief, his Miracles and Suffering, &c. When he had finished, an Indian Orator stood up to thank him. What you have told us, says he, is all very good. It is indeed bad to eat Apples. It is better to make them all into Cyder. We are much obliged by your Kindness in coming so far to tell us those things which you have heard from your Mothers. In Return I will tell you some of those we have heard from ours.

In the Beginning our Fathers had only the Flesh of Animals to subsist on, and if their Hunting was unsuccessful, they were starving. Two of our young Hunters having killed a Deer, made a Fire in the Woods to broil some Parts of it. When they were about to satisfy their Hunger, they beheld a beautiful young Woman descend from the Clouds, and seat herself on that Hill which you see yonder among the blue Mountains. They said to each other, it is a Spirit that perhaps has smelt our broiling Venison, & wishes to eat of it: let us offer some to her. They presented her with the Tongue: She was pleased with the Taste of it, & said, your Kindness shall be rewarded. Come to this Place after thirteen Moons, and you shall find something that will be of great Benefit in nourishing you and your Children to the latest Generations. They did so, and to their Surprise found Plants they had never seen before, but which from that ancient time have been constantly cultivated among us to our great Advantage. Where her right Hand had touch'd the Ground, they found Maize; where her left Hand had touch'd it, they found Kidney-beans; and where her Backside had sat on it, they found Tobacco. The good Missionary, disgusted with this idle Tale, said, what I delivered to you were sacred Truths; but what you tell me is mere Fable, Fiction & Falsehood. The Indian offended, reply'd, my Brother, it seems your Friends have not done you Justice in your Education; they have not well instructed you in the Rules of common Civility. You saw that we who understand and practise those Rules, believed all your Stories; why do you refuse to believe ours?

When any of them come into our Towns, our People are apt to croud round them, gaze upon them, and incommode them where they desire to be private; this they esteem great Rudeness, and the Effect of want of Instruction in the Rules of Civility and good Manners. We have, say they, as much Curiosity as you, and when you come into our Towns we wish for Opportunities of looking at you; but for this purpose we hide ourselves behind Bushes where you are to pass, and never intrude ourselves into your Company.

Their Manner of entring one anothers Villages has likewise its Rules. It is reckon'd uncivil in travelling Strangers to enter a Village abruptly, without giving Notice of their Approach. Therefore as soon as they arrive within hearing, they stop and hollow, remaining there till invited to enter. Two old Men usually come out to them, and lead them in. There is in every Village a vacant Dwelling, called the Strangers House. Here they are placed, while the old Men go round from Hut to Hut acquainting the Inhabitants that Strangers are arrived, who are probably hungry and weary; and every one sends them what he can spare of Victuals and Skins to repose on. When the Strangers are refresh'd, Pipes & Tobacco are brought; and then, but not before, Conversation begins, with Enquiries who they are, whither bound, what News, etc. and it usually ends with Offers of Service, if the Strangers have Occasion of Guides or any Necessaries for continuing their Journey; and nothing is exacted for the Entertainment.

The same Hospitality, esteemed among them as a principal Virtue, is practised by private Persons; of which *Conrad Weiser*, our Interpreter, gave me the following Instance. He had been naturaliz'd among the Six-Nations, and spoke well the Mohock Language. In going thro' the Indian Country, to carry a Message from our Governor to the Council at *Onondaga*, he called at the Habitation of *Canassetego*, an old Acquaintance, who embraced him, spread Furs for him to sit on, placed before him some boiled Beans and Venison, and mixed some Rum and Water for his Drink. When he was well refresh'd, and had lit his Pipe, Canassetego began to converse with him, ask'd how he had fared the many Years since they had seen each other, whence he then came, what occasioned the Journey, &c. &c. Conrad answered all his Questions; and when the Discourse began to flag, the Indian, to continue it, said, Conrad, you have liv'd long among the white People, and know something of their Customs; I have been sometimes at Albany, and have observed that once in seven Days, they shut up their Shops and assemble all in the great House; tell me, what it is for? what do they do there? They meet there, says Conrad, to hear & learn *good things*. I do not doubt, says the Indian, that they tell you so; they have told me the same; but I doubt the Truth of what they say, & I will tell you my Reasons. I went lately to Albany to sell my Skins, & buy Blankets, Knives, Powder, Rum, &c. You know I used generally to deal with Hans Hanson; but I was a little inclined this time to try some other Merchants. However I called first upon Hans, and ask'd him what he would give for Beaver; He said he could not give more than four Shillings a Pound; but, says he, I cannot talk on Business now; this is the Day when we meet together to learn *good things*, and I am going to the Meeting. So I thought to myself since I cannot do any Business to day, I may as well go to the Meeting too; and I went with him. There stood up a Man in black, and began to talk to the People very angrily. I did not understand what he said; but perceiving that he looked much at me, & at Hanson, I imagined he was angry at seeing me there; so I went out, sat down near the House, struck Fire & lit my Pipe; waiting till the Meeting should break up. I thought too, that the Man had mentioned something of Beaver, and I suspected it might be the Subject of their Meeting. So when they came out I accosted any Merchant; well Hans, says I, I hope you have agreed to give more than four Shillings a Pound. No, says he, I cannot give so much. I cannot give more than three Shillings and six Pence. I then spoke to several other Dealers, but they all sung the same Song, three & six Pence, three & six Pence. This made it clear to me that my Suspicion was right; and that whatever they pretended of Meeting to learn *good things*, the real Purpose was to consult, how to cheat Indians in the Price of Beaver. Consider but a little, Conrad, and you must be of my Opinion. If they met so often to learn *good things*, they would certainly have learnt some before this time. But they are still ignorant. You know our Practice. If a white Man in travelling thro' our Country, enters one of our Cabins, we all treat him as I treat you; we dry him if he is wet, we warm him if he is cold, and give him Meat & Drink that he may allay his Thirst and Hunger, & we spread soft Furs for him to rest & sleep on: We demand nothing in return.[8] But if I go into a white Man's House at Albany, and ask for Victuals & Drink, they say, where is your Money? and if I have none, they say, get out, you Indian Dog. You see they have not yet learnt those little *good things*, that we need no Meetings to be instructed in, because our Mothers taught them to us when we were Children. And therefore it is impossible their Meetings should be as they say for any such purpose, or have any such Effect; they are only to contrive *the Cheating of Indians in the Price of Beaver*.

---

8. It is remarkable that in all Ages and Countries, Hospitality has been allowed as the Virtue of those, whom the civiliz'd were pleased to call Barbarians; the Greeks celebrated the Scythians for it. The Saracens possess'd it eminently; and it is to this day the reigning Virtue of the wild Arabs. S. Paul too, in the Relation of his Voyage & Shipwreck, on the Island of Melita, says, *The Barbarous People shew'd us no little Kindness; for they kindled a Fire, and received us every one, because of the present Rain & because of the Cold.* [Franklin's note.]

10. "Alphonzo"

from the *American Magazine*
April 21, 1787

This vignette from the short-lived but influential American Magazine *introduces the subject of the next group of selections, all on the vexed issue of the novel. Maria's demand for truth instead of fiction, and her reproof of "Alphonzo" for flattering her, raise the two central topics in a controversy that preoccupied the colonial literary world. Does the novel do what literature is meant to do, engender a better understanding of life and inspire better living? What about women and the novel? Are they specially connected, and is this a good or a bad thing?*

Will you write another address to the Ladies?" said Maria to me, as I seated myself by her side, and gently took her hand. Maria is in the bloom of fifteen—modest, delicate, sentimental and possessed of exquisite sensibility. She has read a thousand novels, and at the age of ten years, she was so strongly impressed with the romantic tales she had read, that, like the celebrated Mrs. Inchbald, she determined to go abroad in quest of adventures. She persuaded a little companion of hers to accompany her, took a few clothes with her and actually left the house with a design to find a passage to Europe and become an eye witness of the scenes which are described in novels and romances. What a lively imagination must she possess, to be so strongly wrought upon by reading mere fictitious descriptions of life, as to embrace the resolution of crossing the Atlantic to *see* the reality!

Maria's head was once turned with novels—she has now lost her relish for them. Instead of *fiction*, she wishes to find *truth* and to conform to it. She wishes for instruction—young, unsuspecting, susceptible, she begs her friends to point out her faults, and she listens to advice with a lively expression of pleasure that marks the goodness of her heart.

"Perhaps," said I to Maria, "in some future time, I may address your sex a second time. I am their friend, and heaven can witness that every amiable woman is to me like a sister. But I am young—unqualified to direct myself; much less to direct others. Besides, precepts are generally ill received by those that want them most—and where the heart, like Maria's is predisposed to goodness and propriety, precepts are useless."

"This is flattery," said Maria; "and is flattery a proof of the friendship you profess for the ladies?" This interrogatory was accompanied with an air of ingenuous disapprobation—it was very different from the affected frown which is often assumed on such occasions.

"I am reproved," said I, "but it was an inadvertence—when a heart harbors nothing but sincerity, it is not apt to place a centinel over its thoughts, and an untimely truth will sometimes escape from the lips." Maria's cheeks began to be tinged with vermillion—she cast down her eyes—and smiled the pardon of

ALPHONZO.

11. Charles Brockden Brown and Thomas Jefferson

two views of the novel question
1798

> *Upon the publication of his novel* Wieland, *Brown sent a copy to Thomas Jefferson with the letter reproduced here. Jefferson's acknowledgment expressed an appreciation of "works of the imagination" as moral teachers. Later, however, he withdrew even this limited approval in a letter to Nathaniel Burwell, addressing the related issues of the novel and the education of women, and offering a summary of the conservative conventions on both.*

[CHARLES BROCKDEN BROWN: LETTER TO THOMAS JEFFERSON]

December 15, 1798.

SIR:

After some hesitation a stranger to the person, though not to the character of Thomas Jefferson, ventures to entreat his acceptance of the volume by which this is accompanied. He is unacquainted with the degree in which your time and attention is engrossed by your public office; he knows not in what way your studious hours are distributed and whether mere works of imagination and invention are not excluded from your notice. He is even doubtful whether this letter will be opened or read, or, if read, whether its contents will not be instantly dismissed from your memory; so much a stranger is he, though a citizen of the United States, to the private occupations and modes of judging of the most illustrious of his fellow citizens.

To request your perusal of a work which at the same time is confessed to be unworthy of perusal will be an uncommon proof of absurdity. In thus transmitting my book to you I tacitly acknowledge my belief that it is capable of affording you pleasure and of entitling the writer to some portion of your good opinion. If I had not this belief, I should unavoidably be silent.

I am conscious, however, that this form of composition may be regarded by you with indifference or contempt, that social and intellectual theories, that the history of facts in the processes of nature and the operations of government may appear to you the only laudable pursuits; that fictitious narratives in their own nature or in the manner in which they have been hitherto conducted may be thought not to deserve notice, and that, consequently, whatever may be the merit of my book as a fiction, yet it is to be condemned because it is a fiction.

I need not say that my own opinions are different. I am therefore obliged to hope that an artful display of incidents, the powerful delineation of characters and the train of eloquent and judicious reasoning which may be combined in a fictitious work, will be regarded by Thomas Jefferson with as much respect as they are regarded by me.

No man holds a performance which he has deliberately offered to the world in contempt; but, if he be a man of candor and discernment, his favorable judgment of his own work will always be attended by diffidence and fluctuation. I confess I foster the hope that Mr. Jefferson will be induced to open the book that is here offered him; that when he has begun it he will find himself prompted to continue, and that he will not think the time employed upon it tediously or uselessly consumed.

With more than this I dare not flatter myself. That he will be pleased to any uncommon degree, and that, by his recommendation, he will contribute to diffuse the knowledge of its author, and facilitate a favorable reception to future performances, is a benefit far beyond the expectations, though certainly the object of the fondest wishes of

CHARLES B. BROWN

[JEFFERSON: REPLY TO C.B. BROWN]

SIR:

I received on my arrival here some days ago the copy of the book you were so kind as to send me together with your letter, for which be pleased to accept my thanks. As soon as I am in a situation to admit it (which is hardly the case here), I shall read it, and I doubt not with great pleasure. Some of the most agreeable moments of my life have been spent in reading works of imagination, which have this advantage over history, that the incidents of the former may be dressed in the most interesting form, while those of the latter must be confined to fact. They cannot therefore possess virtue in the best and vice in the worst forms possible, as the former may. I have the honor to be with great consideration, Sir.

Your most obed. servt.
TH. JEFFERSON

12. Susanna Haswell Rowson

from *Charlotte Temple*
1794

In her Preface to Charlotte Temple, *Susanna Haswell Rowson (1762–1824) takes
up the novel question and tries to transcend Maria's damaging opposition between
truth and fiction. To be sure, Rowson concedes, the novel is a tale, but it is a "Tale
of Truth": "Not merely the effusion of Fancy, but . . . a reality," Rowson's story
will not recreate life, but rather project life's truthful image. Indeed, she disclaims
story-telling as such. Its truth lies not in the text, admittedly difficult to keep pure
of invention, but in the effect it will have on the actual lives of young women. And,
concluding with a fine fillip, Rowson dismisses literature and all its values in order
to embrace the good she can do in the real world.*

PREFACE

For the perusal of the young and thoughtless of the fair sex, this Tale of Truth is
designed; and I could wish my fair readers to consider it as not merely the effusion of Fancy, but as a reality. The circumstances on which I have founded this
novel were related to me some little time since by an old lady who had personally
known Charlotte, though she concealed the real names of the characters, and likewise
the place where the unfortunate scenes were acted: yet as it was impossible to offer a
relation to the public in such an imperfect state, I have thrown over the whole a slight
veil of fiction, and substituted names and places according to my own fancy. The principal characters in this little tale are now consigned to the silent tomb: it can therefore
hurt the feelings of no one; and may, I flatter myself, be of service to some who are so
unfortunate as to have neither friends to advise, or understanding to direct them,
through the various and unexpected evils that attend a young and unprotected woman
in her first entrance into life.

While the tear of compassion still trembled in my eye for the fate of the unhappy
Charlotte, I may have children of my own, said I, to whom this recital may be of use,
and if to your own children, said Benevolence, why not to the many daughters of
Misfortune who, deprived of natural friends, or spoilt by a mistaken education, are
thrown on an unfeeling world without the least power to defend themselves from the
snares not only of the other sex, but from the more dangerous arts of the profligate of
their own.

Sensible as I am that a novel writer, at a time when such a variety of works are
ushered into the world under that name, stands but a poor chance for fame in the

annals of literature, but conscious that I wrote with a mind anxious for the happiness of that sex whose morals and conduct have so powerful an influence on mankind in general; and convinced that I have not wrote a line that conveys a wrong idea to the head or a corrupt wish to the heart, I shall rest satisfied in the purity of my own intentions, and if I merit not applause, I feel that I dread not censure.

If the following tale should save one hapless fair one from the errors which ruined poor Charlotte, or rescue from impending misery the heart of one anxious parent, I shall feel a much higher gratification in reflecting on this trifling performance, than could possibly result from the applause which might attend the most elegant finished piece of literature whose tendency might deprave the heart or mislead the understanding.

13. Hannah Webster Foster

from *The Coquette*
1797

The real event upon which Hannah Webster Foster (1758–1840) based The Coquette *was commonly known, and her readers would therefore have understood that the sad tale of Eliza Wharton pointed a real-life moral. Yet this moral unfolds almost as if it were a cultural or literary event. In the first letter below, a social evening is both setting and substance for a moral and political disquisition: the characters are creatures of polite society, and the issue of whether women should interest themselves in politics is represented as a question of the definition of cultivated conversation. The second letter casts romantic betrayal in terms of artistic fraud, while its recommended treatment for unhappiness is a change of scene.*

Such artificiality is, of course, precisely the error the novel wishes to expose. A coquette is a poser, an insincere young woman playing a role. But sincerity in the middle-class world of The Coquette *presents the dilemma Franklin lays out in his* Autobiography: *one cannot at the same time be wholly sincere and self-creating, since self-creation requires invention and imagination. The lesson of the novel appears to be that women had better not be self-creating or they will destroy themselves; but this only projects another dilemma, expressed in the virtuous Lucy Sumner's apostrophe against* Romeo and Juliet: *how can there be works of the imagination if one is not to invent stories?*

To the Rev. J. Boyer

NEW-HAVEN

I have executed your commission, and been amply rewarded for my trouble, by the pleasure I enjoyed in the society of the agreeable family to which I was introduced; especially of the amiable and accomplished lady, who is the object of your particular regard. I think she fully justifies your partiality to her. She appears to possess both the virtues and the graces. Her form is fine, and her countenance interests us at once in her favor. There is a mixture of dignity and ease, which commands respect, and conciliates affection. After these encomiums, will you permit me to say, there is an air of gaiety in her appearance and deportment, which favors a little of coquetry. I am persuaded, however, that she has too much good sense to practice its arts. She received your letter very graciously, asked leave to retire a few moments; and returned with a smile of complacency on her brow, which I construe favorably to you.

There was a Mr. Laurence, with his lady and daughter, and a certain Major Sanford, at the house. The latter, I believe, in the modern sense of the phrase, *is much of a gentleman*, that is, a man of show and fashion.

Miss Wharton asked me, when I should leave town, and when I should return, or have an opportunity of conveyance to Hampshire? I told her I should write by the next post, and if she had any commands, would be happy to execute them. She would send a line to her friend, she said, if I would take the trouble to inclose it in my letter. I readily consented; and told her, that I would call and receive her favor to morrow morning. This chit-chat was a little aside, but I could not but observe, that the foresaid Major Sanford had dropped his part in the conversation of the rest of the company, and was attending to us, though he endeavored to conceal his attention, by looking carelessly over a play, which lay on the window by him. Yet he evidently watched every word and action of Miss Wharton, as if he were really interested in her movements.

It is said she has many admirers, and I conceive it very possible that this may be one of them; though, truly, I do not think that she would esteem such a conquest any great honor. I now joined in the general topic of conversation, which was politics. Mrs. Richman and Miss Wharton judiciously, yet modestly bore a part; while the other ladies amused themselves with Major Sanford, who was making his sage remarks on the play, which he still kept in his hand. General Richman at length observed, that we had formed into parties. Major Sanford, upon this, laid aside his book. Miss Laurence simpered; and looked as if she was well pleased with being in a party with so fine a man; while her mother replied, that she never meddled with politics; she thought they did not belong to ladies. Miss Wharton and I, said Mrs. Richman, must beg leave to differ from you, madam. We think ourselves interested in the welfare and prosperity of our country; and, consequently, claim the right of inquiring into those affairs, which may conduce to, or interfere with the common weal. We shall not be called to the senate or the field to assert its privileges, and defend its rights, but we shall feel for the honor and safety of our friends and connections, who are thus employed. If the community flourish and enjoy health and freedom, shall we not share in the happy effects? if it be oppressed and disturbed, shall we not endure our proportion of the evil? Why then should the love of our country be a masculine passion only? Why should government, which involves the peace and order of the society, of which we are a part, be wholly excluded from our observation? Mrs. Laurence made some slight reply and waved the subject. The gentlemen applauded Mrs. Richman's sentiments as truly Roman; and what was more, they said, truly republican.

I rose to take leave, observing to Miss Wharton, that I should call to morrow as agreed. Upon this, Gen. Richman politely requested the favor of my company at dinner. I accepted his invitation, and bid them good night. I shall do the same to you for the present; as I intend, to morrow to scribble the cover, which is to inclose your Eliza's letter.

T. SELBY.

To Miss Eliza Wharton

BOSTON.

My Dear Eliza,

I received yours of the 24th ult.[9] and thank you for it; though it did not afford me those lively sensations of pleasure, which I usually feel at the perusal of your letters. It inspired me both with concern, and chagrin. With concern, lest your dejection of mind should affect your health; and with chagrin at your apparent indulgence of melancholy. Indeed, my friend, your own happiness and honor, require you to dissipate the cloud which hangs over your imagination.

Rise then above it; and prove yourself superior to the adverse occurrences which have befallen you. It is by surmounting difficulties, not by sinking under them, that we discover our fortitude. True courage consists not in flying from the storms of life; but in braving and steering through them with prudence. Avoid solitude. It is the bane of a disordered mind; though of great utility to a healthy one. Your once favorite amusements court your attention. Refuse not their solicitations. I have contributed my mite, by sending you a few books; such as you requested. They are of the lighter kind of reading; yet perfectly chaste; and if I mistake not, well adapted to your taste.

You wish to hear from our theatre. I believe it will be well supplied with performers this winter. Come and see whether they can afford you any entertainment. Last evening I attended a tragedy; but never will I attend another. I have not yet been able to erase the gloom which it impressed upon my mind. It was Romeo and Juliet. Distressing enough to sensibility this! Are there not real woes (if not in our own families, at least among our own friends, and neighbors) sufficient to exercise our sympathy and pity, without introducing fictitious ones into our very diversions? How can that be a diversion, which racks the soul with grief, even though that grief be imaginary. The introduction of a funeral solemnity, upon the stage, is shocking indeed!

Death is too serious a matter to be sported with! An opening grave cannot be a source of amusement to any considerate mind! The closing scene of life can be no pastime, when realized! it must therefore awaken painful sensations, in the representation!

The circus is a place of fashionable resort of late, but not agreeable to me. I think it inconsistent with the delicacy of a lady, even to witness the indecorums, which are practised there; especially, when the performers of equestrian feats are of our own sex. To see a woman depart so far from the female character, as to assume the masculine habit and attitudes; and appear entirely indifferent, even to the externals of modesty, is truly disgusting, and ought not to be countenanced by our attendance, much less by our approbation. But setting aside this circumstance, I cannot conceive it to be a pleasure to sit a whole evening, trembling with apprehension, lest the poor wight of a horseman, or juggler, or whatever he is to be called, should break his neck in contributing to our entertainment.

With Mr. Bowen's museum, I think you were much pleased. He has made a number of judicious additions to it, since you were here. It is a source of rational and refined

9. ult.; of the previous month.

amusement. Here the eye is gratified, the imagination charmed, and the understanding improved. It will bear frequent reviews without palling on the taste. It always affords something new; and for one, I am never a weary spectator.

Our other public, and private places of resort, are much as you left them.

I am happy in my present situation; but when the summer returns, I intend to visit my native home. Again, my Eliza, will we ramble together in those retired shades which friendship has rendered so delightful to us. Adieu, my friend, till then. Be cheerful, and you will yet be happy.

LUCY SUMNER.

14. Charles Brockden Brown

"A Receipt for a Modern Romance," from the *Weekly Magazine* 1798

Brown was very conscious of his role as a founding member of the national literary culture and took up the subject of a distinctive American way of writing in each of his seven novels. In Edgar Huntly *(1799), for instance, he proposed an American form of the gothic that would, to great advantage, replace the theatricalities of medieval castles and family ghosts with the real terrors of the wilderness. His "Receipt for a Modern Romance" makes patriotic fun of the creaking fakeries of the English standard.*

Take an old castle; pull down a part of it, and allow the grass to grow on the battlements, and provide the owls and bats with uninterrupted habitations among the ruins. Pour a sufficient quantity of heavy rain upon the hinges and bolts of the gates, so that when they are attempted to be opened, they may creak most fearfully. Next take an old man and woman, and employ them to sleep in a part of this castle, and provide them with frightful stories of lights that appear in the western or the eastern tower every night, and of music heard in the neighbouring woods, and ghosts dressed in white who perambulate the place.

Convey to this castle a young lady; consign her to the care of the old man and woman, who must relate to her all they know, that is all they do not know, but only suspect. Make her dreadfully terrified at the relation, but dreadfully impatient to behold the reality. Convey her, perhaps on the second night of her arrival, through a trap-door, and from the trap-door to a flight of steps downwards, and from a flight of steps to a subterraneous passage, and from a subterraneous passage, to a door that is shut, and from that to a door that is open, and from that to a cell, and from that to a chapel, and from a chapel back to a subterraneous passage again; here present either a skeleton with a live face, or a living body with the head of a skeleton, or a ghost all in white, or a groan from a distant part of a cavern, or the shake of a cold hand, or a suit of armour moving—fierce "put out the light, and then"—

Let this be repeated for some nights in succession, and after the lady has been dissolved to a jelly with her fears, let her be delivered by the man of her heart, and married—*Probatum est*:

As in medicine there is what physicians call an *elegant* prescription to distinguish it from those incongruous and absurd mixtures of the ancient empirics, so, lest any one should think I have put too many ingredients into the above recipe, let him take the following:

> A novel now, says Will, is nothing more
> Than an old castle, and a creaking door:
> A distant hovel,
> Clanking of chains, a gallery, a light,
> Old armour, and a phantom all in white—,
> And there's a novel.
> ANTI-GHOST.

15. Charles Brockden Brown

"Remarks on Reading," from the *Literary Magazine* 1806

Brown's essay, "Remarks on Reading," was written after the novels (the four most important appeared between 1798 and 1800) and when the author, having in mind the Jacobin radicalism that led the French Revolution to the Terror, had become increasingly doubtful about the future of republican values. Brown's first major intellectual influence had been the radical rationalist William Godwin; history seemed to have belied this mentor, and Brown became an advocate of Federalist political constraint. This, of course, had literary implications and, in the essay, the concluding attack on readers obtusely likely to complain about not understanding, in a work of genius, exactly what the genius has intentionally hidden, bespeaks a growing distrust of the common cultural wisdom. The charge that readers are "capricious" carries more widely, evoking a society prone to disorder or at any rate disappointingly resistant to the order of republican ideals.

"Remarks on Reading" sets out the proper way of a cultivated man with a book, offered ambiguously as a model for the reading public. The ambiguity arises from Brown's relation to this public which he at once invokes and mistrusts. Thus, laying out his own erudition, ranging from the classics to the moderns, he tries to offer ways readers may acquire something like the same. But his instructions are as if coded, intended to be properly deciphered only by those who already possess what they convey. The models cited are the Great: Montaigne, Voltaire, Seneca, Pope; Milton only as poet, not as political writer or historian; the self-consciously middle-class Addison and Steele appear as writers "a great deal unworthy of notice."

Writing during the first moments of the life of the national culture, Brown proposes a pedagogical curriculum made up of the aristocrats of world literature. What lesson should the reader draw from the Richelieu anecdote? Certainly not that writers ought to be democrats. On the contrary, Brown seems to be urging the readers of the new republic to aspire to elite skills and tastes, to the point of a certain dismissive sophistication that would go well at the Tuesday Club. While, as his novels indicate, Brown is interested in the creation of a national tradition, he envisions it as cosmopolitan and universal. The intelligent American reader, and the writer even more so, define themselves for him precisely by their refusal of the narrow demands of a middling nationalism.

Since writing is justly denominated an art, reading may surely claim the same distinction. To adorn ideas with elegance is an act of the mind superior to that of receiving them, and is the province of genius; but to receive them with a happy discrimination is a task not less useful, and can only be the effect of a just taste.

Yet it will be found that a just taste only will not obtain the proper end of reading. Two persons of equal taste rise from the perusal of the same book with very different notions; the one will not only have the ideas of the author at command, and strongly imbibe his manner, but will have enriched his own mind by a new accession of matter, and find a new train of thought awakened and in action. The other quits his author in a pleasing distraction, but of the pleasures of reading, nothing remains but a tumultuous sensation. He has only delighted himself with the brilliant colouring, and the mingled shadows of a variety of objects, while the other receives the impression not only of their colours and shades, but their distinct graces and real forms.

To account for this difference we must recur to a distinction, which appears to reveal one of the great mysteries in the art of reading. Logic distinguishes between perceptions and ideas. Perception is that faculty which notices the simple impression of objects: but it is only when these objects exist in the mind, and are there treasured and arranged as materials for reflection, that they become ideas. A perception is like a transient sunbeam, which just shows the object, but leaves neither light nor warmth; while an idea is like the fervid beam of noon, which throws a settled and powerful light.

Many ingenious readers complain that their memory is defective, and their studies fruitless. This defect, however, arises from their indulging the facile pleasures of perception in preference to the laborious task of forming ideas. We must not deceive ourselves. Perceptions require only the sensibility of taste, and their pleasures are continuous, easy, and exquisite. Ideas not only require the same power of taste, but an art of combination, and an exertion of the reasoning powers, which form no mean operation of the mind. Ideas are therefore labours; and for those who will not undergo the fatigue of labour, it is unjust to complain, if they come from the harvest with scarcely a sheaf in their hands.

The numerous class of readers of taste, who only prefer a book to the odd trick at whist, have, therefore, no reason to murmur, if that which is only taken up as an amusement, should terminate, like all amusements, in temporary pleasure. To be wiser and better is rarely the intention of the gay and frivolous; the complaints of the gay and frivolous are nothing but a new manner of displaying gaiety and frivolity; they are lamentations full of mirth.

There are secrets in the art of reading, which tend to facilitate its purposes, by assisting the memory, and augmenting intellectual opulence. Some, our own ingenuity must form, and perhaps every student has an artificial manner of recollection, and a peculiar arrangement, as, in short hand, almost every writer has a system of his own. There are, however, some regulations which appear of general utility.

The elder Pliny who, having been a voluminous compiler, must have had great experience in the art of reading, tells us, that there is no book, however bad, but which contains something good. Just and obvious as this axiom may seem, it requires some explanation.

To read every book would be fatal to the interest of most readers; men of taste who read variously know that the pains exceed the pleasures; to men of curiosity the pleasures exceed the pains. The reader of erudition, who searches for facts and overlooks opinions, may therefore read every book profitably. He must pick his few flowers from rugged rocks, and pass many days bewildered in wild deserts. But he who only desires to gratify a more delicate sensation, the reader of taste, must be contented to range in more contracted limits, and to restrict himself to the paths of cultured pleasure grounds. Without this distinction in reading, study becomes a labour painful and interminable; and hence readers of taste complain that there is no end of reading, and readers of erudition that books contain nothing but words. When the former confine themselves to works of taste, their complaints cease, and when the latter keep to books of facts, they fix on the proper aliment for their insatiable curiosity.

Nor is it always necessary, in the pursuits of learning, to read every book entire. Perhaps this task has now become impossible, notwithstanding those ostentatious students, who, by their infinite and exact quotations, appear to have read and digested every thing; readers, artless and honest, conceive from such writers splendid ideas of the power and extent of the human faculties. Of many books we need only seize the plan, and examine some of the portions. The quackery of the learned has been often exposed; and the task of quoting fifty books a day is neither difficult nor tedious. Of the little supplement at the close of a volume, few readers conceive the value; but some of the most eminent writers have been great adepts in the art of *index-reading*. An index-reader is, indeed, more let into the secrets of an author, than the other who attends him with all the tedious forms of ceremony. I, for my parts, venerate the inventor of indices; and I know not to whom to yield the preference, either to Hippocrates, who was the first great anatomiser of the human body, or to that unknown labourer in literature, who first laid open the nerves and arteries of a book.

Watts advises the perusal of the prefaces and the index of a book, as they both give light on its contents. Gibbon says, we ought not to attend to the order of our books, so much as of our thoughts. The perusal of a particular work gives birth perhaps to ideas unconnected with the subject it treats; I pursue these ideas and quit my proposed plan of reading. Thus, in the midst of Homer, he read Longinus; a chapter of Longinus led to an epistle of Pliny; and having finished Longinus, he followed the train of his ideas of the sublime and beautiful in the Inquiry of Burke, and concluded by comparing the ancient with the modern Longinus.

It may not be necessary to read all the works of any one author, but only those which have received the approbation of posterity. By this scheme we become acquainted with the finest compositions in half the time those employ, who, attempting to read every thing, are often little acquainted with, and even ignorant of the best. Thus of Machiavel, it may be sufficient to read his Prince and his history of Florence; of Milton nearly all his poetry, little of his prose, and nothing of his history; of Fielding's twelve volumes, six may suffice; and of Voltaire's ninety, perhaps nine is more than enough. One half of the plays of Shakespeare, and one half of each play, is quite enough for one who reads poetry merely for its own sake. All Dryden's fables, two of his satires, one of his odes, with a few of his prefaces, should satisfy a reasonable student, while all his dramas, translations, prologues, and songs, may be left to repose quietly on the shelf. Of the forty volumes of Swift, two or three volumes-full might be culled out, while the dirty or malignant refuse should be doomed to the jakes. The periodical works of Steele and Addison, once so popular, certainly contain a great deal unworthy of notice; and Mrs. Barbauld has lately done a real service to the world, by compressing eighteen or twenty of these into three or four. The best parts of Pope are his translations of Homer and Horace: these, with his moral essays, and his Art of Criticism, should be read, while his pastorals and his odes are forgotten, and his Wife of Bath, his Sappho, and his Eloisa should be reserved for the use of brothels.

A reader is too often a prisoner chained to the triumphal car of an author of great celebrity, and when he ventures not to judge for himself, conceives, while he is reading the bad works of great authors, that the languor which he experiences arises from his own defective taste. But the best writers, when they are voluminous, have a great deal of mediocrity; for whenever an author attains facility in composition, the success of his preceding labours not only stimulates him to new performances, but prejudices the public in their favour; and such being mostly writers by profession, most of their works are the products, not of inclination, but necessity.

On the other side, readers must not imagine that all the pleasures of composition depend on the author; for there is something which a reader himself must bring to the book, that the book may please. There is a literary appetite which the author can no more impart, than the most skilful cook can give appetite to the guests. When Richelieu said to Godeau, that he did not understand his verses, the honest poet replied, it was not his fault. It would indeed be very unreasonable, when a painter exhibits his pictures in public, to expect that he should provide spectacles for the use of the short-sighted. Every man must come prepared as well as he can. Simonides confessed himself incapable of deceiving stupid persons; and Balzac remarked of the girls of his village, that they were too silly to be duped by a man of wit. Dulness is impenetrable; and there are hours when the liveliest taste loses its sensibility. The temporary tone of the mind may be unfavourable to taste a work properly, and we have had many erroneous criticisms from great men, which may be attributed to this circumstance. The mind communicates its infirm dispositions to the book, and an author has not only his own defects to account for, but also those of his reader. There is something in composition like the game of shuttlecock, where, if the reader does not quickly rebound the feathered cork to the author, the game is destroyed, and the whole spirit of the work becomes extinct.

A frequent impediment in reading is a disinclination in the mind to settle on the subject; agitated by incongruous and dissimilar ideas, it is with pain that we admit those of the author. But on applying ourselves, with gentle violence, to the perusal of an interesting work, the mind soon congenealizes with the subject; the disinclination is no more, and like Homer's chariot wheels, we kindle as we roll. The ancient rabbins advised their students to apply themselves to reading, whether they felt an inclination or not, because, as they proceeded, they would find their inclination and their curiosity awakened. We can easily account for this; it is so certain, and acts with such power, that even indifferent works are frequently finished, merely to gratify that curiosity which their early pages have communicated. The ravenous appetite of Johnson for reading is expressed in a strong metaphor, by Mrs. Knowles, who said, "he knows how to read better than any one; he gets at the substance of a book directly; he tears out the heart of it."

We should hesitate to pronounce on a work of some merit, on the first perusal, for that is rarely attended by a proper relish. It is with reading as with wine; for connoisseurs have observed, that the first glass is insufficient to decide on its quality; it is necessary to imbue the palate, to give it that raciness of relish, which communicates every latent quality, and enables us to judge as keenly as the two uncles of Sancho.

There are some mechanical aids in reading, which may prove of great utility, and form a kind of rejuvenescence of our early studies. Montaigne placed at the end of a book which he intended not to re-peruse, the time he had read it, with a concise decision on its merits; that, says he, it may thus represent to me, the air and general idea I had conceived of the author, in reading the work. He has obliged us with giving several of these annotations. Of Young the poet it is told, that whenever he came to a striking passage, he folded the leaf; and that at his death, books have been found in his library, which had long resisted the power of closing: a mode more easy than useful; for, after a length of time, they must be again read to know why they were folded. This difficulty is avoided by those who note in a blank leaf the pages to be referred to, with a word of criticism. Nor let us consider these minute directions as unworthy the most enlarged minds; by these petty exertions at the most distant periods, may learning obtain its authorities, and fancy combine its ideas. Seneca, in sending some volumes to his friend Lucilius, accompanies them with notes of particular passages, that, he observes, you who only aim at the useful, may be spared the trouble of examining the whole. Books are still preserved noted by Voltaire with a word of censure or approbation on the page itself, which was his usual practice. Formey complained that the books he lent Voltaire were returned always disfigured by his remarks; but he was a true German writer of the old class.

A professional student should divide his readings into a *uniform* reading which is useful, and into a *diversified* reading which is pleasant. Guy Patin, an eminent physician and a man of letters, had a just notion of this manner. He says, "I daily read Hippocrates, Galen, Fernel, and other illustrious masters of my profession; this I call my profitable readings. I frequently read Ovid, Juvenal, Horace, Seneca, Tacitus, and others, and these are my recreations." We must observe these distinctions, for it frequently happens that a lawyer or a physician, with great industry and love of study, by giving too much to diversified reading, may utterly neglect what should be his uniform studies.

An author is often cruelly mortified to find his work reposing on a harpsichord or a table, with its virgin pages. It was among the mortifications of Mickle, that the lord to whom he had dedicated his version of the Lusiad, had it long in his possession, in the state he had received it! How often also are authors mortified to perceive, that generally the first volume of their work is fouler than its brother! It is, therefore, an advantage to compose in single volumes; for then they flatter themselves, a second would be acceptable; but most books are more read for curiosity than for pleasure; and are often looked into, but rarely resumed. Authors are vain, but readers are capricious.

Readers may be classed into an infinite number of divisions; but an author is a solitary being, who, for the same reason he pleases one, must consequently displease another. To have too exalted a genius is more prejudicial for his celebrity, than to have a moderate one; for we shall find that the most popular works are not of the highest value, but of the greatest usefulness. I could mention some esteemed writers, whose works have attained a great number of editions, but whose minds were never yet inflamed by an accidental fervour of original genius. They instruct those who require instruction, and they please those, who are yet sufficiently ignorant to discover novelty in their strictures; in a word they form taste, rather than impart genius. A Carlo Marat is a Raphael to those who have not studied a Raphael. They may apply to themselves the same observation Lucilius, the satirist, has made, that he did not write for Persius, for Scipio, and for Rutilius, persons eminent for their science, but for the Tarentines, the Consentines, and the Sicilians. Montaigne has complained, that he found his readers too learned, or too ignorant, and that he could only please a middle class, who have just learning enough to comprehend him. Congreve says, there is in true beauty something which vulgar souls cannot admire. Balzac complains bitterly of readers: a period, he cries, shall have cost us the labour of a day; we shall have distilled into an essay the essence of our minds; it may be a finished piece of art; and they think they are indulgent when they pronounce it to contain some pretty things, and that the style is not bad! There is something in exquisite composition which ordinary readers can never understand.

Some will only read old books, as if there were no valuable truths to be discovered in modern ones, while others will only read new books, as if some valuable truths are not among the old. Some will not read a book, because they are acquainted with the author; by which the reader may be more injured than the author; others not only read the book, but would also read the man; by which the most ingenious author may be injured by the most impertinent reader.

An author would write with refinement and delicacy; the reader has neither; if the author does not succeed he may be an intelligible, but still an indifferent writer; if he succeeds that reader will reject him as an obscure writer; yet the author will then be a highly finished writer. Some readers complain of the obscurity of an author, and often they are right; but there are some eyes to which almost every thing appears misty; for a picture may be hung in its proper light, though for some it may be raised too high. One ought not to see every thing distinctly, but only certain parts of it; the imagination properly supplies the intermediate links. Hence are derived what some consider the obscurities of genius, which indeed are only the *obvious parts* which it wishes to *conceal*.

16. Fisher Ames

American Literature
1803

The historian Thomas P. Slaughter has christened Fisher Ames (1758–1808) "the Jeremiah of conservative American politics." The son of the astronomer and almanac writer Nathaniel Ames (see chapter 10), Fisher Ames was educated at Harvard and became a lawyer. He early distinguished himself by his passionate opposition to popular rule. As a delegate to the Massachusetts state ratification convention, he stood out for his unbending Federalism. He feared that democracy would overrun the republic; and while, as he explains in the essay, this would open the door to literary genius, it would be the end of the political genius embodied in enlightened republicanism.

"American Literature" predicts the demise of an enlightened culture and its replacement by the sophistries of a society polarized by the workings of democracy, between a few rich risen on the backs of their fellows, and many poor who have been deluded into demanding a self-governance they can neither administer nor preserve: "Liberty has never yet lasted long in a democracy; nor has it ever ended in any thing better than despotism."

It is the notion that republican moderation engenders moderate literary achievements, while great art arises in the precincts of despotism, that renders this essay particularly interesting in the context of subsequent history, and also peculiarly difficult. Ames's notion of a republican literature more or less incapable of transcendent distinction seems paradoxically to resemble the later democratic ideal of a widely representative popular culture, while the literature of genius he believes will emerge at the cost of the republic, is what many conservative critics (in the mode of T. S. Eliot) later declared to have been made impossible, exactly, by democracy. Along with Charles Brockden Brown's "Remarks on Reading," Ames's essay raises questions about literary history's fundamental terms. For his part, Fisher Ames suggests that the perennial questions of American criticism—what values should define the nation's literature and how to assess its value as literature—can probably never be answered without contradiction.

Few speculative subjects have exercised the passions more or the judgment less, than the inquiry, what rank our country is to maintain in the world for genius and literary attainments. Whether in point of intellect we are equal to Europeans, or only a race of degenerate creoles; whether our artists and authors have already performed much and promise every thing; whether the muses, like the nightingales, are too delicate to cross the salt water, or sicken and mope without song if they do, are themes upon which we Americans are privileged to be eloquent and loud. It might indeed occur to our discretion, that as the only admissible proof of literary excellence is the measure of its effects, our national claims ought to be abandoned as worthless the moment they are found to need asserting.

Nevertheless, by a proper spirit and constancy in praising ourselves, it seems to be supposed, the doubtful title of our vanity may be quieted in the same manner as it was once believed the currency of the continental paper could, by a universal agreement, be established at par with specie. Yet such was the unpatriotic perverseness of our citizens, they preferred the gold and silver, for no better reason than because the paper bills were not so good. And now it may happen, that from spite or envy, from want of attention or the want of our sort of information, foreigners will dispute the claims of our preëminence in genius and literature, notwithstanding the great convenience and satisfaction we should find in their acquiescence.

In this unmanageable temper or indocile ignorance of Europe, we may be under the harsh necessity of submitting our pretensions to a scrutiny; and as the world will judge of the matter with none of our partiality, it may be discreet to anticipate that judgment, and to explore the grounds upon which it is probable the aforesaid world will frame it. And after all, we should suffer more pain than loss, if we should in the event be stripped of all that does not belong to us; and especially if, by a better knowledge of ourselves, we should gain that modesty which is the first evidence, and perhaps the last, of a real improvement. For no man is less likely to increase his knowledge than the coxcomb, who fancies he has already learned out. An excessive national vanity, as it is the sign of mediocrity, if not of barbarism, is one of the greatest impediments to knowledge.

It will be useless and impertinent to say, a greater proportion of our citizens have had instruction in schools than can be found in any European state. It may be true that neither France nor England can boast of so large a portion of their population who can read and write, and who are versed in the profitable mystery of the rule of three. This is not the footing upon which the inquiry is to proceed. The question is not, what proportion are stone blind, or how many can see, when the sun shines, but what geniuses have arisen among us, like the sun and stars to shed life and splendor on our hemisphere.

This state of the case is no sooner made, than all the firefly tribe of our authors perceive their little lamps go out of themselves, like the flame of a candle when lowered into the mephitic vapor of a well. Excepting the writers of two able works on our politics, we have no authors. To enter the lists in single combat against Hector, the Greeks did not offer the lots to the nameless rabble of their soldiery; all eyes were turned upon Agamemnon and Ajax, upon Diomed and Ulysses. Shall we match Joel Barlow against Homer or Hesiod? Can Thomas Paine contend against Plato? Or could Findley's history of his own insurrection vie with Sallust's narrative of Catiline's? There is no scarcity of spelling-book makers, and authors of twelve-cent pamphlets; and we have a distinguished few, a sort of literary nobility, whose works have grown to the dignity and size of an octavo volume. We have many writers who have read, and who have the sense to understand, what others have written. But a right perception of the genius of others is not genius; it is a sort of business talent, and will not be wanting where there is much occasion for its exercise. Nobody will pretend that the Americans are a stupid race; nobody will deny that we justly boast of many able men, and exceedingly useful publications. But has our country produced one great original work of genius? If we tread the sides of Parnassus, we do not climb its heights; we even creep in our path, by the light that European genius has thrown upon it. Is there one luminary in our firmament that shines with unborrowed rays? Do we reflect how many constellations blend their beams in the history of Greece, which will appear bright to the end of time, like the path of the zodiac, bespangled with stars?

If, then, we judge of the genius of our nation by the success with which American authors have displayed it, our country has certainly hitherto no pretensions to literary fame. The world will naturally enough pronounce its opinion, that what we have not performed we are incapable of performing.

It is not intended to proceed in stripping our country's honors off, till every lover of it shall turn with disgust from the contemplation of its nakedness. Our honors have not faded—they have not been won. Genius no doubt exists in our country, but it exists, like the unbodied soul on the stream of Lethe, unconscious of its powers, till the causes to excite and the occasions to display it shall happen to concur.

What were those causes that have forever consecrated the name of Greece? We are sometimes answered, she owes her fame to the republican liberty of the states. But Homer, and Hesiod, to say nothing of Linus, Orpheus, Musæus, and many others, wrote while kings governed those states. Anacreon and Simonides flourished in the court of Pisistratus, who had overthrown the democracy of Athens. Nor, we may add in corroboration, did Roman genius flourish till the republic fell. France and England are monarchies, and they have excelled all modern nations by their works of genius. Hence we have a right to conclude the form of government has not a decisive, and certainly not an exclusive influence, on the literary eminence of a people.

If climate produces genius, how happens it that the great men who reflected such honor on their country appeared only in the period of a few hundred years before the death of Alexander? The melons and figs of Greece are still as fine as ever; but where are the Pindars?

In affairs that concern morals, we consider the approbation of a man's own conscience as more precious than all human rewards. But in the province of the imagination, the applause of others is of all excitements the strongest. This excitement is the cause; excellence, the effect. When every thing concurs, and in Greece every thing did concur, to augment its power, a nation wakes at once from the sleep of ages. It would seem as if some Minerva, some present divinity, inhabited her own temple in Athens, and by flashing light and working miracles had conferred on a single people, and almost on a single age of that people, powers that are denied to other men and other times. The admiration of posterity is excited and overstrained by an effulgence of glory, as much beyond our comprehension as our emulation. The Greeks seem to us a race of giants, Titans, the rivals, yet the favorites of their gods. We think their apprehension was quicker, their native taste more refined, their prose poetry, their poetry music, their music enchantment. We imagine they had more expression in their faces, more grace in their movements, more sweetness in the tones of conversation than the moderns. Their fabulous deities are supposed to have left their heaven to breathe the fragrance of their groves, and to enjoy the beauty of their landscapes. The monuments of heroes must have excited to heroism; and the fountains, which the muses had chosen for their purity, imparted inspiration.

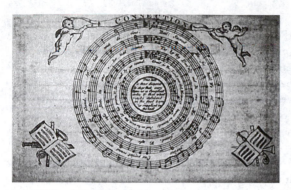

From William Billings, The Continental Harmony, *1794.*

It is indeed almost impossible to contemplate the bright ages of Greece, without indulging the propensity to enthusiasm.

We are ready to suspect the delusion of our feelings, and to ascribe its fame to accident, or to causes which have spent their force. Genius, we imagine, is forever condemned to inaction by having exhausted its power, as well as the subjects upon which it has displayed itself. Another Homer or Virgil could only copy the Iliad and Æneid; and can the second poets, from cinders and ashes, light such a fire as still glows in the writings of the first. Genius, it will be said, like a conflagration on the mountains, consumes its fuel in its flame. Not so. It is a spark of elemental fire that is unquenchable, the contemporary of this creation, and destined with the human soul to survive it. As well might the stars of heaven be said to expend their substance by their lustre. It is to the intellectual world what the electric fluid is to nature, diffused everywhere, yet almost everywhere hidden, capable by its own mysterious laws of action and by the very breath of applause, that like the unseen wind excites it, of producing effects that appear to transcend all power, except that of some supernatural agent riding in the whirlwind. In an hour of calm we suddenly hear its voice, and are moved with the general agitation. It smites, astonishes, and confounds, and seems to kindle half the firmament.

It may be true, that some departments in literature are so filled by the ancients, that there is no room for modern excellence to occupy. Homer wrote soon after the heroic ages, and the fertility of the soil seemed in some measure to arise from its freshness: it had never borne a crop. Another Iliad would not be undertaken by a true genius, nor equally interest this age, if he executed it. But it will not be correct to say, the field is reduced to barrenness from having been overcropped. Men have still imagination and passions, and they can be excited. The same causes that made Greece famous, would, if they existed here, quicken the clods of our valleys, and make our Bœotia sprout and blossom like their Attica.

In analyzing genius and considering how it acts, it will be proper to inquire how it is acted upon. It feels the power it exerts, and its emotions are contagious, because they are fervid and sincere. A single man may sit alone and meditate, till he fancies he is under no influence but that of reason. Even in this opinion, however, he will allow too little for prejudice and imagination; and still more must be allowed when he goes abroad and acts in the world. But masses and societies of men are governed by their passions.

The passion that acts the strongest, when it acts at all, is fear; for in its excess, it silences all reasoning and all other passions. But that which acts with the greatest force, because it acts with the greatest constancy, is the desire of consideration. There are very few men who are greatly deceived with respect to their own measure of sense and abilities, or who are much dissatisfied on that account; but we scarcely see any who are quite at ease about the estimate that other people make of them. Hence it is, that the great business of mankind is to fortify or create claims to general regard. Wealth procures respect, and more wealth would procure more respect. The man who, like Midas, turns all he touches into gold, who is oppressed and almost buried in its superfluity, who lives to get, instead of getting to live, and at length belongs to his own estate and is its greatest encumbrance, still toils and contrives to accumulate wealth, not because he is deceived in regard to his wants, but because he knows and feels, that one of his wants, which is insatiable, is that respect which follows its possession. After engrossing all that the seas and mountains conceal, he would be still unsatisfied, and with some good reason, for of the treasures of esteem who can ever have enough? Who would mar or renounce one half his reputation in the world?

At different times, the opinions of men in the same country will vary with regard to the objects of prime consideration, and in different countries there will ever be a great difference; but that which is the first object of regard will be the chief object of pursuit. Men will be most excited to excel in that department which offers to excellence the highest reward in the respect and admiration of mankind. It was this strongest of all excitements that stimulated the literary ages of Greece.

In the heroic times, it is evident, violence and injustice prevailed. The state of society was far from tranquil or safe. Indeed, the traditional fame of the heroes and demigods is founded on the gratitude that was due for their protection against tyrants and robbers. Thucydides tells us, that companies of travellers were often asked whether they were thieves. Greece was divided into a great number of states, all turbulent, all martial, always filled with emulation, and often with tumult and blood. The laws of war were far more rigorous than they are at present. Each state, and each citizen in the state, contended for all that is dear to man. If victors, they despoiled their enemies of every thing; the property was booty, and the people were made slaves. Such was the condition of the Helots and Messenians under the yoke of Sparta. There was every thing, then, both of terror and ignominy, to rouse the contending states to make every effort to avoid subjugation.

The fate of Platæa, a city that was besieged and taken by the Spartans, and whose citizens were massacred in cold blood, affords a terrible illustration of this remark. The celebrated siege of Troy is an instance more generally known, and no less to the purpose. With what ardent love and enthusiasm the Trojans viewed their Hector, and the Greeks their Ajax and Achilles, is scarcely to be conceived. It cannot be doubted, that to excel in arms was the first of all claims to the popular admiration.

Nor can it escape observation, that in times of extreme danger the internal union of a state would be most perfect. In these days we can have no idea of the ardor of ancient patriotism. A society of no great extent was knit together like one family by the ties of love, emulation, and enthusiasm. Fear, the strongest of all passions, operated in the strongest of all ways. Hence we find, that the first traditions of all nations concern the champions who defended them in war.

This universal state of turbulence and danger, while it would check the progress of the accurate sciences, would greatly extend the dominion of the imagination. It would be deemed of more importance, to rouse or command the feelings of men, than to augment or correct their knowledge.

In this period it might be supposed, that eloquence displayed its power; but this was not the case. Views of refined policy, and calculations of remote consequences were not adapted to the taste or capacity of rude warriors, who did not reason at all, or only reasoned from their passions. The business was not to convince, but to animate; and this was accomplished by poetry. It was enough to inspire the poet's enthusiasm, to know beforehand that his nation would partake it.

Accordingly, the bard was considered as the interpreter and favorite of the gods. His strains were received with equal rapture and reverence as the effusions of an immediate inspiration. They were made the vehicles of their traditions, to diffuse and perpetuate the knowledge of memorable events and illustrious men.

We grossly mistake the matter, if we suppose that poetry was received of old with as much apathy as it is at the present day. Books are now easy of access; and literary curiosity suffers oftener from repletion than from hunger. National events slip from the memory to our records; they miss the heart, though they are sure to reach posterity.

It was not thus the Grecian chiefs listened to Phemius or Demodocus, the bards mentioned by Homer. It was not thus that Homer's immortal verse was received by his countrymen. The thrones of Priam and Agamemnon were both long ago subverted; their kingdoms and those of their conquerors have long since disappeared, and left no wreck nor memorial behind; but the glory of Homer has outlived his country and its language, and will remain unshaken like Teneriffe or Atlas, the ancestor of history, and the companion of time to the end of his course. O! had he in his lifetime enjoyed, though in imagination, but a glimpse of his own glory, would it not have swelled his bosom with fresh enthusiasm, and quickened all his powers? What will not ambition do for a crown? and what crown can vie with Homer's?

Though the art of alphabetic writing was known in the east in the time of the Trojan war, it is nowhere mentioned by Homer, who is so exact and full in describing all the arts he knew. If his poems were in writing, the copies were few; and the knowledge of them was diffused, not by reading, but by the rhapsodists, who made it a profession to recite his verses.

Poetry, of consequence, enjoyed in that age, in respect to the vivacity of its impressions, and the significance of the applauses it received, as great advantages as have ever since belonged to the theatre. Instead of a cold perusal in a closet, or a still colder confinement unread, in a bookseller's shop, the poet saw with delight his work become the instructor of the wise, the companion of the brave and the great. Alexander locked up the Iliad in the precious cabinet of Darius, as a treasure of more value than the spoils of the king of Persia.

But though Homer contributed so much and so early to fix the language, to refine the taste, and inflame the imagination of the Greeks, his work, by its very excellence, seems to have quenched the emulation of succeeding poets to attempt the epic. It was not till long after his age, and by very slow degrees, that Æschylus, Sophocles, and Euripides carried the tragic art to its perfection.

For many hundred years, there seems to have been no other literary taste, and indeed no other literature, than poetry. When there was so much to excite and reward genius, as no rival to Homer appeared, it is a clear proof, that nature did not produce one. We look back on the history of Greece, and the names of illustrious geniuses thicken on the page, like the stars that seem to sparkle in clusters in the sky. But if with Homer's own spirit we could walk the milky-way, we should find that regions of unmeasured space divide the bright luminaries that seem to be so near. It is no reproach to the genius of America, if it does not produce ordinarily such men as were deemed the prodigies of the ancient world. Nature has provided for the propagation of men—giants are rare; and it is forbidden by her laws that there should be races of them.

If the genius of men could have stretched to the giant's size, there was every thing in Greece to nourish its growth and invigorate its force. After the time of Homer, the Olympic and other games were established. All Greece, assembled by its deputies, beheld the contests of wit and valor, and saw statues and crowns adjudged to the victors, who contended for the glory of their native cities as well as for their own. To us it may seem, that a handful of laurel leaves was a despicable prize. But what were the agonies, what the raptures of the contending parties, we may read, but we cannot conceive. That reward, which writers are now little excited to merit, because it is doubtful and distant, "the estate which wits inherit after death," was in Greece a present possession. That public so terrible by its censure, so much more terrible by its neglect, as then assembled in person, and the happy genius who was crowned victor was ready to expire with the transports of his joy.

There is reason to believe, that poetry was more cultivated in those early ages than it ever has been since. The great celebrity of the only two epic poems of antiquity, was owing to the peculiar circumstances of the ages in which Homer and Virgil lived; and without the concurrence of those circumstances their reputation would have been confined to the closets of scholars, without reaching the hearts and kindling the fervid enthusiasm of the multitude. Homer wrote of war to heroes and their followers, to men who felt the military passion stronger than the love of life; Virgil, with art at least equal to his genius, addressed his poem to Romans, who loved their country with sentiment, with passion, with fanaticism. It is scarcely possible, that a modern epic poet should find a subject that would take such hold of the heart, for no such subject worthy of poetry exists. Commerce has supplanted war, as the passion of the multitude; and the arts have divided and contracted the objects of pursuit. Societies are no longer under the power of single passions, that once flashed enthusiasm through them all at once like electricity. Now the propensities of mankind balance and neutralize each other, and, of course, narrow the range in which poetry used to move. Its coruscations are confined, like the northern light, to the polar circle of trade and politics, or like a transitory meteor blaze in a pamphlet or magazine.

The time seems to be near, and perhaps is already arrived, when poetry, at least poetry of transcendent merit, will be considered among the lost arts. It is a long time since England has produced a first rate poet. If America has not to boast at all what our parent country boasts no longer, it will not be thought a proof of the deficiency of our genius.

It is a proof that the ancient literature was wholly occupied by poetry, that we are without the works, and indeed without the names, of any other very ancient authors except poets. Herodotus is called the father of history; and he lived and wrote between four and five hundred years after Homer. Thucydides, it is said, on hearing the applauses bestowed at the public games on the recital of the work of Herodotus, though he was then a boy, shed tears of emulation. He afterwards excelled his rival in that species of writing.

Excellent, however, as these Grecian histories will ever be esteemed, it is somewhat remarkable, that political science never received much acquisition in the Grecian democracies. If Sparta should be vouched as an exception to this remark, it may be replied, Sparta was not a democracy. Lest that however should pass for an evasion of the point, it may be further answered, the constitution of Lycurgus seems to have been adapted to Sparta rather as a camp than a society of citizens. His whole system is rather a body of discipline than of laws whose whole object it was, not to refine manners or extend knowledge but to provide for the security of the camp. The citizens, with whom any portion of political power was intrusted, were a military caste or class; and the rigor of Lycurgus's rules and articles was calculated and intended to make them superior to all other soldiers. The same strictness, that for so long a time preserved the Spartan government, secures the subordination and tranquility of modern armies. Sparta was, of course, no proper field for the cultivation of the science of politics. Nor can we believe, that the turbulent democracies of the neighboring states favored the growth of that kind of knowledge, since we are certain it never did thrive in Greece. How could it be, that the assemblies of the people, convened to hear flattery or to lavish the public treasures for plays and shows to amuse the populace, should be any more qualified, than inclined, to listen to political disquisitions, and especially to the wisdom and necessity of devising and putting in operation systematical checks on their own power, which was threatened with ruin by its licentiousness and excess, and which soon actually overthrew it? It may appear bold, but truth and history seem to warrant the assertion, that political science will never become accurate in popular states; for in *them* the most salutary truths must be too offensive for currency or influence.

It may be properly added, and in perfect consistency with the theory before assumed that fear is the strongest of all passions, that in democracies writers will be more afraid *of* the people, than afraid *for* them. The principles indispensable to liberty are not therefore to be discovered, or if discovered, not to be propagated and established in such a state of things. But where the chief magistrate holds the sword, and is the object of reverence, if not of popular fear, the direction of prejudice and feeling will be changed. Supposing the citizens to have privileges, and to be possessed of influence, or in other words, of some power in the state, they will naturally wish so to use the power they have, as to be secure against the abuse of that which their chief possesses; and this universal propensity of the public wishes will excite and reward the genius, that discovers the way in which this may be done. If we know any thing of the true theory of liberty, we owe it to the wisdom, or perhaps more correctly, to the experience of those nations whose public sentiment was employed to check rather than to guide the government.

It is then little to be expected that American writers will add much to the common stock of political information.

It might have been sooner remarked, that the dramatic art has not afforded any opportunities for native writers. It is but lately that we have had theatres in our cities;

and till our cities become large, like London and Paris, the progress of taste will be slow, and the rewards of excellence unworthy of the competitions of genius.

Nor will it be charged, as a mark of our stupidity, that we have produced nothing in history. Our own is not yet worthy of a Livy; and to write that of any foreign nation where could an American author collect his materials and authorities? Few persons reflect, that all our universities would not suffice to supply them for such a work as Gibbon's.

The reasons why we yet boast nothing in the abstruse sciences, are of a different and more various nature. Much, perhaps all, that has been discovered in these, is known to some of our literati. It does not appear that Europe is now making any advances. But to make a wider diffusion of these sciences, and to enlarge their circle, would require the learned leisure, which a numerous class enjoy in Europe, but which cannot be enjoyed in America. If wealth is accumulated by commerce, it is again dissipated among heirs. Its transitory nature no doubt favors the progress of luxury, more than the advancement of letters. It has among us no uses to found families, to sustain rank, to purchase power, or to pension genius. The objects on which it must be employed are all temporary, and have more concern with mere appetite or ostentation than with taste or talents. Our citizens have not been accustomed to look on rank or titles, on birth or office, as capable of the least rivalship with wealth, mere wealth, in pretensions to respect. Of course the single passion that engrosses us, the only avenue to consideration and importance in our society, is the accumulation of property; our inclinations cling to gold, and are bedded in it, as deeply as that precious ore in the mine. Covered as our genius is in this mineral crust, is it strange that it does not sparkle? Pressed down to earth, and with the weight of mountains on our heads, is it surprising, that no sons of ether yet have spread their broad wings to the sky, like Jove's own eagle, to gaze undazzled at the sun, or to perch on the top of Olympus, and partake the banquet of the gods?

At present the nature of our government inclines all men to seek popularity, as the object next in point of value to wealth; but the acquisition of learning and the display of genius are not the ways to obtain it. Intellectual superiority is so far from conciliating confidence, that it is the very spirit of a democracy, as in France, to proscribe the aristocracy of talents. To be the favorite of an ignorant multitude, a man must descend to their level; he must desire what they desire, and detest all that they do not approve; he must yield to their prejudices, and substitute them for principles. Instead of enlightening their errors, he must adopt them; he must furnish the sophistry that will propagate and defend them.

Surely we are not to look for genius among demagogues; the man who can descend so low, has seldom very far to descend. As experience evinces that popularity, in other words, consideration and power, is to be procured by the meanest of mankind, the meanest in spirit and understanding, and in the worst of ways, it is obvious, that at present the excitement to genius is next to nothing. If we have a Pindar, he would be ashamed to celebrate our chief, and would be disgraced, if he did. But if he did not, his genius would not obtain his election for a selectman in a democratic town. It is party that bestows emolument, power, and consideration; and it is not excellence in the sciences that obtains the suffrages of party.

But the condition of the United States is changing. Luxury is sure to introduce want; and the great inequalities between the very rich and the very poor will be more conspicuous, and comprehend a more formidable host of the latter. The rabble of great cities is the standing army of ambition. Money will become its instrument, and vice its agent. Every step, (and we have taken many,) towards a more complete, unmixed democracy is an advance towards destruction; it is treading where the ground is treacherous and excavated for an explosion. Liberty has never yet lasted long in a democracy; nor has it ever ended in any thing better than despotism. With the change of our government, our manners and sentiments will change. As soon as our emperor has destroyed his rivals, and established order in his army, he will desire to see splendor in his court, and to occupy his subjects with the cultivation of the sciences.

If this catastrophe of our public liberty should be miraculously delayed or prevented, still we shall change. With the augmentation of wealth, there will be an increase of the numbers who may choose a literary leisure. Literary curiosity will become one of the new appetites of the nation; and as luxury advances, no appetite will be denied. After some ages we shall have many poor and a few rich, many grossly ignorant, a considerable number learned, and a few eminently learned. Nature, never prodigal of her gifts, will produce some men of genius, who will be admired and imitated.

Chapter 14

Poetry: The Eighteenth Century

INTRODUCTION

The title of Richard Lewis's 1730 poem "Food for Criticks" speaks volumes about the new aesthetic that appears in the poetry of the eighteenth century. Lewis's poem describes the birds of America as offering a lesson in the forms of poetry. If you want to know how a pastoral sounds, Lewis writes, listen to a quail. If you want love poetry, try the dove. For pindaric odes, the lark; lyric, the robin; etc. Nature sings, but it sings an encyclopedia of poetic genres.

> For every verse a pattern here you have,
> From strains heroic down to humble stave.

Lewis, obviously, had been reading literary criticism. And he expected his readers to have done the same.

It would be hard to imagine any of the authors in chapter 8 making the same assumption. From Dryden in the late seventeenth century to Pope in Lewis's own time, literary criticism had undergone a remarkable explosion. Writers searched for rational principles of aesthetics. Classical literary models were revived, studied, and imitated. The new Lockean psychology was taken by some as a basis for natural laws of aesthetics, as in Edmund Burke's *Philosophical Enquiry into the Origin of our Ideas of the Sublime and Beautiful* (1756). Poetry came to be seen as a marker of politeness, one of the arts of civilization, a means of refinement. Lewis himself was imitating Virgil's *Eclogues*, and his poem, like the song of the birds, is offered as "Food for Criticks."

Yet there is an irony in Lewis's poem: the birds remain birds. Artless, uncivilized birds, without language.

> Not Phoebus self, altho' the god of verse,
> Could hit more fine, more entertaining airs;
> Nor the fair maids who round the fountain sate,
> Such artless heavenly music modulate.

Models of art and artlessness alike, the birds are a sign of ambivalence. (Compare this to the purely artless cricket of Anne Bradstreet's "Contemplations.") The Enlightenment quest for universal laws here shows its flip side, an impulse toward a natural beauty that cannot be duplicated through mere artifice. The progress of civilization and the arts even has a deadly side in the poem, as fowlers appear with "fatal gun" and "artful harms," threatening to turn the birds all too literally into food for critics.

The ambivalence of Lewis's aesthetic may also be that of the colonial: when facing West, he represents the progress of civility; when facing East, he finds himself a provincial in a half-savage world, far from the metropolis. In "Food for Criticks" the figure who most appreciates the beauty of the natural scene is an Indian. But Lewis is not ready to go native. The Indian is a picturesque Indian, a "swarthy ghost." He is the kind of Indian who will be seen later, in Freneau's "On the Emigration to America," tragically but peacefully receding from the landscape as civilization expands. Pastoral landscapes in the colonies tend to have ghosts of this kind, faint shadows of advancing empire.

Like most of the poems in this chapter, "Food for Criticks" was produced for a critical public. The market for verse rapidly expanded in the eighteenth century, particularly in newspapers, which changed the face of the colonial culture after 1719. The inwardness of Puritan devotional verse nearly disappeared from colonial poetry. Poets were increasingly writing on affairs of state and events of the news, as were British poets of the same period. Many wrote publicly useful poems in the form known as georgics: agricultural poems that could sometimes serve as how-to manuals, as in James Grainger's *The Sugar-Cane* (see selection 15 below). Georgics, too, have a public mission, whether through celebrating yeoman virtue or, more commonly in colonial poems, promoting agricultural staples of the Atlantic economy. John Dyer's *The Fleece* (1757) follows the life of a single commodity, wool; it ends with a global vision of "Britain's happy trade." Whether concerned with nature, trade, or politics, eighteenth-century poets increasingly celebrated a vision of empire and commerce. The pattern for this vision was set by Pope, in "Windsor Forest" (1713); it is extended as a theory of the colonies in Berkeley's "On the Prospect of Planting Arts and Learning in America" (1752). Unlike Wigglesworth's "God's Controversy with New-England," such poems see a secular history, a present moving to an expansive future. They look outward on the world of the news.

Poetry had become a public culture in its own right, consumed by a readership educated about the history and formal principles of poetry. This public culture of poetry put its stamp on the new aesthetic even where public issues seem least relevant. William Livingston, author of "Liberty of the Press" in chapter 11, also wrote a long poem called *Philosophical Solitude*; it is *about* solitude, but *for* a public. It is inward only in a universally relevant way.

Many of the poems here touch on subjects of private life, from commercial goods to moral sentiments. And some remained unpublished—particularly among the women writers, who appeared in growing numbers as the eighteenth-century culture of belles lettres gave them a social context for writing. Many major works by colonial women—such as Elizabeth Graeme Fergusson's "The Dream of the Patriotic Philosophical Farmer," a ninety-three page poem inspired by John Dickinson's *Letters from a Farmer in Pennsylvania*—remain unpublished to this day. Yet such works were also written for a critical public, even if it was in practice limited to the new salons and reading circles.

Paradoxically, the exceptions—aside from Lucy Terry's oral composition, "Bars Fight"—are the poems reprinted here from newspapers and other cheap forms of print. They allowed a popular literature of great variety, from the traditional elegy (Tompson); to the sensational execution account ("The Speech of Death to Levi Ames") to bawdy verse, usually male ("Hot Stuff"). Many of these popular writings stem from local literary cultures, isolated from London opinion. The New England elegy continued nearly unchanged through most of the period. But not for everyone. The sixteen-year-old Benjamin Franklin already knew that the Boston elegy did not meet London standards. One of his earliest writings is a parody (see selection 4 below) that tries to bring local traditions into view for urbane criticism.

Poetry that followed the young Franklin's impulse, looking to a critical public, understandably tended to imitate London. Pope and Thomson became the models for nearly every colonial poet with urbane aspirations. This Anglocentric tendency in eighteenth-century poetry would become something of a problem for United States writers in the last quarter of the century. Many responded by writing neoclassical poems to the republic. They found a favorite topic in Columbus, who, as a New World founder, had the distinct advantage of not being British. Though he was seldom mentioned by writers of the colonial period, after the Revolution Columbus inspired a small industry of poetic origin myths. (See also Noah Webster in chapter 10.) "Columbia" became a poeticism for the United States, as in Timothy Dwight's poem of that title. Joel Barlow conceived his *Vision of Columbus*, later revised as *The Columbiad*, as a national epic. In such works the British vision of empire could be transferred almost without revision from "Windsor Forest" or *The Fleece*. As Dwight writes in "Columbia":

A world is thy realm: for a world be thy laws,
Enlarg'd as thine empire, and just as thy cause;
On Freedom's broad basis, that empire shall rise,
Extend with the main, and dissolve with the skies.

M.W.

Suggested reading: Eighteenth-century Anglo-American poetry, like that of the seventeenth century, still awaits a systematic treatment. Much can be learned about the first part of the century from David Shields, *Oracles of Empire*, while a perceptive and far-reaching study of the later period can be found in William Dowling's *Poetry and Ideology in Revolutionary Connecticut*.

1. Ebenezer Cooke

The Sot-Weed Factor
1708

The besotting weed of the title is tobacco. A factor is a commercial agent. So the title could be translated as The Tobacco Agent. *The 1708 title page continues:* The Sot-Weed Factor: Or, a Voyage to Maryland. A Satyr. In which is describ'd, the Laws, Government, Courts and Constitutions of the Country; and also the Buildings, Feasts, Frolicks, Entertainments, and Drunken Humours of the Inhabitants of that Part of America. *Appealing to a London audience that wanted both descriptions of the colonies and a cosmopolitan sense that greater civility lies at home, the poem burlesques the primitive culture of its colonial sots, while supplying local color through Indian words and informative footnotes. It is written in hudibrastic verse (after Samuel Butler's* Hudibras*), an agreeable form for a popular audience: eight-syllable lines, rhyming in couplets, satirical and impious in tone. The verse is occasionally bawdy ("that for which the Ladies linger" to rhyme with "finger"). And much of its comedy derives from the device of the curse: the speaker falls under "way-ward Curse" in the first line, is assailed by untoward events throughout the poem, and concludes with his own curse on America as revenge. Yet through this series of reverses, the poem also burlesques the somewhat bumbling visiting merchant, or factor, who serves as speaker. His anxiety about sliding from civility into the semi-savagism of colonial life, for example, leaves him unprepared to discover that an Indian brave can calmly hold a conversation.*

The poem's author, Ebenezer Cooke (or Cook; 1667?–1732), was the son of a London merchant. Little is known of his early life, but he was in Maryland by 1694. He seems to have divided his life between London and Maryland, inheriting his father's Maryland property in 1712. He wrote a number of other poems, including elegies and the longer poems Sotweed Redivivus *and* The Maryland Muse.

Condemn'd by Fate to way-ward Curse,
Of Friends unkind, and empty Purse;
Plagues worse than fill'd *Pandora's* Box,
I took my leave of *Albion's* Rocks:
With heavy Heart, concern'd that I
Was forc'd my Native Soil to fly,
And the *Old World* must bid good-buy.
But Heav'n ordain'd it should be so,
And to repine is vain we know:
Freighted with Fools, from *Plymouth* sound,
To *Mary-Land* our Ship was bound;
Where we arriv'd in dreadful Pain,

Shock'd by the Terrours of the Main;
For full three Months, our wavering Boat,
Did thro' the surley Ocean float,
And furious Storms and threat'ning Blasts,
Both tore our Sails and sprung our Masts:
Wearied, yet pleas'd, we did escape
Such Ills, we anchor'd at the *Cape*;[1]
But weighing soon, we plough'd the *Bay*,
To Cove[2] it in *Piscato-way*,[3]
Intending there to open Store,
I put myself and Goods a-shore:
Where soon repair'd a numerous Crew,
In Shirts and Drawers of *Scotch-cloth*[4] Blue.
With neither Stockings, Hat, nor Shooe.
These *Sot-weed* Planters Crowd the Shoar,
In Hue as tawny as a Moor:
Figures so strange, no God design'd,
To be a part of Humane Kind:
But wanton Nature, void of Rest,
Moulded the brittle Clay in Jest.
At last a Fancy very odd
Took me, this was the Land of *Nod*;
Planted at first, when Vagrant *Cain*,
His Brother had unjustly slain:
Then conscious of the Crime he'd done,
From Vengeance dire, he hither run;
And in a Hut supinely dwelt,
The first in *Furs* and *Sot-weed* dealt.
And ever since his Time, the Place,
Has harbour'd a destested Race;
Who when they cou'd not live at Home,
For Refuge to these Worlds did roam;
In hopes by Flight they might prevent,
The Devil and his fell intent;
Obtain from Tripple Tree repreive,
And Heav'n and Hell alike deceive:
But e're their Manners I display,
I think it fit I open lay
My Entertainment by the way;
That Strangers well may be aware on,
What homely Diet they must fare on.

---

1. By the *Cape*, is meant the *Capes* of *Virginia*, the first Land on the Coast of *Virginia* and *Mary-Land*. [This and the following notes are Cooke's.]
2. To *Cove* is to lie at Anchor safe in Harbour.

3. The Bay of *Piscato-way*, the usual place where our Ships come to an Anchor in *Mary-Land*.
4. The Planters generally wear Blue *Linnen*.

To touch that Shoar, where no good Sense is found,
But Conversation's lost, and Manners drown'd.
I crost unto the other side,
A River whose impetuous Tide,
The Savage Borders does divide;
In such a shining odd invention,
I scarce can give its due Dimention.
The *Indians* call this watry Waggon
Canoo,[5] a Vessel none can brag on;
Cut from a *Popular-Tree*, or *Pine*,
And fashion'd like a Trough for Swine:
In this most noble Fishing-Boat,
I boldly put myself a-float;
Standing Erect, with Legs stretch'd wide,
We paddled to the other side:
Where being Landed safe by hap,
As *Sol* fell into *Thetis* Lap.
A ravenous Gang bent on the stroul,
Of Wolves[6] for Prey, began to howl;
This put me in a pannick Fright,
Least I should be devoured quite:
But as I there a musing stood,
And quite benighted in a Wood,
A Female Voice pierc'd thro' my Ears,
Crying, *You Rogue drive home the Steers.*
I listen'd to th'attractive sound,
And straight a Herd of Cattel found
Drove by a Youth, and homewards bound:
Cheer'd with the sight, I straight thought fit,
To ask where I a Bed might get.
The surley Peasant bid me stay,
And ask'd from whom I'de[7] run away.
Surpriz'd at such a saucy Word,
I instantly lugg'd out my Sword;
Swearing I was no Fugitive,
But from *Great-Britain* did arrive,
In hopes I better there might Thrive.
To which he mildly made reply,
I beg your Pardon, Sir, that I
Should talk to you Unmannerly;
But if you please to go with me
To yonder House, you'll welcome be.

5. A *Canoo* is an *Indian* Boat, cut out of the body of a
Popler-Tree.
6. Wolves are very numerous in *Mary-Land.*

7. 'Tis supposed by the Planters, that all unknown Persons
are run away from some Master.

Encountring soon the smoaky Seat,
The Planter old did thus me greet:
"Whether you come from Goal or Colledge,
"You're welcome to my certain Knowledge;
"And if you please all Night to stay,
"My Son shall put you in the way.
Which offer I most kindly took,
And for a Seat did round me look:
When presently amongst the rest,
He plac'd his unknown *English* Guest,
Who found them drinking for a whet,
A Cask of Syder[8] on the Fret,
Till Supper came upon the Table,
On which I fed whilst I was able.
So after hearty Entertainment,
Of Drink and Victuals without Payment;
For Planters Tables, you must know,
Are free for all that come and go.
While Pon[9] and Milk, with Mush[10] well stoar'd,
In wooden Dishes grac'd the Board;
With Homine[11] and Syder-pap,
(Which scarce a hungry Dog wou'd lap)
Well stuff'd with Fat, from Bacon fry'd,
Or with *Molossus* dulcify'd.
Then out our Landlord pulls a Pouch,
As greasy as the Leather Couch
On which he sat, and straight begun,
To load with Weed his *Indian* Gun;
In length, scarce longer than ones Finger,
Or that for which the Ladies linger:
His Pipe smoak'd out with aweful Grace,
With aspect grave and solemn pace;
The reverend Sire walks to a Chest,
Of all his Furniture the best,
Closely confin'd within a Room,
Which seldom felt the weight of Broom;
From thence he lugs a Cag of Rum,
And nodding to me, thus begun:
I find, says he, you don't much care,
For this our *Indian* Country Fare;
But let me tell you, Friend of mine,

8. Syder-pap is a sort of Food made of Syder and small
Homine, like our Oat-meal.
9. Pon is Bread made of *Indian*-Corn.
10. Mush is a sort of Hasty-pudding made with Water and
Indian Flower.

11. Homine is a Dish that is made of boiled *Indian*-Wheat,
eaten with Molossus, or Bacon-Fat.

You may be glad of it in time,
Tho' now your Stomach is so fine;
And if within this Land you stay,
You'll find it true what I do say.
This said, the Rundlet up he threw,
And bending backwards strongly drew:
I pluck'd as stoutly for my part,
Altho' it made me sick at Heart,
And got so soon into my Head
I scarce cou'd find my way to Bed;
Where I was instantly convey'd
By one who pass'd for Chamber-Maid;
Tho' by her loose and sluttish Dress,
She rather seem'd a *Bedlam-Bess*:
Curious to know from whence she came,
I prest her to declare her Name.
She Blushing, seem'd to hide her Eyes,
And thus in Civil Terms replies;
In better times, e'er to this Land,
I was unhappily Trapann'd;[12]
Perchance as well I did appear,
As any Lord or Lady here,
Not then a Slave for twice two Year.[13]
My Cloaths were fashionably new,
Nor were my Shifts of Linnen Blue;
But things are changed now at the Hoe,
I daily work, and Bare-foot go,
In weeding Corn or feeding Swine,
I spend my melancholy Time.
Kidnap'd and Fool'd, I hither fled,
To shun a hated Nuptial Bed,[14]
And to my cost already find,
Worse Plagues than those I left behind.
Whate'er the Wanderer did profess,
Good-faith I cou'd not choose but guess
The Cause which brought her to this place,
Was supping e'er the Priest said Grace.
Quick as my Thoughts, the Slave was fled,
(Her Candle left to shew my Bed)
Which made of Feathers soft and good,
Close in the Chimney-corner[15] stood;

12. Trapann'd: kidnapped. [ed.]
13. 'Tis the Custom for Servants to be obliged for four Years to very servile Work; after which time they have their Freedom.
14. These are the general Excuses made by *English* Women, which are sold, or sell themselves to *Mary-Land*.
15. Beds stand in the Chimney-corner in this Country.

I threw me down expecting Rest,
To be in golden Slumbers blest:
But soon a noise disturb'd my quiet,
And plagu'd me with nocturnal Riot;
A Puss which in the ashes lay,
With grunting Pig began a Fray;
And prudent Dog, that Feuds might cease,
Most strongly bark'd to keep the Peace.
This Quarrel scarcely was decided,
By stick that ready lay provided;
But *Reynard* arch and cunning Loon,
Broke into my Appartment soon;
In hot pursuit of Ducks and Geese,
With fell intent the same to seize:
Their Cackling Plaints with strange surprize,
Chac'd Sleeps thick Vapours from my Eyes:
Raging I jump'd upon the Floar,
And like a Drunken Saylor Swore;
With Sword I fiercly laid about,
And soon dispers'd the Feather'd Rout:
The Poultry out of Window flew,
And *Reynard* cautiously withdrew:
The Dogs who this Encounter heard,
Fiercely themselves to aid me rear'd,
And to the Place of Combat run,
Exactly as the Field was won.
Fretting and hot as roasting Capon,
And greasy as a Flitch of Bacon;
I to the Orchard did repair,
To Breathe the cool and open Air;
Expecting there the rising Day,
Extended on a Bank I lay:
But Fortune here, that saucy Whore,
Disturb'd me worse and plagu'd me more,
Than she had done the night before.
Hoarse croaking Frogs[16] did 'bout me ring,
Such Peals the Dead to Life wou'd bring,
A Noise might move their Wooden King.[17]
I stuff'd my Ears with Cotten white
For fear of being deaf out-right,
And curst the melancholy Night:

16. Frogs are called *Virginea* Bells, and make, (both in that Country and *Mary-Land*) during the Night, a very hoarse ungrateful Noise.

17. their Wooden King: a reference to Aesop's *Fables,* in which the frogs ask for a king and receive a log. When they ask for another king, they receive a crane, who eats them. [ed.]

But soon my Vows I did recant,
And Hearing as a Blessing grant;
When a confounded Rattle-Snake,
With hissing made my Heart to ake:
Not knowing how to fly the Foe,
Or whether in the Dark to go;
By strange good Luck, I took a Tree,
Prepar'd by Fate to set me free;
Where riding on a Limb a-stride,
Night and the Branches did me hide,
And I the Devil and Snake defy'd.
Not yet from Plagues exempted quite,
The curst Muskitoes did me bite;
Till rising Morn' and blushing Day,
Drove both my Fears and Ills away;
And from Night's Errors set me free.
Discharg'd from hospitable Tree;
I did to Planters Booth repair,
And there at Breakfast nobly Fare,
On rashier broil'd of infant Bear:
I thought the Cub delicious Meat,
Which ne'er did ought but Chesnuts eat;
Nor was young Orsin's flesh the worse,
Because he suck'd a Pagan Nurse.[18]
Our Breakfast done, my Landlord stout,
Handed a Glass of Rum about;
Pleas'd with the Treatment I did find,
I took my leave of Oast so kind;
Who to oblige me, did provide,
His eldest Son to be my Guide,
And lent me Horses of his own,
A skittish Colt, and aged Rhoan,
The four-leg'd prop of his Wife *Joan*.
Steering our Barks in Trot or Pace,
We sail'd directly for a place
In *Mary-Land* of high renown,
Known by the Name of *Battle-Town*.
To view the Crowds did there resort,
Which Justice made, and Law their sport,
In that sagacious County Court:
Scarce had we enter'd on the way,
Which thro' thick Woods and Marshes lay:

18. In the tale *Valentine and Orson*, Orson is raised by a bear
while Valentine grows up at court. [ed.]

But *Indians* strange did soon appear,
In hot persuit of wounded Deer;
No mortal Creature can express,
His wild fantastick Air and Dress;
His painted Skin in colours dy'd,
His sable Hair in Satchel ty'd,
Shew'd Savages not free from Pride:
His tawny Thighs, and Bosom bare,
Disdain'd a useless Coat to wear,
Scorn'd Summer's Heat, and Winters Air;
His manly Shoulders such as please,
Widows and Wives, were bath'd in Grease
Of Cub and Bear, whose supple Oil,
Prepar'd his Limbs 'gainst Heat or Toil.
Thus naked Pict[19] in Battel faught,
Or undisguis'd his Mistress sought;
And knowing well his Ware was good,
Refus'd to screen it with a Hood;
His Visage dun, and chin that ne'er
Did Raizor feel or Scissers bear,
Or know the Ornament of Hair,
Look'd sternly Grim, surpriz'd with Fear,
I spur'd my Horse, as he drew near:
But Rhoan who better knew than I,
The little Cause I had to fly;
Seem'd by his solemn steps and pace,
Resolv'd I shou'd the Specter face,
Nor faster mov'd, tho' spur'd and lick'd,
Than *Balaam's* Ass by Prophet kick'd.
Kekicknitop[20] the Heathen cry'd:
How is it *Tom,* my Friend reply'd,
Judging from thence the Brute was civel,
I boldly fac'd the Courteous Devil;
And lugging out a Dram of Rum,
I gave his Tawny worship some:
Who in his language as I guess,
(My Guide informing me no less,)
Implored the Devil,[21] me to bless.

---

19. Pict: ancient native of Britain. [ed.]
20. *Kekicknitop* is an *Indian* Expression, and signifies no more than this, *How do you do?*
21. These *Indians* worship the Devil, and pray to him as we do to God Almighty. 'Tis suppos'd, That *America* was peopl'd from *Scythia* or *Tartaria,* which Borders on *China,* by reason the *Tartarians* and *Americans* very much agree in their Manners, Arms and Government. Other Persons are of Opinion, that the *Chinese* first peopled the *West Indies;* imag-ining *China* and the Southern part of *America* to be con-tiguous. Others believe that the *Phoenicians* who were very skilful Mariners, first planted a Colony in the Isles of *America,* and supply'd the Persons left to inhabit there with Women and all other Necessaries; till either the Death or Shipwreck of the first Discoverers, or some other Misfortune occasioned the loss of the Discovery, which had been purchased by the Peril of the first Adventurers.

I thank'd him for his good Intent,
And forwards on my Journey went;
Discoursing as along I rode,
Whether this Race was framed by God
Or whether some Malignant pow'r,
Contriv'd them in an evil hour
And from his own Infernal Look;
Their Dusky form and Image took:
From hence we fell to Argument
Whence Peopled was this Continent,
My Friend suppos'd *Tartarians* wild,
Or *Chinese* from their Home exiled;
Wandring thro' Mountains hid with Snow,
And Rills did in the Vallies flow,
Far to the South of *Mexico*:
Broke thro' the Barrs which Nature cast,
And wide unbeaten Regions past,
Till near those Streams the humane deludge roll'd,
Which sparkling shin'd with glittering Sands of Gold;
And fetch *Pizarro*[22] from the *Iberian*[23] Shoar,
To Rob the Natives of their fatal Stoar.
I Smil'd to hear my young Logician,
Thus Reason like a Politician;
Who ne're by Fathers Pains and Earning
Had got at Mother *Cambridge* Learning;
Where Lubber youth just free from birch
Most stoutly drink to prop the Church;
Nor with *Grey Groat*[24] had taken Pains
To purge his Head and Cleanse his Reines:
And in obedience to the Colledge,
Had pleas'd himself with carnal Knowledge:
And tho' I lik'd the youngester's Wit,
I judg'd the Truth he had not hit;
And could not choose but smile to think
What they could do for Meat and Drink,
Who o'er so many Desarts ran,
With Brats and Wives in *Caravan*;
Unless perchance they'd got the Trick,
To eat no more than Porker sick;
Or could with well contented Maws,
Quarter like Bears[25] upon their Paws.

22. *Pizzarro* was the Person that conquer'd *Peru;* a Man of a most bloody Disposition, base, treacherous, covetous, and revengeful.
23. *Spanish* Shoar.
24. There is a very bad Custom in some Colledges, of giving the Students A *Groat ad purgandas Rhenes*, which is usually employ'd to the use of the *Donor.*
25. Bears are said to live by sucking of their *Paws,* according to the Notion of some Learned Authors.

Thinking his Reasons to confute,
I gravely thus commenc'd Dispute,
And urg'd that tho' a *Chinese* Host,
Might penetrate this *Indian* Coast;
Yet this was certainly most true,
They never cou'd the Isles subdue;
For knowing not to steer a Boat,
They could not on the Ocean float,
Or plant their Sunburnt Colonies,
In Regions parted by the Seas:
I thence inferr'd *Phoenicians*[26] old,
Discover'd first with Vessels bold
These Western Shoars, and planted here,
Returning once or twice a Year,
With *Naval Stoars* and Lasses kind,
To comfort those were left behind;
Till by the Winds and Tempest toar
From their intended Golden Shoar;
They suffer'd Ship-wreck, or were drown'd,
And lost the World so newly found.
But after long and learn'd Contention,
We could not finish our dissention;
And when that both had talk'd their fill,
We had the self same Notion still.
Thus Parson grave well read and Sage,
Does in dispute with Priest engage;
The one protests they are not Wise,
Who judge by Sense[27] and trust their Eyes;
And vows he'd burn for it at Stake,
That Man may God his Maker make;
The other smiles at his Religion,
And vows he's but a learned Widgeon:
And when they have empty'd all their stoar
From Books and Fathers, are not more
Convinc'd or wiser than before.
      Scarce had we finish'd serious Story,
But I espy'd the Town before me,
And roaring Planters on the ground,
Drinking of Healths in Circle round:
Dismounting Steed with friendly Guide,
Our Horses to a Tree we ty'd,

---

26. The *Phoenicians* were the best and boldest Saylors of Antiquity, and indeed the only *Persons*, in former Ages, who durst venture themselves on the Main Sea.

27. The *Priests* argue, That our Senses in the point of *Transubstantiation* ought not to be believed, for tho' the Consecrated Bread has all the accidents of Bread, yet they affirm, 'tis the Body of Christ, and not Bread but Flesh and Bones.

And forwards pass'd amongst the Rout,
To chuse convenient *Quarters* out:
But being none were to be found,
We sat like others on the ground
Carousing Punch in open Air
Till Cryer did the Court declare;
The planting Rabble being met,
Their Drunken Worships likewise set:
Cryer proclaims that Noise shou'd cease,
And streight the Lawyers broke the Peace.
Wrangling for Plaintiff and Defendant,
I thought they ne'er wou'd make an end on't:
With nonsense, stuff and false quotations,
With brazen Lyes and Allegations;
And in the splitting of the Cause,
They us'd such Motions with their Paws,
As shew'd their Zeal was strongly bent,
In Blows to end the Argument.
A reverend Judge, who to the shame
Of all the Bench, cou'd write his Name;[28]
At Petty-fogger took offence,
And wonder'd at his Impudence.
My Neighbour *Dash* with scorn replies,
And in the Face of Justice flies:
The Bench in fury streight divide,
And Scribbles take, or Judges side;
The Jury, Lawyers, and their Clyents,
Contending, fight like earth-born Gyants:
But Sheriff wily lay perdue,
Hoping Indictments wou'd ensue,
And when————
A Hat or Wig fell in the way,
He seiz'd them for the *Queen* as stray:
The Court adjourn'd in usual manner,
In Battle Blood, and fractious Clamour:
I thought it proper to provide,
A Lodging for myself and Guide,
So to our Inn we march'd away,
Which at a little distance lay;
Where all things were in such Confusion,
I thought the World at its conclusion:
A Herd of Planters on the ground,

28. In the County-Court of *Mary-Land*, very few of the
Justices of the *Peace* can write or read.

O'er-whelm'd with Punch, dead drunk we found:
Others were fighting and contending,
Some burnt their Cloaths to save the mending.
A few whose Heads by frequent use,
Could better bare the potent Juice,
Gravely debated State Affairs.
Whilst I most nimbly trip'd up Stairs;
Leaving my Friend discoursing oddly,
And mixing things Prophane and Godly:
Just then beginning to be Drunk,
As from the Company I slunk,
To every Room and Nook I crept,
In hopes I might have somewhere slept;
But all the bedding was possest
By one or other drunken Guest:
But after looking long about,
I found an antient Corn-loft out,
Glad that I might in quiet sleep,
And there my bones unfractur'd keep.
I lay'd me down secure from Fray,
And soundly snoar'd till break of Day;
When waking fresh I sat upright,
And found my Shoes were vanish'd quite,
Hat, Wig, and Stockings, all were fled
From this extended *Indian* Bed:
Vext at the Loss of Goods and Chattel,
I swore I'd give the Rascal battel,
Who had abus'd me in this sort,
And Merchant Stranger made his Sport.
I furiously descended Ladder;
No Hare in *March* was ever madder:
In vain I search'd for my Apparel,
And did with Oast and Servants Quarrel;
For one whose Mind did much aspire
To Mischief,[29] threw them in the Fire:
Equipt with neither Hat nor Shooe,
I did my coming hither rue,
And doubtful thought what I should do:
Then looking round, I saw my Friend
Lie naked on a Tables end;
A Sight so dismal to behold,
One wou'd have judg'd him dead and cold;

---

29. 'Tis the Custom of the Planters, to throw their own, or
any other Persons Hat, Wig, Shooes or Stockings in the Fire.

When wringing of his bloody Nose,
By fighting got we may suppose;
I found him not so fast asleep,
Might give his Friends a cause to weep:
Rise *Oronooko*,[30] rise, said I,
And from this *Hell* and *Bedlam* fly.
My Guide starts up, and in amaze,
With blood-shot Eyes did round him gaze;
At length with many a sigh and groan,
He went in search of aged Rhoan;
But Rhoan, tho' seldom us'd to faulter,
Had fairly this time slipt his Halter;
And not content all Night to stay
Ty'd up from Fodder, ran away:
After my Guide to ketch him ran,
And so I lost both Horse and Man;
Which Disappointment, tho' so great,
Did only Mirth and Jests create:
Till one more Civil than the rest,
In Conversation for the best,
Observing that for want of Rhoan,
I should be left to walk alone;
Most readily did me intreat,
To take a Bottle at his Seat;
A Favour at that time so great,
I blest my kind propitious Fate;
And finding soon a fresh supply,
Of Cloaths from Stoar-house kept hard by,
I mounted streight on such a Steed,
Did rather curb, than whipping need;
And straining at the usual rate,
With spur of Punch which lay in Pate,
E'er long we lighted at the Gate:
Where in an antient *Cedar* House,
Dwelt my new Friend, a Cockerouse;[31]
Whose Fabrick, tho' 'twas built of Wood,
Had many Springs and Winters stood;
When sturdy Oaks, and lofty Pines
Were level'd with Musmelion Vines,[32]
And Plants eradicated were,
By Hurricanes into the air;
There with good Punch and apple Juice,

---

30. Planters are usually call'd by the Name of *Oronooko*, from their Planting *Oronooko-Tobacco*.

31. Cockerouse, is a Man of Quality.

32. Musmilleon Vines are what we call Muskmilleon Plants.

We spent our Hours without abuse:
Till Midnight in her sable Vest,
Persuaded Gods and Men to rest;
And with a pleasing kind surprize,
Indulg'd soft Slumbers to my Eyes.
Fierce *Æthon*[33] courser of the Sun,
Had half his Race exactly run;
And breath'd on me a fiery Ray,
Darting hot Beams the following Day,
When snug in Blanket white I lay:
But Heat and *Chinces*[34] rais'd the Sinner,
Most opportunely to his Dinner;
Wild Fowl and Fish delicious Meats,
As good as *Neptune's* Doxy eats,
Began our Hospitable Treat;
Fat Venson follow'd in the Rear,
And Turkies wild[35] Luxurious Chear:
But what the Feast did most commend,
Was hearty welcom from my Friend.
Thus having made a noble Feast;
And eat as well as pamper'd Priest,
Madera strong in flowing Bowls,
Fill'd with extream, delight our Souls;
Till wearied with a purple Flood,
Of generous Wine (the Giant's blood,
As Poets feign) away I made,
For some refreshing verdant Shade;
Where musing on my Rambles strange,
And Fortune which so oft did change;
In midst of various Contemplations
Of Fancies odd, and Meditations,
I slumber'd long————
Till hazy Night with noxious Dews,
Did Sleep's unwholsom Fetters lose:
With Vapours chil'd, and misty air,
To fire-side I did repair:
Near which a jolly Female Crew,
Were deep engag'd at *Lanctre-Looe*;
In Nightrails white, with dirty Mein,
Such Sights are scarce in *England* seen:
I thought them first some Witches bent,
On Black Designs in dire Convent.

33. *Æthon* is one of the Poetical Horses of the Sun.
34. *Chinces* are a sort of Vermin like our *Bugs* in *England*.
35. Wild Turkies are very good Meat, and prodigiously large in *Maryland*.

Till one who with affected air,
Had nicely learn'd to Curse and Swear:
Cry'd Dealing's lost is but a Flam,
And vow'd by G-d she'd keep her *Pam*.[36]
When dealing through the board had run,
They ask'd me kindly to make one;
Not staying often to be bid,
I sat me down as others did:
We scarce had play'd a Round about,
But that these *Indian* Froes fell out.
D—m you, says one, tho' now so brave,
I knew you late a Four Years Slave;
What if for Planters Wife you go,
Nature design'd you for the Hoe.
Rot you replies the other streight,
The Captain kiss'd you for his Freight;
And if the Truth was known aright,
And how you walk'd the Streets by night,
You'd blush (if one cou'd blush) for shame,
Who from *Bridewell* or *Newgate* came.
From Words they fairly fell to Blows,
And being loath to interpose,
Or meddle in the Wars of Punk,
Away to Bed in hast I slunk.
Waking next day, with aking Head,
And Thirst, that made me quit my Bed;
I rigg'd myself, and soon got up,
To cool my Liver with a Cup
Of *Succahana*[37] fresh and clear,
Not half so good as *English* Beer;
Which ready stood in Kitchin Pail,
And was in fact but *Adam's* Ale;
For Planters Cellars you must know,
Seldom with good *October* flow,
But Perry Quince and Apple Juice,
Spout from the Tap like any Sluce;
Untill the Cask's grown low and stale,
They're forc'd again to Goad[38] and Pail:
The soathing drought scarce down my Throat,
Enough to put a Ship a float,
With Cockerouse as I was sitting,
I felt a Feaver Intermitting;

36. Pam: in the game of loo, the highest card is called Pam. A flam is a cheat. [ed.]
37. *Succahana* is Water.

38. A *Goad* grows upon an *Indian* Vine, resembling a Bottle, when ripe it is hollow; this the Planters make use of to drink water out of.

A fiery Pulse beat in my Veins,
From Cold I felt resembling Pains:
This cursed seasoning I remember,
Lasted from *March* to cold *December;*
Nor would it then its *Quarters* shift,
Until by *Cardus* turn'd a drift,
And had my Doctress wanted skill,
Or Kitchin Physick at her will,
My Father's Son had lost his Lands,
And never seen the *Goodwin-Sands:*
But thanks to Fortune and a Nurse
Whose Care depended on my Purse,
I saw myself in good Condition,
Without the help of a Physitian:
At length the shivering ill relieved,
Which long my Head and Heart had grieved;
I then began to think with Care,
How I might sell my *British* Ware,
That with my Freight I might comply,
Did on my Charter party lie:
To this intent, with Guide before,
I tript it to the Eastern Shoar;
While riding near a Sandy Bay,
I met a *Quaker, Yea* and *Nay;*
A Pious Conscientious Rogue,
As e'er woar Bonnet or a Brogue,
Who neither Swore nor kept his Word,
But cheated in the Fear of God;
And when his Debts he would not pay,
By Light within he ran away.
With this sly Zealot soon I struck
A Bargain for my *English* Truck,
Agreeing for ten thousand weight,
Of *Sot-weed* good and fit for freight,
Broad *Oronooko* bright and sound,
The growth and product of his ground;
In Cask that should contain compleat,
Five hundred of Tobacco neat.
The Contract thus betwixt us made,
Not well acquainted with the Trade,
My Goods I trusted to the Cheat,
Whose crop was then aboard the Fleet;
And going to receive my own,
I found the Bird was newly flown:
Cursing this execrable Slave,

This damn'd pretended Godly Knave;
On due Revenge and Justice bent,
I instantly to Counsel went,
Unto an ambodexter *Quack*,[39]
Who learnedly had got the knack
Of giving Glisters, making Pills,
Of filling Bonds, and forging Wills;
And with a stock of Impudence,
Supply'd his want of Wit and Sense;
With Looks demure, amazing People,
No wiser than a Daw in Steeple;
My Anger flushing in my Face,
I stated the preceding Case:
And of my Money was so lavish,
That he'd have poyson'd half the Parish,
And hang'd his Father on a Tree,
For such another tempting Fee;
Smiling, said he, the Cause is clear,
I'll manage him you need not fear;
The Case is judg'd, good Sir, but look
In *Galen*, No—in my Lord *Cook*,
I vow to God I was mistook:
I'll take out a Provincial Writ,
And Trounce him for his Knavish Wit;
Upon my Life we'll win the Cause,
With all the ease I cure the *Yaws*:[40]
Resolv'd to plague the holy Brother,
I set one Rogue to catch another;
To try the Cause then fully bent,
Up to *Annapolis*[41] I went,
A City Situate on a Plain,
Where scarce a House will keep out Rain;
The Buildings fram'd with Cyprus rare,
Resembles much our *Southwark* Fair:
But Stranger here will scarcely meet,
With Market-place, Exchange, or Street;
And if the Truth I may report,
'Tis not so large as *Tottenham Court*.
St. *Mary's* once was in repute,
Now here the Judges try the Suit,
And Lawyers twice a Year dispute:

39. This Fellow was an Apothecary, and turn'd an Attorney at Law.
40. The *Yaws* is the *Pox.*

41. The chief of *Maryland* containing about twenty four *Houses.*

As oft the Bench most gravely meet,
Some to get Drunk, and some to eat
A swinging share of Country Treat.
But as for Justice right or wrong,
Not one amongst the numerous throng,
Knows what they mean, or has the Heart,
To give his Verdict on a Stranger's part:
Now Court being call'd by beat of Drum,
The Judges left their Punch and Rum,
When Pettifogger Doctor draws,
His Paper forth, and opens Cause:
And least I shou'd the better get,
Brib'd *Quack* supprest his Knavish Wit.
So Maid upon the downy Field,
Pretends a Force, and Fights to yield:
The Byast Court without delay,
Adjudg'd my Debt in Country Pay;
In Pipe staves, Corn, or Flesh of Boar,[42]
Rare Cargo for the *English* Shoar:
Raging with Grief, full speed I ran,
To joyn the Fleet at *Kicketan*;[43]
Embarqu'd and waiting for a Wind,
I left this dreadful Curse behind.

    May Canniballs transported o'er the Sea
Prey on these Slaves, as they have done on me;
May never Merchant's, trading Sails explore
This Cruel, this Inhospitable Shoar;
But left abandon'd by the World to starve,
May they sustain the Fate they well deserve:
May they turn Savage, or as *Indians* Wild,
From Trade, Converse, and Happiness exil'd;
Recreant to Heaven, may they adore the Sun,
And into Pagan Superstitions run
For Vengence ripe————
May Wrath Divine then lay those Regions wast
Where no Man's Faithful,[44] nor a Woman Chast.

---

42. There is a Law in this Country, the Plaintiff may pay his Debt in Country pay, which consists in the produce of his Plantation.

43. The homeward bound Fleet meets here.

44. The Author does not intend by this, any of the *English* Gentlemen resident there.

2. Benjamin Tompson

A Neighbour's Tears Sprinkled on the Dust of the Amiable Virgin, Mrs. Rebekah Sewall
1710

The broadside—a piece of paper printed on one side, like a poster—was the cheapest form of print, and the broadside elegy was one of the most popular forms of poetry, especially in the New England colonies. (For a parody of the form, see selection 4, below.) Benjamin Tompson (1642–1714) was a distinguished and learned Puritan poet and schoolmaster; he published a long poem on King Philip's War, titled New England's Crisis, *as well as many elegies. He trimmed an earlier version of this one down by several lines to fit on the broadside.*

Heav'ns only, in dark hours, can Succour send;
And shew a Fountain, where the cisterns end.
I saw this little One but t'other day
With a small flock of Doves, just in my way:
What New-made Creature's this so bright? thought I
Ah! Pity 'tis such Prettiness should die.
Madam, behold the Lamb of GOD; for there's
Your Pretty Lamb, while you dissolve in Tears;
She lies infolded in her Shepherd's Arms,
Whose Bosom's always full of gracious Charms.
Great JESUS claim'd his own; never begrutch
Your Jewels rare into the Hands of Such.
He, with His Righteousness, has better dress'd
Your Babe, than e're you did, when at your breast.
'Tis not your case alone: for thousands have
Follow'd their sweetest Comforts to the Grave.
Seeking the Plat of Immortality,
I saw no Place Secure; but all must dy.
Death, that stern Officer, takes no denial;
I'm griev'd he found your door, to make a trial.
Thus, be it on the Land, or Swelling Seas,
His Sov'raignty doth what His Wisdom please.
Must then the Rulers of this World's affairs,
By Providence be brought thus into Tears?

A Neighbour's TEARS

Sprinkled on the Dust of the Amiable Virgin,

Mrs. **Rebekah Sewall,**

Who was born **December** 30. 1704. and dyed
suddenly, **August** 3. 1710. 'Ætatis 6.

Heav'ns only, in dark hours, can Succour send ;
And shew a Fountain, where the cisterns end.
I saw this little One but t'other day
With a small flock of Doves, just in my way :
What New-made Creature's this so bright ? thought I
Ah ! Pity 'tis such Prettiness should die.
Madam, behold the Lamb of GOD ; for there's
Your Pretty Lamb, while you dissolve in Tears ;
She lies infolded in her Shepherd's Arms,
Whose Bosom's always full of gracious Charms.
Great JESUS claim'd his own ; never begrutch
Your Jewels rare into the Hands of Such.
He, with His Righteousness, has better dress'd
Your Babe, than e're you did, when at your breast.
'Tis not your case alone ; for thousands have
Follow'd their sweetest Comforts to the Grave.
Seeking the Plat of Immortality,
I saw no Place Secure ; but all must dy.
Death, that stern Officer, takes no denial ;
I'm griev'd he found your door, to make a trial.
Thus, be it on the Land, or Swelling Seas,
His Sov'raignty doth what His Wisdom please.
Must then the Rulers of this World's affairs,
By Providence be brought thus into Tears ?
It is a Lesson hard, I must confess,
For our Proud Wills with Heav'ns to acquiesce.
But when Death goes before ; Unseen, behind,
There's such a One, as may compose the Mind.
Pray, *Madam*, wipe the tears off your fair eyes ;
With your translated Damsel Sympathise :
Could She, from her New School, obtain the leave,
She'd tell you Things would make you cease to grieve.

B. Tompson

It is a Lesson hard, I must confess,
For our Proud Wills with Heav'ns to acquiesce.
But when Death goes before; Unseen, behind,
There's such a One, as may compose the Mind.
Pray, *Madam*, wipe the tears off your fair eyes;
With your translated Damsel Sympathise;
Could She, from her New School, obtain the leave,
She'd tell you Things would make you cease to grieve.

3. Alexander Pope

from "Windsor Forest"
1713

> *Alexander Pope (1688–1744) was the dominant name in eighteenth-century English poetry, almost universally imitated. His* Essay on Man *also has New World references, but this early pastoral poem best articulates the emerging metropolitan consciousness of empire. The poem takes as its occasion the Peace of Utrecht (1713) and the end of Queen Anne's War, in which the British and the French had struggled over Canada. The following passage, with its remarkable dream of being the native at the center of an admiring world, concludes the poem.*

Thy Trees, fair *Windsor!* now shall leave their Woods,
And half thy Forests rush into my Floods,
Bear *Britain*'s Thunder, and her Cross display,
To the bright Regions of the rising Day;
Tempt Icy Seas, where scarce the Waters roll,
Where clearer Flames glow round the frozen Pole;
Or under Southern Skies exalt their Sails,
Led by new Stars, and born by spicy Gales!
For me the Balm shall bleed, and Amber flow,
The Coral redden, and the Ruby glow,
The Pearly Shell its lucid Globe infold,
And *Phœbus* warm the ripening Ore to Gold.
The Time shall come, when free as Seas or Wind
Unbounded *Thames* shall flow for all Mankind,
Whole Nations enter with each swelling Tyde,
And Seas but join the Regions they divide;
Earth's distant Ends our Glory shall behold,
And the new World launch forth to seek the Old.

Then Ships of uncouth Form shall stem the Tyde,
And Feather'd People crowd my wealthy Side,
And naked Youths and painted Chiefs admire
Our Speech, our Colour, and our strange Attire!
Oh stretch thy Reign, fair *Peace!* from Shore to Shore,
Till Conquest cease, and Slav'ry be no more:
Till the freed *Indians* in their native Groves
Reap their own Fruits, and woo their Sable Loves,
Peru once more a Race of Kings behold,
And other *Mexico's* be roof'd with Gold.
Exil'd by Thee from Earth to deepest Hell,
In Brazen Bonds shall barb'rous *Discord* dwell:
Gigantick *Pride*, pale *Terror*, gloomy *Care*,
And mad *Ambition*, shall attend her there.
There purple *Vengeance* bath'd in Gore retires,
Her Weapons blunted, and extinct her Fires:
There hateful *Envy* her own Snakes shall feel,
And *Persecution* mourn her broken Wheel:
There *Faction* roar, *Rebellion* bite her Chain,
And gasping Furies thirst for Blood in vain.
　　　Here cease thy Flight, nor with unhallow'd Lays
Touch the fair Fame of *Albion's* Golden Days.
The Thoughts of Gods let *Granville's* Verse recite,
And bring the Scenes of opening Fate to Light.
My humble Muse, in unambitious Strains,
Paints the green Forests and the flow'ry Plains,
Where Peace descending bids her Olives spring,
And scatters Blessings from her Dove-like Wing.
Ev'n I more sweetly pass my careless Days,
Pleas'd in the silent Shade with empty Praise;
Enough for me, that to the listning Swains
First in these Fields I sung the Sylvan Strains.

4. Benjamin Franklin

Silence Dogood No. 7
1722

Franklin tells us in his autobiography that he began his writing career as a poet, with two broadside ballads, now lost. He also tells us that as an apprentice in his brother's shop he wrote several essays and slipped them under the door, fearing that they would not be taken seriously with his name on them. The pseudonym he used was Mistress Silence Dogood, and the essays begin his lifelong fascination with fictitious personae. This one satirizes both literary criticism and—in an early indication of the aspirations that would shortly lead him to run away—the provinciality of his native Boston. It appeared in James Franklin's paper, the New England Courant, *June 25, 1722.*

> *Give me the Muse, whose generous Force,*
>   *Impatient of the Reins,*
> *Pursues an unattempted Course,*
>   *Breaks all the Cricks Iron Chains.*

Watts.

To the Author of the New-England Courant.
Sir,   No VII.

It has been the Complaint of many Ingenious Foreigners, who have travell'd amongst us, *That good Poetry is not to be expected in* New-England. I am apt to Fancy, the Reason is, not because our Countreymen are altogether void of a Poetical Genius, nor yet because we have not those Advantages of Education which other countries have, but purely because we do not afford that Praise and Encouragement which is merited, when any thing extraordinary of this Kind is produc'd among us: Upon which Consideration I have determined, when I meet with a Good Piece of *New-England* Poetry, to give it a suitable Encomium, and thereby endeavour to discover to the World some of its Beautys, in order to encourage the Author to go on, and bless the World with more, and more Excellent Productions.

There has lately appear'd among us a most Excellent Piece of Poetry, entituled, *An Elegy upon the much Lamented Death of Mrs.* Mehitebell Kitel, *Wife of Mr.* John Kitel *of* Salem, *&c.* It may justly be said in its Praise, without Flattery to the Author, that it is the most *Extraordinary* Piece that ever was wrote in *New-England.* The Language is so soft and Easy, the Expression so moving and pathetick, but above all, the Verse and Numbers so Charming and Natural, that it is almost beyond Comparison,

The Muse *disdains*[45]
Those Links and Chains,
Measures and Rules of vulgar Strains,
And o'er the Laws of Harmony a Sovereign Queen she reigns.

I find no English Author, Ancient or Modern, whose Elegies may be compar'd with this, in respect to the Elegance of Stile, or Smoothness of Rhime; and for the affecting Part, I will leave your Readers to judge, if ever they read any Lines, that would sooner make them *draw their Breath* and Sigh, if not shed Tears, than these following.

Come let us mourn, for we have lost a Wife, a Daughter, and a Sister,
Who has lately taken Flight, and greatly we have mist her.

In another Place,

Some little Time before she yielded up her Breath,
She said, I ne'er shall hear one Sermon more on Earth.
She kist her Husband some little Time before she expir'd,
Then lean'd her Head the Pillow on, just out of Breath and tir'd.

But the Threefold Appellation in the first Line

——*a Wife, a Daughter, and a Sister,*

must not pass unobserved. That Line in the celebrated *Watts,*

GUNSTON *the Just, the Generous, and the Young,*

is nothing Comparable to it. The latter only mentions three Qualifications of *one* Person who was deceased, which therefore could raise Grief and Compassion but for *One.* Whereas the former, (*our most excellent Poet*) gives his Reader a Sort of an Idea of the Death of *Three Persons,* viz.

——*a Wife, a Daughter, and a Sister,*

which is *Three Times* as great a Loss as the Death of *One,* and consequently must raise *Three Times* as much Grief and Compassion in the Reader.

I should be very much straitned for Room, if I should attempt to discover even half the Excellencies of this Elegy which are obvious to me. Yet I cannot omit one Observation, which is, that the Author has (to his Honour) invented a new Species of Poetry, which wants a Name, and was never before known. His Muse scorns to be confin'd to the old Measures and Limits, or to observe the dull Rules of Criticks;

---

45. Watts. [Franklin's note.]

Nor Rapin *gives her Rules to fly, nor* Purcell *Notes to Sing.*

Watts.

Now 'tis Pity that such an Excellent Piece should not be dignify'd with a particular Name; and seeing it cannot justly be called, either *Epic, Sapphic, Lyric,* or *Pindaric,* nor any other Name yet invented, I presume it may, (in Honour and Remembrance of the Dead) be called the *KITELIC.* Thus much in the Praise of *Kitelic Poetry.*

It is certain, that those Elegies which are of our own Growth, (and our Soil seldom produces any other sort of Poetry) are by far the greatest part, wretchedly Dull and Ridiculous. Now since it is imagin'd by many, that our Poets are honest, well-meaning Fellows, who do their best, and that if they had but some Instructions how to govern Fancy with Judgment, they would make indifferent good Elegies; I shall here subjoin a Receipt for that purpose, which was left me as a Legacy, (among other valuable Rarities) by my Reverend Husband. It is as follows,

A RECEIPT to make a New-England *Funeral ELEGY.*

For the Title of your Elegy. *Of these you may have enough ready made to your Hands; but if you should chuse to make it your self, you must be sure not to omit the Words Ætatis Suæ, which will Beautify it exceedingly.*

For the Subject of your Elegy. *Take one of your Neighbours who has lately departed this Life; it is no great matter at what Age the Party dy'd, but it will be best if he went away suddenly, being* Kill'd, Drown'd, *or Froze to Death.*

Having chose the Person, take all his Virtues, Excellencies, &c. and if he have not enough, you may borrow some to make up a sufficient Quantity: To these add his last Words, dying Expressions, &c. if they are to be had; mix all these together, and be sure you strain *them well. Then season all with a Handful or two of Melancholly Expressions, such as,* Dreadful, Deadly, cruel cold Death, unhappy Fate, weeping Eyes, *&c. Have mixed all these Ingredients well, put them into the empty Scull of some* young Harvard; *(but in Case you have ne'er a One at Hand, you may use your own,) there let them Ferment for the Space of a Fortnight, and by that Time they will be incorporated into a Body, which take out, and having prepared a sufficient Quantity of double Rhimes, such as,* Power, Flower; Quiver, Shiver; Grieve us, Leave us; tell you, excel you; Expeditions, Physicians; Fatigue him, Intrigue him; *&c. you must spread all upon Paper, and if you can procure a Scrap of Latin to put at the End, it will garnish it mightily; then having affixed your Name at the Bottom, with a* Mæstus Composuit, *you will have an Excellent Elegy.*

N. B. *This Receipt will serve when a Female is the Subject of your Elegy, provided you borrow a greater Quantity of Virtues, Excellencies, &c.*

SIR,

Your Servant,

SILENCE DOGOOD.

P. S. I shall make no other Answer to *Hypercarpus's* Criticism on my last Letter than this, *Mater me genuit, peperit mox filia matrem.*

The following Lines coming to Hand soon after I had receiv'd the above Letter from Mrs. *Dogood*, I think it proper to insert them in this Paper, that the *Dr.* may at once be paid for his Physical Rhimes administred to the Dead.

To the Sage and Immortal Doctor H——k, *on his Incomparable ELEGY, upon the Death of Mrs.* Mehitebell Kitel, *&c.*

A PANEGYRICK

Thou hast, great Bard, in thy Mysterious Ode,
Gone in a Path which ne'er before was trod,
And freed the World from the vexatious Toil,
Of Numbers, Metaphors, of Wit and Stile,
Those Childish Ornaments, and gravely chose
The middle Way between good Verse and Prose.
Well might the Rhiming Tribe the Work decline,
Since 'twas too great for every Pen but thine.
What Scribbling Mortal dare the Bayes divide?
Thou shalt alone in Fame's bright Chariot ride;
For thou with matchless Skill and Judgment fraught,
Hast, Learned Doggrell, to Perfection brought.
The Loftyest Piece renowned LAW can show,
Deserves less Wonder, than to thine we owe.
No more shall TOM's, but henceforth thine shall be,
The Standard of Eleg'ac Poetry.
The healing Race thy Genius shall admire,
And thee to imitate in vain aspire:
For if by Chance a Patient you should kill,
You can Embalm his Mem'ry with your Quill.
What tho' some captious Criticks discommend
What they with all their Wit, can't comprehend,
And boldly doom to some Ignoble Use,
The Shining Product of thy Fertile Muse?
From your exhaustless Magazine of Sence
To their Confusion keen Replies dispence;
And them behold with a Contemptuous Mien,
Since not a Bard can boast of such a Strain.
By none but you cou'd *Kitel's* Worth be shown;
And none but your great Self can tell your Own;
Then least what is your due should not be said,
Write your own Elegy against you're Dead.

PHILOMUSUS.

5. _____

three versions of Psalm 137

> *The following versions of Psalm 137 vary widely; Dwight's takes most liberty with the source, but all are more verse paraphrases than strict translations. (See also the Bay Psalm Book version in chapter 8.) Taken together, these poems show how much the Bible dominated the literary imagination of Anglo-America; even Benjamin Franklin wrote paraphrases of the Bible, two of which can be found in chapter 9. This psalm was a special favorite in the colonies, perhaps because of its themes of diaspora and conquest. Interestingly, Dwight's version—from the early national period—omits the captivity theme entirely.*

Jane Colman Turell _____

Psalm 137
1725

> *Jane Turell (1708–35) was the precocious daughter of Rev. Benjamin Colman, a distinguished Puritan. Her poetry survives because her husband, Rev. Ebenezer Turell, included some in a biography of her that he published shortly after her death. The poem was written when she was seventeen.*

As on the margin of Euphrate's flood
We wail'd our sins, and mourn'd an angry God:
For God provok'd, to strangers gave our land,
And by a righteous judge condemn'd we stand;
Deep were our groans, our griefs without compare,
With ardent cries, we rent the yielding air.
Born down with woes, no friend at hand was found,
No helper in the waste and barren ground;
Only a mournful willow wither'd there,
its aged arms by winter storms made bare,
On this our lyres, now useless grown, we hung,
Our lyres by us forsaken and unstrung!
We sigh'd in chains, and sunk beneath our woe,
Whilst more insulting our proud tyrants grow.
From hearts opprest with grief they did require
A sacred anthem on the sounding lyre:

Come, now, they cry, regale us with a song,
Music and mirth the fleeting hours prolong.
Shall Babel's daughter hear that blessed sound?
Shall songs divine be sung in heathen ground?
No. Heaven forbid that we should tune our voice,
Or touch the lyre! whilst slaves we can't rejoice.
O Palestina! our once dear abode,
Thou once wert blest with peace, and lov'd by God,
But now art desolate, a barren waste,
Thy fruitful fields by thorns and weeds defac'd.
If I forget Judea's mournful land,
May nothing prosper that I take in hand!
Or if I string the lyre, or tune my voice,
Till thy deliverance cause me to rejoice,
O may my tongue forget her art to move,
And may I never more my speech improve!
Return O Lord! avenge us of our foes,
Destroy the men that up against us rose:
Let Eden's sons thy just displeasure know,
And like us serve some foreign conquering foe,
In distant realms, far from their native home,
To which dear seat O let them never come!
          Thou Babel's daughter! Author of our woe,
Shalt feel the stroke of some revenging blow;
Thy walls and towers be level'd with the ground,
Sorrow and grief shall in each soul be found:
Thrice blest the man, who that auspicious night
Shall seize thy trembling infants in thy sight;
Regardless of thy flowing tears and moans,
And dash the tender babes against the stones.

Lemuel Hopkins

Psalm 137
1785

*Lemuel Hopkins (1750–1801), a physician, was a member of the group known as
the Connecticut Wits. With two others of the group, he wrote* The Anarchiad,
*though he published nothing in his lifetime. This version was long attributed to the
better known Joel Barlow.*

Along the banks where Babel's current flows
      Our captive bands in deep despondence strayed.
While Zion's fall in sad remembrance rose,
      Her friends, her children, mingled with the dead.

The tuneless harp that once with joy we strung,
      When praise employed, and mirth inspired the lay,
In mournful silence on the willows hung,
      And growing grief prolonged the tedious day.

The barbarous tyrants, to increase our woe,
      With taunting smiles a song of Zion claim,
Bid sacred praise in strains melodious flow
      While they blaspheme the great Jehovah's name.

But how, in heathen climes and lands unknown,
      Shall Israel's sons a song of Zion raise?
O hapless Salem, God's terrestial throne,
      Thou land of glory, sacred mount of praise.

If e'er my memory lose thy lovely name,
      If my cold heart neglect my kindred race,
Let dire destruction seize this guilty frame—
      My hand shall perish, and my voice shall cease.

Yet, shall the Lord, who hears when Zion calls,
      O'ertake her foes with terror and dismay;
His arm avenge her desolated walls,
      And raise her children to eternal day.

Timothy Dwight

Psalm 137
1800

Timothy Dwight, a grandson of Jonathan Edwards, was also a member of the Connecticut Wits, along with his brother Theodore. He became a leading light of the Federalists; after becoming president of Yale in 1795, he used all his influence to defend the New England way against encroachments of secular culture—so much so that he came to be known as "old Pope Dwight." See also his "Columbia," in selection 23 below.

I love thy kingdom, Lord,
The house of thine abode,
The church our blest Redeemer sav'd
With his own precious blood.

I love thy Church, O God!
Her walls before thee stand,
Dear as the apple of thine eye,
And graven on thy hand.

If e'er to bless thy sons
My voice, or hands, deny,
These hands let useful skill forsake,
This voice in silence die.

If e'er my heart forget
Her welfare, or her woe,
Let every joy this heart forsake,
And every grief o'erflow.

For her my tears shall fall;
For her my prayers ascend;
To her my care and toils be given,
'Till toils and cares shall end.

Beyond my highest joy
I prize her heavenly ways,
Her sweet communion, solemn vows,
Her hymns of love and praise.

Jesus, thou Friend divine,
Our Saviour and our King,
Thy hand from every snare and foe
Shall great deliverance bring.

Sure as thy truth shall last,
To Zion shall be given
The brightest glories, earth can yield,
And brighter bliss of heaven.

6. Richard Lewis

Food for Criticks
1730

This pastoral vision revalues nature. Gone is the hostile wilderness of the seven-teenth-century settlers' narratives. In its place is an Edenic landscape, clearly reminiscent of promotional literature, but now treated as the setting of a local culture. The final section of the poem sketches (and then tactfully avoids) a ten-sion between use of nature and its enjoyment. The title refers both to the birds of the poem, who are said to model all the modes of classical poetry for the discrimi-nating ear, and to the poem itself, which is offered up as a model of neoclassical accomplishment. This self-consciousness in the poem—Lewis's references to the arts of poetry and criticism, but also his expectation that this will be compared critically to other poems—makes it an early instance of belletristic culture in the colonies. (See chapter 13; for more on the poem, see this chapter's introduction.)

Until recently a nearly forgotten writer, Richard Lewis (1700?–34) was a Welshman who emigrated to Maryland as a young man. He wrote a number of verses for the Maryland Gazette, *and a longer poem called "A Journey from Patapsco to Annapolis, April 4, 1730." Pope, in* The Dunciad, *pokes fun at "A Journey"'s local imagery, particularly its description of hummingbirds. "Food for Criticks" seems to have been published in the* Maryland Gazette *in 1730, but no copy survives; it was republished in Benjamin Franklin's* Pennsylvania Gazette *in 1732. The local references, such as the mention of the Schuylkill in the third line, are likely to have been changes from the lost Maryland original.*

Hic sunt gelidi sontes, hic mollia prata, Lycori
Hic nemus, hic tecum toto consumerer avo.[46]

                                                        Virg.

Of ancient streams presume no more to tell,
The fam'd castalian or pierian well;
SKUYKIL superior, must those springs confess,
As *Pensilvania* yields to *Rome* or *Greece.*
More limpid water can no fountain show,
A fairer bottom or a smoother brow.
A painted world its peaceful gleam contains
The heav'nly arch, the bord'ring groves and plains:
Here in mock silver Cynthia seems to roll,
And trusty pointers watch the frozen pole.

46. "Here are cold springs, here soft meadows, Lycoris / Here woodland, here with thee time alone would wear me away." Virgil, *Eclogues* X: 42–43.

Here sages might observe the wandring stars,
And rudest swains commence astrologers.
Along the brink the lonely plover stalks,
And to his visionary fellow talks:
Amid the wave the vagrant blackbird sees,
And tries to perch upon the imag'd trees:
On flying clouds the simple bullocks gaze,
Or vainly reach to crop the shad'wy grass:
From neighb'ring hills the stately horse espies
Himself a feeding, and himself envies:
Hither pursu'd by op'ning hounds, the hare
Blesses himself to see a forest near;
The waving shrubs he takes for real wood,
And boldly plunges in the yielding flood.
Here bending willows hem the border round,
There graceful trees the promontory crown,
Whose mingled tufts and outspread arms compose
A shade delightful to the lawrel'd brows.
Here mossy couches tempt to pleasing dreams
The love-sick soul; and ease the weary limbs.
No noxious snake disperses poison here,
Nor screams of night-bird rend the twilight air,
Excepting him, who when the groves are still,
Hums am'rous tunes, and whistles whip poor will;
To hear whose carol, elves in circles trip,
And lovers hearts within their bosoms leap;
Whose savage notes the troubled mind amuse,
Banish despair, and hold the falling dews.
        If to the west you turn your ravish'd eyes,
There shaggy hills prop up the bending skies,
And smoaky spires, from lowly cots arise
Tow'rds the northwest the distant mountains wear
In May a green, in June a whit'ning ear,
Or all alive with woolly flocks appear.
Beneath their feet a wide extended plain,
Or rich in cider, or in swelling grain;
Does to the margin of the water stretch,
Bounded by meadows and rushy beach.
The rest a motley mixture, hill and dale,
There open fields here mingled woods prevail:
Here lasting oaks, the hope of navies, stand,
There beauteous poplars hide th'unsightly strand:
In autumn there the full-ripe clusters blush
Around the walnut or the hawthorn bush.
Here fruitful orchards bend their aged boughs,
There sweats the reaper, here the peasant mows.

Each smiling month diversifies the view,
Ev'n hoary winter teams with something new:
A milkwhite fleece does then the lawns o'erspread,
The stream becomes a looking-glass indeed.
A polish'd surface spreads across the deep.
O'er which the youth with rapid vigour slip.
But now the groves the gayest liv'ries wear,
How pleas'd, could it be spring throughout the year!
And in these walks eternity be spent,
Atheists would then to immortality consent.
          The grateful shifting of the colour'd scene,
The rich embroid'ry of the level green;
The trees, and rusling of the branches there,
The silent whispers of the passing air;
Of falling cataracts the solemn roar,
By murmuring eccho sent from shore to shore,
Mix'd with the musick of the winged choir,
Awake the fancy and the poet's fire.
Here rural Maro might attend his sheep,
And the Maeonian with advantage sleep.
Hither ye bards for inspiration come,
Let ev'ry other fount but this be dumb.
Which way soe'er your airy genius leads,
Receive your model from these vocal shades.
Wou'd you in homely pastoral excel,
Take patterns from the merry piping quail;
Observe the bluebird for a roundelay,
The chatt'ring pie, or ever babling jay:
The plaintive dove the soft love verse can teach,
And mimick thrush to imitators preach.
In Pindar's strain the lark salutes the dawn,
The lyrick robin chirps the ev'ning on:
For poignant satyr mind the movis well,
And hear the sparrow for a madrigal;
For every verse a pattern here you have,
From strains heroic down to humble stave.
Not Phoebus self, altho' the god of verse,
Could hit more fine, more entertaining airs;
Nor the fair maids who round the fountain sate,
Such artless heavenly music modulate.
Each thicket seems a paradise renew'd,
The soft vibrations fire the moving blood:
Each sense its part of sweet delusion shares,
The scenes bewitch the eye, the song the ears:
Pregnant with the scent, each wind regales the smell,

Like cooling sheets th' enwrapping breezes feel.
During the dark, if poets eyes we trust,
These lawns are haunted by some swarthy ghost,
Some indian prince, who fond of former joys,
With bow and quiver thro' the shadow flies;
He can't in death his native groves forget,
But leaves elyzium for his ancient seat.
O happy stream! hadst thou in Grecia flow'd,
The bounteous blessing of some wat'ry god
Thou'dst been; or had some Ovid sung thy rise
Distill'd perhaps from slighted virgins eyes.
Well is thy worth in indian story known,
Thy living lymph and fertile borders shown.
The shining roach and yellow bristly breme,
The pick'rel rav'nous monarch of the stream;
The pearch whose back a ring of colours shows;
The horned pout who courts the slimy ooze;
The eel serpentine, some of dubious race;
The tortoise with his golden spotted case;
Thy hairy musk-rat, whose perfume defies
The balmy odours of arabian spice;
The various flocks who shores alternate shun,
Drove by the fowler and the fatal gun.
      Young philadelphians know thy pleasures well,
Joys too extravagant perhaps to tell.
Hither oftimes th'ingenious youth repair,
When Sol returning warms the growing year:
Some take the fish with a delusive bait,
Or for the fowl beneath the arbors wait;
And arm'd with fire, endanger ev'ry shade,
Teaching ev'n unfledg'd innocence a dread.
To gratify a nice luxurious taste
How many pretty songsters breath their last:
Spite of his voice they fire the linnet down,
And make the widow'd dove renew his moan.
But some more humane seek the shady gloom,
Taste nature's bounty and admire her bloom:
In pensive thought revolve long vanish'd toil,
Or in soft song the pleasing hours beguile;
What Eden was, by every prospect told,
Strive to regain the temper of that age of gold;
No artful harms for simple brutes contrive,
But scorn to take a being they cannot give;
To leafy woods resort for health and ease,
Not to disturb their melody and peace.

7. Anonymous

The Cameleon Lover
1732

This poem on miscegenation, like the response that follows, appeared in the South-Carolina Gazette in 1732. Such dialogue poems were a favorite device of the time; a similar pair, also on interracial love, appeared in the Boston Gazette two years later.

If what the *Curious* have observ'd be true,
That the Cameleon will assume the *Hue*
Of all the Objects that approach its *Touch*;
No Wonder then, that the *Amours* of *such*
Whose *Taste* betrays them to a close Embrace
With the *dark* Beauties of the *Sable* Race,
(Stain'd with the Tincture of the *Sooty* Sin,)
Imbibe the *Blackness* of their *Charmer's* Skin.

8. Anonymous

The Cameleon's Defence
1732

All Men have Follies, which they blindly trace
Thro' the dark Turnings of a dubious Maze:
But happy those, who, by a prudent Care,
Retreat betimes, from the fallacious Snare.
The eldest Sons of Wisdom were not free,
From the same Failure you condemn in Me.
If as the Wisest of the Wise have err'd,
I go astray and am condemn'd unheard,
My Faults you too severely reprehend,
More like a rigid Censor than a Friend.
Love is the Monarch Passion of the Mind,
Knows no Superior, by no Laws confin'd;
But triumphs still, impatient of Controul,
O'er all the proud Endowments of the Soul.

9. Joseph Green

The Poet's Lamentation for the Loss of his Cat, which he used to call his Muse
1733

A native of Boston, Joseph Green (1705?–80) graduated from Harvard in 1729. He went into business as a distiller, and thus acquired the nickname of "Stiller Josey." By the time of the Revolution he was wealthy; but he was a loyalist, and left America late in 1774 or early in 1775 to retire in London. In addition to numerous satires, often bawdy, he wrote some works of piety, including an Eclogue on Jonathan Mayhew. *The following poem, published anonymously ("from Boston") in the* London Magazine, *satirizes Green's friend and fellow Bostonian Mather Byles. Byles, whose ardor for poetry was so great that he carried a letter from Alexander Pope in his inner coat pocket until it frayed to bits, owned a cat named Muse.*

Felis quædam Delicium erat cujusdam Adolescentis. —Æsop.

Oppress'd with grief, in heavy strains I mourn
The partner of my studies from me torn:
How shall I sing? what numbers shall I chuse?
For in my fav'rite *cat* I've lost my muse.
No more I feel my mind with raptures fir'd,
I want those airs that *Puss* so oft inspir'd;
No crowding thoughts my ready fancy fill,
Nor words run fluent from my easy quill:
Yet shall my verse deplore her cruel fate,
And celebrate the virtues of my cat.

      In acts obscene she never took delight;
No catterwawls disturb'd our sleep by night;
Chaste as a virgin, free from every stain,
And neighb'ring cats mew'd for her love in vain.

      She never thirsted for the chickens blood;
Her teeth she only us'd to chew her food:
Harmless as satires which her master writes,
A foe to scratching, and unus'd to bites.

      She in the study was my constant mate;
There we together many evenings sat.
Whene'er I felt my tow'ring fancy fail,
I strok'd her head, her ears, her back, and tail;

And, as I strok'd, improv'd my dying song
From the sweet notes of her melodious tongue;
Her purrs and mews so evenly kept time,
She purr'd in metre and she mew'd in rhime.
But when my dullness has too stubborn prov'd
Nor could by *Puss's* musick be remov'd,
Oft to the well-known volumes have I gone,
And stole a line from *Pope* or *Addison*.
    Oftimes, when lost amidst poetic heat,
She leaping on my knee has took her seat;
There saw the throes that rack'd my lab'ring brain,
And lick'd and claw'd me to myself again.
    Then, friends, indulge my grief, and let me mourn;
My cat is gone, ah! never to return.
Now in my study all the tedious night,
Alone I sit, and unassisted write:
Look often round (O greatest cause of pain)
And view the num'rous labours of my brain;
Those quires of words array'd in pompous rhime,
Which brav'd the jaws of all devouring time,
Now undefended, and unwatch'd by cats,
Are doom'd a victim to the teeth of rats.

10. Anonymous

The Lady's Complaint
1736

The following poem was first printed in the Virginia Gazette. *Evidently popular, it was reprinted in 1743 by the* South Carolina Gazette, *and again in 1773 in the* Essex Almanack.

Custom, alas! doth partial prove,
    Nor gives us equal measure;
A pain for us it is to love,
    But is to men a pleasure.

They plainly can their thoughts disclose,
    Whilst ours must burn within:
We have got tongues, and eyes, in vain,
    And truth from us is sin.

Men to new joys and conquests fly,
    And yet no hazard run:
Poor we are left, if we deny,
    And if we yield, undone.

Then equal laws let custom find,
    And neither sex oppress;
More freedom give to womankind,
    Or give to mankind less.

11. Lucy Terry

Bars Fight
c. 1746

> *Lucy Terry (1730–1821) was brought from Africa to New England as a child. Her owner, Ebenezer Wells, lived in Deerfield, Massachusetts, where Terry witnessed an Indian raid in 1746. Sometime thereafter she composed a commemorative verse describing the fight, and recited it, along with other compositions, into old age in the next century. The poem survived in oral tradition until it was published in the middle of the nineteenth century, and is the oldest surviving work by an African woman in the English colonies. It renders a concrete and highly localized memory of what has entered history as King George's War (1744–48), pitched between England and France over the North American continent. In 1756, Lucy Terry married a freeman, Abijah Prince, who later fought in the Revolution.*

August, 'twas the twenty-fifth,
Seventeen hundred forty-six;
The Indians did in ambush lay,
Some very valiant men to slay,
The names of whom I'll not leave out.
Samuel Allen like a hero fout,
And though he was so brave and bold,
His face no more shall we behold.
Eleazer Hawks was killed outright,
Before he had time to fight,—
Before he did the Indians see,
Was shot and killed immediately.
Oliver Amsden he was slain,
Which caused his friends much grief and pain.
Simeon Amsden they found dead,
Not many rods distant from his head.

Adonijah Gillett, we do hear,
Did lose his life which was so dear.
John Sadler fled across the water,
And thus escaped the dreadful slaughter.
Eunice Allen see the Indians coming,
And hopes to save herself by running,
And had not her petticoats stopped her,
The awful creatures had not catched her,
Nor tommy hawked her on her head,
And left her on the ground for dead.
Young Samuel Allen, Oh lackaday!
Was taken and carried to Canada.

12. Charles Hansford

from "My Country's Worth"
1752

The poems of Charles Hansford (1685?–1761) are a rare example of poetry written in the South by someone who was not a member of the planter elite. The grandson of an early Jamestown settler, Hansford was strongly identified with Virginia, and the country of the poem's title is that colony rather than a nation. Little else is known of Hansford other than that he was a blacksmith for most of his life, having also been a schoolteacher, tavern keeper, farmer, and seaman. Though probably self-educated, his poems show that he read widely in ancient and modern history. The only poem he seems to have published in his lifetime was the anonymous "On the Conquest of Cape Breton, by an Honest Tar," in the Virginia Gazette *in 1745; it celebrates a key victory for the British in King George's War. His other works, including "My Country's Worth," survived in manuscripts that were discovered in 1960. Hansford's direct couplets are usually called "rough." He himself wrote out at the top of his manuscript, "A Clumsey Attempt of an Old Man to turn Some of his Serious Thoughts into Verse." Yet his plain style is capable of complexity, as in the opening meditation on patriotism and national difference, in which African slaves—and Hansford himself owned slaves, despite the anxiety that he describes later in the poem—stand as the major example of patriotic feeling. The occasional awkwardness of his style can even be expressive, coming in a poem that celebrates the gentry above him as a source of local pride.*

That most men have a great respect and love
To their own place of birth I need not prove—
Experience shows 'tis true; and the black brood
Of sunburnt Affrick makes the assertion good.
I oft with pleasure have observ'd how they
Their sultry country's worth strive to display

In broken language, how they praise their case
And happiness when in their native place.
Such tales and such descriptions, when I'd leisure,
I often have attended to with pleasure,
And many times with questions would assail
The sable lad to lengthen out his tale.
If, then, those wretched people so admire
Their native place and have so great desire
To reenjoy and visit it again—
Which, if by any means they might attain,
How would they dangers court and pains endure
If to their country they could get secure!
But, barr'd of that, some into madness fly,
Destroy themselves, and wretchedly they die.
Nor is this love to Affrick's race confin'd
But spreads itself (I think) through human kind.
A northern Tartar forc'd from thence would show
The warmest wishes for his ice and snow
Which in that climate doth so much abound
That they for months in caves live underground;
The snow so deep, the cold is so intense
Above ground, houses would be no defense.
For food their case must needs be very bad:
Horse-flesh and milk of mares by them are had
In much esteem. (A loathsome bill of fare—
Methinks t'would poison me did I live there!)
And yet those people love and like it well,
And praise (no doubt) the country where they dwell.

If, then, the torrid and the frozen zone
Are so esteem'd and loved by their own
Home-born inhabitants and natives, we,
Whom Providence hath plac'd in a degree
Of latitude so temperate and a clime
Where neither heat nor cold at any time
Rages to that excess, to that degree,
Where there it does, sure it is fit that we
Should thanks and praise to Providence return,
Who plac'd us where we neither freeze nor burn.
But yet I doubt (it may with truth be said)
Thanks of that kind are very seldom paid.

[In the section following (about 230 lines), omitted here, Hansford praises Virginia's natural convenience for transportation and communication, enumerating its rivers and towns. "Trade makes a place / Greatly to flourish," he writes.]

After this long digression, now I come
Our country's love again to reassume
And mention motives which doth it advance,
Make it tenacious, and will it enhance.
For place alone without society
Will be but dull and joyless, languid, dry.
But if, with worthy men the soil is blest,
The measure's full; for that crowns all the rest.
Who can but love the place that hath brought forth
Such men of virtue, merit, honor, worth?
My countrymen (if I am not too fond)
For parts are by no people gone beyond.

The gentry of Virginia, I dare say,
For honor vie with all America.
Had I great Camden's skill, how freely I
Would celebrate our worthy gentry!
But I am no way equal to that task.
Such a performance certainly doth ask
For a more frequent use of conversation
Than could consist with my low place and station.
Tied down to labor, education wanting,
But yet my busy soul for knowledge panting,
Though struggling hard, I only just could peep
Above the vulgar, but with them must creep.
Neither my time nor means would suffer me
In polish'd conversation much to be,
'Tis true; I have in my declining age
Found courteous treatment from some wise and sage
And most accomplish'd men of the first rank
Whose goodness to me I am bound to thank
And gratefully acknowledge while I live.
'Tis all the tribute in my power to give.
Those men deserve, their worth should mentioned be,
And be display'd unto posterity,
That so their children may example take
And tread in the same path their fathers make.

Could I accomplish this, how gladly I
Would stretch my wit, and all my skill would try!
But, 'tis in vain. I, in my narrow view
Though there be many, yet can mention few,
And those by families (not single men—
That task's too great for my unskillful pen).

The Nelsons, Digges, Carters, Burwells, Pages,
The Grymes and the Robinsons engages
Respect, and reverence to those names be paid!
Blairs Ludwells, Byrds in the same scale are laid.
Randolphs and Wallers, Harrisons likewise—
These all contend for honors, noble prize.
Willises, Wormeleys, Lewises do run
In honor's path, as loath to be outdone.
The Spotswoods, Berkeleys, Armisteads thither bend
Their steps and for the lovely prize contend.
I hope Virginia hath many more
To me unknown—might lengthen out the score.
As stars of the first magnitude these shine
And, in their several stations, do combine
The great support and ornament to be
Of Britain's first and ancient colony.

[Hansford extends his review of the gentry for another hundred lines, omitted here.]

As merchandise and traffic much improve
A country's wealth, many there be that move
Within that circle and with industry
Themselves enrich, their country's wants supply—
A happy thing (no doubt) to any lands
Where public good and private join their hands.
Merchants of all sorts kindly should be us'd,
And just encouragement to none refus'd.
A government that so their laws contrive
Without dispute will flourish, grow, and thrive.
Virginia many worthy merchants yield:
Booth, Holt and Thurston, with the sprightly Shield
Are all her natives. Doubtless many more
Unknown to me might lengthen out the score.

Thus far I have with pleasure gone; but now
A melancholy broods upon my brow.
For, oh, my country, it would not be right
Nor just for me only to show thy bright
And shining side! I fear thou hast a dark
And gloomy one. Attend thee! Do but hark!
The dice-box rattles; cards on tables flow.
I well remember, fifty years ago
This wretched practice scarcely then was known.
Then if a gentleman had lost a crown

At gleek or at backgammon, 'twere a wonder,
And rumbled through the neighborhood like thunder.
But many now do win and lose pistoles
By fifties—nay, by hundreds. In what shoals
Our gentry to the gaming tables run!
Scoundrels and sharpers—nay, the very scum
Of mankind—joins our gentry, wins their cash.
O countrymen! This surely would abash
Our sleeping sires! Should one of them arise,
How would it shock *him*! How would it surprise
An honorable shade to see his boy
His honor, time, and money thus employ!
How could he bear to hear that Sacred Name
From whose dread presence he so lately came
Profan'd and trifled with, their *frauds* to screen?
Methinks he'd wish his son had never been;
Methinks he'd wish for power to destroy
Such wretches and annihilate his boy!

Pardon such warm expressions from a father.
Who would not choose annihilation rather
Than into everlasting flames be press'd?
Oh, hideous thought! O gamesters, think the rest!

Horse racing and cockfighting do much harm
To some estates; 'tis like a spell or charm.
But would our gentry once be pleased to try
The experiment, they would most certainly
More satisfaction find in one pistole
Laid out in putting one poor boy to school
Than five or six expended in no worse
A way than making up a horse-race purse.
'Tis very true; I know some gentlemen
That secretly do this. Their pleasure, then,
Does far exceed the others; they receive
Comfort from this when trifles them will leave.

A gentleman is placed so that he
In his example cannot neuter be:
He's always doing good or doing harm.
And should not this a thinking man alarm?
If he lives ill, the vulgar will him trace;
They fancy his example theirs will grace.
Many are fond to imitate a man
That is above their class; their little span

Of knowledge they consult not. In the way
Their betters walk, they think they safely may.
Thus, both are wrong but may, perhaps, be lost,
And all God's goodness disappointed, cross'd.
For, sure, His goodness always should be prais'd
By those He hath above the vulgar rais'd.
'Tis most ungrateful not to bless that hand
By which we are plac'd above the crowd to stand.

Contrariwise, when gentry do live well,
Their bright example is a kind of spell
Which does insensibly attract the crowd
To follow them in virtue's pleasant road.
In such a way, who would not take delight
To see gentry and commons both unite?
This would true honor to our gentry bring,
And happiness to all would flow and spring.
We find example is of greater force
Than the most famous clergyman's discourse.
None will deny the assertion to be true:
Example always precept will outdo.

I wish our gentry would consider this;
For, sure, much gaming most destructive is.
Honor it stabs; religion it disgraces;
It hurts our trade, and honesty defaces.
But, what is worse, it so much guilt does bring,
That many times distraction thence does spring.

But now Virginia's grand assembly's met
In solemn manner to consult and treat
Of their king's honor and their country's good.
So Rome's great senate, when that city stood
The world's great mistress, in their capitol
Sat to consult the interest of all
Their citizens both as to war and peace.
Their country's wealth and glory to increase,
Good laws to make, the useless to repeal,
Their country's interest and the public weal
Was still the mark at which those sages aim'd,
And yet, sometimes, their ends were not attain'd.

They bought and bred up slaves as we do now
And yet neglected (or they knew not how)

Those slaves to manage. Sometimes they rebell'd,
Which cost much sweat and blood ere they were quell'd.
The Roman legions they did often face
And sometimes rout them, and their masters chase.
For years together they resistance made
And many cities into ruins laid.
Those people found amongst them now and then
Some that were bold, courageous, able men—
Men that could form designs and act them, too,
With courage and discretion; they could view
Advantages and of them make the most.
The Romans often found this to their cost.
None so near ruin brought their capitol
As their own slaves and one-eyed Hannibal.
The Egyptians a much later instance show:
That nation scarce six hundred years ago
By their Circassian slaves were quite bereft
Of regal powers; for they had nothing left.
Their caliph kill'd, a slave usurp'd the throne;
Their slaves, the Mamelukes, made all their own.
Crown'd with success, they modell'd a new state;
In peace and war, the Mamelukes grew great.
Their caliphs (or successors) far extended
Their fame and grandeur; neither was it ended
In a short time. Their regal power lasted
Above two hundred years, till it was blasted
By Selimus, the son of Bajazett,
The Turkish chief—a warlike prince. But yet
They bravely did their monarchy defend,
Disputing every inch, from end to end.
Egypt hath ever since a province been
Unto the Turks, no regal power seen.
That ancient people, deemed once so wise,
Most other nations now contemn, despise.
Their hardships now are greater from the Turks
Than when they subject were to Mamelukes.
A melancholy scene! May Providence
Virginia still preserve, be her defense!

Our church hath taught us in her litany
To beg deliverance from conspiracy.
This was a gloomy view fifty years past;
May Heaven protect Virginia to the last!
Virginia's senate—here you stand alone.
Your Mother Country will admit of none

In her free air in slavery to be.
In England, all—both white and black—are free.
In other things her parliament's example
May you direct; in this, they are no sample.
They give you no direction how to ward
Off such a blow. Have, therefore, a regard
To your own safeties; ponder well the thing.
Neglect doth many times much danger bring.
I know you are wise; that wisdom then employ
In such a manner that you may enjoy
Safety and peace. They very precious are.
Likewise, of your posterity take care;
They, more than you, in this may be concern'd,
And yet the danger not so well discern'd.
'Tis true Great Britain (next to Heaven) would be
Our best support to succor us if we
Under this great calamity should fall.
But the wide ocean surely bars out all
Present assistance she to us could send.
Our neighbors are but weak to serve that end;
At the same time, Indians may them molest.
Nay, by a war Britain may be distress'd.
Oh, shocking thought! If we don't mend our ways,
Who knows how soon we may see wretched days?

Willing, though weak, I have in this essay
Done my endeavor truly to display
My country's worth in several respects
And not conceal'd some of her defects—
A theme deserving a much abler hand.
But, yet, I hope without offense I stand.
An innocent amusement was my end;
Offence to any I did not intend.
To flatter any was not in my view;
But all that here is said (I think) is true.
For flattery I no occasion have;
No place I seek; no office do I crave.
Interest I cannot have and, sure, ambition
Suits very ill with my obscure condition.
'Tis true, the obscure man may honest be,
And have, and practice, great veracity.
If that be granted, I sit down contented;
'Tis in that light I would be represented.

Farewell, my country! May thy happiness,
Thy glory, goodness, virtue, still increase!

13. George Berkeley, Bishop of Cloyne

On the Prospect of Planting Arts and Learning in America
1752

Best known as the great philosopher of idealism, the Irishman George Berkeley (1685–1753) spent three years in Rhode Island trying to raise money for a college in Bermuda. The project failed, and Berkeley returned to London; not long afterward he was named Bishop of Cloyne, in Ireland. The failure of his American plan did not hinder him from publishing, in 1752, one of the most famous celebrations of New World empire. An earlier version appears in a letter of Berkeley's from 1726, two years before he went to America. It was then titled "America or the Muse's Refuge: A Prophecy."

The Muse, disgusted at an Age and Clime
    Barren of every glorious Theme,
In distant Lands now waits a better Time,
    Producing Subjects worthy Fame:

In happy Climes, where from the genial Sun
    And virgin Earth such Scenes ensue,
The Force of Art by Nature seems outdone,
    And fancied Beauties by the true:

In happy Climes the Seat of Innocence,
    Where Nature guides and Virtue rules,
Where Men shall not impose for Truth and Sense
    The Pedantry of Courts and Schools:

There shall be sung another golden Age,
    The rise of Empire and of Arts,
The Good and Great inspiring epic Rage,
    The wisest Heads and noblest Hearts.

Not such as *Europe* breeds in her decay;
    Such as she bred when fresh and young,
When heav'nly Flame did animate her Clay,
    By future Poets shall be sung.

Westward the Course of Empire takes its Way;
    The four first Acts already past,
A fifth shall close the Drama with the Day;
    Time's noblest offspring is the last.

14. John Dyer

from *The Fleece*
1757

The aptly named Welsh poet John Dyer (1699–1758) has traditionally been known as the author of nature poems, especially "Grongar Hill." As historians have begun to pay more attention to the transformation of culture by imperial commerce, interest has grown in his late work The Fleece. *The poem, nominally a paean to wool, offers a digest of the world from the point of view of a commodity. The concluding section, given here, surveys the globe as a favorable market for the British Empire—prophesying, among other things, the Panama Canal. Its vision of empire and America may be compared to Pope's, above.*

    Happy the voyage, o'er th' Atlantic brine,
By active Raleigh made, and great the joy,
When he discern'd, above the foamy surge,
A rising coast, for future colonies,
Op'ning her bays, and figuring her capes,
Ev'n from the northern tropic to the pole.
No land gives more employment to the loom,
Or kindlier feeds the indigent; no land
With more variety of wealth rewards
The hand of labor: thither, from the wrongs
Of lawless rule, the free-born spirit flies;
Thither affliction, thither poverty,
And arts and sciences: thrice happy clime,
Which Britain makes th' asylum of mankind.

    But joy superior far his bosom warms,
Who views those shores in ev'ry culture dress'd;
With habitations gay, and num'rous towns,
On hill and valley; and his countrymen
Form'd into various states, pow'rful and rich,
In regions far remote: who from our looms
Take largely for themselves, and for those tribes
Of Indians, ancient tenants of the land,

In amity conjoin'd, of civil life
The comforts taught, and various new desires,
Which kindle arts, and occupy the poor,
And spread Britannia's flocks o'er ev'ry dale.

    Ye, who the shuttle cast along the loom,
The silkworm's thread inweaving with the fleece,
Pray for the culture of the Georgian tract,
Nor slight the green savannahs, and the plains
Of Carolina, where thick woods arise
Of mulberries, and in whose water'd fields
Up springs the verdant blade of thirsty rice.
Where are the happy regions, which afford
More implements of commerce, and of wealth?

    Fertile Virginia, like a vig'rous bough,
Which overshades some crystal river, spreads
Her wealthy cultivations wide around,
And, more than many a spacious realm, rewards
The fleecy shuttle: to her growing marts
The Iroquese, Cheroques, and Oubacks, come,
And quit their feath'ry ornaments uncouth,
For woolly garments; and the cheers of life,
The cheers, but not the vices, learn to taste.
Blush, Europeans, whom the circling cup
Of luxury intoxicates; ye routs,
Who, for your crimes, have fled your native land;
And ye voluptuous idle, who, in vain,
Seek easy habitations, void of care:
The sons of nature, with astonishment,
And detestation, mark your evil deeds;
And view, no longer aw'd, your nerveless arms,
Unfit to cultivate Ohio's banks.

    See the bold emigrants of Accadie,
And Massachuset, happy in those arts,
That join the polities of trade and war,
Bearing the palm in either; they appear
Better exemplars; and that hardy crew,
Who, on the frozen beech of Newfoundland,
Hang their white fish amid the parching winds:
The kindly fleece, in webs of Duffield woof,
Their limbs, benumb'd, enfolds with cheerly warmth,
And frize of Cambria, worn by those, who seek,
Through gulphs and dales of Hudson's winding bay,

The beaver's fur, though oft they seek in vain,
While winter's frosty rigor checks approach,
Ev'n in the fiftieth latitude. Say why
(If ye, the travell'd sons of commerce, know),
Wherefore lie bound their rivers, lakes, and dales,
Half the sun's annual course, in chains of ice?
While the Rhine's fertile shore, and Gallic realms,
By the same zone encircled, long enjoy
Warm beams of Phœbus, and, supine, behold
Their plains and hilocks blush with clust'ring vines.

  Must it be ever thus? or may the hand
Of mighty labor drain their gusty lakes,
Enlarge the bright'ning sky, and, peopling, warm
The op'ning vallies, and the yellowing plains?
Or rather shall we burst strong Darien's chain,
Steer our bold fleets between the cloven rocks,
And through the great Pacific ev'ry joy
Of civil life diffuse? Are not her isles
Num'rous and large? Have they not harbours calm,
Inhabitants, and manners? haply, too,
Peculiar sciences, and other forms
Of trade, and useful products, to exchange
For woolly vestures? 'Tis a tedious course
By the Antarctic circle: nor beyond
Those sea-wrapt gardens of the dulcet reed,
Bahama and Caribbee, may be found
Safe mole or harbour, till on Falkland's isle
The standard of Britannia shall arise.

   . . . .

  Rejoice, ye nations, vindicate the sway
Ordain'd for common happiness. Wide, o'er
The globe terraqueous, let Britannia pour
The fruits of plenty from her copious horn.
What can avail to her, whose fertile earth
By ocean's briny waves are circumscrib'd,
The armed host, and murd'ring sword of war,
And conquest o'er her neighbours? She ne'er breaks
Her solemn compacts, in the lust of rule:
Studious of arts and trade, she ne'er disturbs
The holy peace of states. 'Tis her delight
To fold the world with harmony, and spread,
Among the habitations of mankind,
The various wealth of toil, and what her fleece,

To clothe the naked, and her skilful looms,
Peculiar give. Ye too rejoice, ye swains;
Increasing commerce shall reward your cares.
A day will come, if not too deep we drink
The cup, which luxury on careless wealth,
Pernicious gift, bestows; a day will come,
When, through new channels sailing, we shall clothe
The Californian coast, and all the realms
That stretch from Anian's streights to proud Japan;
And the green isles, which on the left arise
Upon the glassy brine, whose various capes
Not yet are figur'd on the sailors chart:
Then ev'ry variation shall be told
Of the magnetic steel; and currents mark'd,
Which drive the heedless vessel from her course.

       That portion too of land, a tract immense,
Beneath th' Antarctic spread, shall then be known,
And new plantations on its coast arise.
Then rigid winter's ice no more shall wound
The only naked animal; but man
With the soft fleece shall ev'ry-where be cloath'd.
Th' exulting muse shall then, in vigor fresh,
Her flight renew. Mean while, with weary wing,
O'er ocean's wave returning, she explores
Siluria's flow'ry vales, her old delight,
The shepherd's haunts, where the first springs arise
Of Britain's happy trade, now spreading wide,
Wide as the Atlantic and Pacific seas,
Or as air's vital fluid o'er the globe.

15. James Grainger

from *The Sugar-Cane*
1764

A rather unsuccessful London physician and a member of the literary circle of Dr. Samuel Johnson, James Grainger (1721?–66) left England in 1759 as a paid attendant to a wealthy former pupil with estates in the West Indies. While there, he invested his meager savings in slaves. He also composed his poem on the cultivation of sugar. It is a georgic: an agricultural poem, in this case with an instructional program for those interested in the arts of running a sugar plantation. (Similar

poems exist for other staples of colonial agriculture, such as indigo.) On his return,
he read the poem to Dr. Johnson and other London wits; when he arrived at the
line, "Say, shall I sing of rats?" Johnson thundered, "No!" For a poetic response to
Grainger's georgic, see the excerpt from the anonymous Jamaica, *in selection 24*
below.

[OPENING STATEMENT OF THEME]

What soil the cane affects; what care demands;
Beneath what signs to plant; what ills await;
How the hot nectar best to crystallize;
And Afric's sable progeny to treat:
A Muse, that long hath wander'd in the groves
Of myrtle-indolence, attempts to sing.

[BOOK IV]

Genius of Afric! whether thou bestrid'st
The cattled elephant; or at the source
(While howls the desert fearfully around)
Of thine own Niger, sadly thou reclin'st,
Thy temples shaded by the trem'lous palm,
Or quick papaw, whose top is necklac'd round
With numerous rows of party-colour'd fruit:
Or hear'st thou rather from the rocky banks
Of Rio Grande, or black Sanaga?
Where dauntless thou the headlong torrent brav'st
In search of gold, to brede thy woolly locks,
Or with bright ringlets ornament thine ears,
Thine arms and ankles: O attend my song.
A Muse that pities thy distressful state;
Who sees, with grief, thy sons in fetters bound;
Who wishes freedom to the race of man;
Thy nod assenting craves: dread Genius, come!
        Yet vain thy presence, vain thy favouring nod;
Unless once more the Muses, that erewhile
Upheld me fainting in my past career,
Through Caribbee's cane-isles; kind condescend
To guide my footsteps, through parch'd Libya's wilds,
And bind my sun-burnt brow with other bays,
Than ever deck'd the sylvan bard before.

        . . . .

        In mind and aptitude for useful toil,
The Negroes differ: Muse that difference sing.

Whether to wield the hoe, or guide the plane;
Or for domestic uses thou intend'st
The sunny Libyan: from what clime they spring,
It not imports; if strength and youth be theirs.

Yet those from Congo's wide-extended plains,
Through which the long Zaire winds with crystal stream,
Where lavish Nature sends indulgent forth
Fruits of high flavour, and spontaneous seeds
Of bland nutritious quality, ill bear
The toilsome field; but boast a docile mind,
And happiness of features. These, with care,
Be taught each nice mechanic art: or trained
To household offices: their ductile souls
Will all thy care, and all thy gold repay.

But, if the labours of the field demand
Thy chief attention; and th' ambrosial cane
Thou long'st to see, with spiry frequence, shade
Many an acre: planter, choose the slave,
Who sails from barren climes; where Want alone,
Offspring of rude Necessity, compels
The sturdy native, or to plant the soil,
Or stem vast rivers for his daily food.

Such are the children of the Golden Coast;
Such the Papaws, of Negroes far the best:
And such the num'rous tribes that skirt the shore,
From rapid Volta to the distant Rey.
But, planter, from what coast soe'er they sail,
Buy not the old: they ever sullen prove;
With heart-felt anguish, they lament their home,
They will not, cannot work; they never learn
Thy native language; they are prone to ails:
And oft by suicide their being end.

Must thou from Afric reinforce thy gang? —
Let health and youth their every sinew firm;
Clear roll their ample eye; their tongue be red:
Broad swell their chest; their shoulders wide expand;
Not prominent their belly; clean and strong
Their thighs and legs, in just proportion rise.
Such soon will brave the fervors of the clime;
And free from ails, that kill thy Negro-train,
An useful servitude will long support.

Yet, if thine own, thy children's life, be dear;
Buy not a Cormantee, though healthy, young.
Of breed too generous for the servile field;
They, born to freedom, in their native land,

Choose death before dishonourable bonds:
Or, fir'd with vengeance, at the midnight hour,
Sudden they seize thine unsuspecting watch,
And thine own poniard bury in thy breast.
  At home the men, in many a sylvan realm,
Their rank tobacco, charm of sauntering mines,
From clayey tubes inhale; or, vacant, beat
For prey the forest; or, in war's dread ranks,
Their country's foes affront: while, in the field,
Their wives plant rice, or yams, or lofty maize,
Fell hunger to repel. Be these thy choice:
They, hardy, with the labours of the cane
Soon grow familiar: while unusual toil,
And new severities their husbands kill.
  The slaves from Minnah are of stubborn breed:
But, when the bill, or hammer, they affect,
They soon perfection reach. But fly, with care,
The Moco nation; they themselves destroy.
Worms lurk in all: yet pronest they to worms,
Who from Mundingo sail. When therefore such
Thou buy'st, for sturdy and laborious they,
Straight let some learned leach strong med'cines give,
Till food and climate both familiar grow.
Thus, though from rise to set, in Phoebus' eye,
They toil, unceasing; yet, at night, they'll sleep,
Lapp'd in Elysium; and, each day, at dawn,
Spring from their couch, as blithesome as the Sun.
  One precept more, it much imports to know.
The Blacks, who drink the Quanza's lucid stream,
Fed by ten thousand springs, are prone to bloat,
Whether at home or in these ocean-isles:
And though nice art the water may subdue,
Yet many die; and few, for many a year,
Just strength attain to labour for their lord.
  Would'st thou secure thine Ethiop from these ails,
Which change of climate, change of waters breed,
And food unusual? let Machaon[47] draw
From each some blood, as age and sex require;
And well with vervain, well with sempre-vive,
Unload their bowels.—These, in every hedge,
Spontaneous grow.—Nor will it not conduce
To give what chymists, in mysterious phrase,
Term the white eagle; deadly foe to worms.

---

47. Machaon: physician in *The Iliad*.

But chief do thou, my friend, with hearty food,
Yet easy of digestion, likest that
Which they at home regal'd on; renovate
Their sea-worn appetites. Let gentle work,
Or rather playful exercise, amuse
The novel gang: and far be angry words;
Far pond'rous chains; and far disheart'ning blows.
From fruits restrain their eagerness; yet if
The acajou, haply, in thy garden bloom,
With cherries, or of white or purple hue,
Thrice wholesome fruit in this relaxing clime!
Safely thou may'st their appetite indulge.
Their arid skins will plump, their features shine:
No rheums, no dysenteric ails torment:
The thirsty hydrops flies.—'Tis even averr'd,
(Ah, did experience sanctify the fact,
How many Lybians now would dig the soil,
Who pine in hourly agonies away!)
This pleasing fruit, if turtle join its aid,
Removes that worst of ails, disgrace of art,
The loathsome leprosy's infectious bane.

      There are, the Muse hath oft abhorrent seen,
Who swallow dirt; (so the chlorotic fair
Oft chalk prefer to the most poignant cates).[48]
Such dropsy bloats, and to sure death consigns;
Unless restrain'd from this unwholesome food,
By soothing words, by menaces, by blows:
Nor yet will threats, or blows, or soothing words,
Perfect their cure; unless thou, Paean, deign'st
By med'cines's pow'r their cravings to subdue.

      To easy labour first inure thy slaves;
Extremes are dangerous. With industrious search,
Let them fit grassy provender collect
For thy keen stomach'd herds.—But when the Earth
Hath made her annual progress round the Sun,
What time the conch or bell resounds, they may
All to the cane-ground, with thy gang, repair.

      Nor, Negro, at thy destiny repine,
Though doom'd to toil from dawn to setting Sun.
How far more pleasant is thy rural task,
Than theirs who sweat, sequester'd from the day,
In dark tartarean caves, sunk far beneath
The Earth's dark surface; where sulphureous flames,

48. cates: victuals.

Oft from their vapoury prisons bursting wild,
To dire explosion give the cavern'd deep,
And in dread ruin all its inmates whelm?—
Nor fateful only is the bursting flame;
The exhalations of the deep-dug mine,
Though slow, shake from their wings as sure a death.
With what intense severity of pain
Hath the afflicted Muse, in Scotia, seen
The miners rack'd; who toil for fatal lead?
What cramps, what palsies shake their feeble limbs,
Who on the margin of the rocky Drave,
Trace silver's fluent ore? Yet white men these!
      How far more happy ye, than those poor slaves,
Who, whilom, under native, gracious chiefs,
Incas and emperors, long time enjoy'd
Mild government, with every sweet of life,
In blissful climates? See them dragg'd in chains,
By proud insulting tyrants, to the mines
Which once they call'd their own, and then despis'd!
See, in the mineral bosom of their land,
How hard they toil! how soon their youthful limbs
Feel the decrepitude of age? how soon
Their teeth desert their sockets! and how soon
Shaking paralysis unstrings their frame!
Yet scarce, even then, are they allow'd to view
The glorious god of day, of whom they beg,
With earnest hourly supplications, death;
Yet death slow comes, to torture them the more!
      With these compar'd, ye sons of Afric, say,
How far more happy is your lot? Bland health,
Of ardent eye, and limb robust, attends
Your custom'd labour; and, should sickness seize,
With what solicitude are ye not nurs'd!
Ye Negroes, then, your pleasing task pursue;
And, by your toil, deserve your master's care.

16. Henry Timberlake

"A Translation of the War-Song," from *Memoirs of Lieutenant Henry Timberlake* 1765

This is one of the earliest attempts to render Indian song or oratory as English verse. It appears in a long passage of vivid ethnographic description during Timberlake's narrative of treaty negotiations between the British and the Cherokees on the far Tennessee frontier in the winter of 1761–62. "They have likewise a sort of loose poetry," writes Timberlake, "as the war-songs, love-songs, &c. Of the latter many contain no more than that the young man loves the young woman, and will be uneasy, according to her own expression, if he does not obtain her. Of the former I shall present the following specimen, without the original in Cherokee, on account of the expletive syllables, merely introduced for the music, and not the sense, just like the toldederols of many old English songs."

Lieutenant Henry Timberlake (1730–65), a Virginian, had volunteered to serve as a good faith hostage during the negotiations, and lived with the Cherokees for three months. Later, on two separate occasions, he accompanied Cherokees to England as an intermediary. On the edge of poverty, he wrote his gripping Memoirs *shortly before his death. For the war song given here, Timberlake must have relied for the content of this translation on one of his interpreters. The footnotes are Timberlake's.*

    Caw waw noo dee, &c.
Where'er the earth's enlighten'd by the sun,
Moon shines by night, grass grows, or waters run,
Be't known that we are going, like men, afar,
In hostile fields to wage destructive war;
Like men we go, to meet our country's foes,
Who, woman-like, shall fly our dreaded blows;
Yes, as a woman, who beholds a snake,
In gaudy horror, glisten thro' the brake,
Starts trembling back, and stares with wild surprize,
Or pale thro' fear, unconscious, panting, flies.
[49] Just so these foes, more tim'rous than the hind,
Shall leave their arms and only cloaths behind;

---

49. As the Indians fight naked, the vanquished are constrained to endure the rigours of the weather in their flight, and live upon roots and fruit, as they throw down their arms to accelerate their flight thro' the woods.

"*The Three Cherokees, came over from the head of the River Savanna to London, 1762.*"

Pinch'd by each blast, by ev'ry thicket torn,
Run back to their own nation, now its scorn:
Or in the winter, when the barren wood
Denies their gnawing entrails nature's food,
Let them sit down, from friends and country far,
And wish, with tears, they ne'er had come to war.

[50] We'll leave our clubs, dew'd with their country show'rs,
And, if they dare to bring them back to our's,
Their painted scalps shall be a step to fame,
And grace our own and glorious country's name.
Or if we warriors spare the yielding foe,
Torments at home the wretch must undergo.[51]
But when we go, who knows which shall return,
When growing dangers rise with each new morn?
Farewell, ye little ones, yet tender wives,
For you alone we would conserve our lives!
But cease to mourn, 'tis unavailing pain,
If not fore-doom'd, we soon shall meet again.
But, O ye friends! in case your comrades fall,
Think that on you our deaths for vengeance call;

50. It is the custom of the Indians, to leave a club, something of the form of a cricket-bat, but with their warlike exploits engraved on it, in their enemy's country, and the enemy accepts the defiance, by bringing this back to their country.
51. The prisoners of war are generally tortured by the women, at the party's return, to revenge the death of those that have perished by the wretch's countrymen. This savage custom has been so much mitigated of late, that the prisoners were only compelled to marry, and then generally allowed all the privileges of the natives. This lenity, however, has been a detriment to the nation; for many of these returning to their countrymen, have made them acquainted with the country-passes, weakness, and haunts of the Cherokees; besides that it gave the enemy greater courage to fight against them.

With uprais'd tommahawkes pursue our blood,
And stain, with hostile streams, the conscious wood,
That pointing enemies may never tell
The boasted place where we, their victims, fell.[52]

17. Milcah Martha Moore

The Female Patriots. Addressed to the Daughters of Liberty in America
1768

The following poem appeared in the Pennsylvania Chronicle *late in 1769. Little is known about its author, Milcah Martha Moore (1740–1829). She and her husband, Dr. Charles Moore, were not admitted to the Quaker fellowship because they were first cousins, but they remained loyal to Quakerism. They retreated to the country outside of Philadelphia at the Revolution. There, Milcah Moore taught school, and in 1787 published a compilation called* Miscellanies, Moral and Instructive.

Since the men, from a party or fear of a frown,
Are kept by a sugar-plum quietly down,
Supinely asleep—and depriv'd of their sight,
Are stripp'd of their freedom, and robb'd of their right;
If the sons, so degenerate! the blessings despise,
Let the Daughters of Liberty nobly arise;
And though we've no voice but a negative here,
The use of the taxables, let us forbear:—
(Then merchants import till your stores are all full,
May the buyers be few, and your traffic be dull!)
Stand firmly resolv'd, and bid Grenville to see,
That rather than freedom we part with our tea,
And well as we love the dear draught when a-dry,
As American Patriots our taste we deny—
Pennsylvania's gay meadows can richly afford
To pamper our fancy or furnish our board;
And paper sufficient at home still we have,
To assure the wiseacre, we will not sign slave;
When this homespun shall fail, to remonstrate our grief,
We can speak viva voce, or scratch on a leaf;

---

52. Their custom is generally to engrave their victory on some neighbouring tree, or set up some token of it near the field of battle; to this their enemies are here supposed to point to, as boasting their victory over them, and the slaughter that they made.

Refuse all their colors, though richest of dye,
When the juice of a berry our paint can supply,
To humor our fancy—and as for our houses,
They'll do without painting as well as our spouses;
While to keep out the cold of a keen winter morn,
We can screen the north-west with a well polished horn;
And trust me a woman, by honest invention,
Might give this state-doctor a dose of prevention.
        Joining mutual in this—and but small as it seems,
We may jostle a Grenville, and puzzle his schemes;
But a motive more worthy our patriot pen,
Thus acting—we point out their duty to men;
And should the bound-pensioners tell us to hush,
We can throw back the satire, by biding them blush.

18. Mary Nelson

Forty Shillings Reward
1769

Like Milcah Moore's patriot poem, Mary Nelson's appeared in the Pennsylvania
Chronicle *in 1769. Nelson's, however, was a paid advertisement, and ran in two
issues—with what result no one knows.*

Last Wednesday morn, at break of day,
From Philadelphia run away,
An Irish man, nam'd John M'Keoghn,
To fraud and imposition prone;
About five feet five inches high,
Can curse and swear as well as lie;
How old he is I can't engage,
But forty-five is near his age;
He came (as all reports agree)
From Belfast town in sixty-three,
On board the Culloden, a ship
Commanded by M'Lean that trip;
Speaks like a Scotchman, very broad,
Is round shoulder'd, and meagre jaw'd;
Has thick short hair, of sandy hue,
Breeches and hose of maz'reen blue;

Of lightish cloth an outside vest,
In which he commonly is dress'd;
Inside of which two more I've seen,
One flannel, th'other coarse nankeen.
He stole, and from my house conven'd,
A man's blue coat, of broadcloth made;
A grey great coat, of bearskin stuff,
(Nor had the villain yet enough;)
Some chintz (the ground was pompadour)
I lately purchas'd in a store,
Besides a pair of blue ribb'd hose,
Which he has on as I suppose.
He oft in conversation chatters,
Of scripture and religious matters,
And fain would to the world impart,
That virtue lodges in his heart;
But take the rogue from stem to stern,
The hypocrite you'll soon discern,
And find (though his deportment's civil)
A saint without, within a devil.
Whoe'er secures said John M'Keoghn,
(Provided I should get my own)
Shall have from me, in cash paid down,
Five dollar-bills, and half-a-crown.

The SPEECH of DEATH
TO
LEVI AMES.

Who was Executed on *Boston*-Neck, *October* 21, 1773, for the Crime of Burglary.

I DEATH, Poor *Ames*, pronounce your Fate,
  Thus grining grimly through your Grate.
Remember all the Crimes you've done,
And think how early you begun.
Loft in the grand Apoftacy,
You were at firft condemn'd to die ;
In adding Guilt you ftill went on :
I doubly claim you for my own.
How often you the Sabbath broke !
GOD's Name in vain how often took !
A filthy Drunkard you have been,
And led your Life with the Unclean :
No Thoughts of GOD you ever chofe,
But chas'd them from you when they rofe :
In Idlenefs you did proceed,
And took fmall pains to learn to read :
With vile Companions, your Delight,
You often fpent the guilty Night :
Your Lips fcarce ever breath'd a Prayer,
You gave your Tongue to curfe and fwear :
You've been to all your Friends a Grief,
And from your Infancy a Thief ;
You know the Truth of what I tell,
No Goods were fafe that you could fteal ;
How many Doors you've open broke !
And windows fcal'd, and Money took :
Round Houfes you all Day have been,
To fpy a Place to enter in ;
Thence in the Night, all dark and late,
You've ftole their Goods and Gold and Plate.
Imprifon'd, whip'd, yet you proceed,
The Life you led you ftill would lead.
Your Confcience cry'd, " you'll be undone."—
You ftifl'd Confcience and went on.
And now, behold ! my poifon'd Dart,
I point directly at your Heart.

The Halter and the Gallows view,
Death and Damnation is your due.
Darknefs, and Horror, Fire, and Chains;
Almighty Wrath, and endlefs Pains.
—But lo ! I fee the Preacher come,
Salvation fpeaks——I muft be dumb.

  The Preacher fpeaks—Behold I come,
A voice from Heaven to call you home.
Though you the chief of Sinners were,
I bring the Gofpel ; don't Defpair.
Nor death, nor Hell, fhall do you hurt,
Be JESUS only your Support.
To you he holds His Righteoufnefs,
He bled and dy'd to buy your Peace.
Pardon and Life are His to give,
'Tis thine, Poor Sinner, to believe.
Let Death in all it's Dread appear,
Though public Execution's near,
Of Wrath Divine He bore the Weight,
He fuffer'd too without the Gate,
He betwixt Heaven and Earth was hung,
He conquer'd Hell, and death unftung.

  Now let the Guilty fee and hear,
And all the Congregation fear ;
This Spectacle your Hearts imprefs,
And do no more fuch Wickednefs ;
Hear fuch important Truths as thefe,
Ruin advances by Degrees :
The youth with leffer Crimes begins,
And then proceeds to groffer Sins,
From Step to Step he travels on,
And fees himfelf at once undone :
Surpriz'd ! unthought on ! finds his Fate,
His Ruin final, and compleat.

"The Speech of Death to Levi Ames," 1773. A popular broadside poem commemorating an execution.

19. Phillis Wheatley

Phillis Wheatley (1754?–84) wrote the first of these poems, on Harvard, when she was in her early teens—the age at which white boys then attended college. Born in the Gambia-Senegal region of Africa, she had been taken to Boston in 1761, when she was about seven. There she was bought by John Wheatley, a tailor, as an attendant for his wife. The slave girl mastered English precociously, and began publishing poems in 1767. She achieved some public notice following her broadside elegy on the death of George Whitefield, the English evangelist. Several other broadside elegies followed, and while in England in 1773 she published Poems on Various Subjects—*though not without certification by a committee of white men who testified that she could actually write. At the end of that year she was freed. In 1778 she married John Peters, a freeman, but the couple lived in poverty. All three of their children died in infancy. When she died in December of 1784, Phillis Wheatley was working in a cheap boardinghouse.*

Some critics believe her embrace of English culture to be ironic, speaking of Wheatley's "subtle war" against a slaveowning public. For others, such a reading may seem wishful. Wheatley's argument in "On Being Brought from Africa to America" proceeds without visible sign of hesitation. Her symbolism of light and dark is even more pervasive than in most white poets of the time. And in the poem to the Earl of Dartmouth, who had just been named Secretary of State for the colonies, she even uses slavery as a metaphor for England's control of its colonies. It does seem fair to say that her poetry is marked by tensions between the desire to find a public role as an African woman and her identification with white Christendom. "To the University of Cambridge" and "On Recollection," two seldom read Wheatley poems, are more than usually explicit about that tension.

To the University of Cambridge, in New England
1767, published 1773

While an intrinsic ardor prompts to write,
The muses promise to assist my pen;
'Twas not long since I left my native shore
The land of errors, and *Egyptian* gloom:
Father of mercy, It was thy gracious hand
Brought me in safety from those dark abodes.

Students, to you 'tis giv'n to scan the heights
Above, to traverse the ethereal space,

And mark the systems of revolving worlds.
Still more, ye sons of science ye receive
The blissful news by messengers from heav'n,
How *Jesus'* blood for your redemption flows.
See him with hands out-stretcht upon the cross;
Immense compassion in his bosom glows;
He hears revilers, nor resents their scorn:
What matchless mercy in the Son of God!
When the whole human race by sin had fall'n,
He deign'd to die that they might rise again,
And share with him in the sublimest skies,
Life without death, and glory without end.

     Improve your privileges while they stay,
Ye pupils, and each hour redeem, that bears
Or good or bad report of you to heav'n.
Let sin, that baneful evil to the soul,
By you be shunn'd, nor once remit your guard;
Suppress the deadly serpent in its egg.[53]
Ye blooming plants of human race divine,
An *Ethiop* tells you 'tis your greatest foe;
Its transient sweetness turns to endless pain,
And in immense perdition sinks the soul.

On Being Brought from Africa to America
1768

'Twas mercy brought me from my *Pagan* land,
Taught my benighted soul to understand
That there's a God, that there's a *Saviour* too:
Once I redemption neither sought nor knew.
Some view our sable race with scornful eye,
"Their colour is a diabolic die."
Remember, *Christians*, *Negros*, black as *Cain*,
May be refin'd, and join th' angelic train.

---

53. In one variant of the poem, this line reads, "Suppress the
sable monster in its growth."

Phillis Wheatley, from the 1773 edition of her Poems.

On Recollection
1771

     Mneme begin. Inspire, ye sacred nine,
Your vent'rous *Afric* in her great design.
Mneme, immortal pow'r, I trace thy spring:
Assist my strains, while I thy glories sing:
The acts of long departed years, by thee
Recover'd, in due order rang'd we see:
Thy pow'r the long-forgotten calls from night,
That sweetly plays before the *fancy's* sight.

     Mneme in our nocturnal visions pours
The ample treasure of her secret stores;
Swift from above she wings her silent flight
Through *Phœbe's* realms, fair regent of the night;
And, in her pomp of images display'd,
To the high-raptur'd poet gives her aid,

Through the unbounded regions of the mind,
Diffusing light celestial and refin'd.
The heavenly *phantom* paints the actions done
By ev'ry tribe beneath the rolling sun.

      Mneme, enthron'd within the human breast,
Has vice condemn'd, and ev'ry virtue blest.
How sweet the sound when we her plaudit hear?
Sweeter than music to the ravish'd ear,
Sweeter than *Maro's*[54] entertaining strains
Resounding through the groves, and hills, and plains.
But how is *Mneme* dreaded by the race,
Who scorn her warnings, and despise her grace?
By her unveil'd ear horrid crime appears,
Her awful hand a cup of wormwood bears.
Days, years, mispent, O what a hell of woe!
Hers the worst tortures that our souls can know.

      Now eighteen years their destin'd course have run,
In fast succession round the central sun.
How did the follies of that period pass
Unnotic'd, but behold them writ in brass!
In Recollection see them fresh return,
And sure 'tis mine to be asham'd, and mourn.

      O *Virtue*, smiling in immortal green,
Do thou exert thy pow'r, and change the scene;
Be thine employ to guide my future days,
And mine to pay the tribute of my praise.

      Of *Recollection* such the pow'r enthron'd
In ev'ry breast, and thus her pow'r is own'd.
The wretch, who dar'd the vengeance of the skies,
At last awakes in horror and surprize,
By her alarm'd, he sees impending fate,
He howls in anguish, and repents too late.
But O! what peace, what joys are hers t' impart
To ev'ry holy, ev'ry upright heart!
Thrice blest the man, who, in her sacred shrine,
Feels himself shelter'd from the wrath divine!

54. *Maro's*: Virgil's.

To the Right Honorable William, Earl of Dartmouth
1772

Hail, happy day, when, smiling like the morn,
Fair *Freedom* rose *New-England* to adorn:
The northern clime beneath her genial ray,
Dartmouth, congratulates thy blissful sway:
Elate with hope her race no longer mourns,
Each soul expands, each grateful bosom burns,
While in thine hand with pleasure we behold
The silken reins, and *Freedom's* charms unfold.
Long lost to realms beneath the northern skies
She shines supreme, while hated *Faction* dies:
Soon as appear'd the *Goddess* long desir'd,
Sick at the view, he[55] languish'd and expir'd;
Thus from the splendors of the morning light
The owl in sadness seeks the caves of night.

No more, *America*, in mournful strain
Of wrongs, and grievance unredress'd complain,
No longer shall thou dread the iron chain,
Which wanton *Tyranny* with lawless hand
Had made, and with it meant t'enslave the land.

Should you, my lord, while you peruse my song,
Wonder from whence my love of *Freedom* sprung,
Whence flow these wishes for the common good,
By feeling hearts alone best understood,
I, young in life, by seeming cruel fate
Was snatch'd from *Afric's* fancy'd happy seat:
What pangs excruciating must molest,
What sorrows labour in my parent's breast?
Steel'd was that soul and by no misery mov'd
That from a father seiz'd his babe belov'd:
Such, such my case. And can I then but pray
Others may never feel tyrannic sway?

For favours past, great Sir, our thanks are due,
And thee we ask thy favours to renew,

---

55. he: i.e., *Faction*; the 1773 *Poems* reads "she," apparently a mistake; the text in these lines follows the version published in the *New-York Journal*, June 3, 1773, though otherwise the *Poems* version is taken as Wheatley's preference.

since in thy pow'r, as in thy will before,
To sooth the griefs, which thou did'st once deplore.
May heav'nly grace the sacred sanction give
To all thy works, and thou for ever live
Not only on the wings of fleeting *Fame,*
Though praise immortal crowns the patriot's name,
But to conduct to heav'ns refulgent fane
May fiery coursers sweep th' ethereal plain,
And bear thee upwards to that blest abode,
Where, like the prophet, thou shalt find thy God.

20. attr. Ned Botwood

Hot Stuff
1759

This version of the poem—there are many—comes from Rivington's New-York
Gazetteer, May 5, 1774. *A note following the poem says that the author was a
member of the British-American expedition against Quebec in 1759, which was to
decide the balance between the French and British empires in the New World.
General Wolfe, commander of the English forces, became a hero throughout
Anglo-America after he died outside of Quebec shortly before the English victory.
According to the* Gazetteer, *Ned Botwood also died in the battle.*

[TUNE, LILIES OF FRANCE]

Come, each death-doing dog who dare venture his neck,
Come follow the Hero that goes to Quebec;
Jump aboard of the transports, and loose every sail,
Pay your debts at the tavern by giving leg-bail;
And ye that love fighting, shall soon have enough:
Wolf commands us, my boys, we will give them Hot Stuff.
        Up the River St. Lawrence our troops shall advance;
To the Grenadier's March we will teach them to dance:
Cape-Breton we have taken, and next we will try
At their capital, to give them another black eye.
Vaudreuil, 'tis in vain ye pretend to look gruff,
Those are coming who know how to give you Hot Stuff.
        With powder in his periwig, and snuff in his nose,
Monsieur will run down our descent to oppose;
And the Indians will come; but the light infantry
Will soon oblige them to betake to a tree.

"Quebec, the Capital of New-France."

From such rascals as these may we fear a rebuff?
Advance, Grenadiers, and let fly your Hot Stuff.
　　　　When the forty-seventh regiment is dashing ashore,
While bullets are whistling and cannons do roar,
Says Montcalm, Those are Shirley's, I know the lappells;
You lie, says Ned Botwood, we belong to Lascelles:
Tho' our cloathing is changed, yet we scorn a powder puff,
So at you, ye B———s, here's give you Hot Stuff.
　　　　With Monckton and Townshend, those brave brigadiers,
I think we shall soon knock the town 'bout their ears;
And when we have done with the mortars and guns,
If you please, madam Abbess,—a word with your Nuns;
Each soldier shall enter the Convent in buff,
And then, never fear us,—we will give them Hot Stuff.

21. Anonymous

On the Snake Depicted at the Head of Some American Newspapers
1774

This satire of Franklin's popular "Join or Die" cartoon appeared in Rivington's
New York Gazetteer *in August of 1774. It invokes Genesis 3:15, in which God,
having expelled Adam and Eve from Eden, predicts revenge to the tempter snake:
"And I will put enmity between thee and the woman, and between thy seed and
her seed; it shall bruise thy head, and thou shalt bruise his heel."*

Ye sons of Sedition, how comes it to pass
That America's typ'd by a Snake—in the grass?
Don't you think 'tis a scandalous, saucy reflection,
That merits the soundest, severest correction?
New-England's the Head, too;—New-England's abus'd;
For the Head of the Serpent we know should be bruis'd!

22. Hannah Griffitts

On Reading Some Paragraphs
in 'The Crisis,' April '77
1777

> *The following satire of Thomas Paine, by the Philadelphian Hannah Griffitts*
> *(1727–1817) bears her customary pseudonym, "Fidelia." Although she was a poor,*
> *single woman, Griffitts belonged to a Philadelphia network of women writers,*
> *most of whom belonged to the colonial elite, such as Elizabeth Graeme Fergusson*
> *(see selection 29 below).*

Pane—Though thy tongue may now run glibber,
     Warm'd with thy independent glow,
Thou art indeed the coldest fibber,
     I ever knew, or wish to know.
Here page and page, even num'rous pages,
     Are void of breeding, sense or truth;
I hope thou don't receive thy wages,
     As tutor to our rising youth.

Of female manners, never scribble,
     Nor with thy rudeness wound our ear;
Howe'er thy trimming pen may quibble,
     The delicate is "not thy sphere."

And now, to prove how false thy stories,
     By facts which won't admit a doubt,
Know there are "conscientious tories,"
     And one poor whig, at least, without.

Wilt thou permit the muse to mention
     A whisper, circulated round;
Let Howe increase the scribbler's pension,
     No more will Pane a whig be found;

For not from principle, but lucre,
     He gains his bread from out the fire;
Let court and congress both stand neuter,
     And the poor creature must expire.

                                        Fidelia

23. Timothy Dwight

Columbia
1777

*On Dwight's life see the headnote to selection 5 above. Dwight's major poems—
the epic* Conquest of Canaan *(1785), the georgic* Greenfield Hill *(1787, published
1794), and the mock-epic* Triumph of Infidelity *(1788) are ambitious surveys of the
age in larger neoclassical genres. The* Conquest of Canaan *casts the Biblical story
in eleven books of English verse, with strong overtones of Washington's struggle
against the British.* Greenfield Hill, *modeled on Denham's* Cooper's Hill, *surveys a
scenic countryside from its past, including the war against the Pequot Indians, to
the future, in a concluding vision of "the Future Happiness of America." The*
Triumph of Infidelity *begins ironically, with Satan en route across the Atlantic,
celebrating the advance of universalism and deism. Its hostility to secular visions of
man and history expresses Dwight's fusion of Calvinist and republican thought as
he entered his Federalist, even reactionary period. "Columbia," however, is written
at the height of his optimism for a new order.*

The queen of the world, and child of the skies!
Thy genius commands thee; with rapture behold,
While ages on ages thy splendors unfold.
Thy reign is the last, and the noblest of time,
Most fruitful thy soil, most inviting thy clime;
Let the crimes of the east ne'er encrimson thy name.
Be freedom, and science, and virtue, thy fame.

To conquest, and slaughter, let Europe aspire;
Whelm nations in blood, and wrap cities in fire;
Thy heroes the rights of mankind shall defend,
And triumph pursue them, and glory attend.
A world is thy realm: for a world be thy laws,
Enlarg'd as thine empire, and just as thy cause;
On Freedom's broad basis, that empire shall rise,
Extend with the main, and dissolve with the skies.
Fair Science her gates to thy sons shall unbar,
And the east see thy morn hide the beams of her star.
New bards and new sages, unrival'd shall soar
To fame, unextinguish'd, when time is no more;
To fame, the last refuge of virtue design'd,
Shall fly from all nations the best of mankind;

"American Triumphant and Britannia in Distress." From a 1782 almanac. America invites the commerce of all nations.

Here, grateful to heaven, with transport shall bring
Their incense, more fragrant than odours of spring.

Nor less shall thy fair ones to glory ascend,
And Genius and Beauty in harmony blend;
The graces of form shall awake pure desire,
And the charms of the soul ever cherish the fire;
Their sweetness unmingled, their manners refin'd
And virtue's bright image, instamp'd on the mind,
With peace, and soft rapture, shall teach life to glow,
And light up a smile in the aspect of woe.

Thy fleets to all regions thy pow'r shall display,
The nations admire, and the ocean obey;
Each shore to thy glory its tribute unfold,
And the east and the south yield their spices and gold.
As the day-spring unbounded, thy splendor shall flow,
And earth's little kingdoms before thee shall bow,

While the ensigns of union, in triumph unfurl'd,
Hush the tumult of war, and give peace to the world.

Thus, as down a lone valley, with cedars o'erspread,
From war's dread confusion I pensively stray'd—
The gloom from the face of fair heav'n retir'd;
The winds ceas'd to murmur; the thunders expir'd;
Perfumes, as of Eden, flow'd sweetly along,
And a voice, as of angels, enchantingly sung;
"Columbia, Columbia, to glory arise,
The queen of the world, and the child of the skies."

24. Anonymous

from *Jamaica, a Poem in Three Parts* 1777

The author of Jamaica *inserts this meditation on his muse apparently as a response to poems such as James Grainger's* The Sugar-Cane, *in selection 15 above. A shorter poem appended to* Jamaica *describes the speaker's nightmares and daily unease over the impending crisis of slave society.*

Here could I sing what soils and seasons suit,
Inform the tap'ring arrow how to shoot;
Under what signs to plant the mother cane,
What rums and sugars bring the planter gain;
Teach stubborn oxen in the wain to toil,
And all the culture of a sugar soil:
Th' ungrateful task a British Muse disdains,
Lo! tortures, racks, whips, famine, gibbets, chains,
Rise on my mind, appal my tear-stain'd eye,
Attract my rage, and draw a soul-felt sigh;
I blush, I shudder at the bloody theme,
And scorn on woe to build a baseless fame.

25. The Rector of St. John's, Nevis

The Field Negroe; or the Effect of Civilization 1783

This and several other interesting poems appear in the anonymous Poems, on Subjects Arising in England and the West Indies. *In one footnote, the author mentions a Mr. Powers as "a predecessor of mine in the rectory of St. John's," but surviving records of the parish identify neither the poet nor Mr. Powers. They do place a John Bowen in the rectory in 1767, and a William Jones by 1792. Like* The Sugar-Cane *and so many other works of the period, "The Field Negroe" is intended both as art and as instruction; it introduces vocabulary and information wherever possible, and comes with ample footnotes, only a selection of which are included here.*

Say, lovely muse, what thoughts compel
        Thy poet's partial fire
To sound, uncouth, th'Indian shell,
        Or strike the savage lyre?

From your own lov'd Parnassus smile,
        Ye muses, on my strain;
'Tis you that point a distant isle
        Beyond th' Atlantic main.

And though no laurels there succeed,
        To grace a poet's bier,
My hands, perhaps, shall cull a meed
        From off the prickly pear.

High on my brows this shrub shall stand,
        My humble muse to suit,
And keep, at once, the critic's hand
        From poetry and fruit.

O thither let my footsteps rove,
        Their own peculiar way;
Or lull me in an orange grove,
        Beneath a golden ray.

O, fancy, let me view the toil,
        When drooping, faint with pain,

The panting negroe digs the soil
  Of sugar's sweet domain.

And now I see thy *canes* arise,
  Like blades of springing corn;
And now thy *cocoas* meet my eyes,
  High waving as in scorn.

Here stand the slaves in even rows,
  And, though the season warms,
They throw, at once, their equal hoes,
  Like soldiers under arms.

On skins of goats their children lie,
  Or here and there they run;
And grow, beneath a torrid sky,
  Still blacker in the sun.[56]

Hence, then, the polish'd skin, so meek,
  Of shining glossy black;—
The sable plumes are not so sleek
  Upon a raven's back.

O let me steal upon that soil,
  So long unbless'd by rain,
Which oft, with never-ceasing toil,
  The negroe digs in vain.[57]

'Twas here, as once I stroll'd along,
  With musing steps and slow,
I spied, the other slaves among,
  One leaning on his hoe.

Just by his famish'd side, I think,
  A *yabbah* struck my view;[58]
And, empty quite of meat and drink,
  A *calabash* or two.[59]

---

56. In what part or membrane of the body that humour resides, which tinges the complexion of the negroe with a deep black, it is the business of the anatomists to enquire and describe.

 The powerful operation of heat appears manifestly to be the cause which produces this striking variety in the human species.

 All Europe, almost the whole of Asia, and the temperate parts of Africa, are occupied by men of a fair complexion. All the torrid zone in Africa, some of the warmer regions adjacent to it, and a few countries in Asia, are filled with people of a deep black colour.

57. The allusion here is to the island of Antigua, once a flourishing and wealthy colony, but now desolated by a perpetual sun-shine.

58. An earthen pot or vessel to hold meat, provisions, and the like.

59. Tree as full as big and as spreading as a large apple tree. The fruit is pretty near the size of a maryhead, round like a boys marble, and serves the purposes of a bowl, after the inside, which is not eatable, is carefully scooped out, when it is almost as thin and light as the thickest brown paper. Spoons, bowls, and other utensils for slaves to eat out of are made of them.

Poor Arthur was the wretch's name,
      And Guinea gave him breath;
While he to sad Antigua came,
      To meet, he fear'd, his death.

That negroe near the burning line
      That mov'd the swift canoe,
That stem'd the foamy ocean brine
      With paddle light and true.

Poor Arthur now, aloud cry'd I,
      You are not, sure, dismay'd!
Poor Arthur answer'd with a sigh,
      And scratch'd his woolly head.

I begg'd some water of a maid,
      To give the wretch relief;
He held it, trembling, to his head,
      Within a plantain leaf.

The sweat ran down his sun-burnt face,
      In troubl'd torrents fast;
While not a breeze, with tepid grace,
      Dispell'd it as it past.

I now my silk umbrella spread,
      To screen him from the sun;
And patient held it o'er his head,
      'Till all his work was done.

The slave then stoop'd and kiss'd my feet,[60]
      Low prostrate on the ground,
And made his arms in wonder meet
      My fainting knees around!

The bell of noon now open'd wide,
      The shell a signal sent;
Poor Arthur rubb'd each awkward side,[61]
      And home his footsteps bent.

60. Their usual manner of expressing their gratitude for any great and unlooked for act of kindness.

61. Descriptive of a new negroe, or one who has not been long in the island, after leaving his native country.

But Arthur now has made a hut,[62]
      And little garden wild,
Which keeps, contiguous to a gut,[63]
      Himself, his wife, and child.

'Tis there the Jessamine demure,
      And fav'rite flow'ry fence,
Shall ev'ry holiday allure
      The negroe's simple sense.

'Tis here, oft as the gentle airs
      At morn and eve renew;
So oft a thrilling music bears,
      To tune the *diddledoe*.[64]

There Melancholy lifts her head,
      With soft dejected mien,
And rises from her mountain bed,
      To grace the palmy scene.

On Sunday, oft he joins the throng
      Of India's swarthy dames;
On Sunday, oft he sings the song
      Expressive of his flames.

Now Arthur and the youths advance
      With pleasure-smiling mien,
He leads, at once, the antick dance,
      And beats the *tamboreen*.[65]

At cudgels now, against all blows
      He nicely guards his head;
And boldly meets a thousand foes,
      Beneath the plantain shade.

---

62. Negroes live in huts, on the western side of our dwelling houses; so that every plantation resembles a small town; and the reason why they are seated on the western side, is, that we may breathe the pure eastern air, without being offended with the least nauseous smell. Our kitchens and boiling houses are on the same side, and for the same reason.

63. A gut is a narrow canal, formed by the torrents of rain, which formerly have fallen on the higher parts of the island, in their passage to the sea.

64. The pod in which the seed of the aquasee grows, and which, when blown upon by the mouth or the air, produces a tone.

65. They are great lovers of music, and much pleased with those instruments that make a delightful noise, and a kind of harmony which they accompany with their voices. They had, in the island of St. Christopher, a certain rendezvouz in the midst of the woods, where they met on Sundays and holidays, after divine service, to give some relaxation to their wearied bodies. There they sometimes spent the remainder of that day and the night following, in dancing and pleasant discourses, without any prejudice to the labours imposed upon them by their masters; nay it was commonly observed, that after they had so diverted themselves, they went through their work with greater courage and chearfulness, without expressing any weariness, and did all things better than if they had rested all night long in their huts.

And now the rank *baba* he throws[66]
      From off his polish'd limbs,
And every day he nicer grows,
      Improving in his whims.

A shirt of check that loss supplies,
      And other garbs below;
And rings of horn, or homely guise,
      Compleats the savage beau.

Now, faithful to his master's side,
      He takes his nimble course:
He braids his hair, with decent pride,
      And runs beside his horse.

And now we daily hear him sing,
      The merriest and the best:
He seems, he moves another thing,
      And portly rears his crest.

26. Joseph Stansbury

To Cordelia
c. 1784

Born in London, Joseph Stansbury (1740–1809) moved to Philadelphia in 1767 and became a successful merchant. An outspoken Loyalist, he was arrested in 1780 on charges of spying—he had been an intermediary for Benedict Arnold—and was banished to New York. After the war, he lived in Nova Scotia, where this poem on exile was written. Another poem of the same period, "The United States," pleads for reconciliation of Revolutionaries and loyalists, but when Stansbury tried to move back to Philadelphia he found himself unwelcome. Eventually he returned to New York, where he died in 1809.

Believe me, Love, this vagrant life
      O'er Nova Scotia's wilds to roam,
While far from children, friends, or wife,
      Or place that I can call a home
Delights not me;—another way
My treasures, pleasures, wishes lay.

66. A blanket or loose kind of covering used by the meaner kind of slaves.

In piercing, wet, and wintry skies,
   Where man would seem in vain to toil,
I see, where'er I turn my eyes,
   Luxuriant pasture, trees and soil.
Uncharm'd I see:—another way
My fondest hopes and wishes lay.

Oh could I through the future see
   Enough to form a settled plan,
To feed my infant train and thee
   And fill the rank and style of man:
I'd cheerful be the livelong day;
Since all my wishes point that way.

But when I see a sordid shed
   Of birchen bark, procured with care,
Design'd to shield the aged head
   Which British mercy placed there—
'Tis too, too much: I cannot stay,
But turn with streaming eyes away.

Oh! how your heart would bleed to view
   Six pretty prattlers like your own,
Expos'd to every wind that blew;
   Condemn'd in such a hut to moan.
Could this be borne, Cordelia, say?
Contented in your cottage stay.

'Tis true, that in this climate rude,
   The mind resolv'd may happy be;
And may, with toil and solitude,
Live independent and be free.
So the lone hermit yields to slow decay:
Unfriended lives—unheeded glides away.

If so far humbled that no pride remains,
   But moot indifference which way flows the stream;
Resign'd to penury, its cares and pains;
   And hope has left you like a painted dream;
Then here, Cordelia, bend your pensive way,
And close the evening of Life's wretched day.

27. Joel Barlow

from *The Vision of Columbus*
1787

A member of the Connecticut Wits in his youth, Joel Barlow (1754–1812) later broke with the other members of the circle, exploring ideas that were more liberal, progressive, and French. He graduated from Yale in 1778. After the Revolution, he spent a considerable part of his life abroad, including a stint as consul in Algiers. As emissary to France, he was pursuing Napoleon across Poland to negotiate a treaty when he died in 1812. Barlow befriended Thomas Paine and wrote several radical political tracts, including Advice to the Privileged Orders *(1792, 1794). A poem called "The Hasty Pudding" was long a favorite for its homespun Yankee humor, but Barlow's major work is* The Vision of Columbus, *which he revised twenty years later as* The Columbiad. *An epic modeled loosely after books 11 and 12 of* Paradise Lost, *Barlow's poem presents the history of empire in the New World in the form of a vision offered by an angel to Columbus. The poem begins with Columbus in prison—always a favorite moment for the English in the Discoverer's biography, since it illustrates the Spanish failure to appreciate the promise of the New World, which will only be finally realized by the American republic.*

BOOK I.

Long had the Sage, the first who dared to brave
The unknown dangers of the western wave,
Who taught mankind where future empires lay
In these fair confines of descending day,
With cares o'erwhelm'd, in life's distressing gloom,
Wish'd from a thankless world a peaceful tomb;
While kings and nations, envious of his name,
Enjoy'd his toils and triumph'd o'er his fame,
And gave the chief, from promised empire hurl'd,
Chains for a crown, a prison for a world.
Now night and silence held their lonely reign,
The half-orb'd moon declining to the main;
Descending clouds, o'er varying ether driven,
Obscured the stars and shut the eye from heaven;
Cold mists through opening grates the cell invade,
And deathlike terrors haunt the midnight shade;
When from a visionary, short repose,

The angel visits Columbus in prison, from The Columbiad.

That raised new cares and temper'd keener woes,
Columbus woke, and to the walls address'd
The deep-felt sorrows of his manly breast.
      Here lies the purchase, here the wretched spoil,
Of painful years and persevering toil:
For these dread walks, this hideous haunt of pain,
I traced new regions o'er the pathless main,
Dared all the dangers of the dreary wave,
Hung o'er its clefts and topp'd the surging grave,
Saw billowy seas, in swelling mountains roll,
And bursting thunders rock the reddening pole,
Death rear his front in every dreadful form,
Gape from beneath and blacken in the storm;
Till, tost far onward to the skirts of day,
Where milder suns dispens'd a smiling ray,
Through brighter skies my happier sails descry'd
The golden banks that bound the western tide,
And gave the admiring world that bounteous shore
Their wealth to nations and to kings their power.
      Oh land of transport! dear, delusive coast,
To these fond, aged eyes forever lost!

No more thy gladdening vales I travel o'er,
For me thy mountains rear the head no more,
For me thy rocks no sparkling gems unfold,
Or streams luxuriant wear their paths in gold;
From realms of promised peace forever borne,
I hail dread anguish, and in secret mourn.
   But dangers past, fair climes explored in vain,
And foes triumphant shew but half my pain.
Dissembling friends, each earlier joy who gave,
And fired my youth the storms of fate to brave,
Swarm'd in the sunshine of my happier days,
Pursued the fortune and partook the praise,
Bore in my doubtful cause a twofold part,
The garb of friendship and the viper's heart,
Pass my loath'd cell with smiles of sour disdain,
Insult my woes and triumph in my pain.
   One gentle guardian Heaven indulgent gave,
And now that guardian slumbers in the grave.
Hear from above, thou dear departed shade,
As once my joys, my present sorrows aid,
Burst my full heart, afford that last relief,
Breathe back my sighs and reinspire my grief;
Still in my sight thy royal form appears,
Reproves my silence and demands my tears.
On that blest hour my soul delights to dwell,
When thy protection bade the canvass swell,
When kings and courtiers found their factions vain,
Blind Superstition shrunk beneath her chain,
The sun's glad beam led on the circling way,
And isles rose beauteous in the western day.
But o'er those silvery shores, that fair domain,
What crouds of tyrants fix their horrid reign!
Again fair Freedom seeks her kindred skies,
Truth leaves the world, and Isabella dies.
   Oh, lend thy friendly shroud to veil my sight,
That these pain'd eyes may dread no more the light,
These welcome shades conclude my instant doom,
And this drear mansion moulder to a tomb.
   Thus mourn'd the hapless chief; a thundering sound
Roll'd round the shuddering walls and shook the ground;
O'er all the dome, where solemn arches bend,
The roofs unfold and streams of light descend;
The growing splendor fill'd the astonish'd room,
And gales etherial breathed a glad perfume;
Mild in the midst a radiant seraph shone,

Robed in the vestments of the rising sun;
Tall rose his stature, youth's primeval grace
Moved o'er his limbs and wanton'd in his face,
His closing wings, in golden plumage drest,
With gentle sweep came folding o'er his breast,
His locks in rolling ringlets glittering hung,
And sounds melodious moved his heavenly tongue.
      Rise, trembling Chief, to scenes of rapture, rise,
This voice awaits thee from the approving skies;
Thy just complaints, in heavenly audience known
Call mild compassion from the indulgent throne;
Let grief no more awake the piteous strain,
Nor think thy piety or toils are vain.
Tho' faithless men thy injured worth despise,
Depress all virtue and insult the skies,
Yet look thro' nature, Heaven's own conduct trace,
What power divine sustains the unthankful race!
From that great Source, that life-inspiring Soul,
Suns drew their light and systems learn'd to roll,
Time walk'd the silent round, and life began,
And God's fair image stamp'd the mind of man.
Down the long vale, where rolling years descend,
To thy own days, behold his care extend;
From one eternal Spring, what love proceeds!
Smiles in the seraph, in the Saviour bleeds,
Shines through all worlds, that fill the bounds of space,
And lives and brightens in thy favour'd race.
Yet no return the almighty Power can know,
From earth to heaven no just reward can flow,
Men spread their wants, the all-bounteous hand supplies,
And gives the joys that mortals dare despise.
In these dark vales where blinded faction sways,
Wealth pride and conquest claim the palm of praise,
Aw'd into slaves, while groping millions groan,
And blood-stain'd steps lead upwards to a throne.
      Far other wreaths thy virtuous temples claim,
Far nobler honours build thy sacred name,
Thine be the joys the immortal mind that grace
Pleas'd with the toils, that bless thy kindred race,
Now raise thy ravish'd soul to scenes more bright,
The glorious fruits ascending on thy sight;
For, wing'd with speed, from brighter worlds I came,
To sooth thy grief and show thy distant fame.
      As that great Seer, whose animating rod
Taught Israel's sons the wonder-working God,

Who led, thro' dreary wastes, the murmuring band
To the fair confines of the promised land,
Oppress'd with years, from Pisgah's beauteous height,
O'er boundless regions cast the raptured sight;
The joys of unborn nations warm'd his breast,
Repaid his toils and sooth'd his soul to rest;
Thus, o'er thy subject wave, shalt thou behold
Far happier realms their future charms unfold,
In nobler pomp another Pisgah rise,
Beneath whose foot thine own Canäan lies;
There, rapt in vision, hail the distant clime,
And taste the blessings of remotest time.

28. Annis Boudinot Stockton

Elegy on the Destruction of the Trees by the Icicles, Sunday and Monday of February the 17th and 18th, 1788
1788

Much of the poetry of Annis Boudinot Stockton (1736–1801) is on public themes of the Revolution and early republic, but this lyric signals the beginnings of a shift in poetic temperament. Born in Pennsylvania, Annis Boudinot married the lawyer Richard Stockton around 1755 and settled with him near Princeton, New Jersey. The Stocktons were vocal advocates of independence, and the British sacked their house in 1776. Annis Stockton also belonged to an extensive network of literary women, including Elizabeth Graeme Fergusson ("Laura"), to whom (as "Emilia") she wrote poems of ardent and intimate friendship.

Ah! see them weep! The guardians of the trees,
Dryads and hamadryads, flock around;
Their deep-toned sighs increase the hollow breeze,
And their green hair lies scatter'd on the ground.

Ah! what avails to them this sight sublime!
Though Nature deck'd in crystal looks more gay
Than genial Spring in her soft verdant prime,
Each sprig more dazzling than the new-born day!

Though Iris paints the fields in tints which glow
More variegated than the diamond mine,

Where the bright Queen of Ocean weaves her bow,
And on the clouds suspends the seal divine!

While squadrons of hoar frost from Zembla's cave,
Encrusting all their tender bodies o'er,
Tearing their limbs, their helpless trunks they leave
Expos'd and naked to the tempest's roar!

"Come, Flora, weep with us," the dryads cry,
"For you must too this awful fate deplore;
"Entomb'd in ice our trees in ruins lie,
"Nor their hack'd forms can gentle Spring restore.

"Say, what will shade you when fierce Leo reigns?
"Or where can Pan and Silvius safe retire
"When thirsty Sirius drinks the dewy plains,
"And Phoebus' fiery steeds proclaim his ire?

"Then did our cool recess asylum yield,
"To all the rural powers a sweet retreat;
"And when the ploughman drove his team afield,
"We gave him shelter from the raging heat."

Emelia

29. Elizabeth Graeme Fergusson

On the Mind's Being Engrossed by One Subject 1789

A native of Philadelphia, Elizabeth Graeme (1737–1801) was related to some of the city's most prominent families, and presided over one of the earliest literary salons in English America. She was engaged to marry Benjamin Franklin's son, William, in 1757, but the engagement broke off; much later, in 1772, she married Henry Hugh Fergusson. Suspected of secret loyalism, she remained in Philadelphia, separated from her husband, and was finally forced to sell her family estate before her death in 1801.

When one fond object occupies the mind,
In nature's scenes we still that object find;
And trees, and meads, and sweetly purling rill,
By us made mirrors with ingenious skill,
Reflect the constant subject of our thought;
We view that image in their substance wrought.
The common peasant treads the fresh turn'd soil,
And hopes of future crops his steps beguiles.
The nat'ralist observes each simple's use,
Where lodg'd the healthy, where the baneful juice.
The lover sees his mistress all around
And her sweet voice in vocal birds is found;
He views the brilliant glories of the skies,
But to remind him of her sparkling eyes.
Th' alchemist still anxious seeks the gold,
For this he pierces every cavern's fold:
Trembling to try the magic hazel's pow'r,
Which points attractive to the darling show'r.
While pious Hervey in each plant and tree
Can nought but God and his redeemer see.
When zephyrs play, or when fierce Boreas roars,
The merchant only for his bark implores.
The beau and belle attentive dread the sky,
Lest angry clouds the sprightly scene deny.
But if a coach's procur'd, torrents may pour,
And winds, and tempests, shattered fleets devour.
Thus over all, self-love presides supreme,

It cheers the morn, and gives the ev'ning dream.
Though oft we change through life's swift gliding stage,
And seek fresh objects at each varying age,
Here we are constant, faithful to one cause,
Our own indulgence as a center draws.
That faithful inmate makes our breast its home,
From the soft cradle, to the silent tomb.

30. Sarah Wentworth Morton

Born in Boston, Sarah Apthorp (1759–1846) adopted her mother's maiden name,
Wentworth, out of pride in her Welsh heritage. She knew many of the
Massachusetts elite, including John Adams and John Trumbull. In 1781 she
married Perez Morton, who created a scandal in 1788 by having a liaison with his
sister-in-law, who committed suicide as a result; the story became the basis for
William Hill Brown's novel The Power of Sympathy. *Sarah Morton became known*
as "the Sappho of America" in the 1790s, a decade in which she wrote three long
works: Ouâbi, or The Virtues of Nature; Beacon Hill; *and* The Virtues of Society.
Morton was more conservative on gender than contemporaries such as Judith
Sargent Murray, and denounced Mary Wollstonecraft. But "The African Chief"
(1792) became a favorite of the antislavery movement. Morton published one later
book, My Mind and Its Thoughts, *in 1823.*

Sonnet to the Full Summer Moon

Thou silent traveller, of the glance benign,
 Who from yon crystal car on high
 Shedd'st the full luster of thy moving eye,
While the touched hills and vales reflective shine.

I love the wanderings of thy varied beam,
 What time the pale west bends thy silver wire—
 Till in the gorgeous east, thou bidst the sun retire,
Mingling warm blushes with his parting gleam.

He draws his crimsoned curtain round the main,
 And from the moist earth drinks refreshing dews;
Thou, gently bending o'er the child of pain;
 Canst charm the sadness of the mourning muse.

He, the proud emblem of oppressive power;
Thou, the mild sovereign of the pitying hour!

The African Chief
1792

See how the black ship cleaves the main,
  High bounding o'er the dark blue wave,
Remurmuring with the groans of pain,
  Deep freighted with the princely slave!

Did all the Gods of Afric sleep,
  Forgetful of their guardian love,
When the white tyrants of the deep
  Betrayed him in the palmy grove?

A chief of Gambia's golden shore,
  Whose arm the band of warriors led,
Or more—the lord of generous power,
  By whom the foodless poor were fed.

Does not the voice of reason cry,
  Claim the first right that nature gave,
From the red scourge of bondage fly,
  Nor deign to live a burdened slave?

Has not his suffering offspring clung,
  Desponding round his fettered knee;
On his worn shoulder, weeping hung,
  And urged one effort to be free?

His wife by nameless wrongs subdued,
  His bosom's friend to death resigned;
The flinty path-way drenched in blood,
  He saw with cold and frenzied mind.

Strong in despair, then sought the plain,
  To heaven was raised his steadfast eye,
Resolved to burst the crushing chain,
  Or mid the battle's blast to die.

First of his race, he led the band,
  Guardless of danger, hurling round,
Till by his red avenging hand,
  Full many a despot stained the ground.

When erst Messenia's sons[67] oppressed
      Flew desperate to the sanguine field,
With iron clothed each injured breast,
      And saw the cruel Spartan yield,

Did not the soul to heaven allied,
      With the proud heart as greatly swell,
As when the roman Decius died,
      Or when the Grecian victim fell?

Do later deeds quick rapture raise,
      The boon Batavia's William won,
Paoli's time-enduring praise,
      Or the yet greater Washington?

If these exalt thy sacred zeal,
      To hate oppression's mad control,
For bleeding Afric learn to feel,
      Whose Chieftain claimed a kindred soul.

Ah, mourn the last disastrous hour,
      Lift the full eye of bootless grief,
While victory treads the sultry shore,
      And tears from hope the captive chief.

While the hard race of pallid hue,
      Unpracticed in the power to feel,
Resign him to the murderous crew,
      The horrors of the quivering wheel,

Let sorrow bathe each blushing cheek,
      Bend piteous o'er the tortured slave,
Whose wrongs compassion cannot speak,
      Whose only refuge was the grave.

67. Messenia's sons: slaves of Sparta.

31. Philip Freneau

While an undergraduate at Princeton in 1771, Philip Freneau (1752–1832) wrote "The Rising Glory of America" with his classmate Hugh Henry Brackenridge. This celebration of the western British empire later led Freneau to be the most ardent of the early nationalist poets. He perfected the image of the poetic and voluntarily receding Indian; he sketched visions of ethnic assimilation and westward expansion. His poetry covered a broad range, including humorous sketches and verses on nature.

After graduating from Princeton, Freneau taught school in Long Island, worked in the West Indies, and finally took up privateering against the British before he was caught and confined to a prison ship in 1778; The British Prison Ship was published in 1781. After a return to sea, Freneau became an editor and writer, mostly for Jeffersonian causes, throughout the 1790s. A prolific writer and widely read before 1800, Freneau was largely forgotten by the time he died, having retired to his native New York, in 1832.

On the Emigration to America and Peopling the Western Country
1784

To western woods, and lonely plains,
Palemon from the crowd departs,
Where Nature's wildest genius reigns,
To tame the soil, and plant the arts—
What wonders there shall freedom show,
What mighty STATES successive grow!

From Europe's proud, despotic shores
Hither the stranger takes his way,
And in our new found world explores
A happier soil, a milder sway,
Where no proud despot holds him down,
No slaves insult him with a crown.

What charming scenes attract the eye,
On wild Ohio's savage stream!
There Nature reigns, whose works outvie
The boldest pattern art can frame;

There ages past have rolled away,
And forests bloomed but to decay.

From these fair plains, these rural seats,
So long concealed, so lately known,
The unsocial Indian far retreats,
To make some other clime his own,
When other streams, less pleasing flow,
And darker forests round him grow.

Great Sire[68] of floods; whose varied wave
Through climes and countries takes its way,
To whom creating Nature gave
Ten thousand streams to swell thy sway!
No longer shall *they* useless prove,
Nor idly through the forests rove;

Nor longer shall your princely flood
From distant lakes be swelled in vain,
Nor longer through a darksome wood
Advance, unnoticed, to the main,
Far other ends, the heavens decree—
And commerce plans new freights for thee.

While virtue warms the generous breast,
There heaven-born freedom shall reside,
Nor shall the voice of war molest,
Nor Europe's all-aspiring pride—
There Reason shall new laws devise,
And order from confusion rise.

Forsaking kings and regal state,
With all their pomp and fancied bliss,
The traveller owns, convinced though late,
No realm so free, so blest as this—
The east is half to slaves consigned,
Where kings and priests enchain the mind.

O come the time, and haste the day,
When man shall man no longer crush,
When Reason shall enforce her sway,
Nor these fair regions raise our blush,

68. Mississippi. [Freneau's note.]

Where still the *African* complains,
And mourns his yet unbroken chains.

Far brighter scenes a future age,
The muse predicts, these States will hail,
Whose genius may the world engage,
Whose deeds may over death prevail,
And happier systems bring to view,
Than all the eastern sages knew.

The Wild Honey Suckle
1786

Fair flower, that dost so comely grow,
Hid in this silent, dull retreat,
Untouched thy honied blossoms blow,
Unseen thy little branches greet:
      No roving foot shall crush thee here,
      No busy hand provoke a tear.

By Nature's self in white arrayed,
She bade thee shun the vulgar eye,
And planted here the guardian shade,
And sent soft waters murmuring by;
      Thus quietly thy summer goes,
      Thy days declining to repose.

Smit with those charms, that must decay,
I grieve to see your future doom;
They died—nor were those flowers more gay,
The flowers that did in Eden bloom;
      Unpitying frosts, and Autumn's power
      Shall leave no vestige of this flower.

From morning suns and evening dews
At first thy little being came:
If nothing once, you nothing lose,
For when you die you are the same;
      The space between, is but an hour,
      The frail duration of a flower.

The Indian Burying Ground
1788

In spite of all the learned have said,
I still my old opinion keep;
The *posture*, that *we* give the dead,
Points out the soul's eternal sleep.

Not so the ancients of these lands—
The Indian, when from life released,
Again is seated with his friends,
And shares again the joyous feast.[69]

His imaged birds, and painted bowl,
And venison, for a journey dressed,
Bespeak the nature of the soul,
ACTIVITY, that knows no rest.

His bow, for action ready bent,
And arrows, with a head of stone,
Can only mean that life is spent,
And not the old ideas gone.

Thou, stranger, that shalt come this way,
No fraud upon the dead commit—
Observe the swelling turf, and say
They do not *lie*, but here they *sit*.

Here still a lofty rock remains,
On which the curious eye may trace
(Now wasted, half, by wearing rains)
The fancies of a ruder race.

Here still an aged elm aspires,
Beneath whose far-projecting shade
(And which the shepherd still admires)
The children of the forest played!

There oft a restless Indian queen
(Pale *Shebah*, with her braided hair)

---

69. The North American Indians bury their dead in a sitting posture; decorating the corpse with wampum, the images of birds, quadrupeds, &c: And (if that of a warrior) with bows, arrows, tomahawks and other military weapons. [Freneau's note.]

And many a barbarous form is seen
To chide the man that lingers there.

By midnight moons, o'er moistening dews,
In habit for the chase arrayed,
The hunter still the deer pursues,
The hunter and the deer, a shade!

And long shall timorous fancy see
The painted chief, and pointed spear,
And Reason's self shall bow the knee
To shadows and delusions here.

Epistle to a Student of Dead Languages 1795

I pity him, who, at no small expense,
Has studied sound instead of sense:
He, proud some antique gibberish to attain;
Of Hebrew, Greek, or Latin, vain,
Devours the husk, and leaves the grain.

In *his own language* HOMER writ and read,
Not spent his life in poring on the *dead*:
Why then your native language not pursue
In which all ancient sense (that's worth review)
Glows in translation, fresh and new?

He better plans, who *things*, not *words*, attends,
And turns his studious hours to active ends;
Who ART through every secret maze explores,
Invents, contrives—and Nature's hidden stores
From mirrours, to their object true,
Presents to man's obstructed view,
That dimly meets the light, and faintly soars:—

His strong capacious mind
By fetters unconfin'd
Of Latin lore and heathen Greek,
Takes Science in its way,
Pursues the kindling ray
'Till Reason's morn shall on him break!

The Drunkard's Apology
1795

"You blame the blushes on my nose,
And yet admire the blushing rose;
On CELIA's cheek the bloom you prize,
And yet, on mine, that bloom despise.

"The world of spirits you admire,
To which all holy men aspire:
Yet, me with curses you requite,
Because in *spirits* I delight.

"Whene'er I fall, and crack my crown,
You blame me much for *falling down*—
Yet to some *god*, that you adore,
You, too, fall prostrate on the floor.

"You call me fool, for drinking hard;
And yet old HUDSON you regard,
Who fills his jug from yonder bay,
And drinks his guts-full, every day!"—

The Indian Convert
1797

An Indian, who lived at *Muskingum*, remote,
Was teazed by a parson to join his dear flock,
To throw off his blanket and put on a coat,
And of grace and religion to lay in a stock.

The Indian long slighted an offer so fair,
Preferring to preaching his fishing and fowling;
A *sermon* to him was a heart full of care,
And singing but little superior to howling.

At last by persuasion and constant harassing
Our Indian was brought to consent to be *good*;
He saw that the malice of *Satan* was pressing,
And the *means* to repel him not yet understood.

Of heaven, one day, when the parson was speaking,
And painting the beautiful things of the place,
The *convert*, who something substantial was seeking,
Rose up, and confessed he had doubts in the case.—

Said he, *Master Minister*, this place that you talk of,
Of things for the stomach, pray what has it got;
Has it liquors in plenty?—if so I'll soon walk off
And put myself down in the heavenly spot.

You fool (said the preacher) no liquors are there!
The place I'm describing is most like our meeting,
Good people, all singing, with preaching and prayer;
They live upon these without eating or drinking.

But the doors are all locked against folks that are wicked:
And you, I am fearful, will never get there:—
A life of REPENTANCE must purchase the ticket,
And few of you, Indians, can buy it, I fear.

Farewell (said the Indian) I'm none of your mess;
On victuals, so airy, I faintish should feel,
I cannot consent to be lodged in a place
Where there's nothing to eat and but little to steal.

To the Americans of the United States
1797

Men of this passing age!—whose noble deeds
Honour will bear above the *scum* of Time:
Ere this eventful century expire,
Once more we greet you with our humble rhyme:
Pleased, if we meet your smiles, but—if denied,
Yet, with YOUR sentence, we are satisfied.

Catching our subjects from the varying scene
Of human things; a mingled work we draw,
Chequered with fancies odd, and figures strange,
Such, as no *courtly* poet ever saw;
Who writ, beneath some GREAT MAN'S ceiling placed;
Travelled no lands, nor roved the watery waste.

To seize some *features* from the faithless past;
Be this our care—before the century close:
The colours strong!—for, if we deem aright,
The *coming age will be an age of prose:*
When *sordid cares* will break the muses' dream,
And COMMON SENSE be ranked in seat supreme.

Go, now, dear book; once more expand your wings:
Still to the cause of man *severely true:*
Untaught to flatter *pride,* or fawn on kings;—
Trojan, or Tyrian,—*give them both their due.—*
When they are right, the cause of both we plead,
And both will please us well,—if both will read.

Index